THE HUMANIST TRADITION
IN WORLD LITERATURE

THE HUMANIST TRADITION IN WORLD LITERATURE

An Anthology of Masterpieces
from *Gilgamesh* to *The Divine Comedy*

Stephen L. Harris

Sacramento State College

Charles E. Merrill Publishing Company
A Bell & Howell Company
Columbus, Ohio

ISBN: 0-675-09321-X Clothbound edition
        0-675-09322-8 Paperbound edition

Library of Congress Catalog Number: 77-119517

1 2 3 4 5 6 7 8 9 10–76 75 74 73 72 71 70

Printed in the United States of America

To Marjorie

CONTENTS

THE SPIRIT OF PHILOSOPHY

THE WORLD OF ROME

THE EPIC OF THE MEDIEVAL MIND

Preface

The Humanist Tradition in World Literature ATTEMPTS TO PRESENT A stimulating selection of the best that has been thought and written during the first three thousand years of man's civilized experience. Starting with the Near Eastern beginnings—*Gilgamesh* and the Bible—this volume surveys the masterworks of Greece, Rome, and the Middle Ages.

CONTENTS

The contents have been chosen for their contribution to the history of ideas, their imaginative power, and their ability to delight. To ensure maximum reading pleasure only the finest modern translations available have been used. Besides the "standard classics," such as the *Iliad*, *Oedipus the King*, and the *Aeneid*, which are indispensable to any representative collection of Western masterpieces, this volume includes works of outstanding merit that are, inexplicably, seldom anthologized. The first of these is the Sumero-Babylonian epic of *Gilgamesh*, a strangely poignant narrative whose theme and characters are of archetypal significance. It is anthologized in a text of this kind for perhaps the first time. Plato's *Symposium* and Aristotle's *Ethics* provide an insight into the mental processes and life style of the upper-class Athenian unobtainable elsewhere. Herodotus, with his vivid account of East and West in conflict, is important for the gossipy charm of his style and the fact that the events he describes made possible the Golden Age of Greece. Livy is another historian too often neglected, but enormously influential and helpful in understanding the stuff of which Roman character was made. Plutarch's short biography of Cicero gives a better picture of what life in Rome was like during the last days of the Republic than any number of official white papers. The sensuality and worldliness of Catullus, Juvenal, and Apuleius balance the picture of Stoic idealism and disciplined patriotism given in Virgil and Livy. Selections from the New Testament appear in their proper historical context when juxtaposed with the pagan reaction of Pliny, Trajan, and Symmachus. Jerome's letters illuminate the dilemma of the Christian intellectual during Rome's catastrophic decline. By combining familiar classics with works less well known but of equally high quality, *The Humanist Tradition* hopes to provide material of sufficient scope and variety to interest a wide range of students and teachers.

Several works are included to illustrate certain ethical and spiritual conflicts that characterized early cultures and which remain pertinent today. In Job and the *Prometheus Bound* two great poets, a Hebrew and a Greek, struggle with the same problem of cosmic evil. Both writers question the justice of God, but their conclusions are strikingly divergent; they clearly depict the irreconcilable differences between the Hebraic and Hellenic worldviews. Since the Hebrews and Greeks contributed more toward the formation of the Western mind than any other ancient people, it is instructive to approach their opposing values through the medium of these two supremely representative dramas.

The too-little-known *Philoctetes* provides a thematic link between the *Iliad* and the *Aeneid*. In the course of his sufferings, Sophocles' hero learns to balance the extreme personal pride of Achilles with a sense of community responsibility that foreshadows Aeneas. Although it takes the intervention of a god to transform Philoctetes from a self-engrossed Greek individualist into something resembling a Roman exponent of public duty, Sophocles' tragi-comedy nonetheless manages a reconciliation between the conflicting demands of man and the state. Philoctetes' obedience to the will of Fate is not unworthy of Virgil's hero.

Without exception, the authors included here are represented either by a complete work (all plays are uncut) or by an excerpt long enough to give an adequate impression of the writer's subject and style. Through space limitations Homer's *Iliad* becomes an *Achilleid* (with no loss to its portrait of the hero or his Trojan opponents) and a few tortures are omitted from Dante's *Inferno*, but in no case is a piece of imaginative literature reduced to a snippet. Where abridging has been necessary, the editor has been careful to retain an entire episode and to make each extract as coherent and autonomous as possible.

TRANSLATIONS

Translations were selected for their appeal to the modern ear. Nothing so discourages a reader as the apparently stiff and to him unnatural convolutions of an archaic style. Except where no recent translation can rival the appropriateness or beauty of a standard rendering (such as the King James version of the Creation or Dryden's excerpt from Lucretius), virtually all selections, whether originally written in Sumerian, Hebrew, Greek, Latin, or Italian, appear in a twentieth-century Anglo-American idiom. Thus Augustine is able to confess in the clear direct English of contemporary speech; Dante recounts his journey through the afterlife in John Ciardi's strong, muscular vernacular; and even Achilles speaks a lucid and rhythmic prose unencumbered with archaisms. In fine, translations were chosen for their success in combining clarity, accuracy, and stylistic elegance.

PREFACES

Every selection in the anthology is introduced by a brief critical essay which discusses the author's life, his major themes, his characteristic intellectual and artistic concerns, and the general significance of his work. When it helps the reader to appreciate the writer's philosophic viewpoint or didactic intent, the prefaces give a limited amount of historical background. The emphasis, however, falls on the imaginative and universal aspects of a writer's accomplishment rather than on factual particulars. Besides providing some necessary information, the introductions try to equip the reader with a few suitable literary clues that will prepare him for what to expect in the work to follow. Approaching Sophocles, Plato, and Dante with even the most tentative literary guide will perhaps increase the student's enjoyment by giving him a working point of view.

GLOSSARY

Unique to this anthology is an extensive glossary of mythological, literary, historical, and critical terms. From Aaron the brother of Moses to Zeno the Greek philosopher, the student will find concise definitions of anthologized persons and events, real and fictional. Besides providing a quick reference for particular terms,* the glossary will help augment the student's understanding of the mythological background, intellectual milieu, and critical interpretations of the anthologized material. The reader may find it helpful simply to browse through the glossary before starting the text itself. Prior familiarity with the Olympian gods, Greek heroes, and Roman leaders should make reading Homer or Virgil considerably easier.† In addition to the analytical prefaces and the glossary, *The Humanist Tradition* contains a selective bibliography of authoritative works for those who wish to learn more about a particular author.

---

*The glossary also serves to keep footnoting, particularly of the classical authors, at a minimum. Notes are sometimes a necessary evil, but in general the reader is spared that annoying and repetitious device.

†Because the translators of Dante provide generous annotations, glossary entries for medieval terms and concepts have proven unnecessary. Individual notes and identifications are consequently appended to the text of the *Divine Comedy*.

THE HUMANIST TRADITION IN WORLD LITERATURE

GILGAMESH

LITERALLY THE OLDEST STORY KNOWN TO MAN, THE SUMERO-BABYLONIAN epic of *Gilgamesh* was for twenty-five centuries forgotten in the ruins of a dead civilization. Not until the nineteenth century did British archaeologists discover amid the rubble of an Assyrian palace the twelve clay tablets upon which were inscribed the adventures of King Gilgamesh, the first hero of world literature. Since Layard and Rassam excavated Nineveh and found the Assyrian version of the epic, numerous other, much older, fragments of the poem have come to light. Recent evidence indicates that the oral folk tales lying behind the written version of the epic go back to at least 3000 years before Christ.

What is most striking about *Gilgamesh*, however, is not its extreme antiquity, but its literary excellence. The vivid account of a courageous leader who is so grieved at the death of his beloved friend that he journeys beyond the ends of the earth, beyond the "waters of death" that surround the known world, to find everlasting life, still has the power to fascinate and to move. The heroic quest is unfolded in the deceptively simple, almost naive fashion of an Oriental fairy tale.

The poem opens with a description of mighty Gilgamesh, whose mother is the goddess Ninsun and whose father is the mortal priest Lugulbanda. "Two-thirds god and one third man," Gilgamesh cannot control his enormous energies and tyrannizes over Uruk, the city-state of which he is king. The city elders then beg the gods to create a man whose strength will rival that of Gilgamesh so the city will have some rest. The gods oblige by creating the wild man Enkidu, who lives in the forest and runs with the beasts of the field. When Enkidu releases animals caught in hunters' traps, Gilgamesh is informed and suggests that the wild man be civilized by the love of a temple-prostitute. The woman, as her sacred duty to Ishtar the love-goddess, then goes to the forest, seduces Enkidu, and teaches him the ways of civilization. When he is brought to Uruk, Enkidu battles with Gilgamesh and the two men prove to be matched in strength. Swearing eternal friendship, Gilgamesh and Enkidu embark on a campaign to rid the earth of evil monsters, such as the fire-breathing Humbaba. But Ishtar becomes attracted to Gilgamesh, who rudely spurns her lustful advances. Enraged, the goddess determines to destroy what Gilgamesh loves best, his friend Enkidu. When Enkidu dies because of Ishtar's malice, Gilgamesh is too overwhelmed to carry on his kingly duties. Hearing that the gods had granted immortal life to his ancestor Utnapishtim, the only man to survive the Flood, Gilgamesh sets out on the greatest of his adventures—the search for immortality. The excerpt below contains the complete account of Gilgamesh's journey and return.

Although the epic was lost before Roman times, *Gilgamesh* was extremely popular and influential throughout the ancient Near East. Scholars have even speculated that Enkidu and Gilgamesh provided the prototype of Heracles, the Greek strongman and slayer of monsters, and that their friendship set the pattern for that of Achilles and Patroclus in the *Iliad*. The Bible, too, shows the influence of the common Sumero-Babylonian culture out of which both it and *Gilgamesh* grew. Utnap-ishtim is the Babylonian Noah and his account of the global Deluge closely parallels that given in Genesis. Both flood stories probably derive from the same ancient source.

Like the more sophisticated epics of Greece and Rome, *Gilgamesh* has a heroic sweep, imaginative boldness, and strong feeling for man's strug-gle against nature. It also displays a profound melancholia that springs from a tragic sense of life. The dramatic interest and tension of the poem arise from the conflict between the hero's zestful love of life and the inescapable horror of death that will eventually rob his heroic actions of their meaning. Like the Old Testament writers, the unknown authors of *Gilgamesh* foresaw no afterlife of joy or reward even for good men. Death brings all good things to an end. The poet of Ecclesiastes might in theory have derived his pessimism from a reading of *Gilgamesh*:

> . . . a living dog is better than a dead lion. For the living know that they shall die: but the dead know not anything, neither have they any more a reward; for the memory of them is forgotten. . . .
> Whatsoever thy hand findeth to do, do it with all thy might; for there is no work, nor device, nor knowledge, nor wisdom, in Sheol [the grave], whither thou goest.

This biblical passage is almost identical in sentiment to the advice Siduri, the divine maker of wine, gives to travel-weary Gilgamesh:

> "You will never find that life for which you are looking. When the gods created man they allotted to him death, but life they retained in their own keeping. As for you, Gilgamesh, fill your belly with good things; day and night, night and day, dance and be merry, feast and rejoice . . . and make your wife happy in your embrace; for this too is the lot of man."

The realism of *Gilgamesh* is like that of the *Iliad*. In both epics, the hero's only compensation for his certain death is that future generations will remember and venerate his name. Like Achilles, whom in many respects he foreshadows, Gilgamesh finds immortality only in the memo-ry of other men.

GILGAMESH

THE SEARCH FOR EVERLASTING LIFE

BITTERLY GILGAMESH WEPT FOR HIS FRIEND ENKIDU[1]; HE WANDERED OVER the wilderness as a hunter, he roamed over the plains; in his bitterness he cried, 'How can I rest, how can I be at peace? Despair is in my heart. What my brother is now, that shall I be when I am dead. Because I am afraid of death I will go as best I can to find Utnapishtim whom they call the Faraway, for he has entered the assembly of the gods.' So Gilgamesh travelled over the wilderness, he wandered over the grasslands, a long journey, in search of Utnapishtim, whom the gods took after the deluge; and they set him to live in the land of Dilmun, in the garden of the sun; and to him alone of men they gave everlasting life.

At night when he came to the mountain passes Gilgamesh prayed: 'In these mountain passes long ago I saw lions, I was afraid and I lifted my eyes to the moon; I prayed and my prayers went up to the gods, so now, O moon god Sin, protect me.' When he had prayed he lay down to sleep, until he was woken from out of a dream. He saw the lions round him glorying in life; then he took his axe in hand, he drew his sword from his belt, and he fell upon them like an arrow from the string, and struck and destroyed and scattered them.

So at length Gilgamesh came to that great mountain whose name is Mashu, the mountain which guards the rising and the setting sun. Its twin peaks are as high as the wall of heaven and its paps reach down to the underworld. At its gate the Scorpions stand guard, half man and half dragon; their glory is terrifying, their stare strikes death into men, their shimmering halo sweeps the mountains that guard the rising sun. When Gilgamesh saw them he shielded his eyes for the length of a moment only; then he took courage and approached. When they saw him so undismayed the Man-Scorpion called to his mate, 'This one who comes to us now is flesh of the gods." The mate of the Man-Scorpion answered, 'Two thirds is god but one third is man.'

Then he called to the man Gilgamesh, he called to the child of the gods: 'Why have you come so great a journey; for what have you travelled so far, crossing the dangerous waters; tell me the reason for your coming?' Gilgamesh answered, 'For Enkidu; I loved him dearly, together we endured all kinds of hardships; on his account I have come, for the common lot of man has taken him. I have wept for him day and

---

[1]*Enkidu*—the wild man who became Gilgamesh's faithful companion in the hero's war against evil. Ishtar jealously persuaded the other gods to afflict Enkidu with a fatal illness. For other terms and major characters appearing in *Gilgamesh,* please consult the Glossary.

---

night, I would not give up his body for burial, I thought my friend would come back because of my weeping. Since he went, my life is nothing; that is why I have travelled here in search of Utnapishtim my father; for men say he has entered the assembly of the gods, and has found everlasting life. I have a desire to question him concerning the living and the dead.' The Man-Scorpion opened his mouth and said, speaking to Gilgamesh, 'No man born of woman has done what you have asked, no mortal man has gone into the mountain; the length of it is twelve leagues of darkness; in it there is no light, but the heart is oppressed with darkness. From the rising of the sun to the setting of the sun there is no light.' Gilgamesh said, 'Although I should go in sorrow and in pain, with sighing and with weeping, still I must go. Open the gate of the mountain.' And the Man-Scorpion said, 'Go, Gilgamesh, I permit you to pass through the mountain of Mashu and through the high ranges; may your feet carry you safely home. The gate of the mountain is open.'

When Gilgamesh heard this he did as the Man-Scorpion had said, he followed the sun's road to his rising, through the mountain.[2] When he had gone one league the darkness became thick around him, for there was no light, he could see nothing ahead and nothing behind him. After two leagues the darkness was thick and there was no light, he could see nothing ahead and nothing behind him. After three leagues the darkness was thick, and there was no light, he could see nothing ahead and nothing behind him. After four leagues the darkness was thick and there was no light, he could see nothing ahead and nothing behind him. At the end of five leagues the darkness was thick and there was no light, he could see nothing ahead and nothing behind him. At the end of six leagues the darkness was thick and there was no light, he could see nothing ahead and nothing behind him. When he had gone seven leagues the darkness was thick and there was no light, he could see nothing ahead and nothing behind him. When he had gone eight leagues Gilgamesh gave a great cry, for the darkness was thick and he could see nothing ahead and nothing behind him. After nine leagues he felt the north wind on his face, but the darkness was thick and there was no light, he could see nothing ahead and nothing behind him. Aften ten leagues the end was near. After eleven leagues the dawn light appeared. At the end of twelve leagues the sun streamed out.

There was the garden of the gods; all round him stood bushes bearing gems. Seeing it he went down at once, for there was fruit of carnelian with the vine hanging from it, beautiful to look at; lapis lazuli leaves hung thick with fruit, sweet to see. For thorns and thistles there were haematite and rare stones, agate, and pearls from out of the sea. While Gilgamesh walked in the garden by the edge of the sea Shamash saw him, and he saw that he was dressed in the skins of animals and ate

---

[2] *The mountain*—Gilgamesh traverses a purely mythical landscape to the bejewelled garden of the gods.

their flesh.[3] He was distressed, and he spoke and said, 'No mortal man has gone this way before, nor will, as long as the winds drive over the sea.' And to Gilgamesh he said, 'You will never find the life for which you are searching.' Gilgamesh said to glorious Shamash, 'Now that I have toiled and strayed so far over the wilderness, am I to sleep, and let the earth cover my head for ever? Let my eyes see the sun until they are dazzled with looking. Although I am no better than a dead man, still let me see the light of the sun.'

Beside the sea she lives, the woman of the vine, the maker of wine; Siduri sits in the garden at the edge of the sea, with the golden bowl and the golden vats that the gods gave her. She is covered with a veil; and where she sits she sees Gilgamesh coming towards her, wearing skins, the flesh of the gods in his body, but despair in his heart, and his face like the face of one who has made a long journey. She looked, and as she scanned the distance she said in her own heart, 'Surely this is some felon; where is he going now?' And she barred her gate against him with the cross-bar and shot home the bolt. But Gilgamesh, hearing the sound of the bolt, threw up his head and lodged his foot in the gate; he called to her, 'Young woman, maker of wine, why do you bolt your door; what did you see that made you bar your gate? I will break in your door and burst in your gate, for I am Gilgamesh who seized and killed the Bull of Heaven, I killed the watchman of the cedar forest, I overthrew Humbaba who lived in the forest, and I killed the lions in the passes of the mountain.'

      ✿   ✿   ✿

She answered, 'Gilgamesh, where are you hurrying to? You will never find that life for which you are looking. When the gods created man they allotted to him death, but life they retained in their own keeping. As for you, Gilgamesh, fill your belly with good things; day and night, night and day, dance and be merry, feast and rejoice. Let your clothes be fresh, bathe yourself in water, cherish the little child that holds your hand, and make your wife happy in your embrace; for this too is the lot of man.'

But Gilgamesh said to Siduri, the young woman, 'How can I be silent, how can I rest, when Enkidu whom I love is dust, and I too shall die and be laid in the earth for ever.' He said again, 'Young woman, tell me now, which is the way to Utnapishtim, the son of Ubara-Tutu? What directions are there for the passage; give me, oh, give me directions. I will cross the Ocean[4] if it is possible; if it is not I will wander still

---

[3]*Ate their flesh*—Dependence upon animals for clothing and food was a purely human characteristic. The sun-god Shamash is here registering his surprise at seeing a mortal man in the garden of the gods.

[4]*Ocean*—in the Sumero-Babylonian cosmos, the circular inhabited earth was surrounded by an unknown expanse of ocean. In crossing it, Gilgamesh does what no man has dared to do before.

farther in the wilderness.' The wine-maker said to him, 'Gilgamesh, there is no crossing the Ocean; whoever has come, since the days of old, has not been able to pass that sea. The Sun in his glory crosses the Ocean, but who beside Shamash has ever crossed it? The place and the passage are difficult, and the waters of death are deep which flow between. Gilgamesh, how will you cross the Ocean? When you come to the waters of death what will you do? But Gilgamesh, down in the woods you will find Urshanabi, the ferryman of Utnapishtim; with him are the holy things, the things of stone. He is fashioning the serpent prow of the boat. Look at him well, and if it is possible, perhaps you will cross the waters with him; but if it is not possible, then you must go back.'

✿ ✿ ✿

So Urshanabi the ferryman brought Gilgamesh to Utnapishtim, whom they call the Faraway, who lives in Dilmun at the place of the sun's transit, eastward of the mountain. To him alone of men the gods had given everlasting life.

Now Utnapishtim, where he lay at ease, looked into the distance and he said in his heart, musing to himself, 'Why does the boat sail here without tackle and mast; why are the sacred stones destroyed, and why does the master not sail the boat? That man who comes is none of mine; where I look I see a man whose body is covered with skins of beasts. Who is this who walks up the shore behind Urshanabi, for surely he is no man of mine?' So Utnapishtim looked at him and said, 'What is your name, you who come here wearing the skins of beasts, with your cheeks starved and your face drawn? Where are you hurrying to now? For what reason have you made this great journey, crossing the seas whose passage is difficult? Tell me the reason for your coming.'

✿ ✿ ✿

Oh, father Utnapishtim, you who have entered the assembly of the gods,[5] I wish to question you concerning the living and the dead, how shall I find the life for which I am searching?'

Utnapishtim said, 'There is no permanence. Do we build a house to stand for ever, do we seal a contract to hold for all time? Do brothers divide an inheritance to keep for ever, does the flood-time of rivers endure? It is only the nymph of the dragon-fly who sheds her larva and sees the sun in his glory. From the days of old there is no permanence. The sleeping and the dead, how alike they are, they are like a painted death. What is there between the master and the servant when both have fulfilled their doom? When the Annunaki, the judges, come togeth-

---

[5]*Entered the assembly of the gods—i.e.,* Utnapishtim has been granted immortality.

er, and Mammetun the mother of destinies, together they decree the fates of men. Life and death they allot but the day of death they do not disclose.'

Then Gilgamesh said to Utnapishtim the Faraway, "I look at you now, Utnapishtim, and your appearance is no different from mine; there is nothing strange in your features. I thought I should find you like a hero prepared for battle, but you lie here taking your ease on your back. Tell me truly, how was it that you came to enter the company of the gods and to possess everlasting life?' Utnapishtim said to Gilgamesh, 'I will reveal to you a mystery, I will tell you a secret of the gods.'

THE STORY OF THE FLOOD[6]

'YOU KNOW THE CITY SHURRUPAK, IT STANDS ON THE BANKS OF EUPHRATES? That city grew old and the gods that were in it were old. There was Anu, lord of the firmament, their father, and warrior Enlil their counsellor, Ninurta the helper, and Ennugi watcher over canals; and with them also was Ea. In those days the world teemed, the people multiplied, the world bellowed like a wild bull, and the great god was aroused by the clamour. Enlil heard the clamour and he said to the gods in council, "The uproar of mankind is intolerable and sleep is no longer possible by reason of the babel." So the gods in their hearts were moved to let loose the deluge; but my lord Ea warned me in a dream. He whispered their words to my house of reeds,[7] "Reed-house, reed-house! Wall, O wall, hearken reed-house, wall reflect; O man of Shurrupak, son of Ubara-Tutu; tear down your house and build a boat, abandon possessions and look for life, despise worldly goods and save your soul alive. Tear down your house, I say, and build a boat. These are the measurements of the barque as you shall build her: let her beam equal her length, let her deck be roofed like the vault that covers the abyss; then take up into the boat the seed of all living creatures."

'When I had understood I said to my lord, "Behold, what you have commanded I will honour and perform, but how shall I answer the people, the city, the elders?" Then Ea opened his mouth and said to me, his servant, "Tell them this: I have learnt that Enlil is wrathful against me, I dare no longer walk in his land nor live in his city; I will go down to the Gulf[8] to dwell with Ea my lord. But on you he will rain down abundance, rare fish and shy wild-fowl, a rich harvest-tide. In the evening the rider of the storm will bring you wheat in torrents."

'In the first light of dawn all my household gathered round me, the children brought pitch and the men whatever was necessary. On the

---

[6]Compare Utnapishtim's account of the Flood with that given in Genesis 6:5-8:22.

[7]*To my house of reeds*—Ea, the god of wisdom and benefactor of mankind, speaks to the house rather than to Utnapishtim himself because he does not wish to antagonize the other gods by revealing their secret plans directly to a mere mortal.

[8]*The Gulf*—the Persian Gulf into which the Euphrates and Tigris rivers empty.

fifth day I laid the keel and the ribs, then I made fast the planking. The ground-space was one acre, each side of the deck measured one hundred and twenty cubits, making a square. I built six decks below, seven in all, I divided them into nine sections with bulkheads between. I drove in wedges where needed, I saw to the punt-poles, and laid in supplies. The carriers brought oil in baskets, I poured pitch into the furnace and asphalt and oil; more oil was consumed in caulking, and more again the master of the boat took into his stores. I slaughtered bullocks for the people and every day I killed sheep. I gave the ship-wrights wine to drink as though it were river water, raw wine and red wine and oil and white wine. There was feasting then as there is at the time of the New Year's festival;[9] I myself anointed my head. On the seventh day the boat was complete.

'Then was the launching full of difficulty; there was shifting of ballast above and below till two thirds was submerged. I loaded into her all that I had of gold and of living things, my family, my kin, the beasts of the field both wild and tame, and all the craftsmen. I sent them on board, for the time that Shamash had ordained was already fulfilled when he said, "In the evening, when the rider of the storm sends down the destroying rain, enter the boat and batten her down." The time was fulfilled, the evening came, the rider of the storm sent down the rain. I looked out at the weather and it was terrible, so I too boarded the boat and battened her down. All was now complete, the battening and the caulking; so I handed the tiller to Puzur-Amurri the steersman, with the navigation and the care of the whole boat.

'With the first light of dawn a black cloud came from the horizon; it thundered within where Adad, lord of the storm was riding. In front over hill and plain Shullat and Hanish, heralds of the storm, led on. Then the gods of the abyss rose up; Nergal pulled out the dams of the nether waters, Ninurta the war-lord threw down the dykes, and the seven judges of hell, the Annunaki, raised their torches, lighting the land with their livid flame. A stupor of despair went up to heaven when the god of the storm turned daylight to darkness, when he smashed the land like a cup. One whole day the tempest raged gathering fury as it went, it poured over the people like the tides of battle; a man could not see his brother nor the people be seen from heaven. Even the gods were terrified at the flood, they fled to the highest heaven, the firmament of Anu; they crouched against the walls, cowering like curs. Then Ishtar the sweet-voiced Queen of Heaven cried out like a woman in travail: "Alas the days of old are turned to dust because I commanded evil; why did I command this evil in the council of all the gods? I commanded

---

[9]*New Year's festival*—the chief religious festival of Babylon; the *Enuma Elish,* the Babylonian creation account, was then recited in honor of the creator-god, Marduk, son of Ea.

wars to destroy the people, but are they not my people, for I brought them forth? Now like the spawn of fish they float in the ocean." The great gods of heaven and of hell wept, they covered their mouths.

'For six days and six nights the winds blew, torrent and tempest and flood overwhelmed the world, tempest and flood raged together like warring hosts. When the seventh day dawned the storm from the south subsided, the sea grew calm, the flood was stilled; I looked at the face of the world and there was silence, all mankind was turned to clay. The surface of the sea stretched as flat as a roof-top; I opened a hatch and the light fell on my face. Then I bowed low, I sat down and I wept, the tears streamed down my face, for on every side was the waste of water. I looked for land in vain, but fourteen leagues distant there appeared a mountain, and there the boat grounded; on the mountain of Nisir the boat held fast, she held fast and did not budge. One day she held, and a second day on the mountain of Nisir she held fast and did not budge. A third day, and a fourth day she held fast on the mountain and did not budge; a fifth day and a sixth day she held fast on the mountain. When the seventh day dawned I loosed a dove and let her go. She flew away, but finding no resting-place she returned. Then I loosed a swallow, and she flew away but finding no resting-place she returned. I loosed a raven, she saw that the waters had retreated, she ate, she flew around, she cawed, and she did not come back. Then I threw everything open to the four winds, I made a sacrifice and poured out a libation on the mountain top. Seven and again seven cauldrons I set up on their stands, I heaped up wood and cane and cedar and myrtle. When the gods smelled the sweet savour, they gathered like flies over the sacrifice. Then, at last, Ishtar also came, she lifted her necklace with the jewels of heaven[10] that once Anu had made to please her. "O you gods here present, by the lapis lazuli round my neck I shall remember these days as I remember the jewels of my throat; these last days I shall not forget. Let all the gods gather round the sacrifice, except Enlil. He shall not approach this offering, for without reflection he brought the flood; he consigned my people to destruction."

'When Enlil had come, when he saw the boat, he was wrath and swelled with anger at the gods, the host of heaven, "Has any of these mortals escaped? Not one was to have survived the destruction." Then the god of the wells and canals Ninurta opened his mouth and said to the warrior Enlil, "Who is there of the gods that can devise without Ea? It is Ea alone who knows all things." Then Ea opened his mouth and spoke to warrior Enlil, "Wisest of gods, hero Enlil, how could you so senselessly bring down the flood?

---

[10]*The jewels of heaven*—Ishtar's brightly colored necklace may be the equivalent of the rainbow mentioned at Genesis 9:13-17. In both *Gilgamesh* and the Bible it is a memorial of the Deluge.

*   *   *

It was not I that revealed the secret of the gods; the wise man learned it in a dream. Now take your counsel what shall be done with him."

'Then Enlil went up into the boat, he took me by the hand and my wife and made us enter the boat and kneel down on either side, he standing between us. He touched our foreheads to bless us saying, "In time past Utnapishtim was a mortal man; henceforth he and his wife shall live in the distance at the mouth of the rivers." Thus it was that the gods took me and placed me here to live in the distance, at the mouth of the rivers.'

THE RETURN

UTNAPISHTIM SAID, 'AS FOR YOU, GILGAMESH, WHO WILL ASSEMBLE THE gods for your sake, so that you may find that life for which you are searching? But if you wish, come and put it to the test: only prevail against sleep for six days and seven nights.' But while Gilgamesh sat there resting on his haunches, a mist of sleep like soft wool teased from the fleece drifted over him, and Utnapishtim said to his wife, 'Look at him now, the strong man who would have everlasting life, even now the mists of sleep are drifting over him.' His wife replied, 'Touch the man to wake him, so that he may return to his own land in peace, going back through the gate by which he came.' Utnapishtim said to his wife, 'All men are deceivers, even you he will attempt to deceive; therefore bake loaves of bread, each day one loaf, and put it beside his head; and make a mark on the wall to number the days he has slept.'

So she baked loaves of bread, each day one loaf, and put it beside his head, and she marked on the wall the days that he slept; and there came a day when the first loaf was hard, the second loaf was like leather, the third was soggy, the crust of the fourth had mould, the fifth was mildewed, the sixth was fresh, and the seventh was still on the embers. Then Utnapishtim touched him and he woke. Gilgamesh said to Utnapishtim the Faraway, 'I hardly slept when you touched and roused me.' But Utnapishtim said, 'Count these loaves and learn how many days you slept,[11] for your first is hard, your second like leather, your third is soggy, the crust of your fourth has mould, your fifth is mildewed, your sixth is fresh and your seventh was still over the glowing embers when I touched and woke you.' Gilgamesh said, 'What shall I do, O Utna-pishtim, where shall I go? Already the thief in the night has hold of my limbs, death inhabits my room; wherever my foot rests, there I find death.'

---

[11]*How many days you slept*—by setting out a loaf of bread for each day that the exhausted Gilgamesh slept, Utnapishtim indicates how impossible it is for Gilgamesh to find everlasting life. If man can not resist sleep, how can he hope to conquer death?

Then Utnapishtim spoke to Urshanabi the ferryman: 'Woe to you Urshanabi, now and for ever more you have become hateful to this harbourage; it is not for you, nor for you are the crossings of this sea. Go now, banished from the shore. But this man before whom you walked, bringing him here, whose body is covered with foulness and the grace of whose limbs has been spoiled by wild skins, take him to the washing-place. There he shall wash his long hair clean as snow in the water, he shall throw off his skins and let the sea carry them away, and the beauty of his body shall be shown, the fillet on his forehead shall be renewed, and he shall be given clothes to cover his nakedness. Till he reaches his own city and his journey is accomplished, these clothes will show no sign of age, they will wear like a new garment.' So Urshanabi took Gilgamesh and led him to the washing-place, he washed his long hair as clean as snow in the water, he threw off his skins, which the sea carried away, and showed the beauty of his body. He renewed the fillet on his fore-head, and to cover his nakedness gave him clothes which would show no sign of age, but would wear like a new garment till he reached his own city, and his journey was accomplished.

Then Gilgamesh and Urshanabi launched the boat on to the water and boarded it, and they made ready to sail away; but the wife of Utna-pishtim the Faraway said to him, 'Gilgamesh came here wearied out, he is worn out; what will you give him to carry him back to his own coun-try?" So Utnapishtim spoke, and Gilgamesh took a pole and brought the boat in to the bank. 'Gilgamesh, you came here a man wearied out, you have worn yourself out; what shall I give you to carry you back to your own country? Gilgamesh, I shall reveal a secret thing, it is a mystery of the gods that I am telling you. There is a plant that grows under the water, it has a prickle like a thorn, like a rose; it will wound your hands, but if you succeed in taking it, then your hands will hold that which restores his lost youth to a man.'

When Gilgamesh heard this he opened the sluices so that a sweet-water current might carry him out to the deepest channel; he tied heavy stones to his feet and they dragged him down to the water-bed. There he saw the plant growing; although it pricked him he took it in his hands; then he cut the heavy stones from his feet, and the sea carried him and threw him on to the shore. Gilgamesh said to Urshanabi the ferryman, 'Come here, and see this marvellous plant. By its virtue a man may win back all his former strength. I will take it to Uruk of the strong walls; there I will give it to the old men to eat. Its name shall be "The Old Men Are Young Again"; and at last I shall eat it myself and have back all my lost youth.'[12] So Gilgamesh returned by the gate through which he had come, Gilgamesh and Urshanabi went together. They travelled their twenty leagues and then they broke their fast; after thirty leagues they stopped for the night.

---

[12]*Lost youth*—the magic plant does not confer immortality; it merely restores youth and vigor.

Gilgamesh saw a well of cool water and he went down and bathed; but deep in the pool there was lying a serpent, and the serpent sensed the sweetness of the flower. It rose out of the water and snatched it away, and immediately it sloughed its skin and returned to the well. Then Gilgamesh sat down and wept, the tears ran down his face, and he took the hand of Urshanabi; 'O Urshanabi, was it for this that I toiled with my hands, is it for this I have wrung out my heart's blood? For myself I have gained nothing; not I, but the beast of the earth has joy of it now. Already the stream has carried it twenty leagues back to the channels where I found it. I found a sign and now I have lost it. Let us leave the boat on the bank and go.'

After twenty leagues they broke their fast, after thirty leagues they stopped for the night; in three days they had walked as much as a journey of a month and fifteen days. When the journey was accomplished they arrived at Uruk, the strong-walled city. Gilgamesh spoke to him, to Urshanabi the ferryman, 'Urshanabi, climb up on to the wall of Uruk, inspect its foundation terrace, and examine well the brickwork; see if it is not of burnt bricks; and did not the seven wise men lay these foundations? One third of the whole is city, one third is garden, and one third is field, with the precinct of the goddess Ishtar. These parts and the precinct are all Uruk.'

This too was the work of Gilgamesh,[13] the king, who knew the countries of the world. He was wise, he saw mysteries and knew secret things, he brought us a tale of the days before the flood. He went a long journey, was weary, worn out with labour, and returning engraved on a stone the whole story.

---

[13] *The work of Gilgamesh*—Gilgamesh has learned that he can not escape his mortal nature. But although he must die, he finds compensation in the magnificence of the city he rules and the famous name he will leave behind. Experience has thus taught him the wisdom of Siduri's advice: he must fully enjoy the one life allotted him.

THE OLD TESTAMENT Preface

NO OTHER BOOK HAS EXERTED SO ENORMOUS AN INFLUENCE ON WESTERN CIVilization as the Bible. Three world religions, Jewish, Christian, and Moslem, claim its authority for their teachings. The Bible's strict code of ethics and concept of an Almighty Creator who demands exclusive devotion permeates almost every phase of Western life. Whether or not he belongs to an organized religion, the average westerner has his daily conduct and decisions subtly determined by biblical precepts.

The Bible's continuing moral authority stems directly from the religious genius of the Hebrew people. A tiny nation despised by its powerful neighbors, ancient Israel was repeatedly overwhelmed by the expanding empires of Egypt, Assyria, Babylon, Persia, Macedonian Greece, and Rome. But the Hebrew mind transformed these national defeats into a unique vision of God's relation to human history. The Hebrews not only regarded their national God, Yahweh, as the Creator of heaven and earth but also as the unseen Director of the destiny of all mankind. According to an early interpretation of Hebrew history, Yahweh had made the Israelites his "chosen people" to whom alone He revealed His divine nature and perfect Law. But the later Hebrew prophets, such as Isaiah, expanded Israel's historical mission to one of international significance. In the prophetic view, Israel endured the role of "suffering servant" because she was God's instrument by which He made known to Israel's heathen conquerors His omnipotent will. To the Hebrew writers of the Old Testament, then, the rise and fall of mighty empires was only part of a divine plan which would ultimately culminate in the earthwide triumph of Yahweh's worship. In the meantime Israel was to cherish her ethical monotheism until Yahweh saw fit to impose it upon all nations as the universal faith.

In view of Israel's keen sense of historical purpose, it is not surprising to find the thirty-nine books of the Old Testament strikingly consistent in presenting every event as a manifestation of Yahweh's will. Genesis and Exodus, the first two books of the Bible, are a case in point. From the act of Creation through the giving of the Mosaic Law, the writers take pains to show God in full control of human activity. When Abraham is granted a son in his old age, it is not only to reward his obedience to Yahweh, but also to ensure an heir whose descendants will populate the future nation of Israel. When Yahweh demands that Abraham sacrifice Isaac, it is to test Abraham's worthiness to be the progenitor of the Hebrew people. In repeatedly stating Yahweh's promise that Abraham's progeny will inherit the land of Canaan, the authors of Genesis intend to foreshadow the fulfillment of that promise in Israel's later conquest of Palestine.

The story of Joseph and his brothers, which concludes Genesis, is told not only to teach a moral lesson but to illustrate further Yahweh's manipulation of earthly events according to a pre-arranged pattern. The whole elaborate mechanism of the story—the sale of Joseph into slavery by his jealous brothers, Joseph's unexpected rise to a position of power in Egypt, the international famine that brings Jacob and his eleven other sons into Egypt for food—conspires to reveal the divine will in operation. For purposes known only to himself, Yahweh had determined to bring Abraham's "seed," the twelve sons of Jacob, into the land of Egypt. The adventures of Joseph, then, are not only an entertaining and edifying tale of spiritual virtue rewarded with material success, but also part of the Deity's historical plan.

After passing over a period of several hundred years during which Jacob's twelve sons multiply into populous tribes, Exodus picks up the thread of Yahweh's purpose. Exodus records that a later pharaoh who "knew not Joseph" enslaved the Israelites, whose rapidly increasing numbers he feared. In response to His people's groaning, Yahweh appears to Moses, a Hebrew who had been adopted by an Egyptian princess, and commissions him to appear before Pharaoh and demand Israel's release from captivity. The Ten Plagues which ensue are a dramatic contest between Yahweh, the God of slaves, and the numerous gods of Pharaoh. In the tenth and last plague Yahweh proves His superior might by slaughtering the first-born of every Egyptian, from Pharaoh's son "who was to sit on his throne to the first-born of the captive in the dungeon." Impressed by Yahweh's strength, Pharaoh lets Israel go, only to change his mind and pursue the fleeing tribes. Pharaoh's eagerness to recapture his slaves allows Yahweh yet another opportunity to demonstrate His might. After the Israelites cross the "Sea of Reeds," whose shallow waters are parted by a strong east wind, the tide flows back to engulf the pursuing Egyptians.

The climactic event in the Exodus narrative—in fact the central event in Israel's religious experience—is the giving of the Law on Mount Sinai. According to Exodus 19, Moses ascends the mountain, obscured in clouds and reverberating to thunderclaps, and receives from Yahweh the Ten Commandments, the moral basis of the Hebrew faith. After the presentation of the Law, Yahweh and His people conclude a sacred covenant or agreement by which God vows to protect and guide Israel so long as she obeys His newly-revealed Decalogue. Exodus thus concludes with the establishment of Israel as a *theocracy,* or God-ruled nation.

The authorship of Genesis and Exodus is the subject of much scholarly dispute. Ancient tradition assigned the first five books of the Bible, Genesis through Deuteronomy (the Pentateuch), to Moses in much the same way that the Greeks attributed the *Iliad,* the *Odyssey,* and several other poems to Homer. But many modern scholars have found signs of multiple authorship in both "Homeric" and "Mosaic" writings. Like the early epics of any people, the heroic narratives of both Greeks and Hebrews are probably—to some extent at least—a compilation of traditional folk tales reworked and edited by later hands. The universal significance of these works, however, does not lie in their origin but in their content. The enduring quality of the Old Testament vision is witnessed by the remarkable fact that of all the hundreds of religions known to the ancient world, only that contained in the Bible survives as a living faith.

GENESIS

[THE CREATION]
CHAPTER 1
IN THE BEGINNING GOD CREATED THE heaven and the earth.

2 And the earth was without form, and void; and darkness *was* upon the face of the deep. And the Spirit of God moved upon the face of the waters.

3 And God said, Let there be light: and there was light.

4 And God saw the light, that *it was* good: and God divided the light from the darkness.

5 And God called the light Day, and the darkness he called Night. And the evening and the morning were the first day.

6 And God said, Let there be a firmament in the midst of the waters, and let it divide the waters from the waters.

7 And God made the firmament, and divided the waters which *were* under the firmament from the waters which *were* above the firmament: and it was so.

8 And God called the firmament Heaven. And the evening and the morning were the second day.

9 And God said, Let the waters under the heaven be gathered together unto one place, and let the dry *land* appear: and it was so.

10 And God called the dry *land* Earth; and the gathering together of the waters called he Seas: and God saw that *it was* good.

11 And God said, Let the earth bring forth grass, the herb yielding seed, *and* the fruit tree yielding fruit after his kind, whose seed *is* in itself, upon the earth: and it was so.

12 And the earth brought forth grass, *and* herb yielding seed after his kind, and the tree yielding fruit, whose seed *was* in itself, after his kind: and God saw that *it was* good.

13 And the evening and the morning were the third day.

14 And God said, Let there be lights in the firmament of the heaven to divide the day from the night; and let them be for signs, and for seasons, and for days, and years:

15 And let them be for lights in the firmament of the heaven to give light upon the earth: and it was so.

16 And God made two great lights; the greater light to rule the day, and the lesser light to rule the night: *he made* the stars also.

17 And God set them in the firmament of the heaven to give light upon the earth,

18 And to rule over the day and over the night, and to divide the light from the darkness: and God saw that *it was* good.

19 And the evening and the morning were the fourth day.

20 And God said, let the waters bring forth abundantly the moving

---

From the *King James,* or *Authorized Version* of the Bible, published 1611.

creature that hath life, and fowl *that* may fly above the earth in the open firmament of heaven.

21 And God created great whales, and every living creature that moveth, which the waters brought forth abundantly, after their kind, and every winged fowl after his kind: and God saw that *it was* good.

22 And God blessed them, saying, Be fruitful, and mulitply, and fill the waters in the seas, and let fowl multiply in the earth.

23 And the evening and the morning were the fifth day.

24 And God said, Let the earth bring forth the living creature after his kind, cattle, and creeping thing, and beast of the earth after his kind: and it was so.

25 And God made the beast of the earth after his kind, and cattle after their kind, and every thing that creepeth upon the earth after his kind: and God saw that *it was* good.

26 And God said, Let us make man in our image, after our likeness: and let them have dominion over the fish of the sea, and over the fowl of the air, and over the cattle, and over all the earth, and over every creeping thing that creepeth upon the earth.

27 So God created man in his *own* image, in the image of God created he him; male and female created he them.

28 And God blessed them, and God said unto them, Be fruitful, and multiply, and replenish the earth, and subdue it: and have dominion over the fish of the sea, and over the fowl of the air, and over every living thing that moveth upon the earth.

29 And God said, Behold, I have given you every herb bearing seed, which *is* upon the face of all the earth, and every tree, in the which *is* the fruit of a tree yielding seed; to you it shall be for meat.

30 And to every beast of the earth, and to every fowl of the air, and to every thing that creepeth upon the earth, wherein *there is* life, *I have given* every green herb for meat: and it was so.

31 And God saw every thing that he had made, and, behold, *it was* very good. And the evening and the morning were the sixth day.

CHAPTER 2

THUS THE HEAVENS AND THE EARTH were finished, and all the host of them.

2 And on the seventh day God ended his work which he had made; and he rested on the seventh day from all his work which he had made.

3 And God blessed the seventh day, and sanctified it: because that in it he had rested from all his work which God created and made.

4 These *are* the generations of the heavens and of the earth when they were created, in the day that the LORD God[1] made the earth and the heavens.

5 And every plant of the field before it was in the earth, and every herb of the field before it grew: for the LORD God had not

---

[1]LORD *God*—literally, Yahweh Elohim. The King James translators printed LORD or GOD in small capitals wherever the divine name, Yahweh, occurred in the original Hebrew text.

caused it to rain upon the earth, and *there was* not a man to till the ground.

6 But there went up a mist from the earth, and watered the whole face of the ground.

7 And the Lord God formed man *of* the dust of the ground, and breathed into his nostrils the breath of life; and man became a living soul.

8 And the Lord God planted a garden eastward in E′den; and there he put the man whom he had formed.

9 And out of the ground made the Lord God to grow every tree that is pleasant to the sight, and good for food; the tree of life also in the midst of the garden, and the tree of knowledge of good and evil.

10 And a river went out of E′den to water the garden; and from thence it was parted, and became into four heads.

11 The name of the first *is* Pī′son: that *is* it which compasseth the whole land of Hăv′ĭ-läh, where *there is* gold;

12 And the gold of that land *is* good: there *is* bdellium and the onyx stone.

13 And the name of the second river *is* Gī′hŏn: the same *is* it that compasseth the whole land of Ethiopia.

14 And the name of the third river *is* Hid′dē-kĕl: that *is* it which goeth toward the east of Assyria. And the fourth river *is* Eū-phrā′tēs.

15 And the Lord God took the man, and put him into the garden of E′den to dress it and to keep it.

16 And the Lord God commanded the man, saying, Of every tree of the garden thou mayest freely eat:

17 But of the tree of the knowledge of good and evil, thou shalt not eat of it: for in the day that thou eatest thereof thou shalt surely die.

18 And the Lord God said, *It is* not good that the man should be alone; I will make him a help meet for him.

19 And out of the ground the Lord God formed every beast of the field,[2] and every fowl of the air; and brought *them* unto Adam to see what he would call them: and whatsoever Adam called every living creature, that *was* the name thereof.

20 And Adam gave names to all cattle, and to the fowl of the air, and to every beast of the field; but for Adam there was not found a help meet for him.

21 And the Lord God caused a deep sleep to fall upon Adam, and he slept; and he took one of his ribs, and closed up the flesh instead thereof.

22 And the rib, which the Lord God had taken from man, made he a woman, and brought her unto the man.

23 And Adam said, This *is* now bone of my bones, and flesh of my flesh: she shall be called Woman, because she was taken out of man.

24 Therefore shall a man leave his father and his mother, and shall cleave unto his wife: and they shall be one flesh.

25 And they were both naked, the man and his wife, and were not ashamed.

---

[2]*God formed every beast of the field*—note the different order of creation in Genesis 2. The second creation account apparently comes from a different source.

[THE FALL OF MAN]

CHAPTER 3

Now THE SERPENT WAS MORE SUB-
tile than any beast of the field
which the LORD God had made.
And he said unto the woman, Yea,
hath God said, Ye shall not eat of
every tree of the garden?

2 And the woman said unto the
serpent, We may eat of the fruit of
the trees of the garden:

3 But of the fruit of the tree
which *is* in the midst of the garden,
God hath said, Ye shall not eat of
it, neither shall ye touch it, lest ye
die.

4 And the serpent said unto the
woman, Ye shall not surely die:

5 For God doth know that in the
day ye eat thereof, then your eyes
shall be opened, and ye shall be as
gods, knowing good and evil.

6 And when the woman saw
that the tree *was* good for food,
and that it *was* pleasant to the
eyes, and a tree to be desired to
make *one* wise, she took of the
fruit thereof, and did eat, and gave
also unto her husband with her;
and he did eat.

7 And the eyes of them both
were opened, and they knew that
they *were* naked; and they sewed
fig leaves together, and made themselves aprons.

8 And they heard the voice of
the LORD God walking in the garden in the cool of the day: and
Adam and his wife hid themselves
from the presence of the LORD God
amongst the trees of the garden.

9 And the LORD God called unto
Adam, and said unto him, Where
art thou?

10 And he said, I heard thy voice
in the garden, and I was afraid,
because I *was* naked; and I hid
myself.

11 And he said, Who told thee
that thou *wast* naked? Hast thou
eaten of the tree, whereof I commanded thee that thou shouldest
not eat?

12 And the man said, The
woman whom thou gavest *to be*
with me, she gave me of the tree,
and I did eat.

13 And the LORD God said unto
the woman, What *is* this *that* thou
hast done? And the woman said,
The serpent beguiled me, and I
did eat.

14 And the LORD God said unto
the serpent, Because thou hast done
this, thou *art* cursed above all cattle, and above every beast of the
field; upon thy belly shalt thou go,
and dust shalt thou eat all the days
of thy life:

15 And I will put enmity between thee and the woman, and
between thy seed and her seed; it
shall bruise thy head, and thou
shalt bruise his heel.

16 Unto the woman he said, I
will greatly multiply thy sorrow
and thy conception; in sorrow thou
shalt bring forth children; and thy
desire *shall be* to thy husband, and
he shall rule over thee.

17 And unto Adam he said, Because thou hast hearkened unto
the voice of thy wife, and hast
eaten of the tree, of which I commanded thee, saying, Thou shalt
not eat of it: cursed *is* the ground
for thy sake; in sorrow shalt thou
eat *of* it all the days of thy life;

18 Thorns also and thistles shall
it bring forth to thee; and thou
shalt eat the herb of the field:

19 In the sweat of thy face shalt
thou eat bread, till thou return

unto the ground; for out of it wast thou taken: for dust thou *art*, and unto dust shalt thou return.

20 And Adam called his wife's name Eve; because she was the mother of all living.

21 Unto Adam also and to his wife did the LORD God make coats of skins, and clothed them.

22 And the LORD God said, Behold, the man is become as one of us, to know good and evil: and now, lest he put forth his hand, and take also of the tree of life, and eat, and live for ever:

23 Therefore the LORD God sent him forth from the garden of Ē'den, to till the ground from whence he was taken.

24 So he drove out the man: and he placed at the east of the garden of Ē'den cherubim, and a flaming sword which turned every way, to keep the way of the tree of life.

CHAPTER 4

AND ADAM KNEW EVE HIS WIFE; AND she conceived, and bare Cain, and said, I have gotten a man from the LORD.

2 And she again bare his brother Abel. And Abel was a keeper of sheep, but Cain was a tiller of the ground.

3 And in process of time it came to pass, that Cain brought of the fruit of the ground an offering unto the LORD.

4 And Abel, he also brought of the firstlings of his flock and of the fat thereof. And the LORD had respect unto Abel and to his offering:

5 But unto Cain and to his offering he had not respect. And Cain was very wroth, and his countenance fell.

6 And the LORD said unto Cain, Why art thou wroth? and why is thy countenance fallen?

7 If thou doest well, shalt thou not be accepted? and if thou doest not well, sin lieth at the door: and unto thee *shall be* his desire, and thou shalt rule over him.

8 And Cain talked with Abel his brother: and it came to pass, when they were in the field, that Cain rose up against Abel his brother, and slew him.

9 And the LORD said unto Cain, Where *is* Abel thy brother? And he said, I know not: *Am* I my brother's keeper?

10 And he said, What hast thou done? the voice of thy brother's blood crieth unto me from the ground.

11 And now *art* thou cursed from the earth, which hath opened her mouth to receive thy brother's blood from thy hand.

12 When thou tillest the ground, it shall not henceforth yield unto thee her strength; a fugitive and a vagabond shalt thou be in the earth.

13 And Cain said unto the LORD, My punishment *is* greater than I can bear.

14 Behold, thou hast driven me out this day from the face of the earth; and from thy face shall I be hid; and I shall be a fugitive and a vagabond in the earth; and it shall come to pass, *that* every one that findeth me shall slay me.

15 And the LORD said unto him, Therefore whosoever slayeth Cain, vengeance shall be taken on him sevenfold. And the LORD set a mark

upon Cain, lest any finding him should kill him.

16   And Cain went out from the presence of the LORD, and dwelt in the land of Nod, on the east of Ē′den.

✿   ✿   ✿

[THE STORY OF THE FLOOD][3]

CHAPTER 6

AND IT CAME TO PASS, WHEN MEN began to multiply on the face of the earth, and daughters were born unto them,

2 That the sons of God saw the daughters of men that they *were* fair; and they took them wives of all which they chose.

3 And the LORD said, My Spirit shall not always strive with man, for that he also *is* flesh: yet his days shall be a hundred and twenty years.

4 There were giants in the earth in those days; and also after that, when the sons of God came in unto the daughters of men, and they bare *children* to them, the same *became* mighty men which *were* of old, men of renown.

5   And GOD saw that the wickedness of man *was* great in the earth, and *that* every imagination of the thoughts of his heart *was* only evil continually.

6 And it repented the LORD that he had made man on the earth, and it grieved him at his heart.

7 And the LORD said, I will destroy man whom I have created from the face of the earth; both man, and beast, and the creeping thing, and the fowls of the air; for it repenteth me that I have made them.

8 But Noah found grace in the eyes of the LORD.

9   These *are* the generations of Noah: Noah was a just man *and* perfect in his generations, *and* Noah walked with God.

10 And Noah begat three sons, Shĕm, Ham, and Jā′phĕth.

11 The earth also was corrupt before God; and the earth was filled with violence.

12 And God looked upon the earth, and, behold, it was corrupt; for all flesh had corrupted his way upon the earth.

13 And God said unto Noah, The end of all flesh is come before me; for the earth is filled with violence through them; and, behold, I will destroy them with the earth.

14   Make thee an ark of gopher wood; rooms shalt thou make in the ark, and shalt pitch it within and without with pitch.

15 And this *is the fashion* which thou shalt make it *of*: The length of the ark *shall be* three hundred cubits, the breadth of it fifty cubits, and the height of it thirty cubits.

16 A window shalt thou make to the ark, and in a cubit shalt thou finish it above; and the door of the ark shalt thou set in the side thereof; *with* lower, second, and third *stories* shalt thou make it.

17 And, behold, I, even I, do bring a flood of waters upon the earth, to destroy all flesh, wherein *is* the breath of life, from under heaven; *and* every thing that *is* in the earth shall die.

18 But with thee will I establish my covenant; and thou shalt come

---

[3]Compare the account given in Genesis with that of Utnapishtim in *Gilgamesh*.

into the ark, thou, and thy sons, and thy wife, and thy sons' wives with thee.

19 And of every living thing of all flesh, two of every *sort* shalt thou bring into the ark, to keep *them* alive with thee; they shall be male and female.

20 Of fowls after their kind, and of cattle after their kind, of every creeping thing of the earth after his kind; two of every *sort* shall come unto thee, to keep *them* alive.

21 And take thou unto thee of all food that is eaten, and thou shalt gather *it* to thee; and it shall be for food for thee, and for them.

22 Thus did Noah; according to all that God commanded him, so did he.

CHAPTER 7

❋   ❋   ❋

11   In the six hundredth year of Noah's life, in the second month, the seventeenth day of the month, the same day were all the fountains of the great deep broken up, and the windows of heaven were opened.

12 And the rain was upon the earth forty days and forty nights.

13 In the selfsame day entered Noah, and Shĕm, and Ham, and Jā'phĕth, the sons of Noah, and Noah's wife, and the three wives of his sons with them, into the ark;

14 They, and every beast after his kind, and all the cattle after their kind, and every creeping thing that creepeth upon the earth after his kind, and every fowl after his kind, every bird of every sort.

15 And they went in unto Noah into the ark, two and two of all flesh, wherein *is* the breath of life.

16 And they that went in, went in male and female of all flesh, as God had commanded him: and the LORD shut him in.

17 And the flood was forty days upon the earth; and the waters increased, and bare up the ark, and it was lifted up above the earth.

18 And the waters prevailed, and were increased greatly upon the earth; and the ark went upon the face of the waters.

19 And the waters prevailed exceedingly upon the earth; and all the high hills, that *were* under the whole heaven, were covered.

20 Fifteen cubits upward did the waters prevail; and the mountains were covered.

21 And all flesh died that moved upon the earth, both of fowl, and of cattle, and of beast, and of every creeping thing that creepeth upon the earth, and every man:

22 All in whose nostrils *was* the breath of life, of all that *was* in the dry *land*, died.

23 And every living substance was destroyed which was upon the face of the ground, both man, and cattle, and the creeping things, and the fowl of the heaven; and they were destroyed from the earth: and Noah only remained *alive*, and they that *were* with him in the ark.

24 And the waters prevailed upon the earth a hundred and fifty days.

CHAPTER 8

AND GOD REMEMBERED NOAH, AND every living thing, and all the cattle that *was* with him in the ark: and God made a wind to pass over the earth, and the waters assuaged.

2 The fountains also of the deep and the windows of heaven were stopped, and the rain from heaven was restrained.

3 And the waters returned from off the earth continually: and after the end of the hundred and fifty days the waters were abated.

4 And the ark rested in the seventh month, on the seventeenth day of the month, upon the mountains of Ar′ă-răt.

5 And the waters decreased continually until the tenth month: in the tenth *month*, on the first *day* of the month, were the tops of the mountains seen.

6 And it came to pass at the end of forty days, that Noah opened the window of the ark which he had made:

7 And he sent forth a raven, which went forth to and fro, until the waters were dried up from off the earth.

8 Also he sent forth a dove from him, to see if the waters were abated from off the face of the ground.

9 But the dove found no rest for the sole of her foot, and she returned unto him into the ark; for the waters *were* on the face of the whole earth. Then he put forth his hand, and took her, and pulled her in unto him into the ark.

10 And he stayed yet other seven days; and again he sent forth the dove out of the ark.

11 And the dove came in to him in the evening, and, lo, in her mouth *was* an olive leaf plucked off: so Noah knew that the waters were abated from off the earth.

12 And he stayed yet other seven days, and sent forth the dove, which returned not again unto him any more.

13 And it came to pass in the six hundredth and first year, in the first *month,* the first *day* of the month, the waters were dried up from off the earth: and Noah removed the covering of the ark, and looked, and, behold, the face of the ground was dry.

14 And in the second month, on the seven and twentieth day of the month, was the earth dried.

15 And God spake unto Noah, saying,

16 Go forth of the ark, thou, and thy wife, and thy sons, and thy sons′ wives with thee.

17 Bring forth with thee every living thing that *is* with thee, of all flesh, *both* of fowl, and of cattle, and of every creeping thing that creepeth upon the earth; that they may breed abundantly in the earth, and be fruitful, and multiply upon the earth.

18 And Noah went forth, and his sons, and his wife, and his sons′ wives with him:

18 Every beast, every creeping thing, and every fowl, *and* whatsoever creepeth upon the earth, after their kinds, went forth out of the ark.

20 And Noah builded an altar unto the LORD; and took of every clean beast, and of every clean fowl, and offered burnt offerings on the altar.

21 And the LORD smelled a sweet savor; and the LORD said in his heart, I will not again curse the ground any more for man's sake; for the imagination of man's heart *is* evil from his youth: neither will

I again smite any more every thing living, as I have done.

22 While the earth remaineth, seed-time and harvest, and cold and heat, and summer and winter, and day and night shall not cease.

CHAPTER 9

AND GOD BLESSED NOAH AND HIS sons, and said unto them, Be fruitful, and multiply, and replenish the earth.

2 And the fear of you and the dread of you shall be upon every beast of the earth, and upon every fowl of the air, upon all that moveth *upon* the earth, and upon all the fishes of the sea; into your hand are they delivered.

3 Every moving thing that liveth shall be meat for you; even as the green herb have I given you all things.

4 But flesh with the life thereof, *which is* the blood thereof, shall ye not eat.

5 And surely your blood of your lives will I require: at the hand of every beast will I require it, and at the hand of man; at the hand of every man's brother will I require the life of man.

6 Whoso sheddeth man's blood, by man shall his blood be shed: for in the image of God made he man.

7 And you, be ye fruitful, and multiply; bring forth abundantly in the earth, and multiply therein.

8 And God spake unto Noah, and to his sons with him, saying,

9 And I, behold, I establish my covenant with you, and with your seed after you;

10 And with every living creature that *is* with you, of the fowl, of the cattle, and of every beast of the earth with you; from all that go out of the ark, to every beast of the earth.

11 And I will establish my covenant with you; neither shall all flesh be cut off any more by the waters of a flood; neither shall there any more be a flood to destroy the earth.

12 And God said, This *is* the token of the covenant which I make between me and you, and every living creature that *is* with you, for perpetual generations:

13 I do set my bow in the cloud, and it shall be for a token of a covenant between me and the earth.

14 And it shall come to pass, when I bring a cloud over the earth, that the bow shall be seen in the cloud:

15 And I will remember my covenant, which *is* between me and you and every living creature of all flesh; and the waters shall no more become a flood to destroy all flesh.

16 And the bow shall be in the cloud; and I will look upon it, that I may remember the everlasting covenant between God and every living creature of all flesh that *is* upon the earth.

17 And God said unto Noah, This *is* the token of the covenant, which I have established between me and all flesh that *is* upon the earth.

✿   ✿   ✿

[ABRAHAM'S SACRIFICE][4]

CHAPTER 22

AND IT CAME TO PASS AFTER THESE things, that God did tempt Abraham, and said unto him, Abraham: and he said, Behold, *here* I *am.*

2 And he said, Take now thy son, thine only *son* Isaac, whom thou lovest, and get thee into the land of Mō-rī′àh; and offer him there for a burnt offering upon one of the mountains which I will tell thee of.

3 And Abraham rose up early in the morning, and saddled his ass, and took two of his young men with him, and Isaac his son, and clave the wood for the burnt offering, and rose up, and went unto the place of which God had told him.

4 Then on the third day Abraham lifted up his eyes, and saw the place afar off.

5 And Abraham said unto his young men, Abide ye here with the ass; and I and the lad will go yonder and worship, and come again to you.

6 And Abraham took the wood of the burnt offering, and laid *it* upon Isaac his son; and he took the fire in his hand, and a knife; and they went both of them together.

7 And Isaac spake unto Abraham his father, and said, My father: and he said, Here *am* I, my son. And he said, Behold the fire and the wood: but where *is* the lamb for a burnt offering?

8 And Abraham said, My son, God will provide himself a lamb for a burnt offering: so they went both of them together.

9 And they came to the place which God had told him of; and Abraham built an altar there, and laid the wood in order, and bound Isaac his son, and laid him on the altar upon the wood.

10 And Abraham stretched forth his hand, and took the knife to slay his son.

11 And the Angel of the LORD called unto him out of heaven, and said, Abraham, Abraham: and he said, Here *am* I.

12 And he said, Lay not thine hand upon the lad, neither do thou any thing unto him: for now I know that thou fearest God, seeing thou hast not withheld thy son, thine only *son,* from me.

13 And Abraham lifted up his eyes, and looked, and behold behind *him* a ram caught in a thicket by his horns: and Abraham went and took the ram, and offered him up for a burnt offering in the stead of his son.

14 And Abraham called the name of that place Jehovah-jī′rĕh: as it is said *to* this day, In the mount of the LORD it shall be seen.

15 And the Angel of the LORD called unto Abraham out of heaven the second time,

16 And said, By myself have I sworn, saith the LORD, for because thou hast done this thing, and hast not withheld thy son, thine only *son,*

17 That in blessing I will bless thee, and in multiplying I will multiply thy seed as the stars of the heaven, and as the sand which *is* upon the seashore; and thy seed shall possess the gate of his enemies;

---

[4]The Apostle Paul argued that this episode in Genesis was a prophetic allegory of God's willingness to sacrifice His only son, Jesus Christ.

18 And in thy seed shall all the nations of the earth be blessed; because thou hast obeyed my voice.

19 So Abraham returned unto his young men, and they rose up and went together to Bē′ĕr-shē′bȧ; and Abraham dwelt at Bē′ĕr-shē′bȧ.

[THE STORY OF JOSEPH AND HIS BROTHERS,* (37:2 to 46:7)]

2 The following are the descendants of Jacob.

At the age of seventeen Joseph used to accompany his brothers in looking after the flocks, being a mere lad alongside the sons of Bilhah and Zilpah, his father's wives; and Joseph brought a bad report of them to their father.

3 Now Israel loved Joseph more than any of his other sons, because he was the son of his old age; so he 4 made a long cloak for him. When his brothers saw that their father loved him more than any of his brothers, they hated him, and could not say a good word about him.

5 Joseph had a dream, which he told to his brothers, so that they 6 hated him all the more. He said to them,

"Listen to this dream that I have 7 had. While we were binding sheaves in the field, my sheaf rose up and remained standing, while your sheaves gathered round it, and made obeisance to my sheaf!"

8 His brothers said to him,

"Are you indeed to be king over us; would you actually rule us?"

So they hated him all the more for his dreams and for his words.

Then he had another dream 9 which he recounted to his brothers.

"I have just had another dream," he said, "and the sun, moon, and eleven stars made obeisance to me!"

When he recounted it to his 10 father and his brothers, his father reproved him, saying to him.

"What is this dream that you have had? Am I actually to come with your mother and your brothers, and make obeisance to the earth to you?"

But while his brothers became 11 jealous of him, his father kept the matter in mind.

After his brothers had gone off 12 to pasture their father's flocks at Shechem, Israel said to Joseph, 13

"Are not your brothers pasturing the flocks at Shechem? Come, let me send you to them."

"I am ready," he replied.

So he said to him, 14

"Go and see how your brothers are, and the flocks; and bring me back word."

So he despatched him from the valley of Hebron; and he arrived at Shechem. But a man found him wandering about the country; so 15 the man asked him,

"What are you looking for?"

"I am looking for my brothers," 16 he said; "do tell me where they are pasturing the flocks."

The man said, 17

"They have moved from here; for I heard them say, 'Let us go to Dothan.'"

So Joseph followed his brothers, and found them at Dothan. But 18

---

*From *The Bible, An American Translation,* translated by J. M. Powis Smith. Copyright © 1923, 1927, 1948 by the University of Chicago. Reprinted by permission of the University of Chicago Press.

they saw him in the distance, and before he could reach them, they plotted against him to kill him.

19 "There comes the dreamer yonder!" they said to one another. 20 "Come now, let us kill him, and throw him into one of the pits. We can say that a wild beast devoured him. Then we shall see what his dreams will come to."

21 But when Reuben heard this, he tried to save him from their hands; so he said,

"Let us not take his life."

22 "Do not shed any blood," Reuben said to them; "throw him into the pit here in the wilderness, but do not lay hands on him" (his idea being to save him from their hands, and restore him to his father).

23 As soon as Joseph reached his brothers, they stripped him of his cloak (the long cloak that he was 24 wearing), and seizing him, they thew him into the pit. The pit, however, was empty, with no water in it.

25 Then they sat down to eat a meal; but raising their eyes, they saw a caravan of Ishmaelites coming from Gilead, with their camels carrying gum, balm, and laudanum, which they were engaged in tak- 26 ing down to Egypt. Thereupon Judah said to his brothers,

"What is the good of killing our brother and covering up his blood? 27 Come, let us sell him to the Ishmaelites, and not lay hands on him; for after all he is our brother, our own flesh."

28 His brothers agreed. Some Midianite traders passed by, so pulling Joseph up, they lifted him out of the pit. They sold Joseph to the Ishmaelites for twenty shekels of silver; and they took him to Egypt.

So when Reuben went back to 29 the pit, there was no Joseph in the pit. Then he tore his clothes, and 30 returning to his brothers, said,

"The boy is gone! And I, how can I go home?"

Then they took Joseph's cloak, 31 and killing a goat, they dipped the cloak in the blood. So they soiled 32 the long cloak, and then they brought it to their father, saying,

"We found this; see whether it is your son's cloak or not."

Examining it, he said, 33

"It is my son's cloak! Some wild beast has devoured him; Joseph must be torn to pieces."

Then Jacob tore his clothes, and 34 girded himself with sackcloth, and mourned for his son for a long time. 35 His sons and daughters all tried to console him, but he would not be consoled.

"No," he said, "I will go down mourning to Sheol to my son."

Thus did his father weep for him.

Meanwhile the Midianites had 36 sold him in Egypt to Potiphar, an officer of Pharaoh, his head steward.

*   *   *

When Joseph was taken down to 39 Egypt, Potiphar, an Egyptian, an officer of Pharaoh, his head steward, bought him from the Ishmaelites who had taken him down there. 2 The LORD was with Joseph, so that he became a prosperous man. He lived in the house of his master, the Egyptian; and his master no- 3 ticed that the LORD was with him and that the LORD made everything prosper with him that he undertook; so Joseph found favor with 4 him, and was made his personal attendant; then he made him superintendent of his household, and put him in charge of all his property. 5 From the time that he made him superintendent of his household and all his property, the Lord blessed the house of the Egyptian for Joseph's sake, the Lord's blessing resting on everything that belonged to him, both 6 indoors and outdoors. So he left everything that he had to Joseph's charge, and having him, gave no concern to anything, except the food that he ate.

7 Now Joseph was so handsome and good-looking that some time later the wife of his master took a fancy to Joseph, and said,

"Lie with me."

8 But he refused, saying to his master's wife,

"Having me, my master is giving no concern to anything in the house, but has committed all his property to my charge; there is no 9 one in this house greater than I; he has kept nothing from me except yourself, and that because you are his wife. How then can I commit this great crime, and sin against God?"

10 Though she spoke to Joseph day after day, he would not listen to her solicitations to lie with her, or 11 be with her. One day, however, when into the house to do his work, none of the household servants being anywhere in the house, she 12 caught hold of his coat, saying,

"Lie with me."

But he fled, leaving the coat in 13 her hands, and went outdoors. When she saw that he had fled out- 14 doors, leaving his coat in her hands, she called her household servants, and said to them,

"See how he has brought this Hebrew fellow into our house to violate us! He came into my room to lie with me, but I screamed; and as soon as he heard me scream 15 and call, he fled, leaving his coat beside me, and went outdoors." 16

So she left the coat beside her until his master came home, and then told him this same story. 17

"The Hebrew slave whom you brought into our house came into my room to violate me, but as soon 18 as I screamed and called, he fled outdoors, leaving his coat beside me."

When Joseph's master heard the 19 statements of his wife who said to him, "This is the way your slave treated me," his anged blazed, and 20 Joseph's master took him and threw him into the prison where state prisoners were confined. So he lay there in prison.

The Lord, however, was with 21 Joseph and was kind to him, and got him into the good graces of the 22 jailer, so that the jailer put Joseph in charge of all the prisoners who were in the jail, and he looked after everything that was done there. The jailer exercised no over- 23 sight over anything in his charge, because the Lord was with him, and the Lord made whatever he undertook prosper.

❋   ❋   ❋

Two whole years later Pharaoh 41 dreamed that he was standing beside the Nile, when seven beautiful, fat cows came up out of the Nile, 2 and browsed in the sedge. After

3 them seven other cows came up out of the Nile, ugly and thin, and stood beside the other cows on the 4 bank of the Nile. Then the thin, ugly cows ate up the seven beautiful, fat cows, whereupon Pharaoh 5 awoke. When he fell asleep again, he had a second dream: there were seven ears of grain growing on a 6 single stalk, fine and plump, and after them there sprouted seven other ears, thin and blasted by the 7 east wind. Then the thin ears swallowed up the seven fine, full ears, whereupon Pharaoh awoke, only to find it a dream!

8 Next morning he was so perturbed that he sent for all the magicians and wise men of Egypt. To them Pharaoh recounted his 9 dreams, but no one could interpret them for Pharaoh. Then the chief butler said to Pharaoh,

"I would today recall my offense, 10 how Pharaoh became angry with his servants, and put them in custody in the house of the head stew- 11 ard, myself and the chief baker. On the same night we had dreams, he and I, each of us having a dream of different meaning. With us there 12 was a Hebrew youth, a slave belonging to the head steward, and when we recounted our dreams to him, he interpreted them for us, giving each the proper interpreta- 13 tion of his dream. And it fell out just as he had indicated in the interpretation; I was restored to my position, while the other was hanged."

14 Thereupon Pharaoh sent for Joseph, and he was brought hurriedly from the dungeon. When he had shaved and changed his clothes, he came into Pharaoh's presence.

"I have had a dream," Pharaoh 15 said to Joseph, "but there is no one to interpret it. However, I have heard it said of you that you know how to interpret dreams."

"Apart from God can Pharaoh be 16 given a favorable response?" Joseph answered Pharaoh.

Then Pharaoh said to Joseph, 17 "I dreamed that I was standing on the bank of the Nile, when 18 seven fat and beautiful cows came up out of the Nile, and browsed in 19 the sedge. After them came up seven other cows, thin and very ugly and lean—I have never seen such poor cows in all the land of Egypt. Then the lean, ugly cows 20 ate up the first seven fat cows; they 21 passed right into them, but no one would have known that they had done so—they looked just as bad as before. Then I awoke.

"In another dream I saw seven 22 ears of grain growing on a single stalk, full and plump, and after 23 them there sprouted seven other ears, withered, thin, and blasted by the east wind. Then the thin ears 24 swallowed up the seven plump ears. I told this to the magicians, but there was no one to explain it to me."

Joseph said to Pharaoh, 25 "Pharaoh's dream is simple; God would reveal to Pharaoh what he is about to do. The seven fat cows 26 represent seven years, and the seven plump ears represent seven years—it is a single dream. The seven lean and ugly cows that came 27 up after them represent seven years, and so do the seven empty ears blasted by the east wind; there are to be seven years of famine. It 28 is as I told Pharaoh, God would show Pharaoh what he is about to

29 do. Seven years of great plenty are
coming throughout all the land of
30 Egypt, but following them there
will be seven years of famine, so that
the plenty will all be forgotten in
the land of Egypt; the famine will
31 devastate the land, and the plenty
will become quite unknown in the
land because of that famine which
is to follow; for it will be very
32 severe. The fact that the dream
was sent twice to Pharaoh in two
forms means that the matter is absolutely settled by God, and that
33 God will soon bring it about. Now,
then, let Pharaoh find a shrewd
and prudent man, and put him in
control of the land of Egypt. Let
34 Pharaoh proceed to appoint officials over the land to forearm the
land of Egypt during the seven
35 years of plenty; let them collect all
the food of these good years that
are coming, and under the authority of Pharaoh store up grain for
food in the cities, and hold it there.
36 The food shall serve as a reserve
for the land against the seven years
of famine that are to befall the
land of Egypt, so that the land may
not perish from the famine."
37 The proposal commended itself
38 to Pharaoh and all his courtiers,
and Pharaoh said to his courtiers,
"Can we find a man with the
spirit of God in him like this one?"
39 So Pharaoh said to Joseph,
"Since God has made all this
known to you, there is no one so
shrewd and prudent as you; you
40 shall be in charge of my palace,
and all my people shall be obedient
to your commands; it is only in the
matter of the throne itself that I
shall be your superior."
41 Thereupon Pharaoh said to Joseph,

"I hereby put you in charge of
the whole land of Egypt."
And taking the signet ring from 42
his finger, Pharaoh put it on Joseph's finger; he dressed him in
linen robes, put a gold chain round 43
his neck, and had him ride in the
second of his chariots, with people
shouting "Bow down!" before him,
thus putting him in charge of the
whole land of Egypt.
"Although I continue as Phar- 44
aoh," said Pharaoh to Joseph, "yet
without your consent shall no one
stir hand or foot in all the land of
Egypt."
Then Pharaoh called Joseph's 45
name Zaphenath-paneah, and married him to Asenath, the daughter
of Potiphera, priest of On; and Joseph's fame spread throughout the
land of Egypt.
Joseph was thirty years old when 46
he entered the service of Pharaoh,
king of Egypt.
After leaving the presence of
Pharaoh, Joseph made a tour
through the whole land of Egypt. 47
During the seven years of plenty 48
the land produced abundant crops;
so he collected all the food of the
seven years when there was plenty
in the land of Egypt, and thus
stored food in the cities, storing in
each city the food from the fields
around it. Joseph stored up grain 49
like the sands of the sea, in great
quantities, until he ceased to keep
account of it; for it was past measuring.
Before the years of famine came, 50
two sons were born to Joseph by
Asenath, the daughter of Potiphera,
priest of On. Joseph called the 51
name of the first-born Manasseh
[forgetfulness]; "For," said he,
"God has made me forget all about

my hardships and my father's
52 home." The name of the second he
called Ephraim [fruitfulness]; "For
God has made me fruitful in the
land of my misfortune."

53 When the seven years of plenty
that had prevailed in the land of
54 Egypt came to an end, the seven
years of famine set in, as Joseph
had said.

There was famine in all lands,
but throughout all the land of
Egypt there was food.

55 When all the land of Egypt became famished, the people cried to
Pharaoh for food; so Pharaoh announced to all Egypt,

"Go to Joseph, and do what he
tells you."

56 The famine spread all over the
land, so Joseph threw open all that
he had locked up, and sold grain to
the Egyptians, since the famine was
57 severe in the land of Egypt. People
from all lands came to Joseph in
Egypt to buy grain; for the famine
was severe all over the earth.

42 When Jacob learned that there
was grain in Egypt, he said to his
sons,

"Why do you stare at one
2 another?" "I have just heard," he
said, "that there is grain in Egypt;
go down there, and buy some for
us there, that we may live and not
die."

3 So ten of Joseph's brothers went
4 down to buy grain in Egypt, since
Jacob would not let Joseph's brother Benjamin go with his other
brothers; "Lest," thought he, "harm
5 should befall him." Thus the Israelites came with the rest to buy
grain; for the famine was in the
land of Canaan.

6 Now Joseph was the vizier of the
land; it was he who sold the grain

to all the people of the land. So
Joseph's brothers came and pros-
trated themselves before him, with
their faces to the ground. When 7
Joseph saw his brothers, he recognized them, but he treated them as
if he were a stranger, and spoke
harshly to them.

"Where have you come from?"
he said to them.

"From the land of Canaan to buy
food," they said.

Joseph recognized his brothers, 8
but they did not recognize him. 9
Remembering the dreams that he
had had about them, Joseph said
to them,

"You are spies; you have come to
find out the condition of the land!"

"No, my lord," they said to him, 10
"your servants have come to buy
food. We are all sons of one man; 11
we are honest men; your servants
are not spies."

"Not so," he said to them; "but 12
you have come to find out the condition of the land."

But they said, 13
"Your servants are brothers,
twelve in all; we are sons of a certain man in the land of Canaan; the
youngest is at present with our
father, while the other is no more."

But Joseph said to them, 14
"It is as I told you; you are spies. 15
By this you shall be put to the
proof: as Pharaoh lives, you shall
not leave this place unless your
youngest brother comes here. Send 16
one of your number to fetch your
brother, while the rest of you remain in custody. Thus shall your
statements be put to the proof as
to whether you are truthful or not.
As Pharaoh lives, you are spies!"

So he bundled them off to prison 17
for three days, but on the third 18

day Joseph said to them,

"Since I am one who fears God,
19 you may save your lives, if you do
this: if you are honest men, let one
of you brothers remain confined in
your prison and then the rest of
you, go and take grain home to
20 your starving households; but you
must bring me your youngest
brother. Thus shall your words be
verified, and you shall not die."

21 They proceeded to do so, saying
to one another,

"Unfortunately, we were to
blame about our brother, upon
whose distress, when he pleaded
with us for mercy, we gazed unmoved; that is why this distress has
come to us."

22 Then Reuben spoke up and said
to them,

"Did I not say to you, 'Do not sin
against the lad'? But you paid no
attention; so now comes a reckoning for his blood!"

23 They did not know that Joseph
heard them; for the intermediary
24 was between them. He turned from
them, and wept. On coming back
to them, he spoke to them, took
25 Simeon from them, and imprisoned
him in their presence. Joseph then
ordered their receptacles to be
filled with grain, the money of each
of them to be replaced in his sack,
and provisions to be given them for
26 the journey. This was done for
them. Then they loaded their asses
with their grain, and departed.

*   *   *

43 The famine continued severe in
the land, so when they had finished
2 eating all the grain which they had
brought from Egypt, their father
said to them,

"Go again, and buy us a little
food."

But Judah said to him,   3
"The man strictly warned us:
'You cannot have audience with me
unless your brother is with you.' If 4
you are ready to let our brother go
with us, we will go down and buy   5
food for you; but if you are not
ready to let him go, we cannot go
down; for the man said to us, 'You
cannot have audience with me unless your brother is with you.' "

"Why did you bring this trouble   6
on me," said Israel, "by telling the
man that you had another brother?"

They said,   7
"The man persisted in asking
about ourselves and our family—'Is
your father still living? Have you
another brother?' We only gave
him the information demanded by
these questions of his. How could
we possibly know that he would
say, 'Bring your brother down'?"

"Let the lad go with me," said   8
Judah to his father Israel; "but we
must go at once, if we would save
our lives and not die, both we, you,
and our dependents. I will be
surety for him; you may hold me   9
responsible for him. If I do not
bring him back to you and set him
before you, you may blame me for
it all my life; in fact if we had not 10
wasted so much time, we could
have made a second trip by now."

Then their father Israel said to   11
them,

"If it must be so, then do this:
take some of the country's best in
your receptacles, and take it down
to the man as a present—a little
balm, a little honey, gum, laudanum, pistachio nuts, and almonds.

12 Also take double the money with you, and so take back with you the money that was replaced in the mouths of your sacks—perhaps
13 there was a mistake. Take your
14 brother too, and go, return to the man. May God Almighty grant you such kindness with the man that he will release your other brother for you, as well as Benjamin. As for me, as I am bereaved, I am bereaved.
15 So the men took this present, and taking double the money with them, as well as Benjamin, they started off, went down to Egypt,
16 and stood in the presence of Joseph.

* * *

27 He asked after their health.
"Is your father well," he said, "the old man of whom you spoke? Is he still living?"
28 "Your servant, our father, is well; he is still living," they said, bowing in homage to him.
29 Raising his eyes, he saw his brother Benjamin, the son of his own mother, and said,
"Is this your youngest brother, of whom you told me?"
"May God be gracious to you, my son!" he said.
30 Thereupon Joseph hastily sought a place to weep; for his heart was deeply stirred at sight of his broth-
31 er; he retired to his room, and wept there. Then he bathed his face, and came out, and controlling himself, said,
"Serve the meal."
32 The meal was served, separately for him, for them, and for the Egyptians that were dining with him; for the Egyptians could not eat with the Hebrews, because that would be abhorrent to the Egyptians. They were seated in 33 his presence in order of age, from the oldest to the youngest, so that the men stared at one another in amazement. Portions were carried 34 from his own table to them, but Benjamin's portion was five times as much as any other's. So they feasted, and drank with him.

He then gave orders to his house- 44 steward,
"Fill the men's sacks as full as they will hold with food, and put each man's money in the mouth of his sack; in the mouth of the sack 2 belonging to the youngest put my cup, the silver cup, along with his money for the grain."
He followed the instructions which Joseph gave.
With the dawn of morning the 3 men with their asses were sent on their way. Although they had left 4 the city, they had not gone far, when Joseph said to his house-steward,
"Run at once after the men, and when you overtake them, say to them, 'Why have you returned evil for good? Why have you stolen my silver cup? Is not this the one from 5 which my lord drinks, which in fact he uses for divination? It is a wicked thing that you have done.'"
So he overtook them, and ad- 6 dressed these words to them; but 7 they said to him,
"Why should my lord speak like this? Your servants would never think of doing such a thing! Why, 8 we even brought you back from the land of Canaan the money that we found in the mouths of our sacks. How then could we steal silver or

9 gold from your master's house? That one of your servants in whose possession it is found shall die, and the rest of us will become slaves to my lord."

10 "Although it may indeed be just as you say," he said, "'yet the one in whose possession it is found shall become my slave, but the rest of you shall be held blameless."

11 Then each of them quickly low-

12 ered his sack to the ground, and opened it, and search being made, beginning with the oldest and end-

13 ing with the youngest, the cup was found in Benjamin's sack. There-upon they tore their clothes, and each having reloaded his ass, they returned to the city.

14 Judah and his brothers arrived at the house of Joseph, while he was still there, so they flung them-selves on the ground before him.

15 "What is this that you have done?" Joseph said to them. "Did you not know that a man like me would be sure to use divination?"

16 Judah said,
"What can we say to my lord? What can we urge? How can we prove our innocence? God has dis-covered the crime of your servants; here we are, the slaves of my lord, both we and he in whose possession the cup has been found."

17 "I could not think of doing such a thing," he said; "only the man in whose possession the cup has been found shall be my slave; the rest of you are free to go back to your father."

18 Then Judah went up to him, and said,
"If you please, my lord, let your servant speak a word in the ear of my lord, and your anger not blaze against your servant; for you are the equal of Pharaoh himself. My 19 lord asked his servants, 'Have you a father or a brother?' And we said to my lord, 'We have an aged 20 father, and a young brother, the child of his old age; his brother is dead, so that he alone is left of his mother's children, and his father loves him.' Then you said to your 21 servants, 'Bring him down to me that I may see him.' But we told my lord, 'The boy cannot leave his 22 father; his father would die if he were to leave him.' Whereupon you 23 said to your servants, 'Unless your youngest brother comes down with you, you cannot have audience with me again.'

"When we went back to your 24 servant, my father, we reported to him the words of my lord. Then our 25 father said, 'Go again and buy a little food for us.' But we said, 'We 26 cannot go down; if our youngest brother accompanies us, we can go down; for we shall not be allowed to have audience with the man un-less our youngest brother is with us.' Then your servant, my father, 27 said to us, 'You know that my wife bore me only two children; then one of them left me, and I think 28 he must surely have been torn to pieces; for I have never seen him since. If then you take this one 29 from me too, and harm befall him, you will bring down my gray hairs to Sheol in trouble.'

"And now, when I rejoin your 30 servant, my father, and the boy not with us, his life is so bound up with the boy's that he will die when he 31 sees that there is no boy, and your servants will bring down the gray hairs of your servant, our father,

32 to Sheol[1] in sorrow; for your servant went surety for the boy to my father, saying, 'If I do not bring him back to you, let my father blame me for it all my life.' Now 33 then, pray let your servant remain in the boy's place as my lord's slave, but let the boy go back with his 34 brothers; for how can I go back to my father unless the boy is with me, and witness the agony that would come to my father?"

45 Joseph could no longer control himself before all his attendants, so he cried out,

"Have everyone withdraw from me."

So there was no one with Joseph when he made himself known 2 to his brothers; but he wept so loudly that the Egyptians heard it, 3 and Pharaoh's household heard it. Joseph said to his brothers,

"I am Joseph. Is my father still living?"

But his brothers could not answer him, because they were so 4 dismayed at being in his presence. So Joseph said to his brothers,

"Come nearer to me."

When they came nearer, he said, "I am your brother Joseph whom 5 you sold into Egypt. Now do not be distressed nor angry with yourselves that you sold me here; for it 6 was to save life that God sent me ahead of you; for it is two years now that the famine has prevailed in the land, but there are still five years in which there will be no 7 plowing or reaping. God sent me ahead of you to insure you a remnant in the earth, and to be the 8 means of a remarkable escape for you. So then it was not you, but God who sent me here, and made me a father to Pharaoh, lord of all his house, and ruler over all the land of Egypt. Hurry back to my 9 father and say to him, 'Thus speaks your son Joseph: "Since God has made me lord of all Egypt, come down to me without delay. You 10 shall live in the land of Goshen, and be near me, you, your sons, your grandsons, your flocks, your herds, and all that belong to you; and there I will provide for you, 11 lest you, your household, and all that belong to you come to want; for there are still five years of famine to come."' You can see for 12 yourselves and my brother Benjamin for himself that it is I who 13 speak to you. You must tell my father all about my splendor in Egypt, and all that you have seen; hurry and bring my father here."

Then he fell on the neck of his 14 brother Benjamin and wept, while Benjamin wept on his neck. He 15 kissed all his brothers, and wept on their shoulders, after which his brothers talked with him.

When the news was received at 16 Pharaoh's palace that Joseph's brothers had arrived, Pharaoh was delighted, as were also his courtiers. Pharaoh said to Joseph, 17

"Say to your brothers, 'Do this: load your animals, go back to the land of Canaan, and taking your 18 father and your households, come to me, and I will give you the best of the land of Egypt, so that you shall eat the fat of the land. Also, carry out this order: take wagons 19 from the land of Egypt for your little ones and your wives; convey your father in them, and come 20

---

[1]*Sheol*—domain of the dead, equivalent of the Greek Hades.

back. Never mind your goods; for the best of the whole land of Egypt will be yours.'"

21 The sons of Israel did so. Joseph gave them wagons in accord with the command of Pharaoh, and he 22 also gave them provisions for the journey. To each of them he gave a festal garment, but to Benjamin he gave three hundred shekels of silver and five festal garments. To 23 his father he sent likewise ten asses loaded with the best products of Egypt, and ten she-asses loaded with grain, bread, and provisions 24 for his father on the journey. Then he sent his brothers away; and as they left, he said to them,

"Do not get too excited on the way."

25 So they went up from Egypt, and came to the land of Canaan, to their father Jacob.

26 "Joseph is still living, and he is ruler over all the land of Egypt," they told him.

But he was so stunned that he 27 would not believe them. However, when they told him all that Joseph had said to them, and he saw the wagons that Joseph had sent to convey him, their father Jacob recovered.

"Enough!" said Israel; "my son 28 Joseph is still living; I will go and see him before I die."

So Israel set out with all that be- 46 longed to him. On reaching Beersheba, he offered sacrifices to the God of his father Isaac. In a vision 2 by night God spoke to Israel.

"Jacob! Jacob!" he said.

"Here I am," he said.

"I am El, the God of your fa- 3 ther," he said; "do not be afraid to go down to Egypt; for there I will make you a great nation. I will my- 4 self go down to Egypt with you— yes, and I will bring you up again, when Joseph's hand shall close your eyes."

Then Jacob set out from Beer- 5 sheba; and the sons of Israel conveyed their father Jacob, with their little ones and their wives, in the wagons which Pharaoh had sent to 6 convey them. Taking their live stock and the property which they had acquired in the land of Canaan, Jacob and all his family migrated to Egypt; his sons and his grand- 7 sons accompanied him, as well as his daughters and his grand-daughters; he brought all his family with him into Egypt.

❖   ❖   ❖

EXODUS

THE OPPRESSION OF THE HEBREWS IN EGYPT, 1:1-22

8 Then a new king rose over Egypt, 9 who had no knowledge of Joseph; he said to his people,

"See, the Israelite people have become too numerous and too strong for us; come, let us take precautions against them lest they be- 10 come so numerous that in the case of a war they should join forces with our enemies and fight against us, and so escape from the land."

Accordingly, gang-foremen were 11 put in charge of them, to oppress

them with their heavy labor; and they built Pithom and Raamses as
12 store-cities for Pharaoh. But the more they oppressed them, the more they multiplied and expanded, so that they became apprehensive about the Israelites.
13 The Egyptians reduced the Is-
14 raelites to rigorous slavery; they made life bitter for them in hard work with mortar and bricks, and in all kinds of work in the fields, all the work that they exacted of them being rigorous.
15 Then the king of Egypt spoke to the midwives attending the Hebrew women, of whom the name of one was Shiphrah and that of the other Puah.
16 "When you act as midwives for the Hebrew women," he said, "you are to look at the genitals; if it is a boy, you must kill him, but if it is a girl, she may live."
17 But the midwives stood in awe of God, and so did not do as the king of Egypt told them, but let
18 the male children live. So the king of Egypt summoned the midwives, and said to them,
"Why have you done this: let the male children live?"
19 The midwives said to Pharaoh,
"Because the Hebrew women are not like the Egyptian women; but are animals, in that they are delivered before the midwife reaches them!"
20 So God was good to the midwives; the people multiplied and
21 grew very numerous, and because the midwives stood in awe of God, they established families for them.
22 So Pharaoh commanded all his people,
"Every boy that is born to the Hebrews, you must throw into the

Nile, but you are to let all the girls live."

THE RISE OF THE DELIVERER, MOSES, 2:1–3:18

Now a man belonging to the 2 house of Levi went and married a daughter of Levi. The woman con- 2 ceived and bore a son, and seeing that he was robust, she hid him for three months. When she could no 3 longer hide him, she procured an ark of papyrus reeds for him, and daubing it with bitumen and pitch, she put the child in it, and placed it among the reeds beside the bank of the Nile. His sister posted herself 4 some distance away to see what would happen to him.

Presently Pharaoh's daughter 5 came down to bathe at the Nile, while her maids walked on the bank of the Nile. Then she saw the ark among the reeds and sent her maid to get it. On opening it, she 6 saw the child, and it was a boy crying! She took pity on him, and said,

"This is one of the Hebrews' children."

Thereupon his sister said to Phar- 7 aoh's daughter,

"Shall I go and summon a nurse for you from the Hebrew women, to nurse the child for you?"

"Go," said Pharaoh's daughter to 8 her.

So the girl went and called the 9 child's mother, to whom Pharaoh's daughter said,

"Take this child away and nurse it for me, and I will pay the wages due you."

So the woman took the child and nursed him; and when the child 10 grew up, she brought him to Pharaoh's daughter, and he became her son. She called his name Moses [drawn out]; "For," said she, "I drew him out of the water."

11 It was in those days that Moses, now grown up, went out to visit his fellow-countrymen and noted their heavy labor. He saw an Egyptian

12 kill a Hebrew, one of his own countrymen; so, looking this way and that, and seeing that there was no one in sight, he killed the Egyptian, and hid him in the sand. Another

13 day, when he went out, there were two Hebrews fighting! So he said to him that was in the wrong,

"Why do you strike your companion?"

14 He replied,

"Who made you ruler and judge over us? Are you thinking of murdering me as you did the Egyptian?"

Then was Moses afraid. "The incident must surely be known," he thought.

15 When Pharaoh heard about the matter, he tried to kill Moses, but Moses fled from Pharaoh and went to the land of Midian, and sat down beside a well.

16 Now the priest of Midian had seven daughters, who came to draw water, and fill the troughs to water

17 their father's flock, but some shepherds came and drove them off. So Moses went to their rescue and

18 watered their flock. When they came home to their father Reuel, he said,

"How did you come to get home so soon today?"

19 They said,

"An Egyptian protected us against the shepherds; he even drew water for us, and watered the flock."

"Then where is he?" he said to 20 his daughters. "Why did you leave the man behind? Invite him to have a meal."

When Moses agreed to live with 21 the man, he gave Moses his daughter Zipporah in marriage; and she bore a son, whom he named Ger- 22 shom [immigrant]; "For," said he, "I am an immigrant in a foreign land."

In the course of this long time 23 the king of Egypt died. The Israelites, groaning under their bondage, cried for help, and their cry because of their bondage came up to 24 God. God heard their moaning, and God remembered his covenant with Abraham, Isaac, and Jacob; God saw the plight of Israel, and took 25 cognizance of it.

While Moses was tending the 3 flock of his father-in-law, Jethro, the priest of Midian, he led the flock to the western side of the desert, and came to the mountain of God, Horeb. Then the angel of 2 the LORD appeared to him in a flame of fire, rising out of a bush. He looked, and there was the bush burning with fire without being consumed! So Moses said, 3

"I will turn aside and see this great sight, why the bush is not burned up."

When the LORD saw that he had 4 turned aside to look at it, God called to him out of the bush.

"Moses, Moses!" he said.

"Here I am!" said he.

"Do not come near here," he said; 5 "take your sandals off your feet; for the place on which you are standing is holy ground." "I am the God of your father," he said, 6 "the God of Abraham, Isaac, and Jacob."

Then Moses hid his face; for he was afraid to look at God.

7 "I have indeed seen the plight of my people who are in Egypt," the Lord said, "and I have heard their cry under their oppressors; for I know their sorrows, and I have 8 come down to rescue them from the Egyptians and bring them up out of that land to a land, fine and large, to a land flowing with milk and honey, to the country of the Canaanites, Hittites, Amorites, Per- 9 izzites, Hivvites, and Jebusites. Now the cry of the Israelites has reached me, and I have also seen how the Egyptians are oppressing 10 them; so come now, let me send you to Pharaoh, that you may bring my people, the Israelites, out of Egypt."

11 But Moses said to God, "Who am I, to go to Pharaoh and bring the Israelites out of Egypt?"

12 "I will be with you," he said; "and this shall be the sign for you that I have sent you. When you bring the people out of Egypt, you shall serve God at this mountain."

13 "But," said Moses to God, "in case I go to the Israelites and say to them, 'The God of your fathers has sent me to you,' and they say to me, 'What is his name?' what am I to say to them?"

14 "I am who I am," God said to Moses. Then he said, "Thus you shall say to the Israelites: ' "I am" has sent me to you.' "

15 God said further to Moses, "Thus you shall say to the Israelites:
'Yahweh [the Lord], the God of your fathers, the God of Abraham, Isaac, and Jacob, has sent me to you.' This has always been my name, and this shall remain my title throughout the ages. Go and 16 assemble the elders of Israel, and say to them, 'The Lord, the God of your fathers, the God of Abraham, Isaac, and Jacob, has appeared to me, saying, "I have given careful heed to you and your treatment in Egypt, and I have re- 17 solved to bring you up out of your tribulation in Egypt to the land of the Canaanites, Hittites, Amorites, Perizzites, Hivvites, and Jebusites, to a land flowing with milk and 18 honey." '

* * *

[YAHWEH'S PURPOSE IN AFFLICTING EGYPT WITH THE TEN PLAGUES, 9:14-16]

Then the Lord said to Moses, "Rise early in the morning and present yourself before Pharaoh, and say to him, 'Thus says the Lord, the God of the Hebrews: "Let my people go, that they may serve me; for this time I am going 14 to send all my plagues on you, your courtiers, and your people, in order that you may know that there is no one like me in all the earth. For by 15 now I could have stretched out my hand and struck you and your people with pestilence, so that you would have been effaced from the 16 earth; but this is why I have spared you: to show you my power, and to have my fame recounted throughout all the earth.

* * *

[THE TENTH PLAGUE: THE DEATHS OF THE EGYPTIAN FIRST-BORN, 11:1-8 and 12:21-32]

11   Then the LORD said to Moses,
"One more plague will I bring on Pharaoh and on Egypt; after that he will let you go from here; indeed when he does let you go, he will absolutely drive you out of
2 here. So announce to the people that each man is to ask his neighbor, and each woman her neighbor, for articles of silver and gold."
3   Now the LORD put the people in favor with the Egyptians; besides, the man Moses came to be very greatly esteemed in the land of Egypt by Pharaoh's courtiers and by the people.
4   So Moses said,
"Thus says the LORD: 'At midnight I am going to go forth among
5 the Egyptians, when all the first-born in the land of Egypt shall die, from Pharaoh's first-born who is to sit on his throne to the first-born of the slave-girl who sits behind the mill, as well as the first-born of the
6 live-stock; all through the land of Egypt there shall be loud wailing, such as there never has been and
7 never will be again.' But against none of the Israelites, either man or beast, shall even a dog bark, in order that you may know that the LORD does make a distinction between Egypt and Israel. Then shall
8 all these courtiers of yours come down to me and make obeisance to me, saying, 'Depart, you and all the people that are in your train.' Only after that will I leave."

❊   ❊   ❊

Then Moses summoned all the 21 elders of Israel, and said to them,
"Go and provide yourselves with sheep, family by family, and kill it as a passover-sacrifice. Then you 22 must take a bunch of hyssop, and dipping it in the blood that is in the basin, smear the lintel and the two door-posts with the blood in the basin, and none of you is to go outside his house until morning, in 23 that the LORD will be passing through to strike down the Egyptians, and when he sees the blood on the lintel and the two door-posts, the LORD will pass by that door, and not let the destroyer enter your houses to strike you down. You must observe this as a 24 rite prescribed for you and your descendants forever. And when 25 you enter the land which the LORD shall give you, as he promised, you must observe this service. When your children say to you, 'What do 26 you mean by this service?' you shall say, 'It is the passover-sacrifice to 27 the LORD, who passed by the houses of the Israelites in Egypt when he struck down the Egyptians, but spared our houses.'"

Then the people bowed their heads in reverence. The Israelites 28 went and did so; they did just as the LORD had commanded Moses and Aaron.

At midnight the LORD struck 29 down all the first-born in the land of Egypt, from Pharaoh's first-born who was to sit on his throne to the first-born of the captive in the dungeon, as well as all the first-born of the live stock. Then Pharaoh 30 rose in the night, he and all his courtiers and all the Egyptians, and there arose a loud cry in Egypt; for there was not a house where there was not someone dead.

31 So he summoned Moses and Aaron in the night, and said,

"Withdraw at once from my people, both you and the Israelites,

32 and go, serve the LORD as you suggested. Take both your flocks and herds as you suggested, and be gone; also ask a blessing on me."

❋ ❋ ❋

[PURSUING EGYPTIANS ARE ENGULFED BY THE RED SEA, 14:1-31]

14   Then the LORD said to Moses,
"Tell the Israelites to turn back and camp in front of Pi-hahiroth, between Migdol and the sea, in front of Baal-zephon; you must

3 camp opposite it, beside the sea. Pharaoh will say of the Israelites, 'They are wandering aimlessly in the land; the desert has shut them

4 in.' Then I will make Pharaoh obstinate, so that he will pursue them, and thus I will gain honor through Pharaoh and all his army, and the Egyptians shall know that I am the LORD."

They did so.

5   When the news was brought to the king of Egypt that the people had fled, Pharaoh and his courtiers changed their minds about the people.

"What ever have we done," they said, "to let Israel leave our service?"

6   So he hitched the horses to his
7 chariot, and took his people with him; he took six hundred chariots, picked from all the chariots of Egypt, with charioteers in charge of them all. The LORD made Phar- 8 aoh, king of Egypt, obstinate, so that he pursued the Israelites, as they were going triumphantly out; the Egyptians pursued them, all of 9 Pharaoh's horses and chariots, his cavalry and infantry, and overtook them, camping by the sea, near Pi-hahiroth, in front of Baal-zephon. 10 As Pharaoh drew near, the Israelites raised their eyes, and there were the Egyptians setting out in pursuit of them! The Israelites were terribly afraid, and cried to the LORD. And they said to Moses, 11 "Was it because there were no graves in Egypt that you have taken us away to die in the desert? What a way to treat us, bringing us out of Egypt! Isn't this what we 12 told you in Egypt would happen, when we said, 'Leave us alone and let us serve the Egyptians; for it is better for us to serve the Egyptians than to die in the desert.'"

But Moses said to the people, 13 "Do not be afraid; stand by and see how the LORD is going to save you today; for although you see the Egyptians today, you shall never see them again. The LORD will fight 14 for you, while you have only to keep still."

Then the LORD said to Moses, 15 "Why do you cry to me? Tell the Israelites to set forth; and then 16 raise your staff and stretch out your hand over the sea, and thus divide it in two, so that the Israelites may proceed on dry ground right into the sea. Then I will make 17 the Egyptians obstinate, so that they will go in after them, and thus I will gain honor through Pharaoh and all his infantry, chariotry, and cavalry, so that the Egyptians may 18 know that I am the LORD, when I have gained honor through Pharaoh, his chariotry, and cavalry."

19 Then the angel of God, who was accustomed to go in front of the army of Israel left his position and went behind them; the column of cloud also left its position in front of them and took its place behind 20 them, and came between the army of Egypt and that of Israel, so that the cloud was there with its darkness, and the night passed by without the one coming near the other all night.

21 Then Moses stretched out his hand over the sea, and the LORD moved the sea away by means of a strong east wind all night, and 22 turned the sea into dry land. The waters were divided, so that the Israelites proceeded on dry ground right into the sea, the waters forming a wall for them to right and 23 left of them. Pursuing them, the Egyptians followed them right into the sea, all of Pharaoh's horses, his 24 chariotry and cavalry. At the morning watch the LORD lowered himself toward the Egyptian army in the column of fire and cloud, and 25 threw the Egyptian army into a panic. He clogged their chariot-wheels, and caused them to proceed with such difficulty that the Egyptians said,

"Let us flee from the Israelites; for the LORD is fighting for them against the Egyptians."

26 Then the LORD said to Moses,

"Stretch out your hand over the sea, that the water may flow back upon the Egyptians, upon their chariotry and cavalry."

27 So Moses stretched out his hand over the sea, and as morning broke, the sea returned to its steady flow;

and as the Egyptians fled before it, the LORD shook the Egyptians right into the sea. The water returned, 28 and covered the chariotry and cavalry belonging to the whole army of Pharaoh that had followed them into the sea, not so much as one being left. But the Israelites had 29 walked through the middle of the sea on dry ground, the water forming a wall for them to right and left of them.

Thus did the LORD save Israel 30 that day from the power of the Egyptians. So Israel saw the Egyptians lying dead on the seashore; 31 and when Israel saw the mighty act which the LORD had performed against the Egyptians, the people stood in awe of the LORD and trusted the LORD and his servant Moses.

* * *

[YAHWEH REVEALS THE LAW TO MOSES ON MT. SINAI, 19:9-20:20]

The LORD said to Moses, 9

"See, I am coming to you in a thick cloud, in order that the people may hear me speaking with you, and may then always trust you too."

When Moses reported the words of the people to the LORD, the LORD 10 said to Moses,

"Go to the people, and have them go through a period of consecration today and tomorrow; let them wash their clothes, and be ready 11 by the day after tomorrow; for on the day after tomorrow the LORD is going to descend on Mount Sinai in sight of all the people. You must

12 mark off the mountain all around, saying, 'Take care not to ascend the mountain, nor even to touch the edge of it; whoever touches the 13 mountain must be put to death, having no hand touch him, but being stoned or shot; whether it is man or beast, he shall not be allowed to live. When a long blast is blown on the ram's horn, they may come up to the mountain.'"

14 So Moses descended from the mountain to the people; he consecrated the people, and they washed their clothes.

15 "Be ready by the day after tomorrow," he said to the people; "approach no woman."

16 On the third day, when morning came, there was thunder and lightning, with a heavy cloud over the mountain, and a very loud trumpet-blast, so that all the people that 17 were in the camp trembled. Then Moses brought the people out of the camp to meet God, and they took their stand at the foot of the 18 mountain. Mount Sinai was completely enveloped in smoke, because the LORD had descended upon it in fire; its smoke ascended like the smoke from a kiln, so that the people all trembled violently. 19 As the blast of the trumpet grew louder and louder, Moses spoke, and God answered him with a 20 thunderpeal. The LORD descended upon Mount Sinai, to the top of the mountain; the LORD then summoned Moses to the top of the mountain, and when Moses went 21 up, the LORD said to Moses,

*   *   *

"Since I, the LORD, am your God, 20 who brought you out of the land of 2 Egypt, out of a state of slavery, 3 you must have no other gods beside me.

"You must not carve an image 4 for yourself in the shape of anything that is in the heavens above, or that is on the earth below, or that is in the waters under the earth; you must not pay homage 5 to them, nor serve them; for I, the LORD your God, am a jealous God, punishing children for the sins of their fathers, to the third or fourth generation of those who hate me, 6 but showing kindness to the thousandth generation of those who love me and keep my commands.

"You must not invoke the name 7 of the LORD your God to evil intent; for the LORD will not hold him guiltless who invokes his name to evil intent.

"Remember to keep the sabbath 8 day holy. Six days you are to labor 9 and do all your work, but on the 10 seventh day, a sabbath to the LORD your God, you must not do any work at all, neither you, nor your son, nor your daughter, nor your male or female slave, nor your cattle, nor the alien in your employ residing in your community; for in 11 six days the LORD made the heavens, the earth, and the sea, together with all that is in them, but rested on the seventh day; that is how the LORD came to bless the seventh day and to hallow it.

"Honor your father and mother, 12 that you may live long in the land that the LORD your God is giving you.

"You must not commit murder. 13

14 "You must not commit adultery.

15 "You must not steal.

16 "You must not bring a false charge against your fellow.

17 "You must not covet your neighbor's home; you must not covet your neighbor's wife, nor his male or female slave, nor his ox, nor his ass, nor anything at all that is your neighbor's."

18 As the people all perceived the thunder and lightning, the blast of the trumpet, and the mountain smoking, the people became afraid, and fell back, standing off at a distance.

19 "If you yourself will speak to us," they said to Moses, "we will listen; but do not let God speak to us, lest we die."

20 "Fear not," said Moses to the people, "for it is only to test you that God has come, and in order that the fear of him may be present with you so that you may not sin."

❖   ❖   ❖

HOMER

THE ILIAD IS THE OLDEST AND GREATEST WORK OF WESTERN LITERATURE. An epic poem of unsurpassed artistry, it is also a violent war story, recounting the heroic struggle between two nations for the possession of an incomparably beautiful woman—Helen of Troy. The peoples involved are the Greeks (whom Homer calls Achaeans, Danaans, and Argives) and the Trojans, inhabitants of a trade-rich city on the shores of Asia Minor.

Although Homer's account of the Trojan War may have a basis in historical fact, the events which legend says led to the siege of Troy are pure and delightful fantasy. The conflict began, not with men, but with the Olympian gods. The Greek gods, who dwelt in eternal and carefree bliss on lofty Mount Olympus, were invited to attend the marriage of Thetis, a beautiful sea nymph, to Peleus, a mortal man. Everyone was invited, that is, except the spirit of Discord (Eris). Annoyed at the slight, Discord threw a golden apple into the godly throng. It was marked "for the fairest." Naturally every goddess there claimed that it was intended for her.

The competition was narrowed down to three of the most important Olympians: Here, wife of the head god Zeus; Athene, patroness of wisdom; and Aphrodite, goddess of love. After much quarreling, they decided to call in an authority on feminine good looks to settle the issue. Paris, a Trojan prince and the handsomest man in the world, was asked to judge among them. Not content to be judged on her merits alone, each goddess offered Paris a bribe. Here, as the consort of almighty Zeus, promised power; Athene offered victory and wisdom, but Aphrodite won the contest by promising the love of Helen, the paragon of womanly beauty. When Paris awarded the golden apple to Aphrodite, he unwittingly doomed his people to extinction. For Here and Athene, furious at losing the contest, resolved to destroy Troy and all its people.

Happily unaware of the disaster he was causing, Paris travelled to Sparta, where Helen's husband, Menelaus, received him as an honored guest. While Menelaus was away on a hunting trip, Paris persuaded Helen to flee with him to Troy. But by this act Paris also earned Zeus's anger, for the Chief Olympian always upheld the sacred trust of hospitality, which Paris violated when he seduced his host's wife.

When he discovered that Helen and Paris had eloped, Menelaus called on the help of his brother Agamemnon, ruler of Mycenae, the most powerful of the Achaean (Greek) kingdoms. Agamemnon then organized an expedition of Achaean princes to sail across the Aegean Sea and bring Helen back. Odysseus, the wily king of Ithaca; Diomedes, the warrior-king of Argos; Ajax, the mighty king of Salamis; and the talkative old Nestor, king of Pylos, joined forces not only to retrieve Menelaus' straying wife, but also to seize the gold and treasure of Troy. Such was the legendary beginning of the Trojan War.

The *Iliad,* however, does not include this introductory material. In the ancient epic tradition, Homer begins his poem *in medias res,* in the middle of the action, and refers to earlier events like Helen's infidelity only as his tale unfolds. Homer limits his narrative to a few critical weeks during the tenth year of the war. He does not include the story of the Trojan Horse or the fall of Troy. In spite of the poem's great length—15,000 lines—Homer achieves artistic unity by focusing on a single heroic theme, the "wrath of Achilles" and its disastrous consequences to both Achaeans and Trojans.

After invoking the goddess of poetic inspiration (the Muse Calliope) and posing the *epic question,* Homer begins Book I by dramatizing the fatal quarrel between Agamemnon, commander-in-chief of the Achaean army, and Achilles, the hero of the poem. Through a barrage of scalding insults, Homer skillfully reveals the impulsive, passionate character of both men. The cause of the quarrel is simple, and involves the pride and public reputation of both parties. Agamemnon had captured a slave girl, Chriseis, and refused to give her back to her father, Chryses, a priest of Apollo. Apollo is usually known as the god of masculine beauty and the enlightened intellect, but he is also the "Archer King," shooter of invisible arrows of death. Listening to the prayer of his servant Chryses, Apollo struck the Achaean camp with plague, causing men to die by the hundreds. The devastation of his army forces Agamemnon to end the plague by returning Chriseis to her father.

To compensate for his loss Agamemnon then insults Achilles by commandeering the hero's favorite girl, Briseis. Enraged, Achilles denounces Agamemnon's greed and cowardice. Achilles complains that while he daily risks his life in battle, Agamemnon sits comfortably behind the lines and claims ninety per cent of the captured booty for himself. Angry, wounding words fly until Achilles, cautioned by Athene (Wisdom) not to kill Agamemnon, leaves the general council and stalks to his tent.

Alone with his beloved friend Patroclus, Achilles vows not to aid the Achaeans until Agamemnon comes begging for help. Achilles' mother, the sea-nymph Thetis (at whose marriage Discord had thrown the golden apple), comes to her son and promises to intervene with Zeus so that the Greeks will suffer a series of disastrous defeats until they are made to realize that without Achilles they cannot hope to win the war.

This estrangement between the leader and his indispensable warrior ends Book I. The rest of the epic involves the consequences of Achilles' anger and hurt pride. The personal crisis for Achilles occurs in Book IX when Agamemnon, humbled by Trojan victories, sends the wise Odysseus and soldierly Aias (Ajax) to beg Achilles to return and fight for his fellow Achaeans. At that point in the action the Trojans, led by prince Hector, have pushed the Greeks back to a defensive wall built along the shore, and are about to burn the Achaean ships. Unmoved as Odysseus relates the Achaean position, Achilles proudly rejects Agamemnon's offer of peace. This decision proves fatal: it not only results in the unnecessary deaths of many Achaean soldiers, but in that of Achilles' beloved Patroclus as well.

Because his friend will not fight, Patroclus puts on Achilles' armor and goes to battle in his place. Ignoring Achilles' warning not to go too far, Patroclus is swept away by the excitement of killing and pursues Hector to the walls of Troy. There, already wounded, he falls under Hector's sword.

Grief-stricken at Patroclus' death, for which he rightly holds himself responsible, Achilles transfers his rage from Agamemnon to Hector. Equipped with splendid new armor forged by the god Hephaestus, Achilles re-enters the fighting. Knowing that Fate has decreed that he must die shortly after Hector, he nonetheless kills the Trojan prince to avenge Patroclus.

The poem ends, not with Achilles' shameful humiliation of Hector's corpse, but with a quietly beautiful scene between Achilles and Priam (Book XXIV). The aged King of Troy comes alone by night to claim his son's body, which the gods have miraculously preserved from decay. The confrontation between the dignified old man and the haughty young warrior is an oasis of peace in this great poem of war. Knowing that the body must be buried so that Hector's soul can rest, Priam kneels to kiss the hands that killed his son. Achilles, having also suffered the loss of the person he loved most, recognizes in Priam's grief a bond of common humanity. He finds in Priam the image of his own aged father, Peleus, whom he is destined never to see again. In the *Iliad*'s closing pages Achilles shows a compassion and generosity that make him—at last—as noble in character as he had been courageous in action.

Although Achilles' fiery personality dominates the poem, the *Iliad* is remarkably objective in its sympathetic portrait of the hero's Trojan opponents. Homer narrates the war from the Achaean viewpoint, but—unlike a modern propagandist—he never pictures the enemy as monstrous or sub-human. Homer's Zeus says that Achilles is a better man than Hector, but that judgment refers only to Achilles' almost superhuman ability as a fighter—not to his moral character. In fact, when he describes Hector's parting from his wife Andromache (Book VI), the poet takes pains to show Hector as more mature, more unselfishly dedicated to defending his people than the impulsive Achilles who, until the end of the poem, cares nothing for his fellow Achaeans when his personal honor is at stake. The *Iliad* presents Hector as the responsible man who dies protecting his home and family: Achilles is the born soldier who fights to earn for himself undying glory.

Almost nothing is known of the poet who created this first masterpiece of the Western world. Who he was, where he lived, or when he wrote are unsolved mysteries. Scholars have even argued that "Homer" never existed. A close study of the *Iliad* has led many critics to speculate that it is the product, not of one man the ancients called Homer, but the composite work of countless anonymous "singers" whose contributions to the present epic spanned many generations. The "Homeric Question" is scholarship's attempt to trace the progress of the poem's composition, to date and find the source of its various parts, and to reconstruct a picture of the prehistoric Greek culture out of which the *Iliad* grew.

As late as the last century, most scholars jeered at the notion that Troy had ever existed. The entire Trojan War story, they insisted, was pure legend. But in 1870 a brilliant amateur archaeologist, Heinrich Schliemann, proved the experts wrong by going to Hissarlik, Turkey, the traditional site of Troy, and uncovering there not one, but nine consecutive cities built on the spot. The city which the Achaeans beseiged is thought to be Troy VII, which was sacked and burned about 1250 or 1200 B.C. The latest scientific estimates closely approximate the date of 1184, the year to which classical authorities assigned the fall of Troy.

Having demonstrated that such a war as described in the *Iliad* actually occurred, Schliemann then transported his crew to the Greek mainland where he excavated Mycenae, the "mythical" capitol of Agamemnon. There he found exquisitely formed art objects, pure gold death masks, and other treasures buried in ancient circular tombs. At first Schliemann thought he had discovered the grave of Agamemnon himself, but further research indicated that he had instead unearthed the resting place of Agamemnon's ancestors, Mycenaean royalty who had died centuries before the Trojan War. As later discoveries proved, Mycenae was one of the most powerful centers of a proto-Greek culture-complex that dominated the eastern Mediterranean from about 1500 to 1100 B.C. It included Pylos, Tiryns, and Sparta, as well as Troy and Mycenae, after which it was named.

It is this Mycenaean civilization, together with elements from the poet's own time, that form the social and cultural background of the *Iliad*. Although the Mycenaean cities were destroyed during the Dorian invasions of about 1100 B.C., considerable information about their culture was preserved in their poetry. No written literature as such has survived from the Mycenaean period[1] but it is certain that poems about "the glorious feats of heroes" such as Achilles sings in his tent (Book IX) were composed and transmitted orally. During the four hundred years between the fall of Troy and the probable lifetime of Homer, hundreds of heroic lays about the men who captured Priam's city no doubt circulated throughout the Aegean world. In the meantime the Dorian invasions, which ended the Mycenaean civilization and brought about the Greek Dark Ages (1000-700 B.C.), forced the descendants of Homer's Achaeans from the Greek mainland to the shores of Asia Minor. The Greeks who settled there were called Ionians and were the first to emerge from the chaotic Dark Ages. Within a few centuries the leading Ionian cities, such as Smyrna and Miletus, became the home of a Greek Renaissance, the first flowering of which produced the Homeric epics.

---

[1]Although no literary compositions have been found, the Mycenaean Greeks knew how to write. Linear B, a proto-Greek script, was used on both the mainland and Crete to keep records and take inventories.

Herodotus placed Homer "about four hundred years" before his own time, and most classical and Alexandrian authorities support Smyrna or the island of Chios as his birthplace. This means that Homer, if he lived, was an Ionian poet of about 850 B.C.[2] He may have been an *aoidos*, a professional "singer" who earned his bread and lodging by entertaining Greek princes with exciting tales of their supposed ancestors—the heroes who had fought at Troy. Whoever he was, he probably composed his poems orally, stitching them together from the many legends and folk tales that had accumulated around the Troy saga. From this wealth of previously existing material Homer wove the colorful tapestry of his epic. Such a method of composition accounts for the much older "pre-Homeric" material embedded in the poems.

Whether or not literary critics accept the hypothesis that a single author is responsible for creating the *Iliad* in something like its present state, they are generally agreed that the poem was composed orally and probably not written down in its final form until many years after Homer's death. Milman Parry's work with contemporary Yugoslavian peasants has shown that illiterate shepherds can compose and repeat almost verbatim works of great length. With its often repeated phrases and stock epithets like "swift-footed Achilles," "rosy-fingered dawn," and "Hector tamer of Horses," the *Iliad* shows strong evidence of "formula writing," a device indispensable to poets who composed orally or im-provised new poems from fragments of old ones. The regular rhythms of the *Iliad*'s epic meter, the dactyl hexameter, also provided an aid to oral composition.

After the *aoidos* of Homeric times came the *rhapsode*, who apparently did not create new material but simply recited poems that had already attained wide-spread popularity. To these schools of bards, distinguished by the long staff which they used to mark the beat of the poetry they recited, the Homeric epics are probably indebted for their preservation. During the sixth century B.C. the *rhapsodoi* became so popular that Pisistratus, the Athenian ruler, established their public readings of Homer as a permanent fixture of the Panathenaea, a city-wide festival of music, dancing, and poetry. Pisistratus was also the first to compile an authori-tative edition of the *Iliad* and *Odyssey*. He ordered that all available manuscripts (or, more likely, all oral versions) of the two epics be carefully compared and, from them, an official text be made. Plato's quotations from Homer probably derive from Pisistratus' authorized edi-tion.

So highly was Homer regarded throughout the ancient world that he was designated, by common consent, "the poet." His writings were con-sidered a source of wisdom, a handbook of chivalric conduct, the chief authority on the Olympian gods, and a necessary education to the young. Greek and later Roman children learned to read and to acquire

---

[2]Even those scholars who champion Homer's authorship of the *Iliad* and *Odyssey*, by no means agree on his dates. Some place him about 750 B.C. or later.

standards of decency, heroism, and virtue by studying Homer. Even those who, like Plato, criticized his "immorality" in depicting the all-too-human antics of the gods, recognized him as the unrivaled master of the story-teller's art. In his essay "On Translating Homer," Matthew Arnold defined Homer's salient characteristics as rapidity, plainness in thought and diction, and a noble and profound application of ideas to life. Swiftness, vividness, compassion, and beauty—in these Homer is unequalled.

THE ILIAD

BOOK I

How Achillês and Agamemnon quarreled over Briseïs,
and how Thetis persuaded Zeus to support her son

AN ANGRY MAN—THERE IS MY STORY: THE BITTER RANCOUR OF ACHILLÊS, prince of the house of Peleus, which brought a thousand troubles upon the Achaian* host. Many a strong soul it sent down to Hadês, and left the heroes themselves a prey to dogs and carrion birds, while the will of God** moved on to fulfillment.

It began first of all with a quarrel between my Lord King Agamemnon of Atreus' line and the Prince Achillês.

What god, then, made the feud between them? Apollo, son of Leto† and Zeus. The King had offended him: so he sent a dire pestilence on the camp and the people perished. Agamemnon had affronted his priest Chrysês, when the priest came to the Achaian fleet, bringing a rich treasure to ransom his daughter. He held in his hand a golden staff, twined about with the sacred wreaths of Apollo Shootafar, and made his petition to the Achaian people in general but chiefly to the two royal princes of Atreus' line:

"My lords, and you their subjects, for you I pray that the gods who dwell in Olympos may grant you to sack Priam's city, and to have a happy return home! but my dear daughter—set her free, I beseech you, and accept this ransom, and respect Apollo Shootafar the son of Zeus!"

Then all the people said good words, and bade them respect the priest and accept the ransom; but my lord King Agamemnon was not well pleased. He told the priest to be off, and in harsh words too:

Achaian—The translator has attempted to approximate the original Greek names, rather than use the better-known Latin forms. Hence he uses "Achaian" instead of "Achaean," "Menelaos" instead of "Menelaus," "Aineias" instead of "Aeneas," "Aias" instead of "Ajax," and so on.
**God*—Zeus, head of the Olympian pantheon.
†*Leto*—For identification of the various mythological figures appearing in the *Iliad,* please consult the Glossary.

Abridged. From *The Iliad: The Story of Achilles,* translated by W. H. D. Rouse. First published in 1938 by Thomas Nelson and Sons, Ltd. Reprinted by permission of the publisher.

"Don't let me find you here any more, you; don't stay now and don't come again, or else your staff and sacred wreaths may not protect you. The woman I will not release! She shall live to old age in our house, far away in Argos, working the loom and lying in my bed. Begone now! don't provoke me, or it will be the worse for you."

The old man was afraid, and did as he was told. Silent he passed along the shore of the murmuring sea; and when he came home, he prayed earnestly to Apollo:

"Hear me, Silverbow! thou who dost bestride Chrysè and holy Cilla, thou who art the mighty lord of Tenedos, O Smintheus! If I ever built a temple to thy pleasure, if I have ever burnt for thee fat slices of bulls or of goats, bestow on me this boon: may the Danaäns pay for my tears under thy shafts!"

Phoibos Apollo heard his prayer. Down from Olympos he strode, angry at heart, carrying bow and quiver: the arrows rattled upon his shoulders as the angry god moved on, looking black as night. He sank upon his heel not far from the ships, and let fly a shaft; terrible was the twang of the silver bow. First he attacked the mules and dogs, then he shot his keen arrows at the men, and each hit the mark: pyres of the dead began to burn up everywhere and never ceased.

Nine days the god's arrows fell on the camp; on the tenth day Achillês summoned all to a conference. The goddess Hera put this in his mind, for she was distressed to see the Danaäns dying. And when they were all gathered together, Achillês rose up and spoke.

"My lord King," he said, "I think we shall seem just foiled adventurers when we get home—if indeed we get off with our lives, now you see war and pestilence allied to beat us. Come then, let us inquire of some prophet or priest, or even a diviner of dreams—for God, it seems, doth send our dreams—and let him tell us what has made Phoibos Apollo so angry. Does he find fault with us for prayer or for sacrifice? Does he desire the savour of sheep or goats without blemish, that he may spare us this pestilence?"

He said his say, and sat down. Then up rose Calchas o' Thestor, most excellent diviner of dreams, who knew what is and what will be, and what has been in ancient days; he had guided the fleet to Ilios by the divination which Phoibos Apollo had taught him. He spoke to them from an honest heart, and said:

"Prince Achillês, whom Zeus delights to honour! you bid me explain the wrath of Lord Apollo Shootafar: therefore I will speak. Mark what I say, and swear me an oath that you will defend me with all your might in word and deed. For I think I shall provoke a man who rules all our people, one whom all the people obey. A king when angry always can be stronger than a common man; even if he smothers his anger for the day, yet indeed he keeps a grudge long in his heart until he can pay it off. Consider then if you will hold me safe."

Achillês answered:

"Fear nothing, but speak the word of God which you know. For I swear by Apollo, whom Zeus delights to honour, to whom you pray, Calchas, when you declare God's word to the nation: no man while I live and see the light shall lay heavy hands on you in this fleet, none of all the nation, not even if you name Agamemnon, who now claims to be first and best of us all."

Then the seer took courage and spoke out:

"He finds no fault with us then, for prayer or sacrifice, but for his priest, whom Agamemnon affronted, when he would not accept a ranson and set his daughter free. For his sake Shootafar has sent us trouble, and will send. Nor will he stay the noisome pestilence among our people, until the King gives back to the father his lovely girl, unbought, unransomed, and sends a solemn sacrifice to Chrysê: then we may trust that the god will be appeased."

No sooner had he sat down, than up rose my lord King Agamemnon in his majesty. He was displeased, the dark places in his heart were full of resentment, his eyes were like flashing fire; and he began by rating Calchas:

"Prophet of evil, you have never had a decent word for me! It is always your delight to prophecy evil, but good you have never said and never done! And now you get up and harangue the people with your oracles. So *that* is the reason why Shootafar sends trouble! because of that girl Chryseïs! because I would not accept the ransom—but I want to keep her myself, and take her home! Why, I like her better than my own wife Clytaimnestra, she is just as good in face or figure, brains or fingers. Never mind, I will give her back if that is better. I would rather have the people alive than dead. Only get a prize ready for me at once, or else I shall be the only man in the army without a prize. That is not right! Just look here, all of you, my prize is going away somewhere else!"

Then Achillês answered:

"Your Majesty, gettings are keepings with you, there's no doubt about that. Pray how will our brave men give you a prize? I do not know of any common store anywhere. What we got from the towns we have taken, has been divided, and you cannot expect people to collect it all again in a heap. For the present, then, give the girl up to the god; and we will pay you threefold or fourfold, if Zeus ever allows us to sack the proud city of Troy."

King Agamemnon answered:

"None of that; you may be a great man, Achillês, you may be more than a man, but do not try cheating—you will neither cajole me nor persuade me. Do you want to keep your own prize, and tell me to give up mine and just sit forlorn without any? If our brave men will give me a prize, and satisfy me that I get as much as I give, well and good; but if they will not give, then I will take—I'll come to you, or to Aias, for a prize, or Odysseus, and away I'll go with my gettings! Then it will be his turn to be angry. But we will see about that later. For the time being, let us launch a good ship and find a special crew and put Chryseïs on board; and let one of the princes from our council be in charge, Aias or Idomeneus or Prince Odysseus, or yourself, my young friend, you terror of the world, *you* shall pacify Shootafar by making sacrifice."

Achillês scowled at him, and said:

"Ha! greedyheart, shamelessness in royal dress! How could any man be willing to obey you, whether on some errand or in the battlefield? I cared nothing about the Trojans when I came here to fight; they had done nothing to me, never lifted my cattle, or horses either, never destroyed my fruit or my harvest in Phthia—too many hills and forests between us, and roaring seas. No, it was you I came for, shameless man! to give you pleasure, to revenge Menelaos, and you too, dogface! for the Trojans' wrong. You don't trouble about that, you care nothing for that! And now you threaten to rob me of my prize, which I worked hard to get, which the army gave me. I never get a prize equal to yours if our men capture some town; but most of the hard fighting is done by my hands. Only when sharing-time comes, you get most of the good things, and I have a scrap to comfort me—not much, but all I can get!—as I come back tired out with fighting. Now I will just go home to Phthia, since it is much better to take ship and go, and I don't think I shall fill my hold with riches if I stay here despised."

King Agamemnon answered:

"Do go, if that's what you want, go by all means—I do not sink on my knees and beg you to stay for my sake. I have others in plenty who will honour me, first and foremost Zeus Allwise. I hate you more than any prince on earth, for you are always quarrelling and fighting. If you are such a mighty man, God gave you that, I suppose. Go home with your ships and your men and lord it over your Myrmidons, but I care nothing for you. I don't mind if you *are* in a rage. Now I give you fair warning: since Apollo robs me of Chryseïs, I will send her home with my own ship and crew; but I will take your beautiful Briseïs, and I will come for her myself to your quarters—for your prize! to show you how much stronger I am than you are. Then others will take care not to stand up to me and say they are as good as I am!"

This pierced Achillês to the heart; and he was of two minds, whether he should draw sword from thigh, to push through the crowd and strike down King Agamemnon, or whether he should calm his temper and keep himself in check. As these thoughts went through his mind, and he began to draw the great sword from the sheath, Athena came down from heaven: Queen Hera sent her, loving and anxious at once. She stood behind him, and held him back by his long red hair. No other man saw her, but Achillês alone. Achillês turned round startled—at once he knew Pallas Athenaia. His eyes flashed wildly and he spoke words that winged like arrows to the mark:

"Why have you come again, daughter of Zeus Invincible? To see the insult of my lord King Agamemnon? I'll tell you what, and I will do it too: his own highhandedness one day may be his death!"

Athena replied, with her bright eyes glinting:

"I came to check your passion, if you will listen; and I was sent from heaven by Queen Hera, loving and anxious at once. Come, come, drop the quarrel, don't pull out that sword. Just give him a sound rating and tell him what to expect. For I declare to you that this is what will happen: a time will come when you shall have a magnificent offer, with three times as much offered to make up for this insult. Hold back now, and do what I say."

Achillês answered:

"I must observe the bidding of you both, goddess, angry though I am indeed. It is better so. What the gods command you, do, then the gods will listen to *you*."

So he stayed his heavy hand on the silver hilt, and drove back the sword into the sheath, in obedience to Athena; and she returned to Olympos, where Zeus Invincible dwells with the company of heaven.

But Achillês was angry still. Once more he addressed the King in violent words:

"You drunkard, with eyes like a bitch and heart like a fawn! You never arm yourself with your men for battle, you never go out on a raid with the fighting men—no pluck in you for that! You think that certain death! It is much better, isn't it, to stay in camp and rob any one who tells the truth to your face! The king feeds on his people, for they are a worthless lot—or else, my lord, this would be your last outrage. But one thing I will tell you, and take my solemn oath: as truly as this staff will never grow again, never again will put forth leaves and twigs, after it has been cut from the stump in the mountain forest, and the axe has scraped off leaves and bark, but now it is held in men's hands, men of judgment who guard the statutes of Zeus—hear my solemn oath to you: so truly a time shall come when Achillês will be missed by the nation one and all; then you shall not be able to help them for all your grief, while many are falling and dying before bloodthirsty Hector. Then you shall tear your temper to tatters that you would not respect the best man of all."

As he spoke, Achillês dashed down on the ground the gold-studded staff, and took his seat again; while King Agamemnon opposite fumed with rage. But Nestor rose: a famous orator he was, gracious in speech, whose voice ran off his tongue sweeter than honey. He had seen already in Pylos two generations of men grow up before him and pass away, and he was king still over the third. He now spoke with an honest heart and said:

"For shame, sirs! Here is a great trouble for the Achaian land! How glad Priam would be, and Priam's sons, how all Troy would be in jubilation, if they could only hear you two quarrelling—you, the leaders in wisdom and leaders in war! Now listen to me. You are both younger than I am. Nay more, I have met even better men than you, and they never disregarded me. For never have I seen, and never shall I see, such men as Peirithoös, and that great ruler Dryas, Caineus, and Exadios and the noble Prince Polyphemos.[1] I tell you, those were the mightiest men ever

---

[1] Not the cannibal monster of the Odyssey.

born upon earth, mightiest I say and fought against mightiest foes, the monsters of the mountains,[2] whom they horribly destroyed. Yes, those men I knew well; I travelled all the way from distant Pylos to visit them at their own request. And I fought by their side as a volunteer. Those were men whom no mortal now living on earth could fight! And they heard my advice and took it too. Listen to me then, you also, and take my advice, and you will find it better. You, sir, do not rob this man of the girl, although you are strong; leave her alone, as the army gave her to him at first for his especial prize. And you, Achillês, do not provoke your king, force against force; for greater honour belongs to a sceptred king, when Zeus has given him dignity. If you *are* a mighty man, if your mother *is* divine, yet he is above you for his dominion is greater. Your Grace, forget your bitterness: and I beseech Achillês to let his anger pass, for he is the strong tower of our nation against the horrors of war."

King Agamemnon answered:

"Indeed, sir, all that you say is fair and right. But this man wishes to be above all, to rule every one, to be King over every one, to order every one about—and there is some one who will not obey, I think! If the gods everlasting have set him up as a warrior, does it follow that they have set him on to call ugly names?"

Achillês interposed, and said:

"Yes, for I should be called coward and outcast, if I yield to you in everything you choose to say. Lay your commands on others, don't order me about, for I do not think I shall obey you any more. I tell you one thing, and you will do well to remember it. I will never use my hands to fight for a girl, either with you or with any one—those who gave, may take away; but you shall never carry off anything else of what I have against my will. Just try and see, that these also may know: very soon there will be red blood on the spear-point!"

They finished their bout of hard words, and dismissed the assembly. Achillês with Patroclos and his friends returned to his quarters. Agamemnon launched a good ship, and put on board twenty men with the sacrifice, and brought Chryseïs; Odysseus took charge, and they set sail. Then Agamemnon ordered the people to purify themselves; they cast their peace-offerings into the sea, and slew bulls and goats on the shore to make full sacrifice to Apollo, and the savour went up to heaven through the wreathing smoke.

While all this business was going on, Agamemnon did not forget his quarrel with Achillês and the threats he had made. He called his two trusty servants, the heralds, Talthybios and Eurybatês, and gave them his orders:

"Go to the quarters of Prince Achillês, take Briseïs by the hand and bring her here. If he will not give her up, I will come with a larger party and take her myself, which will be more unpleasant for him."

---

[2]Centaurs.

So he sent his envoys with strict orders. They did not like their errand, but they went along the shore to the place where the Myrmidons had their ships. They found Achillês sitting before his hut, and he was not pleased to see them. They indeed were both afraid and ashamed before the young prince. They only stood, and said nothing to him, and asked nothing; but he understood what they wanted, and spoke:

"Heralds, I greet you, for the envoy is held sacred by gods and men. Come near, I find no fault in you, but in Agamemnon, who has sent you for the girl Briseïs. Here, Patroclos my friend, bring out the girl and let them take her away. Let them both be witnesses before the blessed gods and mortal men, and before this hard-hearted king, if ever the people shall need me to stand between them and dire destruction! Indeed, he is mad with fury and cannot look both before and behind, so that his army may live to fight before our camp."

Patroclos heard him, and brought out the beautiful Briseïs, and handed her over to the envoys. Then they returned to their ships, and the woman followed them unwillingly. But Achillês burst into tears, and went apart from his friends; he threw himself down by the grey salt sea, and gazing over the waters stretched out his hands, calling loudly to his mother:

"O my mother! I was born to die young, it is true, but honour I was to have from Zeus Olympian, Thunderer on high! And now he has not given me one little bit! Yes, my lord King Agamemnon has insulted me! He has taken my prize and keeps it, he has robbed me himself!"

His divine mother heard his sorrowful cry, as she sat in the depths of the sea beside her ancient father. Quickly she shot up like a mist out of the grey sea, and sat down beside her weeping son; she stroked him with her hand, and said:

"My child, why do you weep? What is your trouble? Tell me, don't hide it, then we shall both know."

Achillês answered with a deep groan:

"You know! Why should I talk when you know everything? We attacked Thebê, Eëtion's famous city; we sacked the place and carried off everything. The spoil was divided, and they chose for Agamemnon a beautiful girl, Chryseïs. Chrysês the priest of Apollo Shootafar came to our camp with a heap of treasure, to ransom his daughter; he carried a golden staff twined about with the sacred wreaths of Apollo Shootafar, and made his prayer to the whole people, but especially to the two royal princes. All the people spoke good words, and told them to respect the priest and accept the ransom; but my Lord Agamemnon did not like it. He told him to be off, and rudely too.

"The old man went away very angry, and prayed to Apollo. The god heard him, for he loved the man dearly; he shot us—the deadly shafts fell all over our camp, the people died in heaps. Our prophet knew what it meant, and told us Shootafar's mind. I stood up at once and advised them to pacify the god; but the king fell in a rage and threatened me, and now he has made good his threat. They are sending a ship to Chrysê, with offerings for the god, and the heralds have just gone from my hut and taken away the girl Briseïs whom the people had given to me.

"Do help your son, if you can! Go to Olympos, pray to Zeus, if you have ever pleased him and served him by word or deed! How often have I heard you boasting to father at home, telling how you saved Cronion Thundercloud from violence and ruin, all by yourself, when there was a conspiracy in heaven! The other Olympians wanted to tie him up. Hera and Poseidon and Pallas Athena: but you came and saved him from that, by summoning old Hundredhand, whom the gods call Briareos, but all men call Aigaion—he is stronger than his own father![3] Hundredhand came in and sat down beside Zeus, triumphant—the blessed gods were frightened, and did not tie him up. Remind him of that, mother, fall down and clasp his knees—see if he will help the Trojans and drive the Achaians back to their ships with slaughter! Let them enjoy their king! Let his gracious Majesty King Agamemnon know his own delusion, when he would not respect the best man of all!"

Then Thetis answered, as the tears ran down her cheeks:

"O my poor child, why did I ever bring you up for such a dreadful fate? Why could you not have stayed behind? Why could you not have been spared tears and tribulation, since your life is but a minute, no long day indeed! But now you have both a speedy doom and sorrow beyond all men! Indeed it was a cruel fate you were born for.

"Very well, I will tell your story to Zeus Thunderer—I will go myself to snowy Olympos and see if I can persuade him. Be sure now to stay beside your ships, and be as angry as you like but keep clear of battle altogether. For Zeus went yesterday to the Ocean stream on a visit to the pious Ethiopians, for a feast, and all the other gods with him; but he will be back in twelve days, and then I will go at once to the brazen halls, and make my prayer. I think I can persuade him."

And there she left him, brooding over the loss of his beautiful Briseïs, whom they had torn from him against his will.

But Odysseus came safely to Chrysê with his holy offerings. They entered the deep harbour and furled the sails, and stowed them below; quickly they lowered the mast into the crutch, and rowed the ship to her moorings, where they dropt the anchor stones and made fast the hawsers. Then they landed, and carried out the offerings for Apollo Shootafar. Chryseïs landed, also, and Odysseus led her to the altar and gave her into her father's arms with these words:

"Chyrsês, my lord Agamemnon has sent me to bring your daughter back, with a holy offering for Phoibos on behalf of the Danaäns; that we may propitiate the Lord who has lately sent mourning and trouble upon the people."

He gave her into her father's arms, and he received his daughter with joy. The men quickly set the holy offerings around the altar, then

---

[3]Poseidon.

washed their hands and took up the barley-grains. Chrysês lifted up his hands, and prayed aloud:

"Hear me, Silverbow! thou who dost bestride Chrysê and holy Cilla, thou who art the mighty Lord of Tenedos! Verily thou hast heard my prayer, and done me honour, and smitten hard the Achaian people: grant me now again this boon, even now save the Danaäns from this dire pestilence!"

So he prayed, and Phoibos Apollo heard his prayer. And when they all had prayed and cast the barley-grains, they first drew back the heads, and killed, and flayed, carved out the thigh-slices and rolled them between pieces of fat, and laid more raw flesh upon them: then the old priest burnt them upon sticks of wood, and poured sparkling wine over, while the young men held their five-pronged forks ready by his side. After the thigh-pieces were burnt and the inner parts were divided, they chopt up the rest and ran splits through the meat, roasted all properly and drew it off. This work done, they prepared their meal and enjoyed it, and no one lacked a fair share. When they had all had enough, the lads filled the bowls to the brim, and served the wine to all after spilling the sacred drops.[4]

So all day long the young men of Achaia appeased the god with sweet music, singing the Healer's chant, a hymn to the Farworker; and his heart was glad to hear.

When the sun set and darkness came they lay down to rest beside their moorings; but as soon as Dawn showed her rosy fingers through the mist, at once they rose and sailed for their own camp. Apollo Farworker sent them a following breeze. They lifted the mast, and spread the white sails; the wind filled the great sail, the purple wave swished and poppled against the stem, the ship ran free on her way over the waters. At last they arrived at their camp, and drew the ship ashore high on the sands, and set up the long line of dogshores: then all scattered among the huts and the ships.

But Achillês brooded still over his anger, and did not move from his vessels. He never went to the meeting-place, never to the battlefield, but wore out his heart where he was, although he longed for war and battle.

When the twelfth day dawned, the gods returned to Olympos in a body, led by Zeus.

Thetis did not forget her son's request; but she came out of the sea, and early in the morning she climbed to Olympos in the highest heavens. She found Allseeing Cronidês sitting apart from the rest on the topmost peak of craggy Olympos. There she knelt before him, and threw her left arm about his knees, catching his chin with the right hand as she made her prayer:

"O Father Zeus! If ever I have served you by word or deed, grant me this boon: give honour to my son! He of all others is to die an early

---

[4]The server poured a few drops into each man's goblet, which he then spilled on the ground with a prayer; then the server filled the goblet, and passed on.

death, but now see how my Lord Agamemnon has insulted him. He has taken his prize and keeps it, he has robbed my son himself! Satisfy my son, Zeus Olympian most wise! Let the Trojans prevail, until the Achaian nation shall satisfy my son and magnify him with honour!"

Zeus Cloudgatherer did not answer, but long sat silent; and Thetis— how she clasped his knees, how she clung fast to him and cried out once more:

"Say yes now, and promise me faithfully! Or else say no—for you have nothing to fear! Show me that you care less for me than for any god in heaven!"

Zeus answered in great vexation:

"Bother it all! You'll set me curry-worrying with Hera and make her scold me again! She is always at me as it is before them all, and says I help the Trojans to win. You just go away again now, and don't let Hera see: I will manage to do what you want. Look here, I will bow my head to you that you may believe me. That is my sure and certain sign here among us; when I bow my head, my word can never be recalled, and never deceive, and never fail."

As he spoke, Cronion bowed his black brows; the Lord's ambrosial locks swung forward from his immortal head, and high Olympos quaked.

So they had their talk and parted; Thetis dived from radiant Olympos into the deep sea, and Zeus entered his own hall. All the gods rose up from their seats to receive their father: not one of them dared to sit still, but all rose up to greet him. So he took his seat upon his throne.

But Hera had seen; she knew there had been a confabulation, and a visit from Silverfoot Thetis, the daughter of the Old Man of the Sea. She lost no time in scolding at Zeus Cronion.

"Who is it this time?" she began, "who has been confabulating with you now, you deceiver? You always like to go behind my back and make secret plans, and lay down the law! You never would tell me a word of your notions if you could help it!"

The Father of men and gods made answer:

"My dear Hera, do not expect to know everything I say. You must not expect as much as that, although you are my wife. Whatever is proper for you to hear, you shall be the first to hear before any in heaven or earth; but when I choose to consider things by myself, do not be inquisitive and ask questions about everything."

Queen Hera said at once, opening her fine eyes:

"O you dreadful creature, what a thing to say! I inquisitive? I ask you questions? I never did such a thing in my life! I just leave you alone, and you decide whatever you choose. But I am dreadfully afraid this time. I can't put it out of my mind that you may be cajoled by Silverfoot Thetis, that daughter of the Old Man of the Sea! Early this morning she was kneeling and clasping your knees. I suppose you bowed your head and promised faithfully to honour Achillês and kill crowds on the battlefield."

Zeus Cloudgatherer answered:

"You are a strange creature: always supposing, always watching me. But you shall gain nothing by it. You will only make me dislike you more, and that will only be more unpleasant for you. If this is as you say, it must be my pleasure. Silence please, and sit down, and do what I tell you. All the gods in Olympos will not help you if I come near and lay my heavy hands upon you."

This frightened the Queen; she sat down in silence and took herself in hand. But the other gods were disturbed, and Hephaistos the mastercraftsman was the first to speak. He took his mother's side, and said:

"Bother it all! It is really too bad, if you two quarrel like this about mortals, and make a brawl among the gods. What's the pleasure in good fare with bad manners everywhere? My advice to my mother is this, and she knows it is good; give way to dear Father Zeus, and don't let father scold any more and spoil our breakfast. What if Olympian Flashlightning choose to knock us out of our seats? He is much stronger than we are. Come now, speak him fair and gentle, Olympian will be kind in one minute."

Then he jumped up, and put the double cup in her hand, saying:

"Be patient, mother dear, bear it patiently although it hurts! I love you, and I don't want to see you beaten before my eyes. I shall not be able to help you then, however sorry I am, for Olympian is hard to tackle. Once before I tried to help you, and he caught me by the leg and threw me from the threshold of heaven. All day long I fell, and at sunset down I came in Lemnos, with very little breath left in my body; there I fell, and the Sintians looked after me."

Queen Hera smiled at this, and smiling received the cup from her son's hand. Then he drew sweet nectar from the bowl, and carried it to all the gods, moving round rightways.[5] Laughter unquenchable rose among the blessed gods when they saw Hephaistos butler puffing about the hall.

So they feasted all day until sunset, and there was no lack; plenty to eat and drink, a splendid harp with Apollo to play it, and the Muses singing turn by turn in their lovely voices. But when the bright light of the sun sank down they went each to his room for sleep; for the famous Crookshank Hephaistos had built them each a chamber by his clever skill. And Zeus Olympian Flashlightning went to his own bed, where he used to sleep sound when slumber came upon him; into that bed he climbed and slept, with Queen Hera by his side.

BOOK III

*How Menelaos and Alexandros fought a duel together,
and what came of it*

AND NOW THE TWO ARMIES ADVANCED, EACH UNDER ITS OWN LEADERS.

The Trojans raised a loud din and clamour, like a huge flock of birds. So you may hear cranes honking out of the sky before a storm of rain, as they fly with a great noise towards the Ocean stream, bringing death

---

[5]As the sun goes, as the clock goes, "through the buttonhole": keeping the company on the right hand.

and destruction to the Pygmy men; and in the early morning they open their fight. But the Achaians marched in silence, breathing fury, shoulder to shoulder, with grim determination. The dust rose in clouds under their feet as they marched apace over the plain, as thick as the mist which a south wind spreads over the mountains. Shepherds hate it, the robber likes it better than night; a man can see a stone's throw and no farther.

No sooner had the two armies come near than a champion stept out of the Trojan ranks, the noble prince Alexandros.[1] A leopard-skin hung over his shoulders with bow and sword; he shook his two sharp spears, and challenged all comers to fight him man to man. So he strode out with long steps. Menelaos saw him with joy, as a lion spies a victim, when he is hungry and finds a horned stag or a wild goat: greedily he devours his prey, even if dogs and lusty lads set upon him. So Menelaos was glad when he set eyes on Alexandros, for he thought he was sure to punish the traitor; at once he leapt down from his chariot in his armour.

But as soon as Alexandros saw him come out in front, his heart sank and he slunk back into the ranks to save himself. He might have been some one walking through the woods who suddenly sees a snake, and jumps back all of a tremble pale with fear. So Alexandros jumped back, and so he slunk into safety.

Then Hector rated him with scorn:

"Damn you, Paris, you handsome woman-hunter, you seducer! I wish you had never been born, I wish you had died unwedded! Yes, I wish that! and it would have been much better than to be a public pest, a thing of contempt. What guffaws there must be over there! They thought you a prime champion because you are good-looking. But there's no pluck in you, no fight!

"Were you like this when you got your fine company and set sail over the sea, and travelled in foreign lands, and brought home a handsome woman? She was to marry into a warlike nation, she was to be the ruin of your father and all his people, a joy to your enemies, a disgrace to yourself! So you would not stand up to Menelaos? You ought to find out what sort of fellow he is whose wife you are keeping. There would be little use then for your harp and the gifts of Aphroditê, your fine hair and good looks, when you lie in the dust. Well, the Trojans are all cowards, or you would have had a coat of stone long ago for the evil you have done!"[2]

Alexandros replied:

"That is true enough, Hector, that is true enough. Your heart is always as hard as steel. Like a shipwright's axe, when he slices off a spar from a tree with all the strength of a man! A hard heart indeed! Don't taunt me with Aphroditê's adorable gifts. You can't throw away a god's gifts, offered unasked, which none could win by wishing.

---

[1]That was the name of Paris, who had carried off Helen.
[2]Stoned to death.

"Very well now, if you want me to fight, make both armies sit down on the ground, and put me between them with Menelaos to fight for Helen and all her wealth. Whichever proves the better man, let him take both wealth and woman home with him. Then let both sides swear friendship and peace: you to stay in Troy, they to go back to Argos, where there are plenty of fine women!"

Hector was very well satisfied with this. He went out between the ranks, holding his spear by the middle, and waved back his men. The Trojans sat down in order; but the Achaians at first went on shooting at him and throwing javelins and stones, until King Agamemnon shouted in a loud voice:

"Stop it, men, don't shoot, men! Hector wants to say something."

They stopt at once, and fell silent; and then Hector spoke out between the armies.

"Hear me, Trojans, and you men of Achaia, while I give you a message from Alexandros, who was the cause of our war. He asks that both Trojans and Achaians lay down their arms on the ground, and let Menelaos and himself fight a duel for Helen and all her wealth. Whichever proves the better man shall take both wealth and woman home with him: then let both sides swear friendship and peace."

All heard this in silence; then Menelaos cried out:

"Hear me also! This touches me most nearly, but my mind is, that Achaians and Trojans should now be reconciled. You have suffered enough for this quarrel of mine which Alexandros began. Whichever of us is fated to die, let him die, and let the others make friends forthwith. You bring two lambs—a white ram and a black ewe, for Earth and Sun, and we will bring another ram for Zeus. Call his Grace King Priam that he may take the oath himself, for his sons are overbearing and faithless, and we do not wish anything done to violate the solemn oath. Young men's minds are always a-flutter; but when an old man is there, he looks both before and behind, to see that the best is done for both sides."

Achaians and Trojans were all glad that there was some hope to end that lamentable war. They arranged their chariots in order; the men got out and put off their armour, laying it all upon the ground close together, and leaving a small space between the armies. Hector sent two heralds into the city to fetch the animals and to call Priam; King Agamemnon sent Talthybios to the camp with orders to bring the ram.

Meanwhile Iris had her own errand to Helen. She took the likeness of her goodsister,[3] Laodicè, the most beautiful of Priam's daughters, the wife of Helicaon Antenor's son. Iris found Helen in her room. She was weaving a great web of purple stuff, double size; and embroidering in it pictures of the battles of that war which two armies were waging for her sake. Iris came up to Helen, and said:

---

[3]The traditional English names for the group of relations-in-law are goodfather, goodbrother, etc.

"Come along, my love, and see a wonderful sight! They were all fighting in the plain like fury, and now all of a sudden they are sitting down, not a sound to be heard, no more battle, all leaning upon their shields, and their spears stuck in the ground! But Alexandros and Menelaos are going to fight for you! and you are to be the wife of the winner!"

These words pierced Helen to the heart. She longed for her husband of the old days, for home and family. At once she threw a white veil over her, and left the house quickly with tears running down her cheeks. Two maids were in attendance, Aithra and Clymenê with her great eyes. They made their way to the Scaian Gate.

Priam was sitting over the gatehouse in a group of the city elders, Panthoös and Thymoites, Lampos and Clytios, Hicetaon once well known in the field, and two men of tried wisdom, Ucalegon[4] and Antenor. These were old men long past their fighting days, but excellent speakers. There they all sat on the tower, chirruping in their thin old voices like so many crickets on a tree. As they saw Helen coming up, they whispered to one another in plain words:

"No wonder Achaians and Trojans have been fighting all these years for such a woman! I do declare she is like some divine creature come down from heaven. Well, all the same, I wish she would sail away, and not stay here to be the ruin of us and our children."

But Priam called Helen to his side:

"Come here, my dear child, and sit by me, to see your husband that was, and your family and friends. I don't blame you, my dear, I blame only the gods, for sending that host of enemies to bring tears to our eyes. Tell me the name of that prodigious man yonder? Who is he, that big handsome man? Others there are a head taller, that is true, but so fine a man I never did see, or so royal. He is every inch a king."

Helen answered: "You do me honour, my dear goodfather! How I wish I had died before I followed your son here, and left my bridal chamber and my family, my beloved daughter and all my young friends! But that was not to be; and so I pine away in sorrow. But I must answer your question. That is the great King Agamemnon of the house of Atreus, a good king and a strong spearman, both. He was my own goodbrother, to my shame, as sure as ever he was born."

The old man gazed at him with admiration, and said: "Atreidês, you are blessed indeed, a son of fortune happy in your lot! A great nation indeed is under your sway! I have travelled as far as vine-clad Phrygia, and there I saw hosts of Phrygian men with their dapple nags, the people of Otreus and splendid Mygdon, who were there campaigning on the banks of Sangarios; for I was among them as a volunteer on the day when the Amazons came, those women as good as men. But all those hosts were not so many as the Achaians here."

---

[4]This name means Careless; and Virgil plays upon it neatly in describing the sack of Troy (*Aeneid,* ii. 312), "proximus ardet Ucalegon," Careless is on fire next door.

Next the old man asked about Odysseus.

"Tell me again, dear child, who is that—a head shorter than my lord King Agamemnon but broader in shoulders and chest? His arms lie on the ground, and he is patrolling the ranks of men like a tame wether; indeed, he looks very like a thick-fleeced ram marching through a flock of white ewes."

Helen answered, "That is Odysseus Laertès' son, the man who is never at a loss. He was bred in Ithaca, a rugged rocky land: there is no device or invention which he does not know."

At this Antenor broke in.

"Yes, my lady," he said, "you have spoken nothing but the truth. Odysseus has been here already: he came with Menelaos on a mission concerning yourself. I entertained them both in my house, and I got to know their looks and their many inventions. When they came before our assembly, standing Menelaos was head and shoulders above him; while they both sat, Odysseus was more dignified. But when they put the patterns of their minds and inventions into words before us all, Menelaos ran smoothly on, said not much, but very clearly, for he was not one of many words or one to miss the right word; yet he was the younger man. Then Odysseus rose, this man who is never at a loss: he would stand with his eyes fixt on the ground, didn't move the staff backwards or forwards, but held it stiff, like a dull fellow: you would call him surly and stupid both. But as soon as he let out his great voice from his chest, and a shower of words falling thick and soft like snowflakes in winter time, no other man alive could come near Odysseus. But then we did not think him so very much to look at."

Then the old man saw Aias, and asked again:

"Who is that other big handsome man among the Achaians, standing head and broad shoulders above the rest?"

Helen answered: "That giant of a man is Aias, a real tower of strength. And opposite him is Idomeneus, standing among his Cretan captains like a god. Menelaos often entertained him in our house, when he used to come over from Crete. And now I can see all the others that I know, and I can tell you their names; but two I cannot see, two young princes, Castor, who can tame any horse, and Polydeuces the boxer—my own two brothers, my own mother's sons! I wonder if they never left Lacedaimon? or perhaps they did come, and now they will not show themselves in the field because I have brought all that shame upon them!"

But it was not as she said; already mother earth held them fast, far away in Lacedaimon, their own native land.

[Menelaus and Paris engage in hand-to-hand combat. But when Menelaus seems to be winning, Aphrodite invisibly spirits Paris away to Helen's bedchamber. Frustrated in their attempt to end the war, both sides resume the battle.]

BOOK VI

[After the abortive duel between Menelaus and Paris, the Achaeans fight successfully, even without Achilles. Events go so badly for the Trojans that Hector summons the women of Troy to offer emergency prayers and sacrifices to Athene, the goddess who had vowed to destroy their city.]

When Hector got to the oak tree at the Scaian Gate, the women ran crowding round, asking news of husbands and brothers, sons and friends. He exhorted them each and all to make their prayer to heaven; but sorrows hung over many.

Then Hector went to Priam's noble palace with its portals and galleries of polished stone. There were fifty chambers built of stone standing side by side, where the sons of Priam slept beside their wives; his daughters and their husbands had twelve roofed chambers of stone, standing in a row on the opposite side of the courtyard. Here his gracious mother met him, leading Laodicê the most beautiful of her daughters. She clasped his hand, and said:

"Why have you left the battle, my boy?—They must be pressing you hard, those accursed invaders, and you thought you might lift up your hands in prayer to Zeus from our citadel. Just wait a bit and let me bring you some wine. Pour a libation to Father Zeus and All Gods, and then it will do you good to have a drink yourself. You're tired out with defending your friends, poor dear. When a man is tired out, a drop of wine will make him stout!"

Hector answered:

"No wine for me, my dear mother; you will cripple me, and make me forget that I must fight. And I dare not pour a libation to Zeus with unwashen hands. It is quite impossible to offer prayers to Cronion Thundercloud bespattered like this in blood and mud. You must approach Athena yourself. Gather all the older women, and go to her temple with your burnt offering; take the finest and largest robe you have in your store, the one you prize most, and lay it upon Athena's knees; promise to sacrifice twelve yearling heifers that have never felt the goad, if only she will have compassion upon the wives and children of Troy, if only she will hold off the son of Tydeus from our sacred city, that wild warrior, that strong contriver of defeat!

"I leave you then to visit Athena's temple. Now I must find Paris, and see if he will listen to me. If only the earth would swallow him up! A great trouble the Olympian bred in him, for Troy and for proud Priam, and the sons of Priam! If I could once see that man go down into Hadês, I would say that my heart had forgotten how to grieve."

The Queen called to her servants, and sent them through the city, summoning the older women. She herself went down into her vaulted storeroom, where she kept robes embroidered by the women of Sidon, which Alexandros had brought from Sidon when he went on that voyage across the sea and came back with royal Helen as his bride. She chose one of these for Athena, a great spread of the finest needlework, shining like a star, which lay under the rest.

Bearing this she led the great company of women to Athena's temple upon the citadel. The gates were opened by the priestess, Cisseus' daughter and Antenor's wife, the handsome Theano. All cried aloud the women's alleluia, lifting up their hands. Theano took the robe and laid it on the knees of the goddess, and then she offered her prayer and vow:

"Queen Athena, goddess divine, saviour of our city! Do thou break the spear of Diomedês, and strike him to the ground before the Scaian gates! Then we will sacrifice to thee in this temple twelve yearling heifers that never felt the goad, if only thou wilt have compassion upon our town and the wives and little children of Troy!"

So the priestess prayed, but Athena refused her prayer. Meanwhile Hector had made his way to the mansion of Alexandros, a fine place built by the best workmen in the land—hall and women's room and court-yard; it stood on the citadel next door to Priam and Hector. He entered, holding his great spear eleven cubits long, with a bright blade of bronze made fast with a golden ferrule. He found Alexandros in his wife's room, handling his shield and corselet and fingering his bow. Helen was sitting there with her women and seeing about their work. Hector said to him reproachfully:

"My good man, you should not be sulking here. Men are falling in the fight outside our walls, war and battle is blazing round the city for your sake! You would be the first to attack any one else you might see shirking his part. Up, man! or soon fire will warm up the place!"

Paris answered:

"You are right to reproach me, Hector, quite right indeed! But let me tell you this: I give you my word that I was not sulking. It is not bad temper keeps me here, but simply a bitter heart. Just now my wife has been trying to persuade me with gentle words, and driving me back to the battle. I think it will be better so myself. Victory chops and changes. Just wait a bit, and I will put on my armour.—Or go on, and I will follow; I think I shall catch you up."

Hector answered nothing, but Helen said warmly:

"Brother dear, I am ashamed; I shudder at myself! I can do nothing but evil! I wish a whirlwind had carried me off to the mountains on the day that I was born, or thrown me into the roaring sea—I wish the waves had swept me away before all this was done! But since the gods ordained it so, I wish I had been mated with a better man, one who could feel the contempt and indignation of the world! But this man is unstable, and ever shall be; some day I think this fault will find him out. But do come in now, brother, come in and sit down; I know your heart is most heavy with this world of trouble about us—all for my shame and his infatuation. Indeed, Zeus has laid a cruel fate upon us, to be a byword for generations to come!"

Hector answered:

"Don't ask me to sit, Helen: I thank you all the same, my dear, but I must not stay. They miss me outside, and I must go and do my part. Just keep this man up to the mark; let him make haste himself and catch me up before I go out of the gates, for I am going home first for one look at my wife and my little boy. I don't know if I shall ever see them again. It may be God's will to lay me low by the enemy's hand."

So he took his leave and went to his own house. But he did not find Andromachê there, for she was already upon the battlements with her boy and a servant, weeping in her sorrow. Hector, when he found she was not within, stood at the door, and said to the maids:

"Be so good as to tell me where your mistress has gone. To one of my sisters or to my goodsisters, or to Athena's temple where the women are making supplication?"

The housekeeper said:

"No, sir, not to any of the family, nor to Athena's where the women are all gone to offer their supplication. To tell the truth, she has gone up on the walls, because she heard that our people were in danger and the enemy were getting the best of it. She has just gone off in a great hurry like one distracted, and the nurse carrying the boy."

So Hector went back by the same way along the streets till he reached the Scaian gates, by which he meant to go out into the plain; and there his precious wife came running to meet him. Andromachê was the daughter of Eëtion, the Cilician King, and her home was in Thebê, below the forest of Placos. She came to meet him, and the nurse followed with the boy in her bosom: quite a little child, cheerful and merry—their little Hector, the tiny champion of Troy, like a shining star, whom they dearly loved. Hector called him Scamandrios, but to others he was Astyanax, "his Gracious Majesty"; for Hector was the sole saving help of the city.[1]

The father smiled quietly as he looked at his boy. But Andromachê stood by his side with tears running down her cheeks, and caught his hand fast while she said:

"My dearest, how can you do it? Your courage will be your death! Have you no pity for your baby boy, or your unhappy wife, who will soon be your widow! Soon they will all rush upon you and kill you! And I—if I lose you, it would be better for me to go down into my grave. There will be no more comfort for me if you are taken, but only sorrow.

"I have no father and no mother now. My father was slain by Achillès; he laid waste my home, Thebê with its lofty towers; he killed Eëtion, although he did not despoil him, for he thought that a wicked thing—he burnt him with his armour and raised a barrow upon him, and the divine Oreads of the mountains planted elm-trees round about. My seven brothers all went down to Hadês in one day, for that terrible Achillès killed them all amid their cattle and sheep. My mother who

---

[1]"Hector" means the same as ἄναξ, lord and king.

was queen in that place he brought away a prisoner, with the other spoil; he set her free for a heavy ransom, but Artemis Archeress shot her in her father's house.

"So you are my father and my mother, Hector, you are my brother, you are my loving husband! Then pity me and stay here behind the walls; do not make your boy an orphan and your wife a widow! But post your men by the fig-tree, where the wall may be scaled most easily, where the wall is open to assault—three attacks there have been already in great strength—Aias and the other Aias, then Indomeneus, then the two kings with Diomedês, whether it be some diviner gave them a hint or it may have been their own thought."

Hector answered:

"I have not forgotten all that, my wife, but I could not show my face before the men or the women of Troy if I skulk like a coward out of the way. And I will not do it, for I have learnt how to bear myself bravely in the front of the battle, and to win credit for my father and myself. One thing I know indeed in my heart and soul: a day shall come when sacred Troy shall perish, and Priam and the people of Priam; but my sorrow is not so much for what will happen to the people, or Queen Hecabê herself, or King Priam or my brothers, when all those good men and true shall fall in the dust before their enemies—as for you, when some armed man shall drive you away weeping, and take from you the day of freedom. To think that you should live in a foreign land, and ply the loom at the orders of another woman; that you should carry water from strange fountains, crushed under stern necessity—a hateful task! that some one should see you shedding tears, and say, 'There is Hector's wife, and he was the first and best of the brave Trojans when there was that war about Troy'—and he will make your pain ever fresh, while there is no such man to save you from the day of slavery. May I be dead and buried deep in the earth before I hear your cries and see you dragged away!"

As he spoke, Hector held out his arms for his boy, but the boy shrank back into the nurse's bosom, crying, and scared at the sight of his father; for he was afraid of the gleaming metal and the horsehair crest, when he saw that dreadful thing nodding from the top of the helmet. Father and mother laughed aloud, and Hector took off the helmet and set it down on the ground shining and flashing. Then he kissed his son and dandled him in his hands, and prayed aloud to heaven:

"O Zeus and all ye heavenly gods! Grant that this my son may be as notable among our people as I am, and let him be as strong, and let him rule Ilios in his strength! When he goes to war let them say, This man is much better than his father! May he kill his enemy and bring home the blood-stained spoils, and give joy to his mother's heart!"

Then he gave his boy back into the mother's arms, and she pressed him to her sweet-scented breast, laughing through the tears. Her husband was moved with pity as he saw this; he stroked her with his hand, and said:

"My dearest, do not grieve too much. No man will send me to my grave unless it be so ordained. But destiny is a thing which no man can escape, neither coward nor brave man, from the day he is born. Go home now, and see to your own household work, the loom and the distaff, and keep your servants to their tasks. War shall be men's business, and mine especially of all those who are in Ilios."

Then Hector took up the helmet with its nodding crest; but his wife went on her way home, turning again and again to look, as the tears flowed thick and fast. And when she got to her own house, all the women fell a-weeping too; they mourned for Hector in his own house while he still lived, for they never thought he would escape his enemies and return from the battle again.

Paris made no delay either. As soon as his armour was on, he hurried through the city at the top of his speed. He was like a stallion after a good feed at the manger, who breaks his halter and runs whinnying over the plain to his usual bath in the river; he bears himself proudly, arches his neck, the mane shakes over his shoulders, he knows his own fine looks as he gallops along to the place where the mares graze. Such was Paris Priamidès, as he marched down from Pergamon in armour shining like the sun, chuckling with glee as his quick feet ran.

He caught up his brother just as he was leaving the place where the two loving hearts had spoken. Paris at once said:

"Well, your worship, you see what a drag I am on you when you are in a hurry; I'm late, and I did not come along fair and square as you told me!"

Hector said:

"My good fellow, no fair-minded man could despise your work in battle, for you fight well. But you do not really want to fight, and you are glad to hang back. What I regret is that I hear people speak ill of you, when all their hardships are borne for your sake. But let us go on. We will satisfy them by and by, if Zeus ever grant us to set up a bowl of deliverance in our hall, in gratitude to the deathless gods of heaven, when we have driven the enemy host away from Troy."

✿   ✿   ✿

BOOK IX

How Agamemnon repented of his violence and sent envoys to Achillês

[In answer to Achilles' prayer, Zeus permits the Achaeans to be driven back to their ships along the beach. Fearful of a complete Trojan victory, Agamemnon is now willing to make peace with Achilles.]

So the Trojans kept their watch; but the Achaians were possessed by Panic, the freezing handmaid of Rout, and their strongest were pierced with grief intolerable. Their spirit was torn in pieces, like the sea lashed by those two fierce winds from Thrace, Boreas from the north parts and Zephyros from the west, when they come in a sudden gale, and roll up the dark water into crests, and sweep the seaweed in heaps along the shore.

Atreidês went about crushed with this heavy pain at heart, bidding his heralds summon all to assembly one by one, but not to cry aloud; and he himself did his share with the foremost. They took their seats despondent. Then Agamemnon rose with tears running down his cheeks, as a clear spring trickles over a rock; and groaning deep, he addressed the assembly:

"My friends, my lords and princes, Zeus Cronidês has shackled me in the chains of blind madness. Hard god! Once he promised me that I should sack the fenced city of Ilios before I should return; but now he has contrived a cruel deceit, and he bids me go back to Argos dishonoured, after losing so many lives. Such must be the pleasure of Almighty God, who has brought low the heads of many cities, and will yet bring many low, for his power is greatest of all. Ah well, let us make up our minds to it, and escape with our ships to our native land: for now we never shall take the city of Troy."

They heard him in dead silence. Long they sat silent in their sorrow, until at last Diomedês broke the silence and said:

"My lord King, I must answer you to begin with, where such a thing is lawful, Sir, in public assembly; and I say your advice is foolish: pray do not be angry with me. You attacked me first before the whole nation, and blamed my courage, and said I was unwarlike, a weakling; how that may be every one knows, both young and old. But you, Sir—Cronidês has enriched you by halves. He has given you the sceptre with honour above all others, but courage he has not given you, and that is the true supreme power. Good heavens, do you really think our people are such unwarlike weaklings, as you say? If your own mind is set on retreat, go. There is the road, there are the ships beside the sea, all the great fleet which came with you from Mycenê. But others will yet remain until we utterly destroy that city! Indeed, let them go too, and sail away for happy home! Two of us will go on fighting, Sthenelos and I, until we make our goal! for God has sent us here."

All cheered bold Diomedês in admiration, and Nestor rose to speak:

"Tydeidês, you are first in the hard-fought field, and in counsel you are best of all men of your years. Not one true man of all our nation will find fault with what you say, or gainsay it; but there is something to seek in your words.[1] The truth is, you are young; you might be my own son,

---

[1] You have no policy to propose.

my youngest; yet what you say is right and proper, good advice for our princes. Well, let me speak, and I will put all in proper order, for I am older than you are. No one will disregard what I say, not even my lord King Agamemnon.

"Clanless, lawless, homeless is he who is in love with civil war, that brutal ferocious thing.—But we must think of the present. We must give way to the night. Let us have a good meal; then let bodies of guards be posted outside between wall and moat. This is for the young men; after that, you take command, Atreidês, for you are the paramount king. Call the elder men to dine; that is right and proper for you. There is plenty of wine in your stores, which comes every day in our ships over the sea from Thrace; all entertainment is yours, and your subjects are many. There will be many to help with advice, and you will accept the best advice that is offered. That is the great need for all our nation, good sound advice; for the enemy are near our ships—look at their countless watch-fires! Who could be pleased at that! This night will either break our army to pieces, or save us alive."

❀   ❀   ❀

But Atreidês led all the elder men to his quarters, and gave them a good repast. When they had finished, Nestor was the first to speak, that grand old man whose counsel was always thought the best. He spoke with honesty and good courage, setting out his thoughts neat and clear, like a weaver weaving a pattern upon his loom. This is what he said:

"My lord King Agamemnon, I will begin with your gracious majesty, and I will end with you; for you are lord of many nations, and Zeus has placed in your hands the sceptre and the law, that you may take counsel on their behalf. Therefore it is your duty above all both to speak and to listen, and to act for any other who may have something to say for the common good: another may begin, but the rest depends upon you. Then I will declare what seems best to me. For no one will think of a better plan than this which I have had in mind ever since that day when your Grace took away the girl Briseïs from Achillês, and he was angry. That was not what we wished, not at all. You know I spoke strongly to dissuade you; but you gave way to your proud temper, and insulted a great man whom the gods delighted to honour, for you took and you still keep his prize. But even at this late hour let us consider how we can appease him, and win him with gentle words and kindly gifts."

The King answered:

"Sir, you speak only the truth about my blind madness. I was blind, I do not deny it. Worth more than many thousands is the man whom Zeus loves and honours, as he now has honoured this man and humiliated the Achaian nation. Then since I was blinded and gave way to my wretched passion, it is my wish to appease him and to offer anything in redress.

"Before you all I will proclaim what I have to offer: seven tripods untouched by the fire, ten ingots of gold, twenty bright cauldrons, twelve horses, grand creatures which have won prizes in the race. No man who owned all that my racers have won, could ever be called penniless or pinched for a bit of gold! And I will give seven women skilful in women's work, Lesbians whom I chose when he captured Lesbos himself, the most beautiful women in the world. And along with these I will give back Briseïs, the one whom I took at that time. And I will swear a solemn oath that she has never lain in my bed, and I have never touched her in the way of a man with a woman.

"This is what I offer now. Afterwards, if the gods grant that we sack the city of Priam, let him be there when we are dividing the spoil; he shall load his vessel with piles of gold and bronze, and choose for himself twenty Trojan women, the most beautiful after Helen. Then if we return to Argos, he shall have my daughter to wife; and I will honour him equally with my own son Orestês, my well beloved son, who is now at home living in wealth and luxury. I have three daughters, Chrysothemis, Laodicê, and Iphianassa: any one of these he shall have without bride-price to take to his father's house; and I will give her a dowry greater than ever man gave to a daughter.

"Seven flourishing cities I will give to him, Cardamylê, Enopê, and grassy Hirê, sacred Pherai and meadowy Antheia, lovely Aipeia and Pedasos with its vines. All stand near the sea, on the border of sandy Pylos; and in them inhabit men rich in flocks and rich in cattle, who shall worship him with their tribute and obey his judgments under his sceptre.

"This I will do for him if he will only relent. Let him yield! only Hadês is pitiless and unyielding, and that is why men hate him most of all the gods. Let him give way to me, since I am a greater King, and since I am older than he is."

Gerenian Nestor replied:

"May it please your Grace, my lord King Agamemnon! Such gifts as you offer now to Achillês no one could despise. Then let us choose envoys to send at once—or rather let me look round and choose them. Phoinix first, let him lead the way; then big Aias and Odysseus; heralds— let Odios and Eurybatês go with them. Here, water for our hands if you please, and call a solemn silence, that we may pray to Zeus Chonidês and crave his mercy."

This was approved by all. At once heralds brought the hand-wash, boys filled the mixing bowls to the brim, wine was served all round with the usual solemnity, they poured their drops and drank. Then they separated; and Gerenian Nestor with many a nod and wink told the envoys exactly what to say, especially Odysseus, if they wished to persuade the redoubtable Achillês.

Phoinix had gone on, and the two others paced after him by the sounding sea, with many an earnest prayer to Poseidon Earthholder

Earthshaker that they might successfully persuade that strong will. When they came to the lines of the Myrmidons, they found Achillês amusing himself with his harp; a beautiful thing it was, made by an artist, with a silver bridge and a clear lovely tone, part of the spoils of Thebê.[2] Achillês was playing upon this harp and singing the glorious feats of heroes. Patroclos sat opposite by himself, waiting until his friend should finish. The two envoys came forward, Odysseus first, and stood still.

Achillês jumped up from his seat in surprise, still holding the harp, and Patroclos got up too when he saw visitors. Achillês greeted them, and said:

"Welcome! I am glad to see friends. Just what I wanted! and you are my very best friends, though I am an angry man."

He led them indoors, and found them a comfortable seat with a fine purple rug; then he said to Patroclos by his side:

"A larger bowl, my dear fellow, if you please! stronger wine, and a cup apiece, for very good friends of mine are under my roof."

Patroclos was busy at once. He set a meat-block by the fire, and put on it a shoulder of mutton with another of goat, and the chine of a fine fat hog. Automedon held the meat and Achillês carved. When this was cut up and spitted Patroclos made a good fire, and when the flame had died down, he scattered the ashes, and laid the spits over them on the fire-dogs, sprinkling the grill with salt. Soon all was done brown and set out on platters; Patroclos handed round baskets of bread, and Achillês served the meat.

He sat down himself opposite Odysseus against the other wall, and told Patroclos to do grace to the gods, as he cast the firstlings into the fire.

When they had all had enough, Aias nodded to Phoinix; but Odysseus saw this, and filling his cup with wine he greeted Achillês himself:

"Your health, Achillês! We do not lack good fare and plenty, either at the board of King Agamemnon, or here and now. Indeed you have given us a regular feast.

"But feasting is not our business, bless it! An awful disaster is what we see, my prince, and we are afraid. Life or death is in question for our whole fleet, unless you put on your armour of might. Close beside our ships and wall is the bivouac of the Trojans, with their allies gathered from the wide world, all full of pride. There are the countless watch-fires of their host, and they believe we shall not hold out but be driven back upon our ships. Zeus Cronidês gives them favourable signs with his lightning; Hector in triumphant pride is like a raging madman—he trusts in Zeus, and cares for nothing in heaven or earth while that strong frenzy possesses him. He prays that dawn may soon appear, and vows he will chop the ensigns from our ships and burn them with ravening fire, that he will smother us in the smoke and destroy us beside them.

---

[2]This touch will show how intricate the associations are in the story. Thebê in Mysia was sacked by Achillês, and the King and his seven sons were killed. His daughter was Hector's wife, Andromachê. And Chryseïs, the centre of the whole story, was there at the time, and taken with the spoil.

"This is what terribly affrights me. I fear the gods may fulfil his threats, and it may be our fate to perish in the land of Troy, far from home and Argos. Up, then! if now at last you have a mind to save our people in their extremity. You will be sorry yourself when it is too late, but when mischief is done there is no cure. Think first while you can how to save our people from the evil day.

"Wake up, man! Remember how Peleus your father warned you, on the day when he said goodbye to you on your journey from Phthia to Agamemnon, 'My son, victory will be yours if Athenaia and Hera choose to give it; but your task is to curb that proud temper, for a kind heart is the better part. Avoid quarrels, which go before destruction, and then all the nation will honour you both young and old.' That was the old King's warning, but you have forgotten it. It is not too late to change; let be that rancour which wrings your heart. Agamemnon offers you ample atonement if you will relent.

"Now then listen to me, and I will tell you what Agamemnon promised in his own quarters: Seven tripods untouched by the fire, ten ingots of gold, twenty bright cauldrons, twelve horses, grand creatures which have won prizes in the race. No one who owned all that those horses have won could ever be called penniless or pinched for a bit of gold! And he will give seven women skilful in women's work, the most beautiful women in the world, Lesbians whom he chose when you captured Lesbos yourself. And along with these he will give back Briseïs, the one whom he took away that time. And he will swear a solemn oath that she has never lain in his bed, and he has never touched her in the way of a man with a woman.

"That is what he offers now. Then if the gods grant later that we sack the city of Priam, you shall be there when we are dividing the spoil, and you shall load your ship with piles of gold and bronze, and choose for yourself twenty Trojan women, the most beautiful after Helen. And if we return to Argos, you shall have his daughter to wife, and he will honour you equally with his son Orestês, who is now at home living in wealth and luxury. Three daughters he has, Chrysothemis and Laodicê and Iphianassa; any one of these you shall have without bride-price, to take to your father's house; and he will give her a dowry greater than any man ever gave to a daughter. Seven flourishing cities he will give to you: Cardamylê and Enopê and grassy Hirê, sacred Pherai and meadowy Antheia, lovely Aipeia and Pedasos with its vines. All stand near the sea on the border of sandy Pylos; and in them inhabit men rich in flocks and rich in cattle, who shall worship you with their tribute, and obey your judgments under your sceptre. All this he will do if you will only relent.

"But if you hate and loathe Atreidês too much, him and his gifts, at least pity all the nations of Achaia in their extremity! They will honour you as if you were a god, and a great name you will get among them. For now you may kill Hector! He will come close enough in that furious madness—for now he says there's not a match for himself among all the Danaäns who came to Troy."

Achillês answered:

"Prince Odysseus Laërtiadès, I must speak out without undue respect to you. I must tell you how I feel and how I am resolved, that you two may not sit cooing at me on both sides. I hate that man like the gates of hell who says one thing and hides another thing in his heart! But I will tell you exactly what I have decided. I am not going to be persuaded by my lord King Agamemnon, or by any one else, because it seems one gets no thanks by fighting in battle for ever and for aye. Stay at home, or fight all day, you get only equal pay. Be a coward, or be brave, equal honour you will have. Death is coming if you shirk, death is coming if you work! I get no profit from suffering pain and risking my life for ever in battle. I am like a bird that gives the callow chicks every morsel she can get, and comes off badly herself.

"Just so I have spent many sleepless nights, I have fought through many long bloody days, all for a man to win back his dainty dear! Twelve cities I have destroyed with my ships, eleven fighting on land. Out of all these I have taken treasures rich and rare, and always brought all to my lord King Agamemnon; this Lagamemnon lags behind and takes it, distributes a few trifles and keeps the rest! Some things he gave as prizes to the princes and great men; the others keep theirs safe enough—I am the only one he has robbed! He has a wife of his own, let him sleep by her side and enjoy her.

"Why must Achaians make war on Trojans? Why did my lord King gather an army and bring it here? Was it not for lovely Helen? Are there only two men in the wide world who love their wives, my lord King and his royal brother? Why, every man who is honest and faithful loves his own, as I loved mine in my heart although my spear had won her. But now he has taken my prize from my hands and deceived me, let him not tempt me: I know him too well, he shall never move me. No, Odysseus, you and the other princes must help him to save the ships from the fire. Certainly he has done plenty of things already without me. Just now he built a wall, and ran a deep moat round it, and set stakes along the edge. Yet even so he cannot hold off Hector.

"But when I was in the field, Hector would not dare to show fight away from his walls; he got no farther than the Scaian Gates and the oak-tree. There he did once face me alone, and hardly escaped my attack. But now I don't want to fight with Hector any more. So tomorrow I will do sacrifice to Zeus and All Gods, and launch my ships, and load them full; and early in the morning if you like you shall see them in full sail over the Hellespont, with my men on board quite willing to row; and if the Earthshaker give us a good voyage, in three days I shall be in Phthia.

"I left great wealth behind when I came on this accursed voyage; there is more from these parts, gold and red copper, women and grey steel, which I shall take with me, my share by lot—but my prize, he who gave has taken away, his majesty my lord King Agamemnon. Tell him all that I say, in public, that the whole world may be indignant if he hopes to deceive some one else. He is always clothed in shamelessness, but the dirty dog will not look me in the face. I will not help him with advice or with action, for he has wholly deceived and beguiled me. Never again shall he deceive me with his words; he has done it once too often. Leave him alone to go to the devil, for Zeus has taken away his sense. I loathe his gifts, I value them not one splinter! Not if he offered me ten times as much, or twenty times, or any amount more, all that goes into Orchomenos, all that goes into Egyptian Thebes, the world's greatest treasure-house,—Thebes with its hundred gates, where two hundred men issue forth from each gate with horses and chariots, not if he gave me as much as the sands on the seashore and the dust on the earth, not even then would Agamemnon move me until he shall pay in full for the insult which torments my heart!

"His daughter! I will not marry a daughter of my lord King Agamemnon, not if her beauty challenged golden Aphroditê, not if her skill were a match for Athena Brighteyes. No, even so I will not do it! Let him choose her another man, one of his own rank who is a greater king than I. For if the gods let me live and return home, Peleus no doubt will find me a wife himself. There are women in plenty all over Hellas and Phthia, daughters of princes who have cities under their protection; I will take one of these to be my wife. When I was there, I often used to wish to marry a lawful wife, a mate well suited to me, and to enjoy the possessions which Peleus had gotten. For to me life is worth more than all the wealth of that noble city Ilios in peace time, before our armies came, more than the treasures in rocky Pytho within the doorstone of Phoibos Apollo the Archer. You may seize cattle and sheep, you may get tripods and horses, but for a man's life to come again neither seizing nor catching will help, when once it has passed beyond the fence of the teeth.

"My mother Thetis Silverfoot says, that two different fates are carrying me on the road to death. If I stay here and fight before the city of Troy, there will be no home-coming for me but my fame shall never die; if I go home to my native land, there will be no great fame for me, but I shall live long and not die an early death.

"Indeed, I would advise the others to sail away for home, since you will never make an end of Ilios. Clearly Zeus Allseeing has lifted a protecting hand over her, and the people have grown bold.

"But you return now and give your message to the princes openly, your privilege as counsellors; then let them contrive some better plan than this, if they wish to save the ships and the army. For this plan which they thought of is not for them while I am angry. But let Phoinix stay here and sleep with us, that he may go home with us to-morrow, if he likes; there shall be no compulsion."

They remained silent for some time after this vehement speech. Then old Phoinix spoke, with tears in his eyes, for he was full of fear for the fleet:

"If you have really set your mind on going, Achillês, if you will not help at all to keep the fire away from our ships, if your heart is still full of anger, then how can I part from you, dear boy, how can I be left here alone? You were my charge; your aged father sent me with you on that day when he sent you from Phthia to King Agamemnon, just a child, knowing as yet nothing of the combats of war, nothing of debate, where men can make their mark. So he sent me out to teach you all that, how to be a fine speaker and a man of action too. Then I could not part from you, dear boy, I would not be left behind; not if God himself should promise to scrape off my old age and make me young and strong, such as I was when I first left Hellas with its lovely women.

"I was a banished man; I had to escape from my angry father, Amyntor Ormenidês, and his reproaches. It was all about his concubine; he made much of her, and insulted his wife, my own mother, so she begged and prayed me to take the woman first that she might hate the old man. I did as she asked me; my father came to know it, and cursed me, and prayed the Avenging Spirits that I might never set any son of my own on my knees. The gods have fulfilled his prayer, Underwold Zeus and awful Persephoneia!

"But I could not endure to live in that house with my angry father. Indeed my friends and cousins were all about me, begging me to stay there and trying to hold me back. Many a plump sheep and many an ox they slaughtered, many a fine fat hog they singed and grilled over the fire, many a jar of the old man's wine was drunk. Nine long nights they watched round me as I slept; they took turns in watching, the fire was never out, one fire under the open gallery by the courtyard gates, one in the porch before my bedchamber. But on the tenth night, in the darkness, I broke open the door of my room and got out. I leapt over the courtyard fence easily enough, without being seen by the men on guard or the serving women. Then I went a long way, across the whole breadth of Hellas, until I came to Phthia and to King Peleus. He welcomed me freely, and loved me as a father loves a son, his only beloved son and the heir to his possessions. He made me rich, and put many subjects under my charge, where I lived on the border of Phthia as lord of the Dolopians.

"And I have made you what you are, my magnificent Achillês! I loved you from my heart: you would never go out to dinner without me, or take a bite at home until I sat you down on my knee, and cut off a titbit for you to begin with, and gave you a drop of wine. How often you have wetted my tunic, spluttering out drops of wine like a naughty child! Ah yes, I had much to put up with and I took no end of trouble; but all the time I was thinking that God had given no son to me. You were my son, my magnificent Achillês! I made you mine, hoping that you might save me some time from shame and ruin.

"Come, Achillês, tame that awful temper! You must not let your heart be hard. Even the gods can be moved and they are greater than you in excellence and honour and might. They can be turned by the supplications of mankind, with burnt offerings and tender prayers, and the savour of sacrifice, when there has been transgression and error. Prayers are the daughters of Zeus Almighty. They are lame and wrinkled, and dare not look you in the face, and they follow intent close behind Sin, the spirit of blind madness. But Sin is not lame; she is strong and swift of foot, so she is there first in every part of the world ready to make men fall, and Prayers come after to heal. If any man does reverence to Prayers when they come near, they bless him and hear his supplication but if any one rebuffs them and stubbornly denies them, they go to Zeus Cronion and beseech him that Sin may go with him, so that he may fall and be punished.

"And now you, Achillès, must see to it that reverence attend these daughters of Zeus, the reverence which bends the minds of other good men. For if Atreidès were not offering many gifts and promising others, if he still kept his swelling anger, I should not ask you to forget your resentment and to help your people, however much they might need it. But now he offers much at once, and promises more to follow; he has sent envoys, the noblest he could choose out of all the nation, and your own dearest friends. Do not despise the feet of those who bring good tidings! But you had reason to be angry before.

"Have we not heard the stories of heroes in times past, when one was possessed of swelling anger? They were moved with gifts, they were reconciled with good words. I remember one thing that happened long ago, no new thing indeed, but I know just how it was. You are all my friends, and I will tell you. Curetians and Aitolians were fighting before the city of Calydon, and killing one another; the Aitolians defending their city, the others trying to destroy it. This trouble Artemis Golden-throne had sent upon them. She was offended because Oineus had not offered her the firstfruits in his orchards; when the other gods enjoyed their sacrifices, for her alone there was none. He forgot, or he did not notice; some blind madness possessed him.

"So the offended Archeress sent a ravening wild tusker boar, which did great damage among the orchards: tore up tall trees from the roots, and threw them about in heaps with their roots and their blooming fruits. Oineus' son Meleagros collected huntsmen and hounds from many cities, and killed the boar. A few men could never have mastered him, so huge he was; and many a man he did bring to his funeral!

"But the goddess raised a great turmoil and dispute between Cure-tians and Aitolians, about the boar's head and shaggy hide.[3] So long as Meleagros fought, things went ill for the Curetians, and they could not hold their own outside the wall, though they were many; but anger swells in the hearts of many men, even though they may be sensible enough, and anger took hold of Meleagros.

"So he was angry with his mother Althaia and stayed at home with his wedded wife. She was the beautiful Cleopatra, the daughter of Mar-pessa Eueninè and Idas, the strongest man on earth in those days—he raised his bow against Lord Phoibos Apollo himself when Apollo wanted

---

[3]Meleagros gave the spoils to Atalanta, and his mother's brothers quarrelled with him about it; he killed them, and his mother cursed him, so he sulked like Achillès.

his handsome bride!⁴ The father and mother had a pet name for
Cleopatra at home, 'the little kingfisher,' because Marpessa had wept
like a mourning kingfisher when Phoibos Apollo Shootafar carried her
off.⁵— Well, this was the wife Cleopatra; and Meleagros stayed by her
side and nursed his blighting anger.

"He was angry with his mother, because she had cursed him for killing
her brother. She beat her hands on the earth, calling upon Hadês and
awful Persephoneia, kneeling upon her knees and wetting her bosom
with tears, while she prayed them to give him death. The Avenger that
walks in darkness, that pitiless spirit, heard her from Erebos.

"So then there was din and tumult about the gates as the walls were
assailed; and the Aitolian elders sent the chief priests of the place to
beseech Meleagros to come out and help them with great promises.
They asked him to choose a plot in the richest part of the Calydonian
plain, fifty acres, half vine-land, half cleared arable land, for his own.
Earnestly the old King Oineus entreated him, standing on the threshold
of his lofty chamber and shaking the two leaves of the door; earnestly his
sisters and his mother besought him, but he refused all the more: his
companions, the truest and dearest of all, entreated too. But they could
not move him until his chamber itself began to be battered, and the
Curetians were scaling the walls and setting fire to the great city. Then
at last his own lovely wife entreated him with tears, and recited all the
horrors of a city taken by storm: how the men are slaughtered, the
houses are burnt to the ground, wives and children are driven away by
strangers. Now his heart was torn to hear all these miseries: he put on his
armour, and went out. So his own feelings conquered him, and he saved
his countrymen from the evil day; but he never received those splendid
gifts, and he had to defend them after all.

"Now I pray you do not be of that mind yourself, let not fortune turn
you into that path, my dear! It would be worse to let the ships burn
before you help. While gifts are to be had, come; the people will honour
you as if you were a god. But if without gifts you enter the battle, you
will not have the same honour even if you do save the day."

Achillês answered:

"Phoinix, dear old daddy, this is not the honour I want. I think I have
been honoured by the ordinance of Zeus, and that honour shall be mine
in this fleet as long as the breath remains in my body and as long as my
limbs can move. But now just listen to me. Don't confuse my mind with
lamentations and groans to please the honour of my lord king high and
mighty. You ought not to be kind to him or I shall hate you, and I am
kind to you, so you ought to stand by me and vex any one who vexes
me. Be a prince with me, and take half my honour! These will take the

---

⁴Apollo carried her off, and they fought, until Zeus stopped it. Then Zeus told her
to choose, and she chose Idas.
⁵The hen was supposed to utter her mournful cry when she was separated from
her mate.

message, you stay here for the night and you shall have a soft bed. In the morning we will consider whether to go home or stay here."

He nodded silently to Patroclos to lay a nice bed for Phoinix; a hint to the others that it was time to be going. Aias said then:

"Prince Laërtiadês and my very good friend, let us go; for I do not think we shall achieve our errand this time. We must make our report at once, unwelcome as it is, to our people, who still sit waiting for it, I suppose. But Achillês has worked himself into a savage temper. Hard-hearted man! He does not think of his friends' affection and how we honoured him first and foremost. Cruel man! a man will take blood-price from one who has killed his brother or his own son; the slayer remains in his own country by paying a heavy price, the other controls his heart and temper after accepting the price: but you are implacable, your temper is merciless, such is God's will.—and all for one girl! Now we offer you seven of the best, and a heap of treasure with them. Be reconciled, respect your own roof-tree, for we are under your roof, envoys of the Danaän people; and we would be your nearest and dearest friends of all the Achaian nations."

Achillês answered:

"My lord Telamonian Aias, all you have said is very much what I feel myself, but my heart swells with anger when I remember all that—how Atreidês made me contemptible before the whole nation, as if I were an outcast without rights! However, go now and deliver your message. For I will not think of battle until prince Hector comes as far as the ships and camp of the Myrmidons in his career, and sets our ships in a blaze. Here, I say, beside my own hut and my ship, I think Hector will be held, and his fury stayed."

The envoys took cup in hand, and each poured the sacred drops; then Odysseus led the way back. Patroclos gave orders to the servants to lay a bed for Phoinix without delay, and they made him a comfortable pile of fleeces and rugs with sheets of fine linen. There the old man slept; but Achillês slept in the hut, and beside him the rosy-cheeked Diomedê, a daughter of Phorbas whom he had brought from Lesbos. Patroclos lay opposite, and he also had his companion, Iphis, whom Achillês gave him after the capture of Scyros.

When the envoys reached Agamemnon's quarters, all present rose to their feet, and holding up their cups of gold pledged them standing each in his place. Then they asked what had happened. Agamemnon began:

"Do tell me now, Odysseus—we are most grateful to you, sir—is he willing to defend our ships from the fire, or does he refuse—is he still in the same proud temper?"

Odysseus answered:

"May it please your grace, my lord King Agamemnon, the man will not quench his anger; he is even more full of passion, and rejects you and your gifts. He bids you consider for yourself with your people how you may save the ships and the nation. He threatens to launch his own ships with to-morrow's dawn. He advises us all to sail home, since you will never see the end of Troy city; for Zeus has lifted a protecting hand over it and given courage to the people. That is his message, and here are those to tell you the same who were with me there, Aias and the two excellent heralds. But old Phoinix has stayed behind for the night. Achillês told him to stay, that he might go away with him to-morrow, if he likes, but there shall be no compulsion."

All heard this aghast, in dead silence; it was a heavy blow. They were long silent, but at last Diomedês broke the silence, as usual:

"May it please your Grace, my lord King Agamemnon! It was a great pity to ask Peleion at all or to offer your heaps of treasure. He is always a proud man, and now you have made him prouder than ever. Very well, let us leave him to stay or go as he likes; he shall appear in battle once more whenever he feels inclined or when God makes him go. Now then this is my advice. Let us all have a good meal and a good sleep,—sound sleep and wine and food make the heart and muscles good, you know. And when the dark no longer lingers, but Dawn puts out her rosy fingers, marshal your men and horses betimes, and lead them yourself in the van!"

This pleased them, and all applauded heartily. So they dispersed to their quarters, and enjoyed the boon of sleep.

*   *   *

[Stubbornly persisting in his refusal to fight, Achilles allows Patroclus to borrow his armor and take his place on the battlefield. After an initial success, Patroclus is duped by Apollo and slain by Hector, who strips the body of Achilles' armor. To illustrate the Greeks' need for Achilles, Zeus then permits the Achaeans to be pushed back to a defensive wall they had built to protect their ships.]

BOOK XVIII

*How Achillês received the news, and how his
mother got him new armour from Hephaistos*

WHILE THE BATTLE WENT ON LIKE BLAZING FIRE, ANTILOCHOS HAD BEEN running at the top of his speed to Achillês. He found Achillês in front of the ships anxious and thoughtful. He feared what had really happened, and he was saying to himself:

"Ah, what can this mean? Here are our people again rushing in a rabble towards the camp. I fear the gods may bring bitter grief on me, as my mother told me once. She declared that the best man of the Myrmidons would be killed in battle while I yet lived. It must be the brave Menoitiadês who is dead. Headstrong man! I ordered him strictly to come back as soon as he had got rid of the fire, and not to fight with Hector."

As these thoughts were passing through his mind, there was Antilochos. When he was near enough he told his cruel news, with tears running down his cheeks:

"Bad news, my lord prince! I have very bad news for you, I am sorry to say. Patroclos is dead, they are fighting for his body, only the body, for the armour is lost—Hector has it!"

Sorrow fell on Achillês like a cloud. He swept up the dust with both hands, and poured it over his head and smirched his handsome face, till the black dirt stained his fragrant tunic. He tore his hair and fell flat in the dust, grand in his grandeur. The captive women also whom he and Patroclos had taken, wailed in grief, and ran out to where he lay, beating their breasts and half fainting. Antilochos had taken the hands of Achillês and stood weeping beside him, while he moaned heavily; for he feared Achillês might put the steel to his own throat.

His gracious mother heard his terrible cry, sitting by her old father deep down in the sea. She shrieked, and all the Nereïd nymphs gathered about her in the deep sea: there came Glaucê and Thaleia and Cymodocê, Nesaia and Speio, Thoê and round-eyed Haliê, Cymothoê and Actaia and Limnoraia, Melitê and Iaira, Amphithoê and Agauê, Doto and Proto, Pherusa and Dynamenê, Dexamenê and Amphinomê and Callianeira, Doris and Panopê and famous Galateia, Nemertês and Apseudês and Callianassa; there came Clymenê and Ianeira and Ianassa, Maira and Oreithyia and curly-headed Amatheia, and all the other Nereïds of the deep sea.[1] All beat their breasts and wailed, as Thetis led off the lament:

"Hear me, sister Nereïds, and you all shall know the sorrow of my heart. Woe is me! unhappy mother of a noble son! I bore a lovely boy, perfect and strong, a hero above heroes. He ran up like a slim tree, I tended him like a choice plant in the garden, I let him go in the fleet to fight against Ilios: but I shall never have him back again, he will never return to his father's house. As long as he lives and sees the light of the sun he has only sorrow, and I can do nothing to help him.—But I must go and see my dear child, and hear what trouble has come to him so far from the battle."

She left the cave, and her sisters went with her weeping, through the water, until they came to the Trojan strand. There they stept out upon the beach one after another, not far from the place where the Myrmidons had drawn up their ships, and Thetis sought her son.

---

[1]All these names, like other Greek names, have meanings, many of them connected with the sea. But the effect is very different from the list of Phaiacians in the eighth book of the *Odyssey*. Those are all invented by Homer, with a comic effect, for a company in high spirits. These are traditional, and the effect in this scene of mourning is a soothing echo from the beautiful songs of fairyland. The meaning matters nothing to us, only the sound.

She found him groaning, and clasped his head with a sorrowful cry, saying simply:

"My child, why do you weep? What is your trouble? Tell me, don't hide it. Zeus has done all that for you, all you besought him to do, the whole army has been brought to disaster for want of you and huddled up under their ships!"

Achillês said with a deep groan:

"Yes, my dear mother, the Olympian has done all that for me. But what good do I get of all that now, if my dear friend Patroclos is dead? I cared more for him than all my companions, as much as for my own life. He is lost! my armour is Hector's! Hector killed him, Hector stript off that miraculous armour, that beautiful armour, that wonder of wonders, which the gods gave to Peleus on the day when they laid you in a mortal's bed. I wish you had gone on living with your immortal sisters of the sea, and Peleus had married a mortal wife! But now—it was all to bring a thousand sorrows on you too, for your son's death! You will never have me back again, I shall never go home—for I have no desire myself to live and remain among men, unless I may kill Hector first with my own spear and make him pay the death-price for Patroclos Menoiti-adês!"

Thetis answered weeping:

"You have not long to live, my child, if you say that. Quick after Hector fate is ready for you!"

Achillês burst out in anger:

"Quick let me die, since it seems my friend was killed and I was not there to help him! He perished far from his native land, and I was not there to defend him!

"But now, since I am never to return home, since I brought no hope to Patroclos or my other comrades whom Hector killed, and how many they are! since I only sit idle beside the ships a burden to the earth, although there is none like me in battle—as for debate, others are better there—O that discord might utterly cease to be in heaven or earth! and anger, that makes even the prudent man take offence—anger that is far sweeter than trickling honey, and grows in men's hearts like smoke—just as I was made angry now by my lord King Agamemnon.

"But I will let bygones be bygones, although I am indignant; I will rule my temper because I must. Now I will go and find the destroyer of that dear life, Hector! Fate I will welcome whenever Zeus and All Gods may choose to bring it. Not even the mighty Heraclês escaped fate, and he was one that Lord Zeus Cronion loved best of all; yes, fate brought him low, and the implacable anger of Hera. So with me; if a like fate has been ordained for me, there I shall lie when I am dead; but now may I win a glorious name! May they know that I have been long away from the battle! May I bring sobs and groaning to some wives of Troy and Dardania, and tears to their tender cheeks, which they shall wipe away with both hands! Don't try to keep me from the battle; you love me, I know, but you shall never persuade me."

Silverfoot Thetis answered:

"Yes indeed, my child, that is true, it is no bad thing to defend comrades in distress and danger of death. But your armour is in the enemy's hands. Hector is wearing that fine shining gear on his own shoulders. He is proud enough, yet I don't think he will have it long to boast of, for death is near him! But I do beseech you not to enter the battle until you see me here again. To-morrow I will come back at sunrise, with new armour from Hephaistos himself."

She turned from her son, and said to her sisters as they went away:

"Now you must return to our father's house and tell all to the Old Man of the Sea. I am going to Olympos, to ask Hephaistos the master craftsman if he will kindly make new armour for my son."

And so they dived again into the sea, and Silverfoot Thetis set out for Olympos, to fetch new armour for her dear boy.

But all the while the Achaian rout went on, as Hector chased the fugitives with a terrible noise, until they came to their ships on the Hellespont. They could not get the body of Patroclos clear away; for Hector was on them again with horses and men like a consuming fire. Three times Hector caught him by the legs to drag him away, calling on his men; three times the doughty pair were strong enough to beat him off. Now Hector would make a rush through the press, now he would stand and shout to his men, but never one step backward. Like shepherds who try to keep off a starving lion, the formidable pair could not scare him away from that body.

Indeed, he would have dragged it away in triumph, if Iris had not appeared—Hera sent her to Achillês without a word to Zeus or any other god. She gave her message clear and plain:

"Up, Peleidês! Show them your terrors! Go and help Patroclos! His body is the prize of this awful struggle—Trojans charging to drag him away to Troy, Danaäns fighting to hold him, all killing each other! And Hector most of all—he means to cut off his head and fix it upon the stakes! Up with you, don't lie there! You should be ashamed to let Trojan dogs tumble and tear Patroclos. Yours is the disgrace, if the body is brought in mangled and mutilated!"

Achillês answered:

"My dear goddess, who sent you with this message?"

Iris said:

"Hera sent me—our gracious Queen herself. Cronidês knows nothing about it, nor any other god in Olympos."

Achillês answered:

"And how can I go into the maul? My armour is in the hands of those men, and my mother forbids me to arm until I shall see her again between my eyes. She has promised to bring me fine new armour from Hephaistos. I don't know any other that I could use except the great shield of Aias Telamoniadês. But he is there in the front himself, I believe, using his spear to defend Patroclos."

Iris said:

"We know well enough that they hold your armour. But just go and show yourself at the moat, that the Trojans may be startled into quiet, and your people may have a breathing space. There's little time for breath in face of sudden death!"

Away went Iris at speed, and Achillês rose up. Over his broad shoulders Athena draped the tasselled aegis-cape: over his head she spread a golden haze; from his body shone a white-hot glow. We have seen a city on some island far away in the sea, besieged by enemies: all day long as they fight smoke rises to the sky, but when night falls we can see the beacons one after another signalling to the world for help with fires blazing high. So the light rose from the head of Achillês shining up to the sky, as he stepped from the wall and stood beside the moat. He did not mingle with his people, for he remembered his mother's strict command, but there he stood and shouted, and from far away Pallas Athena lifted up her voice; great was the confusion among the Trojans. The voice of Aiacidês sounded loud and clear, like the loud clear voice of a trumpet when fierce enemies beleaguer a city all about.

The Trojans heard the brazen voice of Aiacidês, and their hearts were filled with consternation. The horses turned away, foreboding evil to come. The charioteers were dumbfounded to see that bright and terrible light blazing above his head, the light which Athena had kindled. Thrice did Achillês shout aloud from the brink of the moat; thrice were confounded the Trojans and all their host. There also perished twelve men of their best, speared upon their own chariots by their own spears.

Then the Achaians were glad indeed to draw back the body of Patroclos out of the turmoil and lay it upon a bier. His companions trooped around it mourning; Achillês followed, weeping hot tears, when he saw his faithful friend stretched on the bier and torn with cruel wounds. He had sent him forth to the war with chariots and horses, hoping to welcome a safe return: but what a return was this!

The sun set unwearied, for Hera sent him unwilling down under the Ocean stream, and the Achaians at last had rest from their desperate struggle.

❖   ❖   ❖

But the Achaians mourned Patroclos all night long. Achillês led their lamentations, sobbing and pressing on his friend's breast those hands which had slain so many; groaning like a lion, when some hunter has robbed him of his cubs and he has come back too late—how he scours the glades in search of the robber's track, and hopes to find him, with bitter bile in his heart! So Achillês cried aloud to his Myrmidons:

"What a fool I was! What empty words I said on that day, when I tried to comfort the noble Menoitios in my home! I said I would bring his son back to Opoeis covered with glory, victor over Troy, laden with spoil! But Zeus does not fulfil all the designs of men. Both of us are destined to make the same earth red, here in Troy; for I shall never return to be welcomed by ancient Peleus in our home, or by Thetis my mother, but earth shall cover me in this place.

"But now, Patroclos, since you have gone down into the grave before me, and I am left, I will not give you burial until I shall bring here Hector's arms, and the head of Hector who killed you. Then before your pyre I will cut the throats of twelve noble sons of Troy in payment for your death. Till then you shall lie as you are beside our ships, and round about you shall weep in lamentation night and day Trojan and Dardanian women, whom we have gotten by our strength and by our long spears in sacking many a rich town."

Then he directed that a large tripod should be set over the fire to wash the blood from his friend's body. They set the tripod accordingly with a cauldron, and filled it with water, and kindled the wood beneath. The flames curled about the cauldron; and when the water boiled they washed him, and rubbed him with oil, and filled the wounds with nine-year-old unguent. Then they laid him on a bier, wrapt in fine white linen from head to foot, with a white sheet spread over him. All night long Achillês and the Myrmidons mourned for Patroclos.

Meanwhile the gods in heaven were talking about it. Zeus said to his Queen:

"So you have had your way after all, my queen! You need not open your fine eyes like that. You have got Achillês up on his quick feet. One would think those bushy-headed Achaians were your own children!"

Queen Hera replied:

"What a thing to say, Cronidês! You shock me. I suppose even a mere man will do what he can for a man, even a mortal who has not my experience of life. I am chief of all goddesses on two counts, because I am eldest, and because I have the honour of being your wife and you are king of heaven: ought not I to damage the Trojans when I hate them?"

By this time Silverfoot Thetis had come to the house of Hephaistos— that brazen starry house incorruptible, preëminent among the immortals, which old Crookshank himself had made. She found him in a sweat, running about among his bellows, very busy; for he had twenty tripods to make which were to stand round by the wall of his room. He put golden wheels under the base of each, that they might run of themselves into any party of the gods and then run back home again. They were a miracle! They were nearly done, only the lugs had to be put on; he was just finishing these and forging the rivets.

While the clever creature was making these, Thetis came up. Charis saw her and ran out at once with her veil flying—pretty Charis whom the famous Crookshank had made his wife. She clasped the visitor's hand and cried out:

"My dear Thetis, what brings you to our humble home in all this finery? This is an honour! I am glad to see you, dear. You don't often come this way! Come in do, and have something to eat."

She led Thetis in and made her sit on a chair covered with silver studs, beautifully carved and inlaid, and set a footstool for her feet. Then she called to Hephaistos:

"Husband! come in here. Thetis wants you!"

The good old hobbler answered:

"Then there's a goddess in our house whom I respect and love. She saved my life when I was laid up after that bad fall I had, all my mother's doing, shameless thing, when she wanted to hide me away because I'm lame. I should have had a bad time of it then, if Eurynomê and Thetis had not taken me to their hearts—you know Eurynomê, the daughter of ebb-and-flow Oceanos. I stayed with them nine years, and I made them no end of lovely things—brooches, twisted spirals, rosettes, necklaces—all in a hollow cave, and Oceanos rolling ever round and round foaming and roaring! Not a soul knew where I was, neither god nor mortal man, only Thetis and Eurynomê, who saved me. And now here she is in our house! I am bound to do anything for Thetis, pretty dear, pretty hair! I have to pay for my life! You just give her something nice to eat and drink while I put away my bellows and tools."

The old nonsuch got up from his anvil puffing and blowing, and limped about on his nimble thin shanks. The bellows he laid away from the fire, and collected all his working tools in a hutch of silver. Then he wiped a sponge over his face and both arms and sturdy neck and hairy chest, and put on his tunic, and limped out leaning on a thick stick, with a couple of maids to support him. These are made of gold exactly like living girls; they have sense in their heads, they can speak and use their muscles, they can spin and weave and do their work by grace of God. These bustled along supporting their master, and he stumbled to a chair beside Thetis, saying:

"My dear Thetis, in all your finery! What brings you to our humble home? This in an honour, and I am glad to see you, my dear; you don't often pay us a visit. Tell me what you want; I shall be pleased to do it if it is doable, and if I can do it."

Thetis answered with tears running down her cheeks:

"My dear Hephaistos, is there any goddess in Olympos who has troubles to bear like mine? Zeus Cronidês has chosen me out of all to make me miserable! Out of all the daughters of the sea he gave *me* to a man, to Peleus Aiacidês, and I had to endure a man's bed against my will. The man lies in his house worn out with the burden of old age, and now there is more for me! He gave me a son to bear and bring up, a hero of heroes. He ran up like a slim tree, I tended him like a rare plant in my garden, I let him go with the fleet to Ilios for the war—but I shall never get him back, he will never come home to his father's house! As long as he lives and sees the light of the sun, he has trouble, and I cannot go to help him.

"There was a girl the army chose for him as a prize—she was taken away from him by my lord Agamemnon! There he was pining away in grief for the girl; then the Trojans drove the Achaians back upon their ships and cooped them up there, would not let them get out; the people sent envoys to him with a petition and promised heaps of fine gifts. He refused to help in the battle himself, but he sent Patroclos in his own armour and strong forces with him. All day long they fought at the Scaian Gates, and he would have taken the city then and there, but Apollo killed Patroclos on the field, after many great exploits though Hector had the credit.

"So now I come to your knees with my prayer for my son, doomed to die so soon—Will you give him spear and helmet and a good pair of greaves with ankle-guards, and a corselet? What he had was lost when the Trojans killed his faithful friend, and there he lies on the ground in misery!"

The famous Crookshank answered:

"Cheer up, don't worry about that. He shall have his fine armour, and every man that sets eyes on it shall be amazed. I wish I could hide him from death as easily when that dreadful doom shall come!"

Without a moment's delay he went off to his bellows, poked them into the fire and told them to get to work. The bellows, twenty in all, blew under their melting-pots, ready to blow or to stop, letting out the blast strong, or weak, or just in any measure he wanted for his work. He put over the fire to melt, hard brass and tin, precious gold and silver. Then he placed a great anvil-stone on the block, and took hammer in one hand and tongs in the other.

First he fashioned a shield large and strong, adorning it with beautiful designs all over. He made a threefold rim round the edge of shining metal, and slung it on a silver baldric. There were five layers of hide in the shield; on the surface he laid his clever designs in metal.[2]

Upon it he wrought the Earth, and the Sky, and the Sea, the untiring Sun and the full Moon, and all the stars that encircle the sky—Pleiades and Hyades, Orion the mighty hunter and the Bear (which men also call the Wain), which revolves in its place and watches Orion, and alone of them all never takes a bath in the ocean.

---

[2]The facing of the shield was of metal. The simplest plan for the pattern is five concentric circles, separated by narrow rims of flat belts, all surrounded by one broader rim or belt (the Ocean stream) and two other narrow rims.

In the middle is the boss (the Earth) surrounded by a small complete circle, with Sun, Moon, and Stars.

Then the first rim or belt, and beyond it a circle or wide belt with the early scenes, the Two Cities (Peace and War).

Then another rim or belt, and beyond it a circle with Vintage, Plowing, Harvest.

Then a third rim or belt, and beyond it a circle with hunting, Sheep, Cattle, and Huts.

Then a fourth rim or belt, and after it a circle with the Dance.

Then a fifth narrow rim, and a broader belt with the Ocean, and narrower rims to finish.

Upon it he fashioned two cities of mortal men, and fine ones. In the first was wedding and feasting, they were leading brides from their chambers along the streets under the light of blazing torches, and singing the bridal song. There were dancing boys twirling about, pipes and harps made a merry noise; the women stood at their doors and watched. A crowd was in the market-place, where a dispute was going on. Two men disputed over the blood-price of a man who had been killed: one said he had offered all, and told his tale before the people, the other refused to accept anything[3]; but both were willing to appeal to an umpire for the decision. The crowd cheered one or other as they took sides, and the heralds kept them in order. The elders sat in the Sacred Circle on the polished stones, and each took the herald's staff as they rose in turn to give judgment. Before them lay two nuggets of gold, for the one who should give the fairest judgment.

The other city had two armies besieging it round about, all in shining armour. They were divided in plan, whether to sack it outright, or to take half the wealth of the city in ransom. But the besieged were by no means ready to agree, and they were preparing an ambush. The wives and little children were left to guard the walls with the old men; the others sallied out, led by Arês and Pallas Athena, both worked in gold with golden robes, fine and tall in their armour like real gods, conspicuous above the men who were much smaller.[4] When they arrived at the place chosen for their ambush, near a river where all the animals came to drink, they settled down to wait under arms. Meanwhile they had sent out two scouts, who sat a long way off to see when the cattle and sheep were coming. Soon they came, with two herdsmen playing on their pipes and suspecting nothing. So the men in ambush had good warning and quickly got round the cattle and fine white sheep, cut out the whole convoy and killed the herdsmen. The besiegers were still sitting in conclave when they heard the news—they were off at once behind their prancers, arrived in no time, stopt and fought their battle along the river-banks with volleys of spears from both sides. And there among them was Discord, there was Tumult, there was cruel Fate, holding one just wounded and still alive, and one unwounded, dragging one dead by the feet; and the cloak she wore on her shoulders was red with the blood of men.

They looked like living men as they struggled and fought and pulled back the dead bodies from either side.

Upon it he placed a rich field of soft fallow land, broad acres already thrice plowed; many plowmen were driving their teams up and down

---

[3]The aggrieved kinsman might refuse any price, and claim death, or outlawry, when any one might kill the offender without price. The parties pleaded, with or without the help of lawmen, and the meeting decided. The Icelandic Sagas describe a state of society where these customs were in use, and they are the most illuminating commentary upon Homer.

[4]I saw long ago a marionette show in a little Indian town, the Siege of Delhi: in which the officers were twice as tall as the men, and the general tallest of all. The Great Mogul stood inside the city, twice as high as the walls.

with a turn at the end. Whenever they came to the headland after a turn, there was a man to receive them and hand them a mug of wine; then they turned again to their furrows and made all haste to the headland. The soil was black behind them, and looked like soil under the plow, although it was gold. That was a wonderful thing!

Upon it he put a royal demesne, where the hands were reaping with sharp sickles. Gavels were falling in a row along the swathe, others the binders were binding into sheaves with wisps of straw. Three sheaf-binders were standing by, and boys behind them were getting the gavels and bringing them up continually; the king was among them standing staff in hand near the swathe, silent and happy. The heralds were under an oak-tree a little way off; they had killed an ox and were getting it ready for supper, while the women were making barley-porridge for the hands' luncheon.

Upon it he put a vineyard heavy with grapes, all of beautiful gold; the place was thick with standing poles of silver and the grapes hanging on them were black. A ditch of blue enamel ran round it, and a fence of tin; there was one path only across, by which the carriers passed when they gathered the vintage. Boys and girls in merry glee carried the honey-sweet fruit in baskets of wickerwork. In the midst a boy with a melodious harp played a delightsome tune, and sang to the harp a dainty ditty in a sweet little voice; the others trippled along behind him singing and shouting and keeping time by the beat of their feet.

Upon it he fashioned a herd of straighthorn cattle. The cattle were made of gold and tin; they made their way from the midden to pasture along the murmuring river side, along the quivering reeds. Golden herdsmen stalked beside them, four men with nine quick-footed dogs. Two grim lions were among the cows in front, holding a roaring bull; they dragged him away bellowing loudly, dogs and men were after him. The lions had torn open the bull's hide, and they were gorging his red blood and bowels: in vain the men tarred on the dogs, which ran up close and barked and jumped back, but as for biting they kept out of reach.

Upon it he made a pasturage for fleecy white sheep, a wide place in a pleasant dell, with folds and pens and roofed huts.

Upon it he worked a dancing-place, like the one that Daidalos made in Cnossos for curly-headed Ariadnê. There young men and maidens of price[5] danced holding one another by the wrist. The maidens were clad in soft linen, the lads in finespun tunics glossy with a touch of oil. The maidens wore pretty chaplets, the lads carried golden daggers hung from silver straps. Now they circled on practised feet, light and smooth as a potter's wheel when he sits and tries with a touch of his hands whether it will run; now they would scamper to meet in opposite lines. A crowd stood round enjoying the lovely dance; a heavenly ministrel

---

[5]Such as would earn a great bride-price from wooers.

twangled his harp, and two tumblers twirled about among them leading the merry sport.

Upon it he placed the mighty River of Oceanos at the extreme edge of the shield.

When the shield was finished, he fashioned a corselet that shone brighter than fire, he fashioned a strong helmet with a golden crest, he fashioned greaves of flexible tin.[6]

Then the famous Crookshank craftsman brought all he had made and laid it before Thetis; and she shot like a falcon from snowy Olympos, bearing the bright armour to her son.

BOOK XIX

*How Achillês made friends with Agamemnon and
armed himself for war*

DAWN IN HER SAFFRON ROBE AROSE OUT OF THE OCEAN STREAM, BRINGING light for heaven and earth; and Thetis came to the Achaian camp with the god's gifts for her son.

He lay with Patroclos in his arms, weeping bitterly, while his comrades were mourning around. The goddess clasped his hand and said:

"My child, we must let this man be, for all our sorrow. He is dead once for all, since that is God's will. Now for you: accept these fine gifts from Hephaistos. See how fine they are. No man has ever worn them!"

She laid them before Achillês in a rattling pile. The Myrmidons were too much startled to look at them and shrank back; but Achillês looked, and when he saw them, how his anger swelled, how his eyes blazed as if with some inward flame! But he was glad when he held in his own hands the glorious gifts of the god.

When he had enjoyed this pleasure for a while, he told her plainly what he meant to do.

"Mother," he said, "this armour is indeed the work of immortal hands, such as no man could make. Now I will get ready at once. But I am very much afraid the flies may get into my dear friend's wounds; worms will breed and make the flesh nasty—there's no life in it—the body will rot."

Thetis answered:

"Do not trouble about that, my child, I will see what I can do to keep off those savage tribes of flies which batten on those killed in war. Even if he lies here a whole twelvemonth his flesh will be as sound as ever, or sounder. What you must do is to call a meeting of the princes, and denounce your feud against King Agamemnon. Then you may arm yourself at once, and clothe you in your valour!"

Then she dropt into the dead man's nostrils red nectar and ambrosia to keep the flesh wholesome.

---

[6]The greaves were not meant to keep off a spear-thrust, but to prevent the edge of the shield from chafing the leg as the man walked. So they were short and pliable.

Achillês felt new courage after his mother's words. He paced along the shore calling aloud in a great voice, and summoned the Achaian princes. Even those who used to stay always about the ships, the pilots who kept the steering-oars, and the stewards who gave out the food, even these came to the assembly; and the two doughty men of war, Tydeidês the indomitable and prince Odysseus, they also came limping and leaning on their spears, for their wounds troubled them still, and then sat down in front. After them came my lord Agamemnon, still suffering from the wound which he owed to Coön Antenor's son.

As soon as the assembly was full, Achillês rose to his feet and spoke.

"Atreidês, what good was it to us both, you and me, to take things to heart so, and to fall into a soul-devouring feud for a girl? I wish Artemis had shot her dead with an arrow on that day when I took Lyrnessos! Then all those brave men would have been saved who bit the dust in battle because I was angry! Hector and the Trojans got all the good there was; and I think the Achaian nation will not soon forget my feud and yours. But we must let bygones be bygones; we must forget our sorrow and control our temper, for we cannot help it. Then here is the end of my resentment, for I must not be angry for ever and ever. Come then, make haste and tell the army to get ready for battle. Let me meet the enemy face to face once more, and see if they would like to spend a quiet night near our ships. But I think there are some who will be glad to bend the knee in rest, if they escape from the battle when my spear shall drive them!"

The assembly was glad indeed to hear Achillês denounce his feud. Then King Agamemnon answered from the place where he was sitting, without coming forward to the front:

"My friends, my brave Danaäns——"

Here he was interrupted by cries and disturbance:

"My friends! it is right to give a hearing to any speaker who rises, it is not fair to break in. That makes it hard for the best of speakers. (Further disturbance.) With all this noise in the crowd how can a man speak? How can you hear? It is too much for the loudest voice.— Peleidês is the man—I want to explain things to him, please listen the rest of you and take note of what I say. (Loud cries: "It was all your fault!") People have said that to me often enough, and reproached me, but it was not *my* fault! Zeus—fate—the Avenger that walketh in darkness—it was *their* fault! *They* put that blind madness in my heart amongst you all, on that day when I robbed Achillês of his prize myself. But what could I do? God bringeth all things to pass! Eldest daughter of Zeus is Atê, the blindness that blindeth all, accursed may she be! Tender are her feet; for she touches not the ground, but she walks upon the heads of men to their harm, and binds fast many a one.

"Aye, before now Zeus himself was blinded, he that is chief of gods and men as they say; yet even he as it seems was deceived by Hera with her woman's wiles, on the day when Alcmenê was to bring forth mighty Heraclês in wall-crowned Thebes.

"Zeus made his boast before the assembled gods. 'Hear me,' he said, 'gods and goddesses all! I have something that I wish to announce. To-day the Lady of Travail will bring a man to the light, one who shall rule all the people round about, one of those men who are sprung from my blood and lineage.'

"Hera made answer in the cunning of her heart, 'You shall prove a liar! Time will show that you cannot make good your words. Swear to me now, Olympian, a solemn oath, that that man shall rule the people round about who this day shall fall between a woman's feet, being of your blood and lineage.'

"Zeus did not understand her cunning; he was wholly blinded, and swore that solemn oath.

"Then Hera darted down from the heights of Olympos, and quickly sped to Achaian Argos. There as she knew was the wife of Sthenelos Perseïadês, seven months gone with child, and she brought forth a son to the light though he lacked the full tale of months. As for Alcmenê, Hera delayed the birth and held back the Ladies of Travail. Then she went herself with tidings to Zeus Cronion:

"'Father Zeus, fiery Thunderbolt! I have news for you. Already the strong man is born who shall rule the people of Argos—Eurystheus, the son of Sthenelos Perseïadês; he is your child, it is unbecoming that he should rule the people of Argos.'

"These words cut him to the heart. Forthwith he seized Atê by the hair of her head in his wrath, and swore a solemn oath that Atê the Blinder who blinds all should never again enter Olympos and the starry sky. He swung her round and cast her out of heaven; quickly she fell down into the world of men. To think of her made him groan, whenever he saw his own son toiling and moiling in disgrace for Eurystheus.

"So it was with me; when now again Hector dealt destruction among our people beside our own ships, I could not forget Atê the Blinder who at the beginning made me blind. But since I was blinded and Zeus took away my sense, I wish to make amends, and to pay anything in atonement.

"To the battle then, sir, I pray! Lead the army to battle! Treasures in plenty are here, and here am I ready to offer all that Odysseus promised you yesterday in your quarters. If you wish, wait now, though you are so fervent to begin. I will send servants to bring the treasures here, and you shall see that they are enough to content you."

Achillês answered:

"My lord King Agamemnon, as for treasures, they are yours to give, if you will, which is right and proper, or to keep; but now let us think of battle and at once. We must not waste time jabberwinding[1] here.

---

[1]κλοτοπεύειν, apparently a word invented for the occasion, in mockery of τολυπεύειν, the women's yarnwinding, which Homer uses regularly in the phrase "winding up the war."

There is a great work yet undone. To see Achillês once more in the field and striking down the battalions of Troy with the spear—let each of you remember what that was, and fight his man!"

Odysseus said to this:

"Wait a bit, Achillês—we know your quality, but do not drive out the army to battle fasting. Fighting lasts a long time, when once the battalions meet, and God breathes courage into both sides.

"First order them all to take food and drink here in camp. Strength and courage both are mine when I have my bread and wine! No man can fight all day from dawn to sunset on an empty belly. Even if his spirit is ardent for battle, yet his limbs grow heavy unawares, hunger and thirst come on him, his knees stagger as he goes. But after plenty of food and wine a man can fight all day; his heart is brave, his limbs are not weary until all take their leave of the battlefield.

"Then dismiss, and tell them to make a proper meal. But first let my lord Agamemnon bring his treasures into this assembly, that every one may see them and you may be consoled yourself. Let the King stand up before all, and swear that he has never gone into that woman's bed, or had to do with her. Be gracious and forgiving yourself, sir, and let him make friends with you in his own quarters over a handsome banquet, that you may lack nothing which is due.

"My lord King, you will be a juster man to others after this. It is no shame for a king to make amends, when he has wronged a man without provocation."

The King answered:

"I am glad to hear what you have said, Laërtiadês. It was all true, and excellently put. I am ready to take my oath, it is my own wish, and I will not speak falsely before God.—But let Achillês wait awhile, wait all the rest of you, until what I offer is brought before you and we swear friendship together.

"For you, sir, this is my request: choose out the first of our young princes to carry the treasures from my ship which I promised yesterday, and to bring the women. My herald Talthybios shall find a boar-pig somewhere for the sacrifice to Zeus and Helios."

Achillês answered at once:

"My lord King Agamemnon Atreidês, another time will do better for that matter, when there shall be some pause in the battle and when there is less passion in my heart. Those men are still lying mangled on the field—the men Hector killed while Zeus gave him victory, and you two are sending us to dinner! What I would say is—Fight, men, fasting and foodless! at sunset we will have a great supper, when we have wiped out our disgrace. Till then not a drop of drink or a bit of food shall pass down my throat; for my friend is dead, he lies in my hut, mangled with spear-thrusts, his feet turned to the door; my friends are mourning around, and I care for no such things, only death, and blood, and the heavy groans of men!"

Odysseus now spoke:

"Prince Achillês," he said, "you are the greatest man in our host, stronger than I am and better far in the field of battle; but I would put myself before you far in judgment, for I am your elder and my experience greater. Then bear with me, and give me a hearing.

"Men soon grow sick of battle; when Zeus the steward of warfare tilts the scales, and cold steel reaps the fields, the grain is very little but the straw is very much. The belly is a bad mourner, and fasting will not bury the dead. Too many are falling, man after man and day after day; how could one ever have a moment's rest from privations? No, we must harden our hearts, and bury the man who dies and shed our tears that day. But those who survive the horrors of war should not forget to eat and drink, and then we shall be better able to wear our armour, which never grows weary, and to fight our enemies for ever and ever.

"Now no one must hang back expecting another summons. This is the summons! There will be trouble if any one stays behind. Let us march all together and waken up war against our enemy!"

No sooner said than done. He called Nestor's two sons, with Megês Phyleus' son, Thoas and Merionês, Lycomedês Creiontiadês and Melanippos, and they went to Agamemnon's quarters, and collected the seven tripods which he had promised, and the burnished cauldrons, and the twelve horses; then they led out the seven skilful work-women, and eighth, beautiful Briseïs. Odysseus weighed out ten nuggets of gold; and carrying these he led the way, followed by the other young princes with their burdens.

These treasures were laid before the assembly; and Agamemnon rose to his feet. Talthybios the herald stood by his side holding the boar in his arms. Then Agamemnon drew out the knife that used to hang by the sheath of his great sword, and cut the firstling hairs from the boar; he lifted up his hands to Zeus and prayed, while the people all sat silent listening, as is meet. He prayed in these words, looking up into the broad heavens:

"Witness first Zeus, highest and greatest of the gods, witness Earth and Sun, and the Avengers who below the earth punish all men that take a lying oath: Never have I laid my hand on the maiden Briseïs, neither desiring her for my bed nor for any other thing. She has remained untouched under my roof. If any word of this is false, may God send upon me all the afflictions which he sends upon one who swears a lying oath."

As he spoke he cut the boar's throat. Then Talthybios swung it round his head and threw it into the deep sea, food for fishes.

Achillês now rose and spoke:

"O Father Zeus, great is the blindness thou sendest upon men! Never would Atreidês have stirred up my temper to last all this time, never would he have carried off the girl against my will deaf to everything, but

Zeus I supposed wished to bring death on many of our people.—Now go to your meal, and then we will fight."

Thus he dismissed the assembly, and they were soon dispersing to their ships. The Myrmidons took charge of the treasures and brought them to the ships of Achillês. They put away the goods in his quarters, and found a place for the women, and the grooms drove off the horses to join the rest.

But when Briseïs, radiant as golden Aphroditê, caught sight of Patroclos manged and pierced with spears, she threw herself on the body and shrieked aloud, tearing her breast and tender neck and lovely face, and cried out through her tears:

"O Patroclos! best beloved of my unhappy heart! Alive I left you when I went from this place, and now I find you dead, my prince of men, when I return! So my life is trouble upon trouble without end. My husband who took me from my father's hands I saw mangled and pierced with spears before the walls; three brothers dear to me, all my own mother's sons, these also met their doom. And when Achillês killed my husband and took the city of prince Mynês, you told me not to weep; you promised that Achillês should take me to Phthia and make me his wedded wife, and hold our wedding feast in the Myrmidons' country! Therefore I weep without ceasing for you dead, since you were always kind!"

She wept, and the women wailed with her, in show for Patroclos, but each also for her own woes.

Round about Achillês was a group of Achaian elders, who begged him to eat, but he refused, groaning:

"I beg you, if any of you my dear comrades will listen, do not ask me to touch food or drink, for I am in deep sorrow. I will wait for sunset and bear it as best I can."

Most of the princes dispersed at this, but the two kings remained, and Odysseus, Nestor and Idomeneus, and the old man Phoinix, trying their best to comfort him in his sorrow; but he would not be comforted before he could plunge into the maw of bloody battle. He could not forget; heaving a deep sigh he said:

"Ah me, time was when *you*, my dearest comrade, now so cruelly lost, when you with your own hands would lay me a tasty meal, quickly and neatly, while all was hurry to get into the battlefield! Now you lie there mangled, and I have not the heart to touch food and drink though there is plenty, because I miss you so. For nothing worse could ever happen to me, not if I heard of my father's death—and now I suppose he is shedding tears in Phthia for want of a son like me, and here I am in a foreign land, battling with Trojans for the sake of that horrible Helen. Or it might be the boy in Scyros, my dear son, if Neoptolemos is still alive. Once I hoped and wished that I alone should perish here far from home, and that you would return to Phthia. You could have picked up my boy

at Scyros and taken him home, you could have showed him my estate
and the servants and my stately house. Peleus would have been dead
and gone by that time—and I think he must be dead already, or perhaps
just alive and unhappy in his old age, always waiting for the cruel news
that I am dead."

He wept as he spoke, and the old men mourned with him, each
thinking of what he had left behind.

❋   ❋   ❋

BOOK XXII

Of the last fight and the death of Hector

[Determined not to rest until he has slain Hector, Achilles sweeps the
battlefield clean of Trojans, who retreat in panic to their city. Only
Hector remains to face the enraged Achilles.]

NOW THE ROUTED MEN WERE HUDDLED TOGETHER IN THE CITY LIKE A LOT
of trembling fawns; and while they cooled off their sweat, and drank to
assuage their thirst, leaning upon the battlements, the Achaians came
near to the walls, and formed up with their shields against their shoulders. But Hector stayed where he was, in front of the Scaian Gate, for
the shackles of fate held him fast.

Then Apollo made himself known to the pursuing Achillês.

"Why are you chasing me, Peleidês?" he said, "mortal man chasing
immortal god? You never knew that I was a god, I see, you are still as
wild as ever. You routed the Trojans, and now you care nothing about
them—just look, they are all collected in the city, and you have wandered away here! You will not kill me, for death cannot come near me."

Achillês answered angrily:

"You have baffled me, Shootafar. Cruel god, to draw me here away
from the walls! Many more should have bit the dust before I reached
Ilios! Now you have saved their lives and robbed me of my victory. Easy
enough, since you have no vengeance to fear. I would certainly have my
revenge if I had the power."

Then he was gone in his angry pride, like a prize race-horse with a car
behind him that gallops over the plain straining every muscle.

The old King Priam was the first to see him speeding over the plain.
His armour shone on his breast, like the star of harvest whose rays are
most bright among many stars, in the murky night: they call it Orion's
Dog. Most brilliant is that star, but he is a sign of trouble, and brings
many fevers for unhappy mankind.

The old man groaned, and lifting up his hands beat them upon his
head as he groaned, and cried aloud to his son entreating him; but his
son was standing before the gates immovable, and determined to meet
Achillês face to face.

"O Hector!" the old man cried in piteous tones as he stretched out his hands. "Hector my beloved son! Do not face that man alone, without a friend, or fate will soon find you out! Do not be so hard-hearted! Peleion will destroy you, for he is stronger than you are. O that the gods loved him as I do! Soon would vultures and dogs feast on him lying on the ground! Then this cruel pain would pass from my heart. He has bereaved me of many sons, and good sons, killing and selling to far-off islands.

"Now again there are two sons that I cannot see amongst those who are crowded here in the city—Lycaon and Polydoros; their mother was the princess Laothoê. If they are alive in the enemy camp, they shall be ransomed; there is gold and bronze enough here, for she had plenty from her old father Altês. If they are dead already and in the house of Hadês, there is grief for their mother and me their father; but for the rest of the people the grief will not last so long if only you do not die with them by the hands of Achillês.

"Do come within these walls, my son! Save the men and women of our city; life is sweet—do not let Achillês rob you of life and win glory for himself! Pity me also—an old man, but not too old to know, not too old to be unhappy! A miserable portion indeed Father Cronidês will give me then—to perish in my old age, after I have lived to see many troubles, seen my sons destroyed and my daughters dragged into slavery, my house ransacked, little children dashed on the ground in fury, my sons' wives dragged away by Achaian hands! And my self last of all—some one shall strike me down or pierce my body, and leave me dead at my door for carrion dogs to devour; my own table-dogs, my watchdogs, which I have fed with my own hands, will go mad and lap my blood, and lie sated by the door where they used to watch. For a young man all is decent when he is killed in battle; he may be mangled with wounds, all is honourable in his death whatever may come. But a hoary head, and a white beard, and nakedness violated by dogs, when an old man is killed, there is the most pitiable sight that mortal eyes can see."

As the old man spoke he tore the white hairs from his head; but Hector would not listen. His mother stood there also, weeping; she loosened the folds of her dress, and with the other hand bared her breast, and through her tears cried out the secrets of her heart:

"O Hector my own child, by *this* I beseech you, have pity on me, if ever I gave you the soothing breast! Remember this, my love, and come behind these walls—let these walls keep off that terrible man! Do not stand out in front against him, do not be so hard! For if he kills you, never shall I lay you on your bier, never shall I mourn over you, my pretty bud, son of my own body! Nor your precious wife—we shall both be far away, and Danaän dogs will devour you in the Danaän camp!"

But their tears and their prayers availed nothing with Hector's proud spirit. He stood fast, and awaited the coming of his tremendous foe. Like a serpent of the mountains over his hole, fed full of poisons and imbued with bitter hate, who lies in wait coiled about the hole and fiercely glaring, so Hector imbued with unquenchable passion would not retreat, but stood, leaning his shield against a bastion of the wall. Then deeply moved he spoke to his own heart:

"What shall I do? If I retreat behind these walls, Polydamas will be the first to heap reproaches on me, for he advised me to lead the army back to the city on that dread night when Achillês rose up. I would not listen—it would have been better if I had! And now that I have ruined them all by my rashness, I am ashamed to face the men and women of Troy, or some base fellows may say—Hector thought too much of his own strength, and ruined us all! They will say that: and my better part is to face him for life and death. Either I shall kill him and return in triumph, or I shall die with honour before the gate.

"Shall I lay down my shield and helmet and lean my spear against the wall, and go to meet him alone, and promise to yield Helen with all her wealth, all that Alexandros brought with her to Troy?—yield the woman who was the cause of the great war, let the princes of Argos take her away, offer to pay besides half the treasure of our city, make the elders of the city take oath to hide nothing but to divide honestly all we possess? But what good would that be? Suppose I should approach him, and then he would not have pity and would not spare me? Suppose I should strip off my armour, and then he should just kill me naked like a woman? This is no place for fairy tales, or lovers' pretty prattle, the way of a man with a maid, when man and maid prattle so prettily together! Better get to work at once; we'll see which of us the Olympian makes the winner!"

So he mused and stood his ground, while Achillês drew near, like Enyalios the warrior god, shaking over his right shoulder that terrible Pelian ashplant: the armour upon him shone like flaming fire or beams of the rising sun. Hector trembled to see him. He could stand no longer but took to flight, and Peleidês was upon him with a leap: Hector fled swiftly under the walls of Troy and Peleidês flew after him furiously, as a falcon swoops without effort after a timid dove, for he is the swiftest of flying things, and he darts upon her with shrieking cries close behind, greedy for a kill. They passed the look-out and the wind-beaten fig tree, keeping ever away from the wall along the cartroad, until they reached the two fountains which are the sources of eddying Scamandros. One is a spring of hot water, with steam rising above it as if it were boiling over a fire, one even in summer is cold as hail or snow or frozen ice. Near these are the tanks of stone, where the Trojan women and girls used to wash their linen in peace-time, before the Achaians came.

So far they came in their race, fleeing and pursuing, a strong man fleeing and a far stronger in pursuit; they ran hard, for Hector's life was the prize of this race, not such prizes as men run for, a beast or an oxhide shield. Thrice round the city of Priam they ran, like champion racehorses running round the turning-post for a tripod or a woman or some great stake, when a man is dead and the games are given in his honour. All the gods were watching, and the Father of gods and men exclaimed:

"Confound it, I love that man whom I see hunted round those walls! I am deeply grieved for Hector, who has sacrificed many an ox on the heights of Ida or the citadel of Troy! and now there is prince Achillês, chasing him round the city of Priam. What do you think, gods? Just consider, shall we save him from death, or shall we let Achillês beat him now? He is a brave man."

Athena Brighteyes replied:

"O Father Flashingbolt, O Thundercloud, you must never say that! A mortal man, long doomed by fate, and you will save him from death? Do as you please, but the rest of us cannot approve."

Zeus Cloudgatherer answered:

"Never mind, Tritogeneia, my love. I did not really mean it and I want to be kind to you. Wait no longer but do what you wish."

Athena was ready enough, and shot away down the slopes of Olympos.

Achillês was now following at full speed and gave Hector no chance. He watched him like a hound which has put up a hart from his lair, and gives chase through the dingles and the dells; let the hart hide and crouch in the brake, the hound tracks him out till he finds. If Hector going by the road made a dash at the city gates for refuge, hoping his friends might help him with a volley from the walls above, Achillês would take a short cut and get before him, running under the walls and turning him back towards the open ground. It was like some race in a dream, where one chases another, and he cannot catch or the other escape; so Achillês could never catch Hector, or Hector escape Achillês. How indeed could Hector have escaped his fleet pursuer so far, if Apollo had not then for the last time been near, to give him strength and speed? And Achillês had signalled to his own men that no one should let fly a shot at Hector, and take his own credit away if he came in second.

But when the fourth time they drew near the two fountains, see now, the Father laid out his golden scales and placed in them two fates of death, one for Achillês and one for Hector. He grasped the balance and lifted it: Hector's doom sank down, sank down to Hadês, and Apollo left him.

At that moment Athena was by the side of Achillês, and she said in plain words:

"Now you and I will win, my splendid Achillês! Now I hope we shall bring great glory to our camp before the Achaian nation, by destroying Hector, for all his insatiable courage. Now there is no chance that he can escape, not if Apollo Shootafar should fume and fret and roll over and over on the ground before Zeus Almighty! Rest and take breath, and I will go and persuade the man to stand up to you."

Achillês was glad of a rest, and stood still leaning on his barbed ashplant.

Athena now took the form and voice of Deïphobos: she went over to Hector and said to him simply:

"Achillês is giving you a hard time, old fellow, chasing you like this round the city. Let us stand and defend ourselves."

Hector answered:

"O Deïphobos, I always liked you best of all the sons of my father and mother! But now I shall think more of you than ever, for daring to come outside for my sake when you saw me here. All the rest keep inside!"

Athena said:

"My dear old fellow, father and mother and all our friends begged and besought me to stay, they are so terribly afraid of him; but I had not the heart to desert you. Now then let us have at him! No sparing of spears—let us see whether he will kill us both and carry off our blood-stained spoils, or if your spear shall bring him down!"

So the deceiver led him towards Achillês; and when they were near him Hector spoke:

"I will fly from you no more, Peleidês. Three times I raced round the city of Priam and would not await your attack; but now my heart bids me stand and face you, for death or for life. But first come near and let us give our troth; the gods shall be the best witnesses and sentinels of our agreement. If Zeus gives me endurance, and if I take your life, I will do no vile outrage to your body; I will take your armour, Achillês, and your body I will give back to your people. You do the same."

Achillês answered with a frowning face:

"Hector, I cannot forget. Talk not to me of bargains. Lions and men make no truce, wolves and lambs have no friendship—they hate each other for ever. So there can be no love between you and me; and there shall be no truce for us, until one of the two shall fall and glut Arês with his blood. Call up all your manhood; now you surely need to be a spearman and a bold man of war. There is no chance of escape now; this moment Pallas Athena shall bring you low by my spear. Now in one lump sum you shall pay for all my companions, whom you have slain and I have mourned."

With the words he poised and cast his long spear. But Hector saw it coming and crouched down, so that it flew over and stuck in the earth. Pallas Athena pulled it out and gave it back to Achillês, but Hector saw nothing. Then Hector said:

"A miss! I am not dead yet as you thought, most magnificent Achillês! So there was something Zeus did not tell you about me, as it seems. You are only a rattletongue with a trick of words, trying to frighten me and make me lose heart. I am not going to run and let you pierce my back—I will charge you straight, and then you may strike me in the breast if it be God's will, but first see if you avoid *my* spear! I pray that you may take it all into your body! The war would be lighter for Troy if you were dead, for you are our greatest danger."

He poised his spear and cast it, and hit the shield fair in the middle; but the spear rebounded and fell away. Hector was troubled that the cast had failed; he had no second spear, and he stood discomfited. Then he shouted to Deïphobos and called for another, but no Deïphobos was there. Now Hector knew the truth, and cried out:

"All is lost! It is true then, the gods have summoned me to death. Deïphobos was by my side I thought—but he is in the city and I have been deceived by Athena. Now then, death is near me, there can be no delay, there is no escape. All this while such must have been the pleasure of Zeus and his son Shootafar, who have kindly protected me so far; but now fate is upon me. Yet I pray that I may die not without a blow, not inglorious. First may I do some notable thing that shall be remembered in generations to come!"

With these words he drew the sword that hung by his side, sharp and strong, gathered himself and sprang, like an eagle flying high and swooping down from the clouds upon a lamb or cowering hare. Achillês moved to meet him full of fury, covering his chest with the resplendent shield while the thick golden plumes nodded upon his flashing helmet. His right hand held poised the great spear, which gleamed like the finest of all the stars of heaven, the star of evening brilliant in the dark night; he scanned Hector with ruthless heart, to see where the white flesh gave the best opening for a blow. Hector was well covered with that splendid armour which he had stript from Patroclos, but an opening showed where the collar-bones join the neck to the shoulder, the gullet, where a blow brings quickest death. There Achillês aimed, and the point went through the soft neck; but it did not cut the windpipe, and Hector could still answer his foe. He fell in the dust, and Achillês cried in triumph:

"There, Hector! You thought no doubt while you were stripping Patroclos that you would be safe; you cared nothing for me far away. Fool! There was an avenger, a stronger man than Patroclos, waiting far away! I was there behind in the camp, and I have brought you low! Now you shall be mauled by vultures and dogs, and he shall be buried by a mourning nation!"

Hector half-fainting answered:

"I beseech you by your soul and by your knees, by your father and your mother, do not leave me for dogs to mangle among your ships— accept a ransom, my father and my mother will provide gold and treasure enough, and let them carry home my body, that my people may give me the fire, which is the rightful due of the dead."

Achillês said with an angry frowning face:

"Knee me no knees, you cur, and father me no fathers! No man living shall keep the dogs from your head—not if they bring ransom ten times and twenty times innumerable, and weigh it out, and promise more, not if Priamos Dardanidès pay your weight in gold—not for that ransom shall your mother lay you out on the bier and mourn for the son of her womb, but carrion dogs and carrion birds shall devour you up! For what you have done to me I wish from the bottom of my heart that I could cut you to pieces and eat you raw myself!"

Hector answered him dying:

"Ah, I know you well, and I forebode what will be. I was not likely to persuade you, for your heart is made of iron. But reflect! or I may bring

God's wrath upon you, on that day when Paris and Phoibos Apollo shall slay you by the Scaian Gate, although you are strong."

As he spoke, the shadow of death encompassed him; and his soul left the body and went down to Hadês, bewailing his fate, bidding a last farewell to manhood and lusty strength. Hector was dead, but even so Achillês again spoke:

"Lie there dead! My fate I will accept, whenever it is the will of Zeus and All Gods to fulfil it."

He drew the spear out of the body and laid it aside. Then he stript off the armour, and the other Achaians came crowding round. How they gazed in wonder at Hector's noble form and looks! Yet no one came near without a stab; they beat him and stabbed him, saying to each other:

"Ha ha! Hector feels very much softer now than when he burnt our ships with his blazing brands!"

Achillês, when he finished stripping the spoils, turned to the crowd, and made them a speech in his downright manner.

"My friends," he said, "princes and captains of the nation, since as you see the gods have granted me to kill this man who has done us more damage than all the rest put together, let us go round the city ready for battle, and find out what they mean to do: whether they will leave their fortress now this man is dead, or whether they will still confront us although they have no Hector.—But stay, what am I thinking about! Patroclos lies beside our ship unmourned, unburied! Patroclos I can never forget so long as I live and move! And even if in the house of Hadês men forget their dead, yet I will remember my dear comrade even there. Come on, my lads, let us march back to our ships singing our hymn of victory, and bring this man with us. We have won a great triumph; we have killed Hector, to whom the Trojans prayed as if he were a god!"

And then he thought of a shameful outrage. He cut behind the sinews of both Hector's feet from ankle to heel and strapt them together with leather thongs, and fastened them to his chariot leaving the head to drag. Then he laid the armour in the car, and got in himself and whipt up the horses. Away they flew: the dust rose as the body was dragged along, the dark hair spread abroad, there in the dirt trailed the head that was once so charming, which now Zeus gave to his enemies to maltreat in his own native land. And as the head was bedabbled thus in the mire, his mother tore her hair and threw away the covering veil, and wailed aloud seeing her son; his father lamented sore, the people wailed, and lamentation filled the city. Such lamentation there might have been, if all frowning Ilios were smouldering in ashes.

The people had much ado to keep the old King in his frenzy from rushing out of the Dardanian Gate. He rolled in the dung-heap and appealed to all, naming each by his name:

"Have done, my friends! I know you love me, but let me go out alone and visit the Achaian camp—let me pray to this terrible violent man! He may have shame before his fellows, and pity an old man—yes, I think he has an old father like me, Peleus, who begat him and bred him to be the ruin of Troy! And for me more than all he has brought trouble—so many of my sons he has killed in their prime! I mourn for them, but not for them all so much as one, who will bring me down with sorrow to the grave, my Hector. Would that he had died in my arms! Then we could have mourned and wept till we could weep no more, the unhappy mother who bore him, and I his father."

As he spoke, he wept, and the people lamented with him. Then Hecabê led the women's lamentation, herself weeping the while:

"My child, I am desolate: how shall I live in sorrow when you are dead? Night and day you were my boast in the city, and a blessing to all, both men and women, who used to welcome you as one divine. Truly you were a great glory to them also while you lived, but now death and fate has come upon you!"

But Hector's wife had not yet heard anything of her husband; no messenger had told her the truth, that he remained outside the gate. She was busy with her loom in a far corner of the house, embroidering pretty flowers on a wide purple web. She called to the servants to put a cauldron to boil on the fire, that Hector might have a warm bath when he came in from the battle. Poor creature, she knew not that he was far away from all baths, brought low by the hands of Achillês and the will of Brighteyes Athena.

But when she heard lamentation and wailing from the wall, her limbs quivered and the shuttle fell to the ground out of her hand, and she called to her maids:

"Here, come with me two of you and let me see what has happened. That was the voice of my honoured goodmother! My heart is in my mouth—my knees are turned to stone! Some trouble is at hand for the sons of Priam! Far from my ear be that word! But I am terribly afraid prince Achillês has cut off my rash Hector by himself and driven him away to the plain! Ah, he will put an end to the fatal pride that always possessed him, for Hector would never stay in the crowd—he would always run out in front and yield in courage to no man!"

She tore out like a mad woman with beating heart, and the maids followed. When she came to the crowd of men on the battlements, she stood peering about—then she saw him dragged along in front of the city; the horses were dragging him at full speed towards the Achaian camp, careless what they did. Then the darkness of night came over her eyes, and she fell backwards fainting and gasping; the coverings fell from her head—diadem, coif, braided circlet, and the veil which golden Aphroditê had given her, on the day when Hector paid his rich bride-gifts and led her away from Eëtion's house. Crowding round her were Hector's sisters and goodsisters holding her up, distracted unto death.

When she came to herself and revived, she cried out amid her sobs:

"O Hector, I am unhappy! So we were both born to one fate, you in Troy in the palace of Priam, I in Thebê under woody Placos, in the house of Eëtion who brought me up as a tiny tot—doomed father, doomed child! Would I had never been born! Now you have gone to the house of Hadês deep down under the earth; but I am left in bitter grief a widow in our home. And our son is still only a baby—O doomed father, doomed mother! Never will you be a blessing to him, Hector, or he to you: for you are dead. Even if he escapes from this miserable war, yet his portion shall be always labour and sorrow, for strangers will rob him of his lands.

"The day of orphanhood makes a child wholly friendless. He must always hang his head, his cheeks are slobbered with tears, he goes begging to his father's friends, and plucks one by the cloak, another by the shirt; if one has pity he puts a cup to his mouth for a sip, wets the lips but not the palate. The boy who has both father and mother slaps him and drives him away from the table with unkind words—'Just get out! Your father does not dine with us.' Then the boy runs crying to his widowed mother—yes, Astyanax, who once sat on his own father's knee and ate only marrow and richest fat of sheep! And when he felt sleepy and did not want to play any more; he slept on a bedstead, with nurse's arms round him, with a soft bed under him, full and satisfied.

"But now he will have plenty to suffer since his father is gone—my Astyanax as they all call him in this city, because you alone saved their gates and walls. And now you are in the enemy camp, far from your father and mother, and when the dogs have had enough, crawling worms will eat your body—naked, although there is nice soft linen in your house made by your own women. But I will make a bonfire of the whole store; it is of no use to you, for your body will not lie out in that, but it will do you honour in the eyes of the people of Troy."

She wept while she spoke, and the women lamented with her.

BOOK XXIII

The funeral rites of Patroclos, and how the games were held in his honour

[Patroclus' ghosts visits Achilles in a dream. He begs to be buried immediately so that his soul can find rest in Hades. After burning Patroclus' body, the Achaeans hold elaborate funeral games in honor of the dead hero.]

IN SLEEP CAME TO HIM THE SOUL OF UNHAPPY PATROCLOS, HIS VERY IMAGE in stature and wearing clothes like his, with his voice and those lovely eyes. The vision stood by his head and spoke:

"You sleep, Achillês, and you have forgotten me! When I lived you were not careless of me, but now that I am dead! Bury me without delay, that I may pass the gates of Hadês. Those phantoms hold me off, the souls of those whose work is done; they will not suffer me to join them beyond the river, but I wander aimlessly about the broad gates of the house of Hadês. And give me that hand, I pray; for never again shall I come back from Hadês when once you have given me my portion of fire. Never again in life shall we go apart from our companions and take counsel together; but I am swallowed up already by that cruel fate which got me on the day I was born; and you also have your portion, my magnificent Achillês, to perish before the walls of this great city. One thing more I say, and I will put it upon you as a charge if you will comply: do not lay my bones apart from yours, Achillês, but with them; as I was brought up with you in your home, when Menoitios brought me quite a little one from Opoeis to your house, for manslaughter, the day when I killed Amphidamas' son—I did not mean it, we had a silly quarrel over the knuckle-bones. Then Peleus received me, and brought me up kindly in his house, and named me as your attendant. Then let one urn cover my bones with yours, that golden two-handled urn which your gracious mother gave you."

Achillês said in answer:

"Why have you come here, beloved one, with all these charges of this and that? Of course I will do as you tell me every bit. But come nearer; for one short moment let us lay our arms about each other and console ourselves with lamentation!"

He stretched out his arms as he spoke, but he could not touch, for the soul was gone like smoke into the earth, twittering. Achillês leapt up in amazement and clapt his hands with solemn words:

"See there now! So there is still something in the house of Hadês, a soul and a phantom but no real life in it at all! For all night long the soul of unhappy Patroclos has been by my side, sorrowing and lamenting and telling me what to do. And it was mightily like himself!"

✿ ✿ ✿

At the place which Achillês had appointed, they laid him down and piled great heaps of firewood. Then Achillês did his part. He stood away from the pile, and cut off the golden tress which he had kept uncut among his thick hair for the river Spercheios, and spoke deeply moved as he gazed over the dark sea:

"O Spercheios! this is not for thee! That vow was vain which Peleus my father made,[1] that when I returned to my native land I would consecrate my hair to thee, and make solemn sacrifice, and that he would sacrifice fifty rams without blemish into thy waters, at the altar which is in thy precinct at the same place. That was my father's vow,

---

[1]A boy kept one part of his hair uncut and this he dedicated to his river-god at puberty: Aeschylus *Choephoroe* 6. Achillês had left home so young that the πλόκαμος θρεπτήριος was still uncut.

but thou didst not fulfil his hope. Now therefore, since I am not to return to my native land, I would give the warrior Patroclos this to carry with him."

Then he laid the hair in the hands of his well-loved companion. All present broke into lamentation with all their hearts; and they would not have ceased while the sun shone, but Achillês drew near to Agamemnon and said to him:

"Atreidês, you are our lord paramont, and it is yours to command. There is plenty of time for the people to mourn, but just now I ask you to dismiss them from this place and tell them to get ready their meal. All this is the business of those who are nearest akin to the dead; and let the chieftains remain with us."

Agamemnon accordingly dismissed the people, while the mourners remained, and piled up the wood, and made a pyre of a hundred feet each way, and upon it they laid the body. They killed flocks of sheep and herds of cattle in front of the pyre, skinned them and cut them up; Achillês took away all the fat, and covered the dead with it from head to foot, and heaped the flayed bodies about him. Jars of honey and oil he placed leaning against the bier. Four horses he laid carefully on the pyre, groaning aloud. Nine dogs the prince had, that fed from his table; two of these Achillês took, and cut their throats and laid beside him. The twelve noble young Trojans he slew without mercy. Then he applied the relentless fire to consume all, and with a groan he called on his comrade's name:

"Fare thee well Patroclos, even in the grave fare thee well! See, I now fulfil all that I promised you before. Here are the twelve noble sons of Trojans—the fire is eating them round about you! Hector Priamidês the fire shall not have to eat, but the dogs!"

But his threat was vain: no dogs were busy about Hector, for the dogs were driven off by the daughter of Zeus, Aphroditê herself, by day and by night. She washed the skin with rose-oil of ambrosia that it might not be torn by the dragging; and Phiobos Apollo drew down a dark cloud from heaven to earth, and covered the place where the body lay, that the sun might not scorch the flesh too soon over the sinews of his limbs.

But the pyre would not burn, and Achillês did not know what to do. At last he stood well away from the smouldering heap, and prayed to North Wind and West Wind promising them good sacrifices; many a libation he poured from his golden goblet, praying them to come and make the wood quickly catch fire, to burn the bodies.

Iris heard his prayers, and flew quickly to the Winds with her message.

They were all in a party at West Wind's, and having a fine feast, when in came Iris flying and stood on the doorstone. As soon as they set eyes on her, up they all jumped and shouted out, every wind of them, "Come and sit by me!" But she said:

"No thank you, no sitting: I'm bound for the Ocean stream. There is a grand sacrifice in the Ethiopian country for us immortals, and I want to have some too. But Achillês is praying to North Wind and West Wind;

he wants them to come and promises a good sacrifice. He wants them to make the pyre burn, where Patroclos lies with the people all mourning around."

Her message given, away she flew, and the Winds rose with a devil of a noise and drove the clouds in a riot before them. They swooped upon the sea and raised the billows under their whistling blasts; they reached the Trojan coast and fell on the pyre till the flames roared again. All night long they beat upon the fire together blowing and whistling; all night long stood Achillês holding his goblet, and dipt into the golden mixer, and poured the wine on the ground, till the place was soaked, calling upon the soul of unhappy Patroclos. As a father laments while he burns the bones of his own son, newly wedded and now dead, to the grief of his bereaved parents, so Achillês lamented as he burnt the bones of Patroclos, stumbling up and down beside the pyre with sobbings and groanings.

But at the time when the morning star goes forth to tell that light is coming over the earth, and after him the saffron mantle of Dawn spreads over the sea, at that hour the flame died down and the burning faded away. Then the Winds returned over the Thracian gulf to their home, while the waters rose and roared.

And then Achillês moved away from the pyre, and sank upon the ground tired out: sleep leapt upon him and gave him peace.

BOOK XXIV

How Priam and Achillês met, and the
funeral of Hector

THE ASSEMBLY WAS DISMISSED, AND THE PEOPLE DISPERSED TO THEIR own ships. Their thoughts were on food and quiet sleep; but Achillês wept, remembering his well-loved friend, and all-conquering sleep did not lay hold upon him. He turned this way and that way, thinking what manhood and fine temper he had lost with Patroclos, how many tasks he had wound up with him, how many hardships they had suffered together, wars with men, and cruel seas they had cloven. As he remembered these things he shed hot tears, now tossing on his side, now on his back, now prone; again he would rise up and roam distracted along the seashore. Never did he fail to see the dawn appear over sea and shore; and then he would harness the horses and fasten Hector to drag behind the car. Three times round the barrow of dead Menoitiadês he would trail him, then return to rest in the hut leaving him stretched prone in the dust. But Apollo kept the skin free from defilement, pitying the poor fellow though dead; he wrapt him all about with his golden cape, that the dragging might never tear him.

Thus Achillês maltreated Hector in his rage. But the blessed gods were offended at this pitiable sight, and wished to send Hermês Argeiphontês to steal him away. Most of the gods approved this; but not Hera nor Poseidon nor the bright-eyed Maiden. They continued as they had been, when first they came to hate sacred Troy, and Priam and his people, for the blind delusion of Alexandros: he had affonted those goddesses, when they came to his farmyard and he preferred the one who granted his shameful lust.

But when the twelfth dawn came, Phiobos Apollo said at last:

"You are hard, you gods, you are torturers! Has not Hector in times past burnt you thigh-pieces of bulls and goats without blemish? Yet you can't bear to save his dead body for his wife to see, and his mother and his son, and Priam his father and his people, to let them burn him in the fire, and perform the rites of burial. But that abominable Achillês—he is the man you want to help, gods—the man who has no sense of decency, no mercy in his mind! Savage as a lion, which is the slave of his strength and furious temper, and hunts the sheep for a dinner! Like him Achillês has lost all pity; he has in him none of that shame which does great good to men as well as harm. A man may have lost some dear one, I suppose, a brother or even a son, but he weeps and laments and there is an end of it; for the Fates have given mankind a patient soul. But this man, after he has taken the life of noble Hector, ties him behind his car and drags him round his comrade's tomb. I declare that is not right or decent. We may well be shocked at him, though he is a brave man; even the senseless clay he insults in his fury."

This made Hera angry, and she retorted:

"That might be all very well, Silverbow, if you are going to put Achillês and Hector in the same rank. Hector's a mortal and sucked a woman's pap, but Achillês had a goddess for his mother—I brought her up myself from a little one, and gave her away as a wife to a man, to Peleus, who was in high favour with the immortals. You were all at the wedding, gods—and you too, there you sat with your harp—but you prefer low company and no one can ever trust you!"

Here Zeus broke in:

"My dear Hera, don't go and get spiky with the gods. They shan't be in the same rank at all, but Hector really was a prime favourite with the gods more than any man in Troy,—at least, I thought so, for he never failed in his friendly offerings. My altar was never without a good feast, or libations and spicy savours, our special prerogative. But let stealing alone—can't be done—we can't steal away Hector so that Achillês won't see, for there is his mother on guard night and day. No, no, let one of you call Thetis before me, and I will give her some good advice. Achillês must accept ransom from Priam and let him have Hector."

This was no sooner said, than stormfoot Iris was off with her message. Midway between Samothrace and rocky Imbros down she plunged into the dark sea with a splash, plunged into the deep like the leaden plummet on a horn-bait which carries death to the greedy fishes.

She found Thetis in a vaulted cave, and the other nymphs of the sea sitting round her. She was lamenting her perfect son, doomed to perish in Troy so far from his native land. Iris stood before her and said:

"Rise up, Thetis, Zeus Allwise summons you before him."

Silverfoot Thetis answered:

"Why does the great god summon me? I am ashamed to show myself among the immortals when my heart is so full of infinite sorrow. However, I will go. No word that he speaks will be spoken in vain."

She took a dark veil as black as any garment could be, and followed Iris, and the water gave way before them; they stept out on the beach and shot up to heaven.

There they found Cronidês Allseeing, and the deathless gods were seated about him in full assembly. Athena was next to Father Zeus, but she gave up her seat to Thetis. Hera placed a golden cup in her hands with friendly words of welcome and Thetis drank and gave back the cup.

Then the Father of gods and men spoke:

"So you have come to Olympos, goddess Thetis, although you are sad and your heart is full of sorrow that will not be comforted. I know that myself, but still I sent for you, and I will tell you why. For nine days there has been quarreling in our family about Hector's body and Achillês. They want Argeiphontês to steal the body away, but I want to keep your respect and affection in time to come, and so I propose to raise your son even higher in men's esteem, and this is how it will be done.[1]

"Go straight to the camp. Tell your son the gods are angry with him, and I most of all have been moved to wrath, because in his mad passion he keeps Hector and has not let him go. I hope he will fear me and let him go. I will send Iris myself to King Priam, and bid him to visit the Achaian camp and ransom his son. He shall bring treasure enough to warm the heart of Achillês."

Thetis lost no time. She made haste to her son's hut, and found him there sobbing and groaning. His companions were busy preparing their meal; they had just killed a shaggy ram which lay in the hut.

His mother sat near him and stroked his head, saying:

"My child, how long will you eat your heart out with sorrow and lamentation? Never a thought for bread or bed? Even a woman to love you is some comfort. And I shall not have you long, but death and cruel fate are at hand!

"Now listen to me quickly—I bear a message from Zeus to you. He says the gods are angry with you, and he most of all has been moved to wrath, because in your mad passion you keep Hector and would not let him go. Make haste now, take ransom and let him go."

Achillês answered:

"Let some one come here with a ransom and take the body, if the Olympian himself commands, and really means it."

Long the mother and the son talked together without concealment heart to heart; and at the same time Cronidês was sending Iris to Ilios:

---

[1] The heroic point of honour lay in the receipt of a *quid pro quo* (Leaf).

"Off with you Iris my quick one! Leave Olympos behind you, and hasten to Troy; announce to King Priam that he is to go into the Achaian camp, and carry treasure enough to warm the heart of Achillês. He must be alone, not another man of the Trojans must go with him. But a herald may attend him, some old man, to drive the mules and the wagon and also to bring back the body of him that Achillês slew. Do not let him fear death or be anxious at all. I will provide for that by sending Argeiphontês as his escort, to lead him as far as Achillês. And when he shall lead him into the hut, neither Achillês nor any one else shall kill him; for Achillês is not stupid or thoughtless or impious—he will be most scrupulous to spare a suppliant man."

Away went stormfoot Iris on her errand. She came to Priam's, and there she found groaning and lamentation. The sons were sitting in the courtyard about their father, soaking their garments in tears; the old man was in their midst, wrapt closely in his mantle, with muck smeared all over head and neck which he had clawed up in handfuls as he grovelled on the ground. In the house his daughters and his gooddaughters were wailing, as they called to mind all those brave men who lay dead by their enemies' hands.

The messenger drew near to Priam; he fell into a fit of trembling, and she spoke softly to him:

"Fear nothing, Priamos Dardanidês, be not anxious at all. I come here with no evil tidings, but with good in my heart for you. I am a messenger from Zeus, who far away cares for you much and pities you. The Olympian bids you ransom Prince Hector. You are to carry treasure to Achillês enough to warm his heart. You must be alone; no other Trojan must go with you, but a herald may attend you, some old man, to drive the mules and wagon and to bring back the body of him that Achillês slew. You are not to fear death or to be anxious at all. Zeus will provide for that by sending Argeiphontês as your escort, and he shall lead you as far as Achillês. Even when he shall lead you into the hut, neither Achillês nor any one else will kill you, for he will prevent them. Achillês is not stupid or thoughtless or impious, and he will be scrupulous to spare a suppliant man."

She gave her message, and she was gone. The old King gave orders at once to get ready a mule-wagon and put on the top-carrier. Meanwhile he went into his treasure chamber, roofed with sweet-smelling cedar, in which he kept many precious things, and called his wife Hecabê:

"My dear, what a surprise! An Olympian messenger has come from Zeus, that I am to go into the Achaian camp and ransom our dear son! I am to carry treasure enough to warm the heart of Achillês. Now then tell me, what do you think about it? As for me, I am terribly anxious to go and visit the Achaian ships and the Achaian camp!"

The woman shrieked and said:

"O misery! where are your wits flown? Once you were famous for good sense throughout your kingdom and even in foreign lands! How can you wish to visit the Achaian ships alone—to meet the eyes of the man who has killed and stript so many of your brave sons! Your heart must be made of steel. If he sets eyes on you—if he gets hold of you—that is a faithless man, a cannibal! He'll never pity, he'll never have mercy! No, no, let us stay in our own house and lament him far away. As for him—that is how inflexible Fate spun her thread for him when I brought him forth from my womb—to be devoured by carrion dogs, far from his father and mother, in the house of a violent man—ah, I could fix my teeth in *his* liver and devour it! That would be some revenge for my son. The man he slew was not playing the coward's part—he was standing to shield Trojan men and Trojan women, and thought neither of shelter nor of flight!"

The old King answered:

"Don't hold me back when I want to go, don't be a bad omen for me yourself. You will never persuade me. If some one else had bidden me go, a mere mortal man such as a priest or seer or diviner, we might think it falsehood and keep clear of the whole thing. But now—I heard a god's voice with my own ears, I saw with my own eyes! Go I will, and his word shall not be in vain. If it is my portion to die in the Achaian camp, I am willing. Let the man kill me on the spot, when once I have held my son in my arms, and lamented him, as I have so longed to do."

Then he opened the store-chests, and took out twelve resplendent robes and twelve singlet cloaks, as many rugs and white sheets, as many tunics. He took out gold and weighed ten nuggets; next two shining tripods and four cauldrons, and a magnificent goblet which a Thracian embassy had presented, a great treasure—not even this did he grudge, for he greatly desired to ransom his son. Lastly he drove away all the people from the corridor with a good rating:

"Get out for shame—don't make yourselves a nuisance here! Have you no mourning at home that you come here to vex me? What good have you gained that Zeus Cronidês has sent trouble upon me, and I have lost the best of my sons? You shall find that out yourselves, when you will be easier than ever to kill now that man is dead. O may I go down to the gates of death, before I see the city wasted and sacked before my eyes!"

He hurried among them driving them out with his staff, and then he cried out to his sons—there were nine of them in the place, Helenos and Paris and Agathon, Pammon and Antiphonos and Politês, Deiphobos and Hippothoös and Dios:

"Make haste there, you worthless sons, I am ashamed of you, hang-dogs! I wish you had all been killed instead of Hector! How unhappy I am! I had the best sons in the broad land of Troy, and I declare not one is left—Mestor too good for this world, and Troilos the famous chariot-fighter, and Hector who was like one come down from heaven to live on earth—he seemed to be no son of mortal man, as if a god must have been his father! These are all killed in battle and only rubbish is left, cheats and tumblers, heroes of the dancing-floor, grand men to raid their neighbours' cattle and sheep! Get ready a wagon, will you, and be quick about it, and put in all this stuff. We have a journey to make."

They were all startled by their father's outburst, and got to work. So they brought out a fine new mule-wagon with its wheels, and fastened on the top-carrier. They took down from the peg a box-wood yoke fitted with knob and rings for the reins. Then they brought out the yoke with its yoke-band, nine cubits long, and fitted it on the pole at the curving end and the ring over the pin; they tied it over the knob with three turns to left and right, and carried the rope back to the car-post tucking the tongue under the rope.

This done they brought out from the treasury all the precious things for Hector's ransom, and packed them on the wagon. They put to a couple of strong-footed mules broken to harness, which had been a gift of the Mysians to Priam. For Priam, they yoked a pair of horses which he had bred himself and fed at the manger.

As Priam and the herald were about these preparations, and considering how they should behave, Hecabê in deep dejection came near. She held a golden goblet of wine in her right hand, that they might pour a libation before they went; and standing before the car she said:

"Take this, and pour to Zeus the Father, and pray for a safe return from our enemies—since your mind is set upon going, although I wished it not. Now pray to Cronion Thundercloud upon Mount Ida, whose eye can see all the Trojan land, and ask for a bird on the right hand—that swift messenger whom he loves more than all the birds, the strongest bird of all; that you may see him with your eyes, and have him to trust in this journey to the Danaän camp. If Zeus Allseeing shall refuse to send his messenger, I at least would bid you not to go to the place, however you may desire it."

King Priam replied:

"My wife, I will not refuse what you ask, for it is well to lift up our hands to Zeus and pray him to have mercy upon us."

The old King called to a waiting-woman for pure water; she brought a jug and bowl and poured the water over his hands. He then took the cup from his wife, and standing in the courtyard poured the wine upon the ground, raising his eyes to heaven as he uttered this prayer:

"O Zeus our Father, most mighty and most glorious, enthroned upon Mount Ida! Grant that Achillês may show me kindness and pity, and send me a bird, that swift messenger whom thou lovest more than all the birds, the strongest bird of all. Show him on my right hand, that I may see him with my eyes and have him to trust in this journey to the Danaän camp!"

So he prayed, and Zeus Allwise heard him. At once he sent an eagle, most unfailing omen among birds that fly, the dark one, the hunter, the one that men also call dapple. The stretch of his outspread wings was as wide as the bolted door of a rich man's lofty treasure-house. They saw him on the right sailing over the city; all that saw him were glad, and their hearts were warmed within them.

Now the old King made haste to mount his car, and drove out of the front gateway from the echoing gallery. The mules went in front drawing their four-wheeled wagon, with Idaios driving, and the horses followed driven by the old King. As they passed quickly through the city, all his kinsfolk followed weeping and wailing as if he were going to his death. But as soon as they had come down from the city upon the plain, these all went back, sons and goodsons together.

Zeus did not fail to see the two men when they appeared upon the plain. He pitied the old King, and said to Hermês his son:

"Hermês, you always like to make friends with a man and have a talk with any one you fancy. Off with you then, and lead Priam to the Achaian camp. Take care that no one sees or takes any notice until you get to Peleion."

Argeiphontês was willing enough. He put on those fine boots, golden, incorruptible, which carry him over moist or dry to the ends of the earth as quick as the wind; and he took the rod that bewitches the eyes of men to sleep, or wakes the sleeping. Holding this, Argeiphontês flew until he reached the Hellespont and the land of Troy. There he took the shape of a young prince with the first down upon his lip, the time when youth is most charming.

The others had just passed beyond the great barrow of Ilos, and they halted by the river to give the animals a drink; for darkness had come by this time. The herald looked out and noticed Hermês not far off, and he said to his master:

" 'Ware man, Dardanidês![2] a wary mind now is what we want. I spy a man! and I surmise he'll soon tear us to pieces. Come, let us take the horse-car and be off—unless you would have us clasp his knees and beg for mercy."

The old man was all confusion and frightened to death; he felt gooseflesh all over his body and stood dazed, but Hermês Luckbringer came up of himself and said, taking him by the hand:

"Whither away, father, with horses and mules in the dead of night, when mortal men are all asleep but you? Have you no fear of the Achaians breathing fury, your enemies, and bad men to meet? If one of them saw you driving all these commodities through the black night, what would you do then? You are not young yourself, and this your follower is old for defence if some one wants to pick a quarrel. But I will do you no harm, indeed I would protect you. You remind me of my own father."

Then the old King replied:

"Things are very much as you say, dear boy. But there is still some god

---

[2] φράζεο is a hunting term, and very likely φραδής is another. This word is unique in Homer, like so many words of common talk.

even for me, who stretched a hand over me when he sent a wayfarer like you to meet me—a good man to meet, if I may judge from your handsome looks and shape, and no unmannerly savage. You must come of a good family."

Argeiphontês answered:

"Quite right, sir, that is true enough. But tell me please if I may ask you, are you exporting all these precious goods to a foreign land just to put them in safety? Or are you all deserting sacred Troy in fear? For the great man has perished, the noblest of them all—your son. He never hung back from the battlefield!"

The old King said:

"And who are you, noble sir, what is your family? How truly you have told me the passing of my ill-fated son!"

Argeiphontês replied:

"You are trying me, sir, when you ask about noble Hector. Often I have seen him with my own eyes in the field of glory—then also when he drove the Achaians upon their ships, and slew and slew, making havoc with his blade! We had to stand and admire, for Achillês would not let us fight because of his rancour against Agamemnon. I am a servant of his, and we came over in the same ship. I am one of the Myrmidons. My father is named Polyctor. He is a rich man, and old just like yourself here; he has six other sons, I was the seventh. We cast lots who should join up, and the lot fell on me. I have just come away from the ships to the plain, for to-morrow the Achaians will open battle against the city. They hate sitting idle, and the princes cannot hold them back.

Then old King Priam said:

"If you are really a servant of Achillês Peleidês, pray tell me the whole truth. Is my son still there by the ships, or has Achillês cut him to pieces and thrown him to the dogs?"

Argeiphontês answered:

"Dear sir, no dogs and vultures have touched him yet, but there he lies beside the ship of Achillês as he was. Twelve days he has been lying there, and his flesh is not decayed, nor do the worms eat him as they eat the dead on the battlefield. It is true Achillês drags him callously round his comrade's barrow at dawn every day, but it does him no harm. You would open your eyes if you could come and see how he lies as fresh as dew, washed clean of blood and nowhere nasty. The wounds have all healed up, and there were many who pierced him. See how the gods care for your son even in death, for he was very dear to them!"

This made the old man happy, and he replied:

"My dear boy, it is good indeed to give the immortals their proper due, for my dead son as truly as he lived never forgot the gods who dwell in Olympos. Therefore they have remembered him, although death is now his portion. But pray do accept from me this pretty cup, and protect me and guide me with God's help, that I may find my way to the hut of Peleidês."

Argeiphontês said:

"You are trying me, sir; you are old, and I am young, but I cannot consent, when you ask me to accept a gift behind the back of Achillês. I fear him, and I should be heartily ashamed to defraud him, or something bad might happen to me. But you shall be my charge. I would guide you carefully as far as Argos, by land or by sea, and no one should despise your guide or attack you."

With this, Luckbringer jumped into the car, and took whip and reins into his hands, and filled horses and mules with spirit. So they went on until they reached the wall and moat. The watchmen were then busy about their supper; but Argeiphontês sent them all to sleep, and in a moment ran back the bars, and opened the gates, and brought in Priam and the wagon with its precious cargo.

They came at last to the hut of Achillês. It was a tall building which the men had made for their prince, walls of fir-planks thatched with a downy roofing of reeds which they had gathered from the meadows. In front was a wide courtyard surrounded by thickset stakes. The door was held by one fir-wood bar; it took three men to push home the bar, and three men to pull it open, but Achillês could push it home by himself. This time, Hermês jumped down and opened the door for the old King, and brought in the precious gifts for Achillês. After that he said:

"I must tell you, sir, that I am an immortal god, Hermês, and my Father sent me to be your guide. But I must go back now, and I must not show myself to Achillês. It would be a shocking thing if a mortal should entertain an immortal god for all to see. You go in and clasp his knees, and beseech him in the name of his father and mother and his son, to touch his heart."

So Hermês took his leave and went back to Olympos.

But Priam dismounted and went towards the house, leaving Idaios where he was, to hold the horses and mules. He found Achillês alone: only two were waiting upon him, ˙Automedon and Alcimos, and he had just finished eating and drinking; the table was still beside him. Priam came in, but they did not see him; he came near Achillês and clasped his knees, and kissed the terrible murderous hands which had killed so many of his sons.

Achillês looked with amazement at royal Priam, and the two men also were amazed and stared at each other, as people stare when some one from a foreign land takes refuge in a rich man's house, after he has killed a man in a fit of madness and has to flee the country.

Then Priam made his prayer:

"Remember your own father, most noble prince Achillês, an old man like me near the end of his days. It may be that *he* is distressed by those who live round about him, and there is no one to defend him from peril and death. But *he* indeed, so long as he hears that you still live, is glad at heart and hopes every day that he will see his well-loved son return home from Troy. But I am all-unhappy, since I had the best sons in the broad land of Troy, and I say not one of them has been left. Fifty I had when the men of Achaia came; nineteen born to me of one womb, the others of women in my household. All those many have fallen in battle; and my only one, who by himself was our safeguard, that one you killed the other day fighting for his country, Hector: for him I come now to your camp, to redeem him from you, and I bring a rich ransom. O Achillês, fear God, and pity me, remembering your own father—but I am even more to be pitied—I have endured to do what no other man in the world has ever done, to lift my hand to the lips of the man who slew my son."[3]

As he said it, he lifted his hand to the face of Achillês, and the heart of Achillês ached with anguish at the thought of his father. He took the old man's hand, and pushed him gently away. So the two thought of their dead and wept, one for his Hector while he crouched before the feet of Achillês, and Achillês for his own father and then for Patroclos. When his agony had passed and he could move again, he got up from his seat and raised the old man by the hand,[4] pitying his white hairs and white beard, and spoke simply from heart to heart:

"Ah, poor man, indeed your heart has borne many sorrows! How could you come to the Achaian camp alone? How could you bear to look on the man who killed all your noble sons, as I have done? Your heart must be made of steel. Come now, sit down upon a seat. We will let our sorrows lie deep in our hearts awhile, for there is no profit in freezing lamentation. This is the way the gods have spun their threads for poor mortals! Our life is all sorrow, but they are untroubled themselves.

"Zeus has two jars of the gifts that he gives, standing upon the floor beside him, one of good things and one of evil things. When the Thunderer mixes and gives, a man meets with good sometimes and bad other times: when he gives all bad, he makes the man despised and rejected; grinding misery drives him over the face of the earth, and he walks without honour from gods or from men. And so with Peleus, the gods gave him glorious gifts from his birth, for he was preëminent in the world for wealth and riches, he was King over the Myrmidons, and although he was mortal they made a goddess his wife. But God gave him evil too, because he got no family of royal princes in his palace, but only one son, to die before his time. And now he is growing old, and I cannot care for him; for I am here in Troy, far from my country, troubling you and your children.

"You also, sir, once were happy, as we hear: upsea as far as Lesbos the seat of Macar, upland to Phrygia, and along the boundless Hellespont, you were paramount with your riches and your sons. But ever since the lords of Heaven brought this calamity upon you, there has been nothing but battle and manslaughter about your city. Endure it, and let not your

---

[3]The suppliants gesture, to touch the chin and caress the lower part of the face. It is clear that Priam does so at this moment, although Homer does not say so; but I have no doubt the minstrel raised his hand, as a Greek would do in reciting such a story, and this would take the place of words.

[4]To raise one by the hand implied accepting him into protection.

heart be uncomforted; for you will have no profit by sorrowing for your son. You will never raise him from the dead; before that, some other trouble will come upon you."

The old King answered:

"Tell me not yet to be seated, gracious prince, while Hector lies here uncared-for. I pray you set him free quickly, that I may look upon him; and accept the ransom that we bring, a great treasure. May you live to enjoy it and return to your own country, since you have spared me first."

Achillês frowned and said:

"Tease me no more, sir, I mean myself to set your Hector free. Zeus sent me a message by my mother, the daughter of the Old Man of the Sea. And I understand quite well, sir, that some god brought you into our camp. For no mere man would dare to come among us, let him be ever so young and strong. He could not escape the guards, and he could not easily lever back the bolt of our doors. Then provoke my temper no more in my sorrow, or I may not spare even you, sir, although you are a suppliant, and that would be sin against the commands of Zeus."

The old man was afraid, and said no more; but Peleidês leapt out like a lion, and the two attendants followed, Automedon and Alcimos, the men whom he trusted most after the dead Patroclos. They unharnessed the horses and mules, and led in the old King's crier to a seat. Then they unpacked Hector's ransom from the wagon, except two sheets and a tunic, which they left to wrap up the body for its journey home. Achillês called out women to wash and anoint the body, but first he moved it out of the way. He did not wish Priam to see his son, and perhaps burst into anger from the sorrow of his heart when he saw him, for then he feared that he might be provoked himself to kill him and sin against the commands of Zeus.

After the women had washed the body and anointed it with oil, and put on the tunic and wrapt the sheet around, Achillês himself lifted him, and laid him upon the bier, and his attendants carried him to the mule-car. Then he cried aloud and called on the name of his lost friend:

"Don't be cross with me, Patroclos, if you hear even in Hadês that I have given back Hector to his father, since the ransom he paid is not unworthy. You shall have your due share of this also."

Then Achillês returned into his hut, and sat down on the bench where he had been before, against the opposite wall, and spoke to Priam:

"Your son, sir, has been set free now as you asked, and he lies on his bier. At break of day you shall see him yourself, on your journey, but just now let us think of supper. Even beautiful Niobê thought of something to eat, after she had lost twelve children in her own house, six daughters and six sons in their prime. Apollo shot the boys with his silver bow, and Artemis Archeress the girls. They were angry because Niobê compared herself with Leto, said she had borne a dozen and Leto only two, so those only two killed them all. They lay nine days in their blood, and there was no one to bury them, for Cronion had turned the people into pebbles⁵; but after all the heavenly ones buried them on the tenth day. So then she thought of something to eat, when she was tired of shedding tears. Now she is somewhere among the rocks, on a lovely mountain in Sipylos, where the beds of the nymphs divine are said to be, the ones that danced about the river Acheloïos; there, stone though she is, she broods over the sorrows which the gods brought on her.

"Well then, venerable prince, let us two also think of something to eat. After that, you may weep for your son again when you have brought him back to Ilios. Many tears he will cost you!"

Then Achillês got up and killed a white lamb, his comrades flayed it and prepared it, cut it up, spitted and broiled it and laid the meat on the table. Automedon brought baskets of bread, and Achillês served the meat.

When they had eaten and drunk all they wanted, Priamos Dardanidês gazed at Achillês, admiring his fine looks and stature—indeed he seemed like some god come down from heaven. And Achillês gazed at Priamos Dardanidês, admiring his noble face and speech. They looked at each other a long time, and then the old King said:

"Put me to bed now quickly, my prince, let us lie down and sleep quietly and rest; for my eyes have never closed under my eyelids since my son lost his life at your hands. All this time I have mourned and brooded over my endless sorrow, tossing about in the muck of my courtyard. Now I have tasted food, and I have let the wine run down my throat; until now I had touched nothing."

Achillês gave orders at once to lay beds in the porch, and strew on them rugs of fine purple with blankets above and woollen robes to wear. The women torch in hand went to get ready two beds, and Achillês said a light word or two:

"You must lie outside, my dear sir, for I may have a visit from one of the councillors from headquarters—they are for ever coming and sitting here and counselling their counsels as if it were a public meeting! If one of them should spy you here in the middle of the night, he would go at once and report it to his majesty King Agamemnon, and there would be delay in releasing the dead.

"But tell me please, if I may ask the question—how many days do you think of to perform the funeral solemnities? I will stay here and keep the people quiet for that time."

The King answered:

"If you are willing to let me do the funeral rites for prince Hector, you will do that for which I shall be deeply grateful. You know how we are crowded into the city; it is a long way for us to get the wood from the mountains, and the people are very much afraid. We would mourn him nine days in the house, on the tenth we would bury him and feast the people, on the eleventh we would build a barrow, and on the twelfth we will fight, if we must."

---

⁵A pun on λαος and λᾶας. Nothing more is known of this part of the story.

Achillês said:

"It shall be as you ask, venerable king. I will hold back the battle for the time you say."

Then he clasped the old man's right wrist, that he might fear nothing, and led him to the porch where he was to sleep with the herald. Achillês himself lay to rest in a corner of the hut, with lovely Briseïs by his side.

All were fast asleep throughout that night both in heaven and on earth, except Hermês, who could not sleep for thinking how he should bring away King Priam out of the camp and keep the watchmen at the gate from seeing. He stood by the old man's bed and said to him:

"Sir! you do not seem to care what happens, sleeping like that in the midst of your enemies because Achillês spared you! Now then: you have redeemed your son, you have paid a heavy ransom: but you alive will cost three times as much for your other sons to get you back, if Agamemnon Atreidês finds out, or the Achaians find out!"

This frightened the old man, and he woke up the herald: Hermês harnessed the horses and mules and drove quickly through the camp, and no one found out.

But when they reached the ford of the Xanthos, Hermês left them and returned to Olympos.

Then the saffron robe of Dawn spread over all the earth, and they drove towards the city mourning and lamenting, while the mules brought the dead. No man and no woman had seen them coming; Cassandra was the first. She had gone up into the citadel, and from there she caught sight of her father standing in his car, and the city-crier, and the other lying on a bier in the mule-wagon. She lifted her voice in wailing, and cried for the whole town to hear:

"Come, all you men and women of Troy! You shall see Hector! Come, if ever you were glad while he lived to welcome his return from battle, for he was a great gladness to the city and all the nation!"

Then grief intolerable came upon every heart. Not a man, not a woman was left behind in the city; all crowded out of the gates and met the dead. First came his wife and his mother tearing their hair; they ran to the wagon and threw their arms over his head, while the people stood mourning around. They would have stayed there all day weeping and wailing, but the old King called out from his car:

"Let the mules pass. When I have brought him into our house you will have plenty of time to lament."

So the people made a way for the wagon to pass.

When he had been brought home, they laid him out on a bier, and posted beside him mourners to lead the dirge, who sang their lamentable dirge while the women wailed in chorus. Andromachê laid her white arms about the head of her dead warrior, and led the lament:

"My husband, you have perished out of life, still young, and left me a widow in the house! The boy is only a baby, your son and my son, doomed father, doomed mother! and he I think will never grow up to manhood; long before that our city will be utterly laid waste! For you have perished, you our watchman, you our only saviour, who kept safe our wives and little children! They will soon be carried off in ships, and I with them. And you, my child!—you will go with me where degrading tasks will be found for you to do, drudging under a merciless master; or some enemy will catch you by the arm, and throw you over the wall to a painful death, in revenge perhaps for some brother that Hector killed, or father, or son maybe, since many a man bit the dust under the hands of Hector; your father was not gentle in the field of battle! Therefore the people throughout the city lament for him,—and you have brought woe and mourning unspeakable upon your parents, Hector! But for me most of all cruel sorrow shall be left. For you did not stretch out to me your dying hands from your deathbed, you said no precious word to me, which I might always remember night and day with tears!"

So Andromachê spoke weeping, and the women wailed in chorus.

Then Hecabê led the lament amid her sobs:

"Hector, best beloved of all my children, dearest to my heart! Living the gods loved you well, therefore they have cared for you even when death is your lot. Other sons of mine Achillês took, and he would sell them over the barren sea, one to Samos, one to Imbros, or to steaming Lamnos; but you—when he had torn out your soul with his sharp blade, he dragged you again and again round the barrow of his comrade whom you slew; but that did not bring him back from the grave! And now you lie in my house fresh as the morning dew, like one that Apollo Silverbow has visited and slain with his gentle shafts!"

So Hecabê spoke weeping, and the women wailed long in chorus.

Helen came third and led the lament:

"Hector, best beloved of all my goodbrothers, and dearest to my heart! Indeed my husband is prince Alexandros, who brought me to Troy—but would that I had died first! Twenty years have passed since I left my country and came here, but I never heard from you one unkind or one slighting word. If any one else reproached me, a sister or brother of yours, or a brother's wife, or your mother—for your father was always as kind as if he were mine—you would reprove them, you would check them, with your gentle spirit and gentle words. Therefore I weep for you, and with you for my unhappy self. For there is no one else in the length and breath of Troy who is kind or friendly; they all shudder at me."

So she spoke weeping, and the people wailed long and loud.

Then old King Priam said:

"Now, Trojans, fetch wood into the city, and have no fear of any ambush of our enemies. For Achillês in parting from me promised that he would do us no harm until the twelfth day shall dawn."

Then they put oxen and mules to their wagons and assembled before the city. Nine days they gathered infinite quantities of wood; when the tenth day dawned, they carried out brave Hector weeping, and laid the body on the pile and set it on fire.

When on the next day Dawn showed her rosy fingers through the mists, the people gathered round about the pyre of Hector. First they quenched the flame with wine wherever the fire had burnt; then his brothers and his comrades gathered his white bones, with hot tears rolling down their cheeks. They placed the bones in a golden casket, and wrapt it in soft purple cloth; this they laid in a hollow space and built it over with large stones. Quickly they piled a barrow, with men on the look-out all round in case the Achaians should attack before their time.

This work done they returned to the city, and the whole assemblage had a famous feast in the palace of Priam their King.

That was the funeral of Hector.

HERODOTUS

HERODOTUS (C. 480-425 B.C.) HAS BEEN CALLED VARIOUSLY THE "FATHER of history" and the "father of lies." He earned the former title as the first writer to describe events realistically and to interpret historical change in terms of men and national character rather than in terms of the gods or other superhuman agencies. Although he is often superstitious and over-fond of recounting doubtful "miracles," Herodotus consistently sees history as the result of purely human actions. He takes considerable trouble to gather and evaluate conflicting accounts of "what actually happened." He was given the less flattering label, not because later writers doubted his truthfulness, but because—from the standpoint of modern scientific method—he is more than a little casual about facts, dates, and statistics. Even so, compared to those who had gone before him, Herodotus manifests a rational, critical spirit worthy of the Age of Pericles. Where he is wrong, it is usually because his sources were untrustworthy.

Although it was in Athens that he won fame by giving public readings from his *History of the Persian Wars*, Herodotus was not a native Athenian. Born in Halicarnassus, a Greek colony on the coast of Asia Minor, he went into exile as a young man and thereafter travelled extensively throughout Egypt, Babylon, Persia, Italy, and Greece. His curiosity and enthusiasm for gathering information were enormous. Apparently he talked to everyone who could tell him about the customs and past of the lands he visited. Conversing with a wide variety of foreigners—an Egyptian priest, a Babylonian magus, a Persian soldier—Herodotus acquired an unusual understanding and tolerance of the "barbarians," as Greeks referred to all non Greek-speaking peoples. Although he lacked the analytic and critical genius of his successor, Thucydides, he recorded with great charm and clarity the most decisive historical movement of his age—the Persian invasion of the West and Greece's role in halting the Oriental advance.

Herodotus defines his purpose as a wish to preserve the "astonishing achievements both of our own and of the Asiatic peoples." The "astonishing" events he records began with the career of Cyrus the Great, a brilliant general who united the Medes and Persians and led them out of Asia on a campaign of world conquest. The story, as Herodotus (with many digressions) tells it, may be summarized as follows. Babylon, an ancient stronghold and the greatest power in the Near East, fell to Cyrus in 539 B.C. Astounding as was Babylon's unexpected collapse, it was only the opening episode on a course of westward expansion that soon brought the Persians into conflict with the Greeks. After conquering Lydia, kingdom of the fabulously wealthy King Croesus, the Persians subjugated the Greek colonies of Ionia, including Athens' sister-city Miletus.

Because of Athenian interference in the seige of Miletus, Cyrus' successor, King Darius, determined to extend his empire into Europe and humiliate the Greeks. Because of his hitherto irresistible power, most

Greek city-states tamely submitted to Darius. Among the major states, only Athens and Sparta resisted.

The Persian attempt to overrun the West underwent a sudden reversal at the famous Battle of Marathon. On that autumn day in 490 B.C., a small band of 10,000 Athenians (including 1000 men from Plataea) defeated a Persian force of perhaps five times their number. (The Spartans did not participate because their priests would not allow the army to march until the next full moon.) According to Herodotus, the Athenians lost 192 men, the "barbarians," 6,400. For the first time in their history, the Persians suffered a military disaster.

After Darius' death, his successor, Xerxes, determined to punish the Athenians for their insolent victory. This time the Spartans had a chance to share in the glory they had missed at Marathon. In 480 B.C., a small company of Spartans under King Leonidas held a crucial mountain pass at Thermopylae until, betrayed by a spy, they were slaughtered to the last man. Sparta's tradition that the brave never surrendered was brilliantly confirmed. The delaying action at Thermopylae allowed Athens to prepare her navy for the decisive sea battle of Salamis (480 B.C.). Under Themistocles' leadership the Athenians abandoned their city, which the Persians sacked and burned, but lured Xerxes' fleet into the narrow straits of Salamis where they utterly destroyed the Persian armada. Two more Greek victories at Plataea and Mycale in Asia Minor ended Persian ambitions for a western empire.

Herodotus, who was born about the time of Salamis, writes of the Greeks at their finest hour. United, they faced a common enemy that the world thought unbeatable, and united they drove him from Europe. The hope and confidence born at Marathon and Salamis inaugurated the famous Golden Age of Athens, a time of creativity and intellectual splendor unmatched elsewhere in world history. By preserving for peoples yet unborn the heroic drama of a relatively tiny nation successfully defending its freedom, Herodotus himself became one of the glories of Greece.

THE HISTORY OF THE PERSIAN WARS

[The following excerpt from Book I illustrates Herodotus' tendency to find a moral in historical events. After writing a new constitution for Athens, Solon, the wise statesman, visits the Near Eastern city of Sardis, capital of wealthy King Croesus. Solon's advice to the over-confident Croesus, that no man can be considered truly fortunate until he had died happily, was later quoted in the final chorus of *Oedipus the King*.]

Abridged. From *Herodotus: The Histories,* translated and with an Introduction by Aubrey de Selincourt. Copyright © 1954 by the Estate of Aubrey de Selincourt. Reprinted by permission of Penguin Books, Ltd. Notes are those of the present editor.

WHEN ALL THESE NATIONS HAD BEEN ADDED TO THE LYDIAN EMPIRE, AND Sardis was at the height of her wealth and prosperity, all the great Greek teachers of that epoch, one after another, paid visits to the capital. Much the most distinguished of them was Solon the Athenian, the man who at the request of his countrymen had made a code of laws for Athens. He was on his travels at the time, intending to be away ten years, in order to avoid the necessity of repealing any of the laws he had made. That, at any rate, was the real reason of his absence, though he gave it out that what he wanted was just to see the world. The Athenians could not alter any of Solon's laws without him, because they had solemnly sworn to give them a ten years' trial.

For this reason, then—and also no doubt for the pleasure of foreign travel—Solon left home and, after a visit to the court of Amasis in Egypt, went to Sardis to see Croesus.

Croesus entertained him hospitably in the palace, and three or four days after his arrival instructed some servants to take him on a tour of the royal treasuries and point out the richness and magnificence of everything. When Solon had made as thorough an inspection as opportunity allowed, Coresus said: 'Well, my Athenian friend, I have heard a great deal about your wisdom, and how widely you have travelled in the pursuit of knowledge. I cannot resist my desire to ask you a question: who is the happiest man you have ever seen?'

The point of the question was that Croesus supposed himself to be the happiest of men. Solon, however, refused to flatter, and answered in strict accordance with his view of the truth. 'An Athenian,' he said, 'called Tellus.'

Croesus was taken aback. 'And what,' he asked sharply, 'is your reason for this choice?'

'There are two good reasons,' said Solon, 'first, his city was prosperous, and he had fine sons, and lived to see children born to each of them, and all these children surviving; and, secondly, after a life which by our standards was a good one, he had a glorious death. In a battle with the neighbouring town of Eleusis, he fought for his countrymen, routed the enemy, and died like a soldier; and the Athenians paid him the high honour of a public funeral on the spot where he fell.'

All these details about the happiness of Tellus, Solon doubtless intended as a moral lesson for the king; Croesus, however, thinking he would at least be awarded second prize, asked who was the next happiest person whom Solon had seen.

'Two young men of Argos,' was the reply; 'Cleobis and Biton. They had enough to live on comfortably; and their physical strength is proved not merely by their success in athletics, but much more by the following incident. The Argives were celebrating the festival of Hera, and it was most important that the mother of the two young men should drive to the temple in her ox-cart; but it so happened that the oxen were late in coming back from the fields. Her two sons therefore, as there was no time to lose, harnessed themselves to the cart and dragged it along, with their mother inside, for a distance of nearly six miles, until they reached the temple. After this exploit, which was witnessed by the assembled crowd, they had a most enviable death—a heaven-sent proof of how much better it is to be dead than alive. Men kept crowding round them and congratulating them on their strength, and women kept telling the mother how lucky she was to have such sons, when, in sheer pleasure at this public recognition of her sons' act, she prayed the goddess Hera, before whose shrine she stood, to grant Cleobis and Biton, who had brought her such honour, the greatest blessing that can fall to mortal man.

'After her prayer came the ceremonies of sacrifice and feasting; and the two lads, when all was over, fell asleep in the temple—and that was the end of them, for they never woke again.

'The Argives had statues made of them, which they sent to Delphi, as a mark of their particular respect.'

Croesus was vexed with Solon for giving the second prize for happiness to the two young Argives, and snapped out: 'That's all very well, my Athenian friend; but what of my own happiness? Is it so utterly contemptible that you won't even compare me with mere common folk like those you have mentioned?'

'My lord,' replied Solon, 'I know God is envious of human prosperity and likes to trouble us; and you question me about the lot of man. Listen then: as the years lengthen out, there is much both to see and to suffer which one would wish otherwise. Take seventy years as the span of a man's life; those seventy years contain 25,200 days, without counting intercalary months. Add a month every other year, to make the seasons come round with proper regularity, and you will have thirty-five additional months, which will make 1050 additional days. Thus the total of days for your seventy years is 26,250, and not a single one of them is like the next in what it brings. You can see from that, Croesus, what a chancy thing life is. You are very rich, and you rule a numerous people; but the question you asked me I will not answer, until I know that you have died happily. Great wealth can make a man no happier than moderate means, unless he has the luck to continue in prosperity to the end. Many very rich men have been unfortunate, and many with a modest competence have had good luck. The former are better off than the latter in two respects only, whereas the poor but lucky man has the advantage in many ways; for though the rich have the means to satisfy their appetites and to bear calamities, and the poor have not, the poor, if they are lucky, are more likely to keep clear of trouble, and will have besides the blessings of a sound body, health, freedom from trouble, fine children, and good looks.

'Now if a man thus favoured dies as he has lived, he will be just the one you are looking for: the only sort of person who deserves to be called happy. But mark this: until he is dead, keep the word 'happy' in reserve. Till then, he is not happy, but only lucky.

'Nobody of course can have all these advantages, any more than a country can produce everything it needs: whatever it has, it is bound to lack something. The best country is the one which has most. It is the same with people: no man is ever self-sufficient—there is sure to be something missing. But whoever has the greatest number of the good things I have mentioned, and keeps them to the end, and dies a peaceful death, that man, my lord Croesus, deserves in my opinion to be called happy.

'Look to the end, no matter what it is you are considering. Often enough God gives a man a glimpse of happiness, and then utterly ruins him.'

These sentiments were not of the sort to give Croesus any pleasure; he let Solon go with cold indifference, firmly convinced that he was a fool. For what could be more stupid than to keep telling him to look at the 'end' of everything, without any regard to present prosperity?

After Solon's departure Croesus was dreadfully punished, presumably because God was angry with him for supposing himself the happiest of men.

*   *   *

The Lydians who were to bring the presents to the temples were instructed by Croesus to ask the oracles if he should undertake the campaign against Persia, and if he should strengthen his army by some alliance. On their arrival, therefore, they offered the gifts with proper ceremony and put their question in the following words: 'Croesus, King of Lydia and other nations, in the belief that these are the only true oracles in the world, has given you gifts such as your power of divination deserves, and now asks you if he should march against Persia and if it would be wise to seek an alliance.' To this question both oracles returned a similar answer; they foretold that if Croesus attacked the Persians, he would destroy a great empire, and they advised him to find out which of the Greek states was the most powerful, and to come to an understanding with it.

Croesus was overjoyed when he learnt the answer which the oracles had given, and was fully confident of destroying the power of Cyrus. To express his satisfaction he sent a further present to Delphi of two gold staters for every man, having first inquired how many men there were. The Delphians in return granted in perpetuity to Croesus and the people of Lydia the right of citizenship for any who wished, together with exemption from dues, front seats at state functions and priority in consulting the oracle.

When Croesus had given the Delphians their presents, he consulted the oracle a third time, for one true answer had made him greedy for more. On this occasion he asked if his reign would be a long one. The Priestess answered:

> When comes the day that a mule shall sit on the Median throne,
> Then, tender-footed Lydian, by pebbly Hermus
> Run and abide not, nor think it shame to be a coward.

This reply gave Croesus more pleasure than anything he had yet heard; for he did not suppose that a mule was likely to become king of the Medes, and that meant that he and his line would remain in power for ever. He then turned his attention to finding out which of the Greek states was the most powerful, with a view to forming an alliance. His inquiries revealed that the Lacedaemonians were the most eminent of the Dorian peoples and the Athenians of the Ionian.[1]

❖   ❖   ❖

What happened to Croesus remains to be told. I have already mentioned his son who was dumb, but in other ways a fine enough young man. In the time of his prosperity—now gone—Croesus had done everything he could for the boy, not even omitting to ask advice from the Delphic oracle. The Priestess had replied:

> *O Lydian lord of many nations, foolish Croesus,*
> *Wish not to hear the longed-for voice within your palace,*
> *Even your son's voice: better for you were it otherwise;*
> *For his first word will he speak on a day of sorrow.*

When the city was stormed, a Persian soldier was about to cut Croesus down, not knowing who he was. Croesus saw him coming; but because in his misery he did not care if he lived or died, he made no effort to defend himself. But this dumb son, seeing the danger, was so terrified by the fearful thing that was about to happen that he broke into speech, and cried: 'Do not kill Croesus, fellow!' Those were the first words he ever uttered—and he retained the power of speech for the rest of his life.

In this way Sardis was captured by the Persians and Croesus taken prisoner, after a reign of fourteen years and a siege of fourteen days. The oracle was fulfilled; Croesus had destroyed a mighty empire—his own.

The Persians brought their prisoner into the presence of the king, and Cyrus chained Croesus and placed him with fourteen Lydian boys on a great pyre that he had built; perhaps he intended them as a choice offering to some god of his, or perhaps he had made a vow and wished to fulfil it; or it may be that he had heard that Croesus was a godfearing man, and set him on the pyre to see if any divine power would save him from being burnt alive. But whatever the reason, that was what he did; and Croesus, for all his misery, as he stood on the pyre, remembered how Solon had declared that no man could be called happy until he was

---

[1]*Lacedaemonians*—the Dorian inhabitants of Lacedaemonia (Laconia), the southeast part of the Peloponnese, of which Sparta was the political center. Whereas the Dorians migrated to the Greek peninsula about 1100 B.C., the Athenians were supposedly native Greeks and related to the Ionians, who, after the Dorian invasion, settled along the coast of Asia Minor.

dead. It was as true as if God had spoken it. Till then Croesus had not uttered a sound; but when he remembered, he sighed bitterly and three times, in anguish of spirit, pronounced Solon's name.

Cyrus heard the name and told his interpreters to ask who Solon was; but for a while Croesus refused to answer the question and kept silent; at last, however, he was forced to speak. 'He was a man,' he said, 'who ought to have talked with every king in the world. I would give a fortune to have had it so.' Not understanding what he meant, they renewed their questions and pressed him so urgently to explain, that he could no longer refuse. He then related how Solon the Athenian once came to Sardis, and made light of the splendour which he saw there, and how everything he said—though it applied to all men and especially to those who imagine themselves fortunate—had in his own case proved all too true.

While Croesus was speaking, the fire had been lit and was already burning round the edges. The interpreters told Cyrus what Croesus had said, and the story touched him. He himself was a mortal man, and was burning alive another who had once been as prosperous as he. The thought of that, and the fear of retribution, and the realization of the instability of human things, made him change his mind and give orders that the flames should at once be put out, and Croesus and the boys brought down from the pyre. But the fire had got a hold, and the attempt to extinguish it failed. The Lydians say that when Croesus understood that Cyrus had changed his mind, and saw everyone vainly trying to master the fire, he called loudly upon Apollo with tears to come and save him from his misery, if any of his gifts had been pleasant to him. It was a clear and windless day; but suddenly in answer to Croesus' prayer clouds gathered and a storm broke with such violent rain that the flames were put out.

This was proof enough for Cyrus that Croesus was a good man whom the gods loved; so he brought him down from the pyre and said, 'Tell me, Croesus; who was it who persuaded you to march against my country and be my enemy rather than my friend?'

'My lord,' Croesus replied, 'the luck was yours when I did it, and the loss was mine. The god of the Greeks encouraged me to fight you: the blame is his. No one is fool enough to choose war instead of peace—in peace sons bury fathers, but in war fathers bury sons. It must have been heaven's will that this should happen.'

Cyrus had his chains taken off and invited him to sit by his side. He made much of him and looked at him with a sort of wonder, as did everyone else who was near enough to see.

For a while Croesus was deep in his thoughts and did not speak. Then he turned, and seeing that the Persians were sacking the town, said: 'Should I tell you, my lord, what I have in my mind, or must I now keep silent?' Cyrus replied that he might say what he pleased without fear, so Croesus put another question: 'What is it,' he asked, 'that all those men of yours are so intent upon doing?'

'They are plundering your city and carrying off your treasures.'

'Not my city or my treasures,' Croesus answered. 'Nothing there any longer belongs to me. It is you they are robbing.'

Cyrus thought this carefully over; then he sent away all the company that was present, and asked Croesus what advice he saw fit to give him in the matter.

'Since the gods have made me your slave,' Croesus said, 'I think it my duty, if I have advice worth giving you, not to withhold it. The Persians are proud—too proud; and they are poor. They are ransacking the town, and if you let them get possession of all that wealth you may be sure that whichever of them gets the most will rebel against you. So do what I advise—if you like the advice: put men from your guard on watch at every gate, and when anyone brings out anything of value, let the sentries take it and say that a tenth part of the spoil must be given to Zeus. If you do that, they will not hate you, as they certainly would if you confiscated the things by mere authority. They will admit that it is an act of justice, and be willing to give up what they have got.'

Cyrus was delighted with this advice, which he thought was excellent. With many compliments to Croesus, he gave orders to the guard to put the proposal into practice. Then turning to Croesus, 'I see,' he said, 'that though you are a king you are ready to do me good service in word and deed. I should like to make you some return: ask, therefore, for whatever you wish, and it shall immediately be yours.'

'Master,' Croesus answered, 'you will please me best if you let me send these chains to the god of the Greeks, whom I most honoured, and ask him if he is accustomed to cheat his benefactors.' Cyrus asked the reason for this request, whereupon Croesus repeated the whole story of what he had hoped to accomplish and of the answers of the oracles, and dwelt at length upon the rich gifts he had sent and on how his belief in the prophecies had emboldened him to invade Persia. Then he ended by repeating his request for permission to reproach Apollo for his deceit. Cyrus laughed, and told Croesus he should have what he wanted, and anything else he might ask for, no matter when. Croesus, therefore, sent to Delphi, and instructed his messengers to lay the chains on the threshold of the temple; then, pointing to the chains, they were to ask the god if, when such things were the fruits of war, he was not ashamed to have encouraged Croesus by his oracles to invade Persia in the confident hope of destroying the power of Cyrus. And they were also to ask if it was the habit of Greek gods to be ungrateful.

It is said that when the Lydian messengers reached Delphi and asked the questions they had been told to ask, the Priestess replied that not God himself could escape destiny. As for Croesus, he had expiated in the fifth generation the crime of his ancestor, who was a soldier in the bodyguard of the Heraclids, and, tempted by a woman's treachery, had murdered his master and stolen his office, to which he had no claim. The God of Prophecy was eager that the fall of Sardis might occur in the time of Croesus' sons rather than in his own, but he had been unable to divert the course of destiny. Nevertheless what little the Fates allowed, he had obtained for Croesus' advantage: he had postponed the capture of Sardis for three years, so Croesus must realize that he had enjoyed three years of freedom more than was appointed for him. Secondly, the god had saved him when he was on the pyre. As to the oracle, Croesus had no right to find fault with it: the god had declared that if he attacked the Persians he would bring down a mighty empire. After an answer like that, the wise thing would have been to send again to inquire which empire was meant, Cyrus' or his own. But as he misinterpreted what was said and made no second inquiry, he must admit the fault to have been his own. Moreover, the last time he consulted the oracle he failed also to understand what Apollo said about the mule. The mule was Cyrus, who was the child of parents of different races—a nobler mother and a baser father. His mother was a Mede and daughter of Astyages, king of Media; but his father was a Persian, subject to the Medes, and had married his queen to whom he was in every way inferior.

When the Lydians returned to Sardis with the Priestess' answer and reported it to Croesus, he admitted that the god was innocent and he had only himself to blame.

Such are the facts about the reign of Croesus and the first conquest of Ionia.

[Cyrus Conquers Babylon (539 B.C.).]

Having subdued the rest of the continent, he[2] turned his attention to Assyria, a country remarkable for the number of great cities it contained, and especially for the most powerful and renowned of them all—Babylon, to which the seat of government was transferred after the fall of Nineveh. Babylon lies in a wide plain, a vast city in the form of a square with sides nearly fourteen miles long and circuit of some fifty-six miles, and in addition to its enormous size it surpasses in splendour any city of the known world. It is surrounded by a broad deep moat full of water, and within the moat there is a wall fifty royal cubits wide and two hundred high (the royal cubit is two inches longer than the ordinary cubit). And now I must describe how the soil dug out to make the moat was used, and the method of building the wall. While the digging was going on, the earth that was shovelled out was formed into bricks, which were baked in ovens as soon as a sufficient number were made; then using hot bitumen for mortar the workmen began by building parapets along each side of the moat, and then went on to erect the actual wall. In both cases they laid rush-mats between every thirty courses of brick. On the top of the wall they constructed, along each edge, a row of one-roomed buildings facing inwards with enough space between for a

---

[2]*He*—Cyrus.

four-horse chariot to turn. There are a hundred gates in the circuit of the wall, all of bronze with bronze uprights and lintels.

Eight days' journey from Babylon there is a city called Is on a smallish river of the same name, a tributary of the Euphrates, and in this river lumps of bitumen are found in great quantity. This was the source of supply for the bitumen used in building the wall of Babylon. The Euphrates, a broad, deep, swift river which rises in Armenia and flows into the Persian Gulf, runs through the middle of the city and divides it in two. The wall is brought right down to the water on both sides, and at an angle to it there is another wall on each bank, but of baked bricks without mortar, running through the town. There are a great many houses of three and four stories. The main streets and the side streets which lead to the river are all dead straight, and for every one of the side streets or alleys there was a bronze gate in the river wall by which the water could be reached.

The great wall I have described is, so to speak, the breastplate or chief defence of the city; but there is a second one within it, not so thick but hardly less strong. There is a fortress in the middle of each half of the city: in one the royal palace surrounded by a wall of great strength, in the other the temple of Bel,[3] the Babylonian Zeus. The temple is a square building, two furlongs each way, with bronze gates, and was still in existence in my time; it has a solid central tower, one furlong square, with a second erected on top of it and then a third, and so on up to eight. All eight towers can be climbed by a spiral way running round the outside, and about half way up there are seats for those who make the ascent to rest on. On the summit of the topmost tower stands a great temple with a fine large couch in it, richly covered, and a golden table beside it. The shrine contains no image, and no one spends the night there except (if we may believe the Chaldeans[4] who are the priests of Bel) one Assyrian woman, all alone, whoever it may be that the god has chosen. The Chaldaeans also say—though I do not believe them—that the god enters the temple in person and takes his rest upon the bed. There is a similar story told by the Egyptians at Thebes, where a woman always passes the night in the temple of the Theban Zeus and is forbidden, so they say, like the woman in the temple at Babylon, to have any intercourse with men; and there is yet another instance in the Lycian town of Patara, where the priestess who delivers the oracles when required (for there is not always an oracle there) is shut up in the temple during the night.

In the temple of Babylon there is a second shrine lower down, in which is a great sitting figure of Bel, all of gold on a golden throne,

---

[3]*Bel*—literally "lord, master," an ancient Babylonian term applied to Enlil and Marduk. Herodotus here follows his usual custom of equating a foreign deity with some member of the Olympian pantheon.

[4]*Chaldeans*—another name for the Babylonians; they were famous to the Greeks for the practice of astrology and magic.

supported on a base of gold, with a golden table standing beside it. I was told by the Chaldaeans that, to make all this, more than twenty-two tons of gold were used. Outside the temple is a golden altar, and there is another one, not of gold, but of great size, on which sheep are sacrificed. The golden altar is reserved for the sacrifice of sucklings only. Again, on the larger altar the Chaldaeans offer something like two and a half tons of frankincense every year at the festival of Bel. In the time of Cyrus there was also in this sacred building a solid golden statue of a man some fifteen feet high—I have this on the authority of the Chaldaeans, though I never saw it myself. Darius the son of Hystaspes had designs upon it, but he never carried it off because his courage failed him; Xerxes, however, did take it and killed the priest who tried to prevent the sacrilege. In addition to the adornments I have described there are also many private offerings in the temple.

✧   ✧   ✧

The Babylonians had taken the field and were awaiting his approach. As soon as he was within striking distance of the city they attacked him, but were defeated and forced to retire inside their defences; they already knew of Cyrus' restless ambition and had watched his successive acts of aggression against one nation after another, and as they had taken the precaution of accumulating in Babylon a stock of provisions sufficient to last many years, they were able to regard the prospect of a siege with indifference. So the siege dragged on and no progress was made by the besieging army. Cyrus was beginning to despair of success when somebody suggested to him a way out of the deadlock. The plan (which may, indeed, have been his own) was as follows: he stationed part of his force at the point where the Euphrates flows into the city and another contingent at the opposite end where it flows out, with orders to both to force an entrance along the river-bed as soon as they saw that the water was shallow enough. Then, taking with him all his non-combatant troops, he withdrew to the spot where Nitocris had excavated the lake, and proceeded to repeat the operation which the queen had previously performed: by means of a cutting he diverted the river into the lake (which was then a marsh) and in this way so greatly reduced the depth of water in the actual bed of the river that it became fordable, and the Persian army, which had been left at Babylon for the purpose, entered the river, now only deep enough to reach about the middle of a man's thigh, and, making their way along it, got into the town. If the Babylonians had learnt what Cyrus was doing or had seen it for themselves in time, they could have let the Persians enter and then, by shutting all the gates which led to the waterside and manning the walls on either side of the river, they could have caught them in a trap and wiped them out. But as it was they were taken by surprise. The Baby-

Ionians themselves say that owing to the great size of the city the outskirts were captured without the people in the centre knowing anything about it; there was a festival going on, and even while the city was falling they continued to dance and enjoy themselves, until hard facts brought them to their senses. That, then, is the story of the first capture of Babylon.[5]

[The Emperor Darius, one of Cyrus' successors, leads the Medo-Persian army into Greece (490 B.C.). As the invaders approach Athens, the Athenians send the runner Pheidippides to bring the Spartans to their aid.]

Before they left the city, the Athenian generals sent off a message to Sparta. The messenger was an Athenian named Pheidippides, a trained runner still in the practice of his profession. According to the account he gave the Athenians on his return, Pheidippides met the god Pan on Mount Parthenium, above Tegea. Pan, he said, called him by name and told him to ask the Athenians why they paid him no attention, in spite of his friendliness towards them and the fact that he had often been useful to them in the past, and would be so again in the future. The Athenians believed Pheidippides' story, and when their affairs were once more in a prosperous state, they built a shrine to Pan under the Acropolis, and from the time his message was received they have held an annual ceremony, with a torch-race and sacrifices, to court his protection.

On the occasion of which I speak—when Pheidippides, that is, was sent on his mission by the Athenian commanders and said that he saw Pan—he reached Sparta the day after he left Athens. At once he delivered his message to the Spartan government. 'Men of Sparta' (the message ran) 'the Athenians ask you to help them, and not to stand by while the most ancient city of Greece is crushed and enslaved by a foreign invader. Already Eretria is destroyed, and her people in chains, and Greece is the weaker by the loss of one fine city.' The Spartans, though moved by the appeal, and willing to send help to Athens, were unable to send it promptly because they did not wish to break their law. It was the ninth day of the month, and they said they could not take the field until the moon was full. So they waited for the full moon, and meanwhile Hippias, the son of Pisistratus,[6] guided the Persians to Marathon.

The previous night Hippias had dreamed that he was sleeping with his mother, and he supposed that the dream meant that he would return to Athens, recover his power, and die peacefully at home in old age. So much for his first interpretation. On the following day, when he was

---

[5]Compare Herodotus' account of the fall of Babylon with that given in the Bible. See *Daniel* 5:1-31.
[6]*Hippias, the son of Pisistratus*—For these and other major historical characters that appear in Herodotus, please consult the Glossary.

acting as guide to the invaders, he put the prisoners from Eretria ashore on Aegilia, an island belonging to the town of Styra, led the fleet to its anchorage at Marathon, and got the troops into position when they had disembarked. While he was busy with all this, he happened to be seized by an unusually violent fit of sneezing and coughing, and, as he was an oldish man, and most of his teeth were loose, he coughed one of them right out of his mouth. It fell somewhere in the sand, and though he searched and searched in his efforts to find it, it was nowhere to be seen. Hippias then turned to his companions, and said with a deep sigh: 'This land is not ours; we shall never be able to conquer it. The only part I ever had in it my tooth possesses.' So he had had to change his mind—and the meaning of the dream was now clear.

The Athenian troops were drawn up on a piece of ground sacred to Heracles, when they were joined by the Plataeans, who came to support them with every available man. Some time before this the Plataeans had surrendered their independence to the Athenians, who had, in their turn, already rendered service to Plataea on many occasions and in difficult circumstances. . . .

[The Battle of Marathon (490 B.C.)]

Amongst the Athenian commanders opinion was divided: some were against risking a battle, on the ground that the Athenian force was too small to stand a chance of success; others—and amongst them Miltiades—urged it. It seemed for a time as if the more faint-hearted policy would be adopted—and so it would have been but for the action of Miltiades. In addition to the ten commanders, there was another person entitled to a vote, namely the polemarch,[7] or War Archon,[8] an official appointed in Athens not by vote but by lot. This office (which formerly carried an equal vote in military decisions with the generals) was held at this time by Callimachus of Aphidne. To Callimachus, therefore, Miltiades turned. 'It is now in your hands, Callimachus,' he said, 'either to enslave Athens, or to make her free and to leave behind you for all future generations a memory more glorious than ever Harmodius and Aristogeiton left. Never in the course of our long history have we Athenians been in such peril as now. If we submit to the Persian invader, Hippias will be restored to power in Athens—and there is little doubt what misery must then ensue; but if we fight and win, then this city of ours may well grow to pre-eminence amongst all the cities of Greece. If you ask me how this can be, and how the decision rests with you, I will tell you: we commanders are ten in number, and we are not agreed upon what action to take; half of us are for a battle, half against it. If we refuse to fight, I have little doubt that the result will be the rise in Athens of bitter

---

[7]Polemarch—Athenian commander-in-chief.

[8]*Archon*—the title of nine civil executives who were elected annually by the Council of the Areopagus.

political dissension; our purpose will be shaken, and we shall submit to Persia. But if we fight before the rot can show itself in any of us, then, if God gives us fair play, we can not only fight but win. Yours is the decision; all hangs upon you; vote on my side, and our country will be free—yes, and the mistress of Greece. But if you support those who have voted against fighting, that happiness will be denied you—you will get the opposite.'

Miltiades' words prevailed. The vote of Callimachus the War Archon was cast on the right side, and the decision to fight was made.

The generals exercised supreme command in succession, each for a day; and those of them who had voted with Miltiades, offered, when their turn for duty came, to surrender it to him. Miltiades accepted the offer, but would not fight until the day came when he would in any case have had the supreme command. When it did come, the Athenian army moved into position for the coming struggle. The right wing was commanded by Callimachus—for it was the regular practice at that time in Athens that the War Archon should lead the right wing; then followed the tribes, one after the other, in an unbroken line; and, finally, on the left wing, was the contingent from Plataea. Ever since the battle of Marathon, when the Athenians offer sacrifice at their quadrennial festival, the herald links the names of Athens and Plataea in the prayer for God's blessing.

One result of the disposition of Athenian troops before the battle was the weakening of their centre by the effort to extend the line sufficiently to cover the whole Persian front; the two wings were strong, but the line in the centre was only a few ranks deep. The dispositions made, and the preliminary sacrifice promising success, the word was given to move, and the Athenians advanced at a run towards the enemy, not less than a mile away. The Persians, seeing the attack developing at the double, prepared to meet it confidently enough, for it seemed to them suicidal madness for the Athenians to risk an assault with so small a force—at the double, too, and with no support from either cavalry or archers. Well, that was what they imagined; nevertheless, the Athenians came on, closed with the enemy all along the line, and fought in a way not to be forgotten. They were the first Greeks, so far as I know, to charge at a run, and the first who dared to look without flinching at Persian dress and the men who wore it; for until that day came, no Greek could hear even the word Persian without terror.

The struggle at Marathon was long drawn out. In the centre, held by the Persians themselves and the Sacae, the advantage was with the foreigners, who were so far successful as to break the Greek line and pursue the fugitives inland from the sea; but the Athenians on one wing and the Plataeans on the other were both victorious. Having got the upper hand, they left the defeated Persians to make their escape, and then, drawing the two wings together into a single unit, they turned their attention to the Persians who had broken through in the centre. Here again they were triumphant, chasing the routed enemy, and cutting them down as they ran right to the edge of the sea. Then, plunging into the water, they laid hold of the ships, calling for fire. It was in this phase of the struggle that the War Archon Callimachus was killed, fighting bravely, and also Stesilaus, the son of Thrasylaus, one of the commanders; Cynegirus,[9] too, the son of Euphorion, had his hand cut off with an axe as he was getting hold of a ship's stern, and so lost his life, together with many other well-known Athenians. Nevertheless the Athenians secured in this way seven ships; the rest managed to get off, and the Persians aboard them, after picking up the Eretrian prisoners whom they had left on Aegilia, laid a course round Sunium for Athens, which they hoped to reach in advance of the Athenian army. In Athens the Alcmaeonidae[10] were accused of suggesting this move; they had, it was said, an understanding with the Persians, and raised a shield as a signal to them when they were on board.

While the Persian fleet was on its way round Sunium, the Athenians hurried back with all possible speed to save their city, and succeeded in reaching it before the arrival of the Persians. Just as at Marathon the Athenian camp had been on a plot of ground sacred to Heracles, so now they fixed their camp on another, also sacred to the same god, at Cynosarges. When the Persian fleet appeared, it lay at anchor for a while off Phalerum (at that time the chief harbour of Athens) and then sailed for Asia.

In the battle of Marathon some 6400 Persians were killed; the losses of the Athenians were 192.

✿ ✿ ✿

After waiting for the full moon, two thousand Spartans set off for Athens. They were so anxious not to be late that they were in Attica on the third day after leaving Sparta. They had, of course, missed the battle; but such was their passion to see the Persians, that they went to Marathon to have a look at the bodies. That done, they complimented the Athenians on their good work, and returned home.

[Ten years after Marathon, the new Persian emperor, Xerxes, begins a second invasion of Greece. He makes elaborate preparations to cross the Hellespont from Asia into Europe (480 B.C.).]

In Sardis Xerxes' first act was to send representatives to every place in Greece except Athens and Sparta with a demand for the usual tokens of submission and a further order to prepare entertainment for him against

---

[9]*Cynegirus*—brother of the playwright Aeschylus, who also fought at Marathon.
[10]*Alcmaeonidae*—an aristocratic family suspected of wishing to establish a dynasty in Athens. Through their mothers, Cleisthenes the law-giver, Pericles, and Alcibiades were Alcmaeonids.

his coming. This renewed demand for submission was due to his confident belief that the Greeks who had previously refused to comply with the demand of Darius would now be frightened into complying with his own. It was to prove whether or not he was right that he took this step.

He then prepared to move forward to Abydos, where a bridge had already been constructed across the Hellespont from Asia to Europe. Between Sestos and Madytus in the Chersonese there is a rocky headland running out into the water opposite Abydos. It was here not long afterwards that the Greeks under Xanthippus the son of Ariphron took Artayctes the Persian governor of Sestos, and nailed him alive to a plank—he was the man who collected women in the temple of Protesilaus at Elaeus and committed various acts of sacrilege. This headland was the point to which Xerxes' engineers carried their two bridges from Abydos—a distance of seven furlongs. One was constructed by the Phoenicians using flax cables, the other by the Egyptians with papyrus cables. The work was successfully completed, but a subsequent storm of great violence smashed it up and carried everything away. Xerxes was very angry when he heard of the disaster, and gave orders that the Hellespont should receive three hundred lashes and have a pair of fetters thrown into it. And I have heard before now that he also sent people to brand it with hot irons. He certainly instructed the men with the whips to utter, as they wielded them, the following words: 'You salt and bitter stream, your master lays this punishment upon you for injuring him, who never injured you. But Xerxes the King will cross you, with or without your permission. No man sacrifices to you, and you deserve the neglect by your acrid and muddy waters'—a highly presumptuous way[11] of addressing the Hellespont, and typical of a barbarous nation. In addition to punishing the Hellespont Xerxes gave orders that the men responsible for building the bridges should have their heads cut off. This unseemly order was duly carried out, and other engineers were appointed to start the work afresh. The method employed was as follows: galleys and triremes were lashed together to support the bridges—360 vessels for the one on the Black Sea side, and 314 for the other. They were moored head-on to the current—and consequently at right angles to the actual bridges they supported—in order to lessen the strain on the cables. Specially heavy anchors were laid out both upstream and downstream— those to the eastward to hold the vessels against winds blowing down the straits from the direction of the Black Sea, those on the other side, to the westward and towards the Aegean, to take the strain when it blew from the west and south. Gaps were left in three places to allow any boats that might wish to do so to pass in or out of the Black Sea.

Once the vessels were in position, the cables were hauled taut by wooden winches ashore. This time the two sorts of cable were not used separately for each bridge, but both bridges had two flax cables and four

---

11*A highly presumptuous way*—Herodotus regards Xerxes as guilty of *hubris*, for which the gods will punish him at the Battle of Salamis.

papyrus ones. The flax and papyrus cables were of the same thickness and quality, but the flax was the heavier—half a fathom of it weighed 114 lb. The next operation was to cut planks equal in length to the width of the floats, lay them edge to edge over the taut cables and then bind them together on their upper surface. That done, brushwood was put on top and spread evenly, with a layer of soil, trodden hard, over all. Finally a paling was constructed along each side, high enough to prevent horses and mules from seeing over and taking fright at the water.

The bridges were now ready; and when news came from Athos that work on the canal was finished, including the breakwaters at its two ends, which had been built to prevent the surf from silting up the entrances, the army, after wintering at Sardis and completing its preparations, started the following spring on its march to Abydos.

No sooner had the troops begun to move than the sun vanished from his place in the sky and it grew dark as night, though the weather was perfectly clear and cloudless. Xerxes, deeply troubled, asked the Magi to interpret the significance of this strange phenomenon, and was given to understand that God meant to foretell to the Greeks the eclipse of their cities—for it was the sun which gave warning of the future to Greece, just as the moon did to Persia. The explanation was satisfactory, and Xerxes continued the march in high spirits.

❊   ❊   ❊

After this conversation Xerxes sent Artabanus[12] back to Susa and then summoned a meeting of his most eminent subjects. 'Gentlemen,' he said to them, 'I have brought you here because I wished to ask you to show courage in what lies before us; you must not disgrace our countrymen, who in former days did so much that was great and admirable. Let each and all of us exert ourselves to the utmost; for the noble aim we are striving to achieve concerns every one of us alike. Fight this war with all your might—and for this reason: our enemies, if what I hear is true, are brave men, and if we defeat them, there is no other army in the world which will ever stand up to us again. And now let us pray to the gods who have our country in their keeping—and cross the bridge.'

All that day the preparations for the crossing continued; and on the following day, while they waited for the sun which they wished to see as it rose, they burned all sorts of spices on the bridges and laid boughs of myrtle along the way. Then sunrise came, and Xerxes poured wine into the sea out of a golden goblet and, with his face turned to the sun, prayed that no chance might prevent him from conquering Europe or turn him back before he reached its utmost limits. His prayer ended, he flung the cup into the Hellespont and with it a golden bowl and a Persian

---

[12]*Artabanus*—a Persian counselor who wisely advised Xerxes against invading Greece.

acinaces, or short sword. I cannot say for certain if he intended the things which he threw into the water to be an offering to the Sun-god; perhaps they were—or it may be that they were a gift to the Hellespont itself, to show he was sorry for having caused it to be lashed with whips.

This ceremony over, the crossing began. The infantry and cavalry went over by the upper bridge—the one nearer the Black Sea; the pack-animals and underlings by the lower one towards the Aegean. The first to cross were the Ten Thousand, all with wreaths on their heads, and these were followed by a mass of troops of all sorts of nationality. Their crossing occupied the whole of the first day. On the next day the first over were the thousand horsemen, and the contingent which marched with spears reversed—these, too, all wearing wreaths. Then came the sacred horses and the sacred chariot, and after them Xerxes himself with his spearmen and his thousand horsemen. The remainder of the army brought up the rear, and at the same time the ships moved over to the opposite shore. According to another account I have heard, the king crossed last.

From the European shore Xerxes watched his troops coming over under the whips. The crossing occupied seven days and nights without a break. There is a story that some time after Xerxes had passed the bridge, a native of the country thereabouts exclaimed: 'Why, O God, have you assumed the shape of a man of Persia, and changed your name to Xerxes, in order to lead everyone in the world to the conquest and devastation of Greece? You could have destroyed Greece without going to that trouble.' . . .

[The Spartans' heroic resistance at Thermopylae]

The Persian army was now close to the pass, and the Greeks, suddenly doubting their power to resist, held a conference to consider the advisability of retreat. It was proposed by the Peloponnesians generally that the army should fall back upon the Peloponnese and hold the Isthmus; but when the Phocians and Locrians expressed their indignation at this suggestion, Leonidas[13] gave his voice for staying where they were and sending, at the same time, an appeal for reinforcements to the various states of the confederacy, as their numbers were inadequate to cope with the Persians.

During the conference Xerxes sent a man on horseback to ascertain the strength of the Greek force and to observe what the troops were doing. He had heard before he left Thessaly that a small force was concentrated here, led by the Lacedaemonians under Leonidas of the house of Heracles. The Persian rider approached the camp and took a thorough survey of all he could see—which was not, however, the whole Greek army; for the men on the further side of the wall which, after its reconstruction, was now guarded, were out of sight. He did, none the

---

[13]*Leonidas*—king of Sparta.

less, carefully observe the troops who were stationed on the outside of the wall. At that moment these happened to be the Spartans, and some of them were stripped for exercise, while others were combing their hair. The Persian spy watched them in astonishment; nevertheless he made sure of their numbers, and of everything else he needed to know, as accurately as he could, and then rode quietly off. No one attempted to catch him, or took the least notice of him.

Back in his own camp he told Xerxes what he had seen. Xerxes was bewildered; the truth, namely that the Spartans were preparing themselves to kill and to be killed according to their strength, was beyond his comprehension, and what they were doing seemed to him merely absurd. Accordingly he sent for Demaratus, the son of Ariston, who had come with the army, and questioned him about the spy's report, in the hope of finding out what the unaccountable behaviour of the Spartans might mean. 'Once before,' Demaratus said, 'when we began our march against Greece, you heard me speak of these men. I told you then how I saw this enterprise would turn out, and you laughed at me. I strive for nothing, my lord, more earnestly than to observe the truth in your presence; so hear me once more. These men have come to fight us for possession of the pass, and for that struggle they are preparing. It is the common practice of the Spartans to pay careful attention to their hair when they are about to risk their lives. But I assure you that if you can defeat these men and the rest of the Spartans who are still at home, there is no other people in the world who will dare to stand firm or lift a hand against you. You have now to deal with the finest kingdom in Greece, and with the bravest men.'

Xerxes, unable to believe what Demaratus said, asked further how it was possible that so small a force could fight with his army. 'My lord,' Demaratus replied, 'treat me as a liar, if what I have foretold does not take place.' But still Xerxes was unconvinced.

For four days Xerxes waited, in constant expectation that the Greeks would make good their escape; then, on the fifth, when still they had made no move and their continued presence seemed mere impudent and reckless folly, he was seized with rage and sent forward the Medes and Cissians with orders to take them alive and bring them into his presence. The Medes charged, and in the struggle which ensued many fell; but others took their places, and in spite of terrible losses refused to be beaten off. They made it plain enough to anyone, and not least to the king himself, that he had in his army many men, indeed, but few soldiers. All day the battle continued; the Medes, after their rough handling, were at length withdrawn and their place was taken by Hydarnes and his picked Persian troops—the King's Immortals—who advanced to the attack in full confidence of bringing the business to a quick and easy end. But, once engaged, they were no more successful than the Medes had been; all went as before, the two armies fighting in a confined space, the Persians using shorter spears than the Greeks and having no advantage from their numbers.

On the Spartan side it was a memorable fight; they were men who understood war pitted against an inexperienced enemy, and amongst the feints they employed was to turn their backs in a body and pretend to be retreating in confusion, whereupon the enemy would come on with a great clatter and roar, supposing the battle won; but the Spartans, just as the Persians were on them, would wheel and face them and inflict in the new struggle innumerable casualties. The Spartans had their losses too, but not many. At last the Persians, finding that their assaults upon the pass, whether by divisions or by any other way they could think of, were all useless, broke off the engagement and withdrew. Xerxes was watching the battle from where he sat; and it is said that in the course of the attacks three times, in terror for his army, he leapt to his feet.

Next day the fighting began again, but with no better success for the Persians, who renewed their onslaught in the hope that the Greeks, being so few in number, might be badly enough disabled by wounds to prevent further resistance. But the Greeks never slackened; their troops were ordered in divisions corresponding to the states from which they came, and each division took its turn in the line except the Phocian, which had been posted to guard the track over the mountains. So when the Persians found that things were no better for them than on the previous day, they once more withdrew.

How to deal with the situation Xerxes had no idea; but while he was still wondering what his next move should be, a man from Malis got himself admitted to his presence. This was Ephialtes, the son of Eurydemus, and he had come, in hope of a rich reward, to tell the king about the track which led over the hills to Thermopylae—and the information he gave was to prove the death of the Greeks who held the pass. . . .

[The traitor Ephialtes shows the Persians the way to ambush Leonidas and his men.]

The ascent of the Persians had been concealed by the oak-woods which cover this part of the mountain range, and it was only when they reached the top that the Phocians became aware of their approach; for there was not a breath of wind, and the marching feet made a loud swishing and rustling in the fallen leaves. Leaping to their feet, the Phocians were in the act of arming themselves when the enemy was upon them. The Persians were surprised at the sight of troops preparing to resist; they had not expected any opposition—yet here was a body of men barring their way. Hydarnes asked Ephialtes who they were, for his first uncomfortable thought was that they might be Spartans; but on learning the truth he prepared to engage them. The Persian arrows flew thick and fast, and the Phocians, supposing themselves to be the main object of the attack, hurriedly withdrew to the highest point of the mountain, where they made ready to face destruction. The Persians, however, with Ephialtes and Hydarnes paid no further attention to them, but passed on along the descending track with all possible speed.

The Greeks at Thermopylae had their first warning of the death that was coming with the dawn from the seer Megistias, who read their doom in the victims of sacrifice; deserters, too, had begun to come in during the night with news of the Persian movement to take them in the rear, and, just as day was breaking, the look-out men had come running from the hills. At once a conference was held, and opinions were divided, some urging that they must on no account abandon their post, others taking the opposite view. The result was that the army split: some dispersed, the men returning to their various homes, and others made ready to stand by Leonidas.

There is another account which says that Leonidas himself dismissed a part of his force, to spare their lives, but thought it unbecoming for the Spartans under his command to desert the post which they had original-ly come to guard. I myself am inclined to think that he dismissed them when he realized that they had no heart for the fight and were unwilling to take their share of the danger; at the same time honour forbade that he himself should go. And indeed by remaining at his post he left a great name behind him, and Sparta did not lose her prosperity, as might otherwise have happened; for right at the outset of the war the Spartans had been told by the oracle, when they asked for advice, that either their city must be laid waste by the foreigner or one of their kings be killed. The prophecy was in hexameter verse and ran as follows:

Hear your fate, O dwellers in Sparta of the wide spaces;
Either your famed, great town must be sacked by Perseus' sons,
Or, if that be not, the whole land of Lacedaemon
Shall mourn the death of a king of the house of Heracles,
For not the strength of lions or of bulls shall hold him,
Strength against strength; for he has the power of Zeus,
And will not be checked till one of these two he has consumed.

I believe it was the thought of this oracle, combined with his wish to lay up for the Spartans a treasure of fame in which no other city should share, that made Leonidas dismiss those troops; I do not think that they deserted, or went off without orders, because of a difference of opinion. Moreover, I am strongly supported in this view by the case of Megistias, the seer from Acarnania who foretold the coming doom by his inspection of the sacrificial victims: this man—he was said to be descended from Melampus—was with the army, and quite plainly received orders from Leonidas to quit Thermopylae, to save him from sharing the army's fate. But he refused to go, sending away instead an only son of his, who was serving with the forces.

Thus it was that the confederate troops, by Leonidas' orders, aban-doned their posts and left the pass, all except the Thespians and the Thebans who remained with the Spartans. The Thebans were detained by Leonidas as hostages very much against their will—unlike the loyal Thespians, who refused to desert Leonidas and his men, but stayed, and died with them. They were under the command of Demophilus the son of Diadromes.

In the morning Xerxes poured a libation to the rising sun, and then waited till about the time of the filling of the market-place, when he began to move forward. This was according to Ephialtes' instructions, for the way down from the ridge is much shorter and more direct than the long and circuitous ascent. As the Persian army advanced to the assault, the Greeks under Leonidas, knowing that the fight would be their last, pressed forward into the wider part of the pass much further than they had done before; in the previous days' fighting they had been holding the wall and making sorties from behind it into the narrow neck, but now they left the confined space and battle was joined on more open ground. Many of the invaders fell; behind them the company commanders plied their whips, driving the men remorselessly on. Many fell into the sea and were drowned, and still more were trampled to death by their friends. No one could count the number of the dead. The Greeks, who knew that the enemy were on their way round by the mountain track and that death was inevitable, fought with reckless desperation, exerting every ounce of strength that was in them against the invader. By this time most of their spears were broken, and they were killing Persians with their swords.

In the course of that fight Leonidas fell, having fought like a man indeed. Many distinguished Spartans were killed at his side—their names, like the names of all the three hundred, I have made myself acquainted with, because they deserve to be remembered. Amongst the Persian dead, too, were many men of high distinction—for instance, two brothers of Xerxes, Habrocomes and Hyperanthes, both of them sons of Darius by Artanes' daughter Phratagune.[14]

There was a bitter struggle over the body of Leonidas; four times the Greeks drove the enemy off, and at last by their valour succeeded in dragging it away. So it went on, until the fresh troops with Ephialtes were close at hand; and then, when the Greeks knew that they had come, the character of the fighting changed. They withdrew again into the narrow neck of the pass, behind the walls, and took up a position in a single compact body—all except the Thebans—on the little hill at the entrance to the pass, where the stone lion in memory of Leonidas stands to-day. Here they resisted to the last, with their swords, if they had them, and, if not, with their hands and teeth, until the Persians, coming on from the front over the ruins of the wall and closing in from behind, finally overwhelmed them.

Of all the Spartans and Thespians who fought so valiantly on that day, the most signal proof of courage was given by the Spartan Diene-

---

[14]Artanes, the son of Hystaspes and grandson of Arsames, was Darius' brother; as Phratagune was his only child, his giving her to Darius was equivalent to giving him his entire estate. [Trans.]

ces. It is said that before the battle he was told by a native of Trachis that, when the Persians shot their arrows, there were so many of them that they hid the sun. Dieneces, however, quite unmoved by the thought of the terrible strength of the Persian army, merely remarked: 'This is pleasant news that the stranger from Trachis brings us: for if the Persians hide the sun, we shall have our battle in the shade.' He is said to have left on record other sayings, too, of similar kind, by which he will be remembered. After Dieneces the greatest distinction was won by the two Spartan brothers, Alpheus and Maron, the sons of Orsiphantus; and of the Thespians the man to gain the highest glory was a certain Dithyrambus, the son of Harmatides.

The dead were buried where they fell, and with them the men who had been killed before those dismissed by Leonidas left the pass. Over them is this inscription, in honour of the whole force:

> *Four thousand here from Pelops' land*
> *Against three million once did stand.*

The Spartans have a special epitaph; it runs:

> *Go tell the Spartans, you who read:*
> *We took their orders, and are dead.*

For the seer Megistias there is the following:

> *I was Megistias once, who died*
> *When the Mede passed Spercheius' tide.*
> *I knew death near, yet would not save*
> *Myself, but share the Spartans' grave.*

The columns with the epitaphs inscribed on them were erected in honour of the dead by the Amphictyons—though the epitaph upon the seer Megistias was the work of Simonides, the son of Leoprepes, who put it there for friendship's sake.

[Following the advice of Themistocles, the Athenians abandon their city and evacuate to the nearby island of Salamis. Xerxes captures and burns Athens, but Themistocles cleverly lures Xerxes' fleet into the narrow Straits of Salamis, where the Greeks destroy the Persian armada (480 B.C.).]

The Persians found Athens itself abandoned except for a few people in the temple of Athene Polias—temple stewards and needy folk, who had barricaded the Acropolis against the invaders with planks and timbers. It was partly their poverty which prevented them from seeking shelter in Salamis with the rest, and partly their belief that they had discovered the real meaning of the Priestess' oracle—that 'the wooden wall would not be taken.' The wooden wall, in their minds, was not the ships but the barricade, and that would save them.

The Persians occupied the hill which the Athenians call the Areopagus, opposite the Acropolis, and began the siege. The method they used was to shoot into the barricade arrows with burning tow attached to them. Their wooden wall had betrayed them, but still the Athenians, though in imminent and deadly peril, refused to give in, or even to listen to the proposals which the Pisistratidae made to them for a truce. All their ingenuity was employed in the struggle to defend themselves; amongst other things, they rolled boulders down the slope upon the enemy as he tried to approach the gates, and the device was so successful that for a long time Xerxes was baffled and unable to take them. It was a difficult problem for the Persians, but at last it was solved: a way of access to the Acropolis was found—and the prophecy fulfilled that all Athenian territory upon the continent of Greece must be overrun by the Persians.

There is a place in front of the Acropolis, behind the usual way up which leads to the gates, where the ascent is so steep that no guard was set, because it was not thought possible that any man would be able to climb it; here, by the shrine of Cecrops' daughter Aglaurus, a few soldiers managed to scramble up the precipitous face of the cliff. When the Athenians saw them on the summit, some leapt from the wall to their death, others sought sanctuary in the inner shrine of the temple. The Persians made straight for the temple gates, flung them open and butchered every man who had hoped to find a refuge there. Having left not one of them alive, they stripped the temple of its treasures and destroyed the whole Acropolis by fire. Xerxes, now absolute master of Athens, despatched a rider to Susa with a letter for Artabanus announcing his success.

On the following day he summoned to his presence the Athenian exiles who were serving with the Persian forces, and ordered them to go up into the Acropolis and offer sacrifice there according to Athenian usage; possibly some dream or other had suggested this course to him, or perhaps his conscience was uneasy for the burning of the temple. The Athenian exiles did as they were bidden. I mention these details for a particular reason: on the Acropolis there is a spot which is sacred to Erechtheus—the 'earth-born', and within it is an olive-tree and a spring of salt water. According to the local legend they were put there by Poseidon and Athene, when they contended for possession of the land, as tokens of their claims to it. Now it happened that this olive was destroyed by fire together with the rest of the sanctuary; nevertheless on the very next day, when the Athenians, who were ordered by the king to offer the sacrifice, went up to that sacred place, they saw that a new shoot eighteen inches long had sprung from the stump. They told the king of this.

Meanwhile at Salamis the effect of the news of what had happened to the Acropolis at Athens was so disturbing, that some of the naval commanders did not even wait for the subject under discussion to be decided, but hurried on board and hoisted sail for immediate flight.

Some, however, stayed; and by these a resolution was passed to fight in defence of the Isthmus.

* * *

Nevertheless everything that ingenuity could contrive had been done to prevent the Persian army from forcing the Isthmus. On the news of the destruction of Leonidas' force at Thermopylae not a moment was lost; and troops from the various towns in the Peloponnese hurried to the Isthmus, where they took up their position under Cleombrotus, the son of Anaxandrides and brother of Leonidas. Their first act was to break up and block the Scironian Way; then, in accordance with a decision taken in council, they began work on a wall across the Isthmus. As there were many thousands there and every man turned to, it was soon finished. Stones, bricks, timbers, sand-baskets—all were used in the building, and the labour went on continuously night and day.

* * *

The Greeks at the Isthmus, convinced that all they possessed was now at stake and not expecting any notable success at sea, continued to grapple with their task of fortification. The news of how they were employed nevertheless caused great concern at Salamis; for it brought home to everyone there not so much his own peril as the imminent threat to the Peloponnese. At first there was whispered criticism of the incredible folly of Eurybiades; then the smothered feeling broke out into open resentment, and another meeting was held. All the old ground was gone over again, one side urging that it was useless to stay and fight for a country which was already in enemy hands, and that the fleet should sail and risk an action in defence of the Peloponnese, while the Athenians, Aeginetans, and Megarians still maintained that they should stay and fight at Salamis.

At this point Themistocles, feeling that he would be outvoted by the Peloponnesians, slipped quietly away from the meeting and sent a man over in a boat to the Persian fleet, with instructions upon what to say when he got there. The man—Sicinnus—was one of Themistocles' slaves and used to attend upon his sons; some time afterwards, when the Thespians were admitting outsiders to citizenship, Themistocles established him at Thespia and made him a rich man. Following his instructions, then, Sicinnus made his way to the Persians and said: 'I am the bearer of a secret communication from the Athenian commander, who is a well-wisher to your king and hopes for a Persian victory. He has told me to report to you that the Greeks have no confidence in themselves and are planning to save their skins by a hasty withdrawal. Only prevent them from slipping through your fingers, and you have at this moment an opportunity of unparalleled success. They are at daggers drawn with each other, and will offer no opposition—on the contrary, you will see the pro-Persians amongst them fighting the rest.'

His message delivered, Sicinnus lost no time in getting away. The Persians believed what he had told them, and proceeded to put ashore a large force on the islet of Psyttaleia, between Salamis and the coast; then, about midnight, they moved one division of the fleet towards the western end of Salamis in order to encircle the enemy, while at the same time the ships off Ceos and Cynosura also advanced and blocked the whole channel as far as Munychia. The object of these movements was to prevent the escape of the Greek fleet from the narrow waters of Salamis, and there to take revenge upon it for the battles at Artemisium.

✿ ✿ ✿

Now I cannot deny that there is truth in prophecies, and I have no wish to discredit them when they are expressed in unambiguous language. Consider the following:

When they shall span the sea with ships from Cynosura
To the holy shore of Artemis of the golden sword,
Wild with hope at the ruin of shining Athens,
Then shall bright Justice quench Excess, the child of Pride,
Dreadful and furious, thinking to swallow up all things.
Bronze shall mingle with bronze, and Ares with blood
Incarnadine the sea; and all-seeing Zeus
And gracious Victory shall bring to Greece the day of freedom.

With that utterance of Bacis in mind, absolutely clear as it is, I do not venture to say anything against prophecies, nor will I listen to criticism from others.

The Greek commanders at Salamis were still at loggerheads. They did not yet know that the enemy ships had blocked their escape at both ends of the channel, but supposed them to occupy the same position as they had seen them in during the day. However, while the dispute was still at its height, Aristides came over in a boat from Aegina. This man, an Athenian and the son of Lysimachus, had been banished from Athens by popular vote, but the more I have learned of his character, the more I have come to believe that he was the best and most honourable man that Athens ever produced. Arrived at Salamis, Aristides went to where the conference was being held and, standing outside, called for Themistocles. Themistocles was no friend of his; indeed he was his most determined enemy; but Aristides was willing, in view of the magnitude of the danger which threatened them, to forget old quarrels in his desire to communicate with him. He was already aware of the anxiety of the Peloponnesian commanders to withdraw to the Isthmus; as soon, therefore, as Themistocles came out of the conference in answer to his call, he said: 'At this moment, more than ever before, you and I should be rivals; and the object of our rivalry should be to see which of us can do most good to our country. First, let me tell you that the Peloponnesians may talk as much or as little as they please about withdrawing from Salamis—it will make not the least difference. What I tell you, I have seen with my own eyes: they *cannot* now get out of here, however much the Corinthians or Eurybiades himself may wish to do so, because our fleet is surrounded. Go back to the conference, and tell them.'

'Good news and good advice,' Themistocles answered; 'what I most wanted has happened—and you bring me the evidence of your own eyes that it is true. It was I who was responsible for this move of the enemy; for as our men would not fight here of their own free will, it was necessary to make them, whether they wanted to do so or not. But take them the good news yourself; if I tell them, they will think I have invented it and will not believe me. Please, then, go in and make the report yourself. If they believe you, well and good; if they do not, it's no odds; for if we are surrounded, as you say we are, escape is no longer possible.' . . .

[The Persians are routed.]

Amongst the killed in this struggle was Ariabignes, the son of Darius and Xerxes' brother, and many other well-known men from Persia, Media, and the confederate nations. There were also Greek casualties, but not many; for most of the Greeks could swim, and those who lost their ships, provided they were not killed in the actual fighting, swam over to Salamis. Most of the enemy, on the other hand, being unable to swim, were drowned. The greatest destruction took place when the ships which had been first engaged turned tail; for those astern fell foul of them in their attempt to press forward and do some service for their king.

❖   ❖   ❖

Xerxes watched the course of the battle from the base of Mt. Aegaleos, across the strait from Salamis; whenever he saw one of his officers behaving with distinction, he would find out his name, and his secretaries wrote it down, together with his city and parentage.

When the Persian rout began and they were trying to get back to Phalerum, the Aeginetan squadron, which was waiting to catch them in the narrows, did memorable service. The enemy was in hopeless confusion; such ships as offered resistance or tried to escape were cut to pieces by the Athenians, while the Aeginetans caught and disabled those which attempted to get clear of the strait, so that any ship which escaped the one enemy promptly fell amongst the other. It happened at this stage that Themistocles, chasing an enemy vessel, ran close aboard the ship which was commanded by Polycritus, the son of Crius, the Aeginetan. Polycritus had just rammed a Sidonian, the very ship which captured the Aeginetan guard-vessel off Sciathus—the one, it will be remembered, which had Pytheas on board, the man the Persians kept with them out of admiration for his gallantry in refusing to surrender in spite of his appalling wounds. When the ship was taken with him and the Persian crew on board, he got safe home to Aegina. When Polycritus noticed the Athenian ship, and recognized the admiral's flag, he shouted to Themistocles and asked him in a tone of ironic reproach if he still thought that the people of Aegina were Persia's friends.

Such of the Persian ships as escaped destruction made their way back to Phalerum and brought up there under the protection of the army.

✿   ✿   ✿

Xerxes, when he realized the extent of the disaster, was afraid that the Greeks, either on their own initiative or at the suggestion of the Ionians, might sail to the Hellespont and break the bridges there. If this happened, he would be cut off in Europe and in danger of destruction. Accordingly, he laid his plans for escape; but at the same time, in order to conceal his purpose both from the Greeks and from his own troops, he began to construct a causeway across the water towards Salamis, lashing together a number of Phoenician merchantmen to serve at once for bridge and breakwater. He also made other preparations, as if he intended to fight again at sea. The sight of this activity made everybody confident that he was prepared to remain in Greece and carry on the war with all possible vigour; there was, however, one exception—Mardonius, who thoroughly understood how his master's mind worked and was in no way deceived. At the same time Xerxes dispatched a courier to Persia with the news of his defeat.

There is nothing in the world which travels faster than these Persian couriers. The whole idea is a Persian invention, and works like this: riders are stationed along the road, equal in number to the number of days the journey takes—a man and a horse for each day. Nothing stops these couriers from covering their allotted stage in the quickest possible time—neither snow, rain, heat, nor darkness. The first, at the end of his stage, passes the dispatch to the second, the second to the third, and so on along the line, as in the Greek torch-race which is held in honour of Hephaestus. The Persian word for this form of post is *angarium*.

Xerxes' first dispatch telling of the capture of Athens caused such rejoicing in Susa amongst the Persians who had not accompanied the expedition, that they strewed the roads with myrtle-boughs, burned incense, and gave themselves up to every sort of pleasure and merry-making; the second, however, coming on top of it, soon put a stop to all this, and such was the distress in the city that there was not a man who did not tear his clothes and weep and wail in unappeasable grief, laying the blame for the disaster upon Mardonius. Nor was it distress for the loss of the ships which caused these demonstrations; it was fear for the personal safety of the king. The demonstrations, moreover, continued without a break until Xerxes himself came home.

✿ ✿ ✿

GREEK TRAGEDY   Preface

According to contemporary newspaper headlines, a tragedy is any-thing from an automobile crash to the death of a president. To the classical Greeks, however, the word had a much more exact meaning. To them a tragedy was a serious play, written in beautiful and majestic language, which dramatized the sufferings of one of their legendary heroes. Greek tragedy always presented a great man in a moment of crisis and conflict that usually destroyed him. The prevailing mood of the play was dignified but not gloomy. Even more important, tragedy compensated for its scenes of grief and terror by revealing the mag-nificence of heroic men and women whom even the worst misfortunes could not strip of their humanity. Then as now, tragedy gave pleasure: a feeling of exultation[1] and reassurance about the worth and dignity of man.

Little is known for certain about the origin and early development of tragedy. In his *Poetics* Aristotle briefly mentions that it "originated with the authors of the Dithyramb" and "advanced by slow degrees" until "it found its natural form, and there it stopped." The brevity of Aristotle's reference probably indicates that even in the fourth century B.C. trage-dy's beginnings were shrouded in mystery. The Dithyramb of which Aristotle speaks was a choral song of wild and ecstatic nature performed in honor of the wine god, Dionysus. Deriving from Asia Minor, it was probably imported to Greece along with the cult of Dionysus, whose alcoholic gifts released his followers from the restraints of reason and convention. As a vegetation deity, Dionysus was worshiped as a manifestation of the life force that rejuvenates growing things in the spring. He was also conceived as a symbol of man's erotic impulses and emotional excess. He was, in short, an incarnation of uncontrollable instincts, a god of both joy and terror.

There are various theories about the precise connection between the Dionysian religion and the development of tragedy, but the almost complete lack of evidence makes it impossible to prove any of them. According to one widely-held hypothesis, tragedy evolved from a ritual depicting the miraculous birth, death, and rebirth of Dionysus, who was viewed as a personification of the cycle of seasons. The ritual theorists maintain that, to the primitive mind, winter's bleakness signified the death of the vegetation god. They argue that prehistoric cultists conse-quently performed an annual ritual that, by a process of sympathetic magic, was intended to bring about the god's resurrection and the return of spring. From this traditional ceremony, which contained improvised

---

[1]Besides presenting the image of indominitable humanity, tragedy also gave plea-sure by eliciting an emotional response which Aristotle described as *catharsis*. *Ca-tharsis* may be defined as a purgation of the feelings of pity and terror which one experiences upon witnessing the hero's unhappy fate. According to a common inter-pretation of Aristotle's metaphor, the pleasure of tragedy derives from its emotionally therapeutic nature. The spectator, purged or relieved of such disturbing emotions as fear and pity, undergoes an agreeable sensation of liberation and renewal.

songs by the leader of the Dithyramb, a formal religious drama gradually developed. To the end, tragedy retained a profoundly religious orientation. The great outdoor theatre in Athens was dedicated to Dionysus, whose priest was given the place of honor at all tragic performances.

The first theatrical presentations were highly musical, probably more like an opera or ballet than a spoken play. Whether the earliest texts were traditional or improvised, they were sung by a chorus of fifty young men, dressed in goat skins and (possibly) smeared with wine lees. The word tragedy may derive from the young men's goat-hair costumes[2] for the Greek *tragoidia* combines *tragos* (he-goat) with *oide* (song). The ancient *goat-song* became a recognizable art form about 535 B.C. when the Athenian ruler Pisistratus reorganized the annual spring festival of Dionysus, called the Great Dionysia. Pisistratus established a city-wide competition among writers to provide plays for the occasion. Each competing author was required to submit a trilogy (three serious plays on a single theme) and a ribald sex comedy known as the satyr play. Judges chosen by lot selected the three best trilogies for performance at the Great Dionysia. The prize-winning dramas were produced by the city itself, although a wealthy *choregus* or patron absorbed most of the expenses.

Thespis, who won the first Athenian competition, also made the first important change in the old tragic ritual. By introducing an "answerer" *(hypokrites)*, who delivered spoken lines in response to musical numbers sung by the chorus, Thespis became the "father of the drama." His invention of the actor made possible a dramatic conflict (*agon*) between the leader of the chorus and another character. For the first time events could be acted out onstage instead of being reported at second hand by a "messenger" who was part of the chorus.

Between Thespis' great innovation and the first extant tragedy by Aeschylus, the oldest of the three tragedians whose plays have survived into modern times, numerous authors contributed to the drama's artistic growth. Only fragments of their works remain. Pratinas, from the northern Peloponnese, is credited with inventing the satyr play, which provided a kind of comic relief to an audience perhaps emotionally exhausted from witnessing several hours of high tragedy. These hilariously obscene farces apparently absorbed the erotic elements that had been purged from Dionysian tragedy early in its history. Of the hundreds of satyr plays written, only one, Euripides' *Cyclops*, survives complete.

The most important tragedian before Aeschylus was Phrynichus of Athens, who won his first victory at the Great Dionysia about 510 B.C. He is credited with being the first to bring female characters onstage (although they were always played by men) and to write the first dramas based on contemporary history. The most famous of these was *The Capture of Miletus*, which depicted in graphic terms the destruction of

---

[2]Notorious for their lust, goats and satyrs (half-men, half-goats) were the traditional companions of Dionysus.

Athens' sister-city by the Persians (494 B.C.). According to Herodotus "the audience in the theatre burst into tears, and the author was fined a thousand drachma for reminding them of a disaster which touched them so closely. A law was subsequently passed forbidding anybody ever to put the play on the stage again" (VI, 21). Phrynichus may also have been the first to write plays on other than Dionysian legends. In spite of the Athenian love of novelty, however, the audiences are said to have complained that the new dramas "had nothing to do with Dionysus." Nonetheless, by the early decades of the fifth century B.C. stories of Dionysus had been superseded by dramas featuring other gods, heroes, and ancient kings, such as Agamemnon and Oedipus. In fact, of the thirty-two serious plays that survive from classical Greece, only one, *The Bacchae* of Euripides, presents the wine god as a major character. In all the others Dionysus is replaced by mortal leaders or noblemen whose very human misfortunes link them with the private sorrows of individual members of the audience.

The enormous popularity of the Homeric epics was another factor that contributed to the change in tragedy's subject matter. Aeschylus, whom Gilbert Murray regards as the actual founder of the tragic drama, boasted that his plays were really "slices from the great banquet of Homer." Homer's probable influence on the theatre becomes clear when one remembers that dramatic recitations of Homeric poems were a prominent feature of the Panathenaea, a companion festival to the Great Dionysia. At about the same time that he established the tragic competition, Pisistratus reorganized the Panathenaea to include public readings of the *Iliad* and *Odyssey*. Not only are such oral recitations akin to the dramatic monologue, but they serve to illustrate Homer's essentially dramatic technique. Homer does not simply narrate events, he reproduces them, complete with action and conversation, as though they were happening before one's eyes. With his emphasis on the personality and psychological motivation of his heroes, his central theme of conflict between protagonist (Achilles) and antagonist (Agamemnon), and his extensive use of dialogue, Homer creates scenes in the *Iliad* that could be lifted out of their epic context and acted in the theatre with very little change. Character, conflict, and dialogue are indispensable to tragedy, and Homer's epics provide them all. Even more important, he created in Achilles the concept of the tragic hero, a man whose pride in his own greatness contains the seeds of his destruction. Of such paradoxes the tragic vision is born, and the Athenian dramatists were not slow to capitalize on Homeric models. One of Aeschylus' lost plays, *The Myrmidons*, celebrated the friendship of Achilles and Patroclus; his finest extant drama, the *Agamemnon*, recounts the tragic homecoming of another Homeric leader.

The oldest of the three master tragedians who dominated the Athenian theatre during the fifth century, Aeschylus (525–456 B.C.) was soldier and religious thinker as well as playwright. Born in Eleusis, home of the Mysteries of Demeter, Aeschylus twice defended his country against the

Persian invaders—at Marathon, where he was wounded and lost a brother, and at Salamis, the sea battle which he vividly described in *The Persians*. He entered the drama competitions about 500 B.C., but did not win a first prize until fifteen years later. Of the ninety plays attributed to him, only seven have been preserved. The earliest of these, *The Persians* (472 B.C.), is a wooden, highly stylized piece that is more like an oratorio than a play. Told entirely from the enemy viewpoint, it is essentially a beautifully orchestrated lament (*threnos*) for Xerxes, the Persian emperor who had proudly invaded Greece only to be defeated at the Battle of Salamis. Like Aeschylus' later work, *The Persians* illustrates one of the author's favorite themes: the tragic fall (*nemesis*) of a hero whose insolence (*hubris*)[3] and ambition the gods check with disaster. In this and the later *Suppliants* (c. 468 B.C.), the chorus still has the main role; choral lyrics comprise most of the text. But in even such relatively primitive works Aeschylus made changes that enormously influenced the development of tragedy. To heighten dramatic conflict he introduced a second actor and, in later plays, considerably reduced the importance and size of the chorus. Although tradition forced him to retain the choral songs and dances, which he had inherited from the Dionysian rites, Aeschylus made them more strictly relevant to the plot. In the *Prometheus Bound* and the *Agamemnon*, the chorus serves a double function of helping to convey the author's theme through its comments on the action and acting as a link between the characters onstage and the audience. Even when it presents only commonplace ideas or a cautious point of view—intended to contrast with the extremes of passion expressed by the tragic actors—the chorus significantly determines the spectators' emotional reactions. To illustrate its role as mediator, the chorus did not appear on the main stage, but stood instead in the circular *orchestra* between the actors and the audience.

Under Aeschylus Greek tragedy achieved its characteristic form and structure. It normally began with a Prologue (*prologus*), the part before the entrance of the chorus. In monologue (as in the *Agamemnon*) or dialogue (as in the *Prometheus Bound*), this opening section introduced the subject, the situation, and whatever background material was necessary to clarify the ensuing action. Next came the *parados*, the song accompanying the chorus' entrance, for which Aeschylus often wrote some of his most beautiful lyrics. Since there was no curtain to raise or lower, the "acts" of the play were really episodes (*epeisodia*), scenes

---

[3]*Hubris* is excessive pride or blind overconfidence that provokes the gods and brings their vengeance upon the offender. It is the most common form of what Aristotle calls *hamartia*, a quality in the otherwise noble character of the tragic hero which makes him vulnerable to disaster. This term, which derives from "missing the mark" in archery, has been variously translated as "fatal error," "flaw," and even "sin." Aristotle, however, regards it rather straightforwardly as an error in judgment, an intellectual miscalculation that plunges the hero into grief. Ironically, the *hamartia* of certain tragic heroes, such as Prometheus, seems to be an excess of virtue which brings an attack from the evil and irrational elements in the universe.

during which the plot unfolded. The episodes usually included an *agon* or conflict between the hero and some other character, such as the debate between Agamemnon and Clytemnestra when she bends the king to her will. The later episodes normally culminate in a sudden reversal (*peripeteia*), which drastically changes the life of the hero. It normally involves a fall from good to evil fortune, such as the *peripeteia* that transforms Agamemnon from a conquering hero into a murder victim. The tragic hero's reversal of fortunes often includes a recognition (*anagnorisis*) of his changed status or of a newly-discovered relationship to the other characters. The recognition may be as literal as finding a lock of hair that identifies a long-lost relative, or it may be as profound as Oedipus' unwilling awareness that he cannot escape his fate. By far the most horrifying *anagnorisis* in Greek tragedy occurs in *The Bacchae*, when Agave gradually realizes that she holds in her hands the severed head of her son.

The *stasima,* or choral songs which separate the episodes, are frequently divided into a *strophe, antistrophe,* and *epode.* These divisions are thought to refer to the position and movement of the chorus, which apparently sang the *strophe* while moving in one direction, reversed its direction for the *antistrophe* and stood still during the *epode.* After the last *stasimon,* came the *exodus,* or final scene in which the complications of the plot were resolved. If the plot had become too complex to unravel through human means, the playwright often introduced a *deus ex machina* (god from the machine) who was lowered onstage by a crane-like device to solve all problems by a show of divine authority. The chariot of the sun which rescues Medea and the appearance of Heracles at the end of the *Philoctetes* are two examples of such mechanical intervention. Euripides frequently added an Epilogue, usually spoken by a god, to point out the moral of the tragedy and to give his drama a cosmic significance.

Aeschylus' supremacy in the theatre was seriously challenged for the first time in 468 B.C., when the youthful Sophocles (c. 496–406) defeated the older poet at the Great Dionysia. Although Aeschylus recovered to win first prize in 458 for his *Oresteia,* Sophocles soon became the most popular tragedian of the fifth century. He was sixteen years old at the time of Salamis and, because of his high birth and personal beauty, was chosen to lead the victory celebration that followed the battle. Good fortune pursued him all his life: he lived through the high tide of the Periclean Golden Age, to which he significantly contributed, and he died, old and honored, just two years before his beloved city fell to Spartan conquerors. Although not a soldier of Aeschylean stature, he nonetheless twice served the state as general. The sensational popularity of his *Antigone* (c. 441) may account for his election to that high office. He wrote about 123 plays, including satyrical farces, and won first prize at least eighteen or twenty times, which gave him as many victories as Aeschylus and Euripides combined.

According to Aristotle, Sophocles made several important innovations which extended the scope of the drama. Besides inventing or extensively developing the use of scene painting, he increased the number of actors to three, fixed the size of the chorus at fifteen, and was the first to present each play as an independent unit rather than as part of a connected series. By introducing a third actor, Sophocles made possible a three-way conflict, a dramatic device he exploits to the full in his *Philoctetes*. Basing each drama on a different tragic situation gave the artist much greater freedom to explore a variety of issues.

Although he upheld the conventional morality and religion, Sophocles placed greater emphasis on the human predicament than on the divine will. Instead of creating abstract figures who act out the historical purpose of Zeus as Aeschylus had done, he usually explained events as the outgrowth of human personality. Even Oedipus' fate is largely determined by his own impulsive nature. In general, the Sophoclean hero, in spite of the fatal flaw (*hamartia*) that causes his downfall, is noble and motivated by lofty ideals. Perhaps Sophocles had this idealization in mind when he observed that he portrayed men as they ought to be, whereas Euripides depicted them as they are. The fact that he did not intend his remark as a compliment to his younger rival indicates that Sophocles viewed the theatre as a place where the highest moral examples were to be seen and imitated.

Sophocles' genius seemed to grow with his years; he wrote two of his finest plays at about the age of 90. The *Philoctetes*, dealing with the righteous anger of an ill-treated old man, was produced in 409 B.C. He completed his last play, the bittersweet *Oedipus at Colonus*, which describes the blinded, beggared Oedipus during his last hours on earth, shortly before his death in 406 B.C. The play was produced posthumously about five years later, earning the poet yet another major award. Dignity, artistic control, and a serene conviction that beyond the chaos of human life there exists an invisible order of justice characterize the Sophoclean drama. Aristotle recognized Sophocles as the master of dramatic form and based his own definition of the perfect tragedy on the Sophoclean model.

Popular legend held that on the day of Salamis when Aeschylus fought and the handsome Sophocles danced in celebration (480 B.C.), Euripides was born. As with most suspiciously neat convergences of date, however, Euripides' birth date was probably contrived to fit the occasion. The youngest of the three major tragedians had probably entered the world at least five years before the Battle of Salamis. He supposedly wrote his first tragedy at eighteen, but did not have a work accepted for performance until he was about thirty (455 B.C.). He obtained only a third prize at his debut, a lack of official recognition that characterized the whole of his long career. Although he composed nearly 100 tragedies and satyr plays, he received a first prize only four times. His influence in literature and philosophy, however, was much more extensive than this record would indicate. It was said that Euripides' were the only dramas that Socrates would consent to sit through.

Unlike the popular and gregarious Sophocles, Euripides lived most of his mature years in retirement. Ensconced in an elaborately equipped cave on the island of Salamis, he devoted his time to thinking, writing, and collecting the first large private library in the ancient world. The reason for Euripides' comparative unpopularity is not difficult to find. In an age when art and literature idealized human form and conduct, Euripides' habit of debunking all kinds of orthodox beliefs was repugnant. His contemporaries particularly criticized his "too-realistic" treatment of women and his undisguised religious scepticism. It is now difficult to understand the charge of misogyny leveled against Euripides, who created some of the most fascinating and sympathetic portraits of the feminine psyche in all drama. Public displeasure with his extremely critical attitude toward the old creeds is more comprehensible. Educated in the same philosophical school that produced Anaxagoras and Socrates, Euripides was an intellectual rebel whose mind was too keen to accept traditional beliefs at face value. His favorite dramatic device was to take a widely-held misconception about the gods, human nature, or the ancient legends and scrutinize it in the light of pure analytical reason. The results were often disastrous for the old myths and offensive to those who believed in them.

Considering his unorthodox opinions, it is not surprising that at the close of his career Euripides went into voluntary exile in Macedonia. Gossip reported that the poet was torn in pieces by Macedonian hunting dogs, but that version of his death may represent only the wishful thinking of his enemies. In any case, Euripides' genius was belatedly recognized when a final tetralogy, which included *The Bacchae*, was produced posthumously in 405 B.C. and won the author his fifth award.

It was not until the more cosmopolitan and cynical Hellenistic period that Euripides fully came into his own. In the chaotic centuries following Alexander's conquests, Euripidean naturalism and disillusionment seemed increasingly congenial. While the plays of Aeschylus and Sophocles were revived less and less frequently, Euripides' works held the stage well into Roman times. This most iconoclastic of playwrights also received the dubious honor of having his writing serve as a textbook for Greek and Roman schoolchildren. His popularity with Alexandrine librarians, who made numerous copies of his plays for teaching purposes, probably accounts for the fact that more of his dramas (nineteen in all) have been preserved than those of Aeschylus and Sophocles put together.

By 406 B.C., two years before Sparta's victory over Athens, both Sophocles and Euripides were dead. Although numerous tragedies continued to be written during the fourth century, no writer comparable to any of the great trio appeared. No more than fragments of these later works remain. What killed tragedy, which had been both the highest and most prolific form of literary art during the Golden Age? Was it the loss of public morale that followed the military collapse of Athens? Was it the increasingly sceptical and scientific spirit of philosophy that dominated the fourth century? Or was it simply the absence of talent that could transform the evil and suffering of human experience into exhilerating poetry?

The fall of tragedy was probably occasioned by a multitude of forces, not the least of which was a steadily declining faith in the old religions and the possibility of human heroism. Exhausted and demoralized by the Peloponnesian War, Greece seems to have lost the conviction that man is intrinsically or at least potentially heroic. Without such belief—that greatness of soul does exist and that the tragic hero is worthy of representing mankind at its best—the hero's defeat and death are robbed of dignity and purpose. Without nobility, tragedy loses its meaning.

Moreover, the new philosophic arguments that the soul was immortal transferred the center of interest from acts of public heroism to themes of personal salvation. In Platonism the troubles of earth were exchanged for promises of joy in Elysium. Among the best minds the tendency was to withdraw from the world, where the tragic vision was to be earned, to a private cultivation of one's virtue. To this shift in emphasis and the consequent failure of the tragic impulse, Euripides, the solitary thinker, was a major contributor. To agree with Nietzsche that Euripides emasculated the drama by overintellectualizing it and that Plato administered the death blow by denying its spiritual relevance would be neither fair nor accurate. Yet the fact that Greek tragedy, as we know it, died with Euripides' last play, gives a certain ironic significance to Aristotle's famous dictum that Euripides was "the most tragic of the poets."

AGAMEMNON   Preface

THE AGAMEMNON IS THE FIRST PLAY IN THE ONLY SURVIVING GREEK TRILogy, the *Oresteia*.[1] Produced at Athens in 458 B.C., just two years before Aeschylus' death, it represents the dramatist's final statement on the problems of evil, inherited guilt, and spiritual redemption that had preoccupied him during his entire creative life. Like nearly all Greek tragedy, the *Agamemnon* dramatizes an ancient legend concerning a famous royal dynasty, in this case the house of Atreus, king of Mycenae. The events described in Aeschylus' tragedy had occurred at least six or

---

[1]The *Oresteia*, so named because Agamemnon's son, Orestes, is the hero of the last two plays in the trilogy, the *Libation-Bearers* and *The Eumenides*.

seven hundred years before the play was written. Clytemnestra's murder of Agamemnon was in fact known to Homer, who referred to the crime in the *Odyssey*.

The theme of the *Agamemnon*, typical of Aeschylus' religious interests, is the will of Zeus that expresses itself through *nemesis*, the retributive justice that strikes down those who sin against divine law. The guilt that dooms Agamemnon is partly inherited and partly of his own making. As the son of Atreus, he was born under the family curse which the gods had placed on his ancestors. The evil deeds which blighted Agamemnon's family had increased with each succeeding generation. Thyestes had committed adultery with the wife of Atreus, his brother. In return Atreus murdered Thyestes' young children, and pretending a reconciliation, served their flesh to him at a banquet. The family evil was compounded when Helen, the wife of Agamemnon's brother, Menelaus, eloped with Paris. The horrors of the Trojan war that followed involved in some way all of Atreus' living descendants.

To ensure fair sailing winds to Troy, Agamemnon ruthlessly sacrificed his daughter Iphigenia, the favorite child of his wife Clytemnestra. Clytemnestra never forgave her husband for this act. During the long years the Greeks were at Troy, she took as her lover Agamemnon's worst enemy, Aegisthus, the only surviving son of Thyestes. Together the adulterous couple plotted the murder of Agamemnon, who had since added to his sins by despoiling the Trojan princess, Cassandra, who had dedicated her viginity to Apollo. Agamemnon's foolishness in bringing Cassandra, now his mistress, home to Mycenae further outrages Clytemnestra.

The catalogue of ancient and recent crimes is a prelude to the action of the tragedy, which opens just as news of Troy's fall reaches Mycenae. Eager to be prepared for her husband's homecoming, Clytemnestra had devised an elaborate system of watchmen and flares that would carry the message of Agamemnon's return from Asia Minor to Greece. The queen is thus aware of events long before the chorus, which is composed of "deserted" men too old to fight at Troy. These aged citizens are deeply suspicious of Clytemnestra, both for her treacherous affair with Aegisthus and for her masculine initiative and intelligence, which they regard as unnatural in a woman. Although their premonitions of disaster help create the dramatic tension that culminates in Agamemnon's murder, the old men are too feeble to prevent the catastrophe. Reduced to the status of mere onlookers powerless to intervene in the action, the chorus nonetheless serves an indispensable thematic function. The chorus not only acts as a mediating link between the tragic characters and the audience, but also speculates upon the meaning of events. In some of the most majestic poetry ever written, the chorus sings of the suffering that brings wisdom and of the inescapable will of Zeus, that, when least expected, punishes all evil-doers. The odes also foreshadow the future vengeance of Agamemnon's son Orestes and the lifting of the curse from the descendants of Atreus.

The choral lyrics, which dominate the first half of the play, largely determine the rhythm of the action. The *parados* and early odes are spacious, contemplative, almost leisurely, but as the plot nears its climax the rhythm quickens, the songs between episodes become increasingly brief, the focus shifts from the ruminations of the chorus to the conflict between Agamemnon and Clytemnestra. The *agon* is magnificently conceived as a battle of wills between husband and wife. Flushed with victory and surrounded by the rich spoils of war, Agamemnon returns as the conquering hero, triumphantly alive when so many others had died. He remains in his chariot while Clytemnestra, standing regally on the palace steps, delivers her long speech of welcome. Then, in rapid one-line exchanges, Clytemnestra subdues Agamemnon to her will. In spite of his other crimes, which she thinks sufficient to condemn him, Clytemnestra wants her husband to commit a last public act of *hubris*. Flattering his vanity, taunting his manhood, she persuades him, against his better judgment, to walk to the palace on a luxurious carpet dyed blood red. In accepting this homage, Agamemnon not only reveals the characteristic arrogance that blinds him to the consequences of his sins, but also takes to himself an honor due only the gods. He thereby dooms himself to just punishment. Once inside the palace, his *hubris* is swiftly met with *nemesis* and he is literally bathed in the blood which the carpet had symbolized.

In this scene, Aeschylus makes striking use of dramatic irony. Clytemnestra's welcoming words are double-edged. Too proud to lie, she is truly glad to see her husband safely home, but only because she herself desires the pleasure of killing him. Her numerous references to the gods and "Justice" are completely sincere. She truly believes herself to be the instrument of divine vengeance, the predestined executioner of Iphigenia's murderer. But Clytemnestra's sense of justice does not, ironically, go far enough. Her eyes are fixed so exclusively on evils of the past that she cannot see her present deed as deserving of future retribution. The audience, however, knows that the gods will require that Clytemnestra's blood be shed to pay for the death of Agamemnon. The "home unhoped-for"—the grave—which she prepared for Agamemnon, is destined to receive her as well.

Clytemnestra's punishment occurs in the second play of the *Oresteia*, *The Libation-Bearers*.[2] Twenty years after his father's murder, the exiled Orestes returns to Mycenae, where, with the encouragement of his sister Electra, he kills Aegisthus and Clytemnestra. But Orestes' matricide evokes the primordial demons of blood vengeance, the hideous Eumenides, who torment and persecute the young prince. The final play in the series, *The Eumenides,* has a happy ending and completes Aeschylus' theme. After expiating his crime by various sufferings, Orestes

---

[2]An interesting but dramatically weak play; neither it nor *The Eumenides* compares artistically to the *Agamemnon*.

receives sanctuary in Athens, where Athene and Apollo organize the first murder trial in history. Apollo testifies that he had commanded Orestes to murder his mother because avenging a father's death is, in the eyes of the Olympian gods, a higher duty than sparing a mother's life. When the Athenian jury splits its votes, Athene, as the voice of wisdom, intervenes to acquit Orestes. In Aeschylus' view, establishing Orestes' innocence represents a victory of civilization over the primitive savagery of blood vengeance. The age-old curse on the house of Atreus ends in reconciliation. The moral order violated by Thyestes and Atreus is at last restored according to the will of Zeus.

AGAMEMNON

Characters   WATCHMAN
                       CHORUS OF OLD MEN
                       CLYTEMNESTRA
                       HERALD
                       AGAMEMNON
                       CASSANDRA
                       AEGISTHUS
                       CAPTAIN OF THE GUARD

The scene is the entrance to the palace of the Atreidae. Before the doors stand shrines of the gods.
[A WATCHMAN *is posted on the roof.*]

WATCHMAN
    I've prayed God to release me from sentry duty
    All through this long year's vigil, like a dog
    Couched on the roof of Atreus, where I study
    Night after night the pageantry of this vast
    Concourse of stars, and moving among them like
    Noblemen the constellations that bring
    Summer and winter as they rise and fall.
    And I am still watching for the beacon signal
    All set to flash over the sea the radiant

Reprinted from *Aeschylus: The Laurel Classical Drama,* edited, with an Introduction, by Robert W. Corrigan. Translated by George Thomson. Copyright © 1965 by Dell Publishing Co., Inc. Used by permission of the publisher. Notes are those of the present editor.

News of the fall of Troy. So confident
Is a woman's spirit,[1] whose purpose is a man's.
Every night, as I turn in to my stony bed,
Quilted with dew, not visited by dreams,
Not mine—no sleep, fear stands at my pillow
Keeping tired eyes from closing once too often;
And whenever I start to sing or hum a tune,
Mixing from music an antidote to sleep,
It always turns to mourning for the royal house,
Which is not in such good shape as it used to be
But now at last may the good news in a flash
Scatter the darkness and deliver us! [*The beacon flashes.*]
O light of joy, whose gleam turns night to day,
O radiant signal for innumerable
Dances of victory! Ho there! I call the queen,
Agamemnon's wife, to raise with all the women
Alleluias of thanksgiving through the palace
Saluting the good news, if it is true
That Troy has fallen, as this blaze portends;
Yes, and I'll dance an overture myself.
My master's dice have fallen out well, and I
Shall score three sixes for this nightwatching. [*A pause.*]
Well, come what will, may it soon be mine to grasp
In this right hand my master's, home again!
    [*Another pause.*]
The rest is secret. A heavy ox has trodden
Across my tongue. These walls would have tales to tell
If they had mouths. I speak only to those
Who are in the know, to others—I know nothing.
[*The* WATCHMAN *goes into the palace. Women's cries are heard. Enter* CHROUS OF OLD MEN.]

CHORUS

    It is ten years since those armed prosecutors of Justice, Menelaus and Agamemnon, twin-sceptred in God-given sovranty, embarked in the thousand ships crying war, like eagles with long wings beating the air over a robbed mountain nest, wheeling and screaming for their lost children. Yet above them some god, maybe Apollo or Zeus, overhears the sky-dweller's cry and sends after the robber a Fury. [CLYTEMNESTRA *comes out of the palace and unseen by the elders places offerings before the shrines.*] Just so the two kings were sent by the greater king, Zeus, for the sake of a promiscuous[2] woman to fight Paris, Greek and Trojan locked fast together in the dusty betrothals of battle. And however it

---

[1] *A woman's spirit*—that of Queen Clytemnestra, who has ordered the watch.
[2] *A promiscuous woman*—Helen, wife of Menelaus.

stands with them now, the end is unalterable; no flesh, no wine can appease God's fixed indignation.

As for us, with all the able-bodied men enlisted and gone, we are left here leaning our strength on a staff, for, just as in infancy, when the marrow is still unformed, the War-god is not at his post, so it is in extreme old age, as the leaves fall fast, we walk on three feet, like dreams in the daylight. [*They see* CLYTEMNESTRA.]

O Queen, what news? what message sets light to the altars? All over the town the shrines are ablaze with unguents drawn from the royal stores and the flames shoot up into the night sky. Speak, let us hear all that may be made public, so healing the anxieties that have gathered thick in our hearts; let the gleam of good news scatter them! [CLYTEMNESTRA *goes out to tend the other altars of the city.*]

Strength have I still to recall that sign which greeted
    the two kings
Taking the road, for the prowess of song is not yet spent.
I sing of two kings united in sovranty, leading
Armies to battle, who saw two eagles
Beside the palace
Wheel into sight, one black, and the other was
    white-tailed,
Tearing a hare with her unborn litter.
Ailinon cry, but let good conquer!

Shrewdly the priest took note and compared each
    eagle with each king,
Then spoke out and prefigured the future in
    these words:
"In time the Greek arms shall demolish the fortress
    of Priam;
Only let no jealous God, as they fasten
On Troy the slave's yoke,
Strike them in anger; for Artemis loathes the rapacious
Beagles of Zeus that have slaughtered the frail hare.
Ailinon cry, but let good conquer!
O Goddess, gentle to the tender whelp of fierce lions
As to all young life of the wild,
So now fulfil what is good in the omen and mend
    what is faulty.
And I appeal unto the Lord Apollo,
Let not the north wind hold the fleet storm-bound,
Driving them on to repay that feast with another,
Inborn builder of strife, feud that fears no man, it
    is still there,

Treachery keeping the house, it remembers, revenges,
    a child's death!"[3]
Such, as the kings left home, was the seer's revelation.
Ailinon cry, but let good conquer!

Zeus, whoe'er he be, if so it best
Please his ear to be addressed,
So shall he be named by me.
All things have I measured, yet
None have found save him alone,
Zeus, if a man from a heart heavy-laden
Seek to cast his cares aside.

Long since lived a ruler of the world,
Puffed with martial pride, of whom
None shall tell, his day is done;
Also, he who followed him
Met his master and is gone.
Zeus the victorious, gladly acclaim him;
Perfect wisdom shall be yours;

Zeus, who laid it down that man
Must in sorrow learn and through
Pain to wisdom find his way.
When deep slumber falls, remembered wrongs
Chafe the bruised heart with fresh pangs, and no
Welcome wisdom meets within.
Harsh the grace dispensed by powers immortal,
Pilots of the human soul.

Even so the elder prince,
Marshal of the thousand ships,
Rather than distrust a priest,
Torn with doubt to see his men
Harbor-locked, hunger-pinched, hard-oppressed,
Strained beyond endurance, still
Watching, waiting, where the never-tiring
Tides of Aulis[4] ebb and flow:

And still the storm blew from mountains far north,
With moorings windswept and hungry crews pent
In rotting hulks,
With tackling all torn and seeping timbers,
Till Time's slow-paced, enforced inaction

---

[3]*A child's death*—the sacrificial murder of Iphigenia by her father Agamemnon.
[4]*Aulis*—the seaport where the Greek fleet assembled before sailing to Troy. Iphigenia was sacrificed there.

Had all but stripped bare the bloom of Greek manhood.
And then was found but one
Cure to allay the tempest—never a blast so bitter—
Shrieked in a loud voice by the priest, "Artemis!"
    striking the Atreidae with dismay, each with
    his staff smiting the ground and weeping.

And then the king spoke, the elder, saying:
"The choice is hard—hard to disobey him,
And harder still
To kill my own child, my palace jewel,
With unclean hands before the altar
Myself, her own father, spill a maid's pure blood.
I have no choice but wrong.[5]
How shall I fail my thousand ships and betray
    my comrades?
So shall the storm cease, and the men eager for war
    clamor for that virginal blood righteously! So
    pray for a happy outcome!"

And when he bowed down beneath the harness
Of cruel coercion, his spirt veering
With sudden sacrilegious change,
He gave his whole mind to evil counsel.
For man is made bold with base-contriving
Impetuous madness, first cause of much grief.
And so then he slew his own child
For a war to win a woman
And to speed the storm-bound fleet from the
    shore to battle.

She cried aloud "Father!", yet they heard not;
A girl in first flower, yet they cared not,
The lords who gave the word for war.
Her father prayed, then he bade his vassals
To seize her where swathed in folds of saffron
She lay, and lift her up like a yearling
With bold heart above the altar,
And her lovely lips to bridle
That they might not cry out, cursing the House
    of Atreus,

With gags, her voice sealed with brute force
    and crushed.

---

[5] *I have no choice but wrong*—This is the attitude that kept alive the curse on the house of Atreus.

And then she let fall her cloak
And cast at each face a glance that dumbly craved
    compassion;
And like a picture she would but could not greet
Her father's guests, who at home
Had often sat when the meal was over,
The cups replenished, with all hearts enraptured
To hear her sing grace with clear unsullied voice for
    her loving father.

The end was unseen and unspeakable.
The task of priestcraft was done.
For Justice first chastens, then she presses home
    her lesson.
The morrow must come, its grief will soon be here,
So let us not weep today.
It shall be made known as clear as daybreak.
And so may all this at last end in good news,
For which the queen prays, the next of kin and stay
    of the land of Argos.[8] [CLYTEMNESTRA *appears*
    at the door of the palace.]
Our humble saluations to the queen!
Hers is our homage, while our master's throne
Stands empty. We are still longing to hear
The meaning of your sacrifice. Is it good news?

CLYTEMNESTRA
Good news! With good news may the morning rise
Out of the night—good news beyond all hope!
My news is this: The Greeks have taken Troy.

CHROUS
What? No, it cannot be true! I cannot grasp it.

CLYTEMNESTRA
The Greeks hold Troy—is not that plain enough?

CHORUS
Joy steals upon me and fills my eyes with tears.

CLYTEMNESTRA
Indeed, your looks betray your loyalty.

CHORUS
What is the proof? Have you any evidence?

---

[8]*Argos*—territory in the north-east Peloponnese of which Agamemnon's capital, Mycenae, was the political center. Its inhabitants were called Argives. The city of Argos was not founded until post-Mycenaean times.

CLYTEMNESTRA
Of course I have, or else the Gods have cheated me.

CHORUS
You have given ear to some beguiling dream.

CLYTEMNESTRA
I would not come screaming fancies out of my sleep.

CHORUS
Rumors have wings—on these your heart has fed.

CLYTEMNESTRA
You mock my intelligence as though I were a girl.

CHORUS
When was it? How long is it since the city fell?

CLYTEMNESTRA
In the night that gave birth to this dawning day.

CHORUS
What messenger could bring the news so fast?

CLYTEMNESTRA
The God of Fire, who from Ida sent forth light
And beacon by beacon passed the flame to me.
From the peak of Ida first to the cliff of Hermes
On Lemnos, and from there a third great lamp
Was flashed to Athos, the pinnacle of Zeus;
Up, up it soared, luring the dancing fish
To break surface in rapture at the light;
A golden courier, like the sun, it sped
Post-haste its message to Macistus, thence
Across Euripus, till the flaming sign
Was marked by the watchers on Messapium,
And thence with strength renewed from piles of heath
Like moonrise over the valley of Asopus,
Relayed in glory to Cithaeron's heights,
And still flashed on, not slow the sentinels,
Leaping across the lake from peak to peak,
It passed the word to burn and burn, and flung
A comet to the promontory that stands
Over the Gulf of Saron, there it swooped
Down to the Spider's Crag above the city,
Then found its mark on the roof of this house of Atreus,
That beacon fathered by Ida's far-off fires.
Such were the stages of our torch relay,

And the last to run is the first to reach the goal.
That is my evidence, the testimony which
My lord has signaled to me out of Troy.

CHORUS

Lady, there will be time later to thank the Gods.
Now I ask only to listen: speak on and on.

CLYTEMNESTRA

Today the Greeks have occupied Troy.
I seem to hear there a very strange street-music.
Pour oil and vinegar into one cup, you will see
They do not make friends. So there two tunes are heard.
Slaves now, the Trojans, brothers and aged fathers,
Prostrate, sing for their dearest the last dirge.
The others, tired out and famished after the
       night's looting,
Grab what meal chance provides, lodgers now
In Trojan houses, sheltered from the night frosts,
From the damp dews delivered, free to sleep
Off guard, off duty, a blissful night's repose.
Therefore, provided that they show due respect
To the altars of the plundered town and are not
Tempted to lay coarse hands on sanctities,
Remembering that the last lap—the voyage home—
Lies still ahead of them, then, if they should return
Guiltless before God, the curses of the bereaved
Might be placated—barring accidents.
That is my announcement—a message from my master.
May all end well, and may I reap the fruit of it!

CHORUS

Lady, you have spoken with a wise man's judgment.
Now it is time to address the gods once more
After this happy outcome of our cares.

Thanks be to Zeus and to gracious Night, housekeeper of heaven's
embroidery, who has cast over the towers of Troy a net so fine as to
leave no escape for old or young, all caught in the snare! All praise to
Zeus, who with a shaft from his outstretched bow has at last brought
down the transgressor!

"By Zeus struck down!" The truth is all clear
With each step plainly marked. He said, Be
It so, and so it was. A man denied once
That heaven pays heed to those who trample
Beneath the feet holy sanctities. He lied wickedly;

For God's wrath soon or late destroys all sinners[6] filled
With pride, puffed up with vain presumption,
And great men's houses stocked with silver
And gold beyond measure. Far best to live
Free of want, without grief, rich in the gift of wisdom.
Glutted with gold, the sinner kicks
Justice out of his sight, yet
She sees *him* and remembers.

As sweet temptation lures him onwards
With childlike smile into the death-trap,
He cannot help himself. His curse is lit up
Against the darkness, a bright baleful light.
And just as false bronze in battle hammered turns
    black and shows
Its true worth, so the sinner time-tried stands condemned.
His hopes take wing, and still he gives chase, with
    foul crimes branding all his people.
He cries to deaf heaven, none hear his prayers.
Justice drags him down to hell as he calls for succor.
Such was the sinner Paris, who
Rendered thanks to a gracious
Host by stealing a woman.[7]

She left behind her the ports all astir
With throngs of men under arms filing onto shipboard;
She took to Troy in lieu of dowry death.
A light foot passed through the gates and fled,
And then a cry of lamentation rose.
The seers, the king's prophets, muttered darkly:
"Bewail the king's house that now is desolate,
Bewail the bed marked with print of love that fled!"
Behold, in silence, without praise, without reproach,
They sit upon the ground and weep.
Beyond the wave lies their love;
Here a ghost seems to rule the palace!
Shapely the grace of statues,
Yet they can bring no comfort,
Eyeless, lifeless and loveless.

Delusive dream shapes that float through the night
Beguile him, bringing delight sweet but unsubstantial;
For, while the eye beholds the heart's desire,

---

[6]*God's wrath . . . destroys all sinners*—The punishment of ancient sin is a major theme of the *Oresteia*.
[7]*A woman*—Helen.

The arms clasp empty air, and then
The fleeting vision fades and glides away
On silent wing down the paths of slumber.
The royal hearth is chilled with sorrows such as these,
And more; in each house from end to end of Greece
That sent its dearest to wage war in foreign lands
The stout heart is called to steel itself
In mute endurance against
Blows that strike deep into the heart's core:
Those that they sent from home they
Knew, but now they receive back
Only a heap of ashes.

The God of War holds the twin scales of strife,
Heartless gold-changer trafficking in men,
Consigning homeward from Troy a jar of dust
    fire-refined,
Making up the weight with grief,
Shapely vessels laden each
With the ashes of their kin.
They mourn and praise them saying, "He
Was practiced well in sword and spear,
And he, who fell so gallantly—
All to avenge another man's wife":
It is muttered in a whisper
And resentment spreads against each of the
    royal warlords.
They lie sleeping, perpetual
Owners each of a small
Holding far from their homeland.

The sullen rumors that pass mouth to mouth
Bring the same danger as a people's curse,
And brooding hearts wait to hear of what the night
    holds from sight.
Watchful are the Gods of all
Hands with slaughter stained. The black
Furies wait, and when a man
Has grown by luck, not justice, great,
With sudden turn of circumstance
He wastes away to nothing, dragged
Down to be food in hell for demons.
For the heights of fame are perilous.
With a jealous bolt the Lord Zeus in a flash shall
    blast them.
Best to pray for a tranquil

Span of life and to be
Neither victor nor vanquished.

—The news has set the whole town aflame.
Can it be true? Perhaps it is a trick.
—Only a child would let such fiery words
Kindle his hopes, then fade and flicker out.
—It is just like a woman
To accept good news without the evidence.
—An old wives' tale, winged with a woman's wishes,
Spreads like wildfire, then sinks and is forgotten.

We shall soon know what the beacon signifies,
Whether it is true or whether this joyful daybreak
Is only a dream sent to deceive us all.
Here comes a messenger breathless from the shore,
Wearing a garland and covered in a cloud
Of dust, which shows that he has news to tell,
And not in soaring rhetoric of smoke and flame,
But either he brings cause for yet greater joy,
Or else,—no, let us abjure the alternative.
Glad shone the light, as gladly break the day!
(*Enter* HERALD)

HERALD
O joy! Argos, I greet you, my fatherland!
Joy brings me home after ten years of war.
Many the shattered hopes, but this has held.
Now I can say that when I die my bones
Will lie at rest here in my native soil.
I greet you joyfully, I greet the Sun,
Zeus the All-Highest, and the Pythian King,
Bending no more against us his fatal shafts,
As he did beside Scamander—that was enough,
And now defend us, Savior Apollo; all
The Gods I greet, among them Hermes, too,
Patron of messengers, and the spirits of our dead,
Who sent their sons forth, may they now prepare
A joyful welcome for those whom war has spared.
Joy to the palace and to these images
Whose faces catch the sun, now, as of old,
With radiant smiles greet your sovran lord,
Agamemnon, who brings a lamp to lighten you
And all here present, after having leveled
Troy with the mattock of just-dealing Zeus,
Great son of Atreus, master and monarch, blest

Above all living men. The brigand Paris
Has lost his booty and brought down the house of Priam.

CHORUS
Joy to you, Herald, welcome home again!

HERALD
Let me die, having lived to see this day!

CHORUS
Your yearning for your country has worn you out.

HERALD
So much that tears spring to the eyes for joy.

CHORUS
Well, those you longed for longed equally for you.

HERALD
Ah yes, our loved ones longed for our safe return.

CHORUS
We have had many anxieties here at home.

HERALD
What do you mean? Has there been disaffection?

CHORUS
Never mind now. Say nothing and cure all.

HERALD
Is it possible there was trouble in our absence?

CHORUS
Now, as you said yourself, it would be a joy to die.

HERALD
Yes, all has ended well. Our expedition
Has been successfully concluded, even though in part
The issue may be found wanting. Only the Gods
Prosper in everything. If I should tell you all
That we endured on shipboard in the night watches,
Our lodging the bare benches, and even worse
Ashore beneath the walls of Troy, the rains
From heaven and the dews that seeped
Out of the soil into lice-infested blankets;
If I should tell of those winters, when the birds
Dropped dead and Ida heaped on us her snows;
Those summers, when unruffled by wind or wave
The sea slept breathless under the glare of noon—

But why recall that now? It is all past,
Yes, for the dead past never to stir again.
Ah, they are all gone. Why count our losses? Why
Should we vex the living with grievance for the dead?
Goodbye to all that for us who have come back!
Victory has turned the scale, and so before
This rising sun let the good news be proclaimed
And carried all over the world on wings of fame:
"These spoils were brought by the conquerors of Troy
And dedicated to the Gods of Greece."
And praise to our country and to Zeus the giver
And thanks be given. That is all my news.
[CLYTEMNESTRA *appears at the palace door.*]

CHORUS
Thank God that I have lived to see this day!
This news concerns all, and most of all the queen.

CLYTEMNESTRA
I raised my alleluia hours ago,
When the first messenger lit up the night,
And people mocked me saying, "Has a beacon
Persuaded you that the Greeks have captured Troy?
Truly a woman's hopes are lighter than air."
But I still sacrificed, and at a hundred
Shrines throughout the town the women chanted
Their endless alleluias on and on,
Singing to sleep the sacramental flames,
And now what confirmation do I need from you?
I wait to hear all from my lord, for whom
A welcome is long ready. What day is so sweet
In a woman's life as when she opens the door
To her beloved, safe home from war? Go and tell him
That he will find, guarding his property,
A wife as loyal as he left her, one
Who in all these years has kept his treasuries sealed,
Unkind only to enemies, and knows no more
Of other men's company than of tempering steel.   [*Exit.*]

HERALD
Such a protestation, even though entirely true,
Is it not unseemly on a lady's lips?

CHORUS
Such is her message, as you understand,
Full of fine phrases plain to those who know.
But tell us now, what news have you of the king's
Co-regent, Menelaus? Is he too home again?

HERALD

Lies cannot last, even though sweet to hear.

CHORUS

Can you not make your news both sweet and true?

HERALD

He and his ships have vanished. They are missing.

CHORUS

What, was it a storm that struck the fleet at sea?

HERALD

You have told a long disaster in a word.

CHORUS

Has no one news whether he is alive or dead?

HERALD

Only the Sun, from whom the whole earth draws life.

CHORUS

Tell us about the storm. How did it fall?

HERALD

A day of national rejoicing must not be marred
By any jarring tongue. A messenger who comes
With black looks bringing the long prayed-against
Report of total rout, which both afflicts
The state in general and in every household leaves
The inmates prostrate under the scourge of war—
With such a load upon his lips he may fitly
Sing anthems to the Furies down in hell;
But when he greets a prospering people with
News of the war's victorious end—how then
Shall I mix foul with fair and find words to tell you
Of the blow that struck us out of that angry heaven?
    Water and Fire, those age-old enemies,
Made common cause against the homebound fleet.
Darkness had fallen, and a northerly gale
Blew up and in a blinding thunderstorm
Our ships were tossed and buffeted hull against hull
In a wild stampede and herded out of sight;
Then, at daybreak, we saw the Aegean in blossom
With a waving crop of corpses and scattered timbers.
Our ship came through, saved by some spirit, it seems,
Who took the helm and piloted her, until

She slipped under the cliffs into a cove.
There, safe at last, incredulous of our luck,
We brooded all day, stunned by the night's disaster.
And so, if any of the others have survived,
They must be speaking of us as dead and gone.
May all yet end well! Though it is most to be expected
That Menelaus is in some great distress,
Yet, should some shaft of sunlight spy him out
Somewhere among the living, rescued by Zeus,
Lest the whole house should perish, there is hope
That he may yet come home. There you have the truth.

CHORUS
Tell us who invented that
Name so deadly accurate?
Was it one who presaging
Things to come divined a word
Deftly tuned to destiny?
Helen—hell indeed she carried
To men, to ships, to a proud city, stealing
From the silk veils of her chamber, sailing seaward
With the Zephyr's breath behind her;
And they set forth in a thousand ships to hunt her
On that path that leaves no imprint,
Bringers of endless bloodshed.

So, as Fate decreed, in Troy,
Turning into keeners kin,
Furies, instruments of God's
Wrath, at last demanded full
Payment for the stolen wife;
And the wedding song that rang out
To greet the bride from beyond the broad Aegean
Was in time turned into howls of imprecation
From the countless women wailing
For the loved ones they had lost in war for her sake,
And they curse the day they gave that
Welcome to war and bloodshed.

An old story is told of an oxherd who reared at his
     hearth a lion-cub, a pet for his children,
Pampered fondly by young and old with dainty
     morsels begged at each meal from his master's table.

But Time showed him up in his true nature after his
     kind—a beast savaging sheep and oxen,

Mad for the taste of blood, and only then they knew
　　what they had long nursed was a curse from
　　heaven.

And so it seemed then there came to rest in Troy
A sweet-smiling calm, a clear sky, seductive,
A rare pearl set in gold and silver,
Shaft of love from a glancing eye.
She is seen now as an agent
Of death sent from Zeus, a Fury
Demanding a bloody bride-price. [*Enter* CLYTEMNESTRA]

From ancient times people have believed that when
A man's wealth has come to full growth it breeds
And brings forth tares and tears in plenty.
No, I say, it is only wicked deeds
That increase, fruitful in evil.
The house built on justice always
Is blest with a happy offspring.

And yet the pride bred of wealth often burgeons anew
In evil times, a cloud of deep night,
Spectre of ancient crimes that still
Walks within the palace walls,
True to the dam that bore it.

But where is Justice? She lights up the smoke-
　　darkened hut.
From mansions built by hands polluted
Turning to greet the pure in heart,
Proof against false praise, she guides
All to its consummation. [*Enter* AGAMEMNON *in a
　　chariot followed by another chariot carrying*
　　CASSANDRA *and spoils of war.*]

Agamemnon, conqueror, joy to our king! How shall my greeting neither
fall short nor shoot too high? Some men feign rejoicing or sorrow with
hearts untouched; but those who can read man's nature in the book of
the eyes will not be deceived by dissembled fidelity. I declare that,
when you left these shores ten years ago to recover with thousands of
lives one woman, who eloped of her own free will, I deemed your
judgment misguided; but now in all sincerity I salute you with joy.
Toil happily ended brings pleasure at last, and in time you shall learn
to distinguish the just from the unjust steward.

AGAMEMNON
　　First, it is just that I should pay my respects
　　To the land of Argos and her presiding Gods,

My partners in this homecoming as also
In the just penalty which I have inflicted on
The city of Troy. When the supreme court of heaven
Adjudicated on our cause, they cast
Their votes unanimously against her, though not
Immediately, and so on the other side
Hope hovered hesitantly before it vanished.
The fires of pillage are still burning there
Like sacrificial offerings. Her ashes
Redolent with riches breathe their last and die.
For all this it is our duty to render thanks
To the celestial powers, with whose assistance
We have exacted payment and struck down
A city for one woman, forcing our entry
Within the Wooden Horse, which at the setting
Of the Pleiads like a hungry lion leapt
Out and slaked its thirst in royal blood.
As to your sentiments, I take due note
And find that they accord with mine. Too few
Rejoice at a friend's good fortune. I have known
Many dissemblers swearing false allegiance.
One only, though he joined me against his will,
Once in the harness, proved himself a staunch
Support, Odysseus, be he now alive or dead.
All public questions and such as concern the Gods
I shall discuss in council and take steps
To make this triumph lasting; and if here or there
Some malady comes to light, appropriate
Remedies will be applied to set it right.
Meanwhile, returning to my royal palace,
My first duty is to salute the Gods
Who led me overseas and home again.
Victory attends me; may she remain with me!

CLYTEMNESTRA

Citizens of Argos, councillors and elders,
I shall declare without shame in your presence
My feelings for my husband. Diffidence
Dies in us all with time. I shall speak of what
I suffered here, while he was away at the war,
Sitting at home, with no man's company,
Waiting for news, listening to one
Messenger after another, each bringing worse
Disasters. If all his rumored wounds were real,
His body was in shreds, shot through and through.
If he had died—the predominant report—
He was a second Geryon,[9] an outstretched giant

---

[9]*Geryon*—a triple-bodied giant killed by Heracles.

With three corpses and one death for each,
While I, distraught, with a knot pressing my throat,
Was rescued forcibly, to endure still more.

And that is why our child is not present here,
As he should be, pledge of our marriage vows,
Orestes. Let me reassure you. He lives
Safe with an old friend, Strophius, who warned me
Of various dangers—your life at stake in Troy
And here a restive populace, which might perhaps
Be urged to kick a man when he is down.

As for myself, the fountains of my tears
Have long ago run dry. My eyes are sore
After so many nights watching the lamp
That burnt at my bedside always for you.
If I should sleep, a gnat's faint whine would shatter
The dreams that were my only company.

But now, all pain endured, all sorrow past,
I salute this man as the watchdog of the fold,
The stay that saves the ship, the sturdy oak
That holds the roof up, the longed-for only child,
The shore despaired-of sighted far out at sea.
God keep us from all harm! And now, dearest,
Dismount, but not on the bare ground! Servants,
Spread out beneath those feet that have trampled Troy
A road of royal purple, which shall lead him
By the hand of Justice into a home unhoped-for,
And there, when he has entered, our vigilant care
Shall dispose of everything as the Gods have ordained.

AGAMEMNON
Lady, royal consort and guardian of our home,
I thank you for your words of welcome, extended
To fit my lengthy absence; but due praise
Should rather come from others; and besides,
I would not have effeminate graces unman me
With barbarous salaams and beneath my feet
Purple embroideries designed for sacred use.
Honor me as a mortal, not as a god.
Heaven's greatest gift is wisdom. Count him blest
Who has brought a long life to a happy end.
I shall do as I have said, with a clear conscience.

CLYTEMNESTRA
Yet tell me frankly, according to our judgment.

AGAMEMNON
My judgment stands. Make no mistake about that.

CLYTEMNESTRA
Would you not in time of danger have vowed such
    an act?

AGAMEMNON
Yes, if the priests had recommended it.

CLYTEMNESTRA
And what would Priam have done, if he had won?

AGAMEMNON
Oh, he would have trod the purple without a doubt.

CLYTEMNESTRA
Then you have nothing to fear from wagging tongues.

AGAMEMNON
Popular censure is a potent force.

CLYTEMNESTRA
Men must risk envy in order to be admired.

AGAMEMNON
A contentious spirit is unseemly in a woman.

CLYTEMNESTRA
Well may the victor yield a victory.

AGAMEMNON
Do you set so much store by your victory?

CLYTEMNESTRA
Be tempted, freely vanquished, victor still!

AGAMEMNON
Well, if you will have it, let someone unlace
These shoes, and, as I tread the purple, may
No far-off god cast at me an envious glance
At the prodigal desecration of all this wealth!
Meanwhile, extend your welcome to this stranger.
Power tempered with gentleness wins God's favor.
No one is glad to be enslaved, and she
Is a princess presented to me by the army,
The choicest flower culled from a host of captives.
And now, constrained to obey you, setting foot
On the sacred purple, I pass into my home.

CLYTEMNESTRA
The sea is still there, nothing can dry it up,

Renewing out of its infinite abundance
Unfailing streams of purple and blood-red dyes.
So too this house, the Gods be praised, my lord.
Has riches inexhaustible. There is no counting
The robes *I* would have vowed to trample on,
Had some oracle so instructed, if by such means
I could have made good the loss of one dear soul.
So now your entry to your hearth and home
Is like a warm spell in the long winter's cold,
Or when Zeus from the virgin grape at last
Draws wine, coolness descends upon the house
(For then from the living root of the new leaves raise
A welcome shelter against the burning Dog-Star)
As man made perfect moves about his home.
        [*Exit* AGAMEMNON.]
Zeus, perfecter of all things, fulfil my prayers
And fulfil also your own purposes! [*Exit.*]

CHORUS
    What is this delirious dread,
    Ominous, oracular,
    Droning through my brain with unrelenting
    Beat, irrepressible prophet of evil?
    Why can I not cast it out
    Planting good courage firm
    On my spirit's empty throne?
    In time the day came
    When the Greeks with anchors plunged
    Moored the sloops of war, and troops
    Thronged the sandy beach of Troy.

    So today my eyes have seen
    Safe at last the men come home.
    Still I hear the strain of stringless music,
    Dirge of the Furies, a choir uninvited
    Chanting in my heart of hearts.
    Mortal souls stirred by God
    In tune with fate divine the shape
    Of things to come; yet
    Grant that these forebodings prove
    False and bring my fears to naught.

    If a man's health be advanced over the due mean,
    It will trespass soon upon sickness, who stands
    Next neighbor, between them a thin wall.
    So does the vessel of life
    Launched with a favoring breeze
    Suddenly founder on reefs of destruction.

Caution seated at the helm
Casts a portion of the freight
Overboard with measured throw;
So the ship may ride the storm.
Furrows enriched each season with showers
    from heaven
Banish hunger from the door.
But if the red blood of a man spatters the ground,
    dripping and deadly, then who
Has the magical power to recall it?
Even the healer who knew
Spells to awaken the dead,
Zeus put an end to his necromancy.
Portions are there preordained,
Each supreme within its own
Province fixed eternally.
That is why my spirit groans
Brooding in fear, and no longer it hopes to unravel
Mazes of a fevered mind.
[*Enter* CLYTEMNESTRA.]

CLYTEMNESTRA
You, too, Cassandra, come inside! The merciful
Zeus gives you the privilege to take part
In our domestic sacrifice[10] and stand
Before his altar among the other slaves there.
Put by your pride and step down. Even Heracles
Submitted once to slavery, and be consoled
In serving a house whose wealth has been inherited
Over so many generations. The harshest masters
Are those who have snatched their harvest out of hand.
You shall receive here what custom prescribes.

CHORUS
She is speaking to you. Caught in the net, surrender.

CLYTEMNESTRA
If she knows Greek and not some barbarous language,
My mystic words shall fill the soul within her.

CHORUS
You have no choice. Step down and do her will.

CLYTEMNESTRA
There is no time to waste. The victims are

---

[10]*Our domestic sacrifice*—Clytemnestra refers not to the usual animal offering made in thanks for a safe homecoming, but to human victims, Agamemnon and Cassandra, whom she plans to sacrifice on the altar of justice.

All ready for the knife to render thanks
For this unhoped-for joy. If you wish to take part,
Make haste, but, if you lack the sense to understand,—
　　[*To the* CHORUS.]
Speak to her with your hands and drag her down.

CHORUS
She is like a wild animal just trapped.

CLYTEMNESTRA
She is mad, the foolish girl. Her city captured,
Brought here a slave, she will be broken in.
I'll waste no words on her to demean myself. [*Exit.*]

CASSANDRA
Oh! oh! Apollo!

CHORUS
What blasphemy, to wail in Apollo's name!

CASSANDRA
Oh! oh! Apollo!

CASSANDRA
Again she cries in grief to the god of joy!

CASSANDRA
Apollo, my destroyer! a second time!

CHORUS
Ah, she foresees what is in store for her.
She is now a slave, and yet God's gift remains.

CASSANDRA
Apollo, my destroyer! What house is this?

CHORUS
Do you not know where you have come, poor girl?
Then let us tell you. This is the House of Atreus.

CASSANDRA
Yes, for its very walls smell of iniquity,
A charnel house that drips with children's blood.[11]

CHORUS
How keen her scent to seize upon the trail!

---

[11]*Children's blood*—that of the sons of Thyestes whom Atreus slew.

CASSANDRA
> Listen to them as they bewail the foul
> Repast of roast meat for a father's mouth!

CHORUS
> Enough! Reveal no more! We know it all.

CASSANDRA
> What is it plotted next? Horror unspeakable,
> A hard cross for kinsfolk.
> The hoped-for savior[12] is far away.

CHORUS
> What does she say? This must be something new.

CASSANDRA
> Can it be so—to bathe one who is travel-tired,
> And then smiling stretch out
> A hand followed by a stealthy hand!

CHORUS
> She speaks in riddles, and I cannot read them.

CASSANDRA
> What do I see? A net!
> Yes, it is she, his mate and murderess!
> Cry alleluia, cry, angels of hell, rejoice,
> Fat with blood, dance and sing!

CHORUS
> What is the Fury you have called upon?
> Helpless the heart faints with the sinking sun.
> Closer still draws the stroke.

CASSANDRA
> Ah, let the bull beware!
> It is a robe she wraps him in, and strikes!
> Into the bath he slumps heavily, drowned in blood.[13]
> Such her skilled handicraft.

CHORUS
> It is not hard to read her meaning now.
> Why does the prophet's voice never have good to tell,
> Only cry woes to come?

---

[12]*The hoped-for savior*—Orestes, who will eventually return to avenge his father's death.

[13]*Drowned in blood*—Cassandra's gift of prophesy allows her to see the murder of Agamemnon as if it were occurring before her eyes. It is presumably taking place within the palace at that very moment.

CASSANDRA
Oh, pitiful destiny! Having lamented his,
Now I lament my own passion to fill the bowl.
Where have you brought me? Must I with him die?

CHORUS
You sing your own dirge, like the red-brown bird
That pours out her grief-stricken soul,
Itys, Itys! she cries, the sad nightingale.

CASSANDRA
It is not so; for she, having become a bird,
Forgot her tears and sings her happy lot,
While I must face the stroke of two-edged steel.

CHORUS
From whence does this cascade of harsh discords
Issue, and where will it at last be calmed?
Calamity you cry—O where must it end?

CASSANDRA
O wedding day, Paris accurst of all!
Scamander, whose clear waters I grew beside!
Now I must walk weeping by Acheron.

CHORUS
Even a child could understand.
The heart breaks, as these pitiful cries
Shatter the listening soul.

CASSANDRA
O fall of Troy, city of Troy destroyed!
The king's rich gifts little availed her so
That she might not have been what she is now.

CHORUS
What evil spirit has possessed
Your soul, strumming such music upon your lips
As on a harp in hell?

CASSANDRA
Listen! My prophecy shall glance no longer
As through a veil like a bride newly-wed,
But bursting towards the sunrise shall engulf
The whole world in calamities far greater
Than these. No more riddles, I shall instruct,
While you shall verify each step, as I
Nose out from the beginning this bloody trail.
Upon this roof—do you see them?—stands a choir—
It has been there for generations—a gallery

Of unmelodious minstrels, a merry troop
Of wassailers drunk with human blood, reeling
And retching in horror at a brother's outraged bed.[14]
Well, have I missed? Am I not well-read in
Your royal family's catalogue of crime?

CHORUS
  You come from a far country and recite
  Our ancient annals as though you had been present.

CASSANDRA
  The Lord Apollo bestowed this gift on me.

CHORUS
  Was it because he had fallen in love with you?

CASSANDRA
  I was ashamed to speak of this till now.

CHORUS
  Ah yes, adversity is less fastidious.

CASSANDRA
  Oh, but he wrestled strenuously for my love.

CHORUS
  Did you come, then, to the act of getting child?

CASSANDRA
  At first I consented, and then I cheated him.

CHORUS
  Already filled with his gift of prophecy?

CASSANDRA
  Yes, I forewarned my people of their destiny.

CHORUS
  Did your divine lover show no displeasure?

CASSANDRA
  Yes, the price I paid was that no one listened to me.

CHORUS
  Your prophecies seem credible enough to us.

CASSANDRA
  Oh!
  Again the travail of the prophetic trance

---

[14]*A brother's . . . bed*—Thyestes had committed adultery with the wife of Atreus.

Runs riot in my soul. Do you not see them
There, on the roof, those apparitions[15]—children
Murdered by their own kin, in their hands
The innards of which their father ate—oh
What a pitiable load they carry! For that crime
Revenge is plotted by the fainthearted lion,
The stay-at-home, stretched in my master's bed
(Being his slave, I must needs call him so),
Lying in wait for Troy's great conqueror.
Little he knows what that foul bitch with ears
Laid back and rolling tongue intends for him
With a vicious snap, her husband's murderess.
What abominable monster shall I call her—
A two-faced amphisbaene or Scylla that skulks
Among the rocks to waylay mariners,
Infernal sea-squib locked in internecine
Strife—did you not hear her alleluias
Of false rejoicing at his safe return?
Believe me or not, what must be will be, and then
You will pity me and say, She spoke the truth.

CHORUS
    The feast of Thyestes I recognized, and shuddered,
    But for the rest my wits are still astray.

CASSANDRA
    Your eyes shall see the death of Agamemnon.

CHORUS
    No, hush those ill-omened lips, unhappy girl!

CASSANDRA
    There is no Apollo present, and so no cure.

CHORUS
    None, if you speak the truth; yet God forbid!

CASSANDRA
    Pray God forbid, while they close in for the kill!

CHORUS
    What man is there who would plot so foul a crime?

CASSANDRA
    Ah, you have altogether misunderstood.

CHORUS
    But how will he do it? That escapes me still.

15*Those apparitions*—Again Cassandra has a vision of Thyestes' murdered children.

CASSANDRA
  And yet I can speak Greek only too well.

CHORUS
  So does Apollo, but his oracles are obscure.

CASSANDRA
  Ah, how it burns me up! Apollo! Now
  That lioness on two feet pours in the cup
  My wages too, and while she whets the blade
  For him promises to repay my passage money
  In my own blood. Why wear these mockeries,
  This staff and wreath, if I must die, then you
  Shall perish first and be damned. Now we are quits!
  Apollo himself has stripped me, looking upon me
  A public laughingstock, who has endured
  The name of witch, waif, beggar, castaway,
  So now the god who gave me second sight
  Takes back his gift and dismisses his servant,
  Ready for the slaughter at a dead man's grave.
  Yet we shall be avenged. Now far away,
  The exile shall return, called by his father's
  Unburied corpse to come and kill his mother.
  Why weep at all this? Have I not seen Troy fall,
  And those who conquered her are thus discharged.
  I name this door the gate of Hades: now
  I will go and knock, I will take heart to die.
  I only pray that the blow may be mortal,
  Closing these eyes in sleep without a struggle,
  While my life blood ebbs quietly away.

CHORUS
  O woman, in whose wisdom is so much grief,
  How, if you know the end, can you approach it
  So gently, like an ox that goes to the slaughter?

CASSANDRA
  What help would it be if I should put it off?

CHORUS
  Yet, while there is life there's hope—so people say.

CASSANDRA
  For me no hope, no help. My hour has come.

CHORUS
  You face your end with a courageous heart.

CASSANDRA
  Yes, so they console those whom life has crossed.

CHORUS
Is there no comfort in an honorable death?

CASSANDRA
O Priam, father, and all your noble sons! [*She approaches the door, then draws back.*]

CHORUS
What is it? Why do you turn back, sick at heart?

CASSANDRA
Inside there is a stench of dripping blood.

CHORUS
It is only the blood of their fireside sacrifice.

CASSANDRA
It is the sort of vapor that issues from a tomb.
I will go now and finish my lament
Inside the house. Enough of life! O friends!
I am not scared. I beg of you only this:
When the day comes for them to die, a man
For a man, woman for woman, remember me!

CHORUS
Poor soul condemned to death, I pity you.

CASSANDRA
Yet one word more, my own dirge for myself.
I pray the Sun, on whom I now look my last,
That he may grant to my master's avengers
A fair price for the slave-girl slain at his side.
O sad mortality! when fortune smiles,
A painted image; and when trouble comes,
One touch of a wet sponge wipes it away. [*Exit.*]

CHORUS
And her case is even more pitiable than his.

Human prosperity never rests but always craves more, till blown up with pride it totters and falls. From the opulent mansions pointed at by all passersby none warns it away, none cries, "Let no more riches enter!" To him was granted the capture of Troy, and he has entered his home as a god, but now, if the blood of the past is on him, if he must pay with his own death for the crimes of bygone generations, then who is assured of a life without sorrow?

AGAMEMNON
Oh me!

CHORUS
Did you hear?

AGAMEMNON
Oh me, again!

CHORUS
It is the King. Let us take counsel!
1 I say, raise a hue and cry!
2 Break in at once!
3 Yes, we must act.
4 *They* spurn delay.
5 They plot a tyranny.
6 Must we live their slaves?
7 Better to die.
8 Old men, what can we do?
9 We cannot raise the dead.
10 His death is not yet proved.
11 We are only guessing.
12 Let us break in and learn the truth!

[*The doors are thrown open and* CLYTEMNESTRA *is seen standing over the bodies of* AGAMEMNON *and* CASSANDRA, *which are laid out on a purple robe.*]

CLYTEMNESTRA
All that I said before to bide my time
Without any shame I shall now unsay. How else
Could I have plotted against an enemy
So near and seeming dear and strung the snare
So high that he could not jump it? Now the feud
On which I have pondered all these years has been
Fought out to its conclusion. Here I stand
Over my work, and it was so contrived
As to leave no loophole. With this vast dragnet
I enveloped him in purple folds, then struck
Twice, and with two groans he stretched his legs,
Then on his outspread body I struck a third blow,
A drink for Zeus the Deliverer of the dead.
There he lay gasping out his soul and drenched me
In these deathly dew-drops, at which I cried
In sheer delight like newly-budding corn
That tastes the first spring showers. And so,
Venerable elders, you see how the matter stands.

Rejoice, if you are so minded. I glory in it.
With bitter tears he filled the household bowl;
Now he has drained it to the dregs and gone.

CHORUS

How can you speak so of your murdered king?

CLYTEMNESTRA

You treat me like an empty-headed woman.
Again, undaunted, to such as understand
I say—commend or censure, as you please—
It makes no difference—here is Agamemnon,
My husband, dead, the work of this right hand,
Which acted justly. There you have the truth.

CHORUS

Woman, what evil brew have you devoured to take
On you a crime that cries out for a public curse?
Yours was the fatal blow, banishment shall be yours,
Hissed and hated of all men.

CLYTEMNESTRA

Your sentence now for me is banishment,
But what did you do then to contravene
His purpose, when, to exorcise the storms,
As though picking a ewe-lamb from his flocks,
Whose wealth of snowy fleeces never fails
To increase and multiply, he killed his own
Child, born to me in pain, my best-beloved?
Why did you not drive *him* from hearth and home?
I bid you cast at me such menaces
As make for mastery in equal combat
With one prepared to meet them, and if, please God,
The issue goes against you, suffering
Shall school those grey hairs in humility.

CHORUS

You are possessed by some spirit of sin that stares
Out of your bloodshot eyes matching your bloody hands.
Dishonored and deserted of your kin, for this
Stroke you too shall be struck down.

CLYTEMNESTRA

Listen! By Justice, who avenged my child,
By the Fury to whom I vowed this sacrament,
No thought of fear shall enter through this door
So long as the hearth within is kindled by
Aegisthus, faithful to me now as always.

Low lies the man who insulted his wedded wife,
The darling of the Chryseids at Troy,
And stretched beside him this visionary seer,
Whom he fondled on shipboard, both now rewarded,
He as you see, and she swanlike has sung
Her dying ditty, his tasty side dish, for me
A rare spice to add relish to my joy.

CHORUS
Oh, for the gift of death
To bring the long sleep that knows no waking,
Now that my lord and loyal protector
Breathes his last. For woman's sake
Long he fought overseas,
Now at home falls beneath a woman's hand.
  Helen, the folly-beguiled, having ravaged the city of
    Troy,
  She has set on the curse of Atreus
  A crown of blood beyond ablution.

CLYTEMNESTRA
Do not pray for death nor turn your anger against one
  woman as the slayer of thousands!

CHORUS
Demon of blood and tears
Inbred in two women single-hearted!
Perched on the roof he stands and preens his
Sable wings, a carrion-crow.
Loud he croaks, looking down
Upon the feast spread before him here below.

CLYTEMNESTRA
Ah now you speak truth, naming the thrice-fed demon,
  who, glutted with blood, craves more, still young
  in his hunger.

CHORUS
When will the feast be done?
Alas, it is the will of Zeus,
Who caused and brought it all to pass.
Nothing is here but was decreed in heaven.

CLYTEMNESTRA
It was not my doing, nor am I Agamemnon's wife, but a
  ghost in woman's guise, the shade of the banqueter
  whom Atreus fed.

CHORUS
How is the guilt not yours?
And yet the crimes of old may well
Have had a hand, and so it drives
On, the trail of internecine murder.

CLYTEMNESTRA
What of *him?* Was the guilt not his, when he killed the
child that I bore him? And so by the sword he
has fallen.

CHORUS
Alas, the mind strays. The house is falling.
A storm of blood lays the walls in ruins.
Another mortal stroke for Justice' hand
Will soon be sharpened.
Oh me, who shall bury him, who sing the dirge?
Who shall intone at the tomb of a blessed spirit
A tribute pure in heart and truthful?

CLYTEMNESTRA
No, I'll bury him, but without mourners. By the waters
of Acheron Iphigenia is waiting for him with a kiss.

CHORUS
The charge is answered with countercharges.
The sinner must suffer: such is God's will.
The ancient curse is bringing down the house
In self-destruction.

CLYTEMNESTRA
That is the truth, and I would be content that the spirit
of vengeance should rest, having absolved the house
from its madness.
[*Enter* AEGISTHUS *with a bodyguard.*]

AEGISTHUS
Now I have proof that there are Gods in heaven,
As I gaze on this purple mesh in which
My enemy lies, son of a treacherous father.
His father, Atreus, monarch of this realm,
Was challenged in his sovran rights by mine,
Thyestes, his own brother, and banished him
From hearth and home. Later he returned
A suppliant and found sanctuary, indeed
A welcome; for his brother entertained him
To a feast of his own children's flesh, of which
My father unsuspecting took and ate.
Then, when he knew what he had done, he fell

Back spewing out the slaughtered flesh and, kicking
The table to the floor, with a loud cry
He cursed the House of Pelops. That is the crime
For which the son lies here. And fitly too
The plot was spun by me; for as a child
I was banished with my father, until Justice
Summoned me home. Now let me die, for never
Shall I live to see another sight so sweet.

CHORUS
Aegisthus, if it was you who planned this murder,
Then be assured, the people will stone you for it.

AEGISTHUS
Such talk from the lower benches! Even in dotage
Prison can teach a salutary lesson.
Better submit, or else you shall smart for it.

CHORUS
You woman, who stayed at home and wallowed in
His bed, you plotted our great commander's death!

AEGISTHUS
Orpheus led all in rapture after him.
Your senseless bark will be snuffed out in prison.

CHORUS
You say the plot was yours, yet lacked the courage
To raise a hand but left it to a woman!

AEGISTHUS
As his old enemy, I was suspect.
Temptation was the woman's part. But now
I'll try my hand at monarchy, and all
Who disobey me shall be put in irons
And starved of food and light till they submit.

CHORUS
Oh, if Orestes yet beholds the sun,
May he come home and execute them both!

AEGISTHUS
Ho, my guards, come forward, you have work to do.

CAPTAIN OF THE GUARD
Stand by, draw your swords!

CHORUS
We are not afraid to die.

AEGISTHUS
    Die! We'll take you at your word.

CLYTEMNESTRA
    Peace, my lord, and let no further wrong be done.
    Captain, sheathe your swords. And you, old men,
    Go home quietly. What has been, it had to be.
    Scars enough we bear, now let us rest.

AEGISTHUS
    Must I stand and listen to their threats?

CHORUS
    Men of Argos never cringed before a rogue.

AEGISTHUS
    I shall overtake you yet—the day is near.

CHORUS
    Not if Orestes should come home again.

AEGISTHUS
    Vain hope, the only food of castaways.

CHORUS
    Gloat and grow fat, blacken justice while you dare!

AEGISTHUS
    All this foolish talk will cost you dear.

CHORUS
    Flaunt your gaudy plumes and strut beside your hen!

CLYTEMNESTRA
    Pay no heed to idle clamor. You and I,
    Masters of the house, shall now direct it well.[16]

PROMETHEUS BOUND   Preface

LIKE THE JOB OF AN UNKNOWN HEBREW POET, THE PROMETHEUS BOUND OF
Aeschylus is a psychological drama raising the most profound of all

---

[16]*Masters . . . direct it well*—Clytemnestra's last words are doubly ironic. She has
gained mastery of Argos by the sword and she is destined to die by the sword, administered by her own son.

questions—the meaning of pain and the uncertainty of divine justice. Aeschylus' tragedy is one of thought in which the gradual revelation of Prometheus' wisdom and courage takes the place of physical action. As Job is rendered immobile upon his dung heap, so the Titan Prometheus is chained to a rocky crag in the Caucasus. But although his body is shackled, his spirit is free and the Promethean mind ranges the heights and depths of the universe. So powerfully does Aeschylus reveal the dynamic intelligence of his hero, that we are caught up in a swiftly flowing current of ideas which mounts irresistibly to the climax of Prometheus' utter rejection of a god who rules not by right or justice but by might alone.

The parallels to Job are instructive. Although technically speaking Prometheus is *not* man, he nevertheless represents a very human spirit of defiance.[1] Like Job, Prometheus perceives that the Deity has brought misfortune upon him unjustly. And, like Job, he is visited by a series of friends who urge him to submit to God's sovereignty. Each visit, however, serves only to elicit further testimony concerning the righteousness of his cause. Each speech born of his pain and consciousness of right widens the gulf between him and the angry god. Prometheus resembles Job too in his complete intellectual honesty: he will not place himself in the wrong merely to make the gods appear just.

The differences between the two dramas are equally significant. Whereas Job suffers in ignorance of his position as a pawn in the personal quarrel between God and Satan, Prometheus is fully aware of the reason for Zeus's displeasure. Job is being tested to prove his loyalty to Yahweh; Prometheus is being punished for having broken Zeus's command and given fire to mankind. His position is therefore morally equivocal: from the purely human standpoint, Prometheus has performed a great and noble deed; but from the viewpoint of universal law (Zeus's will), he has sinned and consequently deserves punishment. In this, Prometheus somewhat resembles Satan, who rebels against God in offering mankind the "knowledge of good and evil."[2] This forbidden knowledge is the symbolic equivalent of the Promethean gift of fire. In resolving to educate mankind against Zeus's will, Prometheus has acted both from charity and from excessive pride (*hubris*), the same presumptuous sin which the Bible attributes to Satan. On the other hand, in his generous determination to suffer on behalf of man, whom he has saved from extinction, Prometheus is not unlike Christ.

The paradox of Prometheus' moral position was also that of Aeschylus' audience. The Athenian spectator was expected to—and no doubt did—identify with the Titan who rebelled to benefit humanity. But at the same time the god against whom Prometheus revolted was the very deity the Athenians worshipped. On the surface it would seem that the two attitudes are completely irreconcilable.

---

[1]The fact that Greek legend credits Prometheus with man's creation closely identifies him with the human position.

[2]See Genesis 3:1-6.

Part of the difficulty is resolved, however, if one remembers that the *Prometheus Bound* is only the first part of a trilogy of which the last two plays have been lost. From ancient writers who quote fragments of the two missing works, it is clear that Aeschylus succeeded in bridging the moral gulf between god and rebel and in reconciling their antithetical positions. It is equally clear that Aeschylus' view of the gods was essentially evolutionary: he saw the newly-enthroned Zeus much as a contemporary would have regarded a parvenu tyrant—arrogant in power and ruling without law or wisdom. Allegorically speaking, Zeus at this stage in his development represents Brute Force, which is unfortunately separated from Prometheus, whose name "Forethought" identifies him as Wisdom. Perhaps the reason Aeschylus set his drama so far back in prehistory is to emphasize the fact that deity, split as it is between Power and Wisdom, must undergo a long evolutionary growth before it achieves the unified maturity of the Olympian Zeus whom the Athenians recognized as their supreme god. Zeus's need of Promethean intelligence had already been demonstrated by his soliciting Prometheus' aid in overthrowing old Cronus and the other Titans. As Prometheus foresees, to continue to rule, Zeus will again be forced to beg help of the Firebearer. In the many millennia that pass between the chaining of Prometheus and his release by Heracles, the prophesied descendant of Io, both mankind and Zeus emerge from primal savagery into the light of civilization.

Perhaps one source of the undiminished appeal which the stories of Job and Prometheus have for the modern mind is the fact that both are dramas of alienation. Both depict a universe which seems governed by arbitrary, unknowable power and which yields no meaning to the questioner except whatever significance he might derive from the fact of his suffering. Both Yahweh and Zeus demonstrate their power through lightning bolt and whirlwind but neither explains his right to inflict pain. Job and Prometheus are forced to substitute their own integrity for that which is absent in their gods. But whereas Job, the submissive Hebrew, grovels before the Voice from the Storm, Prometheus fearlessly shakes his fist at heaven and cries:

> O Holy Mother Earth, O air and sun,
> behold me. I am wronged!

PROMETHEUS BOUND

[Symbolic of the means by which the newly-established Zeus rules the universe, his servants, the allegorical figures of Force and Violence,

Reprinted from *Three Greek Plays,* translated with introductions by Edith Hamilton, by permission of W. W. Norton & Company, Inc. Copyright 1937 by W. W. Norton & Company, Inc.

prepare to crucify Prometheus on a crag in the uninhabited wilds of the
North. Hephaestus, who has a more highly developed ethical sense than
his brutal companions, reluctantly chains the fallen Titan.]

FORCE
Far have we come to this far spot of earth,
this narrow Scythian land, a desert all untrodden.
God of the forge and fire, yours the task
the Father laid upon you.
To this high-piercing, head-long rock
in adamantine chains that none can break
bind him—him here, who dared all things.
Your flaming flower he stole to give to men,
fire, the master craftsman, through whose power
all things are wrought, and for such error now
he must repay the gods; be taught to yield
to Zeus' lordship and to cease
from his man-loving way.

HEPHESTUS
Force, Violence, what Zeus enjoined on you
has here an end. Your task is done.
But as for me, I am not bold to bind
a god, a kinsman, to this stormy crag.
Yet I must needs be bold.
His load is heavy who dares disobey the Father's
    word.
O high-souled child of Justice, the wise counselor,
against my will as against yours I nail you fast
in brazen fetters never to be loosed
to this rock peak, where no man ever comes,
where never voice or face of mortal you will see.
The shining splendor of the sun shall wither you.
Welcome to you will be the night
when with her mantle star-inwrought[1]
she hides the light of day.
And welcome then in turn the sun
to melt the frost the dawn has left behind.
Forever shall the intolerable present grind you
    down,
and he who will release you is not born.
Such fruit you reap for your man-loving way.
A god yourself, you did not dread God's anger,
but gave to mortals honor not their due,
and therefore you must guard this joyless rock—

---

[1]Shelley's adjective is the perfect translation. Anything else would be less exact and
less like Aeschylus. [Translator's note.]

no rest, no sleep, no moment's respite.
Groans shall your speech be, lamentation
your only words—all uselessly.
Zeus has no mind to pity. He is harsh,
like upstarts always.

FORCE

Well then, why this delay and foolish talk?
A god whom gods hate is abominable.

HEPHESTUS

The tie of blood has a strange power,
and old acquaintance too.

FORCE

And so say I—but don't you think
that disobedience to the Father's words
might have still stranger power?

HEPHESTUS

You're rough, as always. Pity is not in you.

FORCE

Much good is pity here. Why all this pother
that helps him not a whit?

HEPHESTUS

O skill of hand now hateful to me.

FORCE

Why blame your skill? These troubles here
were never caused by it. That's simple truth.

HEPHESTUS

Yet would it were another's and not mine.

FORCE

Trouble is everywhere except in heaven.
No one is free but Zeus.

HEPHESTUS

I know—I've not a word to say.

FORCE

Come then. Make haste. On with his fetters.
What if the Father sees you lingering?

HEPHESTUS

The chains are ready here if he should look.

FORCE
    Seize his hands and master him.
    Now to your hammer. Pin him to the rocks.

HEPHESTUS
    All done, and quick work too.

FORCE
    Still harder. Tighter. Never loose your hold.
    For he is good at finding a way out where there is
        none.

HEPHESTUS
    This arm at least he will not ever free.

FORCE
    Buckle the other fast, and let him learn
    with all his cunning he's a fool to Zeus.

HEPHESTUS
    No one but he, poor wretch, can blame my work.

FORCE
    Drive stoutly now your wedge straight through his
        breast,
    the stubborn jaw of steel that cannot break.

HEPHESTUS
    Alas, Prometheus, I grieve for your pain.

FORCE
    You shirk your task and grieve for those Zeus hates?
    Take care; you may need pity for yourself.

HEPHESTUS
    You see a sight eyes should not look upon.

FORCE
    I see one who has got what he deserves.
    But come. The girdle now around his waist.

HEPHESTUS
    What must be shall be done. No need to urge me.

FORCE
    I will and louder too. Down with you now.
    Make fast his legs in rings. Use all your strength.

HEPHESTUS
    Done and small trouble.

FORCE

> Now for his feet. Drive the nails through the flesh.
> The judge is stern who passes on our work.

HEPHESTUS

> Your tongue and face match well.

FORCE

> Why, you poor weakling. Are you one to cast
> a savage temper in another's face?

HEPHESTUS

> Oh, let us go. Chains hold him, hand and foot.

FORCE

> Run riot now, you there upon the rocks.
> Go steal from gods to give their goods to men—
> to men whose life is but a little day.
> What will they do to lift these woes from you?
> Forethought your name means, falsely named.
> Forethought you lack and need now for yourself
> if you would slip through fetters wrought like these.
>   [*Exeunt* FORCE, VIOLENCE, HEPHESTUS.]

PROMETHEUS

> O air of heaven and swift-winged winds,
> O running river waters,
> O never numbered laughter of sea waves,
> Earth, mother of all, Eye of the sun, all seeing,
> on you I call.
> Behold what I, a god, endure from gods.
> See in what tortures I must struggle
> through countless years of time.
> This shame, these bonds, are put upon me
> by the new ruler of the gods.
> Sorrow enough in what is here and what is still to
>   come.
> It wrings groans from me.
> When shall the end be, the appointed end?
> And yet why ask?
> All, all I knew before,
> all that should be.
> Nothing, no pang of pain
> that I did not foresee.
> Bear without struggle what must be.
> Necessity is strong and ends our strife.
> But silence is intolerable here.
> So too is speech.

I am fast bound, I must endure.
I gave to mortals gifts.
I hunted out the secret source of fire.
I filled a reed therewith,
fire, the teacher of all arts to men,
the great way through.
These are the crimes that I must pay for,
pinned to a rock beneath the open sky.
But what is here? What comes?
What sound, what fragrance, brushed me with faint
    wings,
of deities or mortals or of both?[2]
Has someone found a way to this far peak
to view my agony? What else?
Look at me then, in chains, a god who failed,
the enemy of Zeus, whom all gods hate,
all that go in and out of Zeus' hall.
The reason is that I loved men too well.
Oh, birds are moving near me. The air murmurs
with swift and sweeping wings.
Whatever comes to me is terrible.
    [*Enter* CHORUS. *They are sea nymphs. It is clear from what follows
    that a winged car brings them on to the stage.*]

LEADER OF CHORUS
    Oh, be not terrified, for friends are here,
    each eager to be first,
    on swift wings flying to your rock.
    I prayed my father long
    before he let me come.
    The rushing winds have sped me on.
    A noise of ringing brass went through the sea-caves,
    and for all a maiden's fears it drove me forth,
    so swift, I did not put my sandals on,
    but in my winged car I came to you.

PROMETHEUS
    To see this sight—
    Daughters of fertile Tethys,
    children of Ocean who forever flows
    unresting round earth's shores,
    behold me, and my bonds
    that bind me fast upon the rocky height
    of this cleft mountain side,
    keeping my watch of pain.

2This line of Keats is the exact translation. [Translator's note.]

A SEA NYMPH

> I look upon you and a mist of tears,
> of grief and terror, rises as I see
> your body withering upon the rocks,
> in shameful fetters.
> For a new helmsman steers Olympus.
> By new laws Zeus is ruling without law.
> He has put down the mighty ones of old.

PROMETHEUS

> Oh, had I been sent deep, deep into earth,
> to that black boundless place where go the dead,
> though cruel chains should hold me fast forever,
> I should be hid from sight of gods and men.
> But now I am a plaything for the winds.
> My enemies exult—and I endure.

ANOTHER NYMPH

> What god so hard of heart to look on these things
>   gladly?
> Who, but Zeus only, would not suffer with you?
> He is malignant always and his mind
> unbending. All the sons of heaven
> he drives beneath his yoke.
> Nor will he make an end
> until his heart is sated or until
> someone, somehow, shall seize his sovereignty—
> if that could be.

PROMETHEUS

> And yet—and yet—all tortured though I am,
> fast fettered here,
> he shall have need of me,* the lord of heaven,
> to show to him the strange design
> by which he shall be stripped of throne and scepter.
> But he will never win me over
> with honeyed spell of soft, persuading words,
> nor will I ever cower beneath his threats
> to tell him what he seeks.
> First he must free me from this savage prison
> and pay for all my pain.

He shall have need of me—Since Prometheus can foresee the future he has the single advantage of knowing that, unless Zeus changes his ways and learns to rule with justice, the great Olympian will have a son who will grow up to overthrow him, just as Zeus overthrew his Titan father Cronus. This is the secret which Zeus tries to wrest from Prometheus in the final episode.

ANOTHER
  Oh, you are bold. In bitter agony
  you will not yield.
  These are such words as only free men speak.
  Piercing terror stings my heart.
  I fear because of what has come to you.
  Where are you fated to put in to shore
  and find a haven from this troubled sea?
  Prayers cannot move,
  persuasions cannot turn,
  the heart of Kronos' son.

PROMETHEUS
  I know that he is savage.
  He keeps his righteousness at home.
  But yet some time he shall be mild of mood,
  when he is broken.
  He will smooth his stubborn temper,
  and run to meet me.
  Then peace will come and love between us two.

LEADER
  Reveal the whole to us. Tell us your tale.
  What guilt does Zeus impute
  to torture you in shame and bitterness?
  Teach us, if you may speak.

PROMETHEUS
  To speak is pain, but silence too is pain,
  and everywhere is wretchedness:
  When first the gods began to quarrel
  and faction rose among them,
  some wishing to throw Kronos out of heaven,
  that Zeus, Zeus, mark you, should be lord,
  others opposed, pressing the opposite,
  that Zeus should never rule the gods,
  then I, giving wise counsel to the Titans,
  children of Earth and Heaven, could not prevail.
  My way out was a shrewd one, they despised it,
  and in their arrogant minds they thought to conquer
  with ease, by their own strength.
  But Justice, she who is my mother, told me—
  Earth she is sometimes called,
  whose form is one, whose name is many—
  she told me, and not once alone,
  the future, how it should be brought to pass,

that neither violence nor strength of arm
but only subtle craft could win.
I made all clear to them.
They scorned to look my way.
The best then left me was to stand with Zeus
in all good will, my mother with me,
and, through my counsel, the black underworld
covered, and hides within its secret depths
Kronos the aged and his host.
Such good the ruler of the gods had from me,
and with such evil he has paid me back.
There is a sickness that infects all tyrants,
they cannot trust their friends.
But you have asked a question I would answer:
What is my crime that I am tortured for?
Zeus had no sooner seized his father's throne
than he was giving to each god a post
and ordering his kingdom,
but mortals in their misery
he took no thought for.
His wish was they should perish
and he would then beget another race.
And there were none to cross his will save I.
I dared it, I saved men.
Therefore I am bowed down in torment,
grievous to suffer, pitiful to see.
I pitied mortals,
I never thought to meet with this.
Ruthlessly punished here I am
an infamy to Zeus.

LEADER
Iron of heart or wrought from rock is he
who does not suffer in your misery.
Oh, that these eyes had never looked upon it.
I see it and my heart is wrung.*

PROMETHEUS
A friend must feel I am a thing to pity.

LEADER
Did you perhaps go even further still?

PROMETHEUS
I made men cease to live with death in sight.

---

*My heart is wrung—the chorus acts throughout to direct the audience's emotional
response to Prometheus' suffering.

LEADER
What potion did you find to cure this sickness?

PROMETHEUS
Blind hopes I caused to dwell in them.

ANOTHER SEA NYMPH
Great good to men that gift.

PROMETHEUS
To it I added the good gift of fire.

ANOTHER
And now the creatures of a day
have flaming fire?

PROMETHEUS
Yes, and learn many crafts therefrom.

LEADER
For deeds like these Zeus holds you guilty,
and tortures you with never ease from pain?
Is no end to your anguish set before you?

PROMETHEUS
None other except when it pleases him.

LEADER
It pleases him? What hope there? You must see
you missed your mark* I tell you this with pain
to give you pain.
But let that pass. Seek your deliverance.

PROMETHEUS
Your feet are free.
Chains bind mine fast.
Advice is easy for the fortunate.
All that has come I knew full well.
Of my own will I shot the arrow that fell short,
of my own will.
Nothing do I deny.
I helped men and found trouble for myself.
I knew—and yet not all.
I did not think to waste away
hung high in air upon a lonely rock.
But now, I pray you, no more pity

---

*You missed your mark—the chorus here refers to Prometheus' *hamartia*, the intellectual pride and uncompromising virtue that brought him to his present position. Except in the eyes of Zeus, Prometheus' *hubris* is not the usual sin.

for what I suffer here. Come, leave your car,
and learn the fate that steals upon me,
all, to the very end.
Hear me, oh, hear me. Share my pain. Remember,
trouble may wander far and wide
but it is always near.

LEADER

You cry to willing ears, Prometheus.
Lightly I leave my swiftly speeding car
and the pure ways of air where go the birds.
I stand upon this stony ground.
I ask to hear your troubles to the end.
 [*Enter* OCEAN *riding on a four-footed bird. The* CHORUS *draw back,
 and he does not see them.*]

OCEAN

Well, here at last, an end to a long journey.
I've made my way to you, Prometheus.
This bird of mine is swift of wing
but I can guide him by my will,
without a bridle.
Now you must know, I'm grieved at your misfor-
   tunes.
Of course I must be, I'm your kinsman.
And that apart, there's no one I think more of.
And you'll find out the truth of what I'm saying.
It isn't in me to talk flattery.
Come: tell me just what must be done to help you,
and never say that you've a firmer friend
then you will find in me.

PROMETHEUS

Oho! What's here? You? Come to see my troubles?
How did you dare to leave your ocean river,
your rock caves hollowed by the sea,
and stand upon the iron mother earth?
Was it to see what has befallen me,
because you grieve with me?
Then see this sight: here is the friend of Zeus,
who helped to make him master.
This twisted body is his handiwork.

OCEAN

I see, Prometheus. I do wish
You'd take some good advice.
I know you're very clever,

but real self-knowledge—that you haven't got.
New fashions have come in with this new ruler.
Why can't you change your own to suit?
Don't talk like that—so rude and irritating.
Zeus isn't so far off but he might hear,
and what would happen then would make these troubles
seem child's play.
You're miserable. Then do control your temper
and find some remedy
Of course you think you know all that I'm saying.
You certainly should know the harm
that blustering has brought you.
But you're not humbled yet. You won't give in.
You're looking for more trouble.
Just learn one thing from me:
Don't kick against the pricks.
You see he's savage—why not? He's a tyrant.
He doesn't have to hand in his accounts.
Well, now I'm going straight to try
if I can free you from this wretched business.
Do you keep still. No more of this rash talking.
Haven't you yet learned with all your wisdom
the mischief that a foolish tongue can make?

PROMETHEUS

Wisdom? The praise for that is yours alone,
who shared and dared with me and yet were able
to shun all blame.
But—let be now. Give not a thought more to me.
You never would persuade him.
He is not easy to win over.
Be cautious. Keep a sharp look out,
or on your way back you may come to harm.

OCEAN

You counsel others better than yourself,
to judge by what I hear and what I see.
But I won't let you turn me off.
I really want to serve you.
And I am proud, yes, proud to say
I know that Zeus will let you go
just as a favor done to me.

PROMETHEUS

I thank you for the good will you would show me.
But spare your pains. Your trouble would be wasted.

The effort, if indeed you wish to make it,
could never help me.
Now you are out of harm's way. Stay there.
Because I am unfortunate myself
I would not wish that others too should be.
Not so. Even here the lot of Atlas, of my brother,
weighs on me. In the western country
he stands, and on his shoulders is the pillar
that holds apart the earth and sky,
a load not easy to be borne.
Pity too filled my heart when once I saw
swift Typhon overpowered.
Child of the Earth was he, who lived
in caves in the Cilician land,
a flaming monster with a hundred heads,
who rose up against all the gods.
Death whistled from his fearful jaws.
His eyes flashed glaring fire.
I thought he would have wrecked God's sov-
          ereignty.
But to him came the sleepless bolt of Zeus,
down from the sky, thunder with breath of flame,
and all his high boasts were struck dumb.
Into his very heart the fire burned.
His strength was turned to ashes.
And now he lies a useless thing,
a sprawling body, near the narrow sea-way
by Aetna,* underneath the mountain's roots.
High on the peak the god of fire sits,
welding the molten iron in his forge,
whence sometimes there will burst
rivers red hot, consuming with fierce jaws
the level fields of Sicily,
lovely with fruits.
And that is Typhon's anger boiling up,
his darts of flame none may abide,
of fire-breathing spray,
scorched to a cinder though he is
by Zeus' bolt.
But you are no man's fool; you have no need
to learn from me. Keep yourself safe,
as you well know the way.
And I will drain my cup to the last drop,
until Zeus shall abate his insolence of rage.

Aetna—the great Sicilian volcano, under which the Titan Typhon was reputedly buried. Aeschylus may have witnessed Aetna in eruption.

OCEAN

And yet you know the saying,
when anger reaches fever heat
wise words are a physician.

PROMETHEUS

Not when the heart is full to bursting.
Wait for the crisis; then the balm will soothe.

OCEAN

But if one were discreet as well as daring—?
You don't see danger then? Advise me.

PROMETHEUS

I see your trouble wasted,
and you good-natured to the point of folly.

OCEAN

That's a complaint I don't mind catching.
Let be: I'll choose to seem a fool
if I can be a loyal friend.

PROMETHEUS

But he will lay to me all that you do.

OCEAN

There you have said what needs must send me home.

PROMETHEUS

Just so. All your lamenting over me
will not have got you then an enemy.

OCEAN

Meaning—the new possessor of the throne?

PROMETHEUS

Be on your guard. See that you do not vex him.

OCEAN

Your case, Prometheus, may well teach me—

PROMETHEUS

Off with you. Go—and keep your present mind.

OCEAN

You urge one who is eager to be gone.
For my four-footed bird is restless
to skim with wings the level ways of air.
He'll be well pleased to rest in his home stable.
[*Exit* OCEAN. *The* CHORUS *now come forward.*]

CHORUS
　I mourn for you, Prometheus.
　Desolation is upon you.
　My face is wet with weeping.
　Tears fall as waters which run continually.
　The floods overflow me.
　Terrible are the deeds of Zeus.
　He rules by laws that are his own.
　High is his spear above the others,
　turned against the gods of old.
　All the land now groans aloud,
　mourning for the honor of the heroes of your race.
　Stately were they, honored ever in the days of long
　　　ago.
　Holy Asia is hard by.
　Those that dwell there suffer in your trouble, great
　　　and sore.
　In the Colchian land maidens live,
　fearless in fight.
　Scythia has a battle throng,
　the farthest place of earth is theirs,
　where marsh grass grows around Maeotis lake.
　Arabia's flower is a warrior host;
　high on a cliff their fortress stands,
　Caucasus towers near;
　men fierce as the fire, like the roar of the fire
　they shout when the sharp spears clash.
　All suffer with you in your trouble, great and sore.
　Another Titan too, Earth mourns,
　bound in shame and iron bonds.
　I saw him, Atlas the god.
　He bears on his back forever
　the cruel strength of the crushing world
　and the vault of the sky.
　He groans beneath them.
　The foaming sea-surge roars in answer,
　the deep laments,
　the black place of death far down in earth is moved
　　　exceedingly,
　and the pure-flowing river waters grieve for him in
　　　his piteous pain.

PROMETHEUS
　Neither in insolence nor yet in stubbornness
　have I kept silence.
　It is thought that eats my heart,
　seeing myself thus outraged.
　Who else but I, but I myself,

gave these new gods their honors?
Enough of that. I speak to you who know.
Hear rather all that mortals suffered.
Once they were fools. I gave them power to think.
Through me they won their minds.
I have no blame for them. All I would tell you
is my good will and my good gifts to them.
Seeing they did not see, nor hearing hear.
Like dreams they led a random life.
They had no houses built to face the sun,
of bricks or well-wrought wood,
but like the tiny ant who has her home
in sunless crannies deep down in the earth,
they lived in caverns.
The signs that speak of winter's coming,
of flower-faced spring, of summer's heat
with mellowing fruits,
were all unknown to them.
From me they learned the stars that tell the seasons,
their risings and their settings hard to mark.
And number, that most excellent device,
I taught to them, and letters joined in words.
I gave to them the mother of all arts,
hard working memory.
I, too, first brought beneath the yoke
great beasts to serve the plow,
to toil in mortals' stead.
Up to the chariot I led the horse that loves the rein,
the glory of the rich man in his pride.
None else but I first found
the seaman's car, sail-winged, sea-driven.
Such ways to help I showed them, I who have
no wisdom now to help myself.

LEADER
You suffer shame as a physician must
who cannot heal himself.
You who cured others now are all astray,
distraught of mind and faint of heart,
and find no medicine to soothe your sickness.

PROMETHEUS
Listen, and you shall find more cause for wonder.
Best of all gifts I gave them was the gift of healing.
For if one fell into a malady
there was no drug to cure, no draught, or soothing
    ointment.
For want of these men wasted to a shadow

until I showed them how to use
the kindly herbs that keep from us disease.
The ways of divination I marked out for them,
and they are many; how to know
the waking vision from the idle dream;
to read the sounds hard to discern;
the signs met on the road; the flight of birds,
eagles and vultures,
those that bring good or ill luck in their kind,
their way of life, their loves and hates
and council meetings.
And of those inward parts that tell the future,
the smoothness and the color and fair shape
that please the gods.
And how to wrap the flesh in fat
and the long thigh bone, for the altar fire
in honor to the gods.
So did I lead them on to knowledge
of the dark and riddling art.
The fire omens, too, were dim to them
until I made them see.
Deep within the earth are hidden
precious things for men,
brass and iron, gold and silver.
Would any say he brought these forth to light
until I showed the way?
No one, except to make an idle boast.
All arts, all goods, have come to men from me.

LEADER
Do not care now for mortals
but take thought for yourself, O evil-fated.
I have good hope that still loosed from your bonds
you shall be strong as Zeus.

PROMETHEUS
Not thus—not yet—is fate's appointed end,
fate that brings all to pass.
I must be bowed by age-long pain and grief.
So only will my bonds be loosed.
All skill, all cunning, is as foolishness
before necessity.

A SEA NYMPH
Who is the helmsman of necessity?

PROMETHEUS
Fate, threefold, Retribution, unforgetting.

ANOTHER
And Zeus is not so strong?

PROMETHEUS
He cannot shun what is foredoomed.

ANOTHER
And is he not foredoomed to rule forever?

PROMETHEUS
No word of that. Ask me no further.

ANOTHER
Some solemn secret hides behind your silence.

PROMETHEUS
Think of another theme. It is not yet
the time to speak of this.
It must be wrapped in darkness, so alone
I shall some time be saved
from shame and grief and bondage.

CHORUS
Zeus orders all things.
May he never set his might against purpose of mine,
like a wrestler in the match.
May I ever be found where feast the holy gods,
and the oxen are slain,
where ceaselessly flows the pathway
of Ocean, my father.
May the words of my lips forever
be free from sin.
May this abide with me and not depart
like melting snow.
Long life is sweet when there is hope
and hope is confident.
And it is sweet when glad thoughts make the heart
    grow strong,
and there is joy.
But you, crushed by a thousand griefs,
I look upon you and I shudder.
You did not tremble before Zeus.
You gave your worship where you would, to men,
a gift too great for mortals,
a thankless favor.
What help for you there? What defense in those
whose life is but from morning unto evening?
Have you not seen?

Their little strength is feebleness,
fast bound in darkness,
like a dream.
The will of man shall never break
the harmony of God.
This I have learned beholding your destruction.
Once I spoke different words to you
from those now on my lips.
A song flew to me.
I stood beside your bridal bed,
I sang the wedding hymn,
glad in your marriage.
And with fair gifts persuading her,
you led to share your couch
Hesione, child of the sea.
[*Enter* Io.]

Io

What land—what creatures here?
This, that I see—
A form storm-beaten,
bound to the rock.
Did you do wrong?
Is this your punishment?
You perish here.
Where am I?
Speak to a wretched wanderer.
Oh! Oh! he stings again—
the gadfly—oh, miserable!
But you must know he's not a gadfly.
He's Argus, son of Earth, the herdsman.
He has a thousand eyes.
I see him. Off! Keep him away!
No, he comes on.
His eye can see all ways at once.
He's dead but no grave holds him.
He comes straight up from hell.
He is the huntsman,
and I his wretched quarry.
He drives me all along the long sea strand.
I may not stop for food or drink.
He has a shepherd's pipe,
a reed with beeswax joined.
Its sound is like the locust's shrilling,
a drowsy note—that will not let me sleep.
Oh, misery. Oh, misery.

Where is it leading me,
my wandering—far wandering.
What ever did I do,
how ever did I sin,
that you have yoked me to calamity,
O son of Kronos,
that you madden a wretched woman
driven mad by the gadfly of fear.
Oh, burn me in fire or hide me in earth
or fling me as food to the beasts of the sea.
Master, grant me my prayer.
Enough—I have been tried enough—
my wandering—long wandering.
Yet I have found no place
to leave my misery.
—I am a girl who speak to you,
but horns are on my head.

PROMETHEUS

Like one caught in an eddy, whirling round and
    round,
the gadfly drives you.
I know you, girl. You are Inachus' daughter.
You made the god's heart hot with love,
and Hera hates you. She it is
who drives you on this flight that never stops.

Io

How is it that you speak my father's name?
Who are you? Tell me for my misery.
Who are you, sufferer, that speak the truth
to one who suffers?
You know the sickness God has put upon me,
that stings and maddens me and drives me on
and wastes my life away.
I am a beast, a starving beast,
that frenzied runs with clumsy leaps and bounds,
oh, shame,
mastered by Hera's malice.
Who among the wretched
suffer as I do?
Give me a sign, you there.
Tell to me clearly
the pain still before me.
Is help to be found?
A medicine to cure me?
Speak, if you know.

PROMETHEUS
> I will and in plain words,
> as friend should talk to friend.
> —You see Prometheus, who gave mortals fire.

Io
> You, he who succored the whole race of men?
> You, that Prometheus, the daring, the enduring?
> Why do you suffer here?

PROMETHEUS
> Just now I told the tale—

Io
> But will you not still give me a boon?

PROMETHEUS
> Ask what you will. I know all you would learn.

Io
> Then tell me who has bound you to this rock.

PROMETHEUS
> Zeus was the mind that planned.
> The hand that did the deed the god of fire.

Io
> What was the wrong that you are punished for?

PROMETHEUS
> No more. Enough of me.

Io
> But you will tell the term set to my wandering?
> My misery is great. When shall it end?

PROMETHEUS
> Here not to know is best.

Io
> I ask you not to hide what I must suffer.

PROMETHEUS
> I do so in no grudging spirit.

Io
> Why then delay to tell me all?

PROMETHEUS
> Not through ill will. I would not terrify you.

Io
Spare me not more than I would spare myself.

PROMETHEUS
If you constrain me I must speak. Hear then—

LEADER
Not yet. Yield to my pleasure too.
For I would hear from her own lips
what is the deadly fate, the sickness
that is upon her. Let her say—then teach her
the trials still to come.

PROMETHEUS
If you would please these maidens, Io—
they are your father's sisters,
and when the heart is sorrowful, to speak
to those who will let fall a tear
is time well spent.

Io
I do not know how to distrust you.
You shall hear all. And yet—
I am ashamed to speak,
to tell of that god-driven storm
that struck me, changed me, ruined me.
How shall I tell you who it was?
How ever to my maiden chamber
visions came by night,
persuading me with gentle words:
"Oh happy, happy girl,
Why are you all too long a maid
when you might marry with the highest?
The arrow of desire has pierced Zeus.
For you he is on fire.
With you it is his will to capture love.
Would you, child, fly from Zeus' bed?
Go forth to Lerna, to the meadows deep in grass.
There is a sheep-fold there,
an ox-stall, too, that holds your father's oxen—
so shall Zeus find release from his desire."
Always, each night, such dreams possessed me.
I was unhappy and at last I dared
to tell my father of these visions.
He sent to Pytho and far Dodona
man after man to ask the oracle
what he must say or do to please the gods.
But all brought answers back of shifting meaning,

hard to discern, like golden coins unmarked.
At last a clear word came. It fell upon him
like lightning from the sky. It told him
to thrust me from his house and from his country,
to wander to the farthest bounds of earth
like some poor dumb beast set apart
for sacrifice, whom no man will restrain.
And if my father would not, Zeus would send
his thunder-bolt with eyes of flame to end
his race, all, everyone.
He could not but obey such words
from the dark oracle. He drove me out.
He shut his doors to me—against his will
as against mine. Zeus had him bridled.
He drove him as he would.
Straightway I was distorted, mind and body.
A beast—with horns—look at me—
stung by a fly, who madly leaps and bounds.
And so I ran and found myself beside
the waters, sweet to drink, of Kerchneia
and Lerna's well-spring.
Beside me went the herdsman Argus,
the violent of heart, the earth-born,
watching my footsteps with his hundred eyes.
But death came to him, swift and unforeseen.
Plagued by a gadfly then, the scourge of God,
I am driven on from land to land.
So for what has been. But what still remains
of anguish for me, tell me.
Do not in pity soothe me with false tales.
Words strung together by a lie
are like a foul disease.

LEADER
  Oh, shame. Oh, tale of shame.
  Never, oh never, would I have believed that my ears
  would hear words such as these, of strange meaning.
  Evil to see and evil to hear,
  misery, defilement, and terror.
  They pierce my heart with a two-edged sword.
  A fate like that—
  I shudder to look upon Io.

PROMETHEUS
  You are too ready with your tears and fears.
  Wait for the end.

LEADER
Speak. Tell us, for when one lies sick,
to face wth clear eyes all the pain to come
is sweet.

PROMETHEUS
What first you asked was granted easily,
to hear from her own lips her trials.
But for the rest, learn now the sufferings
she still must suffer, this young creature,
at Hera's hands. Child of Inachus,
keep in your heart my words, so you shall know
where the road ends.* First to the sunrise,
over furrows never plowed, where wandering
    Scythians
live in huts of wattles made, raised high
on wheels smooth-rolling. Bows they have,
and they shoot far. Turn from them.
Keep to the shore washed by the moaning sea.
Off to the left live the Chalybians,
workers of iron. There be on your guard.
A rough people they, who like not strangers.
Here rolls a river called the Insolent,
true to its name. You cannot find a ford
until you reach the Caucasus itself,
highest of mountains. From beneath its brow
the mighty river rushes. You must cross
the summit, neighbor to the stars.
Then by the southward road, until you reach
the warring Amazons, men-haters, who one day
will found a city by the Thermodon,
where Salmydessus thrusts
a fierce jaw out into the sea that sailors hate,
stepmother of ships.
And they will bring you on your way right gladly
to the Cimmerian isthmus, by a shallow lake,
Maeotis, at the narrows.
Here you must cross with courage.
And men shall tell forever of your passing.
The strait shall be named for you, Bosporus,
Ford of the Cow. There leave the plains of Europe,

Where the road ends—in the long prophesy of Io's wanderings that follows, Aeschylus presumably appealed to the Athenian love of hearing about remote and exotic geography. Prometheus' speech additionally serves to emphasize the aeons of and immensity of space with which the play deals.

and enter Asia, the great Continent.
—Now does he seem to you, this ruler of the gods,
evil, to all, in all things?
A god desired a mortal—drove her forth
to wander thus.
A bitter lover you have found, O girl,
for all that I have told you is not yet
the prelude even.

Io
Oh, wretched, wretched.

PROMETHEUS
You cry aloud for this? What then
when you have learned the rest?

LEADER
You will not tell her of more trouble?

PROMETHEUS
A storm-swept sea of grief and ruin.

Io
What gain to me is life? Oh, now to fling myself
down from this rock peak to the earth below,
and find release there from my trouble.
Better to die once than to suffer
through all the days of life.

PROMETHEUS
Hardly would you endure my trial,
whose fate it is not ever to find death
that ends all pain. For me there is no end
until Zeus falls from power.

Io
Zeus fall from power?

PROMETHEUS
You would rejoice, I think, to see that happen?

Io
How could I not, who suffer at his hands?

PROMETHEUS
Know then that it shall surely be.

Io
But who will strip the tyrant of his scepter?

PROMETHEUS
He will himself and his own empty mind.

IO
How? Tell me, if it is not wrong to ask.

PROMETHEUS
He will make a marriage that will vex him.

IO
Goddess or mortal, if it may be spoken?

PROMETHEUS
It may not be. Seek not to know.

IO
His wife shall drive him from his throne?

PROMETHEUS
Her child shall be more than his father's match.

IO
And is there no way of escape for him?

PROMETHEUS
No way indeed, unless my bonds are loosed.

IO
But who can loose them against Zeus' will?

PROMETHEUS
A son of yours—so fate decrees.

IO
What words are these? A child of mine shall free
    you?*

PROMETHEUS
Ten generations first must pass and then three more.

IO
Your prophecy grows dim through generations.

PROMETHEUS
So let it be. Seek not to know your trials.

A child . . . shall free you—Heracles, the son of Zeus and the mortal Alcmene, was the descendant of Io who was predestined to liberate Prometheus.

Io

Do not hold out a boon and then withdraw it.

PROMETHEUS

One boon of two I will bestow upon you.

Io

And they are? Speak. Give me the choice.

PROMETHEUS

I give it you: the hardships still before you,
or his name who shall free me. Choose.

LEADER

Of these give one to her, but give to me
a grace as well—I am not quite unworthy.
Tell her where she must wander, and to me
tell who shall free you. It is my heart's desire.

PROMETHEUS

And to your eagerness I yield.
Hear, Io, first, of your far-driven journey.
And bear in mind my words, inscribe them
upon the tablets of your heart.
When you have crossed the stream that bounds
the continents, turn to the East where flame
the footsteps of the sun, and pass
along the sounding sea to Cisthene.
Here on the plain live Phorcys' children, three,
all maidens, very old, and shaped like swans,
who have one eye and one tooth to the three.
No ray of sun looks ever on that country,
nor ever moon by night. Here too their sisters dwell.
And they are three, the Gorgons, winged,
with hair of snakes, hateful to mortals.
Whom no man shall behold and draw again
the breath of life. They garrison that place.
And yet another evil sight, the hounds of Zeus,
who never bark, griffins with beaks like birds.
The one-eyed Arimaspi too, the riders,
who live beside a stream that flows with gold,
a way of wealth. From all these turn aside.
Far off there is a land where black men live,
close to the sources of the sun, whence springs
a sun-scorched river. When you reach it,
go with all care along the banks up to
the great descent. where from the mountains
the holy Nile pours forth its waters

pleasant to drink from. It will be your guide
to the Nile land, the Delta. A long exile
is fated for you and your children here.
If what I speak seems dark and hard to know,
ak me again and learn all clearly.
For I have time to spare and more
than I could wish.

LEADER

If in your story of her fatal journey
there is yet somewhat left to tell her,
speak now. If not, give then to us
the grace we asked. You will remember.

PROMETHEUS

The whole term of her roaming has been told.
But I will show she has not heard in vain,
and tell her what she suffered coming hither,
in proof my words are true.
A moving multitude of sorrows were there,
too many to recount, but at the end
you came to where the levels of Molossa
surround the lofty ridge of Dodona,
seat of God's oracle.
A wonder past belief is there, oak trees that speak.
They spoke, not darkly but in shining words,
calling you Zeus' glorious spouse.
The frenzy seized you then. You fled
along the sea-road washed by the great inlet,
named for God's mother. Up and down you wan-
    dered,
storm-tossed. And in the time to come that sea
shall have its name from you, Ionian,
that men shall not forget your journey.
This is my proof to you my mind can see
farther than meets the eye.
From here the tale I tell is for you all,
and of the future, leaving now the past.
There is a city, Canobus, at the land's end,
where the Nile empties, on new river soil.
There Zeus at last shall make you sane again,
stroking you with a hand you will not fear.
And from this touch alone you will conceive
and bear a son, a swarthy man,
whose harvest shall be reaped on many fields,
all that are washed by the wide-watered Nile.
In the fifth generation from him, fifty sisters
will fly from marriage with their near of kin,

who, hawks in close pursuit of doves, a-quiver
with passionate desire, shall find that death
waits for the hunters on the wedding night.
God will refuse to them the virgin bodies.
Argos will be the maidens' refuge, to their suitors
a slaughter dealt by women's hands,
bold in the watches of the night.
The wife shall kill her husband,
dipping her two-edged sword in blood.
O Cyprian goddess, thus may you come to my foes.
One girl, bound by love's spell, will change
her purpose, and she will not kill
the man she lay beside, but choose the name
of coward rather than be stained with blood.
In Argos she will bear a kingly child—
a story overlong if all were told.
Know this, that from that seed will spring
one glorious with the bow, bold-hearted,
and he shall set me free.
This is the oracle my mother told me,
Justice, who is of old, Earth's daughter.
But how and where would be too long a tale,
nor would you profit.

Io

Oh, misery. Oh, misery.
A frenzy tears me.
Madness strikes my mind.
I burn. A frantic sting—
an arrow never forged with fire.
My heart is beating at its walls in terror.
My eyes are whirling wheels.
Away. Away. A raging wind of fury
sweeps through me.
My tongue has lost its power.
My words are like a turbid stream,
wild waves that dash against a surging sea,
the black sea of madness.
[*Exit* Io.]

Chorus

Wise, wise was he,
who first weighed this in thought
and give it utterance:
Marriage within one's own degree is best,
not with one whom wealth has spoiled,
nor yet with one made arrogant by birth.

Such as these he must not seek
who lives upon the labor of his hands.
Fate, dread deity,
may you never, oh, never behold me
sharing the bed of Zeus.
May none of the dwellers in heaven
draw near to me ever.
Terrors take hold of me
seeing her maidenhood
turning from love of man,
torn by Hera's hate,
driven in misery.
For me, I would not shun marriage nor fear it,
so it were with my equal.
But the love of the greater gods,
from whose eyes none can hide,
may that never be mine.
To war with a god-lover is not war,
it is despair.
For what could I do,
or where could I fly
from the cunning of Zeus?

PROMETHEUS

In very truth shall Zeus, for all his stubborn pride,
be humbled, such a marriage he will make
to cast him down from throne and power.
And he shall be no more remembered.
The curse his father put on him
shall be fulfilled.
The curse that he cursed him with as he fell
from his age-long throne.
The way from such trouble no one of the gods
can show him save I.
These things I know and how they shall come to
       pass.
So let him sit enthroned in confidence,
trust to his crashing thunder high in air,
shake in his hands his fire-breathing dart.
Surely these shall be no defense,
but he will fall, in shame unbearable.
Even now he makes ready against himself
one who shall wrestle with him and prevail,
a wonder of wonders, who will find
a flame that is swifter than lightning,
a crash to silence the thunder,
who will break into pieces the sea-god's spear,

the bane of the ocean that shakes the earth.
Before this evil Zeus shall be bowed down.
He will learn how far apart are a king and a slave.

LEADER
These words of menace on your tongue
speak surely only your desire.

PROMETHEUS
They speak that which shall surely be—
and also my desire.

LEADER
And we must look to see Zeus mastered?

PROMETHEUS
Yes, and beneath a yoke more cruel than this I bear.

LEADER
You have no fear to utter words like these?

PROMETHEUS
I am immortal—and I have no fear.

ANOTHER SEA NYMPH
But agony still worse he might inflict—

PROMETHEUS
So let him do. All that must come I know.

ANOTHER
The wise bow to the inescapable.

PROMETHEUS
Be wise then. Worship power.
Cringe before each who wields it.
To me Zeus counts as less than nothing.
Let him work his will, show forth his power
for his brief day, his little moment
of lording it in heaven.
—But see. There comes a courier from Zeus,
a lackey in his new lord's livery.
Some curious news is surely on his lips.
    [*Enter* HERMES.]

HERMES
You trickster there, you biter bitten,
sinner against the gods, man-lover, thief of fire,
my message is to you.

The great father gives you here his orders:
Reveal this marriage that you boast of,
by which he shall be hurled from power.
And, mark you, not in riddles, each fact clearly.
—Don't make me take a double journey, Prometheus.
    You can see Zeus isn't going to be made kinder
    by this sort of thing.

PROMETHEUS
    Big words and insolent. They well become you,
    O lackey of the gods.
    Young—young—your thrones just won,
    you think you live in citadels grief cannot reach.
    Two dynasties I have seen fall from heaven,
    and I shall see the third fall fastest,
    most shamefully of all.
    Is it your thought to see me tremble
    and crouch before your upstart gods?
    Not so—not such a one am I.
    Make your way back. You will not learn from me.

HERMES
    Ah, so? Still stubborn? Yet this willfulness
    has anchored you fast in these troubled waters.

PROMETHEUS
    And yet I would not change my lot
    with yours, O lackey.

HERMES
    Better no doubt to be slave to a rock
    than be the Father's trusted herald.

PROMETHEUS
    I must be insolent when I must speak to insolence.

HERMES
    You are proud, it seems, of what has come to you.

PROMETHEUS
    I proud? May such pride be
    the portion of my foes.—I count you of them.

HERMES
    You blame me also for your sufferings?

PROMETHEUS
    In one word, all gods are my enemies.
    They had good from me. They return me evil.

HERMES
   I heard you were quite mad.

PROMETHEUS
   Yes, I am mad, if to abhor such foes is madness.

HERMES
   You would be insufferable, Prometheus, if you were
      not so wretched.

PROMETHEUS
   Alas!

HERMES
   Alas? That is a word Zeus does not understand.

PROMETHEUS
   Time shall teach it him, gray time,
   that teaches all things.

HERMES
   It has not taught you wisdom yet.

PROMETHEUS
   No, or I had not wrangled with a slave.

HERMES
   It seems that you will tell the Father nothing.

PROMETHEUS
   Paying the debt of kindness that I owe him?

HERMES
   You mock me as though I were a child.

PROMETHEUS
   A child you are or what else has less sense
   if you expect to learn from me.
   There is no torture and no trick of skill,
   there is no force, which can compel my speech,
   until Zeus wills to loose these deadly bonds.
   So let him hurl his blazing bolt,
   and with the white wings of the snow,
   with thunder and with earthquake,
   confound the reeling world.
   None of all this will bend my will
   to tell him at whose hands he needs must fall.

HERMES
   I urge you, pause and think if this will help you.

PROMETHEUS
I thought long since of all. I planned for all.

HERMES
Submit, you fool. Submit. In agony learn wisdom.

PROMETHEUS
Go and persuade the sea wave not to break.
You will persuade me no more easily.
I am no frightened woman, terrified
at Zeus' purpose. Do you think to see me
ape women's ways, stretch out my hands
to him I hate, and pray him for release?
A world apart am I from prayer for pity.

HERMES
Then all I say is said in vain.
Nothing will move you, no entreaty
soften your heart.
Like a young colt new-bridled,
you have the bit between your teeth,
and rear and fight against the rein.
But all this vehemence is feeble bombast.
A fool, bankrupt of all but obstinacy,
is the poorest thing on earth.
Oh, if you will not hear me, yet consider
the storm that threatens you from which
you cannot fly, a great third wave of evil.
Thunder and flame of lightning will rend
this jagged peak. You shall be buried deep,
held by a splintered rock.
After long length of time you will return
to see the light, but Zeus' winged hound,
an eagle red with blood,
shall come a guest unbidden to your banquet.
All day long he will tear to rags your body,
great rents within the flesh,
feasting in fury on the blackened liver.
Look for no ending to this agony
until a god will freely suffer for you,*
will take on him your pain, and in your stead
descend to where the sun is turned to darkness,
the black depths of death.
Take thought: this is no empty boast
but utter truth. Zeus does not lie.

---

*A god will . . . suffer for you—The centaur Chiron eventually gives his life for that of Prometheus. Hermes, however, does not know this.

Each word shall be fulfilled.
Pause and consider. Never think
self-will is better than wise counsel.

LEADER

To us the words he speaks are not amiss.
He bids you let your self-will go and seek
good counsel. Yield.
For to the wise a failure is disgrace.

PROMETHEUS

These tidings that the fellow shouts to me
were known to me long since.
A foe to suffer at the hands of foes
is nothing shameful.
Then let the twisting flame of forked fire
be hurled upon me. Let the very air
be rent by thunder-crash.
Savage winds convulse the sky,
hurricanes shake the earth from its foundations,
the waves of the sea rise up and drown the stars,
and let me be swept down to hell,
caught in the cruel whirlpool of Necessity.
He cannot kill me.

HERMES

Why, these are ravings you may hear from madmen.
His case is clear. Frenzy can go no further.
You maids who pity him, depart, be swift.
The thunder peals and it is merciless.
Would you too be struck down?

LEADER

Speak other words, another counsel,
if you would win me to obey.
Now, in this place, to urge
that I should be a coward is intolerable.
I choose with him to suffer what must be.
Not to stand by a friend—there is no evil
I count more hateful.
I spit it from my mouth.

HERMES

Remember well I warned you,
when you are swept away in utter ruin.
Blame then yourselves, not fate, nor ever say
that Zeus delivered you
to a hurt you had not thought to see.

With open eyes,
not suddenly, not secretly,
into the net of utter ruin
whence there is no escape,
you fall by your own folly.
   [*Exit* HERMES.]

PROMETHEUS
   An end to words. Deeds now.
   The world is shaken.
   The deep and secret way of thunder
   is rent apart.
   Fiery wreaths of lightning flash.
   Whirlwinds toss the swirling dust.
   The blasts of all the winds are battling in the air,
   and sky and sea are one.
   On me the tempest falls.
   It does not make me tremble.
   O holy Mother Earth, O air and sun,
   behold me. I am wronged.*

---

*I am wronged—Compare Prometheus' refusal to submit to Zeus with Job's contrition before Yahweh.

OEDIPUS THE KING

Preface

IN OEDIPUS THE KING, PRODUCED ABOUT 427 B.C., SOPHOCLES CREATED what is universally acclaimed the most perfectly constructed of all Greek tragedies. The interaction of character and plot, the fusion of form and content, the unity of action and theme, are unique in world drama. With a tremendous economy of means, Sophocles focuses on a single day in the life of Oedipus, king of Thebes, and with almost pitiless clarity analyzes his transformation from the "happiest of mortals" to a blinded, polluted outcast, hated alike by gods and men. Every element in the play is linked to the central issue of Oedipus' self-discovery. Every messenger, every new character appears only to bring the unhappy king a step closer to the long-hidden secret of his identity. A proud, but honest man, Oedipus stops at nothing to learn the truth about himself. His honesty is at once his glory and his downfall, for he cannot survive the revelation of who and what he is.

The dramatic crisis which Oedipus faces lasts only a few hours, but during that short time three irresistible forces converge to destroy him. The first is his own nature—bold, impulsive, and rashly confident. The second is the power of fate, the outworking of a curse placed on Oedipus' father, King Laius. Laius, who had once taken refuge with Pelops, betrayed his host's confidence and violated the divinely ordained laws of hospitality by kidnapping his protector's son, Chrysippus. The third force acting to entangle Oedipus in the web of destiny is the will of Apollo, who, to avenge Pelops, decreed that if Laius had a son, that child would kill him.

Accordingly, when a son was born to Laius and his wife Jocasta, a spike was driven through the baby's feet, and he was exposed on a mountain field to die. There a shepherd found him and took him to Polybus and Merope, king and queen of Corinth, who adopted the infant and called him Oedipus, which means "swollen-foot." When grown to manhood, Oedipus learned of the prophesy that he was destined to murder his father and marry his mother. Thinking that Polybus and Merope were his real parents, Oedipus attempted to avoid fulfilling the oracle and fled from Corinth. At a crossroads leading in one direction to Delphi (the home of Apollo's oracle) and in another to Thebes (his unknown native city), Oedipus encountered Laius (whom of course he could not recognize) and, during a right-of-way struggle, killed him. Having unknowingly fulfilled the first part of Apollo's prediction, Oedipus then proceeded to Thebes where he slew the monster Sphinx that had terrorized the city. His reward was to complete the rest of the prophesy: he married the recently widowed queen, Jocasta, and thereby became king in his father's place.

Sophocles' audience was familiar with the background of Oedipus' story; the interest lay in the skill with which the dramatist unveiled the past and depicted the hero's reaction to his doom. The device which Sophocles uses to heighten the tragedy's impact is to infuse the entire play with examples of dramatic irony. Because the Athenian spectators already knew what Oedipus at the beginning of the action did not, Sophocles could count on an immediate audience response when Oedipus spoke or acted in ignorance of his situation. Since Sophocles gives an ironic twist to virtually every line, it is possible here to cite but a few examples. When he learns that Apollo has afflicted Thebes with plague because Laius' murder has gone unpunished, Oedipus—unaware that he thereby seals his own fate—rashly condemns the unknown assassin to death, exile, or worse. There is further irony in that Oedipus, who had once been the city's saviour, is now its source of pollution. He who had liberated Thebes by his coming can now free it from divine wrath only by leaving it. When the opening chorus addresses Oedipus as "one pre-eminent . . . in man's dealing with the powers above," the words are doubly ironic. For while Oedipus is indeed a supreme example of man controlled by super-human powers, at the same time he has no idea that his life functions as an object lesson in divine manipulation. The ironic tension between the hero's illusions and true insight is introduced with the appearance of the blind prophet Tiresias. Tiresias' cryptic warning that any further inquiry into the cause of the plague and the identity of Laius' slayer will prove catastrophic, not only forecasts the end of the play, but also establishes the metaphor of spiritual blindness which dominates the image patterns throughout. To emphasize that self-knowledge is tantamount to a recognition of one's impotence against the decrees of fate, Sophocles' poetry abounds in eye and sight imagery. Warning Oedipus that though he has eyes he cannot see, Tiresias fore-shadows the king's final self-discovery, which will result in his self-blinding. The ultimate irony is that only when he has lost his physical eyes will Oedipus recognize his true nature. The tragedy is, of course, that Oedipus learns the truth when it is too late to save him.

Although Jocasta, like all the other characters in the play, is subordi-nate to the central figure of Oedipus, she nonetheless embodies an important aspect of Sophocles' theme. Her determined scepticism toward the validity of prophesy probably represents the free-thinking or "modern-ist" trend which Sophocles, a political and religious conservative, so deplored. Even though her only moral guilt is her disbelief in soothsay-ing, it is enough to ensure Jocasta's punishment. Her despair and suicide when she learns that her husband is also her son and that her children have been born of an incestuous union, indicate Sophocles' concern to teach an orthodox respect for Apollo's oracle and to demonstrate the evils that befall those rash enough to defy it.

It is perhaps difficult for a modern reader, reasoning from the assump-tions of contemporary ethics, to feel that Oedipus has in any way deserved his fate. If he was destined from birth to commit the crimes for which he was punished, where does justice lie? The answer, apparently, is nowhere in the Sophoclean moral system. At least not if one defines justice from the purely human standpoint. But granted Sophocles' con-cept of a universe established and ordered by divine law, one can find a certain justice in the restoration of an order which had been upset by Laius' original sin. It is a rather coldly mechanistic theory, but it is philosophically tenable: maintenance of the moral equilibrium demands eye for eye and life for life. It demands that Laius be punished through his son and when that son commits the predestined sin, he too must suffer. It is simple law of cause and effect, totally indifferent to human notions of fairness. The only consolation which Sophocles offers is that man does not stand alone. He inhabits a stable, equitably-governed universe, the balance of which he disturbs at his peril. Since the world was not created to fit man's concept of justice, man's wisdom consists in learning the rules and accommodating himself to them. The process of learning is painful; it is, in fact tragic.

Sophocles' view of the world is undoubtedly bleak, but it is compatible with human experience. It is also characteristically Greek in its refusal to deny either the cruelty of life or the dignity of man. Sophocles' work reflects that brief moment during the Golden Age of Athens when Dionysian vitality and Apollonian serenity achieved a delicate but perfect balance. It was this equilibrium and completeness of vision to which Matthew Arnold referred when he remarked that Sophocles "saw life steadily and saw it whole."

OEDIPUS THE KING

Characters	PRIEST
	OEDIPUS, King of Thebes
	CREON, brother of JOCASTA
	CHORUS of Theban elders
	TEIRESIAS, a blind prophet
	JOCASTA, wife of OEDIPUS
	FIRST MESSENGER
	HERDSMAN
	SECOND MESSENGER

ANTIGONE and ISMENE, daughters of OEDIPUS and JOCASTA (nonspeaking parts)

Citizens of Thebes, Attendants

Reprinted from *Oedipus The King and Antigone* by Sophocles. Translated and Edited by Peter D. Arnott. Copyright © 1960, Meredith Corporation. Reprinted by permission of Appleton-Century-Crofts. Notes are those of the translator.

SCENE: Before the palace of OEDIPUS in Thebes.
[*A crowd of Theban citizens—priests, young men and children—kneel in supplication before the palace, wearing wreaths and carrying branches. Enter* OEDIPUS *from the palace to address them.*]

OEDIPUS

My children, in whom old Cadmus is re-
　　born,
Why have you come with wreathed boughs in your
　　hands.
To sit before me as petitioners?
The town is full of smoke from altar-fires
And voices crying, and appeals to heaven.
I thought it, children, less than just to hear
Your cause at second-hand, but come in person—
I, Oedipus, a name that all men know.
Speak up, old man; for you are qualified
10　To be their spokesman. What is in your minds?
Are you afraid? In need? Be sure I am ready
To do all I can. I should truly be hard-hearted
To have no pity on such prayers as these.

PRIEST

Why, Oedipus, my country's lord and master,
You see us, of all ages, sitting here
Before your altars—some too young to fly
Far from the nest, and others bent with age,
Priests—I of Zeus—and these, who represent
Our youth. The rest sit with their boughs
20　In the city squares, at both of Pallas' shrines,
And where Ismenus' ashes tell the future.
The storm, as you can see, has hit our land
Too hard; she can no longer raise her head
Above the waves of this new sea of blood.
A blight is on the blossoms of the field,
A blight is on the pastured herds, on wives
In childbed; and the curse of heaven, plague,
Has struck, and runs like wildfire through the city,
Emptying Cadmus' house, while black Death reaps

---

1 Cadmus—legendary founder of Thebes. He killed he dragon guarding the site and sowed its teeth in the ground. From them sprang up armed men who fought each other. All were killed except five, who became the ancestors of the Thebans. 2 wreathed boughs—branches entwined with wool, the customary symbol of supplication.
18 Zeus—king of the gods　20 Pallas—Athena, goddess of wisdom　21 Ismenus—river near Thebes. Here the reference is to the prophetic shrine of Apollo by the river, where divination by burnt offerings was practised

30   The harvest of our tears and lamentations.
      Not that we see you as a god, these boys
      And I, who sit there at your feet for favors,
      But as one pre-eminent in life's affairs
      And in man's dealings with the powers above.
      For it was you who came to Cadmus' town
      And freed us from the monster who enslaved us
      With her song, relying on your wits, and knowing
      No more than we. Some god was at your side,
      As men believe, when you delivered us.
40   So now, great Oedipus, giant among men,
      We beg you, all of us who come in prayer,
      Find us some remedy—a whisper heard
      From heaven, or any human way you know.
      In men proved by experience we see
      A living promise, both in word and deed.
      Greatest of men, give our city back its pride!
      Look to your name! This country now remembers
      Your former zeal, and hails you as her savior.
      Never leave us with a memory of your reign
50   As one that raised and let us fall again,
      But lift our city up, and keep it safe.
      You came to make us happy years ago,
      Good omens; show you are the same man still.
      If you continue in your present power
      Better a land with citizens than empty.
      For city walls without their men are nothing,
      Or empty ships, when once the crew has gone.

OEDIPUS
      Poor children, I already know too well
      The desires that bring you here. Yes, I have seen
60   Your sufferings; but suffer as you may,
      There is not one of you who knows my pain.
      Your griefs are private, every man here mourns
      For himself, and for no other; but my heart grieves
      At once for the state, and for myself, and you.
      So do not think you rouse me from my sleep.
      Let me tell you, I have wept, yes, many tears,
      And sent my mind exploring every path.
      My anxious thought found but one hope of cure
      On which I acted—sent Creon, Menoeceus' son,
70   My own wife's brother, to Apollo's shrine
      At Delphi, with commission to enquire
      What I could say or do to save this town.

---

36 the monster . . . her song—the Sphinx and the riddle.
70 Apollo's shrine at Delphi—most famous and prosperous of Greek oracular shrines,
believed to stand at the geographical center of the earth.

Now I am counting the days, and growing anxious
To know what he is doing. It is strange
He should delay so long beyond his time.
But when he comes, I shall be no true man
If I fail to take the course the god has shown us.

PRIEST
Well said, and timely! My friends are signaling
This very moment that Creon is in sight.

OED.
80   O Lord Apollo, let him bring us news
Glad as his face, to give our town good fortune.

PRIEST
I think he brings us comfort; otherwise
He would not wear so thick a crown of Laurel.
    [*Enter* CREON]

OED.
We shall soon know, he is close enough to hear
    us.
Prince, brother of my house, Menoeceus' son,
What is the news you bring us from the god?

CREON
Good news! Our sorrows, heavy as they are,
With proper care may yet end happily.

OED.
What is the oracle? So far you have said noth-
    ing
90   To raise my spirits or to dampen them.

CREON
If you wish to have it here and now, in pub-
    lic,
I am ready to speak; if not, to go inside.

OED.
Speak before all. The sorrows of my people
I count of greater weight than life itself.

CREON
Then, by your leave, I speak as I was told.
Phoebus commands us, in plain terms, to rid
Our land of some pollution, nourished here,
He says, and not to keep a thing past cure.

---

83 crown of laurel—leaves from Apollo's sacred tree   96 Phoebus—Apollo

OED.

How shall we purge ourselves? What stain is
this?

CREON

100 By banishing a man, or taking life
For life, since murder brought this storm on us.

OED.

Who is the man whose fate the god reveals?

CREON

Our country once had Laius for its king,
My lord, before you came to guide this city.

OED.

I have been told as much; I never saw him.

CREON

Laius was murdered. Phoebus tells us plainly
To find his murderers and punish them.

OED.

Where on earth are they? An ancient crime,
A scent grown cold; where shall we find it now?

CREON

110 Here, in this land, he said; seek it, and we
Shall find; seek not, and it shall be hidden.

OED.

And where did Laius meet his bloody end?
In the country? The palace? Traveling abroad?

CREON

He left us on a visit, as he said,
To Delphi, and he never came back home.

OED.

Could no-one tell you? Had he no companion,
No witness, who could give you facts to work on?

CREON

All were killed but one, who ran away in
fright,
And will swear to only one thing that he saw.

OED.

What was that? One thing might give the clue
120   to more
If we had some encouragement, some small beginning.

CREON

    He said they met with bandits; it was not
    By one man's hands that Laius died, but many.

OED.

    What bandit would have taken such a risk
    Unless he were bribed—by someone here, in Thebes?

CREON

    It was suspected; but then our troubles came
    And there was no-one to avenge dead Laius.

OED.

    It must have been great trouble, that could
        make you
    Leave the death of royalty unsolved!

CREON

    The Sphinx, whose riddles made us turn our
130   minds
    To things at home, and abandon mysteries.

OED.

    Then I shall start afresh, and once again
    Find secrets out. Apollo and you too
    Have rightly taken up the dead man's cause.
    You will see me working with you, as is just,
    To avenge the land, and give the god his due.
    It is not on some far-distant friend's behalf
    But on my own, that I shall purge this stain.
    The man whose hand killed Laius might some time
140   Feel a desire to do the same to me,
    And so by avenging him I protect myself.
    Waste no more time, my children, take away
    Your branches and your wreaths, and leave my steps.
    Have Cadmus' people summoned here and tell them
    I will see to everything. We shall be happy now,
    God helping us, or be forever damned.
        [*Exeunt* OEDIPUS *and* CREON]

PRIEST

    Let us arise, my sons. He promises
    The favors that we first came here to ask.
    May Phoebus who has sent this oracle
150   Come to save Thebes, and cure us of the plague!
        [*Exeunt. Enter* CHORUS *of Theban elders*]

CHORUS

    Sweet voice of Zeus, what word do you
        bring

From golden Pytho to glorious Thebes?
I am heart-shaken, torn on the rack of fear.
Apollo, Healer, to whom men cry,
I tremble before you; what will it please you
To send us? Some new visitation?
Or something out of the past, come due
In fullness of time? Tell me, Voice undying,
The child of golden Hope.

160   Daughter of Zeus, to you first I cry,
Immortal Athena; and then her sister
Artemis, guardian of our land, enthroned
In honor in our assemblies; Apollo,
Heavenly archer; now shine on us all three,
Champions strong against death; if ever
In time gone by you stood between Thebes
And threatened disaster, turning the fire
Of pestilence from us, come now!

For my sorrows have grown past counting.
170   The plague is on all our people, and wit
Can devise no armor. No more the good earth
Brings forth its crops; women groan in their barren la-
    bors,
And you may see, like flying birds,
Souls speeding, one by one,
To join the sunset god; their flight
Is faster than the racing flame.

Thebes dies a new death each moment; her children
Lie in the dust, death's agents, and no-one
Spares them a tear; their wives and gray-haired moth-
    ers
Flock screaming to the altars, and pray for their own
180   lives.
Above the counterpoint of tears
There rings out clear the healing chant.
Show us, golden child of Zeus,
The smiling face of comfort!

Grim Death is marching on us, not now with clashing
    shields
But blasts of fiery breath, and the cry goes up around
    him.

---

152 Pytho—Delphi
162 Artemis—goddess of childbirth and of wild things

Turn him away from us, drive him from our land!
Come, fair wind, and blow him away
To the vasty halls of the western ocean
190   Or the Thracian seas, where sailors fear to go.
For if night has left any harm undone
Day treads on its heels to finish the work.
Zeus our Father, lord of the bright lightning,
Come with your thunder and destroy!

And we pray Apollo the archer to string his golden bow
And send invincible arrows to fight for us in the field,
And Artemis' blazing torches, that she carries
To light her way through the Lycian mountains.
On the god with gold-bound hair I call,
200   Bacchus, whose name we have made our own,
Who comes with a cry of maidens dancing.
Bright comforter, bring the joyous light
Of your torch, stand with us against our foe,
The rogue-god, whom his brothers shun!
    [*Enter* OEDIPUS]

OED.
You pray; now for answer. If you are prepared
To accept what I say, and be your own physician,
Cure may be yours, and respite from your pain.
I must speak as a stranger to your story, one
Unacquainted with the facts; I could not press
210   My enquiries far alone, without some clue.
But now I am a Theban among Thebans
And make this proclamation to the sons
Of Cadmus: if anyone among you knows
Who murdered Laius, son of Labdacus,
I order him to make a full disclosure.
If he should fear to implicate himself
By confession, why, nothing unpleasant will happen;
He will leave the land unharmed, and that is all.
If anybody knows another guilty—
220   An alien perhaps—then let him not keep silent.
He will earn a reward and my gratitude besides.
But if you refuse to talk; if anyone
Is frightened into shielding self or friend,
Pay good attention to the consequences.

---

190 Thracian seas—off the north-east coast of Greece, notoriously treacherous. Ares, god of war, was regarded as having his home in this wild region.   198 Lycian mountains—in Asia Minor   200 Bacchus—Dionysus, god of wine, traditionally born in Thebes from the union of Zeus and a mortal woman, Semele.

As lord and master of this land of Thebes
I declare this man, whoever he may be
An outlaw; order you to break off speech
With him, to excommunicate him from your prayers
And sacrifices, to deny him holy water,
230   To drive him from your doors, remembering
That this is our pollution, which the god
This day revealed to me in oracles.
In this I show myself on heaven's side,
One with the murdered man. My solemn curse
Is on the killer, whether he is hiding
In lonely guilt or has accomplices.
May he reap the harm he sowed, and die unblest.
And what is more, I pray that if this man
Should live among my household with my knowledge,
240   The curse I swore just now should fall on me.
I lay the responsibility on you,
For my sake, and the gods', and for our country
Turned to a stricken, god-forsaken waste.
For even if heaven had not shown its hand
Fitness alone forbade such negligence
When one so noble, and your king, had died.
You should have held enquiries. Now since I
Have fallen heir to the power which once was his,
Sleep in his bed, and take his bride to wife,
250   And since, if he had not been disappointed
In his succession, we two would have had
A bond between us, children of one mother,
But as it was, his fortune struck him down,
For all these reasons, I shall fight for him
As I would for my own father, leave no stone
Unturned to find the man who shed his blood
In honor of the son of Labdacus,
Of Polydorus, Cadmus, and Agenor.
For those who disobey my words I pray
260   The gods to send no harvest to their fields,
Their wives no children, but to let them die
In present misery, or worse to come.
But as for you, the rest of Cadmus' children,
Who think as I do, may our ally, Right,
And all the gods be with you evermore.

CHORUS
You put me on my oath and I must speak.
I did not kill him, nor can I point to the man

Who did. It was for Phoebus, who sent the question,
To answer it, and find the murderer.

270 OED.

What you say is fair enough, but no man living
Can force the gods to speak when they do not want to.

CHORUS

By your leave, a second best occurs to
    me. . . .

OED.

Second or third best, do not keep it from us!

CHORUS

I know Teiresias has powers of vision
Second only to Phoebus. A man who asked of him,
My lord, might find his questions answered.

OED.

Another thing that I have not neglected.
On Creon's bidding I have sent men twice
To bring him; it is strange he is not yet come.

CHORUS

We have nothing else but vague and ancient
280   rumors.

OED.

What are they? I must examine every story.

CHORUS

He is said to have been killed by men on the
    road.

OED.

Yes, so I hear; but no-one knows who did it.

CHORUS

If he has any fear in him, a curse
Such as you swore will bring him out of hiding.

OED.

Words will not scare a man when actions do
    not.

CHORUS

But here is one to convict him. They are
    bringing

The prophet here at last, the man of god,
The only one who has the truth born in him.
[*Enter* TEIRESIAS,* *led by a boy*]

OED.

290   Teiresias, all things are known to you,
Open and secret, things of heaven and earth.
Blind though you are, you sense how terrible
A plague is on us; and in you, great prophet,
We find our only means of self-defence.
We sent—perhaps my messengers have told you—
To Phoebus; he replied, by one way only
Could Thebes secure deliverance from the plague,
By hunting down the murderers of Laius
And killing them or driving them abroad.
300   So grudge us nothing of your bird-cry lore
Or any means of prophecy you know.
Come, save the city; save yourself and me,
And heal the foulness spread by Laius' blood.
We are in your hands. Man knows no finer task
Than helping friends with all his might and means.

TEIRESIAS

How terrible is wisdom when it turns
Against you! All of this I know, but let it
Slip from my mind, or I should not have come here.

OED.

What is it? Why have you come in so black a
    mood?

310   TEIR.

Send me home. It will be easiest for each of us
To bear his own burden to the end, believe me.

OED.

A fine way to talk! You do your motherland
No kindness by witholding information.

TEIR.

When I see you opening your mouth at the
    wrong moment
I take care to avoid a like mistake.

OED.

By heaven, if you know something, do not turn
    away!
You see us all on our knees imploring you.

---

300   bird-cry lore—omens were commonly deduced from the flight of birds
*Teiresias—Tiresias, the blind prophet.

TEIR.

 Yes, for you all know nothing. I shall never
 Reveal my sorrows—not to call them yours.

320 OED.

 What do you say? You know and will not talk?
 Do you mean to turn traitor and betray the state?

TEIR.

 I wish to cause no pain—to either of us.
 So why ask useless questions? My lips are sealed.

OED.

 Why, you old reprobate, you could provoke
 A stone to anger! Will you never speak?
 Can nothing touch you? Is there no end to this?

TEIR.

 You blame my temper, but you fail to recognize
 Your own working in you; no, you criticize me!

OED.

 And who would not be angry when he hears
330 you
 Talking like this, and holding Thebes in contempt?

TEIR.

 These things will happen, if I speak or not.

OED.

 Then if they must, it is your duty to tell me.

TEIR.

 This discussion is at an end. Now, if you like,
 You may be as angry as your heart knows how.

OED.

 Then in my anger I will spare you none
 Of my suspicions. This is what I think;
 You helped contrive the plot—no, did it all
 Except the actual killing. If you had
 Your eyesight I should say you did that too.

TEIR.

 Indeed? Then listen to what I say. Obey
340 Your own pronouncement, and from this day on
 Speak not to me or any man here present.
 You are the curse, the defiler of this land.

OED.

> You dare fling this at me? Have you no fear?
> Where can you hope for safety after this?

TEIR.

> I am safe enough. My strength is in my truth.

OED.

> Who put you up to this? No skill of yours!

TEIR.

> You did—by forcing me to speak against my
>   will.

OED.

> What was it? Say it again, I must be sure.

TEIR.

> Did you not understand? Or are you tempting
>   me?

OED.

350 I have not quite grasped it. Tell it me again.

TEIR.

> You hunt a murderer; it is yourself.

OED.

> You will pay for uttering such slanders twice.

TEIR.

> Shall I say something else, to make you angrier
>   still?

OED.

> Say what you like, it is a waste of breath.

TEIR.

> You have been living in unimagined shame
> With your nearest, blind to your own degradation.

OED.

> How long do you think such taunts will go un-
>   punished?

TEIR.

> For ever, if there is any strength in truth.

OED.

> In truth, but not in you. You have no strength,
> Failing in sight, in hearing, and in mind.

TEIR.

360   And you are a fool to say such things to me,
  Things that the world will soon hurl back at you!

OED.

  You live in the dark; you are incapable
  Of hurting me or any man with eyes.

TEIR.

  Your destiny is not to fall by me.
  That is Apollo's task, and he is capable.

OED.

  Who is behind this? You? Or is it Creon?

TEIR.

  Your ruin comes not from Creon, but yourself.

OED.

  Oh wealth! Oh monarchy! Talent which out-
    runs
370   Its rivals in the cutthroat game of life,
  How envy dogs your steps, and with what strength,
  When tempted by the power the city gave
  Into my hands, a gift, and never asked for,
  The man I trusted, Creon, my earliest friend,
  Yearns to depose me, plots behind my back,
  Makes accomplices of conjurers like this
  Who sells his tricks to the highest bidder, who looks
  Only for profits, and in his art is blind.
  Let us hear where you have proved yourself a seer!
380   Why did you not, when the Singing Bitch was here,
  Utter one word to set your people free?
  For this was not a riddle to be solved
  By the first-comer; it cried out for divination.
  You were tried and found wanting; neither birds
  Nor voices from heaven could help you. Then I came,
  I, ignorant Oedipus, and put a stop to her
  By using my wits, no lessons from the birds!
  And it is I you try to depose, assuming
  That you will have a place by Creon's throne.
390   You and your mastermind will repent your zeal
  To purge this land. You are old, by the look of you;
  If not, you would have learnt the price of boldness.

CHORUS

  It seems to me that this man's words were
    spoken

---

380   Singing Bitch—the Sphinx

In anger, Oedipus, and so were yours.
This is not what we need; we ask to know
How we can best obey the oracle.

TEIR.

King though you are, the right of speech must
    be
The same for all. Here, I am my own master.
I live in Apollo's service, not in yours,
400   And have no need of Creon to endorse me.
Listen to me; you taunt me with my blindness,
But you have eyes, and do not see your sorrows,
Or where you live, or what is in your house.
Do you know whose son you are? You are abhorrent
To your kin on earth and under it, and do not know
One day your mother's and your father's curse,
A two-tongued lash, will run you out of Thebes,
And you who see so well will then be blind.
What place will not give shelter to your cries?
410   What corner of Cithairon will not ring with them,
When you have understood the marriage song which
        brought you
From properous voyage to uneasy harbor?
And a throng of sorrows that you cannot guess
Will drag you down and level you with those
You have begotten, and your proper self.
So go your way; heap mockery and insult
On Creon and my message; you will be crushed
More miserably than any man on earth.

OED.

Am I to listen to such things from him
Without protest? Out of my sight this instant! Leave
420   my house!
Go back where you came from, and be damned!

TEIR.

I would never have come here, if you had not
    called me.

OED.

If I had known you would rave like this, it
    would have been
A long time before I asked you to my house.

---

410   Cithairon—mountain near Thebes where Oedipus was exposed

TEIR.

I am what I am. I pass for a fool to you,
But as sane enough for the parents who begot you.

OED.

Who were they? Wait! What is my father's
    name?

TEIR.

This day will give you parents and destroy
    you.

OED.

All the time you talk in riddles, mysteries.

430 TEIR.

And who can decipher riddles better than you?

OED.

Yes, laugh at that! There you will find my
    greatness!

TEIR.

And it is just luck that has destroyed you.

OED.

I saved the city; nothing else can matter.

TEIR.

Very well then, I shall go. Boy, take me home.

OED.

Yes, let him take you. Here you are in the way,
A hindrance; out of sight is out of mind.

TEIR.

I will go when my errand is done. I do not fear
Your frown. There is no way that you can harm me.
Listen to me: the man you have sought so long,
440   Threatening, issuing your proclamations
About the death of Laius—he is here,
Passing for an alien, but soon to be revealed
A Theban born; and he will find no pleasure
In this turn of fortune. He who now has eyes
Will be blind, who now is rich, a beggar,
And wander abroad with a stick to find his way.
He will be revealed as father and as brother
Of the children in his home, as son and husband

Of the woman who bore him, his father's murderer
450   And successor to his bed. Now go away
And think about these things; and if you find I lie
Then you can say that I am no true prophet.
[*Exeunt* TEIRESIAS *and* OEDIPUS]

CHORUS.
Who is the man denounced
By the voice of god from the Delphian rock?
Who is the man with bloody hands
Guilty of horrors the tongue cannot name?
It is time for him to run
Faster of foot than the horses of the storm,
For the Son of Zeus is leaping upon him
460   With fire and lightning, and at his side
The Fates, remorseless avengers.

Fresh from Parnassus' snows
The call blazes forth: the hunt is up!
Search every place for the unknown man!
He doubles among the wild woods for cover,
From hole to hole in the hills,
A rogue bull running a lost race, trying
To shake off the sentence ringing in his ears
Pronounced by the shrine at earth's center, forever
470   Haunting him, goading him on.

The wise man with his birds and omens
Leaves me troubled and afraid,
Unable to believe or disbelieve.
What can I say? I fly from hope to fear.
Dark is the present, dark the days to come.
There is no quarrel that I know of
Now or in the past between
Labdacus' house and the son of Polybus,
480   Nothing that I could use as proof
Against Oedipus' reputation
In avenging Labdacus' line, and solving
The riddle of Laius' death.

To Zeus and Apollo all things are known,
They see the doings of mankind.
But who is to say that a human prophet

---

462 Parnassus—mountain near Delphi celebrated as the home of Apollo and the
Muses, and also as the haunt of Dionysus

Knows any more of the future than I?
Though some men, I know, are wiser than others.
But I shall never join with his accusers
Until they have made good their charge.
490   We saw his wisdom tried and tested
When he fought the girl with wings.
Thebes took him then to her heart, and I
Will never name him guilty.
    [*Enter* CREON]

CREON.
    Citizens, I hear that Oedipus our king
Lays monstrous charges against me, and am here
In indignation. If in the present crisis
He thinks I have injured him in any way
By word or action calculated to harm him,
I would rather die before my time is up
500   Than bear this stigma. Such malicious slander
Touches me on more than one tender spot.
What hurts me most is this—to have my friends
And you and my city brand me as a traitor.

CHORUS
    This insult was probably spoken under
        stress.
In anger, not with deliberate intent.

CREON
    And what about the taunt that the seer was
        coerced
Into lying by my design? Who started it?

CHORUS
    It was said—I do not know how seriously.

CREON
    Did he lay this charge against me steady-
510   eyed?
Did he sound as if he knew what he was saying?

CHORUS
    I know nothing about it. I do not look at
        what
My masters do. Here he comes himself, from the
        palace.
    [*Enter* OEDIPUS]

---

491 the girl with wings—the Sphinx

OED.
> You! And what brings you here? Can you put
>> on
> So bold a face, to visit your victim's house,
> Shown up for what you are, a murderer
> Openly plotting to rob me of my crown?
> In heaven's name, what did you take me for?
> A fool? A coward? to entertain such schemes?
> Do you think I would let you work behind my back
> Unnoticed, or not take precautions once I knew?
> Then is it not senseless, this attempt of yours
> To bid for the throne alone and unsupported?
> It takes men and money to make a revolution.

CREON
> Wait! You have said your say; it is now your
>> turn
> To listen. Learn the facts and then pass judgment.

OED.
> Smooth talker! But I have no inclination
> To learn from you, my bitter enemy.

CREON
> One thing let me say, before we go any
>> further. . . .

OED.
> One thing you must never say—that you are
>> honest!

CREON
> If you think there is any virtue in stub-
>> bornness
> Devoid of reason, you have little sense.

OED.
> If you think you can wrong one of your family
> And get away unpunished, you are mad.

CREON
> Justly said, I grant you. But give me some
>> idea,
> What injury do you say that I have done you?

OED.
> Did you suggest it would be advisable
> To bring the prophet here, or did you not?

CREON
I did; and I am still of the same opinion.

OED.
And how many years ago was it that Laius. . . .

CREON
540   That Laius what? I cannot follow you.

OED.
Was lost to his people by an act of violence.

CREON
That would take us a long way back into
    the past.

OED.
And was the prophet practicing in those days?

CREON
As skillfully as today, with equal honor.

OED.
And did he then make any mention of me?

CREON
Not at any time when I was there to hear
    him.

OED.
But did you not investigate the murder?

CREON
We were bound to, of course, but discovered
    nothing.

OED.
And why did this know-all not tell his story
    then?

CREON
I prefer not to talk about things I do not
550   know.

OED.
You know one thing well enough that you
    could tell me.

CREON
> What is it? If I know, I shall keep nothing
>> back.

OED.
> This: if you had not put your heads together
> We should never have heard about my killing Laius.

CREON
> If he says so, you know best. Now let me ask
> And you must answer as I answered you.

OED.
> Ask what you like. I am innocent of murder.

CREON
> Come now; are not you married to my sister?

OED.
> A question to which I can hardly answer no.

CREON
560 > And you rule the country with her, equally?

OED.
> I give her everything that she could wish for.

CREON
> Do I, the third, not rank with both of you?

OED.
> You do; which makes your treachery the worse.

CREON
> Not if you reason with yourself as I do.
> First ask yourself this question: would any man
> Be king in constant fear, when he could live
> In peace and quiet, and have no less power?
> I want to be a king in everything
> But name—and I have no desire for that,
570 > Nor has any man who knows what is good for him.
> As it is, I am carefree. You give me all I want,
> But as king I should have many tiresome obligations.
> Then why should I find monarchy more desirable
> Than power and influence without the trouble?
> So far I have not been misguided enough
> To hanker after dishonorable gains.
> As it is, all wish me well and greet me kindly,

And people with suits to you call first on me
For there are all their chances of success.
580   So why should I give up one life for the other?
No man with any sense would stoop to treason.
I have no love for such ideas, nor would I
Associate with any man who did.
Do you look for proof of this? Then go to Delphi
And ask if I quoted the oracle correctly.
And another thing; if you find that I have made
A plot with the prophet, there will be two voices
To sentence me to death—yours and my own.
590   But do not convict me out of mere suspicion!
It is hardly just to label good men bad
Or bad men good, according to your whim.
Mark my words: the man who drops an honest friend
Cuts out his heart, the thing he loves the best.
But you will learn this sure enough in time,
For time alone can tell an honest man
While one day is enough to show a villain.

CHORUS
Good advice, my lord, for one who keeps
     a watch
For pitfalls. Hasty thoughts are dangerous.

OED.
When conspirators make haste to set plots
     moving
600   I must make haste myself to counteract them.
If I waited and did nothing it would mean
Success for him and ruin for myself.

CREON
Then what do you want? My banishment
     from Thebes?

OED.
No, not your banishment. I want your death!

CREON
There speaks a man who will not listen to
     reason.

OED.
No, you must show the world what comes of
     envy!

CREON
  I think you must be mad.

OED.
  And I think sane.

CREON
  Then hear me sensibly.

OED.
  Hear you, a traitor?

CREON
  Suppose you are wrong?

OED.
610 Kings must still be obeyed.

CREON
  Kings, but not tyrants.

OED.
  City, oh my city!

CREON
  My city also. I have rights here too.

CHORUS
  Stop this, my lords. I can see Jocasta
        coming
  From the palace just in time. Let her advise you,
  Put your quarrel aside and be friends again.
     [*Enter* JOCASTA]

JOCASTA.
  Have you both gone out of your minds? What
        is the sense
  Of bandying insults? Are you not ashamed
  To start a private feud, when Thebes is ailing?
  Come inside. And Creon, you must go back home.
  Do not make a mortal grievance out of nothing.

CREON
620 Sister, your husband Oedipus thinks fit
  To make me suffer one way or the other—
  To drive me into banishment or kill me.

OED.
  Exactly. I have caught him plotting mischief—
  A criminal attempt on the royal person.

CREON
> May heaven's anger strike me dead this
> > minute
> If I have done anything to deserve this charge!

JOC.
> In the gods' name, Oedipus, believe what he
> > says!
> If not from respect of the oath he has sworn,
> For the sake of your wife and everyone here!

CHORUS
630   Listen to reason, my lord;
> I beg you, be guided by us.

OED.
> You ask for a favor; what is it?

CHORUS
> He has been no fool in the past;
> He is strong in his oath; respect him.

OED.
> Do you know what it is you ask?

CHORUS
> I do.

OED.
> Then explain yourselves; what do you
> > mean?

CHORUS
> Your friends has invoked a curse on his
> > head.
> Do not brand him traitor on rumor alone.

OED.
> You must know, by asking this
640   You are asking my exile or death.

CHORUS
> No, by the Sun, the first among gods!
> May I die the death that men fear most,
> Shunned, unclean in the sight of heaven,
> If I have such thoughts in my mind.
> But my heart is heavy at our country's dying
> If you add new troubles to her present load.

OED.
Let him go then; but I am signing my own
death warrant
Or condemning myself to exile and disgrace.
Your voice has moved me where his oath could not.
650   As for him, wherever he may go, I hate him.

CREON
Now we have seen you—wild when you lose
your temper,
And yielding with bad grace. Such a nature as yours
Is its own worst enemy, and so it should be.

OED.
Get out, and leave me in peace.

CREON
I am going.
They know I am honest, though you will not see it.
[*Exit*]

CHORUS
Now quickly, my lady, take him inside.

JOC.
Not before I know what has happened.

CHORUS
There were words, a vague suspicion,
False, but injustice stings.

JOC.
On both sides?

CHORUS
Yes.

JOC.
660   What was said?

CHORUS
Our country has troubles enough.
Better let sleeping dogs lie.

OED.
You meant well enough, but see where it leads
you,
Checking me, blunting the edge of my anger.

CHORUS

I have said it before and say it again:
Men would think that my wits had wandered,
Would think me insane, to abandon you.
Our beloved country was sinking fast
Till you took the helm; and now you may prove
670   Our guide and salvation again.

JOC.

Tell me as well, my lord, in heaven's name,
What can have set such fury working in you?

OED.

I will tell you; you are more to me than they
      are.
It is Creon, and the way he is plotting against me.

JOC.

Go on, and tell me how this quarrel started.

OED.

He says that I am Laius' murderer.

JOC.

Does he speak from knowledge or from hearsay
      only?

OED.

Neither; he sent a mischief-making prophet.
He is taking care to keep his own mouth clean.

JOC.
680   You can relieve your mind of all such fears.
Listen, and learn from me: no human being
Is gifted with the art of prophecy.
Once an oracle came to Laius—I will not say
From Apollo himself, but from his ministers—
To say a child would be born to him and me
By whose hand it was fated he should die.
And Laius, as rumor goes, was killed by bandits,
From another land, at a place where three roads meet.
And as for our son, before he was in this world
690   Three days, Laius pinned his ankles together
And had him abandoned on the trackless mountain.
So in this case Apollo's purpose failed—
That the child should kill his father, or that Laius
Should be murdered by his son, the fear that haunted
      him.

So much for oracles which map our future!
Then take no notice of such things; whatever the god
Finds needful, he will show without assistance.

OED.
Oh wife, the confusion that is in my heart,
The fearful apprehension, since I heard you speak!

JOC.
700   What is it? What have I said to startle you?

OED.
I thought I heard you telling me that Laius
Was murdered at a place where three roads meet.

JOC.
Such was the story. People tell it still.

OED.
What country was it where the thing was done?

JOC.
In the land called Phocis, at the meeting-point
Of the roads from Delphi and from Daulia.

OED.
And how many years have gone by since it
        happened?

JOC.
It was just before you first appeared in Thebes
To rule us; that is when we heard of it.

OED.
Oh Zeus, what have you planned to do with
710   me?

JOC.
Oedipus, what is it? Why has this upset you?

OED.
Do not ask me yet; but tell me about Laius.
What did he look like? How far gone in years?

JOC.
A tall man, with his hair just turning gray,
To look at, not so different from you.

OED.
Oh, what have I done? I think that I have laid
A dreadful curse on myself and never knew it!

JOC.
What are you saying? It frightens me to look
    at you.

OED.
I am terrified the prophet sees too well.
720   I shall know better if you tell me one thing more.

JOC.
You frighten me; but ask and I will tell you.

OED.
Did he ride with a handful of men, or with a
    band
Of armed retainers, as a chieftain should?

JOC.
There were five in all—a herald one of them.
And a single carriage in which Laius rode.

OED.
Oh, now I see it all. Jocasta, answer me,
Who was the man who told you what had happened?

JOC.
A servant—the only one who returned alive.

OED.
Is he with us? Is he in our household now?

JOC.
730   No, he is not. When he came back and found
You ruling here in Thebes and Laius dead
He wrung me by the hand and begged me send him
Into the country where we graze our sheep
As far as possible from the sight of Thebes.
I let him go away; slave though he was
He could have asked far more and had it granted.

OED.
I want him here, as fast as he can come.

JOC.
That can be seen to. What is in your mind?

OED.

I fear I have already said
740   More than I should; that is why I want to see him.

JOC.

He shall come then; but I too have a right
To know what lies heavy on your heart, my lord.

OED.

I shall keep nothing from you, now my appre-
        hension
Has gone so far. Who else should I confide in
Unless in you, when this crisis is upon me?
My father's name was Polybus of Corinth,
My mother a Dorian, Merope. In that city
I lived as first in honor, till one day
There happened something—worth surprise perhaps,
750   But not such anger as it roused in me.
A man at dinner, too far gone in wine,
Jeered in his cups, I was my father's bastard.
It preyed on my mind; and I restrained myself
That day as best I could, but in the morning
Went questioning my parents. They were angry
At such a taunt, and the man who let it fly,
So on their part I was satisfied; but still
The slander rankled as it spread and grew.
And so I went, without my parents' knowledge,
760   On a journey to Delphi. Phoebus sent me away
No wiser than I came, but something else
He showed me, sad and strange and terrible:
That I was doomed to mate with my own mother,
Bring an abhorrent brood into the world;
That I should kill the father who begat me.
When I heard, I fled from Corinth, ever since
Marking its whereabouts only by the stars,
To find some place where I should never see
This evil oracle's calamities fulfilled,
770   And in my travels reached that very place
Where, as you tell me, Laius met his death.
Wife, I shall tell the truth: I was on my way
And had nearly come to the joining of the roads
When there met me, from the opposite direction,
A herald, and a man in a horse-drawn carriage
Exactly as you described. The fellow in front
And the old man tried to push me out of the way.

---

747 Dorian—one of the oldest Greek tribes; Oedipus says this with some pride

I lost my temper, hit out at the one
Who jostled me, the driver; when the old man saw it,
780   He watched me, from the carriage, coming past
And brought his double goad down on my head—
But took it back with interest! One swift blow
From the good staff in my hand, and over he went
Clean out of the chariot, sprawling on his back,
And I killed every man in sight. If this stranger
Should turn out to have anything to do with Laius,
Who is more wretched than this man before you,
And who could be more hateful to the gods,
A man no citizen, no stranger even,
790   May take into his house or speak with him
But drive him from their doors; and this, this curse
Was laid on me by no-one but myself.
And now my hands, by which he met his death,
Defile his bed. Am I not evil? Am I not
Foul through and through, when I must go to exile
And in that exile never see my people,
Or set foot in my homeland—for if I do
I must marry my mother, murder Polybus,
The father who gave me life and livelihood.
800   Then if you saw in Oedipus the prey
Of some tormenting power, would you be wrong?
Never, oh never, pure and awful gods,
Let me see that day; no, let me rather vanish
Out of sight of men, before I see
This dreadful visitation come upon me.

CHORUS
    This is fearful, my lord; but do not give
        up hope
    Until you have questioned the man who saw it done.

OED.
    Yes, that is all the hope I have left me now,
    To wait the coming of this man, our shepherd.

JOC.
    And when he comes, what would you have from
810   him?

OED.
    I will tell you. If I find his story tallies
    With yours, then it will mean that I am safe.

JOC.
    And what is so important in my story?

OED.

You said that Laius, as he told the tale,
Was killed by robbers. If he stands by this,
That there were more than one, I did not kill him;
You could not make one man a company.
But if he names one solitary traveler
There is no more doubt; the deed swings back to me.

JOC.

820   You can be sure that this is what he said.
He cannot go back on it, all the city heard him.
I was not the only one. But even supposing
We find he tells a different tale today,
My lord, he can never show that Laius' death
Ran true to prophecy. Phoebus expressly said
That he was doomed to die at my child's hands;
But that unhappy babe went to his death
Before he did; then how could he have killed him?
830   So when it comes to oracles, after this
I shall keep both eyes fixed firmly on the front.

OED.

You speak good sense. But all the same, send
    someone
To bring the peasant here; do as I say.

JOC.

I will send at once. Come now, let us go home.
Would I ever fail to do anything you wanted?
    [*Exeunt*]

CHORUS

I pray that this may crown my every day,
In all my words and deeds to walk
Pure-hearted, in proper fear:
For thus we are commanded from on high
By laws created in the shining heavens,
840   Who know no other father but Olympus,
In their birth owing nothing to mortals
Nor sleeping though forgotten; great the god
Within them, and he grows not old.

Out of insolence is born the tyrant,
Insolence grown fat in vain

---

840 Olympus—mountain home of the gods   866 the inviolate . . . world—Delphi;
see n. on v. 70

On things immoderate, unfit.
For a man who has mounted to the highest places
Must fall to meet his destiny below
Where there can be no help, no footing.
850   But honest ambition let us keep,
For thus the state is served; O Lord Apollo
Guide and strenghten me all my days.

But I pray that the man whose hands and tongue
Are arrogant, careless of retribution,
Who blasphemes in the holy places,
May fall upon evil days, the reward
Of the sin of self-conceit.
If he goes the wrong way to gain his ends,
And follows unholy courses, laying
860   Profaning hands on things he should not touch,
Could any man boast his life was safe
From the arrows of angry heaven?
But when such things as these are held in honor
Why should I sing the praises of the gods?

No longer shall I visit with my prayers
The inviolate shrine at the center of the world,
Or Abae's temple, or Olympia,
If the prophecy should fail to come to pass
As spoken, for all the world to see.
870   O Zeus, if you are rightly called
The Almighty, the ruler of mankind,
Look to these things; and let them not escape
Your power eternal; for the oracles
Once told of Laius are forgotten, slighted;
Apollo is divested of his glory
And man turns his face away from heaven.
        [*Enter* Jocasta]

Joc.
Elders of Thebes, I have a mind to pay
A visit to the holy shrines, with gifts
Of incense and wreathed branches in my hands.
880   For Oedipus has let his mind succumb
To all manner of fears, and will not judge the present
By what has gone before, like a sensible man,
But is the prey of every fearful rumor.

---

867 Abae—near Thebes, site of temple and oracle of Apollo   Olympia—home of the temple of Zeus and the famous Olympic Games   876 and man . . . heaven—a fair description of the growing agnosticism of Sophocles' own time

There is nothing more that I can say to help him,
And so I bring offerings to you, Apollo—
The nearest to us—and request this favor;
Show us how we can find a clean way out,
For now we are afraid to see him frightened,
Like sailors who see panic in their steersman.
[*Enter* MESSENGER]

MESSENGER
Could you tell me, my friends, where
890   a man might find
The palace of King Oedipus—better still,
Where the king himself is, if you happen to know?

CHORUS
This is his house, and the king is indoors.
This lady is the mother of his children.

MESS.
May heaven bless Oedipus' honored queen
Her whole life long with every happiness!

JOC.
Stranger, I wish you the same; so fair a greeting
Deserves no less. But tell us why you come.
What have you to ask of us, or tell us?

MESS.
Good news for your house, my lady, and your
900   husband!

JOC.
What news is this? Who sent you here to us?

MESS.
I come from Corinth; what I have to tell
Will please you, no doubt; but there is sadness too.

JOC.
Pleasure and pain at once? What is this mes-
       sage?

MESS.
The people living in the Isthmian land
Will have him for their king; so goes the story.

---

905 Isthmian land—Corinth, situated on the narrow neck of land which joins the two
parts of Greece

Joc.

Why? Is old Polybus no longer king?

Mess.

No, death has claimed him. He is in his grave.

Joc.

What are you saying? Oedipus' father dead?

Mess.

910 If I am lying, may I die myself!

Joc.

Maid, run away and tell this to your master
As fast as you can. Oh gods, where are
Your oracles now? This is the man that Oedipus
Has shunned for years, for fear of killing him,
And now he is dead, and Oedipus never touched him!
[*Enter* Oedipus]

Odeipus.

Jocasta, dearest wife, why have you sent
For me, and called me from the palace?

Joc.

Listen to this man here, and learn from his
words
To what these holy oracles have come!

Oed.

920 This man? Who is he? what has he to say?

Joc.

From Corinth; his message is that Polybus,
Your father, lives no longer—he is dead!

Oed.

What? Stranger, let me have it from your
mouth.

Mess.

If this is where I must begin my message,
I assure you, Polybus is dead and gone.

Oed.

Did it happen by foul play? Or was he sick?

Mess.

When a man is old his life hangs by a thread.

OED.
Poor Polybus. He died of illness, then?

MESS.
That and old age. He had lived a long life.

OED.
930   Oh, wife, why should we ever spare a glance
For the shrine of Delphi, or the birds that scream
Above our heads? On their showing, I was doomed
To be my father's murderer; but he
Is dead and buried, and here am I, who never
Laid hand on sword. Unless perhaps he died
Through pining for me; thus I could have killed him.
But as they stand, the oracles have gone
To join him underground, and they are worthless!

JOC.
Did I not tell you so a long while since?

OED.
940   You did, but I was led astray through fear.

JOC.
Then do not take them any more to heart.

OED.
But my mother's bed . . . how should I not
    fear that?

JOC.
What has a man to fear, when life is ruled
By chance, and the future is unknowable?
The best way is to take life as it comes.
So have no fear of marriage with your mother.
Many men before this time have dreamt that they
Have shared their mother's bed. The man to whom
These things are nothing lives the easiest life.

OED.
950   It would be well enough to talk in such a way
If my mother were not living. As she is,
Though your words make sense, I have good cause to
    fear.

JOC.
But your father's death is a ray of light in dark-
    ness.

OED.
A bright one; but I fear the living woman.

MESS.
Who is this woman that you are afraid of?

OED.
Merope, old man, the wife of Polybus.

MESS.
And what is there in her to make you afraid?

OED.
A terrifying oracle from heaven.

MESS.
May it be told? Or are you sworn to silence?

OED.
960   Why should it not? Apollo told me once
That I was doomed to marry with my mother
And shed my father's blood with these my hands.
And that is why I put my home in Corinth
Behind me—for the best, but all the same
There is nothing so sweet as the sight of parents' faces.

MESS.
Was it for fear of this you left our city?

OED.
It was; and to avoid my father's murder.

MESS.
Then had I better not remove your fear,
My lord, since I am here with friendly purpose?

OED.
970   If so you would deserve reward, and have it.

MESS.
Indeed, this was my principal reason for com-
        ing,
To do myself some good when you came home.

OED.
I shall never come. I must not see my parents.

MESS.
My son, I see you are making a mistake—

OED.
   What do you mean, old man? In god's name
      tell me.

MESS.
   —if you shrink from going home because of
      this.

OED.
   I am terrified of proving Phoebus true.

MESS.
   Of the guilt and shame that will come to you
      through your parents?

OED.
   You have it, old man; that fear is always with
      me.

MESS.
   Then let me tell you that these fears are
      groundless!

OED.
980   How can they be, if I were born their son?

MESS.
   Because there is none of Polybus' blood in
      you.

OED.
   Are you telling me that he was not my father?

MESS.
   No more than I—one thing we had in com-
      mon.

OED.
   What could he have in common with a nobody?

MESS.
   Why, I am not your father, and neither was
      he.

OED.
   But then . . . he called me son . . . what
      made him do it?

MESS.
   He took you as a present from my hands.

OED.
He had such love . . . for an adopted son?

MESS.
990   He had no sons of his own; this moved his
          heart.

OED.
You gave me to him—had you bought me?
Found me?

MESS.
I found you, in the wild woods of Cithairon.

OED.
What led your wanderings to such a place?

MESS.
I was in charge of sheep there, on the moun-
      tain.

OED.
A shepherd, going from place to place for hire?

MESS.
But your preserver at that time, my son.

OED.
Why? What was matter with me when you
found me?

MESS.
Your ankles are best witnesses of that.

OED.
Oh, why do you have to talk of that old
trouble?

MESS.
They were pinned together, and I cut you
loose.

OED.
1000   A shameful mark I carried from my cradle.

MESS.
And from this chance you took the name you
bear.

OED.
Who did this to me? My father or my mother?

MESS.
The man who gave you me knows; I do not.

OED.
You took me from someone else? You did not
    find me?

MESS.
No, another shepherd passed you on to me.

OED.
Who was this man? Can you identify him?

MESS.
We knew him, I think, as one of Laius' people.

OED.
You mean the king who used to rule this
    country?

MESS.
The very same. This man was Laius' herds-
1010   man.

OED.
And is he still alive for me to see him?

MESS.
You in this country would best know of that.

OED.
My people, is there anyone here present
Who knows the herdsman he is talking of,
Who has seen him in the country or the town?
Come, tell me; it is time to solve this riddle.

CHORUS
I think he means no other than the man
You already want to see. Jocasta here
Would be best qualified to tell you that.

OED.
1020   My lady, do you know the man we mean—
The man we just sent for; is he speaking of him?

JOC.
Why ask who he means? Do not bother with it.
This story is not worth thinking of; it is nothing.

OED.
No, that can never be. I have the clues
Here in my hand. I must find out my birth.

JOC.
No, by the gods! If you care for your own
safety
Ask no more questions. I have suffered enough.

OED.
Take courage. If my mother was a slave, and
hers,
And hers before her you are still pure-born.

JOC.
1030 Listen, please listen to me! Do not do this!

OED.
No-one could stop me finding out the truth.

JOC.
It is for your sake; I advise you for the best.

OED.
If this is your best, I have no patience with it.

JOC.
I pray you never find out who you are.

OED.
Go, somebody, and fetch the herdsman here.
Leave her to glory in her wealthy birth!

JOC.
Accursed! Accursed! I have no other name
To call you; you will never hear me again.
[*Exit*]

CHORUS
What can have made her leave you, Oedi-
1040 pus,
In this burst of frantic grief? I have a fear
That from here silence there will break a storm.

OED.
Let break what will! As for my parentage,
Humble though it may be, I want to know it.
She is a woman, with a woman's pride,

And is ashamed, no doubt, of my low birth.
But I proclaim myself the child of Luck,
My benefactress; this is no dishonor.
Yes, Luck is my mother, and the months, my cousins,
Saw me first humble and then saw me great.
1050   With such a parentage I could not be false
To myself again, or let this secret rest.

CHORUS
If I am any judge of the future,
If my mind does not play me false,
Cithairon, tomorrow at the full moon's rising,
By Olympus, you will need no second telling
That Oedipus boasts of your kinship, hailing you
As nurse and mother.
And we shall be there with dances in your honor
Because you have found favor in our king's sight.
1060   Apollo, hear us when we pray,
And bless our good intentions!

Which of the nymphs, the long-lived ones,
Lay with the mountain-wanderer Pan
To bring you to birth? Or was it Loxias?
He is a god who loves the upland pastures.
Or was it Cyllene's lord, or the god
Of the Bacchanals, dwelling
High in the hilltops, who received you,
A new-born treasure, from the arms of a nymph
1070   Of Helicon, the favorite
Companions of his pleasure?
        [*Enter attendants with* HERDSMAN]

OED.
Elders, if who never saw the man,
May make a guess, I think I see the herdsman
We have sought so long; he is well advanced in years—
This answers the description—and besides
I recognize the men escorting him
As servants of my own. But you may well
Have the advantage of me, if you have seen him
        before;

1063 Pan—primitive nature deity, half man, half goat
1064 Loxias—Appolo   1066 Cyllene's lord—Hermes, the messenger god, born on
Mount Cyllene   1067 Bacchanals—frenzied women who worshipped Dionysus   1070
Helicon—mountain sacred to Apollo and the Muses

CHORUS
I know him, no mistake. He worked for
Laius,
As honest a shepherd as you could hope to find.

OED.
1080 First let me hear from you, my Corinthian
friend.
Is this your man?

MESS.
The one you see before you.

OED.
Come here, old man, and look me in the face.
Answer my questions. You once worked for Laius?

HERDSMAN
I did; and I was palace-bred, not bought.

OED.
In what employment? How did you spend your
time?

HERDS.
For the best part of my life I watched the
flocks.

OED.
What part of the country did you mostly work
in?

HERDS.
Sometimes Cithairon, sometimes round about.

OED.
Have you seen this man in those parts, to your
1090 knowledge?

HERDS.
Who? Doing what? What man are you talking about?

OED.
This man in front of you. Have you ever met
him?

HERDS.
Not to remember off-hand. I cannot say.

MESS.

Small wonder, master. But let me refresh
His failing memory. I have no doubt
That he recalls the time we spent together
In the country round Cithairon. He had two flocks,
And I, his mate, had one. Three years we did this,
For six months at a time, from spring to fall.
1100   Then, for the winter, I used to drive my flocks
Home to my fold, he his to that of Laius.
Did it happen as I say, or did it not?

HERDS.

Yes, true; but it was many years ago.

MESS.

Now tell me: do you remember giving me
A boy for me to bring up as my own?

HERDS.

What now? What has put that question in
    your head?

MESS.

That child, my friend, is the man you see
    before you.

HERDS.

Curse you! Do not say another word!

OED.

Old man, do not reprove him. Your words
    stand
1110   In greater need of admonition than his.

HERDS.

And where do I offend, most noble master?

OED.

In not telling of the boy he asks about.

HERDS.

This meddler does not know what he is say-
    ing.

OED.

If you will not speak to oblige me I must make
    you.

HERDS.

No, no, for god's sake; you would not hurt an
    old man?

OED.
Quickly, somebody, tie his arms behind him.

HERDS.
Unhappy man, what more do you want to
know?

OED.
This child he talks of; did you give it him?

HERDS.
I did; and I wish that day had been my last.

OED.
1120   It will come to that, unless you tell the truth.

HERDS.
I shall do myself more harm by telling you.

OED.
It seems he is determined to waste our time.

HERDS.
No, no! I told you once, I gave it him.

OED.
Where did you get it? Your home or another's?

HERDS.
It was not mine. Somebody gave it me.

OED.
Who? Which one of my people? Where does
he live?

HERDS.
No, master, in heaven's name, ask no more
questions.

OED.
You are a dead man if I have to ask again.

HERDS.
It was a child of the house of Laius.

OED.
1130   A slave? Or one of his own family?

HERDS.
I am near to saying what should not be said.

OED.
And I to hearing it; but it must be heard.

HERDS.
They said it was Laius' son. But go inside
And ask your wife; for she could tell you all.

OED.
You mean she gave it you?

HERDS.
She did, my lord.

OED.
But why?

HERDS.
For me to make away with it.

OED.
Her child!

HERDS.
She feared an evil prophecy.

OED.
What was it?

HERDS.
That the son should kill his father.

OED.
Then why did you give him up to this old man?

HERDS.
1140   For pity, master, thinking he would take
The child home, out of Thebes; but he preserved him
For a fate worse than any other. If you are truly
The man he says, then know you were born accursed.
    [*Exit*]

OED.
Oh, oh, then everything has come out true.
Light, I shall not look on you again.
I have been born where I should not be born,
I have married where I should not marry,
I have killed whom I should not kill; now all is clear.
    [*Exit*]

CHORUS
> You that are born into this world,
> 1150   I count you in your lives as nothing worth.
> What man has ever won for himself
> More of happiness than this,
> To seem, and having seemed, to pass?
> For Oedipus, when I look at you
> And the fate which fell upon you, can I
> Call any human being happy?

> Zeus knows, his arrow went straight to its mark
> And all of life's blessings became his prize.
> He killed the girl with the crooked claws,
> 1160   The riddle-monger, and stood up among us
> A tower of strength to drive death from our land,
> For which we called you our king, paid you honors
> The greatest we knew; in the proud land
> Of Thebes you were lord and master.

> Now who has a sadder tale to tell?
> A life turned upside down,
> The door flung wide to misfortune,
> The hounds of fate let loose.
> Oh Oedipus, famous Oedipus,
> 1170   The same ample shelter sufficed
> For father and son, a bed for the mating.
> How could the furrows your father sowed
> Have endured you so long in silence?

> Time sees all, and has found you out
> Despite yourself, passing sentence
> On the marriage that is no marriage,
> Where begetter is one with begotten.
> Laius' child, oh Laius' child,
> Better if I had not seen you,
> 1180   For when all is said, he that gave me new life
> Has taken all my joy in living.
>   [*Enter* SECOND MESSENGER]

MESS.
> Ancestral and most honorable lords,
> Such things you will see and hear of; such a weight
> Of grief is yours, if like true sons of Thebes
> You still care for the sons of Labdacus.
> I think there is no river wide enough
> To wash this palace clean, so many are

The horrors it hides, or soon will bring to light,
Done willfully, from choice; no sufferings
1190 Hurt more than those we bring upon ourselves.

CHORUS
Those that we know already claim their
weight
Of tears. What more have you to add to these?

MESS.
A tale which can be very briefly told
And heard: our royal lady Jocasta is dead.

CHORUS
Oh miserable queen; what was the cause?

MESS.
By her own hand. The worst of what has hap-
pened
You shall be spared, you were not there to see it.
But you shall hear as much as I recall
About the sufferings of the wretched queen.
1200 Past caring what she did, she rushed inside
The hall, and made straight for her marriage bed,
Head in hands, and fingers tearing at her hair.
Once in the room she slammed the doors behind her
And called on Laius rotting in his grave,
Remembering a once begotten child
By whom the father should die, and leave the mother
To bear his son's cursed children; she bewailed
The bed where she had borne a double brood,
Husband by husband, children by her child,
1210 And then she died—I cannot tell you how,
For Oedipus burst on us with a cry
And we had no chance to watch her agonies.
We had eyes for none but him, as he ran from one
To another, demanding a sword, and where
He might find his wife—his mother, not his wife,
The womb that gave him and his children birth.
In his frenzy he was guided by some power
More than human—not by any of us who stood there.
With a dreadful cry, as though a hand had pointed,
1220 He sprang at the double doors, forced back the bolts
Till the sockets gave, and ran into the room.
And there inside we saw the woman hanging,
Her body swinging in a twist of rope.
When he saw, a shuddering cry welled up inside him;

He cut the noose that held her; when she lay
Cold on the ground, we saw a ghastly sight.
He tore away the golden brooches from
Her dress, that she had used as ornaments,
230 And lifted them, and plunged them in his eyes
With words like these: "You shall not see again
Such horrors as I did, saw done to me,
But stare in darkness on forbidden faces,
Meet those I longed to find, and pass them by."
And to this tune he raised his hands and struck
His eyes again and again; with every blow
Blood spurted down his cheeks. It did not fall
In slow and sluggish drops, but all at once
Black blood came pouring like a shower of hail.
This storm has broken on two people's heads,
240 Not one alone; both man and wife have suffered.
Till now, the happiness they inherited
Was happiness indeed; and now, today,
Tears, ruin, death, disgrace, as many ills
As there are names for them; not one is lacking.

CHORUS
How is he now? Is he in peace from pain?

MESS.
He shouts for the doors to be opened, for
      every man
In Thebes to see his father's murderer,
His mother's—heaven forbid I speak that word.
He means to cast himself from Thebes, to stay
250 In this house no more, a self-inflicted curse.
But his strength is gone; he needs someone to guide
His steps, the pain is more than he can bear.
And this too he will show you. See, the doors
Are opening, and soon you will see a sight
To move your tears, though you recoil from it.
      [*Enter* OEDIPUS, *blind*]

CHORUS
Oh sufferings dreadful to see,
Most dreadful of all that ever
Greeted my eyes. Wretched king,
What insanity possessed you?
260 What demon, in one colossal spring
Pounced on your ill-fated life?
Unhappy king,
I cannot even look you in the face,

Though there are still many questions to be asked,
Many things left unsaid, much remaining to be seen,
You fill me with such shuddering.

OED.
Oh, oh, the pain, the pain!
Where do my poor legs take me?
Where do the wild winds scatter my words?
1270   Oh, my fate, where have you leapt with me?

CHORUS
To a dreadful place that must not be
        named,
To a place unfit for the eyes of man.

OED.
Oh, this fog,
This horrible darkness all around me,
Unspeakable visitation
Blown by an evil wind; I am powerless.
Oh, when I remember my sorrows
I feel again the points in my eyes.

CHORUS
No wonder; in such sorrows you must have
1280   Evils redoubled to endure and mourn.

OED.
Oh, my friend,
You are my faithful servant still,
Blind Oedipus' patient nurse.
I know you are here, I can feel your presence.
Although I am in the darkness
I can recognize your voice.

CHORUS
Oh man of wrath, how could you bring
        yourself
To blind your eyes? What demon drove you on?

OED.
It was Apollo, my friends, Apollo
1290   Who contrived my ruin, who worked my fall.
But no-one blinded my eyes
But myself, in my own grief.
What use are eyes to me, who could never
See anything pleasant again?

CHORUS
Yes, it was as you say.

OED.

    What is there left for me to see,
    To love? Who still has a kindly word
    My friends, for me?
    Take me away from this land, my friends,
1300   Take me with all the speed you may,
    For Oedipus is no more,
    Contaminated, cursed,
    Unclean in heaven's sight.

CHORUS

    Knowledge and pain; they hurt you equally
    I wish your path and mine had never crossed.

OED.

    Cursed be the man who struck the cruel chains
    From my feet as I lay abandoned,
    And saved me from death, gave me back
    To the world of the living—why?
1310   If I had died then, I should never
    Have grieved myself or my loved ones so.

CHORUS

    I too would have had it so.

OED.

    I would not have shed my father's blood
    Or heard men call me my mother's husband.
    And now I am
    God-shunned, the son of a mother defiled,
    Have taken my turn in my mother's bed.
    If there is any sorrow
    Greater than all others
1320   It belongs to Oedipus.

CHORUS

    I cannot praise your judgment. You would
        be
    Far better dead than living still and blind.

OED.

    Do not tell me I am wrong. What I have done
    Is best as it is. Give me no more advice.
    If I had sight, I know not with what eyes
    I would have looked upon my father, when
    I walked among the dead, or my sad mother,
    For sins so great cannot be paid by hanging.
    Or do you think the sight of children born
1330   As mine were born could give me any joy?

No, never to these eyes of mine again,
Nor the proud wall of our city, nor the holy
Statues of our gods; these I, ten times accursed,
I, who was noblest of the sons of Thebes,
Have set behind me by my own command
That all cast out the sinner, the man revealed
By heaven as unclean, as Laius' son.
And tainted thus for all the world to see
How could I look my people in the face?
1340   I could not. If I could have stopped my ears,
My fount of hearing, I would not have rested
Till I had made a prison of this body
Barred against sight and sound. How happy the mind
That can so live, beyond the reach of suffering.
Cithairon, why did you shelter me? Why did you not
Kill me there, where you found me, so that I might
     never
Show to mankind the secret of my birth?
Oh Polybus, Corinth, the ancestral home
Men called my father's; oh, how fair of face
1350   Was I, your child, and how corrupt beneath!
For now I am found evil, evil born.
Those three roads, and the hidden clump of trees,
The wood, the narrow place where three paths met,
Who drank from my own hands the father's blood,
And so, my own blood; do you still remember
The things you saw me do? Then I came here
To do other things besides. Oh marriage, marriage,
You gave me birth, and after I was born
Bore children to your child, and brought to light
1360   Sons, fathers, brothers in a web of incest,
Than which men know nothing more abominable.
But what is sin to do is sin to speak of.
For heaven's love, hide me in some wilderness,
Or strike me dead, or throw me in the sea,
Where you will never set eyes on me again.
Come, do not shrink from touching my poor body.
Please; do not be afraid. My sufferings
Are all my own, no-one will be infected.

CHORUS
No. Here is Creon, in time to listen to you,
1370   Ready to act or advise. Now you are gone
He is the only one we have to turn to.

OED.
Oh, what words can I find to say to him?
What proof of my good faith? I have been found

An arrant traitor to him in the past.
[*Enter* CREON *with attendants*]

CREON

Oedipus, I have not come to jeer at you
Or throw your past misconduct in your face.
[*To the* CHORUS]
As for you, if you have no sense of decency
To a fellow man, at least have some respect
For holy sunlight, giver of warmth and life.

1380 Do not leave this pollution uncovered, an offence
To earth, to light, to the pure rain from heaven.
Take him indoors as quickly as you can.
Propriety forbids he should be made
A public spectacle. These things are for his family.

OED.

Listen: since you have removed my apprehen-
sion
And behave so nobly to a man so low
Grant me this favor—for your good, not for mine.

CREON

What is it you are so anxious to have me do?

OED.

Lose no more time; drive me away from Thebes

1390 To some place where nobody will know my name.

CREON

Believe me, I would have done so; but first
I wanted
To find out from the god what I should do.

OED.

The will of god is clear enough already.
Kill the parricide, the sinner; and that am I.

CREON

So he said. But all the same, now things
have gone
So far, it is better that we seek clear guidance.

OED.

You will go to the god? For a poor wretch like
myself?

CREON

I will. Perhaps you will believe him this
time.

OED.

I do. And I will urge your duties on you.
1400 The woman inside—bury her as you would wish
To be buried yourself. It is right, she is your sister.
But as for me, never sentence my father's city
To have me within its walls, as long as I live,
But leave me to the hills, to my Cithairon
As men now call it—destined for my grave
By my father and mother when they were alive.
They tried to kill me; let me die the way they wanted.
But I am sure of one thing; no disease,
Nothing can kill me now. I would not have been saved
1410 From death, unless it were for some strange destiny.
But let my destiny go where it will.
As for my children—Creon, do not trouble youself
About my sons. They are men, they can never lack
A livelihood, wherever they may be.
But my two girls, my poor unhappy daughters,
Who never knew what it was to eat a meal
Away from their father's side, but had their share
Of every little thing I had myself. . . .
1420 Please look after them. And I beg this favor now,
Let me lay my hands on them and weep with them.
Please, my lord,
Please, noble heart. If I could touch them now
I should think they were with me, as if I could see
    them.
    [*Enter* ANTIGONE *and* ISMENE]
What is that?
Oh you gods; is it my darlings that I hear
Sobbing? Has Creon taken pity on me
And sent my darlings, sent my children to me?
Am I right?

CREON

Yes, I had them brought to you; I knew
1430 They would delight you as they always have done.

OED.

Bless you for your trouble. May you find
A kinder fate than what has come to me.
Where are you now, my children? Over here:
Come to these hands of mine, your brother's hands,
Whose offices have made your father's eyes
That were once so bright, to see as they see now.
For the truth is out; your father, stupid, blind,

Begot you in the womb where he was born.
Sight have I none, but tears I have for you
1440 When I think of how you will be forced to live
At men's hands in the bitter days to come.
What gathering of the folk will you attend,
What festival that will not send you home
In tears, instead of making holiday?
And when the time has come for you to marry,
Show me the man, my children, bold enough
To take upon his own head such disgrace,
The stain that you and your brothers will inherit.
What sorrow is not ours? Your father killed
1450 His father, sowed his seed in her
Where he was sown as seed, and did beget you
In the selfsame place where he was once begotten.
That is how men will talk. Then who will marry you?
No-one, my children. Marriage is not for you.
You must be barren till your lives are done.
Son of Menoeceus, you are the only father
These girls have left, for we, their parents,
Are both of us gone. So do not let them wander
Beggared and husbandless. They are your kin.
1460 And do not level them with my misfortunes
But pity them. You see how young they are.
You are the only friend they have in the world.
Touch me, kind heart, in token of your promise.
Children, if you were old enough to understand,
There is much I could say to help you. As it is,
Pray after me—to live with moderation
And better fortune than your father did.

CREON
Your time is up. Dry your tears and go indoors.

OED.
It is hard, but I must obey.

CREON
There must be moderation in all things.

OED.
I shall go on one condition.

CREON
Tell me what it is.

OED.

1470   Send me away from Thebes to live.

CREON
   That is for the gods to say.

OED.
   They will be glad to see me gone.

CREON
   Then your wish will soon be granted.

OED.
   You agree then?

CREON
   When I do not know, I do not speak.

OED.
   Take me away, it is time.

CREON
   Come along. Leave your children here.

OED.
   Never part us!

CREON
   Do not ask to have everything your way.
   Your time for giving orders is over.
   [*Exeunt*]

CHORUS
   People of this city, look, this man is Oedi-
      pus,
   Who guessed the famous riddle, who rose to greatness,
   Envy of all in the city who saw his good fortune.

1480   And now what a fearful storm of disaster has struck
      him.
   That is why we wait until we see the final day,
   Not calling anybody happy who is mortal
   Until he has passed the last milestone without ca-
      lamity.

PHILOCTETES Preface

THE CONFLICT BETWEEN IDEALISTIC YOUTH AND EXPEDIENT MIDDLE AGE
gives the *Philoctetes* a special relevance. The product of Sophocles' extreme old age and mature art, the play, with its happy ending, is a
tragi-comedy in the Euripidean manner. Perhaps influenced by the
younger playwright's psychological realism, Sophocles paints his characters with an immediacy and naturalness that make the ethical problems
they face seem particularly modern.

The interest centers on young Neoptolemus, the son of Achilles, who
must choose between obeying his military superior, the wily Odysseus,
and the dictates of his own conscience. The psychological forces that
determine his decision are so much a part of human nature that young
men of today and the future may undergo a similar testing of their
deepest convictions. On the one hand Neoptolemus' orders command
him to obtain the magic bow of Philoctetes, without which Troy cannot
be taken; on the other, his principles reject the duplicity and outright
betrayal of a helpless and wronged old man that fulfilling his duty
requires. Odysseus, the experienced man of the world, advises that the
end—capturing Troy and returning home—justifies the questionable
means of deceit and theft. Torn between opposite poles of self-interest
and human pity, Neoptolemus is the universal soldier whom his officers
expect to commit an atrocity in order to win the war.

The man Neoptolemus is asked to wrong, Philoctetes, had been abandoned ten years before on the uninhabited island of Lemnos. While en
route to Troy with Agamemnon, Menelaus, and Odysseus, Philoctetes
had been bitten on the foot by a poisonous snake which left an incurable
wound. The stench from the festering sore and Philoctetes' uncontrollable shrieks of anguish proved intolerable to Agamemnon and the other
Achaeans, who consequently left the wounded man to his lonely fate.
During his ten years of unceasing pain and bitter resentment toward his
fellow Greeks, Philoctetes had lived by use of the bow of Heracles, which
the famous hero had give him. Odysseus exploits Neoptolemus' youth
and inexperience to trick Philoctetes into giving up the bow because the
Trojan prophet Helenos has revealed that Troy could not be taken
without it.

Sophocles inspires pity for the deserted Philoctetes not only by graphic
descriptions of his filthy rags, his fetid wound, and his howls of pain, but
also by his pathetic joy when Neoptolemus offers him friendship. After a
decade of unspeakable hardship and suffering, Philoctetes believes that
he has found in the son of his old friend Achilles an incorruptible youth
who will right the wrongs he has endured. When, under Odysseus'
cynical influence, Neoptolemus betrays Philoctetes' trust, steals the bow,
and prepares to desert him forever, Sophocles' drama achieves an intensity of feeling seldom matched in the theatre.

At the beginning of the play Neoptolemus, whose ideals are not yet
tested, expresses an easy and unwarranted optimism about the meaning

289

of Philoctetes' suffering. In response to the sailors' comment that Philoctetes has been reduced to a bestial rather than a human existence, Neoptolemus glibly replies:

> I accept all this because I believe all his sufferings have a meaning. If I am right, there is a higher purpose, an end we do not see, because only a divine power can see it.

Neoptolemus is in fact stating a major Sophoclean theme—that fate, or the gods, give to human pain a "higher purpose" than men can usually foresee—but the dramatist makes clear that Neoptolemus has at that point no right to his facile convictions. The discovery of himself and of his respective obligations to Philoctetes and the Achaean community is still to come. Only when he has proven his moral worth and earned a conscience will he have his original faith confirmed.

The belief that Philoctetes' suffering has not been in vain but in accord with Heaven's will is reaffirmed in the final scene when Heracles appears as the *deus ex machina*. He confronts Philoctetes, who has stubbornly refused to aid his fellow Greeks in taking Troy, to remind him that his extreme disillusionment is unjustified. "Such goodness" as Heracles has done and as Philoctetes will yet live to do "never dies."

> Out of your labors here you will dress your life in glory. You will go to Troy with this young man and there be cured of your terrible disease; then you will be chosen first in valor, first in honor, first in goodness out of Greece. . . .

Emphasizing a characteristically Sophoclean balance between the rights of the individual and the claims of the state, Heracles reminds Odysseus and his men that they have no power to conquer Troy without Philoctetes, just as Philoctetes has no power without them. Each is indispensable to the other.

The intervention of Heracles transforms Philoctetes from a hate-driven and angry old man to one who recognizes that wisdom lies in discovering and obeying the divine will. But Neoptolemus has, on his own, learned both that his nature is not impervious to evil and that he has the strength to triumph over it. Neoptolemus' crucial decision, in which he chooses to stand by Philoctetes, thereby sacrificing his previous ambitions, foreshadows Heracles' final words: "whether one lives or dies, conscience remains, justice remains, right is eternal. . . ."

PHILOCTETES

Characters   ODYSSEUS
                NEOPTOLEMOS
                PHILOCTETES
                MERCHANT
                SPIRIT OF HERCULES
                SAILORS

[*Scene: Lemnos, a volcanic island not far from the coast of Asia Minor. A part of the shore where there is a steep cliff riddled with caves.*]

[*Enter* NEOPTOLEMOS, *a young officer from the Greek army,* ODYSSEUS, *and some* SAILORS *part of the crew of* NEOPTOLEMOS' *ship.*]

ODYSSEUS

The island of Lemnos . . . Sea . . . sand . . . rock! No one comes here, no one lives here—and this is where I put him ashore, Neoptolemos, on this island. Yes, this is where I left Philoctetes all those years ago . . . I had my orders, I carried them out. His foot was a mass of rotting flesh, eaten right down to the bone. The sounds that came from him—we couldn't hold sacrifices, couldn't pray to heaven . . . it would have been blasphemy with him shrieking, screaming . . . But why need we talk of that? We must be quick. The one thing we cannot do is talk. If he knows I'm here, our journey's wasted. I have a plan to catch him—I hope—it's quick and it's clever. Your function here is to carry out that plan . . . Go and see if you can find a cave with two entrances. Look for a place where you could lie in the sun all day in cold weather, or sleep in a cool breeze if the weather was hot . . . And further down to the left you should see a spring of drinking water . . . [NEOPTOLEMOS *has begun to climb.*] Still there? . . . Go in as close as you can . . . [NEOPTOLEMOS *dislodges a stone.*] . . . but keep it *quiet!* . . . If it looks as if he's still living there, wave . . . After that I want you back here, and I'll tell you the rest of my plan. Then our mission can proceed.

NEOPTOLEMOS

Easily done, Odysseus. I think I can see the cave you mean.

ODYSSEUS

Up there, or further down? I can't tell from here . . .

NEOPTOLEMOS

Just above me here . . . No tracks, though, no sign of life . . .

From *Philoctetes* by Sophocles, translated by Kenneth Cavender, published by Chandler Publishing Company, San Francisco. Copyright © 1965 by Chandler Publishing Company. Reprinted by permission.

ODYSSEUS
  Careful! He could be lying there asleep.

[NEOPTOLEMOS *peers into the opening.*]

NEOPTOLEMOS
  No, I can see inside . . . Empty, no one at home.

ODYSSEUS
  Does it seem lived in? . . . Any food?

NEOPTOLEMOS
  A few leaves . . . they've been pressed down flat. Someone slept there last night.

ODYSSEUS
  But otherwise empty. Nothing lying around?

NEOPTOLEMOS
  A cup hollowed out of wood, very rough. Not well made, whoever did it . . . Some pieces of kindling wood . . .

ODYSSEUS
  Yes, all his wealth is in that cave.

NEOPTOLEMOS
  [*letting out a cry of disgust*] These rags left out here to dry— they're stiff with matter . . . pus!

ODYSSEUS
  This is the place. Good. We've found our man. He's living here, may even be close to us now . . . He's a sick man, you see, one limb useless, he can't get far. He probably went looking for food, or perhaps he knows of some leaves that relieve the pain . . . Send one of them to keep watch.

[NEOPTOLEMOS *signals to one of his* SAILORS]

  I mustn't let him find me here. He'd rather lay hands on me than all the Greek army put together!

NEOPTOLEMOS
  One of my men is going now. He'll guard the path . . . Next?

ODYSSEUS
  And now, my boy, you have a mission to fulfill. You are the son of Achilles and I want to see you fulfill it like your father. I don't mean just physical courage. I mean, if what I tell you now comes as a

surprise, appears somewhat ... unusual ... I want complete obedience. Remember, you are here to assist me.

NEOPTOLEMOS
Your orders, sir?

ODYSSEUS
I want Philoctetes. And you must get him for me. And for that you
will tell any lie that may be necessary ... You will be asked who you
are and where you come from. You will say: 'Son of Achilles, from
Skyros.' So far—no deception. But ... you are sailing home, having
withdrawn from the Greek army—the Greeks, remember, you hate,
you loathe! They came to you with an appeal for help, they humbly
asked you to leave your home and sail to Troy where, they assured
you, you were the one man who could take the city for them. You
went to Troy. There, you naturally and correctly asked for the return
of your father's armor. You were most unreasonably refused, and the
armor was handed over to ... Odysseus. Say anything you like about
me, the worst insults you can think of—you won't hurt me . . . But if
you fail me, then I will be hurt, and so will all of us in the Greek
army. You see, without Philoctetes and his bow, you can't take Troy.
Now, Philoctetes hates me, but you he will trust. I'll tell you why. You
took no oath like the rest of us who sailed on the original expedition;
no one forced you to come; ... none of which applies to me. If he
finds me here and that bow is in his hands, I die, and since we are
here together—so will you. . . . No, this requires management, skill.
For the sake of that bow, young man, that invincible weapon, you are
about to become a thief! [*seeing* NEOPTOLEMOS, *about to protest*]
I know, I know, Neoptolemos, it isn't your nature. To you, lying is
wrong, intrigue is wrong. Yes, but victory is sweet—seize it! Dare!
Time will put us in the right—you'll see. Today, just for today, forget
shame, and place yourself in my hands. Then, for the rest of your life
you can be as virtuous as you like.

NEOPTOLEMOS
Odysseus, some things—at the very mention of them I feel disgust—
and when I have to do them, I rebel. Deceit is not my way. I'm not
made like that, nor was my father, so they tell me. If we must use
force to take this man off Lemnos, look I'm ready. But deceive
him—no ... He has one good leg; he can't be strong enough to fight us
all. I was sent here under your command and I shall be accused of
mutiny. I don't enjoy the thought. But if I have to do wrong in order
to succeed, sir, I would rather remain honest—and fail.

ODYSSEUS
How like your father, your upright, honorable father ... When I was
your age, I was the same. I had no use for words, I believed in action.

But now I realize that in this life it is not what you do that counts.
Words are what matters; words have power. I know, believe me.

NEOPTOLEMOS
You are ordering me to tell a lie. Is that the case or not?

ODYSSEUS
I am asking you to bring me Philoctetes by a strategy.

NEOPTOLEMOS
Why strategy? Why not persuade him?

ODYSSEUS
He will never be persuaded. And you can't take him by force.

NEOPTOLEMOS
Why not? Is he so strong, so terrible, so brave?

ODYSSEUS
The arrows. They are deadly and they never miss.

NEOPTOLEMOS
Even to go near him is a risk, then?

ODYSSEUS
Yes, unless you use strategy, as I said.

NEOPTOLEMOS
But don't you think lying is wrong?

ODYSSEUS
Not necessarily . . . Suppose the lie saves my life.

NEOPTOLEMOS
But how does one say the words and not blush?

ODYSSEUS
Think of what you gain and don't be shy. This is no time to be shy.

NEOPTOLEMOS
What do I gain if he goes to Troy . . . ?

ODYSSEUS
His bow will take the city. Nothing else can.

NEOPTOLEMOS
But everyone said I was going to conquer Troy. Wasn't that true?

ODYSSEUS
It was. And that bow can do nothing without you. But you can do
nothing without the bow.

[NEOPTOLEMOS *reflects.*]

NEOPTOLEMOS
I see . . . The bow is essential, then. That is the prize.

ODYSSEUS [*quickly*]
Do what I ask and you win two prizes.

NEOPTOLEMOS
How do you mean? If I could be sure, I think I would agree.

ODYSSEUS
Two prizes, Neoptolemos, one for courage and one for brains.
[*Pause*]

NEOPTOLEMOS
Right, I'll do it! I'm not ashamed. That's gone—

ODYSSEUS
You remember what I said.

NEOPTOLEMOS
Yes, yes, I've told you—I agree to everything.

ODYSSEUS
You wait and meet Philoctetes here. I'll leave you. I don't want him to
catch sight of me. I'll dismiss your sentry back to his ship, but if I
think you're taking too long I'll send the same man back to you
disguised as a merchant so that his uniform isn't recognized. He'll
probably say some puzzling things, my boy, but you improvise as best
you can and take your cue from him. I'm going back to the ship. You
are in charge now . . . May Hermes, patron of all conspirators, assist us
now, and the Goddess Athene of victories, who watches over my
interests always.
[*Exit* ODYSSEUS]

SAILORS
We are strangers in a strange place and this man will be suspicious.
  How much do we say, sir?
How much do we keep quiet?
Give us a lead . . .
Power comes from heaven. Whoever wields power must think faster,
  plan better than other men . . .
You have command, my boy, you are the son of a great king . . .
And you must tell us, sir . . .
Your orders, sir . . .
What do we do now, sir . . . ?

NEOPTOLEMOS
I know you want to search the island, you want to see him, know
where he is. But keep watch, wait, and don't be afraid. And when he

comes, the wandering owner of this mansion, our terrible friend, keep close beside me, and be ready to act the instant I give the command.

SAILORS

We're ready, sir, have been ever since we landed. We'll keep a good watch for you . . . the moment you need us, say so—we're waiting . . . But where has he gone?
Where is he now? It's time we knew . . .
We mustn't be taken by surprise . . .
He might come on us before we see him . . .
Where does he go? Does he go out? Or does he stay indoors?

NEOPTOLEMOS

This rock here, with the two entrances, this is where he lives . . . and this is where he sleeps, too.

SAILORS

Where is he? Not here . . .
What a place! . . .

NEOPTOLEMOS

It's obvious, surely, he's gone in search of food. He has to eat. He's struggling along somewhere near here—if you think, there's only one way he can keep alive—he must use his arrows to bring down wild animals . . . it's a hard and difficult life, no cure for his disease here.

SAILORS

Well, I pity him.
Think of it, no one to care what happens to him.
No one to watch, see that nothing goes wrong, always alone with his misery.
And the disease eating away at him. Barely keeping alive, his strength going . . .
How has he endured it . . . ?
He's still alive . . .
Yes, but how?
Heaven takes us in its hands, and breaks us . . . We're nothing to heaven . . .
We don't get justice here on earth . . . we have to suffer, and suffer we do.
Take him. Perhaps the head of his house, everyone looked up to him, good family, and now a groveling animal, diseased, abandoned, one of the beasts of the forests or the hills, in pain, starving to death, his mind full of terrible thoughts that give him no peace . . .
Only the mountains hear him when he cries out, and the echoes . . . yes, they come back to him—to mock, mock his pain, eavesdrop on his tortured cries . . .

NEOPTOLEMOS
I accept all this because I believe all his sufferings have a meaning. If I am right, there is a higher purpose, an end we do not yet see, because only a divine power can see it. Perhaps this divine power is making sure he doesn't turn his invincible weapon on Troy before a certain time. Many conditions must be fulfilled before the city can be conquered.

SAILORS
Wait! . . . Not a sound! . . .

NEOPTOLEMOS
What is it?

SAILORS
Someone in pain . . .
I heard him . . .
Terrible pain . . .
From over there . . .
No there . . . that way . . . surely . . .
It was, I'm certain it was! I heard a voice . . .
He's dragging himself along the path there, grunting, forcing himself to move, the voice was harsh with pain—I heard it distinctly, sharp, unmistakable . . .
Now my boy, you must have . . .

NEOPTOLEMOS
Yes, what?

SAILORS
Think quickly. The man we came for is here . . .
No longer someone out there in the undergrowth . . .
But here . . . here with us . . .
And he isn't singing on a pipe, either, like some shepherd in the fields . . .
He's stumbling along.
Perhaps he fell and we heard the groan that was forced out of him . . .
Or he's seen our ship at anchor and is trying to make his voice heard on board . . .
He's making enough noise!
I'm frightened!

[*Enter* PHILOCTETES. *A shout from* PHILOCTETES, *hailing the party of* SAILORS.]

PHILOCTETES
Strangers . . . who are you? Where have you come from? You won't find a harbor here, no one lives here . . .

[*The* Sailors *and* Neoptolemos *look at him in silence. His appearance shocks them.*]

Philoctetes
What country are you from? . . . What language do you speak? Are you Greek? Your clothes are Greek—no other clothes could look so dear to me . . .

[*They are still silent.*]

Philoctetes
Well . . . ? I only want to hear a voice! . . . No, don't be afraid, you look at me as if I terrified you—I know, I look wild, fierce, but pity me. This loathsome animal is a man. He's suffered much alone in this desert, no friends, torment, torment . . . Well, speak! Do you come in friendship? At least answer me! I ask no more, but I have a right to that, please! We can at least talk to each other.

Neoptolemos
You ask who we are, stranger. We are Greek.

Philoctetes
The joy . . . the sound of your voice, saying those words—to talk to someone after all this time, just to talk . . . Now, boy, tell me, what brought you here, what's happened to your ship? . . . You're on a journey—where? In what quarter does the wind . . . Oh, I bless the wind that sent you. Tell me everything about yourself, who you are . . .

Neoptolemos
I was born on the island of Skyros, and that is where I'm sailing— home. My name is Neoptolemos, I am the son of Achilles. Now you know everything.

Philoctetes
Your father is my dear friend, my boy, and your country, too, I know well. What are you doing on this island, though, where have you come from?

Neoptolemos
I have just put out from Troy.

Philoctetes
Troy? But you didn't sail with us. I don't remember you when the fleet set out.

Neoptolemos
Were you part of that great expedition?

PHILOCTETES

Look at me . . . Don't you know me, boy?

NEOPTOLEMOS

How could I? I never saw you before in my life.

PHILOCTETES

And you never heard my name, you were never told how I'm slowly dying here, day by day?

NEOPTOLEMOS

No. I have heard nothing, nothing of that, believe me.

PHILOCTETES

Why should it end? I am the eyesore of the gods. My life here—look at it—and nothing reached back home, not a whisper, no one in the whole of Greece knows. Threw me off their ship—did I deserve it? No! A crime, a monstrous crime, but it's their secret, they're safe and well and say nothing, while my disease grows, spreads, blooms . . . Young man, son of Achilles, you see here in front of you the man who was given charge of the weapons of Hercules, yes, perhaps you have heard of me, I am that man, I am . . . Philoctetes! I live here in total isolation because the two generals of the Greek army, Agamemnon and Menelaus, helped by Odysseus, brutally abandoned me here. I was dying, I had a raging fever—a snake bite. The snake had struck deep and the venom was deadly. Discarded, boy, thrown aside. They abandoned me . . . I was exhausted after the voyage to this island, and when we put in here I fell asleep on the shore under the cliff. Exactly what they hoped for. They set sail and left without me. Not without mercy, of course—they flung a few rags down beside me and some scraps of food—I'd like to see them live on that food—Imagine, boy, you imagine what it was like to wake up and find myself alone. I wept. Yes, I shed tears of agony. Not one ship out of my whole fleet was in sight—all gone. The island a desert, no help, no hope of rescue if I collapsed. Wherever I looked I found despair—I could have gorged myself on that, oh yes! . . . The days passed, months, I existed. I eked out a life under that small roof—I had to. My bow here brought me enough to fill my stomach. There were pigeons flying about, and I used to shoot at them. I pulled the string taut, let the arrow go, it never missed! But even then, I still had to haul myself, painfully, dragging my useless wounded foot behind me, to fetch the kill. And if I needed a drink, or there was ice on the ground, and I had to chop wood—that often happened in the winter—well, I managed. I crept out and I managed. Then the fire would die out, and I had to rub two rocks together to get a reluctant spark, just a brief spark but it was all my life to me. And so you see, I have a roof over my head, a fire—I am provided with everything . . . except a cure . . .

Anyway, my boy, let me tell you about this island. No sailor ever comes this way—not intentionally. There's no harbor, no trade, no one to make you welcome. If you have any sense you don't visit this place. Sometimes a ship is forced in shore. Such things happen often enough over the years. But these people, I can tell you, when they do come, they say how sorry they are for me, their pity may even extend to a few bites to eat, or some clothing—but take me home? . . . I've only to say the words and they lose interest . . . Ten years I've rotted here! Ten years I've starved and suffered so that my disease can grow fat! Now do you see, my boy, what the two Greek generals and Odysseus, our great warrior Odysseus, have done to me? May god in heaven punish them with ten such years!

SAILORS

The others who came gave you their pity . . . And we can give no less . . . it is your right, Philoctetes.

NEOPTOLEMOS

I believe you, Philoctetes, every word. I have proof of my own. I met the Greek Generals and Odysseus, too. They're criminals.

PHILOCTETES

So you know. Yes. They rouse everyone against them, those men, they spread chaos everywhere. What did they do to you? I can see you're angry. . . ?

NEOPTOLEMOS

So angry I could . . . Just give me the chance to show how angry I am. Then they'll find out in Mycenae and they'll find out in Sparta that Skyros, too, mothers brave men!

PHILOCTETES

Good, good, my boy! You've cause to hate them too, then. I can see that. You're furious. What did they do?

NEOPTOLEMOS

I'll tell you, Philoctetes, they . . . I can scarcely say it, the way they treated me, the insults, the indignity! . . . You see, when—by the will of heaven—my father died . . .

PHILOCTETES

Wait, stop there! Before you go on . . . Achilles is dead?

NEOPTOLEMOS

No man on this earth killed him. It was said an arrow from the god Apollo ended his life.

PHILOCTETES

Then the one who killed and the one who died were worthy of each other. You make it hard for me, boy. I want to know what happened to you. But when I think of Achilles, my grief for him comes first.

NEOPTOLEMOS

Grieve for yourself, my friend. You have cause. Achilles is far away, and dead.

PHILOCTETES

Yes ... So, the Greeks insulted you. Go back over it, tell me what happened.

NEOPTOLEMOS

The noble Odysseus came to me—brought ships, armament, a full scale expedition. He said—true or not, how can I tell?—that now my father was dead no one in the world except myself was capable of winning the war against Troy. Heaven's will made the task mine. Having been told all this, I could scarcely wait to set sail. More than anything else I longed to see my father, just once before they buried him ... I never really knew him ... And then, it was good to hear that I was to be the one to conquer the fortress of Troy—a great honor. Two days sail and my fleet shipped oars at Sigeion, scene of all that bitter struggle. As I stepped off my ship I was mobbed by the whole army. They swarmed round to greet me, swearing they saw the dead Achilles alive again ... And there he lay, my father. I paid my last respects to him and then went straight to Agamemnon and Menelaus, to my friends, as I naturally thought. I was a fool. I asked for my father's property back, and—of course—the armor he used to wear. When I heard their answer my heart sank. 'Son of Achilles,' they said, 'you are free to take away all your father's possessions except ... except his armor. That has been handed over to someone else, Odysseus.' Choked and trembling with fury I stood up. 'Thieves!' I said. 'How dare you give away my armor—yes, mine!—without consulting me?' Then Odysseus—he happened to be there—spoke up: 'Come, my boy,' he said, 'they had every right to give it to me. I was there when Achilles was killed. I earned the armor when I rescued his body.' I was so enraged that Odysseus, of all people, should take my armor from me that I burst out with a storm of abuse against them all—I spared them nothing. By this time Odysseus was stung into replying— and he doesn't lose his temper easily. 'You were never one of us,' he said. 'You kept well in the background where no fighting was required, you talk too much and too loudly, and I can guarantee you'll never sail back to Skyros with that armor!' I had heard enough, I was sick of insults, so I set off for home, and here I am—robbed of my rightful property by Odysseus, the treacherous, black-hearted scum, Odysseus.

And yet, I blame him less than the commanders-in-chief. Any community and especially any army is represented by its leaders. Men learn bad discipline only from the example of those in charge of them . . . That's my whole story. But anyone who hates the sons of Atreus is my friend, and I hope the friend of heaven.

SAILORS

Yes, I was there, that day, when the full force of the generals' insult struck our leader. I prayed to heaven that day, when they gave his father's armor away. I prayed to the giver of life, the mother of Zeus, to the bountiful Earth herself, who reigns over the mountains and the rich golden streams of the Paktolos, and I call her to witness now, blessed goddess, supreme in power, most high, most awful, ruler of bull-slaying lions, they gave that armor to Odysseus!

PHILOCTETES

Your grievance is enough to recommend you here. Welcome . . . friend! We are in harmony, you and I; the two generals and Odysseus have been at work—I recognize the signs. I know him. The lies slip easily off his tongue—he'll dabble in any crime. Nothing he touches ever comes to good. For me there is one thing in your story hard to believe: Ajax was there and saw it happen and did nothing.

NEOPTOLEMOS

Ajax was dead, my friend. I would have my armor now if he had been alive.

PHILOCTETES

What? Ajax gone . . . dead . . . ?

NEOPTOLEMOS

The light of the sun shines on him no more.

PHILOCTETES

It's wrong, wrong! Agamemnon and Odysseus—their unnecessary lives go on, they are immortal.

NEOPTOLEMOS

True. And I can tell you their influence in the Greek army grows every day.

PHILOCTETES

What happened to my old friend, Nestor—he was a good man. Is he still there? He was always full of wisdom—stood firm when he saw them doing wrong.

NEOPTOLEMOS

This is a bad time for him. His son has been killed, he's quite alone . . .

PHILOCTETES

He lived for his son, so two have died. Neoptolemos, of all men in the world I wish it had not been them. What is one to think, when such men die, and Odysseus lives on? He would have been more use to us dead. Instead it is they we have to mourn.

NEOPTOLEMOS

Odysseus is clever, he wrestles well with life. But even clever wrestlers get tripped, Philoctetes.

PHILOCTETES

Wait, I must ask you—Patroklos! Where is he now? He was your father's dearest friend.

NEOPTOLEMOS

He was killed, too . . . I can tell you one simple fact about war: it never takes the men who deserve to die; its victims are always good.

PHILOCTETES

I know, I've seen it happen. And on that subject, let me ask you about that other useless man, the one with too much to say, but clever . . . what happened to him?

NEOPTOLEMOS

Who answers that description? . . . You don't mean Odysseus?

PHILOCTETES

No, no . . . wasn't there someone called . . . Thersites. Yes, he used to go on speaking when everyone else wanted silence. Do you know whether he came out alive?

NEOPTOLEMOS

I never met him, but I heard he survived.

PHILOCTETES

He would. The evil in this world never dies. No, eternal powers swaddle it in affection; they take pleasure, somehow, in preserving all that is treacherous and corrupt, while they dispatch everything fine and good down into the grave. I can find no sense in it, nothing to revere. How can I feel reverence for heavenly powers whom all the time I see doing wrong?

NEOPTOLEMOS

I tell you this, Philoctetes; from now on my only sight of Troy and the Greek generals will be from a good safe distance. Where corruption is the rule, where fine things die, where all that is mean and shabby has the power—a world like that I cannot love. No, in future the rocks of Skyros will be enough for me; they are my home, I'm happy there . . .

I shall go back to my ship now, and I wish you the best, Philoctetes, the very best. May heaven cure you of your sickness, as you surely wish ... [Neoptolemos *turns to the sailors.*] We must go; we'll weigh anchor as soon as we get a following wind.

[Neoptolemos *and the others make as if to leave.*]

Philoctetes
You're leaving already, my boy ... ?

Neoptolemos
Yes, we must. It's nearly time to sail. I want to be near my ship.

[*They continue on their way back to the ship but* Philoctetes *hobbles after them and blocks their way.*]

Philoctetes
Boy! I'm going to throw myself on your mercy. I'm giving you power of life and death over me. I'm asking you, by your father and your mother, in the name of everything you hold dear at home—don't leave me behind. Don't leave me alone, in this hell, this prison—you've heard what it's like, you've seen it! Give me a corner in your ship, anywhere! It's an ugly sight, I know, an ugly cargo, but try, *try* to forget that ... You're a man of honor, goodness means something to you—the thought of doing wrong appals you. Leave me here, and you earn nothing but disgrace. But if you'll just do what I ask, and I reach my home in Oita alive, you'll have honor, honor everywhere. Come, what does it cost you—scarcely one day's work. Brave it out. You can take me and throw me where you like—in the prow, in the stern, in the bilge, even—wherever I'll be least trouble to your crew. Say yes, boy! In the name of Zeus who pities people in distress, let me persuade you ... Look ... [Philoctetes *kneels.*] this is what I do. Broken in heart and body, lame ... Don't abandon me to this desert where I never see a human being. Save me, take me to your home, or as far as the plains of Chalkedon in Euboea. I can get home easily from there ... I'll get back somehow to Trachis and the Spercheios and because of you I'll see my father again ... and yet, he may be dead by now, I've often thought ... after all this time. When travelers came here I sent him appeals to save me, time and time again I asked him to send a ship to bring me home, but ... either he's dead or ... I don't know, perhaps those messengers didn't think my affairs of much importance and hurried on to their homes. But now, you are my messenger and rescuer all in one, I come to you—be the one to save me, the one to pity me, seeing that man walks in the midst of danger all his life, threatened with sorrow when he is most happy. When you are free from pain then is the time to guard against the troubles you may have; when your life goes well, then is the time for care. You may never know the day of your destruction.

SAILOR

Listen to him, sir . . .

He deserves your pity . . .

He's suffered terribly, you heard what he said . . .

I hope no one I love has to suffer like that!

If you really hate those two generals, sir, we'll give you revenge on
them and do him good at the same time.

We'll put him on board our ship . . . as he asks . . .

She's well supplied . . .

She's fast . . .

Take him back home . . .

And there would be no risk of the gods' displeasure.

NEOPTOLEMOS

[*to* SAILORS] Be sure. You may be ready and willing now. But when
you have to live with this disease, when it fills every moment of your
day—will you stand by what you have just said?

SAILORS

Of course . . . Always! . . . We'll stick by our words . . . You'll never
have cause to say we broke our word . . . it would be foul . . . treacherous . . .

NEOPTOLEMOS

Very well. If you are willing to make sacrifices—so am I. I would be
ashamed for our friend here to think I was less ready than you. Is it
decided then? [*He looks round; they signify assent.*] Right, let's sail,
we leave at once. The ship will carry us all, she won't refuse. I only
pray that heaven stays with us on our voyage out of here and keeps us
safe wherever we sail.

PHILOCTETES

Today happiness has come to me again—you, sir, have become my
dearest friend, and you are my friends too, all of you . . . how can I
ever show my gratitude, what can I do in return for all that I owe
you . . . ? Oh, my friends . . . Come, boy, let us first say goodbye to my
home, though what could be less like a home? You come inside and
see how I lived . . . and what I lived on, then you'll understand my
strength of will. I think the sight of it alone would have defeated
anyone but me. But facts taught me long ago to make friends with
suffering.

SAILORS

Wait! Let's see who this is. There are two men—one from our ship, the
other's a stranger . . . running . . . Find out what they want first . . .

[*One of* NEOPTOLEMOS' *crew and another* SAILOR *disguised as a* MER-
CHANT *come in.*]

MERCHANT

Son of Achilles, Neoptolemos, I asked this man—he was guarding your ship, along with two others—I asked him where you might be, since I met him, quite unexpectedly, but we just happened to put into the same harbor . . . I'm on business, not a big cargo, you know, but I'm on my way home from Troy to Peparethos—we have vineyards there— and I heard that the sailors down on the shore there were your men, so I thought I couldn't sail away just like that without saying a word to you first, and getting from you whatever my news is worth. I presume you don't realize what's going on, or what the Greeks are planning to do about you . . . Well, not just planning, but already getting done, no time wasted there . . .

NEOPTOLEMOS

It is good of you to think of me, stranger; and I would have to be a hard man indeed to forget your kindness . . . Tell me about this. I am always interested in my future. You say the Greeks . . .

MERCHANT

They've left Troy. They're coming after you with a squadron of ships under Phoenix and the sons of Theseus.

NEOPTOLEMOS

How do they propose to get me back? By force? Or will they try talk?

MERCHANT

I don't know. I'm simply telling you now what I've heard.

NEOPTOLEMOS

Why are Phoenix and the others in such a hurry to please the Greek generals?

MERCHANT

Listen, they are on their way now! Their plans have become action!

NEOPTOLEMOS

But Odysseus wasn't prepared to come and say what he had to say in person. Why not? What prevented him? Was he afraid?

MERCHANT

He set out himself, just as I was leaving—he and Diomedes—after someone else.

NEOPTOLEMOS

Odysseus himself! Who is to be honored by a visit from Odysseus?

MERCHANT

Someone called . . . [*He breaks off and glances in the direction of* PHILOCTETES. *He draws* NEOPTOLEMOS *aside and speaks in a whisper.*]

Just a minute, who is this man here? . . . Careful—keep your voice down.

NEOPTOLEMOS
This is Philoctetes, friend, you must have heard of him . . .

MERCHANT [*still in a whisper*]
No more questions, sir! You must get away from here . . . Now! Hurry! Set sail at once!

[PHILOCTETES *has been trying to overhear their conversation. Now he comes up to* NEOPTOLEMOS.]

PHILOCTETES
What's he saying, boy? Why's he whispering? I'm not some of his merchandise, I won't have bargains struck over me!

NEOPTOLEMOS
I'm not sure yet what he's saying. But I want it said out loud so that we can all hear . . .

MERCHANT
Son of Achilles, sir, please, you'll have me in trouble with the generals. I shouldn't be telling you all this. I'm a poor man, I have a business, I make a living from supplying the army . . .

NEOPTOLEMOS
I am a sworn enemy of Agamemnon and Menelaus. And *because* he hates them, too, this man is my friend. If you are here to help me, it is your duty not to conceal any information from us.

MERCHANT
Careful what you do, boy . . .

NEOPTOLEMOS
I am careful, very careful—always have been.

MERCHANT
I hold you responsible for anything that . . .

NEOPTOLEMOS
Do . . . Now, tell me.

MERCHANT
I will, then. It's for Philoctetes that those two I was telling you about—General Diomedes and the mighty Odysseus—have sailed out from Troy. They've taken an oath to bring him back. Either they'll persuade him, or else . . . well, they have the men, they'll use force. Everyone in the Greek army heard Odysseus say so. Odysseus was the confident one—more than Diomedes. He'll do it.

NEOPTOLEMOS

Why, after all this time, should the generals start thinking of Philoctetes? It's years since they cast him away on this island, and now
suddenly they long to see him again. Why? Has the power of justice,
stronger than the power of men, begun to work?

MERCHANT

I'll give you the whole story—you probably haven't heard. In Troy,
there was a man—a prince, he was a son of Priam—called Helenos—
and he had the gift of prophecy. One night Odysseus, whom everyone
calls corrupt, vicious, every kind of bad name—he went out and
captured Helenos singlehanded. Well, it was clever of him ... He
brought back his prisoner, showed him off in the middle of the Greek
camp—a great prize—magnificent. Then Helenos began to prophesy;
he told them many things, but in particular he said they had no hope
of destroying the city of Troy until they persuaded Philoctetes here to
come away from the island where he lives now. When Odysseus heard
the prophet saying this he immediately undertook to bring back
Philoctetes to the Greek army. He hoped, of course, that he would find
him willing to be brought back, but if he wasn't, force would be
applied. And Odysseus let it be known that, if he failed, anyone who
so wishes had permission to cut off his head ... That is all I know,
boy, but my advice to you—and him, and anyone you care about—is,
hurry!

PHILOCTETES

No—this is more than I can bear! That creature, that vermin, he's
sworn, has he, that he'll persuade me back into the Greek army! Oh
yes, I'll be persuaded! I'll be persuaded just about as easily to climb
back out of my grave!

MERCHANT

I don't know about that. I'm going back to my ship now, and may god
keep the rest of you safe and well ... ! [*Exit* MERCHANT.]

PHILOCTETES

Doesn't it make you gasp, boy? Odysseus imagines he's only to say a
few soothing words and I'm on his ship ready to be paraded in front of
the whole Greek army. No. I'd rather have to listen to that snake that
made my leg here useless—and I hate that creature more than anything in the world—but Odysseus cannot relent, he must hound me to
the end. He'll come. I know him ... quick, boy, we must put a good
stretch of sea between us and Odysseus' ship. Let's leave at once.
Speed is everything now. When it's all over there'll be time to sleep
and rest.

NEOPTOLEMOS

As soon as this head wind drops—then we'll leave. At the moment it
stands in the wrong quarter.

PHILOCTETES

Any voyage out of harm's way is good.

NEOPTOLEMOS

Yes, but this wind is blowing just as hard against them.

PHILOCTETES

The bandits of this world find no wind against them, so long as they see a chance to rob and plunder!

NEOPTOLEMOS

It's decided, then. Right, we must hurry. Is there anything you particularly want or need from your cave . . . ?

PHILOCTETES

I don't have much, but there are some things I must have with me.

NEOPTOLEMOS

Anything not on board my ship?

PHILOCTETES

Some leaves which I find ease the pain of this wound—they give me great relief.

NEOPTOLEMOS

Bring them, then. What else would you like to take?

PHILOCTETES

Any arrows I may have forgotten. Nothing must be left.

NEOPTOLEMOS

That is the bow you're holding now? The famous bow?

PHILOCTETES

Yes, this is it, here, in my hands.

NEOPTOLEMOS

May I look more closely? Am I allowed to touch the bow? It fills me with awe. It's power is god-given.

PHILOCTETES

You are indeed allowed, my boy—and anything else of mine if you wish to . . .

NEOPTOLEMOS

Yes, I'm longing to touch it—but only on one condition—that I break no sacred law . . . If I do . . . say no more . . .

PHILOCTETES

Your words show your heart is pure. No, you break no law. You have saved me from the darkness, boy, through you I breathe again, I live, I

will see the earth of my homeland again, my old father, my friends—
and you've taken me out of reach of my enemies.

[NEOPTOLEMOS *has been growing more uneasy, and guilty.*]

Don't worry, you will be allowed to hold this bow, and you may also
boast, when you have given it back, that you alone, out of the whole
world, have been permitted to handle the bow of Hercules. You
deserve it. You are a good man. I won that privilege through doing
good—and so have you.

NEOPTOLEMOS [*hastily*]
Go inside . . . We must hurry!

PHILOCTETES
I'll show you the way ... Here ... [*He leans on* NEOPTOLEMOS'
shoulder.] the disease ... let me lean on you. See how I depend on
you ...

[*Exeunt* PHILOCTETES *and* NEOPTOLEMOS]

SAILORS
I've heard the story . . .
I've never seen the proof . . .
Of the man who tried to come between Zeus and his bride . . .
Tried to defile the union of the greatest power in the universe . . .
And Zeus destroyed him, bound him to a giant wheel that went round
    and round into all eternity. But he is the only one I know of who
    has suffered worse or had a more cruel destiny than Philoctetes
    here.
If there is anyone I've never seen or heard of him.
Why should a man have to suffer like that?
He hurt no one, robbed no one . . .
He was a fair minded man . . .
To those like himself . . .
And yet he is destroyed for nothing.
It amazes me . . . how, how can he survive this terrible existence?
    How can he sit, alone, day after day, hearing only the surge of the
    sea, the crash of the breakers . . .
Only his own company,
Crippled, no one living near to share his troubles, to be there when
    he shrieks in agony, to stay with him in his torment . . . and it is
    torment, the pain's jaws sink deep into his flesh, the blood spurts
    up . . .
Just someone, someone . . .
To stop the flow of steaming blood with gentle leaves . . .
His foot rages like a beast . . .

The wound oozes black pus . . .
You can find leaves, they grow in the forest . . .
But no, he had to creep from place to place, tottering, wavering
    along . . .
Like an infant, without its nurse . . . Looking for something to keep
    him alive, something easily found,
Whenever this thing in his leg, the curse that haunts him, lets him
    go for a time. . .
If he ate, it wasn't anything that grows in the life-giving soil, not any-
    thing which men who live from the earth and by trade, like us, can
    get—it was flesh from birds . . .
If he was lucky enough to have one fly in range of his arrows . . . and
    his arrows are swift . . .
Then he filled his stomach.
But it's a sorry life, barely a life . . .
Ten years without even the pleasure of wine running out of a cup . . .
He had to search for water left standing after rain . . .
But now, he's met a man who comes from a line of heroes.
Now his fortune will change . . .
And after all he's endured he'll regain his strength and sail home . . .
In our ship . . .
After all those months our captain will take him to the shores of Melias
    where the nymphs play . . .
And to the banks of the Spercheios . . .
Where the hero of the bronze shield joined the great company of
    heaven all ablaze over the slopes of Oita in the divine fire of his
    father, Zeus . . .

NEOPTOLEMOS [*into cave*]
    Quickly, then, if you're coming . . . [*Nothing happens.*] Well? . . .
    Philoctetes! [*Silence*] Are you turned to stone? . . . Philoctetes!

[*A sound comes from* PHILOCTETES, *but it is inarticulate.*]

NEOPTOLEMOS
    What is it?

[PHILOCTETES *appears. He is in terrible pain, but trying to suppress the
    signs of it.*]

PHILOCTETES
    Nothing . . . no cause . . . for alarm . . . [*with an effort to seem
    normal*] Come on, let's start, boy.

NEOPTOLEMOS
    It isn't your wound, is it? Is there pain now?

PHILOCTETES
No, no, not at all. No, I think I'm better now . . . [*The next words are forced out of him in spite of himself.*] God in heaven . . . !

NEOPTOLEMOS
Why call on heaven?

PHILOCTETES
I called on heaven to save me. To heal me. [*Another cry is forced out of him.*]

NEOPTOLEMOS
Something's happened! You must tell me . . .

[PHILOCTETES *can't speak for the pain.*]
You must! . . . What's wrong? You can't hide it . . . !

PHILOCTETES
It's killing me, boy, I can't . . . the foul thing's killing me. Look, I . . . oh, it's coming now . . . ! [*He gives another cry. This time he doesn't try to conceal his agony.*] Right through me, right through . . . ! I can't . . . The torture! It . . . death! . . . Eaten alive, boy, *eaten* . . . ! [*He shrieks—a long drawn-out shriek of agony.*] Dear god! . . . Get your sword out, boy! Cut . . . there, cut the foot off . . . Now! Hurry! Chop it away . . . Don't care if I die . . . Come *on,* boy!

NEOPTOLEMOS
What's happening to you? It comes so suddenly, no warning. What is it making you shout and scream like this?

PHILOCTETES
You know, boy.

NEOPTOLEMOS
I don't.

PHILOCTETES
You *know!*

NEOPTOLEMOS
What is it? I don't know!

PHILOCTETES
Why not? You must! [*Once more he screams in pain.*]

NEOPTOLEMOS
The poison! . . . It's working . . . I see . . . yes . . . yes . . . it's terrible . . .

PHILOCTETES
Terrible, boy . . . I can't tell you . . . Pity me!

NEOPTOLEMOS
What shall I do?

PHILOCTETES
Wait, don't be afraid, stay with me. It comes, you see, after a time . . .
It goes, but it always comes back . . .

NEOPTOLEMOS [*in tears*]
My friend . . . look, I . . . your suffering, all that suffering . . . What can
I do, I can't bear to see you like this . . . Do you want me to carry you,
hold you up? Here, let me get you . . . [NEOPTOLEMOS *tries to lift*
PHILOCTETES *but is pushed away.*]

PHILOCTETES
No, no, don't! . . . Here, take the bow . . . You asked me just now. Keep
it till the worst of the attack has passed . . . [*still holding on to it*]
Safely, mind you. Guard it! When the pain goes I must sleep—I get
no relief otherwise. Don't wake me, let me go on sleeping . . . If
Odysseus and the others arrive in the meanwhile don't, in the name of
all that's sacred, don't let that bow leave your hands whatever happens, whatever he tries to make you do, even if you want to . . . and
don't let him trick you! Do you understand? Otherwise we'll both be
corpses. I'm at your mercy, remember that.

NEOPTOLEMOS
Depend on me. I'll be careful. The bow stays with me . . . Bring it
here and good fortune come with it.

[PHILOCTETES *hands the bow over to* NEOPTOLEMOS.]

PHILOCTETES
There, in your hands, boy . . . Pray god its power, the spirit of death it
carries, never brings you my agony—or the labors it brought Hercules.

NEOPTOLEMOS
Heaven grant that prayer. And grant us all a good and prosperous
voyage, wherever destiny and our own mission takes us . . .

PHILOCTETES
I'm afraid, boy, afraid—your prayer may never be answered . . . Look
. . . the wound's open again . . . the blood's scarlet . . . that's from deep
in the flesh . . . Pulse, pulse . . . I can feel it coming . . . worse again . . .
[*He groans.*] That foot! The crimes it commits on me! . . . Coming
now . . . getting closer . . . Damn you, damn you, *damn* you . . . ! Yes,
look! You have it . . . here! . . . No, don't leave me! . . . [*He screams.*]
Odysseus, if only this agony could rip your breast apart! . . . [*He
screams again.*] and you generals . . . Agamemnon, Menelaus, both of
you, just you nurse this disease as long as I have . . . Oh no . . . please

... help me ... Death! Death—every day I call on you ... Why can you never come to me? [*to* NEOPTOLEMOS] My boy ... dear friend, kind ... friend, take me and burn me in the pit of lava on the mountain top ... kind friend ... I did so much for Hercules, and my reward was the bow you're holding now ... What do you say, boy? What do you say ... ?

[NEOPTOLEMOS *is silent, ashamed.*]

Why don't you speak? What are you thinking of?

NEOPTOLEMOS
I can't bear to see you suffer ... All this time—it's terrible to watch ...

PHILOCTETES
Yes, boy, but we must have strength. When the pain comes it breaks me, but it soon goes. All I ask—and this I beg of you—don't leave me alone, not alone!

NEOPTOLEMOS
Trust our promise. We stay.

PHILOCTETES
Will *you* stay?

NEOPTOLEMOS
That you can be sure of.

PHILOCTETES
I won't humiliate you and make you swear, boy.

NEOPTOLEMOS
I can't leave this island without you, I'm bound to stay—it is my duty!

PHILOCTETES
I believe you ... give me your hand. [PHILOCTETES *holds out his hand.* NEOPTOLEMOS *takes it.*]

NEOPTOLEMOS
There, my hand in yours. I stay.

[PHILOCTETES *begins to writhe in pain again.*]

PHILOCTETES
I must ... I ... up there ...

NEOPTOLEMOS
Where?

PHILOCTETES
Up ... !

NEOPTOLEMOS
You're feverish ... delirious. What are you looking up there for? Only the sky's up there.

PHILOCTETES
Let me go, let me *go!*

NEOPTOLEMOS
Where to?

PHILOCTETES
Let me go, can't you?

NEOPTOLEMOS
I won't leave you ... [*He puts out a hand.*]

PHILOCTETES
You kill me every time you touch me!

NEOPTOLEMOS
Look, I'm not touching you now. Is that better?

PHILOCTETES
Earth—receive this—this rotting carcase, this thing, this foul—thing ... I can't stand ... I can't ... [PHILOCTETES *collapses.*]

NEOPTOLEMOS [*to* SAILORS]
He'll sleep now. Look, it won't be long. His head's lolling, his whole body's soaked in sweat ... There's a vein in his foot all black with poisoned blood ... ruptured now ... Leave me, we mustn't disturb him. Let him have his sleep.

SAILORS
Sleep, out of the reach of pain, out of the reach of sorrow, sleep, come down gently, come down sweetly smiling, smiling, and master him. Keep this beam of calm spread over his eyes. Come to us here, come and heal him ...
Now, my boy?
What is it to be?
Have you thought what you do next? You'd better ...
You see how it is ...
We're waiting?
Yes, what for? What are we meant to do?
This is the moment. If we act now, quickly, we shall have the advantage. But it must be now. Grasp the moment—that's the first, the most important lesson ...

NEOPTOLEMOS
He's unconscious, and we have his bow ... But we must bring him to Troy; we still lose all if we sail without him. The chief glory belongs to

him, that is decreed in heaven. He must win it. And if all we have to boast of is frustration, achieved by lies—we are fools, we are criminals, and everyone will know it.

SAILORS

Heaven will decide the outcome, boy . . .
Next time you answer me, keep your voice down, small, small . . . sick men sleep lightly, there's a part of them always on watch . . .
Try and look ahead and tell me . . .
But quietly . . .
What is the plan now?
Can you go on?
Can you persist with your plan . . . ? You know what I mean . . . trouble is bound to come. Think. There's bound to be pain . . . suffering . . .
The wind's in our favor, boy, in our favor . . .
The man's helpless . . .
As good as blind . . .
Stretched out there on his back . . .
Sleep in the sun will make him better . . .
Hands, feet, every muscle . . . idle . . .
He's lying there . . . he could almost be dead—
Careful!
Watch what you say! Careful of words like that now!
One thing I'm sure of, my boy, in my own mind . . .
The best course in life is the one that keeps out of danger.

NEOPTOLEMOS

Silence! Guard your words, and watch . . . He's awake. His eye moved, he's raising his head . . .

PHILOCTETES

Light . . . sun's shining—I've been alseep . . . Thank god! Still there, watching, and I scarcely dared hope—my friends I prayed for this, but I never believed . . . You stayed with me, boy, you had pity, looked after me, bore with the filthy disease. Agamemnon and Menelaus, those two brave generals, they couldn't bear it; they hadn't the spirit to endure such things! But you, my boy, now you have character, strength, the strength of your father, and you made light of all this, the shrieking, the stench, nothing to you. I think it's leaving me now, the pain. I'll have peace for a while. Help me up.

[*The* SAILORS *move forward to obey.*]

. . . no, you, boy, I want you to help me stand. Then, as soon as this exhaustion leaves me, we must get down to the ship and start at once.

NEOPTOLEMOS

Has the pain gone? ... I'm glad. I'd given up hope. But now you're alive, breathing again. Just now, when you collapsed, it looked like death ... Now, try and stand up, or would you rather my men carried you? They will, you know, they won't shirk it—and in any case we have decided, you and I, that it must be done.

PHILOCTETES

Thank you, my boy, yes, lift me up, do as you say. But don't trouble your men, no need for them to be tormented by the stench before they have to. It'll be hard enough for them to live with me when we get to sea ...

NEOPTOLEMOS

Very well. Now stand up, and hold on to me. [NEOPTOLEMOS *holds out his hand and* PHILOCTETES *struggles to his feet.*]

PHILOCTETES

Have courage, boy. My will learnt long ago to force me upright ...

NEOPTOLEMOS [*breaking down*]

What shall I do? How can I go on?

PHILOCTETES

What is it, boy? [NEOPTOLEMOS *is silent.*] You've something to say. Say it!

NEOPTOLEMOS

I don't know how ... it's impossible ... how can I find words to tell you ... ?

PHILOCTETES

What's impossible? Don't say things like that, boy!

NEOPTOLEMOS

Yes, I'm trapped, I see it now, trapped.

PHILOCTETES

I'm not to sail with you, is that it? The disease offends you so much ... you've decided ...

NEOPTOLEMOS

The whole world seems diseased, Philoctetes, when you go against your nature, break every rule of honesty ...

PHILOCTETES

I am a good man and you came to my help. Your father would have said and done exactly the same.

NEOPTOLEMOS

Now they'll know me . . . the shame, the shame! . . . I can't get it out of my head . . . it tortures me!

PHILOCTETES

Shame? You've done nothing wrong. As for what you told me . . . yes, now I *am* afraid.

NEOPTOLEMOS

God in heaven, what am I going to do? Doubly wrong, doubly guilty—I should have told you—and I didn't . . . Then those squalid lies . . .

PHILOCTETES [*to* SAILORS]

Yes, now I know what is to come. He's going back on his word, he's going to sail away and leave me here.

NEOPTOLEMOS

No, believe me, I won't leave you. But suppose I take you, and suppose you hate me for it . . . I can't get it out of my mind, the shame burns me.

PHILOCTETES

What do you mean, boy? I don't understand.

NEOPTOLEMOS

I won't hide it any more. You are bound for Troy, Philoctetes. This voyage takes you straight to the Greek army, the army commanded by Agamemnon and Menelaus.

PHILOCTETES

No, it's not true!

NEOPTOLEMOS

Don't despair, before you've heard what . . .

PHILOCTETES

What is there to hear? . . . Oh, what are you trying to do to me?

NEOPTOLEMOS

To get you cured, Philoctetes—first we'll do that, then, with your help, we'll go out and conquer Troy.

PHILOCTETES

So, it is true—and this was your plan . . . ?

NEOPTOLEMOS

A great and powerful destiny rules our lives. Listen, and control your passion . . .

PHILOCTETES

How can I live after this . . . this cruel betrayal . . . ? What have you done to me, Stranger? Give me back my bow, now! At once!

NEOPTOLEMOS

That's not possible. I have my duty and myself to think of. I must obey the orders of my commanders . . .

PHILOCTETES

You . . . you . . . fire! You all-consuming terror! You foul, scheming, treacherous fiend! Think! Think what you've done, think how you've lied. How can you bear to look at me, after I begged you, went and grovelled to you—don't you sweat for shame . . . thief . . . You take my weapons, steal my very life . . . Give them back, I'll do anything, only give them back, please, please, my boy! By all that's holy to you, don't rob me of life itself . . .

[NEOPTOLEMOS *says nothing.* PHILOCTETES *waits, then lets out a groan of despair.*]

He won't even speak to me now, he looks away, he'll never give them back, I see that . . . Oh, you sandy shores and cliffs, you herds of mountain beasts, you rocky ravines, listen to me. I've lived with you all these years . . . listen, there's no one else to hear—I'm calling to you, *weeping*, do you hear? Look what this boy, this brat of Achilles, look what he's done to me. He swore he would take me home, but no—he's taking me to Troy! He put his hand in mine, he accepted the sacred weapons of Hercules from me, and now he has them he wants to make a present of them to the Greeks. He hauls me off, as if he'd fought and conquered a mighty warrior, never guessing that all he's been fighting is a corpse, a shadow of smoke, a mockery of a man. If I was strong and well, he'd never have won; even now, only a trick gave him victory. Well, the trick has worked and I'm the victim. So what is there for me to do? [PHILOCTETES *turns to* NEOPTOLEMOS *again.*] Give them back! You can still be true to yourself. What do you say, then? . . . Silence I see. Annihilation! I'm lost . . . Well, my rocky home with your two doors, back I come to you, naked, stripped of the means of life. Alone in this cave, I shall shrivel away, never again to kill a bird as it flies overhead, or bring down a mountain animal with my bow. I'll come to my miserable end as food for the beasts on which I once fed myself. Yes, now the hunted become the hunters. I'll pay for my many murders with my own blood, sentenced by a man who seemed to be pure in heart. God curse you and may you—no, first, I'm going to ask you just once more, will you change your mind? If you say no . . . die and be damned to you!

SAILORS [*to* NEOPTOLEMOS]

What are your orders, sir? It is your decision now. Do we sail? He has shown us a way—do we take it?

NEOPTOLEMOS

The only thing I know is—the pity, the terrible pity I feel for him . . .
I didn't tell you, but I felt it . . .

PHILOCTETES

For the love of heaven, show some mercy, boy. Go through with this
deceit, and no one will have a good word for you. Everyone will
condemn you. Don't let that happen!

NEOPTOLEMOS

I can't decide. I don't know. I . . . if only I'd never left Skyros. All this
weighs on me, I can't think . . .

PHILOCTETES

There is good in you—but it is being corrupted. You have taken
instruction from someone else, someone evil. Put yourself in the hands
of better teachers. Give me back my bow and sail out of here.

NEOPTOLEMOS [*to* SAILORS]
What should we do, men?

[*A voice comes from behind them, from the direction of the shore. The
voice belongs to* ODYSSEUS.]

ODYSSEUS

You fool, what are you doing? Hand over that bow to me and get back
to the ship! [ODYSSEUS *comes into view.*]

PHILOCTETES
Who's that? I thought I heard Odysseus.

ODYSSEUS [*coming forward*]
Correct. You heard Odysseus, and now you see him!

PHILOCTETES

Yes, I've been sold for slaughter, and now comes my execution. So he
trapped me, he robbed me of my bow . . .

ODYSSEUS
Yes, guilty, I admit everything!

PHILOCTETES [*to* NEOPTOLEMOS]
Give it back, boy, let me have it, please, the bow! The bow!

ODYSSEUS

That, Philoctetes, is just what he cannot do, even if he wished. And
you must come with us . . . Or must we use force?

PHILOCTETES
Force! That suits you! That satisfies you! Yes, you've reached that low.

ODYSSEUS
 Well, if you refuse to move yourself.

PHILOCTETES
 Earth of Lemnos, all-powerful flame struck from the blazing anvil of
 Hephaistos—can this be allowed to happen? Can Odysseus drag me
 from your land by force?

ODYSSEUS
 It is Zeus—do you understand—Zeus who rules this island, Zeus has
 decreed what must happen—and I am the servant of Zeus.

PHILOCTETES
 You turn my stomach, pretending that god is on your side. Clever! A
 new philosophy! You turn god into a liar.

ODYSSEUS
 No, god reveals the truth to us. Our way is clear—it must be traveled.

PHILOCTETES
 Never!

ODYSSEUS
 Yes. And you will obey.

PHILOCTETES
 Oh yes, yes, indeed, I see now—I've lost my freedom. My state in life
 is to be a slave . . .

ODYSSEUS
 You're wrong. You will be one of the heroes of Troy. In their company
 you will take the city and destroy it.

PHILOCTETES
 Never, never! I don't care, do what you like. I don't care what
 happens, so long as there is one cliff on this island high enough . . .

ODYSSEUS
 What would you do?

PHILOCTETES
 I'll throw myself over—now . . . the rocks below . . . dash my brains
 out . . .

[ODYSSEUS *signals to his men to hold* PHILOCTETES *as he struggles
 towards the edge of the cliff.*]

ODYSSEUS
 Hold him! Don't let him move!

[*Two* SAILORS *pinion* PHILOCTETES]

PHILOCTETES

My arms—now you need the bow you loved to hold, now, when this marauder springs his trap . . . Odysseus, have you ever, in all your life, had a single pure or honest thought? You stalk me like an animal, you hunt me down, using this boy I've never seen before as a screen to skulk behind . . . He's too good for you, he's worth something . . . he should be following me . . . But what does he know about anything except obeying orders? Look at him now. Disgusted with himself . . . He detests the lies he's had to tell, the suffering I've been through . . . But you were clever, because you have an instinct for the tortuous, the crooked, the twisted. He was innocent, he didn't like your corrupt methods—but you closed in on him, and taught him how to operate like you, how to be clever like you. So now, you miserable creature, you've made your capture and you've decided to haul me off. But you flung me on this very beach—don't you remember—years ago, without a friend, without a possession, without a home—a walking corpse! [*His voice rises.*] Heaven strike you dead! Over and over again I've prayed for your death, but heaven never allows me any pleasure and you live on, serene and happy, while I curse the life that brings me nothing but pain and sorrow. Yes, you laugh at me, don't you—you and your two generals? Now you run their errands, you're their servile official, but you joined them in the first place only because you had no choice; you were tricked into coming while I—god, when I think of it!—I came of my own free will, I brought seven ships, I sailed myself. And then they leave me here to rot! Why not just leave me? Why drag me back to life? What can you possibly hope for? I'm nothing to you. I died long ago! . . . Can't you see, you devil—I'm lame, stinking! . . . How are you going to offer your sacrifices to heaven with me on board? Will the wine you pour be sacred? . . . That was your excuse when you threw me off your ship ten years ago! . . . May you all die in agony— and you will die too—if there is justice left in the world—for the things you've done to me . . . I know there is justice. I know that heaven cares. Nothing would induce you to sail out here after a useless wreck of a man like me except the will of some greater power . . . Oh you land of my fathers and you powers that watch over it—take vengeance, vengeance on every last one of them, however late, however delayed, but in the name of pity I must have vengeance! My life is torment, but if I live to see them all destroyed, I'll think I've got the cure for my disease!

SAILORS

Our friend is crushing, Odysseus. His words crush us all. There was no sign of yielding . . . In spite of all—no giving way.

ODYSSEUS

If I had time for argument now I would reply to every word of that. As it is, my defense is simply this. I adapt myself to the needs of the situation, and I change accordingly. Where circumstances demand just and upright men you will find no one with a stronger sense of duty than myself. But whatever I do, I must succeed. I must. I was born so . . . However . . . [ODYSSEUS *turns to* PHILOCTETES.] . . . in your case, I make an exception. I intend, though I am not giving way to pressure, to take no further action over you . . . [*to* SAILORS] Let him go, no one is to touch him . . . he can stay here . . . [*to* PHILOCTETES] We have the bow, we don't need you as well. Teukros is with us, and he knows how to use it. If it comes to that, I think I am at least as capable of looking after it as you. I can aim. I can shoot. Why do you have to be there at all? Goodbye . . . Enjoy your walks on Lemnos. [*to* SAILORS *and* NEOPTOLEMOS] Come on . . . we're leaving . . . [*to* PHILOCTETES] Perhaps the bow you were lucky enough to own will bring me some glory. Remember, it might have been yours. [ODYSSEUS *starts to go.*]

[PHILOCTETES *cries out in despair.*]

PHILOCTETES

What can I do . . . I can't . . . it's cruel, vile . . . [*to* ODYSSEUS] So now you swagger back to the Greek army, show off my bow . . .

ODYSSEUS

I will have no arguments from you. I'm going . . .

[PHILOCTETES *turns to* NEOPTOLEMOS *and holds him back.*]

PHILOCTETES

Son of Achilles, are you going too, just like that, without a word . . . can't I speak to you, either?

ODYSSEUS [*as he sees* NEOPTOLEMOS *wavering*]

Hurry. I know you have fine feelings, but take no notice. You'll spoil it all, ruin our chances.

PHILOCTETES [*to* SAILORS]

My friends, am I just going to be left here? Is no one going to stay, no one to have any pity on me?

SAILORS

He's captain, this young man here. Whatever he says, we say . . .

NEOPTOLEMOS

Odysseus is going to call me softhearted . . . but I was born so . . . [*to* SAILORS] Stay with him if he wishes—but only so long as it takes us to fit out the ship and pray for a good voyage. Perhaps in the meanwhile he'll have some change of heart that will suit our purpose better. [*to* ODYSSEUS] Let's leave them. [*to* SAILORS] . . . and when we call you, back on board immediately. [*Exeunt* NEOPTOLEMOS *and* ODYSSEUS]

PHILOCTETES

My rock, my hollow, my retreat—my fire and frost—you see, we are doomed to each other's company, you and I, for ever, and you will be with me till I die . . . Oh no . . . no . . . no . . . you walls, you've drunk in my tears of pain . . . what will my life be now? How will my days pass . . . ? Is there any hope for me . . . will there be food . . . ? No! Fly up there, you pigeons! The air is yours again. I can't touch you . . . !

SAILORS

You sentenced yourself . . .
You decided it . . .
Yes, you!
It's harsh, but no greater power than yourself decides your fate, not now . . .
You could be safe and well . . .
Look, the choice is open, nothing stops you . . .
And you deliberately chose the hard way.

PHILOCTETES

Damned, damned . . . I'll crawl and howl my life away, rotting to death, alone in filth . . . misery . . . [*He weeps.*] Never find food again, never hold my arrows in my hands again . . . at least my hands were strong . . . Lies! Deceit! They told me lies and . . . their minds! Cunning! Oh cunning . . . got me! I never thought he'd . . . god let him suffer, just let him suffer for what he's done. Let him find out what it feels like, years and years and years.

SAILORS

It was meant, meant to happen, heaven has a purpose—it wasn't lies put you in our power . . .
Save your curses for someone else . . .
They don't sound good, they bring ill luck.
All we ask of you, all we expect is—see we are your friends, accept our friendship . . .

PHILOCTETES

Think of it, oh just to think of it—at this moment, he's sitting on the beach, the sea's gray and foaming, and he's laughing, waving it in his hands—my life, my only source of life—and no one else ever touched it before . . . Oh my bow, my dear bow, they took you away, wrenched you out of my hands, so dear to you . . . Look, here I am . . . you understand, you have feelings, my bow . . . Here I am, the friend of

Hercules, and I can't ever use you again. Now you've a new master, he's so clever, so full of ideas—you'll see his tortuous mind at work, inventing shame. I hate him, god, I loathe him, that man, always breeding his crimes, and what he did to me, the foul detestable . . . Oh god!

SAILORS

A man must stand for justice, he must speak out, yes . . .
But when he does, not bitterly, not angry wounding words . . .
Not spit out abuse . . .
Odysseus acted for all . . .
He was told what to do . . .
He had his orders . . .
All he did was help his friends . . .
Do what was best for everyone.
All are responsible.

PHILOCTETES

Fly up there, birds—every beast of the field, turn your bright eyes here—come down from the mountains, come out of your hiding places, no need to run away, no need to leap away in fear . . . look—empty! My hands are empty. No bow, no power any more. I'm weak now, at your mercy. Forget your fear, there's nothing here to cause fright, not for you at least . . . come on, come on, come near . . . It's your turn now, Justice! Eat as much as you like, fill your stomachs with my rotting flesh. I'll soon be carrion! I'll have nothing from the earth, nothing from my bow—and will the winds nourish me? From nothing there can be no life.

SAILORS

In heaven's name, do you respect friendship, trust, goodwill? If these mean anything, come with us . . .
Yes, we bring you friendship . . .
Embrace it, hug it to you . . .
But remember, be sure and remember, yours is the decision.
You can escape from here . . . nothing keeps you . . .
Except self-pity, your own indulgence . . . Feeding your sorrow on bitterness, keeping it alive with your own tears . . .

PHILOCTETES

Of all the people who have come here—no one has been so good to me—and yet you, even you, bring me back to my agony. You keep reminding me again, again . . . Why did you destroy me? Why did you do this to me?

SAILORS

What do you mean?

PHILOCTETES
Trying to make me go to Troy—whose very name I detest!

SAILORS
Because we believe that is best . . .

PHILOCTETES
Get out of my sight!

SAILORS
Good . . .
I'm glad . . .
I was waiting to hear that . . .
Very willingly, very willingly . . .
Come on, let's go . . .
The ship's down on the shore . . .
Let's go there . . .

PHILOCTETES
No! Wait! In the name of heaven, you swore . . . please don't go, *please!*

SAILORS
Gently, sir . . .
Easy, sir, easy . . .

PHILOCTETES
Friends, stay with me, for god's sake!

SAILORS
Why shout?
What's the need . . . ?

PHILOCTETES
AIAI . . . AIAI . . . ! My soul's hurt, my soul's deep hurt, my heart's sorrow . . . destroyed, cursed, damned! . . . You, you . . . my foot . . . what's left? What do I do—live? How do I live now? . . . Friends, come here, come back, come back again.

SAILORS
Why?
What can we achieve . . . ?
Have you changed your mind . . . ?
Is your temper different . . . ?
Your purpose is fixed, you showed it. Can you alter now?

PHILOCTETES
You shouldn't be angry with me—the pain's a storm, it drowns me. I rave, I'm driven mad . . .

SAILORS
Come then . . .
I know, it's terrible for you . . .
Do what we tell you.

PHILOCTETES
Never, never! I stay here—fixed, firm. Let the lightning come, let the thunderbolt strike me, let fire and flame burn me up—I will not go. Troy can sink in its own damnation and all those men round her, who left me here with my tortured limbs to rot. They flung me aside. They had the heart for it . . . Friends, no, wait, do one thing for me. Let me have this, please, look, I'm pleading for it . . .

SAILORS
What do you mean . . . ?
What do you want . . . ?

PHILOCTETES
A sword, someone, a sword, an axe . . . anything sharp . . . get me . . .

SAILORS
What for . . . ?
What do you want to do . . . ?
Be careful—he'll do something . . .

PHILOCTETES
the mind's murdering now, murdering . . .
I'll cut the flesh off my limbs, the flesh—all of it, myself, with my . . .

SAILORS
Why . . . ?
Listen, sir, wait . . .

PHILOCTETES
I'll find my father, I'll seek him . . .

SAILORS
Where?
Where will you find him . . . ?

PHILOCTETES
In the grave. Never in the sunlight . . . Oh, my city, my country, my home . . . I want to see you. I want to look on you again . . . The fool I was, the stupid fool, leaving you like that, leaving your shores, sailing off from your shore to help the Greeks, the damned Greeks—I hate them! . . . Nothing, I'm nothing now . . .

SAILORS
I can tell you we'd have been well on the way to our ship by now, we'd have been gone long ago . . . if we hadn't seen Odysseus . . .

And the son of Achilles . . .
They're coming this way . . .

[*Enter* NEOPTOLEMOS; *he is running, closely followed by* ODYSSEUS.]

ODYSSEUS
At least give me some reason! All of a sudden you turn round, come running back here, don't even stop to explain . . .

NEOPTOLEMOS
I've done wrong—I mean to make it good.

ODYSSEUS
But this is beyond belief! When did you do wrong?

NEOPTOLEMOS
When I did what you and the rest of our army told me.

ODYSSEUS
You did your duty. Be proud of yourself.

NEOPTOLEMOS
I've used lies, I've used deceit, to trap a man—that makes me ashamed!

ODYSSEUS
What man? . . . Now look, wait, don't do anything rash.

NEOPTOLEMOS
Rash? Oh, no! All I want is that Philoctetes . . .

ODYSSEUS
What? Don't frighten me. Neoptolemos. I'm beginning to think you'd . . .

NEOPTOLEMOS
Philoctetes, from whom I took this bow should once more . . .

ODYSSEUS
God in heaven? You can't give it back. You're mad!

NEOPTOLEMOS
I have no right to the bow. I got it by a lie.

ODYSSEUS
Dear god! This is some cruel joke of yours, it must be!

NEOPTOLEMOS
That's right, if you call the truth a joke.

ODYSSEUS
I don't understand you, my boy. Do you know what you're saying . . . ?

NEOPTOLEMOS
I've told you once—how many times do I have to say it?

ODYSSEUS
I wish I'd never heard it at all—I tell you that!

NEOPTOLEMOS
Good. Then you have everything clear now? Quite understood?

ODYSSEUS
There's a power that can stop you . . . Oh, yes, I assure you there is.

NEOPTOLEMOS [*surprised*]
Who? Who will stop me?

ODYSSEUS
The allied armies of Greece, and as their representative—myself.

NEOPTOLEMOS
I thought you had brains. But now you're talking nonsense.

ODYSSEUS
No, boy. *You* talk brainless, and you act brainless, too.

NEOPTOLEMOS
But I have right on my side! And that is stronger than your brains.

ODYSSEUS
What do you mean, right? I thought this out. I planned it, you got the
bow, and now you're handing it back.

NEOPTOLEMOS
I've done wrong. I am ashamed. I'm trying to make up for that wrong.

ODYSSEUS
And when you think of the Greek army, you can still do it? You're **not**
afraid?

NEOPTOLEMOS
Why should I be afraid? I'm in the right.

ODYSSEUS
But I am here to say you are wrong—and prove it!

NEOPTOLEMOS
Your threats prove nothing to me, Odysseus.

ODYSSEUS
It won't be Troy we are going to war against, but you!

NEOPTOLEMOS
So be it.

ODYSSEUS
You see where my right hand is resting—on my sword? [ODYSSEUS *has half drawn his sword, watching* NEOPTOLEMOS *carefully.* NEOPTOLEMOS *draws his completely.*]

NEOPTOLEMOS
Look—I follow you . . . I'm ready!

[ODYSSEUS *hesitates. For a moment it looks as if the two men will come to blows. Then he abruptly resheathes his sword and starts back in the direction of the ships.*]

ODYSSEUS
Very well, have it your way. I'll go. But you wait till our army hears what you've done. Yes, the army will have your blood for this. *[Exit* ODYSSEUS.*]*

NEOPTOLEMOS [*shouting after him*]
Very wise. Be as careful as this in future, and you may save yourself some painful injuries! [NEOPTOLEMOS *looks up in the direction of the cave where* PHILOCTETES *went.*] Now, Philoctetes . . . are you there? Will you come out? . . . Leave the cave!

PHILOCTETES [*appearing*]
What was all that noise and shouting? Why call me out again? Do you need me for anything, friends . . . ? [*sighs*] You've brought enough misery. Do you have to come and made it worse for me?

NEOPTOLEMOS
Don't be afraid. I've something to tell you—listen . . .

PHILOCTETES
I *am* afraid. Once before you came with something to tell me, the news was good. I listened and was sorry.

NEOPTOLEMOS
A man may change—don't you agree?—have regrets . . .

PHILOCTETES
You sounded just like that when you were stealing my bow—very persuasive, but underneath—the venom, the sting!

NEOPTOLEMOS

That's not so—not now! I want you to tell me—have you made up your mind? Do you stay here and brave it out, or do you sail with us?

PHILOCTETES

No, no . . . You can talk, you can say what you like—it's no use.

NEOPTOLEMOS

That's your final decision?

PHILOCTETES

Absolutely final, more than words can say.

NEOPTOLEMOS

I was hoping I could persuade you, but there seems no point. That finishes it, then.

PHILOCTETES

Good. You would only waste your breath. You will never make a friend of me . . . You trick me out of life itself, leave me destitute, and then you come and lecture me . . . oh, your father was a fine man, but how I hate the very sight of you! Damn, you everlastingly— Agamemnon, Menelaus, Odysseus, all of you!

NEOPTOLEMOS

You can stop your cursing . . . Here, take your bow, it's yours. [NEOPTOLEMOS *holds out the bow.*]

PHILOCTETES

How do you mean? Is this another trick?

NEOPTOLEMOS

I swear by the supreme godhead of almighty Zeus . . .

PHILOCTETES

You mean it—thank god, I'm safe . . . This is the truth now?

NEOPTOLEMOS

Actions speak for themselves. They tell no lies. Watch. [*He holds out the weapons.*] Give me your right hand and become master of your bow again.
[*The voice of* ODYSSEUS *as he enters interrupts them. He is followed by a small force of men.*]

ODYSSEUS

But I say no! In the name of god, who sees all and remembers all, on behalf of the Greek generals and the allied army . . .

[PHILOCTETES *snatches the weapons from* NEOPTOLEMOS.]

PHILOCTETES
Who said that, boy? Odysseus! . . . I thought I heard Odysseus?

ODYSSEUS [*coming forward*]
Yes . . . I have come for you, Philoctetes. I am taking you back to the plains of Troy by force—whether the son of Achilles wishes it or not.

PHILOCTETES
But not alive . . . [*He fits an arrow into the bow.* ODYSSEUS' *men scatter.*] . . . if this bow aims true!

[NEOPTOLEMOS *leaps forward and grabs his arm.*]

NEOPTOLEMOS
No! Don't! Stop it! God in heaven, don't shoot!

PHILOCTETES
Let me go! In heaven's name, let go my arm!

[*While* PHILOCTETES *struggles to free himself,* ODYSSEUS *makes good his escape.*]

NEOPTOLEMOS
I will *not* let go!

[ODYSSEUS *is now safely out of range.*]

PHILOCTETES
Look, why stop me? I could have killed him—my worst enemy, the man I hate most in the world, in range of my bow, and you stop me.

NEOPTOLEMOS
Killing him would do no good—neither to your nor to me.

PHILOCTETES
Well, I can tell you this much anyway. The generals of that army—the lying, so-called heralds of the Greeks—they're cowards in a fight, you see—only brave when it comes to talk.

NEOPTOLEMOS
Perhaps. So now you have your bow, and you've no reason to be angry with me . . . nothing to blame me for.

PHILOCTETES
No, you're right. You've shown your father's spirit, boy. Your father—when he was alive, he was admitted to be our greatest warrior, and now he is the greatest of the dead.

NEOPTOLEMOS

I am proud when a man like you speaks well of my father and myself. But listen, Philoctetes. I want one thing from you and I'm determined to have it. In this life, there are some misfortunes we cannot escape; they are sent by heaven; we must accept them; but there are others we bring upon ourselves, and if a person broods on these, as you do, he deserves no indulgence, no pity. You rise up in fury when someone tries to give you advice—in all good faith—anyone who brings help is at once rejected, gets all your bitter resentment and you treat him like an enemy . . . All the same, I'll say this—and I want you to attend very seriously, because I'm calling god to witness. So chisel it in your brain. You are sick and in pain—for a reason. No man willed it, eternal powers directed it. You trespassed on sacred ground where the snake, guardian of the sanctuary, lies coiled up, waiting in the darkness. You must realize that you will never find a cure for the disease that is killing you . . . no, never, not while the sun rises in the east and sets in the west, unless . . . you go of your own free will to the battlefields of Troy. There you must find the sons of Asklepios—they are there in our army— and let them heal the wounds. You must also help me break the resistance of our enemies with your bow. Now, how do I know all this? Well, we captured someone from Troy, a prophet called Helenos—one of their best men—who told us quite clearly what I've told you. It is bound to happen. What you don't know is—he said that Troy is destined to fall this coming summer. If he is proved wrong, he's willing to forfeit his life. Now you know everything. Come with us and come willingly. The reward . . . oh, it's a fine, it's a great reward—to be a hero, the only Greek, the best of all, to find doctors who will heal you, and then above all, to win eternal glory for yourself by taking the city of Troy, the cause of so much sorrow.

PHILOCTETES

Life—you are my torturer! Why, oh why can't you let me go, sink into darkness and death? What am I to do? I can't just ignore his advice . . . he meant it kindly. And yet, am I going to be so weak? . . . If I give in how could I face people, what could I say to them? How could you, my eyes, having watched all that has happened to me, bear to see me in the same company with Agamemnon and Menelaus, my murderers! Or with that vermin Odysseus? The agonies I've suffered in the past, they can't hurt me now, but the thought of what those men could still do to me—that can, yes it can! The mind, you see, the mind's like a mother; once it's conceived evil in a man, it trains him, fosters him to be evil for the rest of his life. [*to* NEOPTOLEMOS] You surprise me, boy. Your duty is to keep away from Troy, and to make sure I never go there either. They treated you disgracefully, stealing your father's armor. After that insult, are you going to take their side and force me to do the same? No, never, my boy. No, do what you promised, promised on oath, and take me home. Stay in Skyros yourself and let them all perish as they deserve—degraded and defeated. I'll thank you for that. And so will my father—you see, a double reward. Take the side of the evil in this world and you begin to wear its mask, you become what you have sided with. Don't do it!

NEOPTOLEMOS
You're right, you're right, of course. I only wish you would trust in heaven and what I've told you. I'm your friend. Sail out of this place with me . . .

PHILOCTETES
You mean I should go to Troy? Lame and crippled like this? To the Greek generals, to my most hated enemies . . . !

NEOPTOLEMOS
To those who will stop the infection in your foot and heal your sickness and pain.

PHILOCTETES
You call that advice, those terrible words, advice? What do you mean?

NEOPTOLEMOS
The best solution for you and for me—that's what I mean.

PHILOCTETES
Heaven is listening, when you say that. Aren't you ashamed?

NEOPTOLEMOS
Why should a man be ashamed to help his friends?

PHILOCTETES
What do you mean—help? Help me—or the Greek generals?

NEOPTOLEMOS
You, of course, because you are my friend. Everything I say shows that.

PHILOCTETES
How could it? You want to betray me to my enemies.

NEOPTOLEMOS
My friend, please. Listen! You are in great danger, learn not to be so proud, give way!

PHILOCTETES
You'll kill me. I know you, talking like this, you'll kill me!

NEOPTOLEMOS
No, no! But you refuse to learn.

PHILOCTETES
I've learned, boy. I know my lesson. The Greek generals marooned me here.

NEOPTOLEMOS
Can't you see—those very people can save your life!

PHILOCTETES
Never! If being saved means going to Troy—I'll die!

NEOPTOLEMOS
What's to be done, then? I can't persuade you of a single thing I say. The easiest way is for me to spare my breath, and you to go on living as you live now—without hope of cure.

PHILOCTETES
Yes, leave me alone—I'll suffer—but that is my destiny. You promised to see I got home, you gave me your hand on it. So do that for me, and don't waste time by reminding me of Troy. Enough has been heard of Troy; my cries have sung its praises too many times.

NEOPTOLEMOS
If that's your decision . . . let us go.

PHILOCTETES
Well said, now you sound more like your father.

NEOPTOLEMOS
Lean on me as you walk.

PHILOCTETES
As far as my strength will allow . . .

NEOPTOLEMOS [*pausing, worried*]
The Greeks will blame me for this. How shall I defend myself?

PHILOCTETES
Don't think of it . . .

NEOPTOLEMOS
But suppose they attack—overrun my country?

PHILOCTETES
I will be there.

NEOPTOLEMOS
What help can you bring us?

PHILOCTETES
The weapons of Hercules.

NEOPTOLEMOS
How do you mean?

PHILOCTETES
I will keep away all invaders.

NEOPTOLEMOS
Say goodbye to the island. Then come.

[*A voice halts them. They see the spirit of* HERCULES.]

HERCULES
Not yet!

[*They turn to face the vision.*]

First, hear me . . . I speak to you, Philoctetes . . . The voice you are hearing, the vision you see, say they belong to Hercules . . . My place in heaven is empty, I walk on earth for your sake. My mission—to show you how Zeus designs your future, and to halt the journey you are starting . . . Attend, attend, to what I say . . . Before all, remember my destiny—the labors I went through, the sacrifices I made, and the end of all—honor from goodness without self. You see, such goodness never dies—such things never can. And to you, I tell you now, the same reward is due. Out of your labors here you will dress your life in glory. You will go to Troy with this young man and there be cured of your terrible disease; then you will be chosen first in valor, first in honor, first in goodness out of Greece; using my bow you will end the life of Paris, origin of all this suffering; you will turn Troy to smoking ruins, send home costly trophies of your victory, and take the best, the richest spoil of any man in all the army, take them to your father, and your lands in Oita. But all that treasure, Philoctetes, must be brought to my burial place, to stand as memorial of my bow . . . Now, Neoptolemos, I have some words for you; take them to heart. You have no power to take the land of Troy without Philoctetes; and he has none without you; like two lions in the same country he guards you and you guard him. [*to* PHILOCTETES] I will direct Asklepios to Troy, he will end your sickness. Then, for the second time in history, Troy will be taken by my bow—it is destined. But when you have the country at your mercy, helpless, destroyed, you must respect all things sacred. Zeus, the greatest god, father of the universe, places nothing higher than this respect! Conscience follows man through life and into death; whether he lives or dies, conscience remains, justice remains, right is eternal . . .

PHILOCTETES
I longed to hear your voice, and now you have spoken, you have come to me, after so long, so long, and I shall do your will, you are my master.

NEOPTOLEMOS
I stand with him. My mind is made up.

HERCULES
Then hurry, you are late, you must act. The time is now, the voyage is before you, the wind set fair. Go!

[*The vision vanishes;* NEOPTOLEMOS *turns to go.*]

PHILOCTETES
No, look, if I'm leaving, I must say goodbye to the island ... This is where I lived, this was my mansion, where I lay, watching, watching—goodbye to you ... Over there—the meadows and streams with their spirits of the water—goodbye, you spirits ... listen, the roar of the sea pounding on the rocks ... yes, the spray from those breakers often wet my hair as I lay in my cave—goodbye, to the sea ... Up there the mountain of Hermes ... you sent me echoes of my grief when the storm engulfed me—goodbye, goodbye. I am leaving you, I am leaving the springs where the sacred water rises, yes, now, though I never believed this day would come. Goodbye, island of Lemnos, sea-washed Lemnos, and send me on my journey with your blessing ... no regrets, no blame, send me where the great power of my destiny wills, where the resolve of my friends, and the all-conquering spirit of my master, Hercules, carry me—He has decided. Now it must be done.

SAILORS
Hurry ... down to the ship!
Quickly—all of you!
Pray to the spirits of the sea before you leave ...
And ask for a safe voyage home.
[*Exeunt, leaving the island empty.*]

THUCYDIDES

(c. 460-c. 400 B.C.)

HERODOTUS HAD RECORDED THE INSPIRING VISION OF A GREECE UNITED against the common foe. His history of Athenians and Spartans fighting side-by-side to maintain Greek independence by driving the Persians from Europe had shown the Greeks at the height of their achievement, entering the dawn of their Golden Age. To Thucydides, Herodotus' even greater successor, fell the more melancholy task of recording the twilight. In the *History of the Peloponnesian Wars*, Thucydides records the disintegration of the Age of Pericles, the break-up of Greek unity and the disastrous civil conflict between Athens and Sparta.

As Thucydides recognized, the Peloponnesian War marked a turning point in Greek history. Not only did it end a period of unparalleled intellectual and artistic growth, it also revealed the fatal weakness of Greek civilization. In spite of their brilliant experiments with democracy, the Greek city-states proved incapable of cooperating together in a workable government. Whether the problem was one of geographic isolation or a too rugged individualism, the truth is that when the Hellenic states had an opportunity to combine into a power of international importance, they blindly rejected it to engage in suicidal civil wars.

Having been a general in the Athenian army and suffered exile for his failure to relieve a besieged stronghold, Thucydides enjoyed the rare freedom of visiting personally both sides of the war. His intimate knowledge of both Spartan and Athenian camps, with their many attendant allies, enabled him to support his interpretation of events with detailed information not ordinarily available to the historian. With remarkable objectivity, carefully discriminating between propaganda and fact, Thucydides analyzes the national character of both combatants. He admires Spartan discipline, courage, and military organization, but he points out the extreme conservatism and reluctance to act that kept Sparta from playing a creative role in Greek affairs. As a humanist, he admires even more the Athenian democracy with its gracious life and love of freedom, but he is keenly aware of the impulsiveness, ambition, and capriciousness of Athenian politics.

The real reason for the outbreak of the war, Thucydides perceives, was that the swift growth of Athenian power frightened the less venturesome Spartans. After the Persians had withdrawn in 479 B.C., Sparta quietly retired to her traditional sphere of influence in the Peloponnese. But Athens refused to give up the leadership she had enjoyed during the Persian Wars. She therefore organized the Delian League, originally a confederation of independent Greek states formed to resist any future Persian aggression. Athenian ambition, however, soon transformed the nominally autonomous League members into tribute-paying satellites. Enriched by newly-discovered silver mines and possessed of a large naval fleet, Athens became an imperial power. Inevitably, the Athenian Empire elicited a defensive response from Sparta, who belatedly formed a similar confederacy of subject states. Rivalry between the two power blocks was heightened by the interference of Corinth. Like Athens, Corinth was a commercial state whose merchant marine and colonies were the source of her wealth. Bitter economic competition between the two naval powers led Corinth to persuade the Spartans to halt Athenian expansion before it was too late. As Thucydides implies in his dialogue between ambassadors from Corinth and Sparta, Corinthian jealousy of Athens was probably as instrumental in starting the war as Sparta's fear of a too-powerful neighbor.

Without impairing his scientific objectivity, Thucydides seems to present the rise and fall of the Athenian Empire as a kind of Sophoclean drama. Athens, a great and good city but blinded by pride and ambition, is the protagonist. She commits *hubris* both morally and intellectually. Her moral sin Thucydides records in the infamous "Melian Debate," wherein Athens, already corrupted and brutalized by war, argues that neutral Melos, being weak, must submit to the Athenians' superior force. The Melians, expressing Thucydides' own conviction, reply that in breaking the unwritten laws of humanity and decency Athens sets an evil precedent for her own future. The Athenians, however, insist on their doctrine of "political realism"—that might makes right—and destroy the city of Melos. The second example of *hubris* is the Athenians' intellectual error of overexpansion. By trumping up an excuse to attack Syracuse, whose wealth they covet, the Athenians rashly open another warfront. The inescapable consequence of attempting too much occurs when the entire Athenian fleet is annihilated and virtually all the members of the expedition to Syracuse are either killed or imprisoned to await a slow death in the stone quarries. The sensational failure of the Syracuse invasion marks the fatal turning point (*peripeteia*) in Athenian fortunes. *Nemesis* is swift to overtake the proud city and in 404 B.C. she falls to the victorious Spartans.

Viewing the collapse of Athenian imperialism as the historical equivalent of a literary tragedy in no way lessens Thucydides' effectiveness as a historian. Profiting by Herodotus' mistakes, Thucydides is always painstakingly accurate in gathering facts, scrupulously fair in his judgments, and scientifically critical in his evaluation of evidence. His knowledge of military strategy, handling of statistics, and reliability in fixing dates far exceeds Herodotus' competence in these areas.

But even more important than his value as a trustworthy sourcebook for later historians are Thucydides' psychological insight and his firm grasp of political realities. The lasting significance of his record of a particular war, fought at a particular time and place, lies in his perception that since human nature does not change, history must invariably repeat itself. As long as people are motivated by the familiar emotions of economic greed, political ambition, and national pride the events of the past will "at some time or other and in much the same ways, be repeated in the future." Basing his interpretation of history on the bedrock of human frailty, Thucydides produced a work that was "not of an age, but for all time."

THE PELOPONNESIAN WAR

[Thucydides states his purpose in writing and describes his historical method.]

I BEGAN MY HISTORY AT THE VERY OUTBREAK OF THE WAR, IN THE BELIEF that it was going to be a great war and more worth writing about than any of those which had taken place in the past. My belief was based on the fact that the two sides were at the very height of their power and preparedness, and I saw, too, that the rest of the Hellenic world was committed to one side or the other; even those who were not immediately engaged were deliberating on the courses which they were to take later. This was the greatest disturbance in the history of the Hellenes, affecting also a large part of the non-Hellenic world, and indeed, I might almost say, the whole of mankind. For though I have found it impossible, because of its remoteness in time, to acquire a really precise knowledge of the distant past or even of the history preceding our own period, yet, after looking back into it as far as I can, all the evidence leads me to conclude that these periods were not great periods either in warfare or in anything else.

✿　　✿　　✿

In this history I have made use of set speeches some of which were delivered just before and others during the war. I have found it difficult to remember the precise words used in the speeches which I listened to myself and my various informants have experienced the same difficulty; so my method has been, while keeping as closely as possible to the general sense of the words that were actually used, to make the speakers say what, in my opinion, was called for by each situation.

And with regard to my factual reporting of the events of the war I have made it a principle not to write down the first story that came my way, and not even to be guided by my own general impressions; either I was present myself at the events which I have described or else I heard of them from eye-witnesses whose reports I have checked with as much

Abridged. From *Thucydides: The Peloponnesian War,* translated by Rex Warner. Copyright 1964 by Rex Warner. Reprinted by permission of Penguin Books, Ltd., and the Bodley Head.

thoroughness as possible. Not that even so the truth was easy to discover: different eye-witnesses give different accounts of the same events, speaking out of partiality for one side or the other or else from imperfect memories. And it may well be that my history will seem less easy to read because of the absence in it of a romantic element. It will be enough for me, however, if these words of mine are judged useful by those who want to understand clearly the events which happened in the past and which (human nature being what it is) will, at some time or other and in much the same ways, be repeated in the future. My work is not a piece of writing designed to meet the taste of an immediate public, but was done to last forever.

The greatest war in the past was the Persian War; yet in this war the decision was reached quickly as a result of two naval battles and two battles on land. The Peloponnesian War, on the other hand, not only lasted for a long time, but throughout its course brought with it unprecedented suffering for Hellas. Never before had so many cities been captured and then devastated, whether by foreign armies or by the Hellenic Powers themselves; never had there been so many exiles; never such loss of life—both in the actual warfare and in internal revolutions. Old stories of past prodigies, which had not found much confirmation in recent experience, now became credible. Wide areas, for instance, were affected by violent earthquakes; there were more frequent eclipses of the sun than had ever been recorded before; in various parts of the country there were extensive droughts followed by famine; and there was the plague which did more harm and destroyed more life than almost any other single factor. All these calamities fell together upon the Hellenes after the outbreak of war.

War began when the Athenians and the Peloponnesians broke the Thirty Years Truce which had been made after the capture of Euboea. As to the reasons why they broke the truce, I propose first to give an account of the causes of complaint which they had against each other and of the specific instances where their interests clashed: this is in order that there should be no doubt in anyone's mind about what led to this great war falling upon the Hellenes. But the real reason for the war is, in my opinion, most likely to be disguised by such an argument. What made war inevitable was the growth of Athenian power and the fear which this caused in Sparta.

✻   ✻   ✻

[In the following passage, a delegation from Corinth attempts to persuade Sparta to declare war on Athens. The Corinthians emphasize the vast difference between Athenian and Spartan ways of life.]

Then also we think we have as much right as anyone else to point out faults in our neighbours, especially when we consider the enormous difference between you [the Spartans] and the Athenians. To our minds, you are quite unaware of this difference; you have never yet tried to imagine what sort of people these Athenians are against whom you will have to fight—how much, indeed how completely different from you. An Athenian is always an innovator, quick to form a resolution and quick at carrying it out. You, on the other hand, are good at keeping things as they are; you never originate an idea, and your action tends to stop short of its aim. Then again, Athenian daring will outrun its own resources; they will take risks against their better judgement, and still, in the midst of danger, remain confident. But your nature is always to do less than you could have done, to mistrust your own judgement, however sound it may be, and to assume that dangers will last for ever. Think of this, too: while you are hanging back, they never hesitate; while you stay at home, they are always abroad; for they think that the farther they go the more they will get, while you think that any movement may endanger what you have already. If they win a victory, they follow it up at once, and if they suffer a defeat, they scarcely fall back at all. As for their bodies, they regard them as expendable for their city's sake, as though they were not their own; but each man cultivates his own intelligence, again with a view to doing something notable for his city. If they aim at something and do not get it, they think that they have been deprived of what belonged to them already; whereas, if their enterprise is successful, they regard that success as nothing compared to what they will do next. Suppose they fail in some undertaking; they make good the loss immediately by setting their hopes in some other direction. Of them alone it may be said that they possess a thing almost as soon as they have begun to desire it, so quickly with them does action follow upon decision. And so they go on working away in hardship and danger all the days of their lives, seldom enjoying their possessions because they are always adding to them. Their view of a holiday is to do what needs doing; they prefer hardship and activity to peace and quiet. In a word, they are by nature incapable of either living a quiet life themselves or of allowing anyone else to do so.

That is the character of the city which is opposed to you. Yet you still hang back; you will not see that the likeliest way of securing peace is this: only to use one's power in the cause of justice, but to make it perfectly plain that one is resolved not to tolerate aggression. On the contrary, your idea of proper behaviour is, firstly, to avoid harming others, and then to avoid being harmed yourselves, even if it is a matter of defending your own interests. Even if you had on your frontiers a power holding the same principles as you do, it is hard to see how such a policy could have been a success. But at the present time, as we have just pointed out to you, your whole way of life is out of date when compared with theirs. And it is just as true in politics as it is in any art or craft: new methods must drive out old ones. When a city can live in peace and quiet, no doubt the old-established ways are best: but when one is constantly being faced by new problems, one has also to be capable of approaching them in an original way. Thus Athens, because of the very variety of her experience, is a far more modern state than you are. . . .

[Pericles' Funeral Speech]

In the same winter the Athenians, following their annual custom, gave a public funeral for those who had been the first to die in the war. These funerals are held in the following way: two days before the ceremony the bones of the fallen are brought and put in a tent which has been erected, and people make whatever offerings they wish to their own dead. Then there is a funeral procession in which coffins of cypress wood are carried on wagons. There is one coffin for each tribe, which contains the bones of members of that tribe. One empty bier is decorated and carried in the procession: this is for the missing, whose bodies could not be recovered. Everyone who wishes to, both citizens and foreigners, can join in the procession, and the women who are related to the dead are there to make their laments at the tomb. The bones are laid in the public burial-place, which is in the most beautiful quarter outside the city walls. Here the Athenians always bury those who have fallen in war. The only exception is those who died at Marathon, who, because their achievement was considered absolutely outstanding, were buried on the battlefield itself.

When the bones have been laid in the earth, a man chosen by the city for his intellectual gifts and for his general reputation makes an appropriate speech in praise of the dead, and after the speech all depart. This is the procedure at these burials, and all through the war, when the time came to do so, the Athenians followed this ancient custom. Now, at the burial of those who were the first to fall in the war Pericles, the son of Xanthippus, was chosen to make the speech. When the moment arrived, he came forward from the tomb and, standing on a high platform, so that he might be heard by as many people as possible in the crowd, he spoke as follows:

       ✿   ✿   ✿

'I have no wish to make a long speech on subjects familiar to you all: so I shall say nothing about the warlike deeds by which we acquired our power or the battles in which we or our fathers gallantly resisted our enemies, Greek or foreign. What I want to do is, in the first place, to discuss the spirit in which we faced our trials and also our constitution and the way of life which has made us great. After that I shall speak in praise of the dead, believing that this kind of speech is not inappropriate to the present occasion, and that this whole assembly, of citizens and foreigners, may listen to it with advantage.

'Let me say that our system of government does not copy the institutions of our neighbours. It is more the case of our being a model to others, than of our imitating anyone else. Our constitution is called a democracy because power is in the hands not of a minority but of the whole people. When it is a question of settling private disputes, everyone is equal before the law; when it is a question of putting one person before another in positions of public responsibility, what counts is not membership of a particular class, but the actual ability which the man possesses. No one, so long as he has it in him to be of service to the state, is kept in political obscurity because of poverty. And, just as our political life is free and open, so is our day-to-day life in our relations with each other. We do not get into a state with our next-door neighbour if he enjoys himself in his own way, nor do we give him the kind of black looks which, though they do no real harm, still do hurt people's feelings. We are free and tolerant in our private lives; but in public affairs we keep to the law. This is because it commands our deep respect.

'We give our obedience to those whom we put in positions of authority, and we obey the laws themselves, especially those which are for the protection of the oppressed, and those unwritten laws which it is an acknowledged shame to break.

'And here is another point. When our work is over, we are in a position to enjoy all kinds of recreation for our spirits. There are various kinds of contests and sacrifices regularly throughout the year; in our own homes we find a beauty and a good taste which delight us every day and which drive away our cares. Then the greatness of our city brings it about that all the good things from all over the world flow in to us, so that to us it seems just as natural to enjoy foreign goods as our own local products.

'Then there is a great difference between us and our opponents, in our attitude towards military security. Here are some examples: Our city is open to the world, and we have no periodical deportations in order to prevent people observing or finding out secrets which might be of military advantage to the enemy. This is because we rely, not on secret weapons, but on our own real courage and loyalty. There is a difference, too, in our educational systems. The Spartans, from their earliest boyhood, are submitted to the most laborious training in courage; we pass our lives without all these restrictions, and yet are just as ready to face the same dangers as they are. Here is a proof of this: When the Spartans invade our land, they do not come by themselves, but bring all their allies with them; whereas we, when we launch an attack abroad, do the job by ourselves, and, though fighting on foreign soil, do not often fail to defeat opponents who are fighting for their own hearths and homes. As a matter of fact none of our enemies has ever yet been confronted with our total strength, because we have to divide our attention between our navy and the many missions on which our troops are sent on land. Yet, if our enemies engage a detachment of our forces and defeat it, they give themselves credit for having thrown back our entire army; or, if they lose, they claim that they were beaten by us in full strength. There are certain advantages, I think, in our way of meeting danger voluntarily, with an easy mind, instead of with a laborious training, with natural rather than with state-induced courage. We do not have to spend our time practising to meet sufferings which are still in the future; and when they are actually upon us we show ourselves just as brave as these others who are always in strict training. This is one point in which, I think, our city deserves to be admired. There are also others:

'Our love of what is beautiful does not lead to extravagance; our love of the things of the mind does not make us soft. We regard wealth as something to be properly used, rather than as something to boast about. As for poverty, no one need be ashamed to admit it: the real shame is in not taking practical measures to escape from it. Here each individual is interested not only in his own affairs but in the affairs of the state as well: even those who are mostly occupied with their own business are extremely well-informed on general politics—this is a peculiarity of ours: we do not say that a man who takes no interest in politics is a man who minds his own business; we say that he has no business here at all. We Athenians, in our own persons, take our decisions on policy or submit them to proper discussions: for we do not think that there is an incompatibility between words and deeds; the worst thing is to rush into action before the consequences have been properly debated. And this is another point where we differ from other people. We are capable at the same time of taking risks and of estimating them beforehand. Others are brave out of ignorance; and, when they stop to think, they begin to fear. But the man who can most truly be accounted brave is he who best knows the meaning of what is sweet in life and of what is terrible, and then goes out undeterred to meet what is to come.

'Again, in questions of general good feeling there is a great contrast between us and most other people. We make friends by doing good to others, not by receiving good from them. This makes our friendship all the more reliable, since we want to keep alive the gratitude of those who are in our debt by showing continued goodwill to them: whereas the feelings of one who owes us something lack the same enthusiasm, since he knows that, when he repays our kindness, it will be more like paying back a debt than giving something spontaneously. We are unique in this. When we do kindnesses to others, we do not do them out of any calculations of profit or loss: we do them without afterthought, relying on our free liberality. Taking everything together then, I declare that our city is an education to Greece, and I declare that in my opinion each single one of our citizens, in all the manifold aspects of life, is able to show himself the rightful lord and owner of his own person, and do this, moreover, with exceptional grace and exceptional versatility. And to show that this is no empty boasting for the present occasion, but real tangible fact, you have only to consider the power which our city possesses and which has been won by those very qualities which I have mentioned. Athens, alone of the states we know, comes to her testing time in a greatness that surpasses what was imagined of her. In her case, and in her case alone, no invading enemy is ashamed at being defeated, and no subject can complain of being governed by people unfit for their responsibilities. Mighty indeed are the marks and monuments of our empire which we have left. Future ages will wonder at us, as the present age wonders at us now. We do not need the praises of a Homer, or of anyone else whose words may delight us for the moment, but whose estimation of facts will fall short of what is really true. For our adventurous spirt has forced an entry into every sea and into every land; and everywhere we have left behind us everlasting memorials of good done to our friends or suffering inflicted on our enemies.

'This, then, is the kind of city for which these men, who could not bear the thought of losing her, nobly fought and nobly died. It is only natural that every one of us who survive them should be willing to undergo hardships in her service. And it was for this reason that I have spoken at such length about our city, because I wanted to make it clear that for us there is more at stake than there is for others who lack our advantages; also I wanted my words of praise for the dead to be set in the bright light of evidence. And now the most important of these words has been spoken. I have sung the praises of our city; but it was the courage and gallantry of these men, and of people like them, which made her splendid. Nor would you find it true in the case of many of the Greeks, as it is true of them, that no words can do more than justice to their deeds.

'To me it seems that the consummation which has overtaken these men shows us the meaning of manliness in its first revelation and in its final proof. Some of them, no doubt, had their faults; but what we ought to remember first is their gallant conduct against the enemy in defence of their native land. They have blotted out evil with good, and done more service to the commonwealth than they ever did harm in their private lives. No one of these men weakened because he wanted to go on enjoying his wealth: no one put off the awful day in the hope that he might live to escape his poverty and grow rich. More to be desired than such things, they chose to check the enemy's pride. This, to them, was a risk most glorious, and they accepted it, willing to strike down the enemy and relinquish everything else. As for success or failure, they left that in the doubtful hands of Hope, and when the reality of battle was before their faces, they put their trust in their own selves. In the fighting, they thought it more honourable to stand their ground and suffer death than to give in and save their lives. So they fled from the reproaches of men, abiding with life and limb the brunt of battle; and, in a small moment of time, the climax of their lives, a culmination of glory, not of fear, were swept away from us.

'So and such they were, these men—worthy of their city. We who remain behind may hope to be spared their fate, but must resolve to keep the same daring spirit against the foe. It is not simply a question of estimating the advantages in theory. I could tell you a long story (and you know it as well as I do) about what is to be gained by beating the enemy back. What I would prefer is that you should fix your eyes every day on the greatness of Athens as she really is, and should fall in love with her. When you realize her greatness, then reflect that what made her great was men with a spirit of adventure, men who knew their duty, men who were ashamed to fall below a certain standard. If they ever failed in an enterprise, they made up their minds that at any rate the city should not find their courage lacking to her, and they gave to her the best contribution that they could. They gave her their lives, to her and to all of us, and for their own selves they won praises that never grow old, the most splendid of sepulchres—not the sepulchre in which their bodies are laid, but where their glory remains eternal in men's minds, always there on the right occasion to stir others to speech or to action. For famous men have the whole earth as their memorial: it is not only the inscriptions on their graves in their own country that mark them out; no, in foreign lands also, not in any visible form but in peoples' hearts, their memory abides and grows. It is for you to try to be like them. Make up your minds that happiness depends on being free, and freedom depends on being courageous. Let there be no relaxation in face of the perils of the war. The people who have most excuse for despising death are not the wretched and unfortunate, who have no hope of doing well for themselves, but those who run the risk of a complete reversal in their lives, and who would feel the difference most intensely, if things went wrong for them. Any intelligent man would find a humiliation caused by his own slackness more painful to bear than death, when death comes to him unperceived, in battle, and in the confidence of his patriotism.

'For these reasons I shall not commiserate with those parents of the dead, who are present here. Instead I shall try to comfort them. They are well aware that they have grown up in a world where there are many changes and chances. But this is good fortune—for men to end their lives with honour, as these have done, and for you honourably to lament them: their life was set to a measure where death and happiness went hand in hand. I know that it is difficult to convince you of this. When you see other people happy you will often be reminded of what used to make you happy too. One does not feel sad at not having some good thing which is outside one's experience: real grief is felt at the loss of something which one is used to. All the same, those of you who are of the right age must bear up and take comfort in the thought of having more children. In your own homes these new children will prevent you from brooding over those who are no more, and they will be a help to the city, too, both in filling the empty places, and in assuring her security. For it is impossible for a man to put forward fair and honest views about our affairs if he has not, like everyone else, children whose lives may be at stake. As for those of you who are now too old to have children, I would ask you to count as gain the greater part of your life, in which you have been happy, and remember that what remains is not long, and let your hearts be lifted up at the thought of the fair fame of the dead. One's sense of honour is the only thing that does not grow old, and the last pleasure, when one is worn out with age, is not, as the poet said, making money, but having the respect of one's fellow men.

'As for those of you here who are sons or brothers of the dead, I can see a hard struggle in front of you. Everyone always speaks well of the dead, and, even if you rise to the greatest heights of heroism, it will be a hard thing for you to get the reputation of having come near, let alone equalled, their standard. When one is alive, one is always liable to the jealousy of one's competitors, but when one is out of the way, the honour one receives is sincere and unchallenged.

'Perhaps I should say a word or two on the duties of women to those among you who are now widowed. I can say all I have to say in a short word of advice. Your great glory is not to be inferior to what God has made you, and the greatest glory of a woman is to be least talked about by men, whether they are praising you or criticizing you. I have now, as the law demanded, said what I had to say. For the time being our offerings to the dead have been made, and for the future their children will be supported at the public expense by the city, until they come of age. This is the crown and prize which she offers, both to the dead and to their children, for the ordeals which they have faced. Where the rewards of valour are the greatest, there you will find also the best and bravest spirits among the people. And now, when you have mourned for your dear ones, you must depart.'

*   *   *

[The sixteenth year of the war. The Melian Debate.]

Athenians: Then we on our side will use no fine phrases saying, for example, that we have a right to our empire because we defeated the Persians, or that we have come against you now because of the injuries you have done us—a great mass of words that nobody would believe. And we ask you on your side not to imagine that you will influence us by saying that you, though a colony of Sparta, have not joined Sparta in the war, or that you have never done us any harm. Instead we recommend that you should try to get what it is possible for you to get, taking into consideration what we both really do think; since you know as well as we do that, when these matters are discussed by practical people, the standard of justice depends on the equality of power to compel and that in fact the strong do what they have the power to do and the weak accept what they have to accept.

Melians: Then in our view (since you force us to leave justice out of account and to confine ourselves to self-interest)—in our view it is at any rate useful that you should not destroy a principle that is to the general good of all men—namely, that in the case of all who fall into danger there should be such a thing as fair play and just dealing, and that such people should be allowed to use and to profit by arguments that fall short of a mathematical accuracy. And this is a principle which affects you as much as anybody, since your own fall would be visited by the most terrible vengeance and would be an example to the world.

Athenians: As for us, even assuming that our empire does come to an end, we are not despondent about what would happen next. One is not so much frightened of being conquered by a power which rules over others, as Sparta does (not that we are concerned with Sparta now), as of what would happen if a ruling power is attacked and defeated by its own subjects. So far as this point is concerned, you can leave it to us to face the risks involved. What we shall do now is to show you that it is for the good of our own empire that we are here and that it is for the preservation of your city that we shall say what we are going to say. We do not want any trouble in bringing you into our empire, and we want you to be spared for the good both of yourselves and of ourselves.

Melians: And how could it be just as good for us to be the slaves as for you to be the masters?

Athenians: You, by giving in, would save yourselves from disaster; we, by not destroying you, would be able to profit from you.

Melians: So you would not agree to our being neutral, friends instead of enemies, but allies of neither side?

Athenians: No, because it is not so much your hostility that injures us; it is rather the case that, if we were on friendly terms with you, our subjects would regard that as a sign of weakness in us, whereas your hatred is evidence of our power.

Melians: Is that your subjects' idea of fair play—that no distinction should be made between people who are quite unconnected with you and people who are mostly your own colonists or else rebels whom you have conquered?

Athenians: So far as right and wrong are concerned they think that there is no difference between the two, that those who still preserve their independence do so because they are strong, and that if we fail to attack them it is because we are afraid. So that by conquering you we shall increase not only the size but the security of our empire. We rule the sea and you are islanders, and weaker islanders too than the others; it is therefore particularly important that you should not escape.

Melians: But do you think there is no security for you in what we suggest? For here again, since you will not let us mention justice, but tell us to give in to your interests, we, too, must tell you what our interests are and, if yours and ours happen to coincide, we must try to persuade you of the fact. Is it not certain that you will make enemies of all states who are at present neutral, when they see what is happening here and naturally conclude that in course of time you will attack them too? Does not this mean that you are strengthening the enemies you have already and are forcing others to become your enemies even against their intentions and their inclinations?

Athenians: As a matter of fact we are not so much frightened of states on the continent. They have their liberty, and this means that it will be a long time before they begin to take precautions against us. We are more concerned about islanders like yourselves, who are still unsubdued, or subjects who have already become embittered by the constraint which our empire imposes on them. These are the people who are most likely to act in a reckless manner and to bring themselves and us, too, into the most obvious danger.

Melians: Then surely, if such hazards are taken by you to keep your empire and by your subjects to escape from it, we who are still free would show ourselves great cowards and weaklings if we failed to face everything that comes rather than submit to slavery.

Athenians: No, not if you are sensible. This is no fair fight, with honour on one side and shame on the other. It is rather a question of saving your lives and not resisting those who are far too strong for you.

Melians: Yet we know that in war fortune sometimes makes the odds more level than could be expected from the difference in numbers of the two sides. And if we surrender, then all our hope is lost at once, whereas, so long as we remain in action, there is still a hope that we may yet stand upright.

Athenians: Hope, that comforter in danger! If one already has solid advantages to fall back upon, one can indulge in hope. It may do harm, but will not destroy one. But hope is by nature an expensive commodity, and those who are risking their all on one cast find out what it means only when they are already ruined; it never fails them in the period when such a knowledge would enable them to take precautions. Do not let this happen to you, you who are weak and whose fate depends on a single movement of the scale. And do not be like those people who, as so commonly happens, miss the chance of saving themselves in a human and practical way, and, when every clear and distinct hope has left them in their adversity, turn to what is blind and vague, to prophecies and oracles and such things which by encouraging hope lead men to ruin.

Melians: It is difficult, and you may be sure that we know it, for us to oppose your power and fortune, unless the terms be equal. Nevertheless we trust that the gods will give us fortune as good as yours, because we are standing for what is right against what is wrong; and as for what we lack in power, we trust that it will be made up for by our alliance with the Spartans, who are bound, if for no other reason, than for honour's sake, and because we are their kinsmen, to come to our help. Our confidence, therefore, is not so entirely irrational as you think.

Athenians: So far as the favour of the gods is concerned, we think we have as much right to that as you have. Our aims and our actions are perfectly consistent with the beliefs men hold about the gods and with the principles which govern their own conduct. Our opinion of the gods and our knowledge of men lead us to conclude that it is a general and necessary law of nature to rule wherever one can. This is not a law that we made ourselves, nor were we the first to act upon it when it was made. We found it already in existence, and we shall leave it to exist for ever among those who come after us. We are merely acting in accordance with it, and we know that you or anybody else with the same power as ours would be acting precisely the same way. And therefore, so far as the gods are concerned, we see no good reason why we should fear to be at a disadvantage. But with regard to your views about Sparta and your confidence that she, out of a sense of honour, will come to your aid, we must say that we congratulate you on your simplicity but do not envy you your folly. In matters that concern themselves or their own constitution the Spartans are quite remarkably good; as for their relations with others, that is a long story, but it can be expressed shortly and clearly by saying that of all people we know the Spartans are most conspicuous for believing that what they like doing is honourable and what suits their interests is just. And this kind of attitude is not going to be of much help to you in your absurd quest for safety at the moment.

Melians: But this is the very point where we can feel most sure. Their own self-interest will make them refuse to betray their own colonists, the Melians, for that would mean losing the confidence of their friends among the Hellenes and doing good to their enemies.

Athenians: You seem to forget that if one follows one's self-interest one wants to be safe, whereas the path of justice and honour involves one in danger. And, where danger is concerned, the Spartans are not, as a rule, very venturesome.

Melians: But we think that they would even endanger themselves for our sake and count the risk more worth taking than in the case of others, because we are so close to the Peloponnese that they could operate more easily, and because they can depend on us more than on others, since we are of the same race and share the same feelings.

Athenians: Goodwill shown by the party that is asking for help does not mean security for the prospective ally. What is looked for is a positive preponderance of power in action. And the Spartans pay attention to this point even more than others do. Certainly they distrust their own native resources so much that when they attack a neighbour they bring a great army of allies with them. It is hardly likely therefore that, while we are in control of the sea, they will cross over to an island.

Melians: But they still might send others. The Cretan sea is a wide one, and it is harder for those who control it to intercept others than for those who want to slip through to do so safely. And even if they were to fail in this, they would turn against your own land and against those of your allies left unvisited by Brasidas. So, instead of troubling about a country which has nothing to do with you, you will find trouble nearer home, among your allies, and in your own country.

Athenians: It is a possibility, something that has in fact happened before. It may happen in your case, but you are well aware that the Athenians have never yet relinquished a single siege operation through fear of others. But we are somewhat shocked to find that, though you announced your intention of discussing how you could preserve yourselves, in all this talk you have said absolutely nothing which could justify a man in thinking that he could be preserved. Your chief points are concerned with what you hope may happen in the future, while your actual resources are too scanty to give you a chance of survival against the forces that are opposed to you at this moment. You will therefore be showing an extraordinary lack of common sense if, after you have asked us to retire from this meeting, you still fail to reach a conclusion wiser than anything you have mentioned so far. Do not be led astray by a false sense of honour—a thing which often brings men to ruin when they are faced with an obvious danger that somehow affects their pride. For in many cases men have still been able to see the dangers ahead of them, but this thing called dishonour, this word, by its own force of seduction, has drawn them into a state where they have surrendered to an idea, while in fact they have fallen voluntarily into irrevocable disaster, in dishonour that is all the more dishonourable because it has come to them from their own folly rather than their misfortune. You, if you take the right view, will be careful to avoid this. You will see that there is nothing disgraceful in giving way to the greatest city in Hellas when she is offering you such reasonable terms—alliance on a tribute-paying basis and liberty to enjoy your own property. And, when you are allowed to choose between war and safety, you will not be so insensitively arrogant as to make the wrong choice. This is the safe rule—to stand up to one's equals, to behave with deference towards one's superiors, and to treat one's inferiors with moderation. Think it over again, then, when we have withdrawn from the meeting, and let this be a point that constantly recurs to your minds—that you are discussing the fate of your country, that you have only one country, and that its future for good or ill depends on this one single decision which you are going to make.

The Athenians then withdrew from the discussion. The Melians, left to themselves, reached a conclusion which was much the same as they had indicated in their previous replies. Their answer was as follows:

Melians: Our decision, Athenians, is just the same as it was at first. We are not prepared to give up in a short moment the liberty which our city has enjoyed from its foundation for 700 years. We put our trust in the fortune that the gods will send and which has saved us up to now, and in the help of men—that is, of the Spartans; and so we shall try to save ourselves. But we invite you to allow us to be friends of yours and enemies to neither side, to make a treaty which shall be agreeable to both you and us, and so to leave our country.

The Melians made this reply, and the Athenians, just as they were breaking off the discussion said:

Athenians: Well, at any rate, judging from this decision of yours, you seem to us unique in your ability to consider the future as something more certain than what is before your eyes, and to see uncertainties as realities, simply because you would like them to be so. As you have staked most on and trusted most in Spartans, luck, and hopes, so in all these you will find yourselves most completely deluded.

The Athenian representatives then went back to the army, and the Athenian generals, finding that the Melians would not submit, immediately commenced hostilities and built a wall completely round the city of Melos, dividing the work out among the various states. Later they left behind a garrison of some of their own and some allied troops to blockade the place by land and sea, and with the greater part of their army returned home. The force left behind stayed on and continued with the siege.

❀   ❀   ❀

About this same time the Melians again captured another part of the Athenian lines where there were only a few of the garrison on guard. As a result of this, another force came out afterwards from Athens under the command of Philocrates, the son of Demeas. Siege operations were now carried on vigorously and, as there was also some treachery from inside, the Melians surrendered unconditionally to the Athenians, who put to death all the men of military age whom they took, and sold the women and children as slaves. Melos itself they took over for themselves, sending out later a colony of 500 men.

MEDEA

EURIPIDES WROTE THE *Medea* (431 B.C.) JUST AS ATHENS AND SPARTA were plunging into the suicidal Peloponnesian War. As he foresaw, the war-lust that then possessed Athens was to prove fatal to the city's democratic way of life, which Pericles had eulogized in his famous "Funeral Speech."[1] The concepts of freedom in law, governmental order, and individual liberty, upon which the Athenian democracy was based were to be irresistibly undermined by decades of military leadership, war hysteria, and fear-inspired repressions. As Thucydides pointed out, during this turbulent period the veneer of civilization wore dangerously thin and the beast dormant in every man seemed to find release. A savage, barbarian sorceress from the distant wilds of Colchis, Medea was the perfect symbol of the destructive forces that were to hasten the moral disintegration of Athens.

A magic-working princess to whom the restraints of civilized life are meaningless, Medea is the very antithesis of the Greek ideal. While "nothing in excess" was the theoretic principle by which Athenians tried to govern themselves, Medea is ruled entirely by uncontrolled feeling. She has no patience for Jason's political ambitions or his calculating self-interest. She can see him only as the man for whom she sacrificed everything and who now abandons her to marry a Corinthian princess, the daughter of Creon. Although Euripides does not make Jason entirely reprehensible, neither does he picture him as the fearless hero of popular legend. A self-protective exponent of expediency, Euripides' Jason seems far removed from the romantic adventurer who captured the Golden Fleece. His cold rationalizations dwindle into insignificance when pitted against Medea's glowing passion. Throughout the play he remains essentially unheroic even in his grief.

Medea dominates the tragedy by the fierce intensity of her emotions. In the opening scene she appears overcome by sorrow and wounded pride, a cast-off wife facing exile with neither refuge nor hope. Because, for Jason's sake, she had betrayed her father and murdered her brother, she has no home, no friends, no protector. But the energy of her hate for Jason and the other Greeks who despise and fear her barbaric magic, soon transforms her from passive victim to triumphant avenger. With assumed humility, she persuades King Creon to grant her "one more day" to prepare for banishment. Reasoning from the civilized standards that recommend extending mercy to a helpless woman, Creon grants her request. Medea thus has time to prepare for escape and plan her revenge.

In the *Medea* Euripides created not only a portrait of the savage nature latent beneath every civilized exterior, but also the first example in dramatic literature of psychological conflict. Torn between love for her sons and hatred of Jason, Medea agonizes over her decision to kill the children. Maternal feeling wars with the desire for vengeance. But

---

[1]See Thucydides, *History of the Peloponnesian War*, pp. 343-348.

for Medea, hate—the perversion of her original passion for Jason—is stronger than love. She is true to herself and cuts the throats of Jason's sons.

Except for the self-inflicted loss of her children, Medea is not punished for her crime. The ancient gods of her world are a projection of her own savage nature and give their tacit approval to the murder. When, in the final scene, she is swept to safety by the chariot of Helios, the sun god, she has succeeded in reversing every value cherished in Jason's world. Neither wifely subjection, civilized law, nor mother-love is proof against the forces of unreason, disorder, and unbridled emotion which Medea represents. Euripides' final irony, and an example of the poet's prophetic function, is that at the end of the drama Medea takes refuge in Athens. On the eve of the Peloponnesian War, the most catastrophic conflict in Greek history, Euripides clearly saw Medea's violent spirit exercising its murderous spell on the Athenian people.

MEDEA

Characters	
	NURSE
	TUTOR *to Medea's sons*
	MEDEA
	CHORUS *of Corinthian women*
	CREON, *king of Corinth*
	JASON
	AEGEUS, *king of Athens*
	MESSENGER
	MEDEA'S TWO CHILDREN

Scene: *Before Jason's House in Corinth*

NURSE
  If only they had never gone! If the Argo's[1] hull

---

[1]*The Argo*. Jason was the son of Aeson, half-brother of Pelias king of Iolcus in Thessaly. To get rid of Jason, who was a rival for his throne, Pelias persuaded him to go to Colchis, at the Eastern end of the Black sea, and fetch the Golden Fleece. Jason sailed to Colchis in the ship called Argo, and accomplished his task with the help of Medea, daughter of the king of Colchis. Medea drugged the dragon which guarded the treasure; and Jason promised to marry her. They escaped, and Medea's brother came with them. When the king pursued them, Medea killed her brother, cut him in pieces, and threw him into the sea, so that the king might be delayed by the necessity of recovering his son's body. They eventually reached Iolcus. Here Medea contrived the murder of Pelias in the hope that Jason would succeed him; but the people of Iolcus were indignant and expelled Jason and Medea, who subsequently settled in Corinth.

From *Medea and Other Plays*, translated with an Introduction and Notes by Philip Vellacott. Copyright © 1963 by Philip Vellacott. Reprinted by permission of the translator and Penguin Books, Ltd.

Never had winged out through the grey-blue jaws of rock
And on towards Colchis! If that pine on Pelion's slopes
Had never felt the axe, and fallen, to put oars
Into those heroes' hands, who went at Pelias' bidding
To fetch the golden fleece! Then neither would Medea,
My mistress, ever have set sail for the walled town
Of Iolcus, mad with love for Jason; nor would she,
When Pelias' daughters, at her instance, killed their father,
Have come with Jason and her children to live here
In Corinth; where, coming as an exile, she has earned
The citizens' welcome; while to Jason she is all
Obedience—and in marriage that's the saving thing,
When a wife obediently accepts her husband's will.

But now her world has turned to enmity, and wounds her
Where her affection's deepest. Jason has betrayed
His own sons, and my mistress, for a royal bed,
For alliance with the king of Corinth. He has married
Glauce, Creon's daughter. Poor Medea! Scorned and shamed,
She raves, invoking every vow and solemn pledge
That Jason made her, and calls the gods as witnesses
What thanks she has received for her fidelity.
She will not eat; she lies collapsed in agony,
Dissolving the long hours in tears. Since first she heard
Of Jason's wickedness, she has not raised her eyes,
Or moved her cheek from the hard ground; and when her
    friends
Reason with her, she might be a rock or wave of the sea;
For all she hears—unless, maybe, she turns away
Her lovely head, speaks to herself alone, and wails
Aloud for her dear father, her own land and home,
Which she betrayed and left, to come here with this man
Who now spurns and insults her. Poor Medea! Now
She learns through pain what blessings they enjoy who are not
Uprooted from their native land. She hates her sons:
To see them is no pleasure to her. I am afraid
Some dreadful purpose is forming in her mind. She is
A frightening woman; no one who makes an enemy
Of her will carry off an easy victory.

Here come the boys, back from their running. They've no
    thought
Of this cruel blow that's fallen on their mother. Well,
They're young; young heads and painful thoughts don't go
    together.
Enter the TUTOR *with* MEDEA's TWO SONS.

TUTOR
    Old nurse and servant of my mistress's house, tell me,
    What are you doing, standing out here by the door,
    All alone, talking to yourself, harping on trouble?
    Eh? What does Medea say to being left alone?

NURSE
    Old Friend, tutor of Jason's sons, an honest slave
    Suffers in her own heart the blow that strikes her mistress.
    It was too much, I couldn't bear it; I had to come
    Out here and tell my mistress's wrongs to earth and heaven.

TUTOR
    Poor woman! Has she not stopped crying yet?

NURSE
                                    Stopped crying?
    I envy you. Her grief's just born—not yet half grown.

TUTOR
    Poor fool—though she's my mistress and I shouldn't
        say it—
    She had better save her tears. She has not heard the worst.

NURSE
    The worst? What now? Don't keep it from me. What
        has happened?

TUTOR
    Why, nothing's happened. I'm sorry I said anything.

NURSE
    Look—we're both slaves together: don't keep me in
        the dark.
    Is it so great a secret? I can hold my tongue.

TUTOR
    I'd gone along to the benches where the old men play
    At dice, next to the holy fountain of Peirene;
    They thought I was not listening; and I heard one say
    That Creon king of Corinth means to send these boys
    Away from here—to banish them, and their mother too.
    Whether the story's true I don't know. I hope not.

NURSE
    But surely Jason won't stand by and see his sons
    Banished, even if he has a quarrel with their mother?

TUTOR

Old love is ousted by new love. Jason's no friend
To this house.

NURSE

Then we're lost, if we must add new trouble
To old, before we're rid of what we had already.

TUTOR

But listen: it's no time to tell Medea this.
Keep quiet, say nothing about it.

NURSE

Children, do you hear
What sort of father Jason is to you? My curse
On—No! No curse; he is my master. All the same,
He is guilty: he has betrayed those near and dear to him.

TUTOR

What man's not guilty? It's taken you a long time to
learn
That everybody loves himself more than his neighbour.
These boys are nothing to their father: he's in love.

NURSE

Run into the house, boys. Everything will be all
right.
[*The children move away a little.*]
You do your best to keep them by themselves, as long
As she's in this dark mood; don't let them go to her.
I've watched her watching them, her eye like a wild bull's.
There's something that she means to do; and I know this:
She'll not relax her rage till it has found its victim.
God grant she strikes her enemies and not her friends!
MEDEA's *voice is heard from inside the house.*

MEDEA

Oh, oh! What misery, what wretchedness!
What shall I do? If only I were dead!

NURSE

There! You can hear; it is your mother
Racking her heart, racking her anger.
Quick, now, children, hurry indoors;
And don't go within sight of her,
Or anywhere near her; keep a safe distance.
Her mood is cruel, her nature dangerous,
Her will fierce and intractable.
Come on, now, in with you both at once.

[*The* CHILDREN *go in, and the* TUTOR *follows.*]
The dark cloud of her lamentations
Is just beginning. Soon, I know,
It will burst aflame as her anger rises.
Deep in passion and unrelenting,
What will she do now, stung with insult?

MEDEA [*indoors*]
    Do I not suffer? Am I not wronged? Should
      I not weep?
    Children, your mother is hated, and you are cursed:
    Death take you, with your father, and perish his whole
      house!

NURSE
    Oh, the pity of it! Poor Medea!
    Your children—why, what have *they* to do
    With their father's wickedness? Why hate *them?*
    I am sick with fear for you, children, terror
    Of what may happen. The mind of a queen
    Is a thing to fear. A queen is used
    To giving commands, not obeying them;
    And her rage once roused is hard to appease.

    To have learnt to live on the common level
    Is better. No grand life for me,
    Just peace and quiet as I grow old.
    The middle way, neither great nor mean,
    Is best by far, in name and practice.
    To be rich and powerful brings no blessing;
    Only more utterly
    Is the prosperous house destroyed, when the gods are angry.
    Enter the CHORUS *of Corinthian women.*

CHORUS
    I heard her voice, I heard
    That unhappy woman from Colchis
    Still crying, not calm yet.
    Old Nurse, tell us about her.
    As I stood by the door I heard her
    Crying inside the palace.
    And my own heart suffers too
    When Jason's house is suffering;
    For that is where my loyalty lies.

NURSE
    Jason's house? It no longer exists; all that is finished.
    Jason is a prisoner in a princess's bed;

And Medea is in her room
Melting her life away in tears;
No word from any friend can give her comfort.

MEDEA [*still from indoors*]
    Come, flame of the sky,
    Pierce through my head!
    What do I gain from living any longer?
    Oh, how I hate living! I want
    To end my life, leave it behind, and die.

CHORUS
    O Zeus, and Earth, and Light,
    Do you hear the chanted prayer
    Of a wife in her anguish?
    [*turning to the door and addressing* MEDEA]
    What madness is this? The bed you long for—
    Is it what others shrink from?
    Is it death you demand?
    Do not pray that prayer, Medea!
    If your husband is won to a new love—
    The thing is common; why let it anger you?
    Zeus will plead your cause.
    Check this passionate grief over your husband
    Which wastes you away.

MEDEA
    Mighty Themis! Dread Artemis!
    Do you see how I am used—
    In spite of those great oaths I bound him with—
    By my accursed husband?
    Oh, may I see Jason and his bride
    Ground to pieces in their shattered palace
    For the wrong they have dared to do to me, unprovoked!
    O my father, my city, you I deserted;
    My brother I shamefully murdered!

NURSE
    Do you hear what my mistress is saying,
    Clamouring to Themis, hearer of prayer,
    And to Zeus, who is named guardian of men's oaths?
    It is no trifling matter
    That can end a rage like hers.

CHORUS
    I wish she would come out here and let us see her
    And talk to her; if she would listen
    Perhaps she would drop this fierce resentful spirit,

This passionate indignation.
As a friend I am anxious to do whatever I can.
Go, nurse, persuade her to come out to us.
Tell her we are all on her side.
Hurry, before she does harm—to those in there;
This passion of hers is an irresistible flood.

NURSE
I will. I fear I shall not persuade her;
Still, I am glad to do my best.
Yet as soon as any of us servants
Goes near to her, or tries to speak,
She glares at us like a mad bull
Or a lioness guarding her cubs.
[*The* NURSE *goes to the door, where she turns.*]
The men of old times had little sense;
If you called them fools you wouldn't be far wrong.
They invented songs, and all the sweetness of music,
To perform at feasts, banquets, and celebrations;
But no one thought of using
Songs and stringed instruments
To banish the bitterness and pain of life.
Sorrow is the real cause
Of deaths and disasters and families destroyed.
If music could cure sorrow it would be precious;
But after a good dinner why sing songs?
When people have fed full they're happy already.
The NURSE *goes in.*

CHORUS
I heard her sobbing and wailing,
Shouting shrill, pitiful accusations
Against her husband who has betrayed her.
She invokes Themis, daughter of Zeus,
Who witnessed those promises which drew her
Across from Asia to Hellas, setting sail at night,
Threading the salt strait,
Key and barrier to the Pontic Sea.

MEDEA *comes out. She is not shaken with weeping, but cool and self-possessed.*

MEDEA
Women of Corinth, I would not have you censure me,
So I have come. Many, I know, are proud at heart,
Indoors or out; but others are ill spoken of
As supercilious, just because their ways are quiet.
There is no justice in the world's censorious eyes.

They will not wait to learn a man's true character;
Though no wrong has been done them, one look—and they
    hate.
Of course a stranger must conform; even a Greek
Should not annoy his fellows by crass stubbornness.
I accept my place; but this blow that has fallen on me
Was not to be expected. It has crushed my heart.
Life has no pleasure left, dear friends. I want to die.
Jason was my whole life; he knows that well. Now he
Has proved himself the most contemptible of men.

Surely, of all creatures that have life and will, we women
Are the most wretched. When, for an extravagant sum,
We have bought a husband, we must then accept him as
Possessor of our body. This is to aggravate
Wrong with worse wrong. Then the great question: will the
    man
We get be bad or good? For women, divorce is not
Respectable; to repel the man, not possible.

Still more, a foreign woman, coming among new laws,
New customs, needs the skill of magic, to find out
What her home could not teach her, how to treat the man
Whose bed she shares. And if in this exacting toil
We are successful, and our husband does not struggle
Under the marriage yoke, our life is enviable.
Otherwise, death is better. If a man grows tired
Of the company at home, he can go out, and find
A cure for tediousness. We wives are forced to look
To one man only. And, they tell us, we at home
Live free from danger, they go out to battle: fools!
I'd rather stand three times in the front line than bear
One child.
        But the same arguments do not apply
To you and me. You have this city, your father's home,
The enjoyment of your life, and your friends' company.
I am alone; I have no city; now my husband
Insults me. I was taken as plunder from a land
At the earth's edge. I have no mother, brother, nor any
Of my own blood to turn to in this extremity.

So, I make one request. If I can find a way
To work revenge on Jason for his wrongs to me,
Say nothing. A woman's weak and timid in most matters;
The noise of war, the look of steel, makes her a coward.
But touch her right in marriage, and there's no bloodier
    spirit.

CHORUS

I'll do as you ask. To punish Jason will be just.
I do not wonder that you take such wrongs to heart.
[CREON *approaches.*]
But look, Medea; I see Creon, King of Corinth;
He must have come to tell you of some new decision.

CREON

You there, Medea, scowling rage against your husband!
I order you out of Corinth; take your sons and go
Into exile. Waste no time; I'm here to see this order
Enforced. And I'm not going back into my palace
Until I've put you safe outside my boundaries.

MEDEA

Oh! this is the cruel end of my accursed life!
My enemies have spread full sail; no welcoming shore
Waits to receive and save me. Ill-treated as I am,
Creon, I ask: for what offence do you banish me?

CREON

I fear you. Why wrap up the truth? I fear that you
May do my daughter some irreparable harm.
A number of things contribute to my anxiety.
You're a clever woman, skilled in many evil arts;
You're barred from Jason's bed, and that enrages you.
I learn too from reports, that you have uttered threats
Of revenge on Jason and his bride and his bride's father.
I'll act first, then, in self-defence. I'd rather make you
My enemy now, than weaken, and later pay with tears.

MEDEA

My reputation, yet again! Many times, Creon,
It has been my curse and ruin. A man of any shrewdness
Should never have his children taught to use their brains
More than their fellows. What do you gain by being clever?
You neglect your own affairs; and all your fellow citizens
Hate you. Those who are fools will call you ignorant
And useless, when you offer them unfamiliar knowledge.
As for those thought intelligent, if people rank
You above *them*, that is a thing they will not stand.
I know this from experience: because I am clever,
They are jealous; while the rest dislike me. After all,
I am not so clever as all that.
                    So you, Creon,
Are afraid—of what? Some harm that I might do to you?
Don't let *me* alarm you, Creon. I'm in no position—
A woman—to wrong a king. You have done me no wrong.

You've given your daughter to the man you chose. I hate
My husband—true; but you had every right to do
As you have done. So now I bear no grudge against
Your happiness: marry your daughter to him, and good luck
To you both. But let me live in Corinth. I will bear
My wrongs in silence, yielding to superior strength.

CREON

Your words are gentle; but my blood runs cold to
   think
What plots you may be nursing deep within your heart.
In fact, I trust you so much less now than before.
A woman of hot temper—and a man the same—
Is a less dangerous enemy than one quiet and clever.
So out you go, and quickly; no more arguing.
I've made my mind up; you're my enemy. No craft
Of yours will find a way of staying in my city.

MEDEA

I kneel to you, I beseech you by the young bride, your
   child.

CREON

You're wasting words; you'll never make me change
   my mind.

MEDEA

I beg you! Will you cast off pity, and banish me?

CREON

I will: I have more love for my family than for you.

MEDEA

My home, my country! How my thoughts turn to you
   now!

CREON

I love my country too—next only to my daughter.

MEDEA

Oh, what an evil power love has in people's lives!

CREON

That would depend on circumstances, I imagine.

MEDEA

Great Zeus, remember who caused all this suffering!

CREON
Go, you poor wretch, take all my troubles with you!
Go!

MEDEA
I know what trouble is; I have no need of more.

CREON
In a moment you'll be thrown out neck and crop.
Here, men!

MEDEA
No, no, not that! But, Creon, I have one thing to ask.

CREON
You seem inclined, Medea, to give me trouble still.

MEDEA
I'll go. [*She still clings to him.*] It was not *that* I begged.

CREON
Then why resist?
Why will you not get out?

MEDEA
This one day let me stay,
To settle some plan for my exile, make provision
For my two sons, since their own father is not concerned
To help them. Show some pity: you are a father too,
You should feel kindly towards them. For myself, exile
Is nothing. I weep for them; their fate is very hard.

CREON
I'm no tyrant by nature. My soft heart has often
Betrayed me; and I know it's foolish of me now;
Yet none the less, Medea, you shall have what you ask.
But take this warning: if tomorrow's holy sun
Finds you or them inside my boundaries, you die.
That is my solemn word. Now stay here, if you must,
This one day. You can hardly in one day accomplish
What I am afraid of.
Exit CREON.

CHORUS
Medea, poor Medea!
Your grief touches our hearts.
A wanderer, where can you turn?
To what welcoming house?
To what protecting land?

How wild with dread and danger
Is the sea where the gods have set your course!

MEDEA

A bad predicament all round—yes, true enough;
But don't imagine things will end as they are now.
Trials are yet to come for this new-wedded pair;
Nor shall those nearest to them get off easily.

Do you think I would ever have fawned so on this man,
Except to gain my purpose, carry out my schemes?
Not one touch, not one word: yet he—oh, what a fool!
By banishing me at once he could have thwarted me
Utterly; instead, he allows me to remain one day.
Today three of my enemies I shall strike dead:
Father and daughter; and *my* husband.

I have in mind so many paths of death for them,
I don't know which to choose. Should I set fire to the house,
And burn the bridal chamber? Or creep up to their bed
And drive a sharp knife through their guts? There is one
     fear:
If I am caught entering the house, or in the act,
I die, and the last laugh goes to my enemies.
The best is the direct way, which most suits my bent:
To kill by poison.
So—say they are dead: what city will receive me then?
What friend will guarantee my safety, offer land
And home as sanctuary? None. I'll wait a little.
If some strong tower of help appears, I'll carry out
This murder cunningly and quietly. But if Fate
Banishes me without resource, I will myself
Take sword in hand, harden my heart to the uttermost,
And kill them both, even if I am to die for it.

For, by Queen Hecate, whom above all divinities
I venerate, my chosen accomplice, to whose presence
My central hearth is dedicated, no one of them
Shall hurt me and not suffer for it! Let me work:
In bitterness and pain they shall repent this marriage,
Repent their houses joined, repent my banishment.

Come! Lay your plan, Medea; scheme with all your skill.
On to the deadly moment that shall test your nerve!
You see now where you stand. Your father was a king,
His father was the Sun-god: you must not invite
Laughter from Jason and his new allies, the tribe
Of Sisyphus. You know what you must do. Besides—

[*She turns to the Chorus.*]
We were born women—useless for honest purposes,
But in all kinds of evil skilled practitioners.

CHORUS
　Streams of the sacred rivers flow uphill;
　Tradition, order, all things are reversed:
　　Deceit is *men*'s device now,
　　Men's oaths are gods' dishonour.
　Legend will now reverse our reputation;
　A time comes when the female sex is honoured;
　　That old discordant slander
　　Shall no more hold us subject.
　Male poets of past ages, with their ballads
　Of faithless women, shall go out of fashion;
　　For Phoebus, Prince of Music,
　Never bestowed the lyric inspiration
　　Through female understanding—
　　Or we'd find themes for poems,
　We'd counter with our epics against man.
　Oh, Time is old; and in his store of tales
　　Men figure no less famous
　　Or infamous than women.

　So you, Medea, wild with love,
　Set sail from your father's house,
　Threading the Rocky Jaws of the eastern sea;
　And here, living in a strange country,
　Your marriage lost, your bed solitary,
　You are driven beyond the borders,
　An exile with no redress.
　The grace of sworn oaths is gone;
　Honour remains no more
　In the wide Greek world, but is flown to the sky.
　Where can you turn for shelter?
　Your father's door is closed against you;
　Another is now mistress of your husband's bed;
　A new queen rules in your house.
　Enter JASON.

JASON
　I have often noticed—this is not the first occasion—
　What fatal results follow from ungoverned rage.
　You could have stayed in Corinth, still lived in this house,
　If you had quietly accepted the decisions
　Of those in power. Instead, you talked like a fool; and
　　now
　You are banished. Well, your angry words don't upset *me;*

Go on as long as you like reciting Jason's crimes.
But after your abuse of the King and the princess
Think yourself lucky to be let off with banishment.
I have tried all the time to calm them down; but you
Would not give up your ridiculous tirades against
The royal family. So, you're banished. However, I
Will not desert a friend. I have carefully considered
Your problem, and come now, in spite of everything,
To see that you and the children are not sent away
With an empty purse, or unprovided. Exile brings
With it a train of difficulties. You no doubt
Hate me: but I could never bear ill-will to you.

MEDEA

You filthy coward!—if I knew any worse name
For such unmanliness I'd use it—so, you've come!
You, my worst enemy, come to me! Oh, it's not courage,
This looking friends in the face after betraying them.
It is not even audacity; it's a disease,
The worst a man can have, pure shamelessness. However,
It is as well you came; to say what I have to say
Will ease my heart; to hear it said will make you wince.

I will begin at the beginning. When you were sent
To master the fire-breathing bulls,[2] yoke them, and sow
The deadly furrow, then I saved your life; and that
Every Greek who sailed with you in the Argo knows.
The serpent that kept watch over the Golden Fleece,
Coiled round it fold on fold, unsleeping—it was I
Who killed it, and so lit the torch of your success.
I willingly deceived my father; left my home;
With you I came to Iolcus by Mount Pelion,
Showing much love and little wisdom. There I put
King Pelias to the most horrible of deaths
By his own daughters' hands,[3] and ruined his whole house.
And in return for this you have the wickedness
To turn me out, to get yourself another wife,
Even after I had borne you sons! If you had still
Been childless I could have pardoned you for hankering
After this new marriage. But respect for oaths has gone
To the wind. Do you, I wonder, think that the old gods
No longer rule? Or that new laws are now in force?
You must know you are guilty of perjury to me.

---

[2]*The fire-breathing bulls.* The king of Colchis had required this task of Jason, in return for his permission to seek the Golden Fleece.

[3]*By his own daughters' hands.* Medea persuaded the daughters of Pelias that they could renew their father's youth by killing him and boiling his flesh.

My poor right hand, which you so often clasped! My knees
Which you then clung to! How we are besmirched and
  mocked
By this man's broken vows, and all our hopes deceived!

Come, I'll ask your advice as if you were a friend.
Not that I hope for any help from you; but still,
I'll ask you, and expose your infamy. Where now
Can I turn? Back to my country and my father's house,
Which I betrayed to come with you? Or to Iolcus,
To Pelias's wretched daughters? What a welcome they
Would offer me, who killed their father! Thus it stands:
My friends at home now hate me; and in helping you
I have earned the enmity of those I had no right
To hurt. For my reward, you have made me the envy
Of Hellene women everywhere! A marvellous
Husband I have, and faithful too, in the name of pity;
When I'm banished, thrown out of the country without a
  friend,
Alone with my forlorn waifs. Yes, a shining shame
It will be to you, the new-made bridegroom, that your own
  sons,
And I who saved your life, are begging beside the road!

O Zeus! Why have you given us clear signs to tell
True gold from counterfeit; but when we need to know
Bad *men* from good, the flesh bears no revealing mark?

CHORUS
  The fiercest anger of all, the most incurable,
  Is that which rages in the place of dearest love.

JASON
  I have to show myself a clever speaker, it seems.
  This hurricane of recrimination and abuse
  Calls for good seamanship: I'll furl all but an inch
  Of sail, and ride it out. To begin with, since you build
  To such a height your services to me, I hold
  That credit for my successful voyage was solely due
  To Aphrodite, no one else divine or human.
  I admit, you have intelligence; but, to recount
  How helpless passion drove you then to save my life
  Would be invidious; and I will not stress the point.
  Your services, so far as they went, were well enough;
  But in return for saving me you got far more
  Than you gave. Allow me, in the first place, to point out
  That you left a barbarous land to become a resident
  Of Hellas; here you have known justice; you have lived

In a society where force yields place to law.
Moreover, here your gifts are widely recognized,
You are famous; if you still lived at the ends of the earth
Your name would never be spoken. Personally, unless
Life brings me fame, I long neither for hoards of gold,
Nor for a voice sweeter than Orpheus!—Well, *you* began
The argument about my voyage; and that's my answer.

As for your scurrilous taunts against my marriage with
The royal family, I shall show you that my action
Was wise, not swayed by passion, and directed towards
Your interests and my children's.—No, keep quiet! When I
Came here from Iolcus as a stateless exile, dogged
And thwarted by misfortunes—why, what luckier chance
Could I have met, than marriage with the King's daughter?
It was not, as you resentfully assume, that I
Found your attractions wearisome, and was smitten with
Desire for a new wife; nor did I specially want
To raise a numerous family—the sons we have
Are enough, I'm satisfied; but I wanted to ensure
First—and the most important—that we should live well
And not be poor; I know how a poor man is shunned
By all his friends. Next, that I could bring up my sons
In a manner worthy of my descent; have other sons,
Perhaps, as brothers to your children; give them all
An equal place, and so build up a closely-knit
And prosperous family. *You* need no more children, do you?
While *I* thought it worth while to ensure advantages
For those I have, by means of those I hope to have.

Was such a plan, then, wicked? Even you would approve
If you could govern your sex-jealousy. But you women
Have reached a state where, if all's well with your sex-life,
You've everything you wish for; but when *that* goes wrong,
At once all that is best and noblest turns to gall.
If only children could be got some other way,
Without the female sex! If women didn't exist,
Human life would be rid of all its miseries.

CHORUS
Jason, you have set your case forth very plausibly.
But to my mind—though you may be surprised at this—
You are acting wrongly in thus abandoning your wife.

MEDEA
No doubt I differ from many people in many ways.
To me, a wicked man who is also eloquent

Seems the most guilty of them all. He'll cut your throat
As bold as brass, because he knows he can dress up murder
In handsome words. He's not so clever after all.
You dare outface me now with glib high-mindedness!
One word will throw you: if you were honest, you ought
first
To have won me over, not got married behind my back.

JASON

No doubt, if I had mentioned it, you would have
proved
Most helpful. Why, even now you will not bring yourself
To calm this raging temper.

MEDEA

That was not the point;
But you're an ageing man, and an Asiatic wife
Was no longer respectable.

JASON

Understand this:
It's not for the sake of any woman that I have made
This royal marriage, but, as I've already said,
To ensure your future, and to give my children brothers
Of royal blood, and build security for us all.

MEDEA

I loathe your properous future; I'll have none of
it,
Nor none of your security—it galls my heart.

JASON

You know—you'll change your mind and be more
sensible.
You'll soon stop thinking good is bad, and striking these
Pathetic poses when in fact you're fortunate.

MEDEA

Go on, insult me: you have a roof over your head.
I am alone, an exile.

JASON

It was your own choice.
Blame no one but yourself.

MEDEA

My choice? What did I do?
Did I make you my wife and then abandon you?

JASON
> You called down wicked curses on the King and his
>   house.

MEDEA
> I did. On your house too Fate sends me as a curse.

JASON
> I'll not pursue this further. If there's anything else
> I can provide to meet the children's needs or yours,
> Tell me; I'll gladly give whatever you want, or send
> Letters of introduction, if you like, to friends
> Who will help you.—Listen: to refuse such help is mad.
> You've everything to gain if you give up this rage.

MEDEA
> Nothing would induce me to have dealings with your
>   friends,
> Nor to take any gift of yours; so offer none.
> A lying traitor's gifts carry no luck.

JASON
>   Very well.
> I call the gods to witness that I have done my best
> To help you and the children. You make no response
> To kindness; friendly overtures you obstinately
> Reject. So much the worse for you.

MEDEA
>   Go! You have spent
> Too long out here. You are consumed with craving for
> Your newly-won bride. Go, enjoy her!
> [*Exit* JASON.]
>   It may be—
> And God uphold my words—that this your marriage-day
> Will end with marriage lost, loathing and horror left.

CHORUS
> Visitations of love that come
> Raging and violent on a man
> Bring him neither good repute nor goodness.
> But if Aphrodite descends in gentleness
> No other goddess brings such delight.
> Never, Queen Aphrodite,
> Loose against me from your golden bow,
> Dipped in sweetness of desire,
> Your inescapable arrow!
>
> Let Innocence, the gods' loveliest gift,
> Choose me for her own;

Never may the dread Cyprian
Craze my heart to leave old love for new,
Sending to assault me
Angry disputes and feuds unending;
But let her judge shrewdly the loves of women
And respect the bed where no war rages.

O my country, my home!
May the gods save me from becoming
A stateless refugee
Dragging out an intolerable life
In desperate helplessness!
That is the most pitiful of all griefs;
Death is better. Should such a day come to me
I pray for death first.
Of all pains and hardships none is worse
Than to be deprived of your native land.

This is no mere reflection derived from hearsay;
It is something we have seen.
You, Medea, have suffered the most shattering of blows;
Yet neither the city of Corinth
Nor any friend has taken pity on you.
May dishonour and ruin fall on the man
Who, having unlocked the secrets
Of a friend's frank heart, can then disown him!
He shall be no friend of mine.
Enter AEGEUS.

AEGEUS
All happiness to you, Medea! Between old friends
There is no better greeting.

MEDEA
All happiness to you,
Aegeus, son of Pandion the wise! Where have you come
from?

AEGEUS
From Delphi, from the ancient oracle of Apollo.

MEDEA
The centre of the earth, the home of prophecy:
Why did you go?

AEGEUS
To ask for children; that my seed
May become fertile.

MEDEA   Why, have you lived so many years
  Childless?

AEGEUS
  Childless I am; so some fate has ordained.

MEDEA
  You have a wife, or not?

AEGEUS
                    I am married.

MEDEA
                       And what answer
  Did Phoebus give you about children?

AEGEUS
                         His answer was
  Too subtle for me or any human interpreter.

MEDEA
  Is it lawful for me to hear it?

AEGEUS
                    Certainly; a brain
  Like yours is what is needed.

MEDEA
                 Tell me, since you may.

AEGEUS
  He commanded me 'not to unstop the wineskin's
    neck'—

MEDEA
  Yes—until when?

AEGEUS
               Until I came safe home again.

MEDEA
  I see. And for what purpose have you sailed to Corinth?

AEGEUS
  You know the King of Troezen, Pittheus, son of
    Pelops?

MEDEA
  Yes, a most pious man.

AEGEUS
                        I want to ask his advice
About this oracle.

MEDEA
                  He is an expert in such matters.

AEGEUS
Yes, and my closest friend. We went to the wars
   together.

MEDEA
I hope you will get all you long for, and be happy.

AEGEUS
But you are looking pale and wasted: what is the
   matter?

MEDEA
Aegeus, my husband's the most evil man alive.

AEGEUS
Why, what's this? Tell me all about your unhappiness.

MEDEA
Jason has betrayed me, though I never did him wrong.

AEGEUS
What has he done? Explain exactly.

MEDEA
                        He has taken
Another wife, and made her mistress of *my* house.

AEGEUS
But such a thing is shameful! He has never dared—

MEDEA
It is so. Once he loved me; now I am disowned.

AEGEUS
Was he tired of you? Or did he fall in love elsewhere?

MEDEA
Oh, passionately. He's not a man his friends can trust.

AEGEUS
Well, if—as you say—he's a bad lot, let him go.

MEDEA

It's royalty and power he's fallen in love with.

AEGEUS

What?

Go on. Who's the girl's father?

MEDEA

Creon, King of Corinth.

AEGEUS

I see.Then you have every reason to be upset.

MEDEA

It is the end of everything! What's more, I'm banished.

AEGEUS

Worse still—extraordinary! Why, who has banished
you?

MEDEA

Creon has banished me from Corinth.

AEGEUS

And does Jason

Accept this? How disgraceful!

MEDEA

Oh, no! He protests
But he's resolved to bear it bravely.—Aegeus see,
I touch your beard as a suppliant, embrace your knees,
Imploring you to have pity on my wretchedness.
Have pity! I am an exile; let me not be friendless.
Receive me in Athens; give me a welcome in your house.
So may the gods grant you fertility, and bring
Your life to a happy close. You have not realized
What good luck chance has brought you. I know certain
drugs
Whose power will put an end to your sterility.
I promise you shall beget children.

AEGEUS

I am anxious,
For many reasons, to help you in this way, Medea;
First, for the gods' sake, then this hope you've given me
Of children—for I've quite despaired of my own powers.
This then is what I'll do: once you can get to Athens
I'll keep my promise and protect you all I can.
But I must make this clear first: I do not intend

To take you with me away from Corinth. If you come
Yourself to Athens, you shall have sanctuary there;
I will not give you up to anyone. But first
Get clear of Corinth without help; the Corinthians too
Are friends of mine, and I don't wish to give offence.

MEDEA

So be it. Now confirm your promise with an oath,
And all is well between us.

AEGEUS

                              Why? Do you not trust me?
What troubles you?

MEDEA

                    I trust you; but I have enemies—
Not only Creon, but the house of Pelias.
Once you are bound by oaths you will not give me up
If they should try to take me out of your territory.
But if your promise is verbal, and not sworn to the gods,
Perhaps you will make friends with them, and agree to do
What they demand. I've no power on my side, while they
Have wealth and all the resources of a royal house.

AEGEUS

Your forethought is remarkable; but since you
    wish it
I've no objection. In fact, the taking of an oath
Safeguards me; since I can confront your enemies
With a clear excuse; while *you* have full security.
So name your gods.

MEDEA

                    Swear by the Earth under your feet,
By the Sun, my father's father, and the whole race of gods.

AEGEUS

Tell me what I shall swear to do or not to do.

MEDEA

Never yourself to expel me from your territory;
And, if my enemies want to take me away, never
Willingly, while you live, to give me up to them.

AEGEUS

I swear by Earth, and by the burning light of the
    Sun,
And all the gods, to keep the words you have just spoken.

MEDEA

I am satisfied. And if you break your oath, what then?

AEGEUS

Then may the gods do to me as to all guilty men.

MEDEA

Go now, and joy be with you. Everything is well.
I'll reach your city as quickly as I can, when I
Have carried out my purpose and achieved my wish.
AEGEUS *clasps her hand and hurries off.*

CHORUS

May Hermes, protector of travellers, bring you
Safe to your home, Aegeus; may you accomplish
All that you so earnestly desire;
For your noble heart wins our goodwill.

MEDEA

O Zeus! O Justice, daughter of Zeus! O glorious
    Sun!
Now I am on the road to victory; now there's hope!
I shall see my enemies punished as they deserve.
Just where my plot was weakest, at that very point
Help has appeared in this man Aegeus; he is a haven
Where I shall find safe mooring, once I reach the walls
Of the city of Athens. Now I'll tell you all my plans:
They'll not make pleasant hearing.
[*Medea's* NURSE *has entered; she listens in silence.*]
                                    First I'll send a slave
To Jason, asking him to come to me; and then
I'll give him soft talk; tell him he has acted well,
Tell him I think this royal marriage which he has bought
With my betrayal is for the best and wisely planned.
But I shall beg that my children be allowed to stay.
Not that I would think of leaving sons of mine behind
On enemy soil for those who hate me to insult;
But in my plot to kill the princess they must help.
I'll send them to the palace bearing gifts, a dress
Of soft weave and a coronet of beaten gold.
If she takes and puts on this finery, both she
And all who touch her will expire in agony;
With such a deadly poison I'll anoint my gifts.[4]

However, enough of that. What makes me cry with pain
Is the next thing I have to do. I will kill my sons.
No one shall take my children from me. When I have made

---

[4]*I'll anoint my gifts.* When does Medea do this? The action of the play gives her
no opportunity. The dress is brought in a casket, and she sends it off without looking
at it.

Jason's whole house a shambles, I will leave Corinth
A murderess, flying from my darling children's blood.
Yes, I can endure guilt, however horrible;
The laughter of my enemies I will not endure.

Now let things take their course. What use is life to me?
I have no land, no home, no refuge from despair.
My folly was committed long ago, when I
Was ready to desert my father's house, won over
By eloquence from a Greek, whom with God's help I now
Will punish. He shall never see alive again
The sons he had from me. From his new bride he never
Shall breed a son; she by my poison, wretched girl,
Must die a hideous death. Let no one think of me
As humble or weak or passive; let them understand
I am of a different kind: dangerous to my enemies,
Loyal to my friends. To such a life glory belongs.

CHORUS

Since you have told us everything, and since I want
To be your friend, and also to uphold the laws
Of human life—I tell you, you must not do this!

MEDEA

No other thing is possible. You have excuse
For speaking so: you have not been treated as I have.

CHORUS

But—to kill your own children! Can you steel your
heart?

MEDEA

This is the way to deal Jason the deepest wound.

CHORUS

This way will bring you too the deepest misery.

MEDEA

Let be. Until it is done words are unnecessary.
Nurse! You are the one I use for messages of trust.
Go and bring Jason here. As you're a loyal servant,
And a woman, breathe no word about my purposes.
Exit NURSE.

CHORUS

The people of Athens, sons of Erechtheus,
   have enjoyed their prosperity
Since ancient times. Children of blessed gods,
They grew from holy soil unscorched by invasion.

Among the glories of knowledge their souls are pastured;
They walk always with grace under the sparkling sky.
There long ago, they say, was born golden-haired Harmony,
Created by the nine virgin Muses of Pieria.

They say that Aphrodite dips her cup
In the clear stream of the lovely Cephisus;
It is she who breathes over the land the breath
Of gentle honey-laden winds; her flowing locks
She crowns with a diadem of sweet-scented roses,
And sends the Loves to be enthroned beside Knowledge,
And with her to create excellence in every art.

Then how will such a city,
Watered by sacred rivers,
A country giving protection to its friends—
How will Athens welcome
You, the child-killer
Whose presence is pollution?
Contemplate the blow struck at a child,
Weigh the blood you take upon you.
Medea, by your knees,
By every pledge or appeal we beseech you,
Do not slaughter your children!

Where will you find hardness of purpose?
How will you build resolution in hand or heart
To face horror without flinching?
When the moment comes, and you look at them—
The moment for you to assume the role of murderess—
How will you do it?
When your sons kneel to you for pity,
Will you stain your fingers with their blood?
Your heart will melt; you will know you cannot.
Enter JASON *from the palace. Two maids come from the house to
attend Medea.*

JASON
You sent for me: I have come. Although you hate me, I
Am ready to listen. You have some new request; what is it?

MEDEA
Jason, I ask you to forgive the things I said.
You must bear with my violent temper; you and I
Share many memories of love. I have been taking
Myself to task. 'You are a fool,' I've told myself,
'You're mad, when people try to plan things for the best,
To be resentful, and pick quarrels with the King

And with your husband; what he's doing will help us all.
His wife is royal; her sons will be my sons' brothers.
Why not throw off your anger? What is the matter, since
The gods are making kind provision? After all
I have two children still to care for; and I know
We came as exiles, and our friends are few enough.'
When I considered this, I saw my foolishness;
I saw how useless anger was. So now I welcome
What you have done; I think you are wise to gain for us
This new alliance, and the folly was all mine.
I should have helped you in your plans, made it my pleasure
To get ready your marriage-bed, attend your bride.
But we women—I won't say we are bad by nature,
But we are what we are. You, Jason, should not copy
Our bad example, or match yourself with us, showing
Folly for folly. I give in; I was wrong just now,
I admit. But I have thought more wisely of it since.
Children, children! Are you indoors? Come out here.
[*The* CHILDREN *come out. Their* TUTOR *follows.*]
                                            Children,
Greet your father, as I do, and put your arms round him.
Forget our quarrel, and love him as your mother does.
We have made friends; we are not angry any more.
There, children; take his hand.
[*She turns away in a sudden flood of weeping.*]
                            Forgive me; I recalled
What pain the future hides from us.
[*After embracing Jason the* CHILDREN *go back to Medea.*]
                            Oh children! Will you
All your lives long, stretch out your hands to me like this?
Oh, my tormented heart is full of tears and terrors.
After so long, I have ended my quarrel with your father;
And now, see! I have drenched this young face with my tears.

CHORUS
    I too feel fresh tears fill my eyes. May the course
        of evil
    Be checked now, go no further!

JASON
                            I am pleased, Medea,
    That you have changed your mind; though indeed I do not
        blame
    Your first resentment. Only naturally a woman
    Is angry when her husband marries a second wife.
    You have had wiser thoughts; and though it has taken time,
    You have recognized the right decision. This is the act

Of a sensible woman. As for you, my boys, your father
Has taken careful thought, and, with the help of the gods,
Ensured a good life for you. Why, in time, I'm sure,
You with your brothers will be leading men in Corinth.
Only grow big and strong. Your father, and those gods
Who are his friends, have all the rest under control.
I want to see you, when you're strong, full-grown young
      men,
Tread down my enemies.
[*Again* MEDEA *breaks down and weeps.*]
                        What's this? Why these floods of tears?
Why are you pale? Did you not like what I was saying?
Why do you turn away?

MEDEA
                        It is nothing. I was thinking
About these children.

JASON
                        I'll provide for them. Cheer up.

MEDEA
I will. It is not that I mean to doubt your word.
But women—are women; tears come naturally to us.

JASON
Why do you grieve so over the children?

MEDEA
                        I'm their mother.
When you just now prayed for them to live long, I wondered
Whether it would be so; and grief came over me.
But I've said only part of what I had to say;
Here is the other thing. Since Creon has resolved
To send me out of Corinth, I fully recognize
That for me too this course is best. If I lived here
I should become a trouble both to you and him.
People believe I bear a grudge against you all.
So I must go. But the boys—I would like *them* to be
Brought up in your care. Beg Creon to let them stay.

JASON
I don't know if I can persuade him; but I'll try.

MEDEA
Then—get your wife to ask her father to let them
      stay.

JASON
  Why, certainly; I'm pretty sure she'll win him over.

MEDEA
  She will, if she's like other women. But I too
  Can help in this. I'll send a present to your wife—
  The loveliest things to be found anywhere on earth.
  The boys shall take them.—One of you maids, go quickly,
      bring
  The dress and golden coronet.—They will multiply
  Her happiness many times, when she can call her own
  A royal, noble husband, and these treasures, which
  My father's father the Sun bequeathed to his descendants.
  [*A slave has brought a casket, which* MEDEA *now hands to her sons.*]
  Boys, hold these gifts. Now carry them to the happy bride,
  The princess royal; give them into her own hands.
  Go! She will find them all that such a gift should be.

JASON
  But why deprive yourself of such things, foolish
      woman?
  Do you think a royal palace is in want of dresses?
  Or gold, do you suppose? Keep them, don't give them away.
  If my wife values me at all she will yield to *me*
  More than to costly presents, I am sure of that.

MEDEA
  Don't stop me. Gifts, they say, persuade even the
      gods;
  With mortals, gold outweighs a thousand arguments.
  The day is hers; from now on *her* prosperity
  Will rise to new heights. She is royal and young. To buy
  My sons from exile I would give life, not just gold.
  Come, children, go both of you into this rich palace;
  Kneel down and beg your father's new wife, and my mistress,
  That you may not be banished. And above all, see
  That she receives my present into her own hands.
  Go quickly; be successful, and bring good news back,
  That what your mother longs for has been granted you.
  Exit JASON *followed by the* CHILDREN *and the* TUTOR.

CHORUS
  Now I have no more hope,
  No more hope that the children can live;
  They are walking to murder at this moment.
  The bride will receive the golden coronet,
  Receive her merciless destroyer;

With her own hands she will carefully fit
The adornment of death round her golden hair.

She cannot resist such loveliness, such heavenly gleaming;
She will enfold herself
In the dress and the wreath of wrought gold,
Preparing her bridal beauty
To enter a new home—among the dead.
So fatal is the snare she will fall into,
So inevitable the death that awaits her;
From its cruelty there is no escape.

And you, unhappy Jason, ill-starred in marriage,
You, son-in-law of kings:
Little you know that the favour you ask
Will seal your sons' destruction
And fasten on your wife a hideous fate.
O wretched Jason!
So sure of destiny, and so ignorant!

Your sorrow next I weep for, pitiable mother;
You, for jealousy of your marriage-bed,
Will slaughter your children;
Since, disregarding right and loyalty,
Your husband has abandoned you
And lives with another wife.
The TUTOR *returns from the palace with the two* CHILDREN.

TUTOR
Mistress! These two boys are reprieved from banishment.
The princess took your gifts from them with her own hand,
And was delighted. They have no enemies in the palace.
[MEDEA *is silent.*]
Well, bless my soul!
Isn't that good news? Why do you stand there thunder-
  struck?

MEDEA [*to herself*]
How cruel, how cruel!

TUTOR
              That's out of tune with the news I brought.

MEDEA
How cruel life is!

TUTOR
              Have I, without knowing it,
Told something dreadful, then? I thought my news was good.

MEDEA

Your news is what it is. I am not blaming you.

TUTOR

Then why stand staring at the ground, with streaming
eyes?

MEDEA

Strong reason forces me to weep, old friend. The gods,
And my own evil-hearted plots, have led to this.

TUTOR

Take heart, mistress; in time your sons will bring you
home.

MEDEA

Before then, I have others to send home.—Oh, gods!
She weeps.

TUTOR

You're not the only mother parted from her sons.
We are all mortal; you must not bear grief so hard.

MEDEA

Yes, friend. I'll follow your advice. Now go indoors
And get things ready for them, as on other days.
[*Exit* TUTOR. *The* CHILDREN *come to Medea.*]
O children, children! You have a city, and a home;
And when we have parted, there you both will stay for ever,
You motherless, I miserable. And I must go
To exile in another land, before I have had
My joy of you, before I have seen you growing up,
Becoming prosperous. I shall never see your brides,
Adorn your bridal beds, and hold the torches high.
My misery is my own heart, which will not relent.
All was for nothing, then—these years of rearing you,
My care, my aching weariness, and the wild pains
When you were born. Oh, yes, I once built many hopes
On you; imagined, pitifully, that you would care
For my old age, and would yourselves wrap my dead body
For burial. How people would envy me my sons!
That sweet, sad thought has faded now. Parted from you,
My life will be all pain and anguish. You will not
Look at your mother any more with these dear eyes.
You will have moved into a different sphere of life.

Dear sons, why are you staring at me so? You smile
At me—your last smile: why?

[*She weeps. The* CHILDREN *go from her a little, and she turns to the Chorus.*]

Oh, what am I to do?
Women, my courage is all gone. Their young, bright faces—
I can't do it. I'll think no more of it. I'll take them
Away from Corinth. Why should I hurt *them,* to make
Their father suffer, when I shall suffer twice as much
Myself? I won't do it. I won't think of it again.

What is the matter with me? Are my enemies
To laugh at me? Am I to let them off scot free?
I must steel myself to it. What a coward I am,
Even tempting my own resolution with soft talk.
Boys, go indoors.
[*The* CHILDREN *go to the door, but stay there watching her.*]
If there is any here who finds it
Not lawful to be present at my sacrifice,
Let him see to it. My hand shall not weaken.

Oh, my heart, don't, don't do it! Oh, miserable heart,
Let them be! Spare your children! We'll all live together
Safely in Athens; and they will make you happy. . . . No!
No! No! By all the fiends of hate in hell's depths, no!
I'll not leave sons of mine to be the victims of
My enemies' rage. In any case there is no escape,
The thing's done now. Yes, now—the golden coronet
Is on her head, the royal bride is in her dress,
Dying, I know it. So, since I have a sad road
To travel, and send these boys on a still sadder road,
I'll speak to them. Come, children; give me your hand, dear
    son;
Yours too. Now we must say goodbye. Oh, darling hand,
And darling mouth; your noble, childlike face and body!
Dear sons, my blessing on you both—but there, not here!
All blessing here your father has destroyed. How sweet
To hold you! And children's skin is soft, and their breath
    pure.
Go! Go away! I can't look at you any longer;
My pain is more than I can bear.
[*The* CHILDREN *go indoors.*]
I understand
The horror of what I am going to do; but anger,
The spring of all life's horror, masters my resolve.
MEDEA *goes to stand looking towards the palace.*

CHORUS
I have often engaged in arguments,
And become more subtle, and perhaps more heated,

Than is suitable for women;
Though in fact women too have intelligence,
Which forms part of our nature and instructs us—
Not all of us, I admit; but a certain few
You might perhaps find, in a large number of women—
A few not incapable of reflection;

And this is my opinion: those men or women
Who never had children of their own at all
Enjoy the advantage in good fortune
Over those who are parents. Childless people
Have no means of knowing whether children are
A blessing or a burden; but being without them
They live exempt from many troubles.

While those who have growing up in their homes
The sweet gift of children I see always
Burdened and worn with incessant worry,
First, how to rear them in health and saftey,
And bequeath them, in time, enough to live on;
And then this further anxiety:
They can never know whether all their toil
Is spent for worthy or worthless children.

And beyond the common ills that attend
All human life there is one still worse:
Suppose at last they are pretty well off,
Their children have grown up, and, what's more,
Are kind and honest: then what happens?
A throw of chance—and there goes Death
Bearing off your child into the unknown.

Then why should mortals thank the gods,
Who add to their load, already grievous,
This one more grief, for their children's sake,
Most grievous of all?

MEDEA
Friends, I have long been waiting for a message from
    the palace.
What is to happen next? I see a slave of Jason's
Coming, gasping for breath. He must bring fearful news.
Enter a MESSENGER.

MESSENGER
Medea! Get away, escape! Oh, what a thing
    to do!
What an unholy, horrible thing! Take ship, or chariot,
Any means you can, but escape!

MEDEA

Why should I escape?

MESSENGER

She's dead—the princess, and her father Creon
too,
They're both dead, by your poisons.

MEDEA

Your news is excellent.
I count you from today my friend and benefactor.

MESSENGER

What? Are you sane, or raving mad? When
you've committed
This hideous crime against the royal house, you're glad
At hearing of it? Do you not tremble at such things?

MEDEA

I could make suitable reply to that, my friend.
But take your time now; tell me, how did they die? You'll
give
Me double pleasure if their death was horrible.

MESSENGER

When your two little boys came hand in hand,
and entered
The palace with their father, where the wedding was,
We servants were delighted. We had all felt sorry
To hear how you'd been treated; and now the word went
round
From one to another, that you and Jason had made it up.
So we were glad to see the boys; one kissed their hand,
Another their fair hair. Myself, I was so pleased,
I followed with them to the princess's room. Our mistress—
The one we now call mistress in your place—before
She saw your pair of boys coming, had eyes only
For Jason; but seeing them she dropped her eyes, and turned
Her lovely cheek away, upset that they should come
Into her room. Your husband then began to soothe
Her sulkiness, her girlish temper. 'You must not,'
He said, 'be unfriendly to our friends. Turn your head
round,
And give up feeling angry. Those your husband loves
You must love too. Now take these gifts,' he said, 'and ask
Your father to revoke their exile for my sake.'
So, when she saw those lovely things, she was won over,
And agreed to all that Jason asked. At once, before

He and your sons were well out of the house, she took
The embroidered gown and put it round her. Then she
  placed
Over her curls the golden coronet, and began
To arrange her hair in a bright mirror, smiling at
Her lifeless form reflected there. Then she stood up,
And to and fro stepped daintily about the room
On white bare feet, and many times she would twist back
To see how the dress fell in clear folds to the heel.

Then suddenly we saw a frightening thing. She changed
Colour; she staggered sideways, shook in every limb.
She was just able to collapse on to a chair,
Or she would have fallen flat. Then one of her attendants,
An old woman, thinking that perhaps the anger of Pan
Or some other god had struck her, chanted the cry of wor-
  ship.
But then she saw, oozing from the girl's lips, white froth;
The pupils of her eyes were twisted out of sight;
The blood was drained from all her skin. The old woman
  knew
Her mistake, and changed her chant to a despairing howl.
One maid ran off quickly to fetch the King, another
To look for Jason and tell him what was happening
To his young bride; the whole palace was filled with a clatter
Of people running here and there.
                                    All this took place
In a few moments, perhaps while a fast runner might run
A hundred yards; and she lay speechless, with eyes closed.
Then she came to, poor girl, and gave a frightful scream,
As two torments made war on her together: first
The golden coronet round her head discharged a stream
Of unnatural devouring fire: while the fine dress
Your children gave her—poor miserable girl!—the stuff
Was eating her clear flesh. She leapt up from her chair,
On fire, and ran, shaking her head and her long hair
This way and that, trying to shake off the coronet.
The ring of gold was fitted close and would not move;
The more she shook her head the fiercer the flame burned.
At last, exhausted by agony, she fell to the ground;
Save to her father, she was unrecognizable.
Her eyes, her face, were one grotesque disfigurement;
Down from her head dripped blood mingled with flame; her
  flesh,
Attacked by the invisible fangs of poison, melted
From the bare bone, like gum-drops from a pine-tree's
  bark—

A ghastly sight. Not one among us dared to touch
Her body. What we'd seen was lesson enough for us.

But suddenly her father came into the room.
He did not understand, poor man, what kind of death
Had struck his child. He threw himself down at her side,
And sobbed aloud, and kissed her, and took her in his
        arms,
And cried, 'Poor darling child, what god destroyed your life
So cruelly? Who robs me of my only child,
Old as I am, and near my grave? Oh, let me die
With you, my daughter!' Soon he ceased his tears and cries,
And tried to lift his aged body upright; and then,
As ivy sticks to laurel-branches, so he stuck
Fast to the dress. A ghastly wrestling then began;
He struggled to raise up his knee, she tugged him down.
If he used force, he tore the old flesh off his bones.
At length the King gave up his pitiful attempts;
Weakened with pain, he yielded, and gasped out his life.
Now, joined in death, daughter and father—such a sight
As tears were made for—they lie there.
                                To you, Medea,
I have no more to say. You will yourself know best
How to evade reprisal. As for human life,
It is a shadow, as I have long believed. And this
I say without hesitation: those whom most would call
Intelligent, the propounders of wise theories—
Their folly is of all men's the most culpable.
Happiness is a thing no man possesses. Fortune
May come now to one man, now to another, as
Prosperity increases; happiness never.
Exit MESSENGER.

CHORUS
Today we see the will of Heaven, blow after blow,
Bring down on Jason justice and calamity.

MEDEA
Friends, now my course is clear: as quickly as
        possible
To kill the children and then fly from Corinth; not
Delay and so consign them to another hand
To murder with a better will. For they must die,
In any case; and since they must, then I who gave
Them birth will kill them. Arm yourself, my heart: the
        thing
That you must do is fearful, yet inevitable.

Why wait, then? My accursed hand, come, take the sword;
Take it, and forward to your frontier of despair.
No cowardice, no tender memories; forget
That you once loved them, that of your body they were born.
For one short day forget your children; afterwards
Weep: though you kill them, they were your beloved sons.
Life has been cruel to me.
MEDEA *goes into the house.*

CHORUS
Earth, awake! Bright arrows of the Sun,
Look! Look down on the accursed woman
Before she lifts up a murderous hand
To pollute it with her children's blood!
For they are of your own golden race;
And for mortals to spill blood that grew
In the veins of gods is a fearful thing.
Heaven-born brightness, hold her, stop her,
Purge the palace of her, this pitiable
Bloody-handed fiend of vengeance!

All your care for them lost! Your love
For the babes you bore, all wasted, wasted!
Why did you come from the blue Symplegades[5]
That hold the gate of the barbarous sea?
Why must this rage devour your heart
To spend itself in slaughter of children?
Where kindred blood pollutes the ground
A curse hangs over human lives;
And murder measures the doom that falls
By Heaven's law on the guilty house.
A child's scream is heard from inside the house.

CHORUS
Do you hear? The children are calling for help.
O cursed, miserable woman!

CHILDREN'S VOICES
Help, help! Mother, let me go!
Mother, don't kill us!

CHORUS
Shall we go in?
I am sure we ought to save the children's lives.

---

[5]*The blue Symplegades.* The 'Clashing Rocks' (already referred to in line 2), near the mouth of the Bosporus, the gateway to the Black Sea.

CHILDREN'S VOICES

Help, help, for the gods' sake! She is killing us!
We can't escape from her sword!

CHORUS

O miserable mother, to destroy your own increase,
Murder the babes of your body!
Stone and iron you are, as you resolved to be.

There was but one in time past,
One woman that I have heard of,
Raised hand against her own children.
It was Ino, sent out of her mind by a god,
When Hera, the wife of Zeus,
Drove her from her home to wander over the world.
In her misery she plunged into the sea
Being defiled by the murder of her children;
From the steep cliff's edge she stretched out her foot,
And so ended,
Joined in death with her two sons.

What can be strange or terrible after this?
O bed of women, full of passion and pain,
What wickedness, what sorrow you have caused on the
      earth!
Enter JASON, *running and breathless.*

JASON

You women standing round the door there! Is Medea
Still in the house?—vile murderess!—or has she gone
And escaped? I swear she must either hide in the deep earth
Or soar on wings into the sky's abyss, to escape
My vengeance for the royal house.—She has killed the King
And the princess! Does she expect to go unpunished?

Well, I am less concerned with her than with the children.
Those who have suffered at her hands will make her suffer;
I've come to save my sons, before Creon's family
Murder them in revenge for this unspeakable
Crime of their mother's.

CHORUS

                    Jason, you have yet to learn
How great your trouble is; or you would not have spoken so.

JASON

What trouble? Is Medea trying to kill me too?

CHORUS
 Your sons are dead. Their mother has killed both
  your sons.

JASON
 What? Killed my sons? That word kills me.

CHORUS
                                    They are both dead.

JASON
 Where are they? Did she kill them out here, or
  indoors?

CHORUS
 Open that door, and see them lying in their blood.

JASON
 Slaves, there! Unbar the doors! Open, and let me see
 Two horrors: my dead sons, and the woman I will kill.
 JASON *batters at the doors.* MEDEA *appears above the roof, sitting in a
  chariot drawn by dragons, with the bodies of the two children beside
  her.*

MEDEA
 Jason! Why are you battering at these doors,[6] seeking
 The dead children and me who killed them? Stop! Be quiet.
 If you have any business with me, say what you wish.
 Touch us you cannot, in this chariot which the Sun
 Has sent to save us from the hands of enemies.

JASON
 You abomination! Of all women most detested
 By every god, by me, by the whole human race!
 You could endure—a mother!—to lift sword against
 Your own little ones; to leave me childless, my life wrecked.
 After such murder do you outface both Sun and Earth—
 Guilty of gross pollution? May the gods blast your life!
 I am sane now; but I was mad before, when I
 Brought you from your palace in a land of savages
 Into a Greek home—you, a living curse, already
 A traitor both to your father and your native land.

---

 [6]*Battering at these doors.* The Greek apparently means 'battering at these doors
and unbarring them'. But the bars were certainly on the inside, and Jason was calling for someone else to move them. The word could also mean 'prizing them open
with levers'; but this involves further difficulties. So in the translation the second
verb is omitted.

The vengeance due for your sins the gods have cast on me.
You had already murdered your brother at his own hearth
When first you stepped on board my lovely Argo's hull.
That was your beginning. Then you became my wife, and
    bore
My children; now, out of mere sexual jealousy,
You murder them! In all Hellas there is not one woman
Who could have done it; yet in preference to them
I married you, chose hatred and murder for my wife—
No woman, but a tiger; a Tuscan Scylla—but more savage.
Ah, what's the use? If I cursed you all day, no remorse
Would touch you, for your heart's proof against feeling. Go!
Out of my sight, polluted fiend, child-murderer!
Leave me to mourn over my destiny: I have lost
My young bride; I have lost the two sons I begot
And brought up; I shall never see them alive again.

MEDEA

I would if necessary have answered at full length
Everything you have said; but Zeus the father of all
Knows well what service I once rendered you, and how
You have repaid me. You were mistaken if you thought
You could dishonour my bed and live a pleasant life
And laugh at me. The princess was wrong too, and so
Was Creon, when he took you for his son-in-law
And thought he could exile me with impunity.
So now, am I a tiger, Scylla?—Hurl at me
What names you please! I've reached your heart; and that is
    right.

JASON

You suffer too; my loss is yours no less.

MEDEA

                         It is true;
But my pain's a fair price, to take away your smile.

JASON

O children, what a wicked mother Fate gave you!

MEDEA

O sons, your father's treachery cost you your lives.

JASON

It was not my hand that killed my sons.

MEDEA

                       No, not your hand;
But your insult to me, and your new-wedded wife.

JASON
> You thought *that* reason enough to murder them,
>> that I
> No longer slept with you?

MEDEA
>> And is that injury
> A slight one, do you imagine, to a woman?

JASON
>>> Yes,
> To a modest woman; but to you—the whole world lost.

MEDEA
> I can stab too: your sons are dead!

JASON
>>> Dead? No! They live—
> To haunt your life with vengeance.

MEDEA
>>> Who began this feud?
> The gods know.

JASON
>> Yes—they know the vileness of your heart.

MEDEA
> Loathe on! Your bitter voice—how I abhor the
>> sound!

JASON
> As I loathe yours. Let us make terms and part at once.

MEDEA
> Most willingly. What terms? What do you bid me
>> do?

JASON
> Give me my sons for burial and mourning rites.

MEDEA
> Oh, no! I will myself convey them to the temple
> Of Hera Acraea; there in the holy precinct I
> Will bury them with my own hand, to ensure that none
> Of my enemies shall violate or insult their graves.
> And I will ordain an annual feast and sacrifice
> To be solemnized for ever by the people of Corinth,
> To expiate this impious murder. I myself
> Will go to Athens, city of Erechtheus, to make my home

With Aegeus son of Pandion. You, as you deserve,
Shall die an unheroic death, your head shattered
By a timber from the Argo's hull. Thus wretchedly
Your fate shall end the story of your love for me.

JASON
  The curse of children's blood be on you!
  Avenging Justice blast your being!

MEDEA
  What god will hear your imprecation,
  Oath-breaker, guest-deceiver, liar?

JASON
  Unclean, abhorrent child-destroyer!

MEDEA
  Go home: your wife waits to be buried.

JASON
  I go—a father once; now childless.

MEDEA
  You grieve too soon. Old age is coming.

JASON
  Children, how dear you were!

MEDEA
  To their mother; not to you.

JASON
  Dear—and you murdered them?

MEDEA
  Yes, Jason, to break your heart.

JASON
  I long to fold them in my arms;
  To kiss their lips would comfort me.

MEDEA
  Now you have loving words, now kisses for them:
  Then you disowned them, sent them into exile.

JASON
  For God's sake, let me touch their gentle flesh.

MEDEA
  You shall not. It is waste of breath to ask.

JASON

    Zeus, do you hear how I am mocked,
    Rejected, by this savage beast
    Polluted with her children's blood?

    But now, as time and strength permit,
    I will lament this grievous day,
    And call the gods to witness, how
    You killed my sons, and now refuse
    To let me touch or bury them.
    Would God I had not bred them,
    Or ever lived to see
    Them dead, you their destroyer!
    During this speech the chariot has moved out of sight.

CHORUS

    Many are the Fates which Zeus in Olympus dis-
        penses;
    Many matters the gods bring to surprising ends.
    The things we thought would happen do not happen;
    The unexpected God makes possible;
    And such is the conclusion of this story.

THE BACCHAE   **Preface**

IT IS FITTING THAT THE LAST-WRITTEN GREEK DRAMA TO SURVIVE INTO modern times takes as its subject the element from which tragedy originally evolved—the worship of Dionysus. Euripides wrote *The Bacchae,* named for its chorus of female devotees of Bacchus (a popular name for Dionysus), while in his self-imposed Macedonian exile. In 405 B.C., a year after Euripides' death, his son produced it at the Great Dionysia, where it won the author a posthumous first prize. Unlike Euripides' more episodic plays, *The Bacchae* is tightly-knit, dramatically unified, and well-constructed. But while its structure is formal and correct, its content is savage and violent. Although its power and force are undeniable, *The Bacchae* is also the most puzzling and difficult of all Greek plays to interpret.

    The plot is a dramatization of the ancient legend about Pentheus, the rash young king of Thebes who foolishly opposed the establishment of Dionysus' religion. The Pentheus myth is one of many concerning the early introduction of the Dionysian cult into Greece and the opposition with which it was often met by those who considered its irrational and mystic elements un-Greek. The action of the drama is entirely controlled by Dionysus, who appears first in human form to give Pentheus an opportunity to accept the new religion and then, at the denouement, appears in divine glory to punish those who had rejected him. The two contrasting aspects of the god—who is both bestower of ecstatic delight to those who accept his gifts, and a pitiless destroyer of those who deny his divinity—are indicated by the frightening change in his appearance at the end of the play. Dionysus first enters as a gentle, smiling, almost effeminate youth with flowing golden curls and a dainty manner. In this guise, he allows himself to be insulted and imprisoned by Pentheus, who obstinately refuses to acknowledge Dionysus' right to be adored. But after the death of Pentheus, Dionysus manifests the other side of his nature: in the epiphany he stands revealed as a horned beast, the terrible symbol of his awesome power.

In the long prologue which opens the play, Dionysus announces his intention of humbling Pentheus and forcing Thebes to accept the ecstatic cult which the Asian Baccantes have imported from the Near East. The god manifests himself to Thebes before any other Greek city because it is the home of his human mother, the Theban princess Semele, daughter of old Cadmus and sister of Agave.[1] Already, Dionysus says, he has possessed the native Theban women, including Pentheus' mother Agave, and driven them to the mountains, where, clothed in fawnskins and carrying the thyrsus,[2] they dance in god-inspired frenzy. "This town," he says, "must learn, even against their will that the divine can make the human." Like Iago, Dionysus is able to predict in advance how he will manipulate the other characters. In proof of his divinity, the action of the play springs entirely from Dionysus' original intent to demonstrate his godhood and his correct reading of Pentheus' hubristic character.

No play has more puzzled its critics or inspired a wider variety of interpretation. Rationalists of the last century saw it as Euripides' final attack on religious and emotional excess. They cast Pentheus as the upholder of Greek Reason bravely opposing the destructive emotionalism of a foreign cult. According to this view, *The Bacchae* is a bitter condemnation of the irrational forces which Dionysus represents. Unfortunately for this reading of the play, Pentheus is much too narrow and arrogant to embody the cause of Reason. His stubborn resistance to the universal appeal of the new religion is too fanatical and too blind to be an enlightened response.

---

[1]Dionysus is the son of Zeus and Semele. Here, jealous of Zeus's infatuation with the mortal woman, tricked Semele into persuading her divine lover to appear in his full glory. When he did so, Semele was consumed in the lightening flash. From her ashes Zeus saved the unborn infant, who was later reborn as Dionysus. The sacred fire burning at Semele's tomb (mentioned in the prologue) is the eternal flame lit by Zeus's thunderbolt.

[2]A symbol of Dionysus' procreative powers, the thrysus was a short spear garlanded in ivy, an obvious substitute for the phallus.

The significance of Dionysus is no more certain. Perhaps it is helpful to regard him as the personification of certain instinctual drives in man. He is not only a symbol of sexual energy and the ecstasy that springs from throwing off the inhibitions of reason, he is also the gift of life itself: sensuality, joy, intoxication, and illusion. He is what Pentheus rashly tries to live without—a recognition that man is part of the universal life force. It is a bond with nature that must not be reasoned but *felt*. Pentheus' rejection of Dionysian ecstasy is no more "reasonable" than Hippolytus' denial that Love has no hold on him. Both men are wrong and both are destroyed by the power they deny. Pentheus' terrible fate is neither just nor unjust. It is simply a demonstration of pure fact: natural forces, be they within or without the mind of man—lightening bolts or psychological instincts—are amoral and dangerous. Whatever Euripides' intentions in writing *The Bacchae*, its impact is unmistakable, and its meaning magnificently ambiguous.

THE BACCHAE

Characters

DIONYSUS
CHORUS OF ASIAN BACCHAE
TEIRESIAS
KADMUS
PENTHEUS
ATTENDANT
FIRST MESSENGER
SECOND MESSENGER
AGAVE
CORYPHAEUS (CHORUS LEADER)

DIONYSUS
I, Dionysus, son of Zeus, borne by Semele,
And delivered from her womb by the lightning
Fire, have come back here where I was born,
To this land called Thebes.
               Here I stand,
By the two river streams, Ismenos
And limpid Dirke,
               A God, in mortal shape.

The Bacchae, translated by Minos Volanakis, is reprinted from *Euripides* (The Laurel Classical Drama Series), published by Dell Publishing Company, New York. Copyright 1965 by Minos Volanakis. Reprinted by permission of the translator.

Here, I can see my mother's tomb,
—Monument to the bride of thunder—
The ruins of her rooms, still smoldering
Under the living flame
Of Zeus.
            And I have praise for Kadmus,[1]
Her old father, who consecrated the ground,
Untrodden sanctuary to his dead daughter.
And I enshrined it with the green sprays
Of clustering vine.
                    Leaving behind me,
The golden lands of Lydia and Phrygia,
Far behind me, the sun-beaten Persian plains,
Media's harsh winters, blessed Arabia,
And all that part of Asia by the transparent sea,
Where Greeks and Orientals swarm together
In towering, teeming cities,
                            Leaving them
Dancing my sacred dance, and observing
The rituals I have established,
I have come here,
                    To Thebes, before any other
Greek city,
            To unveil myself to mortal eyes,
A God Manifest.
First in Thebes, of all Greek cities,
I have raised my holy cry,
                            From throats
Upturned, the quivering body clothed
In wild fawnskin, the thyrsus, the ivy
Spear I gave them, piercing the sky,
First in Thebes;
                    And this is the reason:
It was first in Thebes that the sisters
Of my mother—Queen Agave and the rest—
They, who ever if true, should be the last
To admit it—said Dionysus is not
The son of Zeus.
                    They said Semele mated
With a mortal man, and, when found pregnant,
Kadmus, her old father, blamed the shame on Zeus
To protect her name.
                    And they proclaimed
Semele's lie drew down on her divine wrath,

---

[1]*Kadmus*—Cadmus, father of Semele and Agave. He is the former king of Thebes,
which his grandson Pentheus now rules.

And that was why Zeus' thunderbolt
Had struck her dead.
                    This is the reason
I goaded these women into frenzy,
Drove them raving from their palace
To the mount'n, their wits unhinged.
And I have stung all the women of this town
Manic, to follow Kadmus' daughters;
And there all live wandering on the roofless rocks,
The fragrant fir trees their only home.
This town must learn, even against their will,
That the divine can make the human,
And I must vindicate Semele, my mortal
Mother, by manifesting myself
To dying eyes,
                    As the God she bore to Zeus.
Now,
        Old King Kadmus has surrendered
His throne and all his kingly honors
To his grandson Pentheus, son of Agave,
One of the royal sisters.
                    And Pentheus
Is fighting a god.
He proscribes me from all libations in his kingdom,
And never whispers my name in his prayers.
And I will prove to him, and the whole town,
            that I am,
                    One of the Powers.
And when I have set everything in order here
I will move to other lands and prove myself.
And if the men of Thebes, in their anger,
Take up arms, and try
To drive the possessed women home by force,
I will join the army of my Bacchae
And lead them into battle.
                    This is the reason
I have confined my divinity
Into a mortal shape, and appear
In the likeness of a
            man.
But you, my Bacchae, my holy band,
Women, who, leaving the golden Tmolus
And the hills of Lydia, have followed me;
My fellow revelers, my companions in rest,
Raise your native rhythm on the Phrygian
Tambourines.

       Surround the palace of Pentheus
With loops of music.
          On, Bacchae,
Make the whole town turn and look!
And I can go to the glens of Cithaeron,[2]
Where the Bacchae of Thebes are reveling,
         And join their dances.

CHORUS
  On, Bacchae, on, Bacchae,
  Bringing Dionysus,
          —On, Bacchae—
  From the Lydian hills,
  To the opening streets
         Of Greece,
  Bringing Bromius,[3]
         —On, Bacchae.
  From the lands of Asia,
  And the sacred Tmolus,
  I have followed the call
         Of my God,
  For him labor is sweet,
  And weariness is strength;
  In his service is
         The only freedom.
  Let my cry resound to
         Iacchos[4]
         IACCHOS!
      Who is here? Who is here?
      Somebody's here!
  On, Bacchae
From the Lydian hills
To the opening streets
         Of Greece—
      Who is here? Who is here?
      Who?
      Somebody's here!
        —Out here in the street
          In there in the palace—
          Somebody's listening!
  Let him withdraw.
  Let every lip
  Keep hallowed silence.

---

[2]*Cithaeron*—mountainous area near Thebes; it was later held sacred to Dionysus.
[3]*Bromius*—"the thunderer," an epithet of Dionysus.
[4]*Iacchos*—another name for Dionysus.

  I will sing
  The ritual hymn
    To Dionysus.
Oh,
Blessed is he,
The fortunate man
Who knows the God-
given mysteries—
And consecrates his life
In holy ritual.
Who breaks the one prison
The one soul,
And joins the holy ecstasy
Up in the mount'n
    in the mount'n
Pure.
  Thyrsus in hand
  Crowned with ivy
  Serving Dionysus.
Oh, Thebes, that gave birth to Semele,
    The mother of God,
Oh, Thebes,
    Now, be crowned with ivy!
    Burst into flower
    Burst, burst
      Into flowering bryony!
   Go wild![5]
   Let wild sprays
   Of fir trees
    And oak,
  Burst
  Shoot through the stones,
  Burst into flower!
  Shake, shake,
Soon the whole land
  Will shake, shake
  And dance!
Dance round the thyrsus,
  In adoration
  Of its power,
  Brute Thyrsus,
  Inhuman rod!
Soon the whole land will shake
    And dance,

---

[5]*Go wild!*—This is the supreme command of the Dionysian religion. Note that the chorus of Asian Bacchae sing and dance with complete ecstatic abandon.

Dionysus,
Dionysus leads the way!
Up to the mount'n!

Mount'n!
The mount'n
Where.

The Women of Thebes, leaving
Their looms and their weaving,
Are dancing already,
Goaded by the sting

Of Dionysus!

—Oh,
What delight in the mount'n,
When from the dancing band

Swift-streaming,
One falls
One flings
Himself

On the ground, warm to touch,
The holy fawnskin clinging
To the body,

And there he hunts,
He hunts for blood,
Of the slaughtered

Hill goat,
The red quick fount'n
The blessing of the raw flesh.

Oh, Bromius, Bromius
On the Lydian Hills!

And the earth is flowing with milk,
Flowing wine and the nectar of bees,
The air sings with the scent of myrrh

Streaming from the flame
Of the pine-torch,
Our leader brandishes,

Oh, Bromius,

Still running, EVOHI,[6]
Still leaping,
Rousing the straggling bands,
EVOHI,
Up, up, from the ground,
Their feet
Ecstatic
The air vibrating
EVOHI,

---

[6]*Evohi*—an ecstatic cry invoking Iacchos (Dionysus).

As he shakes
His delicate tresses to the tender
wind,
Swirling,
EVOHI,
Swirling,
Calling on them:
ON, BACCHAE, ON, BACCHAE,
The Grace of Lydia,
On, Bacchae,
Bring Dionysus,
Thump your thunderous drums
Thump your thunderous drums,
EVOHI,
Bromius,
My God of Joy,
Sing your Phrygian songs
Sing your Phrygian songs
Shout!
While the melodious reeds
Shout!
While the whispering reeds,
Sing
Sacred, sacred games
Shout!
With the pulse of the feet
And the beat of the drum,
EVOHI!
In the Mount'n
Mount'n
Where every Bacchae swirls
And leaps for joy,
Like a foal at pasture,
Free!

TEIRESIAS[7]
Is anybody here? Call Kadmus out
The old man from Siden who, when young and king,
Built this city.
Go on somebody. Tell him.
Teiresias wants him—he knows what for.
Tell him I hold my thyrsus and wear my fawnskin
My head is crowned with sprays of ivy—
To keep the agreement between two very old men.
He is even older.

---

[7]*Teiresias*—Tiresias, the blind prophet, the same who appears in *Oedipus the King*.

KADMUS
                        Sweet friend,
I knew your voice, while still inside the palace.
Wise voice of a wise man, I thought.
Well, here I am, in the apparel the god demands,
Ready to serve him. We must do all we can
To build him up into a very great God indeed,
This Dionysus, born into mortality,
Because he was the son of my own daughter.
Where shall we dance? Where shall we shake a leg,
And stamp, and toss our venerable heads!
Explain it all to me, Teiresias, guide me?
None but the old can lead the old, and you are
The expert. I shall not tire banging the rhythm
With my thyrsus day and night, on the dark earth.
Ah, it is sweet to forget we are old.

TEIRESIAS
I feel I suffered the same transformation.
I'm full of sap; I must attempt the dance.

KADMUS
Could we not take a carriage to the mountain?

TEIRESIAS
That would not show equal reverence to the god.

KADMUS
Must I then guide you by the hand—
Like an old nurse a very old baby?

TEIRESIAS
The god will guide us there, without an effort.

KADMUS
We cross the town then? Dancing? We, alone?

TEIRESIAS
We alone are sensible; the rest are foolish.

KADMUS
We are wasting time. Here take my hand.

TEIRESIAS
Here's mine. Get hold of it. Go on, grip tight.

KADMUS
Be all witness I do not scorn the god.

TEIRESIAS
We do not try to understand the gods.
No, not through mortal cleverness.
And the traditions we have inherited
From our fathers, myths coeval with time,
No argument can spoil no subtlety
From even the most ingenious brains.
You think it's ludicrous at my age
To frisk about with a crown of ivy?
The god makes no distinction between young
And old, who should dance and who should not.
He wants from all equal honor.

KADMUS
                    Teiresias,
As second sight is the only sight you have,
Let me play the seer to you: Pentheus,
My grandson, is coming towards the palace—
King Pentheus, now that I have given him
All power over the state.
                    He looks upset.
Something is going to happen.

PENTHEUS
I was away from this town, when I heard
New evils have descended on our land.
Women have left their homes, pretending
Bacchic ecstasy, and run off to the woods,
Took to the hills, where they dance in honor
Of this upstart god, this Dionysus, whoever that is.
And bowls of wine stand apparently in the middle,
And now the one and now the other woman
Steals off to lonely, god-forgotten places
Where they serve the lust of men, pretending
To be holy maenads, but in fact, they
Offer themselves in sacrifice
To Aphrodite before Bacchus.
Those I have caught already, guards and manacles
Are keeping safe in the state prison.
Those still at large up in the hills,
                    I WILL HUNT,
And I am not going to spare even Agave,
My own mother, let alone her sisters,
Ino and Autonoe. And once they are in chains,
We'll see the end of these obscene orgies.
    I have also heard a stranger has arrived,

A magician from Lydia, fair hair,
A wine-red glow on his face and lips,
The grace of Aphrodite in his eyes,
A charmer, yes. And he manages to be
With our girls, day and night, enticing
Them into the secret joys of this mysterious cult.
If only I ever catch him and bring him
Here, under this floor, I will put an end
To all this thyrsus waving—I will stop
That hair-tossing, those curls perfuming
The winds—unless his head can dance without
His body.
        He is the one who claims Dionysus
To be a god, to have survived sown-up
In the thigh of Zeus—a likely story—
Dionysus, who was just burnt with his mother,
Burnt by lightning, because she'd lied,
She's claimed that Zeus had slept with her.
        But here's another miracle; I see
Teiresias, in the latest fawnskin fashion,
And my own mother's father—sir,
This is ridiculous!—thyrsus in hand,
Playing the Bacchant. Father, I'm deeply ashamed
To see old age without sense. Shake off
That chain of ivy; get rid of that stick;
Your head, your hands should always be free;
You were the king; you are my mother's father!
        You talked him into this, Teiresias,
It's all your doing: how useful, a new god!
More sacrifices, new burnt offerings
And divinations from birds: new profits.
If your extreme old age were not protecting you,
You'd find yourself in chains with your Bacchae,
For introducing such pernicious practices.
When in a women's feast the wine flows,
Believe me, do not expect anything wholesome.

CHORUS
  Oh stranger, oh King, have you no respect
  For the gods! No respect for Kadmus?
  Who sowed the seed of earthborn men? You,
  Son of Echion,
  Will you shame your own roots?

TEIRESIAS
  When in an argument, a clever man
  Is given a good opening, it's no great feat

To speak well. Your tongue is glib, and makes noises
That sound like sense, and yet their sense's unsound.
And a strongheaded man who can speak plausibly
Is a danger to the state, if he has no judgment.
This god, yes, this new god you are making fun of,
I can't begin to say how great he'll prove
Throughout Greece.

      Young man, there are two principles
Supreme in human order:[8] the first is Demeter,
The Mother Earth; by whatever name you call her
She stands for Bread, and feeds our mortal mouths
With solid food.

      And now, here comes the other,
The son of God born to the virgin,
Bringing the counter-gift to bread: wine.
He brought release from the sorrows of flesh;
When replete with blood of grape, sleep comes,
And the oblivion of each day's stale burden,
And there is no other balm for the weariness
Of living.
His blood, a god's blood,
Is poured to the other gods in sacrifice,
And in his name mankind is blessed.

      And this god is also a prophet. His
Ecstasy and bacchic mania have prophecy in it.
When too much god descends into one body
It overshoots time, and the maddened voice
Foretells the future. And he has a share
In the domain of Ares, the God of War.
A whole army in perfect order, with arms
And banners, may break in sudden panic
Before a single spear clangs. This kind
Of madness also comes from Dionysus.
And I predict you'll see this god in Delphi
With pine-torches, dancing on the holy rocks,
Sharing Parnassus' twin mountain peaks
With Apollo himself, shaking and hurling
His drunken bacchic rod, great throughout
Greece. No, listen to me, Pentheus.

                Be not so sure

That force and order rule all-powerful
Over humanity. And be not governed
By one single certainty. That thought is sick,

---

[8]*Two principles supreme in human order*—In the following speech Tiresias argues that the rational man recognizes the power of irrationality and accords it an honorable place in his scheme of things.

Don't think it's wisdom. There is too much
We do not know. And a new god may well be
A very old law, though yet unwritten
And unnamed. Accept this deity in your state;
Submit to his mysteries; pour your libation
To him—come, wreathe your head.

As for the women,
It is not up to Dionysus to force them
To be chaste in love. It should be in their natures.
Kindly consider that. Even in the most
Abandoned figures of the Bacchic dance,
The really pure in heart won't be corrupted.

And then, you see, you are pleased, when
The whole town throngs to the palace gates, and
The people magnify the name of Pentheus: the god
Too, would, I think, delight in receiving honors.
So myself, and Kadmus—whom you find so funny—
Decked in our ivy shoots, are going to dance—
An ancient pair perhaps, yet dance we must—
And I will not be talked into god-fighting,
No, not by anything you say. Your mind
Thrashes about in fever, most painfully,
And it is not a drug would bring relief to it.

CHORUS

Old prophet of Apollo, your words
Bring credit to the god you serve. It is wise
To honor Dionysus.

KADMUS

My son, Teiresias gave you good counsel.
Come, join us, and do not fly against the laws.
Your wits are wandering above your head,
And you only think you are thinking.

And even if
This god did not exist—just as you say—
Still, you should be the first to claim he does.
The credit is worth a lie! Think: Semele,
My own daughter, proclaimed mother to a god,
A great honor to both of us and all our race.
And then, do not forget what has happened
To our house already; you saw the fate
Of my poor Actaion, your cousin, torn to pieces
By his own dogs, the hounds he'd raised and fed,
Because he boasted he was a greater hunter
Than Artemis herself.

You never know who hunts the hunter.
Come here, let me crown your head with ivy.
Honor this god with us—

PENTHEUS
                    Don't touch me!
Go, play the maenad but keep your hands away
From me. Don't try to infect me with your madness.
As for the grand teacher of your folly,
Here is the sentence: Somebody, quick,
Go to the rock, where this blind man divines
The future from the wing-beat of a bird,
And with crowbars and tridents, overthrow
The seat of augury, wreck everything
Upside down, open to the winds and tempests—
To the winds his holy ribans. This will sting him.
The rest of you, go comb, scour the town
For this effeminate stranger, stalk me
The girl-faced thing who introduces
This new disease to women, and preys
On their pollution. And when you catch him,
I want him here, in chains,
                    To meet his death
By stoning, a bitter end to his revelry in Thebes.

TEIRESIAS
Stiff-faced man,[9]
                    You do not know what you are saying.
Just now, you were going mad. Now you are insane.
Kadmus, let us go and pray for this man,
Although he's such a savage, and for the sake
Of the whole city. Pray God move not his arm.
Come, follow me. With your ivied thyrsus.
Now let me help you to redress your body.
Now you help me to stand up—we must support
Each other. It would be doubly shameful
For two old men to fall on their faces.
But let that pass. Now let us serve Dionysus,
And pray that Pentheus brings not mourning,
Kadmus, into your house.
                    I do not say all this
Through prophecy or divination,
But simply because I can face facts.
The blind can. The foolish cannot.

---

[9]*Stiff-faced man*—Pentheus' *hubris* completely blinds him to the merits of the new religion.

CHORUS
Holiness, revered by the Gods,
Holiness, spirit of respect,
Ranging with golden wing
                    Against the earth,
Can you hear Pentheus,
Can you hear his blasphemy
Against the son of Semele?
My god was born from the Joy
                    Of a dying woman,
Yet the immortals
Reclining in evergreen garlands
                    Honor his name.
His kingdom is the unity of souls
                    In the rhythm of dance,
His silence resounds in laughter
                    And the rejoicing reeds,
                    His touch releases from care,
                    When the weary reveler rests
                    And around his head wreathed in ivy
                    Entwine the cool vine-tendrils of sleep.
Holiness, revered by the Gods,
                    Did you hear
                    Pentheus' Hubris?
—Of unbridled mouths
And reckless folly
The end is disaster.
But a life of acceptance
And quiet discretion
Keeps the walls of the city
Unshaken, and the rooms
Of the house,
                    Together.
Far, far, in the undying
                    Ether
Live the heavenly ones
The nonhuman ones;
Yet they keep watch
On human time.
Cleverness is not wisdom.
Life is short.
Man should not wait
His downfall
To measure his height.
And hands that reach—
Beyond the grasp
Of the flesh—

Miss the present.
Life is short.

If I could only be in Pierria,
                    Or Cyprus,
Cyprus, Aphrodite's island,
Haunted by swarms of Eros,
                    The love-boys
Who enchant our mortal lives,
Or Paphos, where the hundred mouths
    Of the fertile river,
        Well out of the transparent sea
        To feed the sun-parched land,
Or Pierria, the gentle half of holy Olympus
    The home of Muses,
                    Oh, take me there,
                    Oh, take me there,
                    Bromius,
                            Bromius,
                    God of Many Voices,
                    God of Joy,
    There,
            There Live the Graces
            There Grows Desire,
    There the Bacchae are free to worship
                    Lead me there.
Dionysus,
    Delights in mirth
    And he loves EIRENE,[10]
                    The Goddess of Peace
                    The Goddess Serene
                    Who breeds him boys.
And wine, the cure of sorrow
He gives alike to rich and poor,
But dislikes the presumptuous man.
Accept each day. Accept the Night
And the friendly Dark; accept the Light.
What the simple, nameless man in the crowd
Believes and does—is enough wisdom for me.

GUARD
    King Pentheus, here's your prey.
                    This
    Is what you sent us hunting—and not in vain,
    As you can see.

---

[10]*Eirene*—one of the three Horae (Hours); daughter of Zeus and Themis, she is a personification of peace.

But this savage beast
Was so gentle to us; he did not try to run away but
Willingly held out his hands; and I cannot say he
Changed color, but smiling, always smiling, he
Asked us tie him up and take him—he even waited
For us; he made it all so easy, I felt ashamed and
Said:
          "Stranger,
"I do not bind you of my own free will,
"But to obey King Pentheus' orders."
And something else:
                    The women you chained,
Those bacchantes you threw into prison,
                                        They are gone,
They disappeared dancing on the meadows
Calling their God,
                  "Bromius, Bromius,
                  "My God of Joy,"
They called, their chains fell by themselves,
Their legs danced free, the prison doors flew back
Untouched—
          King, this man has brought to Thebes
A swarm of miracles, here to this town.
                                        But what
You will do now is your concern. Not mine.

PENTHEUS

Let go his hands. He is in the net.[11]
He may be quick, but not enough to escape me.
                                        Now.

The figure is seductive, I admit,
I mean to women, stranger, no doubt
What you are here for.
                      And not exactly
A wrestler—not with those long curls flowing
Down the line of neck—inviting desire.
The skin is fair—you take great care of your
Complexion. Far from the arrows of the sun, you hunt
In shadows the body's pleasure with that beauty.
First of all, where do you come from?
                                      Answer me.

DIONYSUS

Easy to say. Why should I hesitate?
You must have heard of Tmolus, the Flower-Hills.

---

[11]*He is in the net*—Pentheus' words are ironic: while believing himself to be in control of the situation, he has fallen into Dionysus' trap.

PENTHEUS
That surround the town of Sardis—yes.

DIONYSUS
I come from there. Lydia is my country.

PENTHEUS
And why do you bring these rituals to Greece?

DIONYSUS
A god descended upon us, Dionysus
                               Son of Zeus.

PENTHEUS
Is there another Zeus in Lydia,
                        Who spawns new gods?

DIONYSUS
The same Zeus who loved Semele here.

PENTHEUS
And was it in a dream, or to your open eyes
This god appeared and took possession of you?

DIONYSUS
                          Face to open face.
And he entrusted the signs of his rites to me.

PENTHEUS
What kind of signs?

DIONYSUS
                              I cannot say.
His secrets must be kept from unbelievers.

PENTHEUS
And what do the believers gain from them?

DIONYSUS
That's not for you to hear—although worth hearing.

PENTHEUS
Cleverly coined; to make me want to know.

DIONYSUS
The rites of god abhor the impious.

PENTHEUS
This god of yours; you say you saw him clearly.
What was he like?

DIONYSUS
> What he wished to be;
> I have no command over god's face and shape.

PENTHEUS
> Cleverly sidetracked again; this means nothing.

DIONYSUS
> Wisdom to the unwise means nothing.

PENTHEUS
> And you came straight here, bringing him first
>   to Thebes?

DIONYSUS
> The whole East dances his mysteries.

PENTHEUS
> Oriental mentality is lower than ours.

DIONYSUS
> On this matter, higher. Their ways differ.

PENTHEUS
> Do you worship by day or night?

DIONYSUS
> Mostly by night. Darkness secretes holiness.

PENTHEUS
> Darkness corrupts women to impurity.

DIONYSUS
> You can find impurity by daylight, too.

PENTHEUS
> He's insolent and not unskilled in words.
> You'll pay for this pernicious sophistry.

DIONYSUS
> And you will pay for your ignorance. And blasphemy.
> Tell me what I am to suffer. What will you do?

PENTHEUS
> I will begin with your hair; those delicate curls
> > I'll cut!

DIONYSUS
> It's dedicated to my god; if you touch one hair,
> > You touch him.

PENTHEUS
Give me this thyrsus.

DIONYSUS
Raise your hand and take it.
It's the god's own.

PENTHEUS
As for this body, we'll treasure it,

—In our prison!

DIONYSUS
My god will set me free, whenever I wish.

PENTHEUS
You'd only have to stand amongst the women
And call him?

DIONYSUS
He is not far; even now he sees what I endure.

PENTHEUS
Where is he? I see no sign of him.

DIONYSUS
Where I am, disbelief stops you from seeing the sign.

PENTHEUS
Take him away.
He's shown contempt for us and for our State.

DIONYSUS
Do not bind me.
I, master of my mind, warn you who have lost yours.

PENTHEUS
And I say bind him,
I, who am stronger and master of your body.

DIONYSUS
You do not know what you are doing. What life
You are living.
You do not know who you are.

PENTHEUS
I am PENTHEUS. Son of Agave and Echion.

DIONYSUS
You shall repent even your name.

PENTHEUS

Take him away.
Throw him into the stud-stalls where the beasts breed;
He likes the dark; then let him dance
In the underground night.

As for the women
You lured along to assist you in evil—
I will sell them all as slaves, or keep them
As my property—put them at the looms;—that
Will stop their hands from thumping on those drums.

DIONYSUS

I am ready.
What is not to be I will not have to suffer.
Dionysus—who you say does not exist—
Will not let your hubris pass unpunished.
In wronging me you are leading him to prison.

CHORUS

Dirke, holy river

Virgin river,
Dirke, Acheloos' daughter,

Why do you deny my God?
You first welcomed Dionysus
The holy infant
The son of Zeus
In your always welling water
Cleansing water

Crying:
"Dithyrambos, twice-born[12]
"Enter my thigh, a father's womb,
"Twice-born,
"A day will come
"Under this name you will be blessed."

Yet now
Oh Dirke, blessed river
Virgin river,
My head is crowned with holy ivy
And yet you shun me,
You draw away from my dancing feet,
Why do you fear me?
Why do you reject me?
A time will come
My lord of the clustering vine

---

[12]*Dithyrambos, twice-born*—an epithet of Dionysus; when Semele was consumed in the lightning bolt, Zeus placed their unborn child in his thigh, from which it was "born" a second time as Dionysus.

By your waters
Dionysus name will be blessed.
Oh, what hate,
What hate breeds in Pentheus'
Murderous clay,
The earth-colored King!
He's not in vain
The Dragon's offspring
Challenging the gods!
Oh, in prison
To prison he'll throw me,
In chains these hands
That belong to the god,
My comrade in chains already,
He's already in the dark!

Where are you, my lord?
Can you see, son of Zeus,
Your prophets, your followers
In their hour of need?

Come down
From Olympus, my god,
Brandish your golden thyrsus
And crush this man's impiety,
Come down!
Where are you, my lord?
If only we knew you were dancing on Nyssa,
The mother mount'n the nurse of wild beasts,
Or hurling your thyrsus on Parnassus?
Perhaps on the craggy Corycian heights,
Perhaps in the foliage halls of Olympus,
Green-walled,
Green-roofed,
Where Orpheus' music assembled once
—Humming around his lyre—
The slow trees,
And the beasts of the forest,
Serene.
Oh, blessed is Pierria,
Happy Macedonia,
Dionysus loves you,
Evohi!
Bromius, Bromius,
My God of joy.
He will be there one day,
Crossing the rivers,

Swift flowing Axios,
Curling Aliakmon,
With the winding line of his maenads,
Coiling and uncoiling in their dance.
He will reach Lydias,
The Father river,
Generous to mortals,
Begetter of stallions;
And the prosperous land
That drinks his sweet nourishing stream,
Content.
Where are you, my lord?

DIONYSUS
Io, Io,

Hear me, hear my voice,
Io, Bachae!

CHORUS
What was this,
This voice, wherefrom this voice,
This sudden god?

DIONYSUS
Io, Io,
I call again,
The son of Semele, the son of Zeus!

CHORUS
Io, Io, my Lord,
Come to your company,
Bromius, Bromius,
Lord of Thunder!

DIONYSUS
Oh, holy Earthquake,
Awake
And shake the earth's foundations!

CHORUS
Ah, ah,
The palace will crumble and fall
—Dionysus is in the palace!
—Bow before him!
—We bow before him!
—LOOK!
The lintels on the columns come apart!
—Let the cry of my god burst the roof open!

DIONYSUS
Burn, lightning,
    Blaze,
        Turn
Pentheus' house to a torch!

CHORUS
                        Ah, ah,
Can't you see,
The fire in the tomb of Semele,
                        Leaps up!
The fire of death, gift of heaven!
Down, maenads,
Hurl to the ground those trembling bodies!
The lord is here,
                Wrecking the palace!
                Down!
He comes, the son of Zeus!

DIONYSUS
Women be not afraid.
Has fear struck you into the ground?
                    Why crawl like this?
You felt God shattering the house of Pentheus.
Cast off this trembling from your flesh.
                            Look up!

CHORUS
Ah, what wild great light was your voice to me!
—How good to see your face.
—I was alone and deserted.

DIONYSUS
You lost all hope when I was taken prisoner
And buried into Pentheus' dungeon?

CHORUS
Who will protect me if you meet with evil?
—How did you escape that man of sin?

DIONYSUS
I delivered myself; easily; without effort.

CHORUS
But your arms were bound?

DIONYSUS
                    That's where I fooled him.
He never laid his hands on me, not even touched me,
But fed on fantasies; there, in the manger,

Where they breed the sacrificial animals,
A bull was ready; and there his majesty
Fastened his ropes on horns and hoofs, with great
Sweating and panting and gnashing of the teeth,
Taking the bull for me—while I just stood by,
Watching him,
                        Untouched.
                                    And then all of a sudden,
The god was there, shattering the palace,
And flames flared up out of his mother's tomb.
And the king thinking the palace was on fire,
Rushed here and there, ordering the servants
To bring water and more water, and Acheloos
The river, until it was all confusion,
                                    And all
For nothing.
            Thinking I escaped, he rushed after.
And seeing a phantom, a double of myself
In one of the inner courts, a phantom
Dionysus created—at least, I think created,
How should I know—he sprang triumphantly,
And with his black sword he hacked the air,
The sunny translucent void, happy he was killing me.
                        But Dionysus
Knew more ways of abasing him.
                                    His palace
—Look!—lies in ruins, ghost of a building,
A bitter reminder of the way he tried to
Chain me underground. Bitter
                        Now
In his empty exhaustion he dropped his sword,
A worn-out man, confused. Dog-fighting,
                        god-fighting.
                        —And I just walked out.
But I think I hear the thump of heavy boots.
He's coming out into the courtyard.
                                    Don't be afraid.
I shall be easy with him; let his rage blow high.

PENTHEUS
    Insufferable. Evil.
    Gone. The man was chained but gone—
                                    Ah.
    He's there. Why here? How dare you
    Stand on show outside my palace?
    How did you escape?

DIONYSUS
>   Your anger treads
> Too heavily; a lighter step will get you nearer.

PENTHEUS
> How did you escape from your chains?

DIONYSUS
> Did I not say, or didn't you hear me?
> Someone would set me free?

PENTHEUS
>   Who?
> You always speak mysteriously.

DIONYSUS
> He who makes grow the clustering vine.

PENTHEUS
> Lock the gates of the castle! Guard the ramparts!

DIONYSUS
> You think a god can't overleap a wall?

PENTHEUS
> You know everything except what concerns you.

DIONYSUS
> That I know best.
>   But listen to this man.
> He's coming from the mountain with news for you.
> We shall wait your pleasure—do not worry.
> We shall not try to run away.

HERDSMAN
>   Pentheus,
> King of this land, I've run all the way
> From Cithaeron, the very top of the mountain,
> Where shafts of snow always dazzle the eye!

PENTHEUS
> And what was the reason for such hurry?

HERDSMAN
> I saw the holy Bacchae.
>   Yes, the same women
> Who goaded by sacred madness, vanished
> From this town by night, and nothing was seen

Of their nakedness but a swift white gleam
Of disappearing feet. And I have rushed
My king, to tell you, you and your town,
What fantastic things the maenads do,
Wonders beyond nature.
                              But first,
Can I speak openly or better trim my words?
The truth is, I'm afraid of your quick temper,
My king, and your sharp anger is truly royal.

PENTHEUS

Speak. Nothing to fear from me. You are not
Responsible. It would be unjust to punish
A man simply because he speaks the truth.
But the stranger your story about the maenads,
The more terrible the punishment will be
Of this man here who polluted our women.

HERDSMAN

I was driving my cattle uphill, towards
The meadow near the ridge—just as the first
Morning sunbeam began warming the earth—
When suddenly I saw three bands of women
Sleeping: one led by Ino; the other by Agave
Your mother, my king, the third by Antonoe—
All asleep; their easy limbs sunk into rest;
Their heads light on a bed of oak leaves or fireboughs;
And a sober and modest sight they were, too,
Not, as you said, lured by wine and the sound of flutes
To hunt through the lonely woods the pleasures of
        the body,
                    But your mother, warned
By the lowing of our horned bulls, sprang up; her voice
Rang out calling the Bacchae to heave their bodies
Out of their dreams; and they, brushing
The green leaves of sleep from their eyes, were up,
All in one calm moment, a miracle of order.
And there were old women and young, and girls
Who have not known yet the weight of man.
Hair flowing loose down their necks and arms
They tightened their fawnskins, and some
Were girding their waist with live snakes—yes,
I can still see the flickering tongues.
                                Some,
Cradling in their arms a wild wolf-cub, or
A young fawn, they gave the furry thing their
        milk to suck,
Young mothers, their newborn left at home,

Their breasts still teeming. Others were busy
Wreathing themselves with ivy tendrils
And sprays of oak or flowering bryony.

One of them took a thyrsus and struck the rock;
And a limpid spurt of cool water gushed;
Another hit the ground and a fountain
Of wine sprang out; and those who wanted milk
Had only to scratch the surface of the earth
With their fingertips and the white stream flowed,
And from their ivy-bound thyrsus clear honey dripped.
Ah, if only you were there, my king, this god
You now accuse—you would have prayed to him.

And we, the herdsmen, and all the shepherds
Around there, we put our heads together
And argued about these terrible and strange things;
And one who has lived in town, one who has walked
In streets, a glib one, he said:
"You people, who live up here in Cithaeron
How about hunting Agave, the king's mother,
Lead her away from this madness, and do the king
  a service?"
    And we thought he spoke well,
And hid ourselves, there in the tangled-branched
Bushes, lurking.
    And when the time came,
The women began to whirl their thyrsus
And to sway into their Bacchic state,
And the cry of IACCHOS, IACCHOS, was swelling,
Calling their god, all those mouths with—
Suddenly—one common voice, one common movement:
    IACCHOS! IACCHOS! Lord of Joy!

And the mount'n danced with them, the beasts
Swayed drunk, and nothing remained unstirred
As they streamed by.
    But as it happened
Agave passed so close by me, I leaped out of my
Thicket, hoping to catch her; but she screamed out:
      "Oh, my swift hounds,
We are being hunted by these men,
      Follow me,
Armed with your thyrsus,
      Follow Me!"
And as the possessed women turned as one,
We, few men, fled—it was all we could to escape
Being torn alive.

But they fell barehanded on our
Cattle, browsing the fresh hill grass.
And you could see a woman, her arms outstretched
Tearing a lusty heifer, bellowing,
Her udders swollen. Another rending a calf
To pieces. You could see ribs, or a cloven foot
Thrown to the sky—and lumps of flesh, caught on
A branch, were hanging from the pine trees,
    blood dripping.
        And charging bulls, proud of the anger
Teeming in their horns, were staggered down,
By frail hands of girls, unnumbered—
And clawed clean of hide and flesh faster
Than you could blink your royal eyes—
        They,
Like birds on the wing borne by their own speed,
Swept down the fields by the river Asopos,
Where the Thebans harvest much heavy corn,
Down to the villages of Hyrie and Esythae
Like an enemy army spreading destruction.
They snatched small children from their doorsteps
And carried them on their shoulders without fastening
Without holding them. The children laughed
And did not fall. Nothing could stop them,
Not bronze, not iron, not even fire.
They nested flames on their hair
It did not burn them.
        And the villagers
In fury took up their arms to drive them out.
Then, my king, the terror was:
The sharp spears and javelins, thrown
Against the maenads, drew no blood,
But their thyrsus, hurled, opened wounds!
And women turned men to flight. No, not
Without some God's presence.
        When they returned
To the meadows they started from, where
The god had made his fountains flow for them,
They washed the blood from their hands,
And the stains on their cheeks were licked clean
By whispering serpents.
        This god, whoever
He is, my king, receive in our state.
He's mighty in many ways, and I have heard
He gave us the grape, and cure of sorrow—
That's what they say.
        Oh, let him live, my king,
Without wine we shall not know how to forget

Our small selves—and that will be the end of love,
And every other pleasure for us,
                              Mortals.

CHORUS
  I'm afraid to speak the words of the free
  In front of a king.
                    But it must be said:
  "Dionysus is a great God."

PENTHEUS
                    Here it comes,
  Creeping on us like a spreading fire,
  This Bacchic outrage, a disgrace in the eyes of
                                        Greece.
  There's no time to waste. Run to the Electran Gate.
  Call up all men who can carry a shield,
  Ride a fast horse, hurl a spear,
  Or make a bowstring sing, gather them all
                    —We march against the Bacchae!
  It is too much to suffer this from women.

DIONYSUS
  You hear me, and yet you do not listen
  To my words, Pentheus. But though I suffered
  In your hands, once more I warn you: Do not
  Raise arms against a god, but submit quietly
  To life. Dionysus will not let you drive his
  Bacchae from their hills of joy.

PENTHEUS
  No more from you—you have escaped, you are free,
  Give thanks for that—or back you go to prison.

DIONYSUS
  I'd sacrifice to him, rather than kick
  Against the pricks—a mortal angry with a god.

PENTHEUS
  I'll sacrifice
              Women's blood as they deserve;
  My offering will flood the glens of Cithaeron.

DIONYSUS
  You will all fly in great dishonor;
                              Frail
  Thyrsus will rout your shields of beaten bronze.

PENTHEUS
  This stranger is really impossible
  He will not hold his tongue, free or in prison.

DIONYSUS
Friend,
There's still time to end all this happily.

PENTHEUS
How? By submitting to my own slaves?
                                        Bring my armor!

DIONYSUS
I can lead these women back to Thebes
                                Without weapons.

PENTHEUS
Ha! This is a trap.

DIONYSUS
Why? When I offer to use my power
                                To save you all?

PENTHEUS
It's a conspiracy with them; a truce
Would let you go on with your unholy dancing.

DIONYSUS
The only agreement is between my god and me.

PENTHEUS
Where's my armor?
                        And you, stop talking.

DIONYSUS
Aah.
Wouldn't you like to see those women
                        Up in their mount'n?

PENTHEUS
That I would. I would give anything for that.
                                Any price in gold.

DIONYSUS
And what throws you suddenly into this
                        Great desire?

PENTHEUS
It would be torture for me to see them drunk.

DIONYSUS
And yet sweet to see that bitter sight?

PENTHEUS
>   I must admit it.
> Yes. Sit silently behind the pine trees
>   And just watch them.

DIONYSUS
> Even if you go secretly, they'll find you out.

PENTHEUS
>   I'll go openly.
>   You are right in that.

DIONYSUS
> Shall I, then, show you the way? Are you ready?

PENTHEUS
> Guide me there at once.
>   I cannot wait.

DIONYSUS
> The time has come to dress yourself
>   In a linen robe.

PENTHEUS
> What was this? I am no longer to be a man but
> Dress as a woman?

DIONYSUS
> They'll kill you if they catch you as a man.

PENTHEUS
>   I think you are right
> You really thought of everything
>   From the first moment.

DIONYSUS
> The god himself inspired me.

PENTHEUS
> And what's the best way to carry out
>   Your advice?

DIONYSUS
> Let us go not inside the palace;
>   And let me dress you.

PENTHEUS
> What kind of dress? You don't mean a woman's?
>   I'd be ashamed.

DIONYSUS
                    You changed your mind?
You yearn no longer to watch the maenads?

PENTHEUS
                    What kind of dress?
What did you say you will put on me?

DIONYSUS
First on your head: long flowing hair.

PENTHEUS
And then? What will my costume look like?

DIONYSUS
A long flowing gown; and on top a veil.

PENTHEUS
                    Anything more?

DIONYSUS
Only a thyrsus and a fawnskin.

PENTHEUS
I could never wear women's clothes.

DIONYSUS
If you join battle with the Bacchae,
                    There will be bloodshed.

PENTHEUS
It's true. I should go first alone
                    And spy on them.

DIONYSUS
Better go alone than, using violence, ask for violence.

PENTHEUS
But how can I cross the town
                    Unseen by the people?

DIONYSUS
You shall take lonely and deserted streets;
                    I will lead you.

PENTHEUS
Anything is better than being defied
                    By the Bacchae.
I want to go inside the palace
                    And think about it.

DIONYSUS
As you wish. My preparations are all made.
I am ready.

PENTHEUS
                    I will go in.
Perhaps I shall take arms against them,
Maybe I shall follow your advice.

DIONYSUS
                    Dionysus,
—And you are not far from here—
                                   Now
Demand your retribution.
                         First, drive him
Out of his mind into ecstatic madness.
While he's sane he'll never accept
To dress in women's clothes. But once
Outside the pale of reason, he will.

And the sound of laughter in the streets
At this effeminate sight.
Will repay me for his savage threats.

Now I must go and help him into the dress
He must wear for the visit to the world
Of the dead and prepare him for the hands of his mother
And the kill.
                    And he will know too late
Dionysus,
                    God most benevolent
To mortals, yet if his blessing is scorned
Into curse,
          God of inhuman Terror.

CHORUS
What price wisdom?
And what greater gift from the gods
Than to stretch a conquering arm
Over the enemy's head?
Good has many faces, I know.
Yet, let it always be on my side.

                    It hardly moves.
                         And yet
                         It races!
                    The strength of the gods,
                    A faithful hound!
                    It trails, it trails,
                         And points

At the arrogant two-footed prey,
Who, isolated in his senseless pride,
Does not submit to the god's advice
In the whisper of the leaves.

Time, time, and
Time again,
The hidden gods may well disguise
The creeping foot of lurking time,
Yet it suddenly pounces on the
impious man.
Oh, do not swim against time.
Consent to flow without effort
With the accepted creed.
Consent to truths
Uncreated
Before the stream of natural time
Sprang from the ground
In the spring of things.

Good has many faces—I know—
Yet let it always be on my side.

Oh,
Shall I ever set my foot again
—Ever again—
White feet gleaming in the dark,
Dancing all night long
—Long, long night—
My hair streaming to the dewy wind,
—Air! AIR!
Wind—

Like a foal at pasture, free.
Oh, fawn dancing on the grass
When she escapes the snares
The shouts,
—Listen, listen—
To the sounds of chase!
To the haste of hounds!
—Fast, fast—
Run through the woods
Run by the river,
Reach
The lonely, man-forgotten meadow,
Reach the shadow
Green
Like a foal at pasture,
Free.

> Oh, blessed is the man
> Who escapes the winter sea
> And wins his haven.
> Happy the man who rises free,
> Free above his own striving.
> Let other men in other ways
> Other men surpass in wealth or power.
> He who lives each day
> For the happiness each day offers
>   Him, I call Blessed.

DIONYSUS

You, eager to see what you should never see,
Ready for what you should not do—
                    Pentheus!
Come out of the palace and show yourself to me
Dressed as a woman, a maenad in frenzy to spy
Upon your mother and her company
                    —Come out!
You look exactly like one of Kadmus' daughters.

PENTHEUS

I seem to see a second sun behind the sun,
And I can see a second city behind the city,
And the castle with the seven gates—Look!—is **DOUBLE!**
And you, who lead the way for me, look like a bull,[13]
And horns have sprouted on your head! Were you
An animal before? Now, I am sure you are a bull!

DIONYSUS

The god is now with us, at peace with us,
He, who before was not propitious.
At last, now, you see all you ought to see.

PENTHEUS

How do I look? Don't I stand the way
Women stand? Like Agave, my mother?

DIONYSUS

Looking at you I think I see their very selves!
But wait—this curl is out of place; it should be
Tucked under the hood—as I arranged it.

PENTHEUS

It must have shaken loose as I twirled dancing
Indoors, whirling my head like a maenad.

---

[13]*You . . . look like a bull*—Completely possessed by the god, Pentheus can now recognize the brute power in Dionysus' nature. In the epiphany, Dionysus is probably revealed in animal (irrational) form.

DIONYSUS
>I'll set it straight;
>>It is our duty now
>To attend you and prepare you; lift your head.

PENTHEUS
>You set things right. I'm in your hands.

DIONYSUS
>Your girdle is all loose; the gown
>Should stream down to the feet in even folds.

PENTHEUS
>Perhaps you are right, it does not on this side
>—But on the left, I think, hangs beautifully.

DIONYSUS
>Won't you consider me the best of friends,
>When, to your surprise, you find the maenads
>As self-controlled as you are?

PENTHEUS
>Shall I hold the thyrsus in this hand,
>Or in the right—to look more like a bacchante?

DIONYSUS
>The right hand—and lift it with your right foot,
>Keeping the same time.
>>I like you now,
>You've shaken off your previous mind.

PENTHEUS
>Now I could just heave and shoulder the whole
>Cithaeron—and all those dancing women too—
>You don't believe I could?

DIONYSUS
>>If you wanted.
>Your mind was once diseased; now it has found itself.

PENTHEUS
>Shall we take crowbars? Or I just set
>My shoulder to the cliffs and wrench them out?

DIONYSUS
>Do not destroy the haunts of nymphs,
>>Where Pan is piping.

PENTHEUS

You are right.
It's not through force I must conquer women.
I'll hide my little body behind the fir trees.

DIONYSUS

I'll guide you to an ambush proper for a spy.

PENTHEUS

I shall catch them in the bushes, like mating birds,
Ensnared in the sweet mesh of their embraces.

DIONYSUS

So that is what you are setting out to watch.
You may catch them if they don't catch you first.

PENTHEUS

Lead me through the center of the city!
                    In all Thebes
I, alone, am man enough to dare do this!

DIONYSUS

You alone bear the burden for the city—
And the trial awaits you that you alone
Deserve. Follow me. I will be your guide
And your savior—I'll see you safe there;
Another will bring you home.[14]

PENTHEUS

                    Perhaps my mother!

DIONYSUS

You will be carried high—

PENTHEUS

                    What splendor!

DIONYSUS

A sight for all to see!

PENTHEUS

                    For that I go!

DIONYSUS

High up in your mother's arms!

PENTHEUS

                    You mustn't spoil me!

---

[14]*Another will bring you home*—Dionysus alludes to the imminent murder of Pentheus by his mother, who carries home her son's head as a trophy.

DIONYSUS
   There are ways and ways of spoiling!

PENTHEUS
   I'm ready for what is due me.

DIONYSUS
                           Terrifying,
   Ah, a terrifying man you are, Pentheus,
   And you walk towards a fate most terrifying.
   Your towering fame will pillar up heavens.
   Open your arms for the embrace, Agave,
   And you her sisters, seed of Kadmus.
   To his great Agon this young man I bring!
   I will be the Victor, I, and the God of Joy.
   The event will show the rest.

CHORUS
   Run, swift hounds
              Of Madness,
   Run, to the mount'n
              Where Kadmus'
                           Daughters
   Dance, swift hounds
                           go to them,
              Of Madness,
                           Goad them,
   To hunt, to track down
              The young man
                           Spying on them
                           Hiding
   Dressed as a woman
              The madman,
   Run, swift hounds.
              His own mother will spy him first, perhaps,
              Lurking behind a jagged rock, perhaps,
              Or behind the stump of a tree, perhaps,
                           And she will cry:
              "What man stalks the mountain,
              Maenads,
              What Kadmeian has come to the mount'n
                           Come to the mount'n
                                      Mount'n
                                      Mount'n
              Maenads?
              Who bore him, Bacchae, what brood
                           What mother?
              He did not spring of woman's blood.

A Libyan lioness, perhaps,
Or Gorgons that breed in the desert."
Justice, now reveal thyself!
Visible Justice,
Your visible sword,
Thrust through the throat
—Through and through—
Of the lawless,
Godless,
Unjust son
Of Echion,
Earthborn,
Earthbound!
Justice is balance.
In his unbalanced state
An impious anger rages
Against the almighty wind.
His mind is stark vacant
And his will, unhinged,
Flaps unavailingly
Against the almighty wind.
Death is the only corrective.
But he, who without question
Accepts his share of the possible,
To him a griefless life.
I do not envy knowledge.
I rejoice in hunting it.
But the other, open, staring
Ways that lead into good
I follow, night and day,
Respecting the hidden gods,
And not straying beyond
The pale of Justice.
Justice, now reveal yourself!
Visible justice,
Your visible sword
Thrust through the throat,
—Through and through—
Of the lawless,
Godless,
Unjust son
Of Echion,
Earthborn,
Earthbound.
Come, Dionysus, show yourself.
Come like a bull
—Hunt the hunter—

Or like
A myriad-headed snake,
Or like a flaming lion,
—Hunt the hunter—
Turn round my god, and show your face,
And smiling, always smiling
Throw death on him like a net.
He's down,
—Hunt the hunter—
The herd of maenads closing like a noose!

MESSENGER
Oh, palace,
Once famous for happiness throughout Greece,
—Happy the house of Kadmus, they used to say,
—Who sowed and reaped the earthborn crop—
No I weep for you,
I, a servant,
Yet faithful servants share the fortunes
Of their masters.

CHORUS
What is it?
—You bring news from the Bacchae?

MESSENGER
Pentheus is Dead! Gone is the son of Echion!

CHORUS
Bromius, Bromius,
My Lord of Joy,
Now you prove a great god!

MESSENGER
What was this? What did you say, woman?
You dare rejoice in the death of my king?

CHORUS
I am a foreigner, a girl from the East,
I am just humming a tune of my land,
Meaning nothing,
Meaning joy,
Oh,
I am free!
I am no longer afraid of prison!

MESSENGER
You think no man is left in Thebes—

CHORUS

> Dionysus, not Thebes, is my country.
> He is my State!

MESSENGER

I don't know. I suppose one must forgive you.
But to rejoice over irreparable ills—

> > > > It's evil.

CHORUS

Tell me, what kind of death did he die
The wicked man? Pursuing what wickedness?

MESSENGER

As we left behind us the last farms of Thebes
And crossed the stream of Asopos,
We found ourselves already in the foothills
Of Cithaeron—King Pentheus, and myself,
Following my master, and the stranger,
Who was the guide to our little spying party.

First, we reached a green-lit glen, grass under feet
Saving the sound of steps, sparing our voices,
So that we could see without being seen.
There lies a ravine between two cliffs,
Streams flowing freely, pine trees knitting
Thick shadows overhead, and there the maenads
Were sitting, content with their pleasant tasks,
—Some twining ivy leaves round a thyrsus
That had come loose, others like foals unyoked,
Happily chanting their holy songs
To each other, like answers,

> > > > And questions.

But the ill-fated king just did not see them.
And "Stranger"—he said—"from where we stand,
I cannot reach to see these false worshippers.
But higher up the cliffside, riding, maybe, a tree,
I'd have a proper view of their obscenities."
And then I saw the stranger do the impossible.
He chose the topmost, sky-reaching branch
Of a mountain fir tree, and he bent it;
He brought it down, down,

> > > > Down to the dark earth;

All bent in a half circle like a bow,
Or more like half the curved rim of a wheel,
—And we were looking at his hand. No mortal's.

Then, setting Pentheus astride on that branch,
He let go gradually, gently, through his hands,

Taking good care it would not shake him off.
And the fir tree, straight as a tree,

                          Soared up,
Up, in the upsoaring skies!

But the king on its back was seen more quickly
Than he saw the maenads. Suddenly
The stranger was nowhere,

                      And a voice
—I thought Dionysus'—swooped through the ether:
"Women, this is the man who mocks at me
And you, and my mysteries. Punish him."
And a pillar of unearthly fire flashed
Between the ground and the sky.

                         The forest
Fell silent; silent the weightless wind,
And the leaves sleeping on the trees,
And there was no noise of beasts

                    Or voice.
And they, the women, the call of their god
Still ringing confused in their ears, just stood,
Immobile, their eyes enormous.

                  And then he called again.
                  And the moment
They knew the clear command of the god,
Like doves they darted, like arrows, forward,
The king's mother Agave, and her sisters,
And the rest of the Bacchae,

                Leaping swiftly
Over the torrent-broken ground of the gorge,
Frantic, borne by the very breath of their God—
And they saw Pentheus.

             First, they hurled rocks at him,
—Some climbing on the cliffs towering opposite—
And fir branches, well-aimed like javelins,
Some flung their thyrsus singing through the air
At the wretched king, the sitting target,
But he was too high even for their fury,
Paralyzed by height, helpless on his throne.
Then, the maenads tore oak branches, easy
As thunder, and dug at the feet of the fir,
Levering up the tree, wrenching its roots out.
Suddenly the queen commanded: "Come,
Stand in a circle and heave at the trunk.
We must catch this climbing beast and stop it
From revealing the secrets of our dance."

And, a myriad frail hands gripping the fir,
They pushed, they heaved it right off the ground,
And from its crown,
              Down streamed the man,
                            Reeling.
With one long incessant scream searing the air.
I believe he knew what end was near.
First his mother, being the priestess,
Began the ritual kill.
                 She fell on him.
And he, tearing off the wig,
So that she could recognize and spare him,
Kept mumbling, trying to caress her cheek;
"It's me, Mother, it's Pentheus, Mother, your son
Remember Echion, remember the palace
Where I was born, it's me, don't kill me
Mother, it's me your boy, I've not been good
But don't kill me yet not your own boy."
But she was foaming at the mouth, her eyes
Upturned, showed white, wandering wildly
Like her wits—she was possessed by her god
And words meant nothing.
                   Gripping his left arm,
There, under the elbow, with both her hands,
And setting her foot against his ribs, she burst
His shoulder open—not through her own feeble strength
But through her god's thundering in her veins.
And on his other side Ino, her sister,
Was toiling heavily rending the raucous flesh;
And Autonoe pressed on, and the whole pack
Of the possessed women,
              Tearing.
And there was a continuous noise, confused
In that part of the forest, a man moaning
As long as there was breath in him, some
Women howling.
            One carried an arm,
Another a boot with the foot still in it,
And you could see the ribs, laid bare by clawing,
White, so clean. And the red-stained hands
Were having fun, tossing lumps of Pentheus'
Flesh, to and fro,
            Catch and throw.
Now he lies without a body.
               Some of it
Is under the harsh crags down the precipice;

Some pieces lost in the shadows of the wood,
In the tangled-leaved thickets. They will not
Be easy to find.
>>>>>>>>>>>>>>>And the head. Ah, yes.
That fell in the hands of his mother, and pierced
At the end of a thyrsus, the way hunters
Carry as a trophy the head of a lion;
She is holding it up high, dancing her way
Down Cithaeron.
>>>>>>>>>>>>Leaving her sisters
She's coming towards the palace, already
Past the city walls, exulting in her ill-fated
Prey calling on Bacchus, her Fellow Hunter,
>>>>>>>>>>>>>>>>>>Her Comrade-in-the-Kill
>>>>>>>>>>>>>>>>>>Her Partner-in-Victory
Dionysus, who will give her the triumph of tears.

As for me, I'm going away from this horror
Before the queen gets to the palace.
You see, I don't want to look.
>>>>>>>>>>>>>>>>>Humility
And respect for the gods is the only wisdom.
Yes, and for us mortals, the only weapon
In hand,
>>>>>>>>>—If only we used it.

CHORUS
Dance for Dionysus,
>>>>>>>>>>>EVOHI!
>>>>>>>>>>>>>>>>Sing the fall,
Sing the catastrophe
Of Pentheus, Pentheus,
The Dragonseed!
Dressed as a woman
>>>>>>>>>>>EVOHI!
>>>>>>>>>>>>>>>>Dance his fall
And carrying a thyrsus
A faithful guide to
The nether world!
>>>>>>>>>>>A fair fight, a fair Agon!
>>>>>>>>>>>With loops of ivy
>>>>>>>>>>>To the sacrifice
>>>>>>>>>>>The Bull led the Man!
Kadmeian Bacchae
>>>>>>>>>>>EVOHI!
>>>>>>>>>>>>>>>>You have won!

The Paean of Victory
You sing is ending
In tears and groans!
   A fair fight, a fair Agon!
   With arms still dripping
   His blood, a mother
   Embraces her son.
But look! Agave is running to the palace
Her eyes rolling. Now be ready to receive
The praise of our God of Joy.

AGAVE
Women of Asia, Bacchae, look! Oh!

CHORUS
What do you want me to look at—Oh!

AGAVE
We bring you gifts from the mount'n
A fresh-cut spray of vine shoots
Hallowed prey.

CHORUS
Now we see.
And we accept you in our company.

AGAVE
I, myself caught this, without a net.
Look, this young lion,
   This tender beast, look!
      Look!

CHORUS
In what wilderness—?

AGAVE
      Cithaeron did it.

CHORUS
Cithaeron?

AGAVE
   Yes, the mount'n, the mount'n
    Killed him.

CHORUS
Yes, but whose hands?

AGAVE

               Mine, struck first.
               To me goes the prize.
               "Blessed Agave"
The women were singing,
               "Blessed Agave."

CHORUS
And who else?

AGAVE

          I think Kadmus.

CHORUS

               KADMUS?

AGAVE
Yes, Kadmus' daughters—but after me,
               After me,
Laid their hands to the kill.
Today the gods blessed our hunting.
Now you must share in the feast.

CHORUS
Oh, wretched woman, what feast?

AGAVE
The whelp is young, and the new down still curls
          In soft tendrils,
               On the delicate cheeks.

CHORUS
Indeed it looks like a beast of the woods
               With his long mane.

AGAVE
My god is a skilled hunter,
And skilfully led his pack of maenads
               To hound this quarry.

CHORUS
God is a hunter.

AGAVE

          Have you praise for me?

CHORUS

             Yes, we praise you.

AGAVE
And soon they will,
                    The people of Thebes.

CHORUS
And what about your son, Agave,
                    King Pentheus?

AGAVE
He too will have praise for his mother
                    Who caught this lion.

CHORUS
A strange prey.

AGAVE
                    And strangely caught.

CHORUS
Do you rejoice?

AGAVE
                    I rejoice
In the great and open deeds of the chase!

CHORUS
Show then, poor woman, show to the whole town
The spoils of Victory you carried home!

AGAVE
Look, towers, pride of this city,
                    And you,
Who live in it, look.
                    Here's my trophy!
This is the quarry Kadmus' daughters caught
—And not with nets, or with Thessalian hooks—
But with our bare, white arms, and these our fingers!
Can, after this, men go on boasting? Men.
Who buy from armorers their barren tools?
We,
    Queen of this land,
                    With this very hand
Gave death to him, and tore this pretty
Animal's limbs apart!
                    Where's my father?
Where's that old man? Let him come near and look!
Where's my son?
                    I have a son, his name
                                        Is Pentheus!

I want him here! He may be now the king,
But I gave him life!
                        Tell him his mother
Wants to get strong ladders, set them
Against the face of this arrogant palace
And climb up, high up,
                        To the very top,
And there nail this head, this lovely lion,
My trophy from the hunt,
                        High on the triglyphs—
Top of the palace wall, the highest
Point of this land, to challenge Cithaeron,
                        And for all the town to see!

KADMUS

Follow me, servants,
Carry your wretched burden, bring Pentheus,
—What's left of Pentheus—to his home.
Bring home, what I found in Cithaeron,
Scattered pieces,
                        Lost in the glens and thickets.

I was returning with Teiresias
From the ritual dance, when they broke to me
The news of my daughter's terrible
Action. And I hurried back to the hills
To look for my son, my murdered boy,
Killed by the maenads. Weary search.
And Autonoe I saw there, and I saw Ino,
Still goaded by frenzy among the quiet trees.
But Agave was nowhere. The rumor has it
She ran back here.
                        Now, I see. I can see her.
I only wish I could not.

AGAVE

                        Father,
You can boast now. You can claim
As loudly as you wish, no man alive
Has been so fortunate, so blest in daughters
As you have been. All three of us, but me,
Above the rest.
                        Father, I've left forever
Weaving and looms for something greater:
A better kind of handiwork: hunting.
Hunting in the mountain the wild beasts,
With my bare hands.

Here, I carry in my arms
—As you can see—this trophy I have won,
To hoist above the palace walls.
                    Take it,
Father, hold it in your hands. Why don't you
Take it?
            You should be proud of my catch.
You should invite our friends to celebrate.
Let them call you blessed, and envy you
In your old age for the achievement
Of your daughters.

KADMUS

                    Oh, mourning,
Oh, agony unmeasurable,
                        Unbearable to look at.
Pitiful hands, your handiwork is murder
Oh, what a chosen victim you sacrificed
At the feet of the gods! To what feast
You are inviting Thebes and me!
Ah, me, what grief, first yours, and then what grief
For this old man.
                The god has repaid us
Justly—but too well. The King of Joy.
Born in this house, he has destroyed it.

AGAVE

How difficult old age makes a man! How
Mournfully he scowls at me!
                        I wish my son
Becomes a hunter worthy of his mother;
I wish he were chasing the beasts of the wild
With the young men of Thebes.
                        But he only knows
How to fight the gods. Father, you should speak
To him, make him see reason.
Why do you stare, all? Go someone
Call him here, to admire my good fortune.

KADMUS

                    Woe, woe!
If you ever come to your senses
And understand what you've done, the anguish
Will be inhuman. But if you stay
Forever in this condition, although
Not happy, at least you will be happily
Spared the knowledge of your misfortune.

AGAVE

What is the matter? Has anything gone wrong?
Why do you keep talking of misfortune?

KADMUS

Open your eyes, my daughter. First look that way.
Look at the sky.

AGAVE

There, at the sky. Why d'you want me to look?

KADMUS

Does it seem the same? Or somehow different?

AGAVE

A little brighter than before, and more—translucent.

KADMUS

And this excitement you were living in?
Is it still with you?

AGAVE

I do not know what you mean.
And yet I feel
My thoughts have become a little clearer.
Something has shifted in my mind.

KADMUS

Can you hear me now? And answer clearly?

AGAVE

Yes—Father, what were we talking about?
Now? Just now?

KADMUS

When you were married, to whose house did you come?
Try to remember.

AGAVE

You gave me to the man born from this land.
They called him Echion.

KADMUS

Here, in this palace, you gave a son to him.
Who was he?

AGAVE

Pentheus. That is right. My son and Echion's.

KADMUS
  Now whose head are you cradling in your arms,
                Whose face?

AGAVE
  The head of a lion. That's what the hunters said.

KADMUS
  Look at it, now.
            Go on, it is easy to look.
                        It will soon be over.

AGAVE
  Aah.
  What is this? What am I holding?

KADMUS
  Look steadily at it, until you know it clearly.

AGAVE
  I see a great sorrow. Oh, meee!

KADMUS
  Does it seem, now, the head of a lion?

AGAVE
                                  No.
  Father, this thing looks like the face of my son.

KADMUS
  And you were crying already, before you knew it.

AGAVE
  Father, they killed him! Who did this? How did it
                        Come to my hands?

KADMUS
  Oh, truth, terrible truth, it always comes too soon!

AGAVE
  Go on, Father; say it; my heart has taken already
                A leap in the future.

KADMUS
  It was *you* killed him, *you* and your sisters!

AGAVE
  Where did he die? In the palace? Or where?

KADMUS

In the same spot, where years ago,
His dogs tore Actaion, my other grandson,
Actaion! Actaion!

AGAVE

Cithaeron! What evil hour brought Pentheus
To Cithaeron?

KADMUS

He went there in scorn of the god
And your Bacchic madness.

AGAVE

But why did we all go there?

KADMUS

You went all mad; the whole town was dancing
In ecstasy.

AGAVE

But why was Pentheus responsible?
What part did he play in my madness?

KADMUS

He was like you, contemptuous of the god.
And Dionysus joined us all, in one
Destruction, you, and this boy, and your sisters,
Ruining my house and me;
I had no son;
And this, the only male of my blood,
I had to stand by and see him die,
A horrible and shameful death—you,
My boy, this house looked up to as its head,
My king, who held the city in awe, the bond
Which kept together the walls of this palace.
Nobody dared make fun of the senile old man
Knowing you near; you would punish them.
And now,
I, Kadmus the great,
Who sowed
In the ground the seed of Theban race,
And reaped the envied harvest,
Shall wander,
An outcast, dishonored, far from my home.
Oh, my beloved son, for even now you are no more,
I count you as one of my dearest children,
Never again will you caress my hair,
Call me grandfather, put your arm around me
And say: "Father, has anybody wronged you,

Anybody mocked you? Tell me and I will
Punish them. Anybody troubled you,
Or disturbed your heart?" Never again.
And now you are gone, and I stay here, wretched,
And your mother, and her sisters—pitiful.
If there be anyone who scorns the unknown
Powers, let him consider the death of this man
And accept the gods.

CHORUS
                    Kadmus, I grieve for you.
Your grandson deserved his punishment.
But for you it is cruel.

AGAVE
Father, where is my son?[15] Where is
                    His beloved body?

KADMUS
Here. I have brought it back after long search.

AGAVE
You needn't hide it from me. Father,
I know it is in pieces. I remember.
Is it decently composed? Can I see it?

KADMUS
Help her.

AGAVE
          Father, and you people of this land,
You see how, in one stroke, my whole life
Is changed.
          My son is dead;
What was my pride has turned into shame
And anguish unspeakable.
                    My hands are polluted
With my own blood. The gods goaded me
To this crime against my own flesh,
And yet I know that I'm guilty in their eyes,
And yours.
          The laws of heaven and the holy
Respect we owe to the dead, forbid the killer
To bury his victim.
                    But this flesh grew
In my womb. It is mine, mine.
                    I do not want to live.

---

[15]*Where is my son?*—At about this point there is a long gap in the original manuscript; what follows must be partly reconstructed from fragments of the play quoted by other ancient writers.

I only want to compose my son's body
For the world of the dead, so that my king
Receives the tribute due to his beauty
When he gets there.
                                Then, I want to crawl away
From this town,
                                And die.
I was once queen of this land. Grant me this favor.

KADMUS
My daughter, the cloud of pollution
Is on us, all. The whole town was guilty
Of scorning a god. You and your sisters,
And me. And this boy. Nobody has the right
To keep you away from him.
                                But I warn you
Do not ask for more than mortal eyes
Can survive.
                Help her.

AGAVE
                                Ah.
Who is this dead man?
                                How can I embrace
Him? How can I weep for him and kiss a stranger?
Oh, my son, your skin used to smell so sweetly
When you were a boy,
                                My little boy, my king.
Father, help me. Bring here his beloved head.
Place it here. We must make everything look
Exact.
        Oh, I gave you life once,
        What law forbids me to do it again?
Oh, dearest face,
                        Oh, soft young cheek,
                        Help me.
My boy, see, with this veil I cover you,
Your head, that I shall never see again,
Your bloodstained limbs I myself
Have torn to these unseemly pieces.
            What law?
My king.
            The dead are dead forever.

DIONYSUS[16]
I, Dionysus, son of Zeus have come back
Here, where I was born, to this land of Thebes.

---

[16]*Dionysus*—In the epiphany, Dionysus appears in glory, his godhood undeniably manifest.

And I was thrown in prison,
                                    And insulted
By words and deeds.
                            Now, the end.
Queen Agave and her sisters will leave
This town forever, to save Thebes from cursed
Pollution. The gods cannot accept
Murderers buried with those they killed.
If you had chosen wisdom, when you would not,
The son of Zeus would be now your friend
And your ally, leading you into
                                    Felicity.

KADMUS
    Dionysus,
    Show mercy on us. We have wronged you.

DIONYSUS
    You know me now; it is too late.
    When there was time, you knew me not.

AGAVE
    We have confessed that.
                            But your hand
    Falls on us too heavily.

DIONYSUS
    A god insulted cannot forgive.

AGAVE
    The gods should not be like men[17]
                            In their revenge.

DIONYSUS
    Zeus, my father, and the immutable
    Laws of balance,
                            Have decreed this
    From the beginnings of time.
    Now, you must go.

AGAVE
    Aah.
    Father, the word is spoken: exile.
    The gods are implacable.

---

[17]*The gods should not be like men*—In asserting that the gods should exercise a higher morality than that practiced by men, Agave probably expresses Euripides' own conviction. A fragment from a lost Euripidean play contains the assertion "if the gods do evil, they are not gods."

DIONYSUS
  Why then delay the inevitable?

KADMUS
  Oh, daughter, what terrible end
  Have we all reached, so suddenly.
  You, unfortunate, and your sisters,
  And myself.
                An old man, unnecessary,
  Trying to go on, in foreign lands.
  I shall never find relief from suffering.
  No, not even in death, flowing down Achairon,
  The downward river, to the world of the dark,
  Shall I ever know peace.

AGAVE
  I shall have to go on living.
  Oh, Father, exiled,
                      Separated from you!

KADMUS
  Why throw your arms around my head,
  Poor child,
              Like a swan trying to protect
  Her old and helpless?

AGAVE
  Father, where am I to go, exiled
  From my country?
                    Which way am I
  To turn? The whole world is unnecessary.
  Which way?

KADMUS
  I don't know. Your old father
  Is now of little help to you. I'm tired.

AGAVE
                  Farewell, my home.
  Farewell, my only country.
  For the last time I see
                        This house
  Where, once, I came
                      A bride.
  Oh, Father, I weep for you.

KADMUS
  I still feel pity for you
  And your sisters.

AGAVE

Because so horribly,
HORRIBLY
King Dionysus has punished you, you
And your house.

CHORUS

Because so horribly
You had offended him,
You, and your house,
And shamed his name
In Thebes.

AGAVE

Father, farewell.

KADMUS

This word is cruel irony.
Farewell, my daughter.

AGAVE

Woman, lead me to my sisters
To share their pitiful exile.
And may we find a distant land
Where accursed Cithaeron
Shall never see my face again,
Nor I,
Ever, set eyes again
On Cithaeron.
Take away this Thyrsus
Take away all that may remind me—
Take away memory.
Let that
Be the care
Of other Bacchae

    ✿   ✿   ✿

CHORUS

The gods have many faces.
They manifest themselves
In manifold ways.
What we expected does not happen.
For the Unexpected, gods
Always find a way.
This is what happened here. Today.

ARISTOPHANES

Preface

(c. 448—c. 380 B.C.)

THE ORIGINS OF COMEDY ARE EVEN MORE OBSCURE THAN THOSE OF TRAGEDY. Except for Aristotle's statement that comedy evolved from "phallic songs," presumably associated with the fertility worship of Dionysus, and that it was first performed in rural villages, nothing about its early development is known. The term itself (from the Greek *komoidia*) apparently derives from the combination of *komos* (a revel) and *oide* (song). Revel-songs were featured at various Greek festivals, particularly those of Dionysus, during which a procession of revellers sang, danced, and made indecent jokes about the onlookers. At some indefinite point in its history these improvised lampoons were given a plot and formal comedy was born. Because it was long regarded as not artistically respectable, comedy was not officially sponsored in Athens until about 486 B.C. After that date it was produced annually at the Great Dionysia and (after 450 B.C.) at the Lenaea, a winter wine festival dedicated to comic presentations.

Of the hundreds of comedies that delighted Athenian audiences during the fifth century B.C., only eleven have survived. All these are the work of one man, Aristophanes, whom his contemporaries recognized as the master of the comic mode. While Greek tragedy was stately and noble, the Old Comedy of Aristophanes was farcical, irreverent, and joyously obscene. His plays usually begin with a "happy idea" which the characters and comic chorus work out to a logical—or hilariously illogical—conclusion. In *The Clouds* (423 B.C.) the idea is to ridicule Socrates and the New Learning which people thought was corrupting the youth. *The Frogs* (405 B.C.), the first example of literary criticism in the theatre, cleverly plays on the notion of a drunken Dionysus descending into Hades to bring back to Athens a good poet. (At that time Aeschylus, Sophocles, and Euripides were all dead and Athenian drama-goers were not happy with the inferior successors to the famous trio.)

In the *Lysistrata*, which was produced in 411 B.C., the heroine's ingenius idea is to end the Peloponnesian War by persuading Greek women, Spartan and Athenian alike, to stage an international sex strike. Living up to her name, which may be loosely translated as "Miss Demobilizer," Lysistrata succeeds in proving to everyone's satisfaction that making love is more important than making war. A woman of dignity and purpose, Lysistrata also promotes the rather disturbing theory that women possess minds that sometimes think more clearly than men's. The play's comic effect is heightened, incidentally, by the Greek custom of casting all roles, including those of Lysistrata and her voluptuous companions, with male actors.

For all the sheer fun Aristophanes has in elaborating his scandalous idea, he sharpens the humor by giving it a profoundly serious intent. At the time of the *Lysistrata's* premier, Athens had just suffered the greatest military disaster in her history, the total destruction of a large army and her entire fleet during the Syracuse campaign. The war with Sparta ceased to be a joke. Aristophanes, who had from the beginning fearlessly satirized the war party, took full advantage of the absolute freedom of speech allowed the dramatic poet to expose the folly of Athens' militaristic policy. Like Euripides, he saw war as a meaningless waste, but he differed from the tragic poet by attempting to prove his point not with tears but with laughter. When the *Lysistrata* appeared, the Athenians laughed, the state produced the play at public expense, Aristophanes won his usual prize at the Dionysian festival, but, unfortunately for his country, his pacifist views had no effect on national strategy. After the crushing defeat of Athens, which ended the war in 404 B.C., Aristophanes turned from political satire to invent the New Comedy, a less controversial theatre of manners, romance, and stereotyped lovers.

LYSISTRATA

Characters | LYSISTRATA ⎫
KALONIKE ⎬ Athenian women
MYRRHINA ⎭
LAMPITO, a Spartan woman
CHORUS OF OLD MEN
CHORUS OF WOMEN
ATHENIAN COMMISSIONER
OLD MARKET-WOMEN
CINESIAS, an Athenian, husband of Myrrhina
SPARTAN HERALD
SPARTAN AMBASSADORS
ATHENIAN AMBASSADORS

[*A street in Athens before daylight*]

LYSISTRATA
If anyone had asked them to a festival
of Aphrodite or of Bacchus or of Pan,
you couldn't get through Athens for the tambourines,
but now there's not one solitary woman here.
Except my next-door neighbor. Here she's coming out.
Hello, Kalonike.

From *Lysistrata* by Aristophanes, translated by Donald Sutherland, published by Chandler Publishing Company, San Francisco. Copyright © 1961 by Chandler Publishing Company. Reprinted by permission. Notes are those of the present editor.

KALONIKE

                    Hello, Lysistrata.
What are you so upset about? Don't scowl so, dear.
You're less attractive when you knit your brows and glare.

LYSISTRATA

    I know, Kalonike, but I am smoldering
with indignation at the way we women act.
Men think we are so gifted for all sorts of crime
that we will stop at nothing—

KALONIKE

                      Well, we are, by Zeus!

LYSISTRATA

    —but when it comes to an appointment here with me
to plot and plan for something really serious
they lie in bed and do not come.

KALONIKE

                         They'll come, my dear.
You know what trouble women have in going out:
one of us will be wrapped up in her husband still,
another waking up the maid, or with a child
to put to sleep, or give its bath, or feed its pap.

LYSISTRATA

    But they had other more important things to do
than those.

KALONIKE

    What ever is it, dear Lysistrata?
What have you called us women all together for?
How much of a thing is it?

LYSISTRATA

                Very big.[1]

KALONIKE

                        And thick?

LYSISTRATA

    Oh very thick indeed.

KALONIKE

             Then *how* can we be late?

---

[1]*Very big*—This is the first of many phallic jokes in the *Lysistrata*.

LYSISTRATA

 That's not the way it is. Or we would all be here.
 But it is something I have figured out myself
 and turned and tossed upon for many a sleepless night.

KALONIKE

 It must be something slick you've turned and tossed
 upon!

LYSISTRATA

 So slick that the survival of all Greece depends
 upon the women.

KALONIKE

     On the women? In that case
 poor Greece has next to nothing to depend upon.

LYSISTRATA

 Since now it's we who must decide affairs of state:
 either there is to be no Spartan left alive—

KALONIKE

 A very good thing too, if none were left, by Zeus!

LYSISTRATA

 —and every living soul in Thebes to be destroyed—

KALONIKE

 Except the eels! Spare the delicious eels of Thebes!

LYSISTRATA

 —and as for Athens—I can't bring myself to say
 the like of that for us. But just think what I mean!
 Yet if the women meet here as I told them to
 from Sparta, Thebes, and all of their allies,
 and we of Athens, all together we'll save Greece.

KALONIKE

 What reasonable thing could women ever do,
 or glorious, we who sit around all prettied up
 in flowers and scandalous saffron-yellow gowns,
 groomed and draped to the ground in oriental stuffs
 and fancy pumps?

LYSISTRATA

     And those are just the very things
 I count upon to save us—wicked saffron gowns,
 perfumes and pumps and rouge and sheer transparent frocks.

KALONIKE
But what use can they be?

LYSISTRATA
So no man in our time
will raise a spear against another man again—

KALONIKE
I'll get a dress dyed saffron-yellow, come what may!

LYSISTRATA
—nor touch a shield—

KALONIKE
I'll slip into the sheerest gown!

LYSISTRATA
—nor so much as a dagger—

KALONIKE
I'll buy a pair of pumps!

LYSISTRATA
So don't you think the women should be here by now?

KALONIKE
I don't. They should have *flown* and got here long ago.

LYSISTRATA
You'll see, my dear. They will, like good Athenians,
do everything too late. But from the coastal towns
no woman is here either, nor from Salamis.

KALONIKE
I'm certain those from Salamis have crossed the strait:
they're always straddling *something* at this time of night.

LYSISTRATA
Not even those I was expecting would be first
to get here, from Acharnae, from so close to town,
not even they are here.

KALONIKE
But one of them, I know,
is under way, and three sheets to the wind, by now.
But look—some women are approaching over there.

LYSISTRATA
And over here are some, coming this way—

KALONIKE

Phew! Phew!

Where are they from?

LYSISTRATA

Down by the marshes.

KALONIKE

Yes, by Zeus!

It smells as if the bottoms had been all churned up!
[*Enter* MYRRHINA, *and others.*]

MYRRHINA

Hello Lysistrata. Are we a little late?
What's that? Why don't you speak?

LYSISTRATA

I don't think much of you.

Myrrhina, coming to this business only now.

MYRRHINA

Well, I could hardly find my girdle in the dark.
If it's so urgent, tell us what it is. We're here.

KALONIKE

Oh no. Let's wait for just a little while until
the delegates from Sparta and from Thebes arrive.

LYSISTRATA

You show much better judgment.
[*Enter* LAMPITO, *and others.*]

Here comes Lampito!

LYSISTRATA

Well, darling Lampito! My dearest Spartan friend!
How very sweet, how beautiful you look! That fresh
complexion! How magnificent your figure is!
Enough to crush a bull!

LAMPITO

Ah shorely think Ah could.

Ah take mah exercise. Ah jump and thump mah butt.[2]

KALONIKE

And really, what a handsome set of tits you have!

---

[2]To illustrate the effect of Spartan speech on the Athenian ear, the translator has given Lampito a Texas accent. Needless to add, the Athenians regarded the Doric dialect as a sign of cultural deprivation.

LAMPITO
You feel me ovah lahk a cow fo sacrafahce!

LYSISTRATA
And this other young thing—where ever is *she* from?

LAMPITO
She's prominent, Ah sweah, in Thebes—a delegate
ample enough.

LYSISTRATA
By Zeus, she represent Thebes well,
having so trim a ploughland.

KALONIKE
                              Yes, by Zeus, she does!
There's not a weed of all her field she hasn't plucked.

LYSISTRATA
And who's the other girl?

LAMPITO
                              Theah's nothing small, Ah sweah,
or tahght about her folks in Corinth.

KALONIKE
                              No, by Zeus!—
to judge by this side of her, nothing small or tight.

LAMPITO
But who has called togethah such a regiment
of all us women?

LYSISTRATA
              Here I am. I did.

LAMPITO
                              Speak up,
just tell us what you want.

KALONIKE
                              Oh yes, by Zeus, my dear,
do let us know what the important business is!

LYSISTRATA
Let me explain it, then. And yet . . . before I do . . .
I have one little question.

KALONIKE
                    Anything you like.

LYSISTRATA

Don't you all miss the fathers of your little ones,
your husbands who have gone away to war? I'm sure
you all have husbands in the armies far from home.

KALONIKE

Mine's been away five months in Thrace—a general's
guard,
posted to see his general does not desert.

MYRRHINA

And mine has been away in Pylos seven whole months.

LAMPITO

And mahn, though he does get back home on leave
sometahms,
no soonah has he come than he is gone again.

LYSISTRATA

No lovers either. Not a sign of one is left.
For since our eastern allies have deserted us
they haven't sent a single six-inch substitute
to serve as leatherware replacement for our men.
Would you be willing, then, if I thought out a scheme,
to join with me to end the war?

KALONIKE

                              Indeed I would,
even if I had to pawn this very wrap-around
and drink up all the money in one day, I would!

MYRRHINA

And so would I, even if I had to see myself
split like a flounder, and give half of me away!

LAMPITO

And so would Ah! Ah'd climb up Mount Taÿgetos
if Ah just had a chance of seeing peace from theah!

LYSISTRATA

Then I will tell you. I may now divulge my plan.
Women of Greece!—if we intend to force the men
to make a peace, we must abstain . . .

KALONIKE

                              From what? Speak out!

LYSISTRATA

But will you do it?

KALONIKE

We will, though death should be the price!

LYSISTRATA

Well then, we must abstain utterly from the prick.
Why do you turn your backs? Where are you off to now?
And you—why pout and make such faces, shake your heads?
Why has your color changed? Why do you shed those tears?
Will you do it or will you not? Why hesitate?

KALONIKE

I will not do it. Never. Let the war go on!

MYRRHINA

Neither will I. By Zeus, no! Let the war go on!

LYSISTRATA

How can you say so, Madam Flounder, when just
   now
you were declaiming you would split yourself in half?

KALONIKE

Anything else you like, anything! If I must
I'll gladly walk through fire. That, rather than the prick!
Because there's nothing like it, dear Lysistrata.

LYSISTRATA

How about you?

MYRRHINA

I too would gladly walk through fire.

LYSISTRATA

Oh the complete depravity of our whole sex!
It is no wonder tragedies are made of us,
we have such unrelenting unity of mind!
But you, my friend from Sparta, dear, if you alone
stand by me, only you, we still might save the cause.
Vote on my side!

LAMPITO

They'ah hahd conditions, mahty hahd,
to sleep without so much as the fo'skin of one . . .
but all the same . . . well . . . yes. We need peace just as bad.

LYSISTRATA

Oh dearest friend!—the one real woman of them all!

KALONIKE

And if we really should abstain from what you say—
which Heaven forbid!—do you suppose on that account
that peace might come to be?

LYSISTRATA

I'm absolutely sure.
If we should sit around, rouged and with skins well creamed,
with nothing on but a transparent negligé,
and come up to them with our deltas plucked quite smooth,
and, once our men get stiff and want to come to grips,
we do not yield to them at all but just hold off,
they'll make a truce in no time. There's no doubt of that.

LAMPITO

We say in Spahta that when Menelaos saw
Helen's ba'e apples he just tossed away his swo'd.

KALONIKE

And what, please, if our husbands just toss *us* away?

LYSISTRATA

Well, you have heard the good old saying: Know
Thyself.

KALONIKE

It isn't worth the candle. I hate cheap substitutes.
But what if they should seize and drag us by brute force
into the bedroom?

LYSISTRATA

Hang onto the doors!

KALONIKE

And if—
they beat us?

LYSISTRATA

Then you must give in, but nastily,
and do it badly. There's no fun in it by force.
And then, just keep them straining. They will give it up
in no time—don't you worry. For never will a man
enjoy himself unless the woman coincides.

KALONIKE

If both of you are for this plan, then so are we.

LAMPITO

And we of Spahta shall persuade ouah men to keep
the peace sinceahly and with honah in all ways,
but how could anyone pe'suade the vulgah mob
of Athens not to deviate from discipline?

LYSISTRATA

Don't worry, we'll persuade our men. They'll keep
the peace.

LAMPITO

They won't, so long as they have battleships afloat
and endless money sto'ed up in the Pahthenon.

LYSISTRATA

But that too has been carefully provided for:
we shall take over the Acropolis today.
The oldest women have their orders to do that:
while *we* meet here, *they* go as if to sacrifice
up there, but really seizing the Acropolis.

LAMPITO

All should go well. What you say theah is very smaht.

LYSISTRATA

In that case, Lampito, what are we waiting for?
Let's take an oath, to bind us indissolubly.

LAMPITO

Well, just you show us what the oath is. Then we'll
sweah.

LYSISTRATA

You're right. Where is that lady cop?

[*To the armed* LADY COP *looking around for a* LADY COP]

What do you think
you're looking for? Put down your shield in front of us,
there, on its back. and someone get some scraps of gut.

KALONIKE

Lysistrata, what in the world do you intend
to make us take an oath on?

LYSISTRATA

What? Why, on a shield,
just as they tell me some insurgents in a play
by Aeschylus once did, with a sheep's blood and guts.

KALONIKE
> Oh *don't,* Lysistrata, don't swear upon a *shield,*
> not if the oath has anything to do with peace!

LYSISTRATA
> Well then, what *will* we swear on? Maybe we should
>   get
> a white horse somewhere, like the Amazons, and cut
> some bits of gut from it.

KALONIKE
> 　　　　　　　　*Where* would we get a horse?

LYSISTRATA
> But what kind of an oath *is* suitable for us?

KALONIKE
> By Zeus, I'll tell you if you like. First we put down
> a big black drinking-cup, face up, and then we let
> the neck of a good jug of wine bleed into it,
> and take a solemn oath to—add no water in.

LAMPITO
> Bah Zeus, Ah jest can't tell you how Ah lahk that oath!

LYSISTRATA
> Someone go get a cup and winejug from inside.

[KALONIKE *goes and is back in a flash.*]

KALONIKE
> My dears, my dearest dears—how's *this* for pottery?
> You feel good right away, just laying hold of it.

LYSISTRATA
> Well, set it down, and lay your right hand on this pig.
> O goddess of Persuasion, and O Loving-cup,
> accept this victim's blood! Be gracious unto us.

KALONIKE
> It's not anaemic, and flows clear. Those are good signs.

LAMPITO
> What an aroma, too! Bah Castah it *is* sweet!

KALONIKE
> My dears, if you don't mind—I'll be the first to swear.

LYSISTRATA
By Aphrodite, no! If you had drawn first place
by lot—but now let all lay hands upon the cup.
Yes, Lampito—and now, let one of you repeat
for all of you what I shall say. You will be sworn
by every word she says, and bound to keep this oath:
No lover and no husband and no man on earth—

KALONIKE
No lover and no husband and no man on earth—

LYSISTRATA
shall e'er approach me with his penis up. Repeat.

KALONIKE
shall e'er approach me with his penis up. Oh dear,
my knees are buckling under me, Lysistrata!

LYSISTRATA
and I shall lead an unlaid life alone at home,

KALONIKE
and I shall lead an unlaid life alone at home,

LYSISTRATA
wearing a saffron gown and groomed and beautified

KALONIKE
wearing a saffron gown and groomed and beautified

LYSISTRATA
so that my husband will be all on fire for me

KALONIKE
so that my husband will be all on fire for me

LYSISTRATA
but I will never willingly give in to him

KALONIKE
but I will never willingly give in to him

LYSISTRATA
and if he tries to force me to against my will

KALONIKE
and if he tries to force me to against my will

LYSISTRATA
I'll do it bady and not wiggle in response

KALONIKE
I'll do it badly and not wiggle in response

LYSISTRATA
nor toward the ceiling will I lift my Persian pumps

KALONIKE
nor toward the ceiling will I lift my Persian pumps

LYSISTRATA
nor crouch down as the lions on cheese-graters do

KALONIKE
nor crouch down as the lions on cheese-graters do

LYSISTRATA
and if I keep my promise, may I drink of this—

KALONIKE
and if I keep my promise, may I drink of this—

LYSISTRATA
but if I break it, then may water fill the cup!

KALONIKE
but if I break it, then may water fill the cup!

LYSISTRATA
Do you all swear to this with her?

ALL
                          We do, by Zeus!

LYSISTRATA
I'll consecrate our oath now.

KALONIKE
                   Share alike, my dear,
so we'll be friendly to each other from the start.

LAMPITO
What was that screaming?

LYSISTRATA
                  That's what I was telling you:
the women have already seized the Parthenon
and the Acropolis. But now, dear Lampito,
return to Sparta and set things in order there—
but leave these friends of yours as hostages with us—

And let *us* join the others in the citadel
and help them bar the gates.

KALONIKE

But don't you think the men
will rally to the rescue of the citadel,
attacking us at once?

LYSISTRATA

They don't worry me much:
they'll never bring against us threats or fire enough
to force open the gates, except upon our terms.

KALONIKE

Never by Aphrodite! Or we'd lose our name
for being battle-axes and unbearable!

[*Exeunt. The scene changes to the Propylaea of the Acropolis. A chorus
of very old men struggles slowly in, carrying logs and firepots.*]

ONE OLD MAN

Lead on! O Drakës, step by step, although your
      shoulder's aching
and under this green olive log's great weight
      your back be breaking!

ANOTHER

Eh, life is long but always has
      more surprises for us!
Now who'd have thought we'd live to hear
      this, O Strymodorus?—

The wives we fed and looked upon
as helpless liabilities
now dare to occupy the Parthenon,
our whole Acropolis, for once they seize
the Propylaea, straightway
they lock and bar the gateway.

CHORUS

Let's rush to the Acropolis with due precipitation
and lay these logs down circlewise, till presently we turn them
into one mighty pyre to make a general cremation
of all the women up there—eh! with our own hands we'll burn
      them,
the leaders and the followers, without discrimination!

AN OLD MAN

They'll never have the laugh on me!
      Though I may not look it,

I rescued the Acropolis
    when the Spartans took it
about a hundred years ago.
We laid a siege that kept their king
six years unwashed, so when I made him throw
his armor off, for all his blustering,
in nothing but his shirt he
looked very very dirty.

CHORUS

How strictly I besieged the man! These gates were all
    invested
with seventeen ranks of armored men all equally ferocious!
Shall women—by Euripides and all the gods detested—[3]
not be restrained—with me on hand—from something so
    atrocious?
They shall!—or may our trophies won at Marathon be bested!
        But we must go a long way yet
        up that steep and winding road
    before we reach the fortress where we want to get.
        How shall we ever drag this load,
        lacking pack-mules, way up there?
I can tell you that my shoulder has caved in beyond
    repair!
        Yet we must trudge ever higher,
        ever blowing on the fire,
    so its coals will still be glowing when we get where we
    are going
        Fooh! Fooh!
        Whoo! I choke!
        What a smoke!

        Lord Herakles! How fierce it flies
        out against me from the pot!
and like a rabid bitch it bites me in the eyes!
        It's female fire, or it would not
        scratch my poor old eyes like this.
Yet undaunted we must onward, up the high Acropolis
        where Athena's temple stands
        fallen into hostile hands.
O my comrades! shall we ever have a greater need to
    save her?
        Fooh! Fooh!
        Whoo! I choke!
        What a smoke!

---

[3]*Euripides . . . detested*—Aristophanes was not above getting laughs by exploiting
Euripides' undeserved reputation as a woman-hater.

FIRST OLD MAN
   Well, thank the gods, I see the fire is yet alive and waking!

SECOND OLD MAN
   Why don't we set our lumber down right here in
      handy batches,
   then stick a branch of grape-vine in the pot until it catches

THIRD OLD MAN
   and hurl ourselves against the gate with battering and shaking?

FIRST OLD MAN
   and if the women won't unbar at such an ultimatum
   we'll set the gate on fire and then the smoke will suffocate 'em.

SECOND OLD MAN
   Well, let's put down our load. Fooh fooh, what smoke!
      But blow as needed!

THIRD OLD MAN
   Your ablest generals *these* days would not carry wood
      like *we* did.

SECOND OLD MAN
   At last the lumber ceases grinding my poor back
      to pieces!

THIRD OLD MAN
   These are your orders, Colonel Pot: wake up the coals and
      bid them
   report here and present to me a torch lit up and flaring.

FIRST OLD MAN
   O Victory, be with us! If you quell the women's daring
   we'll raise a splendid trophy of how you and we undid them!

[A CHORUS *of middle-aged women appear in the offing.*]

A WOMAN
   I think that I perceive a smoke in which appears a flurry
   of sparks as of a lighted fire. Women, we'll have to hurry!

CHORUS OF WOMEN
   Oh fleetly fly, oh swiftly flit,
   my dears, e'er Kalykë be lit
   and with Kritylla swallowed up alive
         in flames which the gales dreadfully drive
         and deadly old men fiercely inflate!

Yet one thing I'm afraid of: will I not arrive too late?
for filling up my water-jug has been no easy matter
what with the crowd at the spring in the dusk and the
   clamor and pottery clatter.
  Pushed as I was, jostled by slave-
  women and sluts marked with a brand
  yet with my jug firmly in hand
  here I have come, hoping to save
   my burning friends and brave,

  for certain windy, witless, old,
  and wheezy fools, so I was told,
with wood some tons in weight crept up this path,
  not having in mind heating a bath
  but uttering threats, vowing they will
consume those nasty women into cinders on grill!
But O Athena! never may I see my friends igniting!
Nay!—let them save all the cities of Greece and their
   people from folly and fighting!
  Goddess whose crest flashes with gold,
  they were so bold taking your shine
  only for this—Goddess who hold
  Athens—for *this* noble design,
  braving the flames, calling on you
   to carry water too!

[*One of the old men urinates noisily.*]

CHORUS OF WOMEN
 Be still! What was that noise? Aha! Oh, wicked
  and degraded!
 Would any good religious men have ever done what *they* did?

CHORUS OF MEN
 Just look! It's a surprise-attack! Oh, dear, we're being raided
 by swarms of them below us when we've got a swarm above us!

CHORUS OF WOMEN
 Why panic at the sight of us? This is not many of us.
 We number tens of thousands but you've hardly seen a fraction.

CHORUS OF MEN
 O Phaidrias, shall they talk so big and we not take
  some action?
 Oh, should we not be bashing them and splintering our lumber?

[*The old men begin to strip for combat.*]

CHORUS OF WOMEN
>Let us, too, set our pitchers down, so they will not
>   encumber
>our movements if these gentlemen should care to offer battle.

CHORUS OF MEN
>Oh someone should have clipped their jaws—twice,
>   thrice, until they rattle—
>(as once the poet put it)—then we wouldn't hear their prating.

CHORUS OF WOMEN
>Well, here's your chance. Won't someone hit me?
>   Here I stand, just waiting!
>No other bitch will ever grab your balls, the way I'll treat you!

CHORUS OF MEN
>Shut up—or I will drub you so old age will never reach you!

CHORUS OF WOMEN
>Won't anyone step and lay one finger on Stratyllis?

CHORUS OF MEN
>And if we pulverize her with our knuckles, will you kill us?

CHORUS OF WOMEN
>No, only chew your lungs out and your innards and
>   your eyes, sir.

CHORUS OF MEN
>How clever is Euripides! There is no poet wiser:
>he says indeed that women are the worst of living creatures.

CHORUS OF WOMEN
>Now is the time, Rhodippe: let us raise our brimming
>   pitchers.

CHORUS OF MEN
>Why come up here with water, you, the gods'
>   abomination?

CHORUS OF WOMEN
>And why come here with fire, you tomb? To give
>   yourself cremation?

CHORUS OF MEN
>To set your friends alight upon a pyre erected for them.

CHORUS OF WOMEN
>And so we brought our water-jugs. Upon your pyre
>   we'll pour them.

CHORUS OF MEN
  You'll put my fire out?

CHORUS OF WOMEN
  Any time! You'll see there's nothing to it.

CHORUS OF MEN
  I think I'll grill you right away, with just this torch
    to do it!

CHORUS OF WOMEN
  Have you some dusting-powder? Here's your wedding-
    bath all ready.

CHORUS OF MEN
  You'll bathe me, garbage that you are?

CHORUS OF WOMEN
  Yes, bridegroom, just hold steady!

CHORUS OF MEN
  Friends, you have heard her insolence—

CHORUS OF WOMEN
  I'm free-born, not your slave, sir.

CHORUS OF MEN
  I'll have this noise of yours restrained—

CHORUS OF WOMEN
  Court's out—so be less grave, sir.

CHORUS OF MEN
  Why don't you set her hair on fire?

CHORUS OF WOMEN
  Oh, Water, be of service!

CHORUS OF MEN
  Oh woe is me!

CHORUS OF WOMEN
  Was it too hot?

CHORUS OF MEN
  Oh, stop! What *is* this? Hot? Oh no!

CHORUS OF WOMEN
  I'm watering you to make you grow.

CHROUS OF MEN
  I'm withered from this chill I got!

CHORUS OF WOMEN
> You've got a fire, so warm yourself. You're trembling:
> are you nervous?

[*Enter a* COMMISSIONER, *escorted by four Scythian policemen with bows and quivers slung on their backs.*]

COMMISSIONER
> Has the extravagance of women broken out
> into full fury, with their banging tambourines
> and constant wailings for their oriental gods,
> and on the roof-tops their Adonis festival,
> which I could hear myself from the Assembly once?
> For while Demostratos—that numbskull—had the floor,
> urging an expedition against Sicily,
> his wife was dancing and we heard her crying out
> "Weep for Adonis!"[4]—so the expedition failed
> with such an omen. When the same Demostratos
> was urging that we levy troops from our allies
> his wife was on the roof again, a little drunk:
> "Weep for Adonis! Beat your breast!" says she. At that,
> he gets more bellicose, that god-Damn-ox-tratos.
> To this has the incontinence of women come!

CHORUS OF MEN
> You haven't *yet* heard how outrageous they can be!
> With other acts of violence, these women here
> have showered us from their jugs, so now we are reduced
> to shaking out our shirts as if we'd pissed in them.

COMMISSIONER
> Well, by the God of Waters, what do you expect?
> When we ourselves conspire with them in waywardness
> and give them good examples of perversity
> such wicked notions naturally sprout in them.
> We go into a shop and say something like this:
> "Goldsmith, about that necklace you repaired: last night
> my wife was dancing, when the peg that bolts the catch
> fell from its hole. I have to sail for Salamis,
> but if you have the time, by all means try to come
> towards evening, and put in the peg she needs."
> Another man says to a cobbler who is young
> and has no child's-play of a prick, "Cobbler," he says,

---

[4]*Weep for Adonis*—When the Athenian expedition against Syracuse embarked in 416 B.C., the women were lamenting the death of Adonis—an appropriately evil omen because the expedition proved a national disaster. With Alcibiades, Demostratos was a major supporter of the Sicilian campaign.

"her sandal-strap is pinching my wife's little toe,
which is quite delicate. So please come by at noon
and stretch it for her so it has a wider play."
Such things as that result of course in things like this:
when I, as a Commissioner, have made a deal
to fit the fleet with oars and need the money now,
I'm locked out by these women from the very gates.
But it's no use just standing here. Bring on the bars,
so I can keep these women in their proper place.
What are *you* gaping at, you poor unfortunate?
Where are *you* looking? Only seeing if a bar
is open yet downtown? Come, drive these crowbars in
under the gates on that side, pry away, and I
will pry away on this.

[LYSISTRATA *comes out.*]

LYSISTRATA
No need to pry at all.
I'm coming out, of my own will. What use are bars?
It isn't bolts and bars we need so much as brains.

COMMISSIONER
Really, you dirty slut? Where is that officer?
Arrest her, and tie both her hands behind her back.

LYSISTRATA
By Artemis, just let him lift a hand at me
and, public officer or not, you'll hear him howl.

COMMISSIONER
You let her scare you? Grab her round the middle, you.
Then *you* go help him and between you get her tied.

[KALONIKE *comes out.*]

KALONIKE
By Artemis, if you just lay one hand on her
I have a mind to trample the shit out of you.

COMMISSIONER
It's out already! Look! Now where's the other one?
Tie up *that* woman first. She babbles, with it all.

[MYRRHINA *comes out.*]

MYRRHINA
By Hecatë, if you just lay a hand on her
you'll soon ask for a cup—to get your swellings down!

[*The policeman dashes behind the* COMMISSIONER—*and clings to him for protection.*]

COMMISSIONER
What happened? Where's that bowman, now? Hold
onto *her!*

[*He moves quickly away downhill.*]

I'll see that none of you can get away through here!

LYSISTRATA
By Artemis, you come near her and I'll bereave
your head of every hair! You'll weep for each one, too.

COMMISSIONER
What a calamity! This one has failed me too.
But never must we let ourselves be overcome
by women. All together now, O Scythians!—
let's march against them in formation!

LYSISTRATA
                                        You'll find out
that inside there we have four companies
of fighting women perfectly equipped for war.

COMMISSIONER
Charge! Turn their flanks, O Scythians! and tie
their hands!

LYSISTRATA
O allies—comrades—women! Sally forth and fight!
O vegetable vendors, O green-grocery-
grain-garlic-bread-bean-dealers and inn-keepers all!

[*A group of fierce* OLD MARKET-WOMEN, *carrying baskets of vegetables, spindles, etc. emerges. There is a volley of vegetables. The Scythians are soon routed.*]

Come pull them, push them, smite them, smash them into bits!
Rail and abuse them in the strongest words you know!
Halt, Halt! Retire in order! We'll forego the spoils!

COMMISSIONER [*tragically, like say Xerxes*]
Oh what reverses have my bowmen undergone!

LYSISTRATA
But what did you imagine? Did you think you came
against a pack of slaves? Perhaps you didn't know
that women can be resolute?

COMMISSIONER

        I know they can—
above all when they spot a bar across the way.

CHORUS OF MEN

 Commissioner of Athens, you are spending words
   unduly,
 to argue with these animals, who only roar the louder,
 or don't you know they showered us so coldly and so cruelly,
 and in our undershirts at that, and furnished us no powder?

CHORUS OF WOMEN

 But beating up your neighbor is inevitably bringing
 a beating on yourself, sir, with your own eyes black and bloody.
 I'd rather sit securely like a little girl demurely
 not stirring up a single straw nor harming anybody,
 So long as no one robs my hive and rouses me to stinging.

CHORUS OF MEN

 How shall we ever tame these brutes? We cannot tolerate
 the situation further, so we must investigate
    this occurrence and find
    with what purpose in mind
 they profane the Acropolis, sieze it, and lock
 the approach to this huge and prohibited rock,
    to our holiest ground!
 Cross-examine them! Never believe one word
    they tell you—refute them, confound them!
 We must get to the bottom of things like this
    and the circumstances around them.

COMMISSIONER

 Yes indeed! and I want to know first one thing:
    just *why* you committed this treason,
 barricading the fortress with locks and bars—
    I insist on knowing the reason.

LYSISTRATA

 To protect all the money up there from you—
    you'll have nothing to fight for without it.

COMMISSIONER

 You think it is *money* we're fighting for?

LYSISTRATA

 All the troubles we have are about it.
 It was so Peisander and those in power
    of his kind could embezzle the treasure
 that they cooked up emergencies all the time.

Well, let them, if such is their pleasure,
but they'll never get into this money again,
though you men should elect them to spend it.

COMMISSIONER
And just what will *you* do with it?

LYSISTRATA

Can you ask?
Of course we shall superintend it.

COMMISSIONER
You will superintend the treasury, *you!?*

LYSISTRATA
And why should it strike you so funny?
when we manage our houses in everything
and it's we who look after your money.

COMMISSIONER
But it's not the same thing!

LYSISTRATA

Why not?

COMMISSIONER

It's war,
and *this* money must pay the expenses.

LYSISTRATA
To begin with, you needn't be waging war.

COMMISSIONER
To survive, we don't need our defenses?

LYSISTRATA
You'll survive: we shall save you.

COMMISSIONER

Who? You?

LYSISTRATA

Yes, we.

COMMISSIONER
You absolutely disgust me.

LYSISTRATA
You may like it or not, but you *shall* be saved.

COMMISSIONER
I protest!

LYSISTRATA
If you care to, but, trust me,
this has got to be done all the same.

COMMISSIONER
It has?
It's illegal, unjust, and outrageous!

LYSISTRATA
We must save you, sir.

COMMISSIONER
Yes? And if I refuse?

LYSISTRATA
You will much the more grimly engage us.

COMMISSIONER
And whence does it happen that war and peace
are fit matters for women to mention?

LYSISTRATA
I will gladly explain—

COMMISSIONER
And be quick, or else
you'll be howling!

LYSISTRATA
Now, just pay attention
and keep your hands to yourself, if you can!

COMMISSIONER
But I can't. You can't think how I suffer
from holding them back in my anger!

AN OLD WOMAN
Sir—
if you don't you will have it much rougher.

COMMISSIONER
You may croak that remark to yourself, you hag!
Will *you* do the explaining?

LYSISTRATA
I'll do it.
Heretofore we women in time of war

have endured very patiently through it,
putting up with whatever you men might do,
   for never a peep would you let us
deliver on your unstatesmanly acts
   no matter how much they upset us,
but we knew very well, while we sat at home,
   when you'd handled a big issue poorly,
and we'd ask you then, with a pretty smile
   though our heart would be grieving us sorely,
"And what were the terms for a truce, my dear,
   you drew up in assembly this morning?"
"And what's it to you?" says our husband, "Shut up!"
   —so, as ever, at this gentle warning
I of course would discreetly shut up.

KALONIKE

                    Not me!
You can bet I would never be quiet!

COMMISSIONER
I'll bet, if you weren't, you were beaten up.

LYSISTRATA
I'd shut up, and I do not deny it,
but when plan after plan was decided on,
   so bad we could scarcely believe it,
I would say "This last is so mindless, dear,
   I cannot think how you achieve it!"
And then he would say, with a dirty look,
   "Just you think what your spindle is for, dear,
or your head will be spinning for days on end—
   let the *men* attend to the war, dear."[5]

COMMISSIONER
By Zeus, *he* had the right idea!

LYSISTRATA
                 You fool!
Right ideas were quite out of the question,
when your reckless policies failed, and yet
   we never could make a suggestion.
And lately we heard you say so yourselves:
   in the streets there'd be someone lamenting:
"There's not one man in the country now!"
   —and we heard many others assenting.

---

[5]*Let the men . . . war*—Lysistrata's husband is quoting Hector to Andromache, *Iliad* VI, 492.

After that, we conferred through our deputies
    and agreed, having briefly debated,
to act in common to save all Greece
    at once—for why should we have waited?
So now, when we women are talking sense,
    if you'll only agree to be quiet
and to listen to us as we did to you,
    you'll be very much edified by it.

COMMISSIONER
You will edify *us!* I protest!

LYSISTRATA
                Shut up!

COMMISSIONER
    I'm to shut up and listen, you scum, you?!
Sooner death! And a veil on your head at that!

LYSISTRATA
    We'll fix that. It may really become you:
do accept this veil as a present from me.
Drape it modestly—so—round your head, do you see?
And now—*not* a word more, sir.

KALONIKE
Do accept this dear little wool-basket, too!
Hitch your girdle and card! Here are beans you may chew
the way all of the nicest Athenians do—
and the *women* will see to the war, sir!

CHORUS OF WOMEN
Oh women, set your jugs aside and keep a closer
    distance:
our friends may need from us as well some resolute assistance.

    Since never shall I weary of the stepping of the dance
nor will my knees of treading, for these ladies I'll advance
      anywhere they may lead,
      and they're daring indeed,
    they have wit, a fine figure, and boldness of heart,
    they are prudent and charming, efficient and smart,
      patriotic and brave!

But, O manliest grandmothers, onward now!
    And you matronly nettles, don't waver!
But continue to bristle and rage, my dears,
    for you've still got the wind in your favor!

[*The* Chorus of Women *and the* Old Market-Women *join.*]

LYSISTRATA
But if only the spirit of tender Love
 and the power of sweet Aphrodite
were to breathe down over our breasts and thighs
 an attraction both melting and mighty,
and infuse a pleasanter rigor in men,
 raising only their cudgels of passion,
then I think we'd be known throughout all of Greece
 as makers of peace and good fashion.

COMMISSIONER
Having done just what?

LYSISTRATA
     Well, first of all
 we shall certainly make it unlawful
to go madly to market in armor.

AN OLD MARKET-WOMAN
      Yes!
 By dear Aphrodite, it's awful!

LYSISTRATA
For now, in the midst of the pottery-stalls
 and the greens and the beans and the garlic,
men go charging all over the market-place
 in full armor and beetling and warlike.

COMMISSIONER
They must do as their valor impels them to!

LYSISTRATA
But it makes a man only look funny
to be wearing a shield with a Gorgon's head
 and be wanting sardines for less money.

OLD MARKET-WOMEN
Well, I saw a huge cavalry-captain once
 on a stallion that scarcely could hold him,
pouring into his helmet of bronze a pint
 of pea-soup an old women had sold him,
and a Thracian who, brandishing shield and spear
 like some savage Euripides staged once,
when he'd frightened a vendor of figs to death,
 gobbled up all her ripest and aged ones.

COMMISSIONER
    And how, on the international scale,
        can you straighten out the enormous
    confusion among all the states of Greece?

LYSISTRATA
    Very easily.

COMMISSIONER
    How? Do inform us.

LYSISTRATA
    When our skein's in a tangle we take it thus
        on our spindles, or haven't you seen us?—
    one on this side and one on the other side,
        and we work out the tangles between us.
    And that is the way we'll undo this war,
        by exchanging ambassadors, whether
    you like it or not, one from either side,
        and we'll work out the tangles together.

COMMISSIONER
    Do you really think that with wools and skeins
        and just being able to spin you
    can end these momentous affairs, you fools?

LYSISTRATA
    With any intelligence in you
    you statesmen would govern as we work wool,
        and in everything Athens would profit.

COMMISSIONER
    How so? Do tell.

LYSISTRATA
                        First, you take raw fleece
        and you wash the beshittedness off it:
    just so, you should first lay the city out
        on a washboard and beat out the rotters
    and pluck out the sharpers like burrs, and when
        you find tight knots of schemers and plotters
    who are out for key offices, card them loose,
        but best tear off their heads in addition.
    Then into one basket together card
        all those of a good disposition
    be they citizens, resident aliens, friends,
        an ally or an absolute stranger,

even people in debt to the commonwealth,
       you can mix them all in with no danger.
And the cities which Athens has colonized—
       by Zeus, you should try to conceive them
as so many shreddings and tufts of wool
       that are scattered about and not leave them
to lie around loose, but from all of them
       draw the threads in here, and collect them
into one big ball and then weave a coat
       for the people, to warm and protect them.

COMMISSIONER
       like wool to be beaten and carded,
Now, isn't this awful? They treat the state
who have nothing at all to do with war!

LYSISTRATA
       Yes we do, you damnable hard-head!
We have none of your honors but we have more
       then double your sufferings by it.
First of all, we bear sons whom you send to war.

COMMISSIONER
       Don't bring up our old sorrows! Be quiet!

LYSISTRATA
       And now, when we ought to enjoy ourselves,
       making much of our prime and our beauty,
we are sleeping alone because all the men
       are away on their soldierly duty.
But never mind *us*—when young girls grow old
       in their bedrooms with no men to share them.

COMMISSIONER
       You seem to forget that men, too, grow old.

LYSISTRATA
       By Zeus, but you cannot compare them!
When a man gets back, though he be quite gray,
       he can wed a young girl in a minute,
but the season of woman is very short:
       she must take what she can while she's in it
And you know she must, for when it's past,
       although you're not awfully astute, you're
aware that no man will marry her then
       and she sits staring into the future.

COMMISSIONER
       But he who can raise an erection still—

LYSISTRATA
Is there some good reason you don't drop dead?
We'll sell you a coffin if you but will.
Here's a string of onions to crown your head
and I'll make a honey-cake large and round
you can feed to Cerberus underground!

FIRST OLD MARKET-WOMAN
Accept these few fillets of leek from me!

SECOND OLD MARKET-WOMAN
Let me offer you these for your garland, sir!

LYSISTRATA
What now? Do you want something else you see?
Listen! Charon's calling his passenger—
will you catch the ferry or still delay
when his other dead want to sail away?

COMMISSIONER
Is it not downright monstrous to treat *me* like this?
By Zeus, I'll go right now to the Commissioners
and show myself in evidence, just as I am!

[*He begins to withdraw with dignity and his four Scythian police-men.*]

LYSISTRATA
Will you accuse us of not giving you a wake?
But your departed spirit will receive from us
burnt offerings in due form, two days from now at dawn!

[LYSISTRATA *with the other women goes into the Acropolis. The Co-*MISSIONER *etc. have left. The male chorus and the mixed female chorus are alone.*]

CHORUS OF MEN
No man now dare fall to drowsing, if he wishes
    to stay free!
Men, let's strip and gird ourselves for this eventuality!

To me this all begins to have a smell
of bigger things and larger things as well:
most of all I sniff a tyranny afoot. I'm much afraid
certain secret agents of the Spartans may have come,
meeting under cover here, in Cleisthenes's home,
instigating those damned women by deceit to make a raid
upon our treasury and that great sum
the city paid my pension from.

Sinister events already!—think of lecturing the state,
women as they are, and prattling on of things like shields of
    bronze,
even trying hard to get us reconciled to those we hate—
those of Sparta, to be trusted like a lean wolf when it yawns!
All of this is just a pretext, men, for a dictatorship—
but to me they shall not dictate! Watch and ward! A sword I'll
    hide
underneath a branch of myrtle; through the agora I'll slip,
following Aristogeiton, backing the tyrannicide!

[*The* OLD MEN *pair off to imitate the gestures of the famous group statue
of the tyrannicides Harmodius and Aristogeiton.*]

Thus I'll take my stand beside him! Now my rage is goaded raw
I'm as like as not to clip this damned old woman on the jaw!

CHORUS OF WOMEN
    Your own mother will not know you when
      you come home, if you do!
    Let us first, though, lay our things down, O my dear old friends
      and true.

        For now, O fellow-citizens, we would
        consider what will do our city good.
    Well I may, because it bred me up in wealth and elegance:
      letting me at seven help with the embroidering
      of Athena's mantle, and at ten with offering
    cakes and flowers. When I was grown and beautiful I had my
      chance
      to bear her baskets, at my neck a string
      of figs, and proud as anything.

Must I not, then, give my city any good advice I can?
Need you hold the fact against me that I was not born a man,
when I offer better methods than the present ones, and when
I've a share in this economy, for I contribute men?
But, you sad old codgers, *yours* is forfeited on many scores:
you have drawn upon our treasure dating from the Persian wars,
what they call grampatrimony, and you've paid no taxes back.
Worse, you've run it nearly bankrupt, and the prospect's pretty
    black.
Have you anything to answer? Say you were within the law
and I'll take this rawhide boot and clip you one across the jaw!

CHORUS OF MEN
      Greater insolence than ever!—
      that's the method that she calls
      "better"—if you would believe her.

But this threat must be prevented! Every man with both his balls
must make ready—take our shirts off, for a man must reek of
    male
outright—not wrapped up in leafage like an omelet for sale!

> Forward and barefoot: we'll do it again
> to the death, just as when we resisted
> tyranny out of Leipsydrion, when
> we really existed!

> Now or never we must grow
> young again and, sprouting wings
> over all our bodies, throw
> off this heaviness age brings!

For if any of us give them even just a little hold
nothing will be safe from their tenacious grasp. They are so bold
they will soon build ships of war and, with exorbitant intent,
send such navies out against us as Queen Artemisia[6] sent.
But if they attack with horse, our knights we might as well delete:
nothing rides so well as woman, with so marvelous a seat,
never slipping at the gallop. Just look at those Amazons
in that picture in the Stoa, from their horses bringing bronze
axes down on men. We'd better grab *these* members of the sex
one and all, arrest them, get some wooden collars on their necks!

CHORUS OF WOMEN
> By the gods, if you chagrin me
> or annoy me, if you dare,
> I'll turn loose the sow that's in me

till you rouse the town to help you with the way I've done your
    hair!
Let us too make ready, women, and our garments quickly doff
so we'll smell like women angered fit to bite our fingers off!

> Now I am ready: let one of the men
> come against me, and *he'll* never hanker
> after a black bean or garlic again:
> no woman smells ranker!

> Say a single unkind word,
> I'll pursue you till you drop,
> as the beetle did the bird.
> My revenge will never stop!

---

[6]*Queen Artemisia*—ruler of Halicarnassus, whose fleet fought on the Persian side
at Salamis (480 B.C.).

Yet you will not worry me so long as Lampito's alive
and my noble friends in Thebes and other cities still survive.
You'll not overpower us, even passing seven decrees or eight,
you, poor brutes, whom everyone and everybody's neighbors hate.
Only yesterday I gave a party, honoring Hecatë,
but when I invited in the neighbor's child to come and play,
such a pretty thing from Thebes, as nice and quiet as you please,
just an eel, they said she couldn't, on account of your decrees.
You'll go on forever passing such decrees without a check
till somebody takes you firmly by the leg and breaks your neck!

[LYSISTRATA *comes out. The* CHORUS OF WOMEN *addresses her in the manner of tragedy.*]

Oh Queen of this our enterprise and all our hopes,
wherefore in baleful brooding hast thou issued forth?

LYSISTRATA
The deeds of wicked women and the female mind
discourage me and set me pacing up and down.

CHORUS OF WOMEN
What's that? What's that you say?

LYSISTRATA
The truth, alas, the truth!

CHORUS OF WOMEN
What is it that's so dreadful? Tell it to your friends.

LYSISTRATA
A shameful thing to tell and heavy not to tell.

CHORUS OF WOMEN
Oh, never hide from me misfortune that is ours!

LYSISTRATA
To put it briefly as I can, we are in heat.

CHORUS OF WOMEN
Oh Zeus!

LYSISTRATA
Why call on Zeus? This is the way things are.
At least it seems I am no longer capable
of keeping them from men. They are deserting me.
This morning I caught one of them digging away
to make a tunnel to Pan's grotto down the slope,
another letting herself down the parapet
with rope and pulley, and another climbing down

its sheerest face, and yesterday was one I found
sitting upon a sparrow with a mind to fly
down to some well-equipped whoremaster's place in town.
Just as she swooped I pulled her backward by the hair.
They think of every far-fetched excuse they can
for going home. And here comes one deserter now.
You there, where are you running?

FIRST WOMAN

                    I want to go home,
because I left some fine Milesian wools at home
that must be riddled now with moths.

LYSISTRATA

                Oh, damn your moths!
Go back inside.

FIRST WOMAN
But I shall come back right away,
just time enough to stretch them out upon my bed.

LYSISTRATA
Stretch nothing out, and don't you go away at all.

FIRST WOMAN
But shall I let my wools be ruined?

LYSISTRATA

                   If you must.

SECOND WOMAN
Oh miserable me! I sorrow for the flax
I left at home unbeaten and unstripped!

LYSISTRATA

                  One more—
wanting to leave for stalks of flax she hasn't stripped.
Come back here!

SECOND WOMAN
But, by Artemis, I only want
to strip my flax. Then I'll come right back here again.

LYSISTRATA
Strip me no strippings! If you start this kind of thing
some other woman soon will want to do the same.

THIRD WOMAN
O lady Artemis, hold back this birth until
I can get safe to some unconsecrated place!

LYSISTRATA
What is this raving?

THIRD WOMAN
I'm about to have a child.

LYSISTRATA
But you weren't pregnant yesterday.

THIRD WOMAN
I am today.
Oh, send me home this instant, dear Lysistrata,
so I can find a midwife.

LYSISTRATA
What strange tale is this?
What is this hard thing you have here?

THIRD WOMAN
The child is male.

LYSISTRATA
By Aphrodite, no! You obviously have
some hollow thing of bronze. I'll find what it is.
You silly thing!—you have Athena's helmet here—
and claiming to be pregnant!

THIRD WOMAN
So I am, by Zeus!

LYSISTRATA
In that case, what's the helmet for?

THIRD WOMAN
So if the pains
came on me while I'm still up here, I might give birth
inside the helmet, as I've seen the pigeons do.

LYSISTRATA
What an excuse! The case is obvious. Wait here.
I want to show this bouncing baby helmet off.

[*She passes the huge helmet around the* CHORUS OF WOMEN.]

SECOND WOMAN
But I can't even sleep in the Acropolis,
not for an instant since I saw the sacred snake!

FOURTH WOMAN
The owls are what are killing *me*. How can I sleep
with their eternal whit-to-whoo-to-whit-to-whoo?

LYSISTRATA
You're crazy! Will you stop this hocus-pocus now?
No doubt you miss your husbands: don't you think that they
are missing us as much? I'm sure the nights they pass
are just as hard. But, gallant comrades, do bear up,
and face these gruelling hardships yet a little while.
There is an oracle that says we'll win, if we
only will stick together. Here's the oracle.

CHORUS OF WOMEN
Oh, read us what it says!

LYSISTRATA
                    Keep silence, then and hear:
"Now when to one high place are gathered the fluttering swallows,
Fleeing the Hawk and the Cock however hotly it follows,
Then will their miseries end, and that which is over be under:
Thundering Zeus will decide.

A WOMAN
                    Will *we* lie on top now, I wonder?

LYSISTRATA
But if the Swallows go fighting each other and springing
*   and winging*
Out of the holy and high sanctuary, then people will never
Say there was any more dissolute bitch of a bird whatsoever.

A WOMAN
The oracle is clear, by Zeus!

LYSISTRATA
                    By *all* the gods!
So let us renounce the hardships we endure.
But let us go back in. Indeed, my dearest friends,
it would be shameful to betray the oracle.

[*Exeunt into the Acropolis.*]

CHORUS OF MEN
Let me tell you a story I heard one day when I
    was a child:
There was once a young fellow Melanion by name

who refused to get married and ran away
    to the wild.
    To the mountains he came
    and inhabited there
       in a grove
    and hunted the hare
    both early and late
    with nets that he wove
    and also a hound
and he never came home again, such was his hate,
    all women he found
    so nasty, and we
    quite wisely agree.

Let us kiss you, dear old dears!

CHORUS OF WOMEN
  With no onions, you'll shed tears!

CHORUS OF MEN
  I mean, lift my leg and *kick*.

CHORUS OF WOMEN
  My, you wear your thicket thick!

CHORUS OF MEN
  Great Myronides was rough
    at the front and black enough
    in the ass to scare his foes.
        Just ask anyone who knows:
        it's with hair that wars are won—
        take for instance Phormion.

CHORUS OF WOMEN
  Let me tell you a story in answer to
    Melanion's case.
  There is now a man, Timon, who wanders around
  in the wilderness, hiding his face from view
      in a place
    where the brambles abound
    so he looks like a chip
      off a Fur-
  y, curling his lip.
    Now Timon retired
    in hatred and pure
    contempt of all men
  and he cursed them in words that were truly inspired
    again and again

but women he found
delightful and sound.
Would you like your jaw repaired?

CHORUS OF MEN
Thank you, no. You've got me scared.

CHORUS OF WOMEN
Let me jump and kick it though.

CHORUS OF MEN
You will let your man-sack show.

CHORUS OF WOMEN
All the same you wouldn't see,
old and gray as I may be,
any superfluity
of unbarbered hair on me;
it is plucked and more, you scamp,
since I singe it with a lamp!

[*Enter* LYSISTRATA *on the wall.*]

LYSISTRATA
Women, O women, come here quickly, here to me!

WOMEN
Whatever is it? Tell me! What's the shouting for?

LYSISTRATA
I see a man approaching, shaken and possessed,
seized and inspired by Aphrodite's power.
O thou of Cyprus, Paphos, and Cythera, queen!
continue straight along this way you have begun!

A WOMAN
Whoever he is, where is he?

LYSISTRATA
                                    Near Demeter's shrine.

A WOMAN
Why yes, by Zeus, he is. Who ever can he be?

LYSISTRATA
Well, look at him. Do any of you know him?

MYRRHINA
                                                        Yes.
I do. He's my own husband, too, Cinesias.

LYSISTRATA

Then it's your duty now to turn him on a spit,
cajole him and make love to him and not make love,
to offer everything, short of those things of which
the wine-cup knows.

MYRRHINA

I'll do it, don't you fear.

LYSISTRATA

And I

will help you tantalize him. I will stay up here
and help you roast him slowly. But now, disappear!

[*Enter* CINESIAS.]

CINESIAS

Oh how unfortunate I am, gripped by what spasms,
stretched tight like being tortured on a wheel!

LYSISTRATA

Who's there? Who has got this far past the sentries?

CINESIAS

I.

LYSISTRATA

A man?

CINESIAS

A man, for sure.

LYSISTRATA

Then clear away from here.

CINESIAS

Who're you, to throw me out?

LYSISTRATA

The look-out for the day.

CINESIAS

Then, for god's sake, call Myrrhina out for me.

LYSISTRATA

You don't say! Call Myrrhina out! And who are you?

CINESIAS

Her husband. I'm Cinesias Paionides.

LYSISTRATA

Well, my dear men, hello! Your name is not unknown
among us here and not without a certain fame,

because your wife has it forever on her lips.
She can't pick up an egg or quince but she must say:
Cinesias would enjoy it so!

CINESIAS

How wonderful!

LYSISTRATA

By Aphrodite, yes. And if we chance to talk
of husbands, your wife interrupts and says the rest
are nothing much compared to her Cinesias.

CINESIAS

Go call her.

LYSISTRATA

Will you give me something if I do?

CINESIAS

Indeed I will, by Zeus, if it is what you want.
I can but offer what I have, and I have this.

LYSISTRATA

Wait there. I will go down and call her.

CINESIAS

Hurry up!
because I find no charm whatever left in life
since she departed from the house. I get depressed
whenever I go into it, and everything
seems lonely to me now, and when I eat my food
I find no taste in it at all—because I'm stiff.

MYRRHINA [*offstage*]

I love him, how I love him! But he doesn't want
my love! [*on wall*] So what's the use of calling me to him?

CINESIAS

My sweet little Myrrhina, why do you act like that?
Come down here.

MYRRHINA

There? By Zeus, I certainly will not.

CINESIAS

Won't you come down, Myrrhina, when I'm calling you?

MYRRHINA

Not when you call me without needing anything.

CINESIAS

Not needing anything? I'm desperate with need.

MYRRHINA
I'm going now.

CINESIAS
                    Oh no! No, don't go yet! At least
you'll listen to the baby. Call your mammy, you.

BABY
Mammy mammy mammy!

CINESIAS
What's wrong with you? Have you no pity on your child
when it is six days now since he was washed or nursed?

MYRRHINA
Oh, I have pity. But his father takes no care of him.

CINESIAS
Come down, you flighty creature, for the child.

MYRRHINA
Oh, what it is to be a mother! I'll come down,
for what else can I do?

[MYRRHINA *exits to reenter below.*]

CINESIAS
                              It seems to me she's grown
much younger, and her eyes have a more tender look.
Even her being angry with me and her scorn
are just the things that pain me with the more desire.

MYRRHINA
Come let me kiss you, dear sweet little baby mine,
with such a horrid father. Mammy loves you, though.

CINESIAS
But why are you so mean? Why do you listen to
those other women, giving me such pain?—And you,
you're suffering yourself.

MYRRHINA
                    Take your hands off of me!

CINESIAS
But everything we have at home, my things and yours,
your're letting go to pieces.

MYRRHINA
                    Little do I care!

CINESIAS
Little you care even if your weaving's pecked apart
and carried off by chickens?

MYRRHINA [*bravely*]
                              Little I care, by Zeus!

CINESIAS
You have neglected Aphrodite's rituals
for such a long time now. Won't you come back again?

MYRRHINA
Not I, unless you men negotiate a truce
and make an end of war.

CINESIAS
                         Well, if it's so decreed,
    we will do even that.

MYRRHINA
                         Well, if it's so decreed,
    I will come home again. Not now. I've sworn I won't.

CINESIAS
All right, all right. But now lie down with me once more.

MYRRHINA
No! No!—yet I don't say I'm not in love with you.

CINESIAS
You love me? Then why not lie down, Myrrhina dear?

MYRRHINA
Don't be ridiculous! Not right before the child!

CINESIAS
By Zeus, of course not. Manes, carry him back home.
There now. You see the baby isn't in your way.
Won't you lie down?

MYRRHINA
                    But *where*, you rogue, just where
    is one to do it?

CINESIAS
                Where? Pan's grotto's a fine place.

MYRRHINA
But how could I come back to the Acropolis
in proper purity?

CINESIAS
>   Well, there's a spring below
> the grotto—you can very nicely bathe in that.

[*Ekkyklema or inset-scene with grotto*]

MYRRHINA
>   And then I'm under oath. What if I break my vows?

CINESIAS
>   Let me bear all the blame. Don't worry about your oath.

MYRRHINA
>   Wait here, and I'll go get a cot for us.

CINESIAS
>   No no,
>   the ground will do.

MYRRHINA
>   No, by Apollo! Though you *are*
> so horrid, I can't have you lying on the ground. [*Leaves.*]

CINESIAS
>   You know, the woman loves me—*that's* as plain as day.

MYRRHINA
>   There. Get yourself in bed and I'll take off my clothes.
>   Oh, what a nuisance! I must go and get a mat.

CINESIAS
>   What for? I don't need one.

MYRRHINA
>   Oh yes, by Artemis!
>   On the bare cords? How ghastly!

CINESIAS
>   Let me kiss you now.

MYRRHINA
>   Oh, very well.

CINESIAS
>   Wow! Hurry, hurry and come back.

[MYRRHINA *leaves. A long wait.*]

MYRRHINA
>   Here is the mat. Lie down now, while I get undressed.
>   Oh, what a nuisance! You don't have a pillow, dear.

CINESIAS
But I don't need one, not one bit!

MYRRHINA
                    By Zeus, *I* do [*Leaves.*]

CINESIAS
Poor prick, the service around here is terrible!

MYRRHINA
Sit up, my dear, jump up! Now I've got everything.

CINESIAS
Indeed you have. And now, my golden girl, come here.

MYRRHINA
I'm just untying my brassiere. Now don't forget:
about that treaty—you won't disappoint me, dear?

CINESIAS
By Zeus, no! On my life!

MYRRHINA
                    You have no blanket, dear.

CINESIAS
By Zeus, I do not need one. I just want to screw.

MYRRHINA
Don't worry, dear, you will. I'll be back right away.

[*Leaves.*]

CINESIAS
This number, with her bedding, means to murder me.

MYRRHINA
Now raise yourself upright.

CINESIAS
                    But *this* is upright now!

MYRRHINA
Wouldn't you like some perfume?

CINESIAS
                    By Apollo, no!

MYRRHINA
By Aphrodite, yes! You must—like it or not. [*Leaves.*]

CINESIAS
Lord Zeus! Just let the perfume spill! That's all I ask!

MYRRHINA
Hold out your hand. Take some of this and rub it on.

CINESIAS
This perfume, by Apollo, isn't sweet at all.
It smells a bit of stalling—not of wedding nights!

MYRRHINA
I brought the *Rhodian* perfume! How absurd of me!

CINESIAS
It's fine! Let's keep it.

MYRRHINA
You *will* have your little joke.

[*Leaves.*]

CINESIAS
Just let me at the man who first distilled perfumes!

MYRRHINA
Try this, in the long vial.

CINESIAS
I've got one like it, dear.
But don't be tedious. Lie down. And please don't bring
anything more.

MYRRHINA [*going*]
That's what I'll do, by Artemis!
I'm taking off my shoes. But dearest, don't forget
you're going to vote for peace.

CINESIAS
I will consider it.
She has destroyed me, murdered me, that woman has!
On top of which she's got me skinned and gone away!
What shall I do? Oh, whom shall I screw,
cheated of dear Myrrhina, the first
beauty of all, a creature divine?
How shall I tend this infant of mine?
Find me a pimp: it has to be nursed!

CHORUS OF MEN [*in tragic style, as if to Prometheus or Andromeda bound*]

In what dire woe, how heavy-hearted
I see thee languishing, outsmarted!
  I pity thee, alas I do.
What kidney could endure such pain,
what spirit could, what balls, what back,
what loins, what sacroiliac,
  if they came under such a strain
  and never had a morning screw?

CINESIAS
O Zeus! the twinges! Oh, the twitches!

CHORUS OF MEN
And this is what she did to you,
  that vilest, hatefullest of bitches!

CINESIAS
Oh nay, by Zeus, she's dear and sweet!

CHORUS OF MEN
How can she be? She's vile, O Zeus, she's vile!
  Oh treat her, Zeus, like so much wheat—
  O God of Weather, hear my prayer—
  and raise a whirlwind's mighty blast
  to roll her up into a pile
  and carry her into the sky
  far up and up and then at last
  drop her and land her suddenly
  astride that pointed penis there!

[*The ekkykelma turns, closing the inset-scene. Enter, from opposite sides, a* SPARTAN *and an Athenian official.*]

SPARTAN
Wheah is the Senate-house of the Athenians?
Ah wish to see the chaihman. Ah have news fo him.

ATHENIAN
And who are you? Are you a Satyr or a man?

SPARTAN
Ah am a herald, mah young friend, yes, by the gods,
and Ah have come from Sparta to negotiate.

ATHENIAN
And yet you come here with a spear under your arm?

SPARTAN
Not Ah, bah Zeus, not Ah!

ATHENIAN

                            Why do you turn around?
Why throw your cloak out so in front? Has the long trip
given you a swelling?

SPARTAN

                       Ah do think the man is queah!

ATHENIAN

But you have an erection, oh you reprobate!

SPARTAN

Bah Zeus, Ah've no sech thing! And don't you fool
    around!

ATHENIAN

And what have you got there?

SPARTAN

                        A Spahtan scroll-stick, suh.

ATHENIAN

Well, if it is, *this* is a Spartan scroll-stick, too.
But look, I know what's up: you can tell *me* the truth.
Just how are things with you in Sparta: tell me that.

SPARTAN

Theah is uprising in all Spahta. Ouah allies
are all erect as well. We need ouah milkin'-pails.

ATHENIAN

From where has this great scourge of frenzy fallen on you?
From Pan?

SPARTAN

No, Ah think Lampito began it all,
and then, the othah women throughout Spahta joined
togethah, just lahk at a signal fo a race,
and fought theah husbands off and drove them from theah cunts.

ATHENIAN

So, how're you getting on?

SPARTAN

                    We suffah. Through the town
we walk bent ovah as if we were carrying
lamps in the wind. The women will not let us touch
even theah berries, till we all with one acco'd
have made a peace among the cities of all Greece.

ATHENIAN
    This is an international conspiracy
    launched by the women! Now I comprehend it all!
    Return at once to Sparta. Tell them they must send
    ambassadors fully empowered to make peace.
    And our Assembly will elect ambassadors
    from our side, when I say so, showing them this prick.

SPARTAN
    Ah'll run! Ah'll flah! Fo all you say is excellent!

CHORUS OF MEN
    No wild beast is more impossible than woman is to fight,
    nor is fire, nor has the panther such unbridled appetite!

CHORUS OF WOMEN
    Well you know it, yet you go on warring with me
        without end,
    when you might, you cross-grained creature, have me as a trusty
        friend.

CHORUS OF MEN
    Listen: I will never cease from hating women till I die!

CHORUS OF WOMEN
    Any time you like. But meanwhile is there any reason why
    I should let you stand there naked, looking so ridiculous?
    I am only coming near you, now, to slip your coat on, thus.

CHORUS OF MEN
    That was very civil of you, very kind to treat me so,
    when in such uncivil rage I took it off a while ago.

CHORUS OF WOMEN
    Now you're looking like a man again, and not ridiculous.
    If you hadn't hurt my feelings, I would not have made a fuss,
    I would even have removed that little beast that's in your eye.

CHORUS OF MEN
    That is what was hurting me! Well, won't you take my
        ring to pry
    back my eyelid? Rake the beast out. When you have it, let me see,
    for some time now it's been at my eye and irritating me.

CHORUS OF WOMEN
    Very well, I will—though you were *born* an irritable man.
    What a monster of a gnat, by Zeus! Look at it if you can.
    Don't you see it? It's a native of great marshes, can't you tell?

CHORUS OF MEN
    Much obliged, by Zeus! The brute's been digging at me
        like a well!
    So that now you have removed it, streams of tears come welling
        out.

CHORUS OF WOMEN
    I will dry them. You're the meanest man alive, beyond
        a doubt,
    yet I will, and kiss you, too.

CHORUS OF MEN

Don't kiss me!

CHORUS OF WOMEN

If you will or not!

CHORUS OF MEN
    Damn you! Oh, what wheedling flatterers you
        all are, born and bred!
    That old proberb is quite right and not inelegantly said:
    There's no living *with* the bitches and, without them, even *less*"—
    so I might as well make peace with you, and from now on, I guess
    I'll do nothing mean to you and, from you, suffer nothing wrong.
    So let's draw our ranks together now and start a little song:
        For a change, we're not preparing
        any mean remark or daring
        aimed at any man in town,
    but the very opposite: we plan to do and say
    only good to everyone,
    when the ills we have already are sufficient anyway.
        Any man or woman who
        wants a little money, oh
        say three minas, maybe two,
        kindly let us know.
        What we have is right in here.
        (Notice we have purses, too!)
        And if ever peace appear,
        he who takes our loan today
            never need repay.

        We are having guests for supper,
        allies asked in by our upper
        classes to improve the town.
    There's pea-soup, and I had killed a sucking-pig of mine:
    I shall see it is well done,
    so you will be tasting something very succulent and fine.

Come to see us, then, tonight
early, just as soon as you
have a bath and dress up right:
bring your children, too.
Enter boldly, never mind
asking anyone in sight.
Go straight in and you will find
you are quite at home there, but
all the doors are shut.

And here come the Spartan ambassadors,
  dragging beards that are really the biggest I
have ever beheld, and around their things
    they are wearing some sort of a pig-sty.

  Oh men of Sparta, let me bid you welcome first,
  and then you tell us how you are and why you come.

SPARTAN
  What need is theah to speak to you in many words?
  Fo you may see youahself in what a fix we come.

CHORUS OF MEN
  Too bad! Your situation has become
  terribly hard and seems to be at fever-pitch.

SPARTAN
  Unutterably so! And what is theah to say?
  Let someone bring us peace on any tuhms he will!

CHORUS OF MEN
  And here I see some natives of Athenian soil,
  holding their cloaks far off their bellies, like the best
  wrestlers, who sicken at the touch of cloth. It seems
  that overtraining may bring on this strange disease.

ATHENIAN
  Will someone tell us where to find Lysistrata?
  We're men, and here we are, in this capacity.

CHORUS OF MEN
  This symptom and that other one sound much alike.
  Toward morning I expect convulsions do occur?

ATHENIAN
  By Zeus, we are exhausted with just doing that,
  so, if somebody doesn't reconcile us quick,
  there's nothing for it: we'll be screwing Cleisthenes.

CHORUS OF MEN
> Be careful—put your cloaks on, or you might be seen
> by some young blade who knocks the phalluses off herms.[7]

ATHENIAN
> By Zeus, an excellent idea!

SPARTAN [*having overheard*]
> Yes, bah the gods!
> It altogethah is. Quick, let's put on our cloaks.

[*Both groups cover quick and then recognize each other with full
diplomatic pomp.*]

ATHENIAN
> Greetings, O men of Sparta! [*to his group*] We have
>   been disgraced!

SPARTAN [*to one of his group*]
> Mah dearest fellah, what a dreadful thing fo *us,*
> if these Athenians had seen ouah wo'st defeat!

ATHENIAN
> Come now, O Spartans: one must specify each point.
> Why have you come here?

SPARTAN
>   To negotiate a peace.
> We ah ambassadahs.

ATHENIAN
>   Well put. And so are we.
> Therefore, why do we not call in Lysistrata,
> she who alone might get us to agree on terms?

SPARTAN
> Call her or any man, even a Lysistratus!

CHORUS OF MEN
> But you will have no need, it seems, to call her now,
> for here she is. She heard you and is coming out.

CHORUS OF MEN *and* CHORUS OF WOMEN
> All hail, O manliest woman of all!
>   It is time for you now to be turning

---

[7]*Knocks . . . off herms*—The reference is to a charge against Alcibiades, who was accused of mutilating statues of Hermes the night before he sailed for Syracuse.

into something still better, more dreadful, mean,
    unapproachable, charming, discerning,
for here are the foremost nations of Greece,
    bewitched by your spells like a lover,
who have come to you, bringing you all their claims,
    and to *you* turning everything over.

LYSISTRATA
    The work's not difficult, if one can catch them now
    while they're excited and not making passes at
    each other. I will soon find out. Where's *HARMONY?*

[*A naked maid, perhaps wearing a large ribbon reading HARMONY,
appears from inside.*]

    Go take the Spartans first, and lead them over here,
    not with a rough hand nor an overbearing one,
    nor, as our husbands used to do this, clumsily,
    but like a woman, in our most familiar style:
    If he won't give his hand, then lead him by the prick.
    And now, go bring me those Athenians as well,
    leading them by whatever they will offer you.
    O men of Sparta, stand right here, close by my side,
    and *you* stand over there, and listen to my words.
    I am a woman, yes, but there is mind in me.
    In native judgment I am not so badly off,
    and, having heard my father and my elders talk
    often enough, I have some cultivation, too.
    And so, I want to take and scold you, on both sides,
    as you deserve, for though you use a lustral urn
    in common at the altars, like blood-relatives,
    when at Olympia, Delphi, or Thermopylae—
    how many others I might name if I took time!—
    yet, with barbarian hordes of enemies at hand,
    it is Greek men, it is Greek cities, you destroy.
    That is one argument so far, and it is done.

ATHENIAN
    My prick is skinned alive—that's what's destroying *me.*

LYSISTRATA
    Now, men of Sparta—for I shall address you first—
    do you not know that once one of your kings came here
    and as a suppliant of the Athenians
    sat by our altars, death-pale in his purple robe,
    and begged us for an army? For Messenë then
    oppressed you, and an earthquake from the gods as well.

Then Cimon went, taking four thousand infantry,
and saved the whole of Lacedaemon for your state.[8]
That is the way Athenians once treated you;
you ravage their land now, which once received you well.

ATHENIAN
By Zeus, these men are in the wrong, Lysistrata!

SPARTAN [*with his eyes on* HARMONY]
We'ah wrong . . . What an utterably lovely ass!

LYSISTRATA
Do you suppose I'm letting you Athenians off?
Do you not know that once the Spartans in their turn,
when you were wearing the hide-skirts of slavery,
came with their spears and slew many Thessalians,
many companions and allies of Hippias?[9]
They were the only ones who fought for you that day,
freed you from tyranny and, for the skirt of hide,
gave back your people the wool mantle of free men.

SPARTAN
Ah nevah saw a woman broadah—in her views.

ATHENIAN
And I have never seen a lovelier little nook.

LYSISTRATA
So why, when you have done each other so much good,
go on fighting with no end of malevolence?
Why don't you make a peace? Tell me, what's in your way?

SPARTAN
Wah, *we* ah willin', if *they* will give up to us
that very temptin' cuhve.   [*of* HARMONY, *as hereafter*]

LYSISTRATA
                        What curve, my friend?

SPARTAN
                                                The bay
of Pylos, which we've wanted and felt out so long.

ATHENIAN
No, by Poseidon, you will not get into that!

---

[8]*Saved . . . your state*—Lysistrata reminds Spartans and Athenians of past mutual aid and obligation. When Sparta was endangered by a revolt of her serfs, the Athenians under Cimon led an army to the rescue (462 B.C.).

[9]*Hippias*—In about 510 B.C., the Spartans aided the exiled Athenian democrats in defeating the tyrant Hippias and his Thessalian allies.

LYSISTRATA
Good friend, do let them have it.

ATHENIAN

                                    No! What other town
    can we manipulate so well?

LYSISTRATA

                        Ask them for one.

ATHENIAN
    Damn, let me think! Now first suppose you cede to us
    that bristling tip of land, Echinos, behind which
    the gulf of Malia recedes, and those long walls,
    the legs on which Megara reaches to the sea.

SPARTAN
    No, mah deah man, not *everything*, bah Castah, no!

LYSISTRATA
    Oh, give them up. Why quarrel for a pair of legs?

ATHENIAN
    I'd like to strip and get to plowing right away.

SPARTAN
    And *Ah* would lahk to push manuah, still earliah.

LYSISTRATA
    When you have made a peace, then you will do all that.
    But if you want to do it, first deliberate,
    go and inform your allies and consult with them.

ATHENIAN
    Oh, damn our allies, my good woman! We are stiff.
    Will all of our allies not stand resolved with us—
    namely, to screw?

SPARTAN

                    And so will ouahs, Ah'll guarantee.

ATHENIAN
    Our mercenaries, even will agree with us.

LYSISTRATA
    Excellent. Now to get you washed and purified
    so you may enter the Acropolis, where we
    women will entertain you out of our supplies.
    You will exchange your pledges there and vows for peace.
    And after that each one of you will take his wife,
    departing then for home.

ATHENIAN

SPARTAN

          Lead on, ma'am, anywheah you lahk.
          Let's go in right away.

ATHENIAN
          Yes, and be quick.

[*Exeunt into Acropolis*]

CHORUS OF MEN *and* CHORUS OF WOMEN
      All the rich embroideries, the
      scarves, the gold accessories, the
      trailing gowns, the robes I own
  I begrudge to no man: let him take what things he will
  for his children or a grown
  daughter who must dress for the procession up Athena's hill.
      Freely of my present stocks
      I invite you all to take.
      There are here no seals nor locks
      very hard to break.
      Search through every bag and box,
      look—you will find nothing there
      if your eyesight isn't fine—
      sharper far than mine!

      Are there any of you needing
      food for all the slaves you're feeding,
      all your little children, too?
  I have wheat in tiny grains for you, the finest sort,
  and I also offer you
  plenty of the handsome strapping grains that slaves get by the
      quart.
      So let any of the poor
      visit me with bag or sack
      which my slave will fill with more
      wheat than they can pack,
      giving each his ample share.
      Might I add that at my door
      I have watch-dogs?—so beware.
      Come too close by day or night,
      you will find they bite.

[*Voice of drunken* ATHENIANS *from inside*]

FIRST ATHENIAN
  Open the door! [*shoves the porter aside*]
      And will you get out of my way?

[*A second drunken* ATHENIAN *follows. The first sees the chorus.*]

What are you sitting *there* for? Shall I, with this torch,
burn you alive? [*drops character*]
                          How vulgar! Oh, how commonplace!
I can not do it!

[*Starts back in. The second* ATHENIAN *stops him and remonstrates with
him in a whisper. The first turns and addresses the audience.*]

                          Well, if it really must be done
to please you, we shall face it and go through with it.

CHORUS OF MEN *and* CHORUS OF WOMEN
And *we* shall face it and go through with it with you.

FIRST ATHENIAN [*in character again, extravagantly*]
Clear out of here! Or you'll be wailing for your hair!

[CHORUS OF WOMEN *scours away in mock terror.*]

Clear out of here! so that the Spartans can come out
and have no trouble leaving, after they have dined.

[CHORUS OF MEN *scours away in mock terror.*]

SECOND ATHENIAN
I never saw a drinking-party like this one:
even the Spartans were quite charming, and of course
we make the cleverest company, when in our cups.

FIRST ATHENIAN—
You're right, because when sober we are not quite sane.
If I can only talk the Athenians into it,
we'll always go on any embassy quite drunk,
for now, going to Sparta sober, we're so quick
to look around and see what trouble we can make
that we don't listen to a single word they say—
instead we think we hear them say what they do not—
and none of our reports on anything agree.
But just now everything was pleasant. If a man
got singing words belonging to another song,
we all applauded and swore falsely it was fine!
But here are those same people coming back again
to the same spot! Go and be damned, the pack of you!

[*The* CHORUS, *having thrown off their masks, put on other cloaks, and
rushed back on stage, stays put.*]

SECOND ATHENIAN
  Yes, damn them, Zeus! Just when the party's coming
    out![10]

[*The party comes rolling out.*]

A SPARTAN [*to another*]
  Mah very chahmin friend, will you take up youah flutes?
  Ah'll dance the dipody and sing a lovely song
  of us and the Athenians, of both at once!

FIRST ATHENIAN [*as pleasantly as he can*]
  Oh yes, take up your little reeds, by all the gods:
  I very much enjoy seeing you people dance.

SPARTAN
          Memory, come,
      come inspiah thah young
      votaries to song,
      come inspiah theah dance!

[*other* SPARTANS *join*]
          Bring thah daughtah, bring the sweet
        Muse, fo well she knows
      us and the Athenians,
        how at Ahtemisium
      they in godlike onslaught rose
      hahd against the Puhsian fleet,
          drove it to defeat!
      Well she knows the Spartan waws,
        how Leonidas
        in the deadly pass
        led us on lahk baws
      whettin' shahp theah tusks, how sweat
      on ouah cheeks in thick foam flowahed,
      off ouah legs how thick it showahed,
          fo the Puhsian men were mo'
          than the sands along the sho'.
      Goddess, huntress, Ahtemis,
      slayeh of the beasts, descend:
      vuhgin goddess, come to this
      feast of truce to bind us fast
      so ouah peace may neveh end.
      Now let friendship, love, and wealth
      come with ouah acco'd at last.

---

[10]*The party's coming out*—Athenian Old Comedy traditionally ended in a revel
(*komos*), an extravaganza of music and dancing.

May we stop ouah villainous
wahly foxy stealth!
 Come, O huntress, heah to us,
 heah, O vuhgin, neah to us!

LYSISTRATA
 Come, now that all the rest has been so well arranged,
 you Spartans take these women home; these others, you.
 Let husband stand beside his wife, and let each wife
 stand by her husband: then, when we have danced a dance
 to thank the gods for our good fortune, let's take care
 hereafter not to make the same mistakes again.

ATHENIAN
 Bring on the chorus! Invite the three Graces to follow,
 and then call on Artemis, call her twin brother,
 the leader of choruses, healer Apollo!

CHORUS [*joins*]
 Pray for their friendliest favor, the one and the other.
 Call Dionysus, his tender eyes casting
 flame in the midst of his Maenads ecstatic with dancing.
  Call upon Zeus, the resplendent in fire,
  call on his wife, rich in honor and ire,
 call on the powers who possess everlasting
 memory, call them to aid,
 call them to witness the kindly, entrancing
 peace Aphrodite has made!
   Alalai!
   Bound, leap high! Alalai!
   Cry, as for victory, cry
   Alalai!

LYSISTRATA
 Sing us a new song, Spartans, capping our new song.

SPARTANS
 Leave thah favohed mountain's height,
 Spahtan Muse, come celebrate
 Amyclae's lord with us and great
 Athena housed in bronze;
 praise Tyndareus paih of sons,
 gods who pass the days in spoht
 wheah the cold Eurotas runs.

[*general dancing*]

 Now to tread the dance,
 now to tread it light,

praising Spahta, wheah you find
　　love of singing quickened bah the pounding beat
　　　of dancing feet,
when ouah guhls lahk foals cavoht
wheah the cold Eurotas runs,
when they fleetly bound and prance
　　till theah haih unfilleted shakes in the wind,
as of Maenads brandishin'
ahvied wands and revelin',
　　Leda's daughtah, puah and faiah,
　　leads the holy dances theah.

FULL CHORUS [*as everyone leaves dancing*]

So come bind up youah haih with youah hand,
　　with youah feet make a bound
lahk a deeah; fo the chorus clap out
　　an encouragin' sound,
singin' praise of the temple of bronze
　　housin' her we adaw:
sing the praise of Athena: the goddess unvanquished in waw!

JOB

In form and theme Job more closely resembles a Greek tragedy than any other book of the Bible. Organized like a Euripidean drama, it has a Prologue which features a divine speaker, a series of messengers who bring news of off-stage deaths and other disasters, a central episode which presents a cycle of debates between the hero and his opponents, a *deus ex machina* who intervenes at the end to reveal his power and resolve the action, and an Epilogue which recounts the hero's subsequent fate. But while its structure is Euripidean, the central moral issue of Job is reminiscent of Aeschylean theology. The problem of evil and the conflict between divine power and human concepts of justice strikingly parallel the ethical battle between Might and Right in the *Prometheus Bound*.

It is impossible, however, to determine to what extent, if any, Job was influenced by Greek thought. Scholars are not only unable to date the work with any certainty, they are not even agreed on the number of writers who, at various times, contributed to its composition. Hebrew tradition ascribed the writing of Job to Moses, but both its theological content and language are clearly later than the Mosaic period. In fact, Job seems to be the product of a troubled age when the moral assumptions of the old Mosaic Code had lost much of their former authority. Books of the Mosaic Law, such as Numbers and Deuteronomy, had argued that the good man, obedient to Yahweh's regulations, would automatically enjoy security, prosperity, and long life. Only if he sinned would he suffer catastrophe. Unfortunately, the history of the Hebrew people did not bear out this orthodox belief. In 586 B.C. the nation of Israel was wiped out by its powerful neighbor, Babylon. Under King Nebuchadnezzar the Babylonion armies not only destroyed Jerusalem but also burned the magnificent Temple of Solomon, the holy place of Israel's God, Yahweh. While their sacred temple lay in ruins, the Israelites were taken captive to Babylon. Even when restored by the Persian king Cyrus in 539 B.C., Israel was reduced to a mere province in a Gentile empire. Israel's days of freedom and independence were over.

The question then plaguing every believer was: how could God allow such a catastrophe to overtake his chosen people? How could he permit his center of worship to fall into pagan hands? The prophets and the later biblical historians answered that Israel suffered defeat not because Yahweh was impotent to prevent it or had forgotten his promises to his people, but because the Israelites had, by their sinful disobedience of the Mosaic Law, forfeited their right to divine protection. The prophets' interpretation of history was simple: it was unthinkable that God could do wrong; consequently, man himself must be responsible for whatever evils befell him.

This is the thesis which the anonymous author of Job sets out to refute. He could not agree that the suffering of Israel under a succession of Gentile invaders was justified either by Deuteronomy's simplistic system of rewards and punishments or by the prophets' transference of

517

blame to the people themselves. Combining the traditional Hebrew reverence for Yahweh with a kind of Hellenistic scepticism and demand for moral logic, the author uses the Job story to illustrate the paradox inherent in Israel's religion. Directly stated, the dilemma is this: if God is all-good *and* all-powerful, why is the world a violent and evil place where even God's faithful worshippers suffer through no apparent fault of their own? Must men be held guilty in order for God to be justified in permitting wickedness?

The poet's response to this compelling issue inspires some of the greatest soul-searching poetry in world literature. Most critics agree that Job's opening lament and the long dialogues between Job and his three friends are the work of a single man (with perhaps later additions). The Prologue and Epilogue are in prose, however, and, apparently, not from the same pen. The prose introduction and conclusion probably represent a much older, perhaps original version of the Job story, into which the chief contributor to the present book inserted his poetic elaboration of Job's experiences.

Because it sets the stage for the drama to follow, the Prologue is important. It presents two scenes in Yahweh's heavenly court at which "the Satan" appears to make trouble. Satan challenges Yahweh that Job, a man of exemplary moral character, will not remain faithful to God when he is stripped of all he holds dear: family, property, and livelihood. For reasons known only to Himself, Yahweh accepts Satan's wager and permits the Devil to deprive Job of his possessions and to kill all Job's sons and daughters. But in spite of his losses, Job still blesses Yahweh's name. Satan next persuades Yahweh to test Job's loyalty further by afflicting him with a painful and loathesome disease that renders him unrecognizable. Again Job resists the temptation, suggested by his wife, to "curse God and die!"

It must be remembered that the Prologue gives no hint that Job has in any way deserved his harsh treatment. To the contrary, we have the word of Yahweh himself that Job is a "blameless and upright man who fears God and shuns evil." Yahweh further points out that Satan incites Him against Job "without cause." Not only is there no reference to the Christian doctrine of "Original Sin" to attribute a supposedly inherited guilt to Job, there is also no indication that Job is even guilty of pride or self-rightousness.[1] According to the Prologue, Job's only error is that he is too noticeably "upright" and is therefore singled out as the target of Satan's malice.

In chapter three the action shifts from the heavenly court to Job's dungheap, where, in a long and beautiful monologue, he curses the day he was born. He is joined by three friends, Eliphaz, Bildad, and Zophar, who give little comfort. Following the orthodox argument of the Mosaic

---

[1]Nor is there any indication that Job will be compensated for his earthly sufferings by a future reward in Heaven. The book's import is that Job must receive justice in this life or not at all.

Law, they insist that Job's present misery must be the result of some vile but unknown sin. Each friend gives a speech and Job in turn replies refuting their assumption that his suffering is a punishment for wickedness. As the debates between Job and his friends become more heated, Job's early patience gives way to a dawning realization of two unorthodox truths: (1) his humanity entitles him to certain moral rights, which Yahweh seems to ignore in permitting him to suffer undeservedly; and (2) if he, Job, is guiltless, who then is responsible for the evil which he—and all other men—endure? In chapters nine and ten Job's indignation against the injustice of his position reaches a climax. He challenges Yahweh to appear before him as another man, so that the conflict between them may be settled in terms of human justice. Foreshadowing Yahweh's imminent appearance in the Whirlwind, Job realizes that he has no chance to present the justice of his cause. Man is no match for the glory of God revealed in storm and thunder:

> Though in the right, I could not answer,
> I would have to entreat my opponent . . .
> He would crush with a tempest . . .
> Though righteous, his mouth would condemn me;
> Though guiltless, he would declare me perverse.
> I am innocent. . . .

As Job predicted, when Yahweh does appear it is not in human form to argue rationally the cause of injured innocence. Ignoring the mental anguish which was the chief source of Job's suffering, Yahweh speaks awesomely from the Whirlwind. Almost sardonically, He challenges Job to match Him in wisdom, power, and majesty:

> Would you annul my judgment,
> Condemn me that you may be justified?
> Have you an arm like God?
> Can you thunder with a voice like his?

Faced with Yahweh's irresistible might, Job can only cower before the terror of God revealed:

> Lo, I am small, how can I answer you?
> My hand I lay upon my mouth.

In a similar situation, Prometheus, fiercely convinced of his invincible rights, had shaken his fist at Zeus's Thunder and declared to the heavens that God was wrong so to afflict him. Job, however, is not an immortal Titan. Neither is he a Greek. His tame submission to a Power he does not understand is not necessarily a relinquishing of his own integrity, but may be seen as acknowledgment of his inability to comprehend the mysteries by which the universe is run. In the Epilogue Job is returned to his former comfort and prosperity. Chastened and placed securely in the Hebrew tradition of respect for the authority of God the Father, Job is given no further opportunity to manifest a Hellenic spirit of inquiry.

THE BOOK OF JOB

THE TESTING OF JOB

CHAPTER 1

[1]A MAN THERE WAS IN THE LAND OF UZ, JOB WAS HIS NAME. THAT MAN
was blameless and upright, one who feared God and shunned evil.
[2]Seven sons and three daughters were born to him. [3]His property was
seven thousand sheep, three thousand camels, five hundred yoke of
oxen, five hundred she-asses, and many servants, so that he was the
wealthiest of all the Easterners. [4]His sons used to hold feasts, each in his
house on his day, and they would send and invite their three sisters to
eat and drink with them. [5]When the feast days were over, Job would
send and have them purified. He would get busy in the morning and
offer sacrifices for each of them, for he said,

> "Perhaps my sons have sinned,
> And cursed God in their mind."

This Job did regularly
[6]The day arrived when the gods[1] come and present themselves
before Yahweh, and the Satan also came with them. [7]Yahweh said to
the Satan:

> "Where did you come from?"

The Satan answered Yahweh:

> "From roaming the earth,
> And strolling about in it"

[8]Yahweh said to the Satan:

> "Have you marked my servant Job?
> There is none like him on earth,
> A blameless and upright man
> Who fears God and shuns evil."

[9]The Satan answered Yahweh:

> "Does Job fear God for nought?
> [10]Have you not hedged him round,
> Him and his household
> And everything he has?

---

[1]*The gods*—literally "sons of the gods," perhaps angels.

From *Job* (*The Anchor Bible*), translated with an Introduction and Notes by
Marvin H. Pope. Copyright © 1965 by Doubleday and Company, Inc. Reprinted by
permission of the publisher. Notes are those of the present editor.

His efforts you have blessed,
And his property has increased in the land.
¹¹Just reach out and strike what he has,
And he will curse you to your face."

¹²Yahweh said to the Satan:

"Here, all he has is in your power,
But do not lay hand on him."

Then the Satan went out from Yahweh's presence.
¹³There came a day when Job's sons and daughters were eating and drinking wine in the oldest brother's house. ¹⁴A messenger came to Job and said:

"The oxen were plowing,
The asses grazing beside them,
¹⁵When the Sabeans² attacked and took them.
The boys they put to the sword.
I alone escaped to tell you."

¹⁶While he was still speaking, another came and said;

"Lightning fell from heaven
And burned the sheep and the boys and consumed them.
I alone escaped to tell you."

¹⁷While he was still speaking, another came and said:

"The Chaldeans³ formed three bands
And fell on the camels and took them.
The boys they put to the sword.
I alone escaped to tell you."

¹⁸While he was still speaking, another came and said:

"Your sons and your daughters
Were eating and drinking wine
In the house of their oldest brother,
¹⁹When, lo, a great wind came
From across the desert
And struck the four corners of the house.
It fell on the young folk and they died.
I alone escaped to tell you."

²⁰Then Job rose and tore his robe and shaved his head. He fell on the ground, and worshipped. ²¹He said:

2*Sabeans*—perhaps an Arabian tribe.
3*Chaldeans*—nomadic marauders; probably related to the Babylonians.

"Naked I came from my mother's womb,
And naked shall I return there.
Yahweh gave, Yahweh took away.
Blessed be Yahweh's name."

²²In all this Job did not sin, nor ascribe blame to God.

MORE DRASTIC MEASURES
CHAPTER 2

¹THE DAY ARRIVED WHEN THE GODS COME TO PRESENT THEMSELVES BEFORE Yahweh, and the Satan also came with them to present himself before Yahweh. ²Said Yahweh to the Satan:

"Where did you come from?"

The Satan answered Yahweh:

"From roaming the earth
And strolling about in it."

³Yahweh said to the Satan:

"Have you marked my servant Job?
There is none like him on earth,
A blameless and upright man,
Who fears God and shuns evil?
He still holds fast to his integrity,
Though you incited me against him
To destroy him without cause."

⁴The Satan answered Yahweh:

"Skin after skin.
All that a man has
He will give for his life.
⁵Reach out and strike him,
Touch his bone and flesh,
And he will curse you to your face."

⁶Yahweh said to Satan:

"Here, he is in your power;
Only spare his life."

⁷The Satan went out from Yahweh's presence and afflicted Job with a foul pox from sole to pate. ⁸He took a potsherd to scrape himself, and sat in the ashes.
⁹His wife said to him:

> "Do you still maintain your integrity?
> Curse God and die."

¹⁰Job said to her:

> "You talk like a foolish woman.
> Shall we accept good from God,
> And not accept evil?"

In spite of all this Job did not sin with his lips.
¹¹When Job's three friends heard of all the calamity that had befallen him, they came each from his place, Eliphaz the Temanite, Bildad the Shuhite, and Zophar the Naamathite. They arranged to meet together to go and condole and comfort him. ¹²When they saw him from afar, they could not recognize him, and they raised their voices and wept; each tore his robe and sprinkled dust on his head [heavenward]. ¹³They sat with him on the ground seven days and seven nights, and no one said a word to him, for they saw that his anguish was very great.

JOB'S PROTEST
CHAPTER 3

¹AFTER THIS JOB OPENED HIS MOUTH AND CURSED HIS DAY. ²JOB SPOKE OUT and said:

> ³"Damn the day I was born,
>   The night that said, 'A boy is begot.'
> ⁴That day—let it be darkness.
>   God above ignore it,
>   No light break upon it,
> ⁵Darkness and gloom claim it,
>   Cloud settle over it,
>   Eclipse terrify it.
> ⁶That night—gloom seize it.
>   Include it not in the days of the year,
>   In the roll of the months let it not enter.
> ⁷Yea, that night be sterile,
>   Let no joyful sound come in.
> ⁸Let the Sea-cursers damn it,
>   Those skilled to stir Leviathan.
> ⁹Its twilight stars be darkened,
>   Let it seek light in vain,
>   Nor see the rays of dawn,
> ¹⁰Since it closed not the womb's doors,
>   To hide trouble from my eyes.
> ¹¹Why did I not die at birth,
>
>   Emerge from the womb and expire?

¹⁶Like a stillbirth would I were hidden,
  Like babes that never saw light.
¹²Why did knees receive me,
  Or breasts give me suck?
¹³For now would I be lying quiet;
  I would be asleep and at rest,
¹⁴With kings and counselors of the earth
  Who built themselves ruins,
¹⁵Or with princes who had gold,
  Who filled their houses with silver.

¹⁷There where knaves cease strife,
  Where the weary are at rest,
¹⁸Where prisoners take ease together,
  Heedless of the slave driver's shout.
¹⁹Small and great alike are there,
  And slave is free from master.
²⁰Why gives he light to the wretched,
  Life to the bitter of soul,
²¹Who yearn in vain for death,
  Seek it like a treasure-trove,
²²Glad to reach the burial heap,
  Happy to find the grave?
²³To a man whose way is hidden,
  Whom God has fenced about?
²⁴Instead of my food comes sighs,
  Groans are poured me as water.
²⁵What I most feared has befallen me,
  What I dreaded has o'ertaken me.
²⁶I have no rest, no quiet,
  No repose, but continual agony."

ELIPHAZ REMONSTRATES
CHAPTER 4

¹Eliphaz the Temanite then spoke:
  ²"Should one dare a word, could you bear it?
  But who could be silent now?
  ³Look, you have instructed many,
  Feeble hands you strengthened,
  ⁴Your words encouraged the faint,
  Braced tottering knees.
  ⁵But it befalls you and you falter;
  It strikes you, and you are aghast.
  ⁶Is not your piety your assurance,
  Your hope your perfect conduct?

⁷Consider, what innocent ever perished,
Or where have the righteous been destroyed?
⁸I have observed that they who plow evil
And sow trouble reap the same.
⁹At a breath of God they perish,
A blast of His anger, and they vanish.
¹⁰The lion may roar, the old lion growl,
But the young lion's teeth are broken.
¹¹The lion perishes, robbed of prey,
The lioness' whelps are scattered.
¹²Now a word came to me quietly,
Just a whisper caught my ear.
¹³In a nightmare, in a trance,
When slumber falls upon men,
¹⁴Terror seized me, and trembling,
All my members shuddered.
¹⁵A breath passed over my face,
The hair of my body bristled.
¹⁶It paused, but I could not discern it,
Just a form before my eyes.
A hush, then a voice I heard:
¹⁷'Can mortal be just before God?
A man pure to his Maker?
¹⁸Even his servants he distrusts,
Charges his angels with error.
¹⁹What then of those who dwell in clay houses,
Whose foundations are in the dust,
Who are crushed quick as a moth,
²⁰'Twixt morning and evening shattered?
They perish forever nameless,
²¹Their tent cord pulled up,
They die and not with wisdom.' "

ELIPHAZ'S DISCOURSE
CHAPTER 5

¹"CALL NOW, WILL ANY ANSWER YOU?
To which of the holy ones will you turn?
²Impatience kills the fool,
Passion slays the simpleton.
³I have seen the fool strike root,
Then his abode suddenly accursed,
⁴His children abandoned helpless,
Crushed in the gate, defenseless.
⁵His harvest the hungry consume,
Snatching it among the thorns,
While the thirsty pant for their wealth.

⁶Does not sorrow spring from the soil,
Woe sprout from the very dust?
⁷Man, indeed, is born for trouble,
And Resheph's sons wing high.
⁸Still would I resort to God,
To God I would commit my cause;
⁹Doer of great deeds inscrutable,
Marvels beyond number,
¹⁰Who gives rain to the earth,
Sends water on the face of the field,
¹¹Who exalts the lowly on high,
Lifts the forlorn to safety.
¹²He thwarts the plots of the crafty,
So their hands attain no gain,
¹³Catches the clever in their contrivances,
And their wily schemes collapse.
¹⁴By day they meet with darkness,
Groping at noon as 'twere night.
¹⁵Thus he saves the simple from the sword.
The poor from the clutch of the strong,
¹⁶So that the humble have hope,
And evil's mouth is stopped.
¹⁷Fortunate the man whom God corrects.
Let him not spurn Shaddai's⁴ discipline.
¹⁸He makes a bruise, but he dresses it,
He wounds but his hand also heals.
¹⁹In six disasters he will save you,
In seven no harm will befall you.
²⁰In famine he will save you from death,
In war from the stroke of the sword.
²¹From scourge of tongue you'll be hidden,
Nor fear a demon when he comes.
²²You may laugh at plunder and famine;
Wild beasts you need not fear.
²³You will have a pact with the field-sprites,
Savage beasts will make peace with you.
²⁴You will know that your tent is secure,
Inspect your fold and miss nothing.
²⁵You will know a numerous progeny,
Offspring like the grass of the ground.
²⁶You will come in full vigor to the grave,
Like a sheaf of corn in its season.
²⁷This we have probed: 'tis true.
Now hear it and know it yourself."

---

⁴*Shaddai*—the Almighty; a term of obscure origin, probably referring to God's omnipotence.

JOB'S REPLY TO ELIPHAZ
CHAPTER 6

¹JOB ANSWERED:
2"Could my anguish but be weighed,
My misery heaped on the balances,
3'Twere heavier than the sands of the sea;
Therefore are my words vehement.
4For Shaddai's barbs pierce me,
My soul sucks in their venom;
God's terrors beset me.
5Does the ass bray over his grass?
The bull bellow over his fodder?
6Can flat food be eaten unsalted?
Is there flavor in slimy cream cheese?
7My soul disdains to touch such;
They are putrid as my flesh.
8O that my entreaty might be granted,
That God might reward my hope:
9That it please God to crush me,
Loose his hand and snip me.
10That would even be my comfort;
I would revel in the racking pain;
For I have not denied the Holy One's words.
11What strength have I to endure?
What prospects to bolster my spirit?
12Is my strength that of stones?
Or is my flesh bronze?
13Have I any help within me,
Since success has deserted me?
14A sick man should have the loyalty of his friend,
Even if he renounce fear of Shaddai.
15My friends have betrayed me like a wadi.
Like wadi channels they overflow;
16They run turbid with the thaw,
Covered by the melted snow.
17When it warms they fade;
Comes the heat and they vanish away.
18Caravans change their course,
Go off in the desert and perish.
19Caravans from Tema look,
The trains of Sheba yearn.
20They are tricked that trusted;
They come and are confounded.
21Thus you have been to me.
You see a fright and are panicked.
22Have I said: 'Give me something'?
'Ransom me with your wealth'?

²³'Rescue me from an enemy'?
'Redeem me from brigands'?
²⁴Teach me, and I will be quiet;
Show me where I have erred.
²⁵How pleasant are honest words!
But what does your arguing prove?
²⁶You think to reprove me with words,
But count as wind my words of despair?
²⁷You would cast lots for an orphan,
Barter over your friend.
²⁸Try now to look at me;
Surely I would not lie to your face.
²⁹No more, have done with injustice.
Relent, for my cause is just.
³⁰Is there iniquity on my tongue?
Can my palate not discriminate words?

JOB'S REPLY
CHAPTER 7

¹"HAS NOT MAN HARDSHIP ON EARTH?
Are not his days like those of a hireling?
²Like a slave that gasps for the shade,
Like a hireling that longs for his wage;
³Thus I am allotted empty months,
Weary nights are appointed me.
⁴When I lie down, I say,
'When may I rise?'
But the night drags on,
And I am surfeited with tossing till dawn.
⁵My flesh is clad with worms and dust;
My skin cracks and oozes.
⁶My days go swifter than a shuttle;
They run out without hope.
⁷Remember my life is mere wind;
My eye will not again see good.
⁸The eye that looks will not spy me.
Your eye will be on me, and I'll be gone.
⁹A cloud evaporates and vanishes,
So he that goes down to Sheol does not come up;
¹⁰He returns to his house no more,
His home never sees him again.
¹¹Therefore I'll not restrain my mouth;
I will speak in anguish of spirit,
Complain in the bitterness of my soul.
¹²Am I the Sea or the Dragon,
That you set a guard over me?

¹³If I say, 'My couch will comfort me,
  My bed will ease my complaint,'
¹⁴Then you dismay me with dreams,
  Terrify me with nightmares,
¹⁵Till my soul would choose strangling,
  Death rather than my loathsome pains.
¹⁶I will not live forever.
  Hold off, for my days are a breath.
¹⁷Why do you rear man at all,
  Or pay any mind to him?
¹⁸Inspect him every morning,
  And test him every moment?
¹⁹Will you never look away from me?
  Leave me be till I swallow my spittle?
²⁰What have I done to you, man watcher?
  Why have you made me your target?
  Why am I a burden to you?
²¹Why not pardon my fault,
  Forgive my iniquity,
  That I might now lie in the dust,
  And you seek me but I would not be?"

BILDAD'S FIRST DISCOURSE
CHAPTER 8

¹Bildad the Shuhite answered:
  ²"How long will you prate so?
  Your speech is so much wind.
  ³Does God pervert justice?
  Does Shaddai distort the right?
  ⁴Your children sinned against him,
  And he paid them for their sin.
  ⁵If you will but look to God
  And implore the mercy of Shaddai,
  ⁶If you are pure and upright,
  He will bestir himself for you
  And restore your righteous estate.
  ⁷Then your past will be as nothing,
  And your future will prosper greatly.
  ⁸Only ask past generations,
  Consider the lore of the patriarchs.
  ⁹We are ephemeral and know nothing,
  For our days on earth are a shadow.
  ¹⁰Will they not teach you and tell you,
  And bring forth words from their minds?
  ¹¹Can papyrus grow without marsh?
  Rushes flourish without water?

¹²While still fresh and uncut,
   'Twould wither quicker than grass.
¹³Such is the fate of all who forget God;
   The hope of the impious will perish.
¹⁴His confidence a gossamer thread,
   His trust a spider's house.
¹⁵He leans on his house, it does not stand;
   He grasps it, but it will not hold.
¹⁶Moist is he in the sunlight,
   His roots spread over his garden.
¹⁷Round a rock pile his tendrils twist;
   A house of stone they grasp.
¹⁸When he is swallowed up from his place,
   It disowns him: 'I never saw you.'
¹⁹Lo, this is the joy of his way,
   And from the dust another sprouts.
²⁰God will not reject the upright,
   Nor grasp the hand of evildoers.
²¹He will yet fill your mouth with laughter,
   Your lips with shouts of joy.
²²Your enemies will be clothed with shame.
   The tent of the wicked will vanish."

JOB'S REPLY TO BILDAD
CHAPTER 9

¹JOB ANSWERED:
   ²"Indeed, I know that this is so.
      But how can man be acquitted before God?
   ³If he deigned to argue with him,
      Could he answer him one in a thousand?
   ⁴Be he clever or mighty,
      Who could defy him unharmed?
   ⁵Who moves mountains before one knows it,
      Overturns them in his anger;
   ⁶Who shakes the earth from its place,
      And her pillars tremble;
   ⁷Commands the sun that it rise not,
      Seals up the stars from sight.
   ⁸Alone he stretched out the heavens,
      Trod on the back of Sea;
   ⁹Maker of the Bear, Orion,⁵
      The Pleiades and the Chambers of the South,
   ¹⁰Doer of great deeds inscrutable,
      Marvels beyond number.

---

⁵*Bear, Orion*, etc.—various constellations.

¹¹He passes by and I cannot see him;
 Moves on and I cannot perceive him.
¹²He despoils and who can restrain him?
 Or say to him, 'What are you doing?'
¹³A god could not turn back his anger;
 The cohorts of Rahab⁶ groveled 'neath him.
¹⁴How then could I answer him,
 Or match my words with him?
¹⁵Though in the right, I could not answer;
 I would have to entreat my opponent.
¹⁶If I summoned and he answered,
 I do not believe he would heed me.
¹⁷He would crush with a tempest⁷
 And multiply my wounds without cause.
¹⁸He would not let me draw my breath,
 But would sate me with bitterness.
¹⁹Be it power, he is strongest;
 Or litigation, who could arraign him?
²⁰Though righteous, his mouth would condemn me;
 Though guiltless, he would declare me perverse.
²¹I am innocent;
 I care not for myself;
 I loathe my life.
²²'Tis all the same. Therefore I say,
 'Guiltless as well as wicked he destroys.'
²³When the scourge slays suddenly,
 He mocks the despair of the innocent.
²⁴Earth is given to the control of the wicked.
 The faces of her judges he covers.
 If not he, then who?
²⁵My days go swifter than a courier;
 They flee, they see no good.
²⁶They pass like paper boats,
 As an eagle swoops on its prey.
²⁷If I say, 'I will forget my trouble,
 Change my countenance and be cheerful,'
²⁸I am appalled at my agony.
 I know you will not release me.
²⁹I am already found guilty;
 Why should I struggle in vain?
³⁰Were I to scrub myself with soapwort,
 Cleanse my hands with lye,

---

⁶*Rehab*—a sea monster defeated by Yahweh.
⁷*Crush me with a tempest*—this is exactly what Yahweh does, figuratively, in His speeches from the Storm. Job is here arguing that Yahweh's exalted nature as God does not permit man to deal with Him on rational terms. Only if Yahweh were to appear as another man would Job have a fair opporunity to plead the justice of his cause.

³¹You would douse me in filth,
  And my clothes would abhor me.
³²He is not, like me, a man whom I could challenge,
  'Let us go to court together.'
³³Would there were an umpire between us⁸
  To lay his hand on us both.
³⁴Let him put aside his club,
  Let his terror not dismay me,
³⁵Then I would speak and not fear him.
  But I am not so with him."

JOB'S REPLY
CHAPTER 10

¹"MY SOUL IS SICK OF LIFE;
  I will give vent to my complaint;
  I will speak in the bitterness of my soul.
²I will say to God: 'Don't condemn me;
  Let me know your case against me.
³Is it good for you to oppress,
  To despise your own hands' labor,
  While on the counsel of the wicked you beam?
⁴Do you have eyes of flesh?
  Do you see as humans see?
⁵Are your days as the days of a mortal?
  Your years as men's years?
⁶That you seek out my iniquity,
  And search for my sin?
⁷Though you know that I am not guilty,
  There is no escape from your hand.
⁸Your hands molded and made me,
  And then turned to destroy me.
⁹Remember, it was of mud you made me;
  And back to dust will you return me?
¹⁰Did you not pour me out as milk,
  Curdle me like cheese,
¹¹Clothe me with skin and flesh,
  Knit me with bones and sinews?
¹²Life and love you granted me,
  And your providence guarded my spirit.
¹³Yet these things you hid in your mind;
  I know this is what you did.

---

⁸*Umpire between us*—Job feels confident that an impartial judge would be obliged
to acknowledge his innocence and, by implication, God's guilt in permitting the good
to suffer. In this speech, Job brings his perception of God's responsibility for evil to
a climax.

¹⁴If I should sin, you are watching me,
And would not acquit me of guilt.
¹⁵If I am guilty, woe is me!
Or innocent, I may not lift my head.
Sated with shame,
Drenched in misery.
¹⁶Bold as a lion you stalk me,
Repeat your exploits against me,
¹⁷Renew hostility against me,
Multiply anger against me,
Incessant hardship for me.
¹⁸Why did you bring me from the womb?
I could have expired unseen,
¹⁹Could be as if I had not been,
Carried from womb to tomb.
²⁰Few are my days, let me be.
Hold off, let me smile awhile
²¹Before I go, never to return,
To a land of darkness and gloom,
²²A land of utter darkness,
Of gloom without order,
Which shines like darkness.' "

ZOPHAR'S FIRST DISCOURSE
CHAPTER 11

¹Zophar the Naamathite answered:
²"Shall this spate of words go unanswered?
Shall the glib one be acquitted?
³Shall your babbling silence men?
Shall you mock and none rebuke?
⁴You say, 'My doctrine is pure.'
You are clean in your own eyes.
⁵But would that God might speak,
Might open his lips against you.
⁶He would tell you what is hidden,
For there are two sides to wisdom.
God even forgets part of your guilt.
⁷Can you fathom the depth of God,
Find the limits of Shaddai?
⁸The heights of heaven, what can you do?
Deeper than Sheol, how can you know?
⁹Longer than earth in measure,
Broader than the sea.
¹⁰If he overlook, or shut up,
Or condemn, who can restrain him?

¹¹For he knows false men;
   He sees and ponders evil.
¹²The inane man will get sense,
   When a wild ass is born tame.
¹³If you would order your mind,
   And stretch out your hand toward him,
¹⁴If guilt be in your hand, remove it;
   Let not evil dwell in your tent.
¹⁵Then could you lift up a face unblemished;
   You might be steadfast and undaunted.
¹⁶Trouble you would then forget,
   As water gone by you would remember it.
¹⁷Life would rise brighter than noon,
   Darkness become as morning.
¹⁸You would trust because there is hope,
   Look about and recline in confidence.
¹⁹You would lie down and none disturb.
   Many would court your favor.
²⁰But the eyes of the wicked will dim;
   Refuge will fail them,
   Their hope an expiring breath."

JOB'S REPLY TO ZOPHAR
CHAPTER 12

¹JOB ANSWERED:
   ²"No doubt you are the gentry,
   And with you wisdom will die.
      ³But I have a mind as well as you;
      I am not inferior to you.
      Who does not know such things?
   ⁴A derision to his neighbor I am become,
      One whom God answered when he called,
      The just and perfect a derision.
   ⁵The comfortable hold calamity in contempt,
      Fitting for those whose feet slip.
   ⁶Robbers' households prosper,
      God-provokers are secure,
      One who carries God in his hand.
   ⁷Now ask the beasts, they will teach you;
      The birds of the sky will tell you;
   ⁸Or speak to the earth, it will teach you.
      The fish of the sea will tell you.
   ⁹Who does not know all these things,
      That God's hand has done this?

¹⁰In his hand is every living soul,
   The breath of all human flesh.
¹¹Does not the ear test words,
   The palate taste its food?
¹²Do the aged have wisdom,
   The long-lived understanding?
¹³With him is wisdom and might;
   His are counsel and understanding.
¹⁴If he tear down, there is no rebuilding.
   If he imprison, there is no release.
¹⁵If he withholds the waters, there is drought;
   Or lets them go, they engulf the earth.
¹⁶With him are power and victory;
   Pervert and perverter are his.
¹⁷Earth's counselors he makes foolish;
   Judges he makes mad.
¹⁸He loosens the belt of kings,
   And binds a rag on their loins.
¹⁹He makes priests go bare,
   Overturns the well-established.
²⁰The confident he deprives of speech,
   Takes away the reason of elders,
²¹Pours contempt on princes,
   Loosens the girdle of the mighty,
²²Reveals from darkness mysteries,
   Brings forth dense darkness to light,
²³Makes nations great then destroys them,
   Expands nations and leads them away,
²⁴Deprives leaders of intelligence,
   Makes them wander in a pathless waste.
²⁵They grope in darkness with no light.
   He makes them stagger like a sot."

JOB'S REPLY
CHAPTER 13

¹"Lo, my eye has seen all this,
   My ear has heard and understood it.
²I know as much as you know;
   I am not inferior to you.
³Rather would I speak with Shaddai,
   I wish to remonstrate with God.
⁴But you are daubers of deceit,
   Quack healers, all of you.
⁵I wish you would keep strictly silent.
   That would be wisdom for you.

⁶Hear, now, my argument,
  The plea of my lips attend.
⁷Is it for God's sake you speak evil,
  For him that you utter deceit?
⁸Will you show partiality for him,
  Will you contend for God?
⁹Will it be well when he probes you?
  Can you trick him as men are tricked?
¹⁰He will rebuke you severely,
  If you covertly curry favor.
¹¹Will not his fear overwhelm you,
  And his dread fall upon you?
¹²Your maxims are ashen aphorisms,
  Defenses of clay your defenses.
¹³Be silent before me that I may speak,
  Then come upon me what may.
¹⁴I take my flesh in my teeth,
  My throat I put in my hand.
¹⁵He may slay me, I'll not quaver.
  I will defend my conduct to his face.
¹⁶This might even be my salvation,
  For no impious man would face him.
¹⁷Now listen closely to my speech,
  My declaration be in your ears.
¹⁸See, now, I set forth my case.
  I know I will be acquitted.
¹⁹Who will contend with me?
  I would then be silent and expire.
²⁰Two things only do not do to me,
  Then I will not hide from your face.
²¹Remove your hand from me,
  Let your dread not dismay me.
²²Then challenge and I will answer;
  Or let me speak and you reply.
²³How many are my iniquities and sins?
  Tell me my offense and my sin.
²⁴Why do you hide your face,
  And treat me as a foe?
²⁵Will you harry a fluttering leaf?
  Will you chase withered chaff?
²⁶That you write bitter things against me,
  Make me inherit the iniquities of my youth,
²⁷Put my feet in fetters,
  Make prints on the soles of my feet,
  To mark all my paths."

JOB'S REPLY
CHAPTER 14

¹"MAN SPAWN OF WOMAN,
        Short-lived and sated with strife.
        ²Like a flower he comes out and is cropped;
        Like a shadow he flits never staying.
XIII [²⁸He withers like a rotten thing,
        Like a moth-eaten garment.]
        ³And on such would you turn your gaze,
        Bring me into judgment with yourself?
        ⁴[O that a clean thing could come from an unclean;
        None can.]
        ⁵His days indeed are determined;
        The sum of his months you control.
        You have set him limits he cannot exceed.
        ⁶Look away from him, relent;
        Let him enjoy his hireling day.
        ⁷A tree, though cut down, has hope;
        It may continue and its suckers not cease.
        ⁸Though its root grow old in the ground,
        And its stump die in the dust,
        ⁹At the scent of water it will sprout
        And put forth shoots like a seedling.
        ¹⁰But man dies and is helpless;
        A human expires and where is he?
        ¹¹Water fails from a lake,
        A river parches and dries up,
        ¹²And man lies down and never rises.
        They wake not till the heavens decay;
        They rouse not from their sleep.
        ¹³O that you would hide me in Sheol,
        Conceal me till your anger pass,
        Then set me a time and remember me.
        ¹⁴If a man dies, may he live again?
        All my weary days I would endure,
        I would wait till my relief come.
        ¹⁵You would call me and I would answer;
        You would care for the work of your hands.
        ¹⁶Then you would [not] count my steps,
        Nor be alert for my sins.
        ¹⁷My guilt would be sealed in a bundle,
        You would coat over my iniquity.
        ¹⁸But mountains topple and crumble,
        Rock moves from its place.

¹⁹Water wears away stone,
  Torrents sweep away earth's soil,
  And you destroy man's hope.
²⁰You overwhelm him forever and he passes;
  You change his visage and send him away.
²¹His sons achieve honor, but he never knows;
  They are disgraced, but he perceives not.
²²Only his own flesh pains him,
  And his own soul mourns itself."

* * *

THE THEOPHANY: YAHWEH'S FIRST DISCOURSE
CHAPTER 38

¹Then Yahweh answered Job
  From out of the storm, and said:
²"Who is this that denies Providence
  With words void of knowledge?
³Gird your loins like a hero,
  I will ask you, and you tell me.
⁴Where were you when I founded the earth?
  Tell me, if you know so much.
⁵Who drafted its dimensions? Do you know?
  Who stretched the line over it?
⁶On what are its sockets sunk,
  Who laid its cornerstone,
⁷While the morning stars sang together,
  And all the gods exulted?
⁸Who shut the sea within doors,
  When it came gushing from the womb;
⁹When I made the cloud its garment,
  Dark mist its swaddling bands,
¹⁰When I put bounds upon it,
  Set up bars and doors,
¹¹Saying, 'Thus far come, but no more.
  Here your wild waves halt'?
¹²Did you ever command a morning,
  Post Dawn in his place,
¹³Snatch off Earth's skirts,
  Shaking the wicked out of it?
¹⁴It changes like sealing clay,
  Tinted like a garment.
¹⁵The wicked are robbed of their light,
  The upraised arm is broken.
¹⁶Have you entered the springs of the sea,
  Walked in the recesses of the deep?

¹⁷Have Death's Gates been revealed to you,
Have you seen the Dark Portals?
¹⁸Have you examined earth's expanse?
Tell, if you know all this.
¹⁹Where is the way to light's dwelling,
Darkness, where its abode,
²⁰That you may guide it to its bourne,
Show it the way to go home?
²¹You know, for you were born there,
The sum of your days is great!
²²Have you entered the snow stores,
Or seen the hoards of hail
²³Which I reserve for troublous times,
For the day of attack and war?
²⁴By what power is the flood divided,
The east [wind] spread over the earth?
²⁵Who cleft a channel for the downpour,
A path for the thundershower,
²⁶To bring rain on no-man's land,
The wilderness with no man in it,
²⁷To sate the desolate desert,
Make the thirsty land sprout verdure?
²⁸Does the rain have a father,
Who sired the dew drops?
²⁹From whose womb comes the ice,
The hoarfrost of heaven, who bore it,
³⁰When water hardens like stone,
The surface of the deep imprisoned?
³¹Can you tie Pleiades'⁹ fetters,
Or loose Orions bands?
³²Can you lead out Mazzarot on time,
Guide the Bear with her cubs?
³³Do you know the celestial statutes,
Can you determine his rule on earth?
³⁴Can you raise your voice in the clouds,
And let the streaming water cover you?
³⁵Can you send lightning scurrying,
To say to you, 'Here we are'?
³⁶Who put wisdom in Thoth?¹⁰
Who gave Sekwi¹¹ understanding?
³⁷Who counts the clouds in wisdom,
Tilts the water jars of heaven,

---

⁹*Pleiades, Orion,* etc.—various constellations.
¹⁰*Thoth*—Egyptian god of wisdom. If the translator's rendering is correct, this passage indicates that the author of Job recognized the existence—albeit an inferior one—of gods other than Yahweh.
¹¹*Sekwi*—the meaning is highly uncertain, but perhaps Sekwi can be identified with the planet Mercury. The Greeks identified Mercury (Hermes) with Toth.

³⁸When the dust fuses to lumps,
And the clods cleave together?
³⁹Can you hunt prey for the lioness,
Appease the appetite of her cubs,
⁴⁰When they crouch in their den,
Lie in wait in their lair?
⁴¹Who provides the raven prey,
When its fledglings cry to God,
Frantic for lack of food?

YAHWEH'S FIRST DISCOURSE
CHAPTER 39

¹"Do you know the birth season of the ibex,[12]
Do you watch the calving of the hind,
²Do you count the months they fulfill,
Mark the time they give birth?
³They crouch and squeeze out their young,
Expel their foetus in the field.
⁴Their offspring thrive, they grow;
They leave and do not return.
⁵Who set the wild ass free,
Loosed the onager from his bonds?
⁶His home I made the wilderness,
His dwelling the salt flats.
⁷He scorns the city's tumult;
He hears no driver's shout.
⁸He roams the hills for pasture,
Seeks any bit of green.
⁹Will the buffalo deign to serve you,
Will he stay beside your crib?
¹⁰Can you hold him in the furrow with rope,
Will he harrow the valley after you?
¹¹Can you rely on his great strength,
Can you leave your labor to him?
¹²Can you trust him to return
And gather the grain of your threshing floor?
¹³The ostrich's wings flap wildly,
Though her pinions lack feathers.
¹⁴She lays her eggs on the ground,
Lets them be warmed in the dust.
¹⁵Heedless that foot may crush them,
Some beast trample upon them.
¹⁶Her young she harshly rejects,
Caring not if her labor be vain;

---

¹²*Ibex*—a wild mountain goat.

¹⁷For God deprived her of wisdom,
Apportioned her no understanding.
¹⁸When up she spreads her plumes,
She laughs at horse and rider.
¹⁹Do you give the horse strength,
Clothe his neck with mane?
²⁰Do you make him leap like a locust,
His majestic snort a terror?
²¹He paws violently, exults mightily;
He rushes to meet the fray.
²²He laughs at fear, undaunted;
He shies not from the sword.
²³About him rattles the quiver,
Flash spear and javelin.
²⁴Mid rattle and roar he races,
Unchecked by trumpet sound.
²⁵At the trumpet call he says, 'Aha'!
He scents the battle from afar,
The roar of the captains and shouting.
²⁶Does the hawk soar by your wisdom,
Spread his wings to the south?
²⁷Does the eagle mount at your command,
And make his nest on high?
²⁸On the cliff he dwells and lodges,
The rocky crag his stronghold.
²⁹Thence he spies out the prey,
His eyes see it from afar.
³⁰His young ones suck up blood;
Where the slain are, there is he."

JOB CHALLENGED; YAHWEH'S SECOND DISCOURSE
CHAPTER 40

¹YAHWEH ANSWERED JOB AND SAID:
²"Will the contender with Shaddai yield?
He who reproves God, let him answer for it."

³Job answered Yahweh and said:

⁴"Lo, I am small, how can I answer you?
My hand I lay on my mouth;
⁵I have spoken once, I will not reply;
Twice, but I will say no more."

⁶Then Yahweh answered Job
From out of the storm and said:
⁷"Gird your loins like a hero;
I will ask you, and you tell me.

⁸Would you annul my judgment,
  Condemn me that you may be justified?
⁹Have you an arm like God,
  Can you thunder with a voice like his?
¹⁰Deck now yourself with grandeur and majesty;
  Be arrayed in glory and splendor.
¹¹Let loose your furious wrath;
  Glance at every proud one and humble him.
¹²Glance at every proud one and abase him;
  Tread down the wicked where they stand.
¹³Bury them in the dust together;
  Bind them in the infernal crypt.
¹⁴Then I will acknowledge to you
  That your own right hand can save you.
¹⁵Behold now Behemoth,¹³
  Which I made as well as you;
  Grass he eats like an ox.
¹⁶See the strength in his loins,
  The power in his massive belly.
¹⁷His tail arches like a cedar;
  The thews of his thighs intertwine.
¹⁸His bones are tubes of bronze,
  His gristles like iron bars.
¹⁹He is a primordial production of God;
  His maker may bring near his sword.
²⁰The beasts of the steppe relax;
  All the creatures of the wild play there.
²¹Under the lotus he lies,
  In covert of reed and fen.
²²The lotus gives him shade,
  The wadi willows surround him.
²³Unperturbed though the river rage,
  Though the Jordan surge to his mouth.
²⁴Who is he that with his eyes can take him?
  Can you pierce his nose with barbs?

YAHWEH'S SECOND DISCOURSE
CHAPTER 41

¹CAN YOU DRAW OUT LEVIATHAN¹⁴ WITH A HOOK,
  Press down his tongue with a cord?
  ²Put a cord through his nose,
  Pierce his jaw with a hook?

---

¹³*Behemoth*—a mighty animal, perhaps the hippopotamus.
¹⁴*Leviathan*—a marine monster, perhaps a giant serpent or dragon.

³Will he make long pleas to you,
  Cajole you with tender words?
⁴Will he make a covenant with you,
  Will you take him as eternal slave?
⁵Play with him like a bird,
  Leash him for your girls?
⁶Will mongers haggle over him,
  Divide him among the hucksters?
⁷Will you fill his hide with harpoons,
  His head with fishing spears?
⁸Just lay your hand on him;
  Remember the battle, don't try again.
⁹Lo, any hope is false;
  Were not the gods cast down at sight of him?
¹⁰Is he not fierce when one rouses him?
  Who could stand before him?
¹¹Who could confront him unscathed,
  Under the whole heaven, who?
¹²Did I not silence his boasting,
  By the powerful word Hayyin[15] prepared?
¹³Who can penetrate his outer garment,
  Pierce his double mail?
¹⁴Who can open the doors of his face,
  Ringed round with fearsome fangs?
¹⁵His back row of shields,
  Closed with adamant seal;
¹⁶Each sticks to the other,
  And no space intervenes;
¹⁷Each welded to the other,
  They clasp inseparably.
¹⁸His sneezes flash forth lightning,
  His eyes are like the glow of dawn.
¹⁹From his mouth flames leap,
  Like sparks of fire escaping.
²⁰From his nostrils issues smoke,
  Like a pot seething over brushwood.
²¹From his throat fires blaze,
  Flame pours out his mouth.
²²In his neck dwells strength,
  Before him leaps violence.
²³The folds of his flesh are compact,
  Molded on him immovable.
²⁴His heart is hard as rock,
  Firm as a nether millstone.

---

[15]*Hayyin*—probably a phrase from a magic incantation.

²⁵At his terror the gods are affrighted,
  With consternation prostrate.
²⁶Who attacks, the sword avails not;
  Nor spear, dart, or javelin.
²⁷Iron he regards as straw,
  Bronze as rotten wood.
²⁸No arrow can put him to flight;
  Slingstones change to chaff on him.
²⁹Clubs he counts as splinters;
  Laughs at the javelin's whirr.
³⁰His undersides are sharp shards,
  A threshing sledge dragging the mire.
³¹He seethes the deep like a caldron,
  Makes the sea like an ointment pan.
³²Behind him glistens a wake;
  One would think the deep hoary.
³³On earth is not his equal,
  One formed without fear.
³⁴He looks on all that is lofty,
  Monarch of all proud beings."

JOB RECANTS; EPILOGUE
CHAPTER 42

¹Then Job answered Yahweh:
  ²"I know that you can do all things;
  No purpose of yours can be thwarted.
  [³Who is this who obscures counsel without knowledge?]
  I talked of things I did not know,
  Wonders beyond my ken.
  [⁴Listen, and I will speak;
  I will question you, and you tell me.]
  ⁵I had heard of you by hearsay,
  But now my own eyes have seen you;
  ⁶So I recant and repent¹⁶
  In dust and ashes."

⁷After Yahweh had spoken these words to Job, Yahweh said to Eliphaz the Temanite, "My anger burns against you and your two friends; for you have not spoken truth of me,¹⁷ as did Job, my servant. ⁸So, now, take yourselves seven bullocks and seven rams, and go to Job, my servant, and make a burnt offering for yourselves, and Job, my servant,

---

¹⁶*Recant and repent*—compare Job's submission with the defiances of the hero at the conclusion of *Prometheus Bound.*
  ¹⁷*You have not spoken truth of me*—note that Yahweh credits Job, who had openly questioned God's justice, with a better understanding of Him than that shown by the orthodox friends.

will pray for you, for I will accept him, so that I may not do anything rash to you; for you have not told truth of me, as did Job, my servant. [9]So Eliphaz the Temanite, Bildad the Shuhite, and Zophar the Naamathite went and did as Yahweh commanded them. Yahweh accepted Job [10]and restored Job's fortune when he prayed for his friends and increased what he had twofold. [11]All his brothers and sisters and former acquaintances called on him and had a meal with him in his house; and they consoled and comforted him for all the misfortune Yahweh had inflicted on him. Each one gave him a qesita and a gold ring. [12]Then Yahweh blessed Job's later life more than his earlier life; he now had fourteen thousand sheep, six thousand camels, a thousand yoke of oxen, and a thousand she-asses. [13]He had twice (?) seven sons and three daughters. [14]He named the first daughter Yemimah (Dove); the second's name was Qeziah (Cinnamon); the third's name was Qerenhappuk (Horn of Kohl). [15]In all the land no women were to be found as beautiful as Job's daughters and their father gave them inheritance among their brothers. [16]After this Job lived 140 years and saw his sons and grandsons to four generations. [17]So Job died, old and satisfied with life.

PLATO

(428-348 B.C.)

As HOMER IS THE UNRIVALED POET OF THE ANCIENT WORLD, SO PLATO. IS its supreme thinker. So great is Plato's influence on the history of thought, that Alfred North Whitehead has remarked that all subsequent philosophy is simply "footnotes to Plato." Not only does Plato's work synthesize the major ideas of philosophers who lived before him, it goes beyond the limits of previously existing knowledge to create an entire new mode of speculation.

The turning point in Plato's intellectual life occured shortly before the end of the Peloponnesian War. In about 407 B.C., when he was twenty-one, he came under the influence of Socrates. Until then, as the aristo-cratic son of a politically prominent family, Plato had apparently intended to be a tragic playwright. A famous anecdote tells of Socrates convinc-ing the would-be poet that writing fiction was morally inferior to the philosopher's search for truth. Plato reportedly burned his manuscripts and became a member of the Socratic circle. How intimate he was with the master is not clear, for Plato was not present at Socrates' execution. But regardless of the degree of their friendship, it is a literal fact of history that no student has ever created so magnificent a tribute to his teacher as Plato did for Socrates. With their fascinating portrait of the satyr-faced, slyly humorous, eternally irresistible Socrates, the Platonic dialogues—ironically enough—make the philosopher who distrusted po-etry one of the immortal figures of literature.

Since Socrates himself wrote nothing and since most of the dialogues were composed long after his death, it is almost impossible to determine just what in Plato's writing reflects the master's original teaching and what is the voice of the pupil. In general, it is perhaps safe to assume that relatively early works in which Socrates is the chief speaker, such as the *Apology,* contain a fair representation of Socrates' own ideas. Cer-tainly the emphasis on the undogmatic *search* for truth and the *method* of ironic cross-examination are typical of Socrates' known practice. The middle and later dialogues—the *Symposium, The Republic,* and the *Timeaus*—are probably more the expression of Plato's own mature thought, even when Socrates continues to be the speaker.

Apparently the most decisive event in Plato's experience was the execution of his beloved teacher in 399 B.C. Until then Plato had contem-plated a public life in government, as was the custom of talented young men from the upper classes. But after Socrates' death, Plato left Athens and travelled extensively, possibly visiting Egypt, Sicily, and Italy. As he explains in *Epistle VII,* a kind of apology for his non-participation in the affairs of state, he withdrew from public service because he felt it was impossible to be a politician and escape corruption. Like Socrates, he preferred a private life of contemplation and intense intellectual activity. Devoted to the excellence of philosophy, which then included studies in mathematics, government, ethics, religion, and metaphysics, he sought a philosopher-king who would apply his ideas in the establishment of an ideal state.

Pursuing this goal, Plato three times visited the court of Syracuse. After being first intrigued by the philosopher's theories, the Syracusian tyrant Dionysus I grew irritated with Plato and, according to one colorful legend, had him sold into slavery. Rescued by a friend, Plato returned to Athens, where, in 387 B.C., he founded the Academy, the first institution of higher learning in Europe. When Dionysus II came to the throne, Plato made two more trips to Sicily, in 367 and 361 B.C. The new ruler not only proved mentally incapable of the rigors of philosophy, but degenerated into an unscrupulous demagogue. Disillusioned in his hopes of finding a philospher-king, Plato left the court in disgust.

Fortunately for posterity, Plato did not exhaust his energies in ephemoral political activities. Although most teaching at the Academy was done orally, Plato wrote a long series of dialogues, which were calculated to interest the educated layman in the glories of philosophy. Although he was by choice a philosopher, he never lost his poetic gifts, so that the dialogues are masterpieces of literature as well as monuments to the brilliance of his intellect.

Plato remarks that the essential mysteries of knowledge cannot be recorded on paper. Consequently he at no time composed a straightforward explanation of his central and most characteristic philosophic doctrine—the Theory of Ideas. As noted above, it is impossible to be sure how much of Plato's *idealism* is derived from Socrates and how much of it originates with him.

To try to explain Plato's dualistic cosmos, which is composed of both the familiar material world and an unseen world of spirit, is automatically to distort and oversimplify. As a working approach to his thought, however, the Doctrine of Ideas may be summarized as follows. Perhaps inspired by the Sophists, Plato rejected the physical world as a source of reliable knowledge. As the Ionian philosopher Heraclitus had pointed out, empirical matter is in a constant state of flux: you can not even step into the same river twice. In a mere second the river has changed. Since the world undergoes an endless cycle of birth, growth, and death, it does not meet objective standards of absolute certainty. By definition, ultimate truth must be consistent, permanent, and—if it is to serve the philosopher's purpose—comprehensible to the human mind. The material world, with its multitudinousness and bewildering variety of change, does not offer an acceptable criterion. The physical world, moreover, must of necessity be interpreted by human senses and human judgments, which are notoriously faulty and open to error. What then remains as a possible source of accurate knowledge?

The idea—or, in Plato's untranslatable term, the Ideal Perfect Form— is the source. In spite of the world's physical inconsistencies and the depressing inaccuracy with which men interpret them, there exists in enlightened minds the ability to conceptualize greater perfection than the earth affords. In other words, men can conceive of perfect beauty, perfect justice, perfect love, even though human experience gives them no concrete examples of such values. Whence comes this notion of perfection? To put it briefly, it comes from the immortal part of man which has previously existed in the invisible realm of Ideal Forms. The *Psyche,* or soul, is the source of our intuitive understanding of that unseen world. The soul, which on earth inhabits and animates the human body, is the divine link between the perfect heaven above and the imperfect world here below.

The soul is composed of the same intangible, everlasting substance as the heavenly Forms. According to the *Phaedrus,* the soul leaves her rightful home because she is attracted by curiosity and desire to the material life. When she falls from heaven, she is captured in the life seed of a new human being. She becomes incarnate, imprisoned in a physical body. At first the shock of materialization causes the soul to forget her heavenly origin, but with proper effort and discipline she can be made to remember the truths she beheld in her prehuman existence. That discipline is provided by the study of philosophy.

Socrates likens himself to a midwife who aids in the birth of ideas within men's minds. He visualizes the role of the philosopher as one who turns men away from the mundane, dying world of flesh and directs their thoughts toward their place of origin and their final goal—the invisible home of Perfection. The love of wisdom, which is what "philosophy" means in Greek, is to purify and prepare our souls so that even within earthly bodies they can learn to catch a vision of the ultimate reality, of which this earth is only an imperfect reflection.

Closely connected with Plato's theories of ideas and the soul is his corollary Doctrine of Knowledge. In brief, Plato states that it is a mistake to think that we learn from experiencing material things in this world. To the contrary, we learn to know the essence of a man, tree, state, or concept only because our souls, while in heaven, beheld the Perfect Forms of these things. Objects, people, and governments here on earth are only flawed replicas of Heaven's perfect models. Learning occurs, then, when earthly experience *reminds* us of invisible realities. In fine, we learn by recollection.

Of the dialogues included here, the *Symposium* most clearly reveals Plato's vision of a dualistic universe. Socrates' speech on the motivating force of Eros that impels us to seek beyond earthly beauty to find satisfaction in eternal beauty suggests one important way of climbing the spiritual ladder to the higher realm. Philosophy can channel the creative power of Eros to provide the bridge between this world and the next. What makes the feat possible, according to Socrates, is that the invisible realm is capped by the Idea of the Good, a divine force that irresistibly draws all truth-seekers toward it. Plato's universe is eternally Good, a fact which makes knowledge of it possible.

THE TRADITIONAL INTRODUCTION TO SOCRATES IS THROUGH THE APOLOGY, the work which records the seventy-year old philosopher's defense when he stood trial for his life. After having taught in the streets, marketplaces, and gymnasia of Athens for more than thirty years, Socrates was accused on two serious charges: corrupting youth and atheism.

Although he says at the outset that he will attempt no eloquent speech, Socrates nonetheless demonstrates great skill in confounding his three accusers, Anytus the politician, Meletus the poet, and Lycon the master of rhetoric. With his usual good humor and mocking irony, Socrates defends his life as he had lived it. Avoiding any undignified appeal to the jury's emotions, he shows that far from being irreligious, his whole purpose in life was to obey the will of the gods. He tells the story of a friend who consulted the Oracle of Delphi and learned that "there was no man wiser" than Socrates. Puzzled by the Oracle's answer, Socrates tells how he began his career as a philosopher by attempting to discover what the gods intended by apparently citing him as the wisest man in Greece. After questioning all kinds of men, high and low, Socrates found that no one seemed to know anything that was not subject to doubt. Men's minds, he found, seemed to be clouded by prejudice, false opinion, and general error.

With truly religious humility, Socrates then concluded that the only respect in which he was wiser than other men was that whereas they thought they knew but did not know, Socrates was aware of his ignorance. At this point Socrates realized that the Oracle did not mean that Socrates was truly wise. The divine message really meant that no man could be sure of more than his own fallibility.

Socrates interpreted being singled out by the Oracle as a kind of divine commission. Equipped with a certainty of his own ignorance, he had already taken the first step on a quest for higher truths. He early disassociated himself from the Sophists, professional "wise men" who took money for teaching the Athenian youth. (Socrates always made it a point of pride never to accept a fee for his teaching.) By doubting everything and pointing out the unreliability of human perception and the relative nature of truth, the Sophists had cleared the way for Socrates. By temperament Socrates was unwilling to accept the Sophists' dictum that truth was unattainable. Guided by his wish to understand the Oracle's strange prophesy, he devoted himself to a close examination of what was good, beautiful, and honorable in life and to rejecting the evil, false, and immoral.

At the trial Socrates does not try to explain his theories about the nature of reality to his Athenian judges, most of whom were ordinary men not interested in philosophical speculation. Instead, Socrates emphasizes the fact that rather than being impious or godless, he had deliberately chosen a life that would glorify the gods. For if the gods were true, then the most holy career a man could follow would be the discovery and honoring of Truth. He had accordingly dedicated his career to learning those truths which the immortal gods themselves respected.

Far from corrupting the young men who enjoyed listening to his provocative cross-examinations of their elders, Socrates had in fact acted as a mentor leading them to what was most holy. He brought to birth in youth a desire to set goals higher than the mere pursuit of wealth or political power. He taught them to respect the everlasting rather than the ephemoral, to seek the ideal rather than the mere actual, to live an enlightened and productive life rather than to exist in the spiritual darkness of base and worldly ambition.

But in the eyes of the common men who were suspicious of such critical inquiry, Socrates committed two unpardonable errors. He appealed only to logic and reason and he treated their solemn indictment as a faintly amusing joke. After being found guilty by a narrow margin of jury votes, Socrates was asked to name an alternative to the death penalty. Rather than appear to agree that he was guilty of something deserving punishment, Socrates—with his usual droll wit—proposed that he be given a state pension in recognition of his service to the community. Outraged by his apparent frivolity, the jury overwhelmingly voted that he be put to death.

Before Socrates' time the philosopher Anaxagoras had been driven into exile for his unorthodox scientific opinions. Socrates could easily have arranged for a similar fate. Why he did not and deliberately chose to die rather than leave Athens, escape from his jailors, or stop conducting himself in the irritating manner that had won him such unpopularity is explained in the two short companion pieces to the *Apology*.

An introductory dialogue, the *Euthyphro*, takes place outside the king Archon's office, whence Socrates had been summoned to answer the charges of atheism, for which he was later tried. In conversation with the conventional and dull-witted Euthyphro, Socrates raises the central issue of his moral position. The major problem, Socrates seems to argue, is the relation between man's notion of what is holy and what, in truth, the gods require. Do the gods love the good because it is good, or is it good because the gods love it? Socrates implies that he does not know, of course, but he is moving toward his famous declaration in the *Apology* that he must obey the gods rather than men. Confident of his moral right to seek the holy life regardless of its conflict with public sentiment, Socrates reveals himself as the first man known to history who is willing to die for his freedom to think.

The *Crito* completes Socrates' defense as given in the *Apology*—and illustrates the depth and sincerity of his convictions. The well-meaning but imperceptive Crito has arranged to smuggle Socrates out of prison and help him escape to a place of safety outside Athens. In the dialogue's emotionally charged conclusion, Socrates imagines himself addressed by the personified Spirit of Athenian Law. With a clear vision of ideal justice before him, Socrates determines to die as he had lived, obedient both to the law and to his personal integrity.

THE APOLOGY

Characters   SOCRATES
                  MELETUS

Scene—The Court of Justice

Socrates. I DO NOT KNOW WHAT IMPRESSION MY ACCUSERS HAVE MADE UPON you, Athenians. But I do know that they nearly made me forget who I was, so persuasive were they. And yet they have scarcely spoken one single word of truth. Of all their many falsehoods, the one which astonished me most was their saying that I was a clever speaker, and that you must be careful not to let me deceive you. I thought that it was most shameless of them not to be ashamed to talk in that way. For as soon as I open my mouth they will be refuted, and I shall prove that I am not a clever speaker in any way at all—unless, indeed, by a clever speaker they mean someone who speaks the truth. If that is their meaning, I agree with them that I am an orator not to be compared with them. My accusers, I repeat, have said little or nothing that is true, but from me you shall hear the whole truth. Certainly you will not hear a speech, Athenians, dressed up, like theirs, with fancy words and phrases. I will say to you what I have to say, without artifice, and I shall use the first words which come to mind, for I believe that what I have to say is just; so let none of you expect anything else. Indeed, my friends, it would hardly be right for me, at my age, to come before you like a schoolboy with his concocted phrases. But there is one thing, Athenians, which I do most earnestly beg and entreat of you. Do not be surprised and do not interrupt with shouts if in my defense I speak in the same way that I am accustomed to speak in the market place, at the tables of the money-changers, where many of you have heard me, and elsewhere. The truth is this: I am more than seventy, and this is the first time that I

From Plato: *Euthyphro, Apology, Crito,* translated by F. J. Church, revised by Robert D. Cumming, copyright © 1948, 1956, by The Liberal Arts Press, Inc., reprinted by permission of the publishers, The Bobbs-Merrill Company, Inc. The accompanying footnotes are those of the revisor.

have ever come before a law court; thus your manner of speech here is quite strange to me. If I had really been a stranger, you would have forgiven me for speaking in the language and the manner of my native country. And so now I ask you to grant me what I think I have a right to claim. Never mind the manner of my speech—it may be superior or it may be inferior to the usual manner. Give your whole attention to the question, whether what I say is just or not? That is what is required of a good judge, as speaking the truth is required of a good orator.

I have to defend myself, Athenians, first against the older false accusations of my old accusers, and then against the more recent ones of my present accusers. For many men have been accusing me to you, and for very many years, who have not spoken a word of truth; and I fear them more than I fear Anytus[1] and his associates, formidable as they are. But, my friends, the others are still more formidable, since they got hold of most of you when you were children and have been more persistent in accusing me untruthfully, persuading you that there is a certain Socrates, a wise man, who speculates about the heavens, who investigates things that are beneath the earth, and who can make the worse argument appear the stronger. These men, Athenians, who spread abroad this report are the accusers whom I fear; for their hearers think that persons who pursue such inquiries never believe in the gods. Besides they are many, their attacks have been going on for a long time, and they spoke to you when you were most ready to believe them, since you were all young, and some of you were children. And there was no one to answer them when they attacked me. The most preposterous thing of all is that I do not even know their names: I cannot tell you who they are except when one happens to be a comic poet. But all the rest who have persuaded you, from motives of resentment and prejudice, and sometimes, it may be, from conviction, are hardest to cope with. For I cannot call any one of them forward in court to cross-examine him. I have, as it were, simply to spar with shadows in my defense, and to put questions which there is no one to answer. I ask you, therefore, to believe that, as I say, I have been attacked by two kinds of accusers—first, by Meletus[2] and his associates, and, then, by those older ones of whom I have spoken. And, with your leave, I will defend myself first against my old accusers, since you heard their accusations first, and they were much more compelling than my present accusers are.

Well, I must make my defense, Athenians, and try in the short time allowed me to remove the prejudice which you have been so long a time acquiring. I hope that I may manage to do this, if it be best for you and for me, and that my defense may be successful; but I am quite aware of

---

[1]Anytus is singled out as politically the most influential member of the prosecution. He had played a prominent part in the restoration of the democratic regime at Athens.

[2]Apparently in order to obscure the political implications of the trial, the role of chief prosecutor was assigned to Meletus, a minor poet with fervent religious convictions. Anytus was evidently ready to make political use of Meletus' convictions without entirely sharing his fervor, for in the same year as this trial Meletus also prosecuted Andocides for impiety, but Anytus came to Andocides' defense.

the nature of my task, and I know that it is a difficult one. Be the outcome, however, as is pleasing to god, I must obey the law and make my defense.

Let us begin from the beginning, then, and ask what is the accusation that has given rise to the prejudice against me, on which Meletus relied when he brought his indictment. What is the prejudice which my enemies have been spreading about me? I must assume that they are formally accusing me, and read their indictment. It would run somewhat in this fashion: "Socrates is guilty of engaging in inquiries into things beneath the earth and in the heavens, of making the weaker argument appear the stronger, and of teaching others these same things." That is what they say. And in the comedy of Aristophanes[3] you yourselves saw a man called Socrates swinging around in a basket and saying that he walked on air, and sputtering a great deal of nonsense about matters of which I understand nothing at all. I do not mean to disparage that kind of knowledge if there is anyone who is wise about these matters. I trust Meletus may never be able to prosecute me for that. But the truth is, Athenians, I have nothing to do with these matters, and almost all of you are yourselves my witnesses of this. I beg all of you who have ever heard me discussing, and they are many, to inform your neighbors and tell them if any of you have ever heard me discussing such matters at all. That will show you that the other common statements about me are as false as this one.

But the fact is that not one of these is true. And if you have heard that I undertake to educate men, and make money by so doing, that is not true either, though I think that it would be a fine thing to be able to educate men, as Gorgias of Leontini, and Prodicus of Ceos, and Hippias of Elis do. For each of them, my friends, can go into any city, and persuade the young men to leave the society of their fellow citizens, with any of whom they might associate for nothing, and to be only too glad to be allowed to pay money for the privilege of associating with themselves. And I believe that there is another wise man from Paros residing in Athens at this moment. I happened to meet Callias, the son of Hipponicus, a man who has spent more money on sophists than everyone else put together. So I said to him (he has two sons), "Callias, if your two sons had been foals or calves, we could have hired a trainer for them who would have trained them to excel in doing what they are naturally capable of. He would have been either a groom or a farmer. But whom do you intend to take to train them, seeing that they are men? Who understands the excellence which a man and citizen is capable of attaining? I suppose that you must have thought of this, because you have sons. Is there such a person or not?" "Certainly there is," he replied. "Who is he," said I, "and where does he come from, and what is his fee?" "Evenus, Socrates," he replied, "from Paros, five minae." Then I thought

---

[3] *The Clouds.* The basket was satirically assumed to facilitate Socrates' inquiries into things in the heavens.

that Evenus was a fortunate person if he really understood this art and could teach so cleverly. If I had possessed knowledge of that kind, I should have been conceited and disdainful. But, Athenians, the truth is that I do not possess it.

Perhaps some of you reply: "But, Socrates, what is the trouble with you? What has given rise to these prejudices against you? You must have been doing something out of the ordinary. All these rumors and reports of you would never have arisen if you had not been doing something different from other men. So tell us what it is, that we may not give our verdict arbitrarily." I think that that is a fair question, and I will try to explain to you what it is that has raised these prejudices against me and given me this reputation. Listen, then. Some of you, perhaps, will think that I am joking, but I assure you that I will tell you the whole truth. I have gained this reputation, Athenians, simply by reason of a certain wisdom. But by what kind of wisdom? It is by just that wisdom which is perhaps human wisdom. In that, it may be, I am really wise. But the men of whom I was speaking just now must be wise in a wisdom which is greater than human wisdom, or else I cannot describe it, for certainly I know nothing of it myself, and if any man says that I do, he lies and speaks to arouse prejudice against me. Do not interrupt me with shouts, Athenians, even if you think that I am boasting. What I am going to say is not my own statement. I will tell you who says it, and he is worthy of your respect. I will bring the god of Delphi to be the witness of my wisdom, if it is wisdom at all, and of its nature. You remember Chaerephon. From youth upwards, he was my comrade; and also a partisan of your democracy, sharing your recent exile[4] and returning with you. You remember, too, Chaerephon's character—how impulsive he was in carrying through whatever he took in hand. Once he went to Delphi and ventured to put this question to the oracle—I entreat you again, my friends, not to interrupt me with your shouts—he asked if there was anyone who was wiser than I. The priestess answered that there was no one. Chaerephon himself is dead, but his brother here will witness to what I say.

Now see why I tell you this. I am going to explain to you how the prejudice against me has arisen. When I heard of the oracle I began to reflect: What can the god mean by this riddle? I know very well that I am not wise, even in the smallest degree. Then what can he mean by saying that I am the wisest of men? It cannot be that he is speaking falsely, for he is a god and cannot lie. For a long time I was at a loss to understand his meaning. Then, very reluctantly, I turned to investigate it in this manner: I went to a man who was reputed to be wise, thinking that there, if anywhere, I should prove the answer wrong, and meaning to point out to the oracle its mistake, and to say, "You said that I was the wisest of men, but this man is wiser than I am." So I examined the

---

[4]During the totalitarian regime of The Thirty which remained in power for eight months (404 B.C.), five years before the trial.

man—I need not tell you his name, he was a politician—but this was the result, Athenians. When I conversed with him I came to see that, though a great many persons, and most of all he himself, thought that he was wise, yet he was not wise. Then I tried to prove to him that he was not wise, though he fancied that he was. By so doing I made him indignant, and many of the bystanders. So when I went away, I thought to myself, "I am wiser than this man: neither of us knows anything that is really worth knowing, but he thinks that he has knowledge when he has not, while I, having no knowledge, do not think that I have. I seem, at any rate, to be a little wiser than he is on this point: I do not think that I know what I do not know." Next I went to another man who was reputed to be still wiser than the last, with exactly the same result. And there again I made him, and many other men, indignant.

Then I went on to one man after another, realizing that I was arousing indignation every day, which caused me much pain and anxiety. Still I thought that I must set the god's command above everything. So I had to go to every man who seemed to possess any knowledge, and investigate the meaning of the oracle. Athenians, I must tell you the truth; I swear, this was the result of the investigation which I made at the god's command: I found that the men whose reputation for wisdom stood highest were nearly the most lacking in it, while others who were looked down on as common people were much more intelligent. Now I must describe to you the wanderings which I undertook, like Herculean labors, to prove the oracle irrefutable. After the politicians, I went to the poets, tragic, dithyrambic, and others, thinking that there I should find myself manifestly more ignorant than they. So I took up the poems on which I thought that they had spent most pains, and asked them what they meant, hoping at the same time to learn something from them. I am ashamed to tell you the truth, my friends, but I must say it. Almost any one of the bystanders could have talked about the works of these poets better than the poets themselves. So I soon found that it is not by wisdom that the poets create their works, but by a certain instinctive inspiration, like soothsayers and prophets, who say many fine things, but understand nothing of what they say. The poets seemed to me to be in a similar situation. And at the same time I perceived that, because of their poetry, they thought that they were the wisest of men in other matters too, which they were not. So I went away again, thinking that I had the same advantage over the poets that I had over the politicians.

Finally, I went to the artisans, for I knew very well that I possessed no knowledge at all worth speaking of, and I was sure that I should find that they knew many fine things. And in that I was not mistaken. They knew what I did not know, and so far they were wiser than I. But, Athenians, it seemed to me that the skilled artisans had the same failing as the poets. Each of them believed himself to be extremely wise in matters of the greatest importance because he was skillful in his own art: and this presumption of theirs obscured their real wisdom. So I asked myself, on behalf of the oracle, whether I would choose to remain as I was, without either their wisdom or their ignorance, or to possess both, as they did. And I answered to myself and to the oracle that it was better for me to remain as I was.

From this examination, Athenians, has arisen much fierce and bitter indignation, and as a result a great many prejudices about me. People say that I am "a wise man." For the bystanders always think that I am wise myself in any matter wherein I refute another. But, gentlemen, I believe that the god is really wise, and that by this oracle he meant that human wisdom is worth little or nothing. I do not think that he meant that Socrates was wise. He only made use of my name, and took me as an example, as though he would say to men, "He among you is the wisest who, like Socrates, knows that his wisdom is really worth nothing at all." Therefore I still go about testing and examining every man whom I think wise, whether he be a citizen or a stranger, as the god has commanded me. Whenever I find that he is not wise, I point out to him, on the god's behalf, that he is not wise. I am so busy in this pursuit that I have never had leisure to take any part worth mentioning in public matters or to look after my private affairs. I am in great poverty as the result of my service to the god.

Besides this, the young men who follow me about, who are the sons of wealthy persons and have the most leisure, take pleasure in hearing men cross-examined. They often imitate me among themselves; then they try their hands at cross-examining other people. And, I imagine, they find plenty of men who think that they know a great deal when in fact they know little or nothing. Then the persons who are cross-examined get angry with me instead of with themselves, and say that Socrates is an abomination and corrupts the young. When they are asked, "Why, what does he do? What does he teach?" they do not know what to say. Not to seem at a loss, they repeat the stock charges against all philosophers, and allege that he investigates things in the air and under the earth, and that he teaches people to disbelieve in the gods, and to make the worse argument appear the stronger. For, I suppose, they would not like to confess the truth, which is that they are shown up as ignorant pretenders to knowledge that they do not possess. So they have been filling your ears with their bitter prejudices for a long time, for they are ambitious, energetic, and numerous; and they speak vigorously and persuasively against me. Relying on this, Meletus, Anytus, and Lycon have attacked me. Meletus is indignant with me on behalf of the poets, Anytus on behalf of the artisans and politicians, and Lycon on behalf of the orators. And so, as I said at the beginning, I shall be surprised if I am able, in the short time allowed me for my defense, to remove from your minds this prejudice which has grown so strong. What I have told you, Athenians, is the truth: I neither conceal nor do I suppress anything, trivial or important. Yet I know that it is just this outspokenness which rouses indignation. But that is only a proof that my words are true, and that the prejudice against me, and the causes of it, are what I have said. And whether you investigate them now or hereafter, you will find that they are so.

What I have said must suffice as my defense against the charges of my first accusers. I will try next to defend myself against Meletus, that "good patriot," as he calls himself, and my later accusers. Let us assume that they are a new set of accusers, and read their indictment, as we did in the case of the others. It runs thus: Socrates is guilty of corrupting the youth, and of believing not in the gods whom the state believes in, but in other new divinities. Such is the accusation. Let us examine each point in it separately. Meletus says that I am guilty of corrupting the youth. But I say, Athenians, that he is guilty of playing a solemn joke by casually bringing men to trial, and pretending to have a solemn interest in matters to which he has never given a moment's thought. Now I will try to prove to you that this is so.

Come here, Meletus. Is it not a fact that you think it very important that the young should be as good as possible?

Meletus. It is.

Socrates. Come, then, tell the judges who improves them. You care so much,[5] you must know. You are accusing me, and bringing me to trial, because, as you say, you have discovered that I am the corrupter of the youth. Come now, reveal to the gentlemen who improves them. You see, Meletus, you have nothing to say; you are silent. But don't you think that this is shameful? Is not your silence a conclusive proof of what I say—that you have never cared? Come, tell us, my good man, who makes the young better?

Mel. The laws.

Socr. That, my friend, is not my question. What man improves the young, who begins by knowing the laws?

Mel. The judges here, Socrates.

Socr. What do you mean, Meletus? Can they educate the young and improve them?

Mel. Certainly.

Socr. All of them? Or only some of them?

Mel. All of them.

Socr. By Hera, that is good news! Such a large supply of benefactors! And do the members of the audience here improve them, or not?

Mel. They do.

Socr. And do the councilors?

Mel. Yes.

Socr. Well, then, Meletus, do the members of the assembly corrupt the young or do they again all improve them?

Mel. They, too, improve them.

Socr. Then all the Athenians, apparently, make the young into good men except me, and I alone corrupt them. Is that your meaning?

Mel. Certainly, that is my meaning.

Socr. You have discovered me to be most unfortunate. Now tell me: do you think that the same holds good in the case of horses? Does one

---

[5]Throughout the following passage Socrates plays on the etymology of the name "Meletus" as meaning "the man who cares."

man do them harm and everyone else improve them? On the contrary, is it not one man only, or a very few—namely, those who are skilled with horses—who can improve them, while the majority of men harm them if they use them and have anything to do with them? Is it not so, Meletus, both with horses and with every other animal? Of course it is, whether you and Anytus say yes or no. The young would certainly be very fortunate if only one man corrupted them, and everyone else did them good. The truth is, Meletus, you prove conclusively that you have never thought about the young in your life. You exhibit your carelessness in not caring for the very matters about which you are prosecuting me.

Now be so good as to tell us, Meletus, is it better to live among good citizens or bad ones? Answer, my friend. I am not asking you at all a difficult question. Do not the bad harm their associates and the good do them good?

Mel. Yes.

Socr. Is there anyone who would rather be injured than benefited by his companions? Answer, my good man; you are obliged by the law to answer. Does anyone like to be injured?

Mel. Certainly not.

Socr. Well, then, are you prosecuting me for corrupting the young and making them worse, voluntarily or involuntarily?

Mel. For doing it voluntarily.

Socr. What, Meletus? Do you mean to say that you, who are so much younger than I, are yet so much wiser than I that you know that bad citizens always do evil, and that good citizens do good, to those with whom they come in contact, while I am so extraordinarily ignorant as not to know that, if I make any of my companions evil, he will probably injure me in some way? And you allege that I do this voluntarily? You will not make me believe that, nor anyone else either, I should think. Either I do not corrupt the young at all or, if I do, I do so involuntarily, so that you are lying in either case. And if I corrupt them involuntarily, the law does not call upon you to prosecute me for an error which is involuntary, but to take me aside privately and reprove and educate me. For, of course, I shall cease from doing wrong involuntarily, as soon as I know that I have been doing wrong. But you avoided associating with me and educating me; instead you bring me up before the court, where the law sends persons, not for education, but for punishment.

The truth is, Athenians, as I said, it is quite clear that Meletus has never cared at all about these matters. However, now tell us, Meletus, how do you say that I corrupt the young? Clearly, according to your indictment, by teaching them not to believe in the gods the state believes in, but other new divinities instead. You mean that I corrupt the young by that teaching, do you not?

Mel. Yes, most certainly I mean that.

Socr. Then in the name of these gods of whom we are speaking, explain yourself a little more clearly to me and to these gentlemen here. I cannot understand what you mean. Do you mean that I teach the young to believe in some gods, but not in the gods of the state? Do you accuse me of teaching them to believe in strange gods? If that is your meaning, I myself believe in some gods, and my crime is not that of complete atheism. Or do you mean that I do not believe in the gods at all myself, and that I teach other people not to believe in them either?

Mel. I mean that you do not believe in the gods in any way whatever.

Socr. You amaze me, Meletus! Why do you say that? Do you mean that I believe neither the sun nor the moon to be gods, like other men?

Mel. I swear he does not, judges. He says that the sun is a stone, and the moon earth.

Socr. My dear Meletus, do you think that you are prosecuting Anaxagoras? You must have a very poor opinion of these men, and think them illiterate, if you imagine that they do not know that the works of Anaxagoras of Clazomenae are full of these doctrines. And so young men learn these things from me, when they can often buy them in the theater for a drachma at most, and laugh at Socrates were he to pretend that these doctrines, which are very peculiar doctrines, too, were his own. But please tell me, do you really think that I do not believe in the gods at all?

Mel. Most certainly I do. You are a complete atheist.

Socr. No one believes that, Meletus, not even you yourself. It seems to me, Athenians, that Meletus is very insolent and reckless, and that he is prosecuting me simply out of insolence, recklessness, and youthful bravado. For he seems to be testing me, by asking me a riddle that has no answer. "Will this wise Socrates," he says to himself, "see that I am joking and contradicting myself? Or shall I deceive him and everyone else who hears me?" Meletus seems to me to contradict himself in his indictment: it is as if he were to say, "Socrates is guilty of not believing in the gods, but believes in the gods." This is joking.

Now, my friends, let us see why I think that this is his meaning. You must answer me, Meletus, and you, Athenians, must remember the request which I made to you at the start, and not interrupt me with shouts if I talk in my usual manner.

Is there any man, Meletus, who believes in the existence of things pertaining to men and not in the existence of men? Make him answer the question, gentlemen, without these interruptions. Is there any man who believes in the existence of horsemanship and not in the existence of horses? Or in flute playing and not in flute players? There is not, my friend. If you will not answer, I will tell both you and the judges. But you must answer my next question. Is there any man who believes in the existence of divine things and not in the existence of divinities?

Mel. There is not.

Socr. I am very glad that these gentlemen have managed to extract an answer from you. Well then, you say that I believe in divine things, whether they be old or new, and that I teach others to believe in them. At any rate, according to your statement, I believe in divine things. That you have sworn in your indictment. But if I believe in divine things, I suppose it follows necessarily that I believe in divinities. Is it not so? It is. I assume that you grant that, as you do not answer. But do we not believe that divinities are either gods themselves or the children of the gods? Do you admit that?

Mel. I do.

Socr. Then you admit that I believe in divinities. Now, if these divinities are gods, then, as I say, you are joking and asking a riddle, and asserting that I do not believe in the gods, and at the same time that I do, since I believe in divinities. But if these divinities are the illegitimate children of the gods, either by the nymphs or by other mothers, as they are said to be, then, I ask, what man could believe in the existence of the children of the gods, and not in the existence of the gods? That would be as absurd as believing in the existence of the offspring of horses and asses, and not in the existence of horses and asses. You must have indicted me in this manner, Meletus, either to test me or because you could not find any act of injustice that you could accuse me of with truth. But you will never contrive to persuade any man with any sense at all that a belief in divine things and things of the gods does not necessarily involve a belief in divinities, and in the gods.

But in truth, Athenians, I do not think that I need say very much to prove that I have not committed the act of injustice for which Meletus is prosecuting me. What I have said is enough to prove that. But be assured it is certainly true, as I have already told you, that I have aroused much indignation. That is what will cause my condemnation if I am condemned; not Meletus nor Anytus either, but that prejudice and resentment of the multitude which have been the destruction of many good men before me, and I think will be so again. There is no prospect that I shall be the last victim.

Perhaps someone will say: "Are you not ashamed, Socrates, of leading a life which is very likely now to cause your death?" I should answer him with justice, and say: "My friend, if you think that a man of any worth at all ought to reckon the chances of life and death when he acts, or that he ought to think of anything but whether he is acting justly or unjustly, and as a good or a bad man would act, you are mistaken. According to you, the demigods who died at Troy would be foolish, and among them Achilles, who thought nothing of danger when the alternative was disgrace. For when his mother—and she was a goddess—addressed him, when he was resolved to slay Hector, in this fashion, 'My son, if you avenge the death of your comrade Patroclus and slay Hector, you will die yourself, for fate awaits you next after Hector,' When he heard this, he scorned danger and death; he feared much more to live a coward and not to avenge his friend. 'Let me punish the evildoer and afterwards die,' he said, 'that I may not remain here by the beaked ships jeered at, encumbering the earth.' "[6] Do you suppose that he thought of danger or of death? For this, Athenians, I believe to be the truth. Wherever a

---

[6]Homer, *Iliad,* xviii, 96, 98.

man's station is, whether he has chosen it of his own will, or whether he has been placed at it by his commander, there it is his duty to remain and face the danger without thinking of death or of any other thing except disgrace.

When the generals whom you chose to command me, Athenians, assigned me my station during the battles of Potidaea, Amphipolis, and Delium, I remained where they stationed me and ran the risk of death, like other men. It would be very strange conduct on my part if I were to desert my station now from fear of death or of any other thing when the god has commanded me—as I am persuaded that he has done—to spend my life in searching for wisdom, and in examining myself and others. That would indeed be a very strange thing. Then certainly I might with justice be brought to trial for not believing in the gods, for I should be disobeying the oracle, and fearing death and thinking myself wise when I was not wise. For to fear death, my friends, is only to think ourselves wise without really being wise, for it is to think that we know what we do not know. For no one knows whether death may not be the greatest good that can happen to man. But men fear it as if they knew quite well that it was the greatest of evils. And what is this but that shameful ignorance of thinking that we know what we do not know? In this matter, too, my friends, perhaps I am different from the multitude. And if I were to claim to be at all wiser than others, it would be because, not knowing very much about the other world, I do not think I know. But I do know very well that it is evil and disgraceful to do an unjust act, and to disobey my superior, whether man or god. I will never do what I know to be evil, and shrink in fear from what I do not know to be good or evil. Even if you acquit me now, and do not listen to Anytus' argument that, if I am to be acquitted, I ought never to have been brought to trial at all, and that, as it is, you are bound to put me to death because, as he said, if I escape, all your sons will be utterly corrupted by practicing what Socrates teaches. If you were therefore to say to me, "Socrates, this time we will not listen to Anytus. We will let you go, but on the condition that you give up this investigation of yours, and philosophy. If you are found following these pursuits again, you shall die." I say, if you offered to let me go on these terms, I should reply: "Athenians, I hold you in the highest regard and affection, but I will be persuaded by the god rather than you. As long as I have breath and strength I will not give up philosophy and exhorting you and declaring the truth to every one of you whom I meet, saying, as I am accustomed, 'My good friend, you are a citizen of Athens, a city which is very great and very famous for its wisdom and power—are you not ashamed of caring so much for the making of money and for fame and prestige, when you neither think nor care about wisdom and truth and the improvement of your soul?" If he disputes my words and says that he does care about these things, I shall not at once release him and go away: I shall question him and cross-examine him and test him. If I think that he has not attained excellence, though he says that he has, I shall reproach him for undervaluing the most valuable things, and over-valuing those that are less valuable. This I shall do to everyone whom I meet, young or old, citizen or stranger, but especially to citizens, since they are more closely related to me. This, you must recognize, the god has commanded me to do. And I think that no greater good has ever befallen you in the state than my service to the god. For I spend my whole life in going about and persuading you all to give your first and greatest care to the improvement of your souls, and not till you have done that to think of your bodies or your wealth. And I tell you that wealth does not bring excellence, but that wealth, and every other good thing which men have, whether in public or in private, comes from excellence. If then I corrupt the youth by this teaching, these things must be harmful. But if any man says that I teach anything else, there is nothing in what he says. And therefore, Athenians, I say, whether you are persuaded by Anytus or not, whether you acquit me or not, I shall not change my way of life; no, not if I have to die for it many times.

Do not interrupt me, Athenians, with your shouts. Remember the request which I made to you, and do not interrupt my words. I think that it will profit you to hear them. I am going to say something more to you, at which you may be inclined to protest, but do not do that. Be sure that if you put me to death, I who am what I have told you that I am, you will do yourselves more harm than me. Meletus and Anytus can do me no harm: that is impossible, for I am sure it is not allowed that a good man be injured by a worse. He may indeed kill me, or drive me into exile, or deprive me of my civil rights. Perhaps Meletus and others think those things great evils. But I do not think so. I think it is a much greater evil to do what he is doing now, and to try to put a man to death unjustly. And now, Athenians, I am not arguing in my own defense at all, as you might expect me to do, but rather in yours in order you may not make a mistake about the gift of the god to you by condemning me. For if you put me to death, you will not easily find another who, if I may use a ludicrous comparison, clings to the state as a sort of gadfly to a horse that is large and well-bred but rather sluggish because of its size, so that it needs to be aroused. It seems to me that the god has attached me like that to the state, for I am constantly alighting upon you at every point to arouse, persuade, and reproach each of you all day long. You will not easily find anyone else, my friends, to fill my place; and if you are persuaded by me, you will spare my life. You are indignant, as drowsy persons are when they are awakened, and, of course, if you are persuaded by Anytus, you could easily kill me with a single blow, and then sleep on undisturbed for the rest of your lives, unless the god in his care for you sends another to arouse you. And you may easily see that it is the god who has given me to your city; for it is not human, the way in which I have neglected all my own interests and allowed my private affairs to be neglected for so many years, while occupying myself un-ceasingly in your interests, going to each of you privately, like a father or an elder brother, trying to persuade him to care for human excellence.

There would have been a reason for it, if I had gained any advantage by this, or if I had been paid for my exhortations; but you see yourselves that my accusers, though they accuse me of everything else without shame, have not had the shamelessness to say that I ever either exacted or demanded payment. To that they have no witness. And I think that I have sufficient witness to the truth of what I say—my poverty.

Perhaps it may seem strange to you that, though I go about giving this advice privately and meddling in others' affairs, yet I do not venture to come forward in the assembly and advise the state. You have often heard me speak of my reason for this, and in many places: it is that I have a certain divine guide, which is what Meletus has caricatured in his indictment. I have had it from childhood. It is a kind of voice which, whenever I hear it, always turns me back from something which I was going to do, but never urges me ιo act. It is this which forbids me to take part in politics. And I think it does well to forbid me. For, Athenians, it is quite certain that, if I had attempted to take part in politics, I should have perished at once and long ago without doing any good either to you or to myself. And do not be indignant with me for telling the truth. There is no man who will preserve his life for long, either in Athens or elsewhere, if he firmly opposes the multitude, and tries to prevent the commission of much injustice and illegality in the state. He who would really fight for justice must do so as a private citizen, not as a political figure, if he is to preserve his life, even for a short time.

I will prove to you that this is so by very strong evidence, not by mere words, but by what you value more—actions. Listen, then, to what has happened to me, that you may know that there is no man who could make me consent to commit an unjust act from the fear of death, but that I would perish at once rather than give way. What I am going to tell you may be commonplace in the law court; nevertheless, it is true. The only office that I ever held in the state, Athenians, was that of councilor. When you wished to try the ten admirals who did not rescue their men after the battle of Arginusae as a group, which was illegal, as you all came to think afterwards, the executive committee was composed of members of the tribe Antiochis, to which I belong.[7] On that occasion I alone of the committee members opposed your illegal action and gave my vote against you. The orators were ready to impeach me and arrest me; and you were clamoring and urging them on with your shouts. But I thought that I ought to face the danger, with law and justice on my side, rather than join with you in your unjust proposal, from fear of imprisonment or death. That was when the state was democratic. When the oligarchy came in, The Thirty sent for me, with four others, to the

---

[7]The Council was the administrative body in Athens. Actual administrative functions were performed by an executive committee of the Council, and the members of this committee were recruited from each tribe in turn. The case Socrates is alluding to was that of the admirals who were accused of having failed to rescue the crews of ships which sank during the battle of Arginusae. The six admirals who were actually put on trial were condemned as a group and executed.

council-chamber, and ordered us to bring Leon the Salaminian from Salamis, that they might put him to death. They were in the habit of frequently giving similar orders to many others, wishing to implicate as many as possible in their crimes. But then I again proved, not by mere words, but by my actions, that, if I may speak bluntly, I do not care a straw for death; but that I do care very much indeed about not doing anything unjust or impious. That government with all its power did not terrify me into doing anything unjust. When we left the council-chamber, the other four went over to Salamis and brought Leon across to Athens; I went home. And if the rule of The Thirty had not been overthrown soon afterwards, I should very likely have been put to death for what I did then. Many of you will be my witnesses in this matter.[8]

Now do you think that I could have remained alive all these years if I had taken part in public affairs, and had always maintained the cause of justice like a good man, and had held it a paramount duty, as it is, to do so? Certainly not, Athenians, nor could any other man. But throughout my whole life, both in private and in public, whenever I have had to take part in public affairs, you will find I have always been the same and have never yielded unjustly to anyone; no, not to those whom my enemies falsely assert to have been my pupils. But I was never anyone's teacher. I have never withheld myself from anyone, young or old, who was anxious to hear me converse while I was making my investigation; neither do I converse for payment, and refuse to converse without payment. I am ready to ask questions of rich and poor alike, and if any man wishes to answer me, and then listen to what I have to say, he may. And I cannot justly be charged with causing these men to turn out good or bad, for I never either taught or professed to teach any of them any knowledge whatever. And if any man asserts that he ever learned or heard anything from me in private which everyone else did not hear as well as he, be sure that he does not speak the truth.

Why is it, then, that people delight in spending so much time in my company? You have heard why, Athenians. I told you the whole truth when I said that they delight in hearing me examine persons who think that they are wise when they are not wise. It is certainly very amusing to listen to. And, as I have said, the god has commanded me to examine men, in oracles and in dreams and in every way in which the divine will was ever declared to man. This is the truth, Athenians, and if it were not the truth, it would be easily refuted. For if it were the case that I have already corrupted some of the young men, and am now corrupting others, surely some of them, finding as they grew older that I had given

---

[8]There is evidence that Meletus was one of the four who turned in Leon. Socrates' recalling this earlier lapse from legal procedure is probably also a thrust at Anytus. The Thirty successfully implicated so many Athenians in their crimes that an amnesty was declared, which Anytus strongly favored, in order to enlist wider support for the restored democracy. Thus those who were really implicated could now no longer be prosecuted legally, but Socrates is himself being illegally prosecuted (as he now goes on to suggest) because he was guilty of having associated with such "pupils" as Critias, who was a leader of The Thirty.

them bad advice in their youth, would have come forward today to accuse me and take their revenge. Or if they were unwilling to do so themselves, surely their relatives, their fathers or brothers, or others, would, if I had done them any harm, have remembered it and taken their revenge. Certainly I see many of them in court. Here is Crito, of my own district and of my own age, the father of Critobulus; here is Lysanias of Sphettus, the father of Aeschines; here is also Antiphon of Cephisus, the father of Epigenes. Then here are others whose brothers have spent their time in my company—Nicostratus, the son of Theozotides and the brother of Theodotus—and Theodotus is dead, so he at least cannot entreat his brother to be silent; here is Paralus, the son of Demodocus and the brother of Theages; here is Adeimantus, the son of Ariston, whose brother is Plato here; and Aeantodorus, whose brother is Aristodorus. And I can name many others to you, some of whom Meletus ought to have called as witnesses in the course of his own speech; but if he forgot to call them then, let him call them now—I will yield the floor to him—and tell us if he has any such evidence. No, on the contrary, my friends, you will find all these men ready to support me, the corruptor who has injured their relatives, as Meletus and Anytus call me. Those of them who have been already corrupted might perhaps have some reason for supporting me, but what reason can their relatives have who are grown up, and who are uncorrupted, except the reason of truth and justice—that they know very well that Meletus is lying, and that I am speaking the truth?

Well, my friends, this, and perhaps more like this, is pretty much all I have to offer in my defense. There may be some one among you who will be indignant when he remembers how, even in a less important trial than this, he begged and entreated the judges, with many tears, to acquit him, and brought forward his children and many of his friends and relatives in court in order to appeal to your feelings; and then finds that I shall do none of these things, though I am in what he would think the supreme danger. Perhaps he will harden himself against me when he notices this; it may make him angry, and he may cast his vote in anger. If it is so with any of you—I do not suppose that it is, but in case it should be so—I think that I should answer him reasonably if I said: "My friend, I have relatives, too, for, in the words of Homer, I am 'not born of an oak or a rock'[9] but of flesh and blood." And so, Athenians, I have relatives, and I have three sons, one of them nearly grown up, and the other two still children. Yet I will not bring any of them forward before you and implore you to acquit me. And why will I do none of these things? It is not from arrogance, Athenians, nor because I lack respect for you—whether or not I can face death bravely is another question—but for my own good name, and for your good name, and for the good name of the whole state. I do not think it right, at my age and with my reputation, to do anything of that kind. Rightly or wrongly, men have

[9]Homer, *Odyssey*, xix, 163.

made up their minds that in some way Socrates is different from the multitude of men. And it will be shameful if those of you who are thought to excel in wisdom, or in bravery, or in any other excellence, are going to act in this fashion. I have often seen men of reputation behaving in an extraordinary way at their trial, as if they thought it a terrible fate to be killed, and as though they expected to live for ever if you did not put them to death. Such men seem to me to bring shame upon the state, for any stranger would suppose that the best and most eminent Athenians, who are selected by their fellow citizens to hold office, and for other honors, are no better than women. Those of you, Athenians, who have any reputation at all ought not to do these things, and you ought not to allow us to do them. You should show that you will be much more ready to condemn men who make the state ridiculous by these pathetic performances than men who remain quiet.

But apart from the question of reputation, my friends, I do not think that it is right to entreat the judge to acquit us, or to escape condemnation in that way. It is our duty to teach and persuade him. He does not sit to give away justice as a favor, but to pronounce judgment; and he has sworn, not to favor any man whom he would like to favor, but to judge according to law. And, therefore, we ought not to encourage you in the habit of breaking your oaths; and you ought not to allow yourselves to fall into this habit, for then neither you nor we would be acting piously. Therefore, Athenians, do not require me to do these things, for I believe them to be neither good nor just nor pious; especially, do not ask me to do them today when Meletus is prosecuting me for impiety. For were I to be successful and persuade you by my entreaties to break your oaths, I should be clearly teaching you to believe that there are no gods, and I should be simply accusing myself by my defense of not believing in them. But Athenians, that is very far from the truth. I do believe in the gods as no one of my accusers believes in them; and to you and to the god I commit my cause to be decided as is best for you and for me.

(He is found guilty by 281 votes to 220.)

I am not indignant at the verdict which you have given, Athenians, for many reasons. I expected that you would find me guilty; and I am not so much surprised at that as at the numbers of the votes. I certainly never thought that the majority against me would have been so narrow. But now it seems that if only thirty votes had changed sides, I should have escaped. So I think that I have escaped Meletus, as it is; and not only have I escaped him, for it is perfectly clear that if Anytus and Lycon had not come forward to accuse me, too, he would not have obtained the fifth part of the votes, and would have had to pay a fine of a thousand drachmae.

So he proposes death as the penalty. Be it so. And what alternative penalty shall I propose to you, Athenians?[10] What I deserve, of course, must I not? What then do I deserve to pay or to suffer for having

---

[10]For certain crimes no penalty was fixed by Athenian law. Having reached a verdict of guilty, the court had still to decide between the alternative penalties proposed by the prosecution and the defense.

determined not to spend my life in ease? I neglected the things which most men value, such as wealth, and family interests, and military commands, and public oratory, and all the civic appointments, and social clubs, and political factions, that there are in Athens; for I thought that I was really too honest a man to preserve my life if I engaged in these affairs. So I did not go where I should have done no good either to you or to myself. I went, instead, to each one of you privately to do him, as I say, the greatest of benefits, and tried to persuade him not to think of his affairs until he had thought of himself and tried to make himself as good and wise as possible, nor to think of the affairs of Athens until he had thought of Athens herself; and to care for other things in the same manner. Then what do I deserve for such a life? Something good, Athenians, if I am really to propose what I deserve; and something good which it would be suitable for me to receive. Then what is a suitable reward to be given to a poor benefactor who requires leisure to exhort you? There is no reward, Athenians, so suitable for him as receiving free meals in the prytaneum. It is a much more suitable reward for him than for any of you who has won a victory at the Olympic games with his horse or his chariots. Such a man only makes you seem happy, but I make you really happy; he is not in want, and I am. So if I am to propose the penalty which I really deserve, I propose this—free meals in the prytaneum.

Perhaps you think me stubborn and arrogant in what I am saying now, as in what I said about the entreaties and tears. It is not so, Athenians. It is rather that I am convinced that I never wronged any man voluntarily, though I cannot persuade you of that, since we have conversed together only a little time. If there were a law at Athens, as there is elsewhere, not to finish a trial of life and death in a single day, I think that I could have persuaded you; but now it is not easy in so short a time to clear myself of great prejudices. But when I am persuaded that I have never wronged any man, I shall certainly not wrong myself, or admit that I deserve to suffer any evil, or propose any evil for myself as a penalty. Why should I? Lest I should suffer the penalty which Meletus proposes when I say that I do not know whether it is a good or an evil? Shall I choose instead of it something which I know to be an evil, and propose that as a penalty? Shall I propose imprisonment? And why should I pass the rest of my days in prison, the slave of successive officials? Or shall I propose a fine, with imprisonment until it is paid? I have told you why I will not do that. I should have to remain in prison, for I have no money to pay a fine with. Shall I then propose exile? Perhaps you would agree to that. Life would indeed be very dear to me if I were unreasonable enough to expect that strangers would cheerfully tolerate my discussions and arguments when you who are my fellow citizens cannot endure them, and have found them so irksome and odious to you that you are seeking now to be relieved of them. No, indeed, Athenians, that is not likely. A fine life I should lead for an old man if I were to withdraw from Athens and pass the rest of my days in wandering from city to city, and continually being expelled. For I know very well that the young men will listen to me wherever I go, as they do here. If I drive them away, they will persuade their elders to expel me; if I do not drive them away, their fathers and other relatives will expel me for their sakes.

Perhaps someone will say, "Why cannot you withdraw from Athens, Socrates, and hold your peace?" It is the most difficult thing in the world to make you understand why I cannot do that. If I say that I cannot hold my peace because that would be to disobey the god, you will think that I am not in earnest and will not believe me. And if I tell you that no greater good can happen to a man than to discuss human excellence every day and the other matters about which you have heard me arguing and examining myself and others, and that an unexamined life is not worth living, then you will believe me still less. But that is so, my friends, though it is not easy to persuade you. And, what is more, I am not accustomed to think that I deserve anything evil. If I had been rich, I would have proposed as large a fine as I could pay: that would have done me no harm. But I am not rich enough to pay a fine unless you are willing to fix it at a sum within my means. Perhaps I could pay you a mina, so I propose that. Plato here, Athenians, and Crito, and Critobulus, and Apollodorus bid me propose thirty minae, and they guarantee its payment. So I propose thirty minae. Their security will be sufficient to you for the money.

(He is condemned to death.)

You have not gained very much time, Athenians, and at the price of the slurs of those who wish to revile the state. And they will say that you put Socrates, a wise man, to death. For they will certainly call me wise, whether I am wise or not, when they want to reproach you. If you had waited for a little while, your wishes would have been fulfilled in the course of nature; for you see that I am an old man, far advanced in years, and near to death. I am saying this not to all of you, only to those who have voted for my death. And to them I have something else to say. Perhaps, my friends, you think that I have been convicted because I was wanting in the arguments by which I could have persuaded you to acquit me, if I had thought it right to do or to say anything to escape punishment. It is not so. I have been convicted because I was wanting, not in arguments, but in impudence and shamelessness—because I would not plead before you as you would have liked to hear me plead, or appeal to you with weeping and wailing, or say and do many other things which I maintain are unworthy of me, but which you have been accustomed to from other men. But when I was defending myself, I thought that I ought not to do anything unworthy of a free man because of the danger which I ran, and I have not changed my mind now. I would very much rather defend myself as I did, and die, than as you would have had me do, and live. Both in a lawsuit and in war, there are some things which neither I nor any other man may do in order to escape from death. In battle, a man often sees that he may at least escape from death by throwing down his arms and falling on his knees before the pursuer to beg for his life. And there are many other ways of avoiding death in every danger if a man is willing to say and to do anything. But, my friends, I think that it is a much harder thing to escape from wickedness than from death, for wickedness is swifter than death. And now I, who am old and slow, have been overtaken by the slower pursuer: and my accusers, who are clever and swift, have been overtaken by the swifter pursuer—wickedness. And now I shall go away, sentenced by you to death; they will go away, sentenced by truth to wickedness and injustice. And I abide by this award as well as they. Perhaps it was right for these things to be so. I think that they are fairly balanced.

And now I wish to prophesy to you, Athenians, who have condemned me. For I am going to die, and that is the time when men have most prophetic power. And I prophesy to you who have sentenced me to death that a far more severe punishment than you have inflicted on me will surely overtake you as soon as I am dead. You have done this thing, thinking that you will be relieved from having to give an account of your lives. But I say that the result will be very different. There will be more men who will call you to account, whom I have held back, though you did not recognize it. And they will be harsher toward you than I have been, for they will be younger, and you will be more indignant with them. For if you think that you will restrain men from reproaching you for not living as you should, by putting them to death, you are very much mistaken. That way of escape is neither possible nor honorable. It is much more honorable and much easier not to suppress others, but to make yourselves as good as you can. This is my parting prophecy to you who have condemned me.

With you who have acquitted me I should like to discuss this thing that has happened, while the authorities are busy, and before I go to the place where I have to die. So, remain with me until I go: there is no reason why we should not talk with each other while it is possible. I wish to explain to you, as my friends, the meaning of what has happened to me. An amazing thing has happened to me, judges—for I am right in calling you judges.[11] The prophetic guide has been constantly with me all through my life till now, opposing me even in trivial matters if I were not going to act rightly. And now you yourselves see what has happened to me—a thing which might be thought, and which is sometimes actually reckoned, the supreme evil. But the divine guide did not oppose me when I was leaving my house in the morning, nor when I was coming up here to the court, nor at any point in my speech when I was going to say anything; though at other times it has often stopped me in the very act of speaking. But now, in this matter, it has never once opposed me, either in my words or my actions. I will tell you what I believe to be the reason. This thing that has come upon me must be good; and those of us who think that death is evil must needs be mistaken. I have a clear proof

---

[11]The form of address hitherto has always been "Athenians," or "my friends." The "judges" in an Athenian court were simply the members of the jury.

that that is so; for my accustomed guide would certainly have opposed me if I had not been going to meet with something good.

And if we reflect in another way, we shall see that we may well hope that death is a good. For the state of death is one of two things: either the dead man wholly ceases to be and loses all consciousness or, as we are told, it is a change and a migration of the soul to another place. And if death is the absence of all consciousness, and like the sleep of one whose slumbers are unbroken by any dreams, it will be a wonderful gain. For if a man had to select that night in which he slept so soundly that he did not even dream, and had to compare with it all the other nights and days of his life, and then had to say how many days and nights in his life he had spent better and more pleasantly than this night, I think that a private person, nay, even the Great King of Persia himself, would find them easy to count, compared with the others. If that is the nature of death, I for one count it a gain. For then it appears that all time is nothing more than a single night. But if death is a journey to another place, and what we are told is true—that all who have died are there—what good could be greater than this, my judges? Would a journey not be worth taking, at the end of which, in the other world, we should be delivered from the pretended judges here and should find the true judges who are said to sit in judgment below, such as Minos and Rhadamanthus and Aeacus and Triptolemus, and the other demigods who were just in their own lives? Or what would you not give to converse with Orpheus and Musaeus and Hesiod and Homer? I am willing to die many times if this be true. And for my own part I should find it wonderful to meet there Palamedes, and Ajax the son of Telamon, and the other men of old who have died through an unjust judgment, and to compare my experiences with theirs. That I think would be no small pleasure. And, above all, I could spend my time in examining those who are there, as I examine men here, and in finding out which of them is wise, and which of them thinks himself wise when he is not wise. What would we not give, my judges, to be able to examine the leader of the great expedition against Troy, or Odysseus, or Sisyphus, or countless other men and women whom we could name? It would be an inexpressible happiness to converse with them and to live with them and to examine them. Assuredly there they do not put men to death for doing that. For besides the other ways in which they are happier than we are, they are immortal, at least if what we are told is true.

And you too, judges, must face death hopefully, and believe this one truth, that no evil can happen to a good man, either in life or after death. His affairs are not neglected by the gods; and what has happened to me today has not happened by chance. I am persuaded that it was better for me to die now, and to be released from trouble; and that was the reason why the guide never turned me back. And so I am not at all angry with my accusers or with those who have condemned me to die. Yet it was not with this in mind that they accused me and condemned me, but meaning to do me an injury. So far I may blame them.

Yet I have one request to make of them. When my sons grow up, punish them, my friends, and harass them in the same way that I have harassed you, if they seem to you to care for riches or for any other thing more than excellence; and if they think that they are something when they are really nothing, reproach them, as I have reproached you, for not caring for what they should, and for thinking that they are something when really they are nothing. And if you will do this, I myself and my sons will have received justice from you.

But now the time has come, and we must go away—I to die, and you to live. Which is better is known to the god alone.

THE PHAEDO

[Although illness prevented Plato from attending Socrates' execution, his description of the philosopher's death is one of the most moving passages he ever wrote. In the company of intimate friends, including the young Theban philosophers Simmias and Cebes, and Phaedo, the narrator, Socrates spends his last hours discoursing on the possibilities of the soul's survival after death. He concludes his argument for the soul's immortality with a vivid description of the rewards and punishments of the afterlife. When the executioner brings the lethal drink of hemlock, Socrates reveals that his philosophy has indeed given him the serenity and confidence necessary to bear the final extremity. The purpose of the dialogue is to show that Socrates, to the end, continued the lifelong pursuit of truth for which he had been condemned to death.]

*   *   *

BUT THEN, MY FRIENDS, SAID HE, WE MUST THINK OF THIS. IF IT BE TRUE that the soul is immortal, we have to take care of her, not merely on account of the time which we call life, but also on account of all time. Now we can see how terrible is the danger of neglect. For if death had been a release from all things, it would have been a godsend to the wicked; for when they died they would have been released with their souls from the body and from their own wickedness. But now we have found that the soul is immortal, and so her only refuge and salvation from evil is to become as perfect and wise as possible. For she takes nothing with her to the other world but her education and culture; and

From Plato: *Phaedo,* translated by F. J. Church, copyright © 1951 by the Liberal Arts Press, Inc., reprinted by permission of the publishers, The Bobbs-Merrill Company, Inc. Numbered notes are those of the translator.

these, it is said, are of the greatest service or of the greatest injury to the dead man at the very beginning of his journey thither. For it is said that the genius, who has had charge of each man in his life, proceeds to lead him, when he is dead, to a certain place where the departed have to assemble and receive judgment and then go to the world below with the guide who is appointed to conduct them thither. And when they have received their deserts there, and remained the appointed time, another guide brings them back again after many long revolutions of ages. So this journey is not as Aeschylus describes it in the Telephus, where he says that "a simple way leads to Hades." But I think that the way is neither simple nor single; there would have been no need of guides had it been so; for no one could miss the way if there were but one path. But this road must have many branches and many windings, as I judge from the rites of burial on earth.[1] The orderly and wise soul follows her leader and is not ignorant of the things of that world; but the soul which lusts after the body flutters about the body and the visible world for a long time, as I have said, and struggles hard and painfully, and at last is forcibly and reluctantly dragged away by her appointed genius. And when she comes to the place where the other souls are, if she is impure and stained with evil, and has been concerned in foul murders, or if she has committed any other crimes that are akin to these and the deeds of kindred souls, then everyone shuns her and turns aside from meeting her, and will neither be her companion nor her guide, and she wanders about by herself in extreme distress until a certain time is completed, and then she is borne away by force to the habitation which befits her. But the soul that has spent her life in purity and temperance has the gods for her companions and guides, and dwells in the place which befits her. There are many wonderful places in the earth; and neither its nature nor its size is what those who are wont to describe it imagine, as a friend has convinced me.

What do you mean, Socrates? said Simmias. I have heard a great deal about the earth myself, but I have never heard the view of which you are convinced. I should like to hear it very much.

Well, Simmias, I don't think that it needs the skill of Glaucus to describe it to you, but I think it is beyond the skill of Glaucus to prove it true. I am sure that I could not do so; and besides, Simmias, even if I knew how, I think that my life would come to an end before the argument was finished. But there is nothing to prevent my describing to you what I believe to be the form of the earth and its regions.

Well, said Simmias, that will do.

In the first place then, said he, I believe that the earth is a spherical body placed in the center of the heavens, and that therefore it has no need of air or of any other force to support it; the equiformity of the heavens in all their parts, and the equipoise of the earth itself, are

---

[1]Sacrifices were offered to the gods of the lower world in places where three roads met.

sufficient to hold it up. A thing in equipoise placed in the center of what is equiform cannot incline in any direction, either more or less; it will remain unmoved and in perfect balance. That, said he, is the first thing that I believe.

And rightly, said Simmias.

Also, he proceeded, I think that the earth is of vast extent, and that we who dwell between the Phasis and the pillars of Heracles* inhabit only a small portion of it, and dwell round the sea, like ants or frogs round a marsh; and I believe that many other men dwell elsewhere in similar places. For everywhere on the earth there are many hollows of every kind of shape and size, into which the water and the mist and the air collect; but the earth itself lies pure in the purity of the heavens, wherein are the stars, and which men who speak of these things commonly call ether. The water and the mist and the air, which collect into the hollows of the earth, are the sediment of it. Now we dwell in these hollows though we think that we are dwelling on the surface of the earth. We are just like a man dwelling in the depths of the ocean who thought that he was dwelling on its surface and believed that the sea was the heaven, because he saw the sun and the stars through the water; but who was too weak and slow ever to have reached the water's surface, and to have lifted his head from the sea, and come out from his depths to our world, and seen, or heard from one who had seen, how much purer and fairer our world was than the place wherein he dwelt. We are just in that state; we dwell in a hollow of the earth, and think that we are dwelling on its surface; and we call the air heaven, and think it to be the heaven wherein the stars run their courses. But the truth is that we are too weak and slow to pass through to the surface of the air. For if any man could reach the surface, or take wings and fly upward, he would look up and see a world beyond, just as the fishes look forth from the sea, and behold our world. And he would know that that was the real heaven, and the real light, and the real earth, if his nature were able to endure the sight. For this earth, and its stones, and all its regions have been spoiled and corroded, as things in the sea are corroded by the brine: nothing of any worth grows in the sea, nor, in short, is there anything therein without blemish, but, wherever land does exist, there are only caves, and sand, and vast tracts of mud and slime, which are not worthy even to be compared with the fair things of our world. But you would think that the things of that other world still further surpass the things of our world. I can tell you a tale, Simmias, about what is on the earth that lies beneath the heavens, which is worth your hearing.

Indeed, Socrates, said Simmias, we should like to hear your tale very much.

Between the Phasis and the pillars of Heracles—i.e., from a river (the modern Rion) in the wilds of Russia to the Straits of Gibraltar. Socrates means to indicate the limits of the inhabited earth as they were then known. His view that the world is a much larger place than his contemporaries suspected indirectly supports his argument that there also exists an afterworld of which most men know nothing.

Well, my friend, he said, this is my tale. In the first place, the earth itself, if a man could look at it from above, is like one of those balls which are covered with twelve pieces of leather, and is marked with various colors, of which the colors that our painters use here are, as it were, samples. But there the whole earth is covered with them, and with others which are far brighter and purer ones than they. For part of it is purple of marvelous beauty, and part of it is golden, and the white of it is whiter than chalk or snow. It is made up of the other colors in the same way, and also of colors which are more beautiful than any that we have ever seen. The very hollows in it, that are filled with water and air, have themselves a kind of color, and glisten amid the diversity of the others, so that its form appears as one unbroken and varied surface. And what grows in this fair earth—its trees and flowers and fruit—is more beautiful than what grows with us in the same proportion; and so likewise are the hills and the stones in their smoothness and transparency and color. The pebbles which we prize in this world, our cornelians, and jaspers, and emeralds, and the like, are but fragments of them, but there all the stones are as our precious stones, and even more beautiful still. The reason of this is that they are pure and not corroded or spoiled, as ours are, with the decay and brine from the sediment that collects in the hollows and brings to the stones and the earth and all animals and plants deformity and disease. All these things, and with them gold and silver and the like, adorn the real earth; and they are conspicuous from their multitude and size, and the many places where they are found; so that he who could behold it would be a happy man. Many creatures live upon it; and there are men, some dwelling inland, and others round the air, as we dwell round the sea, and others in islands encircled by the air, which lie near the continent. In a word, they use the air as we use water and the sea, and the ether as we use the air. The temperature of their seasons is such that they are free from disease, and live much longer than we do; and in sight, and hearing, and smell, and the other senses, they are as much more perfect than we, as air is purer than water, and ether than air. Moreover, they have sanctuaries and temples of the gods, in which the gods dwell in very truth; they hear the voices and oracles of the gods, and see them in visions, and have intercourse with them face to face; and they see the sun and moon and stars as they really are; and in other matters their happiness is of a piece with this.

That is the nature of the earth as a whole, and of what is upon it; and everywhere on its globe there are many regions in the hollows, some of them deeper and more open than that in which we dwell; and others also deeper, but with narrower mouths; and others again shallower and broader than ours. All these are connected by many channels beneath the earth, some of them narrow and others wide; and there are passages by which much water flows from one of them to another, as into basins, and vast and never-failing rivers of both hot and cold water beneath the earth, and much fire, and great rivers of fire, and many rivers of liquid mud, some clearer and others more turbid, like the rivers of mud which precede the lava stream in Sicily, and the lava stream itself. These fill each hollow in turn, as each stream flows round to it. All of them are moved up and down by a certain oscillation which is in the earth and which is produced by a natural cause of the following kind. One of the chasms in the earth is larger than all the others, and pierces right through it, from side to side. Homer describes it in the words—

Far away, where is the deepest depth beneath the earth.[2]

And elsewhere he and many others of the poets have called it Tartarus. All the rivers flow into this chasm and out of it again; and each of them comes to be like the soil through which it flows. The reason why they all flow into and out of the chasm is that the liquid has no bottom or base to rest on; it oscillates and surges up and down, and the air and wind around it do the same, for they accompany it in its passage to the other side of the earth, and in its return; and just as in breathing the breath is always in process of being exhaled and inhaled, so there the wind, oscillating with the water, produces terrible and irresistible blasts as it comes in and goes out. When the water retires with a rush to what we call the lower parts of the earth, it flows through to the regions of those streams and fills them, as if it were pumped into them. And again, when it rushes back hither from those regions, it fills the streams here again, and then they flow through the channels of the earth and make their way to their several places, and create seas, and lakes, and rivers, and springs. Then they sink once more into the earth, and after making, some a long circuit through many regions, and some a shorter one through fewer, they fall again into Tartarus, some at a point much lower than that at which they rose, and others only a little lower; but they all flow in below their point of issue. And some of them burst forth again on the side on which they entered; others again on the opposite side; and there are some which completely encircle the earth, twining round it, like snakes, once or perhaps oftener, and then fall again into Tartarus, as low down as they can. They can descend as far as the center of the earth from either side but no farther. Beyond that point on either side they would have to flow uphill.

These streams are many, and great, and various; but among them all are four, of which the greatest and outermost, which flows round the whole of earth, is called Oceanus. Opposite Oceanus, and flowing in the reverse direction, is Acheron, which runs through desert places and then under the earth until it reaches the Acherusian lake, whither the souls of the dead generally go, and after abiding there the appointed time, which for some is longer and for others shorter, are sent forth again to be born as animals. The third river rises between these two, and near its source falls into a vast and fiery region and forms a lake larger than our sea, seething with water and mud. Thence it goes forth turbid and

[2]*Iliad* VIII. 14.

muddy round the earth, and after many windings comes to the end of the Acherusian lake, but it does not mingle with the waters of the lake; and after many windings more beneath the earth, it falls into the lower part of Tartarus. This is the river that men name Pyriphlegethon; and portions of it are discharged in the lava streams, wherever they are found on the earth. The fourth river is on the opposite side; it is said to fall first into a terrible and savage region, of which the color is one dark blue. It is called the Stygian stream, and the lake which its waters create is called Styx. After falling into the lake and receiving strange powers in its waters, it sinks into the earth, and runs winding about in the opposite direction to Pyriphlegethon, which it meets in the Acherusian lake from the opposite side. Its waters, too, mingle with no other waters; it flows round in a circle and falls into Tartarus opposite to Pyriphlegethon. Its name, the poets say, is Cocytus.*

Such is the nature of these regions; and when the dead come to the place whither each is brought by his genius, sentence is first passed on them according as their lives have been good and holy, or not. Those whose lives seem to have been neither very good nor very bad go to the river Acheron, and, embarking on the vessels which they find there, proceed to the lake. There they dwell, and are punished for the crimes which they have committed, and are purified and absolved; and for their good deeds they are rewarded, each according to his deserts. But all who appear to be incurable from the enormity of their sins—those who have committed many and great sacrileges, and foul and lawless murders, or other crimes like these—are hurled down to Tartarus by the fate which is their due, whence they never come forth again. Those who have committed sins which are great, but not too great for atonement, such, for instance, as those who have used violence toward a father or a mother in wrath and then repented of it for the rest of their lives, or who have committed homicide in some similar way, have also to descend into Tartarus; but then when they have been there a year, a wave casts them forth, the homicides by Cocytus, and the parricides and matricides by Pyriphlegethon; and when they have been carried as far as the Acherusian lake they cry out and call on those whom they slew or outraged, and beseech and pray that they may be allowed to come out into the lake, and be received as comrades. And if they prevail, they come out, and their sufferings cease; but if they do not, they are carried back to Tartarus, and thence into the rivers again, and their punishment does not end until they have prevailed on those whom they wronged: such is the sentence pronounced on them by their judges. But such as have been pre-eminent for holiness in their lives are set free and released from this world, as from a prison; they ascend to their pure habitation and dwell on the earth's surface. And those of them who have sufficiently purified themselves with philosophy live thenceforth without bodies

---

*Cocytus—compare Socrates' description of the infernal regions with that given by Virgil (*The Aeneid*, Book VI) and Dante (*The Inferno*).

and proceed to dwellings still fairer than these, which are not easily described, and of which I have not time to speak now.[3] But for all these reasons, Simmias, we must leave nothing undone, that we may obtain virtue and wisdom in this life. Noble is the prize, and great the hope.

A man of sense will not insist that these things are exactly as I have described them. But I think that he will believe that something of the kind is true of the soul and her habitations, seeing that she is shown to be immortal, and that it is worth his while to stake everything on this belief. The venture is a fair one, and he must charm his doubts with spells like these. That is why I have been prolonging the fable all this time. For these reasons a man should be of good cheer about his soul if in his life he has renounced the pleasures and adornments of the body, because they were nothing to him, and because he thought that they would do him not good but harm; and if he has instead earnestly pursued the pleasures of learning, and adorned his soul with the adornment of temperance, and justice, and courage, and freedom, and truth, which belongs to her and is her own, and so awaits his journey to the other world, in readiness to set forth whenever fate calls him. You, Simmias and Cebes, and the rest will set forth at some future day, each at his own time. But me now, as a tragic poet would say, fate calls at once; and it is time for me to betake myself to the bath. I think that I had better bathe before I drink the poison, and not give the women the trouble of washing my dead body.

When he had finished speaking Crito said, Be it so, Socrates. But have you any commands for your friends or for me about your children, or about other things? How shall we serve you best?

Simply by doing what I always tell you, Crito. Take care of your own selves, and you will serve me and mine and yourselves in all that you do, even though you make no promises now. But if you are careless of your own selves, and will not follow the path of life which we have pointed out in our discussions both today and at other times, all your promises now, however profuse and earnest they are, will be of no avail.

We will do our best, said Crito. But how shall we bury you?

As you please, he answered; only you must catch me first and not let me escape you. And then he looked at us with a smile and said, My friends, I cannot convince Crito that I am the Socrates who has been conversing with you and arranging his arguments in order. He thinks that I am the body which he will presently see a corpse, and he asks how he is to bury me. All the arguments which I have used to prove that I shall not remain with you after I have drunk the poison, but that I shall go away to the happiness of the blessed, with which I tried to comfort you and myself, have been thrown away on him. Do you therefore be my sureties to him, as he was my surety at the trial, but in a different way.

---

[3]The account of the rewards and punishments of the next world given in *Republic* X. 614b ff., the story of Er the son of Armenius, is worth comparing with the preceding passage.

He was surety for me then that I would remain; but you must be my sureties to him that I shall go away when I am dead, and not remain with you; then he will feel my death less; and when he sees my body being burned or buried, he will not be grieved because he thinks that I am suffering dreadful things; and at my funeral he will not say that it is Socrates whom he is laying out, or bearing to the grave, or burying. For, dear Crito, he continued, you must know that to use words wrongly is not only a fault in itself, it also creates evil in the soul. You must be of good cheer, and say that you are burying my body; and you may bury it as you please and as you think right.

With these words he rose and went into another room to bathe. Crito went with him and told us to wait. So we waited, talking of the argument and discussing it, and then again dwelling on the greatness of the calamity which had fallen upon us: it seemed as if we were going to lose a father and to be orphans for the rest of our life. When he had bathed, and his children had been brought to him—he had two sons quite little, and one grown up—and the women of his family were come, he spoke with them in Crito's presence, and gave them his last instructions; then he sent the women and children away and returned to us. By that time it was near the hour of sunset, for he had been a long while within. When he came back to us from the bath he sat down, but not much was said after that. Presently the servant of the Eleven came and stood before him and said, "I know that I shall not find you unreasonable like other men, Socrates. They are angry with me and curse me when I bid them drink the poison because the authorities make me do it. But I have found you all along the noblest and gentlest and best man that has ever come here; and now I am sure that you will not be angry with me, but with those who you know are to blame. And so farewell, and try to bear what must be as lightly as you can; you know why I have come." With that he turned away weeping, and went out.

Socrates looked up at him and replied, Farewell, I will do as you say. Then he turned to us and said, How courteous the man is! And the whole time that I have been here, he has constantly come in to see me, and sometimes he has talked to me, and has been the best of men; and now, how generously he weeps for me! Come, Crito, let us obey him; let the poison be brought if it is ready, and if it is not ready, let it be prepared.

Crito replied: But, Socrates, I think that the sun is still upon the hills; it has not set. Besides, I know that other men take the poison quite late, and eat and drink heartily, and even enjoy the company of their chosen friends, after the announcement has been made. So do not hurry; there is still time.

Socrates replied: And those whom you speak of, Crito, naturally do so, for they think that they will be gainers by so doing. And I naturally shall not do so, for I think that I should gain nothing by drinking the poison a little later, but my own contempt for so greedily saving a life which is already spent. So do not refuse to do as I say.

Then Crito made a sign to his slave who was standing by; and the slave went out, and after some delay returned with the man who was to give the poison, carrying it prepared in a cup. When Socrates saw him, he asked, You understand these things, my good man, what have I to do?

You have only to drink this, he replied, and to walk about until your legs feel heavy, and then lie down; and it will act of itself. With that he handed the cup to Socrates, who took it quite cheerfully, Echecrates,* without trembling, and without any change of color or of feature, and looked at the man with that fixed glance of his, and asked, What say you to making a libation from this draught? May I, or not? We only prepare so much as we think sufficient, Socrates, he answered. I understand, said Socrates. But I suppose that I may, and must, pray to the gods that my journey hence may be prosperous. That is my prayer; may it be so. With these words he put the cup to his lips and drank the poison quite calmly and cheerfully. Till then most of us had been able to control our grief fairly well; but when we saw him drinking and then the poison finished, we could do so no longer: my tears came fast in spite of myself, and I covered my face and wept for myself; it was not for him, but at my own misfortune in losing such a friend. Even before that Crito had been unable to restrain his tears, and had gone away; and Apollodorus, who had never once ceased weeping the whole time, burst into a loud wail and made us one and all break down by his sobbing except Socrates himself. What are you doing, my friends? he exclaimed. I sent away the women chiefly in order that they might not behave in this way; for I have heard that a man should die in silence. So calm yourselves and bear up. When we heard that, we were ashamed, and we ceased from weeping. But he walked about, until he said that his legs were getting heavy, and then he lay down on his back, as he was told. And the man who gave the poison began to examine his feet and legs from time to time. Then he pressed his foot hard and asked if there was any feeling in it, and Socrates said, No; and then his legs, and so higher and higher, and showed us that he was cold and stiff. And Socrates felt himself and said that when it came to his heart, he should be gone. He was already growing cold about the groin, when he uncovered his face, which had been covered, and spoke for the last time. Crito, he said, I owe a cock to Asclepius; do not forget to pay it.[4] It shall be done, replied Crito. Is there anything else that you wish? He made no answer to this question; but after a short interval there was a movement, and the man uncovered him, and his eyes were fixed. Then Crito closed his mouth and his eyes.

Such was the end, Echecrates, of our friend, a man, I think, who was the wisest and justest, and the best man I have ever known.

Echecrates—the young man to whom Phaedo relates the story of Socrates' death.
[4]These words probably refer to the offering usually made to Asclepius on recovery from illness. Death is a release from the "fitful fever of life." Another explanation is to make the word refer to the omission of a trifling religious duty.

WHILE THE PHAEDO REVEALS SOCRATES IN DEATH, THE SYMPOSIUM PRESENTS him in life. In fifth-century Athens a symposium was an all-male drinking party where conversation flowed as freely as the wine. The celebration which Socrates attends is held in honor of Agathon, the tragic poet who had just won first prize at the Great Dionysia. The guests, who form a brilliant cross-section of Athens' intelligentsia, decide to send away the flute girls and drink sparingly so they can exercise their wits in good talk. The company votes unanimously to have a round of speeches in praise of Eros, the god of physical love.

The first to speak are young Phaedrus and Pausanias, who seem to take a special interest in the erotic pleasures of Love. Aristophanes the comic playwright, is scheduled next, but has the hiccups, so his turn passes to Eryximachus, a rather literal-minded physician. When Aristophanes recovers from his affliction, he delivers a hilarious theory about the origin of the two sexes and the nature of sexual attraction. He is followed by his host, Agathon, who praises the more flamboyant aspects of Love.

With a gently mocking humility, Socrates then cross-examines Agathon and forces the young man to admit the logical errors in his assumptions about the youth and beauty of Eros. Socrates' discourse is the highlight of the *Symposium*. Putting himself in the position of a mere learner about the mysteries of love, he tells a (probably) fictitious anecdote about Diotima, a wise prophetess of Mantinea. It was she, Socrates confesses, who introduced him to the true nature of Eros. She represented the power of the god in a new light: under the control of reason and philosophy erotic desire becomes the energy and impulse to seek eternal beauty in its heavenly form. In his speech, Socrates enunciates the famous doctrine of Platonic Love, the passion that rises above desire for physical satisfaction to contemplation and possession of the divine, for which earthly attractions are but a poor substitute. Under the guidance of philosophy, the true lover moves step by step up the ladder of love until he attains the vision of perfect beauty, which is identical with the Idea of the Good.

As Socrates concludes, having refuted all the earlier light-minded notions about love, the party is interrupted by the drunken entrance of Alcibiades. Once a disciple of Socrates, Alcibiades swerved from the narrow path of philosophy to pursue a questionable career of political ambition. On the supposed date of the *Symposium* (416 B.C.), Alcibiades had been given command of an unprecedentedly large fleet with which to attack Syracuse. (Readers of Thucydides will remember that Alcibiades was recalled from this post to face charges of religious blasphemy and that, in his absence, the expedition proved a total disaster.) He was suspected by everyone of self-seeking, but his good looks, personal charm, and considerable talent made him the man of the hour. When Plato wrote the *Symposium*, Alcibiades was remembered as a traitor to the state, though perhaps still begrudgingly admired for his undeniable gifts.

Rather than destroy the artistic unity of the dialogue, Alcibiades' raucous appearance serves to provide an opportunity to praise Socrates. In shame-facedly telling of his long-ago attempt to seduce the philosopher, Alcibiades reveals that, in pursuing spiritual rather than physical love, Socrates practiced what he preached.

The guests then propose to follow Alcibiades' example and drink more like celebrants than philosophers. Even in this, Socrates reigns supreme. He literally drinks everyone under the table and, at dawn, quietly leaves to go about his usual tasks of the day.

The following abridged version of the *Symposium* begins with the speech of Aristophanes and then leaps to the conclusion of Agathon's highly rhetorical effort. Apollodorus, who learned the story of what happened at Agathon's party from a friend who was present, narrates the conversation.

BACKGROUND NOTE

The life of the upper-class Athenian male was centered, not in the home and family, but in the typically Greek institutions of the gymnasium, military-fraternal organizations, and the market-place. The Greek democracy demanded that a responsible citizen, even when married and a father, spend much of his time serving the state away from wife and children. The good citizen was also expected to keep his body fit by exercising on the athletic grounds, drilling for war in army camps, and going on extended military campaigns. The strong social insistence on the superiority of the masculine bond, reinforced by athletic, military, and political life, encouraged the Athenian to find emotional and intellectual companionship among other males of like social standing. Except for professional courtesans, women were neither educated nor permitted activities outside the home. The result was that Eros inspired intense friendships, such as Plato describes in the *Symposium*.

THE SYMPOSIUM

'WELL, ERYXIMACHUS,' BEGAN ARISTOPHANES, 'IT IS QUITE TRUE THAT I intend to take a different line from you and Pausanias. Men seem to

Abridged. From *The Symposium*, translated by W. Hamilton. First published 1951 by Penguin Books, Ltd. Reprinted by permission of the publisher. This selection begins with Aristophanes' speech, after Phaedrus, Pausanias, and Eryximachus have already spoken. Notes are those of the translator.

me to be utterly insensible of the power of Love; otherwise he would have had the largest temples and altars and the largest sacrifices. As it is, he has none of these things, though he deserves them most of all. For of all the gods he is the most friendly to man, and his helper and physician in those diseases whose cure constitutes the greatest happiness of the human race. I shall therefore try to initiate you into the secret of his power, and you in turn shall teach others.

'First of all, you must learn the constitution of man and the modifications which it has undergone, for originally it was different from what it is now. In the first place there were three sexes, not, as with us, two, male and female; the third partook of the nature of both the others and has vanished, though its name survives. The hermaphrodite was a distinct sex in form as well as in name, with the characteristics of both male and female, but now the name alone remains, and that solely as a term of abuse. Secondly, each human being was a whole, with its back and flanks rounded to form a circle; it had four hands and an equal number of legs, and two identically similar faces upon a circular neck, with one head common to both the faces, which were turned in opposite directions. It had four ears and two organs of generation and everything else to correspond. These people could walk upright like us in either direction, backwards or forwards, but when they wanted to run quickly they used all their eight limbs, and turned rapidly over and over in a circle, like tumblers who perform a cart-wheel and return to an upright position. The reason for the existence of three sexes and for their being of such a nature is that originally the male sprang from the sun and the female from the earth, while the sex which was both male and female came from the moon, which partakes of the nature of both sun and earth. Their spherical shape and their hoop-like method of progression were both due to the fact that they were like their parents. Their strength and vigour made them very formidable, and their pride was overweening; they attacked the gods, and Homer's story of Ephialtes and Otus attempting to climb up to heaven and set upon the gods is related also to these beings.[1]

'So Zeus and the other gods debated what was to be done with them. For a long time they were at a loss, unable to bring themselves either to kill them by lightning, as they had the giants, and extinguish the race—thus depriving themselves for ever of the honours and sacrifices due from humanity—or to let them go on in their insolence. At last, after much painful thought, Zeus had an idea. "I think," he said, "that I have found a way by which we can allow the human race to continue to exist and also put an end to their wickedness by making them weaker. I will cut each of them in two; in this way they will be weaker, and at the same time more profitable to us by being more numerous. They shall walk upright upon two legs. If there is any sign of wantonness in them

---

[1]Ephialtes and Otus were giants who attempted to scale heaven by piling Mt Ossa on Mt Olympus and Mt Pelion on Mt Ossa. They were killed by Apollo.

after that, and they will not keep quiet, I will bisect them again, and they shall hop on one leg." With these words he cut the members of the human race in half, just like fruit which is to be dried and preserved, or like eggs which are cut with a hair. As he bisected each, he bade Apollo turn round the face and the half-neck attached to it towards the cut side, so that the victim, having the evidence of bisection before his eyes, might behave better in future. He also bade him heal the wounds. So Apollo turned round the faces, and gathering together the skin, like a purse with drawstrings, on to what is now called the belly, he tied it tightly in the middle of the belly round a single aperture which men call the navel. He smoothed out the other wrinkles, which were numerous, and moulded the chest with a tool like those which cobblers use to smooth wrinkles in the leather on their last. But he left a few on the belly itself round the navel, to remind man of the state from which he had fallen.

'Man's original body having been thus cut in two, each half yearned for the half from which it had been severed. When they met they threw their arms round one another and embraced, in their longing to grow together again, and they perished of hunger and general neglect of their concerns, because they would not do anything apart. When one member of a pair died and the other was left, the latter sought after and embraced another partner, which might be the half either of a female whole (what is now called a woman) or a male. So they went on perishing till Zeus took pity on them, and hit upon a second plan. He moved their reproductive organs to the front: hitherto they had been placed on the outer side of their bodies, and the processes of begetting and birth had been carried on not by the physical union of the sexes, but by emission on to the ground, as is the case with grasshoppers. By moving their genitals to the front, as they are now, Zeus made it possible for reproduction to take place by the intercourse of the male with the female. His object in making this change was twofold; if male coupled with female, children might be begotten and the race thus continued, but if male coupled with male, at any rate the desire for intercourse would be satisfied, and men set free from it to turn to other activities and to attend to the rest of the business of life. It is from this distant epoch, then, that we may date the innate love which human beings feel for one another, the love which restores us to our ancient state by attempting to weld two beings into one and to heal the wounds which humanity suffered.

'Each of us then is the mere broken tally of a man, the result of a bisection which has reduced us to a condition like that of flat fish, and each of us is perpetually in search of his corresponding tally. Those men who are halves of a being of the common sex, which was called, as I told you, hermaphrodite, are lovers of women, and most adulterers come from this class, as also do women who are mad about men and sexually promiscuous. Women who are halves of a female whole direct their affections toward women and pay little attention to men; Lesbians belong to this category. But those who are halves of a male whole pursue males, and being slices, so to speak, of the male, love men throughout their boyhood, and take pleasure in physical contact with men. Such boys and lads are the best of their generation, because they are the most manly. Some people say that they are shameless, but they are wrong. It is not shamelessness which inspires their behaviour, but high spirit and manliness and virility, which lead them to welcome the society of their own kind. A striking proof of this is that such boys alone, when they reach maturity, engage in public life. When they grow to be men, they become lovers of boys, and it requires the compulsion of convention to overcome their natural disinclination to marriage and procreation; they are quite content to live with one another unwed. In a word, such persons are devoted to lovers in boyhood and themselves lovers of boys in manhood, because they always cleave to what is akin to themselves.

'Whenever the lover of boys—or any other person for that matter—has the good fortune to encounter his own actual other half, affection and kinship and love combined inspire in him an emotion which is quite overwhelming, and such a pair practically refuse ever to be separated even for a moment. It is people like these who form lifelong partnerships, although they would find it difficult to say what they hope to gain from one another's society. No one can suppose that it is mere physical enjoyment which causes the one to take such intense delight in the company of the other. It is clear that the soul of each has some other longing which it cannot express, but can only surmise and obscurely hint at. Suppose Hephaestus with his tools were to visit them as they lie together, and stand over them and ask: "What is it, mortals, that you hope to gain from one another?" Suppose too that when they could not answer he repeated his question in these terms: "Is the object of your desire to be always together as much as possible, and never to be separated from one another day or night? If that is what you want, I am ready to melt and weld you together, so that, instead of two, you shall be one flesh; as long as you live you shall live a common life, and when you die, you shall suffer a common death, and be still one, not two, even in the next world. Would such a fate as this content you, and satisfy your longings?" We know what their answer would be; no one would refuse the offer; it would be plain that this is what everybody wants, and everybody would regard it as the precise expression of the desire which he had long felt but had been unable to formulate, that he should melt into his beloved, and that henceforth they should be one being instead of two. The reason is that this was our primitive condition when we were wholes, and love is simply the name for the desire and pursuit of the whole. Originally, as I say, we were whole beings, before our wickedness caused us to be split by Zeus, as the Arcadians have been split apart by the Spartans.[2] We have reason to fear that if we do not behave

---

[2] It is almost certain that the reference here is to the punishment inflicted by the Spartans on Mantinea, an Arcadian city, in 385 B.C. The city was broken up and the inhabitants forced to live in four dispersed villages. Mention of this event in a conversation purporting to have taken place in 416 B.C. is of course an anachronism, but it provides valuable evidence for the date of composition.

ourselves in the sight of heaven, we may be split in two again, like dice which are bisected for tallies, and go about like the people represented in profile on tombstones, sawn in two vertically down the line of our noses. That is why we ought to exhort everyone to conduct himself reverently towards the gods; we shall thus escape a worse fate, and even win the blessings which Love has in his power to bestow, if we take him for our guide and captain. Let no man set himself in opposition to Love—which is the same thing as incurring the hatred of the gods—for if we are his friends and make our peace with him, we shall succeed, as few at present succeed, in finding the person to love who in the strictest sense belongs to us. I know that Eryximachus is anxious to make fun of my speech, but he is not to suppose that in saying this I am pointing at Pausanias and Agathon. They may, no doubt, belong to this class, for they are both unquestionably halves of male wholes, but I am speaking of men and women in general when I say that the way to happiness for our race lies in fulfilling the behests of Love, and in each finding for himself the mate who properly belongs to him; in a word, in returning to our original condition. If that condition was the best, it follows that it is best for us to come as near to it as our present circumstances allow; and the way to do that is to find a sympathetic and congenial object for our affections.

'If we are to praise the god who confers this benefit upon us, it is to Love that our praises should be addressed. It is Love who is the author of our well-being in this present life, by leading us towards what is akin to us, and it is Love who gives us a sure hope that, if we conduct ourselves well in the sight of heaven, he will hereafter make us blessed and happy by restoring us to our former state and healing our wounds.

'There is my speech about Love, Eryximachus, and you will see that it is of quite a different type from yours. Remember my request, and don't make fun of it, but let us hear what each of the others has to say. I should have said "each of the other two", for only Agathon and Socrates are left.'

[Like Pausanias and Phaedrus before him, Agathon praises the sensual beauty and voluptuous pleasure of Love. His conclusion, which is supposedly an example of his ornate poetic style, follows.]

❖   ❖   ❖

'In my opinion, then, Phaedrus, Love is in the first place supreme in beauty and goodness himself, and in the second the cause of like qualities in others. Indeed, I feel inspired to express this idea in verse and to say that it is Love who creates

> Peace among men, and calm upon the sea,
> Rest for the winds from strife, and sleep in sorrow.

It is Love who empties us of the spirit of estrangement and fills us with the spirit of kinship; who makes possible such mutual intercourse as this; who presides over festivals, dances, sacrifices; who bestows good-humour and banishes surliness; whose gift is the gift of good-will and never of ill-will. He is easily entreated and of great kindness; contemplated by the wise, admired by the gods; coveted by men who possess him not, the treasure of those who are blessed by his possession; father of Daintiness, Delicacy, Voluptuousness, all Graces, Longing, and Desire; careful of the happiness of good men, careless of the fate of bad; in toil, in fear, in desire, in speech the best pilot, soldier, comrade, saviour; author of order in heaven and earth; loveliest and best of all leaders of song, whom it behoves every man to follow singing his praise, and bearing his part in that melody wherewith he casts a spell over the minds of all gods and all men.

'There is my speech, Phaedrus, a decent compound of playfulness and gravity, and let it be dedicated to the god as the best medley that I can contrive.' . . .

[In a playful but essentially serious manner, Socrates forces Agathon to admit that the young man's understanding of Love is inadequate. Socrates then recalls his (probably fictional) conversation with Diotima, a prophetess of Mantinea, who first opened his eyes to the spiritual vision of Love's significance. (It is a measure of Plato's insight that he presents Eros, the strongest passion known to man, as but a manifestation of the universal energy that compels us to seek the eternal and divine.) At the point where we take up Socrates' speech he is quoting the wise Diotima.]

❖   ❖   ❖

' "All men, Socrates, are in a state of pregnancy, both spiritual and physical, and when they come to maturity they feel a natural desire to bring forth, but they can do so only in beauty and never in ugliness.[3] There is something divine about the whole matter; in pregnancy and bringing to birth the mortal creature is endowed with a touch of immortality. But the process cannot take place in disharmony, and ugliness is out of harmony with everything divine, whereas beauty is in harmony with it. That is why Beauty is the goddess who presides over travail, and why, when a person in a state of pregnancy comes into contact

---

[3]Throughout the whole of the discussion which follows it must be borne in mind that such terms as 'conception', 'pregnancy', 'bringing forth' are used here in a quite general sense and without any reference to the specialized physical functions of male and female.

with beauty, he has a feeling of serenity and happy relaxation which makes it possible to bring forth and give birth. But, when ugliness is near, the effect is just the opposite; he frowns and withdraws gloomily into himself and recoils and contracts and cannot bring forth, but has painfully to retain the burden of pregnancy. So a person who is pregnant and already great with child is violently attracted towards beauty, because beauty can deliver its possessor from the pains of travail. The object of love, Socrates, is not, as you think, beauty." "What is it then?" "Its object is to procreate and bring forth in beauty." "Really?" "It is so, I assure you. Now, why is procreation the object of love? Because procreation is the nearest thing to perpetuity and immortality that a mortal being can attain. If, as we agreed, the aim of love is the perpetual possession of the good, it necessarily follows that it must desire immortality together with the good, and the argument leads us to the inevitable conclusion that love is love of immortality as well as of the good." . . .

* * *

' "Well, if you believe that the natural object of love is what we have more than once agreed that it is, the answer won't surprise you. The same argument holds good in the animal world as in the human, and mortal nature seeks, as far as may be, to perpetuate itself and become immortal. The only way in which it can achieve this is by procreation, which secures the perpetual replacement of an old member of the race by a new. Even during the period for which any living being is said to live and to retain his identity—as a man, for example, is called the same man from boyhood to old age—he does not in fact retain the same attributes, although he is called the same person; he is always becoming a new being and undergoing a process of loss and reparation, which affects his hair, his flesh, his bones, his blood, and his whole body. And not only his body, but his soul as well. No man's character, habits, opinions, desires, pleasures, pains, and fears remain always the same; new ones come into existence and old ones disappear. What happens with pieces of knowledge is even more remarkable; it is not merely that some appear and others disappear, so that we no more retain our identity with regard to knowledge than with regard to the other things I have mentioned, but that each individual piece of knowledge is subject to the same process as we are ourselves. When we use the word recollection we imply by using it that knowledge departs from us; forgetting is the departure of knowledge, and recollection, by implanting a new impression in the place of that which is lost, preserves it, and gives it a spurious appearance of uninterrupted identity. It is in this way that everything mortal is preserved, not by remaining for ever the same, which is the prerogative of divinity, but by undergoing a process in which the losses caused by age are repaired by new acquisitions of a similar kind. This device, Socrates, enables the mortal to partake of immortality, physically as well as in other ways; but the immortal enjoys immortality after another manner. So do not feel surprise that every creature naturally cherishes its own progeny; it is in order to secure immortality that each individual is haunted by this eager desire and love."

'I was surprised at this account and said: "You may be very wise, Diotima, but am I really to believe this?" "Certainly you are," she replied in true professional style; "if you will only reflect you will see that the ambition of men provides an example of the same truth.

❁　　❁　　❁

' "Do you suppose that Alcestis would have died to save Admetus, or Achilles to avenge Patroclus, or your Codrus to preserve his kingdom for his sons,[4] if they had not believed that their courage would live for ever in men's memory, as it does in ours? On the contrary; it is desire for immortal renown and a glorious reputation such as theirs that is the incentive of all actions, and the better a man is, the stronger the incentive; he is in love with immortality. Those whose creative instinct is physical have recourse to women, and show their love in this way, believing that by begetting children they can secure for themselves an immortal and blessed memory hereafter for ever; but there are some whose creative desire is of the soul, and who conceive spiritually, not physically, the progeny which it is the nature of the soul to conceive and bring forth. If you ask what that progeny is, it is wisdom and virtue in general; of this all poets and such craftsmen as have found out some new thing may be said to be begetters; but far the greatest and fairest branch of wisdom is that which is concerned with the due ordering of states and families, whose name is moderation and justice. When by divine inspiration a man finds himself from his youth up spiritually pregnant with these qualities, as soon as he comes of due age he desires to bring forth and to be delivered, and goes in search of a beautiful environment for his children; for he can never bring forth in ugliness. In his pregnant condition physical beauty is more pleasing to him than ugliness, and if in a beautiful body he finds also a beautiful and noble and gracious soul, he welcomes the combination warmly, and finds much to say to such a one about virtue and the qualities and actions which mark a good man, and takes his education in hand. By intimate association with beauty embodied in his friend, and by keeping him always before his mind, he succeeds in bringing to birth the children of which he has been long in

---

[4]Admetus, king of Pherae in Thessaly, was told by Apollo that he must die unless he could induce a substitute to die in his place. When even his parents refused to do so his wife Alcestis offered herself. She was afterwards rescued from Hades by Heracles. . . . Cordus was a legendary king of Attica who in obedience to an oracle voluntarily sacrificed his life to save his country from a Dorian invasion.

labour, and once they are born he shares their upbringing with his friend; the partnership between them will be far closer and the bond of affection far stronger than between ordinary parents, because the children that they share surpass human children by being immortal as well as more beautiful. Everyone would prefer children such as these to children after the flesh. Take Homer, for example, and Hesiod, and the other good poets; who would not envy them the children that they left behind them, children whose qualities have won immortal fame and glory for their parents? Or take Lycurgus the lawgiver,[5] and consider the children that he left at Sparta to be the salvation not only of Sparta but one may almost say of Greece. Among you Athenians Solon is hounoured for the laws which he produced,[6] and so it is in many other places with other men, both Greek and barbarian, who by their many fine actions have brought forth good fruit of all kinds; not a few of them have even won men's worship on account of their spiritual children, a thing which has never yet happened to anyone by reason of his human progeny.

'"So far, Socrates, I have dealt with love-mysteries into which even you could probably be initiated, but whether you could grasp the perfect revelation to which they lead the pilgrim if he does not stray from the right path, I do not know. However, you shall not fail for any lack of willingness on my part: I will tell you of it, and do you try to follow if you can.

'"The man who would pursue the right way to this goal must begin, when he is young, by applying himself to the contemplation of physical beauty, and, if he is properly directed by his guide, he will first fall in love with one particular beautiful person and beget noble sentiments in partnership with him. Later he will observe that physical beauty in any person is closely akin to physical beauty in any other, and that, if he is to make beauty of outward form the object of his quest, it is great folly not to acknowledge that the beauty exhibited in all bodies is one and the same; when he has reached this conclusion he will become a lover of all physical beauty, and will relax the intensity of his passion for one particular person, because he will realize that such a passion is beneath him and of small account. The next stage is for him to reckon beauty of soul more valuable than beauty of body; the result will be that, when he encounters a virtuous soul in a body which has little of the bloom of beauty, he will be content to love and cherish it and to bring forth such notions as may serve to make young people better; in this way he will be compelled to contemplate beauty as it exists in activities and institutions,

---

[5]Lycurgus was the figure to whom later generations ascribed the foundation of the Spartan constitutional and military system in the 9th century B.C., but his historical existence has been questioned. The reference to his system saving Greece is presumably to the part played by Sparta in the Persian Wars.

[6]Solon is unquestionably historical, though many legends collected round him. He was appointed to undertake the work of constitutional reform at Athens in the opening decades of the 6th century B.C., and by his measures laid the foundations of the Athenian democracy.

and to recognize that here too all beauty is akin, so that he will be led to consider physical beauty taken as a whole a poor thing in comparison. From morals he must be directed to the sciences and contemplate their beauty also, so that, having his eyes fixed upon beauty in the widest sense, he may no longer be the slave of a base and mean-spirited devotion to an individual example of beauty, whether the object of his love be a boy or a man or an activity, but, by gazing upon the vast ocean of beauty to which his attention is now turned, may bring forth in the abundance of his love of wisdom many beautiful and magnificent sentiments and ideas, until at last, strengthened and increased in stature by this experience, he catches sight of one unique science whose object is the beauty of which I am about to speak. And here I must ask you to pay the closest possible attention.

' "The man who has been guided thus far in the mysteries of love, and who has directed his thoughts towards examples of beauty in due and orderly succession, will suddenly have revealed to him as he approaches the end of his initiation a beauty whose nature is marvellous indeed, the final goal, Socrates, of all his previous efforts. This beauty is first of all eternal; it neither comes into being nor passes away, neither waxes nor wanes; next, it is not beautiful in part and ugly in part, nor beautiful at one time and ugly at another, nor beautiful in this relation and ugly in that, nor beautiful here and ugly there, as varying according to its beholders; nor again will this beauty appear to him like the beauty of a face or hands or anything else corporeal, or like the beauty of a thought or a science, or like beauty which has its seat in something other than itself, be it a living thing or the earth or the sky or anything else whatever; he will see it as absolute, existing alone with itself, unique, eternal, and all other beautiful things as partaking of it, yet in such a manner that, while they come into being and pass away, it neither undergoes any increase or diminution nor suffers any change.

' "When a man, starting from this sensible world and making his way upward by a right use of his feeling of love for boys, begins to catch sight of that beauty, he is very near his goal. This is the right way of approaching or being initiated into the mysteries of love, to begin with examples of beauty in this world, and using them as steps to ascend continually with that absolute beauty as one's aim, from one instance of physical beauty to two and from two to all, then from physical beauty to moral beauty, and from moral beauty to the beauty of knowledge, until from knowledge of various kinds one arrives at the supreme knowledge whose sole object is that absolute beauty, and knows at last what absolute beauty is.

' "This above all others, my dear Socrates," the woman from Mantinea continued, "is the region where a man's life should be spent, in the contemplation of absolute beauty. Once you have seen that, you will not value it in terms of gold or rich clothing or of the beauty of boys and young men, the sight of whom at present throws you and many people like you into such an ecstasy that, provided that you could always enjoy the sight and company of your darlings, you would be content to go without food and drink, if that were possible, and to pass your whole time with them in the contemplation of their beauty. What may we suppose to be the felicity of the man who sees absolute beauty in its essence, pure and unalloyed, who, instead of a beauty tainted by human flesh and colour and a mass of perishable rubbish, is able to apprehend divine beauty where it exists apart and alone? Do you think that it will be a poor life that a man leads who has his gaze fixed in that direction, who contemplates absolute beauty with the appropriate faculty and is in constant union with it? Do you not see that in that region alone where he sees beauty with the faculty capable of seeing it, will he be able to bring forth not mere reflected images of goodness but true goodness, because he will be in contact not with a reflection but with the truth? And having brought forth and nurtured true goodness he will have the privilege of being beloved of God, and becoming, if ever a man can, immortal himself.'

'This, Phaedrus and my other friends, is what Diotima said and what I believe; and because I believe it I try to persuade others that in the acquisition of this blessing human nature can find no better helper than Love. I declare that it is the duty of every man to honour Love, and I honour and practise the mysteries of Love in an especial degree myself, and recommend the same to others, and I praise the power and valour of Love to the best of my ability both now and always. There is my speech, Phaedrus; if you like, you can regard it as a panegyric delivered in honour of Love; otherwise you can give it any name you please.'

✻   ✻   ✻

[Elegantly dressed and his hair garlanded, Alcibiades breaks into the party uninvited. Settled on a couch beside Socrates, he announces that he will "tell the truth" about the philosopher. First, he compares Socrates to the rustic Silenus and the satyr Marsyas.]

'I propose to praise Socrates, gentlemen, by using similes. He will perhaps think that I mean to make fun of him, but my object in employing them is truth, not ridicule. I declare that he bears a strong resemblance to those figures of Silenus[7] in statuaries' shops, represented holding pipes or flutes; they are hollow inside, and when they are taken apart you see that they contain little figures of gods. I declare also that he is like Marsyas the satyr.[8] You can't deny yourself, Socrates, that you

---

[7]Silenus, to whom Socrates was often compared in appearance, was the constant companion of Dionysus, and was represented as a bald, dissolute old man, with a flattened nose, generally riding upon an ass. In spite of his appearance and habits he was regarded as an inspired prophet, as in Virgil's *Sixth Ecologue*, and he is thus a suitable type of the wisdom which conceals itself beneath an uncouth exterior.

[8]The satyrs were also connected with Dionysus, and were beings with goat-like characteristics addicted to every kind of sensuality. Marsyas, one of their number, to whom, as well as to Silenus and Olympus, the invention of the flute was ascribed, challenged Apollo to a trial of skill in flute-playing, and on being defeated was flayed alive.

have a striking physical likeness to both of these, and you shall hear in a moment how you resemble them in other respects. For one thing you're a bully, aren't you? I can bring evidence of this if you don't admit it. But you don't play the flute, you will say. No, indeed; the performance you give is far more remarkable. Marsyas needed an instrument in order to charm men by the power which proceeded out of his mouth, a power which is still exercised by those who perform his melodies (I reckon the tunes ascribed to Olympus to belong to Marsyas, who taught him); his productions alone, whether executed by a skilled male performer or by a wretched flute-girl, are capable, by reason of their divine origin, of throwing men into a trance and thus distinguishing those who yearn to enter by initiation into union with the gods. But you, Socrates, are so far superior to Marsyas that you produce the same effect by mere words without any instrument. At any rate, whereas we most of us pay little or no attention to the words of any other speaker, however accomplished, a speech by you or even a very indifferent report of what you have said stirs us to the depths and casts a spell over us, men and women and young lads alike. I myself, gentlemen, were it not that you would think me absolutely drunk, would have stated on oath the effect which his words have had on me, an effect which persists to the present time. Whenever I listen to him my heart beats faster than if I were in a religious frenzy, and tears run down my face, and I observe that numbers of other people have the same experience. Nothing of this kind ever used to happen to me when I listened to Pericles and other good speakers; I recognized that they spoke well, but my soul was not thrown into confusion and dismay by the thought that my life was no better than a slave's. That is the condition to which I have often been reduced by our modern Marsyas, with the result that it seems impossible to go on living in my present state. You can't say that this isn't true, Socrates. And even at this moment, I know quite well that, if I were prepared to give ear to him, I should not be able to hold out, but the same thing would happen again. He compels me to realize that I am still a mass of imperfections and yet persistently neglect my own true interests by engaging in public life. So against my real inclination I stop up my ears and take refuge in flight, as Odysseus did from the Sirens; otherwise I should sit here beside him till I was an old man. He is the only person in whose presence I experience a sensation of which I might be thought incapable, a sensation of shame; he, and he alone, positively makes me ashamed of myself. The reason is that I am conscious that there is no arguing against the conclusion that one should do as he bids, and yet that, whenever I am away from him, I succumb to the temptations of popularity. So I behave like a runaway slave and take to my heels, and when I see him the conclusions which he has forced upon me make me ashamed. Many a time I should be glad for him to vanish from the face of the earth, but I know that, if that were to happen, my sorrow would far outweigh my relief. In fact, I simply do not know what to do about him.

'This is the effect which the "piping" of this satyr has had on me and on many other people. But listen and you shall hear how in other respects too he resembles the creatures to which I compared him; and how marvellous is the power which he possesses. You may be sure that none of you knows his true nature, but I will reveal him to you, now that I have begun. The Socrates whom you see has a tendency to fall in love with good-looking young men, and is always in their society and in an ecstasy about them. (Besides, he is, to all appearances, universally ignorant and knows nothing.) But this is exactly the point in which he resembles Silenus; he wears these characteristics superficially, like the carved figure, but once you see beneath the surface you will discover a degree of self-control of which you can hardly form a notion, gentlemen. Believe me, it makes no difference to him whether a person is good-looking—he despises good looks to an almost inconceivable extent—nor whether he is rich nor whether he possesses any of the other advantages that rank high in popular esteem; to him all these things are worthless, and we ourselves of no account, be sure of that. He spends his whole life pretending and playing with people, and I doubt whether anyone has ever seen the treasures which are revealed when he grows serious and exposes what he keeps inside. However, I once saw them, and found them so divine and precious and beautiful and marvellous that, to put the matter briefly, I had no choice but to do whatever Socrates bade me.'

[Using his drunkeness as an excuse for candor, Alcibiades next recalls his unsuccessful attempt to make love to Socrates. By possessing the philosopher's body, Alcibiades had hoped to possess his mind also. He then tells of Socrates' endurance and courage when they served together in the Athenian army.]

❊   ❊   ❊

'It was after these events that we served in the campaign against Potidae together, and were mess-mates there.[9] Of this I may say first that in supporting hardship he showed himself not merely my superior but the whole army's. Whenever we were cut off, as tends to happen on service, and compelled to go without food, the rest of us were nowhere in the matter of endurance. And again, when supplies were abundant, no one enjoyed them more; at drinking especially, though he drank only when he was forced to do so, he was invincible, and yet, what is more remarkable of all, no human being has ever seen Socrates drunk. You will see the proof of this very shortly if I am not mistaken. As for the hardships of winter—and the winters there are very severe—he per-

---

[9]The refusal of Potidea, a tributary of Athens in the peninsula of Chalcidice, to sever its connection with Corinth, its mother-city, was one of the immediate causes of the Peloponnesian War. The seige of the city by the Athenians lasted over two years (432-430 B.C.), and ended in its capitulation.

formed prodigies; on one occasion in particular, when there was a tremendous frost, and everybody either remained indoors or, if they did go out, muffled themselves up in a quite unheard-of-way, and tied and swathed their feet in felt and sheepskin, Socrates went out with nothing on but his ordinary clothes and without anything on his feet, and walked over the ice barefoot more easily than other people in their boots. The soldiers viewed him with suspicion, believing that he meant to humiliate them.

'So much for this subject, but "another exploit that the hero dared"[10] in the course of his military service is worth relating. A problem occurred to him early one day, and he stood still on the spot to consider it. When he couldn't solve it he didn't give up, but stood there ruminating. By the time it was midday people noticed him, and remarked to one another with wonder that Socrates had been standing wrapped in thought since early morning. Finally in the evening after dinner, some Ionians brought their bedding outside—it was summertime—where they could take their rest in the cool and at the same time keep an eye on Socrates to see if he would stand there all night as well. He remained standing until it was dawn and the sun rose. Then he made a prayer to the sun and went away.

'Now, if you please, we will consider his behaviour in battle; we ought to do him justice on this score as well. When the action took place in which I won my decoration for valour,[11] it was entirely to Socrates that I owned my preservation; he would not leave me when I was wounded, but succeeded in rescuing both me and my arms.

✿   ✿   ✿

'But our friend here is so extraordinary, both in his person and in his conversation, that you will never be able to find anyone remotely resembling him either in antiquity or in the present generation, unless you go beyond humanity altogether, and have recourse to the images of Silenus and satyr which I am using myself in this speech. They are as applicable to his talk as to his person; I forgot to say at the beginning that his talk too is extremely like the Silenus-figures which take apart. Anyone who sets out to listen to Socrates talking will probably find his conversation utterly ridiculous at first, it is clothed in such curious words and phrases, the hide, so to speak, of a hectoring satyr. He will talk of pack-asses and blacksmiths, cobblers and tanners, and appear to express the same ideas in the same language over and over again, so that any inexperienced or foolish person is bound to laugh at his way of speaking. But if a man penetrates within and sees the content of Socrates' talk exposed, he will

---

[10]Homer, *Odyssey*, 4.242.
[11]The battle in which Alcibiades distinguished himself was the battle of Potidaea in 432 B.C., immediately before the blockade.

find that there is nothing but sound sense inside, and that this talk is almost the talk of a god, and enshrines countless representatives of ideal excellence, and is of the widest possible application; in fact that it extends over all the subjects with which a man who means to turn out a gentleman needs to concern himself.

'That is what I have to say, gentlemen, in praise of Socrates.'

*   *   *

ARISTOTLE

Preface

(384-322 B.C.)

SECOND ONLY TO PLATO IN HIS INTELLECTUAL ACCOMPLISHMENT AND LATER influence, Aristotle is notable both for the vast number of works he produced and the wide variety of subjects he covered. He was the world's first great scientist, a tireless observer of nature and classifier of knowledge. Of the four hundred treatises attributed to him, only about a fourth survive. These extant materials include the first thoroughly systematic investigations of physics, logic, biology, zoology, ethics, politics, and aesthetics. Aristotle's scientific curiosity and passion for information were enormous. Taking all knowledge as his province, he extended the theoretic philosophy of his master, Plato, to encompass the material world, the phenomena of which he examined with a care and precision hitherto unknown.

Coming to Athens from the cultural backwaters of Macedonia, Aristotle studied for twenty years at Plato's Academy. About five years after Plato's death, Aristotle was recalled to Macedonia, where he was appointed tutor to young Alexander, son of King Philip. The fact that Alexander developed so intense an admiration of Athenian culture, which, as world conqueror, he imposed on nations throughout Asia, is probably due to Aristotle's teaching. In 335 when Alexander began his invasion of Persia, Aristotle returned to Athens and founded the Lyceum, the second university of Europe. This institution for the study of philosophy became known as the "Peripatetic School," from Aristotle's habit of walking up and down the Peripatos or colonnade while conversing with his students. There the philosopher collected the first large private library and established a museum of natural history. Alexander apparently contributed to these establishments by sending back from Asia numerous manuscripts and biological specimens.

When Alexander died suddenly in 323 B.C., the anti-Macedonian sentiment in Athens was sufficient to make Aristotle leave the city. Referring to Socrates' execution two generations earlier, Aristotle remarked that he did not wish the Athenians to "sin a second time against philosophy." He died in self-imposed exile the following year.

Although he eventually rejected various Platonic doctrines, including the Theory of Ideas, Aristotle remained deeply influenced by his master's teaching. He was, however, of a more practical and "realistic" bent of mind than his mentor. His writings, which lack the metaphoric beauty of Plato's dialogues, survive primarily in the form of lecture notes or scientific reports. Many of them may in fact be no more than student-produced outlines of Aristotle's talks at the Lyceum. In any case, such works as the *Nicomachean Ethics* and the *Poetics* reflect a nature more given to painstaking research and classification than to the imaginative flights of an intuitive philosopher. But in spite of Aristotle's stylistic defects, the scope and quality of his achievement are enormously impressive.

During the Middle Ages when Plato was virtually forgotten, Aristotle was universally regarded as "The Philosopher." To Dante he was simply "the Master of those who know."

ETHICS

THE NICOMACHEAN ETHICS, SO NAMED BECAUSE THEY WERE PROBABLY edited after the philosopher's death by his son Nicomachus, reveal Aristotle's characteristic thoroughness and love of systematic analysis. He observes and classifies human moral behavior much as he would the habits of an interesting animal species. Viewing the individual as part of a larger social unit, Aristotle attempts to define the "good life" in terms of man's relation to the external world. The chief good in life is happiness, which is found not in pleasure, wealth or popularity, but in the continuous exercise of the quality unique to human beings—the use of reason. The highest function of reason is the discovery and contemplation of philosophic truth. Unlike Plato, Aristotle argues that man is not born knowing, but learns to know through experience and discipline.

In Book II Aristotle distinguishes between intellectual excellence, which is developed by study, and moral virtue, which is the result of emotional discipline and habit. Moral perfection is acquired through the triumph of reason over instinct. The good man's life is distinguished by his ability to use reason in choosing among alternate courses of action. Practical wisdom lies in learning to recognize and follow the Golden Mean. This, the most famous of Aristotle's ethical doctrines, is a restatement of the ancient Apollonian maxim "moderation in all things." The Mean is the morally acceptable middle ground between two extremes. It is not an absolute standard, but must be adapted to each individual and his situation. Courage, for example, is the Mean between foolhardiness and cowardice, just as generosity is the virtue lying midway between parsimony and prodigality. In Aristotle's philosophy, then, man is a free moral agent who pursues happiness by thinking clearly and living rationally.

THE NICOMACHEAN ETHICS

BOOK II
CHAPTER SIX
[VIRTUE AND THE GOLDEN MEAN]

✿   ✿   ✿

THE MAN WHO KNOWS HIS BUSINESS AVOIDS BOTH TOO MUCH AND TOO LITTLE. It is the mean he seeks and adopts—not the mean of the thing but the relative mean.

Every form, then, of applied knowledge, when it performs its function well, looks to the mean and works to the standard set by that. It is because people feel this that they apply the *cliché*, 'You couldn't add anything to it or take anything from it' to an artistic masterpiece, the implication being that too much and too little alike destroy perfection, while the mean preserves it. Now if this be so, and if it be true, as we say, that good craftsmen work to the standard of the mean, then, since goodness like Nature is more exact and of higher character than any art, it follows that goodness is the quality that hits the mean. By 'goodness' I mean goodness of moral character, since it is moral goodness that deals with feelings and actions, and it is in them that we find excess, deficiency, and a mean. It is possible, for example, to experience fear, boldness, desire, anger, pity, and pleasures and pains generally, too much or too little or to the right amount. If we feel them too much or too little, we are wrong. But to have these feelings at the right times on the right occasions towards the right people for the right motive and in the right way is to have them in the right measure, that is, somewhere between the extremes; and this is what characterizes goodness. The same may be said of the mean and extremes in actions. Now it is in the field of actions and feelings that goodness operates; in them we find excess, deficiency, and, between them, the mean, the first two being wrong, the mean right and praised as such.[1] Goodness, then, is a mean condition in the sense that it aims at and hits the mean.

Consider, too, that it is possible to go wrong in more ways than one. (In Pythagorean terminology evil is a form of the Unlimited, good of the Limited.) But there is only one way of being right. That is why going wrong is easy, and going right difficult; it is easy to miss the bull's-eye and difficult to hit it. Here, then, is another explanation of why the too

---

[1]Being right or successful and being praised are both indicative of excellence.

Abridged From *The Ethics of Aristotle*, translated by J. A. K. Thomson. Copyright © 1953 by the estate of J. A. K. Thomson. Reprinted by permission of George Allen and Unwin, Ltd. The footnotes and chapter summaries are the translator's.

much and the too little are connected with evil and the mean with good. As the poet says,

Goodness is one, evil is multiform.

We are now in a position to state our definition of virtue with more precision. Observe that the kind of virtue meant here is moral, not intellectual, and that Aristotle must not be taken as saying that the kind of virtue which he regards as the highest and truest is any sort of mean.

We may now define virtue as a disposition of the soul in which, when it has to choose among actions and feelings, it observes the mean relative to us, this being determined by such a rule or principle as would take shape in the mind of a man of sense or practical wisdom. We call it a mean condition as lying between two forms of badness, one being excess and the other deficiency; and also for this reason, that, whereas badness either falls short of or exceeds the right measure in feelings and actions, virtue discovers the mean and deliberately chooses it. Thus, looked at from the point of view of its essence as embodied in its definition, virtue no doubt is a mean; judged by the standard of what is right and best, it is an extreme.

Aristotle enters a caution. Though we have said that virtue observes the mean in actions and passions, we do not say this of all acts and all feelings. Some are essentially evil and, when these are involved, our rule to applying the mean cannot be brought into operation.

But choice of a mean is not possible in every action or every feeling. The very names of some have an immediate connotation of evil. Such are malice, shamelessness, envy among feelings, and among actions adultery, theft, murder. All these and more like them have a bad name as being evil in themselves; it is not merely the excess or deficiency of them that we censure. In their case, then, it is impossible to act rightly; whatever we do is wrong. Nor do circumstances make any difference in the rightness or wrongness of them. When a man commits adultery there is no point in asking whether it is with the right woman or at the right time or in the right way, for to do anything like that is simply wrong. It would amount to claiming that there is a mean and excess and defect in unjust or cowardly or intemperate actions. If such a thing were possible, we should find ourselves with a mean quantity of excess, a mean of deficiency, an excess of excess and a deficiency of deficiency. But just as in temperance and justice there can be no mean or excess or deficiency, because the mean in a sense *is* an extreme, so there can be no mean or excess or deficiency in those vicious actions—however done, they are wrong. Putting the matter into general language, we may say that there is no mean in the extremes, and no extreme in the mean, to be observed by anybody.

✻　　✻　　✻

CHAPTER NINE

I HAVE SAID ENOUGH TO SHOW THAT MORAL EXCELLENCE IS A MEAN, AND I have shown in what sense it is so. It is, namely, a mean between two forms of badness, one of excess and the other of defect, and is so described because it aims at hitting the mean point in feelings and in actions. This makes virtue hard of achievement, because finding the middle point is never easy. It is not everybody, for instance, who can find the centre of a circle—that calls for a geometrician. Thus, too, it is easy to fly into a passion—anybody can do that—but to be angry with the right person and to the right extent and at the right time and with the right object and in the right way—that is not easy, and it is not everyone who can do it. This is equally true of giving or spending money. Hence we infer that to do these things properly is rare, laudable and fine.

✻　　✻　　✻

BOOK IV

The following chapter treats of a quality called in Greek megalopsuchia *and in Latin* magnanimitas. *It is not magnanimity in the modern sense, but something like 'justifiable pride'. The translator must be allowed a certain freedom in dealing with so intractable a word, but the reader will soon discover for himself what Aristotle means. The picture here presented of the justifiably proud man has been thought partly humorous or even ironical. The reader may judge for himself. But there is this to be said. Aristotle is here speaking of the quality in isolation from other qualities which would in any actual great man tend to soften and humanize his consciousness of superiority to other people.*

CHAPTER THREE

'MAGNANIMITY', OR 'GREATNESS OF SOUL', IS, AS THE WORD ITSELF LEADS us to infer, concerned with great matters, and before we go further we must try to grasp what sort of matters they are. Not that it will make any difference whether we attend to the quality itself or to the person in whom it is embodied.

Well then, what we mean by a great-souled or superior man is one who claims, and is entitled to claim, high consideration from his fellows. Of course a man who makes such a claim on insufficient grounds is but a silly person, and silliness is not a virtue. The superior man, then, is such as I have described. The man who makes small claims for himself when his merits deserve these and no more shows a wise restraint, but great-souled we must not call him, for that kind of superiority must rest on greatness, just as personal beauty requires that one should be tall; little people may have charm and elegance, but beauty—no. The man who makes lofty but unjustified claims for himself is conceited, but not everybody is conceited who claims more than his due. On the other hand the man who claims less than his due is poor-spirited. It is not a case of claiming much or little or something that is neither too much nor too little. The point is, it must be less than he is entitled to claim. In fact, it is the man who has great deserts that shows the poorest spirit if he does not assert his claim. What would he do if his merits were less? We see, then, that the superior man, while in the extent of his claim going to an extreme, still, by claiming no more than his due, is justified and so avoids both extremes, coming as he does between those who claim too much and those who claim too little—between the vain or conceited and the poor-spirited.

We see, then, that the superior man makes large, even the largest, claims and is entirely justified in doing so. But he must have a particular object in view. What is it? When we say somebody or something has 'worth' or 'value' we are thinking in terms of external goods. The greatest of these we take to be that which we assign to the gods as their due and which is desired by the eminent and awarded as the meed of victory in the most glorious contests, namely, honour. For honour is the greatest of external goods. The superior man, then, has the right attitude to honours and dishonours. Indeed, it goes without saying that he concerns himself with honour; it is what he claims, and claims justly, above all. The small-souled or poor-spirited man errs in the way of deficiency not only by failing to assert his own just claims but also by failing to support the comparison between himself and the superior man in this respect. On the other hand the vain man claims more than his worth.[2] As for the superior man, since nothing is too good for him, he must be the best of men. For the better a man is, the more he deserves, so that he who deserves most is the best. Therefore the truly superior man must be a good man. Indeed, greatness in all the virtues is surely what stamps him for what he is. For instance, it would be totally out of character for such a man to run away helter-skelter, or to be guilty of cheating. For what motive could a man of his standards have to perform dishonourable actions? For honour is the guerdon of goodness and is awarded to the good. It would be nearer the truth to say that greatness of soul is the beautiful completion of the virtues, for it adds to them its own greatness and is inseparable from them. And this makes it hard for a man to be truly great in soul; without a fine moral sense it is impossible.

Well, then, the grand objects of the superior man's ambition are honours; by them he will be gratified, if they are distinguished and are bestowed by estimable persons—but gratified only up to a point, because

---

[2]Not more, however, than the superior man is worth.

he will feel that he is getting no more than his due, or rather less, for no honour can be enough for perfected virtue. Nevertheless he will accept such honours on the ground that they are the highest those men have it in their power to give. But honour coming from men with no special qualities to recommend them and proffered for trifling reasons he will not consider for a moment; that sort of thing is altogether beneath him. And dishonour he will treat in the same way; dishonour and he can never be justly associated. But, while it is true, as has been said, that honour is the main theatre of the great man's activity, still he will also deal in the right spirit with riches, power, every form of good and bad fortune as it may befall him. And when he meets with good fortune he will not be overjoyed, nor will he be excessively depressed when he meets with bad. For even honour does not arouse in him these strong emotions, although it is the chief of external goods. For, while power and riches are desirable, it is for the sake of the honour that surrounds them. At all events the holders of these advantages hope that they may be honoured on account of them. Accordingly the man who sets little store even by honour will set little store by these things. This is the reason why the superior man gives the impression of superciliousness.

❀   ❀   ❀

The superior man will not run petty risks, nor indeed risks of any kind if he can help it, because there are so few things he considers worth while. But he rises to meet a crisis and, so long as that lasts, he will put his life in peril for the cause, since he is not the man to purchase life at any price. It is also part of his character to confer benefits. But he hates receiving them. This is because the former action implies superiority, the latter inferiority. When he does repay a service it is with interest, for in this way the original benefactor will become the beneficiary and debtor in his turn. . . . Another mark of the superior man is his refusal or reluctance to ask anyone to help him, while always ready to bring help himself. And he stands on his dignity with those who are high in public esteem or favourites of fortune, but does not assume airs in his dealings with persons of no great distinction, because to maintain one's superiority in the presence of notabilities is not easy and impresses others, so that here a dignified manner is not unbecoming of a gentleman, though in the worst of taste when one is dealing with humble people—as bad as hustling the weak. . . . He will rarely undertake anything or, if he does, it will be something great and glorious. Since it is an indication of fear to conceal one's feelings, the superior man is bound to be open in his likes and dislikes, and to care more for the truth than for what people think, and to be straightforward in word and deed.[3] He must live his own life uninfluenced by anyone, unless perhaps a friend, since to permit such

---

[3]The poor opinion he has of other people enables him to speak his mind freely, and his language will be sincere, unless when he has recourse to irony, which will be his tone in addressing the generality of men.

influence would involve some degree of complaisance.[4] He is not a gushing person, because nothing strikes him as a subject of mightly admiration.
He does not nurse resentment, for it is not like a superior man to remember things against people, especially the mischief they have tried to do
him—he tends to overlook all that. He does not care for personal talk,
being indisposed to speak either about himself or anyone else. He is not
interested in compliments paid to himself or in uncomplimentary remarks
about his neighbours, although this does not mean that he is himself
given to paying compliments. For the same reason he is not given to
recriminations, even against his ill-wishers, unless he means to be deliberately insulting. In troubles which are unavoidable or of no great
consequence he is not pathetic or pressing, for that would be to give them
too great consequence. He prefers that his possessions should be beautiful
and of no profit to him rather than that they should be profitable and
meant for use, because this goes to show that he is sufficient to himself.
Add that he never hurries (or so people think) and has a deep voice and
a deliberate way of speaking. For the man who believes that there is little
or nothing worth getting excited about will not be prone to hurry or be
high-strung and as a result shrill in his tones and bustling in his movements.

Such, then, is the great-souled or superior man. To him correspond in
one direction the poor-spirited, in the other the vain, man. These, like the
vulgar and paltry, are not generally thought of as evil—for they do no evil
—but as wanderers from the straight path. The poor-spirited man is one
who, though not undeserving, deprives himself of such advantages as he
deserves, the effect of his failure to claim his deserts being to convince
people that there must be something bad about him. . . . For one seeks to
get what one is entitled to, and if one holds aloof from honourable actions
and pursuits, and at the same time makes no claim to external advantages,
it looks as if the reason must be that one is conscious of one's own unworthiness. Vain men, on the other hand, *are* silly, not realizing their own
limitations. This comes out in glaring fashion when they take on an
important job for which they are not qualified, and are proved incompe-
tent. It is a type which affects showy clothes and a smart manner and that
sort of thing. They tell the world what successful men they are, and make
that the topic of their conversation, as if that would win respect for
them. . . .[5]

✿　　✿　　✿

BOOK IX
CHAPTER EIGHT

ANOTHER PROBLEM IS WHETHER ONE OUGHT TO LOVE ONESELF OR ANOTHER
most. The world blames those whose first thoughts are always for them-

---

[4]It is this tendency to servility that makes humble people flatterers, and flatterers
toadies.

[5]Note that poor-spiritedness is more opposed than vanity to greatness of soul. It is
in fact a worse thing and more widespread.

selves and stigmatizes them as self-centered. It is also generally believed that a bad man does everything from a selfish motive, and does this the more, the worse he is.[6] On the other hand the good man is supposed never to act except on some lofty principle—the loftier the principle, the better the man—and to neglect his own interest in order to promote that of his friend. It is a view which is not borne out by the facts. Nor need this surprise us. It is common gound that a man should love his best friend most. But my best friend is the man who in wishing me well wishes it for my sake, whether this shall come to be known or not. Well, there is no one who fulfills this condition so well as I do in my behaviour towards myself; indeed it may be said of every quality which enters into the definition of a friend—I have it in a higher degree than any of my friends. For, as I have already observed, all the affectionate feelings of a man for others are an extension of his feelings for himself. You will find too, that all the popular bywords agree on this point. ('Two bodies and one soul,' 'Amity is parity,' 'The knee is nearer than the shin.') All the proverbs show how close are the ties of friendship, and they all apply best to oneself. For a man is his own best friend. From this it follows that he ought to love himself best.—Which then of these two opinions ought we to accept in practice? It is a reasonable question, since there is a degree of plausibility in both.

No doubt the proper method of dealing with divergent opinions of this sort is to distinguish between them, and so reach a definite conclusion on the point of how far and in what way each of them is true. So the present difficulty may be cleared up if we can discover what meaning each side attaches to the word 'self-love'. Those who make it a term of reproach give the epithet of 'self-loving' to those who assign to themselves more than they are entitled to in money, public distinctions and bodily pleasures, these being what most men crave for and earnestly pursue as the greatest blessings, so that they contend fiercely for the possession of them. Well, the man who grasps at more than his fair share of these things is given to the gratification of his desires and his passions generally and the irrational part of his soul. Now most men are like that, and we see from this that the censorious use of the epithet 'self-loving' results from the fact that the self-love of most men is a bad thing. Applied to them, the censorious epithet is therefore justified. And unquestionably it is people who arrogate too much of such things to themselves who are called 'self-loving' by the ordinary man. For if anybody were to make it his constant business to take the lead himself over everyone else in the performance of just or temperate or any other kind whatever of virtuous actions, generally claiming the honourable role for himself, nobody would stigmatize *him* as 'a self-lover'. Yet the view might be taken that such a man was exceptionally self-loving. At any rate he arrogates to himself the things of greatest moral beauty and excellence, and what he gratifies and obeys throughout is the magistral

---

[6]A bad man is often accused of 'doing nothing until he has to.'

part of himself, his higher intelligence. Now just as in a state or any other composite body it is the magistral or dominant part of it that is considered more particularly to *be* the state or body, so with a man; his intelligence, the governing part of him, *is* the man. Therefore he who loves and indulges this part is to the fullest extent a lover of himself. Further, we may note that the terms 'continent' and 'incontinent' imply that the intellect is or is not in control, which involves the assumption that the intellect is the man. Again, it is our reasoned acts that are held to be more especially those which we have performed ourselves and by our own volition. All which goes to show that a man is, or is chiefly, the ruling part of himself, and that a good man loves it beyond any other part of his nature. It follows that such a man will be self-loving in a different sense from that attached to the word when it is used as a term of reproach. From the vulgar self-lover he differs as far as the life of reason from the life of passion, and as far as a noble purpose differs from mere grasping at whatever presents itself as an expedient. Hence those who are exceptionally devoted to the performance of fine and noble actions receive the approval and commendation of all. And if everyone sought to outdo his neighbour in elevation of character, and laboured strenuously to perform the noblest actions, the common weal would find its complete actualization and the private citizen would realize for himself the greatest of goods, which is virtue.

Therefore it is right for the *good* man to be self-loving, because he will thereby himself be benefited by performing fine actions; and by the same process he will be helpful to others. The bad man on the other hand should not be a self-lover, because he will only be injuring himself and his neighbours by his subservience to base passions. As a result of this subservience what he does is in conflict with what he ought to do, whereas the good man does what he ought to do. For intelligence never fails to choose the course that is best for itself, and the good man obeys his intelligence.

But there is something else which we can truly say about the good man. Many of his actions are performed to serve his friends or his country, even if this should involve dying for them. For he is ready to sacrifice wealth, honours, all the prizes of life in his eagerness to play a noble part. He would prefer one crowded hour of glorious life to a protracted period of quiet existence and mild enjoyment spent as an ordinary man would spend it—one great and dazzling achievement to many small successes. And surely this may be said of those who lay down their lives for others; they choose for themselves a crown of glory. It is also a characteristic trait of the good man that he is prepared to lose money on condition that his friends get more. The friend gets the cash, and he gets the credit, so that he is assigning the greater good to himself. His conduct is not different when it comes to public honours and offices. All these he will freely give up to his friend, because that is the fine and praiseworthy thing for him to do. It is natural then that people should think him virtuous, when he prefers honour to everything else. He may even create opportunities for his friend to do a fine action which he might have done himself, and this may be the nobler course for him to take. Thus in the whole field of admirable conduct we see the good man taking the larger share of moral dignity. In this sense then it is, as I said before, right that he should be self-loving. But in the vulgar sense no one should be so.

It has been questioned whether the possession of friends is necessary to happiness. Aritotle has no doubt that it is so, and gives his reasons.

CHAPTER NINE

ANOTHER DEBATABLE POINT CONCERNING THE HAPPY MAN IS THIS. WILL friends be necessary to his happiness or not? It is commonly said that the happy, being sufficient to themselves, have no need of friends. All the blessings of life are theirs already; so, having all resources within themselves, they are not in need of anything else, whereas a friend, being an *alter ego*, is only there to supply what one cannot supply for oneself. Hence that line of the *Orestes* of Euripides:

When Fortune smiles on us, what need of friends?

Yet it seems a strange thing that in the process of attributing every blessing to the happy man we should not assign him friends, who are thought to be the greatest of all external advantages. Besides, if it is more like a friend to confer than to receive benefits, and doing good to others is an activity which especially belongs to virtue and the virtuous man, and if it is better to do a kindness to a friend than to a stranger, the good man will have need of friends as objects of his active benevolence. Hence a second question. Does one need friends more in prosperity than in adversity? There is a case for either of these alternatives. The unfortunate need people who will be kind to them; the prosperous need people to be kind to.

*   *   *

The good man feels towards his friend as he feels towards himself, since his friend is a second self to him.—If we accept these propositions as true, our conclusion must be that, just as a man's own existence is desirable for that man, so to the same or nearly the same extent is the existence of his friend also desirable for him. But what makes existence desirable is the consciousness of goodness, and such a consciousness is pleasant in itself. So a man ought to have a sympathetic consciousness of his friend's existence, which may be attained by associating with him and conversing and exchanging ideas with him. For that is what is meant when human beings speak of 'living together'—it does not mean grazing together like a herd of cattle.

If then the entirely happy man finds existence desirable in itself as something essentially good and pleasant, and if the existence of his friend is only less desirable for him than his own, then a friend must be considered something to be desired by the happy man. But what is desirable for him he must have, if he is not to suffer some diminution of happiness in that particular. Therefore the man who is to be happy will have need of virtuous friends.

BOOK X
CHAPTER SIX

. . . Almost every objective we choose is chosen for an ulterior purpose. But not happiness; happiness is an end in itself. To make a serious business of amusement and spend laborious days upon it is the height of folly and childishness. The maxim of Anacharsis, *Play so that you may be serious,* may be taken as pointing in the right direction. For amusement is a form of rest or relaxation, and rest we need because we cannot always be working. Rest then is not an end but a means to future activity. Also we believe that it is the life lived in accordance with goodness that is the happy life; and such cannot be divorced from seriousness or spent in amusing oneself. We maintain, too, that serious things are intrinsically better than funny or amusing things, and that the activity of a man, or of some organ or faculty of his, is more serious in proportion as it possesses a higher excellence. Such an activity then is itself superior and therefore more conducive to happiness. We may add another argument. Anybody can enjoy fleshly pleasures—a slave no less than a Socrates. But nobody is prepared to give a slave a life of his own; that is, nobody is prepared to give him a measure of happiness. So—once more—happiness does not consist in pastimes and amusements but in virtuous activities.

In the two following chapters Aristotle gives reasons for thinking that Happiness in its highest and best manifestation is found in cultivating the 'contemplative' life.

CHAPTER SEVEN

But if happiness is an activity in accordance with virtue, it is reasonable to assume that it will be in accordance with the highest virtue; and this can only be the virtue of the best part of us. Whether this be the intellect or something else—whatever it is that is held to have a natural right to govern and guide us, and to have an insight into what is noble and divine, either as being itself also divine or more divine than any other part of us—it is the activity of this part in accordance with the virtue proper to it that will be perfect happiness. Now we have seen already that this activity has a speculative or contemplative character. This is a conclusion which may be accepted as in harmony with our earlier arguments and with the truth. For 'contemplation' is the highest form of activity, since the intellect is the highest thing in us and the objects which come within its range are the highest that can be known. But it is also the most continuous activity, for we can think about intellectual problems more continuously than we can keep up any sort of physical action. Again, we feel sure that a modicum of pleasure must be one of the ingredients of happiness. Now it is admitted that activity along the lines of 'wisdom' is the pleasantest of all the good activities. At all events it is thought that philosophy ('the pursuit of wisdom') has pleasures marvellous in purity and duration, and it stands to reason that those who have knowledge pass their time more pleasantly than those who are engaged in its pursuit. Again, self-sufficiency will be found to belong in an exceptional degree to the exercise of the speculative intellect. The wise man, as much as the just man and everyone else, must have the necessaries of life. But, given an adequate supply of these, the just man also needs people with and towards whom he can put his justice into operation; and we can use similar language about the temperate man, the brave man, and so on. But the wise man can do more. He can speculate all by himself, and the wiser he is the better he can do it. Doubtless it helps to have fellow-workers, but for all that he is the most self-sufficing of men. Finally it may well be thought that the activity of contemplation is the only one that is praised on its own account, because nothing comes of it beyond the act of contemplation, whereas from practical activities we count on gaining something more or less over and above the mere action. Again, it is commonly believed that, to have happiness, one must have leisure; we occupy ourselves in order that we may have leisure, just as we make war for the sake of peace. Now the practical virtues find opportunity for their exercise in politics and in war, but these are occupations which are supposed to leave no room for leisure. Certainly it is true of the trade of war, for no one deliberately chooses to make war for the sake of making it or tries to bring about a war. A man would be regarded as a bloodthirsty monster if he were to make war on a friendly state just to produce battles and slaughter. The business of the politician also makes leisure impossible. Besides the activity itself, politics aims at securing positions of power and honour or the happiness of the politician himself or his fellow-citizens—a happiness obviously distinct from that which we are seeking.

We are now in a position to suggest the truth of the following statements. (*a*) Political and military activities, while pre-eminent among good activities in beauty and grandeur, are incompatible with leisure, and are not chosen for their own sake but with a view to some remoter end, whereas the activity of the intellect is felt to excel in the serious use of leisure, taking as it does the form of contemplation, and not to aim at any end beyond itself, and to own a pleasure peculiar to itself, thereby enhancing its activity. (*b*) In this activity we easily recognize self-sufficiency, the possibility of leisure and such freedom from fatigue as is humanly possible, together with all the other blessings of pure happiness. Now if these statements are received as true, it will follow that it is this intellectual activity which forms perfect happiness for a man—provided of course that it ensures a complete span of life, for nothing incomplete can be an element in happiness.

Yes, but such a life will be too high for *human* attainment. It will not be lived by us in our merely human capacity but in virtue of something divine within us, and so far as this divine particle is superior to man's composite nature, to that extent will its activity be superior to that of the other forms of excellence. If the intellect is divine compared with man, the life of the intellect must be divine compared with the life of a human creature. And we ought not to listen to those who counsel us *O man, think as man should* and *O mortal, remember your mortality.* Rather ought we, so far as in us lies, to put on immortality and to leave nothing unattempted in the effort to live in conformity with the highest thing within us. Small in bulk it may be, yet in power and preciousness it transcends all the rest. We may in fact believe that this is the true self of the individual, being the sovran and better part of him. It would be strange, then, if a man should choose to live not his own life but another's. Moreover, the rule, as I stated it a little before, will apply here—the rule that what is best and pleasantest for each creature is that which intimately belongs to it. Applying it, we shall conclude that the life of the intellect is the best and pleasantest for man, because the intellect more than anything else *is* the man. Thus it will be the happiest life as well.

THE POETICS   **Preface**

IN THE FIRST KNOWN EXAMPLE OF LITERARY CRITICISM, ARISTOTLE subjects poetry to the same kind of rigorous analysis that he applied to the natural sciences. His discussion of tragedy is almost purely descriptive with few attempts at aesthetic judgment. He sees tragedy as developing, like all the other arts, from man's instinctive love of imitation (*mimesis*). In the most famous literary definition of antiquity, Aristotle classifies tragedy as the dramatic imitation of a serious and unified action that inspires *catharsis* in the spectator. Whether by *catharsis* Aristotle means that the audience experiences a spiritual purification of the all-too-mortal feelings of "pity and terror," or whether he means to say that drama produces an artistic pleasure through an almost physical purgation of these emotions, is still warmly debated.

In his treatment of the various parts of tragedy (plot, character, thought, language, spectacle, song), Aristotle is merely *describing* the structure and constituent elements of already existing plays. He is not, as the Renaissance and Neoclassic writers supposed, *prescribing* a slavish adherence to the "three unities." The fact that plays like *Oedipus the King* observed a unity of time, place, and action is the result of the author's wish to gain dramatic impact by focusing on the speedy resolution of a single issue. It is not because "classical" taste demanded a strict obedience to theatrical "rules." (In the *Agamemnon*, for example, Aeschylus allows considerable time to pass between the watchman's opening soliloquy and the entrance of Agamemnon. In *The Eumenides* the action is not restricted to a single locale, but moves freely from Delphi to Athens.) Athenian audiences were apparently as ready as any other to accept the "willing suspension of disbelief" that dramatic illusion requires.

.

POETICS

Poetry in general seems to have sprung from two causes, each of them lying deep in our nature. First, the instinct of imitation is implanted in man from childhood, one difference between him and other animals being that he is the most imitative of living creatures, and through imitation learns his earliest lessons; and no less universal is the pleasure felt in things imitated. We have evidence of this in the facts of experience. Objects which in themselves we view with pain, we delight to contemplate when reproduced with minute fidelity: such as the forms of the most ignoble animals and of dead bodies. The cause of this again is, that to learn gives the liveliest pleasure, not only to philosophers but to men in general; whose capacity, however, of learning is more limited. Thus the reason why men enjoy seeing a likeness is, that in contemplating it they find themselves learning or inferring, and saying perhaps, 'Ah, that is he.' For if you happen not to have seen the original, the pleasure will be due not to the imitation as such, but to the execution, the colouring, or some such other cause.

Imitation, then, is one instinct of our nature. Next, there is the instinct for 'harmony' and rhythm, metres being manifestly sections of rhythm.

Abridged. From *Aristotle's Poetics*, translated by S.H. Butcher. Reprinted by permission of St. Martin's Press, Inc., Macmillan & Co., Ltd. and the Executors of the estate of S.H. Butcher.

Persons, therefore, starting with this natural gift developed by degrees their special aptitudes, till their rude improvisations gave birth to Poetry.

Poetry now diverged in two directions, according to the individual character of the writers. The graver spirits imitated noble actions, and the actions of good men. The more trivial sort imitated the actions of meaner persons, at first composing satires, as the former did hymns to the gods and the praises of famous men.

        ✿   ✿   ✿

As, in the serious style, Homer is pre-eminent among poets, for he alone combined dramatic form with excellence of imitation, so he too first laid down the main lines of Comedy, by dramatising the ludicrous instead of writing personal satire. His Margites bears the same relation to Comedy that the Iliad and Odyssey do to Tragedy. But when Tragedy and Comedy came to light, the two classes of poets still followed their natural bent: the lampooners became writers of Comedy, and the Epic poets were succeeded by Tragedians, since the drama was a larger and higher form of art.

Whether Tragedy has as yet perfected its proper types or not; and whether it is to be judged in itself, or in relation also to the audience,—this raises another question. Be that as it may, Tragedy—as also Comedy—was at first mere improvisation. The one originated with the authors of the Dithyramb, the other with those of the phallic songs, which are still in use in many of our cities. Tragedy advanced by slow degrees; each new element that showed itself was in turn developed. Having passed through many changes, it found its natural form, and there it stopped.

Aeschylus first introduced a second actor; he diminished the importance of the Chorus, and assigned the leading part to the dialogue. Sophocles raised the number of actors to three, and added scene-painting. Moreover, it was not till late that the short plot was discarded for one of greater compass, and the grotesque diction of the earlier satyric form for the stately manner of Tragedy.

        ✿   ✿   ✿

Epic poetry agrees with Tragedy in so far as it is an imitation in verse of characters of a higher type. They differ, in that Epic poetry admits but one kind of metre, and is narrative in form. They differ, again, in their length: for Tragedy endeavours, as far as possible, to confine itself to a single revolution of the sun, or but slightly to exceed this limit; whereas the Epic action has no limits of time.

❀   ❀   ❀

[Definition of Tragedy]

Tragedy, then, is an imitation of an action that is serious, complete, and of a certain magnitude; in language embellished with each kind of artistic ornament, the several kinds being found in separate parts of the play; in the form of action, not of narrative; through pity and fear effecting the proper purgation of these emotions. By 'language embellished,' I mean language into which rhythm, 'harmony,' and song enter. By 'the several kinds in separate parts,' I mean, that some parts are rendered through the medium of verse alone, others again with the aid of song.

Now as tragic imitation implies persons acting, it necessarily follows, in the first place, that Spectacular equipment will be a part of Tragedy. Next, Song and Diction, for these are the medium of imitation. By 'Diction' I mean the mere metrical arrangement of the words: as for 'Song,' it is a term whose sense every one understands.

Again, Tragedy is the imitation of an action; and an action implies personal agents, who necessarily possess certain distinctive qualities both of character and thought; for it is by these that we qualify actions themselves, and these—thought and character—are the two natural causes from which actions spring, and on actions again all success or failure depends. Hence, the Plot is the imitation of the action:—for by plot I here mean the arrangement of the incidents. By Character I mean that in virtue of which we ascribe certain qualities to the agents. Thought is required wherever a statement is proved, or, it may be, a general truth enunciated. Every Tragedy, therefore, must have six parts, which parts determine its quality—namely, Plot, Character, Diction, Thought, Spectacle, Song.

❀   ❀   ❀

But most important of all is the structure of the incidents. For Tragedy is an imitation, not of men, but of an action and of life, and life consists in action, and its end is a mode of action, not a quality. Now character determines men's qualities, but it is by their actions that they are happy or the reverse. Dramatic action, therefore, is not with a view to the representation of character: character comes in as subsidiary to the actions. Hence the incidents and the plot are the end of tragedy; and the end is the chief thing of all. Again, without action there cannot be a tragedy; there may be without character. The tragedies of most of our modern poets fail in the rendering of character; and of poets in general this is often true.

❀   ❀   ❀

Again, if you string together a set of speeches expressive of character, and well finished in point of diction and thought, you will not produce the essential tragic effect nearly so well as with a play which, however deficient in these respects, yet has a plot and artistically constructed incidents. Besides which, the most powerful elements of emotional interest in Tragedy—Peripeteia or Reversal of the Situation, and Recognition scenes—are parts of the plot. The Plot, then, is the first principle, and, as it were, the soul of a tragedy: Character holds the second place. A similar fact is seen in painting. The most beautiful colours, laid on confusedly, will not give as much pleasure as the chalk outline of a portrait. Thus Tragedy is the imitation of an action, and of the agents mainly with a view to the action.

Third in order is Thought,—that is, the faculty of saying what is possible and pertinent in given circumstances. In the case of oratory, this is the function of the political art and of the art of rhetoric: and so indeed the older poets make their characters speak the language of civic life; the poets of our time, the language of the rhetoricians. Character is that which reveals moral purpose, showing what kind of things a man chooses or avoids. Speeches, therefore, which do not make this manifest, or in which the speaker does not choose or avoid anything whatever, are not expressive of character. Thought, on the other hand, is found where something is proved to be or not to be, or a general maxim is enunciated.

      ❖   ❖   ❖

These principles being established, let us now discuss the proper structure of the Plot, since this is the first and most important thing in Tragedy.

Now, according to our definition, Tragedy is an imitation of an action that is complete, and whole, and of a certain magnitude; for there may be a whole that is wanting in magnitude. A whole is that which has a beginning, a middle, and an end. A beginning is that which does not itself follow anything by causal necessity, but after which something naturally is or comes to be. An end, on the contrary, is that which itself naturally follows some other thing, either by necessity, or as a rule, but has nothing following it. A middle is that which follows something as some other thing follows it. A well constructed plot, therefore, must neither begin nor end at haphazard, but conform to these principles.

Unity of plot does not, as some persons think, consist in the unity of the hero. For infinitely various are the incidents in one man's life which cannot be reduced to unity; and so, too, there are many actions of one man out of which we cannot make one action. Hence the error, as it appears, of all poets who have composed a Heracleid, a Theseid, or other poems of the kind. They imagine that as Heracles was one man, the story of Heracles must also be unity. But Homer, as in all else he is of surpassing merit, here too—whether from art or natural genius—seems to have happily discerned the truth. In composing the Odyssey he did not include all the adventures of Odysseus—such as his wound on Parnassus, or his feigned madness at the mustering of the host—incidents between which there was no necessary or probable connexion: but he made the Odyssey, and likewise the Iliad, to centre round an action that in our sense of the word is one. As therefore, in the other imitative arts, the imitation is one when the object imitated is one, so the plot, being an imitation of an action, must imitate one action and that a whole, the structural union of the parts being such that, if any one of them is displaced or removed, the whole will be disjointed and disturbed. For a thing whose presence or absence makes no visible difference, is not an organic part of the whole.

It is, moreover, evident from what has been said, that it is not the function of the poet to relate what has happened, but what may happen,—what is possible according to the law of probability or necessity. The poet and the historian differ not by writing in verse or in prose. The work of Herodotus might be put into verse, and it would still be a species of history, with metre no less than without it. The true difference is that one relates what has happened, the other what may happen. Poetry, therefore, is a more philosophical and a higher thing than history: for poetry tends to express the universal, history the particular. By the universal I mean how a person of a certain type will on occasion speak or act, according to the law of probability or necessity; and it is this universality at which poetry aims in the names she attaches to the personages.

❀   ❀   ❀

But again, Tragedy is an imitation not only of a complete action, but of events inspiring fear or pity. Such an effect is best produced when the events come on us by surprise; and the effect is heightened when, at the same time, they follow as cause and effect. The tragic wonder will then be greater than if they happened of themselves or by accident; for even coincidences are most striking when they have an air of design. We may instance the statue of Mitys at Argos, which fell upon his murderer while he was a spectator at a festival, and killed him. Such events seem not to be due to mere chance. Plots, therefore, constructed on these principles are necessarily the best.

A Complex action is one in which the change is accompanied by such Reversal, or by Recognition, or by both. These last should arise from the internal structure of the plot, so that what follows should be the necessary or probable result of the preceding action.

Reversal of the Situation is a change by which the action veers round to its opposite, subject always to our rule of probability or necessity. Thus in the Oedipus, the messenger comes to cheer Oedipus and free him from his alarms about his mother, but by revealing who he is, he produces the opposite effect.

Recognition, as the name indicates, is a change from ignorance to knowledge, producing love or hate between the persons destined by the poet for good or bad fortune. The best form of recognition is coincident with a Reversal of the Situation, as in the Oedipus. There are indeed other forms. Even inanimate things of the most trivial kind may in a sense be objects of recognition. Again, we may recognise or discover whether a person has done a thing or not. But the recognition which is most intimately connected with the plot and action is, as we have said, the recognition of persons. This recognition, combined with Reversal, will produce either pity or fear; and actions producing these effects are those which, by our definition, Tragedy represents. Moreover, it is upon such situations that the issues of good or bad fortune will depend. Recognition, then, being between persons, it may happen that one person only is recognised by the other—when the latter is already known—or it may be necessary that the recognition should be on both sides.

✿   ✿   ✿

Two parts, then, of the Plot—Reversal of the Situation and Recognition—turn upon surprises. A third part is the Scene of Suffering. The Scene of Suffering is a destructive or painful action, such as death on the stage, bodily agony, wounds and the like.

✿   ✿   ✿

A perfect tragedy should, as we have seen, be arranged not on the simple but on the complex plan. It should, moreover, imitate actions which excite pity and fear, this being the distinctive mark of tragic imitation. It follows plainly, in the first place, that the change of fortune presented must not be the spectacle of a virtuous man brought from prosperity to adversity: for this moves neither pity nor fear; it merely shocks us. Nor, again, that of a bad man passing from adversity to prosperity: for nothing can be more alien to the spirit of Tragedy; it possesses no single tragic quality; it neither satisfies the moral sense nor calls forth pity or fear. Nor, again, should the downfall of the utter villain be exhibited. A plot of this kind would, doubtless, satisfy the moral sense, but it would inspire neither pity nor fear; for pity is aroused by unmerited misfortune, fear by the misfortune of a man like ourselves. Such an event, therefore, will be neither pitiful nor terrible. There remains, then, the character between these two extremes,—that of a man who is not eminently good and just, yet whose misfortune is brought about not by vice or depravity, but by some error or frailty. He must be one who is highly renowned and prosperous,—a personage like Oedipus, Thyestes, or other illustrious men of such families.

A well constructed plot should, therefore, be single in its issue, rather than double as some maintain. The change of fortune should be not from bad to good, but, reversely, from good to bad. It should come about as the result not of vice, but of some great error or frailty, in a character either such as we have described, or better rather than worse. The practice of the stage bears out our view. At first the poets recounted any legend that came in their way. Now, the best tragedies are founded on the story of a few houses,—on the fortunes of Alcmaeon, Oedipus, Orestes, Meleager, Thyestes, Telephus, and those others who have done or suffered something terrible. A tragedy, then, to be perfect according to the rules of art should be of this construction. Hence they are in error who censure Euripides just because he follows this principle in his plays, many of which end unhappily. It is, as we have said, the right ending. The best proof is that on the stage and in dramatic competition, such plays, if well worked out, are the most tragic in effect; and Euripides, faulty though he may be in the general management of his subject, yet is felt to be the most tragic of the poets.

Fear and pity may be aroused by spectacular means; but they may also result from the inner structure of the piece, which is the better way, and indicates a superior poet. For the plot ought to be so constructed that, even without the aid of the eye, he who hears the tale told will thrill with horror and melt to pity at what takes place. This is the impression we should receive from hearing the story of the Oedipus.

* * *

Let us then determine what are the circumstances which strike us as terrible or pitiful.

Actions capable of this effect must happen between persons who are either friends or enemies or indifferent to one another. If an enemy kills an enemy, there is nothing to excite pity either in the act or the intention,—except so far as the suffering in itself is pitiful. So again with indifferent persons. But when the tragic incident occurs between those who are near or dear to one another—if, for example, a brother kills, or intends to kill, a brother, a son his father, a mother her son, a son his mother, or any other deed of the kind is done—these are the situations to be looked for by the poet.

* * *

As in the structure of the plot, so too in the portraiture of character, the poet should always aim either at the necessary or the probable. Thus a person of a given character should speak or act in a given way, by the rule either of necessity or of probability; just as this event should follow that by necessary or probable sequence. It is therefore evident that the unravelling of the plot, no less than the complication, must arise out of the plot itself, it must not be brought about by the *Deus ex Machina*—as in the Medea, or in the Return of the Greeks in the Iliad. The *Deus ex Machina* should be employed only for events external to the drama,—for antecedent or subsequent events, which lie beyond the range of human knowledge, and which require to be reported or foretold; for to the gods we ascribe the power of seeing all things. Within the action there must be nothing irrational. If the irrational cannot be excluded, it should be outside the scope of the tragedy. Such is the irrational element in the Oedipus of Sophocles.

Again, since Tragedy is an imitation of persons who are above the common level, the example of good portrait-painters should be followed. They, while reproducing the distinctive form of the original, make a likeness which is true to life and yet more beautiful.

        ✿   ✿   ✿

LUCRETIUS Preface

(Titus Lucretius Carus, c. 99-55 B.C.)

SCIENTIST, PHILOSOPHER, AND POET, LUCRETIUS IS AT ONCE A BRIL-
liant, sceptical thinker and a master of the epic verse into which he
rendered the ideas of his beloved Epicurus. Lucretius' only known work,
On the Nature of the Universe (De Rerum Natura), is the most complete
statement of the atomic theory of Democritus and the enlightened
materialism of Epicurean philosophy. The author's purpose is to free
his contemporaries from the terrors of superstition and the unnecessary
anxieties imposed by religion. By postulating a morally neutral universe
composed of a chance combination of atoms, Lucretius hoped to reveal a
cosmic system which operated according to predictable laws and which
human reason could fully interpret.

The world-view expressed in *On the Nature of the Universe* is very like
that of contemporary science. According to Lucretius, the entire universe,
including the soul of man, is formed of constantly-moving invisible
atoms. Infinite in number and variety, these atomic particles fall aimlessly through endless space. Occasionally, obeying the immutable laws
of nature, they swerve, collide, and combine to form new worlds. Our
earth and solar system are no more than the result of such an accidental
collision of atoms. The gods, although they exist, had no part in creating
the world and they take no interest in the activities of mankind. Completely removed from the human realm, they pursue a serene existence
of uninterrupted bliss. Although they do not commune with men, their
carefree state provides the model upon which the wise man will base his
life.

The chief premise of Lucretius' "scientific epic" seems to be that, once
he understands the true nature of the universe, the rational man will be
relieved of all anxiety, including the fear of death. The soul, being as
material and temporary as any other pattern of atoms, will simply
dissolve at death along with the body. Since the soul forever perishes, it
is foolish to worry about religious theories of reward or punishment in
the afterlife. The whole duty of man is simply to exercise reason in
adapting himself to a completely material, directionless cosmos.

Lucretius accepts Epicurus' teaching that pleasure is the major goal in
life. Since he defines pleasure as the peace that comes from avoiding
pain and overcoming desire, Lucretius' Epicureanism is more suitable to
a quiet, contemplative existence than to an active life wherein one has
little chance of controlling the degree of pleasure and pain in his
environment. Withdrawal from the world and the peaceful cultivation of
one's private garden may seem a selfish and irresponsible approach to
life, but it has held considerable attraction for the leisured few.

The selections from Book V describing mankind's evolution from savagery to civilization are representative of Lucretius' ability to transform
scientific theories into imaginative literature. The impassioned argument

"against the fear of death" from Book III is, for all its blending of reason and eloquence, a kind of whistling in the dark. The prospect of his mind's everlasting extinction does not really comfort the philosopher.

ON THE NATURE OF THE UNIVERSE
(De rerum natura)

BOOK V

[The natural origin of the world and man's growth to civilization]

THE NEXT STAGE IN THE ARGUMENT IS THIS. I MUST FIRST DEMONSTRATE that the world also was born and is composed of a mortal body. Then I must deal with the concourse of matter that laid the foundation of land, sea and sky, stars and sun and the globe of the moon. I must show what living things have existed on earth, and which have never been born; how the human race began to employ various utterances among themselves for denoting various things; and how there crept into their minds that fear of the gods which, all the world over, sanctifies temples and lakes, groves and altars and images of the gods. After that, I will explain by what forces nature steers the courses of the sun and the journeyings of the moon, so that we shall not suppose that they run their yearly races between heaven and earth of their own free will with the amiable intention of promoting the growth of crops and animals, or that they are rolled round in furtherance of some divine plan. For it may happen that men who have learnt the truth about the carefree existence of the gods fall to wondering by what power the universe is kept going, especially those movements that are seen overhead in the borderland of ether. Then the poor creatures are plunged back into their old superstitions and saddle themselves with cruel masters whom they believe to be all-powerful. All this because they do not know what can be and what cannot: how a limit is fixed to the power of everything and an immovable frontier post. . . .

Furthermore, you must not suppose that the holy dwelling-places of the gods are anywhere within the limits of the world. For the flimsy nature of the gods, far removed from our senses, is scarcely visible even to the perception of the mind. Since it eludes the touch and pressure of our hands, it can have no contact with anything that is tangible to us. For what cannot be touched cannot touch. Therefore their dwelling-places also must be unlike ours, of the same flimsy texture as their bodies, as I will prove to you at length later on.

Next, the theory that they deliberately created the world in all its natural splendour for the sake of man, so that we ought to praise this eminently praiseworthy piece of divine workmanship and believe it eternal and immortal and think it a sin to unsettle by violence the everlasting abode established for mankind by the ancient purpose of the gods and to worry it with words and turn it topsy-turvy—this theory, Memmius;[1] with all its attendant fictions is sheer nonsense. For what benefit could immortal and blessed beings reap from our gratitude, that they should undertake any task on our behalf? Or what could tempt those who had been at peace so long to change their old life for a new? The revolutionary is one who is dissatisfied with the old order. But one who has known no trouble in the past, but spent his days joyfully—what could prick such a being with the itch for novelty? Or again, what harm would it have done us to have remained uncreated? Are we to suppose that our life was sunk in gloom and grief till the light of creation blazed forth? True that, once a man is born, he must will to remain alive so long as beguiling pleasure holds him. But one who has never tasted the love of life, or been enrolled among the living, what odds is it to him if he is never created?

Here is a further point. On what pattern did the gods model their creation? From what source did an image of human beings first strike upon them, so that they might know and see with their minds what they wished to make? How was the power of the atoms made known to them, and the potential effect of their various combinations, unless nature itself provided a model of the creation? So many atoms, clashing together in so many ways as they are swept along through infinite time by their own weight, have come together in every possible way and realized everything that could be formed by their combinations. No wonder, then, if they have actually fallen into those groupings and movements by which the present world through all its changes is kept in being.

Even if I knew nothing of the atoms, I would venture to assert on the evidence of the celestial phenomena themselves, supported by many other arguments, that the universe was certainly not created for us by divine power: it is so full of imperfections. In the first place, of all that is covered by the wide sweep of the sky, part has been greedily seized by mountains and the woodland haunts of wild beasts. Part is usurped by crags and desolate bogs and the sea that holds far asunder the shores of the lands. Almost two-thirds are withheld from mankind by torrid heat and perennial deposits of frost. The little that is left of cultivable soil, if the force of nature had its way, would be choked with briars, did not the force of man oppose it. It is man's way, for the sake of life, to groan over the stout mattock and cleave the earth with down-pressed plough.

---

[1]*Memmius*—Gaius Memmius was a Roman politician and patron of poets. Lucretius addressed *On the Nature of the Universe* to him.

Unless we turn the fruitful clods with the coulter and break up the soil to stimulate the growth of the crops, they cannot emerge of their own accord into the open air. Even so, when by dint of hard work all the fields at last burst forth into leaf and flower, then either the fiery sun withers them with intemperate heat, or sudden showers and icy frosts destroy them and gales of wind batter them with hurricane force. Again, why does nature feed and breed the fearsome brood of wild beasts, a menace to the human race by land and sea? Why do the changing seasons bring pestilence in their train? Why does untimely death roam abroad? The human infant, like a shipwrecked sailor cast ashore by the cruel waves, lies naked on the ground, speechless, lacking all aids to life, when nature has first tossed him with pangs of travail from his mother's womb upon the shores of the sunlit world. He fills the air with his piteous wailing, and quite rightly, considering what evils life holds in store for him. But beasts of every kind, both tame and wild, have no need of rattles or a nurse to lull them with inarticulate babble. They do not want to change their clothes at every change in the weather. They need no armaments or fortifications to guard their possessions, since all the needs of all are lavishly supplied by mother earth herself and nature, the great artificer. . . .

[The evolution of prehistoric man]

The *human beings* that peopled these fields were far tougher than the men of today, as became the offspring of tough earth. They were built on a framework of bigger and solider bones, fastened through their flesh to stout sinews. They were relatively insensitive to heat and cold, to unaccustomed diet and bodily ailments in general. Through many decades of the sun's cyclic course they lived out their lives in the fashion of wild beasts roaming at large. No one spent his strength in building the curved plough. No one knew how to cleave the earth with iron, or to plant young saplings in the soil or lop the old branches from tall trees with pruning hooks. Their hearts were well content to accept as a free gift what the sun and showers had given and the earth had produced unsolicited. Often they stayed their hunger among the acorn-laden oaks. Arbutus berries, whose scarlet tint now betrays their winter ripening, were then produced by the earth in plenty and of a larger size. In addition the lusty childhood of the earth yielded a great variety of tough foods, ample for afflicted mortals. Rivers and springs called to them to slake their thirst, as nowadays a clamorous cataract of water, tumbling out of the high hills, summons from far away the thirsty creatures of the wild. They resorted to those woodland sanctuaries of the nymphs, familiar to them in their wandering, from which they knew that trickling streams of water issued to bathe the dripping rocks in a bountiful shower, sprinkled over green moss, and gushed out here and there over the open plain.

They did not know as yet how to enlist the aid of fire, or to make use of skins, or to clothe their bodies with trophies of the chase. They lived in thickets and hillside caves and forests and stowed their rugged limbs among bushes when driven to seek shelter from the lash of wind and rain.

They could have no thought of the common good, no notion of the mutual restraint of morals and laws. The individual, taught only to live and fend for himself, carried off on his own account such prey as fortune brought him. Venus coupled the bodies of lovers in the greenwood. Mutual desire brought them together, or the male's mastering might and overriding lust, or a payment of acorns or arbutus berries or choice pears. Thanks to their surpassing strength of hand and foot, they hunted the woodland beasts by hurling stones and wielding ponderous clubs. They were more than a match for many of them; from a few they took refuge in hiding-places.

When night overtook them, they flung their jungle-bred limbs naked on the earth like bristly boars, and wrapped themselves round with a coverlet of leaves and branches. It is not true that they wandered panic-stricken over the countryside through the darkness of night, searching with loud lamentations for the daylight and the sun. In fact they waited, sunk in quiet sleep, till the sun with his rose-red torch should bring back radiance to the sky. Accustomed as they were from infancy to seeing the alternate birth of darkness and light, they could never have been struck with amazement or misgiving whether the withdrawal of the sunlight might not plunge the earth in everlasting night. They were more worried by the peril to which unlucky sleepers were often exposed from predatory beasts. Turned out of house and home by the intrusion of a slavering boar or a burly lion, they would abandon their rocky roofs at dead of night and yield up their leaf-strewn beds in terror to the savage visitor.

The proportion of mortal men that relinquished the dear light of life before it was all spent was not appreciably higher then than now. Then it more often happened that an individual victim would furnish living food to a beast of prey: engulfed in its jaws, he would fill thicket and mountainside and forest with his shrieks, at the sight of his living flesh entombed in a living sepulchre. Those who saved their mangled bodies by flight would press trembling palms over ghastly sores, calling upon death in heart-rending voices, till life was wrenched from them by racking spasms. In their ignorance of the treatment that wounds demand, they could not help themselves. But it never happened then that many thousands of men following the standards were led to death on a single day. Never did the ocean levels, lashed into tumult, hurl ships and men together upon the reefs. Here, time after time, the sea would rise and vainly vent its fruitless ineffectual fury, then lightly lay aside its idle threats. The crafty blandishment of the unruffled deep could not tempt any man to his undoing with its rippling laughter. Then, when the mariner's presumptuous art lay still unguessed, it was lack of food that brought failing limbs at last to death. Now it is superfluity that proves too much for them. The men of old, in their ignorance, often served poison to themselves. Now, with greater skill, they administer it to others.

As time went by, men began to build huts and to use skins and fire. Male and female learnt to live together in a stable union and to watch over their joint progeny. Then it was that humanity first began to mellow. Thanks to fire, their chilly bodies could no longer so easily endure the cold under the canopy of heaven. Venus subdued brute strength. Children by their wheedling easily broke down their parents' stubborn temper. Then neighbours began to form *mutual alliances,* wishing neither to do nor to suffer violence among themselves. They appealed on behalf of their children and womanfolk, pointing out with gestures and inarticulate cries that it is right for everyone to pity the weak. It was not possible to achieve perfect unity of purpose. Yet a substantial majority kept faith honestly. Otherwise the entire human race would have been wiped out there and then instead of being propagated, generation after generation, down to the present day.

As for the various sounds of *spoken language,* it was nature that drove men to utter these, and practical convenience that gave a form to the names of objects. We see a similar process at work when babies are led by their speechless plight to employ gestures, such as pointing with a finger at objects in view. For every creature has a sense of the purposes for which he can use his own powers. A bull-calf, before ever his horns have grown and sprouted from his forehead, butts and thrusts with them aggressively when his temper is roused. Panther and lion cubs tussle with paws and jaws when their claws and teeth are scarcely yet in existence. We see every species of winged bird trust in its wings and seek faint-hearted aid from flight. To suppose that someone on some particular occasion allotted names to objects, and that by this means men learnt their first words, is stark madness. Why should we suppose that one man had this power of indicating everything by vocal utterances and emitting the various sounds of speech when others could not do it? Besides, if others had not used such utterances among themselves, from what source was the mental image of its use implanted in him? Whence did this one man derive the power in the first instance of seeing with his mind what he wanted to do? One man could not subdue a greater number and induce them by force to learn his names for things. It is far from easy to convince deaf listeners by any demonstration what needs to be done. They would not endure it or submit for long on any terms to have incomprehensible noises senselessly dinned into their ears. . . .

[The beginning of civilization]

As time went by, men learnt to change their old way of life by means of fire and other new inventions, instructed by those of outstanding ability and mental energy. *Kings began to found cities* and establish citadels for their own safeguard and refuge. They parcelled out cattle and lands, giving to each according to his looks, his strength and his ability; for good looks were highly prized and strength counted for much. Later came the invention of property and the discovery of gold, which speedily robbed the strong and the handsome of their pre-eminence. The man of greater riches finds no lack of stalwart frames and comely faces to follow in his train. And yet, if a man would guide his life by true philosophy, he will find ample riches in a modest livelihood enjoyed with a tranquil mind. Of that little he need never be beggared. Men craved for fame and power so that their fortune might rest on a firm foundation and they might live out a peaceful life in the enjoyment of plenty. An idle dream. In struggling to gain the pinnacle of power they beset their own road with perils. And then from the very peak, as though by a thunderbolt, they are cast down by envy into a foul abyss of ignominy. For envy, like the thunderbolt, most often strikes the highest and all that stands out above the common level. Far better to lead a quiet life in subjection than to long for sovereign authority and lordship over kingdoms. So leave them to the blood and sweat of their wearisome unprofitable struggle along the narrow pathway of ambition. Since they savour life through another's mouth and choose their target rather by hearsay than by the evidence of their own senses, it avails them now, and will avail them, no more than it has ever done.

So the kings were killed. Down in the dust lay the ancient majesty of thrones, the haughty sceptres. The illustrious emblem of the sovereign head, dabbled in gore and trampled under the feet of the rabble, mourned its high estate. What once was feared too much is now as passionately downtrodden. So the conduct of affairs sank back into the turbid depths of mob-rule, with each man struggling to win dominance and supremacy for himself. Then some men showed how to form a constitution, based on fixed rights and recognized laws. Mankind, worn out by a life of violence and enfeebled by feuds, was the more ready to submit of its own free will to the bondage of laws and institutions. This distaste for a life of violence came naturally to a society in which every individual was ready to gratify his anger by a harsher vengeance than is now tolerated by equitable laws. Ever since then the enjoyment of life's prizes has been tempered by the fear of punishment. A man is enmeshed by his own violence and wrong-doing, which commonly recoil upon their author. It is not easy for one who breaks by his acts the mutual compact of social peace to lead a peaceful and untroubled life. Even if he hides his guilt from gods and men, he must feel a secret misgiving that it will not rest hidden for ever. He cannot forget those oft-told tales of men betraying themselves by words spoken in dreams or delirium that drag out long-buried crimes into the daylight.

Let us now consider why *reverence for the gods* is widespread among the nations. What has crowded their cities with altars and inaugurated those solemn rites that are in vogue today in powerful states and busy resorts?

What has implanted in mortal hearts that chill of dread which even now rears new temples of the gods the wide world over and packs them on holy days with pious multitudes? The explanation is not far to seek. Already in those early days men had visions when their minds were awake, and more clearly in sleep, of divine figures, dignified in mien and impressive in stature. To these figures they attributed sentience, because they were seen to move their limbs and give voice to lordly utterances appropriate to their stately features and stalwart frames. They further credited them with eternal life, because the substance of their shapes was perpetually renewed and their appearance unchanging and in general because they thought that beings of such strength could not lightly be subdued by any force. They pictured their lot as far superior to that of mortals, because none of them was tormented by the fear of death, and also because in dreams they saw them perform all sorts of miracles without the slightest effort.

Again, men noticed the orderly succession of celestial phenomena and the round of the seasons and were at a loss to account for them. So they took refuge in handing over everything to the gods and making everything dependent on their whim. They chose the sky to be the home and headquarters of the gods because it is through the sky that the moon is seen to tread its cyclic course with day and night and night's ominous constellations and the night-flying torches and soaring flames of the firmament, clouds and sun and rain, snow and wind, lightning and hail, the sudden thunder-crash and the long-drawn intimidating rumble.

Poor humanity, to saddle the gods with such responsibilities and throw in a vindictive temper! What griefs they hatched then for themselves, what festering sores for us, what tears for our posterity! This is not piety, this oft-repeated show of bowing a veiled head before a graven image; this bustling to every altar; this kow-towing and prostration on the ground with palms outspread before the shrines of the gods; this deluging of altars with the blood of beasts; this heaping of vow on vow. True piety lies rather in the power to contemplate the universe with a quiet mind.

When we gaze up at the supernal regions of this mighty world, at the ether poised above, studded with flashing stars, and there comes into our minds the thought of the sun and moon and their migrations, then in hearts already racked by other woes a new anxiety begins to waken and rear up its head. We fall to wondering whether we may not be subject to some unfathomable divine power, which speeds the shining stars along their various tracks. It comes as a shock to our faltering minds to realize how little they know about the world. Had it a birth and a beginning? Is there some limit in time, beyond which its bastions will be unable to endure the strain of jarring motion? Or are they divinely gifted with everlasting surety, so that in their journey through the termless tract of time they can mock the stubborn strength of illimitable age?

Again, who does not feel his mind quailing and his limbs unnerved with shuddering dread of the gods when the parched earth reels at the dire stroke of the thunderbolt and tumult rolls across the breadth of heaven? Do not multitudes quake and nations tremble? Do not proud monarchs flinch, stricken in every limb by terror of the gods and the thought that the time has come when some foul deed or arrogant word must pay its heavy price? . . .

❁   ❁   ❁

It was the sun and moon, the watchmen of the world, encircling with their light that vast rotating vault, who taught men that the seasons of the year revolve and that there is a constant pattern in things and a constant sequence.

By this time men were living their lives fenced by fortifications and tilling an earth already parcelled out and allotted. The sea was aflutter with flying sails. Societies were bound together by compacts and alliances. Poets were beginning to record history in song. But letters were still a recent invention. Therefore our age cannot look back to see what happened before this stage, except in so far as its traces can be uncovered by reason.

So we find that not only such arts as sea-faring and agriculture, city walls and laws, weapons, roads and clothing, but also without exception the amenities and refinements of life, songs, pictures, and statues, artfully carved and polished, *all were taught gradually by usage* and the active mind's experience as men groped their way forward step by step. So each particular development is brought gradually to the fore by the advance of time, and reason lifts it into the light of day. Men saw one notion after another take shape within their minds until by their arts they scaled the topmost peak.

BOOK III*

Against the Fear of Death

> WHAT HAS THIS BUGBEAR DEATH TO FRIGHTEN MAN,
> If Souls can die, as well as Bodies can?
> For, as before our Birth we felt no pain
> When Punique arms infested Land and Mayn,
> 5   When Heav'n and Earth were in confusion hurl'd
> For the debated Empire of the World,
> Which aw'd with deadful expectation lay,
> Sure to be Slaves, uncertain who shou'd sway:
> So, when our mortal frame shall be disjoyn'd,

---

*Translated by John Dryden. From *The Poems of John Dryden*, Vol. I, edited by James Kinsley. Reprinted by permission of The Clarendon Press, Oxford.

10   The lifeless Lump, uncoupled from the mind,
      From sense of grief and pain we shall be free;
      We shall not feel, because we shall not *Be*.
      Though Earth in Seas, and Seas in Heav'n were lost,
      We shou'd not move, we only shou'd be tost.
15   Nay, ev'n suppose when we have suffer'd Fate,
      The Soul cou'd feel in her divided state,
      What's that to us, for we are only we
      While Souls and bodies in one frame agree?
      Nay, tho' our Atoms shou'd revolve by chance,
20   And matter leape into the former dance;
      Tho' time our Life and motion cou'd restore,
      And make our Bodies what they were before,
      What gain to us wou'd all this bustle bring,
      The new made man wou'd be another thing;
25   When once an interrupting pause is made,
      That individual Being is decay'd.
      We, who are dead and gone, shall bear no part
      In all the pleasures, nor shall feel the smart,
      Which to that other Mortal shall accrew,
30   Whom of our Matter Time shall mould anew.
      For backward if you look, on that long space
      Of Ages past, and view the changing face
      Of Matter, tost and variously combin'd
      In sundry shapes, 'tis easie for the mind
35   From thence t' infer, that Seeds of things have been
      In the same order as they now are seen:
      Which yet our dark remembrance cannot trace,
      Because a pause of Life, a gaping space
      Has come betwixt, where memory lies dead,
40   And all the wandring motions from the sence are fled.
      For who so e're shall in misfortunes live
      Must *Be*, when those misfortunes shall arrive;
      And since the Man who *Is* not, feels not woe,
      (For death exempts him, and wards off the blow,
45   Which we, the living, only feel and bear)
      What is there left for us in death to fear?
      When once that pause of life has come between,
      'Tis just the same as we had never been.
          And therefore if a Man bemoan his lot,
50   That after death his mouldring limbs shall rot,
      Or flames, or jaws of Beasts devour his Mass,
      Know he's an unsincere, unthinking Ass.
      A secret String remains within his mind,
      The fool is to his own cast offals kind;
55   He boasts no sense can after death remain,
      Yet make himself a part of life again:

As if some other He could feel the pain.
If, while he live, this thought molest his head,
What Wolf or Vulture shall devour me dead,
60 He wasts his days in idle grief, nor can
Distinguish 'twixt the Body and the Man:
But thinks himself can still himself survive;
And what when dead he feels not, feels alive.
Then he repines that he was born to die,
65 Nor knows in death there is no other He,
No living He remains his grief to vent,
And o're his senseless Carcass to lament.
If after death 'tis painful to be torn
By Birds and Beasts, then why not so to burn,
70 Or drench'd in floods of honey to be soak'd,
Imbalm'd to be at once preserv'd and choak'd;
Or on an ayery Mountains top to lie
Expos'd to cold and Heav'ns inclemency,
Or crowded in a Tomb to be opprest
75 With Monumental Marble on thy breast?
But to be snatch'd from all thy houshold joys,
From thy Chast Wife, and thy dear prattling boys,
Whose little arms about thy Legs are cast
And climbing for a Kiss prevent their Mothers hast,
80 Inspiring secret pleasure thro' thy Breast,
All these shall be no more: thy Friends opprest,
Thy Care and Courage now no more shall free:
Ah Wretch, thou cry'st, ah! miserable me,
One woful day sweeps children, friends, and wife,
85 And all the brittle blessings of my life!
Add one thing more, and all thou say'st is true;
Thy want and wish of them is vanish'd too,
Which well consider'd were a quick relief,
To all thy vain imaginary grief.
90 For thou shalt sleep and never wake again,
And quitting life, shall quit thy living pain.
But we thy friends shall all those sorrows find,
Which in forgetful death thou leav'st behind,
No time shall dry our tears, nor drive thee from our mind.
95 The worst that can befall thee, measur'd right,
Is a sound slumber, and a long good night.
Yet thus the fools, that would be thought the Wits,
Disturb their mirth with melancholy fits,
When healths go round, and kindly brimmers flow,
100 Till the fresh Garlands on their foreheads glow,
They whine, and cry, let us make haste to live,
Short are the joys that humane Life can give.

Eternal Preachers, that corrupt the draught,
And pall the God that never thinks, with thought;
105 Idiots with all that thought, to whom the worst
Of death, is want of drink, and endless thirst,
Or any fond desire as vain as these.
For ev'n in sleep, the body wrapt in ease,
Supinely lies, as in the peaceful grave,
110 And wanting nothing, nothing can it crave.
Were that sound sleep eternal it were death,
Yet the first Atoms then, the seeds of breath
Are moving near to sense, we do but shake
And rouze that sense, and straight we are awake.
115 Then death to us, and deaths anxiety
Is less than nothing, if a less cou'd be.
For then our Atoms, which in order lay,
Are scatter'd from their heap, and puff'd away,
And never can return into their place,
120 When once the pause of Life has left an empty space.
    And last, suppose Great Natures Voice shou'd call
To thee, or me, or any of us all,
What dost thou mean, ungrateful wretch, thou vain,
Thou mortal thing, thus idly to complain,
125 And sigh and sob, that thou shalt be no more?
For if thy life were pleasant heretofore,
If all the bounteous blessings I cou'd give
Thou hast enjoy'd, if thou hast known to live,
And pleasure not leak'd thro' thee like a Seive,
130 Why dost thou not give thanks as at a plenteous feast
Cram'd to the throat with life, and rise and take thy rest?
But if my blessings thou hast thrown away,
If indigested joys pass'd thro' and wou'd not stay,
Why dost thou wish for more to squander still?
135 If Life be grown a load, a real ill,
And I wou'd all thy cares and labours end,
Lay down thy burden fool, and know thy friend.
To please thee I have empti'd all my store,
I can invent, and can supply no more;
140 But run the round again, the round I ran before.
Suppose thou art not broken yet with years,
Yet still the self same Scene of things appears,
And wou'd be ever, coud'st thou ever live;
For life is still but Life, there's nothing new to give.
145 What can we plead against so just a Bill?
We stand convicted, and our cause goes ill.
But if a wretch, a man opprest by fate,
Shou'd beg of Nature to prolong his date,

She speaks aloud to him with more disdain,
150 Be still thou Martyr fool, thou covetous of pain.
But if an old decrepit Sot lament;
What thou (She cryes) who hast outliv'd content!
Dost thou complain, who hast enjoy'd my store?
But this is still th' effect of wishing more!
155 Unsatisfy'd with all that Nature brings;
Loathing the present, liking absent things;
From hence it comes thy vain desires at strife
Within themselves, have tantaliz'd thy Life,
And ghastly death appear'd before thy sight
160 E're thou hadst gorg'd thy Soul, and sences with delight.
Now leave those joys unsuiting to thy age,
To a fresh Comer, and resign the Stage.
    Is Nature to be blam'd if thus she chide?
No sure; for 'tis her business to provide,
165 Against this ever changing Frames decay,
New things to come, and old to pass away.
One Being worn, another Being makes;
Chang'd but not lost; for Nature gives and takes:
New Matter must be found for things to come,
170 And these must waste like those, and follow Natures doom.
All things, like thee, have time to rise and rot;
And from each others ruin are begot;
For life is not confin'd to him or thee;
'Tis giv'n to all for use; to none for Property.
175 Consider former Ages past and gone,
Whose Circles ended long e're thine begun,
Then tell me Fool, what part in them thou hast?
Thus may'st thou judge the future by the past.
What horrour seest thou in that quiet state,
180 What Bugbear dreams to fright thee after Fate?
No Ghost, no Gobblins, that still passage keep,
But all is there serene, in that eternal sleep.
For all the dismal Tales that Poets tell,[2]
Are verify'd on Earth, and not in Hell.
185 No *Tantalus* looks up with fearful eye,
Or deards th' impending Rock to crush him from on high:
But fear of Chance on earth disturbs our easie hours:
Or vain imagin'd wrath, vain imagin'd Pow'rs.
No *Tityus*[3] torn by Vultures lies in Hell;

---

[2]*Dismal Tales*—Lucretius argues that fears of punishment after death have no basis in fact. The famous stories of Tantalus, Sisiphus, *et al.*, are no more than poets' fancies. Check the Glossary for information about the mythological figures to whom Lucretius alludes.
[3]*Tityus*—a giant punished in Hades for his attempted rape of Artemis (or Leto). Two fierce vultures perpetually fed upon his liver. He was so huge he supposedly covered nine acres.

190 Nor cou'd the Lobes of his rank liver swell
    To that prodigious Mass for their eternal meal.
    Not tho' his monstrous bulk had cover'd o're
    Nine spreading Acres, or nine thousand more;
    Not tho' the Globe of earth had been the Gyants floor.
195 Nor in eternal torments cou'd he lie;
    Nor cou'd his Corps sufficient food supply.
    But he's the *Tityus*, who by Love opprest,
    Or Tyrant Passion preying on his breast,
    And ever anxious thoughts, is robb'd of rest.
200 The *Sisiphus* is he, whom noise and strife
    Seduce from all the soft retreats of life,
    To vex the Government, disturb the Laws;
    Drunk with the Fumes of popular applause,
    He courts the giddy Crowd to make him great,
205 And sweats and toils in vain, to mount the sovereign Seat.
    For still to aim at pow'r, and still to fail,
    Ever to strive and never to prevail,
    What is it, but in reasons true account
    To heave the Stone against the rising Mount;
210 Which urg'd, and labour'd, and forc'd up with pain,
    Recoils and rowls impetuous down, and smoaks along the plain.
    Then still to treat thy ever craving mind
    With ev'ry blessing, and of ev'ry kind,
    Yet never fill thy rav'ning appetite;
215 Though years and seasons vary thy delight,
    Yet nothing to be seen of all the store,
    But still the Wolf within thee barks for more;
    This is the Fables moral, which they tell
    Of fifty foolish Virgins[4] damn'd in Hell
220 To leaky Vessels, which the Liquor spill;
    To Vessels of their Sex, which none cou'd ever fill.
    As for the Dog, the Furies, and their Snakes,
    The gloomy Caverns, and the burning Lakes,
    And all the vain infernal trumpery,
225 They neither are, nor were, nor e're can be.
    But here on Earth the guilty have in view
    The mighty pains to mighty mischiefs due:
    Racks, Prisons, Poisons, the *Tarpeian* Rock,
    Stripes, Hangmen, Pitch, and suffocating Smoak,
230 And last, and most, if these were cast behind,
    Th' avenging horrour of a Conscious mind,
    Whose deadly fear anticipates the blow,
    And sees no end of Punishment and woe:
    But looks for more, at the last gasp of breath:

---

[4]*Foolish Virgins*—fifty daughters of Danaus, who killed their husbands.

235 This makes an Hell on earth, and Life a death.
         Mean time, when thoughts of death disturb thy head;
     Consider, *Ancus*[5] great and good is dead;
     Ancus thy better far, was born to die,
     And thou, dost thou bewail mortality?
240 So many Monarchs with their mighty State,
     Who rul'd the World, were overrul'd by fate.
     That haughty King, who Lorded o're the Main,
     And whose stupendous Bridge[6] did the wild Waves restrain,
     (In vain they foam'd, in vain they threatened wreck,
245 While his proud Legions march'd upon their back:)
     Him death, a greater Monarch, overcame;
     Nor spared his guards the more, for their immortal name.
     The *Roman* chief, the *Carthaginian* dread,
     Scipio the Thunder Bolt of War is dead,
250 And like a common Slave, by fate in triumph led.
     The Founders of invented Arts are lost;
     And Wits who made Eternity their boast;
     Where now is *Homer* who possest the Throne?
     Th' immortal Work remains, the mortal Author's gone.
255 *Democritus* perceiving age invade,
     His Body weakn'd, and his mind decay'd,
     Obey'd the summons with a cheerful face;
     Made hast to welcom death, and met him half the race.
     That stroke, ev'n *Epicurus* cou'd not bar,
260 Though he in Wit surpass'd Mankind, as far
     As does the midday Sun, the midnight Star.
     And thou, dost thou disdain to yield thy breath,
     Whose very life is little more than death?
     More than one half by Lazy sleep possest;
265 And when awake, thy Soul but nods at best,
     Day-Dreams and sickly thoughts revolving in thy breast.
     Eternal troubles haunt thy anxious mind,
     Whose cause and cure thou never hop'st to find;
     But still uncertain, with thy self at strife,
270 Thou wander'st in the *Labyrinth* of Life.
         O, if the foolish race of man, who find
     A weight of cares still pressing on their mind,
     Cou'd find as well the cause of this unrest,
     And all this burden lodg'd within the breast,
275 Sure they wou'd change their course; nor live as now,
     Uncertain what to wish or what to vow.

---

[5]*Ancus*—legendary king of Rome.
[6]*Stupendous Bridge*—bridge which Xerxes, emperor of Persia, built to cross the Hellespont during the second Persian invasion of Greece (480 B.C.) When the waves destroyed his project, he ordered the waters flogged.

Uneasie both in Country and in Town,
They search a place to lay their burden down.
One restless in his Palace, walks abroad,
280 And vainly thinks to leave behind the load.
But straight returns; for he's as restless there;
And finds there's no relief in open Air.
Another to his *Villa* wou'd retire,
And spurs as hard as if it were on fire;
285 No sooner enter'd at his Country door,
But he begins to stretch, and yawn, and snore;
Or seeks the City which he left before.
Thus every man o're works his weary will,
To shun himself, and to shake off his ill;
290 The shaking Fit returns and hangs upon him still.
No prospect of repose, nor hope of ease;
The Wretch is ignorant of his disease;
Which known wou'd all his fruitless trouble spare;
For he wou'd know the World not worth his care:
295 Then wou'd he search more deeply for the cause;
And study Nature well, and Natures Laws:
For in this moment lies not the debate;
But on our future, fix'd, Eternal State;
That never changing state which all must keep,
300 Whom Death has doom'd to everlasting sleep.
    Why are we then so fond of mortal Life,
Beset with dangers and maintain'd with strife.
A Life which all our care can never save;
One fate attends us; and one common Grave.
305 Besides we tread but a perpetual round,
We ne're strike out; but beat the former ground,
And the same Maukish joyes in the same track are found.
For still we think an absent blessing best,
Which cloys, and is no blessing when possest;
310 A new arising wish expells it from the Breast.
The Feav'rish thirst of Life increases still;
We call for more and more and never have our fill:
Yet know not what to morrow we shall try,
What dregs of life in the last draught may lie.
315 Nor, by the longest life we can attain,
One moment from the length of death we gain;
For all behind belongs to his Eternal reign.
When once the Fates have cut the mortal Thred,
The Man as much to all intents is dead,
320 Who dyes to day, and will as long be so,
As he who dy'd a thousand years ago.

CATULLUS

(Gaius Valerius Catullus, c. 84-c. 54 B.C.)

GIVEN CATULLUS' LIFE STYLE AS A GAY YOUNG MAN INTIMATELY ACQUAINTED with Rome's exquisite dissipations and his poetic career as a burning, despairing lover, it was necessary to his reputation that he die young. The finest writer of short lyrics in the Latin tongue, Catullus obliged the demands of his romantic image by dying shortly after he reached thirty. Born of an aristocratic family in Verona, he came to Rome about 62 B.C., where he soon joined an inner circle of fashionable writers and their literary parasites. In this fast-living *demi-monde* of artists, courtesans, and politicians, he met the notorious Clodia Celer, wife of a powerful statesman and sister to the dissolute Clodius. This highly-experienced woman, ten years Catullus' senior, was at first amused and then bored by the young poet's ardor.

While Clodia is known to history through Cicero's angry denunciation of her vices,[1] she is even better known to literature through Catullus' transformation of her into the "Lesbia" of his poems. The affair with "Lesbia" was personally destructive to Catullus, but it inspired some of the most finely wrought, beautifully structured, and deeply felt lyrics of classical times. With unfailing grace and wit, Catullus combined erotic passion, tenderness, and sexual candor, with a technical mastery of meter and poetic form. He employs, in fact, almost every meter known to the ancient world. The combination of yearning and self-contempt which Lesbia aroused is summed up in the famous *odi et amo*, I hate and I love. The tormented lover, pulled between fascination and repulsion, was to become a standard figure in later literature, but Catullus was the first and, in many ways, the most vigorous and charming. There are moments when Catullus seems to enjoy the pose of suffering lover. But even granting an element of self-dramatization in Catullus' poetry, the sincerity of his passion cannot be doubted.

POEMS

5

COME, LESBIA, LET US LIVE AND LOVE,
nor give a damn what sour old men say.

---

[1]Cicero's attack on Clodia's character occurs in the *Pro Caelio*, a speech defending M. Caelius Rufus on a charge of attempted poisoning. See also Plutarch's *Life of Cicero*.

The sun that sets may rise again
but when our light has sunk into the earth,
it is gone forever.
    Give me a thousand kisses,
then a hundred, another thousand,
another hundred
    and in one breath
still kiss another thousand,
another hundred.
    O then with lips and bodies joined
many deep thousands;
    confuse
their number,
    so that poor fools and cuckolds (envious
even now) shall never
learn our wealth and curse us
with their
evil eyes.

51
He is changed to a god he who looks on her,
godlike he shines when he's seated beside her,
immortal joy to gaze and hear the fall of
    her sweet laughter.
All of my senses are lost and confounded;
Lesbia rises before me and trembling
I sink into earth and swift dissolution
    seizes my body.
Limbs are pierced with fire and the heavy tongue fails,
ears resound with noise of distant storms shaking
this earth, eyes gaze on stars that fall forever
    into deep midnight.

          ❂   ❂   ❂

This languid madness destroys you Catullus,
long day and night shall be desolate, broken,
as long ago ancient kings and rich cities
    fell into ruin.

          ❂   ❂   ❂

70
My woman says that she would rather wear the wedding veil for me
than anyone; even if Jupiter himself came storming after her; that's

what she says, but when a woman talks to a hungry, ravenous lover,
her words should be written upon the wind and engraved in rapid
waters.

75

You are the cause of this destruction, Lesbia,
that has fallen upon my mind;
this mind that has ruined itself
by fatal constancy.
And now it cannot rise from its own misery
to wish that you become best of women, nor can it fail
to love you even though all is lost and you destroy all hope.

76

If man can find rich consolation, remembering his good deeds
      and all he has done,
if he remembers his loyalty to others, nor abuses his religion
      by heartless betrayal
of friends to the anger of powerful gods,
then, my Catullus, the long years before you shall not sink
      in darkness with all hope gone,
wandering, dismayed, through the ruins of love.
All the devotion that man gives to man, you have given,
      Catullus,
your heart and your brain flowed into a love that was desolate,
      wasted, nor can it return.
But why, why do you crucify love and yourself through the years?
Take what the gods have to offer and standing serene, rise forth
      as a rock against darkening skies;
and yet you do nothing but grieve, sunken deep in your sorrow,
      Catullus,
for it is hard, hard to throw aside years lived in poisonous love
      that has tainted your brain
and must end.
If this seems impossible now, you must rise
to salvation. O gods of pity and mercy, descend and witness
      my sorrow, if ever
you have looked upon man in his hour of death, see me now
      in despair.
Tear this loathsome disease from my brain. Look, a subtle
      corruption has entered my bones,
no longer shall happiness flow through my veins like a river.
      No longer I pray
that she love me again, that her body be chaste, mine forever.

Cleanse my soul of this sickness of love, give me power to
    rise, resurrected, to thrust love aside,
I have given my heart to the gods, O hear me, omnipotent
    heaven,
and ease me of love and its pain.

85

I HATE and love.
    And if you ask me why,
I have no answer, but I discern,
can feel, my senses rooted in eternal torture.

92

LESBIA, forever spitting fire at me, is never silent. And now
if Lesbia fails to love me, I shall die. Why
do I know in truth her passion burns for me? Because I am
    like her,
because I curse her endlessly. And still, O hear me gods,
I love her.

CICERO

(Marcus Tullius Cicero, 106-43 B.C.)

THE GREATEST ORATOR AND MASTER OF LATIN PROSE OF HIS DAY, CICERO is best remembered as a man of letters. In addition to pursuing a brilliant but hazardous political career, which culminated in his murder by Marc Antony's henchmen, Cicero devoted his later life to studying philosophy and perfecting his famous rhetorical style. A fine example of his clear, melodious prose occurs in the *Dream of Scipio*, which comprises the end of his *De republica*. It was inspired by the conclusion of Plato's *Republic* where the story is told of a man returning from the dead to reveal the condition of souls liberated from their bodies (the Myth of Er). Only part of Cicero's *De republica* is extant, but enough remains to show how much the Roman spirit differs from the Greek. Plato was interested in showing how an ideal state ought to be constituted. Cicero wanted to explain the ideal towards which Rome herself was tending. Scipio's dream emphasizes the importance accorded to public-spirited citizenship in the Roman scale of values. The Ptolemaic description of the universe given during the course of the dream exerted a considerable influence on the imagination of readers from hundreds of years. A commentary by Macrobius, one of the popularizers of neo-Platonism, made the work widely available during the Middle Ages. In creating his vision of Heaven, Dante was undoubtedly influenced by Cicero's representation of the nine celestial orbits, the *primum mobile*, and the "music of the spheres."

ON THE REPUBLIC *(De republica)*

[The Dream of Scipio[1]]

I WANT TO TELL YOU ABOUT A DREAM I HAD SOME TWENTY YEARS AGO WHEN I was just a young officer serving in the fourth legion. It was the first

---

[1]*Scipio*—The Scipio who narrates this dream is the grandson of Publius Scipio Africanus, who had defeated Hannibal at Zama during the second Punic War. The younger Scipio, also known as Africanus, continued the work of his grandfather and brought the long rivalry between Carthage and Rome to an end by obliterating Carthage in 146 B.C. Scipio's policy of genocide was regarded in Rome as proof of exemplary patriotism. For further information, see Livy's *The War with Hannibal* included in this volume.

The following preface and translation are by Paul J. McGinnis and are published here for the first time. For biographical information on Cicero, consult Plutarch's *Life of Cicero* included in this volume.

time I had ever been to North Africa, and following my arrival there was nothing I wanted more than to meet King Masinissa.[2] He was a very close friend of our family dating from the time of his alliance with my grandfather. When I came to visit him, the old man put his arms around me and wept tears of joy. Then he looked up to the heavens and said, "Thanks be to the sun-god and all the other heavenly spirits that I have lived long enough to see in my own kingdom and under this roof the grandson of Publius Cornelius Scipio. By his very name my soul is refreshed. He was a man whose memory I shall always cherish. In all my life I never knew a greater soldier."

Thus did he welcome me, and we spent the whole day discussing questions of government. I made inquiries about the character of his kingdom, and he wanted to know how things were going in our republic. After dinner we prolonged our discussion far into the night. The old king could speak of nothing but my grandfather. He recalled his very words as well as his deeds. Finally I went to bed, and because I was so tired not only from my travels but also from having stayed up so late I slept more soundly than usual. It should be no surprise to you that I dreamed about my grandfather. This often happens. The thoughts we have during our waking hours generate something while we sleep. Be that as it may, my grandfather did not look as he must have looked in person. I would have to say rather that he came to me as a representation of what he was—a statue as it were. On seeing him, I was quite frightened. But he said, "Take heart and do not be afraid. I want you to remember these words of mine."

Then he proceeded to speak. "Do you see Carthage down there?" And from the height where we were standing, in a place illuminated by the radiance of the stars, I was shown which way to look. "I made this city subject to the Roman people, but it is even now at this very moment resuming our ancient rivalry and making hostile preparations. You yourself, though inexperienced in leadership, have come to take part in the impending conflict. I prophesy that in two years' time, during your consulship, you will destroy this city to its very foundations—and that the surname Africanus, now yours by inheritance from me, will also be yours by right of conquest. And so when Carthage is finally laid waste once and for all, you will have your triumph, you will hold the censor's office, you will lead missions to Egypt, Syria, Greece, and Asia Minor. You will be elected in your absence to a second consulship, and you will bring a long war to an end by destroying a stronghold in Spain. But when you return to Rome in your triumphal chariot, you will find the city in turmoil by reason of my grandson's schemes, the machinations of your cousin Tiberius Gracchus. At this point, Africanus, it will be appropriate that you show your country what you are made of, that you display your courage, your character, and your common sense. But when these troubled times do come, I foresee a perilous course laid out for

---

[2]*King Masinissa*—a Numidian ally of Rome.

you, as it were, by the fates. For when you reach the age of fifty-six, this being the product of seven and eight which are both perfect numbers, you will have reached the culminating point of your career. The whole state will turn to you, and to you alone—the senate, the loyal citizens, the people confederated with Rome will all look at you. You will be the one man whose efforts may restore confidence in the republic. In brief, it will be appropriate that you rule for a time with full authority—that is, if you manage to escape the murderous conspiracy of your cousins. But you must go on, nevertheless. And so that you will have the heart to go on, watching out for Rome with a keener sense of doing the right thing, remember this. For all men who serve their country, whether in peace or in war, there is an assured and definite place in heaven where they will enjoy everlasting life. For there is nothing on earth that meets with more approval in the eyes of almighty God than the duly constituted and lawfully ordered gatherings of men which are called states. From heaven their rulers come, and to heaven they return."

Even though I was quite frightened by this time, not so much by fear of death but rather in apprehension of the plots laid against me by my relatives, still I proceeded to inquire whether he and my father Paulus were really alive, and others also who were believed to be dead. And he answered, "Yes, of course they are still living, these men who—as from prison—have escaped from the confinement of their bodies. Indeed, this life so-called of yours is really death. Look up and behold Paulus your father coming to join us here." And when I did look up, I could not keep from shedding tears. But Paulus put his arms around me, and kissed me, and told me not to weep.

When I recovered and was able to speak again, I raised this question. "Tell me, father," I said. "Since this is really life, as Africanus has just described it, why do I linger still on earth? Why not join you here in heaven?" And he replied, "No, it must be otherwise. For unless almighty God, whose temple you see around you on every side, sets you free from the guardianship of your body, the way to heaven will be altogether closed to you. For the law governing human existence requires men to cherish this earthly sphere into which they are born, this world which holds the very center in the temple created by God. But men are given souls composed of those eternal fires which you call stars and planets. These spheres, each animated by its own divine intelligence, complete their circular orbits with incredible swiftness. And so, Publius, you and all good men must keep your souls in the custody of your bodies, and except at the command of him by whom they were bestowed you must not depart from life on earth. It would be unfitting that you should seem to shirk a duty imposed by God. So you must live out your allotted span, my dear son. Follow your grandfather's example, and follow mine. Cultivate justice and devotion to duty. These are worthy virtues in the conduct of our private life, but they are of supreme importance when we are called upon to serve the state. Such is the life leading the way to heaven and to this gathering of blessed spirits, released from the body when their life on earth is over, who live here now and forever in the region known to you as the Milky Way."

As I gazed on the starry spectacle, I could not help but marvel at how bright everything was. There were stars we never see on earth, and we would never guess how huge they are. The moon was the smallest of these bodies, farthest from heaven and nearest the earth, reflecting a light which is not its own. All these heavenly spheres were much larger than the earth. And the earth itself seemed so small that the territory of our empire was hardly more than a speck. Seeing that I had fixed my attention on the earthly sphere, my grandfather spoke up. "How long," he inquired, "are you going to bend your mind on the lowly earth? Do you have no sense of where you are and of what a holy place this is? Listen! It is composed of nine circles or rather spheres. The one farthest away from the earth, encompassing all the rest, is called the *primum mobile*. It is almighty God himself, and it is his power that holds the other spheres under control, that fixes the constellations in their undeviating circular motion. Beneath the *primum mobile* are the seven concentric spheres— each of them rolling in contrary motion with respect to the fixed stars. The first of these is Saturn's sphere. Next comes Jupiter's, which is said to bring health and good fortune to the human race. Then comes the terrible red planet which you call Mars. Just about midway between heaven and earth comes the circuit of the sun. The other spheres submit to his dominion. To the sun belongs the mind and regulating power of the whole world, and his splendid radiance shines everywhere. The planets that come next are Venus and Mercury. After them comes the moon, turning in the lowest circle and borrowing its light from the sun. Beneath the moon everything is mortal—everything is subject to dissolution except for the souls entrusted to us by the ordinance of the gods. Above the moon everything is eternal. Last and least comes the ninth sphere, the earth, fixed and motionless in the very middle of the starry universe."

I began to recover from my amazement, and I posed the following question. "That sweet sound reverberating all around us—would you explain to me where it comes from?" And Africanus said, "What you hear is the music of the spheres. It is caused by their motion. The distance between neighboring spheres is unequal, but all the intervals form an arrangement based on a definite ratio. The unison of high and low tones produces harmonies of various kinds. It is impossible, of course, that such swift motions should continue without setting up correspondent vibrations. Nature ordains that one extreme must produce the tones of lowest pitch, the other those of highest. Therefore the starry sphere, whose revolution is the fastest, produces the most stirring sounds; the lunar sphere, being lowest, produces the vibrations which are lowest. As for the earth, the ninth sphere, it abides forever in its middle station, fixed and motionless. The other eight spheres, two of which move at the same speed, produce seven different sounds. This number, as you know, is the connecting point of just about everything.

Its significance in music is a matter of common knowledge. Composers— their songs and symphonies echoing, as it were, this heavenly harmony— earn for themselves the right of returning to heaven. So do others—men of outstanding talent—who devote their lives to godlike pursuits. But human hearing is so overwhelmed by this sound that it simply cannot be heard on earth. You know well enough how weak, in comparison with the other senses, man's hearing is. The cataracts of the Nile make such a great noise in their precipitous fall that the people living nearby have all become deaf. And so it is with the stupendous sound produced in the heavens by the velocity of these swiftly moving spheres. It simply incapacitates your hearing. You cannot look directly at the sun either because its brightness will make you blind."

I was struck with amazement, but I kept looking back to the earth from time to time. And so Africanus said, "I perceive that you are still attending to the homely habitation of the human race. And if it seems small to you, as indeed it is, learn to look skywards and scorn the lowly earth. For what glory can you gain from the mouths of men? What worldly honors worth the cost and effort expended on them? You can see that the earth is inhabited only in scattered and scarcely noticeable spots and what vast deserts lie between them. You can see that the people living in one of these locations are so widely separated from people living elsewhere that they have almost nothing to do with one another. It is certain that such people will never hear of you nor care in the least about your glorious reputation.

"You will also notice," he continued, "that the earth is encircled by certain zones or weather bands. The two that are farthest apart, extending to the very poles of the earth, are covered with ice and snow. The great equatorial zone is scorched by the heat of the sun. Two zones are habitable by men. The zone in the southern hemisphere, however, is nowhere contiguous with the zone you live in. As for the northern zone, see how small is the part which belongs to the Romans. That great empire you rule over—a narrow strip from north to south with its wider expanse from east to west—what is it really but an inconsiderable island bounded by the Atlantic, or the Great Ocean as you call it on earth? You see, in spite of its great name, how inconsiderable it really is. Now please tell me how your name, or any Roman's name, can possibly transcend these known and settled areas, clambering over peaks in the Caucasus (do you see them?) or swimming to the farther shore of the Ganges. Will anyone in the remote extremes of east or west ever hear of you? Or in the distant regions of the north and south? With these lands left out, you can certainly see how little room there is for your fame to spread.

"Even those who do talk about us, how long will they continue to talk? Suppose our posterity felt it incumbent on them to pass along the stories told of their famous ancestors, how long could this be kept up? Natural catastrophes are bound to happen, floods and fires, which will make it impossible for your glory to last even a relatively short time, much less forever. Besides, what does it matter to be the talk of those born after you when it makes no difference that men of earlier times never heard of your name? These men were not fewer in number than ourselves. And surely they were better men, especially since those among whom our praises are likely to be heard now can scarcely keep our memory fresh for a single year. For men usually measure a year by the return of the sun; that is, by the motion of a single star. But when all the stars return to the same place where they started from and after a long interval form the same configuration in the heavens, then we can properly say that a full year has gone by. In such an immense tract of time it would be impossible to tell how many generations of men will come and go. For it was some seven hundred years ago that the sun suffered an eclipse and was blotted from sight when the soul of Romulus ascended to these heavenly regions. And when the sun fails again at the same point and in the same season, then you may be confident that a great year has gone by and that all the constellations and all the shining lights of heaven have returned to the places where they were once before. But you may rest assured that not even a twentieth part of this great year has yet gone by.

"And thus if you have no hope of returning to this home in the heavens, where good and great men enjoy their true reward, you are not likely to get much consolation from the prospect of earthly fame, which may just barely last for an insignificant fraction of one fleeting year. So if you would just look up here and keep your mind fixed on this blessed place, this everlasting mansion, you would never be anxious about what people might say. Nor would you do great deeds merely in the hope of popular applause. Let virtue be your guiding star in the path which leads to glory. It should make no difference to you what people say. They will say what they please regardless. At any rate, space and time put limits to their prattle. No man's fame spreads very far or lasts very long. It fades with the death of one generation and vanishes in the forgetfulness of posterity."

He stopped, and it seemed fitting for me to reply. "If the gates of heaven admit the men who have justly earned a name for public service, I shall certainly exert even greater efforts on my country's behalf, considering that such a great reward awaits me. Even so, I have always walked in the footsteps of my forefathers, and I have not failed to follow your great example."

Then he said, "Do your best and have faith that you really are an immortal spirit. It is only your body that dies. For it is not your human appearance that constitutes your true self. It is your mind that makes you what you are, not the bodily form to which a man may point with his finger. Be it known therefore that you are a god, if a god is that which lives and thinks, which remembers the past and foresees the future, which rules and guides and moves the body placed in its charge just as almighty God moves the universe. And just as a deity governs the universe (which is partly mortal), so does an enduring soul govern the frail body.

"For that which always moves by its own impulse is everlasting. That which imparts motion to something else as the result of an impulse from outside of itself must cease whenever that impulse ceases. Therefore only that which is self-moved never ceases in its motion. This is because it is never devoid of its motive force or self-determining impulse. Indeed, with respect to other things, it is the very reason why they move, the very source of their motion. Such a source can have no beginnings outside of itself. For all things take from it their own beginnings. As the ultimate source, it does not come into being from anything outside of itself. Nor would it be such a thing if it were generated from something else. And since it had no beginning it will have no end. For if a first cause is annihilated it will not come into being for a second time, nor will it bring anything else into being to take its place since all things must have their beginnings in a first cause. Thus it follows that the cause of movement is to be found in that which is moved by its own impulse. And this is something with no beginning and no end. It is not born, and it cannot die. If it were otherwise, the heavens would fall and nature would come to a standstill. For neither has any force of its own by which it might begin to move.

"When you consider that anything moved by its own impulse must be everlasting, you will have to admit that this is the character exhibited by the operations of the human soul. For everything is inanimate that moves by an impulse from outside of itself; that which is possessed of a soul moves by its own impulse and from within. For this is the essence and the characteristic power of the soul. And since the soul is the one thing out of all things that moves by its own impulse, then surely it had no beginning nor will it have an end. So put it to work in the best causes. The very best, of course, are the enterprises that concern the good of your country. Thus devoted and thus dedicated, your soul will speed with swifter flight to this blessed place which is its destined home for all eternity. An even speedier passage is promised if you keep reaching out, in spite of your enclosure in bodily form, thereby detaching yourself as much as possible from the body to contemplate what lies beyond. As for the souls of those who surrender themselves to the body's pleasures and make themselves mere ministers of vice, who violate all that is right and holy in the service of their lust, the souls of such men are loosed by death to flutter round and round the earth. Only after a buffeting that lasts many hundreds of years do they get back here."

He departed, and I awoke from my dream.

VIRGIL

(Publius Vergilius Maro, 70-19 B.C.)

AFTER A CENTURY OF CIVIL TURMOIL AND BLOODSHED, THE GRANDNEPHEW
of Julius Caesar, Octavian, at last brought peace to Rome. At the Battle
of Actium in 31 B.C., he defeated the combined forces of Antony and
Cleopatra, thereby becoming, in fact if not in name, the absolute ruler of
a vast empire that stretched from Asia to the British Isles. The old
Republic that Cicero and Brutus had defended was gone and with its
passing many of the traditional legal freedoms also vanished. But in
general the Roman people appeared so relieved that Octavian had
restored stability and order to the state that there was no serious opposition to his one-man rule. While he refused the title of emperor and
retained some formal remnants of republican government, Octavian
accepted the supreme power and title "Augustus" which a grateful
Senate bestowed upon him.

Under Augustus the Empire prospered and literature flourished.
Wealthy patrons subsidized the arts and befriended aspiring writers,
particularly those willing to sing the praises of the new political regime.
The most important writer who rose to prominence under this system of
imperial patronage was Virgil, a poet from Gaul (France) who had first
attracted attention by his *Ecologues,* gentle lyrics extolling the beauty
and rustic harmony of nature and country life. With the emperor's
approval and encouragement, Virgil then embarked on his major work, a
long poem celebrating the origin and growth of the Roman Empire and
the peaceful reign of Augustus. He chose as his subject the legends
surrounding Aeneas, a Trojan prince who was supposedly the forefather
of the Roman people. According to ancient tradition, Aeneas fled the
ruins of Troy, wandered for seven years, and at last, under the direction
of the gods, settled in Italy. His descendants included Romulus and
Remus, the twins who, in popular mythology, built the first walls of
Rome and gave the city its name.

The topic was clearly suitable to Virgil's patriotic intent. Like other
writers of his sophisticated age, Virgil was keenly conscious of Rome's
cultural inferiority to Greece. Though Rome had conquered Hellas,
Greek art and literature had taken Rome captive. The Romans did not
innovate, they simply borrowed from Greek models, but if Virgil could
create an epic poem that gave the Romans a heroic ancestry equal to
that of the Homeric Greeks, the poet could not fail to be recognized as a
national benefactor.

In writing the *Aeneid,* then, Virgil hoped to do for Rome what Homer
had done for Greece. He devoted the last ten years of his life to
composing a carefully planned epic that combined the war theme of the
Iliad with the travel-adventure motif of the *Odyssey.* He intended to
create for Augustan Rome a work of literature that would embody two
major elements. Foremost was the power of Fate which had decreed

that Rome was to become an everlasting empire, a political force that first conquered and then united the entire known world. Rome, destined to rule and bring peace to all mankind, is the real hero of the *Aeneid*. The nominal hero, the Trojan prince Aeneas, represents the second major element in Virgilian thought. Aeneas, with his overwhelming sense of filial piety, reverence for the gods, and devotion to country, was created as a symbol of the ideal Roman character, a model of duty, hard work, and patriotism that Virgil wished to see reestablished among the citizens of Augustan Rome.

The adjective which Virgil most frequently applies to his hero is *pius* a term for which there is no adequate English equivalent. To Virgil *pietas* meant more than a mere religiosity, more than a proper sense of awe and respect for the supernatural forces that shape human destiny. In Roman ethics, piety was the supreme virtue, acquired by education and discipline and expressed in action through service to the family, the state, and the gods. It is a thoroughly unromantic virtue: Aeneas is being most pious when he abandons his mistress, Dido, in order to found a city neither he nor his sons will live to see built. Roman duty was a stern master and Aeneas' outstanding characteristic is his unquestioning obedience to its voice.

The clearest way to grasp Virgil's moral purpose in the *Aeneid* is to review the movements of his hero, for the Romans were a practical people who usually expressed their beliefs in *action* rather than in contemplation or speech. The first six books of the epic, which recount the travels of Aeneas, are based on Odysseus' quest for home. But while Odysseus had a kingdom and faithful wife to welcome his return, Aeneas has no homeland and no wife. Both had been lost at the fall of Troy. As with the Homeric epic, whose form and literary conventions Virgil deliberately imitates, the *Aeneid* begins *in medias res*. After invoking the Muse and posing the epic question—a far more provocative one than Homer's[1]—Virgil reveals his hero caught between the opposing powers of two mighty goddesses. Even when Troy lies in ruins, Juno (the Roman version of Here) has not exhausted her hatred for the Trojans. Fearing the prophecy that Aeneas is predestined to future glory, Juno vindictively persecutes the small band of Trojans who escaped their city's destruction. She creates a terrible storm at sea which would have shipwrecked Aeneas and his men had not Neptune (Poseidon) calmed the waves. Furious at Juno's continued interference, Aeneas' divine mother, Venus (Aphrodite), intercedes with Jupiter (Zeus) and reminds him that her son is not fated to die at sea, but is instead to establish a new nation in Italy. As Zeus had granted Thetis' wish in the *Iliad*, so Jupiter yields to the request of Venus.

---

[1]When Virgil, referring to Juno's malice, asks "is vindictiveness an attribute of the celestial mind," he consciously raises the issue of divine justice. By human standards of right and wrong, the universe of the *Aeneid* is horrifyingly capricious. To further the cause of Aeneas and the Roman people he is to father, Fate arbitrarily exterminates his enemies, regardless of their individual merits. Virgil recognizes the inequality of this, but stoically resigns himself to accepting an unanswerable mystery.

Under Venus' supervision, Aeneas and his fleet reach a safe harbor in North Africa. There they are graciously received by Dido, the recently widowed queen of Carthage. Carthage, which is destined to become Rome's mightiest rival, had itself recently been founded by refugees from Tyre, a Phoenician city famous for its commerce and luxury. A kind and generous woman, Dido is ready to welcome the fugitive Trojans, but Venus takes extra measures to make sure that her son is well treated. To protect her favorite from Juno, the patron diety of Carthage, Venus makes Dido—against her will—fall helplessly in love with Aeneas. That love proves to be the greatest test of Aeneas' piety, his willingness to put service to country above personal happiness.

In Book II, Aeneas tells Dido and her court the tragic story of Troy's fall. Aeneas' description of the fatal "Trojan Horse," the Greeks' treacherous infiltration of the city, Priam's murder and—worst of all—the awful moment of truth when Aeneas was granted superhuman vision to see that the very gods were working to annihilate his beloved city, make this section one of the most horrifying and exciting passages in Latin literature. Aeneas recounts leaving the flaming ruin leading his young son Ascanius (Iulus) by the hand and carrying his aged father Anchises on his back. (In Virgil's allegorical scheme, Anchises represents the weight of the past, Troy's ancient cultural legacy which Aeneas takes with him. As the supposed ancestor of Julius and Octavian Caesar, young Ascanius represents the future.)

Aeneas' tale of disaster serves only to heighten Dido's passion for him. Torn between loyalty to her dead husband Sychaeus, and love for Aeneas, Dido suffers great torment until her sister Anna convinces her that, for the sake of Carthage, she should marry the shipwrecked Trojan prince. The gods quickly bring about their union. During a hunting trip in the mountains, Juno brings a sudden storm that forces Dido and Aeneas to take shelter in a cave. Inspired by Venus, the two consummate their love. Now completely overwhelmed by emotion, Dido neglects her queenly duties and her reputation suffers. The great Carthaginian building program stops and rumor spreads that the queen has broken her oath of fidelity to Sychaeus. Finally news of the affair reaches Jupiter himself. The Ruler of Olympus angrily dispatches the winged god Mercury to inform Aeneas that he must linger no more in Carthage but sail immediately to Italy, where his destiny awaits him.

Aeneas' response to Mercury's command has puzzled many readers. Almost without hesitation, Aeneas prepares to abandon Dido. His sense of duty to generations yet unborn is far stronger than his affection for the woman who had wholeheartedly devoted herself to him. In Aeneas' heart, romantic love is no match for piety. To Dido's tears, frantic pleas, and threats of vengeance, Aeneas returns only the cool observation that, while he recognized his indebtedness, he had never promised to marry her.

It may seem difficult to admire a hero who, to the modern reader, appears devoid of normal emotion. But Virgil's contemporaries undoubtedly approved the man who placed his obligation to the community above selfish passion. When service to the state was in question, the noblest Romans were expected to sacrifice personal rights and interests to the higher morality of public duty. Augustan Rome was familiar with the then recent love affair between Marc Antony and another tempting queen of Africa, Cleopatra. Antony's concession to passion had cost him his half of the Roman Empire. By contrast, Octavian's cool rationality gained him control of the whole. The historical lesson taught by Antony's emotional entanglement was not lost on Virgil or his fellow Romans.

Virgil gives the parting of Dido and Aeneas more significance than the mere break-up of a love affair. The end of Book IV becomes, in fact, a historical prophecy of future relations between Carthage and the Roman descendants of Aeneas. When Dido predicts that bitter enmity will exist between the two peoples, that war between them will never cease until one is destroyed, she is correctly forecasting what is already destined. The avenger she predicts is Hannibal, the Carthaginian general who, during the second Punic War, was to invade and lay waste the Italian countryside. The third Punic War, however, was to see Carthage annihilated and the very site sown with salt so that nothing would rise there again. In a sense, Dido's suicide foreshadowed the tragic fate of her people.

In spite of the *Aeneid*'s principal theme being the inevitable growth of Roman power and Roman control of the world, Virgil maintains a kind of double vision which both rejoices at Roman glory and mourns for the conquered peoples whose freedom and happiness must be sacrificed to achieve it. Repeatedly he speaks of the "hard fate" of those who suffer and die through no particular fault of their own. In the last books of the epic, he even shows compassion for the original inhabitants of Italy whom Aeneas and his men must exterminate in order to found their own state. Virgil recognizes the need for Rome to unite the world under a single government, but he laments the cost to humanity it entails.

Virgil's sense of the "unevenness of fate" and the endless injustice which many men suffer, is especially apparent in Book VI. Guided by the Cumean Sibyl, Aeneas descends into the underworld to learn from the spirit of Anchises the future history of Rome. Deep beneath the earth, he encounters the ghost of Dido, and begs her to forgive him. With a look that seems to pierce through her faithless lover, Dido turns her back and, accompanied by the shade of her first husband, wordlessly disappears into the gloom. Dido's silent refusal to absolve Aeneas of his moral crime against her reveals Virgil's civilized awareness of the spiritual price which Rome paid for her power and success.

But Aeneas cannot be allowed even the luxury of conscience or remorse. After skirting the pit of Tartarus where the evil are tormented eternally, the Sibyl brings Aeneas to the Elysian Fields. There among the throngs of blessed souls who dwell in care-free happiness, Aeneas encounters his father. With the power of prophecy given the favored dead, Anchises summons up before his son's living eyes a vision of

Rome's future greatness. From the founding of the city by Romulus and Remus, the dictatorship of the Tarquin kings, and the birth of the Republic, to the rise of Julius Caesar and the establishment of the Empire under Augustus, Aeneas surveys the endless triumphs of the nation he is destined to found. Overwhelmed by the honor and responsibility which the gods and Fate have conferred upon him, Aeneas from this point onward never looks back. When he emerges from the underworld, he is henceforth totally dedicated to the conquest of Italy and to merging his individual will with that of history.

By general consensus, the second half of the *Aeneid* is artistically inferior to the first. At the time of his death Virgil had not finished revising and polishing the last six books, which probably accounts for his instructions that his manuscript was to be destroyed. Fortunately Augustus intervened and Virgil's masterpiece was preserved.

Books VII through XII are based on the battle scenes of the *Iliad*. They record Aeneas' landing in Italy, his marriage to a second wife, Lavinia, and the hero's gradual overthrow of the less-civilized inhabitants of Latium and the surrounding territories. Even with their "Homeric" descriptions of hand-to-hand combat, they are not so exciting or psychologically interesting as the earlier scenes depicting Aeneas' infatuation with Dido and his descent into Hades.

The thematic climax of the *Aeneid* is reached, in fact, at the end of the underworld episode. There Virgil speaks through Anchises' ghost to express the patriotic Roman's view of the role of the Empire in universal history. By implication, distinguishing between the respective contributions of Greece and Rome, Anchises concedes that Hellas reigns supreme in philosophy, science, the arts, and literature. But, he observes, it is Roman Law and the Roman genius for government that have provided the international peace and stability that allowed these delicate fruits of civilization to survive and flourish throughout the world. Anchises' words are not only a tribute to the grandeur of Rome, they are also a solemn reminder of her imperial mission.

> Others, no doubt, will better mould the bronze
> To the semblance of soft breathing, draw, from marble,
> The living countenance, and others plead
> With greater eloquence, or learn to measure
> Better than we, the pathways of the heaven,
> The risings of the stars: remember, Roman,
> To rule the people under law, to establish
> The way of peace, to battle down the haughty,
> To spare the meek. Our fine arts, these, forever.

THE AENEID

BOOK I

THE LANDING NEAR CARTHAGE

ARMS AND THE MAN[1] I SING, THE FIRST WHO CAME,
Compelled by fate, an exile out of Troy,
To Italy and the Lavinian coast,
Much buffeted on land and on the deep
By violence of the gods, through that long rage,
That lasting hate, of Juno's.[2] And he suffered
Much, also, in war, till he should build his town
And bring his gods to Latium, whence, in time,
The Latin race, the Alban fathers, rose
And the great walls of everlasting Rome.

Help me, O Muse, recall the reasons: why,
Why did the queen of heaven drive a man
So known for goodness, for devotion, through
So many toils and perils? Was there slight,
Affront, or outrage? Is vindictiveness
An attribute of the celestial mind?

There was an ancient city, Carthage, once
Founded by Tyrians, facing Italy
And Tiber's mouth, far-off, a wealthy town,
War-loving, and aggressive; and Juno held
Even her precious Samos in less regard.
Here were her arms, her chariot, and here,
Should fate at all permit, the goddess burned
To found the empire of the world forever.
But, she had heard, a Trojan race would come,
Some day, to overthrow the Tyrian towers,
A race would come, imperious people, proud
In war, with wide dominion, bringing doom
For Libya. Fate willed it so. And Juno
Feared, and remembered: there was the old war
She fought at Troy for her dear Greeks; her mind
Still fed on hurt and anger; deep in her heart

---

[1]*Arms and the man*—As Homer announced his theme as "the wrath of Achilles," so Virgil states the subject of his epic in this phrase. "Arms" indicates that the *Aeneid* is a war poem in the tradition of the *Iliad*, while "the man" refers to the hero Aeneas, whose wanderings parallel those of Homer's Odysseus (Ulysses) in the *Odyssey*.

[2]*Juno*—For identification of the leading characters in the *Aeneid*, consult the Glossary.

Paris' decision[3] rankled, and the wrong
Offered her slighted beauty; and the hatred
Of the whole race; and Ganymede's honors—
All that was fuel to fire; she tossed and harried
All over the seas, wherever she could, those Trojans
Who had survived the Greeks and fierce Achilles,
And so they wandered over many an ocean,
Through many a year, fate-hounded. Such a struggle
It was to found the race of Rome!

❖   ❖   ❖

Meanwhile, from the heaven
Jupiter watched the lands below, and the seas
With the white points of sails, and far-off people,
Turning his gaze toward Libya. And Venus
Came to him then, a little sadly, tears
Brimming in those bright eyes of hers. "Great father,"
She said, "Great ruler of the world
Of men and gods, great wielder of the lightning,
What has my poor Aeneas done? what outrage
Could Trojans perpetrate, so that the world
Rejects them everywhere, and many a death
Inflicted on them over Italy?
There was a promise once, that as the years
Rolled onward, they would father Rome and rulers
Of Roman stock, to hold dominion over
All sea and land. That was a promise, father;
What changed it? Once that promise was my comfort;
Troy fell; I weighed one fate against another
And found some consolation. But disaster
Keeps on; the same ill-fortune follows after.
What end of it all, great king? One man, Antenor,
Escaped the Greeks, came through Illyrian waters
Safe to Liburnian regions, where Timavus
Roars underground, comes up nine times, and reaches
The floodland near the seas. One man, Antenor,
Founded a city, Padua, a dwelling
For Trojan men, a resting-place from labor,
And shares their quietude. But we, your children,
To whom heaven's height is granted, we are betrayed,
We have lost our ships, we are kept from Italy,
Kept far away. One enemy—I tell you

---

[3]*Paris' decision*—for the *Judgment of Paris*, consult the preface to the *Iliad* and the Glossary entry.

This is a shameful thing! Do we deserve it?
Is this our rise to power?"

        He smiled, in answer,
The kind of smile that clears the air, and kissed her.
"Fear not, my daughter; fate remains unmoved[4]
For the Roman generations. You will witness
Lavinium's rise, her walls fulfill the promise;
You will bring to heaven lofty-souled Aeneas.
There has been no change in me whatever. Listen!
To ease this care, I will prophesy a little,
I will open the book of fate. Your son Aeneas
Will wage a mighty war in Italy,
Beat down proud nations, give his people laws,
Found them a city, a matter of three years
From victory to settlement. His son,
The boy Ascanius, named Ilus once,
When Troy was standing, and now called Iulus,
Shall reign for thirty years, and great in power
Forsake Lavinium, transfer the kingdom
To Alba Longa, new-built capital.
Here, for three hundred years, the line of Hector
Shall govern, till a royal priestess bears
Twin sons to Mars, and Romulus, rejoicing
In the brown wolf-skin of his foster-mother,
Takes up the tribe, and builds the martial walls
And calls the people, after himself, the Romans.
To these I set no bounds in space or time;
They shall rule forever. Even bitter Juno
Whose fear now harries earth and sea and heaven
Will change to better counsels, and will cherish
The race that wears the toga, Roman masters
Of all the world. It is decreed. The time
Will come, as holy years wheel on, when Troy
Will subjugate Mycenae, vanquish Phthia,
Be lord of Argos. And from this great line
Will come a Trojan, Caesar, to establish
The limit of his empire at the ocean,
His glory at the stars, a man called Julius
Whose name recalls Iulus. Welcome waits
For him in heaven; all the spoils of Asia
Will weigh him down, and prayer be made before him.

---

[4]*Fate remains unmoved*—In the following passage Jupiter not only summarizes the
plot of the *Aeneid*, but also the legendary "history" of Rome's early development.
Virgil is here expounding his Stoic doctrine of Fate, that Rome's growth to world
domination is the product of historical necessity. For a slightly different version of
Rome's mytho-historical past, see Book I of Livy's *History of Rome*.

Then wars will cease, and a rough age grow gentler,
White Faith and Vesta, Romulus and Remus,
Give law to nations. War's grim gates will close,
Tight-shut with bars of iron, and inside them
The wickedness of war sit bound and silent,
The red mouth straining and the hands held tight
In fastenings of bronze, a hundred hundred."
    With that, he sent down Mercury from heaven
That Carthage might be kindly, and her land
And new-built towers receive them with a welcome,
And their queen, Dido, knowing the will of fate,
Swing wide her doors. On the oarage of his wings
He flies through the wide sweep of air to Libya,
Where, at the will of the god, the folk make ready
In kindliness of heart, and their queen's purpose
Is gracious and gentle.

❅   ❅   ❅

[Safely landed on the "Libyan Coast" (North Africa), Aeneas finds
that some of his men, suspected of aggressive intent, have been harassed
by Carthaginian sentries. Rendered invisible by a cloud with which
Venus surrounds him, Aeneas and his faithful companion Acates observe
Dido's gracious reception of the Trojan exiles. She apologizes for her
soldiers' excessive zeal and offers the Trojans a permanent home in
Carthage. At this the protective mist disappears and Aeneas presents
himself to the Carthaginian queen.]

❅   ❅   ❅

And Dido, looking down, made a brief answer:
"I am sorry, Trojans; put aside your care,
Have no more fear. The newness of the kingdom
And our strict need compel to me such measures—
Sentries on every border, far and wide.
But who so ignorant as not to know
The nation of Aeneas, manly both
In deeds and people, and the city of Troy?
We are not as dull as that, we folk from Carthage;
The sun shines on us here. Whether you seek
The land in the west, the sometime fields of Saturn,
Or the Sicilian realms and king Acestes,
I will help you to the limit; should you wish
To settle here and share this kingdom with me,

The city I found is yours; draw up your ships;
 Trojan and Tyrian I treat alike.
Would, also, that your king were here, Aeneas,
Driven by that same wind. I will send good men
Along the coast to seek him, under orders
To scour all Libya; he may be wandering
Somewhere, in woods or town, surviving shipwreck."
    Aeneas and Achates both were eager
To break the cloud; the queen inspired their spirit
With her address. Achates asked Aeneas:—
"What do we do now, goddess-born? You see
They all are safe, our vessels and our comrades,
Only one missing, and we saw him drowning,
Ourselves, beneath the waves; all other things
Confirm what Venus told us." And as he finished,
The cloud around them broke, dissolved in air,
Illumining Aeneas, like a god,
Light radiant around his face and shoulders,
And Venus gave him all the bloom of youth.
Its glow, its liveliness, as the artist adds
Luster to ivory, or sets in gold
Silver or marble. No one saw him coming
Until he spoke:—"You seek me; here I am,
Trojan Aeneas, saved from the Libyan waves.
Worn out by all the perils of land and sea,
In need of everything, blown over the great world,
A remnant left by the Greeks, Dido, we lack
The means to thank our only pitier
For offer of a city and a home.
If there is justice anywhere, if goodness
Means anything to any power, if gods
At all regard good people, may they give
The great rewards you merit. Happy the age,
Happy the parents who have brought you forth!
While rivers run to sea, while shadows move
Over the mountains, while the stars burn on,
Always, your praise, your honor, and your name,
Whatever land I go to, will endure."
His hand went out to greet his men, Serestus,
Gyas, Cloanthus, Ilioneus,
The others in their turn. And Dido marvelled
At his appearance, first, and all that trouble
He had borne up under; there was a moment's silence
Before she spoke: "What chance, what violence,
O goddess-born, has driven you through danger,
From grief to grief? Are you indeed that son
Whom Venus bore Anchises? I remember

When Teucer came to Sidon, as an exile
Seeking new kingdoms, and my father helped him,
My father, Belus, conqueror of Cyprus.
From that time on I have known about your city,
Your name, and the Greek kings, and the fall of Troy
Even their enemies would praise the Trojans,
Or claim descent from Teucer's line. I bid you
Enter my house. I, too, am fortune-driven
Through many sufferings; this land at last
Has brought me rest. Not ignorant of evil,
I know one thing, at least,—to help the wretched.
And so she led Aeneas to the palace,
Proclaiming sacrifice at all the temples
In honor of his welcome, and sent presents
To his comrades at the shore, a score of bullocks,
A hundred swine, a hundred ewes and lambs
In honor of the joyous day. The palace,
Within, is made most bright with pomp and splendor,
The halls prepared for feasting. Crimson covers
Are laid, with fine embroidery, and silver
Is heavy on the tables; gold, engraven,
 Recalls ancestral prowess, a tale of heroes
From the race's first beginnings.

❉   ❉   ❉

BOOK II
THE FALL OF TROY

[Welcoming the Trojans as honored guests, Dido gives a banquet at which Aeneas, at her request, relates the story of Troy's fall. He tells of Odysseus' trick of the Wooden Horse, the mysterious death of Laocoon who tried to warn the Trojans against taking the Achaean gift into the city, and the unexpected night attack of the Greeks. Aeneas describes below the sacrilege of Pyrrhus, the fiery son of Achilles, who broke all laws of chivalry and religion by murdering King Priam at the altar.]

❉   ❉   ❉

"Among the foremost, Pyrrhus, swinging an axe,
 Burst through, wrenched the bronze doors out of their
       hinges,
 Smashed through the panelling, turned it into a window.
 The long halls came to view, the inner chambers

Of Priam and the older kings; they see
Armed warriors at the threshold.
Within, it is all confusion, women wailing,
Pitiful noise, groaning, and blows; the din
Reaches the golden stars. The trembling mothers
Wander, not knowing where, or find a spot
To cling to; they would hold and kiss the doors.
Pyrrhus comes on, aggressive as his father;
No barrier holds him back; the gate is battered
As the ram smashes at it; the doors come down.
Force finds a way: the Greeks pour in, they slaughter
The first ones in their path; they fill the courtyard
With soldiery, wilder than any river
In flood over the banks and dikes and ploughland.
I saw them, Pyrrhus, going mad with murder,
And Atreus' twin sons, and Hecuba
I saw, and all her daughters, and poor old Priam,
His blood polluting the altars he had hallowed.
The fifty marriage-chambers, the proud hope
Of an everlasting line, are violated,
The doors with the golden spoil are turned to splinters.
Whatever the fire has spared the Greeks take over.
  You would ask, perhaps, about the fate of Priam?
When he saw the city fall, and the doors of the palace
Ripped from the hinge, and the enemy pouring in,
Old as he was, he went and found his armor,
Unused so many years, and his old shoulders
Shook as he put it on. He took his sword,
A useless weapon, and, doomed to die, went rushing
Into the midst of the foe. There was an altar
In the open court-yard, shaded by a laurel
Whose shadow darkened the household gods, and here
Hecuba and her daughters had come thronging,
Like doves by a black storm driven. They were praying
Here at the altar, and clinging to the gods,
Whatever image was left. And the queen saw Priam
In the arms of his youth. 'O my unhappy husband,'
She cried, 'have you gone mad, to dress yourself
For battle, so? It is all no use; the time
Needs better help than yours; not even my Hector
Could help us now. Come to me, come to the altar;
It will protect us, or at least will let us
Die all together.' And she drew him to her.
  Just then through darts, through weapons, came Polites,
A son of Priam, fleeing deadly Pyrrhus,
Down the long colonnades and empty hallways,
Wounded, and Pyrrhus after him, vicious, eager

For the last spear-thrust, and he drives it home;
Polites falls, and his life goes out with his blood,
Father and mother watching. And then Priam,
In the very grip of death, cried out in anger:—
'If there is any righteousness in heaven,
To care about such wickedness, the gods
Will have the right reward and thanks to offer
A man like this, who has made a father witness
The murder of his son, the worst pollution!
You claim to be Achilles' son. You liar!
Achilles had some reverence, respected
A suppliant's right and trust; he gave me back
My Hector's lifeless body for the tomb,
 And let me go to my kingdom.' With the word
He flung a feeble spear, which dropped, deflected
From the rough bronze; it had hung there for a moment.
And Pyrrhus sneered: 'So, go and tell my father
The latest news: do not forget to mention,
Old messenger-boy, my villainous behavior,
And what a bastard Pyrrhus is. Now die!'
He dragged the old man, trembling, to the altar,
Slipping in his son's blood; he grabbed his hair
With the left hand, and the right drove home the sword
Deep in the side, to the hilt. And so fell Priam,
Who had seen Troy burn and her walls come down, once
    monarch,
Proud ruler over the peoples and lands of Asia.
He lies, a nameless body, on the shore,
Dismembered, huge, the head torn from the shoulders.
    Grim horror, then, came home to me. I saw
My father when I saw the king, the life
Going out with the cruel wound. I saw Creusa
Forsaken, my abandoned home, Iulus,
My little son. I looked around. They all
Had gone, exhausted, flung down from the walls,
Or dead in the fire, and I was left alone.
    And I saw Helen, hiding, of all places,
At Vesta's shrine, and clinging there in silence,
But the bright flames lit the scene. That hated woman,
Fearing both Trojan anger and Greek vengeance,
A common fury to both lands, was crouching
Beside the altar. Anger flared up in me
For punishment and vengeance. Should she then,
I thought, come home to Sparta safe, uninjured
Walk through Mycenae, a triumphant queen?
See husband, home, parents and children, tended
By Trojan slave-girls? This, with Priam fallen

And Troy burnt down, and the shore soaked in blood?
Never! No memorable name, I knew,
Was won by punishing women, yet, for me,
There might be praise for the just abolition
Of this unholiness, and satisfaction
In vengeance for the ashes of my people.
All this I may have said aloud, in frenzy,
As I rushed on, when to my sight there came
A vision of my lovely mother, radiant
In the dark night, a goddess manifest,
As tall and fair as when she walks in heaven.
She caught me by the hand and stopped me:—'Son,
What sorrow rouses this relentless anger,
This violence? Do you care for me no longer?
Consider others first, your aged father,
Anchises; is your wife Creusa living?
Where is Iulus? Greeks are all around them,
Only my love between them, fire and sword.
It is not for you to blame the Spartan woman,
Daughter of Tyndareus, or even Paris.
The gods are the ones, the high gods are relentless
It is they who bring this power down, who topple
Troy from the high foundation. Look! Your vision
Is mortal dull, I will take the cloud away,—
Fear not a mother's counsel. Where you see
Rock torn from rock, and smoke and dust in billows,
Neptune is working, plying the trident, prying
The walls from their foundations. And see Juno,
Fiercest of all, holding the Scaean gates,
Girt with the steel, and calling from the ships
Implacable companions. On the towers,—
Turn, and be certain—Pallas takes command
Gleaming with Gorgon and storm-cloud. Even Jove,
Our father, nerves the Greeks with fire and spirit,
And spurs the other gods against the Trojans.
Hasten the flight, my son; no other labor
Waits for accomplishment. I promise safety
Until you reach your father's house.' She had spoken
And vanished in the thickening night of shadows.
Dread shapes come into vision, mighty powers,
Great gods at war with Troy, which, so it seemed,
Was sinking as I watched, with the same feeling
As when on mountain-tops you see the loggers
Hacking an ash-tree down, and it always threatens
To topple, nodding a little, and the leaves
Trembling when no wind stirs, and dies of its wounds
With one long loud last groan, and dirt from the ridges
Heaves up as it goes down with roots in air.

Divinity my guide, I leave the roof-top,
I pass unharmed through enemies and blazing,
Weapons give place to me, and flames retire.

At last I reached the house, I found my father,
The first one that I looked for. I meant to take him
To the safety of the hills, but he was stubborn,
Refusing longer life or barren exile,
Since Troy was dead. 'You have the strength,' he told me,
'You are young enough, take flight. For me, had heaven
Wanted to save my life, they would have spared
This home for me. We have seen enough destruction,
More than enough, survived a captured city.
Speak to me as a corpse laid out for burial,
A quick farewell, and go. Death I shall find
With my own hand; the enemy will pity,
Or look for spoil. The loss of burial
Is nothing at all. I have been living too long
Hated by gods and useless, since the time
Jove blasted me with lightning wind and fire.'
He would not move, however we wept, Creusa,
Ascanius, all the house, insistent, pleading
That he should not bring all to ruin with him.
He would not move, he would not listen. Again
I rush to arms, I pray for death; what else
Was left to me? 'Dear father, were you thinking
I could abandon you, and go? what son
Could bear a thought so monstrous? If the gods
Want nothing to be left of so great a city,
If you are bound, or pleased, to add us all
To the wreck of Troy, the way is open for it—
Pyrrhus will soon be here; from the blood of Priam
He comes, he slays the son before the father,
The sire at the altar-stone; O my dear mother,
Was it for this you saved me, brought me through
The fire and sword, to see our enemies
Here in the very house, and wife and son
And father murdered in each other's blood?
Bring me my arms; the last light calls the conquered.
Let me go back to the Greeks, renew the battle,
We shall not all of us die unavenged.'

         ✿   ✿   ✿

[Aeneas' gallant attempt to defend Troy is hopeless and, at the command of Venus, he prepares to leave with Anchises and Ascanias. Aeneas' wife, Creusa, disappears in the confusion. When Aeneas returns to the thick of battle to rescue her, he finds only her ghost, which tells him that he must forget the past and devote himself to what the gods have destined for the future.]

BOOK IV
AENEAS AND DIDO

[By the time Aeneas has finished the tale of Troy's destruction and his wanderings thereafter, Dido has fallen completely in love with him. Both Venus and Juno, for different reasons, conspire to inflame Dido's emotions, which soon become an overmastering passion.]

> But the queen finds no rest. Deep in her veins
> The wound[5] is fed; she burns with hidden fire.
> His manhood, and the glory of his race
> Are an obsession with her, like his voice,
> Gesture and countenance. On the next morning,
> After a restless night, she sought her sister:
> "I am troubled, Anna, doubtful, terrified,
> Or am I dreaming? What new guest is this
> Come to our shores? How well he talks, how brave
> He seems in heart and action! I suppose
> It must be true; he does come from the gods.
> Fear proves a bastard spirit. He has been
> So buffeted by fate. What endless wars
> He told of! Sister, I must tell you something:
> Were not my mind made up, once and for all,
> Never again to marry, having been
> So lost when Sychaeus left me for the grave,
> Slain by my murderous brother at the altar,
> Were I not sick forever of the torch
> And bridal bed, here is the only man
> Who has moved my spirit, shaken my weak will.
> I might have yielded to him. I recognize
> The marks of an old fire. But I pray, rather,
> That earth engulf me, lightning strike me down
> To the pale shades and everlasting night
> Before I break the laws of decency.
> My love has gone with Sychaeus; let him keep it,
> Keep it with him forever in the grave."
> She ended with a burst of tears. "Dear sister,
> Dearer than life," Anna replied, "why must you
> Grieve all your youth away in loneliness,
> Not know sweet children, or the joys of love?

---

[5] *Wound*—the wound of love for Aeneas, inflicted by Venus' son Cupid.

Is that what dust demands, and buried shadows?
So be it. You have kept your resolution
From Tyre to Libya, proved it by denying
Iarbas and a thousand other suitors
From Africa's rich kingdoms. Think a little.
Whose lands are these you settle in? Getulians,
Invincible in war, the wild Numidians,
Unfriendly Syrtes, ring us round, and a desert
Barren with drought, and the Barcaean rangers.
Why should I mention Tyre, and wars arising
Out of Pygmalion's threats? And you, my sister,
Why should you fight against a pleasing passion?
I think the gods have willed it so, and Juno
Has helped to bring the Trojan ships to Carthage.
What a great city, sister, what a kingdom
This might become, rising on such a marriage!
Carthage and Troy together in arms, what glory
Might not be ours? Only invoke the blessing
Of the great gods, make sacrifice, be lavish
In welcome, keep them here while the fierce winter
Rages at sea, and cloud and sky are stormy,
And ships still wrecked and broken."

      So she fanned
The flame of the burning heart; the doubtful mind
Was given hope, and the sense of guilt was lessened.
And first of all they go to shrine and altar
Imploring peace; they sacrifice to Ceres,
Giver of law, to Bacchus, to Apollo,
And most of all to Juno, in whose keeping
The bonds of marriage rest. In all her beauty
Dido lifts up the goblet, pours libation
Between the horns of a white heifer, slowly,
Or, slowly, moves to the rich altars, noting
The proper gifts to mark the day, or studies
The sacrificial entrails for the omens.
Alas, poor blind interpreters! What woman
In love is helped by offerings or altars?
Soft fire consumes the marrow-bones, the silent
Wound grows, deep in the heart.
Unhappy Dido burns, and wanders, burning,
All up and down the city, the way a deer
With a hunter's careless arrow in her flank
Ranges the uplands, with the shaft still clinging
To the hurt side. She takes Aeneas with her
All through the town, displays the wealth of Sidon,
Buildings projected; she starts to speak, and falters

And at the end of the day renews the banquet,
Is wild to hear the story, over and over,
Hangs on each word, until the late moon, sinking,
Sends them all home. The stars die out, but Dido
Lies brooding in the empty hall, alone,
Abandoned on a lonely couch. She hears him,
Sees him, or sees and hears him in Iulus,
Fondles the boy, as if that ruse might fool her,
Deceived by his resemblance to his father.
The towers no longer rise, the youth are slack
In drill for arms, the cranes and derricks rusting,
Walls halt halfway to heaven.

[Hoping that the future glory reserved for Rome will be given instead
to Carthage, Juno suggests to Venus that Dido and Aeneas marry.
Knowing that nothing can change Fate, Venus agrees. Juno then manip-
ulates events so that a storm drives the lovers into a grotto, where their
love is physically fulfilled. From that point on, Dido regards herself as
Aeneas' lawful wife and behaves accordingly. But when Jupiter hears
that a love affair keeps Aeneas in Carthage, the chief Olympian sends
Mercury to order the prince to leave for Italy immediately.]

❃   ❃   ❃

Mercury wastes no time:—"What are you doing,
Forgetful of your kingdom and your fortunes,
Building for Carthage? Woman-crazy fellow,
The ruler of the gods, the great compeller
Of heaven and earth, has sent me from Olympus
With no more word than this: what are you doing,
With what ambition wasting time in Libya?
If your own fame and fortune count as nothing,
Think of Ascanius at least, whose kingdom
In Italy, whose Roman land, are waiting
As promise justly due." He spoke, and vanished
Into thin air. Appalled, amazed, Aeneas
Is stricken dumb; his hair stands up in terror,
His voice sticks in his throat. He is more than eager
To flee that pleasant land, awed by the warning
Of the divine command. But how to do it?
How get around that passionate queen? What opening
Try first? His mind runs out in all directions,
Shifting and veering. Finally, he has it,
Or thinks he has: he calls his comrades to him,
The leaders, bids them quietly prepare
The fleet for voyage, meanwhile saying nothing

About the new activity; since Dido
Is unaware, has no idea that passion
As strong as theirs is on the verge of breaking,
He will see what he can do, find the right moment
To let her know, all in good time. Rejoicing,
The captains move to carry out the orders.
  Who can deceive a woman in love? The queen
Anticipates each move, is fearful even
While everything is safe, foresees this cunning,
And the same trouble-making goddess, Rumor,
Tells her the fleet is being armed, made ready
For voyaging. She rages through the city
Like a woman mad, or drunk, the way the Maenads
Go howling through the night-time on Cithaeron
When Bacchus' cymbals summon with their clashing.
She waits no explanation from Aeneas;
She is the first to speak: "And so, betrayer,
You hoped to hide your wickedness, go sneaking
Out of my land without a word? Our love
Means nothing to you, our exchange of vows,
And even the death of Dido could not hold you.
The season is dead of winter, and you labor
Over the fleet; the northern gales are nothing—
You must be cruel, must you not? Why, even,
If ancient Troy remained, and you were seeking
Not unknown homes and lands, but Troy again,
Would you be venturing Troyward in this weather?
I am the one you flee from: true? I beg you
By my own tears, and your right hand—(I have nothing
Else left my wretchedness)—by the beginnings
Of marriage, wedlock, what we had, if ever
I served you well, if anything of mine
Was ever sweet to you, I beg you, pity
A falling house; if there is room for pleading
As late as this, I plead, put off that purpose.
You are the reason I am hated; Libyans,
Numidians, Tyrians, hate me; and my honor
Is lost, and the fame I had, that almost brought me
High as the stars, is gone. To whom, O guest—
I must not call you husband any longer—
To whom do you leave me? I am a dying woman;
Why do I linger on? Until Pygmalion,
My brother, brings destruction to this city?
Until the prince Iarbas leads me captive?
At least if there had been some hope of children
Before your flight, a little Aeneas playing
Around my courts, to bring you back, in feature

At least, I would seem less taken and deserted."
    There was nothing he could say. Jove bade him keep
Affection from his eyes, and grief in his heart
With never a sign. At last, he managed something:—
"Never, O Queen, will I deny you merit
Whatever you have strength to claim; I will not
Regret remembering Dido, while I have
Breath in my body, or consciousness of spirit.
I have a point or two to make. I did not,
Believe me, hope to hide my flight by cunning;
I did not, ever, claim to be a husband,
Made no such vows. If I had fate's permission
To live my life my way, to settle my troubles
At my own will, I would be watching over
The city of Troy, and caring for my people,
Those whom the Greeks had spared, and Priam's palace
Would still be standing; for the vanquished people
I would have built the town again. But now
It is Italy I must seek, great Italy,
Apollo orders, and his oracles
Call me to Italy. There is my love,
There is my country. If the towers of Carthage,
The Libyan citadels, can please a woman
Who came from Tyre, why must you grudge the Trojans
Ausonian land? It is proper for us also
To seek a foreign kingdom. I am warned
Of this in dreams: when the earth is veiled in shadow
And the fiery stars are burning, I see my father,
Anchises, or his ghost, and I am frightened;
I am troubled for the wrong I do my son,
Cheating him out of his kingdom in the west,
And lands that fate assigns him. And a herald,
Jove's messenger—I call them both to witness—
Has brought me, through the rush of air, his orders;
I saw the god myself, in the full daylight,
Enter these walls, I heard the words he brought me.
Cease to inflame us both with your complainings;
I follow Italy not because I want to."
    Out of the corner of her eye she watched him
During the first of this, and her gaze was turning
Now here, now there; and then, in bitter silence,
She looked him up and down; then blazed out at him:—
"You treacherous liar! No goddess was your mother,
No Dardanus the founder of your tribe,
Son of the stony mountain-crags, begotten
On cruel rocks, with a tigress for a wet-nurse!

Why fool myself, why make pretense? what is there
To save myself for now? When I was weeping
Did he so much as sigh? Did he turn his eyes,
Ever so little, toward me? Did he break at all,
Or weep, or give his lover a word of pity?
What first, what next? Neither Jupiter nor Juno
Looks at these things with any sense of fairness.
Faith has no haven anywhere in the world.
He was an outcast on my shore, a beggar,
I took him in, and, like a fool, I gave him
Part of my kingdom; his fleet was lost, I found it,
His comrades dying, I brought them back to life.
I am maddened, burning, burning: now Apollo
The prophesying god, the oracles
Of Lycia, and Jove's herald, sent from heaven,
Come flying through the air with fearful orders,—
Fine business for the gods, the kind of trouble
That keeps them from their sleep. I do not hold you,
I do not argue, either. Go. And follow
Italy on the wind, and seek the kingdom
Across the water. But if any gods
Who care for decency have any power,
They will land you on the rocks; I hope for vengeance,
I hope to hear you calling the name of Dido
Over and over, in vain. Oh, I will follow
In blackest fire, and when cold death has taken
Spirit from body, I will be there to haunt you,
A shade, all over the world. I will have vengeance,
And hear about it; the news will be my comfort
In the deep world below." She broke it off,
Leaving the words unfinished; even light
Was unendurable; sick at heart, she turned
And left him, stammering, afraid, attempting
To make some kind of answer. And her servants
Support her to her room, that bower of marble,
A marriage-chamber once; here they attend her,
Help her lie down.

       And good Aeneas, longing
To ease her grief with comfort, to say something
To turn her pain and hurt away, sighs often,
His heart being moved by this great love, most deeply,
And still—the gods give orders, he obeys them;
He goes back to the fleet. And then the Trojans
Bend, really, to their work, launching the vessels
All down the shore. The tarred keel swims in the water,

The green wood comes from the forest, the poles are
    lopped
For oars, with leaves still on them. All are eager
For flight; all over the city you see them streaming,
Bustling about their business, a black line moving
The way ants do when they remember winter
And raid a hill of grain, to haul and store it
At home, across the plain, the column moving
In thin black line through grass, part of them shoving
Great seeds on little shoulders, and part bossing
The job, rebuking laggards, and all the pathway
Hot with the stream of work.

       And Dido saw them
With who knows what emotion: there she stood
On the high citadel, and saw, below her,
The whole beach boiling, and the water littered
With one ship after another, and men yelling,
Excited over their work, and there was nothing
For her to do but sob or choke with anguish.
There is nothing to which the hearts of men and women
Cannot be driven by love. Break into tears,
Try prayers again, humble the pride, leave nothing
Untried, and die in vain:—"Anna, you see them
Coming from everywhere; they push and bustle
All up and down the shore: the sails are swelling,
The happy sailors garlanding the vessels.
If I could hope for grief like this, my sister,
I shall be able to bear it. But one service
Do for me first, dear Anna, out of pity.
You were the only one that traitor trusted,
Confided in; you know the way to reach him,
The proper time and place. Give him this message,
Our arrogant enemy: tell him I never
Swore with the Greeks at Aulis to abolish
The Trojan race, I never sent a fleet
To Pergamus, I never desecrated
The ashes or the spirit of Anchises:
Why does he, then, refuse to listen to me?
What is the hurry? Let him give his lover
The one last favor: only wait a little,
Only a little while, for better weather
And easy flight. He has betrayed the marriage,
I do not ask for that again; I do not
Ask him to give up Latium and his kingdom.
Mere time is all I am asking, a breathing-space,
A brief reprieve, until my luck has taught me

To reconcile defeat and sorrow. This
Is all I ask for, sister; pity and help me:
If he grants me this, I will pay it ten times over
After my death." And Anna, most unhappy,
Over and over, told her tears, her pleading;
No tears, no pleading, move him; no man can yield
When a god stops his ears. As northern winds
Sweep over Alpine mountains, in their fury
Fighting each other to uproot an oak-tree
Whose ancient strength endures against their roaring
And the trunk shudders and the leaves come down
Strewing the ground, but the old tree clings to the
      mountain,
Its roots as deep toward hell as its crest toward heaven,
And still holds on—even so, Aeneas, shaken
By storm-blasts of appeal, by voices calling
From every side, is tossed and torn, and steady.
His will stays motionless, and tears are vain.
    Then Dido prays for death at last; the fates
Are terrible, her luck is out, she is tired
Of gazing at the everlasting heaven.
The more to goad her will to die, she sees—
Oh terrible!—the holy water blacken,
Libations turn to blood, on ground and altar,
When she makes offerings. But she tells no one,
Not even her sister. From the marble shrine,
Memorial to her former lord, attended,
Always, by her, with honor, fleece and garland,
She hears his voice, his words, her husband calling
When darkness holds the world, and from the house-top
An owl sends out a long funereal wailing,
And she remembers warnings of old seers,
Fearful, foreboding. In her dreams Aeneas
Appears to hunt her down; or she is going
Alone in a lost country, wandering
Trying to find her Tyrians, mad as Pentheus,
Or frenzied as Orestes, when his mother
Is after him with whips of snakes, or firebrands,
While the Avengers menace at the threshold.
   She was beaten, harboring madness, and resolved
On dying; alone, she plotted time and method;
Keeping the knowledge from her sorrowing sister,
She spoke with calm composure:—"I have found
A way (wish me good luck) to bring him to me
Or set me free from loving him forever.
Near Ocean and the west there is a country,
The Ethiopian land, far-off, where Atlas

Turns on his shoulders the star-studded world;
I know a priestess there; she guards the temple
Of the daughters of the Evening Star; she feeds
The dragon there, and guards the sacred branches.
She sprinkles honey-dew, strews drowsy poppies,
And she knows charms to free the hearts of lovers
When she so wills it, or to trouble others;
She can reverse the wheeling of the planets,
Halt rivers in their flowing; she can summon
The ghosts of night-time; you will see earth shaking
Under her tread, and trees come down from mountains.
Dear sister mine, as heaven is my witness,
I hate to take these arts of magic on me!
Be secret, then; but in the inner courtyard,
Raise up a funeral-pyre, to hold the armor
Left hanging in the bower, by that hero,
That good devoted man, and all his raiment,
And add the bridal bed, my doom: the priestess
Said to do this, and it will be a pleasure
To see the end of all of it, every token
Of that unspeakable knave."

      And so, thought Anna,
Things are no worse than when Sychaeus perished.
She did not know the death these rites portended,
Had no suspicion, and carried out her orders.
   The pyre is raised in the court; it towers high
With pine and holm-oak, it is hung with garlands
And funeral wreaths, and on the couch she places
Aeneas' sword, his garments, and his image,
Knowing the outcome. Round about are altars,
Where, with her hair unbound, the priestess calls
On thrice a hundred gods, Erebus, Chaos,
Hecate, queen of Hell, triple Diana.
Water is sprinkled, from Avernus fountain,
Or said to be, and herbs are sought, by moonlight
Mown with bronze sickles, and the stem-ends running
With a black milk, and the caul of a colt, new-born.
Dido, with holy meal and holy hands,
Stands at the altar, with one sandal loosened
And robes unfastened, calls the gods to witness,
Prays to the stars that know her doom, invoking,
Beyond them, any powers, if there are any,
Who care for lovers in unequal bondage.
   Night: and tired creatures over all the world
Were seeking slumber; the woods and the wild waters

Were quiet, and the silent stars were wheeling
Their course half over; every field was still;
The beasts of the field, the brightly colored birds,
Dwellers in lake and pool, in thorn and thicket,
Slept through the tranquil night, their sorrows over,
Their troubles soothed. But no such blessed darkness
Closes the eyes of Dido; no repose
Comes to her anxious heart. Her pangs redouble,
Her love swells up, surging, a great tide rising
Of wrath and doubt and passion. "What do I do?
What now? Go back to my Numidian suitors,
Be scorned by those I scorned? Pursue the Trojans?
Obey their orders? They were grateful to me,
Once, I remember. But who would let them take me?
Suppose I went. They hate me now; they were always
Deceivers: is Laomedon⁶ forgotten,
Whose blood runs through their veins? What then? At-
    tend them,
Alone, be their companion, the loud-mouthed sailors?
Or with my own armada follow after,
Wear out my sea-worn Tyrians once more
With vengeance and adventure? Better die.
Die; you deserve to; end the hurt with the sword.
It is your fault, Anna; you were sorry for me,
Won over by my tears; you put this load
Of evil on me. It was not permitted,
It seems, for me to live apart from wedlock,
A blameless life. An animal does better.
I vowed Sychaeus faith. I have been faithless."
So, through the night, she tossed in restless torment.
    Meanwhile Aeneas, on the lofty stern,
All things prepared, sure of his going, slumbers
As Mercury comes down once more to warn him,
Familiar blond young god: "O son of Venus,
Is this a time for sleep? The wind blows fair,
And danger rises all around you. Dido,
Certain to die, however else uncertain,
Plots treachery, harbors evil. Seize the moment
While it can still be seized, and hurry, hurry!
The sea will swarm with ships, the fiery torches
Blaze, and the shore rankle with fire by morning.
Shove off, be gone! A shifty, fickle object
Is woman, always." He vanished into the night.

---

⁶*Laomedon*—king of Troy and father of Priam. He accepted help from Neptune and Hercules, but cheated them of their reward. Troy's doom was thus partly of his making.

And, frightened by that sudden apparition,
Aeneas started from sleep, and urged his comrades:—
"Hurry, men, hurry; get to the sails and benches,
Get the ships under way. A god from heaven
Again has come to speed our flight, to sever
The mooring-ropes. O holy one, we follow,
Whoever you are, we are happy in obeying.
Be with us, be propitious; let the stars
Be right in heaven!" He drew his sword; the blade
Flashed, shining, at the hawser; and all the men
Were seized in the same restlessness and rushing.
They have left the shore, they have hidden the sea-water
With the hulls of the ships; the white foam flies, the oars
Dip down in dark-blue water.

      And Aurora
Came from Tithonus' saffron couch to freshen
The world with rising light, and from her watch-tower
The queen saw day grow whiter, and the fleet
Go moving over the sea, keep pace together
To the even spread of the sail; she knew the harbors
Were empty of sailors now; she struck her breast
Three times, four times; she tore her golden hair,
Crying, "God help me, will he go, this stranger,
Treating our kingdom as a joke? Bring arms,
Bring arms, and hurry! follow from all the city,
Haul the ships off the ways, some of you! Others,
Get fire as fast as you can, give out the weapons,
Pull oars! What am I saying? Or where am I?
I must be going mad. Unhappy Dido,
Is it only now your wickedness strikes home?
The time it should have was when you gave him power.
Well, here it is, look at it now, the honor,
The faith of the hero who, they tell me, carries
With him his household gods, who bore on his shoulders
His agèd father! Could I not have seized him,
Torn him to pieces, scattered him over the waves?
What was the matter? Could I not have murdered
His comrades, and Iulus, and served the son
For a dainty at the table of his father?
But fight would have a doubtful fortune. It might have,
What then? I was going to die; whom did I fear?
I would have, should have, set his camp on fire,
Filled everything with flame, choked off the father,
The son, the accursed race, and myself with them.
Great Sun, surveyor of all the works of earth,
Juno, to whom my sorrows are committed,

Hecate, whom the cross-roads of the cities
Wail to by night, avenging Furies, hear me,
Grant me divine protection, take my prayer.
If he must come to harbor, then he must,
If Jove ordains it, however vile he is,
False, and unspeakable. If Jove ordains,
The goal is fixed. So be it. Take my prayer.
Let him be driven by arms and war, an exile,
Let him be taken from his son Iulus,
Let him beg for aid, let him see his people dying
Unworthy deaths, let him accept surrender
On unfair terms, let him never enjoy the kingdom,
The hoped-for light, let him fall and die, untimely,
Let him lie unburied on the sand. Oh, hear me,
Hear the last prayer, poured out with my last blood!
And you, O Tyrians, hate, and hate forever
The Trojan stock. Offer my dust this homage.
No love, no peace, between these nations, ever![7]
Rise from my bones, O great unknown avenger,[8]
Hunt them with fire and sword, the Dardan settlers,
Now, then, here, there, wherever strength is given.
Shore against shore, wave against wave, and war,
War after war, for all the generations."
   She spoke, and turned her purpose to accomplish
The quickest end to the life she hated. Briefly
She spoke to Barce, Sychaeus' nurse; her own
Was dust and ashes in her native country:—
"Dear nurse, bring me my sister, tell her to hurry,
Tell her to sprinkle her body with river water,
To bring the sacrificial beast and offerings,
And both of you cover your temples with holy fillets.
I have a vow to keep; I have made beginning
Of rites to Stygian Jove, to end my sorrows,
To burn the litter of that Trojan leader."
Barce, with an old woman's fuss and bustle,
Went hurrying out of sight; but Dido, trembling,
Wild with her project, the blood-shot eyeballs rolling,
Pale at the death to come, and hectic color
Burning the quivering cheeks, broke into the court,
Mounted the pyre in madness, drew the sword,
The Trojan gift, bestowed for no such purpose,

---

[7]*No love, no peace . . . ever*—Dido's final prayer is prophetic of the historical enmity between Carthage and Rome, which culminated in Carthage's total annihilation by Scipio Africanus the Younger in 146 B.C. Compare Dido's curse with Cicero's *Dream of Scipio*.

[8]*Great unknown avenger*—Hannibal, the Carthaginian general who invaded and devastated Italy during the second Punic War. See Livy's *The War with Hannibal*.

And she saw the Trojan garments, and the bed
She knew so well, and paused a little, weeping,
Weeping, and thinking, and flung herself down on it,
Uttering her last words:—
"Spoils that were sweet while gods and fate permitted,
Receive my spirit, set me free from suffering.
I have lived, I have run the course that fortune gave me,
And now my shade, a great one, will be going
Below the earth. I have built a noble city,
I have seen my walls, I have avenged a husband,
Punished a hostile brother. I have been
Happy, I might have been too happy, only
The Trojans made their landing." She broke off,
Pressed her face to the couch, cried:—"So, we shall die,
Die unavenged; but let us die. So, so,—
I am glad to meet the darkness. Let his eyes
Behold this fire across the sea, an omen
Of my death going with him."

   As she spoke,
Her handmaids saw her, fallen on the sword,
The foam of blood on the blade, and blood on the hands.
A scream rings through the house; Rumor goes reeling,
Rioting, through the shaken town; the palace
Is loud with lamentation, women sobbing,
Wailing and howling, and the vaults of heaven
Echo the outcry, as if Tyre or Carthage
Had fallen[9] to invaders, and the fury
Of fire came rolling over homes and temples.
Anna, half lifeless, heard in panic terror,
Came rushing through them all, beating her bosom,
Clawing her face:—"Was it for this, my sister?
To trick me so? The funeral pyre, the altars,
Prepared this for me? I have, indeed, a grievance,
Being forsaken; you would not let your sister
Companion you in death? You might have called me
To the same fate; we might have both been taken,
One sword, one hour. I was the one who built it,
This pyre, with my own hands; it was my voice
That called our fathers' gods, for what?—to fail you
When you were lying here. You have killed me, sister,
Not only yourself, you have killed us all, the people,
The town. Let me wash the wounds with water,
Let my lips catch what fluttering breath still lingers."

---

[9]*Carthage had fallen*—Dido's suicide foreshadows the ultimate destruction of Carthage.

She climbed the lofty steps, and held her sister,
A dying woman, close; she used her robe
To try to stop the bleeding. And Dido tried
In vain to raise her heavy eyes, fell back,
And her wound made a gurgling hissing sound.
Three times she tried to lift herself; three times
Fell back; her rolling eyes went searching heaven
And the light hurt when she found it, and she moaned.
    At last all-powerful Juno, taking pity,
Sent Iris from Olympus, in compassion
For the long racking agony, to free her
From the limbs' writhing and the struggle of spirit.
She had not earned this death, she had only sought it
Before her time, driven by sudden madness,
Therefore, the queen of Hades had not taken
The golden lock, consigning her to Orcus.
So Iris, dewy on saffron wings, descending,
Trailing a thousand colors through the brightness
Comes down the sky, poises above her, saying,
"This lock I take as bidden, and from the body
Release the soul," and cuts the lock; and cold
Takes over, and the winds receive the spirit.

BOOK VI
THE LOWER WORLD

[After stopping in Sicily to hold funeral games for his father, Anchises, who had died there on his previous visit, Aeneas arrives in western Italy. He then consults the Cumaean Sibyl (a Latin counterpart of the Delphic Oracle), who directs him to find the Golden Bough which will ensure his safe passage through the kingdom of the dead. Guided by the Sibyl, Aeneas descends into the Underworld, where the spirit of Anchises reveals to him the future of the Roman people.]

       ❋   ❋   ❋

    Gods of the world of spirit, silent shadows,
Chaos and Phlegethon, areas of silence,
Wide realms of dark, may it be right and proper
To tell what I have heard, this revelation
Of matters buried deep in earth and darkness!
    Vague forms in lonely darkness, they were going
Through void and shadow, through the empty realm
Like people in a forest, when the moonlight

Shifts with a baleful glimmer, and shadow covers
The sky, and all the colors turn to blackness.
At the first threshold, on the jaws of Orcus,
Grief and avenging Cares have set their couches,
And pale Diseases dwell, and sad Old Age,
Fear, evil-counselling Hunger, wretched Need,
Forms terrible to see, and Death, and Toil,
And Death's own brother, Sleep, and evil Joys,
Fantasies of the mind, and deadly War,
The Furies' iron chambers, Discord, raving,
Her snaky hair entwined in bloody bands.
An elm-tree loomed there, shadowy and huge,
The aged boughs outspread, beneath whose leaves,
Men say, the false dreams cling, thousands on thousands.
And there are monsters in the dooryard, Centaurs,
Scyllas, of double shape, the beast of Lerna,
Hissing most horribly, Briareus,
The hundred-handed giant, a Chimaera
Whose armament is fire, Harpies, and Gorgons,
A triple-bodied giant. In sudden panic
Aeneas drew his sword, the edge held forward,
Ready to rush and flail, however blindly,
Save that his wise companion warned him, saying
They had no substance, they were only phantoms
Flitting about, illusions without body.
    From here, the road turns off to Acheron,
River of Hell; here, thick with muddy whirling,
Cocytus boils with sand. Charon is here,
The guardian of these mingling waters, Charon,
Uncouth and filthy, on whose chin the hair
Is a tangled mat, whose eyes protrude, are burning,
Whose dirty cloak is knotted at the shoulder.
He poles a boat, tends to the sail, unaided,
Ferrying bodies in his rust-hued vessel.
Old, but a god's senility is awful
In its raw greenness. To the bank come thronging
Mothers and men, bodies of great-souled heroes,
Their life-time over, boys, unwedded maidens,
Young men whose fathers saw their pyres burning,
Thick as the forest leaves that fall in autumn
With early frost, thick as the birds to landfall
From over the seas, when the chill of the year compels
    them
To sunlight. There they stand, a host, imploring
To be taken over first. Their hands, in longing,
Reach out for the farther shore. But the gloomy boatman
Makes choice among them, taking some, and keeping

Others far back from the stream's edge. Aeneas,
Wondering, asks the Sibyl, "Why the crowding?
What are the spirits seeking? What distinction
Brings some across the livid stream, while others
Stay on the farther bank?" She answers, briefly:
"Son of Anchises, this is the awful river,
The Styx, by which the gods take oath; the boatman
Charon; those he takes with him are the buried,
Those he rejects, whose luck is out, the graveless.
It is not permitted him to take them over
The dreadful banks and hoarse-resounding waters
Till earth is cast upon their bones. They haunt
These shores a hundred restless years of waiting
Before they end postponement of the crossing."
Aeneas paused, in thoughtful mood, with pity
Over their lot's unevenness. . . .

✿   ✿   ✿

A wailing of thin voices
Came to their ears, the souls of infants crying,
Those whom the day of darkness took from the breast
Before their share of living. And there were many
Whom some false sentence brought to death. Here Minos
Judges them once again; a silent jury
Reviews the evidence. And there are others,
Guilty of nothing, but who hated living,
The suicides. How gladly, now, they would suffer
Poverty, hardship, in the world of light!
But this is not permitted; they are bound
Nine times around by the black unlovely river;
Styx holds them fast.

They came to the Fields of
Mourning,
So-called, where those whom cruel love had wasted
Hid in secluded pathways, under myrtle,
And even in death were anxious. Procris, Phaedra,
Eriphyle, displaying wounds her son
Had given her, Caeneus, Laodamia,
Caeneus, a young man once, and now again
A young man, after having been a woman.
And here, new come from her own wound, was Dido,
Wandering in the wood. The Trojan hero,
Standing near by, saw her, or thought he saw her,
Dim in the shadows, like the slender crescent

Of moon when cloud drifts over. Weeping, he greets
    her:—
"Unhappy Dido, so they told me truly
That your own hand had brought you death. Was I—
Alas!—the cause? I swear by all the stars,
By the world above, by everything held sacred
Here under the earth, unwillingly, O queen,
I left your kingdom. But the gods' commands,
Driving me now through these forsaken places,
This utter night, compelled me on. I could not
Believe my loss would cause so great a sorrow.
Linger a moment, do not leave me; whither,
Whom, are you fleeing? I am permitted only
This last word with you."

         But the queen, unmoving
As flint or marble, turned away, her eyes
Fixed on the ground: the tears were vain, the words,
Meant to be soothing, foolish; she turned away,
His enemy forever, to the shadows
Where Sychaeus, her former husband, took her
With love for love, and sorrow for her sorrow.
And still Aeneas wept for her, being troubled
By the injustice of her doom;[10] his pity
Followed her going.

✿   ✿   ✿

[The Elysian Fields]

    They came to happy places, the joyful dwelling,
The lovely greenery of the groves of the blessèd.
Here ampler air invests the fields with light.[11]
Rose-colored, with familiar stars and sun.
Some grapple on the grassy wrestling-ground
In exercise and sport, and some are dancing,
And others singing; in his trailing robe
Orpheus strums the lyre; the seven clear notes
Accompany the dance, the song. And heroes
Are there, great-souled, born in the happier years,
Ilus, Assaracus; the city's founder,
Prince Dardanus. Far off, Aeneas wonders,

---

[10]*Injustice of her doom*—Note Virgil's frequent references to cosmic injustice, which
is perpetuated in the afterlife. Note, too, that Dido manages a final rebuke to her
faithless lover.

[11]*Invests the fields with light*—Compare Virgil's Elysium with Dante's picture of
Limbo (*Inferno*, Canto IV).

Seeing the phantom arms, the chariots,
The spears fixed in the ground, the chargers browsing,
Unharnessed, over the plain. Whatever, living,
The men delighted in, whatever pleasure
Was theirs in horse and chariot, still holds them
Here under the world. To right and left, they banquet
In the green meadows, and a joyful chorus
Rises through groves of laurel, whence the river
Runs to the upper world. The band of heroes
Dwell here, all those whose mortal wounds were suffered
In fighting for the fatherland; and poets,
The good, the pure, the worthy of Apollo;
Those who discovered truth and made life nobler;
Those who served others—all, with snowy fillets
Binding their temples, throng the lovely valley.
And these the Sibyl questioned, most of all
Musaeus, for he towered above the center
Of that great throng:—"O happy souls, O poet,
Where does Anchises dwell? For him we come here.
For him we have traversed Erebus' great rivers."
And he replied:—"It is all our home, the shady
Groves, and the streaming meadows, and the softness
Along the river-banks. No fixed abode
Is ours at all; but if it is your pleasure,
Cross over the ridge with me; I will guide you there
By easy going." And so Musaeus led them
And from the summit showed them fields, all shining,
And they went on over and down.
    Deep in a valley of green, father Anchises
Was watching, with deep earnestness, the spirits
Whose destiny was light, and counting them over,
All of his race to come, his dear descendants,
Their fates and fortunes and their works and ways,
And as he saw Aeneas coming toward him
Over the meadow, his hands reached out with yearning,
He was moved to tears, and called:—"At last, my son,—
Have you really come, at last? and the long road nothing
To a son who loves his father? Do I, truly,
See you, and hear your voice? I was thinking so,
I was hoping so, I was counting off the days,
And I was right about it. O my son!
What a long journey, over land and water,
Yours must have been! What buffeting of danger!
I feared, so much, the Libyan realm would hurt you."
And his son answered:—"It was your spirit, father,
Your sorrowful shade, so often met, that led me
To find these portals. The ships ride safe at anchor,

Safe in the Tuscan sea. Embrace me, father;
Let hand join hand in love; do not forsake me."
And as he spoke, the tears streamed down. Three times
He reached out toward him, and three times the image
Fled like the breath of the wind or a dream on wings.
　　He saw, in a far valley, a separate grove
Where the woods stir and rustle, and a river,
The Lethe, gliding past the peaceful places,
And tribes of people thronging, hovering over,
Innumerable as the bees in summer
Working the bright-hued flowers, and the shining
Of the white lilies, murmuring and humming.
Aeneas, filled with wonder, asks the reason
For what he does not know, who are the people
In such a host, and to what river coming?
Anchises answers:—"These are spirits, ready
Once more for life; they drink of Lethe's water
The soothing potion of forgetfulness.
I have longed, for long, to show them to you, name them,
Our children's children; Italy discovered,
So much the greater happiness, my son."
"But, O my father, is it thinkable
That souls would leave this blessedness, be willing
A second time to bear the sluggish body,
Trade Paradise for earth? Alas, poor wretches,
Why such a mad desire for light?" Anchises
Gives detailed answer: "First, my son, a spirit
Sustains all matter, heaven and earth and ocean,
The moon, the stars; mind quickens mass, and moves it.
Hence comes the race of man, of beast, of wingèd
Creatures of air, of the strange shapes which ocean
Bears down below his mottled marble surface.
All these are blessed with energy from heaven;
The seed of life is a spark of fire, but the body
A clod of earth, a clog, a mortal burden.
Hence humans fear, desire, grieve, and are joyful,
And even when life is over, all the evil
Ingrained so long, the adulterated mixture,
The plagues and pestilences of the body
Remain, persist. So there must be a cleansing,
By penalty, by punishment, by fire,
By sweep of wind, by water's absolution,
Before the guilt is gone. Each of us suffers
His own peculiar ghost. But the day comes
When we are sent through wide Elysium,
The Fields of the Blessed, a few of us, to linger

Until the turn of time, the wheel of ages,[12]
Wears off the taint, and leaves the core of spirit
Pure sense, pure flame. A thousand years pass over
And the god calls the countless host to Lethe
Where memory is annulled, and souls are willing
Once more to enter into mortal bodies."
    The discourse ended; the father drew his son
And his companion toward the hum, the center
Of the full host; they came to rising ground
Where all the long array was visible,
Anchises watching, noting, every comer.
"Glory to come, my son, illustrious spirits
Of Dardan lineage, Italian offspring,
Heirs of our name, begetters of our future!
These I will name for you and tell our fortunes:
First, leaning on a headless spear, and standing
Nearest the light, that youth, the first to rise
To the world above, is Silvius; his name
Is Alban; in his veins Italian blood
Will run with Trojan; he will be the son
Of your late age; Lavinia will bear him,
A king and sire of kings; from him our race
Will rule in Alba Longa. . . .
    "And there will be a son of Mars; his mother
Is Ilia, and his name is Romulus,
Assaracus' descendant. On his helmet
See, even now, twin plumes; his father's honor
Confers distinction on him for the world.
Under his auspices Rome, that glorious city,
Will bound her power by earth, her pride by heaven,
Happy in hero sons, one wall surrounding
Her seven hills, even as Cybele, riding
Through Phrygian cities, wears her crown of towers,
Rejoicing in her offspring, and embracing
A hundred children of the gods, her children,
Celestials, all of them, at home in heaven.
Turn the eyes now this way; behold the Romans,
Your very own. These are Iulus' children,
The race to come. One promise you have heard
Over and over: here is its fulfillment,
The son of a god, Augustus Caesar,[13] founder
Of a new age of gold, in lands where Saturn

---

[12]*Wheel of ages*—Virgil's doctrine of the reincarnation of souls provides an interesting parallel to that which Plato expresses in the *Phaedo* and the *Myth of Er* (*Republic*, Book X).
[13]*Augustus Caesar*—Virgil's patron, to whom he dedicated his poem.

Ruled long ago; he will extend his empire
Beyond the Indies, beyond the normal measure
Of years and constellations, where high Atlas
Turns on his shoulders the star-studded world.
Maeotia and the Caspian seas are trembling
As heaven's oracles predict his coming,
And all the seven mouths of Nile are troubled.
Not even Hercules, in all his travels,
Covered so much of the world, from Erymanthus
To Lerna;[14] nor did Bacchus, driving his tigers
From Nysa's summit. How can hesitation
Keep us from deeds to make our prowess greater?
What fear can block us from Ausonian land?[15] . . .

[Satisfied that his mission has divine approval, Aeneas returns to the
world of light and begins his conquest of Italy.]

---

[14]*Erymanthus to Lerna*—Erymanthus is a mountain range in Arcadia and Lerna a
swamp near Argos. Virgil means that while Hercules' labors took him to widely
separated points in Greece, the Empire under Augustus far exceeded the extent of
Hercules' legendary travels.
  [15]*Ausonian land*—Italy.

HORACE

(Quintus Horatius Flaccus 65-8 B.C.)

ALTHOUGH HE WAS THE SON OF A FREED SLAVE, HORACE RECEIVED THE FINEST
education available to a young Roman of any class. After studying under
the best tutors in Rome, he was sent to Athens to acquire polish and
master philosophy. While in Greece, along with other idealistic students,
he joined forces with Brutus, defender of the "liberal" Republican cause,
whose armies were crushed at Philippi (42 B.C.). Horace had enlisted in
Brutus' legions, but (as he later ruefully admitted), he threw down his
shield and ran away. He returned home to find his family's property
confiscated by the new government, headed by Marc Antony and the
young Octavian.

Working in Rome as a civil clerk and writing a few verses to increase
his income, he became the friend of Virgil, who introduced him to
Maecenas, a wealthy patron of the arts. Thanks to Maecenas' patronage,
Horace was relieved of financial worries and retired to a small country
estate, the famous "Sabine Farm." There, amid the peace and beauty of
nature which he often praised in his poems, he wrote his books of
Satires, Epistles, and the *Odes.*

Horace's works are marked by a worldly good humor, love of life, and
a gentle but pervasive irony. His philosophy is eclectic but inclines
toward a sunny Epicureanism, epitomized in the command *carpe
diem,* "use up the day," and all its pleasures. Combining the ordinarily
antithetical qualities of sensitivity and common sense, Horace reveals a
personality so eminently civilized and charming that he remains the most
read of the Roman lyricists. Where Virgil impresses with his majesty,
Horace delights with his urbanity and intimate revelations of self. His
picture of Augustan society, high and low, is unsurpassed for its candor
and vivid detail.

While his thinking is seldom profound, he phrases familiar ideas in
graceful, memorable language: "what oft was thought, but n'er so well
expressed." Horace is, in fact, the most quoted of all Latin poets. Besides
the *carpe diem* advice, he expressed the most famous motto of patriotism: *dulce et decorum est pro patria mori* (it is sweet and fitting to die
for one's country). He also coined the phrases *auream mediocritatem*
(the Golden Mean), *ars est celare artem* (art consists in hiding art), and
in medias res (to describe Homer's beginning his epic "in the middle of
the action.") His dictum in the *Art of Poetry*, the most influential example of literary criticism after Aristotle, that poetry should teach or
delight (preferably both), remains a fixed principle of artistic creation.
Horace's ability to summarize literary history and make some keen obser-
vations of his own is nowhere more evident than in this leisurely,
rambling survey of classical literature. But Horace makes his most acute
poetic judgment in evaluating his own accomplishment: *non omnis mori-
ar,* "I shall not altogether perish."

ODES

I, 4*

Winter to Spring: the west wind melts the frozen rancour,
   The windlass drags to sea the thirsty hull;
Byre is no longer welcome to beast or fire to ploughman,
   The field removes the frost-cap from his skull.

Venus of Cythera leads the dances under the hanging
   Moon and the linked line of Nymphs and Graces
Beat the ground with measured feet while the busy Fire god
   Stokes his red-hot mills in volcanic places.

Now is the time to twine the spruce and shining head with myrtle,
   Now with flowers escaped the earthy fetter,
And sacrifice to the woodland god in shady copses
   A lamb or a kid, whichever he likes better.

Equally heavy is the heel of white-faced Death on the pauper's
   Shack and the towers of kings, and O my dear
The little sum of life forbids the ravelling of lengthy
   Hopes. Night and the fabled dead are near

And the narrow house of nothing past whose lintel
   You will meet no wine like this, no boy to admire
Like Lycidas who to-day makes all young men a furnace
   And whom tomorrow girls will find a fire.

I, 11†

What end the gods ordain for thee, for me,
Seek not to know, my dear Leuconoe,
Nor think it aught but wickedness to ask
Soothsaying Babylonians what mask
The future wears. Much better to endure
Whatever comes, content to rest unsure
Whether the gods have willed for thee thy last
Season of wintry storm and northern blast,
Or still to use thou hast a joyful store
Of many days and many seasons more.

Use wisdom, taste of wine, and for a space
Forget thy further hopes. The minutes chase
The hours into years e'en while we borrow
A little time to talk. Trust not tomorrow,
Use up the day that's given thee to spend.
The gods may never thee another lend.

I, 25*

The young men come less often—isn't it so?—
To rap at midnight on your fastened window;
Much less often. How do you sleep these days?

There was a time when your door gave with proficiency
On easy hinges; now it seems apter at being shut.
I do not think you hear many lovers moaning

"Lydia, how can you sleep?
"Lydia, the night is so long!
"Oh, Lydia, I'm dying for you!"

No. The time is coming when you will moan
And cry to scornful men from an alley corner
In the dark of the moon when the wind's in a passion,

With lust that would drive a mare wild
Raging in your ulcerous old viscera.
You'll be alone and burning then

To think how happy boys take their delight
In the new tender buds, the blush of myrtle,
Consigning dry leaves to the winter sea.

IV, 7†

The snows are fled away, leaves on the shaws
    And grasses in the mead renew their birth,
The river to the river-bed withdraws,
    And altered is the fashion of the earth.

The Nymphs and Graces three put off their fear
  And unapparelled in the woodland play.
The swift hour and the brief prime of the year
  Say to the soul, *Thou wast not born for aye.*

Thaw follows frost; hard on the heel of spring
  Treads summer sure to die, for hard on hers
Comes autumn, with his apples scattering;
  Then back to wintertide, when nothing stirs.

But oh, whate'er the sky-led seasons mar,
  Moon upon moon rebuilds it with her beams:
Come *we* where Tullus and where Ancus are,
  And good Aeneas, we are dust and dreams.

Torquatus, if the gods in heaven shall add
  The morrow to the day, what tongue has told?
Feast then thy heart, for what thy heart has had
  The fingers of no heir will ever hold.

When thou descendest once the shades among,
  The stern assize and equal judgment o'er,
Not thy long lineage nor thy golden tongue,
  No, nor thy righteousness, shall friend thee more.

Night holds Hippolytus the pure of stain,
  Diana steads him nothing, he must stay;
And Theseus leaves Pirithöus in the chain
  The love of comrades cannot take away.

THE ART OF POETRY

    That poems should be fine is not enough;
120 They must have charm and lead their hearer's mind
Which way they will. The face of man will smile
With those that smile or mourn with those that weep:
If you would make me weep, you first yourself
Must grieve; then, Telephus or Peleus, I
Shall mourn your fate; but if you speak a part
Ill-suited, I shall fall asleep or laugh.

From *Latin Poetry in Verse Translation,* edited by L. R. Lind. Translated by John G. Hawthorne. Reprinted by permission of Houghton Mifflin Company.

Sad words befit a mourning face and threats
An angry one, and jests belong to sport,
Solemnity of speech to seriousness.
130 For Nature shapes our souls to every phase
Of fortune and she pleases, drives to wrath
Or bows us down with heavy grief and hurts;
Then later uses as interpreter
The tongue to let the feelings be expressed.
So if the speaker's words belie his fate
The Roman audience will raise a laugh.
It matters greatly who it is that speaks:
A god or hero, ripe old man, or youth
Still hot with vigor, or a stately dame,
140 Officious nurse, or merchant travelling,
Or farmer of a happy little plot,
Russian, Assyrian, Argive, or Theban-bred.
Follow tradition or see that you invent
Consistently; should you again portray
The famous man, Achilles, make him hot
And full of wrath, inexorable, keen,
Denying law and claiming all by force
Of arms. Medea should be wildly fierce,
Unconquered, Ino tearful, Ixion
150 Perfidious. Io lost, Orestes sad.
Or if you do put on the stage a thing
Untried and boldly dare to introduce
A novel character, it should proceed
From start to finish with consistency.
  It is not easy to say well-known things
In ways that are peculiarly your own.
You are more sensible to dramatize
The Iliad than be the first to tell
A tale unknown and never yet expressed.
160 A well-known theme allows for private rights,
If you will fly the cheap and hackneyed round
And not translate too closely, word for word,
Nor, like a common imitator, jump
Into a hole from which your shame, if not
The nature of your work, forbids escape.
Do not start as the cyclic writer did:
  "Of Priam's fate I'll sing, and glorious war."
How will a boaster such as he maintain
A level worthy of this gaping phrase?
170 Mountains will labor: born, a silly mouse!
Much better he who suitably begins:
    "Tell of the man, O Muse, who on Troy's fall
    Saw many towns and customs of the world."

He does not plan to give us smoke from fire
But from the smoke a light to let him show
Beautiful wonders, an Antiphates,
A Scylla, Cyclops, a Charybdis too.
He does not trace a Diomede's Return
From Meleager's death, or Trojan War
180 From the twin eggs, but hurries to the end,
Taking his hearer to the midst of things
As if they were well-known and he omits
What cannot by his touch be turned to gold;
He lies so well, so mixes false with true
That start and end and middle harmonize.
      Now hear what I and what the public like
If you would keep your audience in their seats
Until the curtain and the time for cheers,
You must observe the traits of every age
190 And give each changing life and year its due.
A boy, who now can talk and walk aright,
Loves playing with his friends, gets angry soon,
Calms down as soon and changes every hour.
A beardless youth, his tutor gone at last,
Loves horses, hounds, the sunny Campus grass,
Pliant as wax to crime, to counsellors harsh,
Slow to provide for his best interests,
Extravagant, high-minded, amorous,
And quick to change the object of his love.
200 A man, in prime of life, foregoes these tastes,
Seeks wealth and friendships, is ambition's slave,
And shuns what he may soon find hard to change.
Old age has many troubles; for the wretch
Still seeks, but fears and will not use his hoard;
Or else does everything in fear and cold;
He puts things off and spins his hopes out long,
Slow, greedy of the future, difficult,
Full of complaints, a praiser of the past
When he was young, a censor critical
210 Of all the modern generation.
The rising tide of years brings many a joy;
The ebb removes as many. Do not give
Old robes to youth or manhood's part to boys;
Our interest is always fixed on traits
Appropriate and fitted to their age.
      A deed's reported or else done on stage.
The mind is stirred less sharply through the ear
Than if we watch with eyes, our clearest sense,
And as spectators vouch for what we see.
220 You will not put what should be done off-stage

Upon the scene, but keep much out of sight
That soon an eye-witness will tell; let not
Medea's murder of her boys be shown,
Nor wicked Atreus cooking human flesh,
Nor Procne's transformation to a bird
Or Cadmus' to a snake; that kind of sight
I disbelieve and am disgusted at.
A play should have five acts, no less, no more,
To be successful and be staged again.
230 No god should intervene unless the knot
Requires such liberation; and the sum
Of speaking actors should be only three.
The chorus should perform an actor's role
With strength and force; it should not interpose
Ill-fitting songs between the acts which have
No suitable relation to the plot.
Its total duty is to help the good,
Give friendly counsel, temper the irate
And cherish those who fear to do a wrong;
240 Let it praise modest fare, health-giving laws
And justice, and the open gates of peace;
Let it keep secrets; ask the gods in prayer
That fortune help the poor, desert the proud.

     ✿ ✿ ✿

Not every critic sees a faulty verse
And Roman poets have been spared too much.
320 Should I then run amok and write unchecked?
Or should I think that every eye will see
My faults and so stay cautiously and safe
Within the hope of pardon? There, it seems,
I have avoided blame but earned no praise.
So turn the pages of your Greek examples
By night and in the day. Your ancestors,
It will be said, extolled the verse and wit
Of Plautus; yes, and too much tolerance,
Not to say folly, caused their admiration,
330 If only you and I can separate
Vulgarity from charm and tell by ear
Or finger how to scan a proper verse.
  The unknown Muse of tragedy, it's said,
Was found by Thespis first, who carried round
His plays for men with faces smeared with lees
To act and sing from wagons. After him
Aeschylus, who introduced the mask

And robe of honor, built a modest stage
And taught his actors to raise high their voice
340 And wear the buskin. These were followed by
Old Comedy, which earned a wealth of praise.
But soon its freedom turned to viciousness
And violence, that called for legal curbs;
A law was passed; the chorus in disgrace
Was henceforth silent, losing its right to hurt.
Nothing of these our poets left untried;
And when they dared to leave the tracks of Greece
And celebrate Italian themes, they won
Great fame in tragic and in comic dress.
350 In fact the power of Rome would no more rest
On courage and nobility of arms
Than on her native tongue, had not each one
Among her poets all too hastily
Rejected the slow labor of the file.
You, royal blood of King Pompilius,
Should blame a poem which has not been worked
For days on end, through endless alterations,
Ten times corrected by the close-cut nail.
      Democritus believed that innate skill
360 Brought more success than miserable art
And shut sane poets out of Helicon.
Hence a good number do not take the care
To cut their nails or shave their beards or bathe,
But seek out places set apart from men.
They think that they will win the name of poet
And its reward if they will never let
The barber Licinus come near their head
That triple cures for madness will not help.
Fool that I am to purge my bile in spring!
370 If not, none would write better poems, yet
Nothing is worth so much; I shall perform
The part of whetstone, which can sharpen steel
Again but cannot cut a thing itself.
Though I write nothing, still I shall impart
The function and the duty of a poet,
His sources and what trains and fashions him,
What fits him, what does not, and where the path
Of excellence and error will end up.
The spring and fountain-head of writing well
380 Is wisdom; the Socratic dialogues
Will show you matter and, the matter found,
The words will follow not unwillingly.
Who knows his duty to his land and friends
And how to love a parent, guest or brother,

The proper role of senator or judge
Or soldier sent to war, assuredly
He understands the way to represent
The fitting part for every character.
I will command the learned imitator
390 To take real life and manners as his guide,
And hence to draw a language that's alive.
Sometimes a play with brilliant passages
And well-drawn characters, though lacking grace,
Artistic skill and solid weight, will charm
More strongly, hold the people more, than lines
Devoid of substance, trifles with a tune.
     The Muses gave the Greeks their native skill
And power to speak in well-turned, rounded phrase,
The Greeks, whose only avarice was fame.
400 The Roman students with long reasoning
Learn how to split an as a hundred ways.
Albinus' son shall answer: "If a twelfth
Is taken from five-twelfths, what then remains?
You used to know it once." "A third." "Correct;
You won't lose money. Add one, what d'you get?"
"A half." I ask, when once this cankerous love
Of slavish gain has dyed their hearts and minds,
Can we expect them to produce a book
Worth cedar polish and smooth cypress wood?
410   The poet's aim is teaching or delight
Or to speak both with charm and benefit.
When you instruct be brief, so that our minds
May see and learn and faithfully retain
The words that you have briefly said, for all
Superfluous words run off a brimming heart.
If you would please, let fiction follow fact,
So that your work does not demand belief
For anything it will, nor drag alive
A well-digested boy from Lamia's paunch.
420 The older audiences will hiss at plays
Without a moral, while the dry-as-dust
Are passed up by the young aristocrats.
But he who mixes usefulness with charm
By teaching and delighting equally
Wins every vote. This is the book that pays
The publishers, is taken overseas
And brings its famous author lasting life.

       ✻   ✻   ✻

LIVY

(Titus Livius, 59 B.C.-A.D. 17)

WHILE VIRGIL WAS RECREATING ROME'S LEGENDARY ORIGINS IN THE STATELY hexameters of the *Aeneid,* his younger contemporary, the historian Livy, rendered into smoothly-flowing prose the same epic theme of Rome's rise to greatness. Like Virgil, Livy was a friend of the Emperor Augustus and wrote with a similar dedicated patriotism. His 142 volumes, recounting the history of Rome from Aeneas' landing in Italy to the reign of Augustus (approximately 1200 years), are a masterpiece of the storyteller's art. As he states in the introduction, Livy wrote with a national bias and an ethical purpose: to celebrate the high moral character of Rome's energetic founders and, conversely, to record the moral decline which culminated in the collapse of the Republic. By placing examples of their ancestors' noble deeds and unselfish service to the state before the eyes of his fellow Romans, Livy hoped to reverse the process of social decay.

In practice, however, Livy's history is more entertaining than didactic. He never allows an unreasonable respect for facts to interfere with telling a good story. Without the critical faculty or scientific method of Thucydides, Livy often includes material of questionable historicity simply because it is either too delightful to omit or it places Rome in a favorable light. Far more readable than the scrupulously literal Polybius (203–120 B.C.) who was one of his main sources, Livy imaginatively blends "the human and the supernatural." In so doing he achieves an unmatched romantic feeling for ancient customs and a vivid portrait of the Roman psychology. The "old tales" he incorporates into his work have, as he notes, the "charm of poetry." Neither affirming nor denying the legends and miracles attributed to the heroes of the past, Livy tells the story of Rome as the Romans themselves believed (or wished) it to be. In his narrative, Romulus and Remus are as real as Marc Antony and Augustus. Livy so successfully combines the mythological with the historical that he makes mere factual accuracy seem a paltry thing.

The passages from Books I and II which deal with the murderous rivalry between Romulus and Remus, the pragmatic rape of the Sabine women, the heroism of Horatio who defended a strategic bridge against the Etruscans, and the irreproachable purity of Lucretia (an ideal type of the Roman matron) who preferred death to loss of honor, have become a part of the world's mythology, as inspiring to patriots of modern Europe and America as they were to Livy's original audience.

The excerpts from Books XXI through XXX, which present the second war with Carthage and Hannibal's invasion of Italy, reveal Livy's belief in Fate's protection of Rome at its height. The historian's admiration of Hannibal, one of the greatest military geniuses of all time, is probably not a mark of Livy's objectivity. Hannibal's greatness is recognized only to make his defeat the more striking. After bringing his famous elephants across the Alps in 218 B.C., Hannibal laid waste the Italian countryside for fifteen years. But, although coming within three miles of Rome, he never managed to seize the capital. As Livy is fond of noting, Hannibal won every battle against Rome except the last. In 202 B.C. the Roman commander Scipio Africanus defeated Hannibal's troops at the battle of Zama in Africa. Carthage was forced to renounce all her conquests, severely reduce the size of her army, and pay an annual tribute. Thus, by the end of the second Punic War, Rome had eliminated Carthage as a major power. By forcing Carthage into a third conflict (151–146 B.C.), Rome followed a policy of genocide which culminated in Carthage's total extinction. To symbolize eternal barrenness, the site of the once-great city was sown with salt. As Virgil had foreshadowed in Aeneas' treatment of Queen Dido, Rome could triumph only in the utter destruction of her rival. Virgil and Livy were agreed that Rome's survival and growth at the expense of her neighbors was morally justified by the will of Fate.

The heroism, self-denial, love of country, and sense of national destiny which animated the citizens of Livy's Rome not only gave archetypal expression to these qualities, but also provided the model of patriotism upon which the nation-states of the modern world are founded. In spite of his factual errors, Livy's work is universally significant because he instinctively understood and described the unchanging psychological forces that inspire men to create nations and drive them to war with one another.

THE HISTORY OF ROME

[Livy's historical method]

THE TASK OF WRITING A HISTORY OF OUR NATION FROM ROME'S EARLIEST days fills me, I confess, with some misgiving, and even were I confident in the value of my work, I should hesitate to say so. I am aware that for historians to make extravagant claims is, and always has been, all too common: every writer on history tends to look down his nose at his less cultivated predecessors, happily persuaded that he will better them in point of style, or bring new facts to light. But however that may be, I shall find satisfaction in contributing—not, I hope, ignobly—to the labour of putting on record the story of the greatest nation in the world. Countless others have written on this theme and it may be that I shall pass unnoticed amongst them; if so, I must comfort myself with the greatness and splendour of my rivals, whose work will rob my own of recognition.

From *Livy: The Early History of Rome,* translated by Aubrey de Selincourt. Copyright 1960 by Aubrey de Selincourt. Reprinted by permission of Penguin Books, Ltd.

My task, moreover, is an immensely laborious one. I shall have to go back more than seven hundred years, and trace my story from its small beginnings up to these recent times when its ramifications are so vast that any adequate treatment is hardly possible. I am aware, too, that most readers will take less pleasure in my account of how Rome began and in her early history; they will wish to hurry on to more modern times and to read of the period, already a long one, in which the might of an imperial people is beginning to work its own ruin. My own feeling is different; I shall find antiquity a rewarding study, if only because, while I am absorbed in it, I shall be able to turn my eyes from the troubles which for so long have tormented the modern world, and to write without any of that over-anxious consideration which may well plague a writer on contemporary life, even if it does not lead him to conceal the truth.

Events before Rome was born or thought of have come to us in old tales with more of the charm of poetry than of a sound historical record, and such traditions I propose neither to affirm nor refute. There is no reason, I feel, to object when antiquity draws no hard line between the human and the supernatual: it adds dignity to the past, and, if any nation deserves the privilege of claiming a divine ancestry, that nation is our own; and so great is the glory won by the Roman people in their wars that, when they declare that Mars himself was their first parent and father of the man who founded their city, all the nations of the world might well allow the claim as readily as they accept Rome's imperial dominion.

These, however, are comparatively trivial matters and I set little store by them. I invite the reader's attention to the much more serious consideration of the kind of lives our ancestors lived, of who were the men, and what the means both in politics and war by which Rome's power was first acquired and subsequently expanded; I would then have him trace the process of our moral decline, to watch, first, the sinking of the foundations of morality as the old teaching was allowed to lapse, then the rapidly increasing disintegration, then the final collapse of the whole edifice, and the dark dawning of our modern day when we can neither endure our vices nor face the remedies neeeded to cure them. The study of history is the best medicine for a sick mind; for in history you have a record of the infinite variety of human experience plainly set out for all to see; and in that record you can find for yourself and your country both examples and warnings: fine things to take as models, base things, rotten through and through, to avoid.

I hope my passion for Rome's past has not impaired my judgment; for I do honestly believe that no country has ever been greater or purer than ours or richer in good citizens and noble deeds; none has been free for so many generations from the vices of avarice and luxury; nowhere have thrift and plain living been for so long held in such esteem. Indeed, poverty, with us, went hand in hand with contentment. Of late years wealth has made us greedy, and self-indulgence has brought us, through every form of sensual excess, to be, if I may so put it, in love with death both individual and collective.

But bitter comments of this sort are not likely to find favour, even when they have to be made. Let us have no more of them, at least at the beginning of our great story. On the contrary, I should prefer to borrow from the poets and begin with good omens and with prayers to all the host of heaven to grant a successful issue to the work which lies before me.

It is generally accepted that after the fall of Troy the Greeks kept up hostilities against all the Trojans except Aeneas and Antenor. These two men had worked consistently for peace and the restoration of Helen, and for that reason, added to certain personal connexions of long standing, they were allowed to go unmolested. Each had various adventures: Antenor . . . . penetrated to the head of the Adriatic and expelled the Euganei, a tribe living between the Alps and the sea, and occupied that territory with a mixed population of Trojans and Eneti. The spot where they landed is called Troy and the neighbouring country the Trojan district. The combined peoples came to be known as Venetians.

Aeneas was forced into exile by similar troubles; he, however, was destined to lay the foundations of a greater future. He went first to Macedonia, then in his search for a new home sailed to Sicily, and from Sicily to the territory of Laurentum. This part of Italy too, like the spot where Antenor landed, is known as Troy. Aeneas's men in the course of their almost interminable wanderings had lost all they possessed except their ships and their swords; once on shore, they set about scouring the countryside for what they could find, and while thus engaged they were met by a force of armed natives who, under their king Latinus, came hurrying up from the town and the surrounding country to protect themselves from the invaders. There are two versions of what happened next: according to one, there was a fight in which Latinus was beaten; he then came to terms with Aeneas and cemented the alliance by giving him his daughter in marriage. According to the other, the battle was about to begin when Latinus, before the trumpets could sound the charge, came forward with his captains and invited the foreign leader to a parley. He then asked Aeneas who his men were and where they had come from, why they had left their homes and what was their object in landing on Laurentian territory. He was told in reply that the men were Trojans, their leader Aeneas, the son of Anchises and Venus; that their native town had been burnt to the ground and now they were fugitives in search of some place where they could build a new town to settle in. Latinus, hearing their story, was so deeply impressed by the noble bearing of the strangers and by their leader's high courage either for peace or war, that he gave Aeneas his hand in pledge of friendship from that moment onward. A treaty was made; the two armies exchanged signs of mutual respect; Aeneas accepted the hospitality of Latinus, who gave him his daughter in marriage, thus further confirming the treaty of alliance by a private and domestic bond solemnly entered into in the presence of the Gods of his hearth.

The Trojans could no longer doubt that at last their travels were over and that they had found a permanent home. They began to build a settlement, which Aeneas named Lavinium after his wife Lavinia. A child was soon born of the marriage: a boy, who was given the name Ascanius.

The Trojans and the Latins were soon jointly involved in war. Turnus, prince of the Rutuli, to whom Latinus's daughter Lavinia had been pledged before Aeneas's arrival, angered by the insult of having to step down in favour of a stranger, attacked the combined forces of Aeneas and Latinus. Both sides suffered in the subsequent struggle: the Rutuli were defeated, but the victors lost their leader Latinus. Turnus and his people, in their anxiety for the future, then looked for help to Mezentius, king of the rich and powerful Etruscans, whose seat of government was at Caere, at that time a wealthy town. Mezentius needed little persuasion to join the Rutuli, as from the outset he had been far from pleased by the rise of the new settlement, and now felt that the Trojan power was growing much more rapidly than was safe for its neighbours. In this dangerous situation Aeneas conferred the native name of Latins upon his own people; the sharing of a common name as well as a common polity would, he felt, strengthen the bond between the two peoples. As a result of this step the original settlers were no less loyal to their king Aeneas than were the Trojans themselves. Trojans and Latins were rapidly becoming one people, and this gave Aeneas confidence to make an active move against the Etruscans, in spite of their great strength. Etruria, indeed, had at this time both by sea and land filled the whole length of Italy from the Alps to the Sicilian strait with the noise of her name; none the less Aeneas refused to act on the defensive and marched out to meet the enemy. The Latins were victorious, and for Aeneas the battle was the last of his labours in this world. He lies buried on the river Numicus. Was he man or god? However it be, men call him Jupiter Indiges—the local Jove.

Aeneas's son Ascanius was still too young for a position of authority; Lavinia, however, was a woman of great character, and acted as regent until Ascanius came of age and was able to assume power as the successor of his father and grandfather. There is some doubt—and no one can pretend to certainty on something so deeply buried in the mists of time—about who precisely this Ascanius was. Was it the one I have been discussing, or was it an elder brother, the son of Creusa, who was born before the sack of Troy and was with Aeneas in his escape from the burning city—the Iulus, in fact, whom the Julian family claim as their eponym? It is at any rate certain that Aeneas was his father, and—whatever the answer to the other question may be—it can be taken as a fact that he left Lavinium to found a new settlement. Lavinium was by then a populous and, for those days, a rich and flourishing town, and Ascanius left it in charge of his mother (or stepmother, if you will) and went off to found his new settlement on the Alban hills. This town, strung out as it was along a ridge, was named Alba Longa. Its foundation took place about thirty years after that of Lavinium; but the Latins had already grown so strong, especially since the defeat of the Etruscans, that neither Mezentius, the Etruscan king, nor any other neighbouring people dared to attack them, even when Aeneas died and the control of things passed temporarily into the hands of a woman, and Ascanius was still a child learning the elements of kingship. By the terms of the treaty between the Latins and Etruscans the river Albula (now the Tiber) became the boundary between the two territories.

✻   ✻   ✻

But (I must believe) it was already written in the book of fate that this great city of ours should arise, and the first steps be taken to the founding of the mightiest empire the world has known—next to God's. The Vestal Virgin was raped and gave birth to twin boys. Mars, she declared, was their father—perhaps she believed it, perhaps she was merely hoping by the pretence to palliate her guilt. Whatever the truth of the matter, neither gods nor men could save her or her babes from the savage hands of the king. The mother was bound and flung into prison; the boys, by the king's order, were condemned to be drowned in the river. Destiny, however, intervened; the Tiber had overflowed its banks; because of the flooded ground it was impossible to get to the actual river, and the men entrusted to do the deed thought that the floodwater, sluggish though it was, would serve their purpose. Accordingly they made shift to carry out the king's orders by leaving the infants on the edge of the first flood-water they came to, at the spot where now stands the Ruminal fig-tree—said to have once been known as the fig-tree of Romulus. In those days the country thereabouts was all wild and uncultivated, and the story goes that when the basket in which the infants had been exposed was left high and dry by the receding water, a she-wolf, coming down from the neighbouring hills to quench her thirst, heard the children crying and made her way to where they were. She offered them her teats to suck and treated them with such gentleness that Faustulus, the king's herdsman, found her licking them with her tongue. Faustulus took them to his hut and gave them to his wife Larentia to nurse. Some think that the origin of this fable was the fact that Larentia was a common whore and was called Wolf by the shepherds.

Such, then, was the birth and upbringing of the twins. By the time they were grown boys, they employed themselves actively on the farm and with the flocks and began to go hunting in the woods; their strength grew with their resolution, until not content only with the chase they took to attacking robbers and sharing their stolen goods with their friends the shepherds. Other young fellows joined them, and they and the shepherds would fleet the time together, now in serious talk, now in jollity.

❀   ❀   ❀

Romulus and Remus were suddenly seized by an urge to found a new settlement on the spot where they had been left to drown as infants and had been subsequently brought up. There was, in point of fact, already an excess of population at Alba, what with the Albans themselves, the Latins, and the addition of the herdsmen: enough, indeed, to justify the hope that Alba and Lavinium would one day be small places compared with the proposed new settlement. Unhappily the brothers' plans for the future were marred by the same curse which had divided their grandfather and Amulius—jealousy and ambition. A disgraceful quarrel arose from a matter in itself trivial. As the brothers were twins and all question of seniority was thereby precluded, they determined to ask the tutelary gods of the countryside to declare by augury which of them should govern the new town once it was founded, and give his name to it. For this purpose Romulus took the Palatine hill and Remus the Aventine as their respective stations from which to observe the auspices. Remus, the story goes, was the first to receive a sign—six vultures; and no sooner was this made known to the people than double the number of birds appeared to Romulus. The followers of each promptly saluted their master as king, one side basing its claim upon priority, the other upon number. Angry words ensued, followed all too soon by blows, and in the course of the affray Remus was killed. There is another story, a commoner one, according to which Remus, by way of jeering at his brother, jumped over the half-built walls of the new settlement, whereupon Romulus killed him in a fit of rage, adding the threat, 'So perish whoever else shall overleap my battlements.'

This, then, was how Romulus obtained the sole power. The newly built city was called by its founder's name.

❀   ❀   ❀

[The rape of the Sabine women.]

Rome was now strong enough to challenge any of her neighbours; but, great though she was, her greatness seemed likely to last only for a single generation. There were not enough women, and that, added to the fact that there was no intermarriage with neighbouring communities, ruled out any hope of maintaining the level of population. Romulus accordingly, on the advice of his senators, sent representatives to the various peoples across his borders to negotiate alliances and the right of intermarriage for the newly established state. The envoys were instructed to point out that cities, like everything else, have to begin small; in course of time, helped by their own worth and the favour of heaven, some, at least, grow rich and famous, and of these Rome would assuredly be one: Gods had blessed her birth, and the valour of her people would not fail in the days to come. The Romans were men, as they were; why, then, be reluctant to intermarry with them?

Romulus's overtures were nowhere favourably received; it was clear that everyone despised the new community, and at the same time feared, both for themselves and for posterity, the growth of this new power in their midst. More often than not his envoys were dismissed with the question of whether Rome had thrown open her doors to female, as well as to male, runaways and vagabonds, as that would evidently be the most suitable way for Romans to get wives. The young Romans naturally resented this jibe, and a clash seemed inevitable. Romulus, seeing it must come, set the scene for it with elaborate care. Deliberately hiding his resentment, he prepared to celebrate the Consualia, a solemn festival in honour of Neptune, patron of the horse, and sent notice of his intention all over the neighbouring countryside. The better to advertise it, his people lavished upon their preparations for the spectacle all the resources—such as they were in those days—at their command. On the appointed day crowds flocked to Rome, partly, no doubt, out of sheer curiosity to see the new town. The majority were from the neighbouring settlements of Caenina, Crustumium, and Antemnae, but all the Sabines were there too, with their wives and children. Many houses offered hospitable entertainment to the visitors; they were invited to inspect the fortifications, lay-out, and numerous buildings of the town, and expressed their surprise at the rapidity of its growth. Then the great moment came; the show began, and nobody had eyes or thoughts for anything else. This was the Romans' opportunity: at a given signal all the able-bodied men burst through the crowd and seized the young women. Most of the girls were the prize of whoever got hold of them first, but a few conspicuously handsome ones had been previously marked down for leading senators, and these were brought to their houses by special gangs. There was one young woman of much greater beauty than the rest; and the story goes that she was seized by a party of men belonging to the household of someone called Thalassius, and in reply to the many questions about whose house they were taking her to, they, to prevent anyone else laying hands upon her, kept shouting, 'Thalassius, Thalassius!' This was the origin of the use of this word at weddings.

By this act of violence the fun of the festival broke up in panic. The girls' unfortunate parents made good their escape, not without bitter comments on the treachery of their hosts and heartfelt prayers to the God to whose festival they had come in all good faith in the solemnity of the occasion, only to be grossly deceived. The young women were no less indignant and as full of foreboding for the future.

Romulus, however, reassured them. Going from one to another he declared that their own parents were really to blame, in that they had been too proud to allow intermarriage with their neighbours; nevertheless, they need not fear; as married women they would share all the fortunes of Rome, all the privileges of the community, and they would be bound to their husbands by the dearest bond of all, their children. He urged them to forget their wrath and give their hearts to those to whom chance had given their bodies. Often, he said, a sense of injury yields in the end to affection, and their husbands would treat them all the more kindly in that they would try, each one of them, not only to fulfil their own part of the bargain but also to make up to their wives for the homes and parents they had lost. The men, too, played their part: they spoke honied words and vowed that it was passionate love which had prompted their offence. No plea can better touch a woman's heart.

The women in course of time lost their resentment.

✿   ✿   ✿

[The Story of Lucretia]

. . . They were drinking one day in the quarters of Sextus Tarquinius —Collatinus, son of Egerius, was also present—when someone chanced to mention the subject of wives. Each of them, of course, extravagantly praised his own; and the rivalry got hotter and hotter, until Collatinus suddenly cried: 'Stop! What need is there of words, when in a few hours we can prove beyond doubt the incomparable superiority of my Lucretia? We are all young and strong: why shouldn't we ride to Rome and see with our own eyes what kind of women our wives are? There is no better evidence, I assure you than what a man finds when he enters his wife's room unexpectedly.'

They had all drunk a good deal, and the proposal appealed to them; so they mounted their horses and galloped off to Rome. They reached the city as dusk was falling; and there the wives of the royal princes were found enjoying themselves with a group of young friends at a dinner-party, in the greatest luxury. The riders then went on to Collatia, where they found Lucretia very differently employed: it was already late at night, but there, in the hall of her house, surrounded by her busy maid-servants, she was still hard at work by lamplight upon her spinning. Which wife had won the contest in womanly virtue was no longer in doubt.

With all courtesy Lucretia rose to bid her husband and the princes welcome, and Collatinus, pleased with his success, invited his friends to sup with him. It was at that fatal supper that Lucretia's beauty, and proven chastity, kindled in Sextus Tarquinius the flame of lust, and determined him to debauch her.

Nothing further occurred that night. The little jaunt was over, and the young men rode back to camp.

A few days later Sextus, without Collatinus's knowledge, returned with one companion to Collatia, where he was hospitably welcomed in Lucretia's house, and, after supper, escorted, like the honoured visitor he was thought to be, to the guest-chamber. Here he waited till the house was asleep, and then, when all was quiet, he drew his sword and made his way to Lucretia's room determined to rape her. She was asleep. Laying his left hand on her breast, 'Lucretia,' he whispered, 'not a sound! I am Sextus Tarquinius. I am armed—if you utter a word, I will kill you.' Lucretia opened her eyes in terror; death was imminent, no help at hand. Sextus urged his love, begged her to submit, pleaded, threatened, used every weapon that might conquer a woman's heart. But all in vain; not even the fear of death could bend her will. 'If death will not move you,' Sextus cried, 'dishonour shall. I will kill you first, then cut the throat of a slave and lay his naked body by your side. Will they not believe that you have been caught in adultery with a servant—and paid the price?' Even the most resolute chastity could not have stood against this dreadful threat.

Lucretia yielded. Sextus enjoyed her, and rode away, proud of his success.

The unhappy girl wrote to her father in Rome and to her husband in Ardea, urging them both to come at once with a trusted friend—and quickly, for a frightful thing had happened. Her father came with Valerius, Volesus's son, her husband with Brutus, with whom he was returning to Rome when he was met by the messenger. They found Lucretia sitting in her room, in deep distress. Tears rose to her eyes as they entered, and to her husband's question, 'Is it well with you?' she answered, 'No. What can be well with a woman who has lost her honour? In your bed, Collatinus, is the impress of another man. My body only has been violated. My heart is innocent, and death will be my witness. Give me your solemn promise that the adulterer shall be punished—he is Sextus Tarquinius. He it is who last night came as my enemy disguised as my guest, and took his pleasure of me. That pleasure will be my death—and his, too, if you are men.'

The promise was given. One after another they tried to comfort her. They told her she was helpless, and therefore innocent; that he alone was guilty. It was the mind, they said, that sinned, not the body: without intention there could never be guilt.

'What is due to *him*,' Lucretia said, 'is for you to decide. As for me I am innocent of fault, but I will take my punishment. Never shall Lucretia provide a precedent for unchaste women to escape what they deserve.' With these words she drew a knife from under her robe, drove it into her heart, and fell forward, dead.

Her father and husband were overwhelmed with grief. While they stood weeping helplessly, Brutus drew the bloody knife from Lucretia's body, and holding it before him cried: 'By this girl's blood—none more chaste till a tyrant wronged her—and by the gods, I swear that with sword and fire, and whatever else can lend strength to my arm, I will pursue Lucius Tarquinius the Proud, his wicked wife, and all his children, and never again will I let them or any other man be King in Rome.'

He put the knife into Collatinus's hands, then passed it to Lucretius, then to Valerius. All looked at him in astonishment: a miracle had happened—he was a changed man. Obedient to his command, they swore their oath. Grief was forgotten in the sudden surge of anger, and when Brutus called upon them to make war, from that instant, upon the tyrant's throne, they took him for their leader.

Lucretia's body was carried from the house into the public square. Crowds gathered, as crowds will, to gape and wonder—and the sight was unexpected enough, and horrible enough, to attract them. Anger at the criminal brutality of the king's son and sympathy with the father's grief stirred every heart; and when Brutus cried out that it was time for deeds not tears, and urged them, like true Romans, to take up arms against the tyrants who had dared to treat them as a vanquished enemy, not a man amongst them could resist the call. The boldest spirits offered themselves at once for service; the rest soon followed their lead. Lucretia's father was left to hold Collatia; guards were posted to prevent news of the rising from reaching the palace, and with Brutus in command the armed populace began their march on Rome.

In the city the first effect of their appearance was alarm and confusion, but the sight of Brutus, and others of equal distinction, at the head of the mob, soon convinced people that this was, at least, no mere popular demonstration. Moreover the horrible story of Lucretia had had hardly less effect in Rome than in Collatia. In a moment the Forum was packed, and the crowds, by Brutus's order, were immediately summoned to attend the Tribune of Knights—an office held at the time by Brutus himself. There, publicly throwing off the mask under which he had hitherto concealed his real character and feelings, he made a speech painting in vivid colours the brutal and unbridled lust of Sextus Tarquinius, the hideous rape of the innocent Lucretia and her pitiful death, and the bereavement of her father, for whom the cause of her death was an even bitterer and more dreadful thing than the death itself. He went on to speak of the king's arrogant and tyrannical behaviour; of the sufferings of the commons condemned to labour underground clearing or constructing ditches and sewers; of gallant Romans—soldiers who had beaten in battle all neighbouring peoples—robbed of their swords and turned into stone-cutters and artisans. He reminded them of the foul murder of Servius Tullius, of the daughter who drove her carriage over her father's corpse, in violation of the most sacred of relationships—a crime which God alone could punish. Doubtless he told them of other, and worse, things, brought to his mind in the heat of the moment and by the sense of this latest outrage, which still lived in his eye and pressed upon his heart; but a mere historian can hardly record them.

The effect of his words was immediate; the populace took fire, and were brought to demand the abrogation of the king's authority and the exile of himself and his family.

With an armed body of volunteers Brutus then marched for Ardea to rouse the army to revolt. Lucretius, who some time previously had been appointed by the king Prefect of the City, was left in command in Rome. Tullia fled from the palace during the disturbances; wherever she went she was met with curses; everyone, men and women alike, called down upon her head the vengeance of the furies who punish sinners against the sacred ties of blood.

When news of the rebellion reached Ardea, the king immediately started for Rome, to restore order. Brutus got wind of his approach, and changed his route to avoid meeting him, finally reaching Ardea almost at the same moment as Tarquin arrived at Rome. Tarquin found the city gates shut against him and his exile decreed. Brutus the Liberator was enthusiastically welcomed by the troops, and Tarquin's sons were expelled from the camp. Two of them followed their father into exile at Caere in Etruria. Sextus Tarquinius went to Gabii—his own territory, as he doubtless hoped; but his previous record there of robbery and violence had made him many enemies, who now took their revenge and assassinated him.

Tarquin the Proud reigned for twenty-five years. The whole period of monarchical government, from the founding of Rome to its liberation, was 244 years. After the liberation two counsuls were elected by popular vote, under the presidency of the Prefect of the City. . . .

[Horatius at the bridge.]

On the approach of the Etruscan army, the Romans abandoned their farmsteads and moved into the city. Garrisons were posted. In some sections the city walls seemed sufficient protection, in others the barrier of the Tiber. The most vulnerable point was the wooden bridge, and the Etruscans would have crossed it and forced an entrance into the city, had it not been for the courage of one man, Horatius Cocles—that great soldier whom the fortune of Rome gave to be her shield on that day of peril. Horatius was on guard at the bridge when the Janiculum was captured by a sudden attack. The enemy forces came pouring down the hill, while the Roman troops, throwing away their weapons, were behaving more like an undisciplined rabble than a fighting force. Horatius acted promptly: as his routed comrades approached the bridge, he stopped as many as he could catch and compelled them to listen to him. 'By God,' he cried, 'can't you see that if you desert your post escape is hopeless? If you leave the bridge open in your rear, there will soon be more of them in the Palatine and the Capitol than on the Janiculum.' Urging them with all the power at his command to destroy the bridge by fire or steel or any means they could muster, he offered to hold up the Etruscan advance, so far as was possible, alone. Proudly he took his stand at the outer end of the bridge; conspicuous amongst the rout of fugitives, sword and shield ready for action, he prepared himself for close combat, one man against an army. The advancing enemy paused in sheer astonishment at such reckless courage. Two other men, Spurius Lartius and Titus Herminius, both aristocrats with a fine military record, were ashamed to leave Horatius alone, and with their support he won through the first few minutes of desperate danger. Soon, however, he forced them to save themselves and leave him; for little was now left of the bridge, and the demolition squads were calling them back before it was too late. Once more Horatius stood alone; with defiance in his eyes he confronted the Etruscan chivalry, challenging one after another to single combat, and mocking them all as tyrants' slaves who, careless of their own liberty, were coming to destroy the liberty of others. For a while they hung back, each waiting for his neighbour to make the first move, until shame at the unequal battle drove them to action, and with a fierce cry they hurled their spears at the solitary figure which barred their way. Horatius caught the missiles on his shield and, resolute as ever, straddled the bridge and held his ground. The Etruscans moved forward, and would have thrust him aside by the sheer weight of numbers, but their advance was suddenly checked by the crash of the falling bridge and the simultaneous shout of triumph from the Roman soldiers who had done their work in time. The Etruscans could only stare in bewilderment as Horatius, with a prayer to Father Tiber to bless him and his sword, plunged fully armed into the water and swam, through the missiles which fell thick about him, safely to the other side where his friends were waiting to receive him. It was a noble piece of work—legendary, maybe, but destined to be celebrated in story through the years to come.

THE WAR WITH HANNIBAL

A NUMBER OF THINGS CONTRIBUTED TO GIVE THIS WAR ITS UNIQUE CHARACTER: in the first place, it was fought between peoples unrivalled throughout previous history in material resources, and themselves at the peak of their prosperity and power; secondly, it was a struggle between old antagonists, each of whom had learned, in the first Punic War, to appreciate the military capabilities of the other; thirdly, the final issue hung so much in doubt that the eventual victors came nearer to destruction than their adversaries. Moreover, high passions were at work throughout, and mutual hatred was hardly less sharp a weapon than the sword; on the Roman side there was rage at the unprovoked attack by a previously beaten enemy; on the Carthaginian, bitter resentment at what

From *Livy: The War with Hannibal*, translated by Aubrey de Selincourt. Copyright 1965 by the estate of Aubrey de Selincourt. Reprinted by permission of Penguin Books, Ltd.

was felt to be the grasping and tyrannical attitude of their conquerors. The intensity of the feeling is illustrated by an anecdote of Hannibal's boyhood: his father Hamilcar, after the campaign in Africa, was about to carry his troops over into Spain, when Hannibal, then about nine years old, begged, with all the childish arts he could muster, to be allowed to accompany him; whereupon Hamilcar, who was preparing to offer sacrifice for a successful outcome, led the boy to the altar and made him solemnly swear, with his hand upon the sacred victim, that as soon as he was old enough he would be the enemy of the Roman people. Hamilcar was a proud man and the loss of Sicily and Sardinia was a cruel blow to his pride; he remembered, moreover, that Sicily had been surrendered too soon, before the situation had become really desperate, and that Rome, taking advantage of internal troubles in Africa, had tricked Carthage into the loss of Sardinia, and then had added insult to injury by the imposition of a tribute. All this rankled in his mind, and his conduct of affairs during the five years of the war in Africa, following hard upon the signature of peace with Rome, and subsequently during the nine years he spent in extending Carthaginian influence in Spain, made it clear enough that his ultimate object was an enterprise of far greater moment, and that if he had lived the invasion of Italy would have taken place under Hamilcar's leadership, instead of, as actually happened, under Hannibal's. That the war was postponed was due to Hamilcar's timely death and the fact that Hannibal was still too young to assume command.

✿   ✿   ✿

Hannibal was sent to Spain, where the troops received him with unanimous enthusiasm, the old soldiers feeling that in the person of this young man Hamilcar himself was restored to them. In the features and expression of the son's face they saw the father once again, the same vigour in his look, the same fire in his eyes. Very soon he no longer needed to rely upon his father's memory to make himself beloved and obeyed: his own qualities were sufficient. Power to command and readiness to obey are rare associates; but in Hannibal they were perfectly united, and their union made him as much valued by his commander as by his men. Hasdrubal preferred him to all other officers in any action which called for vigour and courage, and under his leadership the men invariably showed to the best advantage both dash and confidence. Reckless in courting danger, he showed superb tactical ability once it was upon him. Indefatigable both physically and mentally, he could endure with equal ease excessive heat or excessive cold; he ate and drank not to flatter his appetites but only so much as would sustain his bodily strength. His time for waking, like his time for sleeping, was never determined by daylight or darkness: when his work was done, then, and then only, he rested, without need, moreover, of silence or a soft bed to woo sleep to his eyes. Often he was seen lying in his cloak on the bare ground amongst the common soldiers on sentry or picket duty. His accoutrement, like the horses he rode, was always conspicuous, but not his clothes, which were like those of any other officer of his rank and standing. Mounted or unmounted he was unequalled as a fighting man, always the first to attack, the last to leave the field. So much for his virtues—and they were great; but no less great were his faults: inhuman cruelty, a more than Punic perfidy, a total disregard of truth, honour, and religion, of the sanctity of an oath and of all that other men hold sacred. Such was the complex character of the man who for three years served under Hasdrubal's command, doing and seeing everything which could help to equip him as a great military leader.

From the very first day of his command Hannibal acted as if he had definite instructions to take Italy as his sphere of operations and to make war on Rome.

✿   ✿   ✿

[Hannibal crosses the Alps]

From the Druentia Hannibal advanced towards the Alps mainly through open country, and reached the foothills without encountering any opposition from the local tribes. The nature of the mountains was not, of course, unknown to his men by rumour and report—and rumour commonly exaggerates the truth; yet in this case all tales were eclipsed by the reality. The dreadful vision was now before their eyes: the towering peaks, the snow-clad pinnacles soaring to the sky, the rude huts clinging to the rocks, beasts and cattle shrivelled and parched with cold, the people with their wild and ragged hair, all nature, animate and inanimate, stiff with frost: all this, and other sights the horror of which words cannot express, gave a fresh edge to their apprehension. As the column moved forward up the first slopes, there appeared, right above their heads, ensconced upon their eminences, the local tribesmen, wild men of the mountains, who, if they had chosen to lurk in clefts of the hills, might well have sprung out from ambush upon the marching column and inflicted untold losses and disaster. . . .

At the head of the column were the cavalry and elephants; Hannibal himself, with the pick of the infantry, brought up the rear, keeping his eyes open and alert for every contingency. Before long the column found itself on a narrowing track, one side of which was overhung by a precipitous wall of rock, and it was suddenly attacked. The natives, springing from their places of concealment, fiercely assaulted front and rear, leaping into the fray, hurling missiles, rolling down rocks from the heights above. The worst pressure was on Hannibal's rear; to meet it, his infantry faced-about—and it was clear enough that, had not the rear of the column been adequately protected, the Carthaginian losses would have been appalling. Even as it was the moment was critical, and disaster only just averted; for Hannibal hesitated to send his own division into the pass—to do so would have deprived the infantry of such support as he was himself providing for the cavalry—and his hesitation enabled the tribesmen to deliver a flank attack, cut the whole column in two, and establish themselves on the track. As a result, Hannibal, for one night, found himself cut off from his cavalry and baggage-train. Next day, however, as enemy activity weakened, a junction was effected between the two halves of the column and the defile was successfully passed, though not without losses, especially amongst the pack-animals.

Thenceforward there was no concerted opposition, the natives confining themselves to mere raids, in small parties, on front or rear, as the nature of the ground dictated, or as groups of stragglers, left behind or pressing on ahead of the column as the case might be, offered a tempting prey. The elephants proved both a blessing and a curse: for though getting them along the narrow and precipitous tracks caused serious delay, they were none the less a protection to the troops, as the natives, never having seen such creatures before, were afraid to come near them.

On the ninth day the army reached the summit.[1] Most of the climb had been over trackless mountain-sides; frequently a wrong route was taken—sometimes through the deliberate deception of the guides, or, again, when some likely-looking valley would be entered by guess-work, without knowledge of whither it led. There was a two days' halt on the summit, to rest the men after the exhausting climb and the fighting. Some of the pack-animals which had fallen amongst the rocks managed, by following the army's tracks, to find their way into camp. The troops had indeed endured hardships enough; but there was worse to come. It was the season of the setting of the Pleiades:[2] winter was near—and it began to snow. Getting on the move at dawn, the army struggled slowly forward over snow-covered ground, the hopelessness of utter exhaustion in every face. Seeing their despair, Hannibal rode ahead and at a point of vantage which afforded a prospect of a vast extent of country, he gave the order to halt, pointing to Italy far below, and the Po Valley beyond the foothills of the Alps. 'My men,' he said, 'you are at this moment passing the protective barrier of Italy—nay more, you are walking over the very walls of Rome. Henceforward all will be easy going—no more hills to climb. After a fight or two you will have the capital of Italy, the citadel of Rome, in the hollow of your hands.'

The march continued, more or less without molestation from the natives, who confined themselves to petty raids when they saw a chance of stealing something. Unfortunately, however, as in most parts of the Alps the descent on the Italian side, being shorter, is correspondingly steeper, the going was much more difficult than it had been during the ascent. The track was almost everywhere precipitous, narrow, and slip-

---

[1]Probably the Col de la Traversette (9,680 feet).
[2]Late October.

pery; it was impossible for a man to keep his feet; the least stumble meant a fall, and a fall a slide, so that there was indescribable confusion, men and beasts stumbling and slipping on top of each other.

Soon they found themselves on the edge of a precipice—a narrow cliff falling away so sheer that even a lightly-armed soldier could hardly have got down it by feeling his way and clinging to such bushes and stumps as presented themselves. It must always have been a most awkward spot, but a recent landslide had converted it on this occasion to a perpendicular drop of nearly a thousand feet. On the brink the cavalry drew rein—their journey seemed to be over. Hannibal, in the rear, did not yet know what had brought the column to a halt; but when the message was passed to him that there was no possibility of proceeding, he went in person to reconnoitre. It was clear to him that a detour would have to be made, however long it might prove to be, over the trackless and untrodden slopes in the vicinity. But even so he was no luckier; progress was impossible, for though there was good foothold in the quite shallow layer of soft fresh snow which had covered the old snow underneath, nevertheless as soon as it had been trampled and dispersed by the feet of all those men and animals, there was left to tread upon only the bare ice and liquid slush of melting snow underneath. The result was a horrible struggle, the ice affording no foothold in any case, and least of all on a steep slope; when a man tried by hands or knees to get on his feet again, even those useless supports slipped from under him and let him down; there were no stumps or roots anywhere to afford a purchase to either foot or hand; in short, there was nothing for it but to roll and slither on the smooth ice and melting snow. Sometimes the mules' weight would drive their hoofs through into the lower layer of old snow; they would fall and, once down, lashing savagely out in their struggles to rise, they would break right through it, so that as often as not they were held as in a vice by a thick layer of hard ice.

When it became apparent that both men and beasts were wearing themselves out to no purpose, a space was cleared—with the greatest labour because of the amount of snow to be dug and carted away—and camp was pitched, high up on the ridge. The next task was to construct some sort of passable track down the precipice, for by no other route could the army proceed. It was necessary to cut through rock, a problem they solved by the ingenious application of heat and moisture; large trees were felled and lopped, and a huge pile of timber erected; this, with the opportune help of a strong wind, was set on fire, and when the rock was sufficiently heated the men's rations of sour wine were flung upon it, to render it friable. They then got to work with picks on the heated rock, and opened a sort of zigzag track, to minimize the steepness of the descent, and were able, in consequence, to get the pack animals, and even the elephants, down it.

Four days were spent in the neighbourhood of this precipice; the animals came near to dying of starvation, for on most of the peaks nothing grows, or, if there is any pasture, the snow covers it. Lower down there are sunny hills and valleys and woods with streams flowing by: country, in fact, more worthy for men to dwell in. There the beasts were put out to pasture, and the troops given three days' rest to recover from the fatigue of their road-building. Thence the descent was continued to the plains—a kindlier region, with kindlier inhabitants.

The march to Italy was much as I have described it. The army reached the frontier in the fifth month, as some records have it, after leaving New Carthage. The crossing of the Alps took fifteen days. There is great difference of opinion about the size of Hannibal's army on his arrival in Italy; the highest recorded estimate puts it at 100,000 infantry and 20,000 cavalry; the lowest at 20,000 infantry and 6,000 cavalry.

[The Battle of Lake Trasimene (217 B.C.)]

Flaminius* had reached the lake at sunset the previous day. On the day following, in the uncertain light of early dawn, he entered the narrow pass. No sort of reconnaissance had been made. When his column began to open out on reaching the wider area of level ground north of the lake, he was aware only of those enemy units which were in the direct line of his advance; of the units concealed in his rear and in the hills above him he had no inkling whatever. Hannibal had achieved his object: as soon as he had his antagonist penned in by the lake and the mountains and surrounded, front, rear, and flank, by his own men, he gave the order for a simultaneous attack by all units. Down they came from the hills, each man by the nearest way, taking the Romans totally unprepared. The unexpectedness of the attack was, moreover, increased by the morning mist from the lake, lying thicker on the low ground than on the hills; the units on the hills could see each other well enough, and were able, in consequence, the better to coordinate their attack.

By the battle-cry which arose on every side of them the Romans knew they were surrounded before they could see that the trap had closed. Fighting began in front and on their flanks before the column had time to form into line of battle, before even their weapons could be made ready, or swords drawn. In the general shock and confusion Flaminius, so far as such an emergency permitted, kept a cool head, and tried as well as time and place allowed to reduce the chaos in the ranks to some sort of order, as each man swung this way or that to face the shouts of triumph or calls for help that met his ears. Wherever he could make his voice heard, or force a way through the press, he encouraged his men and urged them to stand firm, crying out that no prayers would save them now, but only their own strength and their own valour. They must cut their way through with the sword, and the greater their courage the less would be their peril. But the din of the mêlée was so great that not a word either of exhortation or command could be heard. In the

---

Flaminius—Gaius Flaminius, Roman statesman and general.

chaos that reigned not a soldier could recognize his own standard or knew his place in the ranks—indeed, they were almost too bemused to get proper control over their swords and shields, while to some their very armour and weapons proved not a defence but a fatal encumbrance. In that enveloping mist ears were a better guide than eyes: it was sounds, not sights, they turned to face—the groans of wounded men, the thud or ring of blows on body or shield, the shout of onslaught, the cry of fear. Some, flying for their lives, found themselves caught in a jam of their own men still standing their ground; others, trying to return to the fight, were forced back again by a crowd of fugitives. In every direction attempts to break out failed. The mountains on one flank, the lake on the other, hemmed them in, while in front of them and behind stood the formations of the enemy. When at last it was clear to all that the one hope of life lay in their own individual swords, the nature of the struggle was transformed: no man now waited for orders or exhortation: each became his own commander, dependent on his own efforts alone. Familiar tactics, the well-known disposition of forces, were flung to the winds; legion, cohort, company no longer had any significance; if formations there were, chance alone made them, to fight in front or rear was a matter for the spirit in each breast to decide. So great was the fury of the struggle, so totally absorbed was every man in its grim immediacy, that no one even noticed the earthquake which ruined large parts of many Italian towns, altered the course of swift rivers, brought the sea flooding into estuaries and started avalanches in the mountains.

For three long and bloody hours the fight continued, and most furiously of all around the person of Flaminius. His best troops kept constantly at his side, and he was always quick to bring support to any point where he saw his men in trouble or likely to be overwhelmed. His dress and equipment made him a conspicuous figure, and the enemy attacks were as determined as the efforts to save him; and so it continued, until a mounted trooper, an Insubrian named Ducarius, recognized his face. Calling to his fellow-tribesmen, 'There is the counsul,' he cried, 'who destroyed our legions and laid our town and our fields in ruin! I will offer him as a sacrifice to the ghosts of our people foully slain!' Putting spurs to his horse he galloped through the thickest of the press, cut down the armour-bearer who had tried to check his murderous intent, and drove his lance through Flaminius's body. Only the shields of some veterans of the reserve prevented him from stripping the corpse.

For a large part of the Roman army the counsul's death was the beginning of the end. Panic ensued, and neither lake nor mountains could stop the wild rush for safety. Men tried blindly to escape by any possible way, however steep, however narrow; arms were flung away, men fell and others fell on top of them; many, finding nowhere to turn to save their skins, plunged into the edge of the lake till the water was up to their necks, while a few in desperation tried to swim for it—a forlorn hope indeed over that broad lake, and they were either drowned, or, struggling back exhausted into shallow water were butchered wholesale by the mounted troops who rode in to meet them. . . .

All was nearly over when at last the heat of the sun dispersed the mist, and in the clear morning light hills and plain revealed to their eyes the terrible truth that the Roman army was almost totally destroyed. . . .

Such was the famous fight at Lake Trasimene, one of the few memorable disasters to Roman arms. The Roman dead amounted to 15,000; 10,000, scattered in flight throughout Etruria, found their way back to Rome by various ways. Of the enemy 2,500 were killed; many on both sides died of wounds. . . . All prisoners of the Latin name Hannibal liberated without ransom; Roman prisoners he put in chains. He then gave orders that the bodies of his own men should be picked out from the heaps of enemy dead and given burial. He also wished to honour Flaminius with burial, but, though his body was searched for with all diligence, it was never found. . . .

[Scipio and Hannibal before the Battle of Zama (202 B.C.)]

Scipio acceded to Hannibal's request for a conference, and the two generals agreed to advance the position of their respective camps so as to facilitate their meeting. . . .

Exactly half-way between the opposing ranks of armed men, each attended by an interpreter,[1] the generals met. They were not only the two greatest soldiers of their time, but the equals of any king or commander in the whole history of the world. For a minute mutual admiration struck them dumb, and they looked at each other in silence. Hannibal was the first to speak. 'If fate,' he said, 'has decreed that I who was the aggressor in the war with Rome, and so many times have had victory almost within my grasp, should of my own will come to ask for peace, I rejoice at least that destiny has given me you, and no other, from whom to ask it. You have many titles to honour, and amongst them, for you too, it will not be the least to have received the submission of Hannibal, to whom the gods gave victory over so many Roman generals, and to have brought to an end this war which was made memorable by your defeats before ever it was marked by ours. May it not also be a pretty example of the irony of fate that I took up arms when your father was consul, fought against him my first battle with a Roman general, and now come, unarmed, to his son to sue for peace? Assuredly it would have been best if the gods had given our fathers contentment with what was their own—you with ruling Italy, us with ruling Africa. . . .

'Though we sought to win what did not belong to us, we are now fighting to defend our own, and the war has not been, for us, fought only in Italy, any more than for you it has been only in Africa. You too have seen the arms and standards of the enemy almost at your gates, just as

---

[1]Though both spoke Greek and Hannibal probably knew Latin.

now we can hear from Carthage the mutter and stir of a Roman camp. So in discussing terms of peace, it is you who can negotiate from strength—which is precisely what *you* most want, and *we* find most unfortunate. You and I have the most to gain by peace, and our respective governments will ratify whatever terms we decide on; the one essential thing is that we preserve in our negotiations a calm and rational temper.

'As for myself, an old man returning to the homeland I left in boyhood, the years with their burden of success and failure have so taught me that I would rather now follow the dictates of reason than hope for what luck may bring. You are young; fortune has always favoured you; and youth—unbrokenly successful—I fear may be too intolerant for the needs of cool and rational negotiation. The man whom fortune has never deceived cannot easily weigh the changes and chances of coming years: what I was at Trasimene and Cannae, you are today; you accepted a command when you were barely old enough for service; you shrank at nothing—and your luck has never failed you. . . . A man's heart may well long for victory rather than for peace; I better understand the aspiring spirit than the politic brain, and once on me, too, smiled such fortune as is yours. . . . To ignore all else, I alone am sufficient warning of what fate may bring: I, whom but yesterday you saw encamped between the Anio and Rome advancing my standards and on the point of scaling your city's walls—and whom now you see here, bereft of my two brothers—those famous generals, those valiant hearts—before the walls of my native city, already almost under seige, begging that she may be spared the terrors I so nearly inflicted upon yours.

'The greater a man's success, the less it must be trusted to endure. This is your hour of triumph, while for us all is dark; to you peace, if you grant it, will be a splendid thing and fair to look upon, but for us who sue for it, it will carry no honour but only the burden of necessity. Certain peace is better and safer than the uncertain hope of victory: the one is in your hands, the other in the hands of God. Do not stake the success of so many years upon the decision of a single hour; remember not only your own strength but the might of Fortune and the chances of war which we both must share. . . . The luck of an hour can tumble to the ground the honours we have won, the honours we have hoped to win. In making peace, Publius Cornelius,* everything is yours; refuse to make it, and you must take what the gods may please to give you. . . .

'To define terms is the privilege of him who grants a peace, not of him who sues for it; but perhaps we of Carthage are not unworthy to lay a penalty upon ourselves. We do not object to leaving you in possession of everything for which we went to war—Sicily, Sardinia, Spain, and all the islands between Africa and Italy; let us be confined within the shores of Africa, and see you, since such is God's will, extending your sway over foreign countries, both by land and by sea. I would not deny that there was some lack of sincerity in our recent request for peace and our failure

---

Publius Cornelius—Scipio Africanus.

to wait for it, or that therefore the honour of Carthage has become suspect to you. . . . But now it is I, Hannibal, who have come to sue—and I should not seek peace unless I thought it for our good, and for the same reason I shall keep it. I was the aggressor in this war; and just as I did what I could, till the gods envied my success, to ensure that none of my people should regret it, so shall I strive that none may regret the peace obtained through my endeavours.'

To Hannibal's speech the Roman general replied somewhat as follows. 'It did not escape me, Hannibal, that it was the knowledge that you would soon be with them that emboldened the Carthaginians to violate the armistice and wreck the hope of peace. . . . Though you do not deserve peace even on the same terms as before, you are actually asking to better them by your dishonesty. Our fathers were not the aggressors in the war for Sicily, nor we ourselves in the war for Spain; in the former it was the peril of our allies, the Mamertines, in the latter the destruction of Saguntum which induced us to don the armour of loyalty and justice. That you were the aggressors you yourself admit, and the gods are our witnesses in that they granted for that war, even as they are granting and will grant for this, an ending in accordance with divine and human law.

'As for myself, I am aware of human infirmity; I do not ignore the might of Fortune, and I know well that all we do is subject to a thousand chances. If before you came to Africa—if while you were voluntarily evacuating Italy and had already embarked your army—you had come to me and I had turned a deaf ear to your request for peace, then, I confess, I should have been acting with outrageous insolence; but as things are, when on the brink of battle I have forced you to come here in spite of your most bitter reluctance, I am bound by no obligation to consider your feelings. If, therefore, to the terms upon which peace seemed likely to be made you wish to add some compensation for our ships which, with their cargoes, you took by force during the armistice, or for the violence you offered to our envoys, there will be something for me to bring before my council; if, on the contrary, you feel even that to be too great a burden, prepare to fight—for, evidently, you have found peace intolerable.'

Negotiation had failed. The two generals after the conference returned to their armies with the news that words had been in vain and the issue must be decided by blows. Each must accept the fortune which the gods chose to give. . . . Before the next night they would know whether Rome or Carthage was destined to give laws to the nations, for the prize of victory would be not Italy or Africa but the whole world, while a peril as great as the prize would be theirs whom the fortune of war opposed. To the Romans, in an unknown and foreign land, no way of escape was open; Carthage, her last reserves spent, was threatened with instant destruction.

Next day, to decide this great issue, the two most famous generals and the two mightiest armies of the two wealthiest nations in the world advanced to battle, doomed either to crown or to destroy the many triumphs each had won in the past. In all hearts were mixed feelings, confidence alternating with fear. As men surveyed their own and the enemy's ranks, weighing the strength of each merely by what their eyes could tell them, thoughts of joy and of foreboding jostled for preeminence in their minds. Such grounds for confidence as did not readily occur to the rank and file were supplied by the two commanders in words of admonition and encouragement, Hannibal reminding his men of their exploits in Italy during sixteen years of campaigning, of all the Roman generals killed, all the armies wiped out, and, when he came to a man who had distinguished himself in some particular battle, of the heroic deeds of individual soldiers. Scipio, for his part, spoke of the Spanish campaigns, of the recent battles in Africa, and of the enemy's admission of weakness and guilt, in that fear had forced them to sue for a peace which their ineradicable perfidy forbade them to keep. Furthermore, he made good use of his conference with Hannibal, which, as it had taken place without witnesses, he was free to misrepresent in any way he pleased.

* * *

[The Carthaginians are routed]

. . . More than 20,000 of the Carthaginians and their allies were killed on that day, and about the same number captured, together with 132 military standards and eleven elephants. The Romans lost about 1,500 men.

In the confusion Hannibal escaped with a few horsemen and fled to Hadrumetum. He had tried everything he could both before and during the engagement before he withdrew from the battle, and on the admission even of Scipio as well as of all the military experts, he achieved the distinction of having drawn up his line on that day with remarkable skill. . . .

The Senate accordingly decreed that Scipio should make peace with the people of Carthage upon such terms as seemed suitable to him and were in agreement with the opinion of a council of ten members. . . .

The Carthaginians . . . presented themselves to Scipio and made peace. . . . They surrendered their warships, elephants, deserters, and runaway slaves, and 4,000 prisoners-of-war. . . . Scipio ordered the ships to be taken out to sea and burnt: according to some historians there were 500 of them, representing every type of vessel propelled by oars, and the conflagration, seen without warning, was as melancholy a sight for the Carthaginians as it would have been if their own city were in flames. The deserters were more harshly treated than the runaway slaves: Latin citizens were beheaded and Romans crucified.

OVID

(Publius Ovidius Naso, 43 B.C.-A.D. 18)

WITH OVID, AUGUSTAN POETRY LOSES THE DIDACTIC SERIOUSNESS IT HAD under Virgil and Horace. Rather than concern himself with an epic justification of the Empire's role in world history, as Virgil had done, or devote himself like Horace to formulating a theory of the poet's social importance, Ovid was content merely to entertain his readers without feeling any obligation to edify them. A genial figure in the fashionable literary world of Rome, Ovid produced an abundance of delightful, slightly scandalous, erotic poetry that won him a large following among the sophisticated upper classes. But Ovid's urbane, luxurious life among his cosmopolitan friends was brought to an abrupt end in A.D. 8, when the Emperor Augustus banished him to the remote western shores of the Black Sea. The ostensible reason for Ovid's banishment was apparently the frank sensuality of his *Art of Love,* which conflicted with Augustus' desire to elevate the moral tone of his administration. The other "error," though unknown, may have been Ovid's connection with the emperor's licentious daughter, Julia. In spite of his many letters of explanation and pleas to return, Ovid's sentence was never revoked. Miserably unhappy away from the exciting city he loved so well, Ovid died in bleak Tomis after ten years of exile.

Remarking that he could write more easily in verse than in prose, Ovid tended to be prolific rather than profound. His extreme facility and lack of philosophical purpose, brought upon him the charge of shallowness. At his best, however, he shows a sensitive appreciation of the customs and picturesque values of the past. His real genius was for narrative poetry. No one has retold the old myths and legends of Greece and Rome so well as Ovid does in the *Metamorphoses of the Gods.* Within a limited context, he achieves considerable variety of tone and style. The tale of Baucis and Philemon is told with rustic simplicity and evident sincerity. The story of Echo and Narcissus is not only an incomparable depiction of adolescent self-love, it is also a tender and melancholy lament for the inevitable perishing of youth and beauty. Ovid's sheer enjoyment of his gods, their loves, and changes of form gives his poetry a bright charm matched by few storytellers. The exuberance of the lover surprised with delight in *Elegy* V may persuade the reader ask Jove to "send more such poets as this."

THE METAMORPHOSES

[Echo and Narcissus]

                       Now Narcissus
Was sixteen years of age, and could be taken
Either for boy or man; and boys and girls
Both sought his love, but in that slender stripling
Was pride so fierce no boy, no girl, could touch him.
He was out hunting one day, driving deer
Into the nets, when a nymph named Echo saw him,
A nymph whose way of talking was peculiar
In that she could not start a conversation
Nor fail to answer other people talking.
Up to this time Echo still had a body,
She was not merely voice. She liked to chatter,
But had no power of speech except the power
To answer in the words she last had heard.
Juno had done this: when she went out looking
For Jove on top of some nymph among the mountains,
Echo would stall the goddess off by talking
Until the nymphs had fled. Sooner or later
Juno discovered this and said to Echo:
"The tongue that made a fool of me will shortly
Have shorter use, the voice be brief hereafter."
Those were not idle words; now Echo always
Says the last thing she hears, and nothing further.
She saw Narcissus roaming through the country,
Saw him, and burned, and followed him in secret,
Burning the more she followed, as when sulphur
Smeared on the rim of torches, catches fire
When other fire comes near it. Oh, how often
She wanted to come near with coaxing speeches,
Make soft entreaties to him! But her nature
Sternly forbids; the one thing not forbidden
Is to make answers. She is more than ready
For words she can give back. By chance Narcissus
Lost track of his companions, started calling
"Is anybody here?" and "Here!" said Echo.
He looked around in wonderment, called louder
"Come to me!" "Come to me!" came back the answer.
He looked behind him, and saw no one coming;
"Why do you run from me?" and heard his question

Repeated in the woods. "Let us get together!"
There was nothing Echo would ever say more gladly,
"Let us get together!" And, to help her words,
Out of the woods she came, with arms all ready
To fling around his neck. But he retreated:
"Keep your hands off," he cried, "and do not touch me!
I would die before I give you a chance at me."
"I give you a chance at me," and that was all
She ever said thereafter, spurned and hiding,
Ashamed, in the leafy forests, in lonely caverns.
But still her love clings to her and increases
And grows on suffering; she cannot sleep,
She frets and pines, becomes all gaunt and haggard,
Her body dries and shrivels till voice only
And bones remain, and then she is voice only
For the bones are turned to stone. She hides in woods
And no one sees her now along the mountains,
But all may hear her, for her voice is living.

She was not the only one on whom Narcissus
Had visited frustration; there were others,
Naiads¹ or Oreads,² and young men also
Till finally one rejected youth, in prayer,
Raised up his hands to Heaven: "May Narcissus
Love one day, so, himself, and not win over
The creature whom he loves!" Nemesis heard him,
Goddess of Vengeance, and judged the plea was righteous.
There was a pool, silver with shining water,
To which no shepherds came, no goats, no cattle,
Whose glass no bird, no beast, no falling leaf
Had ever troubled. Grass grew all around it,
Green from the nearby water, and with shadow
No sun burned hotly down on. Here Narcissus,
Worn from the heat of hunting, came to rest
Finding the place delightful, and the spring
Refreshing for the thirsty. As he tried
To quench his thirst, inside him, deep within him,
Another thirst was growing, for he saw
An image in the pool, and fell in love
With that unbodied hope, and found a substance
In what was only shadow. He looks in wonder,
Charmed by himself, spell-bound, and no more moving
Than any marble statue. Lying prone
He sees his eyes, twin stars, and locks as comely

---

¹*Naiads*—lovely nymphs who inhabit fresh waters, such as rivers and springs.
²*Oreads*—nymphs who dwell in mountainous areas.

As those of Bacchus or the god Apollo,
Smooth cheeks, and ivory neck, and the bright beauty
Of countenance, and a flush of color rising
In the fair whiteness. Everything attracts him
That makes him so attractive. Foolish boy,
He wants himself; the loved becomes the lover,
The seeker sought, the kindler burns. How often
He tries to kiss the image in the water,
Dips in his arms to embrace the boy he sees there,
And finds the boy, himself, elusive always,
Not knowing what he sees, but burning for it,
The same delusion mocking his eyes and teasing.
Why try to catch an always fleeing image,
Poor credulous youngster? What you seek is nowhere,
And if you turn away, you will take with you
The boy you love. The vision is only shadow,
Only reflection, lacking any substance.
It comes with you, it stays with you, it goes
Away with you, if you can go away.
No thought of food, no thought of rest, can make him
Forsake the place. Stretched on the grass, in shadow,
He watches, all unsatisfied, that image
Vain and illusive, and he almost drowns
In his own watching eyes. He rises, just a little,
Enough to lift his arms in supplication
To the trees around him, crying to the forest:
"What love, whose love, has ever been more cruel?
You woods should know: you have given many lovers
Places to meet and hide in; has there ever,
Through the long centuries, been anyone
Who has pined away as I do? He is charming,
I see him, but the charm and sight escape me.
I love him and I cannot seem to find him!
To make it worse, no sea, no road, no mountain,
No city-wall, no gate, no barrier, parts us
But a thin film of water. He is eager
For me to hold him. When my lips go down
To kiss the pool, his rise, he reaches toward me.
You would think that I could touch him—almost nothing
Keeps us apart. Come out, whoever you are!
Why do you tease me so? Where do you go
When I am reaching for you? I am surely
Neither so old or ugly as to scare you,
And nymphs have been in love with me. You promise,
I think, some hope with a look of more than friendship.
You reach out arms when I do, and your smile
Follows my smiling; I have seen your tears

When I was tearful; you nod and beckon when I do;
Your lips, it seems, answer when I am talking
Though what you say I cannot hear. I know
The truth at last. He is myself! I feel it,
I know my image now. I burn with love
Of my own self; I start the fire I suffer.
What shall I do? Shall I give or take the asking?
What shall I ask for? What I want is with me,
My riches make me poor. If I could only
Escape from my own body! if I could only—
How curious a prayer from any lover—
Be parted from my love! And now my sorrow
Is taking all my strength away; I know
I have not long to live, I shall die early,
And death is not so terrible, since it takes
My trouble from me; I am sorry only
The boy I love must die: we die together."
He turned again to the image in the water,
Seeing it blur through tears, and the vision fading,
And as he saw it vanish, he called after:
"Where are you going? Stay: do not desert me,
I love you so. I cannot touch you; let me
Keep looking at you always, and in looking
Nourish my wretched passion!" In his grief
He tore his garment from the upper margin,
Beat his bare breast with hands as pale as marble,
And the breast took on a glow, a rosy color,
As apples are white and red, sometimes, or grapes
Can be both green and purple. The water clears,
He sees it all once more, and cannot bear it.
As yellow wax dissolves with warmth around it,
As the white frost is gone in morning sunshine,
Narcissus, in the hidden fire of passion,
Wanes slowly, with the ruddy color going,
The strength and hardihood and comeliness,
Fading away, and even the very body
Echo had loved. She was sorry for him now,
Though angry still, remembering; you could hear her
Answer "Alas!" in pity, when Narcissus
Cried out "Alas!" You could hear her own hands beating
Her breast when he beat his. "Farewell, dear boy,
Beloved in vain!" were his last words, and Echo
Called the same words to him. His weary head
Sank to the greensward, and death closed the eyes
That once had marveled at their owner's beauty.
And even in Hell, he found a pool to gaze in,
Watching his image in the Stygian water.

While in the world above, his naiad sisters
Mourned him, and dryads wept for him, and Echo
Mourned as they did, and wept with them, preparing
The funeral pile, the bier, the brandished torches,
But when they sought his body, they found nothing,
Only a flower with a yellow center
Surrounded with white petals.

[The Story of Daedalus and Icarus]

Homesick for homeland, Daedalus hated Crete
And his long exile there, but the sea held him.
"Though Minos[3] blocks escape by land or water,"
Daedalus said, "surely the sky is open,
And that's the way we'll go. Minos' dominion
Does not include the air." He turned his thinking
Toward unknown arts, changing the laws of nature.
He laid out feathers in order, first the smallest,
A little larger next it, and so continued,
The way that pan-pipes rise in gradual sequence.
He fastened them with twine and wax, at middle,
At bottom, so, and bent them, gently curving,
So that they looked like wings of birds, most surely.
And Icarus, his son, stood by and watched him,
Not knowing he was dealing with his downfall,
Stood by and watched, and raised his shiny face
To let a feather, light as down, fall on it,
Or stuck his thumb into the yellow wax,
Fooling around, the way a boy will, always,
Whenever a father tries to get some work done.
Still, it was done at last, and the father hovered,
Poised, in the moving air, and taught his son:
"I warn you, Icarus, fly a middle course:
Don't go too low, or water will weigh the wings down;
Don't go too high, or the sun's fire will burn them.
Keep to the middle way. And one more thing,
No fancy steering by star or constellation,
Follow my lead!" That was the flying lesson,
And now to fit the wings to the boy's shoulders.
Between the work and warning the father found
His cheeks were wet with tears, and his hands trembled.
He kissed his son (*Good-bye*, if he had known it),
Rose on his wings, flew on ahead, as fearful
As any bird launching the little nestlings

---

[3]*Minos*—legendary king of Crete, for whom Daedalus built the labyrinth to house the Minotaur.

Out of high nest into thin air. *Keep on,*
Keep on, he signals, *follow me!* He guides him
In flight—O fatal art!—and the wings move
And the father looks back to see the son's wings moving.
Far off, far down, some fisherman is watching
As the rod dips and trembles over the water,
Some shepherd rests his weight upon his crook,
Some ploughman on the handles of the ploughshare,
And all look up, in absolute amazement,
At those air-borne above. They must be gods!
They were over Samos, Juno's sacred island,
Delos and Paros toward the left, Lebinthus
Visible to the right, and another island,
Calymne, rich in honey. And the boy
Thought *This is wonderful!* and left his father,
Soared higher, higher, drawn to the vast heaven,[4]
Nearer the sun, and the wax that held the wings
Melted in that fierce heat, and the bare arms
Beat up and down in air, and lacking oarage
Took hold of nothing. *Father!* he cried, and *Father!*
Until the blue sea hushed him, the dark water
Men call the Icarian now. And Daedalus,
Father no more, called "Icarus, where are you!
Where are you, Icarus? Tell me where to find you!"
And saw the wings on the waves, and cursed his talents,
Buried the body in a tomb, and the land
Was named for Icarus.[5]

[The Story of Baucis and Philemon]

                    An oak-tree stands
Beside a linden, in the Phrygian hills.
There's a low wall around them. I have seen
The place myself; a prince once sent me there
To land ruled by his father. Not far off
A great marsh lies, once habitable land,
But now a playground full of coots and divers.
Jupiter came here, once upon a time,
Disguised as mortal man, and Mercury,
His son, came with him, having laid aside
Both wand and wings. They tried a thousand houses,
Looking for rest; they found a thousand houses

---

[4]*Drawn to the vast heaven*—Icarus' venturing into a realm forbidden to man in the classic example of *hubris*. The rash youth is soon overtaken by *nemesis*.
[5]*Named for Icarus*—at least a portion of the Aegean Sea was named the *Icarian* in his memory.

Shut in their face. But one at last received them,
A humble cottage, thatched with straw and reeds.
A good old woman, Baucis, and her husband,
A good old man, Philemon, used to live there.
They had married young, they had grown old together
In the same cottage; they were very poor,
But faced their poverty with cheerful spirit
And made its burden light by not complaining.
It would do you little good to ask for servants
Or masters in that household, for the couple
Were all the house; both gave and followed orders.
So, when the gods came to this little cottage,
Ducking their heads to enter, the old man
Pulled out a rustic bench for them to rest on,
As Baucis spread a homespun cover for it.
And then she poked the ashes around a little,
Still warm from last night's fire, and got them going
With leaves and bark, and blew at them a little,
Without much breath to spare, and added kindling,
The wood split fine, and the dry twigs, made smaller
By breaking them over the knee, and put them under
A copper kettle, and then she took the cabbage
Her man had brought from the well-watered garden,
And stripped the outer leaves off. And Philemon
Reached up, with a forked stick, for the side of bacon,
That hung below the smoky beam, and cut it,
Saved up so long, a fair-sized chunk, and dumped it
In the boiling water. They made conversation
To keep the time from being too long, and brought
A couch with willow frame and feet, and on it
They put a sedge-grass mattress, and above it
Such drapery as they had, and did not use
Except on great occasions. Even so,
It was pretty worn, it had only cost a little
When purchased new, but it went well enough
With a willow couch. And so the gods reclined.
Baucis, her skirts tucked up, was setting the table
With trembling hands. One table-leg was wobbly;
A piece of shell fixed that. She scoured the table,
Made level now, with a handful of green mint,
Put on the olives, black or green, and cherries
Preserved in dregs of wine, endive and radish,
And cottage cheese, and eggs, turned over lightly
In the warm ash, with shells unbroken. The dishes,
Of course, were earthenware, and the mixing-bowl
For wine was the same silver, and the goblets
Were beech, the inside coated with yellow wax.

No time at all, and the warm food was ready,
And wine brought out, of no particular vintage,
And pretty soon they had to clear the table
For the second course: here there were nuts and figs
And dates and plums and apples in wide baskets—
Remember how apples smell?—and purple grapes
Fresh from the vines, and a white honeycomb
As centerpiece, and all around the table
Shone kindly faces, nothing mean or poor
Or skimpy in good will.
                              The mixing-bowl,
As often as it was drained, kept filling up
All by itself, and the wine was never lower.
And this was strange, and scared them when they saw it.
They raised their hands and prayed, a little shaky—
'Forgive us, please, our lack of preparation,
Our meagre fare!' They had one goose, a guardian,
Watchdog, he might be called, of their estate,
And now decided they had better kill him
To make their offering better. But the goose
Was swift of wing, too swift for slow old people
To catch, and they were weary from the effort,
And could not catch the bird, who fled for refuge,
Or so it seemed, to the presence of the strangers.
'Don't kill him,' said the gods, and then continued:
'We are gods, you know: this wicked neighborhood
Will pay as it deserves to; do not worry,
You will not be hurt, but leave the house, come with us,
Both of you, to the mountain-top!' Obeying,
With staff and cane, they made the long climb, slowly
And painfully, and rested, where a bowman
Could reach the top with a long shot, looked down,
Saw water everywhere, only their cottage
Standing above the flood. And while they wondered
And wept a little for their neighbors' trouble,
The house they used to live in, the poor quarters
Small for the two of them, became a temple:
Forked wooden props turned into marble columns;
The thatch grew brighter yellow; the roof was golden;
The doors were gates, most wonderfully carved;
The floor that used to be of earth was marble.
Jupiter, calm and grave, was speaking to them:
'You are good people, worthy of each other,
Good man, good wife—ask us for any favor,
And you shall have it.' And they hesitated,
Asked, 'Could we talk it over, just a little?'
And talked together, apart, and then Philemon

Spoke for them both: 'What we would like to be
Is to be priests of yours, and guard the temple,
And since we have spent our happy years together,
May one hour take us both away; let neither
Outlive the other, that I may never see
The burial of my wife, nor she perform
That office for me.' And the prayer was granted.
As long as life was given, they watched the temple,
And one day, as they stood before the portals,
Both very old, talking the old days over,
Each saw the other put forth leaves, Philemon
Watched Baucis changing, Baucis watched Philemon,
And as the foliage spread, they still had time
To say 'Farewell, my dear!' and the bark closed over
Sealing their mouths. And even to this day
The peasants in that district show the stranger
The two trees close together, and the union
Of oak and linden in one. The ones who told me
The story, sober ancients, were no liars,
Why should they be? And my own eyes have seen
The garlands people bring there; I brought new ones,
Myself, and said a verse: *The gods look after*
Good people still, and cherishers are cherished.

ELEGY V

In summer's heat, and mid-time of the day,
To rest my limbs upon a bed I lay;
One window shut, the other open stood,
Which gave such light as twinkles in a wood,
Like twilight glimpse at setting of the sun,
Or night being past, and yet not day begun.
Such light to shamefast maidens must be shown
Where they may sport, and seem to be unknown.
Then came Corinna[1] in her long loose gown,
Her white neck hid with tresses hanging down,   10
Resembling fair Semiramis[2] going to bed,

---

[1]*Corinna*—the poet's mistress, who appears frequently in the *Amores*. Unlike the Lesbia of Catullus, Corinna was probably imaginary.
[2]*Semiramis*—legendary queen of Assyria who founded Babylon. She was noted for her beauty and sensuality.

From the *Amores*. Translated by Christopher Marlowe in *Marlowe's Poems*. Copyright © 1931 by the Gordian Press, Inc. Reprinted by permission of the publisher.

Or Lais[3] of a thousand wooers sped.
I snatch'd her gown; being thin, and harm was small;
Yet striv'd she to be covered therewithal;
And striving thus as one that would be cast,
Betray'd herself, and yielded at the last.
Stark naked as she stood before mine eye,
Not one wen in her body could I spy.
What arms and shoulders did I touch and see,
How apt her breasts were to be press'd by me!   20
How smooth a belly under her waist saw I!
How large a leg, and what a lusty thigh!
To leave the rest, all lik'd me passing well;
I cling'd her naked body, down she fell;
Judge you the rest: being tir'd she bade me kiss;
Jove send me more such afternoons as this.

[3]*Lais*—the name of at least three celebrated Greek courtesans, one of whom was the mistress of Alcibiades. "A thousand wooers" may have won the favors of any or all of the three ladies in question.

PLUTARCH Preface

(Ploutarchos, c. A.D. 46-c. 120)

IRONICALLY, LITTLE IS KNOWN ABOUT THE LIFE OF PLUTARCH, THE MOST distinguished biographer of the classical world. Except for the sparce facts that he travelled extensively in his native Greece, where he served for a time as a priest of Apollo at Delphi, and paid at least two visits to Rome, where he lectured on ethics and philosophy, nothing about him more tangible than the genial personality reflected in his writings survives. Cultivated, sensible, and apparently sympathetic to a wide variety of life styles, Plutarch was the ideal gentleman-scholar to do justice to his major undertaking, the composition of fifty biographies of eminent Greeks and Romans. Plutarch's scheme was to pair a famous Roman general, statesman, or other leader with his Greek counterpart. The *Parallel Lives* include Theseus, Solon, Themistocles, Pericles, Alcibiades, Demosthenes, Alexander the Great, Pompey, Marc Antony, and Julius Caesar.

Writing in Greek for an educated Roman audience, Plutarch wished not only to win popularity for his tributes to Latin heroes, but also to remind the counquering Romans that Greece had produced men with equal claim to be remembered. In spite of his patriotism, Plutarch is balanced and objective. He neither flatters the Romans nor boasts of Greece's past glory.

Plutarch's chief interest in the *Lives* is not to preserve historical statistics but to examine the ethical and psychological nature of his subject and to draw from the life a moral lesson. The biographies are never dry records of births, battles, and deaths, but vital recreations of the subject's character. As a consequence, the *Lives* rely heavily on anecdote and personal detail, in which a man unconsciously reveals his essential disposition.

The *Life of Cicero,* for example, is less concerned with tracing Cicero's rise from middle-class obscurity to the position of leading lawyer, orator, and statesman of his day than with analyzing the personal qualities that accounted for his spectacular success and final tragedy. In Plutarch's finished portrait, Cicero stands revealed as a man of basic integrity and unmatched oratorical gifts, but vain, indecisive, and sometimes foolish. While focusing on Cicero's personal career, Plutarch shows enormous skill in simultaneously depicting the chaotic spirit of the times. Political events are not examined directly, but only insofar as they affect Cicero's life. But since Cicero was intimately connected with virtually every major political figure of the day from Pompey and Julius Caesar to Marc Antony and Octavian, much of Cicero's private life necessarily reflects events of national significance. His exposure of the Catiline Conspiracy, his denunciation of the rebellious Clodius (brother of Catullus' "Lesbia"), his subsequent banishment and triumphal return, his flight after Caesar's assassination, and his murder by Antony's henchmen, all demonstrate that Cicero lived at the heart of Roman history. His *Life* is therefore more than the mere chronicle of an individual career. As Plutarch describes it, Cicero's final agony represents the death throes of the Roman Republic itself.

THE LIFE OF CICERO

HOWEVER, THOUGH HE WAS NOW LAUNCHING HIMSELF ON A POLITICAL CA-reer with the highest hopes, Cicero's eagerness was somewhat blunted by a reply which he received from an oracle. He had consulted the god at Delphi, asking how he could gain the greatest favour, and the Pythian priestess had told him that his guide in life should be, not popular opinion, but his own nature. So during the first part of his time in Rome he behaved with caution; he did not thrust himself forward as a candidate for office and so was passed over unnoticed. People called him 'the Greek' and 'the scholar'—names which came readily enough to the tongues of those Romans who are most lacking in culture or refinement. However, he was ambitious by nature and he was much encouraged by his father and by his friends. So, when he took up his work as an advocate, it was by no means slowly or gradually that he came to the top. He blazed out into fame at once and far surpassed all his competitors at the bar.

❉   ❉   ❉

Both parties, however—that of the nobility and that of the people—combined together to raise him to the consulship. This was done in the interests of the city as a whole, and the reasons were as follows. At first there had seemed to be no sense at all in the change which Sulla* had made in the constitution; but now time had passed and people had got used to it, so that the majority considered that it did offer some kind of stability. There were some, however, who, for the sake of their own private interests and not at all for the general good, wished to disturb the existing state of affairs and make a change. Pompey at this time was still engaged in war with the kings in Pontus and Armenia, and there was no force in Rome capable of dealing with these revolutionaries. They had as their leader Lucius Catiline, a bold and versatile character and one who was ready for anything. He was guilty of many serious

---

Sulla—dictator of Rome who passed many constitutional reforms. He introduced the device of *proscription*—the posting of lists of victims who might be killed without trial and have their property confiscated.

Abridged. From *Plutarch: Fall of the Roman Republic*, translated by Rex Warner. Copyright © 1958 by Rex Warner. Reprinted by permission of Penguin Books, Ltd.

crimes and had once been accused of taking the virginity of his own daughter and of killing his own brother. Fearing that he would be prosecuted for this murder he had induced Sulla to put down his brother's name, as though he were still alive, on the lists of those condemned to death. This, then, was the man whom these scoundrels took as their leader, and they gave pledges of faith to each other which included the sacrificing of a man and the tasting of his flesh. Catiline had also corrupted a great number of the young men in Rome by approaching them individually and supplying them constantly with amusements, drink, and women, pouring out money for them to spend on these dissipations. His agitation had extended to the whole of Etruria, which was now ready for revolt, as was the greater part of Cis-Alpine Gaul. In Rome itself there were most alarming revolutionary tendencies —the result of the unequal distribution of wealth. While men of the highest reputation and the greatest spirit had beggared themselves by their outlay on shows, entertainments, election expenses, and great buildings, money had accumulated in the hands of people whose families were unknown and of no account. So only a spark was needed to set everything on fire and, since the whole state was rotten within itself, it was in the power of any bold man to overthrow it.

Catiline wished nevertheless to obtain first a position of strength from which to start his operations, and so he stood for the consulship. He had great hopes that his colleague in this office would be Caius Antonius, a man with no aptitude for leadership in any direction, good or bad, but one who could be useful in providing additional strength to someone else who did take the lead. Most of the best people in the state realized this and so they put Cicero forward for the consulship; the people accepted him gladly; Catiline was defeated, and Cicero and Caius Antonius were elected as consuls. And this in spite of the fact that of all the candidates Cicero was the only one whose father came not from the senatorial nobility but from the moneyed class outside the senate.

❖   ❖   ❖

Now Catiline and his fellow conspirators, who had been cowed at first and too frightened to act, began to recover their confidence. They got together and encouraged each other by demanding that more daring should be shown; matters should be taken in hand, they said, before the return of Pompey, who was now said to be on his way back with his army. In particular the old soldiers of Sulla kept urging Catiline to take action. These were to be found in all parts of Italy, but the greatest numbers of them and the most formidable fighters were distributed among the cities of Etruria and were now dreaming once more of robbing and looting the wealth that seemed to be lying at their feet. With their leader Manlius, who was one of those who had served with distinction under Sulla, they joined in with Catiline and came to Rome to take part in the consular elections. Catiline was once again standing for the consulship and had planned to kill Cicero in the middle of the general disturbance of election day. Heaven itself, it seemed, was foretelling these events; there were earthquakes, thunderbolts, and apparitions. There was also information available from men, but this information, accurate as it was, was still not sufficient to convict a man like Catiline, who was well known and had very powerful connexions. Cicero therefore postponed the day of the elections, summoned Catiline to appear before the senate, and questioned him closely on the subject of what was being said about him. Catiline, in the belief that there were a number of people in the senate who wanted a revolution and at the same time wishing to show off in front of his fellow-conspirators, was mad enough to answer Cicero as follows: 'I see two bodies,' he said, 'one thin and wasted, but with a head, the other headless, but big and strong. What is there so dreadful about it, if I myself become the head of the body which needs one?' This riddle of his referred to the senate and the people, and Cicero became all the more alarmed. Wearing a breastplate he was escorted down from his house to the Field of Mars by all the nobility and by many of the young men. By loosening the folds of his tunic on his shoulders he purposely allowed people to see that he was wearing a breastplate, thus showing them the danger in which he stood, and the people indignantly rallied round him. Finally, when the votes were taken, they rejected Catiline once again and elected Silanus and Murena cousuls.

Soon afterwards Catiline's soldiers began to gather together in Etruria and to form themselves into companies. The day fixed for going into action was drawing near, and at this time there came to Cicero's house about midnight some of the most powerful and greatest men in Rome— Marcus Crassus, Marcus Marcellus, and Scipio Metellus. They roused the doorkeeper by their knocking and told him to go and tell Cicero that they were there. Their business was as follows: After dinner Crassus's doorkeeper had given him some letters which had been left by an unknown man; they were addressed to various people and one, which had no signature, was addressed to Crassus himself. This was the only one which Crassus had read. It had informed him that there was going to be much bloodshed by Catiline's orders and advised him to slip away secretly from the city. Crassus had therefore left the other letters unopened and had come at once to Cicero, quite overcome by the nature of the news and wishing to do something to clear himself from the suspicion he lay under because of his friendship with Catiline.

After thinking the matter over Cicero convened the senate at dawn. He brought the letters with him, handed them to those to whom they were addressed, and ordered them to read them aloud. Every single letter was found to contain information of a plot. Quintus Arrius, a man of praetorian rank, also made a report on the formation of regular bands of soldiers in Etruria; it was announced too that Manlius with a large force was hovering about the cities in that area in constant expectation of some news from Rome. Then the senate passed a decree that matters should be put into the hands of the consuls, who should accept the responsibility of arranging as best they could for the security of the city. This is a decree that is only rarely passed by the senate and only at times when great danger is feared.

Armed with these powers, Cicero entrusted the conduct of affairs outside Rome to Quintus Metellus. He himself took charge of the city and went out each day with so large a bodyguard that when he entered the forum a great part of the whole area was filled with the men who were escorting him. Catiline now became impatient of any further delay. He decided that he himself would break out of the city and go to join Manlius and his army; but first he instructed Marcius and Cethegus to take their swords and go to Cicero's house at daybreak as though to pay him their respects. They were then to fall on him and make an end of him. This plot was revealed to Cicero by a lady of good family called Fulvia, who came to him by night and told him to be on his guard against Cethegus and those who were with him. At dawn Cethegus and his party arrived and, when they were refused entry, became angry and created a disturbance at the door of the house, thus making themselves more suspect than ever. Cicero then came out and convened a meeting of the senate in the temple of Jupiter Stesius (or Stator, as the Romans say), which was situated at the beginning of the Sacred Way as you go up to the Palatine Hill. Catiline also attended this meeting with the other senators, intending to defend himself. No senator, however, would sit near him; they all moved away from the bench where he was sitting. When he began to speak he was shouted down, and finally Cicero rose up and told him to leave the city. He himself, he said, was a statesman who achieved his results by words, whereas Catiline's method was armed force; it was only right, therefore, that they should be separated from each other by the city wall. And so Catiline, accompanied by 300 armed men, left the city at once. He assumed the rods and axes of a magistrate in office, raised military standards, and marched to join Manlius. By now a force of some 20,000 men had been got together, and with these he marched round to the various cities and attempted to persuade them to revolt. It was now open war and Antonius was sent off with instructions to fight it out to the end.

The remains of Catiline's corrupt crew who had been left behind in Rome were organized and encouraged by Cornelius Lentulus, surnamed Sura. Lentulus came from a distinguished family, but had lived a low life and had once been expelled from the senate for his debauched conduct.

❊   ❊   ❊

There was nothing, then, on a small scale or trivial about Lentulus's plans. In fact he had decided to kill the entire senate and as many other citizens as possible, to burn down the city itself, and to spare no one except the children of Pompey. These were to be seized by the conspirators and held as hostages to secure a peaceful settlement with Pompey; for it was already generally and confidently reported that Pompey was on his way back from his great campaigns. A night—one of the nights of the Saturnalia—had been fixed for the attack, and swords, tow, and brimstone had been carried to the house of Cethegus and hidden there. They had also a force of a hundred men, each of whom had been allotted a particular section of Rome, so that in a short time many people could start fires and the city would be in a blaze on all sides. Others were to cut the aqueducts and to kill anyone who tried to bring water.

There happened to be staying in Rome when these plans were being made two ambassadors of the Allobroges, a nation which was then going through a particularly bad time and was disaffected towards the Roman government. Lentulus and his party thought that these men would be useful in stirring up a revolt in Gaul and so they took them into the conspiracy. They also gave them letters to their own senate and letters for Catiline too. To the senate of the Allobroges they promised freedom from Roman control; and they urged Catiline to set free the slaves and to march on Rome. To accompany the ambassadors on their way to Catiline they sent a man called Titus, a citizen of Croton, who was to carry the letters.

The conspirators, however, were unbalanced characters who seldom met together without wine and women, while Cicero was following their schemes with patient care, with sober judgement, and with exceptional intelligence. He had many agents outside the conspiracy who kept a close watch on what was going on and helped him to collect evidence; and he was also in secret communication with people whom he could trust who were supposed to be in the conspiracy themselves. He therefore heard all about the discussions with the foreign ambassadors and, with the secret cooperation of the Allobroges, laid an ambush by night and arrested the man from Croton with the letters on him.

At dawn he assembled the senate in the temple of Concord, read the letters aloud, and examined the informers. Silanus Iunius also spoke and declared that Cethegus had been heard saying that three consuls and four praetors were going to be killed. Piso too, a man of consular rank, produced more information of much the same kind. Caius Sulpicius, one of the praetors, was sent to the house of Cethegus, where he found apart from spears and armour an enormous quantity of swords and knives, all newly sharpened. Finally, after the senate had voted immunity for the man from Croton on condition that he gave information, Lentulus was convicted. He resigned his office (he was praetor at the time), laid aside his purple-bordered robe in the senate, and put on other clothes more in keeping with his present circumstances. He and his associates were then handed over to the praetors to be kept under arrest, though without chains. . . .

Next day there was a debate in the senate on the punishment of the conspirators. Silanus, who was asked to give his opinion first, said that they should be taken to prison and there should suffer the supreme penalty. All following speakers supported this motion until it came to the turn of Caius Caesar,* who afterwards became dictator. At this time he was still a young man and only at the beginning of his rise to power. He had already committed himself, however, both in his political actions and in his hopes for the future, to the path by which in the end he changed the state of Rome into a monarchy. Others were not aware of this, but Cicero had strong grounds for being suspicious of Caesar, though no evidence strong enough to secure his conviction. Nevertheless there were many who said that Caesar had a very narrow escape from Cicero on this occasion and was nearly caught. Some say, however, that Cicero purposely overlooked and suppressed the information laid against him through fear of his friends and of his power, since it was clear to everyone that, if Caesar were charged with the other conspirators, they were more likely to be acquitted with him than he was to be punished with them.

When it was Caesar's turn to give his opinion he rose and proposed that the conspirators should not be put to death, but that their property should be confiscated and that they themselves should be taken to whatever cities in Italy Cicero might choose and there be kept in chains under close arrest until final victory over Catiline had been secured in the field. The proposal was a reasonable one, Caesar, who made it, was a singularly able speaker, and Cicero also lent some weight to it; for when he rose to speak himself he dealt with the subject from both points of view, now putting forward the arguments for the first proposal and now for Caesar's. All his friends too preferred the second proposal to the first, thinking that Caesar's proposal was to the advantage of Cicero, who would be less open to attack subsequently if he did not put the conspirators to death. Silanus also now took up a different position. He excused himself by saying that in his original proposal he too had never meant death; the 'supreme penalty' in the case of a Roman senator was, of course, prison.

The first to speak against Caesar's proposal was Lutatius Catulus and he was followed by Cato who in a very violent speech joined him in trying to fix suspicion on Caesar. This speech had the effect of making the senate both thoroughly angry and determined to assert itself, so that the death sentence was passed on the conspirators. As for the confiscation of their property, Caesar opposed this, thinking it unfair that they should retain just the one part of his proposal which was most severe while they rejected his recommendation for mercy. When many of the senators wished to force this through, he appealed to the tribunes, but they would not do anything. Cicero himself, however, yielded the point and remitted that part of the sentence which called for the confiscation of their property.

Cicero then went to fetch the conspirators and the members of the senate went with him. The conspirators were not all in the same place;

Caius Caesar—Julius Caesar, greatest of the Roman conquerors and chief rival of General Pompey, whom Cicero supported.

they had been distributed for safe keeping among the praetors. First he called for Lentulus from the Palatine hill and led him down the Sacred Way through the middle of the forum. The most eminent statesmen formed up in ranks and acted as a bodyguard; but the people shuddered at what was being done and passed along in silence—especially the young, who looked as though they were being initiated with fear and trembling into the sacred rites and mysteries of some time-honoured process of aristocratic power. Cicero crossed the forum to the prison and then delivered Lentulus to the public executioner with orders that he should be put to death. Next was the turn of Cethegus, and so he brought down all the rest in order and had them executed. He observed that there were still standing about in bands in the forum many people who were in the conspiracy and who, not knowing what had been done, were waiting for nightfall, with the idea that their leaders were still alive and would be rescued. To these Cicero shouted out in a loud voice: 'They have lived their lives'—this being the Roman way of indicating death without using the ill-omened word.

It was now evening and Cicero went up through the forum to his house. There was no longer the usual silence and regular order in the crowds of citizens who escorted him there. Wherever he passed people shouted aloud and clapped their hands, calling him the saviour and the founder of his country. The streets were brightly lighted, since people had put lamps and torches in their doorways. The women also showed lights from the roofs of the houses in his honour and so that they might see him going up in this splendid procession with the greatest men in Rome escorting him. Most of these had been the victors in famous campaigns, had entered the city in triumph, and had added great areas of land and sea to the Roman dominions; but now as they walked in this procession they acknowledged to each other that the Roman people owed thanks to many commanders and generals of the time for riches and spoils and power, but for the safety and security of the whole their thanks were due to Cicero and to Cicero alone, who had delivered them from this great and terrible danger. What seemed so wonderful was not so much the fact that he had put a stop to the conspiracy and punished the conspirators as that he had succeeded in crushing this greatest of all revolutions by such comparatively painless methods, with no disturbances and no civil strife. For most of those who had flocked to join Catiline deserted him and went off as soon as they heard what had happened to Lentulus and Cethegus; and when Catiline with what was left of his forces joined battle with Antonius, both he and his army were destroyed.

There were, nevertheless, some people who were prepared both in speech and action to attack Cicero for what he had done. Their leaders, among those who were to take up office as magistrates next year, were Caesar, who was to be praetor, and Metellus and Bestia, who were to be tribunes. Cicero still had a few days of his consulship left when they came into office and they refused to allow him to address the people. They set down their benches in front of the rostra and gave him no chance or opportunity to speak, merely telling him that he could, if he wished, just pronounce the oath traditionally taken on leaving office and then come down again from the rostra. Cicero accepted their conditions and came forward to take the oath. When he had obtained silence he pronounced instead of the usual form of words a new oath of his own. 'I swear,' he said, 'in very truth that I have saved my country and maintained her supremacy.' And all the people assented to the oath and confirmed it with him. This made Caesar and the tribunes all the more angry and they tried to put fresh difficulties in Cicero's path. Among these efforts of theirs was a law which they proposed for the recall of Pompey and his army in order, so they said, to put an end to the tyranny of Cicero. Here Cato, who was tribune at the time, was a great help to Cicero, and to the whole state. While his authority was the same as that of the other tribunes, his reputation was a very much better one, and in opposing these measures of theirs he easily put a stop to their further designs. In a speech which he made to the people he so glorified Cicero's consulship that they voted him the greatest honours that had ever been conferred and called him the father of the fatherland.[1]

At this time, then, Cicero was the most powerful man in Rome. However, he made himself obnoxious to a number of people, not because of anything which he did wrong but because people grew tired of hearing him continually praising himself and magnifying his achievements. One could attend neither the senate nor a public meeting nor a session of the law courts without having to listen to endless repetitions of the story of Catiline and Lentulus. He went on to fill his books and writings with these praises of himself and made his style of speaking, which was in itself so very pleasant and so exceedingly charming, boring and tedious to listen to, since this unpleasant habit of his clung to him like fate. Nevertheless, it must be said that although he was so unreservedly fond of his own glory, he was quite free from envy of other people. He was, as can be seen from his writings, most liberal in his praises both of his predecessors and his contemporaries. Many such sayings of his are still remembered. For instance, he said of Aristotle that he was a river of flowing gold, and of the dialogues of Plato that, if it were in the nature of God to converse in human words, this would be how He would do it.

❀   ❀   ❀

Cicero made a number of enemies. In particular Clodius and his party combined against him for the following reasons. Clodius was a member of a noble family, young in years, but bold in spirit and one who was determined to get his own way. He was in love with Caesar's wife, Pompeia, and got into his house secretly by dressing up as a

---

[1]Cicero was the first, it seems, to receive this title. And Cato gave it to him in his speech before the people.

woman lute player. For the women of Rome were celebrating in Caesar's house that mysterious ceremony which men are not allowed to see, and there was no man present. Clodius, however, being still a youth who had not grown a beard, hoped to slip through with the women and get to Pompeia without being noticed. But, as he came in at night and the house was a large one, he lost his way in the passages; and, while he was wandering about, a maid of Caesar's mother Aurelia saw him and asked him what his name was. Since he was forced to speak, he said that he was looking for one of Pompeia's servants called Abra, and the maid, realizing that his voice was not that of a woman, shrieked out and called all the women together. They shut all the doors and carried out a thorough search until they found Clodius hiding in the room of the girl with whom he had come into the house. This affair caused a great scandal and Caesar divorced Pompeia and instituted proceedings against Clodius on the charge of sacrilege.

Cicero was a friend of Clodius and at the time of Catiline's conspiracy had found him most anxious to help and protect him. However, when Clodius, in reply to the charge made against him, insisted that he had never even been in Rome at the time but had been staying at a place a long way away from the city, Cicero gave evidence against him and stated that he had come to his house where he had consulted him on various matters. This was perfectly true, but it was believed that Cicero gave his evidence not so much because of the truth of it as because he wished to put himself in the right with his own wife Terentia, who was very hostile to Clodius on account of his sister Clodia.* Terentia suspected Clodia of wanting to marry Cicero and thought that she was trying to arrange this with the help of a man called Tullus who was on particularly friendly and intimate terms with Cicero. Terentia's suspicions were aroused by the way in which Tullus kept on visiting and paying attentions to Clodia, who lived close by; and since Terentia had a violent will of her own and had gained the ascendancy over Cicero, she urged him on to join in the attack on Clodius and to give evidence against him. Many of the better class of people also gave evidence against Clodius for perjury, fraud, bribing the people, and seductions of women. Lucullus actually produced female slaves who testified that Clodius had had sexual relations with his youngest sister at the time when she was living with Lucullus as his wife. It was generally believed also that Clodius had had intercourse with his other two sisters—Tertia, the wife of Marcius Rex, and Clodia, the wife of Metellus Celer. This last one was called Lady Farthing after the name of the smallest copper coin, because one of her lovers had deceived her by putting copper money instead of silver into a purse and sending it in to her. It was with regard to this sister in particular that Clodius got a bad name. However, the people at this time were united in their opposition to those who had combined to attack Clodius and were giving evidence against him. The members of the jury

---

Clodia—the "Lesbia" of Catullus' poems.

were terrified; they had to be protected by an armed guard, and most of them gave in voting tablets that were undecipherable. Nevertheless, it appeared that the majority had voted for Clodius's acquittal. A certain amount of bribery also was said to have been employed and it was this which prompted Catulus, when he next met the jurymen, to remark: 'You people were quite rightly concerned about your safety when you asked for a guard. Someone might have taken your money from you.' And when Clodius told Cicero that the jury had not believed his evidence, Cicero replied: 'You will find that twenty-five of them trusted in my word since they voted against you, and that the other thirty did not trust yours, since they did not vote for your acquittal until they had actually got your money in their hands.'

Caesar, though called as a witness, gave no evidence against Clodius and said that he had not divorced his wife because he believed her guilty of adultery, but because Caesar's wife should be not only free from guilt but free also from the very suspicion of it.

After Clodius had escaped from this danger he was elected tribune and immediately began to attack Cicero, raking up everything he could and inciting every type of person against him. He won over the people by laws passed in their interest; he had large provinces voted to each of the consuls (Macedonia to Piso and Syria to Gabinius); he organized numbers of the poorer classes into political clubs, and he provided himself with a bodyguard of armed slaves.

The three men with the greatest power in Rome at this time were Crassus, Pompey, and Caesar. Crassus was an open enemy of Cicero; Pompey had a foot in both camps; and Caesar was about to set out with an army to Gaul. Cicero therefore attempted to secure Caesar's favour, though Caesar, so far from being his friend, had incurred his suspicions in connexion with the affair of Catiline. He asked Caesar to give him an appointment on his staff for the forthcoming campaign and Caesar agreed to do so. Clodius, however, seeing that Cicero was escaping from his authority as a tribune, now pretended that he was anxious for a reconciliation. He put most of the blame for the quarrel on Terentia, always referred to Cicero himself with respect and made the most friendly remarks about him, giving the impression that he was without any hatred or illwill for him, indeed had nothing against him except a few minor complaints which one friend might make of another. In this way he entirely dispelled Cicero's fears, so that he declined Caesar's offer of an appointment abroad and again began to take part in public affairs. Caesar was angry at this and encouraged Clodius to renew his attacks. Caesar also turned Pompey completely against Cicero and then in a speech which he made himself to a meeting of the people declared that in his view it was neither right nor lawful for men to be put to death without a trial, as had happened in the cases of Lentulus, Cethegus, and their party. For this was the accusation against Cicero and this was the charge that he was being called upon to meet.

So, finding himself in danger of prosecution, Cicero put on mourning and, with his hair long and unkempt, went about the city approaching the people as a suppliant. However, he could not enter a single street without being accosted by Clodius with a band of insolent ruffians round him, who effectively interfered with his supplications by making all sorts of rude jokes about his change of clothes and his way of carrying himself, and on many occasions pelted him with mud and stones.

In spite of this, in the first place, the members of the class of gentlemen outside the senate, almost without exception, changed into mourning in sympathy with Cicero, and at least 20,000 young men went with him and, with their hair untrimmed like his, joined in his supplications. Then the senate met to pass a vote that the people should go into mourning as at times of public calamity. When this motion was opposed by the consuls and Clodius had surrounded the senate house with armed men, many of the senators ran out, tearing their clothes and crying out aloud. This sight, however, aroused no feelings either of pity or of due respect. It was evident that Cicero would either have to go into exile or else meet Clodius with armed force.

At this point Cicero appealed to Pompey for help, but Pompey had purposely got out of the way and was staying at his country house in the Alban hills. First Cicero sent his son-in-law Piso to plead for him; then he went up there himself. Pompey, however, when he heard of his arrival, could not face seeing him. He was bitterly ashamed when he remembered how in the past Cicero had fought his battles on many important occasions and had often taken a particular line in politics for his sake; but he was Caesar's son-in-law, and at Caesar's request he proved false to the obligations of the past. He slipped out of the house by another door and so avoided the interview.

❊   ❊   ❊

So Cicero came home after an exile of sixteen months. There was such joy among the cities and people were so eager to come out and meet him that what Cicero himself said later—namely, that Italy had taken him on her shoulders and carried him back to Rome—is far from being an exaggeration. And at Rome even Crassus, who had been his enemy before his exile, was now ready enough to come out to meet him and to be reconciled. He did this, he said, to please his son Publius, who was a great admirer of Cicero's.

❊   ❊   ❊

In the senate, when his fellow-members were voting him a triumph, he* said that he would rather follow in Caesar's triumphal procession, if only matters could be settled satisfactorily. And in private he wrote many letters to Caesar, giving him his advice, and had many personal

---

He—Cicero.

interviews in which he interceded with Pompey—trying to calm the feelings of each of them and to bring them to reason. Soon, however, things had gone too far for any remedy. Caesar was advancing on Rome and Pompey did not stay to meet him. With many other good men he abandoned the city. In this exodus Cicero took no part and he was believed to be throwing in his lot with Caesar. It is certainly evident that, with his judgement pulling him in both directions, he was in great distress of mind. He writes in his letters that he does not know which way he ought to turn. 'Pompey,' he says, 'has fair and honourable reasons for going to war; but Caesar has managed his affairs better and is more competent to look after himself and his friends. I know, therefore, whom I should fly from, but not whom I should fly to.' But when Trebatius, one of Caesar's close friends, wrote to him to say that in Caesar's view much the best thing would be for Cicero to range himself on his side and share his hopes, but that, if he felt himself to be too old for this, then he ought to go to Greece and live there quietly without committing himself to either side, Cicero expressed surprise that Caesar had not written to him personally and angrily replied that he would do nothing unworthy of his past career in politics.

So much for the evidence of the letters. When Caesar set out for Spain, Cicero sailed immediately to join Pompey. His appearance was generally welcomed, but when Cato saw him, he spoke to him in private and told him that, in coming over to Pompey's side, he had made a mistake. As for himself, Cato said, he was bound by honour not to forsake the general line in politics which he had taken up from the beginning; but Cicero would be more useful to his country and to his friends if he stayed at home without taking sides and adapted himself to events when he knew what the result would be; now, however, unnecessarily and for no good reason, he had made himself an enemy of Caesar and had come out there and involved himself in the great dangers which threatened them all.

❖   ❖   ❖

Finally the news came that Caesar had landed at Tarentum and was coming round by land from there to Brundisium. Cicero hurried out to meet him. He was not altogether without hope of the result, but he felt ashamed at having to test, as it were, the reactions of an enemy and a conqueror in front of so many witnesses. As it happened there was no need at all for him to do or say anything unworthy of himself. He was some way ahead of the rest when Caesar saw him coming, and he immediately got down and embraced him and then took him along with him for a considerable distance, talking to him privately. Afterwards, too, Caesar always honoured him and showed him kindness, and in his reply to the encomium of Cato which Cicero published, he wrote in the warmest terms of Cicero who, he says, both in his eloquence and in his life, strongly resembled Pericles and Theramenes.[2] It is said too that when Quintus Ligarius was being prosecuted as one of Caesar's enemies and Cicero was defending him, Caesar said to his friends: 'Why should we not hear a speech from Cicero after all this time? As for Ligarius we have long known him to be guilty and an enemy.' But when Cicero began to speak his words were incredibly moving; and as his speech proceeded, ranging in the most wonderfully charming language from one emotion to another, the colour came and went on Caesar's face and it was evident that every passion of his soul was being stirred. And finally, when the orator touched on the battle at Pharsalus, Caesar was so deeply affected that his whole body shook and the papers that he was holding dropped from his hand. So he was, as it were, overpowered and acquitted Ligarius.

After this, when the government had been changed to a monarchy, Cicero retired from public life and gave up his time to those of the young men who wanted to study philosophy. It was chiefly because of his association with these young men, who came from the best and most powerful families, that he once again exercised a great influence in the state.

* * *

In the plot that was taking shape against Caesar he took no part, although he was a particular friend of Brutus, and it was considered that he, more than anyone, was dissatisfied with the present state of affairs and longed for the past. The conspirators, however, were apprehensive about him: he was not very daring by nature, and he had reached an age when even the boldest spirits are apt to lose something of their resolution.

When the deed had been done by Brutus, Cassius, and the rest, the friends of Caesar combined together against them and it was feared that Rome would again be plunged into civil war. At this point Antony, as consul, called a meeting of the senate and said a few words on the subject of preserving peace and concord. Cicero followed with a long speech well suited to the occasion and persuaded the senate to imitate the Athenians and to vote an amnesty for those who had taken part in the killing of Caesar and to assign provinces to Brutus and Cassius. These proposals, however, came to nothing. The people's sympathies were in any case with Caesar, and when they saw his dead body being carried through the forum, and when Antony showed them the garments all drenched with blood and pierced through in every place with swords, they went mad with rage, searched all over the forum for the murderers, and, with torches in their hands, ran to burn down their houses. The conspirators were prepared for this danger beforehand and

---

[2]Cicero's essay was called 'Cato' and Caesar's 'Anti-Cato'.

so escaped it; but, fearing more and greater dangers in the future, they left Rome.

Antony's mood was now one of exultation. Everyone was afraid that he would seek supreme power for himself, and Cicero was more afraid of this than anyone. Antony, realizing that Cicero was once again becoming a power in the state and that he was a friend to Brutus and his party, disliked the idea of his presence in Rome. And even before this time they had been rather suspicious of each other because of the very wide difference in their ways of living. Cicero therefore feared Antony and at first was inclined to take an appointment on Dolabella's staff and sail out with him to Syria. But the consuls elected to succeed Antony were Hirtius and Pansa, both good men and admirers of Cicero. They begged him not to desert them and said that, if Cicero would stay in Rome, they would guarantee to deal with Antony. Cicero, without being entirely confident in these assurances, believed them up to a point and let Dolabella go without him. He agreed with Hirtius and Pansa to spend the summer in Athens and to return again to Rome when they had taken up office. So he set out by himself. His voyage, however, was delayed in some way or other, and, as often happens, the news from Rome suddenly seemed to change. It was now said that there had been an astonishing alteration in Antony's behaviour; all his actions and policies were now directed to please the senate, and it only needed Cicero's presence for everything to be settled in the most satisfactory manner possible. Cicero therefore reproached himself for having been over-cautious. He turned back again to Rome and in his first expectations was not disappointed. People rejoiced to see him and longed for his presence. Such great crowds poured out to meet him that the greetings and speeches of welcome at the city gates and during his entry into the city took up nearly a whole day.

Next day Antony called a meeting of the senate and invited Cicero to attend. Cicero, however, did not come. He stayed in bed, pretending that he was ill after the fatigues of his journey. But the truth seemed to be that, as the result of some suspicion or other and of some information which had suddenly reached him on the road, he was afraid of a plot against him. Antony was extremely angry at the implication and was for sending soldiers with orders either to bring Cicero or to burn down his house. Many people, however, protested against this and begged him not to do anything of the sort; and so he contented himself merely with receiving sureties for Cicero's good behaviour. After this they made no sign of recognition when they met, and they kept up this attitude, each being on his guard against the other, until the time when young Caesar* came from Apollonia to receive the inheritance left to him by the elder Caesar and engaged in a dispute with Antony, who was holding back 25 million drachmas from the estate.

---

*Young Caesar—Octavian, the future Emperor Augustus.

As the result of this Philippus and Marcellus, the husbands respectively of young Caesar's mother and sister, came with the young man to Cicero and made an arrangement by which Cicero was to use his powers of oratory and political influence on Caesar's behalf in the senate and before the people, and Caesar with his wealth and armed forces was to guarantee Cicero's security. The young man had already attached to him many of the soldiers who had served under the elder Caesar. It was thought that there was another and stronger reason, too, which induced Cicero to accept Caesar's friendship so readily. It seems that, while Pompey and Caesar were still alive, Cicero had a dream in which someone invited the sons of the senators to the capitol because Jupiter was going to appoint one of them to be the ruler of Rome. The citizens came running up eagerly and posted themselves round the temple, and the boys in their purple-bordered togas took their places in silence. Suddenly the doors opened and one by one the boys rose up and walked round past the god, who inspected each of them in turn. All, to their sorrow, were dismissed until this young Caesar came into the god's presence. Then the god stretched out his hand and said: 'Romans, you shall have an end of civil wars, when this boy becomes your ruler.' This, they say, was the sort of dream which Cicero had, and from it he received a very vivid impression of the boy's appearance, and retained this impression clearly, though he did not know the boy personally. Next day, however, he was going down to the Field of Mars at the time when the boys had just finished their exercise and were coming away. Among them Cicero saw for the first time the boy who had appeared in his dream. He was amazed and inquired who his parents were. His father was Octavius, who was not a person of great importance, but his mother was Attia, a daughter of Caesar's sister. For this reason Caesar, who had no children of his own, left him in his will his property and his family name. After this, they say, Cicero was always careful to take some notice of the young man whenever they met, and he on his side welcomed these kind attentions; it happened too that he was born in the year of Cicero's consulship.

Though these were the reasons spoken of, what really attached Cicero to young Caesar was, firstly, his hatred of Antony, and secondly, his natural passion for distinction. He imagined that he was adding Caesar's power to his own political influence. And the young man played up to him, going so far as actually to call him 'father'.

*   *   *

Here, certainly Cicero in his old age allowed himself to be carried away by the words of a youth and was utterly taken in by him. He helped Caesar in the canvassing and procured for him the goodwill of the senate. For this he was blamed by his friends at the time, and soon afterwards he too realized that he had ruined himself and betrayed the liberty of his country. Once the young man had established himself and secured the consulship, he paid no further attention to Cicero. Instead he made friends with Antony and Lepidus, joined forces with them, and divided the government with them as though it were a piece of property. A list was drawn up of the names of more than 200 men who were to be put to death. But what caused most trouble at their discussions was the question of including Cicero's name in this list. Antony refused to come to terms unless Cicero was marked down first for death; Lepidus sided with Antony, and Caesar held out against them both. They met secretly by themselves near the city of Bononia, and these meetings lasted for three days. They came together at a place surrounded by a river and at some distance from their camps. It is said that for the first two days Caesar kept up the struggle to save Cicero, but gave in on the third day and abandoned him. The terms of their mutual concessions were as follows: Caesar was to desert Cicero, Lepidus, his brother Paulus, and Antony, Lucius Caesar, who was his uncle on his mother's side. So all considerations of humanity were swept aside by their rage and fury; or was this, rather, a demonstration that no wild beast is more savage than man when his passions are armed with power?

While this was going on, Cicero was at his country estate in Tusculum. He had his brother there with him. When they heard of the proscriptions they decided to move on to Astura, a place belonging to Cicero on the coast, and from there to sail to Brutus in Macedonia. (There was already news of his being there in some strength.) So they were carried on their way in litters. They were quite overwhelmed with grief and on the journey would often stop and, with the litters placed side by side, would condole with each other. Quintus was the more disheartened of the two. He began to think of his destitute condition. He had taken nothing, he said, from the home; and Cicero too had insufficient money for the journey; it was better, therefore, he said, for Cicero to carry on with his flight, and he would hurry after him once he had got from home what he needed. This was the course they decided upon, and so, after they had embraced each other, they parted with many tears.

Only a few days later Quintus was betrayed by his servants to those who were looking for him and was put to death, together with his son. Cicero, however, was carried to Astura, where he found a boat and immediately went on board. He sailed down the coast as far as Circaeum with a following wind. From here the pilots wanted to sail on at once, but Cicero, either because he feared the sea or because he had not yet entirely lost his faith in Caesar, went ashore and travelled on foot about twelve miles in the direction of Rome. Again he lost his resolution and changed his mind, going back to the sea at Astura. Here he passed a night with his mind full of terrible thoughts and desperate plans. He actually decided to go secretly to Caesar's home and to kill himself there on the hearthstone, so as to bring a curse from Heaven upon him; but fear, the fear of torture, turned him from this course also. So, after turning over in his mind all sorts of confused schemes and contradictory projects, he put himself in the hands of his servants to be taken by sea to Caieta. Here he had an estate which was a most agreeable place to go to in the summer, when the Etesian winds are so pleasant.

In this place also there is a temple of Apollo, a little above the sea, and from the temple a flight of crows rose up into the air with a great noise and came flying towards Cicero's ship as it was being rowed to land. They perched on either side of the yard, some croaking and some pecking at the ends of the ropes, and everyone regarded this as a bad omen. Cicero, however, disembarked, went to his villa, and lay down to rest. Then, while most of the crows perched round the window, making a tremendous noise with their cawing, one of them flew down on to the bed where Cicero was lying with his head all covered up, and little by little began to drag away with its bill the garment from his face. When the servants saw this they reproached themselves for standing by as spectators waiting for their master to be murdered, and doing nothing to defend him, while these wild brute creatures were helping him and caring for him in his underserved ill fortune. So, partly by entreaty and partly by force, they took him up and carried him in his litter towards the sea.

Meanwhile, however, the murderers had arrived. These were the centurion Herennius and Popillius, an officer in the army, who had in the past been defended by Cicero when he was prosecuted for having murdered his father. They had their helpers with them. They found the doors shut and broke them down; but Cicero was not to be seen and the people in the house said that they did not know where he was. Then, we are told, a young man who had been educated by Cicero in literature and philosophy, an ex-slave of Cicero's brother Quintus, Philologus by name, told the officer that the litter was being carried down to the sea by a path that was under the cover of the trees. The officer took a few men with him and hurried round to the place where the path came out of the woods, and Herennius went running down the path. Cicero heard him coming and ordered his servants to set the litter down where they were. He himself, in that characteristic posture of his, with his chin resting on his left hand, looked steadfastly at his murderers. He was all covered in dust; his hair was long and disordered, and his face was pinched and wasted with his anxieties—so that most of those who stood by covered their faces while Herennius was killing him. His throat was cut as he stretched his neck out from the litter. He was in his sixty-fourth year. By Antony's orders Herennius cut off his head and his hands—the hands with which he had written the Philippics.[3]

When these severed extremities of Cicero's person were brought to Rome Antony happened to be organizing an election. Hearing the news and seeing the sight, he cried out: 'Now let there be an end of our

---

[3]It was Cicero himself who called these speeches against Antony 'the Philippics'; and they have retained the title to the present day.

proscriptions.' Then he ordered the head and the hands to be fastened up over the ships' rams on the public platform in the forum. It was a sight to make the Romans shudder. They seemed to see there, not so much the face of Cicero, as the image of the soul of Antony.

✿   ✿   ✿

A long time afterwards, so I have been told, Caesar was visiting the son of one of his daughters. The boy had a book of Cicero's in his hands and, terrified of his grandfather, tried to hide it under his cloak. Caesar noticed this and, after taking the book from him, stood there and read a great part of it. He then handed it back to the young man with the words: 'A learned man, my child, a learned man and a lover of his country.'

And directly after the final defeat of Antony, when Caesar was consul himself, he chose Cicero's son to be his colleague. It was thus in his counsulship that the senate took down all the statues of Antony, cancelled all the other honours that had been given to him, and decreed that in the future no member of the family should bear the name of Marcus. In this way Heaven entrusted to the family of Cicero the final acts in the punishment of Antony.

(Decimus Junius Juvenalis, c. A.D. 60-c. 140)

EXCEPT FOR THE PERSISTENT LEGEND THAT HE WAS EXILED, WHICH MAY account for some of his extreme bitterness, nothing is known of Juvenal's life. Whatever his private experience, his sixteen *Satires* reveal an extravagant hatred of many aspects of Roman life. Juvenal professes to aim his malicious attacks on vice, folly, and corruption, not at his contemporaries, but at their ancestors, such as Sejanus and Pompey. It is clear, however, that he intends to excoriate not the dead but the living. No poet has done a more savagely effective job of deflating the pretentions of his generation. At its best, his writing bristles with vitriolic wit, grim humor, and graphic, almost obscene realism.

The *Tenth Satire*, which Samuel Johnson retitled the "Vanity of Human Wishes," is a brilliantly pessimistic condemnation of ambition in virtually every field of endeavor. Its ironic theme is that the gods curse men by granting them their strongest desires. Surveying the gamut of human aspiration: wealth, eloquence, military success, beauty, and political glory, Juvenal cites historical examples to show that every man or woman who achieved his goal suffered cruelly for his success. In answer to his final rhetorical question, what then is worth possessing, he delivers the famous *mens sana in corpore sano* (a sound mind in a sound body). Of the infinite variety of human wishes, only "health of body and content of mind" are safely enjoyed.

SATIRE X

ARGUMENT OF THE TENTH SATYR[1]

The Poet's Design in this Divine Satyr, is to represent the various Wishes and Desires of Mankind; and to set out the Folly of 'em. He runs through all the several Heads of Riches, Honours, Eloquence, Fame for Martial Achievements, Long-Life, and Beauty; and gives Instances in Each, how frequently they have prov'd the Ruin of Those that Own'd them. He concludes therefore, that since we generally chuse so ill for our selves; we shou'd do better to leave it to the Gods, to make the choice for us. All we can safely ask of Heaven, lies within a very small Compass. 'Tis

---

[1]Dryden's seventeenth century spelling is retained throughout.

Translated by John Dryden. From *The Poems of John Dryden*, Vol. II, edited by James Kinsley (1958). Reprinted by permission of the Clarendon Press, Oxford.

but Health of Body and Mind—*And if we have these, 'tis not much matter, what we want besides: For we have already enough to make us Happy.*

The Tenth Satyr

Look round the Habitable World, how few
Know their own Good; or knowing it, pursue.
How void of Reason are our Hopes and Fears!
What in the Conduct of our Life appears
So well design'd, so luckily begun,
But, when we have our wish, we wish undone?
    Whole Houses, of their whole Desires possest,
Are often Ruin'd, at their own Request.
In Wars, and Peace, things hurtful we require,
When made Obnoxious to our own Desire.
    With Laurels some have fatally been Crown'd.
Some who the depths of Eloquence have found,
In that unnavigable Stream were Drown'd.
The Brawny Fool, who did his Vigour boast;
In that Presumeing Confidence was lost:
But more have been by Avarice opprest,
And Heaps of Money crouded in the Chest:
Unwieldly Sums of Wealth, which higher mount
Than Files of Marshall'd Figures can account.
To which the Stores of *Cræsus*, in the Scale,
Wou'd look like little Dolphins, when they sail
In the vast Shadow of the *British* Whale.
    For this, in *Nero's* Arbitrary time,
When Virtue was a Guilt, and Wealth a Crime,
A Troop of Cut-Throat Guards were sent, to seize
The Rich Mens Goods, and gut their Palaces:
The Mob, Commission'd by the Government,
Are seldom to an Empty Garret, sent.
The Fearful Passenger, who Travels late,
Charg'd with the Carriage of a Paltry Plate,
Shakes at the Moonshine shadow of a Rush;
And sees a Red-Coat rise from every Bush:
The Beggar Sings, ev'n when he sees the place
Beset with Thieves, and never mends his pace.
    Of all the Vows, the first and chief Request
Of each, is to be Richer than the rest:
And yet no doubts the Poor Man's Draught controul;
He dreads no Poison in his homely Bowl.

Then fear the deadly Drug, when Gems Divine
Enchase the Cup, and sparkle in the Wine.
  Will you not now, the pair of Sages praise,
Who the same End pursu'd, by several Ways?
One pity'd, one contemn'd the Woful Times:
One laugh'd at Follies, one lamented Crimes:
Laughter is easie; but the wonder lies
What stores of Brine supply'd the Weepers Eyes.
Democritus, cou'd feed his Spleen, and shake
His sides and shoulders till he felt 'em ake;
Tho in his Country Town, no Lictors were;
Nor Rods nor Ax nor Tribune did appear:
Nor all the Foppish Gravity of show
Which cunning Magistrates on Crowds bestow:
  What had he done, had he beheld, on high
Our *Prætor* seated, in Mock Majesty;
His Charriot rowling o're the Dusty place
While, with dumb Pride, and a set formal Face,
He moves, in the dull Ceremonial track,
With *Jove*'s Embroyder'd Coat upon his back:
A Sute of Hangings had not more opprest
His Shoulders, than that long, Laborious Vest.
A heavey Gugaw, (call'd a Crown,) that spred
About his Temples, drown'd his narrow Head:
And wou'd have crush'd it, with the Massy **Freight**,
But that a sweating Slave sustain'd the weight:
A Slave in the same Chariot seem to ride,
To mortifie the mighty Madman's Pride.
Add now th' Imperial Eagle, rais'd on high,
With Golden Beak (the Mark of Majesty)
Trumpets before, and on the Left and Right,
A Cavalcade of Nobles, all in White:
In their own Natures false; and flatt'ring Tribes
But made his Friends, by Places and by Bribes.
  In his own Age *Democritus* cou'd find
Sufficient cause to laugh at Humane kind:
Learn from so great a Wit; a Land of Bogs
With Ditches fenc'd, a Heav'n Fat with Fogs,
May form a Spirit fit to sway the State;
And make the Neighb'ring Monarchs fear their Fate.
  He laughs at all the Vulgar Cares and Fears;
At their vain Triumphs, and their vainer Tears:
An equal Temper in his Mind he found,
When Fortune flatter'd him, and when she frown'd.
'Tis plain from hence that what our Vows request,
Are hurtful things, or Useless at the best.

Some ask for Envy'd Pow'r; which publick Hate
Pursues, and hurries headlong to their Fate:
Down go the Titles; and the Statue Crown'd,
Is by base Hands in the next River Drown'd.
The Guiltless Horses, and the Chariot Wheel
The same Effects of Vulgar Fury feel:
The Smith prepares his Hammer for the Stroke,
While the Lung'd Bellows hissing Fire provoke;
Sejanus[2] almost first of *Roman* Names,
The great *Sejanus* crackles in the Flames:
Form'd in the Forge, the Pliant Brass is laid
On Anvils; and of Head and Limbs are made,
Pans, Cans, and Pispots, a whole Kitchin Trade.
    Adorn your Doors with Laurels; and a Bull
Milk white and large, lead to the Capitol;
Sejanus with a Rope, is drag'd along;
The Sport and Laughter of the giddy Throng!
Good Lord, they Cry, what Ethiop Lips he has,
How foul a Snout, and what a hanging Face:
By Heav'n I never cou'd endure his sight;
But say, how came his Monstrous Crimes to Light?
What is the Charge, and who the Evidence
(The Saviour of the Nation and the Prince?)
Nothing of this; but our Old *Cæsar* sent
A Noisie Letter to his Parliament:
Nay Sirs, if *Cæsar* writ, I ask no more:
He's Guilty; and the Question's out of Door.
How goes the Mob, (for that's a Mighty thing.)
When the King's Trump, the Mob are for the King:
They follow Fortune, and the Common Cry
Is still against the Rogue Condemn'd to Dye.
    But the same very Mob; that Rascal crowd,
Had cry'd *Sejanus*, with a Shout as loud;
Had his Designs, (by Fortune's favour Blest)
Succeeded, and the Prince's Age opprest.
But long, long since, the Times have chang'd their **Face**,
The People grown Degenerate and base:
Not suffer'd now the Freedom of their choice,
To make their Magistrates, and sell their Voice.
    Our Wise Fore-Fathers, Great by Sea and Land,
Had once the Pow'r, and absolute Command;

---

[2]*Sejanus*. Lucius Aelius Sejanus won the confidence of Tiberius Caesar and became virtual master of Rome when the Emperor retired to Capri. But Tiberius grew suspicious of his favorite and denounced Sejanus to the Senate, which condemned him to death. After his execution, Sejanus' body was torn in pieces by the Roman mob. Juvenal cites Sejanus as a model of the ambitious usurper whose failure to seize the imperial throne was a mere accident of Fortune. For Juvenal's other historical allusions, consult the appropriate glossary entries.

All Offices of Trust, themselves dispos'd;
Rais'd whom they pleas'd, and whom they pleas'd, Depos'd.
But we who give our Native Rights away,
And our Inslav'd Posterity betray,
Are now reduc'd to beg an Alms, and go
On Holidays to see a Puppet show.
   There was a Damn'd Design, crys one, no doubt;
For Warrants are already Issued out:
I met *Brutidius* in a Mortal fright:
He's dipt for certain, and plays least in sight:
I fear the Rage of our offended Prince,
Who thinks the Senate slack in his defence!
Come let us haste, our Loyal Zeal to show,
And spurn the Wretched Corps of *Cæsar*'s Foe:
But let our Slaves be present there, lest they
Accuse their Masters, and for Gain betray.
   Such were the Whispers of those jealous Times,
About *Sejanus* Punishment, and Crimes.
   Now tell me truly, wou'dst thou change thy Fate
To be, like him, first Minister of State?
To have thy Levees Crowded with resort,
Of a depending, gaping, servile Court:
Dispose all Honours, of the Sword and Gown,
Grace with a Nod, and Ruin with a Frown;
To hold thy Prince in Pupill-Age and sway,
That Monarch, whom the Master'd World obey?
While he, intent on secret Lusts alone,
Lives to himself, abandoning the Throne;
Coopt in a narrow Isle, observing Dreams
With flatt'ring Wisards, and erecting Schemes!
   I well believe, thou wou'dst be Great as he;
For every Man's a Fool to that Degree:
All wish the dire Prerogative to kill;
Ev'n they wou'd have the Pow'r, who want the Will:
But wou'dst thou have thy Wishes understood,
To take the Bad together with the Good?
Wou'dst thou not rather choose a small Renown,
To be the May'r of some poor Paltry Town,
Bigly to Look, and Barb'rously to speak;
To pound false Weights, and scanty Measures break?
Then, grant we that *Sejanus* went astray,
In ev'ry Wish, and knew not how to pray:
For he who grasp'd the World's exhausted Store
Yet never had enough, but wish'd for more,
Rais'd a Top-heavy Tow'r, of monst'rous height,
Which Mould'ring, crush'd him underneath the Weight.
   What did the mighty *Pompey*'s Fall beget?
And ruin'd him, who Greater than the Great,

The stubborn Pride of *Roman* Nobles broke;
And bent their Haughty Necks beneath his Yoke?
What else, but his immoderate Lust of Pow'r,
Pray'rs made, and granted in a Luckless Hour:
For few Usurpers to the Shades descend
By a dry Death, or with a quiet End.

           ✿   ✿   ✿

    So much the Thirst of Honour Fires the Blood;
So many wou'd be Great, so few be Good.
For who wou'd Virtue for her self regard,
Or Wed, without the Portion of Reward?
Yet this Mad Chace of Fame, by few pursu'd,
Has drawn Destruction on the Multitude:
This Avarice of Praise in Times to come,
Those long Inscriptions, crowded on the Tomb,
Shou'd some Wild Fig-Tree take her Native bent,
And heave below the gaudy Monument,
Wou'd crack the Marble Titles, and disperse
The Characters of all the lying Verse.
For Sepulchres themselves must crumbling fall
In times Abyss, the common Grave of all.
    Great *Hannibal* within the Ballance lay;
And tell how many Pounds his Ashes weigh;
Whom *Affrick* was not able to contain,
Whose length runs Level with th' Atlantick main,
And wearies fruitful *Nilus,* to convey
His Sun-beat Waters by so long a way;
While *Ethiopia*'s double Clime divides,
And Elephants in other Mountains hides.
Spain first he won, the *Pyrenæans* past,
And steepy *Alps,* the Mounds that Nature cast:
And with Corroding Juices, as he went,
A passage through the living Rocks he rent.
Then, like a Torrent, rowling from on high,
He pours his head-long Rage on *Italy;*
In three Victorious Battels overrun;
Yet still uneasie, Cries there's nothing done:
Till, level with the Ground, their Gates are laid;
And *Punick*[3] Flags, on *Roman* Tow'rs displaid.
    Ask what a Face belong'd to this high Fame;
His Picture scarcely wou'd deserve a Frame:
A Sign-Post Dawber wou'd disdain to paint

---

[3]*Punick* (Punic)—*i.e.,* Carthaginian. See Livy's *The War with Hannibal.*

The one Ey'd Heroe on his Elephant.
Now what's his End, O Charming Glory, say
What rare fifth Act, to Crown this huffing Play?
In one deciding Battel overcome,
He flies, is banisht from his Native home:
Begs refuge in a Foreign Court, and there
Attends his mean Petition to prefer:
Repuls'd by surly Grooms, who wait before
The sleeping Tyrant's interdicted Door.
  What wondrous sort of Death, has Heav'n design'd
Distinguish'd from the Herd of Humane Kind,
For so untam'd, so turbulent a Mind!
Nor Swords at hand, nor hissing Darts afar,
Are doom'd t' Avenge the tedious bloody War,
But Poyson, drawn through a Rings hollow plate,
Must finish him; a sucking Infant's Fate.
Go, climb the rugged *Alps,* Ambitious Fool,
To please the Boys, and be a Theme at School.
  How Fortunate an End had *Priam* made,
Among his Ancestors a mighty shade,
While *Troy* yet stood: When *Hector* with the Race
Of Royal Bastards might his Funeral Grace:
Amidst the Tears of *Trojan* Dames inurn'd,
And by his Loyal Daughters, truly mourn'd.
Had Heaven so Blest him, he had Dy'd before
The fatal Fleet to *Sparta Paris* bore.
But mark what Age produc'd; he liv'd to see
His Town in Flames, his falling Monarchy:
In fine, the feeble Syre, reduc'd by Fate,
To change his Scepter for a Sword, too late,
His last Effort before *Jove*'s Altar tries;
A Souldier half, and half a Sacrifice:
Falls like an Oxe, that waits the coming blow;
Old and unprofitable to the Plough.

❊   ❊   ❊

  What then remains? Are we depriv'd of Will?
Must we not Wish, for fear of wishing Ill?
Receive my Counsel, and securely move;
Intrust thy Fortune to the Pow'rs above.
Leave them to manage for thee, and to grant
What their unerring Wisdom sees thee want:
In Goodness as in Greatness they excel;
Ah that we lov'd our selves but half so well!
We, blindly by our headstrong Passions led,
Are hot for Action, and desire to Wed;

Then wish for Heirs: But to the Gods alone
Our future Offspring, and our Wives are known;
Th' audacious Strumpet, and ungracious Son.
   Yet, not to rob the Priests of pious Gain,
That Altars be not wholly built in vain;
Forgive the Gods the rest, and stand confin'd
To Health of Body, and Content of Mind:
A Soul, that can securely Death defie,
And count it Nature's Priviledge, to Dye;
Serene and Manly, harden'd to sustain
The load of Life, and Exercis'd in Pain;
Guiltless of Hate, and Proof against Desire;
That all things weighs, and nothing can admire:
That dares prefer the Toils of *Hercules*
To Dalliance, Banquets, and Ignoble ease.
   The Path to Peace is Virtue: What I show,
Thy Self may freely, on Thy Self bestow:
Fortune was never Worshipp'd by the Wise;
But, set aloft by Fools, Usurps the Skies.

LUCIUS APULEIUS Preface

(c. A.D. 125-?)

APULEIUS, ONE OF THE MOST CURIOUS FIGURES IN ROMAN LITERATURE, was an African who learned Latin as a foreign tongue. Born of a prosperous family at Madaura, a town on the border of Numidia and Gaetulia, about the end of the first quarter of the second century A.D., he set out as a young man for Alexandria, the center of Hellenistic learning. His interest there focused on religion, philosophy, and magic; but he despised the Christianity which was spreading all around him. He held, instead, a form of neo-Platonism, which included an elaborate system of angels and demons; and he was attached, also, to the Isis-Mithras cult then growing popular in the Roman Empire. Leaving Alexandria, he devoted his life to giving philosophical lectures in various African towns. The date of his death is unknown.

Among his many works only one was ever popular, the famous *Golden Ass* (or *Metamorphoses*). Unlike most of his other writings, the *Golden Ass* focuses on subjects other than the author's philosophical teachings. The occasional philosophical passages are far less important than the numerous references to magic, and the story of the transformation of the hero into an ass which is the main thread of the plot. This myth fascinated even Apuleius' Christian contemporaries; several centuries later St. Augustine quoted it. The plot, however, was not original, and was taken from an extant Greek work of uncertain authorship. But Apuleius greatly improved the rather tedious first version, enlarging the threadbare plot with jests and with stories of love and sorcery. His most significant alteration is the insertion, in the middle of the work, of the long and beautiful allegory of Cupid and Psyche.

Apuleius, we must remember, uses Latin as a foreign language; and although he mastered it, he worked out an extraordinary style, with exuberant vigor and strange syntactical patterns startling to readers accustomed to Latin regularity and measured control. And he tells his tales with a rollicking spirit reminiscent of Boccaccio's *Decamaron* and certain of Chaucer's tales.

THE GOLDEN ASS

CUPID AND PSYCHE

[The youngest daughter of a legendary king, Psyche was so dazzlingly beautiful that she aroused the jealousy of Venus. But when Venus sent

---

The preface and translation which follow are by Marc Bertonasco and are published here for the first time.

her son Cupid to make Psyche fall in love with some hideous lout, Cupid himself became her lover. Refusing to disclose his identity, Cupid visited Psyche only in the dark and commanded her never to look upon his face. Psyche's envious sisters convinced her that the unknown lover was a monster and would murder her if she did not kill him first. Frightened and deceived, Psyche then takes a razor and lamp and prepares to carry out her sisters' evil instructions.]

NIGHT ARRIVED, AND WITH IT HER HUSBAND. BUT BEFORE REACHING THE climax of Love's battle, he fell into a deep slumber. Then Psyche (though rather weak both in body and spirit) soon grew brave enough to fetch the lamp and seize the razor; and this courage and aggressiveness transformed her into a male. After the lamp illumined the darkest corners of the bed, Psyche saw the tenderest and sweetest of all animals, the lovely Cupid, a voluptuous sight which made the lamp increase its light in excited joy, and the razor turn its edge. But Psyche, gazing upon this glorious body, grew confused and terrified; pale and trembling, she fell to her knees, hoping to hide the razor, even, if need be, in her own heart. And so she would have done, had not the sharp tool, horrified by the wicked scheme, slipped from those rash hands.

Weak and faint, she turned her gaze toward the heavenly face, and its beauty revived her sagging spirits. She saw his golden hair, damp with ambrosia, pouring forth a sweet perfume; his neck, whiter than milk; his rosy cheeks, over which tumbled his hair, beautifully strewn, and its brightness darkened the lantern's light. And she saw the downy feathers of the flying God covering his shoulders with gleaming shimmer; and though his wings were folded, still the tender down along the edge quivered, disturbingly, yet enticingly. And she saw too the other limbs of that gorgeous body; so soft, so voluptuous, that Venus could not regret having borne such a child. At the foot of the bed lay his bow, quiver, and arrows, the weapons of this powerful God: marvelling at the weapons of her husband, Psyche, consumed with curiosity, removed one of the arrows from its quiver, and, testing its sharpness on her finger, pricked herself. As the little drops of blood flowed, she fell in love with Love. Then, as the love of Cupid seethed more and more furiously within her, she threw herself upon him impulsively, covered him with ravenous kisses, fearing that he might awaken.

But, alas, as she lay enveloped in this rapture, her spirit languishing, suddenly the lamp, either envious, or eager to touch that irresistible body, let fall a drop of scalding oil upon the right shoulder of the god. Oh lamp of rashness! Oh lowly tool of love! How did you dare burn the God of all fire, when surely some lover invented you, to pass his nights in greater pleasure? Awakened by the burn, and recognizing immediately the breach of faith, the broken promise, Cupid flew away speechless from the kisses of his miserable wife. But as he rose, Psyche happened to catch him by the right thigh with both hands, and held on tightly as he flew through the clouds; until, at last overcome by exhaustion, she released her grip and tumbled onto the ground. Cupid did not abandon her, but followed her down: landing on top of a cypress-tree, he angrily berated her: "Oh silly Psyche, remind yourself how I descended from Heaven to love you, disobeying even the commandment of my mother, who had marked you for marriage to a man of lowly and miserable position. To have acted so nobly was foolish, I know; and to hold you as my spouse I even wounded my body with my own weapon. And for all this do you regard me as a beast that you have set about to cut off my head with a razor, this head with its eyes that have loved you so dearly? Have I not always warned you of this danger? Did I not gently urge you to beware? Ah but those accursed counsellors of yours shall be properly rewarded for their efforts! As for you, you will be sufficiently punished by my absence." Having spoken, he soared into the heights.

Then Psyche fell flat on the ground, and for as long as she could see her husband's flying form, gazed up at him, weeping and lamenting pitifully. As he faded out of sight, she hurled herself into the first running river, to drown her anguish. But the gentle stream would not permit her to drown: fearing the wrath of Cupid, who had so often stirred up and boiled its waters, the river took pity on Psyche and cast her up on its banks. Here Pan, the country god, sat teaching the Goddess Echo of the mountains to tune her songs and pipes, as young and tender goats fed upon the grass of the river-bank. As soon as the goat-footed God saw the weeping Psyche, he understood (I know not how) her grief, called her gently beside him, and tried to soothe her: "Oh fair maiden, although I am a crude shepherd, my many years have made me expert in many things: conjecture (which wise men call *divination*) tells me that you are in love. The signs are many—your hesitant, trembling steps; your palor and sobbing sighs; your watery eyes. Ah, then listen to me, and do not weep; but instead worship, adore the great God Cupid and win back that sensitive, voluptuous youth through promise of loving, dedicated service."

[After wandering the earth in search of Cupid and undergoing many hardships and adventures, Psyche is rescued by Jupiter and received into the heavenly court of the gods.]

Then Jupiter began to speak: "Oh ye Gods, registered in the book of the Muses, all of you know this young man Cupid; all of you know that I have nourished him with my own hands, and have thought best to restrain and bridle the raging flames of his adolescence. Suffice it to say that he is everywhere notorious for his adulterous life and numerous shameful vices; for this reason we should remove all opportunity and tie up his boyish wildness with the chains of marriage. He has chosen a maiden who loves him; and he has taken her virginity. So now let him have her, possess her forever, and take his pleasure in her embrace." Turning then to Venus, he urged: "And you, my daughter, do not fear dishonor for your son because of a mortal marriage; for I will make this marriage fully honorable, and legitimate by civil law." Impetuously, then, he commanded Mercury to lift Psyche up into the heavenly palace. Taking the cup of immortality, he commanded: "Take, Psyche, and drink to become immortal, that Cupid may never leave you but live as your everlasting husband."

And then the sumptuous marriage banquet was spread out. Cupid reclined in the highest seat with his beloved bride between his arms; so Juno with Jupiter, and the other gods in order, while Ganymede, the country boy, Jupiter's own page, filled the cup of his master, and Bacchus served the rest; nectar their drink, the wine of immortals. Vulcan prepared the supper, the Hours adorned the palace with roses and purple blossoms, while the Graces sprinkled balm; and the Muses sang with ravishing harmonies as Apollo turned to his harp and Venus danced enchantingly to the music, and Satyr and Pan played on their pipes.

So Psyche was married to Cupid; after due time she gave birth to a daughter, and we call her PLEASURE.

THE NEW TESTAMENT Preface

THE TWENTY-SEVEN BOOKS OF THE NEW TESTAMENT ARE THOSE RECORDS OF Jesus and his disciples which the early Christian Church considered inspired by God. Accepted as a continuation of the divine revelation contained in the Old Testament, the Christian Scriptures are sometimes divided into five categories: (1) the Gospels (literally "good news") of Matthew, Mark, Luke and John, which recount the life and ministry of Jesus; (2) the book of Acts, which describes the organization and missionary activity of Christ's followers immediately after His Resurrection; (3) the letters of St. Paul to the various congregations he had founded or visited, such as his epistles to the Romans, Corinthians, and Thessalonians; (4) the briefer letters of Sts. Peter, James, Jude and other disciples; (5) the Revelation, which is purportedly St. John's vision of the second coming of Christ and the end of the world.

All or nearly all of the New Testament was completed by the end of the first century A.D. Directed at the largest possible audience, it is composed exclusively in the *koine* or common Greek, which was the international language of the Roman Empire. Greek had been spoken in Palestine since the time of Alexander's conquests in the late fourth century B.C. and it had long been the second tongue of educated Romans. Christ himself probably spoke Aramaic, a late form of Hebrew. Consequently none of His words in the exact form he phrased them have survived. It is unlikely, however, that His essential attitudes or moral teachings have been distorted in Greek translation.

Of the four canonical accounts of Christ's life, that of Luke (an early convert but not one of the twelve Apostles) is the most carefully researched and correctly written. By placing events in Jesus' life within the context of secular history, Luke, who seems to have admired Thucydides, is extremely useful in dating at least some of Jesus' actions. Luke tells us, for example, that Jesus' cousin John baptized Him during the "fifteenth year of Tiberius Caesar." Since Tiberius succeeded the Emperor Augustus in A.D. 14, the fifteenth year of his reign would place the beginning of Jesus' ministery about A.D. 29. At that time, Luke states, Jesus "was about thirty years old." Concerning the birth and boyhood of Jesus, Luke includes several facts not mentioned in the other gospels. He alone narrates the visit of the shepherds to the stable where Jesus was born and he is the only New Testament writer to include any reference to Jesus between the time of His birth and His baptism: the famous visit to the Temple in Jerusalem, where the twelve-year-old Jesus amazed the Jewish elders by the insight of His questions.

Matthew, who was a tax collector for Rome before he became one of Christ's original twelve followers, apparently wrote his Gospel to prove that Jesus was the Messiah foretold in the Old Testament. His narrative is full of quotations from the Mosaic Law and the prophets which he applies to events in Jesus' ministry. Almost every detail about Christ's trial, execution, and resurrection Matthew sees as fulfillment of ancient prophecies. He also records Jesus' most famous public speech, the "Sermon on the Mount," in which Jesus outlines His message of love, meekness, and forbearance. This collection contains the "Beatitudes," the injunction to love one's enemies and return good for evil, and the command to forsake worldly ambition and seek first the Kingdom of God. No more lofty moral teachings have ever been expressed.

A major reason for the swift spread of Christianity after Jesus' death was the energy and dedication of St. Paul. Originally a Pharisee named Saul of Tarsus who persecuted the new religion, which he regarded as blasphemous to the Hebrew faith as received from Moses, Saul was converted about A.D. 35 by a vision in which he saw the resurrected Christ. After recovering from this momentous experience, he changed his name from Saul to Paul and became the most zealous defender and preacher of the faith in Christian history. He travelled extensively throughout the Roman Empire, establishing new churches, making converts, and trying desperately to keep the rapidly-expanding followers of Christ unified in doctrine, faith, and good works. Everywhere suffering hardship and persecution—except notably in Athens where he was politely invited to explain his beliefs—Paul was finally martyred in Rome about A.D. 68.

Paul's influence upon Christianity is so enormous as to be incalculable. At the first church council, held in Jerusalem before its destruction by the Romans, Paul boldly opposed St. Peter's conservative position that in order to be accepted as Christians all converts must submit to circumcision and keep the unwieldly legalism of the Jewish ceremonial law. By convincing Church leaders that all men, regardless of race or former creed, should be accepted into the Church as equals, Paul transformed Christianity from a Jewish sect into a universal faith. Although he did not produce a systematic theology as St. Augustine and St. Thomas Aquinas were later to do, Paul contributed more toward the formulation of Christian doctrine than any other man. It has been argued, in fact, that there is more Paul than Christ in Christianity. He was the first to introduce the doctrine of original sin—that all men are born into a just condemnation to eternal death because they are all descendants of the first sinner, Adam—and the first to expand the concept of Christ as a "second Adam" whose sacrificial execution redeemed life for the otherwise damned human race. The Pauline view of sin and redemption is rather mechanical, but it provides the basis for the orthodox Christian interpretation of history.

A multi-faceted personality which combined fanaticism with tenderness and exultation, Paul wrote some of the most inspiring passages in the New Testament, to which he was the major contributor. The thirteenth chapter of his letter to the Corinthians is justly celebrated for its soaring poetry in praise of unselfish love. His hymn is not dedicated to divine love, but to that practiced among human beings. In the fifteenth chapter of the same epistle Paul reveals a "sacred secret" of God's love: the resurrection to everlasting life for those who please Him. In this almost mystical vision of man transcending death, "the last enemy," Paul expresses the universal appeal that was to ensure Christianity's triumph over the religions of the ancient world. The promise of eternal joy beyond that offered in the mystery cults of Isis, Demeter, and Dionysus, created a new hope that the old gods could not satisfy. Christianity filled the emotional need which its new teachings helped to create.

THE GOSPEL OF LUKE

[THE BIRTH AND CHILDHOOD OF JESUS]

CHAPTER 2

AND IT CAME TO PASS IN THOSE DAYS, that there went out a decree from Cæsar Augustus,[1] that all the world should be taxed.

2 (*And* this taxing was first made when Çy-rē'ni-us was governor of Syria.)

3 And all went to be taxed, every one into his own city.

4 And Joseph also went up from Galilee, out of the city of Nazareth, into Judea, unto the city of David,[2] which is called Bethlehem, (because he was of the house and lineage of David,)

5 To be taxed with Mary his espoused wife, being great with child.

6 And so it was, that, while they were there, the days were accomplished that she should be delivered.

7 And she brought forth her firstborn son, and wrapped him in swaddling clothes, and laid him in a manger; because there was no room for them in the inn.

8 And there were in the same country shepherds abiding in the field, keeping watch over their flock by night.

9 And, lo, the angel of the Lord came upon them, and the glory of the Lord shone round about them; and they were sore afraid.

10 And the angel said unto them, Fear not: for, behold, I bring you good tidings of great joy, which shall be to all people.

11 For unto you is born this day in the city of David a Saviour, which is Christ the Lord.

12 And this *shall* be a sign unto you; Ye shall find the babe wrapped in swaddling clothes, lying in a manger.

13 And suddenly there was with the angel a multitude of the heavenly host praising God, and saying,

14 Glory to God in the highest, and on earth peace, good will toward men.

[1]*Augustus*—the first emperor of Rome, patron of Virgil and Horace.
[2]*City of David*—according to the Old Testament prophets, the Messiah or Savior of the Jews was to be a descendant of King David.

From the *King James,* or *Authorized Version* of the Bible, translated 1611.

15 And it came to pass, as the angels were gone away from them into heaven, the shepherds said one to another, Let us now go even unto Bethlehem, and see this thing which is come to pass, which the Lord hath made known unto us.

16 And they came with haste, and found Mary and Joseph, and the babe lying in a manger.

17 And when they had seen *it*, they made known abroad the saying which was told them concerning this child.

18 And all they that heard *it* wondered at those things which were told them by the shepherds.

19 But Mary kept all these things, and pondered *them* in her heart.

20 And the shepherds returned, glorifying and praising God for all the things that they had heard and seen, as it was told unto them.

✿　　✿　　✿

40 And the child grew, and waxed strong in spirit, filled with wisdom; and the grace of God was upon him.

41 Now his parents went to Jerusalem every year at the feast of the passover.

42 And when he was twelve years old, they went up to Jerusalem after the custom of the feast.

43 And when they had fulfilled the days, as they returned, the child Jesus tarried behind in Jerusalem; and Joseph and his mother knew not *of it*.

44 But they, supposing him to have been in the company, went a day's journey; and they sought him among *their* kinsfolk and acquaintance.

45 And when they found him not, they turned back again to Jerusalem, seeking him.

46 And it came to pass, that after three days they found him in the temple, sitting in the midst of the doctors, both hearing them, and asking them questions.

47 And all that heard him were astonished at his understanding and answers.

48 And when they saw him, they were amazed: and his mother said unto him, Son, why hast thou thus dealt with us? behold, thy father and I have sought thee sorrowing.

49 And he said unto them, How is it that ye sought me? wist ye not that I must be about my Father's business?

50 And they understood not the saying which he spake unto them.

51 And he went down with them, and came to Nazareth, and was subject unto them: but his mother kept all these sayings in her heart.

52 And Jesus increased in wisdom and stature, and in favor with God and man.

✿　　✿　　✿

CHAPTER 4

AND JESUS BEING FULL OF THE HOLY Ghost returned from Jordan,[3] and was led by the Spirit into the wilderness.

---

[3] *Jordan*—Jesus had just been baptized by his cousin John the Baptist in the River Jordan.

2 Being forty days tempted of the devil. And in those days he did eat nothing: and when they were ended, he afterward hungered.

3 And the devil said unto him, If thou be the Son of God, command this stone that it be made bread.

4 And Jesus answered him, saying, It is written, That man shall not live by bread alone, but by every word of God.

5 And the devil, taking him up into a high mountain, showed unto him all the kingdoms of the world in a moment of time.

6 And the devil said unto him, All this power will I give thee, and the glory of them: for that is delivered unto me; and to whomsoever I will, I give it.

7 If thou therefore wilt worship me, all shall be thine.

8 And Jesus answered and said unto him, Get thee behind me, Satan: for it is written, Thou shalt worship the Lord thy God, and him only shalt thou serve.

9 And he brought him to Jerusalem, and set him on a pinnacle of the temple, and said unto him, If thou be the Son of God, cast thyself down from hence:

10 For it is written, He shall give his angels charge over thee, to keep thee:

11 And in *their* hands they shall bear thee up, lest at any time thou dash thy foot against a stone.

12 And Jesus answering said unto him, It is said, Thou shalt not tempt the Lord thy God.

13 And when the devil had ended all the temptation, he departed from him for a season.

14 And Jesus returned in the power of the Spirit into Galilee: and there went out a fame of him through all the region round about.

15 And he taught in their synagogues, being glorified of all.

16 And he came to Nazareth, where he had been brought up: and, as his custom was, he went into the synagogue on the sabbath day, and stood up for to read.

17 And there was delivered unto him the book of the prophet Ē-sa′ias.[4] And when he had opened the book, he found the place where it was written,

18 The Spirit of the Lord *is* upon me, because he hath anointed me to preach the gospel to the poor; he hath sent me to heal the brokenhearted, to preach deliverance to the captives, and recovering of sight to the blind, to set at liberty them that are bruised,

19 To preach the acceptable year of the Lord.

20 And he closed the book, and he gave *it* again to the minister, and sat down. And the eyes of all them that were in the synagogue were fastened on him.

21 And he began to say unto them, This day is this Scripture fulfilled in your ears.

22 And all bare him witness, and wondered at the gracious words which proceeded out of his mouth. And they said, Is not this Joseph's son?

* * *

---

[4]*Esaias*—Isaiah, the most famous of the Old Testament prophets. Jesus read aloud *Isaiah* 61:1-2, omitting the reference to divine vengeance.

THE GOSPEL OF MATTHEW

[THE SERMON ON THE MOUNT]

CHAPTER 5

AND SEEING THE MULTITUDES, HE went up into a mountain: and when he was set, his disciples came unto him:

2 And he opened his mouth, and taught them, saying,

3 Blessed *are* the poor in spirit: for theirs is the kingdom of heaven.

4 Blessed *are* they that mourn: for they shall be comforted.

5 Blessed *are* the meek: for they shall inherit the earth.

6 Blessed *are* they which do hunger and thirst after righteousness: for they shall be filled.

7 Blessed *are* the merciful: for they shall obtain mercy.

8 Blessed *are* the pure in heart: for they shall see God.

9 Blessed *are* the peacemakers: for they shall be called the children of God.

10 Blessed *are* they which are persecuted for righteousness' sake: for their is the kingdom of heaven.

11 Blessed are ye, when *men* shall revile you, and persecute *you,* and shall say all manner of evil against you falsely, for my sake.

12 Rejoice, and be exceedingly glad: for great *is* your reward in heaven: for so persecuted they the prophets which were before you.

13 Ye are the salt of the earth: but if the salt have lost his savor, wherewith shall it be salted? it is thenceforth good for nothing, but to be cast out, and to be trodden under foot of men.

14 Ye are the light of the world. A city that is set on a hill cannot be hid.

15 Neither do men light a candle, and put it under a bushel, but on a candlestick; and it giveth light unto all that are in the house.

16 Let your light so shine before men, that they may see your good works, and glorify your Father which is in heaven.

17 Think not that I am come to destroy the law, or the prophets: I am not come to destroy, but to fulfil.

18 For verily I say unto you, Till heaven and earth pass, one jot or one tittle shall in no wise pass from the law, till all be fulfilled.

19 Whosoever therefore shall break one of these least commandments, and shall teach men so, he shall be called the least in the kingdom of heaven: but whosoever shall do and teach *them,* the same shall be called great in the kingdom of heaven.

20 For I say unto you, That except your righteousness shall exceed *the righteousness* of the scribes and Phar'i-sees, ye shall in no case enter into the kingdom of heaven.

21 Ye have heard that it was said by them of old time, Thou shalt not kill; and whosoever shall kill shall be in danger of the judgment:

22 But I say unto you, That whosoever is angry with his brother without a cause shall be in danger of the judgment: and whosoever shall say to his brother, Rā'ca, shall

be in danger of the council: but whosoever shall say, Thou fool, shall be in danger of hell fire.

23 Therefore if thou bring thy gift to the altar, and there rememberest that thy brother hath aught against thee;

24 Leave there thy gift before the altar, and go thy way; first be reconciled to thy brother, and then come and offer thy gift.

25 Agree with thine adversary quickly, while thou art in the way with him; lest at any time the adversary deliver thee to the judge, and the judge deliver thee to the officer, and thou be cast into prison.

26 Verily I say unto thee. Thou shalt by no means come out thence, till thou hast paid the uttermost farthing.

27 Ye have heard that it was said by them of old time, Thou shalt not commit adultery:

28 But I say unto you, That whosoever looketh on a woman to lust after her hath committed adultery with her already in his heart.

29 And if thy right eye offend thee, pluck it out, and cast *it* from thee: for it is profitable for thee that one of thy members should perish, and not *that* thy whole body should be cast into hell.

30 And if thy right hand offend thee, cut it off, and cast *it* from thee: for it is profitable for thee that one of thy members should perish, and not *that* thy whole body should be cast into hell.

31 It hath been said, Whosoever shall put away his wife, let him give her a writing of divorcement:

32 But I say unto you, That whosoever shall put away his wife, saving for the cause of fornication, causeth her to commit adultery: and whosoever shall marry her that is divorced committeth adultery.

33 Again, ye have heard that it hath been said by them of old time, Thou shalt not forswear thyself, but shalt perform unto the Lord thine oaths:

34 But I say unto you, Swear not at all; neither by heaven; for it is God's throne:

35 Nor by the earth; for it is his footstool: neither by Jerusalem; for it is the city of the great King.

36 Neither shalt thou swear by thy head, because thou canst not make one hair white or black.

37 But let your communication be, Yea, yea; Nay, nay: for whatsoever is more than these cometh of evil.

38 Ye have heard that it hath been said, An eye for an eye, and a tooth for a tooth:

39 But I say unto you, That ye resist not evil: but whosoever shall smite thee on thy right cheek, turn to him the other also.

40 And if any man will sue thee at the law, and take away thy coat, let him have *thy* cloak also.

41 And whosoever shall compel thee to go a mile, go with him twain.

42 Give to him that asketh thee, and from him that would borrow of thee turn not thou away.

43 Ye have heard that it hath been said, Thou shalt love thy neighbor, and hate thine enemy.

44 But I say unto you, Love your enemies, bless them that curse you, do good to them that hate you, and pray for them which despitefully use you, and persecute you;

45 That ye may be the children of your Father which is in heaven: for he maketh his sun to rise on the evil and on the good, and sendeth rain on the just and on the unjust.

46 For if ye love them which love you, what reward have ye? do not even the publicans the same?

47 And if ye salute your brethren only, what do ye more *than others?* do not even the publicans so?

48 Be ye therefore perfect, even as your Father which is in heaven is perfect.

CHAPTER 6

TAKE HEED THAT YE DO NOT YOUR alms before men, to be seen of them: otherwise ye have no reward of your Father which is in heaven.

2 Therefore when thou doest *thine* alms, do not sound a trumpet before thee, as the hypocrites do in the synagogues and in the streets, that they may have glory of men. Verily I say unto you, They have their reward.

3 But when thou doest alms, let not thy left hand know what thy right hand doeth:

4 That thine alms may be in secret: and thy Father which seeth in secret himself shall reward thee openly.

5 And when thou prayest, thou shalt not be as the hypocrites *are:* for they love to pray standing in the synagogues and in the corners of the streets, that they may be seen of men. Verily I say unto you, They have their reward.

6 But thou, when thou prayest, enter into thy closet, and when thou hast shut thy door, pray to thy Father which is in secret; and thy Father which seeth in secret shall reward thee openly.

7 But when ye pray, use not vain repetitions, as the heathen *do:* for they think that they shall be heard for their much speaking.

8 Be not ye therefore like unto them: for your Father knoweth what things ye have need of, before ye ask him.

9 After this manner therefore pray ye: Our Father which art in heaven, Hallowed be thy name.

10 Thy kingdom come. Thy will be done in earth, as *it is* in heaven.

11 Give us this day our daily bread.

12 And forgive us our debts, as we forgive our debtors.

13 And lead us not into temptation, but deliver us from evil: For thine is the kingdom, and the power, and the glory, for ever. Amen.

14 For if ye forgive men their trespasses, your heavenly Father will also forgive you:

15 But if ye forgive not men their trespasses, neither will your Father forgive your trespasses.

16 Moreover when ye fast, be not, as the hypocrites, of a sad countenance: for they disfigure their faces, that they may appear unto men to fast. Verily I say unto you, They have their reward.

17 But thou, when thou fastest, anoint thine head, and wash thy face;

18 That thou appear not unto men to fast, but unto thy Father which is in secret: and thy Father which seeth in secret shall reward thee openly.

19 Lay not up for yourselves treasures upon earth, where moth

and rust doth corrupt, and where thieves break through and steal:

20 But lay up for yourselves treasures in heaven, where neither moth nor rust doth corrupt, and where thieves do not break through nor steal:

21 For where your treasure is, there will your heart be also.

22 The light of the body is the eye: if therefore thine eye be single, thy whole body shall be full of light.

23 But if thine eye be evil, thy whole body shall be full of darkness. If therefore the light that is in thee be darkness, how great *is* that darkness!

24 No man can serve two masters: for either he will hate the one, and love the other; or else he will hold to the one, and despise the other. Ye cannot serve God and mammon.

25 Therefore I say unto you, Take no thought for your life, what ye shall eat, or what ye shall drink; nor yet for your body, what ye shall put on. Is not the life more than meat, and the body than raiment?

26 Behold the fowls of the air: for they sow not, neither do they reap, nor gather into barns; yet your heavenly Father feedeth them. Are ye not much better than they?

27 Which of you by taking thought can add one cubit unto his stature?

28 And why take ye thought for raiment? Consider the lilies of the field, how they grow; they toil not, neither do they spin:

29 And yet I say unto you, That even Solomon in all his glory was not arrayed like one of these.

30 Wherefore, if God so clothe the grass of the field, which to-day is, and to-morrow is cast into the oven, *shall he* not much more *clothe* you, O ye of little faith?

31 Therefore take no thought, saying, What shall we eat? or, What shall we drink? or, Wherewithal shall we be clothed?

32 (For after all these things do the Gentiles seek:) for your heavenly Father knoweth that ye have need of all these things.

33 But seek ye first the kingdom of God, and his righteousness; and all these things shall be added unto you.

34 Take therefore no thought for the morrow: for the morrow shall take thought for the things of itself. Sufficient unto the day *is* the evil thereof.

CHAPTER 7

JUDGE NOT, THAT YE BE NOT JUDGED.

2. For with what judgment ye judge, ye shall be judged: and with what measure ye mete, it shall be measured to you again.

3 And why beholdest thou the mote that is in thy brother's eye, but considerest not the beam that is in thine own eye?

4 Or how wilt thou say to thy brother, Let me pull out the mote out of thine eye; and, behold, a beam *is* in thine own eye?

5 Thou hypocrite, first cast out the beam out of thine own eye; and then shalt thou see clearly to cast out the mote out of thy brother's eye.

6 Give not that which is holy unto the dogs, neither cast ye your pearls before swine, lest they trample them under their feet, and turn again and rend you.

7 Ask, and it shall be given you; seek, and ye shall find; knock, and it shall be opened unto you:

8 For every one that asketh receiveth; and he that seeketh findeth; and to him that knocketh it shall be opened.

9 Or what man is there of you, whom if his son ask bread, will he give him a stone?

10 Or if he ask a fish, will he give him a serpent?

11 If ye then, being evil, know how to give good gifts unto your children, how much more shall your Father which is in heaven give good things to them that ask him?

12 Therefore all things whatsoever ye would that men should do to you, do ye even so to them: for this is the law and the prophets.

13 Enter ye in at the strait gate: for wide *is* the gate, and broad *is* the way, that leadeth to destruction, and many there be which go in thereat:

14 Because strait *is* the gate, and narrow *is* the way, which leadeth unto life, and few there be that find it.

15 Beware of false prophets, which come to you in sheep's clothing, but inwardly they are ravening wolves.

16 Ye shall know them by their fruits. Do men gather grapes of thorns, or figs of thistles?

17 Even so every good tree bringeth forth good fruit; but a corrupt tree bringeth forth evil fruit.

18 A good tree cannot bring forth evil fruit, neither *can* a corrupt tree bring forth good fruit.

19 Every tree that bringeth not forth good fruit is hewn down, and cast into the fire.

20 Wherefore by their fruits ye shall know them.

21 Not every one that saith unto me, Lord, Lord, shall enter into the kingdom of heaven; but he that doeth the will of my Father which is in heaven.

22 Many will say to me in that day, Lord, Lord, have we not prophesied in thy name? and in thy name have cast out devils? and in thy name done many wonderful works?

23 And then will I profess unto them, I never knew you: depart from me, ye that work iniquity.

24 Therefore whosoever heareth these sayings of mine, and doeth them, I will liken him unto a wise man, which built his house upon a rock:

25 And the rain descended, and the floods came, and the winds blew, and beat upon that house; and it fell not: for it was founded upon a rock.

26 And every one that heareth these sayings of mine, and doeth them not, shall be likened unto a foolish man, which built his house upon the sand:

27 And the rain descended, and the floods came, and the winds blew, and beat upon that house; and it fell: and great was the fall of it.

28 And it came to pass, when Jesus had ended these sayings, the people were astonished at his doctrine:

29 For he taught them as *one* having authority, and not as the scribes.

✿ ✿ ✿

THE GOSPEL OF LUKE

THE TRIAL AND CRUCIFIXION OF JESUS (*LUKE* 22:1-24:53)

22 Now THE FESTIVAL OF UNLEAVENED Bread, which is called the Passover, was approaching. And the high
2 priests and the scribes were casting about for a way to put him to death, for they were afraid of the people.
3 But Satan entered into Judas, who was called Iscariot, a member
4 of the Twelve. And he went off and discussed with the high priests and captains of the Temple how he could betray him to them. And they
5 were delighted and agreed to pay
6 him for it. And he accepted their offer, and watched for an opportunity to betray him to them without a disturbance.
7 When the day of Unleavened Bread came, on which the Passover
8 lamb had to be sacrificed, Jesus sent Peter and John, saying to them, "Go and make preparations for us to eat the Passover."
9 They said to him, "Where do you want us to pre-
10 pare it?"
He said to them,
"Just after you enter the city, you will meet a man carrying a pitcher of water. Follow him to the house
11 to which he goes, and say to the man of the house, 'Our Master says to you, "Where is the room where I can eat the Passover supper with
12 my disciples?"' And he will show you a large room upstairs with the necessary furniture. Make your preparations there."
13 So they went and found every-

thing just as he had told them, and they prepared the Passover supper.
When the time came, he took his 14 place at the table, with the apostles about him. And he said to them, 15 "I have greatly desired to eat this Passover supper with you before I suffer. For I tell you, I will never 16 eat one again until it reaches its fulfilment in the Kingdom of God."
And when he was handed a cup, 17 he thanked God, and then said, "Take this and share it among 18 you, for I tell you, I will not drink the product of the vine again until the Kingdom of God comes."
And he took a loaf of bread and 19 thanked God, and broke it in 20 pieces, and gave it to them, saying, "This is my body. Yet look! The 21 hand of the man who is betraying me is beside me on the table! For 22 the Son of Man is going his way, as it has been decreed, but alas for the man by whom he is betrayed!"
And they began to discuss with 23 one another which of them it was who was going to do this. A dispute 24 also arose among them, as to which one of them ought to be considered the greatest. But he said to them, 25 "The kings of the heathen lord it over them, and their authorities are given the title of Benefactor. But 26 you are not to do so, but whoever is greatest among you must be like the youngest, and the leader like a 27 servant. For which is greater, the man at the table, or the servant who waits on him? Is not the man at the table? Yet I am like a servant 28 among you. But it is you who have 29

stood by me in my trials. So just as
30 my Father has conferred a kingdom
on me I confer on you the right to
eat and drink at my table in my
kingdom, and to sit on thrones and
31 judge the twelve tribes of Israel! O
Simon, Simon! Satan has obtained
32 permission to sift all of you like
wheat, but I have prayed that your
own faith may not fail. And afterward you yourself must turn and
strengthen your brothers."

33 Peter said to him,
"Master, I am ready to go to
prison and to death with you!"

34 But he said,
"I tell you, Peter, the cock will
not crow today before you deny
three times that you know me!"

35 And he said to them,
"When I sent you out without
any purse or bag or shoes, was
there anything you needed?"
They said,
"No, nothing."

36 He said to them,
"But now, if a man has a purse
let him take it, and a bag too. And
a man who has no sword must sell
37 his coat and buy one. For I tell you
that this saying of Scripture must
find its fulfilment in me: 'He was
rated an outlaw.' Yes, that saying
about me is to be fulfilled!"

38 But they said,
"See, Master, here are two
swords!"
And he said to them,
"Enough of this!"

39 And he went out of the city and
up on the Mount of Olives as he
was accustomed to do, with his
disciples following him. And when
40 he reached the spot, he said to
them,
"Pray that you may not be subjected to trial."

And he withdrew about a stone's 41
throw from them, and kneeling
down he prayed and said, 42
"Father, if you are willing, take
this cup away from me. But not my
will but yours be done!" 45
When he got up from his prayer,
he went to the disciples and found
them asleep from sorrow. And he 46
said to them,
"Why are you asleep? Get up,
and pray that you may not be subjected to trial!" 47
While he was still speaking, a
crowd of people came up, with the
man called Judas, one of the
Twelve, at their head, and he
stepped up to Jesus to kiss him.
Jesus said to him, 48
"Would you betray the Son of
Man with a kiss?"
Those who were about him saw 49
what was coming and said,
"Master, shall we use our
swords?"
And one of them did strike at the 50
high priest's slave and cut his right
ear off. But Jesus answered, 51
"Let me do this much!"
And he touched his ear and
healed him. And Jesus said to the 52
high priests, captains of the Temple, and elders who had come to
take him,
"Have you come out with swords
and clubs as though I were a rob- 53
ber? When I was among you day
after day in the Temple you never
laid a hand on me! But you choose
this hour, and the cover of darkness!"
Then they arrested him and led 54
him away and took him to the
house of the high priest. And Peter
followed at a distance. And they 55
kindled a fire in the middle of the
courtyard and sat about it, and

56 Peter sat down among them. A maid saw him sitting by the fire and looked at him and said,
"This man was with him too."
57 But he denied it, and said,
"I do not know him."
58 Shortly after, a man saw him and said,
"You are one of them too!"
But Peter said,
"I am not!"
59 About an hour later, another man insisted,
"This man was certainly with him too, for he is a Galilean!"
60 But Peter said,
"I do not know what you mean." And immediately, just as he
61 spoke, a cock crowed. And the Lord turned and looked at Peter, and Peter remembered the words the Lord had said to him—"Before the cock crows today, you will disown
62 me three times." And he went outside and wept bitterly.
63 The men who had Jesus in cus-
64 tody flogged him and made sport of him, and they blindfolded him, and asked him,
"Show that you are a prophet!
65 Who was it that struck you?" And they said many other abusive things to him.
66 As soon as it was day, the elders of the people, the high priests and scribes, assembled, and brought him before their council, and said to him,
67 "If you are the Christ, tell us so." But he said to them,
"If I tell you, you will not be-
68 lieve me, and if I ask you a question, you will not answer me. But
69 from this time on, the Son of Man will be seated at the right hand of God Almighty!"
70 And they all said,

"Are you the Son of God then?"
And he said to them,
"I am, as you say!"
Then they said, 71
"What do we want of testimony now? We have heard it ourselves from his own mouth!"
Then they arose in a body and 23
took him to Pilate, and they made 2
this charge against him:
"Here is a man whom we have found misleading our nation, and forbidding the payment of taxes to the emperor, and claiming to be an anointed king himself."
And Pilate asked him, 3
"Are you the king of the Jews?"
He answered,
"Yes."
And Pilate said to the high priests 4
and the crowd,
"I cannot find anything criminal about this man."
But they persisted and said, 5
"He is stirring up the people all over Judea by his teaching. He began in Galilee and he has come here."
When Pilate heard this, he asked 6
if the man were a Galilean and 7
learning that he belonged to Herod's jurisdiction he turned him over to Herod, for Herod was in Jerusalem at that time. When Herod 8
saw Jesus he was delighted, for he had wanted for a long time to see him, because he had heard about him and he hoped to see some wonder done by him. And he ques- 9
tioned him at some length, but he made him no answer. Meanwhile 10
the high priests and the scribes stood by and vehemently accused him. And Herod and his guards 11
made light of him and ridiculed him, and they put a gorgeous robe on him and sent him back to Pilate. 12

And Herod and Pilate became friends that day, for they had been at enmity before.

13 Pilate summoned the high priests and the members of the council 14 and the people, and said to them,

"You brought this man before me charged with misleading the people, and here I have examined him before you and not found him guilty of any of the things that you 15 accuse him of. Neither has Herod, for he has sent him back to us. You see he has done nothing to call for 16 his death. So I will teach him a lesson and let him go."

18 But they all shouted out.

"Kill him, and release Barabbas for us!"

19 (He was a man who had been put in prison for a riot that had taken place in the city and for 20 murder.) But Pilate wanted to let 21 Jesus go, and he called out to them again. But they kept on shouting,

"Crucify him! Crucify him!"

22 And he said to them a third time,

"Why, what has he done that is wrong? I have found nothing about him to call for his death. So I will teach him a lesson and let him go."

23 But they persisted with loud outcries in demanding that he be cru- 24 cified, and their shouting won. And Pilate pronounced sentence that 25 what they asked for should be done. He released the man they asked for, who had been put in prison for riot and murder, and handed Jesus over to their will.

26 As they led him away, they seized a man named Simon, from Cyrene, who was coming in from the country, and put the cross on 27 his back, for him to carry behind Jesus. He was followed by a great crowd of people and of women who were beating their breasts and la- menting him. But Jesus turned to 28 them and said,

"Women of Jerusalem, do not weep for me but weep for your- selves and for your children, for a 29 time is coming when they will say, 'Happy are the childless women, and those who have never borne or 30 nursed children!' Then people will begin to say to the mountains, 'Fall on us!' and to the hills, 'Cover us 31 up!' For if this is what they do when the wood is green, what will happen when it is dry?"

Two criminals were also led out 32 to execution with him.

When they reached the place 33 called the Skull, they crucified him there, with the criminals one at his right and one at his left. But Jesus 34 said,

"Father, forgive them, for they do not know what they are doing!"

And they divided up his clothes among them by drawing lots for them, while the people stood look- 35 ing on. Even the councilors jeered at him, and said,

"He has saved others, let him save himself, if he is really God's Christ, his Chosen One!"

The soldiers also made sport of 36 him, coming up and offering him sour wine, saying, 37

"If you are the king of the Jews, save yourself!" For there was a notice above his head, "This is the 38 king of Jews!"

One of the criminals who were 39 hanging there, abused him, saying,

"Are you not the Christ? Save yourself and us too!"

But the other reproved him and 40 said,

"Have you no fear even of God when you are suffering the same

penalty? And we are suffering it
41 justly, for we are only getting our
deserts, but this man has done
nothing wrong."
42 And he said,
"Jesus, remember me when you
come into your kingdom!"
43 And he said to him,
"I tell you, you will be in Paradise with me today!"
44 It was now about noon, and
darkness came over the whole country, and lasted until three in the
45 afternoon, as the sun was in eclipse.
And the curtain before the sanctuary was torn in two. Then Jesus
46 gave a loud cry, and said,
"Father, I intrust my spirit to
your hands!"
With these words he expired.
47 When the captain saw what had
happened he praised God, and said,
"This man must really have been
innocent!"
48 And all the crowds that had collected for the sight, when they saw
what happened, returned to the
city beating their breasts. And all
49 his acquaintances and the women
who had come with him from Galilee, stood at a distance looking on.
50 Now there was a man named
Joseph, a member of the council, a
good and upright man, who had
51 not voted for the plan or action of
the council. He came from the Jewish town of Arimathea and lived in
expectation of the Kingdom of God.
52 He went to Pilate and asked for
53 Jesus' body. Then he took it down
from the cross and wrapped it in
linen and laid it in a tomb hewn in
54 the rock, where no one had yet
been laid. It was the Preparation
Day, and the Sabbath was just be-
55 ginning. The women who had come
with Jesus from Galilee followed
and saw the tomb and how his
body was put there. Then they
went home, and prepared spices
and perfumes.

[THE RESURRECTION]

On the Sabbath they rested in 24
obedience to the commandment,
but on the first day of the week, at
early dawn, they went to the tomb,
taking spices they had prepared. 2
But they found the stone rolled 3
back from the tomb, and when
they went inside they could not
find the body. They were in great 4
perplexity over this, when suddenly
two men in dazzling clothing stood
beside them. The women were 5
frightened and bowed their faces
to the ground, but the men said to
them,
"Why do you look among the
dead for him who is alive? Remem- 6
ber what he told you while he was
still in Galilee, when he said that 7
the Son of Man must be handed
over to wicked men and be crucified and rise again on the third
day."
Then they remembered his 8
words, and they went back from 9
the tomb and told all this to the
eleven and all the rest. They were
Mary of Magdala and Joanna and 10
Mary, the mother of James; the
other women with them also told
this to the apostles. But the story 11
seemed to them to be idle talk and
they would not believe them.
That same day two of them were 13
going to a village called Emmaus,
about seven miles from Jerusalem, 14
and they were talking together
about all these things that had
happened. And as they were talk- 15

ing and discussing them, Jesus himself came up and went with them, 16 but they were prevented from recognizing him. 17 And he said to them,

"What is all this that you are discussing with each other on your way?"

18 They stopped sadly, and one of them named Cleopas said to him,

"Are you the only visitor to Jerusalem who does not know what has happened there lately?" 19

And he said,

"What is it?"

They said to him,

"About Jesus of Nazareth, who in the eyes of God and of all the people was a prophet mighty in 20 deed and word, and how the high priests and the members of our council gave him up to be sentenced to death, and had him cru- 21 cified. But we were hoping that he was to be the deliverer of Israel. Why, besides all this, it is three 22 days since it happened. But some women of our number have astounded us. They went to the tomb 23 early this morning and could not find his body, but came back and said that they had actually seen a vision of angels who said that he 24 was alive. Then some of our party went to the tomb and found things just as the women had said, but they did not see him."

25 Then he said to them,

"How foolish you are and how slow to believe, after all that the prophets have said! Did not the 26 Christ have to suffer thus before entering upon his glory?"

27 And he began with Moses and all the prophets and explained to them the passages all through the 28 Scriptures that referred to himself. When they reached the village to which they were going, he acted as though he were going on, but they 29 urged him not to, and said,

"Stay with us, for it is getting toward evening, and the day is nearly over."

So he went in to stay with them. 30 And when he took his place with them at table, he took the bread and blessed it and broke it in pieces and handed it to them. Then their eyes were opened and they knew 31 him, and he vanished from them. And they said to each other, 32

"Did not our hearts glow when he was talking to us on the road, and was explaining the Scriptures to us?"

And they got up immediately and 33 went back to Jerusalem, and found the eleven and their party all to- 34 gether, saying that the Master had really risen and had been seen by Simon. And they told what had 35 happened on the road, and how they had known him when he broke the bread in pieces.

While they were still talking of 36 these things, he himself stood among them. They were startled 37 and panic-stricken, and thought they saw a ghost. But he said to 38 them,

"Why are you so disturbed, and why do doubts arise in your minds? 39 Look at my hands and feet, for it is I myself! Feel of me and see, for a ghost has not flesh and bones, as you see I have."

But they could not yet believe it 41 for sheer joy and they were amazed. And he said to them,

"Have you anything here to eat?"

And they gave him a piece of 42 broiled fish, and he took it and ate 43 it before their eyes.

Then he said to them, 44

"This is what I told you when I was still with you—that everything that is written about me in the Law of Moses and the Prophets and the Psalms must come true."

45 46 Then he opened their minds to the understanding of the Scriptures, and said to them,

"The Scriptures said that Christ should suffer as he has done, and 47 rise from the dead on the third day, and that repentance leading to the forgiveness of sins should be 48 preached to all the heathen in his name. You are to be witnesses to all this, beginning at Jerusalem. And I will send down upon you 49 what my Father has promised. Wait here in the city until you are clothed with power from on high."

And he led them out as far as 50 Bethany. Then he lifted up his hands and blessed them. And as he 51 was blessing them, he parted from them. And they went back with 52 great joy to Jerusalem, and were constantly in the Temple, blessing 53 God.

THE FIRST LETTER TO THE CORINTHIANS

[ST. PAUL ON LOVE]

13 I WILL SHOW YOU A FAR BETTER WAY. If I can speak the languages of men and even of angels, but have no love, I am only a noisy gong or a 2 clashing cymbal. If I am inspired to preach and know all the secret truths and possess all knowledge, and if I have such perfect faith that I can move mountains, but 3 have no love, I am nothing. Even if I give away everything I own, and give myself up, but do it in pride, 4 not love, it does me no good. Love is patient and kind. Love is not 5 envious or boastful. It does not put on airs. It is not rude. It does not insist on its rights. It does not become angry. It is not resentful. It is 6 not happy over injustice, it is only 7 happy with truth. It will bear anything, believe anything, hope for anything, endure anything. Love 8 will never die out. If there is inspired preaching, it will pass away. If there is ecstatic speaking, it will 9 cease. If there is knowledge, it will pass away. For our knowledge is imperfect and our preaching is imperfect. But when perfection comes, 10 what is imperfect will pass away. When I was a child, I talked like 11 a child, I thought like a child, I reasoned like a child. When I became a man, I put aside my child- 12 ish ways. For now we are looking at a dim reflection in a mirror, but then we shall see face to face. Now my knowledge is imperfect, but then I shall know as fully as God knows me. So faith, hope, and love 13 endure. These are the great three, and the greatest of them is love.

❊   ❊   ❊

[ST. PAUL ON THE RESURRECTION]

❊   ❊   ❊

Now I WANT TO REMIND YOU, 15 brothers, of the form in which I presented to you the good news I brought, which you accepted and 2 have stood by, and through which you are to be saved, if you hold on, unless your faith has been all for 3 nothing. For I passed on to you, as of first importance, the account I had received, that Christ died for 4 our sins, as the Scriptures foretold, that he was buried, that on the third day he was raised from the 5 dead, as the Scriptures foretold, 6 and that he was seen by Cephas, and then by the Twelve. After that he was seen by more than five hundred brothers at one time, most of whom are still alive, although some 7 of them have fallen asleep. Then he was seen by James, then by all the 8 apostles, and finally he was seen by me also, as though I were born at 9 the wrong time. For I am the least important of the apostles, and am not fit to be called an apostle, because I once persecuted God's 10 church. But by God's favor I have become what I am, and the favor he showed me has not gone for nothing, but I have worked harder than any of them, although it was 11 not really I but the favor God showed me. But whether it was I or they, this is what we preach, and this is what you believed.

12   Now if what we preach about Christ is that he was raised from the dead, how can some of you say that there is no such thing as a resurrection of the dead? If there is 13 no resurrection of the dead, then 14 Christ was not raised, and if Christ was not raised, there is nothing in our message; there is nothing in our 15 faith either, and we are found guilty of misrepresenting God, for we have testified that he raised Christ, when he did not do it, if it is true that the dead are never raised. For if the dead are never raised, 16 Christ was not raised; and if Christ 17 was not raised, your faith is a delusion; you are still under the control of your sins. Yes, and those 18 who have fallen asleep in trust in Christ have perished. If we have centered our hopes on Christ in this 19 life, and that is all, we are the most pitiable people in the world.

But the truth is, Christ was raised 20 from the dead, the first to be raised of those who have fallen asleep. 21 For since it was through a man that we have death, it is through a man also that we have the raising of the 22 dead. For just as because of their relation to Adam all men die, so because of their relation to Christ they will all be brought to life again. But each in his own turn; 23 Christ first, and then at Christ's coming those who belong to him. 24 After that will come the end, when he will turn over the kingdom to God his Father, bringing to an end all other government, authority, and power, for he must retain the 25 kingdom until he puts all his enemies under his feet. The last enemy 26 to be overthrown will be death, for 27 everything is to be reduced to subjection and put under Christ's feet. But when it says that everything is subject to him, he is evidently excepted who reduced it all to sub- 28 jection to him. And when everything is reduced to subjection to him, then the Son himself will also become subject to him who has reduced everything to subjection to him, so that God may be everything to everyone.

Otherwise, what do people mean 29 by having themselves baptized on behalf of their dead? If the dead do not rise at all, why do they have themselves baptized on their be-

30 half? Why do we ourselves run

31 such risks every hour? By the very pride I take in you, brothers,

32 through our union with Christ Jesus our Lord, I face death every day. From the human point of view, what good is it to me that I have fought wild animals here in Ephesus? If the dead do not rise at all, "Let us eat and drink, for we will

33 be dead tomorrow!" Do not be misled. Bad company ruins character.

34 Return to your sober sense as you ought, and stop sinning, for some of you are utterly ignorant about God. To your shame I say so.

35 But someone will say, "How can the dead rise? What kind of a body

36 will they have when they come back?" You foolish man, the very

37 seed you sow never comes to life without dying first; and when you sow it, it has not the form it is going to have, but is a naked kernel, perhaps of wheat or something else;

38 and God gives it just such a form as he pleases, so that each kind of

39 seed has a form of its own. Flesh is not all alike; men have one kind,

40 animals another, birds another, and fish another. There are heavenly bodies, and there are earthly bodies, but the beauty of the heavenly bodies is of one kind, and the beauty of the earthly bodies is of an-

41 other. The sun has one kind of beauty, and the moon another, and the stars another; why, one star

42 differs from another in beauty. It is

43 so with the resurrection of the dead. The body is sown in decay, it is raised free from decay. It is sown in humiliation, it is raised in splendor. It is sown in weakness, it is

44 raised in strength. It is a physical body that is sown, it is a spiritual body that is raised. If there is a physical body, there is a spiritual 45 body also. This is also what the Scripture says: "The first man Adam became a living creature." The last Adam has become a life- 46 giving Spirit. It is not the spiritual that comes first, but the physical, and then the spiritual. The first man 47 is of the dust of the earth; the second man is from heaven. Those who 48 are of the earth are like him who was of the earth, and those who are of heaven are like him who is from heaven, and as we have been like 49 the man of the earth, let us also be like the man from heaven. But I can 50 tell you this, brothers: flesh and blood cannot share in the Kingdom of God, and decay will not share in what is imperishable. I will tell you 51 a secret. We shall not all fall asleep, but we shall all be changed, in a 52 moment, in the twinkling of an eye, at the sound of the last trumpet. For the trumpet will sound, and the dead will be raised free from decay, and we shall be changed. For this 53 perishable nature must put on the imperishable, and this mortal nature must put on immortality. And when this mortal nature puts on 54 immortality, then what the Scripture says will come true—"Death has been triumphantly destroyed. 55 Where, Death, is your victory? Where, Death, is your sting?" Sin is 56 the sting of death, and it is the Law that gives sin its power. But thank God! He gives us victory through 57 our Lord Jesus Christ. So my dear brothers, be firm and unmoved, and 58 always devote yourselves to the Lord's work, for you know that through the Lord your labor is not thrown away.

PLINY

(Gaius Plinius Caecilius Secundus) (c. A.D. 61/62-113)

A LEISURED ARISTOCRAT WITH A TASTE FOR LITERATURE, PLINY THE Younger is best remembered for his ten volumes of letters. The most famous of these are those sent to the historian Tacitus describing the spectacular eruption of Vesuvius in A.D. 79. That catastrophe not only buried the thriving cities of Pompeii and Herculaneum, thus hermetically sealing them for the archaeologist's spade, but also cost the life of Pliny's uncle, the eminent naturalist. Of particular interest is Pliny's letter to the Emperor Trajan in which he, as governor of Bithynia, asked for instruction on the imperial policy toward Christians. Then an illegal religious sect, the Christians were popularly regarded as "haters of mankind" for their refusal to engage in military service, hold public office, or participate in the state cult of emperor worship. In this as in his other voluminous correspondence, Pliny reveals himself as intelligent and well-meaning, but rather timid. He was probably too much the cultivated gentleman to be an effective administrator. Trajan, who was apparently weary of being solicited on every issue, trivial or great that worried Pliny, replied rather curtly. Even so, Trajan's answer is an exemplary statement of governmental moderation.

PLINY TO TRAJAN ON THE CHRISTIANS

IT IS MY WONT, SIRE, TO REFER TO YOU ALL MATTERS CONCERNING WHICH I am in doubt; for who better than you can guide me in my hesitations, or, if you please, instruct me in my ignorance? The trials of the Christians—I have never had to do with them, and so have no idea as to how far the sect should be held subject either to punishment or to examination. And I have felt no slight hesitation as to whether time of life should be taken into account, or no distinction should be made between those of very tender age and those of more years and strength; and as to whether the repentant should receive pardon, or renunciation should count for nothing if one at any time has been a Christian; and as to whether the mere name unattended by criminal conduct should constitute cause for punishment, or whether it is the crime inhering in the name that is to be punished.

---

[1]Gaius Plinius Secundus (A.D. 23/24-79), called Pliny the Elder.

From *Century Readings in Ancient Classical and Modern European Literature,* I and II, edited by John W. Conliffe and Grant Showerman. Copyright © 1925, Meredith Corporation. Reprinted by permission of Appleton-Century-Crofts.

In the meantime, in the cases brought before me with the charge of being Christians, I have followed this method of procedure. I have asked them whether they were Christians. On their confession of the fact, I have asked them a second and a third time, with threats of punishment. If they have persisted, I have ordered their execution; for I have had no doubt that, whatever they confessed, their pertinacity and their inflexible obstinacy at least ought to bring punishment upon them. There have been some afflicted with the same madness whom, because of their being citizens, I have taken steps to have sent to Rome for trial. Before long, by the very fact of measures being taken against it, as is usually the result, accusations began to be heard in various quarters, and a greater number of cases were brought before me. Anonymous information, with the names of many persons, has been lodged with me.

When those who have denied that they either were or had been Christians have called upon the gods in my presence, and have gone through the forms of worship, with incense and wine, before your likeness, which, with the images of the gods, I have ordered brought in for the purpose, and in addition to this have cursed Christ,—none of which acts those who are in real truth Christians can be brought to perform,—I have thought them deserving of discharge. Some have said that they were Christians, and then presently denied it, saying that they had been but had ceased to be, some many years before, a few even twenty years. These also, all of them, have both worshipped your likeness and the images of the gods and cursed Christ. They have affirmed, moreover, that the worst crime, or rather mistake, of which they had been guilty, had consisted in their custom of coming together before dawn on stated days to sing together a hymn to Christ, as if to God, and to bind themselves by an oath not to commit theft, robbery, or adultery, and not to deny a deposit when called upon. After this, according to their statement, they had been wont to separate. They had been accustomed to come together again to partake of a meal, common to all, and without blame; but they had discontinued even this after the edict in which, in obedience to your instructions, I had forbidden the existence of secret societies. For this reason I thought it all the more necessary to try to get at the truth by the examination of two female slaves said to be deaconesses, and I even had them put to the torture. I have been able to discover nothing except a distorted and exaggerated outside cult, and so have postponed the hearings and resorted to you for counsel. The matter seemed to me to demand consultation, especially on account of the number of those who are in danger. For many, of every age, of every rank, and of both sexes, are being called into jeopardy, and will continue to be in the future. Not merely cities, but villages, too, and the country districts, have been thoroughly infected with the contagion of these wretched non-conformists—who I nevertheless think may be stayed and corrected. At least it is certain that the temples, already almost deserted, have begun to be much frequented again, and that the usual sacrifices, long neglected, are again being performed, and the fodder for the victims is on sale—there were very few buyers of it heretofore.

From this it is easy to form an opinion of the throngs who can be set right if only allowed the opportunity for recantation.

TRAJAN TO PLINY

In dealing with the cases of the Christians brought before you, my dear Secundus, you have followed the proper mode of procedure.

No definite rule, to apply in all cases, can be laid down. The Christians are not to be sought out. If brought before you and found guilty, they are to be punished, but on this condition, that whosoever denies that he is a Christian, and makes good his assertion by performing acts of worship to our gods, is to have full pardon, however greatly suspected in the past. Anonymous charges are in no case to be admitted as evidence; this would be a very bad precedent, and besides not in the spirit of our times.

SYMMACHUS

(Quintus Aurelius Symmachus, A.D. 345-405)

EVEN AFTER CHRISTIANITY BECAME THE STATE RELIGION OF ROME, NOT all men of stature and distinction were willing to accept the new cult. Chief among the rebels who defended the old pagan gods which had been worshipped during the great days of empire, was Symmachus, a Roman aristocrat noted for his eloquence. In 384, as prefect of Rome, an important government office, he appealed to the young emperor Valentinian to restore the ancient Altar of Victory that had for generations stood in the Roman Senate. The Christians, upon whose insistence the altar had been removed, argued that their "jealous God" could permit no such abomination in a Christian nation. The disposition of this symbol of imperial Victory therefore became a center of violent controversy between the new faith and the dying pagan creed.

Less than a century after Constantine had legalized its status, the Church was as vigorously persecuting pagans and the non-conformists within its own ranks as heathen Rome had persecuted Christians during the reigns of Nero and Diocletian. Symmachus' *Plea for Paganism* is not only the work of a highly cultivated nobleman asking that the "rites of his forefathers" be respected, it is also a plea for civilized tolerance. He reminds the Christians, who adamantly denied freedom of worship to those who disagreed with them, that the universe is too vast and unknown a quantity to permit such narrow parochialism. The fact that all men share the same world, Symmachus points out, should be enough to make all religions aware that "it is not by one path alone that we can penetrate to so great a mystery."

St. Ambrose, the powerful bishop of Milan, successfully opposed Symmachus' appeal for universal tolerance. The following year Symmachus was able to return good for evil by recommending to the same Ambrose a talented young Christian, albeit then a wavering one, for the post of professor of rhetoric in Milan. The Christian whose career Symmachus advanced was the future St. Augustine.

A PLEA FOR PAGANISM

To OUR LORDS VALENTINIAN, THEODOSIUS, AND ARCADIUS, ALWAYS Augusti, Symmachus the Senator, Prefect of the City.

Let us at least give to the name the honor which has been denied the deity. Your Eternities owe much to Victory and will owe still more. Let

From *Century Readings in Ancient Classical and Modern European Literature,* I and II, edited by John W. Conliffe and Grant Showerman. Copyright © 1925, Meredith Corporation. Reprinted by permission of Appleton-Century-Crofts.

those turn away from this source of power who have had from it no advantage; you cannot afford to give up the protection of a deity friendly to triumphs. Hers is a power for whose favor everyone prays. No one would deny that a deity whose aid he professes is to be desired should be the object of religious attention. But if the avoidance of this omen were not a just thing to ask, at any rate it would have been but decency to keep hands off the ornaments of the senate house.

Enable us, we supplicate you, to leave as old men to our children what as children we received from our fathers. Deep is the affection men feel for that to which they are accustomed. The act of Deified Constantine did not long hold, and deservedly. All precedents should be shunned by you which are found soon to have lost their force. We are concerned for the lasting renown of your names; we desire that time to come shall find nothing there to correct.

Where are we to swear allegiance to your laws and your words? With what shall the minds of the false be made to fear so that they will not lie in the giving of testimony? It is true, of course, that all creation is full of deity, and that no place is safe for the perjurer, but the fear of playing false is greatly magnified if he is constrained also by deity actually at hand. That altar stands for the concord of all our body, that altar is the pledge of good faith for individuals; there is nothing makes for authority in our decrees so much as the fact that our body votes them all as it were under oath to the gods. Shall perjury therefore have an unconsecrated place at which to take oath, and will my illustrious Princes, who owe protection to the public oath, find this a thing they can approve?

But Deified Constantine will be said to have done this. Let us rather emulate other acts of that emperor, who would have entered upon no such policy as this had any other made the mistake before him; for the lapse of the predecessor serves as correction for the follower, and it is from the disregard of precedent that improvement springs. It may have been right for him, the example of Your Clemencies, in a matter still untried not to make sure he did nothing invidious; but can that same defense apply in our case if we imitate an act we have seen proved wrong? Let Your Eternities listen to other acts of this same emperor which you will find more worthy of appropriation. He took from the Sacred Virgins not a single one of their privileges, he decreed priesthoods to nobles, he did not deny moneys to meet the expense of the ceremonies in Rome, he accompanied the happy senate through all the streets of the Eternal City, looking with placid eye on our altars and shrines and on the names of the gods carved on the façades, inquiring into the origins of the temples, and marveling at their founders; and, although he professed another religion, gave ours his guarantee. For every man has his own ways, and every man has his own manner of worship; divine purpose has assigned various cults as protectors to cities. Just as souls are partitioned among human beings at birth, so to peoples are allotted the divine spirits that rule their fates.

There is the matter of benefits, too, which most of all justifies the gods to men. For when we bring every argument into the open, on what basis can we better judge of the gods than from the record and proof of prospering circumstances? Farther, if long existence confers authority upon religions, the faith of so many generations is worthy of preservation, and we ought to follow our fathers as they with such good results followed theirs.

Let us imagine Rome now present and pleading with you after this fashion: 'Best of princes, fathers of your country, have respect for my years—years to which my devotion to religion has brought me. Let me continue in the rites of my forefathers; for I have no reason for regret. Let me live, since I am free, in my own ways. The religion I profess brought the whole world under my sway, the cult I practise repulsed Hannibal from my walls and the Senones from the Capitol. Have I then been preserved for this, to be denied in my old age? What new ways are to be entered upon, should be mine to judge. Change in old age is tardy and disgraceful.'

And so we ask for peace to the gods of our fathers, and to the gods of our native soil. It is but fair that what all men worship should be regarded as one and the same. We gaze upon the same stars, the heavens are common to us, the same universe wraps us round. Why should it be a concern as to what manner of search for the truth another employs? It is not by one path alone that we can penetrate to so great a mystery.

ST. JEROME

Preface

(Hieronymus, A.D. 340-420)

THE LIFE AND WORKS OF ST. JEROME ARE SUPREMELY REPRESENTATIVE OF
that uneasy period in later Roman history when the Empire was crumbling under the shock of repeated barbarian invasions and the classical
impulse, apparently exhausted, was being replaced by the Judaeo-
Christian tradition. Jerome's own divided personality symbolizes the
tension and conflict between the dying classical spirit and the austere
demands of the new religion. Shortly before Jerome's birth the Emperor
Constantine had transformed the despised and persecuted faith into the
state religion of Rome. Although born into a Christian family, Jerome
had received the finest possible education in the philosophy, literature,
and rhetoric of the pagan world. Gifted with a keen intellect, but
plagued by a debilitating guilt, the young Jerome underwent an agoniz-
ing struggle between his love and appreciation of classical authors,
particularly Cicero, and his compulsive sense of sinful unworthiness in
the eyes of Christ. According to a literal reading of the New Testament,
the world and all its works were of the Devil. The beauties of classical
thought were merely snares to entrap the minds of the unwary. Only
total rejection of all life's goods and pleasures could provide a way of
pleasing Christ, who demanded that his followers sacrifice all temporal
ambitions. Torn between an emotional and intellectual allegiance to
pagan wisdom and his equally powerful yearning for salvation and
purity which only God could satisfy, Jerome's personal struggle reached
a climax in his vision of an angry Christ. The Lord appeared to Jerome
in a dream and demanded to know who he was. "A Christian," Jerome
meekly replied. "Liar," Christ snapped back. "You are not a Christian
but a Ciceronian." From that moment on Jerome was seized by a
passionate conviction that to admire any non-biblical writer was to deny
Christ. Depreciating the glories of pagan civilization as so much "filth,"
he transferred his abundant energies to the study of Scripture and soon
became recognized as the most learned theologian of his time. His 63
books of commentary on the Old Testament prophets, his interpretations
of biblical texts, and his monumental translation of the Bible from
Hebrew and Greek into Latin make Jerome one of the most influential
"Doctors" of the Church. His version of the Bible, called the *Vulgate*
because it rendered Scripture into the common or "vulgar" language, is
still the official text of the Roman Catholic Church.

Proud of his immense erudition and yet (sometimes) terrified lest his
intellectual pursuits offend the Christ, Jerome presents one of the most
complex personalities of Christian history. Although he could be a generous and loyal friend, he was an irascible and vituperative enemy. His
satirical letters to relapsed priests, luxury-loving monks, and other
clergymen who earned his disapproval are scathing in their biting wit
and bitter criticism. A saint who mortified his flesh and humiliated his

780

natural desires to win the blessing of God, Jerome was capable of verbally lascerating his victims with a withering scorn reminiscent of Martial and Juvenal. Even St. Augustine, who had disputed a passage of Jerome's biblical exegesis, was not spared a generous dose of venom. Jerome's letter to Augustine is a strange mixture of gentle irony, assumed humility, and violent arrogance. Jerome gives us, in fact, the curious example of a hermit and scholar who uses his mastery of classical rhetoric not only to attack the ideals of classical learning but also to castigate his fellow Christians.

Along with his phenomenal scholarship, intense friendships, and acid disposition, Jerome is distinguished by a fanatical asceticism. For years he lived as a hermit in the Syrian desert, his body unwashed and skeleton-thin, despising supposed followers of Christ who lived comfortably, ate well, and enjoyed the patronage of Roman officials. Jerome's uncompromising insistence on celibacy (marriage is good only because it produces virgins), the abuse of his physical nature (the skin develops mange because no true Christian bathes), and his unaccountable predilection for the diseased, the filthy, and the death-haunted, inspired considerable criticism from less ascetically inclined members of the Church. But Jerome damned them all.

The long epistle to Eustochium, the first member of the Roman aristocracy to become a nun, shows Jerome's opposition to the world, the flesh, and the Devil at its most eloquent. Sex, comfort, the mere enjoyment of food and drink, he condemns as insidious enemies of salvation. He flees from earthly joy as if it were Satan himself, as, indeed, Jerome believed it was. He approves of no one who tries to accommodate the Christian message to an ordinary life in the world. He also decries the increasing corruption of the Church. Security and freedom from persecution, inevitably gave birth to heresy and theological dissention; they also led to a luxurious undermining of the Christian ascetic ideal. Safe, repectable, and prosperous, the Roman Church stood in danger of becoming as dissolute as pagan Rome, whose temporal authority it was rapidly usurping. Pope Damasus, who authorized Jerome's work on the *Vulgate*, had ascended the papal throne only after persuading the Emperor Valentinian I to intervene and eliminate Damasus' competitors.

Taking with him a group of irreproachably chaste nuns, Jerome withdrew from Rome and retired to Bethlehem, where he spent his last years teaching monks to copy sacred manuscripts. While in Bethlehem, he learned of Alaric's sack of Rome. Horrified that the "eternal city" had fallen into barbarian hands, Jerome seems to have regarded the event as a defeat for Christ. It is perhaps the final irony of Jerome's paradoxical career that it should be he, a Christian saint, who most articulately lamented the fall of pagan Rome, an eventuality which the persecuted writers of the New Testament had looked for so ardently.

THE LETTERS

TO EUSTOCHIUM: HOW TO LIVE AS A NUN IN A PROFLIGATE SOCIETY*

BECAUSE THE FLESH STINGS AND ENTICES TO SIN, THE APOSTLE PAUL, a chosen vessel set apart to preach Christ's Gospel, subjected his flesh and bones to slavery, lest in preaching to others he himself might be found a sinner. Despite his efforts, he recognizes that there is another law in his limbs and organs fighting against the law of his will, bringing him into captivity. This law was the law of sin. Even after being stripped, starved, imprisoned, lashed, tortured, Paul recoils upon himself, crying, "Wretched creature that I am! Who shall deliver me from the body of this death?" Do you still think you should cease being vigilant?

❖   ❖   ❖

Let not the faithful city of Sion[1] become a prostitute. Devils must not dance or sirens and satyrs roost in the place that once sheltered the Holy Trinity. Never loosen the garment confining your breasts. Lust tickling the senses, the gentle fires of pleasure radiating a delightful glow—this is when we must break out and cry, "The Lord is with me, I shall not fear what flesh can do." And when the inner man for a moment shows signs of fluctuating between vice and virtue, exclaim, "Why are you sad, O my soul, why do you contend with you? Hope in the Lord, for I shall continue to praise Him Who is the health of my countenance and my God." Thoughts like these must never arise in you, my dear Eustochium. Babylonian[2] confusions must never grow and flourish in your heart. While an enemy is still small, massacre him. Evil must be uprooted while still in the bud. Hear the Psalmist, "O miserable daughter of Babylon, blessed be the man who rewards you as you have rewarded us: blessed the man who takes and dashes your children against rocks."

Now it is impossible that the body's natural heat should not occasionally attack a man in his marrow. However, he is praised and thought blessed who, whenever sensual thoughts arise, murders them by dashing them against a rock. That rock is Christ.

How often while I was living in the desert—that savage, vast, solitary place for hermits which is scorched by the broiling sun—how often did I

[1]*Sion* (Zion)—literally the hill upon which Jerusalem was built, hence a synonym for the holy city itself. In Christian usage, Zion symbolizes the community of the faithful, the Church and those dedicated to it.

[2]*Babylon*—the city which conquered Jerusalem and took Israel captive (586 B.C.). It is therefore symbolic of the Devil's world.

*From *The Satirical Letters of St. Jerome*, translated by Paul Carroll. Copyright © 1956 by Henry Regnery Company. Reprinted by permission of the publisher. Since Eustochium was only fifteen when Jerome wrote her (384 A.D.), it is likely that he intended his missive as a general statement about the holy life and the corrupting influences of Roman society.

imagine that I was among the pleasures of Rome! Bitterly I sat alone in the sands. Rough sackcloths covered my unshapely frame, making it seem disfigured; through long neglect my skin wrinkled, coarse and black as an Ethiopian's. Every day groans of complaint and tears, and if sleep happened to break down my resistance, my naked bones, scarcely hanging together, knocked against the ground. Of my food and drink I say nothing, for even in illness hermits take nothing but cold water, any cooked dishes being considered a great indulgence. Terrified by the thought of hell, I had condemned myself to this prison, my sole companions being wild beasts and scorpions. Often, however, a chorus of dancing girls cavorted around me. Emaciated, pale, my limbs cold as ice, still my mind boiled with desire. Lust's fires bubbled about me even when my flesh was as good as dead. Completely helpless, I would fling myself at the feet of Jesus, water them with my tears, wiping them with my hair. Weeks of abstinence had to subdue my rebellious body. This miserable experience does not embarrass me, my dear Eustochium. Only I do complain because I am no longer what once I was. How many times I cried out violently at night, and would not stop beating my breast until, at the Lord's request, a measure of peace returned. My very cell was fearful to me, for it seemed to know my secret thoughts. Angry, stern with myself, I would wander alone far into the wilderness, and whenever I happened to come into a valley or discovered craggy mountains or steep cliffs, there I established a place to pray, a house of correction, as it were, for this wretched bone and flesh. After much lamentation, much straining towards heaven in those desolate places— here the Lord is my witness—sometimes I experienced the presence of angelic hosts, and from joy and gladness I would sing out, "Because of the fragrance of Your ointments, we shall pursue You, O Lord."

Fierce temptations like these attack men whose bodies are emaciated and have but evil thoughts and fancies to fight. What will it be like, then, for a young girl who delights in pleasant, sophisticated living? Truly, in the Apostle's phrase, "she is dead while she exists." Have I the right to advise you, my dear, has experience given my opinion some weight? If so, my advice would begin with a warning. As a bride of Christ, you must avoid wine as you would poison; it is the very first weapon which devils employ to assault youth. Greed does not agitate, nor pride inflate, nor ambition infatuate the young the way wine does. Other vices one manages to do without, but wine's potentiality to breed evil is like having the enemy within the walls, for wherever we happen to go, we carry this potentiality with us. Youth and wine between them kindle the flames of voluptuousness. Why throw oil on fire? Why add fuel to a body already miserable and burning with desire?

When Timothy is advised by the Apostle "to abstain from water, and take a little wine for your stomach's sake and for your other ailments," notice the reasons why wine is permitted: to cure an aching digestive tract and other physical ailments. On the other hand, only a little wine is prescribed, so that illness may not be an excuse for indulgence. Here

Paul speaks more as a physician than an apostle, though, indeed, an apostle is a spiritual physician. What he feared was that Timothy might collapse and not have strength enough to take the many trips necessary to spread the Gospel. Moreover, Paul remembered that in other passages he had said, "Debauchery is in wine," and "To neither drink wine nor eat meat is good for a man." Wine intoxicated father Noah; but he lived in the primitive age after the Flood, and since grapes had only recently been planted, perhaps he was unaware that their drink could inebriate. Permit me to develop this point, for I want you to understand Scripture in all its mystery, the word of God being a pearl able to be pierced on all sides. After Noah's drunkenness came the uncovering of his thighs: lust joins indulgence. First the belly swells, then the other organs. "The people sat down to eat and drink, then rose up to play." After Sodom was destroyed, and Lot had been saved in the mountains because he was the only honest man among so many thousands, his daughters saw to it that Lot, the friend of God, became intoxicated. Although they may have been justified, believing that the human race was in danger of extinction, and not acting from lustful desires, they were well aware that their father, an extremely honest man, would not impregnate them unless he were unconscious and drunk. The fact is that Lot did not realize what he was doing. Nevertheless, his error, though unconscious, was sinful, for it produced sons like Moab and Ammon, enemies of Israel, whose children "even to the fourteenth generation shall not enter into the Lord's congregation."

❖   ❖   ❖

Married women should not be your companions, nor should you visit the residences of the nobility. I would not have you gazing too often on the kind of life you spurned in order to take the veil. Women of the world, as you know, preen themselves if their husbands are judges or hold other high, dignified positions. Surrounding the Emperor's wife is a crowd of ambitious women; but why should you pay court for the sake of your Husband? God's bride, why do you scamper to court the wife of a mere man? In matters of this sort, cultivate a holy pride, by realizing that a nun is better than the worldly kind of wife.

But it is not enough merely to avoid friendship with women inflated by their husband's position and honors, who surround themselves with eunuchs and dress in robes embroidered with fine, gold material. I desire more from you than this. Eustochium, you must also shun those ladies who are widows from necessity, not from choice. Not that these widows should have longed for their husbands' deaths; but they have failed to welcome the opportunity for chastity once it came. As it is, they simply change their clothes. Old ambitions remain with them.

Here comes one of them. Rouged cheeks and plump skin, she travels in a spacious sedan-chair in front of which stroll eunuchs. One would suppose she was looking for a husband, not mourning one. Parasites and guests swarm about her house; and the very priests who ought to inspire respect and authority smack her on the forehead, then stretch out their hands—to give a blessing you would think if you knew no better—to accept money for their visit. Knowing priests need her assistance, our lady swells with pride. Experience having taught her what a husband is like, she much prefers her widow's freedom. Ladies like this call themselves 'chaste nuns', and after consuming a tremendous dinner, they sprawl on their couches, dreaming of the blessed Apostles.

Instead of this type, your companions should be pale and thin from fasting, their characters proven through long decorous lives, ladies who sing in their hearts, "Where do You feed Your flock? Where do You rest at noon?" and exclaim with love, "To be free and with Christ is all that I desire."

Imitating your Husband's example, be obedient to your parents. Above all, seldom go out in public. When you wish to seek help from the martyrs and saints, remain at home and pray. If you only leave the house when it is absolutely necessary, you will never need excuses. Always eat with moderation. Many women are quite temperate with drink, but so intemperate with food. When you rise in the middle of night to pray, the eructation of your breath should come from an empty stomach, not from indigestion. Read and learn as much as you can. Sleep should overcome you with a book in your hand, the sacred pages a pillow for your nodding head. Moderate refreshment should break your daily fast, for it is foolish to keep your stomach empty for days, and then compensate by gorging. When the mind is cloyed with food, it grows sluggish: watered earth encourages the thorns of lust. If ever your body begins to sigh for the flower of youth, and lying on your couch after meals you begin to tremble as a parade of delicious lusts march by, then seize the shield of Faith, and it will quench the devil's flaming arrows. "Adulterers all," storms the Prophet, "they have turned their hearts into a furnace."

In all things, stay close to Christ's footsteps, and always pay attention to what He says. Repeat to yourself, "Did our hearts not blaze on the journey to Emmaus when Christ opened the Scriptures to us?" and, "How Your eloquent words burn, how Your servant loves them."

How very difficult it is for the human soul not to love something. Of necessity our minds and wills must be drawn to some kind of affection. Carnal love is overcome by spiritual love. Desire is extinguished by a deeper desire. Whatever is taken from carnal love is given to the higher love. Therefore, as you lie on your bed, mumur this over and over again, "On my bed at night I have sought Him Whom my soul adores."

❖ ❖ ❖

THE CHARM OF CICERO*

WHEN YEARS AGO I HAD TORN MYSELF FROM HOME AND PARENTS, SISTER and friends, for the kingdom of heaven's sake, and had taken my journey for Jerusalem, I could not part with the books which I had collected at Rome with very great care and labor. And so, unhappy man that I was, I followed up my fasting by reading Cicero; after a night of watching, after shedding tears, which the remembrance of my past sins drew from my inmost soul, I took up Plautus. If sometimes, coming to myself, I began to read the prophets, their inartistic style repelled me. When my blinded eyes could not see the light, I thought the fault was in the sun, not in my eyes. While the old serpent thus deceived me, about the middle of Lent a fever seized me, and so reduced my strength that my life scarce cleaved to my bones. They began to prepare for my funeral. My whole body was growing cold, only a little vital warmth remained in my breast; when suddenly I was caught up in spirit, and brought before the tribunal of the Judges. So great was the glory of his presence, and such the brilliancy of the purity of those who surrounded Him, that I cast myself to the earth, and did not dare to raise my eyes. Being asked who I was, I answered that I was a Christian. 'Thou liest,' said the Judge, 'thou art a Ciceronian, and not a Christian; for where thy treasure is, there is thy heart also.' Thereupon, I was silent. He ordered me to be beaten, but I was tormented more by remorse of conscience than by the blows; I said to myeslf, 'Who shall give thee thanks in hell?' Then I cried, 'Have mercy upon me, O Lord, have mercy upon me!' My cry was heard above the sound of the blows. Then they who stood by, gliding to the knees of the Judge, prayed Him to have mercy on my youth, and He gave me time for repentance, on pain of more severe punishment if I should read pagan books in the future. I, who in such a strait would have promised even greater things, made oath, and declared by His sacred Name, 'O Lord, if ever I henceforth possess profane books or read them, let me be treated as if I had denied thee.' After this oath, they let me go, and I returned to the world. To the wonder of all who stood by, I opened my eyes, shedding such a shower of tears that my grief would make even the incredulous believe in my vision. And this was not mere sleep, or a vain dream, such as often deludes us. The tribunal before which I lay is witness, so may I never come into a like judgment. I protest that my shoulders were livid, that I felt the blows after I awoke, and thenceforward I studied divine things with greater ardor than ever I had studied the things of the world.

THE RUIN OF THE ROMAN WORLD

IT IS NOT THE CALAMITIES OF WRETCHED MEN THAT I AM SPEAKING OF, but the fragile state of human conditions. My soul shrinks from reciting

---

*This and the following two excerpts are from *Century Readings in Ancient Classical and Modern European Literature,* I and II, edited by John W. Conliffe and Grant Showerman. Copyright © 1925, the Meredith Corporation. Reprinted by permission of Appleton-Century-Crofts.

the ruins of our times. For twenty years and more, the blood of Rome has been poured out daily between the city of Constantine and the Julian Alps. In Scythia, Thrace, Macedonia, Thessaly, Dardania, Dacia, Epirus, Dalmatia, and all the Pannonias, the Goth, Sarmatian, Quade, Alan, Hun, Vandal, and Marcoman lay waste, pillage, and drag away. How many matrons, how many virgins of God, how many of the free-born and noble have been used for the mirth of these beasts! Bishops have been seized, elders and other officials slain, churches overthrown, horses stabled at the altars of Christ, the mortal relics of the martyrs dug up. Everywhere are lamentations, everywhere groanings, and on every hand the image of death. The Roman world is tumbling in ruins. And yet our head is erect and unbent. In what state of mind and soul now do you suppose are the people of Corinth, of Athens, of Lacedæmon, of Arcadia, and of entire Greece, all of them in the control of barbarians? and indeed I have named only a few cities that once had no slight power. The East seemed immune from these misfortunes, and thrown into consternation merely by rumors—when, look you, in the past year from the farthest cliffs of the Caucasus the wolves of the North came sweeping down on us, and in this short time have ranged over these big provinces. How many monasteries have been seized, how many rivers have had their waters changed to human blood!

✿   ✿   ✿

ALARIC IN ROME[3]

A TERRIFYING RUMOR COMES TO ME FROM THE WEST THAT ROME HAS been besieged and her citizens' safety bought with gold; that, once despoiled, they were again beset, so that after losing their substance they might yield up life as well. My voice is stopped, and sobs cut off the words as I try to speak. Captive is the city which once took captive all the world; yea, it perished from famine ere touched by the sword, and few were found to be rendered captive. Maddening hunger drove to the use of meats unspeakable; they tore their own members, the one the other, mothers not sparing the sucking babe, and consuming again the fruits of their own bosoms. In the night was Moab taken, in the night its walls fell. O God, the heathen are come into thine inheritance; Thy holy temple have they defiled, they have laid Jerusalem on heaps. The dead bodies of thy servants have they given to be meat unto the fowls of the heaven, the flesh of thy saints unto the beasts of the earth. Their blood have they shed like water round about Jerusalem; and there was none to bury them. What voice could tell of that night's destruction and of its deadly woes, or what tears equal its sorrows? The city of old, the queen of the world for many years, is fallen to ruin, and the lifeless bodies of men lie thickly scattered in its streets and homes, and everywhere is the spectre of death.

---

[3]*Alaric* (c. A.D. 370-410)—the first Teutonic conqueror to sack Rome (410).

ST. AUGUSTINE

(Aurelius Augustinus, A.D. 354-430)

THE LIFE AND WORKS OF ST. AUGUSTINE MARK A CRUCIAL TRANSITION from the spirit of the classical world to the Christian Ideal of the Middle Ages. Born in Numidia to a pagan father and Christian mother, Augustine was thoroughly educated in the literature and philosophy of Greece and Rome. For more than thirty years he resisted the ceaseless entreaties of his mother, St. Monica, to become a follower of Christ. First a Manichean and ultimately a neo-Platonist, Augustine taught rhetoric successively at Thagaste, Carthage, and Rome, which he visited in 383. Thanks to the recommendation of Symmachus, the leading defender of the old pagan religions, St. Ambrose, then bishop of Milan, appointed the still-unconverted Augustine to a professorship of rhetoric in that city.

Under the influence of Ambrose, who was one of the most learned and versatile men of his time, Augustine began to study the Scriptures in earnest. After much wavering and soul-searching, he was baptized in the faith in 387. Within days after her son's conversion, St. Monica died, having realized her dearest wish. Augustine then returned to Africa and became a priest. In 395 he was made bishop of Hippo, a position he retained until his death. His last years were devoted to preaching, contemplation, and the production of an astonishingly prolific body of writing. Besides his autobiographical *Confessions,* he wrote numerous treatises on Christian doctrine, criticisms of pagan philosophy, speculative essays on the immortality of the soul and a dissertation on the problems of free will and predestination. Augustine's later works are more exclusively concerned with Christian theology. The *Confessions,* for example, is an attempt to demonstrate that God's grace can redeem even the blackest sinner; Augustine cites his own conversion as proof of divine mercy. The *City of God,* the longest and last of his major works, was written to defend Christianity against the charge that Rome's catastrophic decline was due to its neglect of the old pagan gods. Instead, Augustine insisted, the "eternal city" of Rome was only a brief manifestation of God's heavenly city which, like a Platonic Ideal, abides forever. The concept of an invisible "city of God" of which the Roman Church is the visible reflection was enormously influential in later Christian thought. It was also the "death-blow to paganism."

The greatest of the Church Fathers, Augustine used his vast erudition to develop a systematic philosophy of the Christian religion, incorporating into it the best of his classical heritage. In spite of his neo-Platonism, however, Augustine's concern is not to discover new truth through the exercise of reason, but to use the techniques and accepted tenets of pagan philosophy to justify and rationalize the divinely revealed truths of Christianity. Like the medieval scholastics who were his intellectual descendants, Augustine regards philosophy, not as an independent means of investigation, but as "the handmaiden of the Church." From his time onward, all science, logic, and philosophy are subordinate to the Faith given to the saints and upheld by the Catholic or "universal" Church.

Despite his subjection of reason to revelation, Augustine achieves a creative synthesis of the three most enduring cultures of the ancient world. In him the Hebraic devotion to law and conscience, Greek sensitivity and psychological insight and Roman love of order and respect for authority, meet and find a new expression. Combining practicality, mortality, and dialectic, Augustine provides the spiritual bond between the classical and medieval views of life. His work is the indispensable link between Virgil and Dante.

THE CONFESSIONS

BOOK I

7

HEAR ME, O GOD! HOW WICKED ARE THE SINS OF MEN! MEN SAY THIS AND you pity them, because you made man, but you did not make sin in him.

Who can recall to me the sins I committed as a baby? For in your sight no man is free from sin, not even a child who has lived only one day on earth. Who can show me what my sins were? Some small baby in whom I can see all that I do not remember about myself? What sins, then, did I commit when I was a baby myself? Was it a sin to cry when I wanted to feed at the breast? I am too old now to feed on mother's milk, but if I were to cry for the kind of food suited to my age, others would rightly laugh me to scorn and remonstrate with me. So then too I deserved a scolding for what I did; but since I could not have understood the scolding, it would have been unreasonable, and most unusual, to rebuke me. We root out these faults and discard them as we grow up, and this is proof enough that they are faults, because I have never seen a man purposely throw out the good when he clears away the bad. It can hardly be right for a child, even at that age, to cry for everything, including things which would harm him; to work himself into a tantrum against people older than himself and not required to obey him; and to try his best to strike and hurt others who know better than he does, including his own parents, when they do not give in to him and refuse to pander to whims which would only do him harm. This shows that, if

Abridged. From *Saint Augustine: The Confessions,* translated with an introduction by R. S. Pine-Coffin. Copyright © 1961 by R. S. Pine-Coffin. Reprinted by permission of Penguin Books, Ltd.

babies are innocent, it is not for lack of will to do harm, but for lack of strength.

I have myself seen jealousy in a baby and know what it means. He was not old enough to talk, but whenever he saw his foster-brother at the breast, he would grow pale with envy. This much is common knowledge. Mothers and nurses say that they can work such things out of the system by one means or another, but surely it cannot be called innocence, when the milk flows in such abundance from its source, to object to a rival desperately in need and depending for his life on this one form of nourishment? Such faults are not small or unimportant, but we are tender-hearted and bear with them because we know that the child will grow out of them. It is clear that they are not mere peccadilloes, because the same faults are intolerable in older persons.

You, O Lord my God, gave me my life and my body when I was born. You gave my body its five senses; you furnished it with limbs and gave it its proper proportions; and you implanted in it all the instincts necessary for the welfare and safety of a living creature. For these gifts you command me to acknowledge you and *praise you and sing in honour of your name*,[1] because you are Almighty God, because you are good, and because I owe you praise for these things, even if you had done nothing else. No one but you can do these things, because you are the one and only mould in which all things are cast and the perfect form which shapes all things, and everything takes its place according to your law.

I do not remember that early part of my life, O Lord, but I believe what other people have told me about it and from watching other babies I can conclude that I also lived as they do. But, true though my conclusions may be, I do not like to think of that period as part of the same life I now lead, because it is dim and forgotten and, in this sense, it is no different from the time I spent in my mother's womb. But if *I was born in sin and guilt was with me already when my mother conceived me*,[2] where, I ask you, Lord, where or when was I, your servant, ever innocent? But I will say no more about that time, for since no trace of it remains in my memory, it need no longer concern me.

8

The next stage in my life, as I grew up, was boyhood. Or would it be truer to say that boyhood overtook me and followed upon my infancy— not that my infancy left me, for, if it did, where did it go? All the same, it was no longer there, because I ceased to be a baby unable to talk, and was now a boy with the power of speech. I can remember that time, and later on I realized how I had learnt to speak. It was not my elders who showed me the words by some set system of instruction, in the way that they taught me to read not long afterwards; but, instead, I taught myself

---

[1] Ps. 91:2 (92:1).
[2] Ps. 50:7 (51:5).

by using the intelligence which you, my God, gave to me. For when I tried to express my meaning by crying out and making various sounds and movements, so that my wishes should be obeyed, I found that I could not convey all that I meant or make myself understood by everyone whom I wished to understand me. So my memory prompted me. I noticed that people would name some object and then turn towards whatever it was that they had named. I watched them and understood that the sound they made when they wanted to indicate that particular thing was the name which they gave to it, and their actions clearly showed what they meant, for there is a kind of universal language, consisting of expressions of the face and eyes, gestures and tones of voice, which can show whether a person means to ask for something and get it, or refuse it and have nothing to do with it. So, by hearing words arranged in various phrases and constantly repeated, I gradually pieced together what they stood for, and when my tongue had mastered the pronunciation, I began to express my wishes by means of them. In this way I made my wants known to my family and they made theirs known to me, and I took a further step into the stormy life of human society, although I was still subject to the authority of my parents and the will of my elders.

9

But, O God my God, I now went through a period of suffering and humiliation. I was told that it was right and proper for me as a boy to pay attention to my teachers, so that I should do well at my study of grammar and get on in the world. This was the way to gain the respect of others and win for myself what passes for wealth in this world. So I was sent to school to learn to read. I was too small to understand what purpose it might serve and yet, if I was idle at my studies, I was beaten for it, because beating was favoured by tradition. Countless boys long since forgotten had built up this stony path for us to tread and we were made to pass along it, adding to the toil and sorrow of the sons of Adam.

But we found that some men prayed to you, Lord, and we learned from them to do the same, thinking of you in the only way that we could understand, as some great person who could listen to us and help us, even though we could not see you or hear you or touch you. I was still a boy when I first began to pray to you, my Help and Refuge. I used to prattle away to you, and though I was small, my devotion was great when I begged you not to let me be beaten at school. Sometimes, for my own good, you did not grant my prayer, and then my elders and even my parents, who certainly wished me no harm, would laugh at the beating I got—and in those days beatings were my one great bugbear.

O Lord, throughout the world men beseech you to preserve them from the rack and the hook and various similar tortures which terrify them. Some people are merely callous, but if a man clings to you with great devotion, how can his piety inspire him to find it in his heart to make light of these tortures, when he loves those who dread them so fearfully? And yet this was how our parents scoffed at the torments which we boys suffered at the hands of our masters. For we feared the whip just as much as others fear the rack, and we, no less than they, begged you to preserve us from it. But we sinned by reading and writing and studying less than was expected of us. We lacked neither memory nor intelligence, because by your will, O Lord, we had as much of both as was sufficient for our years. But we enjoyed playing games and were punished for them by men who played games themselves. However, grown-up games are known as 'business', and even though boys' games are much the same, they are punished for them by their elders. No one pities either the boys or the men, though surely we deserved pity, for I cannot believe that a good judge would approve of the beatings I received as a boy on the ground that my games delayed my progress in studying subjects which would enable me to play a less creditable game later in life. Was the master who beat me himself very different from me? If he were worsted by a colleague in some petty argument, he would be convulsed with anger and envy, much more so than I was when a playmate beat me at a game of ball.

10

And yet I sinned, O Lord my God, creator and arbiter of all natural things, but arbiter only, not creator, of sin. I sinned, O Lord, by disobeying my parents and the masters of whom I have spoken. For, whatever purpose they had in mind, later on I might have put to good use all the things which they wanted me to learn. I was disobedient, not because I chose something better than they proposed to me, but simply from the love of games. For I liked to score a fine win at sport or to have my ears tickled by the make-believe of the stage, which only made them itch the more. As time went on my eyes shone more and more with the same eager curiosity, because I wanted to see the shows and sports which grown-ups enjoyed. The patrons who pay for the production of these shows are held in esteem such as most parents would wish for their children. Yet the same parents willingly allow their children to be flogged if they are distracted by these displays from the studies which are supposed to fit them to grow rich and give the same sort of shows themselves. Look on these things with pity, O Lord, and free us who now call upon you from such delusions. Set free also those who have not yet called upon you, so that they may pray to you and you may free them from this folly.

✱   ✱   ✱

12

These temptations were thought to be less of a danger in boyhood than in adolescence. But even as a boy I did not care for lessons and I disliked being forced to study. All the same I was compelled to learn and good came to me as a result, although it was not of my own making. For I would not have studied at all if I had not been obliged to do so, and what a person does against his will is not to his own credit, even if what he does is good in itself. Nor was the good which came of it due to those who compelled me to study, but to you, my God. For they had not the insight to see that I might put the lessons which they forced me to learn to any other purpose than the satisfaction of man's insatiable desire for the poverty he calls wealth and the infamy he knows as fame. But you, who *take every hair of our heads into your reckoning,*[3] used for my benefit the mistaken ideas of all those who insisted on making me study; and you used the mistake I made myself, in not wishing to study, as a punishment which I deserved to pay, for I was a great sinner for so small a boy. In this way you turned their faults to my advantage and justly punished me for my own. For this is what you have ordained and so it is with us, that every soul that sins brings its own punishment upon itself.

13

Even now I cannot fully understand why the Greek language, which I learned as a child, was so distasteful to me. I loved Latin, not the elementary lessons but those which I studied later under teachers of literature. The first lessons in Latin were reading, writing, and counting, and they were as much of an irksome imposition as any studies in Greek. But this, too, was due to the sinfulness and vanity of life, since I was *flesh and blood, no better than a breath of wind that passes by and never returns.*[4] For these elementary lessons were far more valuable than those which followed, because the subjects were practical. They gave me the power, which I still have, of reading whatever is set before me and writing whatever I wish to write. But in the later lessons I was obliged to memorize the wanderings of a hero named Aeneas, while in the meantime I failed to remember my own erratic ways. I learned to lament the death of Dido, who killed herself for love, while all the time, in the midst of these things, I was dying, separated from you, my God and my Life, and I shed no tears for my own plight.

What can be more pitiful than an unhappy wretch unaware of his own sorry state, bewailing the fate of Dido, who died for love of Aeneas, yet shedding no tears for himself as he dies for want of loving you? O God, you are the Light of my heart, the Bread of my inmost soul, and the Power that weds my mind and the thoughts of my heart. But I did not love you. *I broke my troth with you*[5] and embraced another while applause echoed about me. For to love this world is to break troth with you,[6] yet men applaud and are ashamed to be otherwise. I did not

[3] Matt. 10:30.
[4] Ps. 77:39 (78:39).
[5] Ps. 72:27 (73:27).
[6] See James 4:4.

weep over this, but instead I wept for Dido, who surrendered her life to the sword, while I forsook you and surrendered myself to the lowest of your created things. And if I were forbidden to read these books, I was sad not to be able to read the very things that made me sad. Such folly is held to be a higher and more fruitful form of study than learning to read and write.

But now, my God, let your voice ring in my soul and let your truth proclaim to me that it is wrong to think this. Tell me that reading and writing are by far the better study. This must be true, for I would rather forget the wanderings of Aeneas and all that goes with them, than how to read and write. It is true that curtains are hung over the entrances to the schools where literature is taught, but they are not so much symbols in honour of mystery as veils concealing error. The schoolmasters need not exclaim at my words, for I no longer go in fear of them now that I confess my soul's desires to you, my God, and gladly blame myself for my evil ways so that I may enjoy the good ways you have shown me. Neither those who traffic in literature nor those who buy their wares need exclaim against me. For if I put to them the question whether it is true, as the poet* says, that Aeneas once came to Carthage, the less learned will plead ignorance and the better informed will admit that it is not true. But if I ask how the name of Aeneas is spelt, anyone who has learnt to read will give me the right answer, based on the agreed convention which fixes the alphabet for all of us. If I next ask them whether a man would lose more by forgetting how to read and write or by forgetting the fancies dreamed up by the poets, surely everyone who is not out of his wits can see the answer they would give. So it was wrong of me as a boy to prefer empty romances to more valuable studies. In fact it would be truer to say that I loved the one and hated the other. But in those days 'one and one are two, two and two are four' was a loathsome jingle, while the wooden horse and its crew of soldiers, the burning of Troy and even the ghost of Creusa made a most enchanting dream, futile though it was.

14

If this was so, why did I dislike Greek literature, which tells these tales, as much as the Greek language itself? Homer, as well as Virgil, was a skilful spinner of yarns and he is most delightfully imaginative. Nevertheless, as a boy, I found him little to my taste. I suppose that Greek boys think the same about Virgil when they are forced to study him as I was forced to study Homer. There was of course the difficulty which is found in learning any foreign language, and this soured the sweetness of the Greek romances. For I understood not a single word and I was constantly subjected to violent threats and cruel punishments to make me learn. As a baby, of course, I knew no Latin either, but I learned it

---

The Poet—Virgil. See the *Aeneid*, Book IV.

without fear and fret, simply by keeping my ears open while my nurses fondled me and everyone laughed and played happily with me. I learned it without being forced by threats of punishment, because it was my own wish to be able to give expression to my thoughts. I could never have done this if I had not learnt a few words, not from schoolmasters, but from people who spoke to me and listened when I delivered to their ears whatever thoughts I had conceived. This clearly shows that we learn better in a free spirit of curiosity than under fear and compulsion. But your law, O God, permits the free flow of curiosity to be stemmed by force. From the schoolmaster's cane to the ordeals of martyrdom, your law prescribes bitter medicine to retrieve us from the noxious pleasures which cause us to desert you.

15

Grant my prayer, O Lord, and do not allow my soul to wilt under the discipline which you prescribe. Let me not tire of thanking you for your mercy in rescuing me from all my wicked ways, so that you may be sweeter to me than all the joys which used to tempt me; so that I may love you most intensely and clasp your hand with all the power of my devotion; so that you may save me from all temptation until the end of my days.

You, O Lord, are my King and my God, and in your service I want to use whatever good I learned as a boy. I can speak and write, read and count, and I want these things to be used to serve you, because when I studied other subjects you checked me and forgave me the sins I committed by taking pleasure in such worthless things. It is true that these studies taught me many useful words, but the same words can be learnt by studying something that matters, and this is the safe course for a boy to follow.

* * *

BOOK II

1

I MUST NOW CARRY MY THOUGHTS BACK TO THE ABOMINABLE THINGS I did in those days, the sins of the flesh which defiled my soul. I do this, my God, not because I love those sins, but so that I may love you. For love of your love I shall retrace my wicked ways. The memory is bitter, but it will help me to savour your sweetness, the sweetness that does not deceive but brings real joy and never fails. For love of your love I shall retrieve myself from the havoc of disruption which tore me to pieces when I turned away from you, whom alone I should have sought, and lost myself instead on many a different quest. For as I grew to manhood I was inflamed with desire for a surfeit of hell's pleasures. Foolhardy as I was, I ran wild with lust that was manifold and rank. In your eyes my beauty vanished and I was foul to the core, yet I was pleased with my own condition and anxious to be pleasing in the eyes of men.

2

I cared for nothing but to love and be loved. But my love went beyond the affection of one mind for another, beyond the arc of the bright beam of friendship. Bodily desire, like a morass, and adolescent sex welling up within me exuded mists which clouded over and obscured my heart, so that I could not distinguish the clear light of true love from the murk of lust. Love and lust together seethed within me. In my tender youth they swept me away over the precipice of my body's appetites and plunged me in the whirlpool of sin. More and more I angered you, unawares. For I had been deafened by the clank of my chains, the fetters of the death which was my due to punish the pride in my soul. I strayed still farther from you and you did not restrain me. I was tossed and spilled, floundering in the broiling sea of my fornication, and you said no word. How long it was before I learned that you were my true joy! You were silent then, and I went on my way, farther and farther from you, proud in my distress and restless in fatigue, sowing more and more seeds whose only crop was grief.

Was there no one to lull my distress, to turn the fleeting beauty of these new-found attractions to good purpose and set up a goal for their charms, so that the high tide of my youth might have rolled in upon the shore of marriage? The surge might have been calmed and contented by the procreation of children, which is the purpose of marriage, as your law prescribes, O Lord. By this means you form the offspring of our fallen nature, and with a gentle hand you prune back the thorns that have no place in your paradise. For your almighty power is not far from us, even when we are far from you. Or, again, I might have listened more attentively to your voice from the clouds, saying of those who marry that they will *meet with outward distress, but I leave you your freedom;*[7] that *a man does well to abstain from all commerce with women,*[8] and that *he who is unmarried is concerned with God's claim, asking how he is to please God; whereas the married man is concerned with the world's claim, asking how he is to please his wife.*[9] These were the words to which I should have listened with more care, and if I had made myself *a eunuch for love of the kingdom of heaven,*[10] I should have awaited your embrace with all the greater joy.

✿   ✿   ✿

---

[7]I Cor. 7:28.
[8]I Cor. 7:1.
[9]I Cor. 7:32,33.
[10]Matt. 19:12.

3

In the meanwhile, during my sixteenth year, the narrow means of my family obliged me to leave school and live idly at home with my parents. The brambles of lust grew high above my head and there was no one to root them out, certainly not my father. One day at the public baths he saw the signs of active virility coming to life in me and this was enough to make him relish the thought of having grandchildren. He was happy to tell my mother about it, for his happiness was due to the intoxication which causes the world to forget you, its Creator, and to love the things you have created instead of loving you, because the world is drunk with the invisible wine of its own perverted, earthbound will. But in my mother's heart you had already begun to build your temple and laid the foundations of your holy dwelling, while my father was still a catechumen and a new one at that. So, in her piety, she became alarmed and apprehensive, and although I had not yet been baptized, she began to dread that I might follow in the crooked path of those who do not keep their eyes on you but turn their backs instead.

How presumptuous it was of me to say that you were silent, my God, when I drifted father and farther away from you! Can it be true that you said nothing to me at that time? Surely the words which rang in my ears, spoken by your faithful servant, my mother, could have come from none but you? Yet none of them sank into my heart to make me do as you said. I well remember what her wishes were and how she most earnestly warned me not to commit fornication and above all not to seduce any man's wife. It all seemed womanish advice to me and I should have blushed to accept it. Yet the words were yours, though I did not know it. I thought that you were silent and that she was speaking, but all the while you were speaking to me through her, and when I disregarded her, your handmaid, I was disregarding you, though I was both her son and your servant. But I did this unawares and continued headlong on my way. I was so blind to the truth that among my companions I was ashamed to be less dissolute than they were. For I heard them bragging of their depravity, and the greater the sin the more they gloried in it, so that I took pleasure in the same vices not only for the enjoyment of what I did, but also for the applause I won.

Nothing deserves to be despised more than vice; yet I gave in more and more to vice simply in order not to be despised. If I had not sinned enough to rival other sinners, I used to pretend that I had done things I had not done at all, because I was afraid that innocence would be taken for cowardice and chastity for weakness. These were the companions with whom I walked the streets of Babylon.* I wallowed in its mire as if it were made of spices and precious ointments, and to fix me all the faster in the very depths of sin the unseen enemy trod me underfoot and enticed me to himself, because I was an easy prey for his seductions.

Babylon—Mesopotamian city-state which destroyed Jerusalem (586 B.C.); hence a synonym for the Devil's world.

For even my mother, who by now had escaped from the centre of Babylon, though she still loitered in its outskirts, did not act upon what she had heard about me from her husband with the same earnestness as she had advised me about chastity. She saw that I was already infected with a disease that would become dangerous later on, but if the growth of my passions could not be cut back to the quick, she did not think it right to restrict them to the bounds of married love. This was because she was afraid that the bonds of marriage might be a hindrance to my hopes for the future—not of course the hope of the life to come, which she reposed in you, but my hopes of success at my studies. Both my parents were unduly eager for me to learn, my father because he gave next to no thought to you and only shallow thought to me, and my mother because she thought that the usual course of study would certainly not hinder me, but would even help me, in my approach to you. To the best of my memory this is how I construe the characters of my parents. Furthermore, I was given a free rein to amuse myself beyond the strict limits of discipline, so that I lost myself in many kinds of evil ways, in all of which a pall of darkness hung between me and the bright light of your truth, my God. What malice proceeded from my pampered heart!

BOOK III

1

I WENT TO CARTHAGE, WHERE I FOUND MYSELF IN THE MIDST OF A HISSING cauldron of lust. I had not yet fallen in love, but I was in love with the idea of it, and this feeling that something was missing made me despise myself for not being more anxious to satisfy the need. I began to look around for some object for my love, since I badly wanted to love something. I had no liking for the safe path without pitfalls, for although my real need was for you, my God, who are the food of the soul, I was not aware of this hunger. I felt no need for the food that does not perish, not because I had had my fill of it, but because the more I was starved of it the less palatable it seemed. Because of this my soul fell sick. It broke out in ulcers and looked about desperately for some material, worldly means of relieving the itch which they caused. But material things, which have no soul, could not be true objects for my love. To love and to have my love returned was my heart's desire, and it would be all the sweeter if I could also enjoy the body of the one who loved me.

So I muddied the stream of friendship with the filth of lewdness and clouded its clear waters with hell's black river of lust. And yet, in spite of this rank depravity, I was vain enough to have ambitions of cutting a fine figure in the world. I also fell in love, which was a snare of my own choosing. My God, my God of mercy, how good you were to me, for you mixed much bitterness in that cup of pleasure! My love was returned and finally shackled me in the bonds of its consummation. In the midst of my joy I was caught up in the coils of trouble, for I was lashed with the cruel, fiery rods of jealousy and suspicion, fear, anger, and quarrels.

2

I was much attracted by the theatre, because the plays reflected my own unhappy plight and were tinder to my fire. Why is it that men enjoy feeling sad at the sight of tragedy and suffering on the stage, although they would be most unhappy if they had to endure the same fate themselves? Yet they watch the plays because they hope to be made to feel sad, and the feeling of sorrow is what they enjoy. What miserable delirium this is! The more a man is subject to such suffering himself, the more easily he is moved by it in the theatre. Yet when he suffers himself, we call it misery: when he suffers out of sympathy with others, we call it pity. But what sort of pity can we really feel for an imaginary scene on the stage? The audience is not called upon to offer help but only to feel sorrow, and the more they are pained the more they applaud the author. Whether this human agony is based on fact or is simply imaginary, if it is acted so badly that the audience is not moved to sorrow, they leave the theatre in a disgruntled and critical mood; whereas, if they are made to feel pain, they stay to the end watching happily.

This shows that sorrow and tears can be enjoyable. Of course, everyone wants to be happy; but even if no one likes being sad, is there just the one exception that, because we enjoy pitying others, we welcome their misfortunes, without which we could not pity them? If so, it is because friendly feelings well up in us like the waters of a spring. But what course do these waters follow? Where do they flow? Why do they trickle away to join that stream of boiling pitch, the hideous flood of lust? For by their own choice they lose themselves and become absorbed in it. They are diverted from their true course and deprived of their original heavenly calm.

✳   ✳   ✳

However, in those unhappy days I enjoyed the pangs of sorrow. I always looked for things to wring my heart and the more tears an actor caused me to shed by his performance on the stage, even though he was portraying the imaginary distress of others, the more delightful and attractive I found it. Was it any wonder that I, the unhappy sheep who strayed from your flock, impatient of your shepherding, became infected with a loathsome mange? Hence my love of things which made me sad. I did not seek the kind of sorrow which would wound me deeply, for I had no wish to endure the sufferings which I saw on the stage; but I enjoyed fables and fictions, which could only graze the skin. But where the fingers scratch, the skin becomes inflamed. It swells and festers with hideous pus. And the same happened to me. Could the life I led be called true life, my God?

BOOK IV

4

DURING THOSE YEARS, WHEN I FIRST BEGAN TO TEACH IN THAGASTE, MY native town, I had found a very dear friend. We were both the same age, both together in the heyday of youth, and both absorbed in the same interests. We had grown up together as boys, gone to school together, and played together. Yet ours was not the friendship which should be between true friends, either when we were boys or at this later time. For though they cling together, no friends are true friends unless you, my God, bind them fast to one another through that love which is sown in our hearts by the Holy Ghost, who is given to us. Yet there was sweetness in our friendship, mellowed by the interests we shared. As a boy he had never held firmly or deeply to the true faith and I had drawn him away from it to believe in the same superstitious, soul-destroying fallacies which brought my mother to tears over me. Now, as a man, he was my companion in error and I was utterly lost without him. Yet in a moment, before we had reached the end of the first year of a friendship that was sweeter to me than all the joys of life as I lived it then, you took him from this world. For you are the God of vengeance[11] as well as the fountain of mercy. You follow close behind the fugitive and recall us to yourself in ways we cannot understand.

No man can count your praises, even though he is but one man and reckons only the blessings he has received in his own life. How can I understand what you did at that time, my God? How can I plumb the unfathomable depth of your judgement? My friend fell gravely ill of a fever. His senses were numbed as he lingered in the sweat of death, and when all hope of saving him was lost, he was baptized as he lay unconscious. I cared nothing for this, because I chose to believe that his soul would retain what it had learnt from me, no matter what was done to his body when it was deprived of sense. But no such thing happened. New life came into him and he recovered. And so soon as I could talk to him—which was as soon as he could talk to me, for I never left his side since we were so dependent on each other—I tried to chaff him about his baptism, thinking that he too would make fun of it, since he had received it when he was quite incapable of thought or feeling. But by this time he had been told of it. He looked at me in horror as though I were an enemy, and in a strange, new-found attitude of self-reliance he warned me that if I wished to be his friend, I must never speak to him like that

---

[11]See Ps. 93:1 (94:1).

again. I was astonished and confused, but I did not tell him what I felt, hoping that when he was better and had recovered his strength, he would be in a condition to listen to what I had to say. But he was rescued from my folly and taken into your safe keeping, for my later consolation. For a few days after this, while I was away from him, the fever returned and he died.

My heart grew sombre with grief, and wherever I looked I saw only death. My own country became a torment and my own home a grotesque abode of misery. All that we had done together was now a grim ordeal without him. My eyes searched everywhere for him, but he was not there to be seen. I hated all the places we had known together, because he was not in them and they could no longer whisper to me 'Here he comes!' as they would have done had he been alive but absent for a while. I had become a puzzle to myself, asking my soul again and again 'Why are you downcast? Why do you distress me?'[12] But my soul had no answer to give. If I said 'Wait for God's help', she did not obey. And in this she was right because, to her, the well-loved man whom she had lost was better and more real than the shadowy being in whom I would have her trust. Tears alone were sweet to me, for in my heart's desire they had taken the place of my friend.

❋ ❋ ❋

BOOK VIII

10

❋ ❋ ❋

WHEN I WAS TRYING TO REACH A DECISION ABOUT SERVING THE LORD MY God, as I had long intended to do, it was I who willed to take this course and again it was I who willed not to take it. It was I and I alone. But I neither willed to do it nor refused to do it with my full will. So I was at odds with myself. I was throwing myself into confusion. All this happened to me although I did not want it, but it did not prove that there was some second mind in me besides my own. It only meant that my mind was being punished. *My action did not come from me, but from the sinful principle that dwells in me.*[13] It was part of the punishment of a sin freely committed by Adam, my first father. . . .

In this way I wrangled with myself, in my own heart, about my own self. And all the while Alypius* stayed at my side, silently awaiting the outcome of this agitation that was new in me.

---

[12]See Ps. 41:12 (42:12).
[13]Rom. 7:17.
*Alypius—a close friend and fellow scholar who shared Augustine's spiritual growth.

12

I probed the hidden depths of my soul and wrung its pitiful secrets from it, and when I mustered them all before the eyes of my heart, a great storm broke within me, bringing with it a great deluge of tears. I stood up and left Alypius so that I might weep and cry to my heart's content, for it occurred to me that tears were best shed in solitude. I moved away far enough to avoid being embarrassed even by his presence. He must have realized what my feelings were, for I suppose I had said something and he had known from the sound of my voice that I was ready to burst into tears. So I stood up and left him where we had been sitting, utterly bewildered. Somehow I flung myself down beneath a fig tree and gave way to the tears which now streamed from my eyes, the sacrifice that is acceptable to you.[14] I had much to say to you, my God, not in these very words but in this strain: *Lord, will you never be content?*[15] *Must we always taste your vengeance? Forget the long record of our sins.*[16] For I felt that I was still the captive of my sins, and in my misery I kept crying 'How long shall I go on saying "tomorrow, tomorrow"? Why not now? Why not make an end of my ugly sins at this moment?'

I was asking myself these questions, weeping all the while with the most bitter sorrow in my heart, when all at once I heard the sing-song voice of a child in a nearby house. Whether it was the voice of a boy or a girl I cannot say, but again and again it repeated the refrain 'Take it and read, take it and read'. At this I looked up, thinking hard whether there was any kind of game in which children used to chant words like these, but I could not remember ever hearing them before. I stemmed my flood of tears and stood up, telling myself that this could only be a divine command to open my book of Scripture and read the first passage on which my eyes should fall. For I had heard the story of Antony, and I remembered how he had happened to go into a church while the Gospel was being read and had taken it as a counsel addressed to himself when he heard the words *Go home and sell all that belongs to you. Give it to the poor, and so the treasure you have shall be in in heaven; then come back and follow me.*[17] By this divine pronouncement he had at once been converted to you.

So I hurried back to the place where Alypius was sitting, for when I stood up to move away I had put down the book containing Paul's Epistles. I seized it and opened it, and in silence I read the first passage on which my eyes fell: *Not in revelling and drunkenness, not in lust and wantonness, not in quarrels and rivalries. Rather, arm yourselves with the Lord Jesus Christ; spend no more thought on nature and nature's appetites.*[18] I had no wish to read more and no need to do so. For in an

---

[14]See Ps. 50:19 (51:17).
[15]Ps. 6:4 (6:3).
[16]Ps. 78:5, 8 (79:5, 8).
[17]Matt. 19:21.
[18]Rom. 13:13, 14. Saint Augustine does not quote the whole passage, which begins 'Let us pass our time honourably, as by the light of day, not in revelling and drunkenness,' etc.

instant, as I came to the end of the sentence, it was as though the light of confidence flooded into my heart and all the darkness of doubt was dispelled.

I marked the place with my finger or by some other sign and closed the book. My looks now were quite calm as I told Alypius what had happened to me. He too told me what he had been feeling, which of course I did not know. He asked to see what I had read. I showed it to him and he read on beyond the text which I had read. I did not know what followed, but it was this: *Find room among you for a man of over-delicate conscience.*[19] Alypius applied this to himself and told me so. This admonition was enough to give him strength, and without suffering the distress of hesitation he made his resolution and took this good purpose to himself. And it very well suited his moral character, which had long been far, far better than my own.

Then we went in and told my mother, who was overjoyed. And when we went on to describe how it had all happened, she was jubilant with triumph and glorified you, *who are powerful enough, and more than powerful enough, to carry out your purpose beyond all our hopes and dreams.*[20] For she saw that you had granted her far more than she used to ask in her tearful prayers and plaintive lamentations. You converted me to yourself, so that I no longer desired a wife or placed any hope in this world but stood firmly upon the rule of faith, where you had shown me to her in a dream so many years before. And you *turned her sadness into rejoicing,*[21] into joy far fuller than her dearest wish, far sweeter and more chaste than any she had hoped to find in children begotten of my flesh.

BOOK IX

8

THERE ARE MANY THINGS WHICH I DO NOT SET DOWN IN THIS BOOK, SINCE I am pressed for time. My God, I pray you to accept my confessions and also the gratitude I bear you for all the many things which I pass over in silence. But I will omit not a word that my mind can bring to birth concerning your servant, my mother. In the flesh she brought me to birth in this world: in her heart she brought me to birth in your eternal light. It is not of her gifts that I shall speak, but of the gifts you gave to her. For she was neither her own maker nor her own teacher. It was you who made her, and neither her father nor her mother knew what kind of woman their daughter would grow up to be. It was by Christ's teaching, by the guidance of your only Son, that she was brought up to honour and obey you in one of those good Christian families which form the body of your Church. Yet she always said that her good upbringing had

---

[19]Rom. 14:1.
[20]Eph. 3:20.
[21]Ps. 29:12 (30:11).

been due not so much to the attentiveness of her mother as to the care of an aged servant, who had carried my grandfather on her back when he was a baby, as older girls do with small children. Her master and mistress, out of gratitude for her long service and respect for her great age and unexceptionable character, treated her as an honoured member of their Christian household. This was why they placed their daughters in her care. She was conscientious in attending to her duties, correcting the children when necessary with strictness, for the love of God, and teaching them to lead wise and sober lives. . . .

10

Not long before the day on which she was to leave this life—you knew which day it was to be, O Lord, though we did not—my mother and I were alone, leaning from a window which overlooked the garden in the courtyard of the house where we were staying at Ostia. We were waiting there after our long and tiring journey, away from the crowd, to refresh ourselves before our sea-voyage. I believe that what I am going to tell happened through the secret working of your providence. For we were talking alone together and our conversation was serene and joyful. *We had forgotten what we had left behind and were intent on what lay before us.*[22] In the presence of Truth, which is yourself, we were wondering what the eternal life of the saints would be like, that life which *no eye has seen, no ear has heard, no human heart conceived.*[23] But we laid the lips of our hearts to the heavenly stream that flows from your fountain, *the source of all life* which is *in you,*[24] so that as far as it was in our power to do so we might be sprinkled with its waters and in some sense reach an understanding of this great mystery.

Our conversation led us to the conclusion that no bodily pleasure, however great it might be and whatever earthly light might shed lustre upon it, was worthy of comparison, or even of mention, beside the happiness of the life of the saints. As the flame of love burned stronger in us and raised us higher towards the eternal God, our thoughts ranged over the whole compass of material things in their various degrees, up to the heavens themselves, from which the sun and the moon and the stars shine down upon the earth. Higher still we climbed, thinking and speaking all the while in wonder at all that you have made. At length we came to our own souls and passed beyond them to that place of everlasting plenty, where you feed Israel for ever with the food of truth. There life is that Wisdom by which all these things that we know are made, all things that ever have been and all that are yet to be. But that Wisdom is not made: it is as it has always been and as it will be for ever—or, rather, I should not say that it *has been* or *will be,* for it simply *is,* because eternity is not in the past or in the future. And while we spoke

---

[22]Philipp. 3:13.
[23]I Cor. 2:9.
[24]Ps. 35:10 (36:10).

of the eternal Wisdom, longing for it and straining for it with all the strength of our hearts, for one fleeting instant we reached out and touched it. Then with a sigh, leaving *our spiritual harvest*[25] bound to it, we returned to the sound of our own speech, in which each word has a beginning and an ending—far, far different from your Word, our Lord, who abides in himself for ever, yet never grows old and gives new life to all things.

And so our discussion went on. Suppose, we said, that the tumult of a man's flesh were to cease and all that his thoughts can conceive, of earth, of water, and of air, should no longer speak to him; suppose that the heavens and even his own soul were silent, no longer thinking of itself but passing beyond; suppose that his dreams and the visions of his imagination spoke no more and that every tongue and every sign and all that is transient grew silent—for all these things have the same message to tell, if only we can hear it, and their message is this: We did not make ourselves, but he who abides for ever made us. Suppose, we said, that after giving us this message and bidding us listen to him who made them, they fell silent and he alone should speak to us, not through them but in his own voice, so that we should hear him speaking, not by any tongue of the flesh or by an angel's voice, not in the sound of thunder or in some veiled parable, but in his own voice, the voice of the one whom we love in all these created things; suppose that we heard him himself, which none of these things between ourselves and him, just as in that brief moment my mother and I had reached out in thought and touched the eternal Wisdom which abides over all things; suppose that this state were to continue and all other visions of things inferior were to be removed, so that this single vision entranced and absorbed the one who beheld it and enveloped him in inward joys in such a way that for him life was eternally the same as that instant of understanding for which we had longed so much—would not this be what we are to understand by the words *Come and share the joy of your Lord?*[26] But when is it to be? Is it to be when *we all rise again, but not all of us will undergo the change?*[27]

This was the purport of our talk, though we did not speak in these precise words or exactly as I have reported them. Yet you know, O Lord, that as we talked that day, the world, for all its pleasures, seemed a paltry place compared with the life that we spoke of. And then my mother said, 'My son, for my part I find no further pleasure in this life. What I am still to do or why I am here in the world, I do not know, for I have no more to hope for on this earth. There was one reason, and one alone, why I wished to remain a little longer in this life, and that was to see you a Catholic Christian before I died. God has granted my wish and more besides, for I now see you as his servant, spurning such happiness as the world can give. What is left for me to do in this world?'

[25]Rom. 8:23.
[26]Matt. 25:21.
[27]I Cor. 15:51.

11

I scarcely remember what answer I gave her. It was about five days after this, or not much more, that she took to her bed with a fever. One day during her illness she had a fainting fit and lost consciousness for a short time. We hurried to her bedside, but she soon regained consciousness and looked up at my brother and me as we stood beside her. With a puzzled look she asked 'Where was I?' Then watching us closely as we stood there speechless with grief, she said 'You will bury your mother here.' I said nothing, trying hard to hold back my tears, but my brother said something to the effect that he wished for her sake that she would die in her own country, not abroad. When she heard this, she looked at him anxiously and her eyes reproached him for his worldly thoughts. She turned to me and said, 'See how he talks!' and then, speaking to both of us, she went on, 'It does not matter where you bury my body. Do not let that worry you! All I ask of you is that, wherever you may be, you should remember me at the altar of the Lord.'

Although she hardly had the strength to speak, she managed to make us understand her wishes and then fell silent, for her illness was becoming worse and she was in great pain. But I was thinking of your gifts, O God. Unseen by us you plant them like seeds in the hearts of your faithful and they grow to bear wonderful fruits. This thought filled me with joy and I thanked you for your gifts, for I had always known, and well remembered now, my mother's great anxiety to be buried beside her husband's body in the grave which she had provided and prepared for herself. Because they had lived in the greatest harmony, she had always wanted this extra happiness. She had wanted it to be said of them that, after her journeyings across the sea, it had been granted to her that the earthly remains of husband and wife should be joined as one and covered by the same earth. How little the human mind can understand God's purpose! I did not know when it was that your good gifts had borne their full fruit and her heart had begun to renounce this vain desire, but I was both surprised and pleased to find that it was so. And yet, when we talked at the window and she asked, 'What is left for me to do in this world?', it was clear that she had no desire to die in her own country. Afterwards I also heard that one day during our stay at Ostia, when I was absent, she had talked in a motherly way to some of my friends and had spoken to them of the contempt of this life and the blessings of death. They were astonished to find such courage in a woman—it was your gift to her, O Lord—and asked whether she was not frightened at the thought of leaving her body so far from her own country. 'Nothing is far from God,' she replied, 'and I need have no fear that he will not know where to find me when he comes to raise me to life at the end of the world.'

And so on the ninth day of her illness, when she was fifty-six and I was thirty-three, her pious and devoted soul was set free from the body.

12

I closed her eyes, and a great wave of sorrow surged into my heart. It would have overflowed in tears if I had not made a strong effort of will and stemmed the flow, so that the tears dried in my eyes. What a terrible struggle it was to hold them back! As she breathed her last, the boy Adeodatus began to wail aloud and only ceased his cries when we all checked him. I, too, felt that I wanted to cry like a child, but a more mature voice within me, the voice of my heart, bade me keep my sobs in check, and I remained silent. For we did not think it right to mark my mother's death with weeping and moaning, because such lamentations are the usual accompaniment of death when it is thought of as a state of misery or as total extinction. But she had not died in misery nor had she wholly died. Of this we were certain, both because we knew what a holy life she had led and also because our faith was real and we had sure reasons not to doubt it.

What was it, then, that caused me such deep sorrow? It can only have been because the wound was fresh, the wound I had received when our life together, which had been so precious and so dear to me, was suddenly cut off. I found comfort in the memory that as I did what I could for my mother in the last stages of her illness, she had caressed me and said that I was a good son to her. With great emotion she told me that she could not remember ever having heard me speak a single hard or disrespectful word against her. And yet, O God who made us both, how could there be any comparison between the honour which I showed to her and the devoted service she had given me? It was because I was now bereft of all the comfort I had had from her that my soul was wounded and my life seemed shattered, for her life and mine had been as one.

❖   ❖   ❖

You knew, O Lord, how I suffered, but my friends did not, and as they listened intently to my words, they thought that I had no sense of grief. But in your ears, where none of them could hear, I blamed myself for my tender feelings. I fought against the wave of sorrow and for a while it receded, but then it swept upon me again with full force. It did not bring me to tears and no sign of it showed in my face, but I knew well enough what I was stifling in my heart. It was misery to feel myself so weak a victim of these human emotions, although we cannot escape them, since they are the natural lot of mankind, and so I had the added sorrow of being grieved by my own feelings, so that I was tormented by a twofold agony.

When the body was carried out for burial, I went and returned without a tear. I did not weep even during the prayers which we recited while the sacrifice of our redemption was offered for my mother and her body rested by the grave before it was laid in the earth, as is the custom there. Yet all that day I was secretly weighed down with grief. With all my heart I begged you to heal my sorrow, but you did not grant my prayer. I believe that this was because you wished to impress upon my memory, if only by this one lesson, how firmly the mind is gripped in the bonds of habit, even when it is nourished on the world of truth. I thought I would go to the baths, because I had been told that the Latin name for them was derived from the Greek βαλανειον, so called because bathing rids the mind of anxiety. And I acknowledge your mercy in this too, O Father of orphans,[28] for I went to the baths and came back in the same state as before. Water could not wash away the bitter grief from my heart. Then I went to sleep and woke up to find that the rest had brought me some relief from my sorrow. As I lay alone in bed, I remembered the verses of your servant Ambrose and realized the truth of them:

> Deus, Creator omnium,
> polique Rector, vestiens
> diem decoro lumine,
> noctem sopora gratia,
>
> Artus solutos ut quies
> reddat laboris usui,
> mentesque fessas allevet,
> luctusque solvat anxios.[29]

Then little by little, my old feelings about your handmaid came back to me. I thought of her devoted love for you and the tenderness and patience she had shown to me, like the holy woman that she was. Of all this I found myself suddenly deprived, and it was a comfort to me to weep for her and for myself and to offer my tears to you for her sake and for mine. The tears which I had been holding back streamed down, and I let them flow as freely as they would, making of them a pillow for my heart. On them it rested, for my weeping sounded in your ears alone, not in the ears of men who might have misconstrued it and despised it.

And now, O Lord, I make you my confession in this book. Let any man read it who will. Let him understand it as he will. And if he finds

---

[28]See Ps. 67:6 (68:5).
[29]Maker of all things! God most high!
Great Ruler of the starry sky!
Who, robing day with beauteous light,
Hath clothed in soft repose the night,

That sleep may wearied limbs restore,
And fit for toil and use once more;
May gently soothe the careworn breast,
And lull our anxious griefs to rest.
—From Saint Ambrose's 'Evening Hymn',
trs. J. D. Chambers, 1854.

that I sinned by weeping for my mother, even if only for a fraction of an hour, let him not mock at me. For this was the mother, now dead and hidden awhile from my sight, who had wept over me for many years so that I might live in your sight. Let him not mock at me but weep himself, if his charity is great. Let him weep for my sins to you, the Father of all the brothers of your Christ.

13

Now that my soul has recovered from that wound, in which perhaps I was guilty of too much worldly affection, tears of another sort stream from my eyes. They are tears which I offer to you, my God, for your handmaid. They flow from a spirit which trembles at the thought of the dangers which await every soul that *has died with Adam.*[30] For although she was alive in Christ even before her soul was parted from the body, and her faith and the good life she led resounded to the glory of your name, yet I cannot presume to say that from the time when she was reborn in baptism no word contrary to your commandments ever fell from her lips. Your Son, the Truth, has said: *Any man who says to his brother, You fool, must answer for it in hell fire,*[31] and however praiseworthy a man's life may be, it will go hard with him if you lay aside your mercy when you come to examine it. But you do not search out our faults ruthlessly, and because of this we hope and believe that one day we shall find a place with you. Yet if any man makes a list of his deserts, what would it be but a list of your gifts? If only men would know themselves for what they are! If only *they who boast would make their boast in the Lord!*[32]

And so, my Glory and my Life, God of my heart, I will lay aside for a while all the good deeds which my mother did. For them I thank you, but now I pray to you for her sins. Hear me through your Son, who hung on the cross and now *sits at your right hand and pleads for us,*[33] for he is the true medicine of our wounds. I know that my mother always acted with mercy and that she forgave others with all her heart when they trespassed against her. Forgive her too, O Lord, if ever she trespassed against you in all the long years of her life after baptism. Forgive her, I beseech you; *do not call her to account.*[34] Let *your mercy give your judgement an honourable welcome,*[35] for your words are true and you have promised mercy to the merciful. If they are merciful, it is by your gift; and *you will show pity on those whom you pity; you will show mercy where you are merciful.*[36]

---

[30] I Cor. 15:22.
[31] Matt. 5:22.
[32] II Cor. 10:17.
[33] Rom. 8:34.
[34] Ps. 142:2 (143:2).
[35] James 2:13.
[36] Rom. 9:15.

I believe that you have already done what I ask of you, but, *Lord, accept these vows of mine.*[37] For on the day when she was so soon to be released from the flesh she had no care whether her body was to be buried in a rich shroud or embalmed with spices, nor did she wish to have a special monument or a grave in her own country. These were not the last wishes she passed on to us. All she wanted was that we should remember her at your altar, where she had been your servant day after day, without fail. For she knew that at your altar we receive the holy Victim, who *cancelled the decree made to our prejudice,*[38] and in whom we have triumphed over the enemy who reckons up our sins, trying to find some charge to bring against us, yet can find no fault in him in whom we conquer. Who shall restore to him his innocent blood? Who shall take us from him by repaying him the price for which he bought us? By the strong ties of faith your handmaid had bound her soul to this sacrament of our redemption. Let no one tear her away from your protection. Let not the devil, who is *lion and serpent*[39] in one, bar her way by force or by guile. For she will not answer that she has no debt to pay, for fear that her cunning accuser should prove her wrong and win her for himself. Her reply will be that her debt has been paid by Christ, to whom none can repay the price which he paid for us, though the debt was not his to pay.

Let her rest in peace with her husband. He was her first husband and she married no other after him. She served him, *yielding you a harvest,*[40] so that in the end she also won him for you. O my Lord, my God, inspire your servants my brothers—they are your sons and my masters, whom I serve with heart and voice and pen—inspire those of them who read this book to remember Monica, your servant, at your altar and with her Patricius, her husband, who died before her, by whose bodies you brought me into this life, though how it was I do not know. With pious hearts let them remember those who were not only my parents in this light that fails, but were also my brother and sister, subject to you, our Father, in our Catholic mother the Church, and will be my fellow citizens in the eternal Jerusalem for which your people sigh throughout their pilgrimage, from the time when they set out until the time when they return to you. So it shall be that the last request that my mother made to me shall be granted in the prayers of the many who read my confessions more fully than in mine alone.

---

[37]Ps. 118:108 (119:108).
[38]Col. 2:14.
[39]Ps. 90:13 (91:13).
[40]Luke 8:15.

DANTE ALIGHIERI

(1265-1321)

Preface

THE GREATEST POET BETWEEN HOMER AND SHAKESPEARE, DANTE IS THE authentic voice of medieval Europe. His *Divine Comedy*[1] so comprehensively embodies the thought and aspirations of ten Christian centuries that it is the unrivaled masterpiece of the Middle Ages. One of the supreme feats of imaginative creation, Dante's poem traces the journey of a soul through the terror of Hell and the hope of Purgatory to the dazzling glory of Heaven. With Promethean vision, Dante incorporates into his work literally all that was known in his time about the world, man, and God. In the sense of giving total expression to the spirit of an age, no other poet approaches Dante's achievement.

Born in Florence, Italy, to an ancient but impoverished family, Dante was both poet and aspiring statesman. His political career was cut short, however, when in 1302 he was exiled from his native city on a false charge of embezzlement. According to the harsh laws of the age, he was condemned to be burned alive if ever he came under the jurisdiction of the Florentine republic. His life thereafter was a sad record of wandering from city to city, earning his bread by teaching and political counseling, and yearning for a return to his beloved Florence. After nearly twenty years of labor and disappointment, Dante died in Ravenna. Florence has since attempted to claim the remains of her most distinguished native son, but his bones remain in the city that offered him refuge.

Only seven cantos of the *Inferno,* the first section of the three-part *Divine Comedy,* were completed when Dante was banished; consequently, the bulk of the work is, among many other things, the spiritual autobiography of an unhappy man looking for deliverance from the wreck of his private life. But Dante, who appears as the chief character of his narrative, also stands for every man on his bewildering journey through life. The poem, part epic, part drama, and something beyond either of these genres, is an allegorical quest in which literal characters and events are symbols of unseen realities. In Dante's allegory—one of the most elaborate ever written—Hell, Purgatory, and Heaven are not only literal places the narrator visits, but also states of mind, conditions of the soul, and images of sin, repentance, and salvation. Virgil, who guides Dante through the Inferno and to the gates of paradise atop Mount Purgatory, is both the ghost of a dead Latin poet and a manifestation of human reason. Beatrice, whose intervention in heaven makes possible Dante's journey through the after-life, is both the girl Dante loved[2] and a symbol of divine revelation. When Dante, purified

---

[1]Because it began in misery but ended happily, Dante simply called his work a *Commedia.* Later generations added the adjective "divine."

[2]In *La Vita Nuova* (*The New Life*), Dante tells of the famous incident when he, at age nine, met the eight-year-old daughter of Folco Portinari, a wealthy Florentine. He glimpsed her only a few times thereafter, but she became for him the image of all that was gracious, holy, and beautiful. When she died in 1290, Dante resolved "to write of her what never yet was written of any woman." She became the heroine of his *Divine Comedy.*

by the fires of suffering, reaches a state of sinless perfection represented
by his entrance into the Garden of Eden (*Purgatory, XXX*). Beatrice
replaces Virgil as Dante's guide and escorts him to the celestial paradise.
The change of mentors is itself symbolic of the fact that while reason can
bring men to a knowledge of error (Hell) and a desire for spiritual
cleansing (Purgatory) it can not reveal to him the nature and abode of
God (Heaven).

Since the translators' excellent notes and chapter headings give an
illuminating discussion of particular symbols as the reader encounters
them on his excursion through the afterworld, it is unnecessary to do
more here than to mention the system of correspondences upon which
Dante's imaginative cosmos is structured. Although there were several
astronomical theories current in Dante's time, the Roman Church upheld
the Ptolemaic hypothesis that the earth, because it was the stage where-
center of the universe. In a series of concentric circles, the moon, sun,
upon God and Satan fought for possession of man's soul, was the literal
planets and stars revolved about the earth. It is this geocentric theory
that Dante adopts as most suitable to his poetic vision. His picture of Hell
is a kind of inverted reflection of the solar system as conceived by the
medieval mind. Just as there are nine planetary orbits circling the
physical earth, so within the earth are the nine circles of Hell. Formed by
Satan and his demons when they were hurled from Heaven to earth, Hell
is a funnel-shaped hollow or an inverted cone, twisting like a corkscrew
into the heart of the globe. Because each level is a step further removed
from God, the sins are blacker and the punishment more severe as
Dante descends into the pit. But whatever the nature of the sin, it is
invariably assigned a fitting penalty.

In the vestibule of Hell are the Opportunists, the souls of men and
women who had been indifferent to good and evil alike. Because they
existed for neither God nor the Devil, they are condemned to an eternity
of homelessness. The first circle of Hell proper, across the River Acheron
which marks Hell's boundary, is Limbo, the realm of unbaptized babies
and virtuous pagans. Church doctrine taught that only those dedicated
to Christ could enter Heaven, so all good men who died before Jesus'
resurrection are permanently relegated to Limbo.[3] Illuminated by human reason and inhabited by the great thinkers and poets of antiquity,
this circle is like the Elysian Fields of pagan philosophy. There is no
pain, but neither is there hope of receiving God's grace. At Beatrice's
request, Virgil himself has left this area to guide Dante.

According to a comprehensive scheme of retributive justice, the rest of
the *Inferno* is divided into three general areas of mortal sin and their
appropriate punishments. First are sins of Incontinence or self-
indulgence, which include those of lust, gluttony, and savage anger. The
tortures increase sharply on level VI, where sins of the will and intellect,

---

[3]All except members of God's chosen race, the Israelites. After His crucifixion,
Christ descended into Hell and removed from Limbo the souls of those Jews who
had faithfully awaited His earthly coming.

as opposed to more "instinctive" crimes of the flesh, are punished. Those who corrupted their minds endure worse anguish than illicit lovers like Paolo and Francesca, who merely succumbed to carnal desire. The Inferno's second general category includes crimes of Violence: murder, violations of nature and self-slaughter. The third classification, that of Fraud, encompasses the worst sinners: hypocrites, thieves, evil counselors, and traitors. Symbolic of the three most heinous treacheries of all time, Judas (who betrayed Christ), Cassius and Brutus (who betrayed Julius Caesar), are gnawed eternally in the three maws of Satan, who sits frozen in the ice of hate at the nadir of Hell.

At this point Dante's use of mystically significant numbers requires some explanation. Almost all numbers in the *Divine Comedy* are some multiple or combination of three. The reason for this is that Dante follows medieval theology in regarding the universe as an extension of God's triune nature. According to the doctrine of the Holy Trinity, God was One but manifested Himself through three aspects: God the Father (the Creator), God the Son (the Christ), and God the Holy Ghost (the divine Spirit). Dante even describes Satan, a fallen angel who rebelled because he wanted to equal God, as a distortion of the Trinity: his three faces are a grotesque parody of God. His wish to honor the Trinity accounts for Dante's division of his poem into three parts: Hell (revealing God's justice), Purgatory (demonstrating His mercy), and Heaven (showing His love). Each realm of the afterworld is subdivided into nine sections (the square of three) and each section of the poem contains thirty-three cantos (a double symbol of the Trinity). Adding the introductory canto to the three sections of the thirty-three cantos each, gives a mystical total of 100, which is both the symbol of perfection and a multiple of God's unity. Even the verse form which Dante invented for his purpose, the *terza rima*, contains three lines in each stanza. In the highly structured universe which Dante wishes to reproduce in his poem, nothing is without significance.

On the side of the earth opposite the entrance to Hell is the Mount of Purgatory, built of earth thrown up when the ground fled from Satan's approach during his fall from Heaven. Since according to medieval geography all land masses were grouped in the northern hemisphere, Purgatory, on the southern half of the globe, is therefore entirely surrounded by water. Like Hell, it is divided into nine sections, in which the seven deadly sins (Pride, Envy, Wrath, Sloth, Avarice, Gluttony, and Lust) are punished. The chief difference between the Inferno and Purgatory is that while consignment to Hell is eternal and without hope, placement in Purgatory is only temporary. The damned of Hell died without repentance while souls in Purgatory, though they were sinful, died abhorring the moral crimes they had committed and had received absolution from the Church. The atmosphere is consequently different from the oppressive gloom of Hell. On the Mount of Purgatory the souls rejoice in their agony, delighted to suffer a pain that will cleanse them of sin and prepare them for entrance into Heaven. Symbolic of the sinless state which purified souls eventually attain is the presence of the Garden of Eden on Purgatory's summit. Once the paradisiac home of the first human couple, Eden represents the fact that souls who reach it have returned to the innocence which Adam and Eve possessed before their fall into original sin. After drinking of Eden's River Lethe, an act which washes away all memory of past evil, the souls joyfully ascend to their rightful place in Heaven.

At this stage of Dante's journey, Virgil disappears. Beatrice descends from Heaven to replace him and conducts Dante to a vision of the celestial paradise. Like Hell and Purgatory, Heaven consists of nine concentric circles, symbolized by the orbits of the sun, moon, planets, and stars which wheel about the immobile earth. As Dante progresses upward through increasingly blessed ranks of martyrs and saints, he approaches the ineffable source of all goodness, light, and love, the universal center about which all creation endlessly revolves. With the help of St. Bernard, who appeals to the Virgin Mary (a manifestation of divine mercy), Dante finally beholds the beatific vision of God. Because the sight is untranslatable into mere words, Dante depicts God by the metaphor of three concentric circles of radiant light which represent the mystery of Trinity in Unity. Having experienced the reality and beauty of God, with whom he has momentarily become one, Dante has imparted to Him the hope of Grace by which his soul will be saved after he returns to earth.

Dante's fleeting glimpse of Immortality is the culmination, in Christian terms, of the search for meaning that had begun with Gilgamesh and the Greek philosophers. But while Gilgamesh sought a literal plant that would restore his youth and Socrates hoped through reason to mount the ladder of Love and embrace the eternal Ideal, Dante attains the goal through neither reason nor the labors of his quest. After the experiences of Hell and Purgatory had transformed and purified his soul, Dante receives the ultimate revelation as a gift—the unmerited Grace of God. Momentary as the vision was, it provided the supreme image of that which has and will forever attract man to the stars.

THE DIVINE COMEDY

INFERNO

CANTO I

THE DARK WOOD OF ERROR

Midway in his allotted threescore years and ten, Dante comes to himself with a start and realizes that he has strayed from the True Way into the Dark Wood of Error (Worldliness). As soon as he has realized his loss, Dante lifts his eyes and sees the first light of the sunrise (the Sun is the Symbol of Divine Illumination) lighting the shoulders of a little hill (The Mount of Joy). It is the Easter Season, the time of resurrection, and the sun is in its equinoctial rebirth. This juxtaposition of joyous symbols fills Dante with hope and he sets out at once to climb directly up the Mount of Joy, but almost immediately his way is blocked by the Three Beasts of Worldliness: THE LEOPARD OF MALICE AND FRAUD, THE LION OF VIOLENCE AND AMBITION, and THE SHE-WOLF OF INCONTINENCE. These beasts, and especially the She-Wolf, drive him back despairing into the darkness of error. But just as all seems lost, a figure appears to him. It is the shade of VIRGIL, Dante's symbol of HUMAN REASON.

Virgil explains that he has been sent to lead Dante from error. There can, however, be no direct ascent past the beasts: the man who would escape them must go a longer and harder way. First he must descend through Hell (The Recognition of Sin), then he must ascend through Purgatory (The Renunciation of Sin), and only then may he reach the pinnacle of joy and come to the Light of God. Virgil offers to guide Dante, but only as far as Human Reason can go. Another guide (BEATRICE, symbol of DIVINE LOVE) must take over for the final ascent, for Human Reason is self-limited. Dante submits himself joyously to Virgil's guidance and they move off.

Midway in our life's journey, I went astray
    from the straight road and woke to find myself
    alone in a dark wood. How shall I say

what wood that was! I never saw so drear,
    so rank, so arduous a wilderness!
    Its very memory gives a shape to fear.

Death could scarce be more bitter than that place!
    But since it came to good, I will recount
    all that I found revealed there by God's grace.

How I came to it I cannot rightly say,
    so drugged and loose with sleep had I become
    when I first wandered there from the True Way.

But at the far end of that valley of evil
    whose maze had sapped my very heart with fear!
    I found myself before a little hill

and lifted up my eyes. Its shoulders glowed
    already with the sweet rays of that planet
    whose virtue leads men straight on every road,

and the shining strengthened me against the fright
    whose agony had wracked the lake of my heart
    through all the terrors of that piteous night.

Just as a swimmer, who with his last breath
    flounders ashore from perilous seas, might turn
    to memorize the wide water of his death—

so did I turn, my soul still fugitive
    from death's surviving image, to stare down
    that pass that none had ever left alive.

And there I lay to rest from my heart's race
    till calm and breath returned to me. Then rose
    and pushed up that dead slope at such a pace

each footfall rose above the last. And lo!
    almost at the beginning of the rise
    I faced a spotted Leopard, all tremor and flow

and gaudy pelt. And it would not pass, but stood
    so blocking my every turn that time and again
    I was on the verge of turning back to the wood.

This fell at the first widening of the dawn
    as the sun was climbing Aries with those stars
    that rode with him to light the new creation.

Thus the holy hour and the sweet season
    of commemoration did much to arm my fear
    of that bright murderous beast with their good omen.

Yet not so much but what I shook with dread
    at sight of a great Lion that broke upon me
    raging with hunger, its enormous head   (45)

held high as if to strike a mortal terror
    into the very air. And down his track,
    a She-Wolf drove upon me, a starved horror

ravening and wasted beyond all belief.
    She seemed a rack for avarice, gaunt and craving.
    Oh many the souls she has brought to endless grief!

She brought such heaviness upon my spirit
    at sight of her savagery and desperation,
    I died from every hope of that high summit.

And like a miser—eager in acquisition
    but desperate in self-reproach when Fortune's wheel
    turns to the hour of his loss—all tears and attrition

I wavered back; and still the beast pursued,
    forcing herself against me bit by bit
    till I slid back into the sunless wood.   (60)

And as I fell to my soul's ruin, a presence
    gathered before me on the discolored air,
    the figure of one who seemed hoarse from long silence.

At sight of him in that friendless waste I cried:
    "Have pity on me, whatever thing you are,
    whether shade or living man." And it replied:

"Not man, though man I once was, and my blood
    was Lombard, both my parents Mantuan.
    I was born, though late, *sub Julio,* and bred

in Rome under Augustus in the noon
    of the false and lying gods. I was a poet
    and sang of old Anchises' noble son

who came to Rome after the burning of Troy.
    But you—why do *you* return to these distresses
    instead of climbing that shining Mount of Joy   (75)

which is the seat and first cause of man's bliss?"
    "And are you then that Virgil and that fountain
    of purest speech?" My voice grew tremulous:

"Glory and light of poets! now may that zeal
  and love's apprenticeship that I poured out
  on your heroic verses serve me well!

For you are my true master and first author,
  the sole maker from whom I drew the breath
  of that sweet style whose measures have brought me honor.

See there, immortal sage, the beast I flee.
  For my soul's salvation, I beg you, guard me from her,
  for she has struck a mortal tremor through me."

And he replied, seeing my soul in tears:
  "He must go by another way who would escape
  this wilderness, for that mad beast that fleers   (90)

before you there, suffers no man to pass.
  She tracks down all, kills all, and knows no glut,
  but, feeding, she grows hungrier than she was.

She mates with any beast, and will mate with more
  before the Greyhound comes to hunt her down.
  He will not feed on lands nor loot, but honor

and love and wisdom will make straight his way.
  He will rise between Feltro and Feltro, and in him
  shall be the resurrection and new day

of that sad Italy for which Nisus died,
  and Turnus, and Euryalus, and the maid Camilla.
  He shall hunt her through every nation of sick pride

till she is driven back forever to Hell
  whence Envy first released her on the world.
  Therefore, for you own good, I think it well   (105)

you follow me and I will be your guide
  and lead you forth through an eternal place.
  There you shall see the ancient spirits tried

in endless pain, and hear their lamentation
  as each bemoans the second death of souls.
  Next you shall see upon a burning mountain

souls in fire and yet content in fire,
  knowing that whensoever it may be
  they yet will mount into the blessed choir.

To which, if it is still your wish to climb,
   a worthier spirit shall be sent to guide you.
   With her shall I leave you, for the King of Time,

who reigns on high, forbids me to come there
   since, living, I rebelled against his law.
   He rules the waters and the land and air   (120)

and there holds court, his city and his throne.
   Oh blessed are they he chooses!" And I to him:
   "Poet, by that God to you unknown,

lead me this way. Beyond this present ill
   and worse to dread, lead me to Peter's gate
   and be my guide through the sad halls of Hell."

And he then: "Follow." And he moved ahead
in silence, and I followed where he led.

NOTES

1. *midway in our life's journey:* The Biblical life span is three-score years and ten. The action opens in Dante's thirty-fifth year, i.e., 1300 A.D.

17. *that planet:* The sun. Ptolemaic astronomers considered it a planet. It is also symbolic of God as He who lights man's way.

31. *each footfall rose above the last:* The literal rendering would be: "So that the fixed foot was ever the lower." "Fixed" has often been translated "right" and an ingenious reasoning can support that reading, but a simpler explanation offers itself and seems more competent: Dante is saying that he climbed with such zeal and haste that every footfall carried him above the last despite the steepness of the climb. At a slow pace, on the other hand, the rear foot might be brought up only as far as the forward foot. This device of selecting a minute but exactly-centered detail to convey the whole of a larger action is one of the central characteristics of Dante's style.

THE THREE BEASTS: These three beasts undoubtedly are taken from *Jeremiah* v, 6. Many additional and incidental interpretations have been advanced for them, but the central interpretation must remain as noted. They foreshadow the three divisions of Hell (incontinence, violence, and fraud) which Virgil explains at length in Canto XI, 16-111. I am not at all sure but what the She-Wolf is better interpreted as Fraud and the Leopard as Incontinence. Good arguments can be offered either way.

38-9. *Aries . . . that rode with him to light the new creation:* The medieval tradition had it that the sun was in Aries at the time of the Creation. The significance of the astronomical and religious conjunction is an important part of Dante's intended allegory. It is just before dawn of Good Friday 1300 A.D. when he awakens in the Dark Wood. Thus his new life begins under Aries, the sign of creation, at dawn (rebirth) and in the Easter season (resurrection). Moreover the moon is full and the sun is in the equinox, conditions that did not fall together on any Friday of 1300. Dante is obviously constructing poetically the perfect Easter as a symbol of his new awakening.

69. *sub Julio:* In the reign of Julius Caesar.

95. *The Greyhound . . . Feltro and Feltro:* Almost certainly refers to Can Grande della Scala (1290-1329), great Italian leader born in Verona, which lies between the towns of Feltre and Montefeltro.

100-101. *Nisus, Turnus, Euryalus, Camilla:* All were killed in the war between the Trojans and the Latians when, according to legend, Aeneas led the survivors of Troy into Italy. Nisus and Euryalus (*Aeneid* IX) were Trojan comrades-in-arms who died together. Camilla (*Aeneid* XI) was the daughter of the Latian king and one of the warrior women. She was killed in a horse charge against the Trojans after displaying great gallantry. Turnus (Aeneid XII) was killed by Aeneas in a duel.

110. *the second death:* Damnation. "This is the second death, even the lake of fire." (*Revelation* xx, 14)

118. *forbids me to come there since, living, etc.:* Salvation is only through Christ in Dante's theology. Virgil lived and died before the establishment of Christ's teachings in Rome, and cannot therefore enter Heaven.

125. *Peter's gate:* The gate of Purgatory. (*See Purgatorio* IX, 76 ff.) The gate is guarded by an angel with a gleaming sword. The angel is Peter's vicar (Peter, the first Pope, symbolized all Popes; i.e., Christ's vicar on earth) and is entrusted with the two great keys.
  Some commentators argue that this is the gate of Paradise, but Dante mentions no gate beyond this one in his ascent to Heaven. It should be remembered, too, that those who pass the gate of Purgatory have effectively entered Heaven.
  The three great gates that figure in the entire journey are: the gate of Hell (Canto III, 1-11), the gate of Dis (Canto VIII, 79-113, and Canto IX, 86-87); and the gate of Purgatory, as above.

CANTO II

THE DESCENT

It is evening of the first day (Friday). Dante is following Virgil and finds himself tired and despairing. How can he be worthy of such a vision as Virgil has described? He hesitates and seems about to abandon his first purpose.

To comfort him Virgil explains how Beatrice descended to him in Limbo and told him of her concern for Dante. It is she, the symbol of Divine Love, who sends Virgil to lead Dante from error. She has come into Hell itself on this errand, for Dante cannot come to Divine Love unaided; Reason must lead him. Moreover Beatrice has been sent with the prayers of the Virgin Mary (COMPASSION), and of Saint Lucia (DIVINE LIGHT). Rachel (THE CONTEMPLATIVE LIFE) also figures in the heavenly scene which Virgil recounts.

Virgil explains all this and reproaches Dante: how can he hesitate longer when such heavenly powers are concerned for him, and Virgil himself has promised to lead him safely?

Dante understands at once that such forces cannot fail him, and his spirits rise in joyous anticipation.

The light was departing. The brown air drew down
    all the earth's creatures, calling them to rest
    from their day-roving, as I, one man alone,

prepared myself to face the double war
    of the journey and the pity, which memory
    shall here set down, nor hesitate, nor err.

O Muses! O High Genius! Be my aid!
    O Memory, recorder of the vision,
    here shall your true nobility be displayed!

Thus I began: "Poet, you who must guide me,
    before you trust me to that arduous passage,
    look to me and look through me—can I be worthy?

You sang how the father of Sylvius, while still
    in corruptible flesh won to that other world,
    crossing with mortal sense the immortal sill. (15)

But if the Adversary of all Evil
    weighing his consequence and who and what
    should issue from him, treated him so well—

that cannot seem unfitting to thinking men,
    since he was chosen father of Mother Rome
    and of her Empire by God's will and token.

Both, to speak strictly, were founded and foreknown
    as the established Seat of Holiness
    for the successors of Great Peter's throne.

In that quest, which your verses celebrate,
    he learned those mysteries from which arose
    his victory and Rome's apostolate.

There later came the chosen vessel, Paul,
    bearing the confirmation of that Faith
    which is the one true door to life eternal. (30)

But I—how should I dare? By whose permission?
    I am not Aeneas. *I* am not Paul.
    Who could believe me worthy of the vision?

How, then, may I presume to this high quest
    and not fear my own brashness? You are wise
    and will grasp what my poor words can but suggest."

As one who unwills what he wills, will stay
    strong purposes with feeble second thoughts
    until he spells all his first zeal away—

so I hung back and balked on that dim coast
    till thinking had worn out my enterprise,
    so stout at starting and so early lost.

"I understand from your words and the look in your eyes,"
    that shadow of magnificence answered me,
    "your soul is sunken in that cowardice   (45)

and resolution by imagained perils,
that bears down many men, turning their course
    as his own shadow turns the frightened horse.

To free you of this dread I will tell you all
    of why I came to you and what I heard
    when first I pitied you. I was a soul

among the souls of Limbo, when a Lady
    so blessed and so beautiful, I prayed her
    to order and command my will, called to me.

Her eyes were kindled from the lamps of Heaven.
    Her voice reached through me, tender, sweet, and low.
    An angel's voice, a music of its own:

'O gracious Mantuan whose melodies
    live in earth's memory and shall live on
    till the last motion ceases in the skies,   (60)

my dearest friend, and fortune's foe, has strayed
    onto a friendless shore and stands beset
    by such distresses that he turns afraid

from the True Way, and news of him in Heaven
    rumors my dread he is already lost.
    I come, afraid that I am too-late risen.

Fly to him and with your high counsel, pity,
    and with whatever need be for his good
    and soul's salvation, help him, and solace me.

It is I, Beatrice, who send you to him.
    I come from the blessed height for which I yearn.
    Love called me here. When amid Seraphim

I stand again before my Lord, your praises
    shall sound in Heaven.' She paused, and I began:
    'O Lady of that only grace that raises   (75)

feeble mankind within its mortal cycle
    above all other works God's will has placed
    within the heaven of the smallest circle;

so welcome is your command that to my sense,
    were it already fulfilled, it would yet seem tardy.
    I understand, and am all obedience.

But tell me how you dare to venture thus
    so far from the wide heaven of your joy
    to which your thoughts yearn back from this abyss.'

'Since what you ask,' she answered me, 'probes near
    the root of all, I will say briefly only
    how I have come through Hell's pit without fear.

Know then, O waiting and compassionate soul,
    that is to fear which has the power to harm,
    and nothing else is fearful even in Hell.   (90)

I am so made by God's all-seeing mercy
    your anguish does not touch me, and the flame
    of this great burning has no power upon me.

There is a Lady in Heaven so concerned
    for him I send you to, that for her sake
    the strict decree is broken. She has turned

and called Lucia to her wish and mercy
    saying: 'Thy faithful one is sorely pressed;
    in his distresses I commend him to thee.'

Lucia, that soul of light and foe of all
    cruelty, rose and came to me at once
    where I was sitting with the ancient Rachel,

saying to me: 'Beatrice, true praise of God,
    why dost thou not help him who loved thee so
    that for thy sake he left the vulgar crowd?   (105)

Dost thou not hear his cries? Canst thou not see
    the death he wrestles with beside that river
    no ocean can surpass for rage and fury?

No soul of earth was ever as rapt to seek
    its good or flee its injury as I was—
    when I had heard my sweet Lucia speak—

to descend from Heaven and my blessed seat
    to you, laying my trust in that high speech
    that honors you and all who honor it.'

She spoke and turned away to hide a tear
    that, shining, urged me faster. So I came
    and freed you from the beast that drove you there,

blocking the near way to the Heavenly Height.
    And now what ails you? Why do you lag? Why
    this heartsick hesitation and pale fright   (120)

when three such blessed Ladies lean from Heaven
    in their concern for you and my own pledge
    of the great good that waits you has been given?"

As flowerlets drooped and puckered in the night
    turn up to the returning sun and spread
    their petals wide on his new warmth and light—

just so my wilted spirits rose again
    and such a heat of zeal surged through my veins
    that I was born anew. Thus I began:

"Blesséd be that Lady of infinite pity,
    and blesséd be thy taxed and courteous spirit
    that came so promptly on the word she gave thee.

Thy words have moved my heart to its first purpose.
    My Guide! My Lord! My Master! Now lead on:
    one will shall serve the two of us in this."   (135)

He turned when I had spoken, and at his back
I entered on that hard and perilous track.

NOTES

13-30. AENEAS AND THE FOUNDING OF ROME.
    Here is a fair example of the way in which Dante absorbed pagan themes into his Catholicism.
    According to Virgil, Aeneas is the son of mortal Anchises and of Venus. Venus, in her son's interest, secures a prophecy and a promise from Jove to the effect that Aeneas is to found a royal line that shall rule the world. After the burning of Troy, Aeneas is directed by various signs to sail for the Latian lands (Italy) where his destiny awaits him. After many misadventures, he is compelled (like Dante) to descend to the underworld of the dead. There he finds his father's shade, and there he is shown the shades of the great kings that are to stem from him. (*Aeneid* VI,

921 ff.) Among them are Romulus, Julius Caesar, and Augustus Caesar. The full glory of the Roman Empire is also foreshadowed to him.

Dante, however, continues the Virgilian theme and includes in the predestination not only the Roman Empire but the Holy Roman Empire and its Church. Thus what Virgil presented as an arrangement of Jove, a concession to the son of Venus, becomes part of the divine scheme of the Catholic God, and Aeneas is cast as a direct forerunner of Peter and Paul.

13. *father of Sylvius:* Aeneas.

51-52. *I was a soul among the souls in Limbo:* See Canto IV, lines 31-45, where Virgil explains his state in Hell.

78. *the heaven of the smallest circle:* The moon. "Heaven" here is used in its astronomical sense. All within that circle is the earth. According to the Ptolemaic system the earth was the center of creation and was surrounded by nine heavenly spheres (nine heavens) concentrically placed around it. The moon was the first of these, and therefore the smallest. A cross section of this universe could be represented by drawing nine concentric circles (at varying distances about the earth as a center). Going outward from the center these circles would indicate, in order, the spheres of

> The Moon
> Mercury
> Venus
> The Sun
> Mars
> Jupiter
> Saturn
> The Fixed Stars
> The Primum Mobile

Beyond the Primum Mobile lies the Empyrean.

97. *Lucia:* (Loo-TCHEE-yah) Allegorically she represents Divine Light. Her name in Italian inevitably suggests "luce" (light), and she is the patron saint of eyesight. By a process quite common in medieval religion, the special powers attributed to Lucia seem to have been suggested by her name rather than her history. (In France, by a similar process, St. Clair is the patroness of sight.)

102. *Rachel:* Represents the Contemplative Life.

A note on "thee" and "thou": except for the quotations from the souls in Heaven, and for Dante's fervent declamation to Virgil, I have insisted on "you" as the preferable pronoun form. I have used "thee" and "thou" in these cases with the idea that they might help to indicate the extraordinary elevation of the speakers and of the persons addressed.

CANTO III

THE VESTIBULE OF HELL   THE OPPORTUNISTS

The Poets pass the Gate of Hell and are immediately assailed by cries of anguish. Dante sees the first of the souls in torment. They are THE OPPORTUNISTS, those souls who in life were neither for good nor evil but only for themselves. Mixed with them are those outcasts who took no sides in the Rebellion of the Angels. They are neither in Hell nor out of it. Eternally unclassified, they race round and round pursuing a wavering banner that runs forever before them through the dirty air; and as they run they are pursued by swarms of wasps and hornets, who sting them and produce a constant flow of blood and putrid matter which trickles down the bodies of the sinners and is feasted upon by loathsome worms and maggots who coat the ground.

The law of Dante's Hell is the law of symbolic retribution. As they sinned so are they punished. They took no sides, therefore they are given no place. As they pursued the ever-shifting illusion of their own advantage, changing their courses with every changing wind, so they pursue eternally an elusive, ever-shifting banner. As their sin was a darkness, so they move in darkness. As their own guilty conscience pursued them, so they are pursued by swarms of wasps and hornets. And as their actions were a moral filth, so they run eternally through the filth of worms and maggots which they themselves feed.

Dante recognizes several, among them POPE CELESTINE V, but without delaying to speak to any of these souls, the Poets move to ACHERON, the first of the rivers of Hell. Here the newly-arrived souls of the damned gather and wait for monstrous CHARON to ferry them over to punishment. Charon recognizes Dante as a living man and angrily refuses him passage. Virgil forces Charon to serve them, but Dante swoons with terror, and does not reawaken until he is on the other side.

I AM THE WAY INTO THE CITY OF WOE.
I AM THE WAY TO A FORSAKEN PEOPLE.
I AM THE WAY INTO ETERNAL SORROW.

SACRED JUSTICE MOVED MY ARCHITECT.
I WAS RAISED HERE BY DIVINE OMNIPOTENCE,
PRIMORDIAL LOVE AND ULTIMATE INTELLECT.

ONLY THOSE ELEMENTS TIME CANNOT WEAR
WERE MADE BEFORE ME, AND BEYOND TIME I STAND.
ABANDON ALL HOPE YE WHO ENTER HERE.

These mysteries I read cut into stone
    above a gate. And turning I said: "Master,
    what is the meaning of this harsh inscription?"

And he then as initiate to novice:
    "Here must you put by all division of spirit
    and gather your soul against all cowardice.   (15)

This is the place I told you to expect.
    Here you shall pass among the fallen people,
    souls who have lost the good of intellect."

So saying, he put forth his hand to me,
    and with a gentle and encouraging smile
    he led me through the gate of mystery.

Here sighs and cries and wails coiled and recoiled
    on the starless air, spilling my soul to tears.
    A confusion of tongues and monstrous accents toiled

in pain and anger. Voices hoarse and shrill
    and sounds of blows, all intermingled, raised
    tumult and pandemonium that still

whirls on the air forever dirty with it
    as if a whirlwind sucked at sand. And I,
    holding my head in horror, cried: "Sweet Spirit,   (30)

what souls are these who run through this black haze?"
    And he to me: "These are the nearly soulless
    whose lives concluded neither blame nor praise.

They are mixed here with that despicable corps
    of angels who were neither for God nor Satan,
    but only for themselves. The High Creator

scourged them from Heaven for its perfect beauty,
    and Hell will not receive them since the wicked
    might feel some glory over them." And I:

"Master, what gnaws at them so hideously
    their lamentation stuns the very air?"
    "They have no hope of death," he answered me,

"and in their blind and unattaining state
    their miserable lives have sunk so low
    that they must envy every other fate.   (45)

No word of them survives their living season.
    Mercy and Justice deny them even a name.
    Let us not speak of them: look, and pass on."

I saw a banner there upon the mist.
    Circling and circling, it seemed to scorn all pause.
    So it ran on, and still behind it pressed

a never-ending rout of souls in pain.
    I had not thought death had undone so many
    as passed before me in that mournful train.

And some I knew among them; last of all
    I recognized the shadow of that soul
    who, in his cowardice, made the Great Denial.

At once I understood for certain: these
 were of that retrograde and faithless crew
 hateful to God and to His enemies.   (60)

These wretches never born and never dead
 ran naked in a swarm of wasps and hornets
 that goaded them the more the more they fled,

and made their faces stream with bloody gouts
 of pus and tears that dribbled to their feet
 to be swallowed there by loathsome worms and maggots.

Then looking onward I made out a throng
 assembled on the beach of a wide river,
 whereupon I turned to him: "Master, I long

to know what souls these are, and what strange usage
 makes them as eager to cross as they seem to be
 in this infected light." At which the Sage:

"All this shall be made known to you when we stand
 on the joyless beach of Acheron." And I
 cast down my eyes, sensing a reprimand   (75)

in what he said, and so walked at his side
 in silence and ashamed until we came
 through the dead cavern to that sunless tide.

There, steering toward us in an ancient ferry
 came an old man with a white bush of hair,
 bellowing: "Woe to you depraved souls! Bury

here and forever all hope of Paradise:
 I come to lead you to the other shore,
 into eternal dark, into fire and ice.

And you who are living yet, I say begone
 from these who are dead." But when he saw me stand
 against his violence he began again:

"By other windings and by other steerage
 shall you cross to that other shore. Not here! Not here!
 A lighter craft than mine must give you passage." (90)

And my Guide to him: "Charon, bite back your spleen:
 this has been willed where what is willed must be,
 and is not yours to ask what it may mean."

The steersman of that marsh of ruined souls,
    who wore a wheel of flame around each eye,
    stifled the rage that shook his woolly jowls.

But those unmanned and naked spirits there
    turned pale with fear and their teeth began to chatter
    at sound of his crude bellow. In despair

they blasphemed God, their parents, their time on earth,
    the race of Adam, and the day and the hour
    and the place and the seed and the womb that gave them birth.

But all together they drew to that grim shore
    where all must come who lose the fear of God.
    Weeping and cursing they come for evermore,   (105)

and demon Charon with eyes like burning coals
    herds them in, and with a whistling oar
    flails on the stragglers to his wake of souls.

As leaves in autumn loosen and stream down
    until the branch stands bare above its tatters
    spread on the rustling ground, so one by one

the evil seed of Adam in its Fall
    cast themselves, at his signal, from the shore
    and streamed away like birds who hear their call.

So they are gone over that shadowy water,
    and always before they reach the other shore
    a new noise stirs on this, and new throngs gather.

"My son," the courteous Master said to me,
    "all who die in the shadow of God's wrath
    converge to this from every clime and country.   (120)

And all pass over eagerly, for here
    Divine Justice transforms and spurs them so
    their dread turns wish: they yearn for what they fear.

No soul in Grace comes ever to this crossing;
    therefore if Charon rages at your presence
    you will understand the reason for his cursing."

When he had spoken, all twilight country
    shook so violently, the terror of it
    bathes me with sweat even in memory:

the tear-soaked ground gave out a sigh of wind
that spewed itself in flame on a red sky,
and all my shattered senses left me. Blind,

like one whom sleep comes over in a swoon,
I stumbled into darkness and went down.

NOTES

7-8. *Only those elements time cannot wear:* The Angels, the Empyrean, and the First Matter are the elements time cannot wear, for they will last to all time. Man, however, in his mortal state, is not eternal. The Gate of Hell, therefore, was created before man. The theological point is worth attention. The doctrine of Original Sin is, of course, one familiar to many creeds. Here, however, it would seem that the preparation for damnation predates Original Sin. True, in one interpretation, Hell was created for the punishment of the Rebellious Angels and not for man. Had man not sinned, he would never have known Hell. But on the other hand, Dante's God was one who knew all, and knew therefore that man would indeed sin. The theological problem is an extremely delicate one.

It is significant, however, that having sinned, man lives out his days on the rind of Hell, and that damnation is forever below his feet. This central concept of man's sinfulness, and, opposed to it, the doctrine of Christ's ever-abounding mercy, are central to all of Dante's theology. Only as man surrenders himself to Divine Love may he hope for salvation, and salvation is open to all who will surrender themselves.

8. *and to all time I stand:* So odious is sin to God that there can be no end to its just punishment.

9. *Abandon all hope ye who enter here:* The admonition, of course, is to the damned and not to those who come on Heaven-sent errands. The Harrowing of Hell (see Canto IV, note to 1.53) provided the only exemption from this decree, and that only through the direct intercession of Christ.

57. *who, in his cowardice, made the Great Denial:* This is almost certainly intended to be Celestine V, who became Pope in 1294. He was a man of saintly life, but allowed himself to be convinced by a priest named Benedetto that his soul was in danger since no man could live in the world without being damned. In fear for his soul he withdrew from all worldly affairs and renounced the papacy. Benedetto promptly assumed the mantle himself and became Boniface VIII, a Pope who became for Dante a symbol of all the worst corruptions of the church. Dante also blamed Boniface and his intrigues for many of the evils that befell Florence. We shall learn in Canto XIX that the fires of Hell are waiting for Boniface in the pit of the Simoniacs, and we shall be given further evidence of his corruption in Canto XXVII. Celestine's great guilt is that his cowardice (in selfish terror for his own welfare) served as the door through which so much evil entered the church.

80. *an old man:* Charon. He is the ferryman of dead souls across the Acheron in all classical mythology.

88-90. *By other windings:* Charon recognizes Dante not only as a living man but as a soul in grace, and knows, therefore, that the Infernal Ferry was not intended for him. He is probably referring to the fact that souls destined for Purgatory and Heaven assemble not at his ferry point, but on the banks of the Tiber, from which they are transported by an Angel.

100. *they blasphemed God:* The souls of the damned are not permitted to repent, for repentance is a divine grace.

123. *they yearn for what they fear:* Hell (allegorically Sin) is what the souls of the damned really wish for. Hell is their actual and deliberate choice, for divine grace is denied to none who wish for it in their hearts. The damned must, in fact,

deliberately harden their hearts to God in order to become damned. Christ's grace is sufficient to save all who wish for it.

133-34. DANTE'S SWOON: This device (repeated at the end of Canto V) serves a double purpose. The first is technical: Dante uses it to cover a transition. We are never told how he crossed Acheron, for that would involve certain narrative matters he can better deal with when he crosses Styx in Canto VII. The second is to provide a point of departure for a theme that is carried through the entire descent: the theme of Dante's emotional reaction to Hell. These two swoons early in the descent show him most susceptible to the grief about him. As he descends, pity leaves him, and he even goes so far as to add to the torments of one sinner. The allegory is clear: we must harden ourselves against every sympathy for sin.

CANTO IV

CIRCLE ONE: LIMBO   THE VIRTUOUS PAGANS

Dante wakes to find himself across Acheron. The Poets are now on the brink of Hell itself, which Dante conceives as a great funnel-shaped cave lying below the northern hemisphere with its bottom point at the earth's center. Around this great circular depression runs a series of ledges, each of which Dante calls a CIRCLE. Each circle is assigned to the punishment of one category of sin.

As soon as Dante's strength returns, the Poets begin to cross the FIRST CIRCLE. Here they find the VIRTUOUS PAGANS. They were born without the light of Christ's revelation, and, therefore, they cannot come into the light of God, but they are not tormented. Their only pain is that they have no hope.

Ahead of them Dante sights a great dome of light, and a voice trumpets through the darkness welcoming Virgil back, for this is his eternal place in Hell. Immediately the great Poets of all time appear— HOMER, HORACE, OVID, and LUCAN. They greet Virgil, and they make Dante a sixth in their company.

With them Dante enters the Citadel of Human Reason and sees before his eyes the Master Souls of Pagan Antiquity gathered on a green, and illuminated by the radiance of Human Reason. This is the highest state man can achieve without God, and the glory of it dazzles Dante, but he knows also that it is nothing compared to the glory of God.

A monstrous clap of thunder broke apart
    the swoon that stuffed my head; like one awakened
    by violent hands, I leaped up with a start.

And having risen; rested and renewed,
    I studied out the landmarks of the gloom
    to find my bearings there as best I could.

And I found I stood on the very brink of the valley
    called the Dolorous Abyss, the desolate chasm
    where rolls the thunder of Hell's eternal cry,

so depthless-deep and nebulous and dim
    that stare as I might into its frightful pit
    it gave me back no feature and no bottom.

Death-pale, the Poet spoke: "Now let us go
    into the blind world waiting here below us.
    I will lead the way and you shall follow."   (15)

And I, sick with alarm at his new pallor,
    cried out, "How can I go this way when you
    who are my strength in doubt turn pale with terror?"

And he: "The pain of these below us here,
    drains the color from my face for pity,
    and leaves this pallor you mistake for fear.

Now let us go, for a long road awaits us."
    So he entered and so he led me in
    to the first circle and ledge of the abyss.

No tortured wailing rose to greet us here
    but sounds of sighing rose from every side,
    sending a tremor through the timeless air,

a grief breathed out of untormented sadness,
    the passive state of those who dwelled apart,
    men, women, children—a dim and endless congress.   (30)

And the Master said to me: "You do not question
    what souls these are that suffer here before you?
    I wish you to know before you travel on

that these were sinless. And still their merits fail,
    for they lacked Baptism's grace, which is the door
    of the true faith *you* were born to. Their birth fell

before the age of the Christian mysteries,
    and so they did not worship God's Trinity
    in fullest duty. I am one of these.

For such defects are we lost, though spared the fire
    and suffering Hell in one affliction only:
    that without hope we live on in desire."

I thought how many worthy souls there were
    suspended in that Limbo, and a weight
    closed on my heart for what the noblest suffer.   (45)

"Instruct me, Master and most noble Sir,"
 I prayed him then, "better to understand
 the perfect creed that conquers every error:

has any, by his own or another's merit,
 gone ever from this place to blessedness?"
 He sensed my inner question and answered it:

"I was still new to this estate of tears
 when a Mighty One descended here among us,
 crowned with the sign of His victorious years.

He took from us the shade of our first parent,
 of Abel, his pure son, of ancient Noah,
 of Moses, the bringer of law, the obedient.

Father Abraham, David the King,
 Israel with his father and his children,
 Rachel, the holy vessel of His blessing,   (60)

and many more He chose for elevation
 among the elect. And before these, you must know,
 no human soul had ever won salvation."

We had not paused as he spoke, but held our road
 and passed meanwhile beyond a press of souls
 crowded about like trees in a thick wood.

And we had not traveled far from where I woke
 when I made out a radiance before us
 that struck away a hemisphere of dark.

We were still some distance back in the long night,
 yet near enough that I half-saw, half-sensed,
 what quality of souls lived in that light.

"O ornament of wisdom and of art,
 what souls are these whose merit lights their way
 even in Hell. What joy sets them apart?"   (75)

And he to me: "The signature of honor
 they left on earth is recognized in Heaven
 and wins them ease in Hell out of God's favor."

And as he spoke a voice rang on the air:
 "Honor the Prince of Poets; the soul and glory
 that went from us returns. He is here! He is here!"

The cry ceased and the echo passed from hearing;
    I saw four mighty presences come toward us
    with neither joy nor sorrow in their bearing.

"Note well," my Master said as they came on,
    "that soul that leads the rest with sword in hand
    as if he were their captain and champion.

It is Homer, singing master of the earth.
    Next after him is Horace, the satirist,
    Ovid is third, and Lucan is the fourth. (90)

Since all of these have part in the high name
    the voice proclaimed, calling me Prince of Poets,
    the honor that they do me honors them."

So I saw gathered at the edge of light
    the masters of that highest school whose song
    outsoars all others like an eagle's flight.

And after they had talked together a while,
    they turned and welcomed me most graciously,
    at which I saw my approving Master smile.

And they honored me far beyond courtesy,
    for they included me in their own number,
    making me sixth in that high company.

So we moved toward the light, and as we passed
    we spoke of things as well omitted here
    as it was sweet to touch on there. At last (105)

we reached the base of a great Citadel
    circled by seven towering battlements
    and by a sweet brook flowing round them all.

This we passed over as if it were firm ground.
    Through seven gates I entered with those sages
    and came to a green meadow blooming round.

There with a solemn and majestic poise
    stood many people gathered in the light,
    speaking infrequently and with muted voice.

Past that enameled green we six withdrew
    into a luminous and open height
    from which each soul among them stood in view.

And there directly before me on the green
    the master souls of time were shown to me.
    I glory in the glory I have seen!   (120)

Electra stood in a great company
    among whom I saw Hector and Aeneas
    and Caesar in armor with his falcon's eye.

I saw Camilla, and the Queen Amazon
    across the field. I saw the Latian King
    seated there with his daughter by his throne.

And the good Brutus who overthrew the Tarquin:
    Lucrezia, Julia, Marcia, and Cornelia;
    and, by himself apart, the Saladin.

And rising my eyes a little I saw on high
    Aristotle, the master of those who know,
    ringed by the great souls of philosophy.

All wait upon him for their honor and his.
    I saw Socrates and Plato at his side
    before all others there. Democritus   (135)

who ascribes the world to chance, Diogenes,
    and with him there Thales, Anaxagoras,
    Zeno, Heraclitus, Empedocles.

And I saw the wise collector and analyst—
    Dioscorides I mean. I saw Orpheus there,
    Tully, Linus, Seneca the moralist,

Euclid the geometer, and Ptolemy,
    Hippocrates, Galen, Avicenna,
    and Averrhoës of the Great Commentary.

I cannot count so much nobility;
    my longer theme pursues me so that often
    the word falls short of the reality.   (150)

The company of six is reduced by four.
    My Master leads me by another road
    out of that serenity to the roar

and trembling air of Hell. I pass from light
into the kingdom of eternal night.

NOTES

13 ff. *death-pale:* Virgil is most likely affected here by the return to his own place in Hell. "The pain of these below" then (line 19) would be the pain of his own group in Limbo (the Virtuous Pagans) rather than the total of Hell's suffering.

31 ff. *You do not question:* A master touch of characterization. Virgil's *amour propre* is a bit piqued at Dante's lack of curiosity about the position in Hell of Virgil's own kind. And it may possibly be, by allegorical extension, that Human Reason must urge the soul to question the place of reason. The allegorical point is conjectural, but such conjecture is certainly one of the effects inherent in the use of allegory; when well used, the central symbols of the allegory continue indefinitely to suggest new interpretations and shades of meaning.

53. *a Mighty One:* Christ. His name is never directly uttered in Hell.

53. *descended here:* The legend of the Harrowing of Hell is Apocryphal. It is based on I *Peter* iii, 19: "He went and preached unto the spirits in prison." The legend is that Christ in the glory of His resurrection descended into Limbo and took with Him to Heaven the first human souls to be saved. The event would, accordingly, have occurred in 33 or 34 A.D. Virgil died in 19 B.C.

102. *making me sixth in that high company:* Merit and self-awareness of merit may well be a higher thing than modesty. An additional point Dante may well have had in mind, however, is the fact that he saw himself as one pledged to continue in his own times the classic tradition represented by these poets.

103-105. These lines amount to a stylistic note. It is good style (*'l tacere è bello* where *bello* equals "good style") to omit this discussion, since it would digress from the subject and, moreover, his point is already made. Every great narrator tends to tell his story from climax to climax. There are times on the other hand when Dante delights in digression.

106. A GREAT CITADEL. The most likely allegory is that the Citadel represents philosophy (that is, human reason without the light of God) surrounded by seven walls which represent the seven liberal arts, or the seven sciences, or the seven virtues. Note that Human Reason makes a light of its own, but that it is a light in darkness and forever separated from the glory of God's light. The *sweet brook flowing* round them all has been interpreted in many ways. Clearly fundamental, however, is the fact that it divides those in the Citadel (those who wish to know) from those in the outer darkness.

109. *as if it were firm ground:* Since Dante still has his body, and since all others in Hell are incorporeal shades, there is a recurring narrative problem in the *Inferno* (and through the rest of the *Commedia*): how does flesh act in contact with spirit? In the *Purgatorio* Dante attempts to embrace the spirit of Casella and his arms pass through him as if he were empty air. In the Third Circle, below (Canto VI, 34-36), Dante steps on some of the spirits lying in the slush and his foot passes right through them. (The original lines offer several possible readings of which I have preferred this one.) And at other times Virgil, also a spirit, picks Dante up and carries him bodily.

It is clear, too, that Dante means the spirits of Hell to be weightless. When Virgil steps into Phlegyas' bark (Canto VIII) it does not settle into the water, but it does when Dante's living body steps aboard. There is no narrative reason why Dante should not sink into the waters of this stream and Dante follows no fixed rule in dealing with such phenomena, often suiting the physical action to the allegorical need. Here, the moat probably symbolizes some requirement (The Will to Know) which he and the other poets meet without difficulty.

THE INHABITANTS OF THE CITADEL. They fall into three main groups:

1. *The heroes and heroines:* All of these it must be noted were associated with the Trojans and their Roman descendants. (See note on AENEAS AND THE FOUNDING OF ROME, Canto II.) The Electra Dante mentions here is not the sister of Orestes (see Euripides' *Electra*) but the daughter of Atlas and the mother of Dardanus, the founder of Troy.

2. *The philosophers:* Most of this group is made up of philosophers whose teachings were, at least in part, acceptable to church scholarship. Democritus, however, "who ascribed the world to chance," would clearly be an exception. The group is best interpreted, therefore, as representing the highest achievements of Human Reason unaided by Divine Love. *Plato and Aristotle:* Through a considerable part of the Middle Ages Plato was held to be the fountainhead of all scholarship, but in Dante's time practically all learning was based on Aristotelian theory as interpreted through the many commentaries. *Linus:* the Italian is "Lino" and for it some commentators read "Livio" (Livy).

3. *The naturalists:* They are less well known today. In Dante's time their place in scholarship more or less corresponded to the role of the theoretician and historian of science in our universities. *Avicenna* (his major work was in the eleventh century) and *Avverhoës* (twelfth century) were Arabian philosophers and physicians especially famous in Dante's time for their commentaries on Aristotle. *Great Commentary:* has the force of a title, i.e., The Great Commentary as distinguished from many lesser commentaries.

The Saladin: This is the famous Saladin who was defeated by Richard the Lion-Heart, and whose great qualities as a ruler became a legend in medieval Europe.

CANTO V

CIRCLE TWO   THE CARNAL

The Poets leave Limbo and enter the SECOND CIRCLE. Here begin the torments of Hell proper, and here, blocking the way, sits MINOS, the dread and semi-bestial judge of the damned who assigns to each soul its eternal torment. He orders the Poets back; but Virgil silences him as he earlier silenced Charon, and the Poets move on.

They find themselves on a dark ledge swept by a great whirlwind, which spins within it the souls of the CARNAL, those who betrayed reason to their appetites. Their sin was to abandon themselves to the tempest of their passions: so they are swept forever in the tempest of Hell, forever denied the light of reason and of God. Virgil identifies many among them. SEMIRAMIS is there, and DIDO, CLEOPATRA, HELEN, ACHILLES, PARIS, and TRISTAN. Dante sees PAOLO and FRANCESCA swept together, and in the name of love he calls to them to tell their sad story. They pause from their eternal flight to come to him, and Francesca tells their history while Paolo weeps at her side. Dante is so stricken by compassion at their tragic tale that he swoons once again.

So we went down to the second ledge alone;
    a smaller circle of so much greater pain
    the voice of the damned rose in a bestial moan.

There Minos sits, grinning, grotesque, and hale.
    He examines each lost soul as it arrives
    and delivers his verdict with his coiling tail.

That is to say, when the ill-fated soul
    appears before him it confesses all,
    and that grim sorter of the dark and foul

decides which place in Hell shall be its end,
    then wraps his twitching tail about himself
    one coil for each degree it must descend.

The soul descends and others take its place:
    each crowds in its turn to judgment, each confesses,
    each hears its doom and falls away through space. (15)

"O you who come into this camp of woe."
    cried Minos when he saw me turn away
    without awaiting his judgment, "watch where you go

once you have entered here, and to whom you turn!
    Do not be misled by that wide and easy passage!"
    And my Guide to him: "That is not your concern;

it is his fate to enter every door.
    This has been willed where what is willed must be,
    and is not yours to question. Say no more."

Now the choir of anguish, like a wound,
    strikes through the tortured air. Now I have come
    to Hell's full lamentation, sound beyond sound.

I came to a place stripped bare of every light
    and roaring on the naked dark like seas
    wracked by a war of winds. Their hellish flight (30)

of storm and counterstorm through time foregone,
    sweeps the souls of the damned before its charge.
    Whirling and battering it drives them on,

and when they pass the ruined gap of Hell
    through which we had come, their shrieks begin anew.
    There they blaspheme the power of God eternal.

And this, I learned, was the never ending flight
    of those who sinned in the flesh, the carnal and lusty
    who betrayed reason to their appetite.

As the wings of wintering starlings bear them on
    in their great wheeling flights, just so the blast
    wherries these evil souls through time foregone.

Here, there, up, down, they whirl and, whirling, strain
    with never a hope of hope to comfort them,
    not of release, but even of less pain.   (45)

As cranes go over sounding their harsh cry,
    leaving the long streak of their flight in air,
    so come these spirits, wailing as they fly.

And watching their shadows lashed by wind, I cried:
    "Master, what souls are these the very air
    lashes with its black whips from side to side?"

"The first of these whose history you would know,"
    he answered me, "was Empress of many tongues.
    Mad sensuality corrupted her so

that to hide the guilt of her debauchery
    she licensed all depravity alike,
    and lust and law were one in her decree.

She is Semiramis of whom the tale is told
    how she married Ninus and succeeded him
    to the throne of that wide land the Sultans hold.   (60)

The other is Dido; faithless to the ashes
    of Sichaeus, she killed hereslf for love.
    The next whom the eternal tempest lashes

is sense-drugged Cleopatra. See Helen there,
    from whom such ill arose. And great Achilles,
    who fought at last with love in the house of prayer.

And Paris. And Tristan." As they whirled above
    he pointed out more than a thousand shades
    of those torn from the mortal life by love.

I stood there while my Teacher one by one
    named the great knights and ladies of dim time;
    and I was swept by pity and confusion.

At last I spoke: "Poet, I should be glad
    to speak a word with those two swept together
    so lightly on the wind and still so sad."   (75)

And he to me: "Watch them. When next they pass,
    call to them in the name of love that drives
    and damns them here. In that name they will pause."

Thus, as soon as the wind in its wild course
    brought them around, I called: "O wearied souls!
    if none forbid it, pause and speak to us."

As mating doves that love calls to their nest
    glide through the air with motionless raised wings,
    borne by the sweet desire that fills each breast—

Just so those spirits turned on the torn sky
    from the band where Dido whirls across the air;
    such was the power of pity in my cry.

"O living creature, gracious, kind, and good,
    going this pilgrimage through the sick night,
    visiting us who stained the earth with blood,   (90)

were the King of Time our friend, we would pray His peace
    on you who have pitied us. As long as the wind
    will let us pause, ask of us what you please.

The town where I was born lies by the shore
    where the Po descends into its ocean rest
    with its attendant streams in one long murmur.

Love, which in gentlest hearts will soonest bloom
    seized my lover with passion for that sweet body
    from which I was torn unshriven to my doom.

Love, which permits no loved one not to love,
    took me so strongly with delight in him
    that we are one in Hell, as we were above.

Love led us to one death. In the depths of Hell
    Caïna waits for him who took our lives."
    This was the piteous tale they stopped to tell.   (105)

And when I had heard those world-offended lovers
    I bowed my head. At last the Poet spoke:
    "What painful thoughts are these your lowered brow covers?"

When at length I answered, I began: "Alas!
    What sweetest thoughts, what green and young desire
    led those two lovers to this sorry pass."

Then turning to those spirits once again,
    I said: "Francesca, what you suffer here
    melts me to tears of pity and of pain.

But tell me: in the time of your sweet sighs
    by what appearances found love the way
    to lure you to his perilous paradise?"

And she: "The double grief of a lost bliss
    is to recall its happy hour in pain.
    Your Guide and Teacher knows the truth of this.   (120)

But if there is indeed a soul in Hell
    to ask of the beginning of our love
    out of his pity, I will weep and tell:

On a day for dalliance we read the rhyme
    of Lancelot, how love had mastered him.
    We were alone with innocence and dim time.

Pause after pause that high old story drew
    our eyes together while we blushed and paled;
    but it was one soft passage overthrew

our caution and our hearts. For when we read
    how her fond smile was kissed by such a lover,
    he who is one with me alive and dead

breathed on my lips the tremor of his kiss.
    That book, and he who wrote it, was a pander.
    That day we read no further." As she said this,   (135)

the other spirit, who stood by her, wept
    so piteously, I felt my senses reel
    and faint away with anguish. I was swept

by such a swoon as death is, and I fell,
as a corpse might fall, to the dead floor of Hell.

NOTES

2. *a smaller circle:* The pit of Hell tapers like a funnel. The circles of ledges accordingly grow smaller as they descend.

4. *Minos:* Like all the monsters Dante assigns to the various offices of Hell, Minos is drawn from classical mythology. He was the son of Europa and of Zeus who descended to her in the form of a bull. Minos became a mythological king of Crete, so famous for his wisdom and justice that after death his soul was made judge of the dead. Virgil presents him fulfilling the same office at Aeneas' descent to the underworld. Dante, however, transforms him into an irate and hideous monster with a tail. The transformation may have been suggested by the form Zeus assumed for the rape of Europa—the monster is certainly bullish enough here—but the obvious pur-

pose of the brutalization is to present a figure symbolic of the guilty conscience of the wretches who come before it to make their confessions. Dante freely reshapes his materials to his own purposes.

8. *it confesses all:* Just as the souls appeared eager to cross Acheron, so they are eager to confess even while they dread. Dante is once again making the point that sinners elect their Hell by an act of their own will.

27. *Hell's full lamentation:* It is with the second circle that the real tortures of Hell begin.

34. *the ruined gap of Hell:* See note to Canto II, 53. At the time of the Harrowing of Hell a great earthquake shook the underworld shattering rocks and cliffs. Ruins resulting from the same shock are noted in Canto XII, 34, and Canto XXI, 112 ff. At the beginning of Canto XXIV, the Poets leave the *bolgia* of the Hypocrites by climbing the ruined slabs of a bridge that was shattered by this earthquake.

THE SINNERS OF THE SECOND CIRCLE (THE CARNAL): Here begin the punishments for the various sins of Incontinence (The sins of the She-Wolf). In the second circle are punished those who sinned by excess of sexual passion. Since this is the most natural sin and the sin most nearly associated with love, its punishment is the lightest of all to be found in Hell proper. The Carnal are whirled and buffeted endlessly through the murky air (symbolic of the beclouding of their reason by passion) by a great gale (symbolic of their lust).

53. *Empress of many tongues:* Semiramis, a legendary queen of Assyria who assumed full power at the death of her husband, Ninus.

61. *Dido:* Queen and founder of Carthage. She had vowed to remain faithful to her husband, Sichaeus, but she fell in love with Aeneas. When Aeneas abandoned her she stabbed herself on a funeral pyre she had had prepared.
According to Dante's own system of punishments, she should be in the Seventh Circle (Canto XIII) with the suicides. The only clue Dante gives to the tempering of her punishment in his statement that "she killed herself for love." Dante always seems readiest to forgive in that name.

65. *Achilles:* He is placed among this company because of his passion for Polyxena, the daughter of Priam. For love of her, he agreed to desert the Greeks and to join the Trojans, but when he went to the temple for the wedding (according to the legend Dante has followed) he was killed by Paris.

74. *those two swept together:* Paolo and Francesca (PAH-oe-loe: Frahn-CHAY-ska).
Dante's treatment of these two lovers is certainly the tenderest and most sympathetic accorded any of the sinners in Hell, and legends immediately began to grow about this pair.
The facts are these. In 1275 Giovanni Malatesta (Djoe-VAH-nee Mahl-ah-TEH-stah) of Rimini, called Giovanni the Lame, a somewhat deformed but brave and powerful warrior, made a political marriage with Francesca, daughter of Guido da Polenta of Ravenna. Francesca came to Rimini and there an amour grew between her and Giovanni's younger brother Paolo. Despite the fact that Paolo had married in 1269 and had become the father of two daughters by 1275, his affair with Francesca continued for many years. It was sometime between 1283 and 1286 that Giovanni surprised them in Francesca's bedroom and killed both of them.
Around these facts the legend has grown that Paolo was sent by Giovanni as his proxy to the marriage, that Francesca thought he was her real bridegroom and accordingly gave him her heart irrevocably at first sight. The legend obviously increases the pathos, but nothing in Dante gives it support.

102. *that we are one in Hell, as we were above:* At many points of *The Inferno* Dante makes clear the principle that the souls of the damned are locked so blindly into their own guilt that none can feel sympathy for another, or find any pleasure in the presence of another. The temptation of many readers is to interpret this line romantically: *i.e.,* that the love of Paolo and Francesca survives Hell itself. The more

Dantean interpretation, however, is that they add to one another's anguish (a) as mutual reminders of their sin, and (b) as insubstantial shades of the bodies for which they once felt such great passion.

104. *Caïna waits for him:* Giovanni Malatesta was still alive at the writing. His fate is already decided, however, and upon his death, his soul will fall to Caïna, the first ring of the last circle (Canto XXXII), where lie those who performed acts of treachery against their kin.

124-5. *the rhyme of Lancelot:* The story exists in many forms. The details Dante makes use of are from an Old French version.

126. *dim time:* The original simply reads "We were alone, suspecting nothing." "Dim time" is rhyme-forced, but not wholly outside the legitimate implications of the original, I hope. The old courtly romance may well be thought of as happening in the dim ancient days. The apology, of course, comes after the fact: one does the possible then argues for justification, and there probably is none.

134. *that book, and he who wrote it, was a pander:* "Galeotto," the Italian word for "pander," is also the Italian rendering of the name of Gallehault, who, in the French Romance Dante refers to here, urged Lancelot and Guinevere on to love.

[In Cantos VI and VII the poets traverse the Third and Fourth Circles, wherein the Gluttons and the Hoarders and Wasters are punished. At the beginning of Canto VIII they come to a dismal marsh formed by the River Styx, which marks the boundary of Upper Hell. Across the marsh are the Wrathful and the Sullen.]

CANTO VIII

CIRCLE FIVE: STYX	THE WRATHFUL, PHYLEGYAS
CIRCLE SIX: DIS	THE FALLEN ANGELS

The Poets stand at the edge of the swamp, and a mysterious signal flames from the great tower. It is answered from the darkness of the other side, and almost immediately the Poets see PHLEGYAS, the Boatman of Styx, racing toward them across the water, fast as a flying arrow. He comes avidly, thinking to find new souls for torment, and he howls with rage when he discovers the Poets. Once again, however, Virgil conquers wrath with a word and Phlegyas reluctantly gives them passage.

As they are crossing, a muddy soul rises before them. It is FILIPPO ARGENTI, one of the Wrathful. Dante recognizes him despite the filth with which he is covered, and he berates him soundly, even wishing to see him tormented further. Virgil approves Dante's disdain and, as if in answer to Dante's wrath, Argenti is suddenly set upon by all the other sinners present, who fall upon him and rip him to pieces.

The boat meanwhile has sped on, and before Argenti's screams have died away, Dante sees the flaming red towers of Dis, the Capital of Hell. The great walls of the iron city block the way to the Lower Hell. Properly speaking, all the rest of Hell lies within the city walls, which separate the Upper and the Lower Hell.

Phlegyas deposits them at a great Iron Gate which they find to be guarded by the REBELLIOUS ANGELS. These creatures of Ultimate Evil, rebels against God Himself, refuse to let the Poets pass. Even Virgil is powerless against them, for Human Reason by itself cannot cope with the essence of Evil. Only Divine Aid can bring hope. Virgil accordingly sends up a prayer for assistance and waits anxiously for a Heavenly Messenger to appear.

Returning to my theme, I say we came
    to the foot of a Great Tower; but long before
    we reached it through the marsh, two horns of flame

flared from the summit, one from either side,
    and then, far off, so far we scarce could see it
    across the mist, another flame replied.

I turned to that sea of all intelligence
    saying: "What is this signal and counter-signal?
    Who is it speaks with fire across this distance?"

And he then: "Look across the filthy slew:
    you may already see the one they summon,
    if the swamp vapors do not hide him from you."

No twanging bowstring ever shot an arrow
    that bored the air it rode dead to the mark
    more swiftly than the flying skiff whose prow   (15)

shot toward us over the polluted channel
    with a single steersman at the helm who called:
    "So, do I have you at last, you whelp of Hell?"

"Phlegyas, Phlegyas," said my Lord and Guide,
    "this time you waste your breath: you have us only
    for the time it takes to cross to the other side."

Phlegyas, the madman, blew his rage among
    those muddy marshes like a cheat deceived,
    or like a fool at some imagined wrong.

My Guide, whom all the fiend's noise could not nettle,
    boarded the skiff, motioning me to follow:
    and not till I stepped aboard did it seem to settle

into the water. At once we left the shore,
    that ancient hull riding more heavily
    than it had ridden in all of time before.   (30)

And as we ran on that dead swamp, the slime
    rose before me, and from it a voice cried:
    "Who are you that come here before your time?"

And I replied: "If I come, I do not remain.
    But you, who are *you*, so fallen and so foul?"
    And he: "I am one who weeps." And I then:

"May you weep and wail to all eternity,
    for I know you, hell-dog, filthy as you are."
    Then he stretched both hands to the boat, but warily

the Master shoved him back, crying, "Down! Down!
    with the other dogs!" Then he embraced me saying:
    "Indignant spirit, I kiss you as you frown.

Blessed be she who bore you. In world and time
    this one was haughtier yet. Not one unbending
    graces his memory. Here is his shadow in slime.   (45)

How many living now, chancellors of wrath,
    shall come to lie here yet in this pigmire,
    leaving a curse to be their aftermath!"

And I: "Master, it would suit my whim
    to see the wretch scrubbed down into the swill
    before we leave this stinking sink and him."

And he to me: "Before the other side
    shows through the mist, you shall have all you ask.
    This is a wish that should be gratified."

And shortly after, I saw the loathsome spirit
    so mangled by a swarm of muddy wraiths
    that to this day I praise and thank God for it.

"After Filippo Argenti!" all cried together.
    The maddog Florentine wheeled at their cry
    and bit himself for rage. I saw them gather.   (60)

And there we left him. And I say no more.
    But such a wailing beat upon my ears,
    I strained my eyes ahead to the far shore.

"My son," the Master said, "the City called Dis
    lies just ahead, the heavy citizens,
    the swarming crowds of Hell's metropolis."

And I then: "Master, I already see
the glow of its red mosques, as if they came
hot from the forge to smolder in this valley."

And my all-knowing Guide: "They are eternal
flues to eternal fire that rages in them
and makes them glow across this lower Hell."

And as he spoke we entered the vast moat
of the sepulchre. Its wall seemed made of iron
and towered above us in our little boat.   (75)

We circled through what seemed an endless distance
before the boatman ran his prow ashore
crying: "Out! Out! Get out! This is the entrance."

Above the gates more than a thousand shades
of spirits purged from Heaven for its glory
cried angrily: "Who is it that invades

Death's Kingdom in his life?" My Lord and Guide
advanced a step before me with a sign
that he wished to speak to some of them aside.

They quieted somewhat, and one called, "Come,
but come alone. And tell that other one,
who thought to walk so blithely through death's kingdom,

he may go back along the same fool's way
he came by. Let him try his living luck.
You who are dead can come only to stay."   (90)

Reader, judge for yourself, how each black word
fell on my ears to sink into my heart:
I lost hope of returning to the world.

"O my beloved Master, my Guide in peril,
who time and time again have seen me safely
along this way, and turned the power of evil,

stand by me now," I cried, "in my heart's fright.
And if the dead forbid our journey to them,
let us go back together toward the light."

My Guide then, in the greatness of his spirit:
"Take heart. Nothing can take our passage from us
when such a power has given warrant for it.

Wait here and feed your soul while I am gone
    on comfort and good hope; I will not leave you
    to wander in this underworld alone."   (105)

So the sweet Guide and Father leaves me here,
    and I stay on in doubt with yes and no
    dividing all my heart to hope and fear.

I could not hear my Lord's words, but the pack
    that gathered round him suddenly broke away
    howling and jostling and went pouring back,

slamming the towering gate hard in his face.
    That great Soul stood alone outside the wall.
    Then he came back; his pain showed in his pace.

His eyes were fixed upon the ground, his brow
    had sagged from its assurance. He sighed aloud:
    "Who has forbidden me the halls of sorrow?"

And to me he said: "You need not be cast down
    by my vexation, for whatever plot
    these fiends may lay against us, we will go on.   (120)

This insolence of theirs is nothing new:
    they showed it once at a less secret gate
    that still stands open for all that they could do—

the same gate where you read the dead inscription;
    and through it at this moment a Great One comes.
    Already he has passed it and moves down

ledge by dark ledge. He is one who needs no guide,
and at his touch all gates must spring aside."

NOTES

1. *Returning to my theme:* There is evidence that Dante stopped writing for a longer or shorter period between the seventh and eighth Cantos. None of the evidence is conclusive but it is quite clear that the plan of the *Inferno* changes from here on. Up to this point the Circles have been described in one canto apiece. If this was Dante's original plan, Hell would have been concluded in five more Cantos, since there are only Nine Circles in all. But in the later journey the Eighth Circle alone occupies thirteen Cantos. Dante's phrase may be simply transitional, but it certainly marks a change in the plan of the poem.

19. *Phlegyas:* Mythological King of Boeotia. He was the son of Ares (Mars) by a human mother. Angry at Apollo, who had seduced his daughter (Aesculapius was born of this union), he set fire to Apollo's temple at Delphi. For this offense, the God killed him and threw his soul into Hades under sentence of eternal torment.

Dante's choice of a ferryman is especially apt. Phlegyas is the link between the Wrathful (to whom his paternity relates him) and the Rebellious Angels who menaced God (as he menaced Apollo).

27. *and not till I stepped aboard did it seem to settle:* Because of his living weight.

32. *Filippo Argenti:* (Ahr-DJEN-tee) One of the Adimari family, who were bitter political enemies of Dante. Dante's savagery toward him was probably intended in part as an insult to the family. He pays them off again in the Paradiso when he has Cacciaguida (Kah-tchah-GWEE-da) call them "The insolent gang that makes itself a dragon to chase those who run away, but is sweet as a lamb to any who show their teeth—or their purse."

43. *Blessed be she who bore you:* These were Luke's words to Christ. To have Virgil apply them to Dante after such violence seems shocking, even though the expression is reasonably common in Italian. But Dante does not use such devices lightly. The *Commedia*, it must be remembered, is a vision of the progress of man's soul toward perfection. In being contemptuous of Wrath, Dante is purging it from his soul. He is thereby growing nearer to perfection, and Virgil, who has said nothing in the past when Dante showed pity for other sinners (though Virgil will later take him to task for daring to pity those whom God has shut off from pity), welcomes this sign of relentless rejection. Only by a ruthless enmity toward evil may the soul be purified, and as Christ is the symbol of ultimate perfection by rejection of Evil, so the birth of that rejection in Dante may aptly be greeted by the words of Luke, for it is from this that the soul must be reborn. Righteous indignation, moreover (*giusto sdegno*), is one of the virtues Christ practiced (e.g., against the money changers) and is the golden mean of right action between the evil extremes of wrath and sullenness.

64. *Dis:* Pluto, King of the Underworld of ancient mythology, was sometimes called Dis. This, then, is his city, the metropolis of Satan. Within the city walls lies all the Lower Hell; within it fire is used for the first time as a torment of the damned; and at its very center Satan himself stands fixed forever in a great ice cap.

68. *mosques:* To a European of Dante's time a mosque would seem the perversion of a church, the impious counterpart of the House of God, just as Satan is God's impious counterpart. His city is therefore achitecturally appropriate, a symbolism that becomes all the more terrible when the mosques are made of red-hot iron.

70-71. *they are eternal flues to eternal fire:* The fires of Hell are all within Dis.

80. *spirits purged from Heaven for its glory:* The Rebellious Angels. We have already seen, on the other side of Acheron, the Angels who sinned by refusing to take sides.

95. *time and time again:* A literal translation of the original would read "more than seven times." "Seven" is used here as an indeterminate number indicating simply "quite a number of times." Italian makes rather free use of such numbers.

106. *leaves me:* Dante shifts tenses more freely than English readers are accustomed to.

113. *That Great Soul stood alone:* Virgil's allegorical function as Human Reason is especially important to an interpretation of this passage.

122. *a less secret gate:* The Gate of Hell. According to an early medieval tradition, these demons gathered at the outer gate to oppose the descent of Christ into Limbo at the time of the Harrowing of Hell, but Christ broke the door open and it has remained so ever since. The service of the Mass for Holy Saturday still sings *Hodie portas mortis et seras pariter Salvator noster disrupit.* (On this day our Saviour broke open the door of the dead and its lock as well.)

125. *a Great One:* A Messenger of Heaven. He is described in the next Canto.

CANTO IX

CIRCLE SIX   THE HERETICS

At the Gate of Dis the Poets wait in dread. Virgil tries to hide his anxiety from Dante, but both realize that without Divine Aid they will surely be lost. To add to their terrors THREE INFERNAL FURIES, symbols of Eternal Remorse, appear on a near-by tower, from which they threaten the Poets and call for MEDUSA to come and change them to stone. Virgil at once commands Dante to turn and shut his eyes. To make doubly sure, Virgil himself places his hands over Dante's eyes, for there is an Evil upon which man must not look if he is to be saved.

But at the moment of greatest anxiety a storm shakes the dirty air of Hell and the sinners in the marsh begin to scatter like frightened Frogs. THE HEAVENLY MESSENGER is approaching. He appears walking majestically through Hell, looking neither to right nor to left. With a touch he throws open the Gate of Dis while his words scatter the Rebellious Angels. Then he returns as he came.

The Poets now enter the gate unopposed and find themselves in the Sixth Circle. Here they find a countryside like a vast cemetery. Tombs of every size stretch out before them, each with its lid lying beside it, and each wrapped in flames. Cries of anguish sound endlessly from the entombed dead.

This is the torment of the HERETICS of every cult. By Heretic, Dante means specifically those who did violence to God by denying immortality. Since they taught that the soul dies with the body, so their punishment is an eternal grave in the fiery morgue of God's wrath.

My face had paled to a mask of cowardice
    when I saw my Guide turn back. The sight of it
    the sooner brought the color back to his.

He stood apart like one who strains to hear
    what he cannot see, for the eye could not reach far
    across the vapors of that midnight air.

"Yet surely we were meant to pass these tombs,"
    he said aloud. "If not . . . so much was promised . . .
    Oh how time hangs and drags till our aid comes!"

I saw too well how the words with which he ended
    covered his start, and even perhaps I drew
    a worse conclusion from that than he intended.

"Tell me, Master, does anyone ever come
  from the first ledge, whose only punishment
  is hope cut off, into this dreary bottom?"   (15)

I put this question to him, still in fear
  of what his broken speech might mean; and he:
  "Rarely do any of us enter here.

Once before, it is true, I crossed through Hell
  conjured by cruel Erichtho who recalled
  the spirits to their bodies. Her dark spell

forced me, newly stripped of my mortal part,
  to enter through this gate and summon out
  a spirit from Judaïca. Take heart,

that is the last depth and the darkest lair
  and the farthest from Heaven which encircles all,
  and at that time I came back even from there.

The marsh from which the stinking gasses bubble
  lies all about this capital of sorrow
  whose gates we may not pass now without trouble."   (30)

All this and more he expounded; but the rest
  was lost on me, for suddenly my attention
  was drawn to the turret with the fiery crest

where all at once three hellish and inhuman
  Furies sprang in view, bloodstained and wild.
  Their limbs and gestures hinted they were women.

Belts of greenest hydras wound and wound
  about their waists, and snakes and horned serpents
  grew from their heads like matted hair and bound

their horrid blows. My Master, who well knew
  the handmaids of the Queen of Woe, cried: "Look:
  the terrible Erinyes of Hecate's crew.

That is Megaera to the left of the tower.
  Alecto is the one who raves on the right.
  Tisiphone stands between." And he said no more.   (45)

With their palms they beat their brows, with their nails they clawed
  their bleeding breasts. And such mad wails broke from them
  that I drew close to the Poet, overawed.

And all together screamed, looking down at me:
    "Call Medusa that we may change him to stone!
    Too lightly we let Theseus go free."

"Turn your back and keep your eyes shut tight;
    for should the Gorgon come and you look at her,
    never again would you return to the light."

This was my Guide's command. And he turned me about
    himself, and would not trust my hands alone,
    but, with his placed on mine, held my eyes shut.

Men of sound intellect and probity,
    weigh with good understanding what lies hidden
    behind the veil of my strange allegory!   (60)

Suddenly there broke on the dirty swell
    of the dark marsh a squall of terrible sound
    that sent a tremor through both shores of Hell;

a sound as if two continents of air,
    one frigid and one scorching, clashed head on
    in a war of winds that stripped the forests bare,

ripped off whole boughs and blew them helter skelter
    along the range of dust it raised before it
    making the beasts and shepherds run for shelter.

The Master freed my eyes. "Now turn," he said,
    "and fix your nerve of vision on the foam
    there where the smoke is thickest and most acrid."

As frogs before the snake that hunts them down
    churn up their pond in flight, until the last
    squats on the bottom as if turned to stone—   (75)

so I saw more than a thousand ruined souls
    scatter away from one who crossed dry-shod
    the Stygian marsh into Hell's burning bowels.

With his left hand he fanned away the dreary
    vapors of that sink as he approached;
    and only of that annoyance did he seem weary.

Clearly he was a Messenger from God's Throne,
    and I turned to my Guide; but he made me a sign
    that I should keep my silence and bow down.

Ah, what scorn breathed from that Angel-presence!
  He reached the gate of Dis and with a wand
  he waved it open, for there was no resistance.

"Outcasts of Heaven, you twice-loathsome crew,"
  he cried upon that terrible sill of Hell,
  "how does this insolence still live in you?   (90)

Why do you set yourselves against that Throne
  whose Will none can deny, and which, times past,
  has added to your pain for each rebellion?

Why do you butt against Fate's ordinance?
  Your Cerberus, if you recall, still wears
  his throat and chin peeled for such arrogance."

Then he turned back through the same filthy tide
  by which he had come. He did not speak to us,
  but went his way like one preoccupied

by other presences than those before him.
  And we moved toward the city, fearing nothing
  after his holy words. Straight through the dim

and open gate we entered unopposed.
  And I, eager to learn what new estate
  of Hell those burning fortress walls enclosed,   (105)

began to look about the very moment
  we were inside, and I saw on every hand
  a countryside of sorrow and new torment.

As at Arles where the Rhone sinks into stagnant marshes,
  as at Pola by the Quarnaro Gulf, whose waters
  close Italy and wash her farthest reaches,

the uneven tombs cover the even plain—
  such fields I saw here, spread in all directions,
  except that here the tombs were chests of pain:

for, in a ring around each tomb, great fires
  raised every wall to a red heat. No smith
  works hotter iron in his forge. The biers

stood with their lids upraised, and from their pits
  an anguished moaning rose on the dead air
  from the desolation of tormented spirits.   (120)

And I: "Master, what shades are these who lie
   buried in these chests and fill the air
   with such a painful and unending cry?"

"These are the arch-heretics of all cults,
   with all their followers," he replied. "Far more
   than you would think lie stuffed into these vaults.

Like lies with like in every heresy,
   and the monuments are fired, some more, some less;
   to each depravity its own degree."

He turned then, and I followed through that night
between the wall and the torments, bearing right.

NOTES

1-15. DANTE'S FEAR AND VIRGIL'S ASSURANCE. Allegorically, this highly dramatic scene once more represents the limits of the power of Human Reason. There are occasions, Dante makes clear, in which only Divine Aid will suffice. The anxiety here is the turmoil of the mind that hungers after God and awaits His sign in fear and doubt, knowing that unless that sign is given, the final evil cannot be surmounted.

Aside from the allegorical significance the scene is both powerfully and subtly drawn. Observing Dante's fear, Virgil hides his own. Dante, however, penetrates the dissimulation, and is all the more afraid. To reassure himself (or to know the worst, perhaps) he longs to ask Virgil whether or not he really knows the way. But he cannot ask bluntly; he has too much respect for his Guide's feelings. Therefore, he generalizes the question in such a way as to make it inoffensive.

Having drawn so delicate a play of cross-motives in such brief space, Dante further seizes the scene as an opportunity for reinforcing Virgil's fitness to be his Guide. The economy of means with which Dante brings his several themes to assist one another is in the high tradition of dramatic poetry.

14. *from the first ledge:* Limbo.

20. *Erichtho:* A sorceress drawn from Lucan (*Pharsalia* VI, 508ff).

24. *a spirit from Judaïca . . . :* Judaïca (or Judecca) is the final pit of Hell. Erichtho called up the spirit in order to foretell the outcome of the campaign between Pompey and Caesar. There is no trace of the legend in which Virgil is chosen for the descent; Virgil, in fact, was still alive at the time of the battle of Pharsalia.

34ff. THE THREE FURIES: (or Erinyes) In classical mythology they were especially malignant spirits who pursued and tormented those who had violated fundamental taboos (desecration of temples, murder of kin, etc.). They are apt symbols of the guilty conscience of the damned.

41. *the Queen of Woe:* Proserpine (or Hecate) was the wife of Pluto, and therefore Queen of the Underworld.

50. *Medusa:* The Gorgon. She turned to stone whoever looked at her. Allegorically she may be said to represent Despair of ever winning the Mercy of God. The further allegory is apparent when we remember that she is summoned by the Furies, who represent Remorse.

51. *too lightly we let Theseus go free:* Theseus and Pirithous tried to kidnap Hecate. Pirithous was killed in the attempt and Theseus was punished by being chained to a great rock. He was later set free by Hercules, who descended to his rescue in defiance of all the powers of Hell. The meaning of the Furies' cry is that Dante must be made an example of. Had they punished Theseus properly, men would have acquired more respect for their powers and would not still be attempting to invade the Underworld.

59-60. *my strange allegory:* Most commentators take this to mean the allegory of the Three Furies, but the lines apply as aptly to the allegory that follows. Dante probably meant both. Almost certainly, too, "my strange allegory" refers to the whole *Commedia*.

61ff. *THE APPEARANCE OF THE MESSENGER:* In Hell, God is expressed only as inviolable power. His messenger is preceded by great storms, his presence sends a terror through the damned, his face is the face of scorn.

95. *Cerberus:* When Cerberus opposed the fated entrance of Hercules into Hell, Hercules threw a chain about his neck and dragged him to the upperworld. Cerberus' throat, according to Dante, is still peeled raw from it.

104. THE SIXTH CIRCLE: Once through the gate, the Poets enter the Sixth Circle and the beginning of the Lower Hell.

109ff. *Arles . . . Pola:* Situated as indicated on the Rhone and the Quarnaro Gulf respectively, these cities were the sites of great cemeteries dating back to the time of Rome. The Quarnaro Gulf is the body of water on which Fiume is situated.

114. *The Heretics:* Within the Sixth Circle are punished the Heretics. They lie in chests resembling great tombs, but the tombs are made of iron and are heated red-hot by great fires. The tombs are uncovered, and the great lids lie about on the ground. As we shall learn soon, these lids will be put into place on the Day of Judgment and sealed forever. Thus, once more the sin is refigured in the punishment, for as Heresy results in the death of the soul, so the Heretics will be sealed forever in their death within a death.
It must be noted, however, that Dante means by "heretic" specifically those skeptics who deny the soul's immortality. They stand in relation to the Lower Hell as the Pagans stood in relation to the Upper Hell. The Pagans did not know how to worship God: the Heretics denied His existence. Each group, in its degree, symbolizes a state of blindness. (Other varieties of Heretics are in Bolgia 9 of Circle VIII.) Moreover, in Dante's system, to deny God is the beginning of Violence, Bestiality, and Fraud; and it is these sins which are punished below.

131. *bearing right:* Through all of Hell the Poets bear left in their descent with only two exceptions, the first in their approach to the Heretics, the second in their approach to Geryon, the monster of fraud. Note that both these exceptions occur at a major division of the *Inferno*. There is no satisfactory explanation of Dante's allegorical intent in making these exceptions.

CANTO X

CIRCLE SIX   THE HERETICS

As the Poets pass on, one of the damned hears Dante speaking, recognizes him as a Tuscan, and calls to him from one of the fiery tombs. A moment later he appears. He is FARINATA DEGLI UBERTI, a great war-chief of the Tuscan Ghibellines. The majesty and power of his bearing seem to diminish Hell itself. He asks Dante's lineage and recognizes him as an enemy. They begin to talk politics, but are interrupted by another shade, who rises from the same tomb.

*This one is CAVALCANTE DEI CAVALCANTI, father of Guido
Cavalcanti, a contemporary poet. If it is genius that leads Dante on his
great journey, the shade asks, why is Guido not with him? Can Dante
presume to a greater genius than Guido's? Dante replies that he comes
this way only with the aid of powers Guido has not sought. His reply is a
classic example of many-leveled symbolism as well as an overt criticism
of a rival poet. The senior Cavalcanti mistakenly infers from Dante's
reply that Guido is dead, and swoons back into the flames.*

*Farinata, who has not deigned to notice his fellowsinner, continues
from the exact point at which he had been interrupted. It is as if he
refuses to recognize the flames in which he is shrouded. He proceeds to
prophesy Dante's banishment from Florence, he defends his part in
Florentine politics, and then, in answer to Dante's question, he explains
how it is that the damned can foresee the future but have no knowledge
of the present. He then names others who share his tomb, and Dante
takes his leave with considerable respect for his great enemy, pausing
only long enough to leave word for Cavalcanti that Guido is still alive.*

We go by a secret path along the rim
    of the dark city, between the wall and the torments.
    My Master leads me and I follow him.

"Supreme Virtue, who through this impious land
    wheel me at will down these dark gyres," I said,
    "speak to me, for I wish to understand.

Tell me, Master, is it permitted to see
    the souls within these tombs? The lids are raised,
    and no one stands on guard." And he to me:

"All shall be sealed forever on the day
    these souls return here from Jehosaphat
    with the bodies they have given once to clay.

In this dark corner of the morgue of wrath
    lie Epicurus and his followers,
    who make the soul share in the body's death. (15)

And here you shall be granted presently
    not only your spoken wish, but that other as well,
    which you had thought perhaps to hide from me."

And I: "Except to speak my thoughts in few
    and modest words, as I learned from your example,
    dear Guide, I do not hide my heart from you."

"O Tuscan, who go living through this place
    speaking so decorously, may it please you pause
    a moment on your way, for by the grace

of that high speech in which I hear your birth,
    I know you for a son of that noble city
    which perhaps I vexed too much in my time on earth."

These words broke without warning from inside
    one of the burning arks. Caught by surprise,
    I turned in fear and drew close to my Guide.   (30)

And he: "Turn around. What are you doing? Look there:
    it is Farinata rising from the flames.
    From the waist up his shade will be made clear."

My eyes were fixed on him already. Erect,
    he rose above the flame, great chest, great brow;
    he seemed to hold all Hell in disrespect.

My Guide's prompt hands urged me among the dim
    and smoking sepulchres to that great figure,
    and he said to me: "Mind how you speak to him."

And when I stood alone at the foot of the tomb,
    the great soul stared almost contemptuously,
    before he asked: "Of what line do you come?"

Because I wished to obey, I did not hide
    anything from him: whereupon, as he listened,
    he raised his brows a little, then replied: (45)

"Bitter enemies were they to me,
    to my fathers, and to my party, so that twice
    I sent them scattering from high Italy."

"If they were scattered, still from every part
    they formed again and returned both times," I answered,
    "but yours have not yet wholly learned that art."

At this another shade rose gradually,
    visible to the chin. It had raised itself,
    I think, upon its knees, and it looked around me

as if it expected to find through that black air
    that blew about me, another traveler.
    And weeping when it found no other there,

turned back. "And if, " it cried, "you travel through
    this dungeon of the blind by power of genius,
    where is my son? why is he not with you?"   (60)

And I to him: "Not by myself am I borne
    this terrible way. I am lead by him who waits there,
    and whom perhaps your Guido held in scorn."

For by his words and the manner of his torment
    I knew his name already, and could, therefore,
    answer both what he asked and what he meant.

Instantly he rose to his full height:
    "He *held?* What is it you say? Is he dead, then?
    Do his eyes no longer fill with that sweet light?"

And when he saw that I delayed a bit
    in answering his question, he fell backwards
    into the flame, and rose no more from it.

But that majestic spirit at whose call
    I had first paused there, did not change expression,
    nor so much as turn his face to watch him fall.   (75)

"And if," going on from his last words, he said,
    "men of my line have yet to learn that art,
    that burns me deeper than this flaming bed.

But the face of her who reigns in Hell shall not
    be fifty times rekindled in its course
    before you learn what griefs attend that art.

And as you hope to find the world again,
    tell me: why is that populace so savage
    in the edicts they pronouce against my strain?"

And I to him: "The havoc and the carnage
    that dyed the Arbia red at Montaperti
    have caused these angry cries in our assemblage."

He sighed and shook his head. "I was not alone
    in that affair," he said, "nor certainly
    would I have joined the rest without good reason.   (90)

But I *was* alone at that time when every other
    consented to the death of Florence; I
    alone with open face defended her."

"Ah, so may your soul sometime have rest,"
 I begged him, "solve the riddle that pursues me
 through this dark place and leaves my mind perplexed:

you seem to see in advance all time's intent,
 if I have heard and understood correctly;
 but you seem to lack all knowledge of the present."

"We see asquint, like those whose twisted sight
 can make out only the far-off," he said,
 "for the King of All still grants us that much light.

When things draw near, or happen, we perceive
 nothing of them. Except what others bring us
 we have no news of those who are alive.   (105)

So may you understand that all we know
 will be dead forever from that day and hour
 when the Portal of the Future is swung to."

Then, as if stricken by regret, I said:
 "Now, therefore, will you tell that fallen one
 who asked about his son, that he is not dead,

and that, if I did not reply more quickly,
 it was because my mind was occupied
 with this confusion you have solved for me."

And now my Guide was calling me. In haste,
 therefore, I begged that mighty shade to name
 the others who lay with him in that chest.

And he: "More than a thousand cram this tomb.
 The second Frederick is here, and the Cardinal
 of the Ubaldini. Of the rest let us be dumb."   (120)

And he disappeared without more said, and I
 turned back and made my way to the ancient Poet,
 pondering the words of the dark prophecy.

He moved along, and then, when we had started,
 he turned and said to me, "What troubles you?
 Why do you look so vacant and downhearted?"

And I told him. And he replied: "Well may you bear
 those words in mind." Then, pausing, raised a finger:
 "Now pay attention to what I tell you here:

when finally you stand before the ray
    of that Sweet Lady whose bright eye sees all,
    from her you will learn the turnings of your way."

So saying, he bore left, turning his back
    on the flaming walls, and we passed deeper yet
    into the city of pain, along a track   (135)

that plunged down like a scar into a sink
    which sickened us already with its stink.

NOTES

11. *Jehosaphat:* A valley outside Jerusalem. The popular belief that it would serve as the scene of the Last Judgment was based on *Joel* iii, 2, 12.

14. *Epicurus:* The Greek philosopher. The central aim of his philosophy was to achieve happiness, which he defined as the absence of pain. For Dante this doctrine meant the denial of the Eternal life, since the whole aim of the Epicurean was temporal happiness.

17. *not only your spoken wish, but that other as well:* "All knowing" Virgil is frequently presented as being able to read Dante's mind. The "other wish" is almost certainly Dante's desire to speak to someone from Florence with whom he could discuss politics. Many prominent Florentines were Epicureans.

22. *Tuscan:* Florence lies in the province of Tuscany. Italian, to an extent unknown in America, is a language of dialects, all of them readily identifiable even when they are not well understood by the hearer. Dante's native Tuscan has become the main source of modern official Italian. Two very common sayings still current in Italy are: *"Lingua toscana, lingua di Dio"* (the Tuscan tongue is the language of God) and—to express the perfection of Italian speech—*"Lingua Toscana in bocca romana* (the Tuscan tongue in a Roman mouth).

32-51. *Farinata:* Farinata degli Uberti (DEH-lyee Oob-EHR-tee) was head of the ancient noble house of the Uberti. He became leader of the Ghibellines of Florence in 1239, and played a large part in expelling the Guelphs in 1248. The Guelphs returned in 1251, but Farinata remained. His arrogant desire to rule singlehanded led to difficulties, however, and he was expelled in 1258. With the aid of the Manfredi of Siena, he gathered a large force and defeated the Guelphs at Montaperti on the River Arbia in 1260. Re-entering Florence in triumph, he again expelled the Guelphs, but at the Diet of Empoli, held by the victors after the battle of Montaperti, he alone rose in open counsel to resist the general sentiment that Florence should be razed. He died in Florence in 1264. In 1266 the Guelphs once more returned and crushed forever the power of the Uberti, destroying their palaces and issuing special decrees against persons of the Uberti line. In 1283 a decree of heresy was published against Farinata.

26. *that noble city:* Florence.

39. *"Mind how you speak to him":* The surface interpretation is clearly that Virgil means Dante to show proper respect to so majestic a soul. But the allegorical level is more interesting here. Virgil (as Human Reason) is urging Dante to go forward on his own. These final words then would be an admonition to Dante to guide his speech according to the highest principles.

52. *another shade:* Cavalcante dei Cavalcanti was a famous Epicurean ("like lies with like"). He was the father of Guido Cavalcanti, a poet and friend of Dante. Guido was also Farinata's son-in-law.

61. *Not by myself:* Cavalcanti assumes that the resources of human genius are all that are necessary for such a journey. (It is an assumption that well fits his character as an Epicurean.) Dante replies as a man of religion that other aid is necessary.

63. *whom perhaps your Guido held in scorn:* This reference has not been satisfactorily explained. Virgil is a symbol on many levels—of Classicism, of religiosity, of Human Reason. Guido might have scorned him on any of these levels, or on all of them. One interpretation might be that Dante wished to present Guido as an example of how skepticism acts as a limitation upon a man of genius. Guido's skepticism does not permit him to see beyond the temporal. He does not see that Virgil (Human Reason expressed as Poetic Wisdom) exists only to lead one to Divine Love, and therefore he cannot undertake the final journey on which Dante has embarked.

70. *and when he saw that I delayed:* Dante's delay is explained in lines 112-114.

79. *her who reigns in Hell:* Hecate or Proserpine. She is also the moon goddess. The sense of his prophecy, therefore, is that Dante will be exiled within fifty full moons. Dante was banished from Florence in 1302, well within the fifty months of the prophecy.

83. *that populace:* The Florentines.

97-108. THE KNOWLEDGE OF THE DAMNED: Dante notes with surprise that Farinata can foresee the future, but that Cavalcanti does not know whether his son is presently dead or alive. Farinata explains by outlining a most ingenious detail of the Divine Plan: the damned can see far into the future, but nothing of what is present or *of what has happened.* Thus, after Judgment, when there is no longer any Future, the intellects of the damned will be void.

119. *the second Frederick:* The Emperor Frederick II. In Canto XIII Dante has Pier delle Vigne speak of him as one worthy of honor, but he was commonly reputed to be an Epicurean.

119-120. *the Cardinal of the Ubaldini:* In the original Dante refers to him simply as "il Cardinale." Ottaviano degli Ubaldini (born *circa* 1209, died 1273) became a Cardinal in 1245, but his energies seem to have been directed exclusively to money and political intrigue. When he was refused an important loan by the Ghibellines, he is reported by many historians as having remarked: "I may say that if I have a soul, I have lost it in the cause of the Ghibellines, and no one of them will help me now." The words "If I have a soul" would be enough to make him guilty in Dante's eyes of the charge of heresy.

131. *that Sweet Lady:* Beatrice.

CANTO XI

CIRCLE SIX   THE HERETICS

The Poets reach the inner edge of the SIXTH CIRCLE and find a great jumble of rocks that had once been a cliff, but which has fallen into rubble as the result of the great earthquake that shook Hell when Christ died. Below them lies the SEVENTH CIRCLE, and so fetid is the air that arises from it that the Poets cower for shelter behind a great tomb until their breaths can grow accustomed to the stench.

Dante finds an inscription on the lid of the tomb labeling it as the place in Hell of POPE ANASTASIUS.

Virgil takes advantage of the delay to outline in detail THE DIVISION OF THE LOWER HELL, a theological discourse based on The Ethics *and* The Physics *of Aristotle with subsequent medieval interpreta-*

tions. Virgil explains also why it is that the Incontinent are not punished within the walls of Dis, and rather ingeniously sets forth the reasons why Usury is an act of Violence against Art, which is the child of Nature and hence the Grandchild of God. [By "Art," Dante means the arts and crafts by which man draws from nature, i.e., Industry.]

As he concludes he rises and urges Dante on. By means known only to Virgil, he is aware of the motion of the stars and from them he sees that it is about two hours before Sunrise of Holy Saturday.

We came to the edge of an enormous sink
    rimmed by a circle of great broken boulders.
    Here we found ghastlier gangs. And here the stink

thrown up by the abyss so overpowered us
    that we drew back, cowering behind the wall
    of one of the great tombs; and standing thus,

I saw an inscription in the stone, and read:
    "I guard Anastasius, once Pope,
    he whom Photinus led from the straight road."

"Before we travel on to that blind pit
    we must delay until our sense grows used
    to its foul breath, and then we will not mind it,"

my Master said. And I then: "Let us find
    some compensation for the time of waiting."
    And he: "You shall see I have just that in mind.   (15)

My son," he began, "there are below this wall
    three smaller circles, each in its degree
    like those you are about to leave, and all

are crammed with God's accurst. Accordingly,
    that you may understand their sins at sight,
    I will explain how each is prisoned, and why.

Malice is the sin most hated by God.
    And the aim of malice is to injure others
    whether by fraud or violence. But since fraud

is the vice of which man alone is capable,
    God loathes it most. Therefore, the fraudulent
    are placed below, and their torment is more painful.

The first below are the violent. But as violence
    sins in three persons, so is that circle formed
    of three descending rounds of crueler torments.   (30)

Against God, self, and neighbor is violence shown.
>   Against their persons and their goods, I say,
>   as you shall hear set forth with open reason.

Murder and mayhem are the violation
>   of the person of one's neighbor: and of his goods;
>   harassment, plunder, arson, and extortion.

Therefore, homicides, and those who strike
>   in malice—destroyers and plunderers—all lie
>   in that first round, and like suffers with like.

A man may lay violent hands upon his own
>   person and substance; so in that second round
>   eternally in vain repentance moan

the suicides and all who gamble away
>   and waste the good and substance of their lives
>   and weep in that sweet time when they should be gay.   (45)

Violence may be offered the deity
>   in the heart that blasphemes and refuses Him
>   and scorns the gifts of Nature, her beauty and bounty.

Therefore, the smallest round brands with its mark
>   both Sodom and Cahors, and all who rail
>   at God and His commands in their hearts' dark.

Fraud, which is a canker to every conscience,
>   may be practiced by a man on those who trust him,
>   and on those who have reposed no confidence.

The latter mode seems only to deny
>   the bond of love which all men have from Nature;
>   therefore within the second circle lie

simoniacs, sycophants, and hypocrites,
>   falsifiers, thieves, and sorcerers,
>   grafters, pimps, and all such filthy cheats.   (60)

The former mode of fraud not only denies
>   the bond of Nature, but the special trust
>   added by bonds of friendship or blood-ties.

Hence, at the center point of all creation,
>   in the smallest circle, on which Dis is founded,
>   the traitors lie in endless expiation."

"Master," I said, "the clarity of your mind
    impresses all you touch; I see quite clearly
    the orders of this dark pit of the blind.

But tell me: those who lie in the swamp's bowels,
    those the wind blows about, those the rain beats,
    and those who meet and clash with such mad howls—

why are *they* not punished in the rust-red city
    if God's wrath be upon them? and if it is not,
    why must they grieve through all eternity?"   (75)

And he: "Why does your understanding stray
    so far from its own habit? or can it be
    your thoughts are turned along some other way?

Have you forgotten that your *Ethics* states
    the three main dispositions of the soul
    that lead to those offenses Heaven hates—

incontinence, malice, and bestiality?
    and how incontinence offends God least
    and earns least blame from Justice and Charity?

Now if you weigh this doctrine and recall
    exactly who they are whose punishment
    lies in that upper Hell outside the wall,

you will understand at once why they are confined
    apart from these fierce wraiths, and why less anger
    beats down on them from the Eternal Mind."   (90)

"O sun which clears all mists from troubled sight,
    such joy attends your rising that I feel
    as grateful to the dark as to the light.

Go back a little further," I said, "to where
    you spoke of usury as an offense
    against God's goodness. How is that made clear?"

"Philosophy makes plain by many reasons,"
    he answered me, "to those who heed her teachings,
    how all of Nature,—her laws, her fruits, her seasons,—

springs from the Ultimate Intellect and Its art:
    and if you read your *Physics* with due care,
    you will note, not many pages from the start,

that Art strives after her by imitation,
   as the disciple imitates the master;
   Art, is it were, is the Grandchild of Creation.   (105)

By this, recalling the Old Testament
   near the beginning of Genesis, you will see
   that in the will of Providence, man was meant

to labor and to prosper. But usurers,
   by seeking their increase in other ways,
   scorn Nature in herself and her followers.

But come, for it is my wish now to go on:
   the wheel turns and the Wain lies over Caurus,
   the Fish are quivering low on the horizon,

and there beyond us runs the road we go
down the dark scarp into the depths below."

NOTES

   2. *broken boulders:* These boulders were broken from the earthquake that shook Hell at the death of Christ.

   3. *the stink:* The stink is, of course, symbolic of the foulness of Hell and its sins. The action of the poets in drawing back from it, and their meditations on the nature of sin, are therefore subject to allegorical as well as to literal interpretation.

   8-9. ANASTASIUS and PHOTINUS: Anastasius II was Pope from 496 to 498. This was the time of schism between the Eastern (Greek) and Western (Roman) churches. Photinus, deacon of Thessalonica, was of the Greek church and held to the Acacian heresy, which denied the divine paternity of Christ. Dante follows the report that Anastasius gave communion to Photinus, thereby countenancing his heresy. Dante's sources, however, had probably confused Anastasius II, the Pope, with Anastasius I, who was Emperor from 491 to 518. It was the Emperor Anastasius who was persuaded by Photinus to accept the Acacian heresy.

   17. *three smaller circles:* The Poets are now at the cliff that bounds the Sixth Circle. Below them lies Circles Seven, Eight, and Nine. They are smaller in circumference, being closer to the center, but they are all intricately subdivided, and will be treated at much greater length than were the Circles of Upper Hell.

LOWER HELL: The structure of Dante's Hell is based on Aristotle (as Virgil makes clear in his exposition), but with certain Christian symbolisms, exceptions, and misconstructions of Aristotle's text. The major symbolisms are the three beasts met in Canto I. The exceptions are the two peculiarly Christian categories of sin: Paganism and Heresy. The misconstructions of Aristotle's text involve the classification of "bestiality." Aristotle classified it as a different thing from vice or malice, but medieval commentators construed the passage to mean "another sort of malice." Dante's intent is clear, however; he understood Aristotle to make three categories of sin: Incontinence, Violence and Bestiality, and Fraud and Malice. Incontinence is punished in the Upper Hell. The following table sets forth the categories of the Lower Hell.

THE CLASSIFICATIONS OF SIN IN LOWER HELL

Heresy . . . . Circle   VI

THE VIOLENT
AND BESTIAL
(Circle VII)
(SINS OF THE
LION)

⎧ Round 1. Against Neighbors.
⎪ (Murderers and war-makers)
⎨ Round 2. Against Self.
⎪ (Suicides and destroyers of their
⎪ own substance)
⎩ Round 3. Against God, Art, and Nature.
(Blasphemers, perverts, and usurers)

THE FRAUDULENT
AND MALICIOUS
(SINS OF THE
LEOPARD)

(Circle VIII)
(Simple
Fraud)

Bolgia 1.	Seducers and panderers.
Bolgia 2.	Flatterers.
Bolgia 3.	Simoniacs.
Bolgia 4.	Fortune tellers and diviners.
Bolgia 5.	Grafters.
Bolgia 6.	Hypocrites.
Bolgia 7.	Thieves.
Bolgia 8.	Evil counselors.
Bolgia 9.	Sowers of discord.
Bolgia 10.	Counterfeiters and alchemists.

(Circle IX)
(Compound
Fraud)

Caïna.	Treachery against kin.
Antenora.	Treachery against country.
Ptolemea.	Treachery against guests and hosts.
Judaïca.	Treachery against lords and benefactors.

50. *Sodom and Cahors:* Both these cities are used as symbols for the sins that are said to have flourished within them. Sodom (*Genesis* xix) is, of course, identified with unnatural sex practices. Cahors, a city in southern France, was notorious in the Middle Ages for its usurers.

64. *the center point of all creation:* In the Ptolemaic system the earth was the center of the Universe. In Dante's geography, the bottom of Hell is the center of the earth.

70. *those who lie, etc.:* These are, of course, the sinners of the Upper Hell.

73. *the rust-red city: Dis.* All of Lower Hell is within the city walls.

79. *your* Ethics: *The Ethics* of Aristotle.

101. *your* Physics: *The Physics* of Aristotle.

113. *the Wain lies over Caurus etc.:* The Wain is the constellation of the Great Bear. Caurus was the northwest wind in classical mythology. Hence the constellation of the Great Bear now lies in the northwest. The Fish is the constellation and zodiacal sign of Pisces. It is just appearing over the horizon. The next sign of the zodiac is Aries. We know from Canto I that the sun is in Aries, and since the twelve signs of the zodiac each cover two hours of the day, it must now be about two hours before dawn. It is, therefore, approximately 4:00 A.M. of Holy Saturday.

The stars are not visible in Hell, but throughout the *Inferno* Virgil reads them by some special power which Dante does not explain.

CANTO XII

CIRCLE SEVEN: ROUND ONE

THE VIOLENT
AGAINST NEIGHBORS

The Poets begin the descent of the fallen rock wall, having first to evade the MINOTAUR, who menaces them. Virgil tricks him and the Poets hurry by.

*Below them they see the RIVER OF BLOOD, which marks the First
Round of the Seventh Circle as detailed in the previous Canto. Here are
punished the VIOLENT AGAINST THEIR NEIGHBORS, great war-
makers, cruel tyrants, highwaymen—all who shed the blood of their
fellowmen. As they wallowed in blood during their lives, so they are
immersed in the boiling blood forever, each according to the degree of
his guilt, while fierce Centaurs patrol the banks, ready to shoot with
their arrows any sinner who raises himself out of the boiling blood
beyond the limits permitted him. ALEXANDER THE GREAT is here,
up to his lashes in the blood, and with him ATTILA, THE SCOURGE
OF GOD. They are immersed in the deepest part of the river, which
grows shallower as it circles to the other side of the ledge, then deepens
again.*

*The Poets are challenged by the Centaurs, but Virgil wins a safe
conduct from CHIRON, their chief, who assigns NESSUS to guide them
and to bear them across the shallows of the boiling blood. Nessus carries
them across at the point where it is only ankle deep and immediately
leaves them and returns to his patrol.*

The scene that opened from the edge of the pit
    was mountainous, and such a desolation
    that every eye would shun the sight of it:

a ruin like the Slides of Mark near Trent
    on the bank of the Adige, the result of an earthquake
    or of some massive fault in the escarpment—

for, from the point on the peak where the mountain split
    to the plain below, the rock is so badly shattered
    a man at the top might make a rough stair of it.

Such was the passage down the steep, and there
    at the very top, at the edge of the broken cleft,
    lay spread the Infamy of Crete, the heir

of bestiality and the lecherous queen
    who hid in a wooden cow. And when he saw us,
    he gnawed his own flesh in a fit of spleen.   (15)

And my Master mocked: "How you do pump your breath!
    Do you think, perhaps, it is the Duke of Athens,
    who in the world above served up your death?

Off with you, monster; this one does not come
    instructed by your sister, but of himself
    to observe your punishment in the lost kingdom."

As a bull that breaks its chains just when the knife
    has struck its death-blow, cannot stand nor run
    but leaps from side to side with its last life—

so danced the Minotaur, and my shrewd Guide
    cried out: "Run now! While he is blind with rage!
    Into the pass, quick, and get over the side!"

So we went down across the shale and slate
    of that ruined rock, which often slid and shifted
    under me at the touch of living weight.   (30)

I moved on, deep in thought; and my Guide to me:
    "You are wondering perhaps about this ruin
    which is guarded by that beast upon whose fury

I played just now. I should tell you that when last
    I came this dark way to the depths of Hell,
    this rock had not yet felt the ruinous blast.

But certainly, if I am not mistaken,
    it was just before the coming of Him who took
    the souls from Limbo, that all Hell was shaken

so that I thought the universe felt love
    and all its elements moved toward harmony,
    whereby the world of matter, as some believe,

has often plunged to chaos. It was then,
    that here and elsewhere in the pits of Hell,
    the ancient rock was stricken and broke open.   (45)

But turn your eyes to the valley; there we shall find
    the river of boiling blood in which are steeped
    all who struck down their fellow men." Oh blind!

Oh ignorant, self-seeking cupidity
    which spurs us so in the short mortal life
    and steeps us so through all eternity!

I saw an arching fosse that was the bed
    of a winding river circling through the plain
    exactly as my Guide and Lord had said.

A file of Centaurs galloped in the space
    between the bank and the cliff, well armed with arrows
    riding as once on earth they rode to the chase.

And seeing us descend, that straggling band
    halted, and three of them moved out toward us,
    their long bows and their shafts already in hand.   (60)

And one of them cried out while still below:
    "To what pain are you sent down that dark coast?
    Answer from where you stand, or I draw the bow!"

"Chiron is standing there hard by your side;
    our answer will be to him. This wrath of yours
    was always your own worst fate," my Guide replied.

And to me he said: "That is Nessus, who died in the wood
    for insulting Dejanira. At his death
    he plotted his revenge in his own blood.

The one in the middle staring at his chest
    is the mighty Chiron, he who nursed Achilles:
    the other is Pholus, fiercer than all the rest.

They run by that stream in thousands, snapping their bows
    at any wraith who dares to raise himself
    out of the blood more than his guilt allows."   (75)

We drew near those swift beasts. In a thoughtful pause
    Chiron drew an arrow, and with its notch
    he pushed his great beard back along his jaws.

And when he had thus uncovered the huge pouches
    of his lips, he said to his fellows: "Have you noticed
    how the one who walks behind moves what he touches?

That is not how the dead go." My good Guide,
    already standing by the monstrous breast
    in which the two mixed natures joined, replied:

"It is true he lives; in his necessity
    I alone must lead him through this valley.
    Fate brings him here, not curiosity.

From singing Alleluia the sublime
    spirit who sends me came. He is no bandit.
    Nor am I one who ever stooped to crime.   (90)

But in the name of the Power by which I go
    this sunken way across the floor of Hell,
    assign us one of your troop whom we may follow,

that he may guide us to the ford, and there
    carry across on his back the one I lead,
    for he is not a spirit to move through air."

Chiron turned his head on his right breast
    and said to Nessus: "Go with them, and guide them,
    and turn back any others that would contest

their passage." So we moved beside our guide
    along the bank of the scalding purple river
    in which the shrieking wraiths were boiled and dyed.

Some stood up to their lashes in that torrent,
    and as we passed them the huge Centaur said:
    "These were the kings of bloodshed and despoilment.   (105)

Here they pay for their ferocity.
    Here is Alexander. And Dionysius,
    who brought long years of grief to Sicily.

That brow you see with the hair as black as night
    is Azzolino; and that beside him, the blonde,
    is Opizzo da Esti, who had his mortal light

blown out by his own stepson." I turned then
    to speak to the Poet but he raised a hand:
    "Let him be the teacher now, and I will listen."

Further on, the Centaur stopped beside
    a group of spirits steeped as far as the throat
    in the race of boiling blood, and there our guide

pointed out a sinner who stood alone:
    "That one before God's altar pierced a heart
    still honored on the Thames." And he passed on.   (120)

We came in sight of some who were allowed
    to raise the head and all the chest from the river,
    and I recognized many there. Thus, as we followed

along the stream of blood, its level fell
    until it cooked no more than the feet of the damned.
    And here we crossed the ford to deeper Hell.

"Just as you see the boiling stream grow shallow
    along this side," the Centaur said to us
    when we stood on the other bank, "I would have you know

that on the other, the bottom sinks anew
more and more, until it comes again
full circle to the place where the tyrants stew.

It is there that Holy Justice spends its wrath
on Sextus and Pyrrhus through eternity,
and on Attila, who was a scourge on earth: (135)

and everlastingly milks out the tears
of Rinier da Corneto and Rinier Pazzo,
those two assassins who for many years

stalked the highways, bloody and abhorred."
And with that he started back across the ford.

NOTES

4. *the slides of Mark: Li Slavoni di Marco* are about two miles from Rovereto (between Verona and Trent) on the left bank of the River Adige.

9. *a man at the top might, etc.:* I am defeated in all attempts to convey Dante's emphasis in any sort of a verse line. The sense of the original: "It might provide some sort of a way down for one who started at the top, but (by implication) would not be climbable from below."

12-18. *the Infamy of Crete:* This is the infamous Minotaur of classical mythology. His mother was Pasiphaë, wife of Minos, the King of Crete. She conceived an unnatural passion for a bull, and in order to mate with it, she crept into a wooden cow. From this union the Minotaur was born, half-man, half-beast. King Minos kept him in an ingenious labyrinth from which he could not escape. When Androgeos, the son of King Minos, was killed by the Athenians, Minos exacted an annual tribute of seven maidens and seven youths. These were annually turned into the labyrinth and there were devoured by the Minotaur.

The monster was finally killed by Theseus, Duke of Athens. He was aided by Ariadne, daughter of Minos (and half-sister of the monster). She gave Theseus a ball of cord to unwind as he entered the labyrinth and a sword with which to kill the Minotaur.

The Minotaur was, thus, more beast than human, he was conceived in a sodomitic union, and he was a devourer of human flesh—in all ways a fitting symbol of the souls he guards.

34 ff. THE BROKEN ROCKS OF HELL: According to *Matthew* xxvii, 51, an earthquake shook the earth at the moment of Christ's death. These stones, Dante lets us know, were broken off in that earthquake. We shall find other effects of the same shock in the Eighth Circle. It is worth noting also that both the Upper (See Canto V, 34) and the Lower Hell begin with evidences of this ruin. For details of Virgil's first descent see notes to Canto IX.

38. *the coming of Him, etc.:* For details of Christ's descent into Hell see notes to Canto IV.

40-42. *the universe felt love . . . as some believe:* The Greek philosopher, Empedocles, taught that the universe existed by the counter-balance (discord or mutual repulsion) of its elements. Should the elemental matter feel harmony (love or mutual attraction) all would fly together into chaos.

47. *the river of boiling blood:* This is Phlegethon, the river that circles through the First Round of the Seventh Circle, then sluices through the wood of the suicides (the Second Round) and the burning sands (Third Round) to spew over the Great Cliff into the Eighth Circle, and so, eventually, to the bottom of Hell (Cocytus).

The river is deepest at the point at which the Poets first approach it and grows shallower along both sides of the circle until it reaches the ford, which is at the opposite point of the First Round. The souls of the damned are placed in deeper or shallower parts of the river according to the degree of their guilt.

55. THE CENTAURS: The Centaurs were creatures of classical mythology, half-horse, half-men. They were skilled and savage hunters, creatures of passion and violence. Like the Minotaur, they are symbols of the bestial-human, and as such, they are fittingly chosen as the tormentors of these sinners.

65. *Chiron:* The son of Saturn and of the nymph Philira. He was the wisest and most just of the Centaurs and reputedly was the teacher of Achilles and of other Greek heroes to whom he imparted great skill in bearing arms, medicine, astronomy, music, and augury. Dante places him far down in Hell with the others of his kind, but though he draws Chiron's coarseness, he also grants him a kind of majestic understanding.

67. *Nessus:* Nessus carried travelers across the River Evenus for hire. He was hired to ferry Dejanira, the wife of Hercules, and tried to abduct her, but Hercules killed him with a poisoned arrow. While Nessus was dying, he whispered to Dejanira that a shirt stained with his poisoned blood would act as a love charm should Hercules' affections stray. When Hercules fell in love with Iole, Dejanira sent him a shirt stained with the Centaur's blood. The shirt poisoned Hercules and he died in agony. Thus Nessus revenged himself with his own blood.

72. *Pholus:* A number of classical poets mention Pholus, but very little else is known of him.

88-89. *the sublime spirit:* Beatrice.

97. *Chiron turned his head on his right breast:* The right is the side of virtue and honor. In Chiron it probably signifies his human side as opposed to his bestial side.

107. *Alexander:* Alexander the Great. *Dionysius:* Dionysius I (died 367 B.C.) and his son, Dionysius II (died 343), were tyrants of Sicily. Both were infamous as prototypes of the bloodthirsty and exorbitant ruler. Dante may intend either or both.

110. *Azzolino (or Ezzelino):* Ezzelino da Romano, Count of Onora (1194-1259). The cruelest of the Ghibelline tyrants. In 1236 Frederick II appointed Ezzelino his vicar in Padua. Ezzelino became especially infamous for his bloody treatment of the Paduans, whom he slaughtered in great numbers.

111. *Opizzo da Esti:* Marquis of Ferrara (1264-1293). The account of his life is confused. One must accept Dante's facts as given.

119-120. *that one . . . a heart still honored on the Thames:* The sinner indicated is Guy de Montfort. His father, Simon de Montfort, was a leader of the barons who rebelled against Henry III and was killed at the battle of Evesham (1265) by Prince Edward (later Edward I).
In 1271, Guy (then Vicar General of Tuscany) avenged his father's death by murdering Henry's nephew (who was also named Henry). The crime was openly committed in a church at Viterbo. The murdered Henry's heart was sealed in a casket and sent to London, where it was accorded various honors.

134. *Sextus:* Probably the younger son of Pompey the Great. His piracy is mentioned in Lucan (*Pharsalia*, VI, 420-422). *Pyrrhus:* Pyrrhus, the son of Achilles, was especially bloodthirsty at the sack of Troy. Pyrrhus, King of Epirus (319-372 B.C.), waged relentless and bloody war against the Greeks and Romans. Either may be intended.

135. *Attila:* King of the Huns from 433 to 453. He was called the Scourge of God.

137. *Rinier da Corneto, Rinier Pazzo:* (Rin-YAIR PAH-tsoe) Both were especially bloodthirsty robber-barons of the thirteenth century.

CANTO XIII

CIRCLE SEVEN: ROUND TWO   THE VIOLENT
                                                AGAINST THEMSELVES

Nessus carries the Poets across the river of boiling blood and leaves them
in the Second Round of the Seventh Circle. THE WOOD OF THE
SUICIDES. Here are punished those who destroyed their own lives and
those who destroyed their substance.

The souls of the Suicides are encased in thorny trees whose leaves are
eaten by the odious HARPIES, the overseers of these damned. When the
Harpies feed upon them, damaging their leaves and limbs, the wound
bleeds. Only as long as the blood flows are the souls of the trees able to
speak. Thus, they who destroyed their own bodies are denied a human
form; and just as the supreme expression of their lives was self-destruc-
tion, so they are permitted to speak only through that which tears
and destroys them. Only through their own blood do they find voice.
And to add one more dimension to the symbolism, it is the Harpies—
defilers of all they touch—who give them their eternally recurring
wounds.

The Poets pause before one tree and speak with the soul of PIER
DELLE VIGNE. In the same wood they see JACOMO DA SANT'
ANDREA, and LANO DA SIENA, two famous SQUANDERERS and
DESTROYERS OF GOODS pursued by a pack of savage hounds. The
hounds overtake SANT' ANDREA, tear him to pieces and go off carry-
ing his limbs in their teeth, a self-evident symbolic retribution for the
violence with which these sinners destroyed their substance in the
world. After this scene of horror, Dante speaks to an UNKNOWN
FLORENTINE SUICIDE whose soul is inside the bush which was torn
by the hound pack when it leaped upon Sant' Andrea.

Nessus had not yet reached the other shore
    when we moved on into a pathless wood
    that twisted upward from Hell's broken floor.

Its foliage was not verdant, but nearly black.
    The unhealthy branches, gnarled and warped and tangled,
    bore poison thorns instead of fruit. The track

of those wild beasts that shun the open spaces
    men till between Cecina and Corneto
    runs through no rougher nor more tangled places.

Here nest the odious Harpies of whom my Master
    wrote how they drove Aeneas and his companions
    from the Strophades with prophecies of disaster.

Their wings are wide, their feet clawed, their huge bellies
    covered with feathers, their necks and faces human.
    They croak eternally in the unnatural trees.   (15)

"Before going on, I would have you understand,"
    my Guide began, "we are in the second round
    and shall be till we reach the burning sand.

Therefore look carefully and you will see
    things in this wood, which, if I told them to you
    would shake the confidence you have placed in me."

I heard cries of lamentation rise and spill
    on every hand, but saw no souls in pain
    in all that waste; and, puzzled, I stood still.

I think perhaps he thought that I was thinking
    those cries rose from among the twisted roots
    through which the spirits of the damned were slinking

to hide from us. Therefore my Master said:
    "If you break off a twig, what you will learn
    will drive what you are thinking from your head."   (30)

Puzzled, I raised my hand a bit and slowly
    broke off a branchlet from an enormous thorn:
    and the great trunk of it cried: "Why do you break me?"

And after blood had darkened all the bowl
    of the wound, it cried again: "Why do you tear me?
    Is there no pity left in any soul?

Men we were, and now we are changed to sticks;
    well might your hand have been more merciful
    were we no more than souls of lice and ticks."

As a green branch with one end all aflame
    will hiss and sputter sap out of the other
    as the air escapes—so from that trunk there came

words and blood together, gout by gout.
    Startled, I dropped the branch that I was holding
    and stood transfixed by fear, half turned about   (45)

to my Master, who replied: "O wounded soul,
    could he have believed before what he has seen
    in my verses only, you would yet be whole,

for his hand would never have been raised against you.
    But knowing this truth could never be believed
    till it was seen, I urged him on to do

what grieves me now; and I beg to know your name,
    that to make you some amends in the sweet world
    when he returns, he may refresh your fame."

And the trunk: "So sweet those words to me that I
    cannot be still, and may it not annoy you
    if I seem somewhat lengthy in reply.

I am he who held both keys to Frederick's heart,
    locking, unlocking with so deft a touch
    that scarce another soul had any part   (60)

in his most secret thoughts. Through every strife
    I was so faithful to my glorious office
    that for it I gave up both sleep and life.

That harlot, Envy, who on Caesar's face
    keeps fixed forever her adulterous stare,
    the common plague and vice of court and palace,

inflamed all minds against me. These inflamed
    so inflamed him that all my happy honors
    were changed to mourning. Then, unjustly blamed,

my soul, in scorn, and thinking to be free
    of scorn in death, made me at last, though just,
    unjust to myself. By the new roots of this tree

I swear to you that never in word or spirit
    did I break faith to my lord and emperor
    who was so worthy of honor in his merit.   (75)

If either of you return to the world, speak for me,
    to vindicate in the memory of men
    one who lies prostrate from the blows of Envy."

The Poet stood. Then turned. "Since he is silent,"
    he said to me, "do not you waste this hour,
    if you wish to ask about his life or torment."

And I replied: "Question him for my part,
    on whatever you think I would do well to hear;
    I could not, such compassion chokes my heart."

The Poet began again: "That this man may
    with all his heart do for you what your words
    entreat him to, imprisoned spirit, I pray,

tell us how the soul is bound and bent
    into these knots, and whether any ever
    frees itself from such imprisonment." (90)

At that the trunk blew powerfully, and then
    the wind became a voice that spoke these words:
    "Briefly is the answer given: when

out of the flesh from which it tore itself,
    the violent spirit comes to punishment,
    Minos assigns it to the seventh shelf.

It falls into the wood, and landing there,
    wherever fortune flings it, it strikes root,
    and there it sprouts, lusty as any tare,

shoots up a sapling, and becomes a tree.
    The Harpies, feeding on its leaves then, give it
    pain and pain's outlet simultaneously.

Like the rest, we shall go for our husks on Judgment Day,
    but not that we may wear them, for it is not just
    that a man be given what he throws away. (105)

Here shall we drag them and in this mournful glade
    our bodies will dangle to the end of time,
    each on the thorns of its tormented shade."

We waited by the trunk, but it said no more;
    and waiting, we were startled by a noise
    that grew through all the wood. Just such a roar

and trembling as one feels when the boar and chase
    approach his stand, the beasts and branches crashing
    and clashing in the heat of the fierce race.

And there on the left, running so violently
    they broke off every twig in the dark wood,
    two torn and naked wraiths went plunging by me.

The leader cried, "Come now, O Death! Come now!"
    And the other, seeing that he was outrun
    cried out: "Your legs were not so ready, Lano, (120)

in the jousts at the Toppo." And suddenly in his rush,
    perhaps because his breath was failing him,
    he hid himself inside a thorny bush

and cowered among its leaves. Then at his back,
    the wood leaped with black bitches, swift as greyhounds
    escaping from their leash, and all the pack

sprang on him; with their fangs they opened him
    and tore him savagely, and then withdrew,
    carrying his body with them, limb by limb.

Then, taking me by the hand across the wood,
    my Master led me toward the bush. Lamenting,
    all its fractures blew out words and blood:

"O Jacomo da Sant' Andrea!" it said,
    "what have you gained in making me your screen?
    What part had I in the foul life you led?"   (135)

And when my Master had drawn up to it
    he said: "Who were you, who through all your wounds
    blow out your blood with your lament, sad spirit?"

And he to us: "You who have come to see
    how the outrageous mangling of these hounds
    has torn my boughs and stripped my leaves from me,

O heap them round my ruin! I was born
    in the city that tore down Mars and raised the Baptist.
    On that account the God of War has sworn

her sorrow shall not end. And were it not
    that something of his image still survives
    on the bridge across the Arno, some have thought

those citizens who of their love and pain
    afterwards rebuilt it from the ashes
    left by Attila, would have worked in vain.   (150)

I am one who has no tale to tell:
I made myself a gibbet of my own lintel."

NOTES

6-10. The reference here is to the Maremma district of Tuscany which lies between the mountains and the sea. The river Cecina is the northern boundary of this
district; Corneto is on the river Marta, which forms the southern boundary. It is a
wild district of marsh and forest.

10-15. THE HARPIES: These hideous birds with the faces of malign women were often associated with the Erinyes (Furies). Their original function in mythology was to snatch away the souls of men at the command of the Gods. Later, they were portrayed as defilers of food, and, by extension, of everything they touched. The islands of the Strophades were their legendary abode. Aeneas and his men landed there and fought with the Harpies, who drove them back and pronounced a prophecy of unbearable famine upon them.

18. *The burning sand:* The Third Round of this Circle.

25. *I think perhaps he thought that I was thinking:* The original is *"Cred' io ch'ei credette ch'io credesse."* This sort of word play was considered quite elegant by medieval rhetoricians and by the ornate Sicilian School of poetry. Dante's style is based on a rejection of all such devices in favor of a sparse and direct diction. The best explanation of this unusual instance seems to be that Dante is anticipating his talk with Pier delle Vigne, a rhetorician who, as we shall see, delights in this sort of locution. (An analogous stylistic device is common in opera, where the musical phrase identified with a given character may be sounded by the orchestra when the character is about to appear.)

48. *in my verses only:* The *Aeneid,* Book III, describes a similar bleeding plant. There, Aeneas pulls at a myrtle growing on a Thracian hillside. It bleeds where he breaks it and a voice cries out of the ground. It is the voice of Polydorus, son of Priam and friend of Aeneas. He had been treacherously murdered by the Thracian king.

58. *I am he, etc.:* Pier delle Vigne (Pee-YAIR deh-leh VEE-nyeh), 1190-1249. A famous and once-powerful minister of Emperor Frederick II. He enjoyed Frederick's whole confidence until 1247 when he was accused of treachery and was imprisoned and blinded. He committed suicide to escape further torture. (For Frederick see Canto X.) Pier delle Vigne was famous for his eloquence and for his mastery of the ornate Provençal-inspired Sicilian School of Italian Poetry, and Dante styles his speech accordingly. The double balanced construction of line 59, the repetition of key words in lines 67-69, and 70-72 are characteristic of this rhetorical fashion. It is worth noting, however, that the style changes abruptly in the middle of line 72. There, his courtly preamble finished, delle Vigne speaks from the heart, simply and passionately.

58. *who held both keys:* The phrasing unmistakably suggests the Papal keys; delle Vigne may be suggesting that he was to Frederick as the Pope is to God.

64. *Caesar:* Frederick II was of course Caesar of the Roman Empire, but in this generalized context "Caesar" seems to be used as a generic term for any great ruler, *i.e.,* "The harlot, Envy, never turns her attention from those in power."

72. *new roots:* Pier delle Vigne had only been in Hell fifty-one years, a short enough time on the scale of eternity.

98. *wherever fortune flings it:* Just as the soul of the suicide refused to accept divine regulation of its mortal life span, so eternal justice takes no special heed of where the soul falls.

102. *pain and pain's outlet simultaneously:* Suicide also gives pain and its outlet simultaneously.

117 ff. THE VIOLENT AGAINST THEIR SUBSTANCE. They are driven naked through the thorny wood pursued by ravening bitches who tear them to pieces and carry off the limbs. (Obviously the limbs must re-form at some point so that the process can be repeated. For a parallel see Canto XXVIII, the Schismatics. Boccaccio uses an identical device in the Decameron V, vi.) The bitches may be taken as symbolizing conscience, the last besieging creditors of the damned who must satisfy their claims by dividing their wretched bodies, since nothing else is left them. It is not simply prodigality that places them here but the *violence* of their wasting. This fad of violent wasting, scandalously prevalent in Dante's Florence, is hard to imagine today.

120. *Lano:* Lano da Siena, a famous squanderer. He died at the ford of the river Toppo near Arezzo in 1287 in a battle against the Aretines. Boccaccio writes that he deliberately courted death having squandered all his great wealth and being unwilling to live on in poverty. Thus his companion's jeer probably means: "You were not so ready to run then, Lano: why are you running now?"

133. *Jacomo da Sant' Andrea* (YAH-coe-moe): A Paduan with an infamous lust for laying waste his own goods and those of his neighbors. Arson was his favorite prank. On one occasion, to celebrate the arrival of certain noble guests, he set fire to all the workers' huts and outbuildings of his estate. He was murdered in 1239, probably by assassins hired by Ezzolino (for whom see Canto XII).

131-152. AN ANONYMOUS FLORENTINE SUICIDE: All that is known of him is what he says himself.

143. *the city that tore down Mars and raised the Baptist:* Florence. Mars was the first patron of the city and when the Florentines were converted to Christianity they pulled down his equestrian statue and built a church on the site of his temple. The statue of Mars was placed on a tower beside the Arno. When Totila (see note to line 150) destroyed Florence the tower fell into the Arno and the statue with it. Legend has it that Florence could never have been rebuilt had not the mutilated statue been rescued. It was placed on the Ponte Vecchio but was carried away in the flood of 1333.

150. *Attila:* Dante confuses Attila with Totila, King of the Ostrogoths (died 552). He destroyed Florence in 542. Attila (d. 453), King of the Huns, destroyed many cities of northern Italy, but not Florence.

[In Canto XIV Dante enters the Burning Plain, where the Violent against God, Nature, and Art suffer under a ceaseless rain of fire.]

CANTO XV

CIRCLE SEVEN: ROUND THREE   THE VIOLENT
                                        AGAINST NATURE

Protected by the marvelous powers of the boiling rill, the Poets walk along its banks across the burning plain. The WOOD OF THE SUI-CIDES is behind them; the GREAT CLIFF at whose foot lies the EIGHTH CIRCLE is before them.

They pass one of the roving bands of SODOMITES. One of the sinners stops Dante, and with great difficulty the Poet recognizes him under his baked features as SER BRUNETTO LATINO. This is a reunion with a dearly-loved man and writer, one who had considerably influenced Dante's own development, and Dante addresses him with great and sorrowful affection, paying him the highest tribute offered to any sinner in the Inferno. *BRUNETTO prophesies Dante's sufferings at the hands of the Florentines, gives an account of the souls that move with him through the fire, and finally, under Divine Compulsion, races off across the plain.*

We go by one of the stone margins now
    and the steam of the rivulet makes a shade above it,
    guarding the stream and banks from the flaming snow.

As the Flemings in the lowland between Bruges
    and Wissant, under constant threat of the sea,
    erect their great dikes to hold back the deluge;

as the Paduans along the shores of the Brent
    build levees to protect their towns and castles
    lest Chiarentana drown in the spring torrent—

to the same plan, though not so wide nor high,
    did the engineer, whoever he may have been,
    design the margin we were crossing by.

Already we were so far from the wood
    that even had I turned to look at it,
    I could not have made it out from where I stood,   (15)

when a company of shades came into sight
    walking beside the bank. They stared at us
    as men at evening by the new moon's light

stare at one another when they pass by
    on a dark road, pointing their eyebrows toward us
    as an old tailor squints at his needle's eye.

Stared at so closely by that ghostly crew,
    I was recognized by one who seized the hem
    of my skirt and said: "Wonder of wonders! You?"

And I, when he stretched out his arm to me,
    searched his baked features closely, till at last
    I traced his image from my memory

in spite of the burnt crust, and bending near
    to put my face closer to his, at last
    I answered: "Ser Brunetto, are *you* here?"   (30)

"O my son! may it not displease you," he cried,
    "if Brunetto Latino leave his company
    and turn and walk a little by your side."

And I to him: "With all my soul I ask it.
    Or let us sit together, if it please him
    who is my Guide and leads me through this pit."

"My son!" he said, "whoever of this train
    pauses a moment, must lie a hundred years
    forbidden to brush off the burning rain.

Therefore, go on; I will walk at your hem,
    and then rejoin my company, which goes
    mourning eternal loss in eternal flame."

I did not dare descend to his own level
    but kept my head inclined, as one who walks
    in reverence meditating good and evil.   (45)

"What brings you here before your own last day?
    What fortune or what destiny?" he began.
    "And who is he that leads you this dark way?"

"Up there in the happy life I went astray
    in a valley," I replied, "before I had reached
    the fullness of my years. Only yesterday

at dawn I turned from it. This spirit showed
    himself to me as I was turning back,
    and guides me home again along this road."

And he: "Follow your star, for if in all
    of the sweet life I saw one truth shine clearly,
    you cannot miss your glorious arrival.

And had I lived to do what I meant to do,
    I would have cheered and seconded your work,
    observing Heaven so well disposed toward you.   (60)

But that ungrateful and malignant stock
    that came down from Fiesole of old
    and still smacks of the mountain and the rock,

for your good works will be your enemy.
    And there is cause: the sweet fig is not meant
    to bear its fruit beside the bitter sorb-tree.

Even the old adage calls them blind,
    an envious, proud, and avaricious people:
    see that you root their customs from your mind.

It is written in your stars, and will come to pass,
    that your honours shall make both sides hunger for you:
    but the goat shall never reach to crop that grass.

Let the beasts of Fiesole devour their get
    like sows, but never let them touch the plant,
    if among their rankness any springs up yet,   (75)

in which is born again the holy seed
    of the Romans who remained among their rabble
    when Florence made a new nest for their greed."

"Ah, had I all my wish," I answered then,
    "you would not yet be banished from the world
    in which you were a radiance among men,

for that sweet image, gentle and paternal,
    you were to me in the world when hour by hour
    you taught me how man makes himself eternal,

lives in my mind, and now strikes to my heart;
    and while I live, the gratitude I owe it
    will speak to men out of my life and art.

What you have told me of my course, I write
    by another text I save to show a Lady
    who will judge these matters, if I reach her height.   (90)

This much I would have you know: so long, I say,
    as nothing in my conscience troubles me
    I am prepared for Fortune, come what may.

Twice already in the eternal shade
    I have heard this prophecy; but let Fortune turn
    her wheel as she please, and the countryman his spade."

My guiding spirit paused at my last word
    and, turning right about, stood eye to eye
    to say to me: "Well heeded is well heard."

But I did not reply to him, going on
    with Ser Brunetto to ask him who was with him
    in the hot sands, the best-born and best known.

And he to me: "Of some who share this walk
    it is good to know; of the rest let us say nothing,
    for the time would be too short for so much talk.   (105)

In brief, we all were clerks and men of worth,
    great men of letters, scholars of renown;
    all by the one same crime defiled on earth.

Priscian moves there along the wearisome
    sad way, and Francesco d'Accorso, and also there,
    if you had any longing for such scum,

you might have seen that one the Servant of Servants
    sent from the Arno to the Bacchiglione
    where he left his unnatural organ wrapped in cerements.

I would say more, but there across the sand
   a new smoke rises and new people come,
   and I must run to be with my own band.

Remember my *Treasure,* in which I still live on:
   I ask no more." He turned then, and he seemed,
   across that plain, like one of those who run   (120)

for the green cloth at Verona; and of those,
more like the one who wins, than those who lose.

NOTES

4-9. Dante compares the banks of the rill of Phlegethon to the dikes built by the Flemings to hold back the sea, and to those built by the Paduans to hold back the spring floods of the river Brent. Chiarentana (Latin: Clarentana) was a Duchy of the Middle Ages. Its territory included the headwaters of the Brent (Brenta).

10. *though not so wide nor high:* Their width is never precisely specified, but we shall see when Dante walks along speaking to Ser Brunetto (line 40) that their height is about that of a man.

23-119. *Ser Brunetto Latino:* or Latini. (Born between 1210 and 1230, died 1294.) A prominent Florentine Guelph who held, among many other posts, that of notary, whence the title *Ser* (sometimes *Sere*). He was not Dante's schoolmaster as many have supposed—he was much too busy and important a man for that. Dante's use of the word "master" is to indicate spiritual indebtedness to Brunetto and his works. It is worth noting that Dante addresses him in Italian as "voi" instead of using the less respectful "tu" form. Farinata is the only other sinner so addressed in the *Inferno.* Brunetto's two principal books, both of which Dante admires, were the prose *Livre dou Tresor* (*The Book of the Treasure*) and the poetic *Tesoretta* (*The Little Treasure*). Dante learned a number of his devices from the allegorical journey which forms the *Tesoretto.*
   Dante's surprise at finding Brunetto here is worth puzzling about. So too is the fact that he did not ask Ciacco about him (Canto VI) when he mentioned other prominent Florentines. One speculation is that Dante had not intended to place him in Hell, and that he found reason to believe him guilty of this sin only years after Brunetto's death (the *Inferno* was written between 1310 and 1314, in all probability). This answer is not wholly satisfactory.

40. *I will walk at your hem:* See also line 10. Dante is standing on the dike at approximately the level of Brunetto's head and he cannot descend because of the rain of fire and the burning sands.

61-67. *that ungrateful and malignant stock:* The ancient Etruscan city of Fiesole was situated on a hill about three miles north of the present site of Florence. According to legend, Fiesole had taken the side of Catiline in his war with Julius Caesar. Caesar destroyed the town and set up a new city called Florence on the Arno, peopling it with Romans and Fiesolans. The Romans were the aristocracy of the new city, but the Fiesolans were a majority. Dante ascribes the endless bloody conflicts of Florence largely to the internal strife between these two strains. His scorn of the Fiesolans is obvious in this passage. Dante proudly proclaimed his descent from the Roman strain.

66. *sorb-tree:* A species of tart apple.

67. *calls them blind:* The source of this proverbial expression, "Blind as a Florentine," can no longer be traced with any assurance, though many incidents from Florentine history suggest possible sources.

71. *shall make both sides hunger for you:* Brunetto can scarcely mean that both sides will hunger to welcome the support of a man of Dante's distinction. Rather, that both sides will hunger to destroy him. (See also lines 94-95. Dante obviously accepts this as another dark prophecy.)

73. *the beasts of Fiesole:* The Fiesolans themselves.

89. *to show a Lady:* Beatrice.

94-99. *twice already . . . I have heard:* The prophecies of Ciacco (Canto VI) and of Farinata (Canto X) are the other two places at which Dante's exile and suffering are foretold. Dante replies that come what may he will remain true to his purpose through all affliction; and Virgil turns to look proudly at his pupil uttering a proverb: *"Bene ascolta chi la nota,"* i.e., "Well heeded is well heard."

109. *Priscian:* Latin grammarian and poet of the first half of the sixth century.

110. *Francesco d'Accorso:* (Frahn-CHAY-skoe dah-KAWR-soe) A Florentine scholar. He served as a professor at Bologna and, from 1273 to 1280, at Oxford. He died in Bologna in 1294.

112-13. *that one the Servant of Servants . . . Arno to the Bacchiglione etc.:* "The Servant of Servants" was Dante's old enemy, Boniface VIII. *Servus servorum* is technically a correct papal title, but there is certainly a touch of irony in Dante's application of it in this context. In 1295 Boniface transferred Bishop Andrea de' Mozzi from the Bishopric of Florence (on the Arno) to that of Vicenza (on the Bacchiglione). The transference was reputedly brought about at the request of the Bishop's Brother, Tommaso de' Mozzi of Florence, who wished to remove from his sight the spectacle of his brother's stupidity and unnatural vices.

114. *unnatural organ:* The original, *mal protesi nervi*, contains an untranslatable word-play. *Nervi* may be taken as "the male organ" and *protesi* for "erected"; thus the organ aroused to passion for unnatural purposes (*mal*). Or *nervi* may be taken as "nerves" and *mal protesi* for "dissolute." Taken in context, the first rendering strikes me as more Dantean.

121. *the green cloth:* One the first Sunday of Lent all the young men of Verona ran a race for the prize of green cloth. The last runner in was given a live rooster and was required to carry it through the town.

[Leaving Circle Seven (Cantos XVI and XVII), Dante and Virgil are flown by the winged monster Geryon to the Eighth Circle, which is named Malebolge. Like the seventh level of Hell, Malebolge is sub-divided into areas of special punishment. The travellers pass from the Panderers, Seducers, and Flatterers to the Simoniacs.]

CANTO XIX

CIRCLE EIGHT: BOLGIA THREE   THE SIMONIACS

Dante comes upon the SIMONIACS [sellers of ecclesiastic favors and offices] and his heart overflows with the wrath he feels against those who corrupt the things of God. This bolgia is lined with round tube-like holes and the sinners are placed in them upside down with the soles of their feet ablaze. The heat of the blaze is proportioned to their guilt.

The holes in which these sinners are placed are debased equivalents of the baptismal fonts common in the cities of Northern Italy and the sinners' confinement in them is temporary: as new sinners arrive, the souls drop through the bottoms of their holes and disappear eternally into the crevices of the rock.

As always, the punishment is a symbolic retribution. Just as the Simoniacs made a mock of holy office, so are they turned upside down in a mockery of the baptismal font. Just as they made a mockery of the holy water of baptism, so is their hellish baptism by fire, after which they are wholly immersed in the crevices below. The oily fire that licks at their soles may also suggest a travesty on the oil used in Extreme Unction (last rites for the dying).

Virgil carries Dante down an almost sheer ledge and lets him speak to one who is the chief sinner of that place, POPE NICHOLAS III. Dante delivers himself of another stirring denunciation of those who have corrupted church office, and Virgil carries him back up the steep ledge toward the FOURTH BOLGIA.

O Simon Magus! O you wretched crew
    who follow him, pandering for silver and gold
    the things of God which should be wedded to

love and righteousness! O thieves for hire,
    now must the trump of judgment sound your doom
    here in the third fosse of the rim of fire!

We had already made our way across
    to the next grave, and to that part of the bridge
    which hangs above the mid-point of the fosse.

O Sovereign Wisdom, how Thine art doth shine
    in Heaven, on Earth, and in the Evil World!
    How justly doth Thy power judge and assign!

I saw along the walls and on the ground
    long rows of holes cut in the livid stone;
    all were cut to a size, and all were round.   (15)

They seemed to be exactly the same size
    as those in the font of my beautiful San Giovanni,
    built to protect the priests who come to baptize;

(one of which, not so long since, I broke open
    to rescue a boy who was wedged and drowning in it.
    Be this enough to undeceive all men.)

From every mouth a sinner's legs stuck out
    as far as the calf. The soles were all ablaze
    and the joints of the legs quivered and writhed about.

Withes and tethers would have snapped in their throes.
　　As oiled things blaze upon the surface only,
　　so did they burn from the heels to the points of their toes.

"Master," I said, "who is that one in the fire
　　who writhes and quivers more than all the others?
　　From him the ruddy flames seem to leap higher."　　　　(30)

And he to me: "If you wish me to carry you down
　　along that lower bank, you may learn from him
　　who he is, and the evil he has done."

And I: "What you will, I will. You are my lord
　　and know I depart in nothing from your wish;
　　and you know my mind beyond my spoken word."

We moved to the fourth ridge, and turning left
　　my Guide descended by a jagged path
　　into the strait and perforated cleft.

Thus the good Master bore me down the dim
　　and rocky slope, and did not put me down
　　till we reached the one whose legs did penance for him.

"Whoever you are, sad spirit," I began,
　　"who lie here with your head below your heels
　　and planted like a stake—speak if you can."　　　　(45)

I stood like a friar who gives the sacrament
　　to a hired assassin, who, fixed in the hole,
　　recalls him, and delays his death a moment.

"Are you there already, Boniface? Are you there
　　already?" he cried. "By several years the writ
　　has lied. And all that gold, and all that care—

are you already sated with the treasure
　　for which you dared to turn on the Sweet Lady
　　and trick and pluck and bleed her at your pleasure?"

I stood like one caught in some raillery,
　　not understanding what is said to him,
　　lost for an answer to such mockery.

Then Virgil said. "Say to him: 'I am not he,
　　I am not who you think.'" And I replied
　　as my good Master had instructed me.　　　　(60)

The sinner's feet jerked madly; then again
    his voice rose, this time choked with sighs and tears,
    and said at last: "What do you want of me then?

If to know who I am drives you so fearfully
    that you descend the bank to ask it, know
    that the Great mantle was once hung upon me.

And in truth I was a son of the She-Bear,
    so sly and eager to push my whelps ahead,
    that I pursed wealth above, and myself here.

Beneath my head are dragged all who have gone
    before me in buying and selling holy office;
    there they cower in fissures of the stone.

I too shall be plunged down when that great cheat
    for whom I took you comes here in his turn.
    Longer already have I baked my feet   (75)

and been planted upside-down, than he shall be
    before the west sends down a lawless Shepherd
    of uglier deeds to cover him and me.

He will be a new Jason of the Maccabees;
    and just as that king bent to his high priests' will,
    so shall the French king do as this one please."

Maybe—I cannot say—I grew too brash
    at this point, for when he had finished speaking
    I said: "Indeed! Now tell me how much cash

our Lord required of Peter in guarantee
    before he put the keys into his keeping?
    Surely he asked nothing but 'Follow me!'

Nor did Peter, nor the others, ask silver or gold
    of Matthew when they chose him for the place
    the despicable and damned apostle sold.   (90)

Therefore stay as you are; this hole well fits you—
    and keep a good guard on the ill-won wealth
    that once made you so bold towards Charles of Anjou.

And were it not that I am still constrained
    by the reverence I owe to the Great Keys
    you held in life, I should not have refrained

from using other words and sharper still;
>   for this avarice of yours grieves all the world,
>   tramples the virtuous, and exalts the evil.

Of such as you was the Evangelist's vision
>   when he saw She who Sits upon the Waters
>   locked with the Kings of earth in fornication.

She was born with seven heads, and ten enormous
>   and shining horns strengthened and made her glad
>   as long as love and virtue pleased her spouse.   (105)

Gold and silver are the gods you adore!
>   In what are you different from the idolator,
>   save that he worships one, and you a score?

Ah Constantine, what evil marked the hour—
>   not of your conversion, but of the fee
>   the first rich Father took from you in dower!"

And as I sang him this tune, he began to twitch
>   and kick both feet out wildly, as if in rage
>   or gnawed by conscience—little matter which.

And I think, indeed, it pleased my Guide: his look
>   was all approval as he stood beside me
>   intent upon each word of truth I spoke.

He approached, and with both arms he lifted me,
>   and when he had gathered me against his breast,
>   remounted the rocky path out of the valley,   (120)

nor did he tire of holding me clasped to him,
>   until we reached the topmost point of the arch
>   which crosses from the fourth to the fifth rim

of the pits of woe. Arrived upon the bridge,
>   he tenderly set down the heavy burden
>   he had been pleased to carry up that ledge

which would have been hard climbing for a goat.
Here I looked down on still another moat.

NOTES

1. *Simon Magus:* Simon the Samarian magician (see *Acts* viii, 9-24) from whom the word "Simony" derives. Upon his conversion to Christianity he offered to buy the power to administer the Holy Ghost and was severely rebuked by Peter.

8. *the next grave:* The next *bolgia.*

9. *that part of the bridge:* The center point. The center of each span is obviously the best observation point.

11. *Evil World:* Hell.

17-18. *the font of my beautiful San Giovanni:* It was the custom in Dante's time to baptize only on Holy Saturday and on Pentecost. These occasions were naturally thronged, therefore, and to protect the priests a special font was built in the Baptistry of San Giovanni with marble stands for the priests, who were thus protected from both the crowds and the water in which they immersed those to be baptized. The Baptistry is still standing, but the font is no longer in it. A similar font still exists, however, in the Baptistry at Pisa.

19-21. In these lines Dante is replying to a charge of sacrilege that had been rumored against him. One day a boy playing in the baptismal font became jammed in the marble tube and could not be extricated. To save the boy from drowning, Dante took it upon himself to smash the tube. This is his answer to all men on the charge of sacrilege.

29. *more than all the others:* The fire is proportioned to the guilt of the sinner. These are obviously the feet of the chief sinner of this *bolgia.* In a moment we shall discover that he is Pope Nicholas III.

46-47. *like a friar, etc.:* Persons convicted of murdering for hire were sometimes executed by being buried alive upside down. If the friar were called back at the last moment, he should have to bend over the hole in which the man is fixed upside down awaiting the first shovelful of earth.

POPE NICHOLAS III: Giovanni Gaetano degli Orsini, Pope from 1277-1280. His presence here is self-explanatory. He is awaiting the arrival of his successor, Boniface VIII, who will take his place in the stone tube and who will in turn be replaced by Clement V, a Pope even more corrupt than Boniface. With the foresight of the damned he had read the date of Boniface's death (1303) in the Book of Fate. Mistaking Dante for Boniface, he thinks his foresight has erred by three years, since it is now 1300.

66. *the Great Mantle:* of the Papacy.

67. *son of the She-Bear:* Nicholas' family name, degli Orsini, means in Italian "of the bear cubs."

69. *pursed:* A play on the second meaning of *bolgia* (*i.e.,* "purse"). "Just as I put wealth in my purse when alive, so am I put in this foul purse now that I am dead."

77-79. *a lawless Shepherd . . . Jason of the Maccabees . . . the French King:* The reference is to Clement V, Pope from 1305 to 1314. He came from Gascony (the West) and was involved in many intrigues with the King of France. It was Clement V who moved the Papal See to Avignon where it remained until 1377. He is compared to Jason (see *Maccabees* iv, 7ff.) who bought an appointment as High Priest of the Jews from King Antiochus and thereupon introduced pagan and venal practices into the office in much the same way as Clement used his influence with Philip of France to secure and corrupt his high office.

Clement will succeed Boniface in Hell because Boniface's successor, Benedictus XI (1303-1304), was a good and holy man. The terms each guilty Pope must serve in this hellish baptism are:

Nicholas III 1280-1303
(four good Popes intervene)

Boniface VIII 1303-1314
(one good Pope intervenes)

Clement V 1314—not stated

88-89. *nor did Peter . . . of Matthew:* Upon the expulsion of Judas from the band of Apostles, Matthew was chosen in his place.

93. *Charles of Anjou:* The seventh son of Louis VIII of France. Charles became King of Naples and of Sicily largely through the good offices of Pope Urban IV and later of Clement IV. Nicholas III withdrew the high favor his predecessors had shown Charles, but the exact nature and extent of his opposition are open to dispute. Dante probably believed, as did many of his contemporaries, that Nicholas instigated the massacre called the Sicilian Vespers, in which the Sicilians overthrew the rule of Charles and held a general slaughter of the French who had been their masters. The Sicilian Vespers, however, was a popular and spontaneous uprising, and it did not occur until Nicholas had been dead for two years.

Dante may have erred in interpreting the Sicilian question, but his point is indisputably clear when he laments the fact that simoniacally acquired wealth had involved the Papacy in war and political intrigue, thereby perverting it from its spiritual purpose.

95. *the Great Keys:* of the Papacy.

100-105. *the Evangelist . . . She Who Sits upon the Waters:* St. John the Evangelist. His vision of She who sits upon the waters is set forth in *Revelations* xvii. The Evangelist intended it as a vision of Pagan Rome, but Dante interprets it as a vision of the Roman Church in its simoniacal corruption. The seven heads are the seven sacraments; the ten horns, the ten commandments.

109-11. *Ah Constantine, etc.:* The first rich Father was Silvester (Pope from 314 to 355). Before him the Popes possessed nothing, but when Constantine was converted and Catholicism became the official religion of the Empire, the church began to acquire wealth. Dante and the scholars of his time believed, according to a document called "The Donation of Constantine," that the Emperor had moved his Empire to the East in order to leave sovereignty of the West to the Church. The document was not shown to be a forgery until the fifteenth century. Knowledge of the forgery would not, however, have altered Dante's view; he was unwavering in his belief that wealth was the greatest disaster that had befallen the Church, for in wealth lay the root of the corruption which Dante denounced so passionately.

[Canto XX is primarily a catalogue of Fortune Tellers and Diviners, including the Theban prophet Tiresias.]

CANTO XXI

CIRCLE EIGHT: BOLGIA FIVE   THE GRAFTERS

The Poets move on, talking as they go, and arrive at the FIFTH BOL-GIA. Here the GRAFTERS are sunk in boiling pitch and guarded by DEMONS, who tear them to pieces with claws and grappling hooks if they catch them above the surface of the pitch.

The sticky pitch is symbolic of the sticky fingers of the Grafters. It serves also to hide them from sight, as their sinful dealings on earth were hidden from man's eyes. The demons, too, suggest symbolic possibilities, for they are armed with grappling hooks and are forever ready to rend and tear all they can get their hands on.

The Poets watch a demon arrive with a grafting SENATOR of LUC-CA and fling him into the pitch where the demons set upon him.

To protect Dante from their wrath, Virgil hides him behind some jagged rocks and goes ahead alone to negotiate with the demons. They set upon him like a pack of mastiffs, but Virgil secures a safe-conduct from their leader, MALACODA. Thereupon Virgil calls Dante from hiding, and they are about to set off when they discover that the

BRIDGE ACROSS THE SIXTH BOLGIA *lies shattered. Malacoda tells them there is another further on and sends a squad of demons to escort them. Their adventures with the demons continue through the next Canto.*

These two Cantos may conveniently be remembered as the GAR-GOYLE CANTOS. If the total Commedia *is built like a cathedral (as so many critics have suggested), it is here certainly that Dante attaches his grotesqueries. At no other point in the* Commedia *does Dante give such free rein to his coarsest style.*

Thus talking of things which my Comedy does not care
    to sing, we passed from one arch to the next
    until we stood upon its summit. There

we checked our steps to study the next fosse
    and the next vain lamentations of Malebolge;
    awesomely dark and desolate it was.

As in the Venetian arsenal, the winter through
    there boils the sticky pitch to caulk the seams
    of the sea-battered bottoms when no crew

can put to sea—instead of which, one starts
    to build its ship anew, one plugs the planks
    which have been sprung in many foreign parts;

some hammer at a mast, some at a rib;
    some make new oars, some braid and coil new lines;
    one patches up the mainsail, one the jib—   (15)

so, but by Art Divine and not by fire,
    a viscid pitch boiled in the fosse below
    and coated all the bank with gluey mire.

I saw the pitch; but I saw nothing in it
    except the enormous bubbles of its boiling,
    which swelled and sank, like breathing, through all the pit.

And as I stood and stared into that sink,
    my Master cried, "Take care!" and drew me back
    from my exposed position on the brink.

I turned like one who cannot wait to see
    the thing he dreads, and who, in sudden fright,
    runs while he looks, his curiosity

competing with his terror—and at my back
  I saw a figure that came running toward us
  across the ridge, a Demon huge and black.   (30)

Ah what a face he had, all hate and wildness!
  Galloping so, with his great wings outspread
  he seemed the embodiment of all bitterness.

Across each high-hunched shoulder he had thrown
  one haunch of a sinner, whom he held in place
  with a great talon round each ankle bone.

"Blacktalons of our bridge," he began to roar,
  "I bring you one of Santa Zita's Elders!
  Scrub him down while I go back for more:

I planted a harvest of them in that city:
  everyone there is a grafter except Bonturo.
  There 'Yes' is 'No' and 'No' is 'Yes' for a fee."

Down the sinner plunged, and at once the Demon
  spun from the cliff; no mastiff ever sprang
  more eager from the leash to chase a felon.   (45)

Down plunged the sinner and sank to reappear
  with his backside arched and his face and both his feet
  glued to the pitch, almost as if in prayer.

But the Demons under the bridge, who guard that place
  and the sinners who are thrown to them, bawled out:
  "You're out of bounds here for the Sacred Face:

this is no dip in the Serchio: take your look
  and then get down in the pitch. And stay below
  unless you want a taste of a grappling hook."

Then they raked him with more than a hundred hooks
  bellowing: "Here you dance below the covers.
  Graft all you can there: no one checks your books."

They dipped him down into that pitch exactly
  as a chef makes scullery boys dip meat in a boiler,
  holding it with their hooks from floating free.   (60)

And the Master said: "*You* had best not be seen
  by these Fiends till I am ready. Crouch down here.
  One of these rocks will serve you as a screen.

And whatever violence you see done to me,
    you have no cause to fear. I know these matters:
    I have been through this once and come back safely."

With that, he walked on past the end of the bridge;
    and it wanted all his courage to look calm
    from the moment he arrived on the sixth ridge.

With that same storm and fury that arouses
    all the house when the hounds leap at a tramp
    who suddenly falls to pleading where he pauses—

so rushed those Fiends from below, and all the pack
    pointed their gleaming pitchforks at my Guide.
    But he stood fast and cried to them: "Stand back!   (75)

Before those hooks and grapples make too free,
    send up one of your crew to hear me out,
    then ask yourselves if you still care to rip me."

All cried as one: "Let Malacoda go."
    So the pack stood and one of them came forward,
    saying: "What good does he think *this* will do?"

"Do you think, Malacoda," my good Master said,
    "you would see me here, having arrived this far
    already, safe from you and every dread,

without Divine Will and propitious Fate?
    Let me pass on, for it is willed in Heaven
    that I must show another this dread state."

The Demon stood there on the flinty brim,
    so taken aback he let his pitchfork drop;
    then said to the others: "Take care not to harm him!"   (90)

"O you crouched like a cat," my Guide called to me,
    "among the jagged rock piles of the bridge,
    come down to me, for now you may come safely."

Hearing him, I hurried down the ledge;
    and the Demons all pressed forward when I appeared,
    so that I feared they might not keep their pledge.

So once I saw the Pisan infantry
    march out under truce from the fortress at Caprona,
    staring in fright at the ranks of the enemy.

I pressed the whole of my body against my Guide,
    and not for an instant did I take my eyes
    from those black fiends who scowled on every side.

They swung their forks saying to one another:
    "Shall I give him a touch in the rump?" and answering:
    "Sure; give him a taste to pay him for his bother."   (105)

But the Demon who was talking to my Guide
    turned round and cried to him: "At ease there Snatcher!"
    And then to us: "There's no road on this side:

the arch lies all in pieces in the pit.
    If you *must* go on, follow along this ridge;
    there's another cliff to cross by just beyond it.

In just five hours it will be, since the bridge fell,
    a thousand two hundred sixty-six years and a day;
    that was the time the big quake shook all Hell.

I'll send a squad of my boys along that way
    to see if anyone's airing himself below:
    you can go with them: there will be no foul play.

Front and center here, Grizzly and Hellken,"
    he began to order them. "You too, Deaddog.
    Curlybeard, take charge of a squad of ten.   (120)

Take Grafter and Dragontooth along with you.
    Pigtusk, Catclaw, Cramper, and Crazyred.
    Keep a sharp lookout on the boiling glue

as you move along, and see that these gentlemen
    are not molested until they reach the crag
    where they can find a way across the den."

"In the name of heaven, Master," I cried, "what sort
    of guides are these? Let us go on alone
    if you know the way. Who can trust such an escort!

If you are as wary as you used to be
    you surely see them grind their teeth at us,
    and knot their beetle brows so threateningly."

And he: "I do not like this fear in you.
    Let them gnash and knot as they please; they menace only
    the sticky wretches simmering in that stew."   (135)

They turned along the left bank in a line;
　　but before they started, all of them together
　　had stuck their pointed tongues out as a sign

to their Captain that they wished permission to pass,
and he had made a trumpet of his ass.

NOTES

A GENERAL NOTE ON DANTE'S TREATMENT OF THE GRAFTERS AND THEIR GUARDS
(CANTOS XXI and XXII).

Dante has been called "The Master of the Disgusting" with the stress at times on the mastery and at times on the disgust. The occasional coarseness of details in other Cantos (especially in Cantos XVIII and XXVIII) has offended certain delicate readers. It is worth pointing out that the mention of bodily function is likely to be more shocking in a Protestant than in a Catholic culture. It has often seemed to me that the offensive language of Protestantism is obscenity; the offensive language of Catholicism is profanity or blasphemy: one offends on a scale of unmentionable words for bodily function, the other on a scale of disrespect for the sacred. Dante places the Blasphemous in Hell as the worst of the Violent against God and His Works, but he has no category for punishing those who use four-letter words.

The difference is not, I think, national, but religious. Chaucer, as a man of Catholic England, took exactly Dante's view in the matter of what was and what was not shocking language. In "The Pardoner's Tale," Chaucer sermonized with great feeling against the rioters for their profanity and blasphemy (for the way they rend Christ's body with their oaths) but he is quite free himself with "obscenity." Modern English readers tend to find nothing whatever startling in his profanity, but the schoolboys faithfully continue to underline the marvels of his Anglo-Saxon monosyllables and to make marginal notes on them.

7. *the Venetian arsenal:* The arsenal was not only an arms manufactory but a great center of shipbuilding and repairing.

37. *Blacktalons:* The original is Malebranche, i.e., "Evil Claws."

38. *Santa Zita:* The patron saint of the city of Lucca. "One of Santa Zita's Elders" would therefore equal "One of Lucca's Senators" (i.e., Aldermen). Commentators have searched the records of Luccan Aldermen who died on Holy Saturday of 1300, and one Martino Bottaio has been suggested as the newcomer, but there is no evidence that Dante had a specific man in mind. More probably he meant simply to underscore the fact that Lucca was a city of grafters, just as Bologna was represented as a city of panderers and seducers.

41. *Bonturo:* Bonturo Dati, a politician of Lucca. The phrase is ironic: Bonturo was the most avid grafter of them all.

51. *Sacred Face: Il volto santo* was an ancient wooden image of Christ venerated by the Luccanese. These ironies and the grotesqueness of the Elder's appearance mark the beginning of the gargoyle dance that swells and rolls through this Canto and the next.

52. *Serchio:* A river near Lucca.

61. You *had best not be seen:* It is only in the passage through this Bolgia, out of the total journey, that Dante presents himself as being in physical danger. Since his dismissal from office and his exile from Florence (on pain of death if he return) was based on a false charge of grafting, the reference is pointedly autobiographical. Such an autobiographical interpretation is certainly consistent with the method of Dante's allegory.

79. *Malacoda:* The name equals "Bad Tail," or "Evil Tail." He is the captain of these grim and semi-military police. I have not translated his name at I have those of the other fiends, since I cannot see that it offers any real difficulty to an English reader.

97-99. *Pisan infantry . . . Caprona, etc.:* A Tuscan army attacked the fortress of Caprona near Pisa in 1289 and after fierce fighting the Pisan defenders were promised a safe-conduct if they would surrender. Dante was probably serving with the Tuscans (the opening lines of the next Canto certainly suggest that he had seen military service). In some accounts it is reported that the Tuscans massacred the Pisans despite their promised safe-conduct—an ominous analogy if true. In any case the emerging Pisans would be sufficiently familiar with the treacheries of Italian politics to feel profoundly uneasy at being surrounded by their enemies under such conditions.

110-11. *If you* must *go on, etc.:* Malacoda is lying, as the Poets will discover: all the bridges across the Sixth Bolgia have fallen as a result of the earthquake that shook Hell at the death of Christ. The great rock fall between the Sixth and Seventh Circle (see Canto IX) was caused by the same shock, as was the ruin at the entrance to the Second Circle (see Canto V).

112-14. *in just five hours . . . a thousand two hundred and sixty six years and a day:* Christ died on Good Friday of the year 34, and it is now Holy Saturday of the year 1300, five hours before the hour of his death. Many commentators (and Dante himself in the *Convivio*) place the hours of Christ's death at exactly noon. Accordingly, it would now be 7:00 A.M. of Holy Saturday—exactly eight minutes since the Poets left the bridge over the Fourth Bolgia (at moonset).

In the gospels of Matthew, Mark, and Luke, however, the hour of Christ's death is precisely stated as 3:00 P.M. Dante would certainly be familiar with the Synoptic Gospels, and on that authority it would now be 10:00 A.M.

As far as the action of the poem is concerned the only question of consequence is the time-lapse from the bridge over the Fourth Bolgia to the talk with Malacoda, a matter of eight minutes or of three hours and eight minutes. One certainly seems too short, the other needlessly long, and while either answer can be supported with good arguments, this may be another case of literal worrying of "poetic" accuracy.

138-40. *tongues . . . trumpet:* The fiends obviously constitute a kind of debased military organization and these grotesqueries are their sign and countersign. Dante, himself, in his present satyr-like humor, finds them quite remarkable signals, as he goes on to note in the next Canto.

CANTO XXII

CIRCLE EIGHT: BOLGIA FIVE   THE GRAFTERS

The poets set off with their escorts of demons. Dante sees the GRAFTERS lying in the pitch like frogs in water with only their muzzles out. They disappear as soon as they sight the demons and only a ripple on the surface betrays their presence.

One of the Grafters, AN UNIDENTIFIED NAVARRESE, ducks too late and is seized by the demons who are about to claw him, but CURLYBEARD holds them back while Virgil questions him. The wretch speaks of his fellow sinners, FRIAR GOMITA and MICHEL ZANCHE, while the uncontrollable demons rake him from time to time with their hooks.

The Navarrese offers to lure some of his fellow sufferers into the hands of the demons, and when his plan is accepted he plunges into the pitch and escapes. HELLKEN and GRIZZLY fly after him, but too late. They start a brawl in mid-air and fall into the pitch themselves. Curlybeard immediately organizes a rescue party and the Poets, fearing the bad temper of the frustrated demons, take advantage of the confusion to slip away.

I have seen horsemen breaking camp. I have seen
    the beginning of the assault, the march and muster,
    and at times the retreat and riot. I have been

where chargers trampled your land, O Aretines!
    I have seen columns of foragers, shocks of tourney,
    and running of tilts. I have seen the endless lines

march to bells, drums, trumpets, from far and near.
    I have seen them march on signals from a castle.
    I have seen them march with native and foreign gear.

But never yet have I seen horse or foot,
    nor ship in range of land nor sight of star,
    take its direction from so low a toot.

We went with the ten Fiends—ah, savage crew!—
    but "In church with saints; with stewpots in the tavern,"
    as the old proverb wisely bids us do.   (15)

All my attention was fixed upon the pitch:
    to observe the people who were boiling in it,
    and the customs and the punishments of that ditch.

As dolphins surface and begin to flip
    their arched backs from the sea, warning the sailors
    to fall-to and begin to secure ship—

So now and then, some soul, to ease his pain,
    showed us a glimpse of his back above the pitch
    and quick as lightning disappeared again.

And as, at the edge of a ditch, frogs squat about
    hiding their feet and bodies in the water,
    leaving only their muzzles sticking out—

so stood the sinners in that dismal ditch;
    but as Curlybeard approached, only a ripple
    showed where they had ducked back into the pitch.   (30)

I saw—the dread of it haunts me to this day—
    one linger a bit too long, as it sometimes happens
    one frog remains when another spurts away;

and Catclaw, who was nearest, ran a hook
    through the sinner's pitchy hair and hauled him in.
    He looked like an otter dripping from the brook.

I knew the names of all the Fiends by then;
    I had made a note of them at the first muster,
    and, marching, had listened and checked them over again.

"Hey, Crazyred," the crew of Demons cried
    all together, "give him a taste of your claws.
    Dig him open a little. Off with his hide."

And I then: "Master, can you find out, please,
    the name and history of that luckless one
    who has fallen into the hands of his enemies?"   (45)

My Guide approached that wraith from the hot tar
    and asked him whence he came. The wretch replied:
    "I was born and raised in the Kingdom of Navarre.

My mother placed me in service to a knight;
    for she had borne me to a squanderer
    who killed himself when he ran through his birthright.

Then I became a domestic in the service
    of good King Thibault. There I began to graft,
    and I account for it in this hot crevice."

And Pigtusk, who at the ends of his lower lip
    shot forth two teeth more terrible than a boar's,
    made the wretch feel how one of them could rip.

The mouse had come among bad cats, but here
    Curlybeard locked arms around him crying;
    "While I've got hold of him the rest stand clear!"   (60)

And turning his face to my Guide: "If you want to ask him
    anything else," he added, "ask away
    before the others tear him limb from limb."

And my Guide to the sinner: "I should like to know
    if among the other souls beneath the pitch
    are any Italians?" And the wretch: "Just now

I left a shade who came from parts near by.
    Would I were still in the pitch with him, for then
    these hooks would not be giving me cause to cry."

And suddenly Grafter bellowed in great heat:
    "We've stood enough!" And he hooked the sinner's arm
    and, raking it, ripped off a chunk of meat.

Then Dragontooth wanted to play, too, reaching down
    for a catch at the sinner's legs; but Curlybeard
    wheeled round and round with a terrifying frown,   (75)

and when the Fiends had somewhat given ground
    and calmed a little, my Guide, without delay,
    asked the wretch, who was staring at his wound:

"Who was the sinner from whom you say you made
    your evil-starred departure to come ashore
    among these Fiends?" And the wretch: "It was the shade

of Friar Gomita of Gallura, the crooked stem
    of every Fraud: when his master's enemies
    were in his hands, he won high praise from them.

He took their money without case or docket,
    and let them go. He was in all his dealings
    no petty bursar, but a kingly pocket.

With him, his endless crony in the fosse,
    is Don Michel Zanche of Logodoro;
    they babble about Sardinia without pause.   (90)

But look! See that fiend grinning at your side!
    There is much more that I should like to tell you,
    but oh, I think he means to grate my hide!"

But their grim sergeant wheeled, sensing foul play,
    and turning on Cramper, who seemed set to strike,
    ordered: "Clear off, you buzzard. Clear off, I say!"

"If either of you would like to see and hear
    Tuscans or Lombards," the pale sinner said,
    "I can lure them out of hiding if you'll stand clear

and let me sit here at the edge of the ditch,
    and get all these Blacktalons out of sight;
    for while they're here, no one will leave the pitch.

In exchange for myself, I can fish you up as pretty
    a mess of souls as you like. I have only to whistle
    the way we do when one of us gets free."   (105)

Deaddog raised his snout as he listened to him;
    then, shaking his head, said, "Listen to the grafter
    spinning his tricks so he can jump from the brim!"

And the sticky wretch, who was all treachery:
　　"Oh I am more than tricky when there's a chance
　　to see my friends in greater misery."

Hellken, against the will of all the crew,
　　could hold no longer. "If you jump," he said
　　to the scheming wretch, "I won't come after you

at a gallop, but like a hawk after a mouse.
　　We'll clear the edge and hide behind the bank:
　　let's see if you're trickster enough for all of us."

Reader, here is new game! The Fiends withdrew
　　from the bank's edge, and Deaddog, who at first
　　was most against it, led the savage crew.　　　　　　　　(120)

The Navarrese chose his moment carefully:
　　and planting both his feet against the ground,
　　he leaped, and in an instant he was free.

The Fiends were stung with shame, and of the lot
　　Hellken most, who had been the cause of it.
　　He leaped out madly bellowing: "You're caught!"

but little good it did him; terror pressed
　　harder than wings; the sinner dove from sight
　　and the Fiend in full flight had to raise his breast.

A duck, when the falcon dives, will disappear
　　exactly so, all in a flash, while he
　　returns defeated and weary up the air.

Grizzly, in a rage at the sinner's flight,
　　flew after Hellken, hoping the wraith would escape,
　　so he might find an excuse to start a fight.　　　　　　(135)

And as soon as the grafter sank below the pitch,
　　Grizzly turned his talons against Hellken,
　　locked with him claw to claw above the ditch.

But Hellken was sparrowhawk enough for two
　　and clawed him well; and ripping one another,
　　they plunged together into the hot stew.

The heat broke up the brawl immediately,
　　but their wings were smeared with pitch and they could not rise.
　　Curlybeard, upset as his company,

commanded four to fly to the other coast
    at once with all their grapples. At top speed
    the Fiends divided, each one to his post.

Some on the near edge, some along the far,
    they stretched their hooks out to the clotted pair
    who were already cooked deep through the scar   (150)

of their first burn. And turning to one side
we slipped off, leaving them thus occupied.

NOTES

4. *Aretines:* The people of Arezzo. In 1289 the Guelphs of Florence and Lucca defeated the Ghibellines of Arrezo at Campaldino. Dante was present with the Guelphs, though probably as an observer and not as a warrior.

5-6. *tourney . . . tilts:* A tourney was contested by groups of knights in a field; a tilt by individuals who tried to unhorse one another across a barrier.

7. *bells:* The army of each town was equipped with a chariot on which bells were mounted. Signals could be given by the bells and special decorations made the chariot stand out in battle. It served therefore as a rallying point.

8. *signals from a castle:* When troops were in sight of their castle their movements could be directed from the towers—by banners in daytime and by fires at night, much as some naval signals are still given today.

19-21. *dolphins, etc.:* It was a common belief that when dophins began to leap around a ship they were warning the sailors of an approaching storm.

31 ff. *The Navarrese grafter:* His own speech tells all that is known about him. The recital could serve as a description of many a courtier. Thibault II was King of Navarre, a realm that lay in what is now northern Spain.

54. *and I account:* Dante's irony is certainly intentional: the accounts of the Grafters can not be concealed from God's Justice.

66. *Italians:* Dante uses the term *Latino* strictly speaking, a person from the area of ancient Latium, now (roughly) Lazio, the province in which Rome is located. It was against the Latians that Aeneas fought on coming to Italy. More generally, Dante uses the term for any southern Italian. Here, however, the usage seems precise, since the sinner refers to "points near by" and means Sardinia. Rome is the point in Italy closest to Sardinia.

82. *Friar Gomita of Gallura* (GHAW-mee-ta): In 1300 Sardinia was a Pisan possession, and was divided into four districts, of which Galluria was the northeast. Friar Gomita administered Gallura for his own considerable profit. He was hanged by the Pisan governor when he was found guilty of taking bribes to let prisoners escape.

89. *Michel Zanche de Logodoro* (Mee-KELL ZAHN-keh): He was made Vicar of Logodoro when the King of Sardinia went off to war. The King was captured and did not return. Michel maneuvered a divorce for the Queen and married her himself. About 1290 he was murdered by his son-in-law, Branca d'Oria (see Canto XXXIII).

CANTO XXIII

CIRCLE EIGHT: BOLGIA SIX   THE HYPOCRITES

The Poets are pursued by the Fiends and escape them by sliding down the sloping bank of the next pit. They are now in the SIXTH BOLGIA. Here the HYPOCRITES, weighed down by the great leaden robes, walk eternally round and round a narrow track. The robes are brilliantly gilded on the outside and are shaped like a monk's habit, for the hypocrite's outward appearance shines brightly and passes for holiness, but under that show lies the terrible weight of his deceit which the soul must bear through all eternity.

The Poets talk to TWO JOVIAL FRIARS and come upon CAIAPHAS, the chief sinner of that place. Caiaphas was the High Priest of the Jews who counseled the Pharisees to crucify Jesus in the name of public expedience. He is punished by being himself crucified to the floor of Hell by three great stakes, and in such a position that every passing sinner must walk upon him. Thus he must suffer upon his own body the weight of all the world's hypocrisy, as Christ suffered upon his body the pain of all the world's sins.

The Jovial Friars tell Virgil how he may climb from the pit, and Virgil discovers that Malacoda lied to him about the bridges over the Sixth Bolgia.

Silent, apart, and unattended we went
    as Minor Friars go when they walk abroad,
    one following the other. The incident

recalled the fable of the Mouse and the Frog
    that Aesop tells. For compared attentively
    point by point, "pig" is no closer to "hog"

than the one case to the other. And as one thought
    springs from another, so the comparison
    gave birth to a new concern, at which I caught

my breath in fear. This thought ran through my mind:
    "These Fiends, through us, have been made ridiculous,
    and have suffered insult and injury of a kind

to make them smart. Unless we take good care—
    now rage is added to their natural spleen—
    they will hunt us down as greyhounds hunt the hare."   (15)

Already I felt my scalp grow tight with fear.
    I was staring back in terror as I said:
    "Master, unless we find concealment here

and soon, I dread the rage of the Fiends: already
    they are yelping on our trail: I imagine them
    so vividly I can hear them now." And he:

"Were I a pane of leaded glass, I could not
    summon your outward look more instantly
    into myself, than I do your inner thought.

Your fears were mixed already with my own
    with the same suggestion and the same dark look;
    so that of both I form one resolution:

the right bank may be sloping: in that case
    we may find some way down to the next pit
    and so escape from the imagined chase."   (30)

He had not finished answering me thus
    when, not far off, their giant wings outspread,
    I saw the Fiends come charging after us.

Seizing me instantly in his arms, my Guide—
    like a mother wakened by a midnight noise
    to find a wall of flame at her bedside

(who takes her child and runs, and more concerned
    for him than for herself, does not pause even
    to throw a wrap about her) raised me, turned,

and down the rugged bank from the high summit
    flung himself down supine onto the slope
    which walls the upper side of the next pit.

Water that turns the great wheel of a land-mill
    never ran faster through the end of a sluice
    at the point nearest the paddles—as down that hill   (45)

my Guide and Master bore me on his breast,
    as if I were not a companion, but a son.
    And the soles of his feet had hardly come to rest

on the bed of the depth below, when on the height
    we had just left, the Fiends beat their great wings.
    But now they gave my Guide no cause for fright;

for the Providence that gave them the fifth pit
    to govern as the ministers of Its will,
    takes from their souls the power of leaving it,

About us now in the depth of the pit we found
    a painted people, weary and defeated.
    Slowly, in pain, they paced it round and round.

All wore great cloaks cut to as ample a size
    as those worn by the Benedictines of Cluny.
    The enormous hoods were drawn over their eyes.   (60)

The outside is all dazzle, golden and fair;
    the inside, lead, so heavy that Frederick's capes,
    compared to these, would seem as light as air.

O weary mantle for eternity!
    We turned to the left again along their course,
    listening to their moans of misery,

but they moved so slowly down that barren strip,
    tired by their burden, that our company
    was changed at every movement of the hip.

And walking thus, I said: "As we go on,
    may it please you to look about among these people
    for any whose name or history may be known."

And one who understood Tuscan cried to us there
    as we hurried past: "I pray you check your speed.
    you who run so fast through the sick air: (75)

it may be I am one who will fit your case."
    And at his words my Master turned and said:
    "Wait now, then go with him at his own pace."

I waited there, and saw along that track
    two souls who seemed in haste to be with me;
    but the narrow way and their burden held them back.

When they had reached me down that narrow way
    they stared at me in silence and amazement,
    then turned to one another. I heard one say:

"This one seems, by the motion of his throat,
    to be alive; and if they are dead, how is it
    they are allowed to shed the leaden coat?"

And then to me "O Tuscan, come so far
    to the college of the sorry hypocrites,
    do not disdain to tell us who you are."   (90)

And I: "I was born and raised a Florentine
on the green and lovely banks of Arno's waters,
I go with the body that was always mine.

But who are *you*, who sighing as you go
distill in floods of tears that drown your cheeks?
What punishment is this that glitters so?"

"These burnished robes are of thick lead," said one,
"and are hung on us like counterweights, so heavy
that we, their weary fulcrums, creak and groan.

Jovial Friars and Bolognese were we.
We were chosen jointly by your Florentines
to keep the peace, an office usually

held by a single man; near the Gardingo
one still may see the sort of peace we kept.
I was called Catalano, he, Loderingo."   (105)

I began: "O Friars, your evil . . ."—and then I saw
a figure crucified upon the ground
by three great stakes, and I fell still in awe.

When he saw me there, he began to puff great sighs
into his beard, convulsing all his body;
and Friar Catalano, following my eyes,

said to me: "That one nailed across the road
counselled the Pharisees that it was fitting
one man be tortured for the public good.

Naked he lies fixed there, as you see,
in the path of all who pass; there he must feel
the weight of all through all eternity.

His father-in-law and the others of the Council
which was a seed of wrath to all the Jews,
are similarly staked for the same evil."   (120)

Then I saw Virgil marvel for a while
over that soul so ignominiously
stretched on the cross in Hell's eternal exile.

Then, turning, he asked the Friar: "If your law permit,
can you tell us if somewhere along the right
there is some gap in the stone wall of the pit

through which we two may climb to the next brink
    without the need of summoning the Black Angels
    and forcing them to raise us from this sink?"

He: "Nearer than you hope, there is a bridge
    that runs from the great circle of the scarp
    and crosses every ditch from ridge to ridge,

except that in this it is broken; but with care
    you can mount the ruins which lie along the slope
    and make a heap on the bottom." My Guide stood there   (135)

motionless for a while with a dark look.
    At last he said: "He lied about this business,
    who spears the sinners yonder with his hook."

And the Friar: "Once at Bologna I heard the wise
    discussing the Devil's sins; among them I heard
    that he is a liar and the father of lies."

When the sinner had finished speaking, I saw the face
    of my sweet Master darken a bit with anger:
    he set off at a great stride from that place,

and I turned from that weighted hypocrite
to follow in the prints of his dear feet.

NOTES

4. *the fable of the Mouse and the Frog:* The fable was not by Aesop, but was attributed to him in Dante's time: A mouse comes to a body of water and wonders how to cross. A frog, thinking to drown the mouse, offers to ferry him. but the mouse is afraid he will fall off. The frog thereupon suggests that the mouse tie himself to one of the frog's feet. In this way they start across, but in the middle the frog dives from under the mouse, who struggles desperately to stay afloat while the frog tries to pull him under. A hawk sees the mouse struggling and swoops down and seizes him; but since the frog is tied to the mouse, it too is carried away, and so both of them are devoured.

6. *point by point:* The mouse would be the Navarrese Grafter. The frog would be the two fiends, Grizzly and Hellken. By seeking to harm the Navarrese they came to grief themselves.

22. *a pane of leaded glass:* A mirror. Mirrors were backed with lead in Dante's time.

43. *land-mill:* As distinguished from the floating mills common in Dante's time and up to the advent of the steam engine. These were built on rafts that were anchored in the swift-flowing rivers of Northern Italy.

44-45. *ran faster . . . at the point nearest the paddles:* The sharp drop of the sluice makes the water run fastest at the point at which it hits the wheel.

59. *the Benedictines of Cluny:* The habit of these monks was especially ample and elegant. St. Bernard once wrote ironically to a nephew who had entered this monastery: "If length of sleeves and amplitude of hood made for holiness, what could hold me back from following [your lead]."

62. *Frederick's capes:* Frederick II executed persons found guilty of treason by fastening them into a sort of leaden shell. The doomed man was then placed in a cauldron over a fire and the lead was melted around him.

68-9. *our company was changed, etc.:* Another tremendous Dantean figure. Sense: "They moved so slowly that at every step (movement of the hip) we found ourselves beside new sinners."

100. *Jovial Friars:* A nickname given to the military monks of the order of the Glorious Virgin Mary founded at Bologna in 1261. Their original aim was to serve as peacemakers, enforcers of order, and protectors of the weak, but their observance of their rules became so scandalously lax, and their management of worldly affairs so self-seeking, that the order was disbanded by Papal decree.

101-2. *We were chosen jointly . . . to keep the peace:* Catalano dei Malavolti (c. 1210-1285), a Guelph, and Loderingo degli Andolo (c. 1210-1293), a Ghibelline, were both Bolognese and, as brothers of the Jovial Friars, both had served as *podestà* (the chief officer charged with keeping the peace) of many cities for varying terms. In 1266 they were jointly appointed to the office of *podestà* of Florence on the theory that a bipartisan administration by men of God would bring peace to the city. Their tenure of office was marked by great violence, however; and they were forced to leave in a matter of months. Modern scholarship has established the fact that they served as instruments of Clement IV's policy in Florence, working at his orders to overthrow the Ghibellines under the guise of an impartial administration.

103. *Gardingo:* The site of the palace of the Ghibelline family degli Uberti. In the riots resulting from the maladministration of the two Jovial Friars, the Ghibellines were forced out of the city and the Uberti palace was razed.

107 ff. *a figure crucified upon the ground:* Caiaphas. His words were: "It is expedient that one man shall die for the people and that the whole nation perish not." (*John* xi, 50).

118. *his father-in-law and the others:* Annas, father-in-law of Caiaphas, was the first before whom Jesus was led upon his arrest. (*John* xviii, 13). He had Jesus bound and delivered to Caiaphas.

121. *I saw Virgil marvel:* Caiaphas had not been there on Virgil's first descent into Hell.

137-38. *he lied . . . who spears the sinners yonder:* Malacoda.

143. *darken a bit:* The original is *turbato un poco d'ira.* A bit of anger befits the righteous indignation of Human Reason, but immoderate anger would be out of character. One of the sublimities of Dante's writing is the way in which even the smallest details reinforce the great concepts.

✿　　✿　　✿

[Cantos XXIV and XXV describe the punishment of the Thieves, who are entwined about and crushed by hideous reptiles. In Bolgia Eight Dante encounters the Evil Counselors, who are hidden in tongues of searing flame. Two of those who perverted their organs of speech with malicious deception are the Homeric heroes Ulysses and Diomede.]

CANTO XXVI

I stood on the bridge, and leaned out from the edge;
   so far, that but for a jut of rock I held to
   I should have been sent hurtling from the ledge   (45)

without being pushed. And seeing me so intent,
    my Guide said: "There are souls within those flames;
    each sinner swathes himself in his own torment."

"Master," I said, "your words make me more sure,
    but I had seen already that it was so
    and meant to ask what spirit must endure

the pains of that great flame which splits away
    in two great horns, as if it rose from the pyre
    where Eteocles and Polynices lay?"

He answered me: "Forever round his path
    Ulysses and Diomede move in such dress,
    united in pain as once they were in wrath;

there they lament the ambush of the Horse
    which was the door through which the noble seed
    of the Romans issued from its holy source;   (60)

there they mourn that for Achilles slain
    sweet Deidamia weeps even in death;
    there they recall the Palladium in their pain."

"Master," I cried, "I pray you and repray
    till my prayer becomes a thousand—if these souls
    can still speak from the fire, oh let me stay

until the flame draws near! Do not deny me:
    You see how fervently I long for it!"
    And he to me: "Since what you ask is worthy,

it shall be. But be still and let me speak;
    for I know your mind already, and they perhaps
    might scorn your manner of speaking, since they were Greek."

And when the flame had come where time and place
    seemed fitting to my Guide. I heard him say
    these words to it: "O you two souls who pace   (75)

together in one flame!—if my days above
    won favor in your eyes, if I have earned
    however much or little of your love

in writing my High Verses, do not pass by,
    but let one of you be pleased to tell where he,
    having disappeared from the known world, went to die."

As if it fought the wind, the greater prong
　　of the ancient flame began to quiver and hum;
　　then moving its tip as if it were the tongue

that spoke, gave out a voice above the roar.
　　"When I left Circe," it said, "who more than a year
　　detained me near Gaëta long before

Aeneas came and gave the place that name,
　　not fondness for my son, nor reverence
　　for my aged father, nor Penelope's claim   (90)

to the joys of love, could drive out of my mind
　　the lust to experience the far-flung world
　　and the failings and felicities of mankind.

I put out on the high and open sea
　　with a single ship and only those few souls
　　who stayed true when the rest deserted me.

As far as Morocco and as far as Spain
　　I saw both shores; and I saw Sardinia
　　and the other islands of the open main.

I and my men were stiff and slow with age
　　when we sailed at last into the narrow pass
　　where, warning all men back from further voyage,

Hercules' Pillars rose upon our sight.
　　Already I had left Ceuta on the left;
　　Seville now sank behind me on the right.   (105)

'Shipmates,' I said, 'who through a hundred thousand
　　perils have reached the West, do not deny
　　to the brief remaining watch our senses stand

experience of the world beyond the sun.
　　Greeks! You were not born to live like brutes,
　　but to press on toward manhood and recognition!

With this brief exhortation I made my crew
　　so eager for the voyage I could hardly
　　have held them back from it when I was through;

and turning our stern toward morning, our bow toward night,
　　we bore southwest out of the world of man;
　　we made wings of our oars for our fool's flight.

That night we raised the other pole ahead
    with all its stars, and ours had so declined
    it did not rise out of its ocean bed. (120)

Five times since we had dipped our bending oars
    beyond the world, the light beneath the moon
    had waxed and waned, when dead upon our course

we sighted, dark in space, a peak so tall
    I doubted any man had seen the like.
    Our cheers were hardly sounded, when a squall

broke hard upon our bow from the new land:
    three times it sucked the ship and the sea about
    as it pleased Another to order and command.

At the fourth, the poop rose and the bow went down
    till the sea closed over us and the light was gone."

NOTES

53-54. *the pyre where Eteocles and Polynices lay:* Eteocles and Polynices, sons of Oedipus, succeeded jointly to the throne of Thebes, and came to an agreement whereby each one would rule separately for a year at a time. Eteocles ruled the first year and when he refused to surrender the throne at the appointed time, Polynices led the Seven against Thebes in a bloody war. In single combat the two brothers killed one another. Statius (*Thebaid* XII, 429 ff.) wrote that their mutual hatred was so great that when they were placed on the same funeral pyre the very flame of their burning drew apart in two great raging horns.

56-63. *Ulysses and Diomede, etc.:* They suffer here for their joint guilt in counseling and carrying out many stratagems which Dante considered evil, though a narrator who was less passionately a partisan of the Trojans might have thought their actions justifiable methods of warfare. They are in one flame for their joint guilt, but the flame is divided, perhaps to symbolize the moral that men of evil must sooner or later come to a falling out, for there can be no lasting union except by virtue.

    Their first sin was the stratagem of the Wooden Horse, as a result of which Troy fell and Aeneas went forth to found the Roman line. The second evil occurred at Scyros. There Ulysses discovered Achilles in female disguise, hidden by his mother, Thetis, so that he would not be taken off to the war. Deidamia was in love with Achilles and had borne him a son. When Ulysses persuaded her lover to sail for Troy, she died of grief. The third count is Ulysses' theft of the sacred statue of Pallas from the Palladium. Upon the statue, it was believed, depended the fate of Troy. Its theft, therefore, would result in Troy's downfall.

72. *since they were Greek:* Dante knew no Greek, and these sinners might scorn him, first, because he spoke what to them would seem a barbarous tongue, and second, because as an Italian he would seem a descendant of Aeneas and the defeated Trojans. Virgil, on the other hand, appeals to them as a man of virtuous life (who therefore has a power over sin) and as a poet who celebrated their earthly fame. (Prof. MacAllister suggests another meaning as well: that Dante [and his world] had no direct knowledge of the Greeks, knowing their works through Latin intermediaries. Thus Virgil stood between Homer and Dante.)

80-81. *one of you:* Ulysses. He is the figure in the larger horn of the flame (which symbolizes that his guilt, as leader, is greater than that of Diomede). His memorable account of his last voyage and death is purely Dante's invention.

86. *Circe:* Changed Ulysses' men to swine and kept him a prisoner, though with rather exceptional accommodations.

87. *Gaëta:* Southeastern Italian coastal town. According to Virgil (*Aeneid,* VII, 1ff.) it was earlier named Caieta by Aeneas in honor of his aged nurse.

90. *Penelope:* Ulysses' wife.

98. *both shores:* Of the Mediterranean.

101. *narrow pass:* The Straits of Gibraltar, formerly called the Pillars of Hercules. They were presumed to be the Western limit beyond which no man could navigate.

104. *Ceuta:* In Africa, opposite Gibraltar.

105. *Seville:* In Dante's time this was the name given to the general region of Spain. Having passed through the Straits, the men are now in the Atlantic.

115. *morning . . . night:* East and West.

118. *we raised the other pole ahead:* i.e., They drove south across the equator, observed the southern stars, and found that the North Star had sunk below the horizon. The altitude of the North Star is the easiest approximation of latitude. Except for a small correction, it is directly overhead at the North Pole, shows an altitude of 45° at North latitude 45, and is on the horizon at the equator.

124. *a peak:* Purgatory. They sight it after five months of passage. According to Dante's geography, the Northern hemisphere is land and the Southern is all water except for the Mountain of Purgatory which rises above the surface at a point directly opposite Jerusalem.

[Having passed through the ten bolgias of the Eighth Circle (Cantos XXVII-XXXI), the poets reach the ninth and lowest level of Hell, Cocytus, the pit of ultimate guilt.]

CANTO XXXII

CIRCLE NINE: COCYTUS	COMPOUND FRAUD
ROUND ONE: CAÏNA	THE TREACHEROUS TO KIN
ROUND TWO: ANTENORA	THE TREACHEROUS TO COUNTRY

At the bottom of the well Dante finds himself on a huge frozen lake. Thus is COCYTUS, the NINTH CIRCLE, the fourth and last great water of Hell, and here, fixed in the ice, each according to his guilt, are punished sinners guilty of TREACHERY AGAINST THOSE TO WHOM THEY WERE BOUND BY SPECIAL TIES. The ice is divided into four concentric rings marked only by the different positions of the damned within the ice.

This is Dante's symbolic equivalent of the final guilt. The treacheries of these souls were denials of love (which is God) and of all human warmth. Only the remorseless dead center of the ice will serve to express their natures. As they denied God's love, so are they furthest removed from the light and warmth of His Sun. As they denied all human ties, so are they bound only by the unyielding ice.

The first round is CAINA, named for Cain. Here lie those who were treacherous against blood ties. They have their necks and heads out of the ice and are permitted to bow their heads—a double boon since it allows them some protection from the freezing gale and, further, allows their tears to fall without freezing their eyes shut. Here Dante sees ALESSANDRO and NAPOLEONE DEGLI ALBERTI, and he speaks to CAMICION, who identifies other sinners of this round.

The second round is ANTENORA, named for Antenor, the Trojan who was believed to have betrayed his city to the Greeks. Here lie those guilty of TREACHERY TO COUNTRY. They, too, have their heads above the ice, but they cannot bend their necks, which are gripped by the ice. Here Dante accidentally kicks the head of BOCCA DEGLI ABBATI and then proceeds to treat him with a savagery he has shown to no other soul in Hell. Bocca names some of his fellow traitors, and the Poets pass on to discover two heads frozen together in one hole. One of them is gnawing the nape of the other's neck.

If I had rhymes as harsh and horrible
 as the hard fact of that final dismal hole
 which bears the weight of all the steeps of Hell,

I might more fully press the sap and substance
 from my conception; but since I must do
 without them, I begin with some reluctance.

For it is no easy undertaking, I say,
 to describe the bottom of the Universe;
 nor is it for tongues that only babble child's play.

But may those Ladies of the Heavenly Spring
 who helped Amphion wall Thebes, assist my verse,
 that the word may be the mirror of the thing.

O most miscreant rabble, you who keep
 the stations of that place whose name is pain,
 better had you been born as goats or sheep!   (15)

We stood now in the dark pit of the well,
 far down the slope below the Giant's feet,
 and while I still stared up at the great wall,

I heard a voice cry: "Watch which way you turn:
 take care you do not trample on the heads
 of the forworn and miserable brethren."

Whereat I turned and saw beneath my feet
 and stretching out ahead, a lake so frozen
 it seemed to be made of glass. So thick a sheet

never yet hid the Danube's winter course,
    nor, far away beneath the frigid sky,
    locked the Don up in its frozen source:

for were Tanbernick and the enormous peak
    of Pietrapana to crash down on it,
    not even the edges would so much as creak.   (30)

The way frogs sit to croak, their muzzles leaning
    out of the water, at the time and season
    when the peasant woman dreams of her day's gleaning—

Just so the livid dead are sealed in place
    up to the part at which they blushed for shame,
    and they beat their teeth like storks. Each holds his face

bowed toward the ice, each of them testifies
    to the cold with his chattering mouth, to his heart's grief
    with tears that flood forever from his eyes.

When I had stared about me, I looked down
    and at my feet I saw two clamped together
    so tightly that the hair of their heads had grown

together. "Who are you," I said, "who lie
    so tightly breast to breast?" They strained their necks,
    and when they had raised their heads as if to reply,   (45)

the tears their eyes had managed to contain
    up to that time gushed out, and the cold froze them
    between the lids, sealing them shut again

tighter than any clamp grips wood to wood,
    and mad with pain, they fell to butting heads
    like billy-goats in a sudden savage mood.

And a wraith who lay to one side and below,
    and who had lost both ears to frostbite, said,
    his head still bowed: "Why do you watch us so?

If you wish to know who they are who share one doom,
    they owned the Bisenzio's valley with their father,
    whose name was Albert. They sprang from one womb,

and you may search through all Caïna's crew
    without discovering in all this waste
    a squab more fit for the aspic than these two;   (60)

not him whose breast and shadow a single blow
    of the great lance of King Arthur pierced with light;
    nor yet Focaccia; nor this one fastened so

into the ice that his head is all I see,
    and whom, if you are Tuscan, you know well—
    his name on the earth was Sassol Mascheroni.

And I—to tell you all and so be through—
    was Camicion de' Pazzi. I wait for Carlin
    beside whose guilt my sins will shine like virtue."

And leaving him, I saw a thousand faces
    discolored so by cold, I shudder yet
    and always will when I think of those frozen places.

As we approached the center of all weight,
    where I went shivering in eternal shade,
    whether it was my will, or chance, or fate,   (75)

I cannot say, but as I trailed my Guide
    among those heads, my foot struck violently
    against the face of one. Weeping, it cried:

"Why do you kick me? If you were not sent
    to wreak a further vengeance for Montaperti,
    why do you add this to my other torment?"

"Master," I said, "grant me a moment's pause
    to rid myself of a doubt concerning this one;
    then you may hurry me at your own pace."

The Master stopped at once, and through the volley
    of foul abuse the wretch poured out, I said:
    "Who are you who curse others so?" And he:

"And who are *you* who go through the dead larder
    of Antenora kicking the cheeks of others
    so hard, that were you alive, you could not kick harder?"   (90)

"I *am* alive," I said, "and if you seek fame,
    it may be precious to you above all else
    that my notes on this descent include your name."

"Exactly the opposite is my wish and hope,"
    he answered. "Let me be; for it's little you know
    of how to flatter on this icy slope."

I grabbed the hair of his dog's-ruff and I said:
    "Either you tell me truly who you are,
    or you won't have a hair left on your head."

And he: "Not though you snatch me bald. I swear
    I will not tell my name nor show my face.
    Not though you rip until my brain lies bare."

I had a good grip on his hair; already
    I had yanked out more than one fistful of it,
    while the wretch yelped, but kept his face turned from me;   (105)

when another said: "Bocca, what is it ails you?
    What the Hell's wrong? Isn't it bad enough
    to hear you bang your jaws? Must you bark too?"

"Now filthy traitor, say no more?" I cried,
    "for to your shame, be sure I shall bear back
    a true report of you." The wretch replied:

"Say anything you please but go away.
    And if you *do* get back, don't overlook
    that pretty one who had so much to say

just now. Here he laments the Frenchman's price.
    'I saw Buoso da Duera,' you can report,
    'where the bad salad is kept crisp on ice.'

And if you're asked who else was wintering here,
    Beccheria, whose throat was slit by Florence,
    is there beside you. Gianni de' Soldanier   (120)

is further down, I think, with Ganelon,
    and Tebaldello, who opened the gates of Faenza
    and let Bologna steal in with the dawn."

Leaving him then, I saw two souls together
    in a single hole, and so pinched in by the ice
    that one head made a helmet for the other.

As a famished man chews crusts—so the one sinner
    sank his teeth into the other's nape
    at the base of the skull, gnawing his loathsome dinner.

Tydeus in his final raging hour
    gnawed Menalippus' head with no more fury
    than this one gnawed at skull and dripping gore.

"You there," I said, "who show so odiously
　　your hatred for that other, tell me why
　　on this condition: that if in what you tell me　　(135)

you seem to have a reasonable complaint
　　against him you devour with such foul relish,
　　I, knowing who you are, and his soul's taint,

may speak your cause to living memory,
God willing the power of speech be left to me."

NOTES

3. *which bears the weight of all the steeps of Hell:* Literally, it is the base from which all the steeps rise; symbolically, it is the total and finality of all guilt.

10. *those Ladies of the Heavenly Spring, etc.:* The Muses. They so inspired Amphion's hand upon the lyre that the music charmed blocks of stone out of Mount Cithaeron, and the blocks formed themselves into the walls of Thebes.

28-29. *Tanbernick . . . Pietrapana:* There is no agreement on the location of the mountain Dante called Tanbernick, Pietrapana, today known as *la Pania*, is in Tuscany.

32-33. *season . . . gleaning:* The summer.

35. *the part at which they blushed:* The cheeks. By extension, the whole face.

41-61. *two clamped together:* Alessandro and Napoleone, Counts of Mangona. Among other holdings, they inherited a castle in the Val di Bisenzio. They seemed to have been at odds on all things and finally killed one another in a squabble over their inheritance and their politics (Alessandro was a Guelph and Napoleone a Ghibelline).

61. *him whose breast and shadow, etc.:* Modred, King Arthur's traitorous nephew. He tried to kill Arthur, but the king struck him a single blow of his lance, and when it was withdrawn, a shaft of light passed through the gaping wound and split the shadow of the falling traitor.

63. *Focaccia:* (Foh-KAH-tcha) Of the Cancellieri of Pistoia. He murdered his cousin (among others) and may have been the principal cause of a great feud that divided the Cancellieri, and split the Guelphs into the White and Black parties.

66. *Sassol Mascheroni:* Of the Toschi of Florence. He was appointed guardian of one of his nephews and murdered him to get the inheritance for himself.

68. *Camicion de' Pazzi:* (Kah-mih-TCHONE day PAH-tsee) Alberto Camicion de' Pazzi of Valdarno. He murdered a kinsman. *Carlin:* Carlino de' Pazzi, relative of Alberto. He was charged with defending for the Whites the castle of Piantravigne (Pyahn-trah-VEE-nyeh) in Valdarno but surrendered it for a bribe. He belongs therefore in the next lower circle, Antenora, as a traitor to his country, and when he arrives there his greater sin will make Alberto seem almost virtuous by comparison.

70. *And leaving him:* These words mark the departure from Caïna to Antenora.

73. *the center of all weight:* In Dante's cosmology the bottom of Hell is at the center of the earth, which is in turn the center of the universe; it is therefore the center of all gravity. Symbolically, it is the focal point of all guilt. Gravity, weight, and evil are equivalent symbols on one level; they are what ties man to the earth,

what draws him down. At the center of all, Satan is fixed forever in the eternal ice. The journey to salvation, however, is up from that center, once the soul has realized the hideousness of sin.

78. *against the face of one:* Bocca degli Abbati, a traitorous Florentine. At the battle of Montaperti (cf. Farinata, Canto X) he hacked off the hand of the Florentine standard bearer. The cavalry, lacking a standard around which it could rally, was soon routed.

107. *What the Hell's wrong?:* In the circumstances, a monstrous pun. The original is *"qual diavolo ti tocca?"* (what devil touches, or molests, you?) a standard colloquialism for "what's the matter with you?" A similar pun occurs in line 117 "kept crisp (cool) on ice." Colloquially *"stare fresco"* (to be or to remain cool) equals "to be left out in the cold," i.e., to be out of luck.

116. *Buoso da Duera:* Of Cremona. In 1265 Charles of Anjou marched against Manfred and Naples (see Canto XIX), and Buoso da Duera was sent out in charge of a Ghibelline army to oppose the passage of one of Charles' armies, but accepted a bribe and let the French pass unopposed. The event took place near Parma.

119. *Beccheria:* Tesauro dei Beccheria of Pavia, Abbot of Vallombrosa and Papal Legate (of Alexander IV) in Tuscany. The Florentine Guelphs cut off his head in 1258 for plotting with the expelled Ghibellines.

120. *Gianni de' Soldanier:* A Florentine Ghibelline of ancient and noble family. In 1265, however, during the riots that occurred under the Two Jovial Friars, he deserted his party and became a leader of the commoners (Guelphs). In placing him in Antenora, Dante makes no distinction between turning on one's country and turning on one's political party, not at least if the end is simply for power.

121. *Ganelon:* It was Ganelon who betrayed Roland to the Saracens.

122. *Tebaldello:* Tebaldello de' Zambrasi of Faenza. At dawn on November 13, 1280, he opened the city gates and delivered Faenza to the Bolognese Guelphs in order to revenge himself on the Ghibelline family of the Lambertazzi who, in 1274, had fled from Bologna to take refuge in Faenza.

130-1. *Tydeus . . . Menalippus:* Statius recounts in the *Thebaid* that Tydeus killed Menalippus in battle but fell himself mortally wounded. As he lay dying he had Menalippus' head brought to him and fell to gnawing it in his dying rage.

CANTO XXXIII

CIRCLE NINE: COCYTUS	COMPOUND FRAUD
ROUND TWO: ANTENORA	THE TREACHEROUS
	TO COUNTRY
ROUND THREE: PTOLOMEA	THE TREACHEROUS TO
	GUESTS AND HOSTS

In reply to Dante's exhortation, the sinner who is gnawing his companion's head looks up, wipes his bloody mouth on his victim's hair, and tells his harrowing story. He is COUNT UGOLINO and the wretch he gnaws is ARCHBISHOP RUGGIERI. Both are in Antenora for treason. In life they had once plotted together. Then Ruggieri betrayed his fellowplotter and caused his death, by starvation, along with his four "sons." In the most pathetic and dramatic passage of the Inferno, *Ugolino details how their prison was sealed and how his "sons" dropped dead before him one by one, weeping for food. His terrible tale serves only to renew his grief and hatred, and he has hardly finished it before he begins to gnaw Ruggieri again with renewed fury. In the immutable Law of Hell, the killer-by-starvation becomes the food of his victim.*

The Poets leave Ugolino and enter PTOLOMEA, so named for the Ptolomaeus of Maccabees, *who murdered his father-in-law at a banquet. Here are punished those who were TREACHEROUS AGAINST THE TIES OF HOSPITALITY. They lie with only half their faces above the ice and their tears freeze in their eye sockets, sealing them with little crystal visors. Thus even the comfort of tears is denied them. Here Dante finds FRIAR ALBERIGO and BRANCA D'ORIA, and discovers the terrible power of Ptolomea: so great is its sin that the souls of the guilty fall to its torments even before they die, leaving their bodies still on earth, inhabited by Demons.*

The sinner raised his mouth from his grim repast
    and wiped it on the hair of the bloody head
    whose nape he had all but eaten away. At last

he began to speak: "You ask me to renew
    a grief so desperate that the very thought
    of speaking of it tears my heart in two.

But if my words may be a seed that bears
    the fruit of infamy for him I gnaw,
    I shall weep, but tell my story through my tears.

Who you may be, and by what powers you reach
    into this underworld, I cannot guess,
    but you seem to me a Florentine by your speech.

I was Count Ugolino, I must explain;
    this reverend grace is the Archbishop Ruggieri:
    now I will tell you why I gnaw his brain.   (15)

That I, who trusted him, had to undergo
    imprisonment and death through his treachery,
    you will know already. What you cannot know—

that is, the lingering inhumanity
    of the death I suffered—you shall hear in full:
    then judge for yourself if he has injured me.

A narrow window in that coop of stone
    now called the Tower of Hunger for my sake
    (within which others yet must pace alone)

had shown me several waning moons already
    between its bars, when I slept the evil sleep
    in which the veil of the future parted for me.

This beast appeared as master of a hunt
    chasing the wolf and his whelps across the mountain
    that hides Lucca from Pisa. Out in front   (30)

of the starved and shrewd and avid pack he had placed
    Gualandi and Sismondi and Lanfranchi
    to point his prey. The father and sons had raced

a brief course only when they failed of breath
    and seemed to weaken; then I thought I saw
    their flanks ripped open by the hounds' fierce teeth.

Before the dawn, the dream still in my head,
    I woke and heard my sons, who were there with me,
    cry from their troubled sleep, asking for bread.

You are cruelty itself if you can keep
    your tears back at the thought of what foreboding
    stirred in my heart; and if you do not weep,

at what are you used to weeping?—The hour when food
    used to be brought, drew near. They were now awake,
    and each was anxious from his dream's dark mood.   (45)

And from the base of that horrible tower I heard
    the sound of hammers nailing up the gates:
    I stared at my sons' faces without a word.

I did not weep: I had turned stone inside.
    They wept. 'What ails you, Father, you look so strange,'
    my little Anselm, youngest of them, cried.

But I did not speak a word nor shed a tear:
    not all that day nor all that endless night,
    until I saw another sun appear.

When a tiny ray leaked into that dark prison
    and I saw staring back from their four faces
    the terror and the wasting of my own,

I bit my hands in helpless grief. And they,
    thinking I chewed myself for hunger, rose
    suddenly together. I heard them say: (60)

'Father, it would give us much less pain
 if you ate us: it was you who put upon us
 this sorry flesh; now strip it off again.'

I calmed myself to spare them. Ah! hard earth,
 why did you not yawn open? All that day
 and the next we sat in silence. On the fourth,

Gaddo, the eldest, fell before me and cried,
 stretched at my feet upon that prison floor:
 'Father, why don't you help me?' There he died.

And just as you see me, I saw them fall
 one by one on the fifth day and the sixth.
 Then, already blind, I began to crawl

from body to body shaking them frantically.
 Two days I called their names, and they were dead.
 Then fasting overcame my grief and me."   (75)

His eyes narrowed to slits when he was done,
 and he seized the skull again between his teeth
 grinding it as a mastiff grinds a bone.

Ah, Pisa! foulest blemish on the land
 where "si" sounds sweet and clear, since those nearby you
 are slow to blast the ground on which you stand,

may Caprara and Gorgona drift from place
 and dam the flooding Arno at its mouth
 until it drowns the last of your foul race!

For if to Ugolino falls the censure
 for having betrayed your castles, you for your part
 should not have put his sons to such a torture:

you modern Thebes! those tender lives you split—
 Brigata, Uguccione, and the others
 I mentioned earlier—were too young for guilt!   (90)

We passed on further, where the frozen mine
 entombs another crew in greater pain;
 these wraiths are not bent over, but lie supine.

Their very weeping closes up their eyes;
 and the grief that finds no outlet for its tears
 turns inward to increase their agonies:

for the first tears that they shed knot instantly
    in their eye-sockets, and as they freeze they form
    a crystal visor above the cavity.

And despite the fact that standing in that place
    I had become as numb as any callus,
    and all sensation had faded from my face,

somehow I felt a wind begin to blow,
    whereat I said: "Master, what stirs this wind?
    Is not all heat extinguished here below?"   (105)

And the Master said to me: "Soon you will be
    where your own eyes will see the source and cause
    and give you their own answer to the mystery."

And one of those locked in that icy mall
    cried out to us as we passed: "O souls so cruel
    that you are sent to the last post of all,

relieve me for a little from the pain
    of this hard veil; let my heart weep a while
    before the weeping freeze my eyes again."

And I to him: "If you would have my service,
    tell me your name; then if I do not help you
    may I descend to the last rim of the ice."

"I am Friar Alberigo," he answered therefore,
    "the same who called for the fruits from the bad garden.
    Here I am given dates for figs full store."   (120)

"What! Are you dead already?" I said to him.
    And he then: "How my body stands in the world
    I do not know. So privileged is this rim

of Ptolomea, that often souls fall to it
    before dark Atropos has cut their thread.
    And that you may more willingly free my spirit

of this glaze of frozen tears that shrouds my face,
    I will tell you this: when a soul betrays as I did,
    it falls from flesh, and a demon takes its place,

ruling the body till its time is spent.
    The ruined soul rains down into this cistern.
    So, I believe, there is still evident

in the world above, all that is fair and mortal
   of this black shade who winters here behind me.
   If you have only recently crossed the portal   (135)

from that sweet world, you surely must have known
   his body: Branca D'Oria is its name,
   and many years have passed since he rained down."

"I think you are trying to take me in," I said,
   "Ser Branca D'Oria is a living man;
   he eats, he drinks, he fills his clothes and his bed."

"Michel Zanche had not yet reached the ditch
   of the Black Talons," the frozen wraith replied,
   "there where the sinners thicken in hot pitch,

when this one left his body to a devil,
   as did his nephew and second in treachery,
   and plumbed like lead through space to this dead level.

But now reach out your hand, and let me cry."
   And I did not keep the promise I had made,
   for to be rude to him was courtesy.

Ah, men of Genoa! souls of little worth,
   corrupted from all custom of righteousness,
   why have you not been driven from the earth?

For there beside the blackest soul of all
   Romagna's evil plain, lies one of yours
   bathing his filthy soul in the eternal

glacier of Cocytus for his foul crime,
while he seems yet alive in world and time!

NOTES

1-90. *Ugolino and Ruggieri:* (Oog-oh-LEE-noe: Roo-DJAIR-ee) Ugolino, Count
of Donoratico and a member of the Guelph family della Gherardesca. He and his
nephew, Nino de' Visconti, led the two Guelph factions of Pisa. In 1288 Ugolino
intrigued with Archbishop Ruggieri degli Ubaldini, leader of the Ghibellines, to get
rid of Visconti and to take over the command of all the Pisan Guelphs. The plan
worked, but in the consequent weakening of the Guelphs, Ruggieri saw his chance
and betrayed Ugolino, throwing him into prison with his sons and his grandsons. In
the following year the prison was sealed up and they were left to starve to death.
The law of retribution is clearly evident: in life Ruggieri sinned against Ugolino by
denying him food; in Hell he himself becomes food for his victim.

18. *you will know already:* News of Ugolino's imprisonment and death would certainly have reached Florence, *what you cannot know:* No living man could know what happened after Ugolino and his sons were sealed in the prison and abandoned.

22. *coop:* Dante uses the word *muda*, in Italian signifying a stone tower in which falcons were kept in the dark to moult. From the time of Ugolino's death it became known as The Tower of Hunger.

25. *several waning moons:* Ugolino was jailed late in 1288. He was sealed in to starve early in 1289.

28. *This beast:* Ruggieri.

29-30. *the mountain that hides Lucca from Pisa:* These two cities would be in view of one another were it not for Monte San Giuliano.

32. *Gualandi and Sismondi and Lanfranchi:* (Gwah-LAHN-dee . . . Lahn-FRAHN-kee) Three Pisan nobles, Ghibellines and friends of the Archbishop.

51-71. UGOLINO'S "SONS": Actually two of the boys were grandsons and all were considerably older than one would gather from Dante's account. Anselm, the younger grandson, was fifteen. The others were really young men and were certainly old enough for guilt despite Dante's charge in line 90.

75. *Then fasting overcame my grief and me:* i.e., He died. Some interpret the line to mean that Ugolino's hunger drove him to cannibalism. Ugolino's present occupation in Hell would certainly support that interpretation but the fact is that cannibalism is the one major sin Dante does not assign a place to in Hell. So monstrous would it have seemed to him that he must certainly have established a special punishment for it. Certainly he could hardly have relegated it to an ambiguity. Moreover, it would be a sin of bestiality rather than of fraud, and as such it would be punished in the Seventh Circle.

79-80. *the land where "sì" sounds sweet and clear:* Italy.

82. *Caprara and Gorgona:* These two islands near the mouth of the Arno were Pisan possessions in 1300.

86. *betrayed your castles:* In 1284, Ugolino gave up certain castles to Lucca and Florence. He was at war with Genoa at the time and it is quite likely that he ceded the castles to buy the neutrality of these two cities, for they were technically allied with Genoa. Dante, however, must certainly consider the action as treasonable, for otherwise Ugolino would be in Caïna for his treachery to Visconti.

88. *you modern Thebes:* Thebes, as a number of the foregoing notes will already have made clear, was the site of some of the most hideous crimes of antiquity.

91. *we passed on further:* Marks the passage into Ptolomea.

105. *is not all heat extinguished:* Dante believed (rather accurately, by chance) that all winds resulted from "exhalations of heat." Cocytus, however, is conceived as wholly devoid of heat, a metaphysical absolute zero. The source of the wind, as we discover in the next Canto, is Satan himself.

117. *may I descend to the last rim of the ice:* Dante is not taking any chances; he has to go on to the last rim in any case. The sinner, however, believes him to be another damned soul and would interpret the oath quite otherwise than as Dante meant it.

118. *Friar Alberigo:* (Ahl-beh-REE-ghoe) Of the Manfredi of Faenza. He was another Jovial Friar. In 1284 his brother Manfred struck him in the course of an argument. Alberigo pretended to let it pass, but in 1285 he invited Manfred and his son to a banquet and had them murdered. The signal to the assassins was the words: "Bring in the fruit." "Friar Alberigo's bad fruit," became a proverbial saying.

125. *Atropos:* The Fate who cuts the thread of life.

137. *Branca d'Oria:* (DAW-ree-yah) A Genoese Ghibelline. His sin is identical in kind to that of Friar Alberigo. In 1275 he invited his father-in-law, Michel Zanche (see Canto XXII), to a banquet and had him and his companions cut to pieces. He was assisted in the butchery by his nephew.

CANTO XXXIV

NINTH CIRCLE: COCYTUS
ROUND FOUR: JUDECCA

THE CENTER

COMPOUND FRAUD
THE TREACHEROUS TO
THEIR MASTERS
SATAN

"On march the banners of the King," Virgil begins as the Poets face the last depth. He is quoting a medieval hymn, and to it he adds the distortion and perversion of all that lies about him. "On march the banners of the King—of Hell." And there before them, in an infernal parody of Godhead, they see Satan in the distance, his great wings beating like a windmill. It is their beating that is the source of the icy wind of Cocytus, the exhalation of all evil.

All about him in the ice are strewn the sinners of the last round, JUDECCA, named for Judas Iscariot. These are the TREACHEROUS TO THEIR MASTERS. They lie completely sealed in the ice, twisted and distorted into every conceivable posture. It is impossible to speak to them, and the Poets move on to observe Satan.

He is fixed into the ice at the center to which flow all the rivers of guilt; and as he beats his great wings as if to escape, their icy wind only freezes him more surely into the polluted ice. In a grotesque parody of the Trinity, he has three faces, each a different color, and in each mouth he clamps a sinner whom he rips eternally with his teeth. JUDAS ISCARIOT is in the central mouth: BRUTUS and CASSIUS in the mouths on either side.

Having seen all, the Poets now climb through the center, grappling hand over hand down the hairy flank of Satan himself—a last supremely symbolic action—and at last, when they have passed the center of all gravity, they emerge from Hell. A long climb from the earth's center to the Mount of Purgatory awaits them, and they push on without rest, ascending along the sides of the river Lethe, till they emerge once more to see the stars of Heaven, just before dawn on Easter Sunday.

"On march the banners of the King of Hell,"
    my Master said. "Toward us. Look straight ahead:
    can you make him out at the core of the frozen shell?"

Like a whirling windmill seen afar at twilight,
    or when a mist has risen from the ground—
    just such an engine rose upon my sight

stirring up such a wild and bitter wind
    I cowered for shelter at my Master's back,
    there being no other windbreak I could find.

I stood now where the souls of the last class
    (with fear my verses tell it) were covered wholly;
    they shone below the ice like straws in glass.

Some lie stretched out; others are fixed in place
    upright, some on their heads, some on their soles;
    another, like a bow, bends foot to face.　　　　　　　(15)

When we had gone so far across the ice
    that it pleased my Guide to show me the foul creature
    which once had worn the grace of Paradise,

he made me stop, and, stepping aside, he said:
    "Now see the face of Dis! This is the place
    where you must arm your soul against all dread."

Do not ask, Reader, how my blood ran cold
    and my voice choked up with fear. I cannot write it:
    this is a terror that cannot be told.

I did not die, and yet I lost life's breath:
    imagine for yourself what I became,
    deprived at once of both my life and death.

The Emperor of the Universe of Pain
    jutted his upper chest above the ice;
    and I am closer in size to the great mountain　　　　(30)

the Titans make around the central pit,
    than they to his arms. Now, starting from this part,
    imagine the whole that corresponds to it!

If he was once as beautiful as now
    he is hideous, and still turned on his Maker,
    well may he be the source of every woe!

With what a sense of awe I saw his head
    towering above me! for it had three faces:
    one was in front, and it was fiery red;

the other two, as weirdly wonderful,
    merged with it from the middle of each shoulder
    to the point where all converged at the top of the skull;

the right was something between white and bile;
    the left was about the color that one finds
    on those who live along the banks of the Nile.   (45)

Under each head two wings rose terribly,
    their span proportioned to so gross a bird:
    I never saw such sails upon the sea.

They were not feathers—their texture and their form
    were like a bat's wings—and he beat them so
    that three winds blew from him in one great storm:

it is these winds that freeze all Cocytus.
    He wept from his six eyes, and down three chins
    the tears ran mixed with bloody froth and pus.

In every mouth he worked a broken sinner
    between his rake-like teeth. Thus he kept three
    in eternal pain at his eternal dinner.

For the one in front the biting seemed to play
    no part at all compared to the ripping: at times
    the whole skin of his back was flayed away.   (60)

"That soul that suffers most," explained my Guide,
    "is Judas Iscariot, he who kicks his legs
    on the fiery chin and has his head inside.

Of the other two, who have their heads thrust forward,
    the one who dangles down from the black face
    is Brutus: note how he writhes without a word.

And there, with the huge and sinewy arms, is the soul
    of Cassius.—But the night is coming on
    and we must go, for we have seen the whole."

Then, as he bade, I clasped his nesk, and he,
    watching for a moment when the wings
    were opened wide, reached over dexterously

and seized the shaggy coat of the king demon;
    then grappling matted hair and frozen crusts
    from one tuft to another, clambered down.   (75)

When we had reached the joint where the great thigh
    merges into the swelling of the haunch,
    my Guide and Master, straining terribly,

turned his head to where his feet had been
    and began to grip the hair as if he were climbing;
    so that I thought we moved toward Hell again.

"Hold fast!" my Guide said, and his breath came shrill
    with labor and exhaustion. "There is no way
    but by such stairs to rise above such evil."

At last he climbed out through an opening
    in the central rock, and he seated me on the rim;
    then joined me with a nimble backward spring.

I looked up, thinking to see Lucifer
    as I had left him, and I saw instead
    his legs projecting high into the air.   (90)

Now let all those whose dull minds are still vexed
    by failure to understand what point it was
    I had passed through, judge if I was perplexed.

"Get up. Up on your feet," my Master said.
    "The sun already mounts to middle tierce,
    and a long road and hard climbing lie ahead."

It was no hall of state we had found there,
    but a natural animal pit hollowed from rock
    with a broken floor and a close and sunless air.

"Before I tear myself from the Abyss,"
    I said when I had risen, "O my Master,
    explain to me my error in all this:

where is the ice? and Lucifer—how has he
    been turned from top to bottom: and how can the sun
    have gone from night to day so suddenly?"   (105)

And he to me: "You imagine you are still
    on the other side of the center where I grasped
    the shaggy flank of the Great Worm of Evil

which bores through the world—you *were* while I climbed down,
    but when I turned myself about, you passed
    the point to which all gravities are drawn.

You are under the other hemisphere where you stand;
 the sky above us is the half opposed
 to that which canopies the great dry land.

Under the mid-point of that other sky
 the Man who was born sinless and who lived
 beyond all blemish, came to suffer and die.

You have your feet upon a little sphere
 which forms the other face of the Judecca.
 There it is evening when it is morning here. (120)

And this gross Fiend and Image of all Evil
 who made a stairway for us with his hide
 is pinched and prisoned in the ice-pack still.

On this side he plunged down from heaven's height,
 and the land that spread here once hid in the sea
 and fled North to our hemisphere for fright;

and it may be that moved by that same fear,
 the one peak that still rises on this side
 fled upward leaving this great cavern here."

Down there, beginning at the further bound
 of Beelzebub's dim tomb, there is a space
 not known by sight, but only by the sound

of a little stream descending through the hollow
 it has eroded from the massive stone
 in its endlessly entwining lazy flow." (135)

My Guide and I crossed over and began
 to mount that little known and lightless road
 to ascend into the shining world again.

He first, I second, without thought of rest
 we climbed the dark until we reached the point
 where a round opening brought in sight the blest

and beauteous shining of the Heavenly cars.
And we walked out once more beneath the Stars.

NOTES

1. *On march the banners of the King:* The hymn (*Vexilla regis prodeunt*) was written in the sixth century by Venantius Fortunatus, Bishop of Poitiers. The original

celebrates the Holy Cross, and is part of the service for Good Friday to be sung at the moment of uncovering the cross.

17. *the foul creature:* Satan.

38. *three faces:* Numerous interpretations of these three faces exist. What is essential to all explanation is that they be seen as perversions of the qualities of the Trinity.

54. *blody froth and pus.* The gore of the sinners he chews which is mixed with his slaver.

62. *Judas:* Note how closely his punishment is patterned on that of the Simoniacs (Canto XIX).

67. *huge and sinewy arms:* The Cassius who betrayed Caesar was more generally described in terms of Shakespeare's "lean and hungry look." Another Cassius is described by Cicero (*Catiline* III) as huge and sinewy. Dante probably confused the two.

68. *the night is coming on:* It is now Saturday evening.

82. *his breath came shrill:* CF Canto XXIII, 85, where the fact that Dante breathes indicates to the Hypocrites that he is alive. Virgil's breathing is certainly a contradiction.

95. *middle tierce:* In the canonical day tierce is the period from about six to nine A.M. Middle tierce therefore, is seven-thirty. In going through the center point, they have gone from night to day. They have moved ahead twelve hours.

128. *the one peak:* The Mount of Purgatory.

129. *this great cavern:* The natural animal pit of line 98. It is also "Beelzebub's dim tomb," line 131.

133. *a little stream:* Lethe. In classical mythology, the river of forgetfulness, from which souls drank before being born. In Dante's symbolism it flows down from Purgatory, where it has washed away the memory of sin from the souls who are undergoing purification. That memory it delivers to Hell, which draws all sin to itself.

143. *Stars:* As part of his total symbolism Dante ends each of the three divisions of the *Commedia* with this word. Every conclusion of the upward soul is toward the stars, God's shining symbols of hope and virtue. It is just before dawn of Easter Sunday that the Poets emerge—a further symbolism.

PARADISE

[In the third and concluding part of the *Divine Comedy,* Beatrice guides Dante upward through the nine circles of Paradise until the two reach the Empyrean, the highest heaven, a place or state of being far beyond and different from the physical world. After bathing his eyes in a river of light, which symbolic act enables him to look on celestial glory,

Abridged. From *Dante Alighieri: The Divine Comedy.* Translated and Edited by Thomas G. Bergin. Copyright © 1955, Meredith Corporation. Reprinted by permission of Appleton-Century-Crofts.

Dante beholds the saints of heaven ranked in tiers which form the petals of a radiant white rose.]

CANTO XXX

    Splendor of God, through whom I there did see
The lofty triumph of the realm of truth,
Give me the power to tell how I could see.
100 There is a light up yonder, making visible
The Creator to that creature which can find
Its peace only in looking upon Him;
In figure of a circle it extends
So vast that its circumference would be
Too wide a girdle for the very sun.
All of its splendor flows from one ray glancing
Off the high pole of the first moving sphere
Which thence derives its power and its life;
And as a cliff gives its own image back
110 From water at the base, as 't were to see
Its own rich mantle of green shrubs and flowers,
So, high above the light and all around
In row on mirrored row, I saw arrayed
All of mankind which has returned up there.
And if the lowest step takes to itself
Splendor so great, what then must be this rose
In amplitude of its most wide spread leaves?
My sight was not dismayed by sweep of breadth
Nor altitude but could embrace alike
130 The scope and nature of that gladsomeness.
Up yonder "near" and "far" do nothing add
Nor take away; where God directly rules
The law of nature has no relevance.
Into the gold of the eternal rose,
Unfolding as it rises and breathes forth
Perfume of praise to that Sun who creates
Eternal springtime, Beatrice led me—
Like one yet wordless and who yet would speak—
And cried: "Behold how vast a company
120 Wears the white stole. Behold how spaciously
Our city sweeps, see our seats so well filled
That but a few are now awaited here."

NOTES

106-108. One ray of God's grace strikes the summit of the outermost sphere of the material universe (the *Primum Mobile*) and so sets it in motion, reflected from the sphere the ray takes on the appearance of the circular light (100-105) which Dante sees as the floor of his vision of Heaven.

[Dazzled by the splendor of the snow-white rose, Dante finds that Beatrice has disappeared. Allegorically, Beatrice has served her purpose in teaching Dante all that intellect can know of revealed theology. Hence she is replaced by St. Bernard, the contemplative mystic, who has appeared to bring Dante to the ultimate experience of his long journey— a vision of God.]

CANTO XXXI

Thus in the semblance of a pure white rose
That sacred host displayed itself to me
Which, in His own blood, Christ had made His spouse;
The other army which beholds and sings
The glory of the One who stirs its love
And the high Good that gave it such degree,
Even as a swarm of bees that penetrates
Within the flower and thence makes swift return
Whither their toil yields savorous reward,
10 So it descended into that great flower adorned
With leaves so plenteous, and coming forth
Sped back to where its love forever dwells.
They had their faces all of living flame
And wings of gold and all the rest so white
That never snow has known such purity.
Descending in the flower, from row to row
They gave forth of the ardor and the peace
Which they acquired by fanning of their flanks,
Nor did that multitude, though still in flight
20 Between the flower and the upper space,
Hinder the sight nor mar the splendor; nay,
For light divine must ever penetrate
The universe in measure to its worth,
Nor is there anything that may resist.

This kingdom ever joyful and secure,
Thronging with folk of olden times and new,
Had look and love all on one mark intent.
Oh, threefold light which in a single star
So satisfies them, shining on their sight,
30 Look down upon our earthly tempest here!
If the Barbarians, hailing from such parts
As every day are spanned by Helice,
Wheeling in company with her beloved son,
On seeing Rome and her stupendous works,
(While yet the Lateran stood high above
All mortal things)—if they were stupefied,
With what amaze must I be overcome,

I who had come to things divine from works
Of man, from time to wide eternity,
40   From Florence to a just and wholesome folk.
Indeed between astonishment and joy
I wanted to hear nothing and be still.
And, as the pilgrim who feels strength renewed
As he surveys the temple of his vow,
Planning to give account of how it stands,
So passing slowly through that living light
I brought my eyes to dwell in every step
With glances up and down and round about.
And faces I beheld suasive to love,
50   All by their smile and light not theirs adorned
And movements of the chastest dignity.

    My glance already had absorbed in full
The form, in general, of Paradise,
Nor had my sight yet rested anywhere,
So with rekindled will I turned again
To inquire of my lady of some things
Concerning which my mind was in suspense.
But one I sought, another gave response;
I looked for Beatrice but beheld instead
60   An ancient clothed like all the glorious folk.
He bore his eyes and cheeks with joy benign
Suffused, and gentle was his attitude
As would befit a father's tender care.
At once "Where is she?" I inquired, and he
Made answer: "To accomplish your desire
Beatrice moved me from my appointed place;
And if you look up into the third gyre
From the highest rank, you will see her again,
Upon the throne her merits have assigned."
70   Without replying I raised up my eyes
And saw her making for herself a crown,
Reflecting from herself the eternal beams.
From that place whence the highest thunder peals
No mortal vision is so far remote,
However deeply plunged beneath the sea,
As there my sight was far from Beatrice;
But that counted as nought; her image came
Downward to me by no medium obscured.

    "O lady in whom my hope takes its root,
80   Who didst suffer for my soul's weal to let
The traces of thy feet remain in Hell,
The grace and virtue of such mighty things

As I have looked upon I recognize
As by thy power and excellence bestowed.
Thou hast brought me, a slave, to freedom's state,
Through all those roads, by use of every means
Which thou didst have the power to employ.
Preserve thy great munificence toward me,
So that my soul, which thou hast now made whole,
90   May leave the body, pleasing unto thee."
So I made prayer, and she, so far remote
As she appeared, smiling glanced down at me,
Then turned her to the Fount forever flowing.
Then spoke the saintly elder: "That you may
In full perfection consummate your course—
To which end prayer and holy love sent me—
Throughout this garden let your vision rove,
For seeing it will better fit your glance
To mount above up to the ray divine;
100   And Heaven's queen, for whom I am consumed
In ardent love, will grant us every grace
Because I am her faithful son Bernard."
As one who comes—from Croatia it may be
To gaze on our Veronica and cannot,
For reverence of its history, sate his eyes
But in his thought says, while it is displayed:
"My Lord Christ Jesus, God of very truth,
And was this then the semblance of Thy face?"
Even so was I the while I looked upon
110   The living charity of him who here
In contemplation tasted of that peace.
"O child of grace"—so he began, "this world
Of gladsomeness will not be known to you
Through eyes fixed only on its base down here;
Look on the circles, search the most remote
Until your eyes behold the Queen enthroned
Who holds as subject this devoted realm."
Upward I raised my eyes and, as at dawn
The marches of the sky-rim on the East
120   Surpass the region of the setting sun,
So as from valley rising to the peaks,
I could see with my eyes a frontier zone
Outglow in splendor all that glowing front.
And as on earth the greater is the light
Where we await the chariot once steered ill
By Phaethon, while lesser is the glow
On either hand, so that great oriflamme
Of peace shone at the center mightily
And with like tempered brightness on each side.

130   At that mid-point I saw a myriad host
      Of angels, festive all with wings unfurled,
      Each one distinct in brightness and in kind.
      And smiling on their games and canticles
      I saw a beauty which as a deep content
      Filled the rapt gaze of all the other saints.
      Had I such wealth in talent to set down
      As to conceive, yet so I would not dare
      To attempt the least part of her loveliness.
      Bernard then, seeing that my eyes were fixed
140   Upon the shining source of his own warmth,
      With such devotion turned his eyes on her
      As to make mine more ardent in their gaze.

NOTES

4. *other army:* the angels

31-32. *parts . . . son:* the north; *Helice* is the Great Bear (or Big Dipper), her son Boötes is the Little Bear (Dipper).

35-36. while the Lateran, the old papal palace, said to have been given to Sylvester by Constantine, still exemplified the magnificence of unconquered Rome.

69. see Canto xxxii, 8-9.

102. *Bernard:* founder of the abbey Clairvaux, preacher of the second crusade, celebrated for his devotion to the Virgin (1091-1153).

104. *the Veronica:* the *sudarium* or towel kept in St. Peter's and regularly exposed for veneration in the Middle Ages, supposed to retain the outlines of Jesus' features as He wiped the sweat from His face with it on His way to Calvary.

126. *Phaethon:* son of Apollo, who attempted to drive the chariot of the Sun. His inability to manage the horses would have led to the destruction of the earth had Jove not slain him by a thunderbolt.

CANTO XXXII

[After identifying the principal redeemed souls enthroned in the white rose, St. Bernard explains that the degree of their blessedness was predestined. He then leads Dante in a prayer to the Virgin.]

    Enraptured with his joy, he then assumed,
  That great contemplative, the generous role
  Of teacher, opening thus his saintly speech:
  "The wound which Mary salved and closed again
  Was opened by the cutting thrust of her
  Who—mark how lovely—sits beneath her there.
  Disposed in order in the third rank sit
    Below her Rachel with, as you perceive,
  Beatrice, and Sarah, Rebecca, Judith too

10   And she that was great granddam to the singer
      Who for remorse cried *Miserere mei.*
      You may mark each from tier to lower tier
      As I, while calling out their proper names,
      Go by descending petals down the rose.
      And from the seventh rank down, as likewise reaching
      Up to it, falls a line of Hebrew dames
      Dividing all the tresses of the flower;
      For in accordance with the way Faith looked
      Toward Christ, they indicate the boundary wall
20   Partitioning these banks of sacred steps.
      On this side where the flower is mature
      In every petal are enthroned all souls
      Who trusted in the Christ to come, yon side
      With vacant places interspersed they sit
      Whose eyes were turned to the incarnate Word.
      And as on this side the siege glorious
      Of Heaven's lady and the other seats
      Below it make so great a cleaving line,
      So, facing her, the place of John the Great,
30   Who ever saintly dared the wilderness
      And Martyrdom and two years' span of Hell
      Makes a like line with those assigned beneath him:
      Francis and Benedict and Augustine,
      And others down to here from row to row.
      Now marvel at the providence profound:
      For one and the other aspect of the faith
      Shall fill this garden and in shares alike.
      Know too that downward from the rank that cleaves
      The two divisions at their middle line,
40   Not through one's merits is a seat assigned
      But through another's, under certain laws:
      For all of these are spirits who were freed
      Before they could themselves make a true choice.
      You may indeed perceive it by their faces
      And by their childrens' voices, if you will
      But look on them and listen as they sing.
      Now you have doubts and doubting say no word:
      But I will solve for you the tangled knot
      Wherein your subtle thoughts hold you enmeshed.
50   Through all the vastness of this ample realm,
      No point of chance may find a place, no more
      Than may such things as hunger, thirst or grief.
      For everything you see has been decreed
      By law eternal so that here the ring
      And finger in perfection correspond.
      Therefore these swift sped souls, not without cause

Are come to the true life, in excellence
Of varying degrees among themselves.
The King for whom this kingdom rests in peace
60 Of such great love and of such ecstasy,
That never will could dare desire more,
Creating every mind in His glad sight,
Endows diversely as it pleases Him
Each one—and here let the effect suffice.
This is by Holy Writ set down for you
Clear and expressly, speaking of the twins
Whose wrath was stirred while in their mother's womb.
Wherefore according to the color of
Their locks of grace, so must the loftiest Light
70 Encircle them with garland suitable.
So, without reference to their way of life,
And differing only in their first insight
They are placed here in varying degrees.
In the first centuries the parents' faith
sufficed—with innocence—to win them weal;
But when the primal ages were complete,
By circumcision young males were obliged
To gather virtue to their sinless wings.
However when the time of grace had come,
80 Then without perfect baptism in Christ
Such innocence was held back there below.
Now on the face that is most like to Christ's
Look closely, for its clarity alone
Has power to prepare you to see Christ."

I saw upon that face rain down such joy,
Borne of the holy minds that had been made
To spread their wings in heavens so supreme,
That all the wonders I had seen before
Had held me not in such amazement rapt
90 Nor shown me such a great semblance of God.
That love which first descended unto her
Singing "Hail Mary full of Grace" now came
And in her aspect spread his pinions wide.
Responses to that canticle divine
Came forth from all parts of that blessed court,
Whereby each face became yet more serene.
"O holy father, for my sake consenting
To stay down here and leave the pleasant place
Wherein by lot eternal thou dost sit,
100 Who is yon angel who with such delight
Gazes so deeply into our Queen's eyes,
Seeming enflamed in his enamorment?"

Seeking his teaching thus I had recourse
Once more to him who waxed in Mary's sight
More fair, as with the sun the morning star.
He answered: "All the blithesomeness and charm
That any soul or angel may contain
Are found in him—and we would have it so,
For he it was who downward bore the palm
110 To Mary when the Son of God decreed
To take our human burden on Himself.
But now come, let thine eyes accompany
My discourse and remark the mighty peers
Of this our empire, loyal and most just.
Happiest are the twain who sit up there;
Since they are nearest to our Emperor's spouse
They are twin roots, one may say, of the rose.
The one who sits beside her on her left
Is the sire through whose taste presumptuous
120 Mankind goes savoring so much bitterness;
Behold the ancient father, on the right,
Of Holy Church to whom Christ did commend
The keys unto this flower so passing fair.
He that, before he died, did witness all
The times of hardship of the beauteous bride
Won by the lance and nails, sits next to him.
Along the other's flank that leader rests
Under whose guidance lived, by manna fed,
The fickle, wilful and ungrateful folk.
130 Opposite Peter see how Anna sits,
Eyeing her child with such content that ne'er
Her glances stray the while she sings Hosanna.
Facing the greatest family father sits
Lucía who did stir thy lady's steps
When thou wast bending ruinward thy brows.
But since the time that holds thee fast asleep
Is passing, here we'll pause, as the good tailor
Cuts out the gown according to his cloth,
And to the First Love we shall raise our eyes,
140 So that, there gazing, thou mayest penetrate
Into His splendor as deeply as may be.
However, lest perchance, trying thy wings,
Thou movest backward, thinking to advance,
By prayer behoveth grace to be acquired,
Grace of her giving, who can lend thee aid.
Do thou with thy affection follow me
So that thy heart depart not from my speech . . ."
Thus he began the holy orison.

NOTES

4-5. *wound:* [of original sin, which Mary healed by giving birth to Jesus—Ed.]

5. *her:* Eve.

8. *Rachel:* [in Genesis, wife of Jacob, mother of Joseph and Benjamin—Ed.] see *Inf.* ii.

9. *Sarah:* wife of Abraham, mother of Isaac, ancestress of all believers in Christ to come; see Hebrews xi, 11; *Rebecca:* wife of Isaac; *Judith:* Hebrew heroine who slew Holofernes.

10. *granddam:* Ruth *singer:* David 11 *Miserere mei:* "Have mercy on me" (Psalm li).

29. *John:* the Baptist.

32. *Francis:* [(1181/82-1226) St. Francis of Assisi—Ed.] *Benedict:* [(480-543) founder of the Benedictine monastic order—Ed.]; *Augustine:* (354-430) Bishop of Hippo and founder of Christian theology.

43. *Before . . . choice:* i.e., before reaching the age of reason.

56-64. the souls of the children who are saved find their proper place in heaven according to their potential merits. This working of predestination is beyond mortal understanding.

66. *twins:* Jacob and Esau, see Genesis xxv, 22-25.

74. *in . . . centuries:* before Abraham.

77. *circumcision:* under the Hebraic law.

81. *there below:* in Limbo, see *Inf.* iv.

82. *the face:* of the Virgin.

91. *the love:* Gabriel.

119. *the sire:* Adam.

121. *the . . . father:* St. Peter.

125. *bride:* the Church.

127. *the other's:* Adam's *leader:* Moses.

130. *Anna:* Mary's mother.

134-135 see *Inf.* ii.

145. *her:* Mary.

CANTO XXXIII

[St. Bernard's prayer is granted and Dante is permitted to gaze directly upon the Supreme Being, whose triune nature is represented by three concentric spheres of light. Dante begs that he be allowed to communicate some memory of this vision in his poetry.]

"Virgin mother, daughter of thy son,
Humble and high above all creatures made,
Foreordained goal of the eternal plan,
Thou didst endow with such nobility

Our human nature that He did not scorn,
Who was its Maker, to be made of it.
Within thy womb enkindled once again
Was that love through whose warmth in peace eternal
This flower hath burgeoned forth to such effect.
10 For us here thou art as the meridian torch
Of love, and for the mortals down below
Thou art the living fountain of their hope.
Lady, so great art thou, of such avail,
That one who wishes grace and seeks not thee,
Lo, his desire essays flight without wings.
Not only does thy bounty succor him
Who asks of thee, but oftentimes also
Foreruns the prayer, in liberality.
In thee is mercy, pity dwells in thee,
20 And all magnificence and every good
That any thing created may possess.
Now this man, who hath seen one after one
The spirit lives, from out the deepest pit
Of all the universe upwards to here,
Implores thee, of thy grace, such virtue as
Therewith he may uplift him with his eyes
Yet higher toward the final bliss of all;
And I, who for my vision never burned
More than I burn for his, I proffer all
30 My prayers and pray they be not scant, that thou
With thine own prayer may dissipate for him
Each and all clouds of his mortality
That he may look upon the Highest Joy.
Further, I ask of thee, O Queen, whose power
Is as thy will, that after his great vision,
Thou keep all his affections hale in him.
Let thy care check his human impulses;
See Beatrice and so many sainted souls
Who with me join their hands in prayer to thee."

40   The eyes beloved and revered of God
Fixed on the orator made manifest
How pleasing in their sight are prayers devout.
Then they were turned to the eternal light
Wherein we may believe no creature else
May delve with vision of such clarity.
And I who was now drawing to the end
Of each and all desiring, as I should,
Brought warmth of wishing to an end in me.
Bernard, smiling the while, made me a sign
50 To look above, but of my own accord

I was already such as he would have me.
For my eyes' vision, clear and clearer growing
Was piercing ever deeper in the beam
Of light sublime which of itself is truth.
From that point on my strength to see surpassed
Our mortal speech which yields to such a sight
As memory must yield to such excess.
As one who dreaming sees a vision clear
And afterwards the feeling it aroused
60 Remains, while all the rest forsakes the mind;
Even such am I for here my vision fades
Almost away, while yet the sweetness borne
Thereof is in my heart distilled. Even so
The snow disintegrates beneath the sun,
And, as the wind stirred all the fragile leaves,
The sentences of Sybil were dispersed.
O Light Supreme that raisest up Thyself
Far above mortal concepts, lend again
A little of Thy semblance to my mind,
70 And make my tongue so potent that at least
I may bequeath to folk as yet unborn
The glory of one little spark of Thine.
For by in part returning to my mind
And hence resounding somewhat in these verses
More of thy victory will be conceived.
I would have been confounded, I believe,
By very keenness of that living ray
If my regard had turned aside from it,
Wherefore, so I recall, on that account
80 More boldly I sustained it and so joined
My mortal glance with Virtue infinite.
O grace abundant wherein I presumed
To plunge my glance into the eternal Light,
Till I consumed my strength of sight thereon!
Lodged in its deep recess I could behold
All in the one same volume bound with love
The scattered leaves of all the universe;
Substance and accident and their effects,
As it were fused together in such wise
90 That what I speak of is one simple flame.
I think I saw the universal form
Of this complexity for as I speak
I feel a larger welling-up of joy.
One moment makes a deeper wonderment
In me than five and twenty centuries have wrought
Upon the enterprise that long ago
Made Neptune marvel at the Argo's shade.

So my mind, held in high suspense remained
Fixed in its gaze, intent and motionless
100 And by its gazing more and more inflamed.
Under that light a man is altered so
That to turn from it to another sight
Is not an action possible to allow.
For the good which is the object of the will
Is therein wholly gathered, what is there
Most perfect is defective out of it.
My speech shall now, against what little part
I yet remember, fall below the babe's
Whose tongue is still bathed at his mother's breast.
110 Not that more than one simple semblance was
Within the living Light I looked upon
Which is forever what it was before,
But rather by the sight that waxed in strength
As I kept gazing, one aspect alone
Continually altered as I changed.
In the profound and deep subsistence of
The lofty Light, three whirling gyres appeared
Having three colors and one measurement;
One from another seemed to be reflected
120 As Iris out of Iris, whilst the third
Was as a fire breathing alike on each.
Alas, how short and feeble is the word
For my conception,—nay, 'gainst what I saw
"Short" gives scant measure of the word's default.
Eternal Light, in Thyself only dwelling
And Who in understanding pourest forth
Radiant Love upon Thyself, for Thou
Alone dost understand Thyself and art
Full comprehended by Thyself alone!
130 That circling motion which in Thee appeared
To be conceived as a reflected light,
When my eyes had considered it somewhat,
Within itself and of its own color seemed
To be depicted with our effigy
Wherefore my sight was given over to it.
As the geometer who bends all his strength
To measuring of the circle, finding not,
For all his thought, the principle he lacks—
Even so stood I before that vision rare:
140 How might the image with the gyre accord,
And how it found its place, that would I see
But my own wings were not for such a flight:
Save that my mind was smitten by a flash
Wherein its longing was achieved. And here

Further strength failed my high imagining;
But like a wheel, that as a whole rotates
My yearning and my will were borne along
By the Love that moves the sun and all the stars.

NOTES

65-66. the prophecies of the Cumaean Sybil, written on fallen leaves, were dispersed by the wind. *Aeneid* iii, 441-451.

88. *substance and accident:* here used in the scholastic sense.

94-97. i.e., one moment of the sublime vision creates in the poet an amazement more profound than 25 centuries of reflecting on the voyage of the Argo (the first ship ever launched; hence a source of wonder to Neptune, the Ocean God) have made on mankind's memory (following Scartazzini).

119. *One:* the Son. *another:* the Father.

120. *the third:* the Holy Ghost.

134. *our effigy:* the likeness of man.

136-138. a reference to the old problem of "squaring" the circle.

Glossary of Helpful Terms

Aaron—brother of the prophet Moses and the first high priest of Israel. Because Moses had a speech defect, Aaron acted as his spokesman when they appeared before the Pharaoh of Egypt.

Abel and Cain—in Genesis the first sons of Adam and Eve. When God preferred Abel's animal sacrifice to Cain's grain offering, Cain became the first murderer by killing his brother. The "mark of Cain" was not a curse but a symbol of God's protection.

Abraham (*Abram*)—according to Genesis the supreme example of obedience to God and the progenitor of the Hebrew nation. By divine command Abraham left his adopted city of Ur in Mesopotamia and journeyed to Canaan (Palestine), which God promised to give his descendants. In extreme old age he had an only son, Isaac, by his wife Sarah. To test Abraham's faith, God demanded that he sacrifice Isaac. At the last moment, an angel intervened and substituted a sacrificial ram in place of the boy. Because of Abraham's willingness to give up what was dearest to him, God reaffirmed His promise that Abraham's "seed" (progeny) would become "as the sands of the sea" in number and a source of blessing to all men. The twelve tribes of Israel descended from Abraham's grandson Jacob.

Academy—the first university of Europe. It was so called because in 387 B.C. Plato founded his famous school of philosophy in the groves of Academe, near Athens. The Academy, where Plato and his successors taught mathematics, geometry, rhetoric, logic, music, and oratory, continued until A.D. 529 when the Christian emperor Justinian closed all centers of pagan learning.

Achaeans—Homer's name for the Greeks who besieged Troy. In a strict sense Achaean applies to the people of Achilles' kingdom in Thessaly, but in a broader way it refers to the whole Greek expedition. Almost interchangeably, Homer also calls the Greeks Argives or Danaans.

Achates—faithful friend and companion of Aeneas.

Acheron—(1) in Greek and Roman myth, one of the rivers of Hades; (2) in Dante's *Inferno,* it marks the upper boundary of Hell, flowing between the Opportunists and Limbo.

Achilles—hero of Homer's *Iliad* and for centuries the Greek ideal of the warrior-prince. His anger against the Achaean commander-in-chief, Agamemnon, with its disastrous consequences to both Greeks and Trojans, is the main theme of Homer's epic. Achilles is the supreme example of the classical hero: brave, proud, tremendously effective in warfare, keenly conscious of his honor and public reputation. Rejecting a safe, obscure life, he deliberately chooses a short, violent existence which will earn him undying fame. (According to some legends, his mother, the sea nymph Thetis, dipped the infant Achilles in the River Styx, which rendered him invulnerable, except for the heel by which he was held.) Shortly after Hector's death, Achilles is killed by Paris' shooting a poisoned arrow into his unprotected heel. Homer does not include this incident in the *Iliad*.

Acropolis—the fortified hill of Athens on which Pericles built the Parthenon and other public and religious buildings whose ruins still give Greece her chief architectural distinction.

Adam—according to Genesis, the first man created by God, the forefather of the entire human race. According to Christian theology, his "original sin" of eating the forbidden fruit not only caused his expulsion from Eden but also brought the curse of sin and death upon all his descendants.

Admetus—legendary Greek king, fated to an early death unless someone could be found to die in his place. Only his young wife, Alcestis, was willing to make the sacrifice. At the last moment, Admetus' friend Heracles saved Alcestis by wresting her from Death (Thanatos) and restoring her to life.

Adonai—the Hebrew word for "Lord," used as a title for God in the Old Testament.

Adonis—the beautiful youth beloved by Aphrodite and slain by a wild boar. Moved by Aphrodite's tears, Zeus permitted Adonis to return to earth for six months of every year. His annual return signals the advent of spring. Originally Adonis was probably a male fertility god, whose name derives from the Semetic word *Adon,* meaning "lord." He can be equated with Dionysus or the Canaanite Tammuz.

Aegis—fear-producing breastplate worn by Zeus and Athene.

Aegisthus—son of Thyestes, cousin and mortal enemy of Agamemnon. While Agamemnon was fighting at Troy, Aegisthus became Clytemnestra's lover and helped her kill her husband upon his return home. Years later he and Clytemnestra were slain by Agamemnon's son, Orestes.

Aeneas—Trojan prince, minor character in the *Iliad* and hero of the *Aeneid.* According to Virgil, Aeneas is the son of Anchises and Venus (Aphrodite), who acts as her son's guide and protector on his long journey from Troy to Italy where he is destined to found the Roman nation. Aeneas exemplifies the ideal Roman virtues of patience, endurance, hard work, and complete obedience to the divine Providence that directs his life.

Aeolus—Greek god of the winds.

Aeropagus—the "hill of Ares (Mars)," a spur of the Athenian Acropolis, where, in legend, Orestes was tried for murdering his mother. St. Paul delivered a famous speech to the Athenians there (see *Acts* 17).

Agamemnon—son of Atreus and brother of Menelaus. By his wife Clytemnestra he fathered Iphigenia, Electra, Chrysothemis, and Orestes. As king of Mycenae and the territory of Argos, he is the most powerful of the Achaean chieftans who besiege Troy. His quarrel with his leading fighter, Achilles, provides the major conflict of the *Iliad.* Both Homer and Aeschylus portray him as capable and dignified, but pompous and overbearing.

Agathon—popular Athenian dramatist and friend of Socrates. In Plato's *Symposium,* the action of which occurs in 416 B.C., he hosts an all-night drinking party to celebrate his first victory in the tragic competition. None of Agathon's plays survive, but from ancient sources we know that he invented his own plots and wrote in a highly florid style. The comic playwright Aristophanes later wrote a comedy ridiculing Agathon's excesses.

Agave—daughter of Cadmus, mother of King Pentheus of Thebes. In Euripides' *The Bacchae,* Dionysus drives her temporarily insane, causing her to murder her own son. For this crime she goes into exile.

Agon—(1) athletic, musical, or dramatic contest; (2) term in Greek tragedy for the struggle or conflict between the hero and some other character.

Aias (*Ajax*)—the name of two heroes in the *Iliad*. (1) The "great" or Telamonian Aias, despite his fighting power, is defeated by Odysseus in the contest for dead Achilles' armor. Later poets, such as Sophocles, record that Aias then went mad from shame and disappointment and killed himself. (2) The "lesser" Aias is called the "runner." Noted for conceit and insolence, he is punished by Athene for raping Cassandra and dies by drowning.

Alaric (c. A.D. 370-410)—leader of the Gothic invaders of Italy and Greece during the last years of the Roman Empire. He was the first Germanic conqueror to sack Rome, preparing the way for the city's total collapse in A.D. 476.

Alba Longa—in the *Aeneid*, Italian city founded by Aeneas' son Ascanius.

Alcestis—heroine of Euripides' earliest surviving play. When the Fates decree that her husband, Admetus, must die young, she volunteers to die in his place. Heracles then rescues her from Death and restores her to her family.

Alcibiades—(c. 450-404 B.C.)—brilliant Athenian of extraordinary beauty, intelligence, and political talent. He was also self-seeking, arrogant, and untrustworthy. Educated by Pericles and a one-time disciple of Socrates, Alcibiades played an important role in the Peloponnesian War.

Alexander the Great (356-323 B.C.)—son of King Philip of Macedonia, conqueror of the world from Greece to India. In a series of spectacular military victories, he brought the huge Persian Empire, Egypt, Palestine, Mesopotamia, Anatolia and western India under Greek control. He turned back from marching into China only because his troops threatened to revolt, unless they returned home. Although his empire was soon divided among his four generals after his death in Babylon, Alexander's permanent achievement was to spread Greek ideas and culture throughout the Near East. It is possible that Alexander envisioned a one-world government, dominated by Greek customs but assimilating Oriental influences. The period after his reign is called "Hellenistic."

Ambrosia—the food of the Olympian gods.

Anaxagoras (c. 500-c. 428 B.C.)—Greek philosopher, friend of Pericles and Euripides. A scientist who taught that the sun and moon were not gods but physical bodies like the earth, he was also the first to teach that Mind *(Nous)* exists independently of matter. For his revolutionary ideas he was exiled from Athens.

Anchises—Trojan prince, father of the hero Aeneas by Aphrodite (Venus). Virgil records that Aeneas carried his father on his back out of burning Troy and took him on his wanderings. Anchises died and was buried in Sicily.

Andromache—wife of Hector, model of the virtuous, domestic woman. In Euripides' *Trojan Women,* her son Astyanax is murdered by Odysseus' orders and she is given in slavery to Neoptolemus, son of Achilles.

Anna—in the *Aeneid,* devoted sister of Dido.

Antenor—an elder nobleman of Troy, famous for his wisdom. According to legend, because he had urged Helen's return to the Greeks, he was spared when the town was destroyed.

Antilochus—in the *Iliad,* son of Nestor and friend of Achilles.

Antony, Marc (*Marcus Antonias*), (c. 82-30 B.C.)—Roman commander, supporter of Julius Caesar, member of the second Triumvirate, lover and later husband of

Cleopatra. Rivalry between Octavian and Antony led to the latter's defeat at the Battle of Actium (31 B.C.). Antony, having lost his half of the empire, then committed suicide.

Anytus—one of the three accusers at Socrates' trial.

Aphrodite—daughter of Zeus, goddess of love and fertility. In the *Iliad* she favors the Trojans, especially Paris, to whom she had given Helen. In Virgil's *Aeneid* she is known by her Latin name Venus and she acts as the guide and patroness of Aeneas, with whom she inspires the Queen of Carthage, Dido, to fall in love. Although officially married to Hephaestus (Vulcan), she fulfills her nature as love incarnate by having affairs with many gods and men, including Aeneas' father, Anchises. She was originally a Near-Eastern fertility goddess; her worship was probably introduced into Greece via the island of Cyprus for which reason Greek poets sometimes call her "the Cypriote."

Apollo—son of Zeus and Leto, called Phoebus (the Shining One), god of light, music, healing, and sickness. His chief shrine was at Delphi where a priestess (the Pythia) would answer questions and deliver prophecies inspired by Apollo. In later times Apollo became identified with Helios, god of the sun; he was then pictured as driving the chariot of the sun across the heavens from dawn to sunset. He is the most beautiful of the male gods and his symbol is either the bow and arrow or the lyre. He is the protector of the nine Muses, goddesses of poetry and the arts.

Apostle—New Testament title given to the twelve original followers of Jesus Christ. After Judas committed suicide, he was replaced by Saul of Taursus, who became St. Paul the new twelfth Apostle. According to Roman Catholic tradition, St. Peter was the chief Apostle and his office was passed on to his spiritual heirs—the popes of Rome. The term means literally "a messenger or ambassador (of God)."

Aquinas, St. Thomas (A.D. 1225-1274)—influential theologian and scholar of the medieval Roman Catholic Church. His major work, the *Summa Theologica,* was an attempt to reconcile Aristotelian philosophy with Christian belief. His thought greatly influenced the composition of Dante's *Divine Comedy.*

Arcadia—a mountainous region in the south of Greece, sacred to Pan, Hermes and Apollo. Its inhabitants claimed to be descended from the Achaeans about whom Homer wrote. Poets later made Arcadia a symbol of the peaceful, simple life of shepherds, a kind of paradise.

Archetype—the primal form or original pattern from which all other things of a like nature are descended. In literary study it refers to characters, ideas, or actions which represent the supreme and/or essential examples of a universal type. Gilgamesh and Odysseus are archetypes of the wandering hero, as Oedipus is of the incest taboo, and Yahweh of the stern Father-God. According to psychologist Carl Jung, we inherit racial memories of our earliest ancestors' basic emotions, attitudes, and goals. These become directive forces in our subconscious minds so that when we encounter an act or situation in literature it stimulates our inherited memory and we recognize it as "archetypal."

Ares—son of Zeus and Here, god of war and human aggresson, whom Zeus describes as "most hated" of all the gods. He is often shown as the illicit lover of Aphrodite. He figures most prominently in war-loving Roman times when he was called Mars.

Argive—Homer's name for the Greeks who besieged Troy. It is interchangeable with Achaean and Danaan. In later usage it may mean "people of Argos."

Argonauts—fifty Greek heroes who sailed with Jason to obtain the Golden Fleece (q.v.). Their ship was called the *Argo*.

Aristides (c. 530-c. 468 B.C.)—Athenian democratic leader during the Persian Wars, known as "the Just" for his patriotism and excellent character. He fought at Marathon and held high office, but politically opposed Themistocles (q.v.), for which he was exiled in 482. He returned to fight at Salamis and Plataea, and organized the Delian League, a confederation of Greek city-states formed to resist future Persian invasions. Because of his honesty, he was given the job of deciding how much each member state was to pay in taxes.

Ark—(1) large chest-like boat which Noah built to contain his family and pairs of all animals during the biblical flood. (2) Ark of the Covenant refers to the ornamental chest which contained sacred symbols of the Hebrew religion, such as Moses' staff and the two stone tablets of the Mosaic Law. It was kept in the innermost sanctuary of Solomon's temple in Jerusalem.

Artaphernes—in Herodotus, commander of the Persian expedition against Greece in 490 B.C.

Artemis—daughter of Zeus and Leto, twin sister of Apollo. She is a virgin goddess devoted to the hunt and protectress of wild animals. Like Apollo, she carries a bow and arrow and her "gentle darts" can cause disease among women. To the Romans she was Diana, to whom the moon was sacred.

Ascanius—son of Aeneas by the Trojan princess Creusa. He is also called Iulus.

Asclepius (Greek *Asklepios*)—human son of Apollo and the maid Coronis, later deified as the Greek god of medicine and healing. Raised by the wise centaur Chiron, he was able not only to cure the sick but also to raise the dead. When he restored Hippolytus to life, Zeus jealously killed him with a thunderbolt. His most famous temple was at Epidaurus, where patients slept overnight to be told in dreams how to cure themselves.

Ashur—Assyrian god of war, who combined the functions of the earlier Sumero-Babylonian gods Enlil and Marduk. Kings were named after him, such as Ashur-banipal, in the ruins of whose palace the tablets of *Gilgamesh* were found.

Assur—ancient capital of Assyria.

Assyria—empire of the ancient Near East which conquered large parts of Mesopotamia, Palestine, Egypt, and Ionia. Notorious for its military might and cruelty, Assyria was overthrown in 612 B.C. by a coalition of Medes, Persians, and Babylonians. Assyria's last great king, Ashurbanipal, collected the world's first major library, consisting of clay tablets inscribed in the cuneiform script. This collection, excavated from the ruins of Nineveh, includes our most complete copy of the epic of *Gilgamesh*.

Astarte—an ancient Canaanite mother and fertility goddess, analogous to the Sumero-Babylonian Ishtar. In the Old Testament, she was called Ashtoreth and her worship condemned by the prophets.

Ate—Greek goddess personifying moral blindness.

Athene—virgin daughter of Zeus, goddess of wisdom, military victory, and psychological craft. Athens chose her as its patron deity and erected the magnificent Parthenon in her honor. Severe, chaste, and masculine-minded, she is the exact opposite of Aphrodite. Her Roman name is Minerva.

Atlantis—mythological kingdom supposed to have sunk beneath the Atlantic Ocean, giving rise to legends of a lost continent. The story is given in Plato's dialogue the *Timaeus*.

Atlas—Titan brother of Prometheus; after Zeus deposed Cronos, Atlas was made to bear the heavens on his shoulders.

Atonement—Hebrew annual day of fasting and sacrifice on which an animal was offered to atone for the sins of the people. In Christian terminology, Christ became the sacrificial animal which permanently expiated human sins.

Atrapos—one of the three Fates, who blindly cuts the thread of life spun and measured by her sisters Clotho and Lachesis. She is the "dread" goddess because her decisions are irrevocable.

Atreides—Homeric term describing either one or both sons of Atreus, Menelaus and Agamemnon. The plural is Atreidae.

Attica—province in east-central Greece; Athens is the chief city.

Attila (A.D. 406-453)—King of the Huns who invaded and ravaged Europe just prior to the final fall of Rome. To Dante and other Christians, Attila was "the scourge of God." He was finally bribed to leave Italy by Pope Leo I.

Augustus—title assumed by Octavian when he received imperial power. See *Octavian.*

Aulis—Greek seaport at which the Achaean expedition assembled before sailing to Troy. Agamemnon sacrificed his daughter Iphigenia there.

Baal—in ancient Near Eastern religion, a fertility god worshiped in Canaan (Palestine), a major rival of the Hebrew deity Yahweh. Mythologically, he is equivalent to dying and resurrected gods like Dionysus of Greece, Tammuz of Babylon, and Osiris of Egypt.

Babylon—ancient city in Mesopotamia dating from Sumerian times, which achieved its greatest fame under King Nebuchadnezzar in the sixth century B.C. In 586 Nebuchadnezzar captured Jerusalem, burned Solomon's temple, and carried a portion of the Jewish population into the "Babylonian Captivity." Babylon fell to Cyrus of Persia in 539 B.C., and the Jews were restored to their homeland. Alexander of Macedon intended to restore the city to its former glory, but died there before he could make it his Near Eastern capital.

Bacchus—an epithet for *Dionysus* (q.v.).

Beatrice (A.D. 1266-1290)—daughter of the Florentine Folco Portinari, married to Simone dei Bardi. To Dante, Beatrice was the epitome not only of beauty and graciousness but also the purity of true religion. In the *Divine Comedy* she functions as a symbol of heavenly love, revealed religion, and divine grace. At her wish Virgil is sent to guide Dante through Hell and Purgatory. In the garden of Eden at the top of the Mount of Purgatory, Beatrice replaces Virgil as Dante's guide and teacher. This suggests that human reason can take man to a knowledge of sin and the need for purification, but only heaven-sent grace can raise man to a knowledge of ultimate Truth.

Beelzebub—a corruption of the Canaanite term Baal-Zebul, or "Prince Baal," distorted by the Hebrews and interpreted as "Lord of the Flies." In popular medieval theology he was regarded as a demon-prince of Satan. He so appears in Dante's Hell.

Benjamin—twelfth and youngest son of the patriarch Jacob by his wife Rachael. His descendants became one of the twelve tribes of Israel.

Bethlehem—birthplace of David, second King of Israel, hence called "the city of David." A tiny hamlet in the hill country of Palestine, it was the prophesied birthplace of the Messiah (Christ) (Micah 5:2). There Jesus (later of Nazareth) was born to Mary and Joseph (see Matthew 2:5).

Bible—collection of writings in Hebrew, Aramaic, and Greek sacred to Jews and Christians, the authority for many of their religious beliefs. The Old Testament contains 39 books divided into three categories: The Mosaic Law, the Prophets, and the Writings, such as Job and the Psalms. The Christians add to this the 27 books of the New Testament which they consider inspired. The term Bible comes from the Greek *biblos* (book) which in turn was derived from the Phoenician city Byblos, an ancient exporter of papyrus *(byblos)* from which writing paper was made. Beginning in about 280 B.C. the Jews of Alexandria, Egypt began a translation of the Hebrew scriptures into Greek; known as the Septuagint, it was used by writers of the New Testament. In the fourth century A.D. St. Jerome made the first translation of all 66 books into Latin, the Vulgate, so called because it used the "vulgar" or common language of the time. The Apochrypha (hidden writings) are late books in Hebrew and Aramaic, included in Catholic Bibles but not considered inspired by Protestants.

Bildad—friend of the afflicted Job who argues that only the guilty are punished.

Bion (about 100 B.C.)—Greek poet whose lament for the dead Adonis established the form of the pastoral elegy.

Bishop—literally an "overseer" of Church affairs; in medieval Europe the official head of a district, superior to all monks and priests under his administration.

Bloodguilt—in ancient Greece, Israel, and other cultures, the kind of pollution a man incurred if he willfully or accidentally committed a murder. In some mythologies, such as that associated with Agamemnon's family, the guilt passed on from father to son, always bringing disaster to the killer's descendants. Oedipus brings bloodguilt upon all Thebes for his unpunished murder of Laius.

Boeotia—Greek territory northwest of Athens; its principal city was Thebes.

Boethius, Anicius Manlius Severinus (A.D. 480-524)— scholar and philosopher whose great work, *Consolations of Philosophy,* occupies a transitional position between the collapse of Roman civilization and the rise of the Middle Ages. Trained in Greek and Latin, deeply influenced by Plato's Theory of Ideas and Aristotelian logic, Boethius attempted to reconcile classical learning with Christian belief. He wrote the *Consolations* while in prison.

Briseis—daughter of Brises, ally of the Trojans, Achilles' captive of war, whom Agamemnon takes to compensate himself for the loss of Chryseis. This act ignites the "wrath of Achilles" and starts the quarrel between him and Agamemnon. When the two Achaeans are reconciled, Briseis is returned to Achilles.

Brutus, Marcus Junius (c. 78-42 B.C.)—an idealistic Roman republican who conspired with Cassius to murder Julius Caesar in 44 B.C. Instead of preserving Roman liberty, however, this act led to civil war and Brutus' defeat at Philippi, where he committed suicide. Dante places Brutus and Cassius as supreme examples of treachery in the very jaws of Satan.

Byzantine Empire—the eastern or Greek-speaking half of the Roman Empire, which survived as a (steadily diminishing) center of power and culture until the Moslem

Turks took it in A.D. 1453. The capital, Constantinople, was founded in A.D. 330 by the Christian Emperor Constantine. A later emperor, Justinian, built the magnificent Church of Holy Wisdom (Hagia Sophia) which survives today as a mosque.

Cadmus—mythological king of Thebes, husband of Harmonia (daughter of Ares and Aphrodite) and father of Agave and Semele (q.v.). As a young man Cadmus slew a dragon and (by Athene's direction) planted its teeth from which warriors sprang up. These fought among themselves until only five remained alive. These five "sown men" then helped build the citadel of Thebes and were the ancestors of the Theban aristocracy.

Caesar, Gaius Julius (c. 102-44 B.C.)—Roman general whose conquest of western Europe and Britain made him—along with his chief military rival, General Pompey—one of the most powerful men in Rome. He formed the first Triumvirate with Pompey and the enormously rich Crassus, but civil war broke out between the two generals, ending with Pompey's murder in Egypt in 48 B.C. Caesar then became entangled with the Egyptian queen, Cleopatra, who was with him in Rome when Brutus and Cassius (ardent republicans who feared Caesar would make himself dictator) murdered him on March 15, 44 B.C. Caesar was a leader of amazing energy and genius, whose military victories were matched by his political and administrative ability. His *History of the Gallic Wars* is a model of Latin prose. The Roman emperors called themselves "Caesar" in his memory.

Calchas—prophet who accompanied the Achaeans to Troy.

Calliope—Muse of epic poetry, the goddess whom Homer invokes at the beginning of the *Iliad* and *Odyssey*.

Calypso—minor goddess who held Odysseus captive for seven years on the remote island of Ogygia. She promised her lover immortality if he would stay with her, but when compelled by Zeus she helped Odysseus build a raft and sent him away.

Canon—a critical standard, a criterion, especially that by which certain books of the Bible were judged genuine and inspired and added to the list of accepted Scripture. Canon laws refers to decrees of the Church made in council and endorsed by the Pope.

Canto—literally a song, or a section of a long poem, as in Dante's *Divine Comedy,* which is divided into 100 cantos.

Carthage—a powerful colony of Tyre on the north coast of Africa, opposite the boot of Italy. It became the chief rival of Rome for domination of the Mediterranean, resulting in the three Punic Wars which ended with Carthage's total destruction in 146 B.C. During the second Punic War the Carthaginian general Hannibal crossed the Alps into Italy and devastated the countryside. He was finally defeated by Scipio at the battle of Zama in 202 B.C. In the *Aeneid*, Hannibal is the foretold avenger of Carthage's legendary founder, Queen Dido.

Cassandra—daughter of Priam and Hecuba, sister of Hector, priestess of Apollo. Cassandra illustrates the paradox of divine favor. Apollo gave her the gift of prophecy, but decreed that no one would believe her. After the fall of Troy she was carried off as Agamemnon's mistress and was murdered with him by Clytemnestra. A tragic, half-mad figure, she appears in the *Iliad*, the *Agamemnon,* and the *Trojan Women.*

Cassius, Gaius—Roman soldier and politician, partner with Brutus in the slaying of Julius Caesar, for which Dante condemned him to the lowest pit of the *Inferno*. He was killed at Philippi in 42 B.C.

Castor and Pollux (Polydeuces)—mythological twin brothers, born like their sisters Helen and Clytemnestra of Leda's union with Zeus in the form of a swan. They went with Jason on the voyage of the Argonauts. Famous for their loyalty to each other, they were allowed after death to spend alternating days in Hades and Heaven. According to later tradition, they were identified with the constellation Gemini. They were also known as the *Dioscuri* (youths of Zeus).

Catharsis—the emotional effect of tragedy, the purgation of "pity and terror" which Aristotle described as the result of witnessing the sufferings of the tragic hero.

Catiline, Lucius Sergius (c. 108-62 B.C.)—impoverished Roman politician and former governor of Africa who attempted to overthrow the government of Rome. In 63 B.C. he plotted to burn the city, murder leading statesmen and senators and seize power either for himself or for Julius Caesar, who may have backed the conspiracy. Cicero, then chief Consul, discovered the plot and denounced it publicly both in the Senate and the forum. He also supervised the rounding up and execution of several important conspirators. Catiline fled Rome with a small army, but was defeated and killed in 62 B.C.

Cato—(1) Cato "the Censor" (234-149 B.C.), model of the austere, frugal, incorruptible Roman, skilled speaker, and "father" of Roman prose. His most famous speeches were against Greek influence in Roman life, which he saw as weakening the old simple virtues, and against Carthage, archenemy of Roman expansion. His most famous maxim was "Carthage must be destroyed," with which he is said to have ended every speech regardless of its subject; (2) Marcus Cato (95-46 B.C.), great-grandson of the first Cato, equally stern and an unyielding opponent of Julius Caesar. He committed suicide when Caesar's legions won in the civil war against Pompey. He appears in Dante's *Purgatorio.*

Centaur—in classical myths, a creature who was half-man, half-horse.

Cerberus—the "hound of hell," who appears as a serpent-tailed monster in Dante's *Inferno.*

Ceres—Roman name for Demeter, the ancient earth goddess.

Chaos—in Greek legend, the original Void that existed before Heaven and Earth came into being. It was not only confusion of matter, in the modern sense, but a horrible vacuum which nature itself abhorred.

Charlemagne (A.D. 742-814)—"Charles the Great," ruler of the Franks, crowned Holy Roman Emperor of the West by Pope Leo III in 800. Charlemagne's reign gave rise to many heroic tales, such as the *Song of Roland.* His dealings with the Church expressed the dual nature of medieval politics: the pope was accorded honorific titles and "spiritual" supremacy, while the emperor insisted on control of the national Church and absolute sovereignty over his own domains. Duels for power between emperor and pope continued throughout the Middle Ages and Renaissance. See the notes to Dante's *Divine Comedy.*

Charon—ancient god of the underworld who ferries souls of the dead across the River Styx. Dante differs from Virgil in making Charon convey spirits across the Achaeron.

Charybdis—female monster who, with Scylla, guarded the Straits of Messina between Italy and Sicily. In the *Odyssey,* she was like a giant whirlpool that sucked ships under water.

Cherubim—in Jewish and Christian terminology, winged angels who surrounded the throne of God.

Chimaera—in Greek legend, a fire-breathing monster with a lion's head, goat's body, and dragon's tail. He is part of the demonic zoo in Dante's Hell.

Chiron (*Cheiron*)—the wise and just Centaur who educated Jason, Achilles, etc. He also taught Asclepius the art of medicine.

Choregus—the title given to the man selected to produce or pay for the presentation of plays in Athens. He equipped the chorus.

Chorus—indispensable element in Greek drama, usually a group of twelve to fifteen men representing a commonsense medium between the extremes set by the tragic figures. It sometimes acts as a link between the drama and the audience, sometimes as a mouthpiece for the views of the author. In plays like *The Bacchae* the chorus is part of the action, whereas in the *Oedipus* and *Agamemnon* it consists of mere spectators, whose function is to sing the lyric odes that comment on the action and divide the play into scenes. Choral songs were usually accompanied by music, sometimes by dancing. In comedy the chorus numbered twenty-four (two semi-choruses) and, when gorgeously costumed, it provided the "spectacle" which Aristotle mentioned.

Christ—Greek translation of the Hebrew *Messiah*, which means "Anointed (of God)." As the early kings of Israel were anointed with holy oil signifying their divine right to rule, so it was believed that the coming Messiah would be a prophet divinely appointed to shepherd his people. The Christians believed Jesus of Nazareth to be the foretold king and regarded him as "the Christ," which through use became part of his personal name.

Chryseis—daughter of Chryses, priest of Apollo. When Agamemnon takes her as his mistress, her father begs the god to bring a plague upon the Greek camp. Forced to return Chryseis, Agamemnon then kindles the "wrath of Achilles" by taking the latter's slave girl, Briseis.

Chrysothemis—daughter of Agamemnon, sister of Electra, generally a passive figure.

Circe—enchantress in the *Odyssey* who turns men into swine. Protected by the magical moly plant, given him by Hermes, Odysseus resists transformation. Circe directs him to Hades to consult the prophet Tiresias. According to some legends, Odysseus fathered a son, Telegonus, by Circe.

Cleisthenes—Greek statesman, founder of the Athenian democracy (508 B.C.).

Cleopatra (68-30 B.C.)—Greek queen of Egypt, mistress of Julius Caesar by whom she had a son, Caesarion, and later paramour of Marc Antony. Famous for her beauty, charm, and sensuality, she may have seduced her Roman lovers in order to preserve Egypt's independence. During the crucial Battle of Actium between Octavian and Antony, Cleopatra inexplicably withdrew her fleet. Antony abandoned his command to follow her, thus forfeiting his half of the Roman Empire. After Antony's death, Cleopatra committed suicide. Dante placed her among the lustful in his *Inferno*.

Clio—Muse of history.

Clodia—Roman matron involved in many scandals, the "Lesbia" whom Catullus loved and to whom he addressed many of his poems. Cicero denounced her in an infamous court trial.

Clotho—one of the three Fates; see *Atrapos*.

Clouds, The—the comedy in which Aristophanes satirized the new Athenian philosophies, especially Sophism. It falsely depicts Socrates as a conniving rogue who, for money, teaches young men to outwit their fathers. At his trial, Socrates dated his unpopularity from the time of the play (423 B.C.).

Clytemnestra—daughter of Zeus and Leda, sister of Helen, wife of Agamemnon, queen of Mycenae. To avenge Agamemnon's sacrifice of her daughter, Iphigenia, she takes his worst enemy, Aegisthus, as her lover and murders her husband upon his homecoming from Troy. Later her son Orestes avenges his father's death by killing her and Aegisthus.

Cocles, Publius Horatius—legendary Roman soldier who, single-handedly, defended a bridge leading to Rome against the entire Etruscan army. He held his position while the bridge behind him was being destroyed, then leapt into the river and swam to safety. "Horatio at the bridge" became a favorite topic of patriotic literature.

Colchis—barbaric home of Medea, located on the remote shores of the Black Sea.

Colonus—suburb of Athens, birthplace of Sophocles, site of Oedipus' death.

Comedy—from *komoidia,* a festal song. According to Aristotle, comedy evolved from primitive village revels and phallic songs and to the end retained its obscene character. The eleven plays of Aristophanes are all that survive of the many hundreds produced in Athens during the fifth and fourth centuries B.C. Aristophanic Old Comedy observed a fairly strict format: a *prologue* which introduced the action, a *parados* or entry song of the chorus, an *agon* or contest between two opponents (the main subject of the play), several *episodes* separated by choral songs, and the *exodos* or final scene, usually involving a *komos* or celebration.

Commedia—term Dante applied to his masterpiece because it fit the medieval definition of comedy as a work that begins unhappily and ends happily. Dante's journey through the afterworld started in Hell but culminated in Heaven.

Constantine (A.D. 280-337)—first Christian emperor of Rome, who in 314 issued the Edict of Milan which proclaimed toleration for all religions in the Empire. In 325 he called the Church Council of Nicaea at which the doctrine of the Trinity (that God exists in three equal persons, Father, Son, and Holy Ghost) was decided upon and became official Roman Catholic dogma.

Constantinople—capital of the eastern Roman Empire, established by Constantine in A.D. 330 on the site of the Greek colony, Byzantium. It remained a center of classical learning until captured by the Moslem Turks in 1453 and renamed Istanbul.

Constitution of the Lacedaemonians—a minor political work of Xenophon in which he praises the rigorous Spartan way of life, including the training of the young, the marriage system, the holding of property in common, and the willingness to die rather than to live a cowardly or dishonorable life. He also laments the passing of these virtues.

Consul—Roman executive political office to which an outstanding citizen was elected annually.

Corinth—city of classical Greece, famous for its wealth and luxury. It was one of Athens' chief enemies during the Peloponnesian War. St. Paul wrote two epistles to the Christians there.

Coryphaeus—leader of the chorus in Greek drama.

Covenant—literally a contract between two parties, as that between Abraham and Yahweh. In the Mosaic Covenant Israel agreed to obey Yahweh's religious laws and He agreed to protect and enrich them.

Cratinas (c. 520-c. 423 B.C.)—Athenian writer of the Old Comedy, a rival of the young Aristophanes. He often attacked Pericles.

Cimon (c. 507-449 B.C.)—Athenian commander and statesman who favored cooperation with Sparta and played an important role in the second Persian invasion (480-479 B.C.). After Themistocles' exile and Aristides' death, he led Athenian imperial expansion in the Aegean. When Pericles rose to power, Cimon was exiled for ten years.

Creon—(1) Greek word for king, applied indiscriminately to various rules such as Creon of Corinth in Euripides' *Medea*; (2) in Sophocles' *Oedipus*, Jocasta's brother who assumes power after Oedipus' exile.

Crete—largest island in the Mediterranean, home of the pre-Greek Minoan civilization that dominated the eastern Mediterranean from about 2000 to 1400 B.C. According to Homer, King Idomeneus of Crete was an important Achaean ally in the Trojan War.

Creusa—daughter of Priam, first wife of Aeneas, mother of Ascanias (Iulus). She is killed in the fall of Troy.

Critias (460-403 B.C.)—leader of the notorious Thirty Tyrants who misruled Athens toward the end of the Peloponnesian War. For a while he was associated with Socrates, and Plato named a dialogue after him.

Crito—friend of Socrates who urged him to escape from prison, but to whom the philosopher replied that even unjust laws must be obeyed.

Croesus (ruled 560-546 B.C.)—king of Lydia (country in western Asia Minor), famous for his wealth and his impulsiveness. According to Herodotus, he sent to Delphi to ask if he should go to war with Persia. When the oracle replied that if he did so a great empire would fall, Croesus foolishly assumed that Persia was doomed. When captured by the Persians and about to be burned alive, he was spared at the last moment by Cyrus' clemency.

Cronus (*Kronos*)—chief god of the Titans, son of Uranus and Gaea (Heaven and Earth). According to Hesiod's *Theogony*, Cronus castrated his father and assumed rule of the universe. By Rhea he had six divine children, Zeus, Here, Hestia, Demeter, Poseidon, and Hades. Like Uranus, Cronus was overthrown by his son, Zeus, who hurled the Titans into Tartarus and introduced a third generation of gods, the Olympians. These are the gods of Homer and the classical Greeks.

Cumaean Sibyl—Roman equivalent of the Greek prophetess of Delphi, inspired by Apollo to predict the future. In the *Aeneid* she guides Aeneas through the underworld.

Cupid—the Roman name for Eros, son of Aphrodite (Venus), who mischievously uses his arrows to inspire love. He was the lover of Psyche (Soul).

Cybele—an Asiatic earth mother whom the Greeks identified with Rhea, wife of the Titan Cronus. Her worship was introduced into Athens in 430 B.C. in the hope that she would end the plague that then ravaged the city. Although she had a large temple in Rome, her religion was never officially condoned there. Cybele's priests were eunuchs.

Cyclopes—giant, one-eyed monsters, sons of Poseidon or Uranus but abhorred alike by gods and men. In the *Odyssey*, the Cyclops Polyphemus traps and devours Odysseus' men until they put out the creature's eye. Euripides renders this episode comically in the *Cyclops*, the only surviving satyr play.

Cynic—school of philosophy founded in Athens by Antisthenes in the late fifth century B.C. The Cynics held that virtue was happiness and could be gained by self-denial. Their most famous exponent was Diogenes who lived in a barrel, ate scraps, and, to show his contempt for common morality, went about in daylight with a lantern looking for "an honest man."

Cynthia—another name for the moon.

Cypris—epithet for Aphrodite, who was supposed to have emerged from the sea on the shores of the island Cyprus.

Cyrus the Great (600-529 B.C.)—king of Persia who captured Babylon in 539, released the Jewish captives, overthrew Croesus of Lydia, subdued the Greek cities of Asia Minor (Ionia) and otherwise greatly extended the Persian Empire.

Cyrus the Younger (c. 424/23-401 B.C.)—a royal contender for the Persian throne who hired Greek mercenaries to fight against his brother Artaxerxes. Xenophon described the Greeks' experience in Asia and their retreat after Cyrus' death in his *March of the Ten Thousand*.

Daedalus—legendary master architect who constructed the Labyrinth for King Minos, from whom he escaped by making wings of wax and feathers for himself and his son Icarus. When Icarus flew too near the sun its heat melted his wings and he fell to his death.

Daemon (*Daimon, Demon*)—a Greek term meaning deity in general, but in later times denoting lesser spirits which inhabited particular locales. In the Christian view, they became imps of Satan.

Damascus—oldest continuously inhabited town in Syria, on the road to which Saul of Tarsus was converted by beholding a vision of the resurrected Christ. He then became St. Paul, missionary to the non-Jewish peoples (Gentiles).

Danae—mother of the Greek hero Perseus, whom she conceived when Zeus appeared in a shower of gold. Her father, Acrisius, King of Argos, feared that the child would grow up to kill him, so he imprisoned Danae and her infant son in a chest, which was cast upon the sea and borne to the island of Seriphos. The mother and child were then rescued.

Daphne—Greek nymph who, when pursued by Apollo, prayed that she might escape him. Just as the god embraced her, she was changed into a laurel tree, thereafter sacred to Apollo.

Dardanus—legendary ancestor of Trojan kings. Because he was born of Zeus's love affair with a mortal woman, Here persecuted him and his descendants. Her hatred culminated in the fall of Troy.

Darius—king of Persia whose troops invaded Greece and were defeated at Marathon in 490 B.C. Darius III was the Persian emperor whom Alexander the Great overthrew.

Datis—Persian commander defeated at Marathon in 490 B.C.

David—second king of the Hebrew nation, successor to Saul. Originally a poor shepherd boy, he won fame by singlehandedly killing the giant Goliath and by playing the harp at King Saul's court. Later, his military victories and popularity won Saul's jealous fear so that he was declared an outlaw. After Saul's death, the prophet Samuel anointed David king of Israel. Because he was a man of war, Yahweh did not permit David to build the temple at Jerusalem, the construction of which was left to his son and successor, Solomon. David became one of the most popular figures in Hebrew history; the hoped-for national savior or *Messiah* was to be born of his line.

Deimos—Greek personification of fear, depicted as the son of Ares (Mars).

Deiphobus—son of Priam and Hecuba, prince of Troy, who married Helen after Paris' death. Menelaus killed him when the Greeks captured Troy.

Delos—Greek island sacred to Apollo and Artemis, who were supposedly born there. It served as the treasury of the Delian League (formed to protect Greece against Persian invasion) until Pericles removed the treasure to Athens, where part of it was spent in rebuilding the Acropolis.

Delphi—ancient holy place of Apollo on the lower slopes of Mt. Parnassus. There the young god slew a giant serpent (the Python), overthrew the primitive earth-mother cult that had flourished on the spot, and established his own worship. Apollo then appointed a priestess with power to foresee the future whom his worshipers could consult. On the altar of his Delphian temple were inscribed such famous examples of Greek wisdom as "nothing in excess" and "know thyself." Dionysus also had an important shrine at Delphi.

Delphic Oracle—the most famous center of prophecy in ancient Greece. Men came to inquire the will of the gods from Apollo's virgin priestess, called the Pythia or Pythoness after the great snake the god had killed there. Oedipus, King Croesus, and Socrates' friends sought advice from the Oracle, who was chiefly an authority on religious issues. When consulted about politics or the future, her answers tended to be obscure or "oracular."

Deluge—the world-wide flood of Noah's day described in Genesis. *Gilgamesh* gives another account of the legendary event.

Demeter—most powerful earth-goddess in ancient Greece, the daughter of Cronus and Rhea, and mother of Persephone. The center of her worship was Eleusis, near Athens, where mystery religions in her honor abounded. The Eleusinian rituals also concerned her daughter Persephone, whom Hades kidnapped and held in the underworld. Mourning for her daughter, Demeter withheld fertility from the earth, and no grain grew. At Zeus's command, Persephone was returned to her mother for six months out of the year, during which time spring and summer make the land fruitful. In the fall Persephone returns to Hades and winter desolates the earth. This seasonal myth, with its death-resurrection theme, was the heart of the Eleusinian Mysteries. See *Mysteries.*

Democritus (c. 460 B.C.)—Greek philosopher who adopted and expanded the atomic theory of his master Leucippus. Epicurus and Lucretius further developed his materialistic cosmology.

Demodocus—a singer of tales at the court of King Alcinous in the *Odyssey.*

Demosthenes (383-322 B.C.)—an Athenian statesman, the most famous orator of classical Greece, best known for his impassioned warnings against the rise of King Philip of Macedon (the *Philippics*). His speeches are marked by nobility of thought and simplicity of language.

Denouement—in drama, the final unraveling of the plot, the resolution of the action. It means literally the "untying of the knot" of a complex situation.

Deus ex machina—literally, the "god from the machine," referring to the practice in the Greek and Roman theatre of introducing a god into the action by hoisting him onstage by means of a crane. In literary terms, it means the unexpected appearance of a character or event to bring a hopelessly complicated plot to a satisfactory conclusion. In the *Philoctetes*, Heracles acts as a *deus ex machina* to make the stubborn hero change his mind.

Deuteronomy—literally the "second law," the fifth book of the Bible in which Moses summarizes Israel's divinely-given legislation and promises that if the laws are kept the nation will never suffer evil.

Devil—from the Greek *diabolos*, meaning "adversary, prosecutor," a translation of the Hebrew "Satan." In Christian theology, the Devil was originally an important angel who through pride rebelled against the Creator and was then cast from heaven. In Dante, the Devil is frozen at the bottom of Hell, but his evil influence as Tempter of man permeates the earth.

Diadochi—the name applied to the successors of Alexander the Great, particularly his generals Ptolemy, Seleucis and Antigonus.

Dialectic—form of logical argument developed by Socrates and Plato. It uses reason to discover truth.

Dialogue—(1) in the drama, a conversation between two or more people which reveals their characters and advances the action; (2) in philosophy, a literary form in which a teacher and his pupils or opponents discuss a theory for the purpose of conveying information or establishing the truth. Plato developed the form and it was used later by Xenophon, Aristotle, Cicero, and Plutarch.

Diana—the Roman name for Artemis, virgin goddess of the hunt.

Diction—literally "word choice," referring to the appropriateness or exactitude of an author's language and style.

Dido—mythical founder and queen of Carthage who received Aeneas and his men on their wanderings from Troy. Venus caused her to fall in love with Aeneas, who soon abandoned her in order to found the Roman nation in Italy. Dido then committed suicide on a funeral pyre.

Dike—Greek deity personifying justice, daughter of Zeus and Themis.

Dilmun—the Sumerian paradise where Utnapishtim and his wife live; it lies beyond the "waters of death."

Diogenes (4th cent. B.C.)—a famous Cynic philosopher, reputed to have shown his contempt for civilized life by living in a tub and going about by day with a lantern "to find an honest man." He is also supposed to have asked the conquering Alexander the Great "to step out of his light."

Diomede(s)—youngest and one of the most effective Greek fighters in the war against Troy, leader of forces from Argos and Tiryns, important cities in southern Greece. Fiery and impulsive, he even fought with the gods, wounding Ares and Aphrodite. In revenge, the latter made his wife unfaithful to him.

Dionysus—Greek god of wine, ecstasy, and the life force which gives earth its fertility. Not native to Greece, his cult was probably imported from Asia Minor or Thrace, where he was worshiped with wild dancing, violent music, and midnight orgies. He was the son of Zeus by Semele, a Theban princess who was deceived by the jealous Here into asking her divine lover to appear in his full glory. Zeus manifested himself in a lightning flash, consuming Semele, but rescuing the unborn child and concealing it in his thigh, from which it was later born as Dionysus. When grown, the young god roamed the world establishing his worship and bestowing the gift of wine on those who accepted him. Since his cult of irrationality and mystic ecstasy often met with strong opposition in Greece, he would sometimes assume a bestial form, utterly destroying all enemies. (See the case of King Pentheus in Euripides' *The Bacchae.*) Because his power sprang from nature he often appeared as a bull, serpent, or panther. His followers included the satyrs, Sileni, and his fanatical priestesses, the Maenads. Goats, for their sexual energies, were associated with his orgiastic worship and were often torn in pieces and eaten raw by intoxicated bacchants. According to some legends, he descended into Hades to rescue his mother, which may explain the mystery cults which recognized him as a dying and resurrected god. More likely, the seasonal nature of his powers over growing things equated him with the life-death-rebirth cycle of all vegetation so that he was interpreted as dying in winter and being reborn in spring. It is generally believed that the old rituals which reenacted his resurrection gave rise to Tragedy (q.v.). Among his many names were Bromius and Bacchus, by which the Romans knew him. He was also a god of prophecy and had a shrine near Apollo's at Delphi.

Dioscuri—literally the "youths of god," the twin brothers Castor and Pollux, born of Zeus and Leda. Famous for their bravery and loyalty to each other, one legend has Zeus reward them by placing their spirits among the stars as the Gemini constellation.

Diotima—prophetess of Mantinea whom Socrates in the *Symposium* cites as his source for the doctrine of ideal love.

Dirae—Roman name for the Eumenides, the Furies who persecute murderers.

Dis—a name for Hades or Pluto (the "wealthy one"), Greek god of the underworld. Dante's "City of Dis" is in the lower regions of Hell.

Dithyramb—an ecstatic dance or choral song performed in honor of Dionysus, from which, according to Aristotle, tragedy developed.

Divination—the practice of trying to foretell the future from such things as the flight of birds or the condition of the internal organs of sacrificial animals.

Donation of Constantine—medieval forgery purporting to be the Emperor Constantine's recognition of the spiritual supremacy of the papacy over all other bishoprics and a grant of temporal and political power over Italy and western Europe to Pope Silvester and his successors. In spite of its falsity, it was sometimes invoked to justify the pope's intervention in secular affairs.

Dorians—a Greek-speaking people whose invasion of the Greek peninsula about 1100 B.C. supposedly caused the collapse of Mycenaean civilization. The Dorians settled in the Peloponnese and were ancestors of the classical Spartans.

Draconic Code—the body of law formulated by the Athenian Draco, who in 621 received special authority to revise the city's legal system. He replaced private vengeance with public justice, entrusting trials for murder to the Areopagus (q.v.). Famous for its severity, his code was replaced by that of Solon a generation later.

Dragon—mythical monster usually resembling a serpent or giant lizard, sometimes having wings and breathing fire. In medieval religion it became a symbol of Satan.

Drama—a term from Greek meaning a "thing done," usually referring to a serious play in poetic language intended for public performance, a tragedy rather than comedy.

Dramatic irony—the element present when the audience knows something a character onstage does not know, as when Oedipus condemns the murderer of Laius, unaware that he himself is the criminal. See **Irony**.

Ea (*Enki*)—the Sumero-Babylonian god of magic and wisdom, one of the creators of mankind. In *Gilgamesh*, he warns Utnapishtim of the oncoming flood. With Anu and Enlik he makes up the triad of the most powerful Mesopotamian gods. His son is Marduk.

Echo—wood nymph who pined away to a mere repetitious voice for the unrequited love of Narcissus.

Ecologue—literally a "choice selection," a poem from a larger collection. It usually refers to short verses praising nature, a shepherd's life, the pastoral scene. Virgil's are famous.

Eden—in Hebrew myth, the "garden of delight" in which Yahweh placed Adam and Eve after their creation. When they ate the forbidden fruit, they were expelled from this paradise. To symbolize the state of innocence to which former sinners' souls have been returned after their purgation, Dante places Eden at the summit of Mount Purgatory.

El—Semitic word for God, the Hebrew plural of which is *Elohim,* the term used in Genesis 1:1 to denote the Creator.

Electra—daughter of Agamemnon and Clytemnestra, princess of Mycenae. After Agamemnon's murder she plots for years to avenge his death by killing her mother. When her brother Orestes returns after a long exile, she persuades him to kill Clytemnestra and her lover Aegisthus. Aeschylus, Sophocles, and Euripides all wrote tragedies based on the Electra-Orestes legend.

Eliphaz—one of Job's three unsympathetic friends.

Elis—democratic state in southern Greece in which Olympia was located. Sparta conquered her in 399 B.C.

Elysium (*Elysian Fields*)—an earthly paradise mentioned in the *Odyssey* as the eternal home of some of Zeus's favorites, such as Menelaus. In later myth, it was that part of Hades in which the souls of good men were rewarded. Aeneas interviews his father's spirit there.

Endymion—a handsome shepherd boy with whom the moon-goddess Selene fell in love.

Enkidu—the faithful friend of Gilgamesh. He was originally created as a wild man who lived among forest animals, but was civilized by a temple prostitute and brought to live in Uruk. After discovering that they were matched in strength, Gilgamesh and Enkidu set out as a team to rid the world of evil monsters like Humbaba. But Enkidu insulted the love goddess Ishtar, who cursed him with a fatal illness. Gilgamesh then went on his long journey to find Utnapishtim and learn the secret of immortality.

Enlil—Sumero-Babylonian god of air, wind, and storm who causes the great flood that destroys all mankind except Utnaphishtim and his household.

Ennius, Quintus (239-169 B.C.)—"father of Roman literature," first Latin writer to compose a Homeric epic, the *Annales,* 18 hexameter books which presented the history of Rome from its legendary origins to his own time. Only fragments survive, but these 600 extant lines indicate the seriousness and patriotism which influenced later authors like Cicero and Virgil.

Enuma Elish—the Babylonian creation epic which celebrates the powers of Marduk, the son of Ea, who battles and defeats an older generation of gods and assumes supreme control of the universe. He then creates heaven and earth out of the body of Tiamat, an evil goddess who had tried to kill the younger deities. Marduk forms man out of the blood of Tiamat's accomplice, Kingu.

Eos—Greek goddess personifying the dawn, sister of Helios, the sun and Selene, the moon. Her Roman name is Aurora.

Epic—a long narrative poem telling in vivid, majestic language the great deeds of a larger-than-life hero who excels all ordinary men in adventure and noble action. Defining "epic" is really an attempt to describe Homer's *Iliad,* which is the supreme example of the form and the one on which all later epics are modeled. Although of great length, the epic achieves artistic unity by use of a basic theme that ties all its parts into one whole. "The wrath of Achilles," for example, is the unifying theme in the *Iliad.* It determines events for almost all the other characters: a temporary Trojan military triumph, the humiliation of Agamemnon, the deaths of Patroclus and Hector. The *Odyssey* and the *Aeneid* follow the *Iliad* in presenting a relatively simple plot with many side-incidents such as the attempts of Odysseus to return home to Ithaca and Aeneas to reach Italy and found the Roman nation. Both involve ancient legendary material. Their themes deal with problems—war, love, identity—of universal human significance and their heroes embody the major values of the society they represent. Achilles is the ideal soldier in a military aristocracy, Odysseus the curious explorer who survives by his wits, and Aeneas the stern exponent of duty and patriotism. The world of the epic usually has three levels: (1) the earth in which the hero and his companions fight their battles and win everlasting fame; (2) an underworld of the dead into which the hero may descend to learn of the future; and (3) an invisible heaven inhabited by gods who live in ease and pleasure, interfering in human affairs only to help their favorites, vent their anger, or see that what is fated takes place. The epic poet usually begins by calling on the aid of a "heavenly muse" to inspire his work, poses the *epic question,* and begins *in medias res,* at a point just before the climax and then, by a series of flashbacks, recounts the action leading to the crisis. Extended similes, and stock epithets, such as "rosy-fingered dawn," "fleet-footed Achilles," the "wine-dark sea" are common. The style is elevated yet simple, swift yet complete in its painting of human emotions, motives, and behavior. Though no longer fashionable, it is helpful to draw a distinction between the "natural" epics of Homer, which grew up gradually out of ancient legends and folk-tales, and the "artificial" epics of Virgil and his successors, who consciously wrote in sophisticated imitation of Homeric models.

Epicureanism—a philosophy that makes pleasure (or the absence of pain) the supreme good in life. It is based on the ideas of Epicurus (341-270 B.C.) who taught that wisdom was attained by relying on the evidence of the senses, avoiding pain, and eliminating the fear of supernatural or religious powers. He was not a hedonist, however, and insisted that the wise man would cultivate those pleasures which were of longest duration—those of the mind and spirit. He used the atomic theory of Democritus (q.v.) to explain the material universe and held that every event has a natural, material cause. Lucretius was his most famous disciple.

Epigram—a short poem, originally carved on tombs and temples as a solemn memorial, usually to dead heroes. In Roman times, especially under the poet Martial, it became a brief, satirical verse distinguished by cleverness and a stinging wit.

Epilogue—in drama, the final address to the audience at the conclusion of the action. In Greek drama, it includes anything occuring after the last choral song.

Epiphany—from the Greek "showing forth"; in drama, the manifestation of a god, as when Dionysus triumphantly reveals his divinity at the end of Euripides' *Bacchae*. On the human level it may apply to the sudden revelation of some unsuspected truth, as when Oedipus learns his true identity.

Episode—in Greek drama, the scene occurring between two choral odes; an act.

Epistle—a formal letter, such as the messages of St. Paul in the New Testament.

Epitaph—usually a serious tomb inscription, like the terse memorial to the Spartans who died at Thermopylae.

Epithet—a descriptive word or phrase such as those Homer uses to identify and typify a character—*swift-footed* Achilles and *man-slaying* Hector.

Epode—in Greek drama, the part of a choral song that followed the strophe and antistrophe. It was sung standing still.

Erebus—primeval Darkness, offspring of Chaos. In later myths, the dark region beneath the earth through which souls passed to reach Hades. Eventually it came to stand for Hades itself.

Erechtheus—legendary king or early founder of Athens, to whom a temple on the Acropolis was dedicated.

Equestrian Order—the aristocratic knights of Rome, who in later times controlled much of the Empire's wealth and its civil service.

Erinyes—an old name for the Furies or Eumenides.

Eris—Greek personification of strife and disorder, the sister of Ares. She threw the golden apple of discord at Thetis' marriage to Peleus. In another sense, *eris* (uncapitalized) can mean good competition, striving toward what is excellent.

Eros—Greek god of love and sexual desire. In some legends, he is the winged son of Aphrodite who shoots his arrows into gods and men alike, inspiring in them uncontrollable passions. In older myths, he is the most ancient of the gods, sprung from primordial Chaos, the force that urges all creation toward unity. Greek artists usually picture him as a beautiful adolescent boy. The Romans made a chubby infant of him and called him Cupid.

Eteocles—son of Oedipus and Jocasta who assumed the control of Thebes after his father's banishment. He had agreed to divide power with his brother Polynices by ruling in alternate years, but after his first year on the throne he refused to relinquish it to his brother. Polynices then mustered an army which attacked the seven gates of Thebes. During the fighting the brothers killed each other, thus fulfilling the curse Oedipus put upon them for having left their father in exile.

Etruscans—a little-known people of Greek-influenced civilization who after about 1000 B.C. controlled much of north Italy before Roman expansion destroyed or absorbed their culture. It is thought that the Tarquins, early kings of Rome, were Etruscans.

Euclid—Greek mathematician who flourished at Alexandria about 300 B.C. His six books on plane geometry summarized and expanded the work of early thinkers, including Thales and Pythagoras. His work is still authoritative.

Eumenides—the Kindly Ones, a euphemistic name for the Furies, the undying avengers of those murdered by a relative. They pursue Orestes after he slays Clytemnestra.

Europa—mythical princess of Tyre whom Zeus in the form of a bull kidnapped and took to Crete where she became mother of Minos and Rhadamanthus.

Eurydice—beloved wife of the legendary musician Orpheus, who was so grieved at her death that the gods permitted him to descend into Hades to bring her back. When Eurydice's pleading made Orpheus break his vow not to look at her until they had reached the daylight, she died in his arms. Her second demise was final.

Euryximachus—Athenian physician, one of the speakers in Plato's *Symposium*.

Exodos—in Greek drama, the final speech of the chorus, sung as they leave the stage.

Exodus—the second book of the Bible; supposedly written by Moses, it records the Ten Plagues, the escape of the Israelites from Egypt, the parting of the Red Sea, and the giving of the law at Mt. Sinai.

Fate—in Greek and Roman belief it is the power of historical necessity, sometimes the will of the gods (as in the Oedipus story), sometimes a force that predestines men and action and is superior even to Zeus (as in *Prometheus Bound*). The *Three Fates (Moirai)* are Clotho, Lachesis, and Atropos, blind old hags who eternally weave a gigantic tapestry, each thread of which symbolizes a human life. When Atropos cuts a thread, the man it represents dies. Her blindness stands for the sheer irrationality and arbitrariness of human destiny.

Fauna—a Roman goddess with the qualities of Faunus (q.v.).

Faunus—a Roman woodland god who presided over crops and herds and had the power to foresee the future. He was identified with Pan.

Flora—a Roman goddess of fertility, associated with spring and flowers.

Fortuna—Roman goddess, the "first-born daughter" of Jupiter, a personification of Destiny. As *Fors Fortuna* she symbolized chance and luck.

Furies—the ancient Greek goddesses of blood vengeance who rose from beneath the earth to pursue anyone who had murdered a relative. They are also known as the Erinyes and Eumenides (q.v.).

Gaea (*Ge, Gaia*)—the earth, the ancient Greek goddess sprung from original Chaos. She produced Uranus (Sky), mated with him, and bore the Titans and Cyclopes.

Galen (A.D. 129-199)—the most famous physician of Roman times; he left an enormous number of essays on medicine which had a great influence on the history of medical science.

Ganymede—a beautiful Trojan shepherd boy with whom Zeus fell in love. In the shape of an eagle, Zeus carried the boy to Mount Olympus, where Ganymede replaced Hebe as cupbearer of the gods. Hebe was furious at Zeus's infatuation; her jealousy of Ganymede contributed toward her determination to punish Troy.

Gehenna—a refuse dump outside Jerusalem into which the bodies of executed criminals were thrown. It became a symbol of eternal destruction and was used as such in Jesus' parables. Originally it was "the valley of the son of Hinnom," where Canaanites had performed human sacrifices and other rituals abhorrent to the Jews.

Gemini—Castor and Pollux, the twins whom Zeus changed into a constellation of stars.

Genius—in Roman religion the indwelling procreative spirit of a man or place. There was a genius of the house, field, family, and even of the collective Roman people.

Geryon—a three-headed giant whom Heracles killed.

Ghibelline—an aristocratic Florentine political party which supported the policies of the Germanic emperor and opposed the growing temporal powers of the papacy. They were in constant conflict with the Guelphs (q.v.).

Gilgamesh—legendary Sumero-Babylonian hero, fifth king of Uruk after the Flood, famous as a builder of cities and conqueror of evil monsters. A whole cycle of epic poems has collected about his name. As son of the goddess Ninsun and a human priest of Kullab, he was two-thirds god and one-third man.

Glaucon—brother of Plato, a speaker in the *Republic.*

Glaucus—a grandson of Bellerophon, co-leader of the Lycian allies of the Trojans. He is a gallant but simple-minded soldier who foolishly exchanges his golden armor for Diomedes' bronze.

Golden Age—(1) according to Hesiod, the legendary period of excellence and innocence that prevailed during Cronus' (or Saturn's) reign as king of the gods, which was followed by progressively inferior ages of silver, bronze, and iron; (2) of Athens, the era of the Periclean democracy (461-429 B.C.); (3) of Latin literature, the period covering the Ciceronian and Augustan ages (70 B.C.–A.D. 14).

Golden Bough—in the *Aeneid* a magical tree branch, sacred to Persephone, which Aeneas plucks and uses as his passport into the underworld. Only the sight of the Golden Bough persuades Charon to ferry Aeneas across the River Styx.

Golden Fleece—the wool of a golden ram given to the king of Colchis and later stolen by Jason and his Argonauts.

Gorgons—three hideous sisters with snakes for hair and hypnotic eyes. The one mortal sister, Medusa, had a gaze so terrifying that whoever beheld her was turned to stone. From Medusa's blood sprang the winged horse Pegasus. The gorgon's head was often pictured on armor to frighten enemies.

Gospel—literally "good news"; in the New Testament it refers to the four lives of Christ by Matthew, Mark, Luke, and John.

Gothic—(1) a soaring style of architecture dominant in the Middle Ages, it applies particularly to castles, cathedrals, and churches characterized by lofty towers, pointed arches, and attenuated sculpture; (2) originally a pejorative term, referring to the "barbarous" culture of the Dark Ages after the Goths (a German tribe) had invaded and destroyed the Roman Empire, it can also be applied to literature that makes a cult of medieval mysteriousness and superstition.

Gracchi, The *(Tiberius Sempronius* and *Gaius Sempronius Gracchus)*—aristocratic brothers who tried to reform the oppressive legal and social institutions of the decaying Roman Republic. Their attempts at reform were bitterly opposed by the Senate and other vested interests, resulting in Tiberius' murder during an election riot in 133 B.C. and Gaius' forced suicide in 121 B.C. In later times the Gracchi became famous as examples of a heroic struggle against political and social injustice.

Graces, The—three lovely goddesses who personify beauty and charm; like the Muses, they inspire poetry and the arts.

Guelph—a Florentine political party to which Dante belonged and which worked for a constitutional form of government. The Guelfs opposed the more aristocratic Ghibellines and supported the power of the Pope.

Gymnasium—one of the most important social institutions of classical Greece, a kind of private athletic club where men and boys exercised and practiced sports such as wrestling, boxing, running, and throwing the discus. It was also a place for relaxation, conversation, and music. Philosophy was born there from the heated debates between teachers and disciples over matters of logic, religion, and ethics. Socrates often recruited followers from intelligent but idle young men of the gymnasium.

Hades—son of Cronos and Rhea, brother of Zeus and Poseidon, god of the dead. He is wed to Persephone, a young goddess whom he abducted to reign with him in the underworld, which itself is called Hades. His Roman name is Pluto, "the wealthy one."

Hagar—Egyptian slave girl who bears a son, Ishmael, to Abraham when his wife Sarah is barren. Because of Sarah's jealousy Hagar and son are driven into the wilderness, where they are rescued by an angel.

Ham—in Genesis, the youngest of Noah's three sons, from whom the Egyptians and Ethiopians were supposedly descended.

Hamartia—in his *Poetics* Aristotle uses this term to describe the "fatal flaw" in the otherwise noble character of the tragic hero, a flaw which brings about his downfall *(nemesis)*. Hamartia has variously been translated as "error," "weakness," or even "sin." Ultimately it derives from a term in archery meaning "to miss the mark." It is used in the New Testament to denote a sin or vice which offends God. In Greek tragedy the most common form of *hamartia* is excessive pride or hubris (q.v.) which antagonizes the gods and dooms the hero. It is normally an error in judgment, an intellectual rather than a moral failure. However, "missing the mark" can also refer to the hero's excessive virtue, his incautious clinging to principle as in the *Prometheus Bound* or *Oedipus the King.*

Hannibal (247-183 B.C.)—general who led Carthage in the second Punic War against Rome. Although he won many victories, even in Italy, he failed to capture Rome and was decisively beaten by Scipio Africanus at the battle of Zama in 202. The historian Livy regarded him as the greatest single threat to Rome.

Harmodius—Athenian youth who rejected the love of Hipparchus, brother of the tyrant Hippias. He became a popular champion of political liberty by conspiring with his lover Aristogiton to kill the two tyrants at the Panathenaea. By bad luck only Hipparchus was slain and his guards murdered Harmodius on the spot. Hippias had

Aristogiton tortured to death, but became so hated for this act that he was eventually driven into exile.

Harmonia—daughter of Ares and Aphrodite, wife of Cadmus, founder and king of Thebes.

Harpies—three vicious winged demonesses believed to steal people and leave no trace.

Hebe—cupbearer of the Olympian gods until Zeus chose Ganymede to replace her. As a symbol of blossoming youth, she was called Juventas (Youth) by the Romans.

Hebrew—language of the Israelites, in which most of the Old Testament was written.

Hecate—Greek goddess of night and the underworld, the patroness of witchcraft and magic.

Hector—son of King Priam and Hecuba, champion of the Trojan cause, sworn enemy of Achilles, whose friend Patroclus he slays. With the help of Athene, Achilles avenges Patroclus' death by killing Hector and dragging his body (preserved from decay by Apollo) around the walls of Troy. As defender of home and family, Hector is perhaps the most sympathetic hero in the *Iliad*. The epic reaches its climax when aged Priam comes to Achilles' tent to ransom Hector's corpse.

Hecuba *(Hecabe)*—wife of Priam, Queen of Troy, mother of Hector, Paris, Cassandra, and many other children. In Euripides' *Trojan Women* she becomes the prototype of suffering endurance, bearing nobly the loss of husband, children, and homeland.

Helen—wife of Menelaus, Queen of Sparta, daughter of Zeus by Leda, legendary cause of the Trojan War. In the Homeric version of her story, Aphrodite promises Helen to Paris as his reward for choosing the love goddess as more beautiful than all the other Olympians, including Athene and Here. Since Helen is already Menelaus' wife, Paris illegally abducts her from Sparta and carries her to Troy, where her incomparable beauty excites universal admiration but where the trouble she brings makes her an unwelcome guest. Upon her heels come the Achaean forces destined to retrieve her and sack Troy. The *Odyssey* shows her comfortably restored to her former position as Menelaus' consort.

Hellas—classical name for mainland Greece, whose citizens were called Hellenes after the legendary hero Hellen. *Hellenism* is the cultivation of Greek culture, attitudes, and learning. After the time of Alexander the Great (d. 323 B.C.), Greek civilization was mixed with Oriental influences and called *Hellenistic*.

Hellespont—the Dardanelles, a narrow waterway connecting the Black Sea with the Mediterranean and separating Europe from Asia.

Helios—Greek god of the sun, son of Hyperion and brother of Eos (the Dawn). In later mythology, Apollo assumed his functions.

Helots—native population of the Peloponnese, enslaved by the Spartans.

Hephaestus—son of Zeus and Here, husband of Aphrodite, the god of fire and metalwork, master architect of Olympus. In the *Iliad* he is on the Greek side and forges the splendid armor and shield with which Achilles defeats Hector. The Romans called him Vulcan, from which the term "volcano" derives.

Heracles *(Hercules)*—strongest and hardest-working of the earthly heroes. Although the son of Zeus, he is mortal and at Here's instigation dies horribly by being chemically burned to death in a poisoned robe. Noted for courage, loyalty, endurance, and good nature, Heracles became the most popular hero in folk mythology. Most famous are his Twelve Labors, which included slaying such monsters as the Nemean lion and the many-headed Hydra. He is the foretold descendant of Zeus and Io who is destined to liberate Prometheus.

Heraclitus (c. 540-480 B.C.)—Greek philosopher of Ephesus (in Asia Minor) who taught that fire is the basic substance of the universe and that "all is flux." By insisting that the world is in a constant process of change or "becoming" and therefore not knowable, he anticipated Plato's rejection of the material world as a source of reliable knowledge.

Here (*Hera*)—wife of Zeus, Queen of the gods, patroness of marriage and domesticity. As daughter of Cronos and Rhea, she is Zeus's sister as well as his consort. In most legends she is consistently vindictive and unpleasant, as when she vows to exterminate Troy and all its inhabitants. Juno is her Roman equivalent.

Heresy—the intellectual sin of holding a religious opinion contrary to the accepted doctrine of a Church, usually the Roman Catholic. Dante punishes heretics more severely than adulterers, because persons with false beliefs, however sincere, tend to corrupt the innocent, subvert Church authority, and create dissension.

Hermaphroditus—son of Hermes and Aphrodite, beloved of the Nymph Salmacis, whose love he rejected. When Salmacis prayed that she and the boy might become "one flesh," the gods obliged, creating a being who possessed the attributes of both sexes. This legend had been taken to symbolize the basically bisexual nature of man.

Hermes—son of Zeus and Maia, the messenger and ambassador of the gods, as well as the god of luck, gambling, and travel. One of his duties is to convey the souls of the dead to Hades.

Hermione—daughter of Menelaus and Helen, princess of Sparta. According to some legends, she married Orestes.

Herod—the name of several Roman-appointed kings of Palestine, one of whom commanded the deaths of all male infants under age two when he heard of Christ's birth. A later Herod executed John the Baptist.

Hesiod—Greek epic poet, second in importance only to Homer. Like Homer, Hesiod lived during the "Dark Ages" that followed the Dorian invasion, but whereas the *Iliad* glorifies a military aristocracy, Hesiod's poetry is concerned with the daily life of the average poor farmer. His *Works and Days* is a rich source of early agricultural customs, superstitions, and the values and attitudes of small landowners. In the more ambitious *Theogony* he attempted a coherent and organized account of the origin and development of the universe, including its gods. Like Homer he helped systemize Greek mythology and religion and his influence was enormous. Hesiod was the first to record such myths as the birth of Aphrodite, the war of the Titans, and Zeus's punishment of fire-stealing Prometheus.

Hesperides—legendary "daughters of the evening" who lived far to the west, near the Atlas mountains, and who guarded a tree bearing golden apples.

Hestia—sister of Zeus, goddess of the hearth and protectress of the sacred temple fires. She was worshiped as Vesta in Roman times by a cult of virgin priestesses who tended the eternal flame of Rome.

Hexameter—the poetic meter used by Homer and Virgil in their epics. It consists of six feet of dactyls and spondees.

Hippias—son of the Athenian tyrant Pisistratus whom Harmodius and his lover Aristogiton conspired to kill in 514 B.C. Hippias escaped, but was later exiled. Hoping to regain his power, he treacherously aided the Persians during their first invasion of Greece (490 B.C.).

Hippolytus—son of Theseus and Antiope, queen of the Amazons. Like his mother he worshiped the virgin Artemis, to whom he vowed a life of chastity. His step-mother, Phaedra, fell in love with him and when he rejected her advances, she accused him of attempted rape. Cursed by his father, Hippolytus was dragged to death when his horses were frightened by a monster from the sea.

Hittites—a Near Eastern people who flourished in central Turkey (Anatolia) and north Mesopotamia from about 1900 to 1200 B.C. They attained a high civiliaztion and are frequently mentioned in the Bible.

Homeric Question—the academic problem concerning the authorship and composition of the *Iliad* and *Odyssey*, including conjecture about the dates, birthplace and very existence of a poet named Homer.

Horae—the three daughters of Zeus and Themis who personified Justice *(Dike)*, Order *(Eunomia)*, and Peace *(Eirene)*. Guardians of the laws of nature, they regulated the seasons and the smooth working of the cosmos.

Hubris *(Hybris)*—excessive pride, such as that which dooms the tragic hero to a disastrous fall. It is the most common form of hamartia (q.v.), the fatal flaw within the otherwise admirable character of the hero. The earliest example of *hubris* occurs in Book IX of the *Iliad* when Achilles refuses to accept Agamemnon's overtures of peace. This proud refusal to compromise not only allows the needless slaughter of many Achaean soldiers but also personal catastrophe for Achilles. The single most famous example of *hubris* is that of Icarus (q.v.). The erecting of the infamous Tower of Babel, recorded in Genesis, is another instance of *hubris* that offends the Deity. Overweening pride is also the sin attributed to Satan when he rebels against God.

Hyacinthus—beautiful youth whom both Apollo and Zephyrus (the West Wind) loved. When he returned Apollo's love and rejected that of Zephyrus, the jealous suitor caused Apollo accidentally to strike Hyacinthus' head with a discus, instantly killing him. From the boy's blood Apollo caused a flower to grow, the hyacinth.

Hydra—a seven-headed monster that ravaged Argos and was slain by Heracles.

Hylas—boy beloved of Heracles, lost while looking for water on the voyage of the Argonauts. Heracles remained behind to look for the youth, while the others sailed on to find the Golden Fleece.

Hymen—son of Apollo and one of the Muses, the god of marriage.

Hypokrites—literally, an "answerer," the Greek word for actor, who originally "answered" or responded to lines from the tragic chorus.

Icarus—in Greek myth, the son of Daedalus who flew from Crete on artificial wings his father had constructed. Ignoring Daedalus' instructions, Icarus flew too near the sun, which melted the wax holding together his wings and caused him to fall to his death in the Aegean Sea. By venturing into a realm reserved for the gods alone, Icarus became a famous example of *hubris*, dangerous pride.

Ichor—the colorless liquid which flows instead of blood in the veins of the Greek gods.

Ida, Mount—(1) the mountain in Crete where Zeus was born; (2) a mountain near Troy.

Ideas, Theory of—Plato's doctrine that the idea (or perfect ideal form) has a greater reality than does the world of matter, which is subject to change and destruction. See Preface on pages 547-548.

Idomeneus—grandson of King Minos of Crete, an ally of the Greeks in their war against Troy.

Ilium (*Ilios*)—Latinized name of Troy. The *Iliad* is a "song about Ilios."

Image—the mental picture as well as the physical sensation evoked by a verbal description—such as Homer's vivid portrait of Patroclus spearing an enemy through the jaw as a man hooks a fish. This image appeals to our senses of sight and memory, and our moral judgment simultaneously.

Invocation of the Muse—a literary convention summoning help from a deity. Homer was the first to use it in both the *Iliad* and the *Odyssey,* and all later epic poets, including Virgil and Dante, employed it.

Io—lovely young girl, beloved of Zeus but whom he changed into a heifer to allay Here's jealous suspicions. Undeceived, Here sent a stinging gadfly to drive Io into a mad frenzy. The fly pursued Io across Asia, where she met the chained Prometheus. Heracles was Io's promised descendant, whom Prometheus predicted would overthrow Zeus unless the tyrant God learned wisdom.

Iocasta—variant spelling of Jocasta, mother and wife of Oedipus.

Ion—son of Apollo and Creusa who, according to some legends, became the ancestor of the Ionian Greeks. Euripides wrote a tragi-comedy based on his story.

Ionia—central coast of Asia Minor, settled by Greek colonists after the Dorian invasion of 1100 B.C. Its chief cities were Miletus, Ephesus, Smyrna, and Halicarnassus.

Iphigenia—daughter of Clytemnestra and Agamemnon whom the latter sacrificed to ensure fair sailing winds to Troy. According to other legends, Artemis rescued Iphigenia at the last minute, and carried her off to Taurus (the Crimea), where her brother Orestes later found her.

Iris—a personification of the rainbow and messenger of the gods, particularly of Here. She is married to Zepherus, the West Wind.

Irony—a literary term based on the Greek word *eironeia,* meaning a pretense or dissimilation in speech. Cicero called it "saying one thing and meaning another." The ambiguity of the Delphic Oracle often had an ironic twist, as in the case of her prediction that if King Croesus went to war a great empire would fall. Misinterpreting her meaning, King Croesus rashly attacked the Persian Empire, only to discover that the fall of his own kingdom was meant. Aeschylus uses a similar irony of hidden intent in the *Agamemnon,* when Clytemnestra welcomes Agamemnon home. She is truly glad to see her husband, but not for the reason he thinks. His safe return pleases her because she may now have the pleasure of killing him herself. Aeschylus here approaches *Dramatic* or *Sophoclean Irony* (q.v.), in which the audience knows something about a character that he himself does not. Statements based on misunderstanding or partial knowledge—when seen in their true significance by the audience but not by the characters involved—increase the tension and horror of the drama. *Irony of Fate* involves the disparity between man's hopes or expectations and what Fate or the gods bring about. Job, for example, as a good man who pleases an all-powerful God can reasonably expect to have a happy life. It is ironic that he does not. A further Irony of Fate occurs in the *Prometheus Bound* when Zeus is forced to send Hermes to inquire of the prophesied son who is destined to overthrow Zeus. It is the unexpected situation of the master having to beg of the slave. *Socratic Irony* is usually used in argument or debate; it is the ruse of pretending ignorance and humility in order to trap and expose an unwary opponent.

Isaac—in Genesis, the long-awaited son of Abraham and Sarah, miraculously born in their old age. To test Abraham's loyalty, God later commands Abraham to sacrifice his only legal son, but at the last moment sends an angel to stop the slaughter and substitutes a lamb in Isaac's place. Isaac and his wife Rebekah have twin sons, Jacob and Esau. Old and blind, Isaac is tricked into giving second-born Jacob the paternal blessing.

Ishtar (Innina)—Sumero-Babylonian fertility goddess, consort of Tammuz, characterized by her lust, cruelty, and destructiveness. As patron of both love and war, she had many temples in Babylon, Uruk, and other Mesopotamian cities.

Israel—in the Bible the term is used in at least three different ways: (1) to denote the whole Hebrew nation, consisting of the twelve tribes descended from the twelve sons of Jacob, whose name was changed to Israel; (2) to denote the ten northern Hebrew tribes which revolted and formed a separate nation after King Solomon's death. (These became the "lost" tribes of Israel when the Assyrians destroyed the northern kingdom and deported the population in 722 B.C. The northern capital was Samaria, so that the non-Jewish inhabitants which the Assyrians settled in the area were called Samaritans. They were looked down upon by the orthodox Jews of Jerusalem.); (3) after the destruction of northern Israel in 722, the two-tribe kingdom in the south, with its capital at Jerusalem, was often referred to as Israel. (This is the "Israel" of the New Testament.)

Iulus—son of Aeneas and his Trojan wife Creusa. He was also called Ascanius.

Ithaca—island kingdom of Odysseus; its location is unknown. There Penelope, beseiged by 100 unruly suitors, faithfully waited during her husband's twenty-year absence.

Ixion—in Greek myth, a murderer whom Zeus mercifully pardoned. He then treacherously tried to seduce Here, but Zeus deluded him with a cloud in Here's shape, by which he became father of the Centaurs. For his crimes he was thrown into Hades where he was bound to an eternally revolving wheel.

Jacob—son of the Hebrew patriarch Isaac and his wife Rebekah; he fathered twelve sons whose descendants became the Twelve Tribes of Israel. Besides having a dream in which he saw a ladder connecting heaven with earth, he is most famous for tricking his twin-brother Esau out of his birthright. By his favorite wife Rachel he had two sons, Joseph and Benjamin. After wrestling an angel, Jacob had his name changed to Israel.

James—(1) a brother of the Apostle John; (2) a brother of Jesus and a leader of the early Christian Church. He is the reputed author of the New Testament epistle bearing his name.

Janus—Roman god of doorways, always pictured with a double-faced head, each face looking in opposite directions. The month January is named after him.

Japheth—one of the three sons of Noah; according to Genesis the Greeks descended from him.

Jason—Greek adventurer who led the 50 Argonauts to Colchis on the Black Sea to obtain the Golden Fleece. He succeeded and escaped with the help of the Colchian princess Medea, by whom he had two sons. When he deserted her, Medea avenged her honor by slaying their children. Jason later died of grief.

Jehovah—English version of Yahweh (q.v.), God of the Hebrews.

Jerusalem—sacred city and ancient capital of the Hebrew nation, site of Solomon's temple to Yahweh. It was destroyed in 586 B.C. when the Babylonians invaded Palestine. Rebuilt, it was burned by the Romans in A.D. 70.

Jesus—English version of the Greek name Iesous, derived from the Hebrew Joshua ("Yahweh is Salvation"), the personal name given to the son of Mary and Joseph of Nazareth, recognized by Christians as the Son of God and Savior of Mankind. He is called Jesus Christ because *Christ* is the Greek word for *Messiah*, the chosen or "Anointed One" of God. His earthly history is recorded in the four New Testament Gospels and books of Acts. He was born during the reign of the Roman Emperor Augustus, practiced his three-year ministry in Palestine during the reign of the Emperor Tiberius, and was crucified during the governorship of Pontius Pilate about A.D. 33.

Job—central character of the biblical book of Job. He was famous for his honesty, moral goodness, and religious faith. His story explores the mystery of God's permitting good men to suffer evil and records Job's doubts about Yahweh's justice. Job is not a study of patience under affliction: it is a profound questioning of God's responsibility for undeserved suffering and cosmic evil.

Jocasta (*Iocasta*)—Queen of Thebes, mother and wife of Oedipus. When the Oracle of Apollo predicted that Jocasta's first husband, King Laius, would be murdered by his own son, Joscasta had the infant Oedipus put out in a field to die (a common custom in the ancient world). The boy was rescued, however, and returned as a man to Thebes, where he solved the riddle of the Sphinx and married the recently widowed Jocasta, by whom he had Antigone, Ismene, Eteocles, and Polynices. When she discovered that her second husband was also her lost son, she hanged herself.

John the Apostle—one of the original twelve disciples of Jesus Christ, called the "well-beloved" because he was his Master's favorite. Tradition ascribes to him the Gospel John, the three letters of I, II, and III John, as well as Revelation, although there is doubt about his authorship of the last work. His writings emphasize the merciful and loving aspects of Jesus' ministry.

Joseph—eleventh son of Jacob by his favorite wife Rachel. According to Genesis, Joseph's jealous brothers sold him into slavery in Egypt, where he eventually became the Pharoah's chief aid by successfully predicting and preparing for seven years of famine. When his brothers came to Egypt seeking food, Joseph generously forgave their early treachery, thus becoming a model of forbearance.

Jove—shortened form of Jupiter, the Roman equivalent of Zeus, king of the gods.

Judah—(1) the fourth of the twelve sons of Jacob (Israel), whose symbol was the lion; (2) the tribe descended from Judah; (3) the southern part of the Hebrew nation, with its capital at Jerusalem; (4) the two-tribe kingdom (Judah and part of Benjamin) left after the Assyrians destroyed the larger ten-tribe kingdom of Israel (Samaria) in 722 B.C. *Judaea* is a geographical term for the province of Judah when it was successively under the administration of the Romans.

Judgment Day—according to Scripture, the day on which history comes to an end, when God destroys the wicked and judges the dead, whether for reward or damnation. The medieval world lived in constant dread of Judgment Day.

Judgment of Paris—refers to the occasion when Paris, a prince of Troy, judged the beauty competition among Athene, Here, and Aphrodite. When he gave Aphrodite the prize, the two slighted goddesses resolved to avenge themselves on the Trojans by destroying Troy.

Juno—queen of the Roman gods, wife of Jupiter, equivalent of Here (q.v.).

Jupiter—king of the Roman gods, equivalent to Zeus (q.v.).

Justinian (A.D. 483-565)—most important of the eastern Roman emperors, famous for his reorganization of Roman law, conquest of Italy, construction of the then largest Christian temple (the Church of Holy Wisdom at Constantinople).

Labyrinth—the underground maze which the master architect Daedalus built for King Minos of Crete. It housed the Minotaur, half-man, half-bull, which fed on human victims. Theseus found his way to slay the Minotaur by unwinding the spool of thread given him by Ariadne.

Lacedaemonia *(Laconia)*—an ancient name for the south-east Peloponnese, the political center of which was Sparta, whose inhabitants were known as Lacedaemonians.

Laius—legendary king of Thebes, father of Oedipus, first husband of Jocasta. He brought a curse upon himself and his son by eloping with the boy Chrysippos, son of Pelops, in whose palace Laius had been raised. This ingratitude toward his benefactor brought Apollo's prophesy that if Laius had a son, that child would grow up to kill him, as Oedipus unwittingly did.

Lamia—in Greek myth, a serpent-like female monster who stole unwary children.

Laocoon—the Trojan priest who warned his people against taking the Greek's Wooden Horse into their city, but was suddenly attacked by giant serpents that rose from the sea to crush him and his two sons. Pallas Athene (Minerva) was presumably responsible for his death.

Lares—in Roman religion, the deified spirits of family ancestors which were worshiped along with the Penates, the household gods whose powers protected the family. They were kept in the innermost part of the house, often near the hearth.

Latinus—the king of Latium and father of Lavinia, whom Aeneas married.

Latium—that section of western Italy where the Latins lived. Rome lies within its northern border.

Lavinia—daughter of King Latinus and Queen Amata. She became Aeneas' second wife.

Lay—short lyric or story in verse, often recited with musical accompaniment.

Leda—wife of Tyndareus, king of Sparta. Zeus visited her in the form of a swan, causing her to give birth to Helen, Clytemnestra, and the twins Castor and Pollux.

Legends vary, and in some only Pollux and Helen were actual children of Zeus while Clytemnestra and Castor were Tyndareus' offspring.

Lemnos—a volcanic island in the north of the Aegean Sea, site of Philoctetes' ten-year sufferings.

Lenaea—Athenian drama festival held annually in January in honor of Dionysus. Comedies were presented then.

Leonidas—courageous Spartan king who led the 300 Greeks massacred at Thermopylae (480 B.C.).

Lesbia—the poetic name which Catullus gave his beloved mistress, Clodia Metelli, wife of Metellus Celer.

Lesbos—large Greek-inhabited island off the coast of Asia Minor, site of Sappho's famous marriage school for young girls.

Lethe—the river of forgetfulness that ran through Hades. Dante places it atop Mount Purgatory; redeemed souls drinking its waters forget their previous sins before entering Heaven.

Leto—Titan goddess, mother of Apollo and Artemis by Zeus.

Leucippus (c. 440 B.C.)—Greek philosopher, originator of the theory that the world is composed of minute atoms mechanically arranged. His materialist views were developed by Democritus and adopted by Epicurus and Lucretius.

Leviathan—Biblical term for legendary monsters of the sea. They are symbols of Yahweh's power.

Lex talionis—law of retaliation, "eye for eye, life for life," a feature of the Mosaic Law and early Roman code.

Library—famous ancient libraries included that of the Assyrian king Ashurbanipal at Nineveh, whose ruins yielded our most complete copy of *Gilgamesh* and that at Alexandria, Egypt, which contained the largest and most complete collection of manuscripts in the classical world. The Alexandrian librarians were also noted scholars and critics, whose commentaries upon ancient authors often form the basis of modern criticism. Pisistratus was said to have begun a public library in sixth century Athens, but the private collections of Euripides and Aristotle were more famous. The various Athenian gymnasia usually contained libraries, as did the larger public baths in imperial Rome.

Linear A and B—the form of writing used in Minoan Crete. B was deciphered in 1952 by the British architect Michael Ventris, who found it to be a form of archaic Greek; A, the earlier script, may be of west Semitic origin.

Logos—"the Word," the creative intellectual principle of the universe, used to describe the pre-human existence of Jesus Christ in John 1:1. The notion that the *Logos,* or abstract utterance of God, is the mediating link between man and the divine, was evolved by the Hellenistic Jew, Philo Judaeus, in an attempt to reconcile Greek learning with the Hebrew religion. The concept was later adopted by the Christian apologists to make belief in Jesus' incarnation philosophically intelligible.

Lot—nephew of the Hebrew patriarch Abraham. According to Genesis, Lot and his family fled from Sodom when an angel warned them of its imminent destruction. Lot's wife looked back and was turned into a pillar of salt.

Loxias—another name for Apollo.

Lucifer—"the light-bearer," the planet Venus as a morning star. The name is often erroneously applied to the rebel angel, Satan.

Lucretia (*Lucrece*)—legendary Roman matron who committed suicide after her virtue had been assaulted by Sextus, son of Tarquinius Superbus. This incident caused the insurrection in which the Tarquins were expelled from Rome.

Luke—"the beloved physician" of the New Testament, reputed author of the gospel bearing his name and the Acts of the Apostles. He was apparently a Greek-educated Jew with a larger vocabulary, better style, and greater sense of historical accuracy than most of the other Gospel writers.

Lyceum—school of philosophy which Aristotle founded in Athens (335 B.C.). It was called "Peripatetic" because of Aristotle's habit of walking about as he lectured.

Lycia—grain-raising country in Asia Minor; in the *Iliad*, the Lycian king Sarpedon was a leading ally of Troy.

Lycon—an accuser of Socrates mentioned in the *Apology*.

Lycurgus—(1) (probably) legendary lawgiver to whom the Spartan constitution and military system were attributed: (2) a famous Attic orator of the fourth century B.C.

Lydia—country in west central Asia Minor famous for its wealth and the invention of coinage. It was conquered by the Persians under Cyrus the Great in the sixth century B.C. Herodotus describes the fall of the Lydian capital, Sardis, and the fate of its last king, Croesus (q.v.).

Lyre—Greek musical instrument resembling a small harp, which all well born young men of classical times learned to play. It was also a symbol of Apollo, patron god of music.

Lyric—originally a poem to be sung to a lyre, but later any non-narrative short poem of intense personal feeling. In drama the chorus often sings or chants lyrics which describe their emotional responses to onstage action.

Lysistrata—strong-minded heroine of Aristophanes' comedy about the folly of war.

Macedonia (*Macedon*)—territory in northern Greece, less civilized than Athens, Corinth, or Thebes, which rose to enormous political power during the reigns of Philip II (c. 383-336 B.C.) and his son Alexander (356-323 B.C.), who led the Macedonians and allied Greeks on a world conquest as far east as India. After Alexander's death, Macedonia was ruled by the Antigonid dynasty, until, after three disastrous wars with Rome, it was incorporated as a Roman province in 148 B.C.

Maecenas—friend and counselor of Augustus; literary patron of Virgil and Horace.

Maenads—female worshippers of Dionysus, often called *Bacchae* and *Bacchantes*. They follow the wandering god dressed in fawnskins, crowned in wine leaves, and carrying the phallic thrysus. When inspired, they dance in wild frenzy, tear animals apart, and eat their raw flesh.

Mammon—literally "money," a personification of material greed, often pictured as a demon in Hell.

Manes—in Roman religion, the spirits of the dead, thought to be hostile to the living and euphemistically called "the kindly ones."

Manna—food miraculously supplied the Israelites during their forty-year wandering in the Sinai wilderness. Manna means "gift."

Marcellus—the name of two Roman heroes mentioned in Book VI of the *Aeneid*: (1) a general in the second Punic War who also defeated the Gauls in 222 B.C.; (2) son of Octavia, the sister of Augustus. Intended to succeed to the imperial throne, he died while still a youth.

Marduk—chief god of Babylon, hero of the Babylonian creation account (*Enuma Elish*) in which he receives power from his father Ea (Enki) to slay the evil Tiamat, goddess of watery chaos. He then creates heaven and earth from Tiamat's body and makes man from the blood of one of her slain allies.

Mark—Christian disciple of St. Peter, under whose influence he composed the brief gospel bearing his name.

Mars—in Roman religion, the personification of human aggression and military might and the god of war. See Ares.

Marsyas—satyr who foolishly challenged Apollo to a contest in flute-playing. When he lost, Apollo had him flayed alive for his insolence.

Matthew—one of Jesus' original twelve Apostles, formerly a "publican" or tax-collector for Rome. He is probably the author of the Gospel bearing his name, though some scholars have doubted this.

Medea—sorceress daughter of Aeetes, king of Colchis. She used her magic to help Jason capture the Golden Fleece and return to Greece. When, disgusted by her savage nature, Jason abandoned her to marry a princess of Corinth, Medea avenged herself by murdering his two sons.

Medusa—one of the three Gorgons. Medusa grew snakes instead of hair and her face was so terrifying that whoever looked at her was turned into stone. She was slain by the Greek hero Perseus.

Melos—small island city-state which, during the Peloponnesian War, resisted Athens' demands that she become a tribute-paying ally. Refusing to recognize Melian neutrality, Athens destroyed the city and sold its inhabitants into slavery.

Melpomene—Greek Muse of tragedy, usually shown in a tragic mask.

Menelaus—son of Atreus, younger brother of Agamemnon, husband of Helen. When Paris elopes with Helen to Troy, Menelaus and Agamemnon organize the Achaean expedition to retrieve her. After the war, Menelaus takes Helen back to Sparta, where, according to the *Odyssey*, they live as examples of domestic bliss.

Mercury—Roman name for Hermes, messenger of the Olympian gods.

Metaphor—a figure of speech in which one object is used to describe the quality of another, a direct comparison of one thing to another, implying that the first has a hitherto unrecognized likeness to the second. For example, Achilles is a lion—meaning that Achilles has the courage, strength, and aggressiveness of the king of beasts. By contrast, Christ is a metaphoric lamb, personifying the gentle meekness of that animal.

Metis—Greek personification of wise advice, Zeus' first wife, whom he swallowed when it was prophesied that she would bear a child wiser and stronger than he. Since he had already impregnated Metis, Zeus then gave birth to their daughter, Athene, who sprang fully grown and armed from her father's head.

Midas—in Greek legend, a king of Phrygia whose wish that everything he touched would turn to gold was fulfilled. He nearly starved to death before the gods revoked his foolish wish.

Miletus—important Greek city in Asia Minor, birthplace of philosophy. Its sack by the Persians in 494 B.C. was dramatized in a lost tragedy of Phrynichus.

Miltiades—commander of the Athenian troops at Marathon in 490 B.C.

Mimesis—Aristotle's term for imitation, the mother of all of the arts.

Minoan Civilization—elaborate, luxurious pre-Greek culture that flourished on Crete and other Aegean islands from about 3000 to 1400 B.C., when it was apparently destroyed by earthquakes and volcanic eruptions. The Mycenean settlements on the Greek mainland seem to be later offshoots of Minoan Crete.

Minos—legendary king of Knossos, after whom the Minoan civilization is named. The son of Zeus and Europa, Minos married Pasiphae, whose unnatural union with a bull produced the Minotaur. Because of his just laws, Minos, with his brother Rhadamanthus, was made a judge in Hades.

Minotaur—legendary monster, half-man, half-bull, produced from Pasiphae's union with the sacred bull of Poseidon. It was confined in the labyrinth, where annually seven youths and seven maidens, offered from cities paying tribute to Crete, were sacrificed to it. It was slain by Theseus.

Mnemosyne—Greek personification of Memory, daughter of Uranus and Gaea, and by Zeus the mother of the Muses.

Moira—Greek word for Fate or Destiny, a universal power that determines the lives of men. The plural *Moirae* was applied to the three Fates, old hags who spun, wove, and cut short individual lives.

Monody—in Greek poetry, a song or lament sung by one person.

Monologue—in dramatic or narrative poetry, a speech by one person. A *soliloquy* is a monologue given when the speaker is alone, when he reveals his innermost thoughts.

Morpheus—Greek god of sleep and dreams.

Moses—Hebrew leader and lawgiver who, by Yahweh's command, led the twelve tribes of Israel out of Egypt to Mt. Sinai, where they received the Ten Commandments and other legislation upon which the Hebrew theocracy was founded. According to Exodus, Moses, a Levite, was born during a period of persecution when the Egyptian Pharaoh commanded that all male Hebrew infants be put to death. The baby Moses was put in a waterproofed cradle and set afloat among the Nile reeds, where he was found by Pharaoh's daughter, who adopted him as her son. At age forty, Moses fled Egypt and for forty years was a shepherd for Jethro, his father-in-law. When eighty years old he heard a voice from a burning bush command him to return to Egypt and demand that Pharaoh release Yahweh's people from bondage. After a miraculous crossing of the Red Sea (or shallow "Sea of Reeds") and receiving of the Law, Moses led Israel for forty years through the Sinai desert. Punished for an act of pride, Moses died at age 120, just before Israel crossed the River Jordan to enter the Promised Land. Tradition credits Moses with writing the first five books of the Bible, Genesis through Deuteronomy (the Pentateuch), though many scholars dispute this claim.

Motivation in literature—the psychological cause or reason that moves a character to perform a particular act.

Musaeus—legendary pre-Homeric poet, reputed to have been the pupil of Orpheus.

Muses—in Greek myth, the nine patron goddesses of literature and the fine arts. They inspired poets, painters, musicians, and thinkers to create their works. Daughters of Zeus and Mnemosyne (Memory), they are often led by Apollo and said to dwell on Mt. Helicon or Mt. Parnassus. They are: Calliope, Muse of epic poetry; Clio, Muse of history; Euterpe, Muse of lyric poetry and music; Erato, Muse of erotic poetry; Melpomene, Muse of tragedy; Polyhymnia, Muse of sacred song; Terpsichore, Muse of dancing; Thalia, Muse of comedy; and Urania, Muse of astronomy.

Mycenae—capital city ruled by Agamemnon in the Peloponnessus. Famous for its wealth in pre-Homeric times, the city apparently held sway over many lesser kingdoms of the Achaean Greeks. It was overthrown by the Dorian invasion about 1100 B.C. Its massive walls, Lion Gate, and rich tombs were excavated in modern times.

Mycenaean Civilization—the earliest mainland Greek civilization, apparently derived from the Minoan culture on Crete. Named after Mycenae, Agamemnon's capital, the Mycenaean culture-complex included Argos, Sparta, Pylos, and Tiryns. The civilization was destroyed during the Dorian invasions about 1100 B.C.

Myrmidons—in the *Iliad*, Achilles' faithful troops who accompany him to Troy.

Mysteries—"underground" Greek religions, mostly based on cults of the earth-mothers Demeter, Persephone, and Cybele, or on young dying and resurrected gods and heroes like Dionysus, Adonis, and Orpheus. Members of these secret brotherhoods were called "initiates" and underwent strange rituals in the hope of gaining hidden knowledge and/or immortality. The Mysteries were extremely popular in Rome, where cults of Isis, Osiris, and other Egyptian and Persian deities rivaled the official state religion. So well were their occult secrets guarded that we know almost nothing of their beliefs or ceremonies.

Myth—from Greek *mythos*, a fable or story: (1) the term which Aristotle used to denote the plot of a tragedy; (2) widely repeated stories of gods, legendary kings, and heroes whose origins lie hidden in the remote past but whose content exerts a universal emotional appeal and becomes part of the racial consciousness of any given people. Some experts have argued that myths arose to explain the origin of some common practice or otherwise inexplicable natural phenomenon, such as the lightning bolt and thunderclap, which Greek myth interprets as the angry shaft and roar of Zeus. Similarly, the sun travels across the sky from dawn to dusk because Helios (later Apollo) drives a fiery chariot across the arc of heaven. Other scholars see myth as an attempt to interpret ancient magical rites, such as the stories derived from the cult of Dionysus, whose death and rebirth were acted out annually. Myths may not be historically true, but they often express a psychological or poetic truth. Psychologists like Carl Jung see myths as stories that embody a universal desire, fear, or anxiety—such as the father-son rivalry or the revenge motif—which appear again and again in the mythologies of different races and peoples. A folk tale or saga may have a historical basis in fact, such as the cycle of legends about the Trojan War.

Naiads—Greek nymphs who dwell in springs, rivers, and lakes.

Narcissus—beautiful Greek youth beloved by Echo but enamored of his own reflection, for the love of which he pined away and died.

Narrative—a story relating a series of events, not necessarily structured into a formal plot.

Nausicaa—beautiful daughter of Alcinous, king of the mythical Phaeacians, who hospitably receive Odysseus when he is shipwrecked on their shores. Although Nausicaa and the Greek hero do not have a love affair, the charm of their mutual admiration has made this a popular episode in the *Odyssey*.

Nazareth—a town of Galilee in Palestine, where Jesus was raised by Mary and Joseph. It did not have the reputation of being a brilliant center of civilization.

Nebuchadnezzar—king of Babylon and military conqueror who besieged and destroyed Jerusalem about 586 B.C., taking many upper-class Jews into the famous Babylonian Captivity. He was noted for building the great walls and hanging gardens of Babylon.

Necessity—the power of Fate or Destiny which decreed the nature of the universe, superior to both gods and men.

Nectar—the drink of the Olympian gods.

Nemesis—(1) in Homer, the power of retributive justice, the punishment that catches up with wrong-doers. (2) Although the spirit of inflexible vengeance was personified as a goddess (Nemesis) in early thought, Aristotle uses the term to describe the fall of the tragic hero which is brought on by some fault in his character.

Neoplatonism—a late Greek school of philosophy based on the teachings of Plato, but emphasizing the mystical, other-wordly, ascetic aspects of his thought. Plotinus (A.D. 205-270), its most famous exponent, taught the superiority of the soul to the body and the necessity of forsaking earthly interests to contemplate the invisible realm of spiritual ideals.

Neoptolemus—son of Achilles and Deidamia, known as Pyrrhus ("yellow-haired"). During the Trojan War he went with Odysseus to Lemnos to bring Philoctetes and his magic bow to the seige. When Troy fell he murdered Priam and took Andromache captive. According to some accounts, he later married Hermione, daughter of Helen and Menelaus, but was slain by Orestes.

Nephilim—according to Genesis, giant offspring of rebel angels and mortal women. Their violence apparently incited Yahweh to cause the Flood.

Neptune—Roman name of Poseidon, god of the sea.

Nereus—in Homer, the "Old Man of the Sea," father of the Nereids, or sea nymphs, the most famous of which was Thetis, wife of Peleus and mother of Achilles.

Nero—(A.D. 37-68)—Roman emperor, famous for his artistic talents and corrupt nature, which expressed itself in numerous murders and persecutions of the early Christians. When the army and his guards revolted, Nero committed suicide.

Nestor—aged king of Pylos who did much organizing but little fighting in the siege of Troy. Because of his experience and reputation for statesmanship, he was listened to with respect by the other Achaean leaders.

Nicias (d. 413 B.C.)—an earnest but ineffective Athenian leader during the Peloponnesian Wars. Opposing Cleon's war party, he negotiated the Peace of Nicias (421), which temporarily halted the conflict. Against his will, he was eventually put in charge of the expedition against Syracuse, which he handled badly. It ended in the destruction of the Athenian fleet and his own capture and execution.

Nike—personified Greek goddess of Victory, to whom a temple was dedicated on the Athenian Acropolis.

Nimrod—a powerful king and mighty hunter mentioned in Genesis. Except that he somehow opposed Yahweh and that his realm included Babel and other Mesopotamian cities, nothing about him is known.

Nineveh—capital of the Assyrian Empire, located on the Tigris River in Mesopotamia. In the ruins of Ashurbanipal's palace there were found the clay tablets in which were inscribed the epic of *Gilgamesh.*

Ninlil—Sumero-Babylonian goddess of earth, heaven, and (sometimes) the underworld, wife of Enlil and mother of the Moon.

Ninsun—mother of Gilgamesh, a minor Sumero-Babylonian goddess known for her wisdom. She was married to Lugulbanda, a Sumerian king-priest, and her temple was in Uruk.

Niobe—daughter of Tantalus, sister of Pelops, and wife of Amphion, king of Thebes. Because she had twelve (or fourteen) children, she boasted she was superior to Leto, who had only two, Apollo and Artemis. In punishment, Apollo and his sister killed all Niobe's children. Weeping eternally, she was changed into stone.

Noah—patriarch of Genesis who pleased Yahweh and, with his wife and children, built an ark to survive the universal Deluge. Having preserved all kinds of animals and birds through the Flood, he concluded the "Rainbow Covenant" with God, who promised never again to destroy the world by water. In Babylonian mythology, his counterpart is Utnapishtim.

Nous—Greek word for mind, the intellect, the understanding.

Numen—in Roman religion, the force or spirit inhabiting each earthly object—a cave, a tree, a spring—and also each man.

Nymphs—female spirits dwelling in aspects of nature, such as rivers, trees, mountains, or fields. Young and beautiful, they are long-lived but not necessarily immortal. Nymphs of trees are Dryads, those of fresh water, Naiads.

Ocean (*Oceanus*)—(1) in early Greek thought, a gigantic river that encircled the earth; (2) one of the Titans, son of Uranus and Gaea.

Octavia—sister of Octavian (Augustus) and second wife of Marc Antony.

Octavian (*Gaius Octavius*) (63 B.C.-A.D. 14)—grandnephew, adopted son, and heir of Julius Caesar. The first of the Roman emperors, he later received the title of Augustus (q.v.).

Ode (from the Greek *oide*, a song)—(1) in Greek drama, the lyrics sung by the chorus. The choral ode is usually divided into several stanzas, each containing three parts: a *strophe* (which the chorus sang while dancing in one direction), an *antistrophe* (which the chorus chanted while moving in the opposite direction), and an *epode* (sung while the chorus stood still). Choral, tragic, and Pindaric odes were originally set to music, none of which has survived. (2) a stately, dignified song performed in honor of gods or legendary heroes, such as the odes of Pindar (c. 522-443 B.C.). The most famous Pindaric odes were written to celebrate the victories of Greek athletes at the Olympic and Pythian Games. Horace (65-8 B.C.) is the master of the Latin ode, which by his time had become a formal lyric poem recited without musical accompaniment.

Odysseus *(Ulysses)*—legendary king of Ithaca, a leading character in the *Iliad* and hero of the *Odyssey*. Happy with his wife Penelope and new-born son Telemachus, Odysseus reluctantly left his island kingdom to fight with the Achaeans in the expedition against Troy. Although a brave fighter and athlete, he was most noted for his cunning and quick wit, a cleverness that sometimes bordered on treachery. After Troy had fallen, he earned Poseidon's hatred by blinding the sea god's son, Polyphemus, after which he was shipwrecked several times and wandered for ten years before reaching home. His return found Penelope faithful but besieged by one hundred eager suitors, whom Odysseus, with the help of his patron goddess Athene, slew. In the *Philoctetes* Sophocles presents Odysseus as much less noble than he appeared in the Homeric poems. Sophocles' play contrasts the expediency and moral pragmatism of Odysseus with the youthful idealism of Neoptolemus.

Oedipus—legendary son of Laius and Jocasta, rulers of Thebes. To avoid Apollo's prophecy that his son would murder him, Laius exposed the infant Oedipus, but the baby was taken by shepherds to Corinth, where he was adopted by the royal family. See Preface on pages 232-234. Sophocles' second drama on the subject, *Oedipus at Colonus*, depicts the aged king after twenty years of exile when only his daughter Antigone has remained faithful to him. In the groves of Colonus, near Athens, he is mysteriously spirited away by the gods, who at last forgive him his unwilling sin.

Ogygia—the island home of Calypso, who held Odysseus captive there.

Oligarchy—rule by the few; Sparta was a traditional oligarchy.

Olympia—Greek religious center, where every four years nation-wide athletic contests were held, dating from about 776 B.C.

Olympus—(1) a high mountain along the northern boundary between Thessaly and Greece proper, near the Vale of Tempe, sacred to Apollo; (2) the mythological home of the Greek gods, more a heavenly dwelling-place than a literal mountaintop.

Oracle—the *word* of a god, usually a command or prophecy about the future. The most famous Oracle was that at Delphi, where the priestess of Apollo issued ambiguous statements in answer to questions posed by worshippers. Near the Bay of Naples in Italy, was established the most popular Roman oracle, the Cumaean Sibyl, whom Aeneas consulted.

Oratory—the art of effective public speaking, which in ancient times was studied by all young men who hoped to engage in politics or the military. The most famous Greek orator was Demosthenes of Athens, who repeatedly warned Greece against the rise of Philip of Macedon (the *Philippics*). In Rome, Cicero earned a great reputation for his rhetorical powers.

Orchestra—the circular arena of the theatre, lower than the main stage, where chorus sang and danced.

Oresteia—three connected plays by Aeschylus depicting Agamemnon's murder and the revenge by Orestes, his son. The only surviving trilogy, it includes the *Agamemnon, The Libation Bearers (Choephoroe),* and *The Eumenides.* Produced in 458 B.C., it was Aeschylus' last and greatest work.

Orestes—son of Clytemnestra and Agamemnon, brother of Electra and Iphigenia. See Preface on pages 158-161.

Orion—in Greek legend, a giant hunter who was transformed into a major constellation.

Orpheus—legendary singer whose music could enchant wild beasts and cause stones to speak. Grieved by the death of his beloved wife, Eurydice, he charmed open the gates of Hades and rescued her. The gods had stipulated, however, that he could not look on Eurydice's face until he reached the earth's surface. But at his wife's pleading he looked back at her, causing her instant and permanent death. He then renounced the love of women and went to Thrace where the young men flocked to hear him sing and play. Because of his supposed resurrection (in the manner of Dionysus), he was regarded as the founder of the mystery religions.

Orphism—a mystery religion celebrating the death and resurrection of the legendary poet, Orpheus. The worshippers practiced a ritual purity and believed in the transmigration of souls. The cult flourished in superstitious Roman times.

Osiris—the most widely worshiped Egyptian god, brother and husband of Isis, the principal Egyptian fertility goddess. Since he was torn in pieces by his evil brother Set but later restored to life, the Greeks regarded him as the equivalent of Dionysus.

Paean—(1) a song of thanksgiving or triumph, a hymn of praise to some god; (2) originally a choral ode invoking the healing powers of Apollo, later a song chanted to Ares before marching into war.

Palestine—an area in south-west Asia Minor lying on the Mediterranean coast north of Egypt and south of modern Lebanon. In Biblical times it was inhabited by the Canaanites and (later) Philistines, until the nomadic Hebrews drove out the native tribes and established their own kingdom. The modern state of Israel now occupies part of this territory.

Palladium—a small wooden statue of Pallas Athene which the Trojans held in the belief that as long as they kept it their city would be safe. Odysseus stole it, after which Troy fell to the Achaeans.

Pallas—(1) part of the title of Athene, goddess of wisdom; its meaning is unknown; (2) the name of a Titan who by Styx fathered Nike, the personification of victory.

Pan—Greek god of nature, usually pictured as a goat from the waist down, with human torso, a goat's horns and pointed ears. A son of Hermes, he is patron of goatherds and flocks. He spends his time playing wild music on the "pipes of Pan" and pursuing lovely woodland Nymphs. Sudden, unreasoning fear among crowds or armies was attributed to him, and hence called "panic."

Panathenaea—an Athenian festival held yearly to honor the city's patron goddess. Celebrations included horseracing, musical contests, and a public recitation of Homer's poetry, the last instituted by Pisistratus. The festival climaxed with a magnificent parade of leading citizens and beautiful maidens and youths who carried gifts to

Athene's temple atop the Acropolis. The Parthenon frieze depicts this stately procession.

Pandarus—a Trojan commander who foolishly breaks the truce with the Achaeans by piercing Menelaus. Diomedes kills him shortly thereafter.

Pandora—in Greek myth the first woman on earth, corresponding to the Hebrew Eve. Zeus had Hephaestus create her to bring misery to mankind, in retaliation for Prometheus' having given fire to man. Given a box she was told not to open, she disobeyed and released evil, sickness, and unhappiness to pollute the world. She was married to Epimetheus (After-thought), brother of Prometheus. Her name means "all-gifted."

Pantomime—a popular form of entertainment in classical Rome; while a soloist or (later) full chorus sang, a single male performer silently acted out or danced all roles in the story, wearing an appropriate mask for each part.

Papyrus (pl., *Papyri*)—an Egyptian river plant which, when processed, made a writing material much used in Egypt, Greece, and Rome; most classical works survive on papyrus rolls. Our word "paper" derives from this fact.

Parabasis—a feature of the Greek Old Comedy in which the chorus moves toward the audience to address it directly, usually to ridicule a public figure or to lecture an audience for its political or social errors. It was a dramatic convention by which a comic author could fearlessly air his views.

Parable—a short, simple narrative in which a speaker compares the familiar actions of daily life to some deeper spiritual truth. Jesus, for example, used the parable of the sheep and goats to illustrate his work of separating good men from bad.

Paradise—a Greek word of Persian origin, meaning an enclosed, cultivated garden or park. In Scripture, the term refers to the Garden of Eden, but in Greek and Roman religion it often applies to the Elysian Fields (Elysium), a place where the souls of good men enjoy an afterlife of earth-like beauty and pleasure. Dante places the Edenic paradise atop the Mount of Purgatory to illustrate that souls which have been purged of sin have returned to the state of innocence enjoyed by Adam and Eve before their Fall.

Parados—the song which the tragic chorus sings during its first entrance.

Paradox—a statement which, on close inspection, may be true in fact but which *seems* to be contradictory to normal opinion or common sense. Jesus' assertion that "the first must be the last" seems a paradox, but it expresses the Christian belief that humility exalts one in divine approval.

Parallelism—the arrangement of the parts of a sentence or composition so that key words or ideas are placed in grammatically similar positions. It is a device that balances equivalent words or expressions in equal and coordinate verbal structures. Hebrew poetry relies heavily on parallelism for its effect; as in the famous passage from Job: "Naked I came from my mother's womb/And naked shall I return there./Yahweh gave, Yahweh/took away. Blessed be Yahweh's name."

Paris (also called *Alexander, Alexandros*)—handsome pleasure-loving son of Priam and Hecuba, king and queen of Troy, younger brother of Hector. Near the end of the Trojan War, Paris shot a poisoned arrow into Achilles' unprotected heel, thus killing the Greek hero. Paris in turn was slain by the arrows of Philoctetes, who had rejoined the Achaean forces. See also Judgment of Paris.

Parnassus—an 8,000 foot mountain near Delphi, sacred to Apollo and the Muses.

Parody—an imitation of a literary work that deliberately distorts or ridicules the style, subject-matter or other qualities of that work. Aristophanes, for example, often Parodies the characteristic elements of tragedy which, in a comic context, sound absurdly funny.

Parthenon—the marble temple of Athene Parthenos (the Virgin) built atop the Athenian Acropolis and completed in 438 B.C. In the severe Doric style, it is considered the most beautifully proportioned building in the world.

Pasiphae—daughter of Helios, sister of Circe, wife of King Minos of Crete, and mother of Ariadne and Phaedra. She fell in love with the white bull of Poseidon, mated with it, and produced the monstrous Minotaur.

Passion—religious term referring to the last agonies and crucifixion of Jesus Christ.

Pastoral—literary form that uses quaint shepherds and poets in an unnaturally idyllic country setting. Begun by Theocritus (3rd cent. B.C.), the convention was used by Virgil and Horace.

Pathos—that part of a Greek tragedy which depicts the suffering and/or death of the hero.

Patricians—the upper class of Rome, distinguished from the plebeians, or common people. Much of Roman history is a struggle between these two hereditary groups for economic and political dominance. The patricians, descended from ancient noble families, traditionally controlled the Senate.

Patroclus—son of Menoetius, in some legends one of Helen's original suitors, famous as the faithful companion of Achilles, whom he accompanied to Troy. Although Patroclus may have been older than Achilles, popular legend makes him the great warrior's young squire and their relationship the perfect model of noble friendship.

Paul, St.—originally a zealous Jewish Pharisee and persecutor of the new Christian religion. On the road to Damascus, however, he experienced a vision of the resurrected Christ, after which he became the most active of Christian missionaries. He traveled all over the Roman world until he was imprisoned and beheaded in Rome about A.D. 67-68. His letters (epistles) to the various Christian congregations he had founded or visited form a large part of the New Testament. He was generally accepted as the Apostle who replaced Judas, Christ's betrayer. His teachings are thought by some historians to have had a greater effect on Christian doctrine than those of Christ Himself.

Pausanias—(1) Spartan general who led the Greeks to victory against the Persians at Plataea (479 B.C.) but who was later buried alive for treason; (2) Greek historian and traveller of the second century A.D. who wrote a *Description of Hellas*, an extant guidebook listing points of historical and artistic interest for Graeco-Roman tourists; (3) young guest at Plato's *Symposium*.

Pax Romana—the political peace which Roman imperial efficiency brought to the Mediterranean world from the reign of Augustus (31 B.C.–A.D. 14) until the death of Marcus Aurelius in A.D. 180. Although the Roman legions were often at war defending imperial frontiers against Germanic invaders, the various parts of the empire itself were internally at peace.

Pegasus—a winged horse which grew from the blood of Medusa after Perseus had beheaded her. The famous spring of the Muses on Mt. Helicon was said to have been formed by a thrust of his hooves.

Pelasgians—term for the people who inhabited Greece before the Achaean or Dorian invasions (before 2000-1100 B.C.).

Peleus—a mortal man who married the sea-nymph Thetis and fathered Achilles. When he grew old and ugly, the immortal Thetis abandoned him to a lonely old age as king of Phthia.

Peloponnese—the southern peninsula of Greece, connected with central Greece by the Isthmus of Corinth. Here were located the cities of Sparta, Mycenae, Tiryns, and Pylos and the provinces of Arcadia, Laconia, and Argos.

Peloponnesian War (431-404 B.C.)—disastrous conflict between the rival states of Athens and Sparta and their respective allies, ending with Sparta's victory in 404 B.C. The war, which blighted an entire generation and weakened Greek strength generally, arose not only from Spartan envy of Athenian economic and political expansion, but also from an ideological conflict.

Pelops—son of Tantalus, king of Phrygia. When he was a boy, his father tested the gods' omniscience by serving them his own children's flesh at a banquet. Only Demeter, absorbed in her grief for Persephone, failed to notice the nature of her food and ate Pelops' shoulder. Tantalus was punished in Hades for his sin and Pelops was restored to life, being given an ivory shoulder to replace what Demeter had eaten. Pelops later founded a kingdom in southern Greece and the whole Peloponnesian Peninsula was named after him. His sons included Atreus and Thyestes.

Penelope—the faithful wife of Odysseus, king of Ithaca, for whom she waited twenty years while he fought at Troy. During Odysseus' absence Penelope was besieged by one hundred young suitors who hoped to seize Ithaca. She kept them waiting by promising to marry one of their number as soon as she finished weaving a shroud for Laertes, her father-in-law. Each night she unraveled what she had woven by day until her trick was discovered. Odysseus arrived soon thereafter and killed all the suitors.

Pentateuch—the first five books of the Bible, often called the "Law of Moses."

Pentecost—holy day on which, according to the book of Acts, spirit from Heaven impowered the newly formed Christian church to begin its missionary expansion.

Pentheus—youthful king of Thebes who resisted the establishment of Dionysus' worship, for which he was torn to pieces by the maddened Theban women, including his own mother, Agave. One of the earliest legends about the introduction of Dionysian rites into Greece, it was the subject of Euripides' last tragedy, *The Bacchae.*

Pericles (c. 500-429 B.C.)—leader of the Athenian democracy, a great statesman, general, and orator whose influence was so profound that the period of his rule has been called the Age of Pericles. Pericles' most enduring monuments are the principles of an ideal democracy which he set forth in his "Funeral Oration" during the first year of the war with Sparta (recorded by Thucydides) and his public building program, which included the incomparable Parthenon and other temples on the Acropolis.

Peripatetic School—Aristotle's Lyceum, a school of philosophy which he opened in Athens in 335 B.C. It received its name from Aristotle's habit of lecturing as he strolled up and down the Lyceum gardens. Peripatetic comes either from the Greek "to walk about" or from the Peripatos, or colonnade, where he taught.

Peripeteia *(Peripety)*—sudden reversal of the hero's fortunes in Greek tragedy, as when Agamemnon, who had survived all dangers of war and returned home victorious, is unexpectedly cut down by his wife.

Persephone *(Proserpina)*—daughter of Zeus and Demeter (mother earth), also known as Kore (the Maiden). She was loved by Hades, who carried her down to the underworld. Demeter went into such deep mourning that all living things died, causing the Olympian gods to decree that Persephone be allowed to return to earth for six months out of the year, thus bringing spring to the world. This myth, which symbolizes the seasonal cycle of vegetation's death and rebirth, was central to the Eleusinian Mysteries.

Perseus—son of Zeus and Danae. He beheaded the Gorgon Medusa, whose face turned men to stone. He married Andromeda and in some legends had a son named Perses, after whom the Persian nation was named. In other stories, he was the founder of Mycenae.

Persian Wars—a series of three Persian invasions into Greece which continued the westward expansion of the Persian empire begun by Cyrus the Great, who had conquered Lydia and Babylon. The first movement into Greece was abortive, the Persian fleet being wrecked off Mt. Athos, but a second invasion under King Darius in 490 B.C. succeeded in bringing most northern Greek states under Persian rule. Only Athens and Sparta resisted. But since their prophet warned that the time was unripe, the Spartans left the Athenians alone to meet the assembled Persian armies at Marathon, in September, 490. A third invasion in 480-479 B.C. succeeded in burning Athens (the population having fled to Salamis). At the decisive sea battle of Salamis, the Athenians under Themistocles destroyed King Xerxes' huge fleet. Two later Greek victories at Plataea and Mycale completely ended Persian ambitions in Europe. The Spartans meanwhile had regained their honor by fighting to the last man at the mountain pass of Thermopylae.

Personification—a literary device by which an abstract quality is given human or divine form, as when Homer makes Panic (the sudden fear that seizes a crowd) and Rout (the impulse to flee the battlefield) actual personages. Many of the Greek and Roman gods are personifications either of natural forces or human emotions: Aphrodite is the erotic instinct and Poseidon the power of the sea.

Peter, St.—a Judean fisherman, one of the twelve original Apostles of Jesus Christ and traditionally author of two New Testament epistles. According to Roman Catholic theology Christ appointed him His substitute on earth, an office that was passed on to Peter's successors, the bishops of Rome. After the fall of pagan Rome, the Christian bishop there acquired great power and became the acknowledged head of the Church, the Pope.

Phaedo—young disciple of Socrates after whom Plato's dialogue describing Socrates' last hours was named. Phaedo came to Athens as a slave, but, at Socrates' urging, was purchased by a wealthy friend and set free, after which he became a philosopher. His extensive writings have been lost.

Phaedra—daughter of Pasiphae and Minos, king of Crete. She married Theseus, king of Athens, but fell in love with his son, Hippolytus, who rejected her offers.

Phaedra then killed herself, leaving a note falsely accusing Hippolytus of attempted rape. Deceived, Theseus cursed his son, who was slain by a monster from the sea.

Phaedrus—a young disciple of Socrates, famous for his beauty. He appears as an erotically inclined guest at the *Symposium* and as the subject of Plato's second dialogue on love, the *Phaedrus*.

Phalanx—a Macedonian military formation developed by King Philip and used extensively by his son Alexander the Great. A group of soldiers interlocked shields from which pointed spears 13 to 18 feet long, forming an unapproachable mass of sharp points.

Pharaoh—ancient title of the rulers of Egypt.

Pharisees—a sect of Jewish religious leaders prominent in the first century A.D., who believed in strict obedience to the Mosaic Law and in the resurrection of the dead. Jesus often cited them as examples of tradition-bound self-righteousness. Their religious rivals were the Sadducees, who denied the resurrection.

Phidias—Athenian artist of the fifth-century B.C., best known for his three statues of Athene on the Acropolis and for his colossal ivory and gold statue of Zeus at Olympia. He was also responsible for the frieze of the Parthenon. Accused of impiety, he died in prison.

Philemon and Baucis—a poor old couple famous in Greek legend for having received Zeus and Hermes hospitably when they visited the earth disguised as men. Ovid tells their story in his *Metamorphoses*.

Philip of Macedon (c. 382-336 B.C.)—king of Macedonia who organized his armies into the most efficient fighting force in Greece. He brought most of the Greek states under Macedonian influence and intended to reverse the movement of the Persian Wars by leading Greek troops eastward into Persia, but was murdered before he could unify Greece sufficiently for a Persian expedition. Philip's unfinished work was completed by his son Alexander, who conquered Asia as far east as India.

Philippides—in Herodotus, the professional runner sent to Sparta to warn that the Persians were advancing toward Marathon.

Philo Judaeus (c. 30 B.C.-A.D. 40)—the Greek-educated Jewish philosopher of Alexandria who developed the doctrine of the *Logos,* or "Word of God" which was the Deity's first creation and by which all other things were created. In the gospel of *John* this doctrine is applied to Jesus, who "in the beginning" was "the Word (Logos)."

Philoctetes—Greek hero to whom Heracles, when about to die, gave his magical bow and arrows. On the expedition to Troy, Philoctetes directed the Achaeans to an island where they might offer sacrifices for military success. There he was bitten on the foot by a poisonous snake, creating a festering wound that refused to heal. The stench from this wound was so intolerable that the Achaean leaders abandoned Philoctetes on the barren island of Lemnos, where he remained alone for nearly ten years. Sophocles' play on the subject explores the bitter resentment of the forsaken hero.

Philosophy—literally, the "love of wisdom," a Greek mode of thought which applied logic and speculative reason to explain the world, to discover "the Good" or moral way of life, and to bring the mind to its highest attainments. The movement began with Thales of Miletus, the first thinker to interpret the cosmos in purely rational terms. At first indistinguishable from science, philosophy reached its height in the Athens of Socrates, Plato, and Aristotle.

Phoebus—an epithet of Apollo, meaning "the shining one," referring to his connection with the sun.

Phoenicians—an eastern-Mediterranean sea-going people whose principal cities were Tyre and Sidon and from whom the Greeks borrowed the alphabet. Carthage was their most important colony.

Phoenix—(1) mythological Egyptian bird which lived for 500 years and then consumed itself in flames; from its ashes rose a new bird. (2) in the *Iliad*, Achilles' old teacher who tries to persuade the hero to give up his anger and rejoin the siege of Troy.

Phrynichus—early tragedian, the first to produce plays about contemporary history. His most famous was the *Capture of Miletus*, in which he depicted the sufferings of Athens' sister-city when she was destroyed by the Persians (494 B.C.). Phrynichus is regarded as the most important predecessor of Aeschylus.

Pietas—supreme Roman virtue of duty toward the family, state, and gods, expressed in action rather than thought.

Pilate, Pontius—Roman governor of Judea (c. A.D. 33) who gave Jesus of Nazareth His civil trial and, when pressed by the rabble, condemned Him to death. His act of public handwashing was to disclaim responsibility for Jesus' crucifixion.

Pillars of Hercules—the rocks of Gibraltar, which guard the entrance to the Mediterranean Sea and beyond which almost no ancient sailor cared to travel.

Pindar (518-438 B.C.)—Greek lyric poet, whose compositions celebrating victories of famous athletes at the Olympic and Pythian games are supreme examples of the classical ode, later imitated by Horace.

Piraeus—chief seaport of Athens, about five miles southwest of the city, to which it was joined by the Long Walls, parallel fortifications built about 460 B.C. to protect Athens' access to the sea.

Pisistratus—the benevolent Athenian tyrant during whose reign (560-527 B.C.) were instituted the public readings of Homer at the Panathenaea, the tragic competitions at the Great Dionysia, and other public works.

Plataea—city of Boeotia on the frontier of Attica, the scene of the great land battle in 479 B.C. when the Greeks defeated the invading Persian army. At Marathon (490) the Plataeans were the only other Greeks who helped the Athenians resist the Persians.

Plautus, Titus Maccus (254-184 B.C.)—Roman writer of comedies which adapted to cruder Roman taste the Greek "New Comedy" of Menander and his successors. Twenty of his plays survive, including the *Amphitruo* and the *Menaechmi,* upon which Shakespeare based his *Comedy of Errors.* Much of our knowledge of Roman social life and customs of the third century B.C. comes from Plautus.

Plebeians *(Plebs)*—the common people of Rome, freemen but socially inferior to the privileged patrician class, hence "the vulgar," "the mob."

Pleiades—in Greek myth, a constellation of seven stars, supposedly the daughters of Atlas who were pursued by Orion and changed into heavenly bodies.

Plot—the arrangement of incidents in a play or other literary work so that they conform to a coherent pattern and illustrate the author's theme. A plot forms a unified structure of characters and events, as opposed to a narrative or story-line which merely relates a series of incidents without binding them into an artistic whole. Aristotle calls plot (*mythos*) the "heart and soul" of tragedy.

Plotinus (A.D. 205-270)—Greek-educated philosopher of Alexandria and Rome, chief exponent of Neoplatonism. He emphasized the spiritual, other-worldly aspect of Plato's teaching, combining it with eastern mysticism and a desire to escape from the physical world to the invisible realm of pure existence. He saw the cosmos as a hierarchy culminating in God (Plato's supreme Idea of the Good) and accessible only by disciplined contemplation. So intense was Plotinus' will to achieve union with the universal abstract that, according to his disciple and biographer Porphyry, he "seemed ashamed to be in a body."

Pluto—"the wealthy one," another name for Hades, god of the underworld.

Poet—from the Greek *poietes*, a maker or composer of verse; the term implies both the craftsmanship and creative ability of the artist. To the classical world Homer was "the Poet."

Polis—Greek term for a "city-state," always relatively small and independent of its neighbors, the characteristic political organization of the classical Greeks.

Pollution—in the ancient world, a state of religious or ceremonial uncleanness incurred when one had offended the gods by some crime. Until one had expiated his sin by the proper ceremony or ritual, he was often driven from his fellows' company or even sent into exile.

Pollux (Polydeuces)—brother of Castor, one of the Dioscuri (youths of Zeus) who, with his brother, became the constellation Gemini (the Twins).

Polybius (202-120 B.C.)—Greek historian who wrote a *Universal History* of Rome's wars with Carthage (264-146 B.C.) in forty volumes, of which five survive complete. He greatly admired the government of Republican Rome and advocated Greek submission to Roman supremacy.

Polyphemus—one of the giant Cyclopes, one-eyed cannibalistic sons of Poseidon.

Pompey (Pompeius, Gnaeus) (106-48 B.C.)—Roman general and conqueror of Asia Minor, chief rival of Julius Caesar, with whom he formed the first Triumvirate. When the Civil War broke out between the two leaders, Pompey was defeated and murdered in Egypt.

Pontifex Maximus—(1) title given the chief religious leader in ancient Rome who was responsible for the state cults and ceremonies. (2) the title, once held by Caesar and all the emperors, was assumed by the Pope, who became "supreme pontiff" of the Roman Catholic church.

Poseidon—Greek god of the sea, brother of Zeus and Hades, son of Cronus and Rhea. He is also god of the earthquake and sea storm, which he usually brings to punish his enemies. The three-pronged trident and horse are his symbols.

Potidaea—city-state in north Greece; subject of the Athenian Empire; its refusal to sever connections with Corinth and the intervention of Sparta into the affair was an immediate cause of the Peloponnesian War.

Praetorian Guard—the Roman emperor's special bodyguard, the only armed troops allowed in the capital; they frequently used their power to make or unmake emperors.

Pratinas—early fifth-century poet said to have invented the satyr play.

Praxiteles—Athenian sculptor of the fourth century B.C., famous for his graceful, naturalistic statues of Eros, Apollo, and Aphrodite. Only his "Hermes Holding the Infant Dionysus" survives.

Priam—in the *Iliad*, the aged king of Troy, husband of Hecuba, father of Hector, Paris, Cassandra, and (by various concubines) about fifty other sons.

Princeps—Latin term for "leader," a title taken by the Roman emperor Augustus and his successors.

Prologue—in Greek drama, a speech introducing the action or theme of the play, usually given by a god or minor character who takes no direct part in the events to follow.

Prometheus ("Forethought")—Titan god who disobeyed Zeus by stealing fire from heaven and giving it to man, to whom he also taught the arts of civilization. Zeus then cast Prometheus from Heaven and imprisoned him on a craig in the Caucasus where daily an eagle came to tear out his liver, which miraculously grew back again each night.

Prophet—(1) in classical Greece and Rome, a man or woman whom the gods inspired to see the future or to reveal the divine will. Zeus gave Apollo charge of human oracles, the most famous of which were institutionalized at Delphi and Cumae. (2) in ancient Israel, a "speaker for the Lord," a man who felt himself chosen to preach and interpret the will of God. The role of Hebrew prophet was never institutionalized.

Proscenium—in the Greek theatre, the term for the facade of the skene building which formed a backdrop to the stage; it usually represented the front of a temple or palace.

Protagonist—"first actor," the chief character in a Greek tragedy.

Protagoras—fifth century B.C. Greek philosopher, most famous of the Sophists.

Proteus—son of Poseidon or Ocean (Oceanus); he had to tell the future of anyone who captured him, but tried to avoid capture by changing his form.

Psyche—(1) in Greek legend, a king's daughter with whom Eros (Cupid) fell in love. (2) Greek term for the human soul which, according to Plato, is immortal, existing in heaven before being born in a human body (to which it gives life) and surviving death for reward or punishment in the spirit world.

Ptolemy (c. 367-283 B.C.)—Macedonian general of Alexander the Great who established a royal dynasty which ruled Egypt from 323 until 31 B.C., when the Roman Octavian (Augustus) defeated the last of the Ptolemies, Queen Cleopatra.

Punic Wars—series of three wars between Rome and Carthage for control of the Mediterranean. The first (264-241 B.C.) gave Rome Sicily; during the second (218-201 B.C.) the great Carthaginian general Hannibal invaded Italy and, though he did not capture Rome, won every encounter except the decisive battle of Zama, after which Carthage was forced to give up her fleet and pay a huge indemnity. Carthage's continued prosperity again aroused Roman fears, causing Rome to declare the third war (151-146 B.C.) in which Carthage was utterly destroyed. The result was Roman supremacy throughout the Mediterranean world.

Purgatory—in Roman Catholic theology, the spiritual realm where, after death, souls are temporarily punished for their sins until through suffering and repentance they earn a state of salvation. Dante pictures Purgatory as a high mountain in the earth's southern hemisphere where souls are joyfully purged of sin until they reach a state of innocence and can ascend to heaven.

Pylades—faithful friend of Orestes who accompanies him to Mycenae.

Pylos—(1) kingdom of Nestor, aged Achaean leader in the *Iliad.* (2) city in southern Greece where the Spartans were defeated by the Athenians in 425 B.C.

Pyrrhus—a name of Neoptolemus, son of Achilles; it means "yellow-haired."

Pythagoras—(c. 580-c. 497 B.C.)—Greek philosopher who founded a school or brotherhood devoted to strict rules and the study of mathematics, especially mystical theories of numbers. His doctrines of the prehuman existence and transmigration of souls and his emphasis on the abstract, ideal perfection of numerical relationships may have influenced Plato. His geometric theorem on the right-angled triangle is still studied.

Pythia *(Pythian Oracle)*—the priestess of Apollo at Delphi, so named in memory of the giant serpent (Python) which Apollo slew there. The Pythian Games, athletic competitions second only to the Olympics, were supposedly founded to celebrate Apollo's ancient victory.

Rachael—wife of the Hebrew patriarch, Jacob, to whom she bore two sons, Joseph and Benjamin.

Rebekah—wife of the patriarch Isaac, mother of twin sons, Jacob and Esau. To ensure that her favorite, Jacob, received his dying father's blessing, she arranged a deception by which the younger twin received the birthright due the elder.

Recognition—from the Greek *anagnorisis,* a term used in drama to denote the point at which the hero discovers an important truth, either about another character, about himself, or about the nature of his world—as when Oedipus recognizes that his wife is also his mother. In Aristotle's *Poetics,* a *Recognition* or *Disclosure* usually involves a simple realization of who is who. But, as in the *Philoctetes,* it can also be a more general discovery, such as Neoptolemus' awareness that his nature will not permit him to live by deceit.

Remus—twin brother of Romulus, mythical founder of Rome.

Republic, The—Plato's major work on the nature of the ideal state, as discussed by Socrates and his disciples. Based partly on the ideal of philosopher-kings, partly on the rigid stability of the Spartan oligarchy, the *Republic* is the first carefully thought-out political utopia.

Resurrection—Judaeo-Christian belief that after death the soul and/or body will be brought back to life to face reward or punishment. The doctrine is first developed in the Hebrew book of Daniel and elaborated in the Gospels and epistles of St. Paul. The resurrection is usually associated with the "last day," when Christ judges the world.

Reversal—in Greek tragedy, the point at which the hero's fortunes suddenly change or an action produces the opposite of what was expected. Aristotle uses the term *peripeteia* (anglicized to peripety) to describe the unexpected change in the tragic hero's life.

Rhadamanthus—son of Zeus and Europa, who, with his brother Minos, became a judge of the dead and ruler of Elysium.

Rhapsode, Rhapsodist—originally, a poet who recited his own works; later, a professional singer of Homeric poems. The term means "one who stitches songs together," a bard who collects and assembles traditional heroic tales.

Rhea—Titan wife of Cronus, mother of Zeus, Poseidon, Hades, Here, and Hestia. Sometimes identified with either Gaea (Gaia) or the Asiatic fertility goddess Cybele.

Rhea Silvia—in some legends, the mother by Mars of Romulus and Remus.

Rhetoric—the art of effective speaking or writing, a major subject of study in classical education.

Rhodes—island in the Aegean Sea famous for the enormous Colossus at the entrance to its harbor.

Romulus—mythical founder of Rome who, with his twin brother Remus, built the original walls of the capital. Abandoned as infants, they were raised by a she-wolf and later adopted by the shepherd Faustulus.

Roxana—wife of Alexander the Great.

Rubicon—river which divides Italy from Cisalpine Gaul and which Julius Caesar illegally crossed with his army in 49 B.C. The expression "crossing the Rubicon" denotes taking an irrevocable step.

Sabbath—seventh day of the Jewish week on which the Mosaic Law decreed no labor was to be done. See *Exodus* 20: 8-11.

Sabines—a tribe from the hills of west Italy.

Salamis—island across a narrow channel from Athen's port, Piraeus, into which the Athenians (under Themistocles) lured the Persian fleet and destroyed them at the Battle of Salamis in 480 B.C.

Sappho—greatest of the Greek lyric poets, whom Plato called the "tenth Muse." She lived in the sixth century B.C. on the island of Lesbos, where according to legend she ran a school for unmarried girls.

Sarah—wife and half-sister of the Hebrew patriarch Abraham, by whom she had a son, Isaac.

Sardis—capital of the kingdom of Lydia, later part of the Persian Empire.

Satan—a Hebrew word meaning "Adversary" or "Opposer" of Yahweh. In the New Testament Satan is identified with the Devil (the "Slanderer") and is regarded as the source of all sin and wickedness.

Satire—the only form of literature invented by the Romans. Horace's satires were gentle; Juvenal's poems were noted for their biting wit and scathing ridicule of human vice, folly, and hypocrisy.

Saturn—the Roman name for Cronus, Titan king of the gods, overthrown by Zeus.

Saturnalia—a Roman festival celebrated from December 17 to 19 in honor of Saturn, the rebirth of the sun after the winter solstice, and the sowing of crops. It was a licentious holiday so popular with the people that the Roman Catholic Church later scheduled the celebration of Christ's birth to coincide with its observance.

Satyr—in Greek mythology, a creature half-goat, half-man characterized by lust and cowardice. Satyrs, led by Silenus, accompanied Dionysus on his revels, hence the presence of the satyr play at tragic festivals.

Satyr play—a short, obscene comedy that followed the presentation of three tragedies at the Great Dionysia. Only Euripides' *Cyclops* and part of Sophocles' *Trackers* survive.

Scipio Africanus (235-183 B.C.)—Roman general who in the Second Punic War drove the Carthaginians out of Spain and defeated Hannibal at Zama in 202.

Scylla and Charybdis—the two female monsters that guard the narrow straits of Messina between Sicily and the tip of Italy. Scylla snatches up sailors from any ship that passes; Charybdis is a powerful whirlpool that sucks men and ships into the depths of the sea.

Sejanus, Lucius Aelius—favorite of the Emperor Tiberius; while the Emperor lived in retirement on Capri, Sejanus attempted to usurp the throne, for which he was executed. His treachery and ambition are satirized by Juvenal.

Seleucus—General of Alexander the Great who, after the latter's death, established a dynasty that ruled over Syria, Palestine, and Asia Minor. His territories were eventually absorbed by Rome.

Semele—daughter of Cadmus and a mistress of Zeus by whom she conceived Dionysus.

Seneca, Lucius Annaeus (c. 4 B.C.-A.D. 65) Stoic philosopher, dramatist, and tutor to Nero. Nine of his tragedies, all based on Greek models, survive.

Serpent—usually a symbol of evil, but, because the serpent loses its skin and seems to renew itself, it is also a symbol of healing.

Shamash—Sumero-Babylonian sun god, husband and brother of Ishtar, worshipped for his power, wisdom, and justice.

Shem—son of Noah from whom the Semitic peoples, including the Babylonians, Assyrians, and Hebrews, were supposedly descended.

Sheol—in Hebrew religion, the land or state of the dead, roughly equivalent to the Greek Hades, to which all men, good and evil alike, are doomed.

Sibyl—Roman prophetess, who guides Aeneas through the underworld.

Silenus—wise leader of the satyrs and tutor to the young Dionysus.

Simile—an explicit comparison between two unlike objects, using "as" or "like."

Simony—the sin of selling church offices for money, a practice common in the Middle Ages and Renaissance.

Sin—a moral crime, usually conceived as an act of disobedience to some deity. The Greek word for sin is *hamartia,* which is an archery term, meaning literally "to miss the mark." Aristotle uses it in a more technical sense as the "tragic flaw" or fatal weakness that brings the hero's downfall. In the New Testament and in Dante it is both an act and a state of mind alienated from God that, without repentance, brings damnation. Original sin is that inherited from Adam which makes the entire human race guilty in the eyes of God.

Sinai, Mount—a mountain on the Arabian Peninsula on which Moses received the Ten Commandments from Yahweh. See *Exodus* 19-20.

Sinon—in the *Aeneid,* a Greek spy who persuades the Trojans to take the Wooden Horse into their city.

Sirens—Greek nymphs, half-bird, half-woman, who by the charm of their songs lured sailors to their deaths.

Sisyphus—Greek founder of Corinth who, for his greed and deceit, was condemned in Hades to roll a huge stone uphill forever, from whence it always rolled down again.

Skene—in the Greek theatre, the building in back of the stage used as the actors' dressing room.

Socrates—Athenian philosopher, friend and teacher of Plato, condemned to death in 399 B.C. for his unorthodox teaching methods.

Sodom and Gomorrah—in Genesis the notoriously sinful "cities of the plain," destroyed by fire from heaven.

Soliloquy—a speech, usually in drama, in which a character "thinks out loud" while alone.

Solon (c. 640-c. 558 B.C.)—Athenian statesman, poet, and lawgiver, famous for his just revision of the Athenian constitution.

Sophists—literally "wise men," a school of philosophers and teachers who used (and sometimes abused) logic to undermine old beliefs and traditions. In Athens they earned a reputation for "making the better argument appear the worse" and for twisting facts in order to win a debate. They taught for money and, to the popular mind, seemed more concerned about clever victories in the law courts than in the objective pursuit of truth. Aristophanes mocks them in *The Clouds,* but unfortunately he confuses Socrates with the Sophist movement and thereby discredits him.

Sparta—in Mycenaean times, the luxurious capital of Menelaus and Helen, but after the Dorian invasion (c. 1100 B.C.) an increasingly austere and totalitarian state. In classical times it was Athens' chief rival and political opposite. Whereas Athens was a democracy, Sparta was ruled by a hereditary aristocracy which rigidly suppressed all other classes and tolerated no arts or sciences that did not prepare the citizens for war. The harsh, comfortless life of the ruling military caste was a marvel to other Greeks, some of whom admired the stability of its government and the efficiency of its war machine. Plato based his ideal republic partly on Spartan models.

Sphinx—mythical creature with head of a woman, body of a lion, and wings of an eagle.

Stichomythia—in drama, a dialogue in which two speakers exchange rapid one-line speeches, usually in the form of a verbal duel.

Stoicism—school of philosophy founded by Zeno at Athens (c. 315 B.C.). It teaches the use of reason to discipline the emotions, the necessity of virtue and right conduct to achieve happiness, and the cultivation of a spiritual independence from the world, a tough indifference to good or evil fortune, and the ability to endure whatever life brings with equal poise and calm. It was the most popular philosophy among the more thoughtful and educated Romans.

Strophe—in Greek drama, the choral ode sung while the chorus moved from one side of the orchestra to the other. The anti-strophe was the part sung while the chorus rotated in another direction.

Styx—mythical river of the underworld across which the dead passed to enter Hades.

Symbol—in literature, a symbol is anything—person, object, or place—that stands for something besides itself. It often suggests a higher meaning than one ordinarily associates with the character or object in question. In the *Divine Comedy*, for example, the figure of Beatrice functions as a symbol of heavenly grace.

Symposium—literally, a "drinking together," an all-male banquet at which guests conversed on a chosen topic.

Syracuse—wealthy colony of Corinth and largest city on the island of Sicily, famous for its defeat of the Athenian navy during the Peloponnesian War and for imprisoning the survivors in open stone quarries.

Tacitus, Publius Cornelius (c. A.D. 55-117)—Roman historian whose *Histories* cover the reigns of the emperors from Galba to Domitian and whose *Annals* concern the earlier period from Tiberius to Nero. Only parts of his works survive; these emphasize the corruption rather then the beneficial aspects of imperial government.

Tammuz (Thammuz)—ancient Sumero-Babylonian fertility god whose death and resurrection correspond to the seasonal change from winter to spring.

Tantalus—son of Zeus, father of Pelops, whose flesh he served to the gods to test their omniscience. For this he was condemned to eternal torture in Hades, where he stood in water he was unable to drink and where fruit growing above his head withdrew when he attempted to eat it. Hence the term to "tantalize," to hold something desperately desired just out of reach.

Tarquin—the name of two Etruscan kings of ancient Rome.

Tartarus—in classical myth, the deep abyss under Hades where the wicked were tortured and where the fallen Titans were imprisoned.

Telemachus—son of Odysseus and Penelope.

Ten Commandments (the *Decalogue*)—the laws inscribed on tablets of stone, given to Moses by Yahweh on Mt. Sinai, as recorded in Exodus 19-20. These commands formed the basis of the *Torah,* or Jewish religious doctrine.

Terza Rima—interlocking rhyme scheme invented by Dante for use in the *Divine Comedy.* The verse is composed of tercets, the second line rhyming with the first and succeeding triplet; in the first triplet lines one and three rhyme; in the last there is an extra line rhyming with its second. This metrical use of three is part of Dante's elaborate numerological scheme celebrating the Trinity.

Tetragrammaton—literally, the four letters of the divine name of God, YHWH.

Tetrology—in Greek drama, a series of three tragedies plus an accompanying satyr play.

Teucer—son of Telamon, greatest Greek archer in the war against Troy.

Thales (c. 625-c. 546 B.C.)—first known Greek philosopher; also a political leader, engineer, mathematician, and astronomer.

Thanatos—Greek personification of Death, twin brother of Hypnos (Sleep).

Thebes—the major city in Boeotia, supposedly founded by Cadmus; home of Oedipus and Antigone.

Themis—a Titan goddess personifying Justice and Law, the mother of Prometheus.

Themistocles (c. 527-c. 459 B.C.)—Athenian statesman and general whose policy of building a strong navy saved Athens during the Persian invasion of 480-479 B.C.

Thermopylae—narrow mountain pass in eastern Greece where King Leonidas and a heroic band of 300 Spartans held back the invading Persian army in 480 B.C.

Thersites—in the *Iliad*, a deformed and mean-spirited common soldier who dares to argue with his commanders and is beaten by Odysseus.

Theseus—son of Aegeus (for whom the Aegean Sea was named), legendary king of Athens; in his youth he went to Crete to participate in the infamous bull dances at King Minos' court. Aided by Ariadne, Minos' daughter, he found the way through the labyrinth, slew the Minotaur, and escaped to Greece, abandoning Ariadne on the island of Naxos. He later had a son, Hippolytus, by Antiope, Queen of the Amazons. After her death he married Ariadne's sister, Phaedra.

Thespis (c. 534 B.C.)—Athenian dramatist, known as father of the drama for having created the first role for an actor.

Thessaly—northern section of classical Greece; location of Mt. Olympus.

Thetis—a sea nymph married to the mortal king Peleus, mother of Achilles.

Thrace—area north and east of Greece along the northern Aegean Sea.

Three Unities—neo-classic theory of dramatic construction which held that a well-made play must observe (1) unity of time—all action must occur during one day; (2) unity of place—there can be no change of scene; and (3) unity of action—there must be no sub-plot to detract from the main story. It was based on a misunderstanding of Aristotle.

Thyestes—brother of Atreus and father of Aegisthus.

Tiber—river of western Italy upon whose banks Rome was founded.

Tiberius, Claudius Nero Caesar (42 B.C.-A.D. 37)—the second Roman emperor; during his reign Jesus performed his ministry and was crucified (c. A.D. 33).

Tiresias—Theban prophet who for a time was changed into a woman for having killed a snake. When questioned by Zeus and Here whether male or female has more pleasure in the act of love, he supported Zeus' contention that the woman does, for which Here struck him blind. In compensation Zeus gave Tiresias long life and the ability to foresee the future.

Titans—twelve ancient Greek gods, children of the primordal Uranus and Gaea (Heaven and Earth). Their chief was Cronus, who married Rhea, and by her fathered Zeus, Poseidon, Hades, Hestia, and Here.

Titus, Flavius Sabinus Vespasianus (c. A.D. 40-81)—Roman conqueror who destroyed Jerusalem in A.D. 70. A triumphal arch commemorating his victory still stands in the Roman forum. Titus succeeded his father Vespasian as emperor in A.D. 79.

Torah—literally, "instruction"; the Law of Moses contained in the first five books of the Bible.

Trajan (Marcus Ulpius Trajanus) (c. A.D. 52-117)—Roman emperor who enlarged the Empire to its greatest extent.

Trilogy—in Greek tragedy, a series of three plays on the same theme.

Troy (Ilios, Ilium)—in the *Iliad,* the city ruled by Priam and Hecuba that guarded the travel routes between the Black Sea and the Mediterranean. Modern Hissarlik, Turkey, occupies the ancient site.

Trojan Horse—the hollow wooden horse that concealed Odysseus and other Achaeans and was left as a parting gift when the Greeks pretended to leave Troy. It was so large that the Trojans had to tear down their walls to drag it into the city. At night the Greeks emerged and slaughtered the unsuspecting Trojans. Homer does not describe the incident, but Virgil includes it in the *Aeneid.*

Trojan War—the ten-year siege of Troy by the Achaeans (Greeks) led by Agamemnon to retrieve Helen who had eloped with Paris, prince of Troy.

Twelve Tables, The—a code of Roman law, published in 451-450 B.C., and inscribed on stone monuments in the Roman forum for all citizens to read, to meet the plebeian demand for written laws consistently applied.

Tyrant—in early Greek terminology, the ruler of a city-state who took over, rather than inherited, political power. Later, the term applied to a despised, oppressive autocrat.

Tyre—important Phoenician city. A major center of trade and commerce in the ancient world, it founded Carthage as its leading colony.

Ulysses—Roman name for Odysseus (q.v.).

Ur—ancient city in Mesopotamia from which Abraham made his journey to Palestine.

Uranus—ancient Greek sky-god, mated to Gaea (the Earth), who fathered the Titans and the Furies. According to Hesiod, Cronus, the son of Uranus, overthrew his father and established the Titans as rulers of the universe.

Urshanabi—the boatman who ferried Gilgamesh across the waters of death to the paradise where Utnapishtim dwelt and later accompanied Gilgamesh back to Uruk.

Uruk (Biblical *Erech*)—city in southern Babylonia near Ur; home of Gilgamesh, who is credited with building its walls and temples.

Usury—the practice of charging interest on loaned money, condemned by the medieval Roman Catholic Church as the unnatural growth of inanimate matter.

Utnapishtim—in *Gilgamesh,* the Sumero-Babylonian version of Noah; the man who survived the Great Flood when Ea instructed him to build a ship that would carry his family, servants, and livestock through the disaster.

Venus—Roman name for Aphrodite (q.v.).

Vespasian (A.D. 9-79)—Roman emperor during whose reign Jerusalem was destroyed (A.D. 70) and the Jews scattered throughout the world.

Vesta—Roman name for Hestia (q.v.).

Vulcan—Roman name for Hephaestus (q.v.).

Xanthus—Achilles' horse; he prophesies his master's death.

Xenophon (c. 430-355 B.C.)—Greek historian who completed Thucydides' narrative of the Peloponnesian Wars. He also wrote memoirs of Socrates' trial which provide an interesting contrast to Plato's somewhat idealized account. Xenophon's most famous work is the *Anabasis* or *March of the Ten Thousand,* which records the adventures of a Greek army's retreat through hostile territory.

Xerxes—Persian emperor who invaded Greece (480-479 B.C.) and whose fleet was destroyed at the sea battle of Salamis (480).

Yahweh—English translation of the tetragrammaton, the four Hebrew consonants (YHWH) of the Hebrew name for God, probably derived from a Hebrew verb, meaning "He causes to be."

Zeno—(1) of Elea (born c. 500 B.C.), a disciple of Parmenides the Philosopher, after whom a Platonic dialogue is named. He taught that the world is a single, eternal, unchanging unity and that change and division are only illusions. Socrates and Plato seem to have been influenced by these doctrines. (2) Zeno (c. 320-250 B.C.) the founder of Stoicism; he stressed discipline, restraint, and endurance. See Stoicism.

Zeus—king of Olympus, head of the Greek pantheon, a sky god whose symbol was the thunderbolt. Married to his sister Here, the model of the nagging wife, he engaged in numerous infidelities and had many mortal children, such as Heracles, Helen, and Castor. His divine offspring were Apollo, Artemis, Ares, Hephaestus, Hermes, and Athene. Although he began his rule by overthrowing his father Cronus and the other Titans, he became the most morally developed deity in Greek religion. He was the guardian of justice, law, order, kingship and the punisher of evil-doing.

Zephyrus—Greek personification of the West Wind.

Zophar—one of Job's three friends who argues that God punishes only the guilty.

Suggestions for Further Reading

Gilgamesh and the Sumero-Babylonian Culture

N. K. Sandars' Introduction to *The Epic of Gilgamesh* (1960) gives a readable and scholarly summary of the poem's background and history. In *Middle Eastern Mythology* (1963) S. H. Hooke surveys the ancient culture out of which *Gilgamesh* and the Bible developed. *The Babylonian Genesis,* second edition (1951), translated by Alexander Heidel, includes a complete version of the *Enuma Elish,* the Babylonian creation story. Heidel's *The Gilgamesh Epic and Old Testament Parallels* (1949) is also of interest. Samuel Noah Kramer has several relevant works on the Mesopotamian origins of civilization, including *Sumerian Mythology*, revised (1961), and *History Begins at Sumer* (1959).

The Old Testament

"The History of the Religion of Israel" by James Mullenberg in *The Interpreters Bible,* Vol. I, 292-389 (1951), is a good introduction to biblical studies. Harry M. Orlinsky, *Ancient Israel* (1964), gives an excellent brief history of Israel. Samuel Sandmel's *The Hebrew Scriptures* (1963) is clear, perceptive, and enthusiastically written. *From the Stone Age to Christianity,* revised (1957), by W. F. Albright, places Israel's religious experience in the context of other ancient Near Eastern civilizations. *World of the Old Testament,* revised (1958), by Cyrus H. Gordon, provides general information. Gordon's *The Common Background of Greek and Hebrew Civilizations,* revised (1965), argues that prehistoric Greece and Israel evolved from the same Near Eastern cultural complex. Robert H. Pfeiffer's *Introduction to the Old Testament,* revised (1948), is perhaps too detailed for beginners, but it is thorough, authoritative, and satisfying. *The Bible as History* (1956) by Werner Keller summarizes archaeological confirmations of the Bible's historical accuracy.

Greek Civilization

Mythology: Gods and Heroes of the Greeks (1958) and *A Handbook of Greek Mythology* (1959) by H. J. Rose provide an excellent introduction to Greek legends. A more ambitious and detailed analysis is *The Greeks and Their Gods* (1955) by W. K. C. Guthrie.

History: The Pelican History of Greece (1965) by A. R. Burn briefly surveys Greek history from Minoan Crete to the rise of Rome. In *The Will of Zeus* (1961) Stringfellow Barr enthusiastically discusses Greece's historical and cultural achievement. These are both highly readable one-volume paperbacks.

General: Edith Hamilton's *The Greek Way* (1930) is a classic appreciation of Greek literature and thought. H. D. F. Kitto's *The Greeks* revised (1957) is not so readable but perhaps more balanced. *The Greek Experience* (1957) by C. M. Bowra is a standard work.

Literature: A Literary History of Greece (1964) by Robert Flaceliere is a lucid, relevant analysis of the classical authors and their cultural milieu. Albin Lesky's

A History of Greek Literature (1966) is an enjoyable and thorough recent study. Werner Jaeger's *Paideia: The Ideals of Greek Culture*, 3 Vols. (1939-44) is an insightful and almost exhaustive analysis of the relation between literature and Greek education. Moses Hadas has an urbane *History of Greek Literature* (1950).

Homer

Most recent publications have concentrated on the "Homeric Question": Denys L. Page, *History and the Homeric Iliad* (1959); M. P. Nilsson, *Homer and Mycenae* (1933); G. S. Kirk, *The Songs of Homer* (1962); H. L. Lorimer, *Homer and the Monuments* (1950). *A Companion to Homer* (1963), edited by A. J. B. Wace and F. H. Stubbings, is a collection of scholarly essays on theories of composition, language, religion, and social culture. In *The Poet of the Iliad* (1952), H. T. Wade-Gery supports the minority opinion that Homer is the single author of the *Iliad*.

Criticism: C. M. Bowra, *Tradition and Design in the Iliad* (1930); J. P. Shephard, *The Pattern of the Iliad* (1922); C. H. Whitman, *Homer and the Heroic Tradition* (1958); G. Steiner and Robert Fagles, *Homer, A Collection of Critical Essays* (1962). Simone Weil's *The Iliad, or, The Poem of Force*, translated by Mary McCarthy, is a provocative essay.

Herodotus

Aubrey de Selincourt has translated the complete *Histories* (1954) with an Introduction and extremely helpful index. See also: T. R. Glover, *Herodotus* (1924); F. R. B. Godolphin, *The Greek Historians*, 2 Vols. (1942); J. L. Myres, *Herodotus, Father of History* (1953).

Greek Tragedy

For a comprehensive study of the origin and development of the drama, see *Dithyramb, Tragedy and Comedy*, 2nd edition (1962), by A. W. Pickard-Cambridge. The same author's *Theatre of Dionysus* (1946) and *The Dramatic Festivals of Athens* (1953) contain valuable material about stagecraft and machinery of the Athenian theatre. For a brilliant analysis of some philosophical implications of tragedy, see *The Spirit of Tragedy* (1956) by H. J. Muller. Other useful works: Gilbert Norwood, *Greek Tragedy* (1960); Albin Lesky, *Greek Tragedy* (1963); T. B. L. Webster, *Greek Theater Production* (1956); Peter Arnott, *An Introduction to the Greek Theatre* (1959).

Criticism: D. W. Lucas, *The Greek Tragic Poets*, 2nd edition (1959), and H. D. F. Kitto, *Greek Tragedy, A Literary Study*, 3rd edition (1961).

Aeschylus

Paul Roche's edition of *The Orestes Plays of Aeschylus* (1962) contains the complete *Oresteia* as well as an appendix of questions and answers about the Greek theatre; the latter is an excellent aid for students. Gilbert Murray's *Aeschylus, Creator of Tragedy* (1940) includes a section comparing Job with *Prometheus Bound*. Other helpful works: George Thomson, *Aeschylus and Athens,* 2nd edition (1948); E. T. Owen, *The Harmony of Aeschylus* (1952); H. Weir Smith, *Aeschylean Tragedy* (1924).

Sophocles

All seven of Sophocles' plays are included in *The Complete Greek Tragedies,* Vol. II, edited by David Grene and Richmond Lattimore (1957). Good critical studies include: C. M. Bowra, *Sophoclean Tragedy* (1944); J. A. Moore, *Sophocles and Arete* (1938); S. M. Adams, *Sophocles the Playwright* (1957); C. H. Whitman, *Sophocles, A Study in Heroic Humanism* (1951); J. T. Shephard, *Aeschylus and Sophocles, Their Work and Influence* (1927).

Thucydides

Recent critical studies include: F. E. Adcock, *Thucydides and His History* (1963); J. H. Finley, Jr., *Thucydides* (1947); J. de Rosmilly, *Thucydides and Athenian Imperialism* (1963). F. M. Cornford's *Thucydides Mythhistoricus* (1907) is old but still illuminating.

Euripides

Philip Vellacott has translated several Euripidean dramas in various Penguin editions: *Medea and Other Plays* (1963), *Alcestis and Other Plays,* and *The Bacchae and Other Plays* (1954). All nineteen of Euripides' plays are included in paperback volumes of *The Complete Greek Tragedies* (1957), edited by David Grene and Richmond Lattimore. The best analysis of *The Bacchae* is that of R. P. Winnington-Ingram, *Euripides and Dionysus* (1948).

General Criticism: Gilbert Murray, *Euripides and His Age,* 2nd edition (1946); G. M. A. Grube, *The Drama of Euripides* (1941, 1960); Gilbert Norwood, *Essays on Euripidean Drama* (1954); F. L. Lucas, *Euripides and His Influence* (1928).

Aristophanes

Three of Aristophanes' best comedies are delightfully translated by David Barrett in *The Frogs and Other Plays* (1964). F. M. Cornford, *The Origin of Attic Comedy* (1914) and A. W. Pickard-Cambridge, *Dithyramb, Tragedy and Comedy,* 2nd edition (1962), explore the beginning and early development of comedy.

Criticism: V. Ehrenberg, *The People of Aristophanes: A Sociology of Old Attic Comedy* (1943); Gilbert Murray, *Aristophanes, A Study* (1933); Gilbert Norwood, *Greek Comedy* (1931); K. Lever, *The Art of Greek Comedy* (1956).

Job

For a general discussion and thorough annotation of the text see Job (*The Anchor Bible*) (1965), translated and edited by Marvin H. Pope. For critical interpretations see Samuel Terrien, *Job: Poet of Existence* (1957) and *The Book of Job, A Collection of Critical Essays* (1968), edited by P. S. Sanders. In *The Book of Job as a Greek Tragedy Restored* (1918), H. M. Kallen presents an acting version of the drama.

Plato

Although a bit old fashioned, the standard translation of the complete works remains that of Benjamin Jowett, *The Dialogues of Plato*, 4th edition (1953). A more recent version of several dialogues is that of W. H. D. Rouse, *Great Dialogues of Plato* (1956). The best translation of *The Republic* is by F. M. Cornford (1945). Cornford has also written some important critical studies: *Plato's Cosmology* (1937) and *Plato's Theory of Knowledge* (1951). Paul Shorey's *What Plato Said* (1933) and *Plato's Theory of Ideas* (1951) are good introductions. A. E. Taylor, *Plato, The Man and His Work*, 6th edition (1955), is the standard reference.

Aristotle

The Oxford edition, edited by W. D. Ross, contains the complete *Works of Aristotle* (1931). Ross gives a classic account of Aristotelian philosophy in *Aristotle*, 5th edition (1949). In *Aristotle*, revised edition (1943), A. E. Taylor writes from the viewpoint of a dedicated Platonist. Werner Jaeger, *Aristotle: Fundamentals of the History of his Development*, 2nd edition (1950), studies chronologically the evolution of Aristotelian thought. J. A. K. Thomson writes a biographical and critical Introduction to his translation of *The Ethics of Aristotle* (1953). Thomson also published a comparative study, *Plato and Aristotle* (1928). Francis Ferguson offers an introductory essay to *Aristotle's Poetics* (1961). *Aristotle, A Collection of Critical Essays* (1967), edited by J. M. E. Moravcsik, surveys numerous aspects of Aristotelian logic, metaphysics, and ethics.

Roman Civilization

Mythology: Michael Grant, *Myths of the Greeks and Romans* (1962); *A Handbook of Greek Mythology* (1959) by H. J. Rose has been extended to include Roman legends.

History: A. E. R. Boak, *A History of Rome to 565 A.D.*, 3rd edition (1943); C. E. Robinson, *A History of Rome from 753 to 410 A.D.* (1935); J. C. Stobart, *The Grandeur That Was Rome*, 3rd edition (1935).

General: Edith Hamilton's *The Roman Way* (1932) is a pleasant introduction to Roman mores and literature. Michael Grant, *The World of Rome* (1960), Donald R. Dudley, *The Civilization of Rome* (1960), and R. H. Barrow, *The Romans* (1949) are appropriate for the beginning student and available in paperback. The English edition of *Daily Life in Ancient Rome* (1956) by Jerome Carcopino gives a clear summary of information about the period.

Literature: Moses Hadas, *A History of Latin Literature* (1952); Michael Grant, *Roman Literature*, revised edition (1958); H. J. Rose, *A Handbook of Latin Literature* (1949) are excellent introductions. Others: J. W. Duff, *A Literary History of Rome from the Origins to the Close of the Golden Age*, 2nd edition (1953), and *The Literary History of Rome in the Silver Age, from Tiberius to Hadrian*, 2nd edition

(1932); C. Bailey, ed., *The Mind of Rome* (1926); W. A. Laidlaw, *Latin Literature* (1941). *The Classical Heritage and its Beneficiaries* (1954) by R. R. Bolgar discusses the Graeco-Roman accomplishment.

Lucretius

R. E. Latham provides a lucid introduction and helpful index to his prose translation of *On the Nature of the Universe* (1951). George Santayana has an essay on Lucretius in *Three Philosophical Poets* (1910). Other useful works: E. E. Sikes, *Lucretius, Poet and Philosopher* (1936); G. D. Hadzsits, *Lucretius and his Influence* (1935); C. Bailey, *The Greek Atomists and Epicurus* (1928); W. J. Oates, *The Stoic and Epicurean Philosophers* (1940).

Catullus

Horace Gregory, *The Poems of Catullus* (1956), is by far the best translation available. Good books on Catullus include: K. P. Harrington, *Catullus and his Influence* (1923); E. A. Havelock, *The Lyric Genius of Catullus* (1939); T. Frank, *Catullus and Horace: Two Poets in their Environment* (1928); A. L. Wheeler, *Catullus and the Traditions of Ancient Poetry* (1934). Peter Whigham's Introduction to *The Poems of Catullus* (1966) contains a penetrating analysis of the poet's psychology.

Cicero

The Loeb Classical Library gives the original text (and an English translation on opposite pages) of almost all Cicero's works. L. P. Wilkinson has edited selected *Letters of Cicero* (1949). F. R. Cowell's *Cicero and the Roman Republic* (1948, 1967) is a thorough analysis of Cicero and his historical milieu. E. G. Sihler's *Cicero of Arpinum* (1914) is the standard biography. See also: T. H. Dorey and D. R. Dudley, eds., *Cicero* (1965); H. J. Haskell, *This Was Cicero* (1942); H. A. K. Hunt, *The Humanism of Cicero* (1954).

Virgil

For commentary on the *Aeneid*, as well as the *Bucolics, Georgics,* and other Virgilian poems, see: Brooks Otis, *Virgil, A Study in Civilized Poetry* (1964); Viktor Poschl, *The Art of Vergil: Image and Symbolism in the Aeneid* (1962); H. W. Prescott, *The Development of Virgil's Art* (1927); Cyril Bailey, *Religion in Virgil* (1935); D. L. Drew, *The Allegory of the Aeneid* (1927); W. F. J. Knight, *Roman Vergil* (1944).

Livy

In *The Early History of Rome* (1960), Aubrey de Selincourt translates the first five books of Livy's work, with an Introduction and index. De Selincourt's edition of *The War with Hannibal* (1965) (Books XXI-XXX) includes a chronological index and introductory essay by Betty Radice. For Livy's achievement as a historican, see P. G. Walsh, *Livy: his Historical Aims and Methods* (1961).

Horace

Translations of Horace abound, but no single translator has done justice to all the Horatian poems. Some recent paperback versions that include introductions and glossaries: James Michie, *The Odes of Horace* (1964) and J. P. Clancy, *The Odes and Epodes of Horace* (1960). Good critical works include: T. R. Glover, *Horace: A Return to Allegiance* (1932); E. A. Haight, *Horace and his Art of Enjoyment* (1925); C. N. Smiley, *Horace, his poetry and Philosophy* (1945); Grant Showerman, *Horace and his Influence* (1925); T. Frank, *Catullus and Horace: Two Poets in their Environment* (1928).

Ovid

Rolfe Humphries has made verse translations of both the complete *Metamorphoses* (1955) and *The Art of Love* (1957). Miss Mary M. Innes introduces her prose translation of the *Metamorphoses* (1955) with a long critical essay. General studies of Ovid include: L. P. Wilkinson, *Ovid Recalled* (abridged as *Ovid Surveyed*, 1962) and *Ovidiana* (1958); H. Frankel, *Ovid: A Poet Between Two Worlds* (1945).

Plutarch

Penguin Books has an excellent series of paperback reprints of Plutarch's *Lives: The Rise and Fall of Athens* (1960) (Theseus, Solon, Themistocles, Pericles, Alcibiades, etc.), and the *Makers of Rome* (1965) (Cato the Elder, Tiberius and Gaius Gracchus, Brutus, Mark Antony, etc.), translated with an Introduction by Ian Scott-Kilvert; and *Fall of The Roman Republic* (1958) (Marius, Sulla, Crassus, Pompey, Caesar, Cicero), translated by Rex Warner. Moses Hadas published seven little-known but rewarding essays from Plutarch's *Moralia: On Love, The Family, and the Good Life* (1957).

Juvenal

Dryden's epigrammatic translations of the *Satires* are found in *The Poems of John Dryden*, Vol. II, (1958), edited by James Kinsley. J. W. Duff, *Roman Satire: its Outlook on Social Life* (1936), offers interesting comment. Other works: E. Walford, *Juvenal* (1872) and I. G. Scott, *The Grand Style in the Satires of Juvenal* (1927).

Apuleius

The Loeb Classical Library contains a complete translation of *The Golden Ass (The Metamorphoses)* by W. Adlington (1566), revised by S. Gaselee (1915). The best edition of *Cupid and Psyche* is still that by L. C. Purser (1910).

The New Testament

One of the most stimulating discussions of the Judaeo-Christian religion occurs in H. J. Muller's *The Uses of the Past* (1952); see ch. IV "The Legacy of Israel" and ch. VI "The Rise of Christianity," in which Muller criticizes Hebraic monotheism and Christianity from the humanist's point of view. Conventional introduction to Christ's ministry is *The Life and Teachings of Jesus* (1955) by C. M. Laymon. *The Abingdon Bible Commentary* (1929) by F. C. Eiselen and Edwin Lewis, is probably the best single volume commentary; *Harper's Bible Dictionary* (1959) by M. S. Miller and J. L. Miller is also useful. Good general works are: H. C. Kee and F. W. Young, *Understanding the New Testament* (1957); D. W. Riddle and H. H. Hutson, *New Testament Life and Literature* (1947); C. W. Quimby, *Paul for Everyone* (1944); William Manson, *The Gospel of Luke,* in the *Moffat New Testament Commentary* (1930). *The Interpreter's Bible* (1951-57), which uses the King James text, contains 12 volumes of commentary, introductions, and essays by various Bible scholars.

Christianity and the Pagan Reaction

F. Van der Meer and C. Mohrmann, *Atlas of the Early Christian World* (1958) summarize recent information on the subject. C. N. Cochrane, *Christianity and Classical Culture* (1940) and W. Barclay, *Educational Ideals in the Ancient World* discuss the relation of Christianity to paganism. Other good sources: A. D. Nock, *Conversion: The Old and New in Religion from Alexander the Great to Augustine of Hippo* (1933); P. Carrington *The Early Christian Church,* 2 vols. (1957); T. R. Glover, *The Conflict of Religions in the Early Roman Empire,* 10th edition (1923); A. H. M. Jones, *Constantine and the Conversion of Europe* (1962); Anne Fremantle, ed., *A Treasury of Early Christianity* (1953).

Jerome

Paul Carroll creates a vivid portrait of Jerome's personality in *The Satirical Letters of St. Jerome* (1956). F. A. Wright has published other *Selected Letters of St. Jerome* (1933). F. X. Murphy has edited a collection of critical essays, *A Monument to St. Jerome* (1952).

Augustine

R. S. Pine-Coffin's translation of the complete *Confessions* (1961) contains a short critical introduction. Both Marcus Dodes and John Healey have published translations of *The City of God* (1948 and 1945). See also: Whitney J. Oates, ed., *Basic Writings of St. Augustine,* 2 vols. (1948).

Criticism: R. W. Battenhouse, *A Companion to the Study of St. Augustine* (1955); R. J. O'Connell, *St. Augustine's Confessions: The Odyssey of a Soul* (1969); J. J. O'Meara, *Charter of Christendom: The Significance of the City of God* (1961); P. R. L. Brown, *Augustine of Hippo, A Biography* (1967).

Dante

Dorothy Sayers has translated the complete *Divine Comedy* in fluent *terza rima*, 3 vols. (1949, 1955, 1962); her comprehensive notes and introductions are splendid. *La Divina Commedia* (Italian text with prefaces and annotations in English), edited by C. H. Grandgent, revised edition (1933), provides excellent summaries of each canto as well as an enormous bibliography. T. G. Bergin's translation of *The Divine Comedy* (1955) is in blank verse. John Ciardi's versions of *The Inferno* (1954) and *The Purgatorio* (1957) are rendered in vigorous and colloquial English. *The New Life (La Vita Nouva)*, which contains Dante's original account of his love for Beatrice, has recently been translated by William Anderson in a Penguin edition.

Criticism and background: There are almost as many critical studies of Dante as of Shakespeare. The following, though of varying difficulty, are excellent: Dorothy L. Sayers, *Introductory Papers on Dante* and *Further Papers on Dante* (1954, 1957); Umberto Cosmo, *A Handbook to Dante Studies* (1950); T. G. Bergin, *Dante* (1965); Charles Williams, *The Figure of Beatrice* (1943); George Santayana, *Three Philosophical Poets* (1910); Francis Fergusson, *Dante's Drama of the Mind: A Modern Reading of the Purgatorio* (1953); C. S. Singleton, *Dante Studies 1, Commedia: Elements of Structure* (1954) and *Dante Studies 2, Journey to Beatrice* (1958); Irma Brandeis, *The Ladder of Vision* (1961); P. H. Wicksteed, *From Vita Nuova to Paradiso;* Erich Auerbach, *Dante, Poet of the Secular World* (1962). For background in the medieval world consult Ernst Curtius, *European Literature and the Latin Middle Ages* (1953); Karl Vossler, *Medieval Culture: An Introduction to Dante and His Times,* 2 vols. (reprinted 1958); Etienne Gilson, *Dante the Philosopher* (1948); F. J. Powicke, *Christian Life in the Middle Ages* (1935).

INDEX

INDEX